Negotiation, Decision Making and Conflict Management
Volume III

The International Library of Critical Writings on Business and Management

Wherever possible, the articles in these volumes have been reproduced as originally published using facsimile reproduction, inclusive of footnotes and pagination to facilitate ease of reference.

For a list of all Edward Elgar published titles visit our site on the World Wide Web at
www.e-elgar.com

Negotiation, Decision Making and Conflict Management Volume III

Edited by

Max H. Bazerman

Jesse Isidor Straus Professor of Business Administration
Harvard Business School, USA

THE INTERNATIONAL LIBRARY OF CRITICAL WRITINGS ON BUSINESS AND MANAGEMENT

An Elgar Reference Collection
Cheltenham, UK • Northampton, MA, USA

Published by
Edward Elgar Publishing Limited
Glensanda House
Montpellier Parade
Cheltenham
Glos GL50 1UA
UK

Edward Elgar Publishing, Inc.
136 West Street
Suite 202
Northampton
Massachusetts 01060
USA

A catalogue record for this book is available from the British Library.

ISBN   1 84376 377 X (3 volume set)

Printed and bound in Great Britain by MPG Books Ltd, Bodmin, Cornwall

Contents

Acknowledgements

The editor and publishers wish to thank the authors and the following publishers who have kindly given permission for the use of copyright material.

Administrative Science Quarterly for articles: J. Keith Murnighan, Jae Wook Kim and A. Richard Metzger (1993), 'The Volunteer Dilemma', *Administrative Science Quarterly*, **38** (4), December, 515–38; Philip E. Tetlock (2000), 'Cognitive Biases and Organizational Correctives: Do Both Disease and Cure Depend on the Politics of the Beholder?', *Administrative Science Quarterly*, **45**, 293–326.

American Economic Association for articles: John H. Kagel and Dan Levin (1986), 'The Winner's Curse and Public Information in Common Value Auctions', *American Economic Review*, **76** (5), December, 894–920; Alvin E. Roth and Xiaolin Xing (1994), 'Jumping the Gun: Imperfections and Institutions Related to the Timing of Market Transactions', *American Economic Review*, **84** (4), September, 992–1044.

American Psychological Association for articles: Robyn M. Dawes, Jeanne McTavish and Harriet Shaklee (1977), 'Behavior, Communication, and Assumptions About Other People's Behavior in a Commons Dilemma Situation', *Journal of Personality and Social Psychology*, **35** (1), 1–11; J. Keith Murnighan (1978), 'Models of Coalition Behavior: Game Theoretic, Social Psychological, and Political Perspectives', *Psychological Bulletin*, **85** (5), September, 1130–53; Robyn M. Dawes (1979), 'The Robust Beauty of Improper Linear Models in Decision Making', *American Psychologist*, **34** (7), July, 571–82; Richard P. Larrick and Sally Blount (1997), 'The Claiming Effect: Why Players Are More Generous in Social Dilemmas Than in Ultimatum Games', *Journal of Personality and Social Psychology*, **72** (4), April, 810–25.

Annual Reviews (www.annualreviews.org) for article: Robyn M. Dawes (1980), 'Social Dilemmas', *Annual Review of Psychology*, **31**, 169–93.

Basic Books, a member of Perseus Books, LLC for excerpt: Robert Axelrod (1984), 'The Success of TIT FOR TAT in Computer Tournaments', in *The Evolution of Cooperation*, Chapter 2, 27–54, 217, references.

Cambridge University Press and the Russell Sage Foundation for excerpt: Colin F. Camerer (2000), 'Prospect Theory in the Wild: Evidence from the Field', in Daniel Kahneman and Amos Tversky (eds), *Choices, Values and Frames*, Chapter 16, 288–300, references.

Econometric Society for article: Alvin E. Roth (2002), 'The Economist as Engineer: Game Theory, Experimentation, and Computation as Tools for Design Economics', *Econometrica*, **70** (4), July, 1341–78.

Elsevier for articles and excerpts: Margaret A. Neale (1984), 'The Effects of Negotiation and Arbitration Cost Salience on Bargainer Behavior: The Role of the Arbitrator and Constituency on Negotiator Judgment', *Organizational Behavior and Human Performance*, **34** (1), August, 97–111; Margaret A. Neale and Gregory B. Northcraft (1990), 'Experience, Expertise, and Decision Bias in Negotiation: The Role of Strategic Conceptualization', in Blair H. Sheppard, Max Bazerman and Roy J. Lewicki (eds), *Research in Negotiation in Organizations*, Volume 2, 55–75; Sheryl B. Ball, Max H. Bazerman and John S. Carroll (1991), 'An Evaluation of Learning in the Bilateral Winner's Curse', *Organizational Behavior and Human Decision Processes*, **48** (1), February, 1–22; Elizabeth A. Mannix (1991), 'Resource Dilemmas and Discount Rates in Decision Making Groups', *Journal of Experimental Social Psychology*, **27** (4), July, 379–91; Harris Sondak and Max H. Bazerman (1991), 'Power Balance and the Rationality of Outcomes in Matching Markets', *Organizational Behavior and Human Decision Processes*, **50** (1), October, 1–23; Roderick M. Kramer (1991), 'The More the Merrier? Social Psychological Aspects of Multiparty Negotiations in Organizations', in M.H. Bazerman, R.J. Lewicki and B.H. Sheppard (eds), *Research on Negotiation in Organizations*, Volume 3: *Handbook of Negotiation Research*, 307–32; Ann E. Tenbrunsel, Kimberly A. Wade-Benzoni, Joseph Moag and Max H. Bazerman (1999), 'The Negotiation Matching Process: Relationships and Partner Selection', *Organizational Behavior and Human Decision Processes*, **80** (3), December, 252–83; Leigh Thompson, Dedre Gentner and Jeffrey Loewenstein (2000), 'Avoiding Missed Opportunities in Managerial Life: Analogical Training More Powerful Than Individual Case Training', *Organizational Behavior and Human Decision Processes*, **82** (1), May, 60–75; Kathleen Valley, Leigh Thompson, Robert Gibbons and Max H. Bazerman (2002), 'How Communication Improves Efficiency in Bargaining Games', *Games and Economic Behavior*, **38**, 127–55.

Industrial and Labor Relations Review, Cornell University for articles: Henry S. Farber (1981), 'Splitting-the-difference in Interest Arbitration', *Industrial and Labor Relations Review*, **35** (1), October, 70–7; Max H. Bazerman (1985), 'Norms of Distributive Justice in Interest Arbitration', *Industrial and Labor Relations Review*, **38** (4), July, 558–70.

Institute for Operations Research and the Management Sciences (INFORMS) for article: Daniel Kahneman and Dan Lovallo (1993), 'Timid Choices and Bold Forecasts: A Cognitive Perspective on Risk Taking', *Management Science*, **39** (1), January, 17–31.

Psychology Press Ltd, Taylor and Francis Ltd for article: Robyn M. Dawes and David M. Messick (2000), 'Social Dilemmas', *International Journal of Psychology*, Special Issue: Diplomacy and Psychology, **35** (2), 111–16.

Sage Publications, Inc. for articles and excerpt: Max H. Bazerman and William F. Samuelson (1983), 'I Won the Auction But Don't Want the Prize', *Journal of Conflict Resolution*, **27** (4), December, 618–34; David M. Messick and Marilynn B. Brewer (1983), 'Solving Social

Dilemmas: A Review', in Ladd Wheeler and Phillip Shaver (eds), *Review of Personality and Social Psychology*, Volume 4, 11–44; Jonathan Bendor, Roderick M. Kramer and Suzanne Stout (1991), 'When in Doubt … Cooperation in a Noisy Prisoner's Dilemma', *Journal of Conflict Resolution*, **35** (4), December, 691–719.

Tribune Media Services International for article: Max H. Bazerman and Henry S. Farber (1985), 'Analyzing the Decision-Making Processes of Third Parties', *Sloan Management Review*, **27** (1), Fall, 39–48.

John Wiley and Sons, Inc. for excerpt: William L. Ury, Jeanne M. Brett and Stephen B. Goldberg (1988), 'Three Approaches to Resolving Disputes: Interests, Rights, and Power', in *Getting Disputes Resolved: Designing Systems to Cut the Costs of Conflict*, Chapter 1, 3–19, 177–81.

Every effort has been made to trace all the copyright holders but if any have been inadvertently overlooked the publishers will be pleased to make the necessary arrangement at the first opportunity.

In addition the publishers wish to thank the Marshall Library of Economics, Cambridge University, the Library of the University of Warwick and the Library of Indiana University at Bloomington, USA for their assistance in obtaining these articles.

Part I
Prisoner and Social Dilemmas

[1]

Journal of Personality and Social Psychology
1977, Vol. 35, No. 1, 1-11

Behavior, Communication, and Assumptions About Other People's Behavior in A Commons Dilemma Situation

Robyn M. Dawes, Jeanne McTavish, and Harriet Shaklee
University of Oregon and Oregon Research Institute

Two experiments investigated effects of communication on behavior in an eight-person commons dilemma of group versus individual gain. Subjects made a single choice involving a substantial amount of money (possible outcomes ranging from nothing to $10.50). In Experiment 1, four communication conditions (no communication, irrelevant communication, relevant communication, and relevant communication plus roll call) were crossed with the possibility of losing money (loss, no loss). Subjects chose self-serving (defecting) or cooperating responses and predicted responses of other group members. Results showed defection significantly higher in the no-communication and irrelevant-communication conditions than in relevant-communication and relevant-communication plus roll call conditions. Loss had no effect on decisions. Defectors expected much more defection than did cooperators. Experiment 2 replicated irrelevant communication and cooperation effects and compared predictions of participants with those of observers. Variance of participants' predictions was significantly greater than that of observers, indicating that participants' decisions were affecting their expectations about others' behavior.

When first discussing the prisoner's dilemma, Luce and Raiffa wrote (1957, p. 97) that there ought to be a law against it. There are laws against some prisoner's dilemmas, but modern societies seem to be inventing new ones at an alarming rate. It is, for example, to each individual's rational self-interest to exploit the environment, pollute, and (in some countries) overpopulate, while the collective effect is worse for everyone than if each individual exercised restraint.

Thus, individual behavior when faced with such dilemmas is a matter of increasing interest to both social scientists and people in general.

Social dilemmas—such as that in the Prisoner's Dilemma Game—are characterized by two conditions (Dawes, 1975): (a) the antisocial, or defecting, response is dominating for each individual; that is, no matter what other people do, each individual is best off behaving in an antisocial manner:

(b) the result is an *equilibrium* that is *deficient*. It is an equilibrium because no player is motivated to change, and it is deficient because all individuals would prefer an outcome in which all cooperated to one in which all chose their dominant strategy of defection. Within the context of these conditions, it is possible to define a number of different social dilemmas. It turns out, however, that the most common experimental games that have been devised for studying behavior in a dilemma situation are all structurally identical, although often stated differently by different authors. These games are (a) *N*-person separable prisoner's dilemma (e.g., Hamburger, 1973), (b) games in which payoffs for cooperation and defection are linear functions with equal slopes of the number of cooperators (e.g., Kelley & Grzelak, 1972), and (c) games devised according to the principle that profit for defection accrues directly to the defector while loss (which is greater than gain) is spread out equally among all the players [1] (Dawes, 1975). The purpose of the present research is to examine behavior in such an experimental game—specifically, to look at the roles of communication about the dilemma and at the relationship between one's own behavior and one's expectations about how other people will behave.

Before proceeding to the empirical study, let us first explain the game as characterized by the gain-to-self-loss-spread-out principle. The game is constructed on the basis of Hardin's (1968) analysis of the "tragedy of the commons." Each player can receive a certain amount c for cooperating, but each

player can in addition receive an amount d if he or she chooses to defect. The group as a whole is fined $d + \lambda$, with $\lambda > 0$, for each defecting choice, each player's share of the fine being $(d + \lambda)/N$ where N is the number of players. Thus, each player's motive for defection is $d - (d + \lambda)/N$ which will be greater than 0 provided that $d > \lambda/(N-1)$, a side condition. Note that if there are m cooperators, then the payoff for cooperation is $c - (N - m)(d + \lambda)/N = [(d + \lambda)/N] m + c - d - \lambda$; the payoff for defection is the same amount incremented by d. Hence, the payoffs for cooperation and defection are linear functions with equal slopes of the number of cooperators, and as Hamburger (1973) has shown, such payoff functions define games that are equivalent to N-person separable prisoner's dilemmas.

Subjects in the experiments described in this paper met in eight-person groups and were faced with the following choices. A cooperative response earned \$2.50 with no fine to anyone. A defecting response earned \$12.00 with a fine of \$1.50 to each group member including the defector. Thus, each player had an \$8.00 motive to defect ([\$12.00 − \$1.50] − \$2.50). Of course, if all defect, no one receives anything. If someone cooperates and two or more other group members defect, the cooperator has a negative payoff. This investigation is the first of a series of experiments to identify situational and personal variables important to group or self-interested decisions in this dilemma. Two major variables were of interest here.

Opportunity for communication was the first major variable and was manipulated with the expectation that people faced with this dilemma would have a better chance of resolving it if they could communicate with each other. Communication commonly results in increased cooperation in two-person prisoner's dilemmas (e.g., Deutsch, 1960; Loomis, 1959; Radlow & Weidner, 1966; Swensson, 1967; Wichman, 1972) and had a similar effect in a five-person social dilemma

Experiment 1 was presented at the 1975 West Coast Conference on Small Group Research in Victoria, British Columbia on April 16, 1975. The entire research was supported by the Advanced Research Projects Agency of the Department of Defense (ARPA Order No. 2449); it was partially monitored by Office of Naval Research under Contract N00014-75-C-0093. We would like to thank Sol Fulero, Lita Furby, Phil Hyman, Mike Moore, Len Rorer, and Myron Rothbart for their help in this project.

Reprint requests should be sent to Robyn M. Dawes, Department of Psychology, University of Oregon, Eugene, Oregon 97403.

[1] Messick's (1973) union dilemma game also is structurally identical, although in a probabilistic context.

involving hypothetical business decisions (Jerdee & Rosen, 1974). Caldwell (1976) found that communication alone did not seem to be sufficient to affect subjects' decisions; nevertheless, his findings were in the right direction (although not significant) and as he notes (p. 279), "Perhaps with real money subjects would be less inclined to treat the experiment as a competitive game." (The same possibility applies to most of the other research as well.)

Communication effects could have at least three sources. First, the opportunity to communicate allows group members to get acquainted, which could raise their concern for each others' welfare. Second, the relevant information raised through the discussion and appeals for mutual cooperation could persuade group members to cooperate. Third, group members' statements of their own intended decisions could assure other members of their good intentions, leading to higher rates of cooperation.

To distinguish between these possibilities, four communication conditions were included in the present design. The no-communication (N) groups worked silently on an unrelated topic before making their decision in the game. The irrelevant-communication (I) groups were allowed to get acquainted with each other through a group discussion of an unrelated topic, but were not permitted to discuss the group dilemma decision. The relevant-communication (C) groups discussed the dilemma situation before making their decisions, and the relevant-communication plus vote (C + V) groups ended their discussion with a roll call in which each group member made a nonbinding declaration of intended decision. If a role call vote were suggested in the C groups, it was stopped by the experimenters. Thus, considering groups ordered N, I, C, C + V, each of the possible sources of communication effects were systematically added to the conditions of the previous group to see if it incremented the level of cooperation in the group.

A second major variable of interest concerned possible individual differences in cooperators' and defectors' expectations about others' decisions. Prior work by Kelley and Stahelski (1970) on the prisoner's dilemma indicated that cooperators and competitors maintain different world views, with competitors expecting competition from other players and cooperators expecting either cooperation or competition. Subjects in Experiment 1 were asked to predict other group members' decisions to see if similar individual differences occur in the commons dilemma. Further research in Experiment 2 suggests an alternative to Kelley and Stahelski's interpretation of these differences in expectations.

A final variable manipulation was the possibility of losing money in the game. The possibility for cooperators to lose money might increase the risk associated with a cooperative decision, leading to less cooperation. Alternatively, defectors might be more reluctant to defect if their decision caused other group members to lose money. The net effect of these contrary forces was difficult to predict. Equally difficult, however, was the task of designing an experiment where loss of money was possible without violating experimental ethics.

The solution used in the experimental work was to have subjects pool their winnings or losses with friends, truncating pooled losses at zero. Thus, an individual subject could be put in a condition where he or she could lose money. Subjects came to the experiment in groups of four friends. Two of the four went to a loss condition where they individually could lose money; two went to a condition in which their potential personal losses were truncated at zero. When the four friends returned from their decision groups, their earnings were pooled and shared equally. If the net total was negative, money was not taken from the group. Thus, subjects' losses could detract from their other friends' gains, but subjects would never owe the experimenter money by the end of the experiment. In sum, communication (N, I, C, C + V) and loss (loss, no loss) conditions were crossed in a 4×2 factorial design.

Subjects' decisions and their expectations about others' decisions were the two dependent variables of interest.

Table 1
Payoff Matrix

Payoff to X	Number choosing		Payoff to O
	X	O	
	Loss condition		
—	0	8	2.50
10.50	1	7	1.00
9.00	2	6	−.50
7.50	3	5	−2.00
6.00	4	4	−3.50
4.50	5	3	−5.00
3.00	6	2	−6.50
1.50	7	1	−8.00
.00	8	0	—
	No-loss condition		
—	0	8	2.50
10.50	1	7	1.00
9.00	2	6	0
7.50	3	5	0
6.00	4	4	0
4.50	5	3	0
3.00	6	2	0
1.50	7	1	0
.00	8	0	—

Experiment 1

Method

Subjects

Subjects were recruited from newspaper advertisements asking for groups of four friends. Eight such groups were scheduled for each time, so that one member from each "friendship group" could participate in separate "decision-making groups" of eight strangers. Since scheduled groups occasionally did not show up, a total of 284 subjects were run in 40 decision-making groups, rather than the anticipated 320.

Friendship Groups

Friendship groups met initially with an experimenter who informed them that each person would go to a different decision group where she or he would make a decision with seven other people. The four friends would then return to their friendship group, pool their earnings, and divide them equally among themselves. If the total were negative, no member of the friendship group would receive anything (although people who did not win at least $2.00 were contacted later and paid from $1.00 to $2.50 depending on their initial earnings). One member from each friendship group was sent to each of the four communication conditions. Two went to groups in which it was possible to lose money, two to groups in which negative payoffs

were truncated at zero. Thus, the eight groups of four friends separated and formed four groups of eight strangers to play the commons dilemma game.

Decision-making Groups

Payoff matrices were determined according to the rule that each member of the decision group would earn $2.50 for a cooperative choice (O) or $12.00 for a defecting choice (X). All group members were fined $1.50 for each person in the group who chose X.

When fewer than eight friendship groups showed up for the experiment, the defectors' payoff was reduced by an appropriate amount: to $10.50 for seven-person groups, $9.00 for six-person groups, etc.

Two payoff conditions were included in the experiment. In the loss condition, payoff to a cooperator was reduced by $1.50 for every defector in the group; in the no-loss condition, cooperators' negative payoffs were truncated at zero. Table 1 indicates all possible outcomes to decision makers under these two conditions.

Opportunity for communication was manipulated in four communication conditions. In the no-communication condition, (N) subjects were not permitted to talk to each other. Subjects in this condition worked silently for 10 minutes on an irrelevant task (estimating the percentage of people at certain income levels in Eugene, Oregon, in the United States, etc.) before making their decisions. In the irrelevant-communication condition, (I) subjects discussed the same irrelevant topic for 10 minutes before making their decisions. In the relevant-communication condition, (C) subjects discussed the commons dilemma decision for 10 minutes before making their decisions. They were not, however, permitted to take a roll call. In the communication-plus-vote condition, (C + V) subjects' 10-minute discussion of the commons dilemma decision ended in a roll call—a nonbinding declaration of intended decision.

The two loss conditions were crossed with the four communication conditions in a 2 × 4 factorial design. Five groups were run in each condition.

Procedure

Instructions were read to the decision groups as follows:

I would like to explain the decision-making task in which you will now be participating. To insure that all of our subjects receive exactly the same information, I will have to read the instructions. Please listen carefully. I can answer questions at the end.

This table (Table 1) indicates the possible consequences of the decision each of you will be asked to make. You must decide whether to choose an X or an O. You will have to mark an X or an O on the card in private. If you choose an O, you will earn $2.50 minus a $1.50 fine for every person who chooses X. If you choose X,

BEHAVIOR, COMMUNICATION, AND ASSUMPTIONS   5

you will earn $2.50 plus $9.50 minus $1.50 fine for each person, including yourself, who chooses X. (However, as you can see, your payoffs do not go below zero.) By looking at the first row, for example, you can see that if seven of you choose O and one of you chooses X, then those choosing O will earn $1.00 and the person choosing X will earn $10.50.

You will write your code number and decision on the top of the sheet in your envelope. Your decision will be totally private and none of the other participants in this group will know what you decided. You will each be paid and dismissed separately. On the sheet please indicate what decision you believe each other person here to be making. Beside the code number of each person, mark X or O to indicate the choice you believe that person to be making. Then indicate your confidence level for each judgment with a number from 50 to 100, with 100 indicating complete confidence. If you are just guessing, the probability is 50–50 that you are correct, so you should mark 50 if you have no confidence at all in your predictions. Questions?

Once questions had been answered and group members understood the decision, they proceeded to 10 minutes of discussion or interpolated task, depending on the communication condition. When the 10 minutes were up, subjects made their decisions and predictions of other group members' decisions. Once outcomes had been determined, subjects returned to their friendship groups where they divided any net gain between themselves.

Results

Because the groups differed in size, results of defection and predicted defection are presented in percentages. Table 2 shows the average proportion of defectors in each of the eight conditions.

An analysis of variance based on arc sine transformations of the proportions (where the *group* is the unit of analysis) indicates that the effect of communication is extremely significant, $F(3, 32) = 9.36$, $p < .001$. The loss manipulation was not only insignificant, but accounted for virtually no variance as did the Communication × Loss interaction. As can be seen from Table 2, there is a great deal more defection when subjects cannot communicate about the dilemma, even if they interact for 10 minutes about an irrelevant topic. Moreover, the structured communication with the vote did not elicit any more cooperation than did the unstructured communication (73% versus 72% on the average), *despite the fact that every subject*

Table 2
Proportion of Subjects Defecting

	Condition			
Condition	No communication	Irrelevant communication	Unrestricted communication	Communication plus vote
Loss	.73	.65	.26	.16
No loss	.67	.70	.30	.42

in the structured communication condition announced an intention to cooperate.

The possible loss manipulation was not only ineffective in eliciting differential cooperation, it was ineffective in eliciting differential predictions about others' behavior as well. In the results about such prediction, potential loss will therefore not be included as a variable. What will be included is the variable concerning whether the individual making the prediction is a cooperator or a defector.

The correlation between the proportion of defections the subject predicted (not including himself or herself) and whether the subject actually defected was .60 ($p < .001$). Table 3 presents the average proportion of predicted defection on the part of *other* subjects made by defectors and cooperators in the four different communication conditions (collapsed across loss versus no loss). An analysis of variance—again on these proportions transformed to arc sines, and again with the group as the unit of analysis—revealed two strong main effects, one for communication condition and one for defectors versus cooperators.[2] Overall, more defection is predicted when people cannot communicate, $F(3, 31) = 9.86$, $p < .001$, and defectors predict almost four times as much defection as do cooperators, $F(1, 31) = 35.93$, $p < .001$). When the subject's own behavior is included in the prediction (i.e., the defector predicts himself or herself to defect and the cooperator to cooperate), the overall predic-

---

[2] Some groups had to be omitted because they consisted entirely of cooperators or defectors; hence the number of degrees of freedom is attenuated to 31. Analyses were also performed using the individuals as the unit of analysis; the conclusions were virtually identical.

Table 3
Proportion of Subjects Predicted to Defect (Subjects not Included)

| | Condition | | | | |
| | No communication | Irrelevant communication | Unrestricted communication | Communication plus vote | Overall |
Subject					
Defectors	.65	.61	.29	.30	.54
Cooperators	.35	.42	.08	.04	.16

tions become even more discrepant—.60 versus .13. The analysis of variance shows virtually identical results; neither it nor the proportions with the subjects included in each condition are presented here. In the results that follow, all predictions do not include the subjects themselves.

Table 4 presents the proportion of correct predictions made by defectors and cooperators in the four conditions. Again, the analysis of variance was based on the arc sine transformations of these proportions with the group as the unit of analysis.

Subjects overall are more accurate at predicting in the communications conditions, $F(3, 31) = 11.30$, $p < .001$, which is not exactly surprising.

The overall accuracy of each subject as measured by proportion correct is directly affected by the match between the subject's base-rate prediction of defection and the actual base rate of defection. If, for example, a subject predicted r percentage of defection and p occurred, then even if the predictions were *noncontingent*—that is, if the subject could not accurately predict which subjects would defect and which wouldn't—the expected proportion of correct predictions would be $rp + (1 - r) (1 - p)$. Each subject's actual proportion of correct predictions was corrected for this base-rate accuracy, and the *residuals* subjected to an analysis of condition by defection. These residual scores are tiny, averaging .03, but significant, $F(1, 248) = 8.69$, $p < .01$.

The data were analyzed for sex differences. Across conditions, there were no significant sex differences in subjects' decisions, $\chi^2(1) = 1.78$, $p > .10$.

Finally, the data were analyzed for differ-

ences in defection as a function of group size. Due to no-shows, there were groups of size 5 ($n = 12$), size 6 ($n = 5$), size 7 ($n = 10$), and size 8 ($n = 13$); the overall proportion of defectors was .46, .30, .52, and .54, respectively. The data were subjected to a 4×2 analysis of variance with unequal cells (Winer, 1962, p. 242) where the two levels of the second factor were defined by collapsing conditions N and I (which elicited little cooperation) and C and C + V (which elicited much). The effect of group size on proportion of defection was nill, $F(3, 32) = 1.50$, as was the interaction of group size by condition, $F(3, 32) = 1.47$.[3]

Discussion

It is not surprising that when people can communicate, they can solve a dilemma better than when they cannot. Simply getting to know other people did not make much of a difference, at least in the 10-minute discussion of the irrelevant-communication condition. Whether subjects in more contact or longer lasting groups would be better able to elicit implicit cooperation is an open question. For reasons described later in this discussion, that question may remain unanswered. At any rate, groups of strangers can in fact elicit cooperative behavior from each other if they are permitted to communicate about the dilemma for 10 minutes. Even in these groups, however, many people lied about their intentions; although every vote was

---

[3] A linear trend analysis using coefficients -3, -1, $+1$, $+3$ and the same error term used in the Winer analysis revealed even less evidence for a size effect. The F value was 1.44. (See Hays, 1973, p. 587, for a description of such a trend analysis.)

Table 4
Proportion of Subjects Correctly Predicted to Defect (Subjects not Included)

| | Condition | | | | |
| | No communication | Irrelevant communication | Unrestricted communication | Communication plus vote | Overall |
Subject					
Defectors	.56	.57	.67	.74	.60
Cooperators	.35	.54	.73	.76	.66

unanimous in favor of cooperating, there was only a single group in which all people actually cooperated. Nevertheless, the overall rate of cooperation in communicating groups was about 75%. (Interestingly enough, if the rate in each group was 75%, each cooperator would end up with no money or losing 50¢).

A much more striking finding concerns the expectations about others' behavior. Defectors predict approximately four times as much defection as do cooperators. The present study is purely correlational, so it is not possible to determine the degree to which perception of others' intentions influences the decision to cooperate or defect and the degree to which such a decision influences judgment about other peoples' behavior. Experiment 2 assesses the degree of such influence by comparing the judgments of people who are actually making the decisions in such groups with the judgments of observers.

The data concerning the prediction of defection indicate that people can accurately predict overall defection and even the sources of defection. But the prediction of the individual source—when corrected for base rate—is pretty feeble.

One of the most significant aspects of this study, however, did not show up in the data analysis. It is the extreme seriousness with which the subjects take the problems. Comments such as, "If you defect on the rest of us, you're going to have to live with it the rest of your life," were not at all uncommon. Nor was it unusual for people to wish to leave the experimental building by the back door, to claim that they did not wish to see the "sons of bitches" who doublecrossed them, to become extremely angry at other

subjects, or to become tearful. For example, one subject just assumed that everyone else would cooperate in the no-communication condition, and she ended up losing $8.00 which matched the amount of money her friends had won. She was extremely upset, wishing to see neither the other members of the decision group, nor her friends. We are concerned that her experience may have had a very negative effect on her expectations about other people (although, alas, making her more realistic).

The affect level was so high that we are unwilling to run any intact groups because of the effect the game might have on the members' feelings about each other. The affect level also mitigates against examining choice visibility. In pretesting, we did run one group in which choices were made public. The three defectors were the target of a great deal of hostility ("You have no idea how much you alienate me!" one cooperator shouted before storming out of the room); they remained after the experiment until all the cooperators were presumably long gone. With the exception of the one cooperator who left hurriedly, the experimenters calmed all cooperators who were upset. There was, however, no general "debriefing" procedure because there was no deception in the experiment.[4]

Experiment 2

The purposes of Experiment 2 were to replicate the findings of Experiment 1 and

---

[4] But subjects who received less than $2.00 for participation were contacted later and paid handsomely (up to $2.00) for filling out a brief questionnaire.

8 R. DAWES, J. McTAVISH, AND H. SHAKLEE

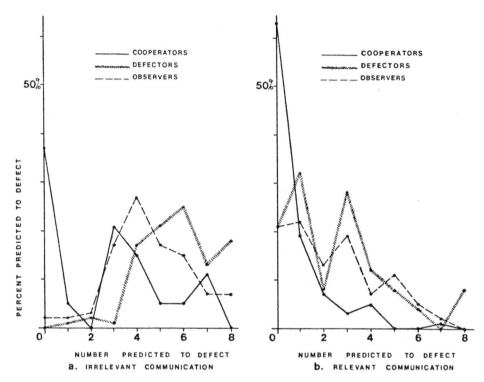

Figure 1. Predictions of participant defectors, participant cooperators, and observers.

to explore further the source of the high correlation between subjects' own behavior and their expectations about others. Kelley and Stahelski (1970) attributed similar differences between cooperators and defectors in a prisoner's dilemma to stable differences in world view. According to them, competitive people elicit competition from both cooperative and competitive people. Their consistent experience is that people are competitive, leading to a generalized expectancy that others are like themselves. Cooperators' experience is differentiated according to the behavior of others. Cooperative people meet with cooperation from other cooperators and competition from competitive people, resulting in a belief that others are heterogeneous with respect to the competitive dimension. According to this theory, then, defectors come to the experiment with a pre-

disposition to expect others to behave similarly; cooperative people have no such consistent expectation.

Our interest was in the alternative possibility that the decision itself was affecting subjects' expectations about others. A couple of explanations were plausible. One source may be motivational. Subjects may feel the need to justify their decision—defectors in order to assuage possible guilt over their decision, cooperators to avoid feeling duped. A second source is cognitive. Given the belief that people tend to behave similarly in the same situation, a subject who decides to cooperate or to defect may have a rational basis for believing others will do likewise. Whichever the source, the subjects' decisions themselves would lead them to believe that others' decisions would be like theirs.

The expectation, then, is that predictions

of people who actually make the decision will be different from those of people who observe the same process but make no decision. Participant cooperators should expect more cooperation; participant defectors should expect defection, if the decision is affecting participants' expectations. The observers who make no decision should not be similarly biased. Since participants' decisions would distort cooperators' and defectors' predictions in opposite directions, the variance of all participants' predictions should be greater than the variance of observers' predictions.

On the other hand, if Kelley and Stahelski are correct, observers and participants should have similar world views and should have the same expectations about others' decisions. Thus, the variance of predictions should be roughly the same for participants and observers, since the proportion of potential cooperators and defectors should be the same in each group (given, of course, random assignment to the role of participant and observer).

Method

The number of conditions in Experiment 2 was reduced to two. Because potential money loss had no effect in Experiment 1, all losses were truncated at zero. Further, because there was no difference between the no-communication and irrelevant-communication conditions and between the communication and communication-plus-vote conditions, only an irrelevant-communication condition and a relevant-communication condition were run— with subjects in the relevant one being free to have a roll call vote or not, depending upon the group interaction. Further, there was no need to use "friendship groups" because there was no necessity of having potential monetary loss.

Subjects

Subjects were recruited from newspaper ads, and 16 were scheduled for each session: 8 were to be assigned to be participants, the remaining 8 as observers who viewed the interaction through a one-way mirror. Because subjects sometimes failed to appear at the experiment, 8 were randomly chosen to be participants with the remainder observers. The result was that there were 160 participants and 149 observers, 10 groups being run in the irrelevant-communication condition and 10 in the relevant-communication condition. Because the previous results have indicated no effect of sex, no attempt was made to balance men and women equally in the roles of participant and observer.

Procedure

Procedure for decision groups was identical to that of the corresponding conditions in Experiment 1. Instructions to observers were as follows:

> You will be observing a decision-making task in which the participants must individually decide between two choices: X and O. The outcome of the individuals in the group depends on the number of individuals choosing X and O. [Copies of the matrix and prediction sheets are distributed.] This will also be explained to the participants and should be clear to you. Before the participants make their decisions, you will have an opportunity to observe a 10-minute discussion. Your task will be to predict what each individual in the group will choose: either X or O. In addition, we will ask you to indicate your confidence level for each prediction with a number from 50 to 100, with 100 indicating complete confidence. If you are just guessing, the probability is 50–50 that you are correct, so you should mark 50 if you have no confidence at all in your predictions. Please make these predictions and confidence ratings individually, without consulting one another. In addition, please refrain from commenting about the group as you observe. I will now instruct the decision-making group and will return shortly. Questions?

Observers were placed behind a one-way mirror and made their predictions at the same time as the participants made their predictions and decisions.

Results

The difference between irrelevant-communication and relevant-communication was replicated. In the irrelevant-communication condition, 76% of the subjects defected, while in the relevant communication only 31% did so. Since all groups contained eight people, a one-way analysis of variance was performed on the number of defectors in the two conditions, the groups themselves again being the unit of analysis. The results were significant, $F(1, 18) = 41.51, p < .001$. (Only one group in the irrelevant-communication condition had fewer defectors than did any of the groups in the relevant condition.)

Analysis of sex differences in subjects' decisions showed that females were more likely to cooperate than were males $\chi^2(1) = 3.6$, $p < .10$. Considering the decisions within each condition, this sex difference was strong in the relevant-communication condition χ^2

$(1) = 7.6$, $p < .01$, but nonexistent in the irrelevant-communication condition.[5]

All the other effects for participants replicated. As before, there is more predicted defection in the irrelevant-communication condition (.53 vs. .20; $F(1, 16) = 16.65$, $p < .001$), and defectors predict more defection than do cooperators (.56 vs. .18; $F(1, 16) = 37.86$, $p < .001$).

Also, as before, there is a higher proportion of correct predictions in the relevant-communication condition than in the irrelevant-communication condition, but the result is not significant, $F(1, 16) = 1.72$. The findings of positive residual accuracy, however, was not replicated; in fact, the residual accuracy was negative, averaging $-.02$.

Figure 1 presents the number of defections predicted by cooperators, defectors, and observers, broken down by conditions. In order to make the predictions of participants and observers comparable, each participant was assumed to have made an (implicit) prediction for himself or herself; in addition, each observer was randomly paired with a participant, and the prediction of the observer for that participant was changed if it was incorrect. Thus, the observers and participants were put in the same situation—guessing about seven of the choices and knowing about one.[6] The variance of predictions for the participants was 7.50, whereas that for the observers was 4.60; for testing the null hypothesis of equal variance, $F(159, 148) = 1.63$, $p < .01$. In the irrelevant-communication condition, the variances are 5.24 for participants and 3.20 for observers, $F(79, 75) = 1.64$, $p < .05$, while in the relevant-communication condition the respective variances were 3.84 and 3.65, $F(79, 72) = 1.05$, *ns*.

Discussion

The most important finding of this experiment was that having to make the cooperative or defective choice apparently did affect the estimates of what other people would do, as well as vice versa. Thus, one's choices in such a dilemma situation not only reflect beliefs about others, but also affect these beliefs. There are a number of possible explanations.

First, the effect may be pure rationalization. Having decided to cooperate or defect, the group member may attempt to justify the choice by his or her estimates of what others will do. Clearly, a cooperative choice is not very wise if any other people are going to defect, while a defecting choice may be considered downright immoral if most other people cooperate. Thus, the group member may have a motivational reason for believing that other people will behave in a similar manner; specifically, such a belief helps the individual maintain an image of being a rational, moral person.

Second, there may be two closely related cognitive reasons for the behavior to affect the belief. Individuals may decide to use their own behavior as information about what other people would do; after all, if people from similar cultures tend to behave in similar ways in similar situations, and if I do this, it follows that my peers may do so also. In addition, there is the possibility that as I make up my mind to defect or cooperate, the reasons leading to the choice I finally make become more salient, while those leading to the other choice become less so. Then, when attempting to evaluate what other people will do, I see compelling reasons for

---

[5] Subsequent research—not supported here supports the findings of Experiment 1; we have never been able to replicate the sex effect.

[6] The rationale for this procedure may best be explained by example. Suppose that four of the eight group members defect. A cooperator is facing seven other group members, of whom four (57%) defect; a defector is facing seven other group members, of whom three (43%) defect; an observer is facing eight group members of whom four (50%) defect. By including the participants' own choice in the predictions, cooperators, defectors, and observers are all facing the same situation—eight group members of whom four defect. Such an inclusion, however, means that for the participants, one of the "predictions" (of their own behavior) is not a guess but a certainty. To make the choices of the observers strictly comparable to the participants, one of their predictions was turned into a certainty by randomly pairing them with a group member and changing the predictions of that group member if it were wrong. Many other means of achieving comparability were considered over a 4-month period, and all were rejected. The reasons for such rejection would be too lengthy to detail here.

doing what I do and less compelling ones for doing the opposite.

As suggested by our colleague, David Messick (Note 1), one such reason may involve the ethical implication of the choice—that when people perceive an ethical dimension or component in a particular social choice, they may have a tendency to assume that other people will have the same perception. (For example, the individual who perceives a particular social choice in terms of a fundamental religious struggle between good and evil tends to believe that others would view it along the same dimension and that the atheist or agnostic who denies such a perception is simply lying or deluding himself.) Thus, the act of making a choice considered ethical or rational may define the situation for the chooser as one requiring ethicality or rationality and hence bias the chooser to believe that others will behave in a similar ethical or rational manner.

Reference Note

1. Messick, D. Personal communication, 1975.

References

Caldwell, M. Communication and sex effects in a five-person Prisoner's Dilemma Game. *Journal of Personality and Social Psychology,* 1976, *33,* 273–280.

Dawes, R. M. Formal models of dilemmas in social decision making. In M. Kaplan & S. Schwartz (Eds.), *Human judgment and decision processes: Formal and mathematical approaches.* New York: Academic Press, 1975.

Deutsch, M. The effect of motivational orientation upon trust and suspicion. *Human Relations,* 1960, *13,* 123–139.

Hamburger, H. N-person prisoner's dilemmas. *Journal of Mathematical Sociology,* 1973, *3,* 27–48.

Hardin, G. The tragedy of the commons. *Science,* 1968, *162,* 1243–1248.

Hays, W. L. *Statistics for the social scientist* (2nd ed.). New York: Holt, Reinhart & Winston, 1973.

Jerdee, T. H., & Rosen, B. Effects of opportunity to communicate and visibility of individual decisions on behavior in the common interest. *Journal of Applied Psychology,* 1974, *59,* 712–716.

Kelley, H. H., & Grzelak, J. Conflict between individual and common interest in an *n*-person relationship. *Journal of Personality and Social Psychology,* 1972, *21,* 190–197.

Kelley, H. H., & Stahelski, A. V. Social interaction basis of cooperators' and competitors' beliefs about others. *Journal of Personality and Social Psychology,* 1970, *16,* 66–91.

Loomis, J. Communication: The development of trust and cooperative behavior. *Human Relations,* 1959, *12,* 305–315.

Luce, R. D., & Raiffa, H. *Games and decision: Introduction and critical survey.* London: Wiley, 1957.

Messick, D. M. To join or not to join: An approach to the unionization decision. *Organizational Behavior and Human Performance,* 1973, *10,* 145–156.

Radlow, R., & Weidner, M. Unenforced commitments in "cooperative" and "noncooperative" non-constant-sum games. *Journal of Conflict Resolution,* 1966, *10,* 497–505.

Swensson, R. Cooperation in a Prisoner's Dilemma Game: I. The effects of asymmetric payoff information and explicit communication. *Behavioral Science,* 1967, *12,* 314–322.

Winer, B. J. *Statistical principles in experimental design.* New York: McGraw-Hill, 1962.

Wichman, H. Effects of communication on cooperation in a 2-person game. In L. Wrightsman, J. O'Connor, & N. Baker (Eds.), *Cooperation and competition.* Belmont, Calif.: Brooks/Cole, 1972.

Received November 18, 1976 ∎

[2]

Ann. Rev. Psychol. 1980. 31:169–93

SOCIAL DILEMMAS

Robyn M. Dawes[1]

Department of Psychology, University of Oregon, Eugene, Oregon 97403

CONTENTS

Interest in social dilemmas—particularly those resulting from overpopulation, resource depletion, and pollution—has grown dramatically in the past 10 years among humanists, scientists, and philosophers. Such dilemmas are defined by two simple properties: (*a*) each individual receives a higher payoff for a socially defecting choice (e.g. having additional children, using all the energy available, polluting his or her neighbors) than for a socially cooperative choice, no matter what the other individuals in society do, but (*b*) all individuals are better off if all cooperate than if all defect. While

[1]This paper was written while I was a James McKeen Cattel Sabbatical Fellow at the Research Center for Group Dynamics at the Institute for Social Research at the University of Michigan and at the psychology department there. I thank these institutions for their assistance and especially all my friends there who helped.

0066-4308/80/0201-0169$01.00

many thinkers have simply pointed out that our most pressing societal problems result from such dilemmas, most have addressed themselves to the question of how to get people to cooperate. Answers have ranged from imposition of a dictatorship (Leviathan) to "mutual coercion mutually agreed upon," to appeals to conscience.

This paper reviews the structure and ubiquity of social dilemma problems, outlines proposed "solutions," and then surveys the contributions of psychologists who have studied dilemma behavior in the context of N-person games ($N > 2$). The hypothesis that follows from this survey and review is that there are two crucial factors that lead people to cooperate in a social dilemma situation. First, people must "think about" and come to understand the nature of the dilemma, so that moral, normative, and altruistic concerns as well as external payoffs can influence behavior. Second, people must have some reason for believing that others will not defect, for while the difference in payoffs may always favor defection no matter what others do, the absolute payoff is higher if others cooperate than if they don't. The efficacy of both factors—and indeed the possibility of cooperative behavior at all in a dilemma situation—is based upon rejecting the principle of "nonsatiety of economic greed" as an axiom of actual human behavior. And it is rejected.

INTRODUCTION TO THE LOGIC OF SOCIAL DILEMMAS

Social dilemmas are characterized by two properties: (a) the social payoff to each individual for defecting behavior is higher than the payoff for cooperative behavior, regardless of what the other society members do, yet (b) all individuals in the society receive a lower payoff if all defect than if all cooperate.

Examples abound. People asked to keep their thermostats low to conserve energy are being asked to suffer from the cold without appreciably conserving the fuel supply by their individual sacrifices; yet if all keep their thermostats high, all may run out of fuel and freeze. During pollution alerts in Eugene, Oregon, residents are asked to ride bicycles or walk rather than to drive their cars. But each person is better off driving, because his or her car's contribution to the pollution problem is negligible, while a choice to bicycle or walk yields the payoff of the drivers' exhausts. Yet all the residents are worse off driving their cars and maintaining the pollution than they would be if all bicycled or walked. Soldiers who fight in a large battle can reasonably conclude that no matter what their comrades do they personally are better off taking no chances; yet if no one takes chances, the result will be a rout and slaughter worse for all the soldiers than is taking chances. Or consider the position of a wage earner who is asked to use restraint in his or her salary demands. Doing so will hurt him or her and have a minute effect on the overall rate of inflation; yet if all fail to exercise restraint, the result is runaway inflation from which all will suffer. Women in India will almost certainly outlive their husbands, and for the vast majority who can't work, their only source of support in their old age is their male sons. Thus each individual woman achieves the highest social payoff by having as many children as possible. Yet the resulting overpopulation makes a social security or old-age benefit system impossible, so that all the women are worse off than they would have been if they had all practiced restraint in having children. Untenured assistant professors are best off publishing every article possible, no matter how mediocre or in how obscure a journal. (The deans' committees never actually read articles.) Yet the result is an explosion of dubious information and an expectation that anyone worthwhile will have published 10 or 15 articles within 5 years of obtaining a PhD, a result from which we all suffer (except those of us who own paper pulp mills).

Some of these examples come from the three crucial problems of the modern world: resource depletion, pollution, and overpopulation. In most societies, it is to each individual's advantage to use as much energy, to pollute as much, and to have as many children as possible.[2] (This statement should not be interpreted as meaning that these three phenomena are independent—far from it.) Yet the result is to exceed the "carrying capacity" (Hardin 1976) of "spaceship earth," an excess from which all people suffer, or will suffer eventually. These problems have arisen, of course, because the checks on energy use, pollution, and population that existed until a hundred years or so ago have been all but destroyed by modern technology—mainly industrial and medical. And use of new energy sources or new agricultural techniques for increasing harvests often exacerbate the problems (see Wade 1974a,b). While many societies throughout history have faced their members with social dilemmas, it is these dilemmas that are particularly global and pressing that have attracted the most attention among social thinkers (from an extraordinarily wide variety of fields).

Perhaps the most influential article published recently was Garrett Hardin's "Tragedy of the Commons," which appeared in *Science* in 1968. In it Hardin argued that modern humanity as the result of the ability to overpopulate and overuse resources faces a problem analogous to that faced by herdsmen using a common pasture (1968, p. 1244).

---

[2]People in affluent or in Communist societies do not contribute to world overpopulation, but in most societies in the world the payoff remains greatest for having as many children as possible.

As a rational being, each herdsman seeks to maximize his gain. Explicitly or implicitly, more or less consciously he asks, "What is the utility to *me* of adding one more animal to my herd?" This utility has one negative and one positive component.

   1. The positive component is a function of the increment of one animal. Since the herdsman receives all the proceeds from the sale of the additional animal, the positive utility is nearly +1.

   2. The negative component is a function of the additional overgrazing created by one more animal. Since, however, the effects of overgrazing are shared by all the herdsmen, the negative utility for any particular decision-making herdsman is only a fraction of −1.

   Adding together the component partial utilities, the rational herdsman concludes that the only sensible course for him to pursue is to add another animal to his herd. And another; and another ... But this is the conclusion reached by every rational herdsman sharing the commons. Therein is the tragedy. Each man is locked into a system that compels him to increase his herd without limit—in a world that is limited. Ruin is the destination toward which all men rush, each pursuing his own best interest in a society that believes in the freedom of the commons.[3,4]

The gain-to-self harm-spread-out situation does indeed result in a social dilemma, although not all social dilemmas have that precise form (Dawes 1975).

Contrast Hardin's analysis of herdsmen rushing toward their own destruction with Adam Smith's (1776, 1976) analysis of the individual worker's unintended beneficence in a laissez-faire capitalistic society.

It is not from the benevolence of the butcher, the brewer, or the baker, that we expect our dinner, but from their regard to their own interest. We address ourselves, not to their humanity but to their self-love, and never talk to them of our own necessities but of their advantages (Book 1, p. 18).

As every individual, therefore, endeavors as much as he can both to employ his capital in the support of domestic industry, and so to direct that industry that its produce may be of the greatest value; every individual necessarily labors to render the annual revenue of the society as great as he can ... By preferring the support of domestic to that of foreign industry, he intends his own security; and by directing that industry in such a manner as its produce may be for the greatest value, he intends only his own gain, and he is in this, as in many other cases, led by an invisible hand to promote an end which was no part of his intention (Book 4, p. 477).

[3]Actually, the negative payoff must be more negative than −1 for a true dilemma to exist. Hardin clearly implies a greater value when he discusses the destruction of the commons. If, for example, the commons can maintain 10,000 pounds of cattle when 10 1000-pound bulls are grazed on it, but only 9900 pounds when 11 bulls are grazed, then the herdsman who introduces an additional bull has two 900-pound bulls—a gain of 800 pounds over one 1000-pound one—while the total wealth of the commons has decreased by 100 pounds.

[4]Hardin uses the term "utility" to refer to social economic payoff. As will be emphasized in the next section of this article, there may be other utilities that determine behavior, so it does not follow from his analysis that "freedom in a commons brings ruin to all" (1968, p. 1244).

Hardin and Smith are not social theorists with diametrically opposed views about the effects of self-interested behavior. Rather, they are discussing different situations. Hardin's is a dilemma situation in which the external consequences of each herdsman's trying to maximize his profits are negative, and the negative consequences outweigh the positive ones to him. [Hardin specifically "exorcises" Smith's "invisible hand" in resolving population problems (p. 1244).] Smith's situation is a nondilemma one, in which maximizing individual profit does not hurt others more than it benefits the individual; in fact, it helps them. This difference is captured in the economic concept of an *externality* (Buchanan 1971, p. 7): "we can define an externality as being present whenever the behavior of a person affects the situation of other persons without the explicit agreement of that person or persons." In Hardin's commons the externalities are negative and greater than the individual's payoffs; in Smith's Scotland they are positive.

To define social dilemmas in terms of magnitudes of externalities would, however, involve interpersonal comparisons of payoffs. In most cases such a comparison is simple, but not in all. For example, it is difficult to compare the drivers' positive payoffs for driving during a pollution alert to the bike riders' negative payoffs for breathing polluted air. In contrast, the definition of a social dilemma proposed at the beginning of this paper involves payoff comparison only *within* an individual (who receives a ·higher payoff for defecting but whose payoff for universal defection is lower than that for universal cooperation). It is enough to note that most economic writing about negative externalities that has come to my attention has in fact been about dilemma situations.

Finally, Platt's (1973) concept of *social traps* is closely related to the concept of a dilemma. He defines a social trap as occurring when a behavior that results in immediate reward leads to long-term punishment. For example, many observers have noted that many modern technological advances may be traps; e.g. the good effects of DDT usage were immediately evident, while the disastrous effects took years to ascertain. Moreover, even when the long-term ill effects are known at the beginning, they may be "time discounted." ("If we're still around, we'll jump off that bridge when we come to it.") On an individual level, cigarette smoking, overeating, and excessive alcohol ingestion are traps. On the social level, most social dilemmas are social traps. But again not all—for dilemmas exist in which even defecting behavior is punished (because enough other people are bound to defect)—although not as badly as cooperative behavior would be. Further, not all social dilemmas involve a time lag.

We return then to the original definition of a social dilemma. Each individual receives a higher payoff for a socially defecting choice than for a socially cooperative one, yet all individuals have a higher payoff if all cooperate than if all defect. All the examples discussed earlier meet these two conditions.

Given the ubiquity of social dilemmas—and the global importance of some of them—the question arises of how individuals and societies can deal with them. One answer is that they can't. The role of the social theorist is to point out where dilemmas exist and then to watch everyone defect—verifying the hypothesis that a social dilemma indeed is there. A far more common answer has been to propose mechanisms by which cooperation may be engendered in people facing social dilemmas.

PROPOSALS FOR ELICITING COOPERATIVE BEHAVIOR

Changing the Payoffs

Social dilemmas are defined in terms of the social payoff structure. The simplest proposal for eliciting cooperative behavior is to change that structure. That is, when analysis reveals that a social dilemma exists, an effort can be made to obliterate it by appropriate choices of rewards and punishments for cooperative and defecting behavior respectively. Then it is no longer a social dilemma.

The simplicity of this approach is appealing until we ask who will change the payoffs and how. The almost universal answer to the first question is government, and—somewhat surprisingly given the cultural background of the writers—the most common answer to the second question is: through coercion. Thus, for example, Hardin (1968, p. 1247) advocates "mutual coercion mutually agreed upon," and Ophuls (1977) and Heilbroner (1974) advocate coercion from an authoritarian government in order to avoid the most pressing social dilemmas. These solutions are essentially the same as Hobbes's (1651) Leviathan, constructed to avoid the social dilemma of the "warre of all against all." But there is *empirical* evidence that those societies where people are best off—currently at any rate—are those whose governments correspond least to Hobbes's authoritarian Leviathan (Orbell & Rutherford 1973). The counterargument (Robertson 1974) is that these societies are those that have been fortunate enough to have ample natural resources, or to have evolved from a more authoritarian state originating at a time when pressing social dilemmas did in fact exist. And if new dilemmas—in the form of overpopulation, pollution, and energy depletion —come as expected, Leviathan will again be necessary.

Most of us would prefer reward to coercion, although there are those who are willing to pay complex and expensive governmental bureaucracies to make sure that only the "deserving" achieve governmental rewards, rather than to allow "giveaways." The problem with both reward and coercion, however, is that they are very costly. The society faced with the potential dilemma must deplete its resources either to reward those tempted to defect, or to establish a policing authority that is sufficiently effective that those tempted will not dare do so. This depletion is paid by some or all society members. In effect, the dilemma has been turned into a new situation where everyone must cooperate but where the payoffs to everyone are less than they would be if everyone were to cooperate freely in the original situation. Sometimes, in fact, it is not even possible to avoid a dilemma by reward or coercion, because the costs of rewarding people for cooperating or effectively coercing them to do so exceed the gain the society derives from having everyone cooperate rather than defect.

Moreover, societal change in the payoffs by introducing rewards and punishments can be terribly inefficient. Consider, for example, the worker on a collective farm whose productivity is used in part to pay for a police agent whose job is to make sure that that worker does not sell the farm produce privately. Not only does that result in wasted productivity of the worker, but this police agent himself could instead be doing something productive for the society—such as working on the farm. Finally, coercive systems—and some governmental reward systems—apparently create, or at least exacerbate, a motivation to get around the rules.

From Payoffs to Utilities

Many of us would not rob a bank, even if we knew that we could get away with it, and even if we could be assured that none of our friends or neighbors would know. Many of us give money to public television or to the United Fund, even though we know that our paltry contribution will make no difference in terms of the services rendered. Most of us take the trouble to vote, even though we know that the probability that an election will be decided by a single ballot is effectively zero. And some couples desiring a large family do in fact limit its size not out of desire but out of a belief that it is not moral to have too many children.

All these behaviors involve rejecting a payoff that is larger for one that is smaller. The potential bank robbers could be wealthy, the contributors could save their money, the voters could save themselves inconvenience, and the couples who want children could have them. The point is that the people making these decisions have *utilities* that determine their behavior, utilities associated with aspects of their behavior other than the external payoffs they would receive. The question of whether all behavior is "ultimately selfish" because it reflects *some* utilities is beside the point, just as the question of whether such selfishness is a primary human motivator is irrelevant to the question of whether society members facing a dilemma are doomed to defect. The point is that if a person chooses action A over action B, then A must (by definition) have greater utility; if simultaneously action B provides a higher social payoff in terms of economic benefits or security, then (again by definition) other utilities must be guiding the individual's choice. The problem is to assess what these utilities are and to study their role in encouraging cooperative behavior.

Thus it is possible to have a social dilemma represented by a payoff structure and yet have people cooperate. The reason would be that the individuals' utilities do not present them with a dilemma. The utilities most important in eliciting cooperation are those associated with altruism, following social norms, and obeying dictates of conscience. These will be considered in turn.

ALTRUISM   It is a demonstrable fact that people take account of others' payoffs as well as of their own in reaching decisions. Good Samaritans exist. (Whether this behavior is "ultimately selfish" in light of some hope of Heaven is again irrelevant.) Few of us would accept $500 with nothing for our friend in lieu of $498 for each of us. The importance of payoffs to others has been demonstrated experimentally by Messick and McClintock (Messick & McClintock 1968, Messick 1969, McClintock et al 1973)—albeit in some competitive experimental contexts where subjects apparently wish to minimize the payoffs to others, or at least to maximize the discrepancy between own and others' payoffs (Messick & Thorngate 1967).

The question is whether altruism can lead to cooperative behavior in the face of a social dilemma. If concern for others' payoffs is merely a *tactical* consideration for obtaining future rewards from that other, then utility for behaving altruistically cannot be counted upon as a factor that could outweigh external social payoffs. In most social dilemmas, individuals must behave privately, and the problem occurs because the social outcome results from the aggregate social behavior across a large number of people who do *not* interact. Thus, few people would be motivated to cooperate by tactical altruism.

Does altruism exist other than as a tactic? That question is difficult to answer experimentally, or on the basis of naturalistic observation, but it has been addressed recently by sociobiologists and others interested in the implications of evolutionary theory for modern human behavior. They do not agree about altruism. On the one hand, some see it as occurring in the face of natural genetic selection toward pure selfishness, because societies support the long-term reproductive success of altruists, even though altruistic behavior itself would be deleterious in a context outside the society. Thus, Campbell (1975), for example, believes in a "social evolution" toward altruistic and cooperative norms and morals, one that must be carefully guarded against rampant individualism and the consequent genetic success of those most selfish. Blany (1976) notes that for whatever reason (the selfish interests of those shaping a society's beliefs?) women in all societies prefer men who are altruistic and brave to those who are self-centered and cowardly. So socially trained sexual preference may involve a social breeding of altruistic traits, again those that might not fare well in a "warre of all against all." Finally, Trivers (1971) proposes that altruism is a tactical advantage due to socially imposed norms of reciprocity.

In contrast, other sociobiologists hypothesize mechanisms by which altruism in and of itself may result in genetic propagation, even if not through direct propagation. Those proposing that such survival works through "group selection" ultimately benefiting the individual currently (1980) have few adherents. Many others (e.g. Alexander 1980) have proposed "kin altruism" as a plausible genetic link to all altruism. People share genes with their close relatives, and to the degree to which they—even in the celibate roles of priest and maiden aunt—help relatives survive, they enhance the probability that their own genes are propagated. Evidence for such kin altruism is most easily found in a mother's sacrifice for her children. Hence, to the degree to which altruistic concern is focused primarily on close kin ("nepotistic") and partially genetically based, it would be expected to increase through genetic selection. Whether such kin altruism would lead to a general altruistic concern for surrounding people, or for a whole tribe or society, is a moot question.

This literature does not provide a clear indication of whether altruism is purely tactical—nor does any other literature to my knowledge. Nevertheless, it may not be limited to tactical concerns, in which case it could be an important factor in leading people to cooperate in a social dilemma situation. There is one important proviso: people have to *know* about the payoffs to others if altruistic utilities are to be effective. This proviso is not trivial.

CONSCIENCE AND NORMS   Even though conscience may often be only "the inner voice which warns us that someone may be looking" (Mencken, quoted in Cooke 1955), it has been a powerful force throughout history in motivating human behavior. People die for it. Tyrants use it to demand behavior of people that other people believe unconscionable. Desperate appeals are made to it—sometimes successfully—by potential victims of aggression.

Hardin (1968, pp. 1246–47) specifically dismisses appeals to conscience as a means of eliciting cooperative behaviors in social dilemmas. He first hypothesizes that such an appeal is a "double bind," because the person making the appeal may regard the person swayed as a "simpleton." Not necessarily so. For if the person making the appeal also has a regard for his own "clear conscience" (perhaps as his "only sure reward"), then he is equally bound. A second argument of Hardin's confuses morality with neurotic guilt and concludes that appeals to conscience are "psychologically pathogenic" (and may, like everything else, be misused by unscrupulous individuals).

But Hardin's is the main discussion of appeals to conscience in the literature—or at least in the literature which has come to my attention. Psychologists, economists, political scientists, and sociobiologists do not tend to use "conscience" as an explanatory construct, perhaps because it is often considered secondary to other factors. But secondary or not, it does appear to have an important place in determining everyday behavior, and as one paper to be reviewed in the fourth section of this article suggests, it may be efficacious in eliciting cooperation.

Norms are somewhere between conscience and coercion. Most norms that exist may elicit punishment if violated. But norms have the ability to motivate people in the absence of any threat of censure. If we fight bravely because we are in Caesar's Legions, it is true that we may be decimated if we do not. But it is not the fear of decimation that leads most of us to fight bravely. We fight because of what we are. Similarly, people may cooperate in social dilemmas because of what they are; they are not "the kind of people" who profit at others' expense, or who contribute to a holocaust.

THE MATHEMATICAL STRUCTURE OF DILEMMA GAMES

A game is simply a system of payoffs depending on the combination of choices made by the players. (An additional "choice" may be made by a random element that receives no payoff.) In dilemma games, each player makes one of two choices: D (for defecting) or C (for cooperating). The payoff to each player depends wholly on his or her choice of D or C and on the number of other players who choose C or D.

Let $D(m)$ be the payoff to the defectors in an N-person game where m players cooperate, and let $C(m)$ be the payoff to the cooperators when m players (including themselves) cooperate. A social dilemma game is characterized by two simple inequalities.

1. $D(m) > C(m + 1)$

That is, the payoff when m other people cooperate is always higher for an individual who remains a defector than for one who becomes the m plus first cooperator (m goes from 0 to $N - 1$).

2. $D(0) < C(N)$

That is, universal cooperation among the N players leads to a greater payoff than does universal defection.

The statement of condition No. 1 in game theory language is that defection *is a dominating strategy.* But if everyone chooses that dominating strategy, the outcome that results is one that is less preferred by all players to at least one other (e.g. that resulting from universal cooperation). Since according to game theory all players should choose a dominating strategy, the result is termed an *equilibrium.* (No player would want to switch his or her choice.) Because the outcome dictated by the dominating strategy is less preferred by all players to the outcome of unanimous cooperation, this outcome is termed *deficient.* Hence, *a dilemma game is one in which all players have dominating strategies that result in a deficient equilibrium.* Two games developed for experimental research are illustrative.

The "Take Some" Game

Each of three players simultaneously holds up a red or blue poker chip. Each player who holds up a red chip receives $3.00 in payoff, but each of the three players *including that player* is fined $1.00 for that choice. This is the negative externality. Each player who holds up a blue chip receives $1.00 with no resultant fine. Three blue chips being held up provides a $1.00 payoff to all players (and a social product of $3.00) while three red chips being held up provides a zero payoff for all (and a zero social product). At the same time, however, each player reasons that he or she is best off holding up a red chip, because that increases the fines he or she must pay by only $1.00 while increasing the immediate amount received by $2.00 ($3.00 − $1.00). In effect, the player gets $2.00 from the other two players' $1.00 fines. In this game, one can *take some* from others. Such a choice is analogous to that involved in the decision to pollute (Dawes, Delay & Chaplin 1974).

The "Give Some" Game

Each of five players may keep $8.00 from the experimenter for himself or herself, or give $3.00 from the experimenter to each of the other players. Again it is a dilemma because if all *give,* all get $12.00 (4 X $3.00) while if all *keep,* all get $8.00; yet it is clearly in each player's individual interest to keep. In fact, each player is getting $8.00 more by keeping than by giving. This game is based on the research of Bonacich (1972). The *give some* game presents the subjects with a choice analogous to that of deciding whether to contribute to a public good (Olsen 1965). (Each of us can reap the benefit of others' contributions while withholding ours.)

The "take some" and "give some" games can be presented in matrix form displaying the payoffs to defectors and cooperators as a function of the number of cooperators (Table 1).

180   DAWES

Table 1 Payoffs for the two games

The "Take Some" Game			The "Give Some" Game		
Number of cooperators	Payoffs to defectors	Payoffs to cooperators	Number of cooperators	Payoffs to defectors	Payoffs to cooperators
3	—	$1.00	5	—	$12.00
2	$2.00	0	4	$20.00	$ 9.00
1	$1.00	−$1.00	3	$17.00	$ 6.00
0	0	—	2	$14.00	$ 3.00
			1	$11.00	0
			0	$ 8.00	—

In addition to properties 1 and 2 (above), the "take some" and the "give some" games have three further properties:

A. $D(m+1) - D(m) = c_1 > 0$

B. $C(m+1) - C(m) = c_2 > 0$

C. $D(m) - C(m+1) = c_3 > 0$

In the "take some" game, $c_1 = \$1.00$, $c_2 = \$1.00$, and $c_3 = \$1.00$. In the "give some" game, $c_1 = \$3.00$, $c_2 = \$3.00$, and $c_3 = \$8.00$.

If we were to plot the payoffs for defection and cooperation as a function of the number of cooperators, properties A and B state that both functions are straight lines with positive slopes (see Schelling 1973, Hamburger 1973). Property C states that these slopes are equal. Condition No. 1 (that an additional cooperator makes less than had he or she remained a defector) follows directly from property C, and condition No. 2 states that the right hand extreme of the cooperating function is above the left hand extreme of the defecting function.[5] Graphically, a social dilemma exists when the D payoff function is above the C function for its entire length and the right extremity of the C function is higher than the left extremity of the D function. It is apparent that a very wide range of configurations will meet this specification. Schelling (1973) has discussed many such configurations and has given a host of imaginative examples.

Hamburger (1973) has shown that dilemma games having properties A through C are equivalent to games in which each participant simultaneously

---

[5] Properties A and B do not imply property C unless $c_1 = c_2$, because it is possible that payoffs for cooperation and defection are linear but do not have equal slopes. On the other hand, properties A and C not only imply property B, but that c_1 is equal to c_2 as well. Properties B and C yield the same implication. Property C by itself has no implication other than condition No. 1, because it does not specify that the payoff functions need be straight lines.

plays identical two-person prisoners' dilemma games having property C (termed "separable" in the literature) against each of the remaining $N - 1$ participants. Dawes (1975) has shown that they are also equivalent to the algebraic expression of the "commons dilemma" described by Hardin (1968). Figure 1 plots the payoffs for the "take some" game and the "give some" game respectively.

In the literature to be described here, most of the dilemma games have properties A–C. We shall term these *uniform games,* following Kahan (1973) and Goehring & Kahan (1976). One group of experimenters, work- ing primarily at Arizona State University in the 1970s, uses much different games—those in which subjects may draw points from a pool that can "replenish itself" (i.e. be increased by the experimenter) at varying intervals in amounts depending upon the subjects' behavior (e.g. restraint or self- sacrifice). This paradigm, which defies a simple mathematical description, is similar to a card game devised by Rubenstein in his doctoral dissertation (cf Rubenstein et al 1975). Such games will be referred to as *variable.*

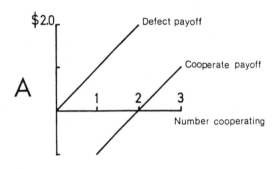

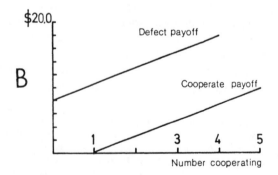

Figure 1   Graphs of payoffs for the two games.

REVIEW OF THE LITERATURE ABOUT EXPERIMENTAL N-PERSON DILEMMA GAMES

The *prisoner's dilemma* is a two-person dilemma game. The name derives from an anecdote concerning two prisoners who have jointly committed a felony and who have been apprehended by a District Attorney who cannot prove their guilt. The District Attorney holds them incommunicado and offers each the chance to confess. If one confesses and the other doesn't, the one who confesses will go free while the other will receive a maximum sentence. If both confess they will both receive a moderate sentence, while if neither confesses both will receive a minimum sentence. In this situation, confession is a dominant strategy. (If the other confesses, confession leads to a moderate sentence rather than to a maximum one; if the other doesn't, it leads to freedom rather than to a minimum sentence.) But confession leads to a deficient equilibrium, because dual confession results in moderate sentences, whereas a minimum sentence could be achieved by neither confessing. Hence, the dilemma.

In the experimental gaming literature prisoner's dilemmas are often played repeatedly. That leads to an additional constraint on the payoffs so that the players cannot take turns playing the defecting strategy. (The sum of the payoffs for one defecting and one cooperating choice must be less than the sum for two cooperating choices.) Uniform dilemma games satisfy this constraint, but so do many others.

The overwhelming majority of experimental investigations of behavior in social dilemma games have studied subjects' responses in two-person prisoner's dilemmas that are played repeatedly by the same subjects (or by subjects who believe that they are playing against the same other subject— who may be a computer program). Payoffs for these two-person games have usually been in small amounts of money (e.g. mils); in virtually all experiments, subjects have been told that their purpose should be to maximize their own gain—although we suspect that many other motives such as maximizing relative gain (Messick & Thorngate 1967) or minimizing boredom may have been involved. There may well be over 1000 experiments reported in the psychological literature documenting how college students behave in such iterated prisoner's dilemmas.

The two-person iterated prisoner's dilemma has three characteristics, however, that make it unique—and hence unrepresentative of the social dilemmas discussed in this article.

1. In the two-person prisoner dilemma (iterated or not) all harm for defection is visited completely on the other player; harm is focused rather than spread out. In most social dilemmas in contrast, harm for defecting behavior is diffused over a considerable number of players.

2. In most social dilemmas defecting behavior may be anonymous; it is not necessarily so, but the possibility is there. In the two-person iterated game, in contrast, each player knows with certainty how the other has behaved. This necessary knowledge is unique to the two-person situation.

3. Each player has total reinforcement control over the other in the iterated two-person dilemma. That is, each player can "punish" the other for defection or cooperation (behavior that is socially optimal if individually suboptimal) by choosing defection on the subsequent choice, and can "reward" the previous choice of the other by choosing cooperation. Thus, each player can attempt to shape the other's behavior by choice of defection and cooperation, while partially determining his or her own outcome by that same choice. The situation is very complicated. Each "game" is analogous to a play in chess which has meaning only within the metagame of the entire match. In fact, Amnon Rapoport (1967) has shown that if subjects really can influence each others' subsequent choices, then the iterated prisoner's dilemma isn't a dilemma at all! So if subjects believe that they have such influence it is not a dilemma to them. This characteristic is unique to the two-person iterated dilemma; when there are more people involved it is not possible to attempt to shape a particular other person's behavior by judicious (or believed to be judicious) choice of one's own behavior. (There may be some element of such attempted shaping when the number of people involved approaches two—i.e. three or four—but the potential effectiveness of doing so is clearly diluted.)

Due to the specificity of harm, the lack of possible anonymity, and the potential use of one's own behavior as a strategy to shape the other, two-person iterated prisoner's dilemmas cannot be considered to be representative social dilemmas *in general.* The review of the literature and its findings that follow will be limited to investigations of dilemmas involving three or more people.

Findings

INVOLVEMENT   While any correlation between the "ecological validity" of an experiment and the degree of subject involvement is far from perfect, the assessment of such involvement is certainly an important factor in evaluating a domain of studies. When social dilemma games are played for substantial amounts of money, subjects are *extremely* involved. In 1972, Bonacich ran two conditions of 5-person "give some" games; in both conditions $c_1 = c_2 = \$.25$; in a "low temptation" condition c_3 ranged from \$.01 to \$.20 across five trials, while in a "high temptation" condition it ran from \$.01 to \$.75, with a special trial at the end where subjects could win up to

$16 by betraying their groups. In both conditions, communication was allowed, and the subjects made ample use of evaluative terms ("cheat," "screw," "greed," "fink" being the four most common). In a later study (1976) Bonacich used larger amounts of money, which resulted in even more striking involvement. All subjects, in 5-person groups, played two games; in the first $c_1 = c_2 = c_3 = \$.30$, while in the second, which was not a uniform game, any defection resulted in no payoff to cooperators and a payoff as high as $9.00 to a single defector.

Bonacich writes (1976, p. 207):

> During the coding of the tapes we noticed occasional joking threats about what the group would do to a noncooperator; he would not leave the place alive, they would push him down the stairs as he left, they would beat him up, they would write a letter to the student newspaper exposing his perfidy, or they would take him to small claims court. These threats could be intimidating and could suggest how angry the group would be toward the noncooperator.

Dawes, McTavish & Shaklee (1977) conducted an experiment involving even larger amounts of money; subjects played just once. Total cooperation resulted in $2.50 for each member of their 8-person groups, total defection resulted in no payment to anyone, $c_1 = c_2 = \$1.50$, and $c_3 = \$8.00$, a substantial monetary incentive to defect. Some groups could communicate while others could not. Dawes, McTavish & Shaklee (p. 7) write:

> One of the most significant aspects of this study, however, did not show up in the data analysis. It is the extreme seriousness with which the subjects take the problems. Comments such as, "If you defect on the rest of us, you're going to have to live with it the rest of your life," were not at all uncommon. Nor was it unusual for people to wish to leave by the back door, to claim that they did not wish to see the "sons of bitches" who double-crossed them, to become extremely angry at other subjects, or to become tearful. . . .
>
> The affect level was so high that we are unwilling to run intact groups because of the effect the game might have on the members' feelings about each other. The affect level also mitigates against examining choice visibility [NB in experiments involving high stakes]. In pretesting we did run one group in which choices were made public. The three defectors were the target of a great deal of hostility ("You have no idea how much you alienate me!," one cooperator shouted before storming out of the room); they remained after the experiment until all the cooperators were presumably long gone.

Experimenters whose payoffs consist of points to be converted to trivial amounts of cash or course credits do not report the affect level of their subjects. It may also be high, but I suspect that if it were it would be mentioned.

Whether or not high stakes and affect are necessary to reach valid conclusions about behavior in social dilemmas is a question that cannot be answered a priori, but depends in part upon a general finding of congruent or disparate results across high involvement and low involvement studies. As yet there are not enough investigations in the field to know.

Certainly most of the dilemma situations in which we are interested involve high affect—e.g. that experienced by the author during the 1973 gasoline crisis as friend and neighbor after friend and neighbor finked out to become a "regular customer" of some service station.

COMMUNICATION   The salutary effects of communication on cooperation are ubiquitous. In the first experiment by Bonacich reported above, communication was allowed in all groups, and 93% of the choices were cooperative. In the second experiment, there was a 94% cooperation rate. Bonacich did not run a no-communication control group (because he was not studying the effects of communication per se), but Dawes, McTavish, and Shaklee did. They found 72% cooperation in their communicating groups (which consisted of two different types to be described shortly) as opposed to 31% in their no-communication groups (which also consisted of two types).

Using points as payoffs, Rapoport et al (1962) and Bixenstine et al (1966) found that communicating groups cooperated more.[6] Using variable games with points taken from a replenishing pool, Brechner (1977), Edney & Harper (1978, 1979), and Harper (1977) all found that groups able to communicate cooperated more, with the result that more points were "harvested" from the pool.

Using a hypothetical uniform business game (in which manufacturers could cooperate against consumers), Jerdee & Rosen (1974) found that communication enhanced cooperation, but in a uniform game in which subjects "should act as if each point were worth $1," Caldwell (1976) did not. Caldwell did find, however, that a communication condition in which subjects could sanction defectors resulted in greater cooperation. Moreover, he found that communication per se did yield higher cooperation, although not significantly so, and as he wrote (p. 279), "Perhaps with real money subjects would be less inclined to treat the experiment as a competitive game."

What is it about communication that leads to more cooperation? While most of the studies mentioned above simply pitted communication against

---

[6]These results require qualification. The communication that was effective in the Rapoport et al study was unintended; it occurred during a break between two 3–4 hour sessions, and because the experimenters' (p. 40) "main interest was in the distribution of choices in the *absence* of communication;" the results after the break were ignored except for noting the high degree of cooperation. The game in the Bixenstine et al study was not strictly a dilemma, because there were some points at which defection did not dominate cooperation.

no communication, Dawes, McTavish, and Shaklee attempted to study the effects of various aspects of communication. They argued that there is a hierarchy of at least three aspects involved in any face-to-face communication about dilemma problems. First, subjects get to know each other as human beings (humanization); second, they get to discuss the dilemma with which they are faced (discussion); third, they have the opportunity to make commitments about their own behavior, and to attempt to elicit such commitments from others (commitment). Commitment entails discussion, and discussion in turn entails humanization. What Dawes, McTavish, and Shaklee did was to run four types of groups: those that couldn't communicate at all, those that communicated for 10 minutes about an irrelevant topic (they were asked to estimate the proportion of people at various income levels in Eugene, Oregon), those that could discuss the problem but couldn't ask for public commitments, and those that were required to "go around the table" and make public commitments after discussion. The first two types yielded cooperation rates of 30% and 32% respectively, while the last two had rates of 72% and 71%. Thus, humanization made no difference —at least not personal acquaintance based on a 10 minute discussion (the average amount of time that the discussion and commitment groups spent on the problem). Surprisingly, commitment made no difference, but it must be remembered that this commitment was one forced by the experimenters rather than one arising spontaneously from the group process. (Moreover, *every* subject promised to cooperate, which is the only reasonable statement to make no matter what one's intentions.)

GROUP SIZE   All experimenters who have made explicit or implicit comparisons of dilemma games with varying number of players have concluded that subjects cooperate less in larger groups than in smaller ones. Rapoport et al (1962) and Bixenstine et al (1966) simply noted the low degree of cooperation in their three- and six-person games and stated that it is less than in comparable two-person prisoner's dilemmas. But they had no strict criterion of comparability. Marwell & Schmidt (1972) studied two- and three-person uniform games with c_3 equal in each and found less cooperation in the three-person game. Unfortunately, c_1 and c_2 were not equated, being twice as large in the two-person as in the three-person game (which resulted in the "expected values" of cooperation and defection being identical *if* the other players were to respond in a 50–50 random manner). Harper et al (unpublished) compared one-, three-, and six-person groups in the variable dilemma involving pool replacement; they found cooperation decreased with group size, but it is not clear what the results were for a "one-person group" test—other than the intellectual ability of a single individual to solve the replenishment problem in an optimal manner given the experimenter's replenishment rule.[7]

The problem is, of course, how to "equate" N and N' person dilemma games, or even whether such an equating is desirable (from the standpoint of "ecological validity"). Could it not be argued, for example, that the motive to defect (e.g. c_3) should "naturally" increase with more players because the harm from defection—i.e. negative externality—should be diffused among more people?

The most careful job of equating we have found is in one game from a larger study by Bonacich et al (1976). These investigators set c_1, c_2, and c_3 equal in three-, six-, and nine-person games, and they discovered that cooperation decreased with increasing size (contrary to their theoretical expectations, which was that these parameters alone would determine rate of defection).

PUBLIC DISCLOSURE OF CHOICE VERSUS ANONYMITY   Three studies have compared private with public choice (Bixenstine et al 1966, Jerdee & Rosen 1974, Fox & Guyer 1978); all found higher rates of cooperation when choice was public. While the difference between anonymity and public disclosure in these studies is not striking, they used minimal payoffs—and given the involvement obtained with significant amounts of money, we suspect that the difference would be much greater were the payoffs more significant.

EXPECTATIONS ABOUT OTHERS' BEHAVIOR   There are three studies that collected subjects' expectations about whether others playing the games would cooperate or defect (Tyszka & Grzelak 1976, Dawes, McTavish & Shaklee 1977, Marwell & Ames 1979). There are two possible predictions. To the degree to which a subject believes others *won't* defect, he or she may feel it is possible to obtain a big payoff without hurting others too much. This desire to be a "free rider" [or "greed" as Coombs (1973) terms it] could result in a negative correlation between the propensity to cooperate and beliefs that others will. To the degree to which a subject believes that others *will* defect, he or she may feel that it is necessary to avoid a big loss by defecting himself or herself. The desire to "avoid being a sucker" [or "fear" as Coombs (1973) terms it] could result in a positive correlation

[7]Interestingly, there *is* an optimal solution for harvesting animals in their natural environment. Determine the maximal population size where there is no harvesting, and then keep the population at precisely half that size. See Dawes, Delay & Chaplin (1974) and Anderson (1974).

between the propensity to cooperate and beliefs that others will. In fact, all three studies report strong *positive* correlations. This finding is compatible with those reviewed by Pruitt & Kimmel (1977) in the area of iterated games.

There is one other interesting finding in the Dawes et al and the Tyszka and Grzelak studies. Defectors are more accurate at predicting cooperation rates than are cooperators. But Dawes, McTavish, and Shaklee found that they were *not* more accurate at predicting specifically who would cooperate and who would not. This apparent discrepancy between base rate accuracy and specific accuracy can be best understood by considering the predictions of the outcome of coin tosses. A person who predicts heads 50% of the time will be correct only 50% of the time despite a perfect base rate accuracy; a person who predicts heads 100% of the time will also be correct 50% of the time despite making the worst possible base rate prediction. In fact, in the Dawes, McTavish, and Shaklee study subjects were *very* poor at predicting who would and who would not cooperate.

MORALIZING Noting that the subjects in the Dawes, McTavish, and Shaklee study often raised moral issues in the discussion and commitment groups Dawes et al (unpublished) ran two experiments in which the experimenters themselves moralized at the subjects. These two studies, one conducted at Santa Barbara, California, and one conducted at Eugene, Oregon, contrasted a no-communication condition with a no-communication condition in which the experimenter delivered a 938 word sermon about group benefit, exploitation, whales, ethics, and so on. At both locations, the sermon worked—yielding rates of cooperation comparable to those found in the discussion and commitment groups of the earlier experiments. Of course, these sermons confounded logic, social pressure, experimental demand, emotional appeal, and so on.

A FINAL HYPOTHESIS ABOUT ELICITING COOPERATIVE BEHAVIOR

The experiments reviewed in this article are lousy *simulations* of the social dilemmas with which most of us are concerned. In our current overpopulated world, the dilemmas of greatest import involve thousands to millions of people, large-scale communication or public disclosure is impossible, and most of the people choosing do not share the cultural background of American high school or college students. Findings about how small groups of such students behave in contrived situations cannot be generalized to statements about how to save the world (even though as part of our own research-finding dilemma game, we often pretend that they can, thereby leading granting agencies to expect such statements).

What must be assumed is that the psychological and social factors that lead to defection or cooperation in small-scale dilemmas are roughly the same as those that influence behavior in large dilemmas. (Of course, small N dilemmas may be studied in their own right, in which case no such assumption is necessary.) This assumption cannot be based purely on the formal (i.e. mathematical) identity of small and large dilemmas. Rather, such an assumption must be based on broader theoretical ideas about human behavior—ideas that imply what might lead people to cooperate or defect in general, and which may then be tested in the small dilemma situation. Most of the studies reviewed in this article are based on such ideas. (Those, for example, that merely examine the effect of changing mathematical parameters in the experimental situation have been omitted.)

This distinction between experimental dilemmas as simulations and as hypotheses-testing devices is not just one of regard. For example, most simulation studies vary parameters of the dilemma itself (following the precedent of numerous iterated prisoner's dilemma studies); such studies are based on the assumption that these parameters (e.g. a mathematically defined "degree of conflict") have counterparts in the "real world," although it is difficult if not impossible to identify them with any precision. In contrast, those studies that investigate variables outside the structure of the game—e.g. communication, public disclosure, moralizing—vary these; such studies are based on the assumption that the experimental dilemma is (just) another "real" dilemma to the subjects, and that their behavior will be affected by these variables in the same way (more or less) as it would be affected in other dilemma situations.[8] And the expectation that these variables will affect behavior must always be based on some theoretical orientation or belief.

The analysis and literature reported thus far support a very simple theoretical proposition, one derived from extensive literature documenting that people have very limited abilities to process information on a conscious level, particularly social information. This ability is "limited" relative to what we naively believe; that is, study after study has shown a surprising inability to process information correctly on what appear to be the simplest tasks, provided they are not overlearned or automatic. The literature supporting this limited processing phenomenon is too vast to be referenced here without doubling the bibliography, but see Dawes (1976).

---

[8]I grant that it is always possible to attempt to construct a meta-game incorporating such variables, although their exact role and parameterization is extremely difficult to determine.

Such cognitive limitation may often result in an inablity to understand or fully grasp the utilities in a social dilemma situation other than those that are most obvious, i.e. those connected with the payoffs. But it is precisely the payoff utilities that lead the players to defect, while the other utilities —e.g. those connected with altruisms, norms, and conscience—lead the players to cooperate. It follows that manipulations that enhance the salience and understanding of these utilities should increase cooperation. Communication (with or without commitment), public disclosure, and moralizing are precisely such manipulations.

Moreover, there are two additional studies—one mentioned briefly and one involving an iterated game—that support this hypothesis that greater knowledge yields greater cooperation. Marwell & Ames (1979) contacted high school students both by telephone and mail and asked them to invest a number of "tokens" supplied by the experimenter in either a "private" or "public" stock. The tokens invested in the private stock resulted in a fixed monetary yield per token. Those invested in the public stock resulted in a payoff to *all* members of the subject's group (of 4 or 80 members whom the subject didn't know); this payoff was an accelerating function of the number of people who invested their tokens in this public stock. The dilemma occurred because subjects received money from the public investment whether or not they personally contributed tokens to it. (It was not, however, strictly a dilemma situation, because if enough other group members invested in the public stock a "provision point" was reached, beyond which the public stock was also personally more rewarding than was the private stock.)

Marwell and Ames obtained a much higher rate of cooperation (public investment) than would be predicted from economic theory; their subjects were as much concerned with "fairness" as with monetary return. Why? The hypothesis proposed here suggests that the concern with the internal utility of fairness could have been brought about by the *length of time* the subjects had to consider their choice. They had a minimum of 3 days. (The time in the typical no-communication experiment is 10 minutes.) It follows that they had time to think about factors other than the external payoffs —e.g. to think about "fairness." Note that this study was done under a condition of total anonymity, a factor most common in large-scale social dilemmas.

The other study supporting the general hypothesis presented here is that of Kelley & Grzelak (1972). When interviewing subjects who had played an iterated social dilemma game in groups of 13 subjects, these investigators found that subjects who had made a (relatively) high proportion of cooperative responses were better able to identify the response best for the group than were those who made a low proportion of cooperative responses. While the hypothesis stated here is the converse of that finding, direction (not magnitude) of statistical association is symmetric.

Is knowledge *all* that is necessary? No, for while utilities associated with altruism, norms, and conscience may be made salient by knowledge, they do not necessarily overwhelm those associated with the payoffs. Repugnant as it may be from a normative point of view, moral and monetary (or survival) utilities combine in a compensatory fashion for most people.

He: Lady, would you sleep with me for 100,000 pounds?
She: Why, yes. Of course.
He: Would you sleep with me for 10 shillings?
She: (angrily) What do you think I am, a prostitute?
He: We have already established that fact, madam. What we are haggling about is the price.

Everyone may not have his or her price, but it does not require a systematic survey to establish that most people in the world will compromise his or her altruistic or ethical values for money or survival. Thus, the negative payoffs for cooperative behavior must not be too severe if people are to cooperate. It may be for precisely this reason that the expectation that others will cooperate is so highly correlated with cooperation itself. If others cooperate, then the expected payoff for cooperation is not too low, even though—in a uniform game, for example—the *difference* between the payoff for cooperation and that for defection is still quite large. People may be greedy, may prefer more to less, but their greed is not "insatiable" when other utilities are involved.

Thus, three important ingredients for enhancing cooperation in social dilemma situations may be: knowledge, morality, and trust. These ancient virtues were not discovered by the author—or by the United States Government, which invested millions of dollars in research grants over the years to have subjects play experimental games. But the above analysis indicates that they may be the particular virtues relevant to the noncoercive (and hence efficient) resolution of the social dilemmas we face.

192   DAWES

Literature Cited

Alexander, R. D. 1980. *Darwinism and Human Affairs.* Seattle: Univ. Washington Press

Anderson, J. M. 1974. A model for the "tragedy of the commons." *IEEE Trans. Syst. Man Cybern.* pp. 103–5

Bixenstine, V. E., Levitt, C. A., Wilson, K. R. 1966. Collaboration among six persons in a prisoner's dilemma game. *J. Conflict Resolut.* 10:488–96

Blany, P. H. 1976. Genetic basis of behavior —especially of altruism. *Am. Psychol.* 31:358

Bonacich, P. 1972. Norms and cohesion as adaptive responses to political conflict: an experimental study. *Sociometry* 35:357–75

Bonacich, P. 1976. Secrecy and solidarity. *Sociometry* 39:200–8

Bonacich, P., Shure, G. H., Kahan, J. P., Meeker, R. J. 1976. Cooperation and group size in the N-person prisoner's dilemma. *J. Conflict Resolut.* 20:687–705

Brechner, K. C. 1977. An experimental analysis of social traps. *J. Exp. Soc. Psychol.* 13:552–64

Buchanan, J. M. 1971. *The Bases for Collective Action.* New York: Gen. Learn. Press

Caldwell, M. D. 1976. Communication and sex effects in a five-person prisoner's dilemma. *J. Pers. Soc. Psychol.* 33:273–81

Campbell, D. T. 1975. On the conflict between biological and social evolution and between psychology and the moral tradition. *Am. Psychol.* 30:1103–26

Cooke, A. 1955. *The Vintage Mencken,* p. 231. New York: Vantage

Coombs, C. A. 1973. A reparameterization of the prisoner's dilemma game. *Behav. Sci.* 18:424–28

Dawes, R. M. 1975. Formal models of dilemmas in social decision-making. In *Human Judgment and Decision Processes,* ed. M. F. Kaplan, S. Schwartz, pp. 88–107. New York: Academic

Dawes, R. M. 1976. Shallow psychology. In *Cognitions and Social Behavior,* ed. J. Carroll, J. Payne, pp. 3–12. Hillsdale NJ: Erlbaum

Dawes, R. M., Delay, J., Chaplin, W. 1974. The decision to pollute. *Environment and Planning,* pp. 2–10

Dawes, R. M., McTavish, J., Shaklee, H.1977. Behavior, communication and assumptions about other people's behavior in a commons dilemma situation. *J. Pers. Soc. Psychol.* 35:1–11

Dawes, R. M., Shaklee, H., Talarowski, F. On getting people to cooperate when facing a social dilemma: moralizing helps. Unpublished manuscript

Edney, J. J., Harper, C. S. 1978. The effects of information in a resource management problem: A social trap analog. *Hum. Ecol.* 6:387–95

Edney, J. J., Harper, C. S. 1979. Heroism in a resource crisis: a simulation study. *Environmental Management.* In press

Fox, J., Guyer, M. 1978. "Public" choice and cooperation in n-person prisoner's dilemma. *J. Conflict Resolut.* 22:468–81

Goehring, D. J., Kahan, J. P. 1976. The uniform n-person prisoner's dilemma game. *J. Conflict Resolut.* 20:111–28

Hamburger, H. 1973. N-person prisoners dilemmas. *J. Math. Sociol.* 3:27–48

Hardin, G. R. 1968. The tragedy of the commons. *Science* 162:1243–48

Hardin, G. R. 1976. Carrying capacity as an ethical concept. *Soundings: Interdiscip. J.* 59:121–37

Harper, C. S. 1977. Competition and cooperation in a resource management task: a social trap analogue. In *Priorities for Environmental Design Research,* ed S. Weidman, J. R. Anderson, pp. 305–12. Washington DC: Environ. Res. Assoc.

Harper, C. S., Gregory, W. L., Edney, J. J., Lindner, D. Group size effects in a simulated commons dilemma. Unpublished manuscript

Heilbroner, R. 1974. *An Inquiry into the Human Prospect.* New York: Norton

Hobbes, T. 1651, 1947. *Leviathan.* London: Dent

Jerdee, T. H., Rosen, B. 1974. Effects of opportunity to communicate and visibility of individual decisions on behavior in the common interest. *J. Appl. Psychol.* 59:712–16

Kahan, J. P. 1973. Noninteraction in an anonymous three-person prisoner's dilemma game. *Behav. Sci.* 18:124–27

Kelley, H. H., Grzelak, J. 1972. Conflict between individual and common interest in an n-person relationship. *J. Pers. Soc. Psychol.* 21:190–97

Marwell, G., Ames, R. E. 1979. Experiments on the provision of public goods I: resources, interest, group size, and the free rider problem. *Am. J. Sociol.* 84:1335–60

Marwell, G., Schmidt, D. R. 1972. Cooperation in a three-person prisoner's dilemma. *J. Pers. Soc. Psychol.* 31:376–83

McClintock, C. G., Messick, D. M., Kuhleman, D. M., Campos, F. T. 1973. Motivational bases of choice in three-choice decomposed games. *J. Exp. Soc. Psychol.* 9:572–90

Messick, D. M. 1969–1970. Some thoughts on the nature of human competition. *Hypothese: Tijdschr. Psychol. Opvoedkunde.* 14:38–52

Messick, D. M., McClintock, C. G. 1968. Motivational bases of choice in experimental games. *J. Exp. Soc. Psychol.* 4:1–25

Messick, D. M., Thorngate, W. B. 1967. Relative gain maximization in experimental games. *J. Exp. Soc. Psychol.* 3: 85–101

Olsen, M. 1965. *The Logic of Collective Action.* Cambridge, Mass: Harvard Press

Ophuls, W. 1977. *Ecology and the Politics of Scarcity.* San Francisco: Freeman

Orbell, J. M., Rutherford, B. 1973. Can Leviathan make the life of man less solitary, poor, nasty, brutish, and short? *Br. J. Polit. Sci.* 3:383–407

Platt, G. 1973. Social traps. *Am. Pyschol.* 28:641–51

Pruitt, D. G., Kimmel, M. J. 1977. Twenty years of experimental gaming: critique, synthesis, and suggestions for the future. *Ann. Rev. Psychol.* 28:363–92

Rapoport, Amnon. 1967. Optimal policies for the prisoner's dilemma. *Psychol. Rev.* 74:136–48

Rapoport, Anatol, Chammah, A., Dwyer, J., Gyr, J. 1962. Three-person non-zero-sum nonnegotiable games. *Behav. Sci.* 7:30–58

Robertson, D. 1974. Well, does Leviathan . . . ? *Br. J. Polit. Sci.* 4:245–50

Rubinstein, F. D., Watzke, G., Doctor, R. H., Dana, J. 1975. The effect of two incentive schemes upon the conservation of shared resource by five-person groups. *Organ. Behav. Hum. Perform.* 13:330–38

Schelling, T. C. 1973. Hockey helmets, concealed weapons, and daylight saving: a study of binary choices with externalities. *J. Conflict Resolut.* 17:381–428

Smith, A. 1776, 1976. *The Wealth of Nations.* Chicago: Univ. Chicago Press

Trivers, R. L. 1971. The evolution of reciprocal altruism. *Q. Rev. Biol.* 46:35–57

Tyszka, T., Grzelak, J. L. 1976. Criteria of choice in non-constant zero-sum games. *J. Conflict Resolut.* 20:357–76

Wade, N. 1974a. Sahelian drought: No victory for Western aid. *Science* 185: 234–37

Wade, N. 1974b. Green revolution (1): a just technology, often unjust in use. *Science* 186:1094–96

[3]

The Success of
TIT FOR TAT in
Computer Tournaments

SINCE the Prisoner's Dilemma is so common in everything from personal relations to international relations, it would be useful to know how best to act when in this type of setting. However, the proposition of the previous chapter demonstrates that there is no one best strategy to use. What is best depends in part on what the other player is likely to be doing. Further, what the other is likely to be doing may well depend on what the player expects *you* to do.

To get out of this tangle, help can be sought by combing the research already done concerning the Prisoner's Dilemma for useful advice. Fortunately, a great deal of research has been done in this area.

Psychologists using experimental subjects have found

The Emergence of Cooperation

that, in the iterated Prisoner's Dilemma, the amount of cooperation attained—and the specific pattern for attaining it—depend on a wide variety of factors relating to the context of the game, the attributes of the individual players, and the relationship between the players. Since behavior in the game reflects so many important factors about people, it has become a standard way to explore questions in social psychology, from the effects of westernization in Central Africa (Bethlehem 1975) to the existence (or nonexistence) of aggression in career-oriented women (Baefsky and Berger 1974), and to the differential consequences of abstract versus concrete thinking styles (Nydegger 1974). In the last fifteen years, there have been hundreds of articles on the Prisoner's Dilemma cited in *Psychological Abstracts*. The iterated Prisoner's Dilemma has become the *E. coli* of social psychology.

Just as important as its use as an experimental test bed is the use of the Prisoner's Dilemma as the conceptual foundation for models of important social processes. Richardson's model of the arms race is based on an interaction which is essentially a Prisoner's Dilemma, played once a year with the budgets of the competing nations (Richardson 1960; Zinnes 1976, pp. 330–40). Oligopolistic competition can also be modeled as a Prisoner's Dilemma (Samuelson 1973, pp. 503–5). The ubiquitous problems of collective action to produce a collective good are analyzable as Prisoner's Dilemmas with many players (G. Hardin 1982). Even vote trading has been modeled as a Prisoner's Dilemma (Riker and Brams 1973). In fact, many of the best-developed models of important political, social, and economic processes have the Prisoner's Dilemma as their foundation.

There is yet a third literature about the Prisoner's Dilem-

28

Computer Tournaments

ma. This literature goes beyond the empirical questions of the laboratory or the real world, and instead uses the abstract game to analyze the features of some fundamental strategic issues, such as the meaning of rationality (Luce and Raiffa 1957), choices which affect other people (Schelling 1973), and cooperation without enforcement (Taylor 1976).

Unfortunately, none of these three literatures on the Prisoner's Dilemma reveals very much about how to play the game well. The experimental literature is not much help, because virtually all of it is based on analyzing the choices made by players who are seeing the formal game for the first time. Their appreciation of the strategic subtleties is bound to be restricted. Although the experimental subjects may have plenty of experience with everyday occurrences of the Prisoner's Dilemma, their ability to call on this experience in a formal setting may be limited. The choices of experienced economic and political elites in natural settings are studied in some of the applied literature of Prisoner's Dilemma, but the evidence is of limited help because of the relatively slow pace of most high-level interactions and the difficulty of controlling for changing circumstances. All together, no more than a few dozen choices have been identified and analyzed this way. Finally, the abstract literature of strategic interaction usually studies variants of the iterated Prisoner's Dilemma designed to eliminate the dilemma itself by introducing changes in the game, such as allowing interdependent choices (Howard 1966; Rapoport 1967), or putting a tax on defection (Tideman and Tullock 1976; Clarke 1980).

To learn more about how to choose effectively in an iterated Prisoner's Dilemma, a new approach is needed. Such an approach would have to draw on people who have

The Emergence of Cooperation

a rich understanding of the strategic possibilities inherent in a non-zero-sum setting, a situation in which the interests of the participants partially coincide and partially conflict. Two important facts about non-zero-sum settings would have to be taken into account. First, the proposition of the previous chapter demonstrates that what is effective depends not only upon the characteristics of a particular strategy, but also upon the nature of the other strategies with which it must interact. The second point follows directly from the first. An effective strategy must be able at any point to take into account the history of the interaction as it has developed so far.

A computer tournament for the study of effective choice in the iterated Prisoner's Dilemma meets these needs. In a computer tournament, each entrant writes a program that embodies a rule to select the cooperative or noncooperative choice on each move. The program has available to it the history of the game so far, and may use this history in making a choice. If the participants are recruited primarily from those who are familiar with the Prisoner's Dilemma, the entrants can be assured that their decision rule will be facing rules of other informed entrants. Such recruitment would also guarantee that the state of the art is represented in the tournament.

Wanting to find out what would happen, I invited professional game theorists to send in entries to just such a computer tournament. It was structured as a round robin, meaning that each entry was paired with each other entry. As announced in the rules of the tournament, each entry was also paired with its own twin and with RANDOM, a program that randomly cooperates and defects with equal probability. Each game consisted of exactly two hundred moves.[1] The payoff matrix for each move was the familiar

Computer Tournaments

one described in chapter 1. It awarded both players 3 points for mutual cooperation, and 1 point for mutual defection. If one player defected while the other player cooperated, the defecting player received 5 points and the cooperating player received 0 points.

No entry was disqualified for exceeding the allotted time. In fact, the entire round robin tournament was run five times to get a more stable estimate of the scores for each pair of players. In all, there were 120,000 moves, making for 240,000 separate choices.

The fourteen submitted entries came from five disciplines: psychology, economics, political science, mathematics, and sociology. Appendix A lists the names and affiliations of the people who submitted these entries, and it gives the rank and score of their entries.

One remarkable aspect of the tournament was that it allowed people from different disciplines to interact with each other in a common format and language. Most of the entrants were recruited from those who had published articles on game theory in general or the Prisoner's Dilemma in particular.

TIT FOR TAT, submitted by Professor Anatol Rapoport of the University of Toronto, won the tournament. This was the simplest of all submitted programs and it turned out to be the best!

TIT FOR TAT, of course, starts with a cooperative choice, and thereafter does what the other player did on the previous move. This decision rule is probably the most widely known and most discussed rule for playing the Prisoner's Dilemma. It is easily understood and easily programmed. It is known to elicit a good degree of cooperation when played with humans (Oskamp 1971; W. Wilson 1971). As an entry in a computer tournament, it has the

The Emergence of Cooperation

desirable properties that it is not very exploitable and that it does well with its own twin. It has the disadvantage that it is too generous with the RANDOM rule, which was known by the participants to be entered in the tournament.

In addition, TIT FOR TAT was known to be a powerful competitor. In a preliminary tournament, TIT FOR TAT scored second place; and in a variant of that preliminary tournament, TIT FOR TAT won first place. All of these facts were known to most of the people designing programs for the Computer Prisoner's Dilemma Tournament, because they were sent copies of a description of the preliminary tournament. Not surprisingly, many of them used the TIT FOR TAT principle and tried to improve upon it.

The striking fact is that *none* of the more complex programs submitted was able to perform as well as the original, simple TIT FOR TAT.

This result contrasts with computer chess tournaments, where complexity is obviously needed. For example, in the Second World Computer Chess Championships, the least complex program came in last (Jennings 1978). It was submitted by Johann Joss of the Eidgenossishe Technische Hochschule of Zurich, Switzerland, who also submitted an entry to the Computer Prisoner's Dilemma Tournament. His entry to the Prisoner's Dilemma Tournament was a small modification of TIT FOR TAT. But his modification, like the others, just lowered the performance of the decision rule.

Analysis of the results showed that neither the discipline of the author, the brevity of the program—nor its *length*—accounts for a rule's relative success. What does?

Before answering this question, a remark on the interpretation of numerical scores is in order. In a game of 200 moves, a useful benchmark for very good performance is

32

Computer Tournaments

600 points, which is equivalent to the score attained by a player when both sides always cooperate with each other. A useful benchmark for very poor performance is 200 points, which is equivalent to the score attained by a player when both sides never cooperate with each other. Most scores range between 200 and 600 points, although scores from 0 to 1000 points are possible. The winner, TIT FOR TAT, averaged 504 points per game.

Surprisingly, there is a single property which distinguishes the relatively high-scoring entries from the relatively low-scoring entries. This is the property of being *nice*, which is to say never being the first to defect. (For the sake of analyzing this tournament, the definition of a nice rule will be relaxed to include rules which will not be the first to defect before the last few moves, say before move 199.)

Each of the eight top-ranking entries (or rules) is nice. None of the other entries is. There is even a substantial gap in the score between the nice entries and the others. The nice entries received tournament averages between 472 and 504, while the best of the entries that were not nice received only 401 points. Thus, not being the first to defect, at least until virtually the end of the game, was a property which, all by itself, separated the more successful rules from the less successful rules in this Computer Prisoner's Dilemma Tournament.

Each of the nice rules got about 600 points with each of the other seven nice rules and with its own twin. This is because when two nice rules play, they are sure to cooperate with each other until virtually the end of the game. Actually the minor variations in end-game tactics did not account for much variation in the scores.

Since the nice rules all got within a few points of 600

The Emergence of Cooperation

with each other, the thing that distinguished the relative rankings among the nice rules was their scores with the rules which are not nice. This much is obvious. What is not obvious is that the relative ranking of the eight top rules was largely determined by just two of the other seven rules. These two rules are *kingmakers* because they do not do very well for themselves, but they largely determine the rankings among the top contenders.

The most important kingmaker was based on an "outcome maximization" principle originally developed as a possible interpretation of what human subjects do in the Prisoner's Dilemma laboratory experiments (Downing 1975). This rule, called DOWNING, is a particularly interesting rule in its own right. It is well worth studying as an example of a decision rule which is based upon a quite sophisticated idea. Unlike most of the others, its logic is not just a variant of TIT FOR TAT. Instead it is based on a deliberate attempt to understand the other player and then to make the choice that will yield the best long-term score based upon this understanding. The idea is that if the other player does not seem responsive to what DOWNING is doing, DOWNING will try to get away with whatever it can by defecting. On the other hand, if the other player does seem responsive, DOWNING will cooperate. To judge the other's responsiveness, DOWNING estimates the probability that the other player cooperates after it (DOWNING) cooperates, and also the probability that the other player cooperates after DOWNING defects. For each move, it updates its estimate of these two conditional probabilities and then selects the choice which will maximize its own long-term payoff under the assumption that it has correctly modeled the other player. If the two conditional probabilities have similar values, DOWNING deter-

34

Computer Tournaments

mines that it pays to defect, since the other player seems to be doing the same thing whether DOWNING cooperates or not. Conversely, if the other player tends to cooperate after a cooperation but not after a defection by DOWNING, then the other player seems responsive, and DOWNING will calculate that the best thing to do with a responsive player is to cooperate. Under certain circumstances, DOWNING will even determine that the best strategy is to alternate cooperation and defection.

At the start of a game, DOWNING does not know the values of these conditional probabilities for the other players. It assumes that they are both .5, but gives no weight to this estimate when information actually does come in during the play of the game.

This is a fairly sophisticated decision rule, but its implementation does have one flaw. By initially assuming that the other player is unresponsive, DOWNING is doomed to defect on the first two moves. These first two defections led many other rules to punish DOWNING, so things usually got off to a bad start. But this is precisely why DOWNING served so well as a kingmaker. First-ranking TIT FOR TAT and second-ranking TIDEMAN AND CHIERUZZI both reacted in such a way that DOWNING learned to expect that defection does not pay but that cooperation does. All of the other nice rules went downhill with DOWNING.

The nice rules did well in the tournament largely because they did so well with each other, and because there were enough of them to raise substantially each other's average score. As long as the other player did not defect, each of the nice rules was certain to continue cooperating until virtually the end of the game. But what happened if there was a defection? Different rules responded quite dif-

The Emergence of Cooperation

ferently, and their response was important in determining their overall success. A key concept in this regard is the forgiveness of a decision rule. *Forgiveness* of a rule can be informally described as its propensity to cooperate in the moves after the other player has defected.[2]

Of all the nice rules, the one that scored lowest was also the one that was least forgiving. This is FRIEDMAN, a totally unforgiving rule that employs permanent retaliation. It is never the first to defect, but once the other defects even once, FRIEDMAN defects from then on. In contrast, the winner, TIT FOR TAT, is unforgiving for one move, but thereafter is totally forgiving of that defection. After one punishment, it lets bygones be bygones.

One of the main reasons why the rules that are not nice did not do well in the tournament is that most of the rules in the tournament were not very forgiving. A concrete illustration will help. Consider the case of JOSS, a sneaky rule that tries to get away with an occasional defection. This decision rule is a variation of TIT FOR TAT. Like TIT FOR TAT, it always defects immediately after the other player defects. But instead of always cooperating after the other player cooperates, 10 percent of the time it defects after the other player cooperates. Thus it tries to sneak in an occasional exploitation of the other player.

This decision rule seems like a fairly small variation of TIT FOR TAT, but in fact its overall performance was much worse, and it is interesting to see exactly why. Table 1 shows the move-by-move history of a game between JOSS and TIT FOR TAT. At first both players cooperated, but on the sixth move, JOSS selected one of its probabilistic defections. On the next move JOSS cooperated again, but TIT FOR TAT defected in response to JOSS's previous defection. Then JOSS defected in response to TIT FOR

36

Computer Tournaments

TABLE 1
Illustrative Game Between TIT FOR TAT and JOSS

moves	1–20	11111	23232	32323	23232
moves	21–40	32324	44444	44444	44444
moves	41–60	44444	44444	44444	44444
moves	61–80	44444	44444	44444	44444
moves	81–100	44444	44444	44444	44444
moves	101–120	44444	44444	44444	44444
moves	121–140	44444	44444	44444	44444
moves	141–160	44444	44444	44444	44444
moves	161–180	44444	44444	44444	44444
moves	181–200	44444	44444	44444	44444

Score in this game: TIT FOR TAT 236; JOSS 241.
Legend: 1 both cooperated
2 TIT FOR TAT only cooperated
3 JOSS only cooperated
4 neither cooperated

TAT's defection. In effect, the single defection of JOSS on the sixth move created an *echo* back and forth between JOSS and TIT FOR TAT. This echo resulted in JOSS defecting on all the subsequent even numbered moves and TIT FOR TAT defecting on all the subsequent odd numbered moves.

On the twenty-fifth move, JOSS selected another of its probabilistic defections. Of course, TIT FOR TAT defected on the very next move and another reverberating echo began. This echo had JOSS defecting on the odd numbered moves. Together these two echoes resulted in both players defecting on every move after move 25. This string of mutual defections meant that for the rest of the game they both got only one point per turn. The final score of this game was 236 for TIT FOR TAT and 241 for JOSS. Notice that while JOSS did a little better than TIT FOR TAT, both did poorly.[3]

The problem was a combination of an occasional defec-

The Emergence of Cooperation

tion after the other's cooperation by JOSS, combined with
a short-term lack of forgiveness by both sides. The moral is
that if both sides retaliate in the way that JOSS and TIT
FOR TAT did, it does not pay to be as greedy as JOSS was.

A major lesson of this tournament is the importance of
minimizing echo effects in an environment of mutual
power. When a single defection can set off a long string of
recriminations and counterrecriminations, both sides suffer.
A sophisticated analysis of choice must go at least three
levels deep to take account of these echo effects. The first
level of analysis is the direct effect of a choice. This is easy,
since a defection always earns more than a cooperation.
The second level considers the indirect effects, taking into
account that the other side may or may not punish a defection. This much of the analysis was certainly appreciated by
many of the entrants. But the third level goes deeper and
takes into account the fact that in responding to the defections of the other side, one may be repeating or even ampli-
fying one's own previous exploitative choice. Thus a single
defection may be successful when analyzed for its direct
effects, and perhaps even when its secondary effects are
taken into account. But the real costs may be in the tertiary
effects when one's own isolated defections turn into unending mutual recriminations. Without their realizing it,
many of these rules actually wound up punishing themselves. With the other player serving as a mechanism to
delay the self-punishment by a few moves, this aspect of
self-punishment was not picked up by many of the decision
rules.

Despite the fact that none of the attempts at more or less
sophisticated decision rules was an improvement on TIT
FOR TAT, it was easy to find several rules that would have
performed substantially better than TIT FOR TAT in the

38

Computer Tournaments

environment of the tournament. The existence of these rules should serve as a warning against the facile belief that an eye for an eye is necessarily the best strategy. There are at least three rules that would have won the tournament if submitted.

The sample program sent to prospective contestants to show them how to make a submission would in fact have won the tournament if anyone had simply clipped it and mailed it in! But no one did. The sample program defects only if the other player defected on the previous two moves. It is a more forgiving version of TIT FOR TAT in that it does not punish isolated defections. The excellent performance of this TIT FOR TWO TATS rule high-lights the fact that a common error of the contestants was to expect that gains could be made from being relatively less forgiving than TIT FOR TAT, whereas in fact there were big gains to be made from being even more forgiving. The implication of this finding is striking, since it suggests that even expert strategists do not give sufficient weight to the importance of forgiveness.

Another rule which would have won the tournament was also available to most of the contestants. This was the rule which won the preliminary tournament, a report of which was used in recruiting the contestants. Called LOOK AHEAD, it was inspired by techniques used in arti-ficial intelligence programs to play chess. It is interesting that artificial intelligence techniques could have inspired a rule which was in fact better than any of the rules designed by game theorists specifically for the Prisoner's Dilemma.

A third rule which would have won the tournament was a slight modification of DOWNING. If DOWNING had started with initial assumptions that the other players would be responsive rather than unresponsive, it too would

The Emergence of Cooperation

have won and won by a large margin. A kingmaker could have been king. DOWNING's initial assumptions about the other players were pessimistic. It turned out that optimism about their responsiveness would not only have been more accurate but would also have led to more successful performance. It would have resulted in first place rather than tenth place.[4]

These results from supplementary rules reinforce a theme from the analysis of the tournament entries themselves: the entries were too competitive for their own good. In the first place, many of them defected early in the game without provocation, a characteristic which was very costly in the long run. In the second place, the optimal amount of forgiveness was considerably greater than displayed by any of the entries (except possibly DOWNING). And in the third place, the entry that was most different from the others, DOWNING, floundered on its own misplaced pessimism regarding the initial responsiveness of the others.

The analysis of the tournament results indicate that there is a lot to be learned about coping in an environment of mutual power. Even expert strategists from political science, sociology, economics, psychology, and mathematics made the systematic errors of being too competitive for their own good, not being forgiving enough, and being too pessimistic about the responsiveness of the other side.

The effectiveness of a particular strategy depends not only on its own characteristics, but also on the nature of the other strategies with which it must interact. For this reason, the results of a single tournament are not definitive. Therefore, a second round of the tournament was conducted.

The results of the second round provide substantially

40

Computer Tournaments

better grounds for insight into the nature of effective choice in the Prisoner's Dilemma. The reason is that the entrants to the second round were all given the detailed analysis of the first round, including a discussion of the supplemental rules that would have done very well in the environment of the first round. Thus they were aware not only of the outcome of the first round, but also of the concepts used to analyze success, and the strategic pitfalls that were discovered. Moreover, they each knew that the others knew these things. Therefore, the second round presumably began at a much higher level of sophistication than the first round, and its results could be expected to be that much more valuable as a guide to effective choice in the Prisoner's Dilemma.

The second round was also a dramatic improvement over the first round in sheer size of the tournament. The response was far greater than anticipated. There was a total of sixty-two entries from six countries. The contestants were largely recruited through announcements in journals for users of small computers. The game theorists who participated in the first round of the tournament were also invited to try again. The contestants ranged from a ten-year-old computer hobbyist to professors of computer science, physics, economics, psychology, mathematics, sociology, political science, and evolutionary biology. The countries represented were the United States, Canada, Great Britain, Norway, Switzerland, and New Zealand.

The second round provided a chance both to test the validity of the themes developed in the analysis of the first round and to develop new concepts to explain successes and failures. The entrants also drew their own lessons from the experience of the first round. But different people drew

The Emergence of Cooperation

different lessons. What is particularly illuminating in the second round is the way the entries based on different lessons actually interact.

TIT FOR TAT was the simplest program submitted in the first round, and it won the first round. It was the simplest submission in the second round, and it won the second round. Even though all the entrants to the second round knew that TIT FOR TAT had won the first round, no one was able to design an entry that did any better.

This decision rule was known to all of the entrants to the second round because they all had the report of the earlier round, showing that TIT FOR TAT was the most successful rule so far. They had read the arguments about how it was known to elicit a good degree of cooperation when played with humans, how it is not very exploitable, how it did well in the preliminary tournament, and how it won the first round. The report on the first round also explained some of the reasons for its success, pointing in particular to its property of never being the first to defect ("niceness") and its propensity to cooperate after the other player defected ("forgiveness" with the exception of a single punishment).

Even though an explicit tournament rule allowed anyone to submit any program, even one authored by someone else, only one person submitted TIT FOR TAT. This was Anatol Rapoport, who submitted it the first time.

The second round of the tournament was conducted in the same manner as the first round, except that minor endgame effects were eliminated. As announced in the rules, the length of the games was determined probabilistically with a 0.00346 chance of ending with each given move.[5] This is equivalent to setting $w = .99654$. Since no one knew

42

Computer Tournaments

exactly when the last move would come, end-game effects were successfully avoided in the second round.

Once again, none of the personal attributes of the contestants correlated significantly with the performance of the rules. The professors did not do significantly better than the others, nor did the Americans. Those who wrote in FORTRAN rather than BASIC did not do significantly better either, even though the use of FORTRAN would usually indicate access to something more than a bottom-of-the-line microcomputer. The names of the contestants are shown in the order of their success in appendix A along with some information about them and their programs.

On average, short programs did not do significantly better than long programs, despite the victory of TIT FOR TAT. But on the other hand, neither did long programs (with their greater complexity) do any better than short programs.

The determination of what does account for success in the second round is not easy because there were 3969 ways the 63 rules (including RANDOM) were paired in the round robin tournament. This very large tournament score matrix is given in Appendix A along with information about the entrants and their programs. In all, there were over a million moves in the second round.

As in the first round, it paid to be nice. Being the first to defect was usually quite costly. More than half of the entries were nice, so obviously most of the contestants got the message from the first round that it did not pay to be the first to defect.

In the second round, there was once again a substantial correlation between whether a rule was nice and how well

43

The Emergence of Cooperation

it did. Of the top fifteen rules, all but one were nice (and that one ranked eighth). Of the bottom fifteen rules, all but one were not nice. The overall correlation between whether a rule was nice and its tournament score was a substantial .58.

A property that distinguishes well among the nice rules themselves is how promptly and how reliably they responded to a challenge by the other player. A rule can be called *retaliatory* if it immediately defects after an "uncalled for" defection from the other. Exactly what is meant by "uncalled for" is not precisely determined. The point, however, is that unless a strategy is incited to an immediate response by a challenge from the other player, the other player may simply take more and more frequent advantage of such an easygoing strategy.

There were a number of rules in the second round of the tournament that deliberately used controlled numbers of defections to see what they could get away with. To a large extent, what determined the actual rankings of the nice rules was how well they were able to cope with these challengers. The two challengers that were especially important in this regard I shall called TESTER and TRANQUILIZER.

TESTER was submitted by David Gladstein and came in forty-sixth in the tournament. It is designed to look for softies, but is prepared to back off if the other player shows it won't be exploited. The rule is unusual in that it defects on the very first move in order to test the other's response. If the other player ever defects, it apologizes by cooperating and playing tit-for-tat for the rest of the game. Otherwise, it cooperates on the second and third moves but defects every other move after that. TESTER did a good job of exploiting several supplementary rules that would have

44

Computer Tournaments

done quite well in the environment of the first round of the tournament. For example, TIT FOR TWO TATS defects only after the other player defects on the preceding two moves. But TESTER never does defect twice in a row. So TIT FOR TWO TATS always cooperates with TESTER, and gets badly exploited for its generosity. Notice that TESTER itself did not do particularly well in the tournament. It did, however, provide low scores for some of the more easygoing rules.

As another example of how TESTER causes problems for some rules which had done well in the first round, consider the three variants of Leslie Downing's outcome maximization principle. There were two separate submissions of the REVISED DOWNING program, based on DOWNING, which looked so promising in round one. These came from Stanley F. Quayle and Leslie Downing himself. A slightly modified version came from a youthful competitor, eleven-year-old Steve Newman. However, all three were exploited by TESTER since they all calculated that the best thing to do with a program that cooperated just over half the time after one's own cooperation was to keep on cooperating. Actually they would have been better off doing what TIT FOR TAT and many other high-ranking programs did, which was to defect immediately on the second move in response to TESTER's defection on the first move. This would have elicited TESTER's apology and things would have gone better thereafter.

TRANQUILIZER illustrates a more subtle way of taking advantage of many rules, and hence a more subtle challenge. It first seeks to establish a mutually rewarding relationship with the other player, and only then does it cautiously try to see if it will be allowed to get away with something. TRANQUILIZER was submitted by Craig

45

The Emergence of Cooperation

Feathers and came in twenty-seventh in the tournament. The rule normally cooperates but is ready to defect if the other player defects too often. Thus the rule tends to cooperate for the first dozen or two dozen moves if the other player is cooperating. Only then does it throw in an unprovoked defection. By waiting until a pattern of mutual cooperation has been developed, it hopes to lull the other side into being forgiving of occasional defections. If the other player continues to cooperate, then defections become more frequent. But as long as TRANQUILIZER is maintaining an average payoff of at least 2.25 points per move, it does not defect twice in succession, and it does not defect more than one-quarter of the time. It tries to avoid pressing its luck too far.

What it takes to do well with challenging rules like TESTER and TRANQUILIZER is to be ready to retaliate after an "uncalled for" defection from the other. So while it pays to be nice, it also pays to be retaliatory. TIT FOR TAT combines these desirable properties. It is nice, forgiving, and retaliatory. It is never the first to defect; it forgives an isolated defection after a single response; but it is always incited by a defection no matter how good the interaction has been so far.

The lessons of the first round of the tournament affected the environment of the second round, since the contestants were familiar with the results. The report on the first round of the Computer Prisoner's Dilemma Tournament (Axelrod 1980*a*) concluded that it paid to be not only nice but also forgiving. The contestants in the second round knew that such forgiving decision rules as TIT FOR TWO TATS and REVISED DOWNING would have done even better than TIT FOR TAT in the environment of the first round.

46

Computer Tournaments

In the second round, many contestants apparently hoped that these conclusions would still be relevant. Of the sixty-two entries, thirty-nine were nice, and nearly all of them were at least somewhat forgiving. TIT FOR TWO TATS itself was submitted by an evolutionary biologist from the United Kingdom, John Maynard Smith. But it came in only twenty-fourth. As mentioned earlier, REVISED DOWNING was submitted twice. But in the second round, it was in the bottom half of the tournament.

What seems to have happened is an interesting interaction between people who drew one lesson and people who drew another from the first round. Lesson One was: "Be nice and forgiving." Lesson Two was more exploitative: "If others are going to be nice and forgiving, it pays to try to take advantage of them." The people who drew Lesson One suffered in the second round from those who drew Lesson Two. Rules like TRANQUILIZER and TESTER were effective at exploiting rules which were too easygoing. But the people who drew Lesson Two did not themselves do very well either. The reason is that in trying to exploit other rules, they often eventually got punished enough to make the whole game less rewarding for *both* players than pure mutual cooperation would have been. For example, TRANQUILIZER and TESTER themselves achieved only twenty-seventh and forty-sixth place, respectively. Each surpassed TIT FOR TAT's score with fewer than one-third of the rules. None of the other entries that tried to apply the exploitative conclusion of Lesson Two ranked near the top either.

While the use of Lesson Two tended to invalidate Lesson One, no entrants were able to benefit more than they were hurt in the tournament by their attempt to exploit the easygoing rules. The most successful entries tended to be

47

The Emergence of Cooperation

relatively small variations on TIT FOR TAT which were designed to recognize and give up on a seemingly RANDOM player or a very uncooperative player. But the implementations of these ideas did not do better than the pure form of TIT FOR TAT. So TIT FOR TAT, which got along with almost everyone, won the second round of the tournament just as it had won the first round.

Would the results of the second round have been much different if the distribution of entries had been substantially different? Put another way, does TIT FOR TAT do well in a wide variety of environments? That is to say, is it *robust*?

A good way to examine this question is to construct a series of hypothetical tournaments, each with a very different distribution of the types of rules participating. The method of constructing these drastically modified tournaments is explained in appendix A. The results were that TIT FOR TAT won five of the six major variants of the tournament, and came in second in the sixth. This is a strong test of how robust the success of TIT FOR TAT really is.

Another way to examine the robustness of the results is to construct a whole sequence of hypothetical future rounds of the tournament. Some of the rules were so unsuccessful that they would be unlikely to be tried again in future tournaments, while others were successful enough that their continued presence in later tournaments would be likely. For this reason, it would be helpful to analyze what would happen over a series of tournaments if the more successful rules became a larger part of the environment for each rule, and the less successful rules were met less often. This analysis would be a strong test of a rule's performance, because continued success would require a rule to do well with other successful rules.

48

Computer Tournaments

Evolutionary biology provides a useful way to think about this dynamic problem (Trivers 1971; Dawkins 1976, pp. 197–202; Maynard Smith 1978). Imagine that there are many animals of a single species which interact with each other quite often. Suppose the interactions take the form of a Prisoner's Dilemma. When two animals meet, they can cooperate with each other, not cooperate with each other, or one animal could exploit the other. Suppose further that each animal can recognize individuals it has already interacted with and can remember salient aspects of their interaction, such as whether the other has usually cooperated. A round of the tournament can then be regarded as a simulation of a single generation of such animals, with each decision rule being employed by large numbers of individuals. One convenient implication of this interpretation is that a given animal can interact with another animal using its own decision rule, just as it can run into an animal using some other rule.

The value of this analogy is that it allows a simulation of future generations of a tournament. The idea is that the more successful entries are more likely to be submitted in the next round, and the less successful entries are less likely to be submitted again. To make this precise, we can say that the number of copies (or offspring) of a given entry will be proportional to that entry's tournament score. We simply have to interpret the average payoff received by an individual as proportional to the individual's expected number of offspring. For example, if one rule gets twice as high a tournament score in the initial round as another rule, then it will be twice as well-represented in the next round.[6] Thus, RANDOM, for example, will be less important in the second generation, whereas TIT FOR TAT and the other high-ranking rules will be better represented.

The Emergence of Cooperation

In human terms, a rule which was not scoring well might be less likely to appear in the future for several different reasons. One possibility is that a player will try different strategies over time, and then stick with what seems to work best. Another possibility is that a person using a rule sees that other strategies are more successful and therefore switches to one of those strategies. Still another possibility is that a person occupying a key role, such as a member of Congress or the manager of a business, would be removed from that role if the strategy being followed was not very successful. Thus, learning, imitation, and selection can all operate in human affairs to produce a process which makes relatively unsuccessful strategies less likely to appear later.

The simulation of this process for the Prisoner's Dilemma tournament is actually quite straightforward. The tournament matrix gives the score each strategy gets with each of the other strategies. Starting with the proportions of each type in a given generation, it is only necessary to calculate the proportions which will exist in the next generation.[7] The better a strategy does, the more its representation will grow.

The results provide an interesting story. The first thing that happens is that the lowest-ranking eleven entries fall to half their initial size by the fifth generation while the middle-ranking entries tend to hold their own and the top-ranking entries slowly grow in size. By the fiftieth generation, the rules that ranked in the bottom third of the tournament have virtually disappeared, while most of those in the middle third have started to shrink, and those in the top third are continuing to grow (see figure 2).

This process simulates survival of the fittest. A rule that is successful on average with the current distribution of

50

Computer Tournaments

FIGURE 2
Simulated Ecological Success of the Decision Rules

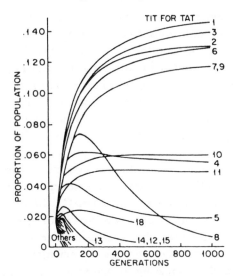

rules in the population will become an even larger proportion of the environment of the other rules in the next generation. At first, a rule that is successful with all sorts of rules will proliferate, but later as the unsuccessful rules disappear, success requires good performance with other successful rules.

This simulation provides an ecological perspective because there are no new rules of behavior introduced. It differs from an evolutionary perspective, which would allow mutations to introduce new strategies into the environment. In the ecological perspective there is a changing distribution of given types of rules. The less successful rules become less common and the more successful rules proliferate. The statistical distribution of types of individuals changes in each generation, and this changes the environ-

51

The Emergence of Cooperation

ment with which each of the individual types has to interact.

At first, poor programs and good programs are represented in equal proportions. But as time passes, the poorer ones begin to drop out and the good ones thrive. Success breeds more success, provided that the success derives from interactions with other successful rules. If, on the other hand, a decision rule's success derives from its ability to exploit other rules, then as these exploited rules die out, the exploiter's base of support becomes eroded and the exploiter suffers a similar fate.

A good example of ecological extinction is provided by HARRINGTON, the only non-nice rule among the top fifteen finishers in the second round. In the first two hundred or so generations of the ecological tournament, as TIT FOR TAT and the other successful nice programs were increasing their percentage of the population, HARRINGTON was also increasing its percentage. This was because of HARRINGTON's exploitative strategy. By the two hundredth generation or so, things began to take a noticeable turn. Less successful programs were becoming extinct, which meant that there were fewer and fewer prey for HARRINGTON to exploit. Soon HARRINGTON could not keep up with the successful nice rules, and by the one thousandth generation HARRINGTON was as extinct as the exploitable rules on which it preyed.

The ecological analysis shows that doing well with rules that do not score well themselves is eventually a self-defeating process. Not being nice may look promising at first, but in the long run it can destroy the very environment it needs for its own success.

The results also provide yet another victory for TIT FOR TAT. TIT FOR TAT had a very slight lead in the

52

Computer Tournaments

original tournament, and never lost this lead in simulated generations. By the one-thousandth generation it was the most successful rule and still growing at a faster rate than any other rule.

The overall record of TIT FOR TAT is very impressive. To recapitulate, in the second round, TIT FOR TAT achieved the highest average score of the sixty-two entries in the tournament. It also achieved the highest score in five of the six hypothetical tournaments which were constructed by magnifying the effects of different types of rules from the second round. And in the sixth hypothetical tournament it came in second. Finally, TIT FOR TAT never lost its first-place standing in a simulation of future generations of the tournament. Added to its victory in the first round of the tournament, and its fairly good performance in laboratory experiments with human subjects, TIT FOR TAT is clearly a very successful strategy.

Proposition 1 says that there is no absolutely best rule independent of the environment. What can be said for the empirical successes of TIT FOR TAT is that it is a very robust rule: it does very well over a wide range of environments. Part of its success might be that other rules anticipate its presence and are designed to do well with it. Doing well with TIT FOR TAT requires cooperating with it, and this in turn helps TIT FOR TAT. Even rules like TESTER that were designed to see what they could get away with, quickly apologize to TIT FOR TAT. Any rule which tries to take advantage of TIT FOR TAT will simply hurt itself. TIT FOR TAT benefits from its own nonexploitability because three conditions are satisfied:

1. The possibility of encountering TIT FOR TAT is salient.
2. Once encountered, TIT FOR TAT is easy to recognize.

53

The Emergence of Cooperation

3. Once recognized, TIT FOR TAT's nonexploitability is easy to appreciate.

Thus TIT FOR TAT benefits from its own *clarity*.

On the other hand, TIT FOR TAT foregoes the possibility of exploiting other rules. While such exploitation is occasionally fruitful, over a wide range of environments the problems with trying to exploit others are manifold. In the first place, if a rule defects to see what it can get away with, it risks retaliation from the rules that are provocable. In the second place, once mutual recriminations set in, it can be difficult to extract oneself. And, finally, the attempt to identify and give up on unresponsive rules (such as RANDOM or excessively uncooperative rules) often mistakenly led to giving up on rules which were in fact salvageable by a more patient rule like TIT FOR TAT. Being able to exploit the exploitable without paying too high a cost with the others is a task which was not successfully accomplished by any of the entries in round two of the tournament.

What accounts for TIT FOR TAT's robust success is its combination of being nice, retaliatory, forgiving, and clear. Its niceness prevents it from getting into unnecessary trouble. Its retaliation discourages the other side from persisting whenever defection is tried. Its forgiveness helps restore mutual cooperation. And its clarity makes it intelligible to the other player, thereby eliciting long-term cooperation.

Notes to pages 30–56

Chapter 2. *The Success of TIT FOR TAT in Computer Tournaments*

1. The second round of the tournament used a variable game length, as described in the text.

2. This is a broader definition of forgiveness than the one used by Rapoport and Chammah (1965, pp. 72–73), which is the probability of cooperation on the move after receiving the sucker's payoff, S.

3. In the five games between them, the average scores were 225 for TIT FOR TAT and 230 for JOSS.

4. In the environment of the 15 rules of the tournament, REVISED DOWN-ING averages 542 points. This compares to TIT FOR TAT, which won with 504 points. TIT FOR TWO TATS averages 532 in the same environment, and LOOK AHEAD averages 520 points.

5. This probability of ending the game at each move was chosen so that the expected median length of a game would be 200 moves. In practice, each pair of players was matched five times, and the lengths of these five games were determined once and for all by drawing a random sample. The resulting random sample from the implied distribution specified that the five games for each pair of players would be of lengths 63, 77, 151, 156, and 308 moves. Thus the average length of a game turned out to be somewhat shorter than expected at 151 moves.

6. This reproduction process creates a simulated second generation of the tournament in which the average score achieved by a rule is the *weighted* average of its score with each of the rules, where the weights are proportional to the success of the other rules in the initial generation.

7. This simulation of future rounds of the tournament is done by calculating the weighted average of the scores of a given rule with all other rules, where the weights are the numbers of the other rules which exist in the current generation. The numbers of a given rule in the next generation are then taken to be proportional to the product of its numbers in the current generation and its score in the current generation. This procedure assumes cardinal measurement of the payoff matrix. It is the only instance in this book where the payoff numbers are given a cardinal, rather than merely interval, interpretation.

References

Axelrod, Robert. 1980*a*. 'Effective Choice in the Prisoner's Dilemma.' *Journal of Conflict Resolution* 24:3–25.

Baefsky, P., and S. E. Berger. 1974. 'Self-Sacrifice, Cooperation and Aggression in Women of Varying Sex-Role Orientations.' *Personality and Social Psychology Bulletin* 1:296–98.

Bethlehem, D. W. 1975. 'The Effect of Westernization on Cooperative Behavior in Central Africa.' *International Journal of Psychology* 10:219–24.

Clarke, Edward H. 1980. *Demand Revelation and the Provision of Public Goods.* Cambridge, Mass.: Ballinger.

Dawkins, Richard. 1976. *The Selfish Gene.* Oxford: Oxford University Press.

Downing, Leslie L. 1975. 'The Prisoner's Dilemma Game as a Problem-Solving Phenomenon: an Outcome Maximizing Interpretation.' *Simulation and Games* 6:366–91.

Friedman, James W. 1971. 'A Non-Cooperative Equilibrium for Supergames.' *Review of Economic Studies* 38:1–12.

Hardin, Garrett. 1968. 'The Tragedy of the Commons.' *Science* 162:1243–48.

Hardin, Russell. 1982. *Collective Action.* Baltimore: Johns Hopkins University Press.

Howard, Nigel. 1966. 'The Mathematics of Meta-Games.' *General Systems* 11 (no. 5):187–200.

Jennings, P. R. 1978. 'The Second World Computer Chess Championships.' *Byte* 3 (January):108–18.

Luce, R. Duncan, and Howard Raiffa. 1957. *Games and Decisions.* New York: Wiley.

Maynard Smith, John. 1978. 'The Evolution of Behavior.' *Scientific American* 239:176–92.

Nydegger, Rudy V. 1974. 'Information Processing Complexity and Gaming Behavior: The Prisoner's Dilemma.' *Behavioral Science* 19:204–10.

Oskamp, Stuart. 1971. 'Effects of Programmed Strategies on Cooperation in the Prisoner's Dilemma and Other Mixed-Motive Games.' *Journal of Conflict Resolution* 15:225–29.

Rapoport, Anatol. 1967. 'Escape from Paradox.' *Scientific American* 217 (July):50–56.

Rapoport, Anatol, and Albert M. Chammah. 1965. *Prisoner's Dilemma.* Ann Arbor: University of Michigan Press.

Richardson, Lewis F. 1960. *Arms and Insecurity.* Chicago: Quadrangle.

Riker, William, and Steve J. Brams. 1973. 'The Paradox of Vote Trading.' *American Political Science Review* 67:1235–47.

Samuelson, Paul A. 1973. *Economics.* New York: McGraw-Hill

Schelling, Thomas C. 1973. 'Hockey Helmets, Concealed Weapons, and Daylight Saving: A Study of Binary Choices with Externalities.' *Journal of Conflict Resolution* 17:381–428.

Taylor, Michael. 1976. *Anarchy and Cooperation.* New York: Wiley.

Tideman, T. Nicholas, and Gordon Tullock. 1976. 'A New and Superior Process for Making Social Choices.' *Journal of Political Economy* 84:1145–59.

Trivers, Robert L. 1971. 'The Evolution of Reciprocal Altruism.' *Quarterly Review of Biology* 46:35–57.

Wilson, Warner. 1971. 'Reciprocation and Other Techniques for Inducing Cooperation in the Prisoner's Dilemma Game.' *Journal of Conflict Resolution* 15:167–95.

Zinnes, Dina A. 1976. *Contemporary Research in International Relations.* New York: Macmillan.

[4]

When in Doubt . . .

COOPERATION IN A NOISY PRISONER'S DILEMMA

JONATHAN BENDOR
RODERICK M. KRAMER
SUZANNE STOUT
Stanford University

In the last decade, there has been a resurgence of interest in problems of cooperation, stimulated largely by Axelrod's work. Using an innovative tournament approach, Axelrod found that a simple strategy, tit-for-tat (TFT), was most successful in playing the repeated prisoner's dilemma (PD) in a noiseless environment. However, recent analytical work has shown that monitoring problems caused by noise significantly impair TFT's effectiveness. The primary purpose of the present research is to discover whether there exist alternative strategies that perform well in noisy PDs. To investigate this question, the authors conducted a computer tournament. The results of the tournament demonstrated that, consistent with analytical work, TFT performed rather poorly. In contrast, strategies that were generous (i.e., cooperated more than their partners did) were quite effective.

In the last decade, few works in social science have had the general impact of *The Evolution of Cooperation* (Axelrod 1984). A beautiful synthesis of deductive reasoning and empirical inferences, *Evolution* examined the conditions under which cooperation can emerge among a population of self-interested decision makers. It also exploited a powerful new approach to investigate this problem: computer tournaments of strategies playing a binary choice prisoner's dilemma game (PD).

AUTHORS' NOTE: For helpful comments we would like to thank Jim Baron, Rob Boyd, Peter Reiss, Gene Webb, Bruce Russett, two anonymous reviewers, and participants in the Politics and Organizations seminar (Stanford), the Charles Merriam seminar (University of Illinois), and the Jacob Marschak Colloquium (UCLA). Elizabeth Martin and Warren Redlich helped greatly with data analysis, and Dao-Lin Mao and Michael Pich provided invaluable programming assistance.

JOURNAL OF CONFLICT RESOLUTION, Vol. 35 No. 4, December 1991 691-719
© 1991 Sage Publications, Inc.

692   JOURNAL OF CONFLICT RESOLUTION

One of the striking and far from obvious results of Axelrod's tournaments was the finding that tit-for-tat (TFT), the simplest strategy submitted in the tournament, emerged as the most successful. TFT, which cooperates on the first move and thereafter does whatever its partner did on the previous move, outperformed even highly sophisticated strategies. This result is all the more striking given that all of the strategies had been submitted by game theorists, economists, and psychologists who were intimately familiar with the nuances of the PD.

The impressive performance of TFT suggested that there may exist a number of basic attributes, such as niceness and provocability, that are necessary and/or sufficient for the emergence and survival of cooperation. Axelrod (1980a) suggested, for example that "reciprocity is not only a social norm, but can also be an extremely successful operating rule for an individ-ualistic pragmatist" (p. 18).

Any important work attracts critical scholarly attention that probes the limits of its findings. We believe that one significant limitation of *Evolution* — and of most investigations, both empirical and theoretical, of the PD — is that virtually throughout the book it is assumed that each player has perfect information about her or his partner's actions.[1] In classical experiments on the PD, subjects can either monitor one another directly, or there is a one-to-one correspondence between moves and payoffs, allowing flawless inferences. Models of the PD frequently incorporate similar assumptions. In many real situations, however, decision makers, unprotected by an experi-menter's careful design, suffer from a measure of uncertainty about col-leagues' actions. For example, in large and complex firms, division chiefs are often physically removed from each other, and are consequently unable to observe each other's behavior directly. Moreover, the payoffs they obtain may reflect exogenous shocks — the economy, the behavior of customers, suppliers, the workforce — that may not be perfectly known by their col-leagues. Due to these disturbances that are external to the dyadic relation-ships, the decision makers may occasionally draw incorrect inferences about their peers' actions.[2]

The primary aim of the present research is to investigate how such uncertainty or "noise" affects cooperation. In particular, we reevaluate the performance of reciprocating strategies such as TFT in the presence of

---

1. The exception to this pattern, reported on pp. 182-83 and in footnote 5, p. 222 of Axelrod (1984), concerns the results of rerunning one of the tournaments with a small chance of misperception added. TFT won this tournament as well.

2. Indeed, in complex strategic situations it would be surprising if decision makers never erred in making such inferences.

random shocks. Our research thus examines the robustness of TFT and the attributes it embodies in a noisy environment. Prior work has shown analytically that even when the shocks are small, they can, in the long run, significantly impair reciprocating strategies such as TFT (Bendor 1987; Molander 1985; Mueller 1987). For example, if cooperation can vary continuously between some lower (C_{min}) and upper bound (C_{max}), and small positive and negative errors occur with equal probability, then it has been shown that a pair of TFT strategies will wander all over the strategy space of (C_{min}, C_{max}), creating a random walk whose steady state distribution is symmetric around the average level of feasible cooperation, $\frac{C_{min} + C_{max}}{2}$ (Bendor 1987). Thus in the presence of uncertainty, TFT cannot stabilize itself at high levels of cooperation.[3]

Although these results are suggestive of the difficulties TFT might encounter in a strategically diverse ecology, they were confined to the behavior of TFT and of other reciprocating strategies with longer memories. To broaden the scope of these findings and to probe further the relative performance of strategies in the face of uncertainty, we created a tournament for a noisy prisoner's dilemma. If it turns out that strict reciprocators such as TFT do perform less well in the face of uncertainty, then it becomes important to investigate other general strategies that might fare better. Thus, another major aim of this research is to identify alternative strategies (and their attributes) that can sustain cooperation in a noisy setting.

METHODS

To enhance comparability, much of the tournament was structured in a manner similar to Axelrod's original tournaments (Axelrod 1980a, 1980b). We recruited potential participants from several departments across the university and from a university seminar. Each person was invited to submit a strategy that would be programmed and played pairwise in a round robin tournament.[4] The tournament would last a random number of periods.[5]

In order to create uncertainty, each player's cooperation level was obscured by adding a small random term during each period of play. The "noise" was a random variable, distributed normally, with a mean of zero and a

---

3. This instability of a pair of TFT strategies also holds in the binary choice game under either discrete or continuous noise (Bendor 1990). See also Downs, Rocke and Siverson (1985), and Molander (1985).

4. Unlike Axelrod, we chose not to enter the RANDOM strategy.

5. With a probability of .0067, the play would stop after any given period.

TABLE 1

Cooperation Level X	Cooperation Level Y	Error Level X	Error Level Y	Payoff Level X	Payoff Level Y
100	100	0	0	20	20
100	0	0	0	−80	100
0	0	0	0	0	0
100	100	20	−20	0	40
100	0	20	−20	−100	120
0	0	20	−20	−20	20

standard deviation of eight. We generated the error term by a normal transformation of a uniform random variable.[6] The noise was independent across players and over periods.

Because the normal is continuously distributed, we thought it would be more natural for the decision variable to also range continuously. Accordingly, either player could choose to cooperate anywhere in the interval [0, 100].

A player's payoff or benefit therefore was equal to his/her partner's cooperation minus a cost factor of cooperation plus a random error term:

$$V_t(i|j) = C_t(j,i) - \alpha C_t(i,j) + \varepsilon_t(j,i)$$

where $V_t(i|j)$ denotes i's payoff in period t in its pairing with j, $C_t(j,i)$ denotes j's cooperation level vis-à-vis i in period t, $C_t(i,j)$ refers to i's choice, and $\varepsilon_t(j,i)$ symbolizes the disturbance added to j's choice.

To ensure that the game meets the requirements of a PD, the cost-of-cooperation parameter, α, must be between zero and one; we fixed it at 0.80. With this structure, the maximum average symmetric per period payoff is 20; the minimum, zero. (The entire set of feasible average per period payoffs is displayed in Figure 1.) Of course in the presence of the random shocks, both payoffs can fall outside this region of feasible expected payoffs. Table 1 gives some sample values of $V(i|j)$, $V(j|i)$, $C(i,j)$, $C(j,i)$, $\varepsilon(i,j)$, and $\varepsilon(j,i)$.

In each round of play the computer generated two normally distributed error terms to determine the value of ε_x and ε_y. The computer also generated a uniform random number which was used to determine whether the sample path would end after that particular period of play. Each strategy then played all other strategies, including itself, using the generated error terms for each period. Each strategy therefore played using both sets of error terms in each

6. The error term distribution was truncated to the interval [−100, 100].

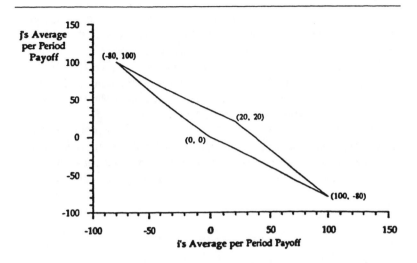

Figure 1:   Feasible Average Payoffs in the Noisy Tournament

sample path. (That is, initially Strategy 1 was assigned ε_x, and it played Strategy 2, assigned ε_y. Then the strategies were assigned the other error term, and played again.) To assure stable results, each pair of strategies played 100 games, with each game of random length.

Before they submitted their strategies, the participants were given all of the previously described information about the payoff equation, the distribution of the disturbances, and the stopping probability of the game. They were also instructed that they (or more precisely their strategies) would not be told the realized values of the disturbances, their partner's cooperation level, or the rules defining their partner's strategy.

Participants were informed that there was a chance to receive monetary rewards. At the end of the tournament, a lottery would be conducted: three of the strategies would be selected to win money. The amount each lottery-winner would take home would equal $50 plus a variable component, the latter being proportional to the strategy's payoffs. This incentive scheme heightened the variable sum character of the game: one's financial reward was dependent only on one's own payoff, and was not diminished by someone else doing well.[7]

7. Assuming, of course, that the researchers' budget was not busted! However, it is unlikely that participants worried about this; because there were to be only a few lottery winners, the odds were that most of the time one's strategy would be playing another strategy that was not competing for the researcher's kitty.

To investigate how decision makers revised their strategies in the light of performance information, we informed participants that at the end of the tournament they would be given a summary description of the results and an opportunity to revise and resubmit their strategies. A second round of the tournament would then be held, under the same conditions as the first. (If participants did not revise their strategies, they would be played unchanged.) The prize money would be awarded after the second round.

Thirteen strategies were submitted. In some cases, participants also included brief verbal descriptions or comments about the conceptual motivation or assumptions underlying their strategy. Because the participants were guaranteed anonymity, only the strategies' names are mentioned in the results described below.

RESULTS AND ANALYSIS

The results of the first round of the tournament are displayed in Table 2.

The first point to make about Table 2 is that TFT did not perform very well, either absolutely or relatively. Because one would expect most strategies' absolute performance to suffer in the presence of noise,[8] we are more interested in their relative performance, that is, the rankings. Measured this way, TFT's performance was mediocre, placing eighth out of the 13 strategies. Based on the earlier analytical work (Bendor 1987), one suspects that this mediocre performance is due to TFT's hair-trigger provocability that, given noise, causes it to fall into unintended vendettas with other nice, but provocable strategies. We shall examine this suspicion systematically below; for now we merely note that TFT averaged, when playing itself, a cooperation level of only 71 (out of a maximum of 100), indicating that it was unable to stabilize at a high level of cooperation when playing an equally provocable (though nice!) partner.[9]

The winning strategy in the tournament, NICE AND FORGIVING, differed in several significant ways from TFT. First, instead of reciprocating by returning an unbiased estimate of its partner's action, NICE tended to be *generous*, which for now we loosely define as returning more cooperation than one had received.[10] NICE's generosity took the form of a benign indifference: as long as its partner's observed cooperation level exceeded 80, NICE would continue to play *maximal* cooperation. Thus, within this range

8. However, recent work has shown that some strategies — even some nice ones — perform *better* in the presence of noise (Bendor 1990).

9. Without noise, TFT would cooperate forever when it encountered itself.

10. We will stipulate a more precise definition of generosity shortly.

TABLE 2

Rank	Name	Average per Period Payoff
1	NICE AND FORGIVING	17.05
2	DRIFTING	16.55
3	BIASED TFT	16.17
4	MENNONITE	16.13
5	Wtd. Avg. Recip.	16.00
6	TF2T	15.67
7	Staying Even	15.39
8	TFT	15.00
9	Normal	14.78
10	Running Average	14.06
11	Deviations w/ Anchor	13.74
12	CHEATING TFT	12.88
13	VIGILANT	8.99

NICE would intentionally be more cooperative than its partner. Second, although NICE would retaliate if its partner's observed cooperation fell below 80, it was willing to revert to full cooperation *before* its partner did, so long as the partner satisfied certain thresholds of acceptable behavior.

Both of these features counteracted unintentionally triggered vendettas that plagued TFT when it played itself in our noisy world. For example, suppose NICE accidentally (due to noise) delivered a cooperation level of 95 in the first period. TFT would infer C_1(NICE, TFT) = 95, and in period two TFT would set its own cooperation level at 95. Suppose it delivers $95 - 1 = 94$. In period three, instead of reciprocating, NICE would generously set its own cooperation level at 100. This would shortcircuit an impending vendetta, and "restart" the relationship as if it were period one all over again.

More generally, we infer from Table 3 that NICE's average cooperation level with its clone was 99 — just short of the maximum feasible average — in contrast to TFT's average with itself of only 71.

However, this generosity creates a risk: other strategies may exploit NICE AND FORGIVING's willingness to give more than it receives. Moreover, considered in isolation, cooperating is costly: ceteris paribus, a strategy's payoff falls the more it cooperates, following one of the fundamental properties of the prisoner's dilemma. It is therefore possible that the success of NICE AND FORGIVING was anomalous to this particular ecology.

Certainly one can readily imagine strategic ecologies in which this strategy would do very badly. In this environment, however, its success was consistent with the performance of most of the other strategies. We show this

TABLE 3

	NICE	DRIFT.	BTFT	MENN.	W.A.	TF2T	Even	TFT	Norm.	Run.	Dev.	CTFT	VIG.
NICE	19.8	12.0	19.5	19.5	18.5	18.2	19.3	17.4	18.4	14.0	17.1	13.0	14.9
DRIFTING	26.0	16.8	23.7	23.7	18.1	20.5	17.6	17.5	19.2	12.3	12.4	6.7	0.7
BTFT	20.0	13.5	19.7	19.7	18.7	18.5	19.4	17.5	18.5	13.0	15.9	12.6	3.1
MENNONITE	20.0	13.5	19.7	19.7	18.7	18.5	19.4	17.5	18.5	12.1	15.7	12.6	3.8
Wtd. avg.	20.8	15.7	20.4	20.4	17.9	19.3	18.4	17.0	18.7	12.5	18.0	7.3	1.7
TF2T	21.0	15.1	20.5	20.5	18.7	18.9	19.0	17.1	18.3	10.4	13.7	10.6	-0.2
Staying even	20.2	16.2	19.9	19.9	18.3	19.0	19.3	15.4	18.0	13.4	12.1	6.2	2.2
TFT	21.7	16.2	21.1	21.1	17.7	19.1	15.9	14.2	15.9	13.1	11.5	6.6	1.0
Normal	20.9	15.2	20.3	20.3	18.3	18.6	18.1	14.8	16.4	11.3	11.9	7.4	-1.4
Running avg.	17.0	11.5	18.0	19.1	14.8	18.3	14.3	14.4	17.0	12.8	6.2	10.4	9.0
Deviations	21.9	11.6	20.0	20.4	17.8	16.5	12.8	12.4	15.0	7.4	14.4	7.2	1.2
CHEATING TFT	25.1	7.8	22.7	22.7	12.3	17.4	8.7	9.4	11.4	13.7	10.9	5.8	-0.4
VIGILANT	23.6	3.2	9.9	9.0	9.1	9.8	5.2	6.5	10.7	13.9	8.3	10.7	2.6

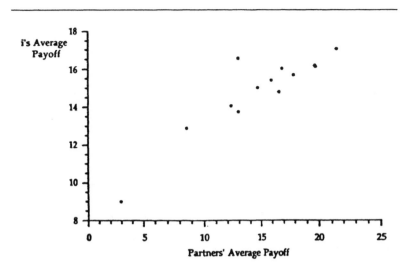

Figure 2

via two simple quantitative patterns. First, consider Figure 2, which depicts the relation between a strategy's average per period payoff and that of its partners. The scatter plot reveals a strong positive relationship. The regression equation echoes this theme:

$$V(i|\bar{j}) = 9.15 + 0.38 \times V(\bar{j}|i) \qquad \text{(adjusted } R^2 = 80.6\%)$$

where $V(i|\bar{j})$ is defined as strategy i's per period payoff averaged over all its partners, and $V(\bar{j}|i)$ is defined as the average per period payoff received by i's partners when they played i.

Thus, in general in this tournament, strategies did better when their partners did better.[11] This relationship reflects another fundamental feature of the prisoner's dilemma: because mutual cooperation is pareto-superior to mutual defection, there are joint gains that could be reaped by moving away from the noncooperative outcome. Of course there is also the everpresent

11. A similar relation was manifested in Axelrod's (1984) first tournament where $V(i|\bar{j}) = 51.6 + 0.866 \times V(\bar{j}|i)$, with an $R^2 = 65.1\%$, once the unresponsive RANDOM had been deleted. (These figures are based on the data in Table 3, p. 194.) Of course neither in Axelrod's nor in our tournament can one regard $V(i|\bar{j})$ as being a function of an exogenous variable called $V(\bar{j}|i)$, because $V(\bar{j}|i)$ is determined by the play of the game just as much as $V(i|\bar{j})$ is. Therefore, the above regression equation and corresponding R^2 are intended to show only the degree of association between the two variables; they are not supposed to support causal claims.

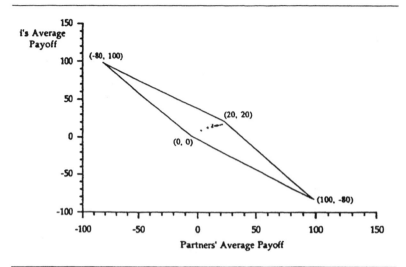

Figure 3

danger of exploitation, of being suckered by a nasty strategy that is disinterested in joint gains. Indeed, given the payoff structure of this tournament, the graph of the feasible set of average per period payoffs (recall Figure 1) gives a visual impression of a negative sum game. Empirically, however, this danger was not realized in our tournament: Figure 3 shows how the actual payoffs of $V(i|\bar{j})$ and $V(\bar{j}|i)$ are positively associated, despite the latent negative sum context of the feasible average per period payoffs.

However, this positive association between $V(i|\bar{j})$ and $V(\bar{j}|i)$ might indicate only pure reciprocity rather than generosity. Note that the payoffs of strategies in Axelrod's first tournament exhibited a similar positive relation with their partners, yet generosity was not a prominent feature in his tournament. For example, TFT is designed to be a pure reciprocator after the first round. Indeed, in a deterministic, binary choice PD, it is not altogether clear what would be the analog to the continuum-based generosity of NICE. In the classical PD environment, one always knows what one's partner did in the previous round. Accordingly one can only be generous by turning the other cheek, that is, by responding to a known doublecross with cooperation. In the noisy and continuous setting of our tournament, generosity can sensibly be interpreted as giving one's partner the benefit of the doubt; there is no such retrospective doubt in the deterministic game.

A closer inspection of the scatter plot of $V(i|\bar{j})$ versus $V(\bar{j}|i)$ reveals that generosity was indeed a pattern in our noisy tournament. NICE was not an outlier in this regard. Observe that the high scoring strategies tended to fall below the 45° line, whereas the low-scoring ones tended to be above that line, indicating that being generous — allowing your partner to do better than yourself — was adaptive in this environment.[12]

Consider, then, a simple index of generosity: $V(\bar{j}|i) - V(i|\bar{j})$. A strategy plays generously, on average, in a particular ecology if this index is positive; it plays stingily if it is negative; a pure reciprocator would have an index of zero. Regressing the strategies' payoffs on this index would reveal a strong positive relationship. However, causal claims would be inappropriate for two reasons. First, because the generosity index contains $V(i|\bar{j})$, one would be regressing a "dependent" variable on an index that incorporates that dependent variable. Second, because interdependence is the essence of the prisoners' dilemma, this generosity index is endogenous: the second component of the index, $V(\bar{j}|i)$, is determined by the play of the game just as much as the first component — $V(i|\bar{j})$ — is. To ameliorate this problem, it would be desirable to measure strategies' generosity independently of their play in a given ecology. One such measure would be the following:

Definition: a strategy's generosity index $\equiv C_{t+1}(i,j) - \hat{C}_t(j,i)$ where $\hat{C}_t(j,i)$ is an unbiased estimate of its partner's move in round t.

Thus regardless of the mix of strategies it encounters, TFT would have an index of zero.

Unfortunately, however, this measure could be used on only one of the strategies (TFT) in this tournament; the conditional structures of the other strategies were too complex to be measured by this simple index. For example, NICE's generosity measure could change from period-to-period, depending on whether its partner's observed cooperation level was above or below the threshold of 80. Similarly, BIASED TIT-FOR-TAT (BTFT), another strategy that was submitted, would have a generosity index of eight so long as $\hat{C}(j,i)$ exceeded 25. If it fell below this criterion, BTFT became a pure reciprocator, and its index would fall to zero.

As a second-best alternative, we use TFT as a baseline. Because we know that TFT is a pure reciprocator, with an ecology-free generosity index of zero, it is reasonable to say that the generosity of strategy i is indexed by the sign and magnitude of $V(\text{TFT}|i) - V(i|\text{TFT})$. Thus the better TFT does with i, compared to i's score against TFT, the more i can be considered generous.

---

12. The same point can be seen by noting that the regression line, $V(i|\bar{j}) = 8.49 + 0.420\ V(\bar{j}|i)$, crosses the 45° line.

702   *JOURNAL OF CONFLICT RESOLUTION*

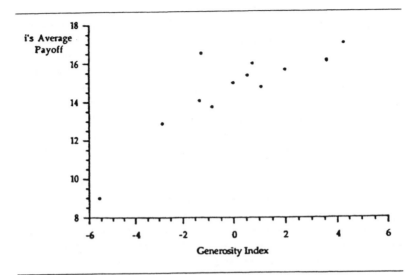

Figure 4

Further, because in our tournament (as in others), payoffs are additive across partners—play between i and j does not affect play between j and k—how strategy i performs with TFT will not affect how it performs with j.

Using $V(TFT|i) - V(i|TFT)$ as our index of generosity, Figure 4 shows the distribution of the strategies' payoffs, and again a strong positive relationship is evident. Letting our index of generosity be called generosity$_{(i,TFT)}$, the regression equation is

$$V(i|\bar{j}) = 14.6 + 0.653 \times generosity_{(i, TFT)} \qquad \text{(adjusted } R^2 = 70.3\%).$$

In this tournament, it pays not only to reciprocate, but to overcompensate.

In a sense one can view this as an extension, in a stochastic environment, of Axelrod's interesting insight that in a deterministic setting TFT cannot outscore any partner and can be beaten by many nasty strategies, but overall it can do very well indeed. This insight strikes many readers as paradoxical; how could a strategy only tie or lose to all its partners yet rank first in a tournament? We believe this reaction reflects an underlying bias toward zero sum thinking (Bazerman 1986). The answer that dispels the paradox rests on (1) the variable sum nature of prisoner's dilemma, (2) the difference between absolute and relative performance, and (3) ecological effects. Although nasty strategies can beat TFT, their absolute scores will be mediocre, because TFT retaliates in the very next period. Therefore in the binary choice PD, the most edge a nasty strategy can get on TFT is the one period gain of $(T - R)$; thereafter, however it loses $(R - P)$ — the cost of being mired in mutual defection instead of enjoying mutual cooperation — in every period.[13] In addition, nasty strategies tend to do badly against each other, whereas TFT in a noiseless environment enjoys unending cooperation with all other nice strategies (the ecological effect). Naturally, it does not beat these partners either, but, again, we must focus on TFT's absolute payoff, not its relative one.

WHY GENEROSITY WORKS

Having noted the power of pure reciprocity in the deterministic game, why does it work less well in a noisy setting? Or, to put the question more positively, why does generosity tend to work better than pure reciprocity? Again, there is an apparent paradox. Indeed, it seems sharper here; due to its generosity NICE *lost* in its pairwise play with every one of its partners (except, of course, itself). And in contrast to NICE's pattern, VIGILANT, the strategy that placed dead last in our tournament, *beat* every one of its partners in bilateral play.[14]

Much of the answer can be found by reanalyzing how a pure reciprocator, TFT, behaves when it plays itself in the presence of noise. Because TFT is nice, it starts off by cooperating fully. Sooner or later, however, a bad realization of the disturbance occurs, say in period t. TFT's move in period $t + 1$ will reflect this unlucky event. Its clone will, in turn, react in $t + 2$ to what TFT chose in $t + 1$, plus a new sample of the disturbance. And although good bounces are just as likely as bad, good luck helps less than bad luck hurts so long as the pair is nearer to the upper barrier of maximum feasible cooperation than to the lower barrier of minimum feasible cooperation. An example of this asymmetric effect is displayed in Figure 5. (Because the shocks are independent across players, it suffices to show a single sequence of behavior when the players use TFT.)

With neutral, symmetrically distributed shocks, this process continues until the feasibility limits are equidistant from TFT's expected choice of cooperation. Thus in our tournament, when TFT played itself, its expected

13. By convention, T, R, and P symbolize the one-shot payoffs of $V(defect \mid cooperate)$, $V(cooperate \mid cooperate)$, and $V(defect \mid defect)$, respectively, in the binary choice PD.

14. VIGILANT was a highly provocable and unforgiving strategy that retaliated sharply if it inferred that its partner was playing anything less than maximal cooperation.

Period	K		K+1		K+2		K+3		K+4		K+5	
TFT	choice	noise	choice	noise	choice	noise	choice	noise	choice	noise	choice	noise
Clone	100	-3	97	+4	100	-2	98	-3	95	0	95	+1

Figure 5

704

Period	K		K+1		K+2		K+3		K+4		K+5	
	choice	noise	choice	noise	choice	noise	choice	noise	choice	noise	choice	noise
TFT	100	-3			100	-2			97	0		
BTFT			100	+4			100	-3			100	+1

Figure 6

level of cooperation fell monotonically to 50.

A more generous strategy slows down this degradation by returning more than an unbiased estimate of its partner's move. Consider, for example, how BTFT would have responded to the same sample path described in the previous figure. Thus generosity seems to dampen unintended vendettas.

If this is indeed an important part of the explanation for generosity's effect on performance, then we would expect that the longer a tournament lasts, the bigger the difference in payoffs between generous and stingy entries. Why? Because the longer the tournament, the more opportunities for unintended vendettas between nice but provocable strategies, thus degrading their scores. Since each pair of strategies played 100 games, and because the lengths of the games are geometrically distributed with a large variance,[15] we have a substantial body of evidence relevant to this claim. Figure 7 contrasts TFT's performance in the 100 different tournaments with that of BTFT. The comparison is a clean one because the two strategies are virtually identical, except for BTFT's generosity in returning $\hat{C}(j,\text{BTFT}) + 8$ instead of merely $\hat{C}(j,\text{BTFT})$. Observe that time not only is more damaging to TFT, it explains more as well (at least in the sense of a higher R^2).

The next figures compare the overtime performance of the highly generous winner, NICE AND FORGIVING, with that of the very stingy loser, VIGILANT. Whereas NICE is insensitive to time (the slope of the regression line is .00052 and the R^2 is virtually zero), the effect on VIGILANT is dramatically nonlinear, most of the damage being done in the first 75 periods.

Table 4 shows that this pattern holds for most of the other strategies as well. Thus the evidence strongly supports our hypothesis that generosity works by dampening the occurrence and effects of unintended vendettas that threaten to unfold over time.

IMPLEMENTING GENEROSITY

We know what it means for a strategy to *be* generous — giving more to TFT than one receives — but so far we have said relatively little about how a strategy *achieves* generosity. The diverse approaches of the seven generous strategies in this tournament indicate that the property can be realized in many different ways. We will briefly describe the methods of the four most generous strategies: NICE, BTFT, MENNONITE, and TF2T.

---

15. The variance of a geometric distribution is $\frac{1-p}{p^2}$; here p denotes the probability that the tournament will stop at the end of a period. Note that the variance increases as p falls, becoming very large for p close to zero.

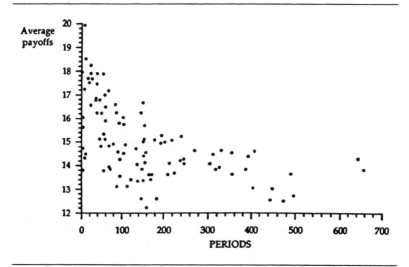

Figure 7a: TFT over Time

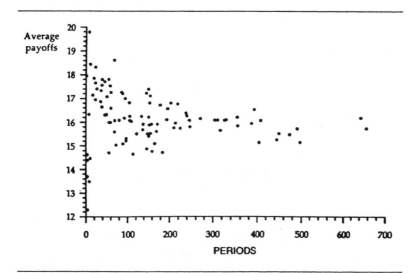

Figure 7b: BTFT over Time

NICE's approach can best be summarized as insensitivity: it simply ignored its partner's observed levels of cooperation between 80 and 100,

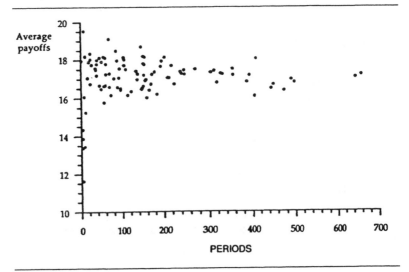

Figure 8a: NICE AND FORGIVING over Time

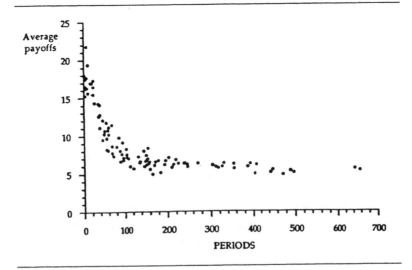

Figure 8b: VIGILANT over Time

cooperating fully so long as its partner stayed in this range. Indeed, NICE also ignored the first time it saw a $\hat{C}(j,\text{NICE})$ below 80, and would only

TABLE 4

Rank	Strategy	Generosity Index	Slope of Time Equation	R^2 in Time Equation
1	NICE	4.24	.00052	.004
2	DRIFTING	−1.25	−.00445	.040
3	BTFT	3.57	−.00159	.042
4	MENNONITE	3.57	−.00160	.043
5	Wtd. Avg. Recip.	0.73	−.00403	.201
6	TF2T	1.97	−.00280	.108
7	Staying Even	0.54	−.00466	.256
8	TFT	0.00	−.00611	.314
9	Normal	1.07	−.00548	.236
10	Running Average	−1.31	−.01060	.456
11	Deviations	−0.83	−.01228	.510
12	CHEATING TFT	−2.84	−.01312	.340
13	VIGILANT	−5.58	−.01904	.454

reduce its cooperation setting by five points in subsequent periods when $\hat{C}(j,\text{NICE})$ fell below 80.[16] Due to this insensitivity, it was quite likely that NICE would mostly choose 100 against the pure reciprocating strategy of TFT. And because 80 is two and a half standard deviations below 100, it was quite unlikely that NICE's choice of 100 would, when combined with a random shock, result in TFT inferring that NICE had played less than 80 two periods in a row. Thus NICE's behavior was likely to keep TFT in the [80, 100] range. Hence, because NICE allowed TFT substantial shortfalls below full cooperation, whereas it itself maintained complete cooperation, it achieved a high score on the TFT-based index of generosity.

The main thrust of the other three strategies was to return a fixed amount more in period $t + 1$ than the unbiased estimate of their partner's cooperation in period t.[17] BTFT and MENNONITE added eight to this estimate; TF2T added four. The latter's generosity score was correspondingly lower. This Markovian approach is exceedingly simple, requiring (by definition) a memory of only one period. And it can be adjusted to parametric changes in the variance of the disturbance: It was probably no coincidence that BTFT and

16. For example, suppose the $\hat{C}(j,\text{NICE})$ was 83, 78, 72, 76, and 81 in periods $t, t + 1, t + 2, t + 3$, and $t + 4$, respectively. Then in periods $t + 1$ through $t + 5$, NICE would set its cooperation at 100, 100, 95, 90, and 100, respectively.

17. For each of these strategies, this main rule was subject to one or more provisos. For example, if MENNONITE inferred that its partner played less than 50 for three periods consecutively, it would play zero for the rest of the game. These qualifications did not appear to affect the strategies' behavior vis-à-vis TFT.

710   *JOURNAL OF CONFLICT RESOLUTION*

	Nice	Not-Nice
Generous	6	1
Stingy	2	3

Figure 9
NOTE: TFT, being a pure reciprocator, is neither generous nor stingy. It is, of course, nice.

MENNONITE gave their partners a "benefit of the doubt" gift that exactly equalled the standard deviation of the random shocks.

Both of the above approaches refer to a strategy's behavior in the steady state, when it has settled down into a stable longrun pattern of behavior, rather than to its behavior in the first period, when one must behave unconditionally. The property that covers this unconditional behavior is *niceness*: As defined by Axelrod, a nice strategy is one that in a deterministic game never defects first. (As a plausible extension of this concept to noisy games, a nice strategy is one that never defects first so long as it infers that its partner cooperated fully.) Thus a nice strategy in our tournament would cooperate maximally in period one.

It turns out that NICE, BTFT, MENNONITE, and TF2T are all nice in this sense. And overall, niceness and generosity were positively correlated in this tournament (see Figure 9). There were some exceptions, however. Most dramatic of these was VIGILANT, a nice strategy that achieved the stingiest record. This highlights the fact that the two properties are not related in a simple way, particularly in an environment with unpredictable shocks. In a deterministic setting, all nice strategies cooperate indefinitely with other nice strategies. Consequently, in a completely nice ecology, all strategies will be pure reciprocators, neither generous nor nice. But once random shocks are introduced, heretofore latent properties — especially the degree of provocability and the willingness to let bygones be bygones — become manifest, as some nice strategies punish their nice partners for unintended bad outcomes.

ANALYZING THE OUTLIER

An impressive exception to the patterns connecting generosity and outcomes was the performance of a strategy called DRIFTING MAXIMUM LIKELIHOOD ESTIMATOR. As indicated by Table 4, DRIFTING was

TABLE 5

Rank	Strategy	Payoff
1	DRIFTING	16.496
2	BTFT	15.932
3	NICE	15.904
4	Weighted Average	15.869
5	MENNONITE	15.838
6	TF2T	15.685
7	Staying Even	15.221
8	TFT	14.923
9	Normal	14.888
10	Deviations	13.648
11	Running Average	13.368
12	CHEATING TFT	8.790

rather stingy, with a generosity index of –1.25; despite this, it placed second in the tournament. This combination of solid performance and stinginess made DRIFTING the largest outlier in the regression of score on generosity.

Interestingly, the success of DRIFTING is not based on exploiting the weakest entries in the tournament. We can see this by reinspecting the pairwise averages between strategies, reported in Table 3: DRIFTING did worse than average against the bottom two strategies, but better than average against the *strongest* strategies. Suppose, then, we were to create a simple (and draconian) ecological dynamic by rerunning the tournament several times, each time dropping the strategy that finished last. VIGILANT would then disappear in generation two. Recomputing the average per period payoffs in generation two, we obtain the rankings shown in Table 5. Observe that DRIFTING has now moved from second into first place. Further, the pairwise averages of Table 3 indicate that further ecological changes, such as the demise of CHEATING TFT, the worst strategy in generation two, would only strengthen DRIFTING's hold on first place.

The performance of DRIFTING is sufficiently good so that the strategy warrants closer examination. In some ways DRIFTING is the most interesting entry in the tournament. It incorporates a pessimistic bias about the meaning of high observed values of its partner's cooperativeness, that is of $C(j,\text{DRIFTING}) + \varepsilon(j,\text{DRIFTING})$. In the author's own words: "If [the] opponent appears to have been extremely cooperative, chances are that noise made him [sic] look more altruistic than he really is."[18] And this statement is

18. This is from a comment inserted with the author's program.

made despite the fact that the noise is neutral $-E(\varepsilon) = 0$ — which participants knew. (For this reason most strategies used $\hat{C}(j,i) = C(j,i) + \varepsilon(j,i)$ as an estimator of their partner's true cooperation level.)[19]

The quantitative implication of this pessimistic inference is that, against a nice opponent who plays maximal cooperation constantly, DRIFTING will settle down into playing 94 indefinitely. It therefore "cheats" although apparently its author does not think it is doing so. This cheating is rather mild — a phenomenon that cannot be easily replicated in the classical (deterministic, binary choice) game — and generous strategies such as MENNONITE, BTFT, and NICE usually let DRIFTING get away with it. Thus DRIFTING inadvertently "hides under the noise," getting the benefit of the doubt from strategies that are designed to avoid unintended cycles of retaliation.[20] Because the other top strategies are, within limits, generous, and because DRIFTING happens to stay within those limits, it does very well with/against them.

This however, is not the end of the story. CHEATING TFT also scored well against MENNONITE, BTFT, and NICE for similar reasons, but it did poorly overall. What accounts for this difference? The explanation is that DRIFTING's cheating is a pessimistic inference about the meaning of higher values of $C(j, \text{DRIFTING}) + \varepsilon(j, \text{DRIFTING})$; if $C(j, \text{DRIFTING}) + \varepsilon(j, \text{DRIFTING})$ falls below 88, then DRIFTING turns into a reciprocator in the steady state. And in early rounds, when $C(j, \text{DRIFTING}) + \varepsilon(j, \text{DRIFTING})$ is below 88, DRIFTING is slightly generous. It is therefore less vulnerable to the downward spirals that plague pure TFT.

CONCLUSIONS

The results of our tournament suggest several conclusions. First, generosity was clearly adaptive in this tournament. It seems plausible that in tournaments with similar strategic ecologies but more noise (greater variance in the disturbance), even more generosity would have been appropriate. However, as Axelrod and Dion (1988) aptly noted, "for larger amounts of noise, there is a trade-off: unnecessary conflict can be avoided by generosity, but generosity invites exploitation" (p. 1387). Thus strategies that are unilaterally generous will not fare well in every ecology.

19. It is clear, therefore, that the second part of DRIFTING's name is a misnomer: it is not a maximum likelihood estimator.

20. While designing the tournament, we had wondered whether any strategy would try to cheat by hiding under noise's cloak. Ironically, the strategy that did it most successfully did so unintentionally.

In the present tournament, several strategies tied the generosity of their responses directly to the disturbance's standard deviation. Thus these strategies were preadapted to changing in response to altered shocks. This method suggests a simple heuristic for designing strategies for PD tournaments: cooperate fully in period one, and thereafter set $C_{t + 1}(i, j) = \hat{C}_t(j,i)+$ (the standard deviations of ε). Note that this is a biased TFT that reduces to ordinary TFT in the special case of the noiseless game.[21]

On the other hand, holding fixed the disturbance, a nastier ecology would mandate cutting back on generosity. Giving one's partner the benefit of the doubt does make one vulnerable to intentional exploitation, and this vulnerability will exact a greater penalty as the proportion of the ecology that defects without cause rises.[22]

Thus these points display a fundamental tension or trade-off inherent in designing strategies for noisy ecologies. In such environments, bad things can happen to a player either by chance or malice. Ideally, the former should be ignored; the latter should evoke swift retaliation. But in our normally imperfect world (or, as game theorists would say, a second-best world), these inferences can be confounded. One may mistake bad luck for malice or vice versa. One must therefore trade off type 1 and type 2 errors. The optimal balance between these errors inevitably depends on two key parameters of a strategy's environment: the strategic mix it encounters, and the nature of the random shocks.

In the context of a specific tournament, such as the one reported here, one could of course be more precise about the exact nature of this trade-off. Indeed, with sufficient effort, one might be able to design the optimal strategy for a specific ecology and noise distribution. Normally, however, we are more interested in ascertaining the broad features of strategies that work "reasonably well" in a wider class of tournaments. The loss in precision is compen-

21. In more realistic tournaments, participants would be told neither the mean nor the variance of the noise; indeed, the disturbance may not be stationary. In such circumstances the heuristic for creating Biased TFT must include a subroutine for making inferences about these parameters.

22. Like most rules, this one has exceptions. Consider, in the noiseless, binary choice PD, the following ecology: TFT, MutantTFT, GRIM TRIGGER. MutantTFT is defined as play C in periods one *and* two, and thereafter mimic your opponent's move of the preceding period. GRIM TRIGGER is defined conventionally as play C in period one, thereafter cooperating if and only if one's partner has always cooperated. Holding the noise constant at zero, increase the ecology's nastiness by changing GRIM TRIGGER to SUSPICIOUS GRIM TRIGGER, defined as play D in period one, thereafter cooperating if and only if one's partner has always cooperated. In this example, the increased nastiness in the ecology implies that TFT's author would do better to make his/her strategy more generous, because the slightly more forgiving MutantTFT does much better with SUSPICIOUS GRIM TRIGGER than TFT does. (Note that MutantTFT would, in a noisy game, have a slightly higher TFT-based generosity index than TFT itself would.)

sated by the greater generality. We have touched on properties — generosity versus provocability — that we believe should vary in systematic ways in response to a strategy's environment. But much work remains to be done if we are to discover what (if anything) can make strategies robust, in the above sense of doing tolerably well across a wide variety of ecologies.[23]

Although generosity emerged as an important ingredient of success in the present tournament, we should consider the generalizability and external validity of this finding.[24] One question that immediately suggests itself is the extent to which generosity is likely to be observed among human decision makers in such situations. To what extent might we expect human strategists to display generosity? To address this question, we need to consider both those processes that inhibit generosity, as well as those that foster it. Because we have found no studies that directly examined generosity as a general disposition of strategic actors, we will attempt to draw some reasonable, albeit admittedly tentative, inferences from previous studies.[25]

Laboratory research on the PD has identified several psychological factors that might diminish generosity among human strategists. These factors can be categorized in terms of decision makers' a priori *expectations* about the other party's behavior, their *causal attributions* about the intentions or motives underlying the other party's behavior, and their *motivational orientation*.

Several studies have found that individuals' expectations regarding the likelihood that their cooperative initiatives will be reciprocated influence whether or not they themselves cooperate. Messick et al. (1983), for example, found that when individuals' a priori expectations of reciprocity are low in a PD situation, they are less likely to cooperate. This general pattern has also been observed in studies that have examined the relationship between trust and cooperation (Deutsch 1973; Brann and Foddy 1988). Extrapolating from these studies, we suggest that individuals will be less likely to be generous

23. Recent analytical work (Bendor and Swistak 1990) has proven that for tournaments of the repeated deterministic PD, "lethal" ecologies exist for every strategy, that is, for every possible strategy there exist tournaments in which (a) the strategy in question places last, and (b) the strategy's tournament score can fall behind the tournament winner's score by an arbitrarily large amount. This result places an upper bound on the degree of robustness that is feasible in PD tournaments.

24. When we began our empirical investigations on the effects of noise on cooperation in 1987, we hypothesized, based on extant theoretical work, that noise would degrade TFT's performance. However, the merits of generosity emerged only subsequently, when we analyzed the data from our tournament. In writing our results, we have been careful to preserve the inductive history underlying our conclusions about generosity. We would like to acknowledge, however, that Axelrod and Dion's (1988) review of PD research suggested that generosity might be an important attribute of effective strategies in at least some noisy environments.

25. Many of the studies discussed in this section used n-person versions of the PD. However, there is no reason to think that their results would not apply to dyadic PDs as well.

when they expect low levels of generosity from others.

The causal attributions that individuals make when trying to interpret another party's behavior may also influence how generous they are in PDs. The results of several recent studies suggest that individuals' willingness to continue to cooperate with another party depends, at least in part, on whether they attribute the outcomes of their interaction to the other party or to environmental factors beyond the other party's control (Messick 1986). Specifically, when an unfavorable outcome is attributed to the other party's greed, individuals abandon cooperation. When the unfavorable outcome can be blamed on external factors that are uncontrollable, however, individuals may continue to cooperate with each other.

Attributional processes may be especially important in noisy environments, because the greater the noise, the more uncertain or ambiguous is any given signal. Moreover, in trying to interpret ambiguous signals in noisy environments, decision makers may rely on preexisting theories or stereotypes about the other party (Jervis 1976). If those preexisting theories are based on negative stereotypes about the other party (Kramer 1989) or pessimistic/worst case assumptions (Kramer, Meyerson, and Davis 1990), then individuals may be especially reluctant to be generous. Attributional biases, such as the tendency to overattribute intentionality to the other party (Heider 1958) and to underestimate the impact of situational factors on their behavior (Ross 1977) may lead decision makers to underestimate the generosity or cooperativeness of the other party. Indeed, previous research suggests that, even under the best of circumstances, there may be considerable ambiguity regarding the motives or intentions of the other party (Nemeth 1972). A particularly relevant study by Solomon (1960) found that individuals even had trouble interpreting the motives of another actor who always cooperated. We offer as a general hypothesis the proposition that these attributional biases will directly affect individuals' willingness to give the other party the benefit of the doubt in noisy environments. In particular, they may lead decision makers to overestimate the stinginess of the other party, leading to a reluctance to be generous one's self.

There are also several motivational considerations that may inhibit generosity. First, the fear of exploitation or desire to avoid the so-called sucker's payoff may make it difficult for individuals to risk generosity (Coombs 1973; Kuhlman, Camac, and Cunha 1986). Experimental studies of the PD have found that players will often cooperate until they have evidence or even the mere suspicion that the other party is taking advantage of them (see discussions in Dawes and Thaler 1988; Deutsch 1973; Messick et al. 1983). Because of the fear of exploitation, individuals may engage in a kind of defensive "stinginess" even though they recognize the merits of generosity.

Research on the motivational underpinnings of choice in PDs suggests another reason why generosity might not be the dominant or modal orientation among decision makers. A large number of studies have shown that individuals approach PDs with a variety of distinct motivational orientations or outcome preferences. Of particular relevance to the present discussion is the motivational orientation called competitiveness. Competitiveness is defined as a preference for outcomes that maximize the difference between one's own outcomes and those obtained by the other party. Experimental research suggest that competitors evaluate their outcomes in terms of their relative gain over others, even when this means smaller absolute individual gains for themselves (Knight and Dubro 1984; Kramer, McClintock, and Messick 1986; Kuhlman and Marshello 1975; Liebrand 1984; Messick and McClintock 1968). Players with a competitive motive may be particularly unlikely to regard generosity as an attractive or viable strategy in a PD.

There is also research suggesting that individuals generally prefer equal outcomes and regard unequal outcomes as aversive or undesirable (see Messick 1990). If so, then they may be particularly sensitive and reactive to any indications that the other party is doing better or coming out ahead.

We have identified three general psychological factors that may discourage generosity among decision makers in a PD. Are there factors that might facilitate or promote generosity? Reversing the logic of the arguments presented above, one might imagine that if individuals' expectations about the other party's behavior were more positive or the welfare of the other party weighted more heavily, then they would be more likely to behave generously.

One way in which a willingness to be generous may develop is a history of gradual, sustained reciprocated exchanges. Empirical studies have shown that such exchanges can lead to the emergence of a relatively stable trust in the other party (Lindskold 1978; Rotter 1980). A limitation of this form of trust, of course, is that it depends on a rather specific history of interpersonal reciprocity; consequently, it may be limited in its generality (i.e., it may not be extended to other parties in one's ecology).

There are other variants of trust that may not suffer from this limitation. Brewer (1981) proposed that there may exist a form of group-based trust (i.e., trust predicated on common membership in a social group) which is extended — without requiring prior interaction — to other members of one's group or community. Such a generalized trust enables individuals to initiate cooperation with the expectation that others will respond favorably to these initiatives. Of course, if reciprocity is not forthcoming, cooperation can be abandoned. The important point is that group-based trust is a social mechanism for initiating cooperative behavior without lengthy or explicit negotiations with each member of one's community.

Previous research has also identified two general motivational orientations that might lead to generous behavior in PDs. We noted above that there is evidence that some players, when confronted with a PD situation, will subjectively transform the game into a competitive one because they seek to maximize their relative gain over other parties. This same research suggests that another common motive is for players to maximize their joint gain. These individuals, who are labeled *cooperators* in these studies, will characteristically choose whichever alternative maximizes the combined outcomes of the two parties, even if this means a lesser gain for self. Along similar lines, Dawes and others have posited that altruistic motives may also lead to cooperative behavior (Dawes and Thaler 1988; Etzioni 1988; Mansbridge 1990).

In summary, the results of our computer tournament provide empirical support for the analytical arguments of Molander (1985), Downs, Rocke, and Siverson (1985) and Bendor (1987) regarding constraints on the robustness of TFT. Just as these authors argued, when noise is introduced into a PD situation, TFT fares less well than in the comparatively certain world of Axelrod's original tournament study. Our results also suggest some nuances about those attributes of strategies that might prosper in noisy PDs. In particular, giving one's partner the benefit of the doubt may avoid costly vendettas that neither partner wants. However, in generalizing such findings, it is critical that we incorporate insights from psychological and behavioral research in order to more fully "humanize" our strategies. Thus, although the tournament methodology provides a rich ecological setting in which to develop, hone, and test our intuitions and formal theories about cooperation, such results should be subjected to validation in behavioral studies as well.

REFERENCES

Axelrod, R. 1980a. Effective choice in the prisoner's dilemma. *Journal of Conflict Resolution* 24:3-25.

———. 1980b. More effective choice in the prisoner's dilemma. *Journal of Conflict Resolution* 24:379-403.

———. 1984. *The evolution of cooperation.* New York: Basic Books.

Axelrod, R., and D. Dion. 1988. The further evolution of cooperation. *Science* 242:1385-90.

Bazerman, M. 1986. *Judgment in managerial decision making.* New York: Wiley.

Bendor, J. 1987. In good times and bad: Reciprocity in an uncertain world. *American Journal of Political Science* 31:531-58.

———. 1990. Uncertainty's effect on the repeated prisoner's dilemma: Four false conjectures — and five true propositions. Unpublished manuscript, Graduate School of Business, Stanford University.

Bendor, J., and P. Swistak. 1990. The evolutionary stability of cooperation in the iterated prisoner's dilemma. Research paper no. 1115, Graduate School of Business, Stanford University.

Brann, P., and M. Foddy. 1988. Trust and the consumption of a deteriorating common resource. *Journal of Conflict Resolution* 31:614-630.

Brewer, M. B. 1981. Ethnocentrism and its role in interpersonal trust. In *Scientific inquiry and the social sciences*, edited by M. B. Brewer and B. E. Collins. New York: Jossey-Bass.

Coombs, C. H. 1973. A re-parameterization of the prisoner's dilemma game. *Behavioral Science* 18:424-28.

Dawes, R. M., and R. H. Thaler. 1988. Anomalies: Cooperation. *Journal of Economic Perspectives* 2:187-97.

Deutsch, M. 1973. *The resolution of conflict: Constructive and destructive processes.* New Haven, CT: Yale University Press.

Downs, G. W., D. M. Rocke, and R. M. Siverson. 1985. Arms races and cooperation. *World Politics* 38:118-46.

Etzioni, A. 1988. *The moral dimension: Toward a new economics.* New York: Free Press.

Heider, F. 1958. *The psychology of interpersonal relations.* New York: Wiley.

Jervis, R. 1976. *Perception and misperception in international politics.* Princeton, NJ: Princeton University Press.

Knight, G. P., and A. F. Dubro. 1984. Cooperative, competitive, and individual social values: An individualized regression and clustering approach. *Journal of Personality and Social Psychology* 46:98-105.

Kramer, R. M. 1989. Windows of vulnerability or cognitive illusions? Cognitive processes in the nuclear arms race. *Journal of Experimental Social Psychology* 25:79-100.

Kramer, R. M., C. G. McClintock, and D. M. Messick. 1986. Social values and cooperative response to a simulated resource conservation crisis. *Journal of Personality* 54:576-91.

Kramer, R. M., D. Meyerson, and G. Davis. 1990. How much is enough? Psychological components of "guns versus butter" decisions in a security dilemma. *Journal of Personality and Social Psychology* 58:984-93.

Kuhlman, D. M., C. Camac, and D. Cunha. 1986. Individual differences in social orientation. In *Experimental social dilemmas*, edited by H. Wilke, D. Messick, & C. Rutte. Frankfurt, Germany: Peter Lang.

Kuhlman, D. M., and A. Marshello. 1975. Individual differences in game motivation as moderators of preprogrammed strategic effects in prisoner's dilemma. *Journal of Personality and Social Psychology* 32:922-31.

Liebrand, W. B. 1984. The effect of social motives, communication, and group size on behavior in an n-person multi-stage mixed-motive game. *European Journal of Social Psychology* 14:239-64.

Lindskold, S. 1978. Trust development, the GRIT proposal, and the effects of conciliatory acts on conflict and cooperation. *Psychological Bulletin* 85:7972-93.

Mansbridge, J. 1990. *Beyond self-interest.* Chicago: University of Chicago Press.

Messick, D. M. 1986. Decision making in social dilemmas: Some attributional effects. In *New directions in research on decision making*, edited by B. Brehmer, H. Jungerman, P. Lourens, and G. Sevon. North-Holland: Elsevier Science.

———. 1990. The preference for equality. Unpublished manuscript.

Messick, D. M., & C. G. McClintock. 1968. Motivational basis of choice in experimental games. *Journal of Experimental and Social Psychology* 4:1-25.

Messick, D. M., H. Wilke, M. B. Brewer, R. M. Kramer, P. Zemke, and L. Lui. 1983. Individual adaptations and structural change as solutions to social dilemmas. *Journal of Personality and Social Psychology* 44:294-309.

Molander, P. 1985. The optimal level of generosity in a selfish, uncertain environment. *Journal of Conflict Resolution* 29:611-18.

Mueller, U. 1987. Optimal retaliation for optimal cooperation. *Journal of Conflict Resolution* 31:692-724.

Nemeth, C. 1972. A critical analysis of research utilizing the prisoner's dilemma paradigm for the study of bargaining. In *Advances in experimental social psychology* Vol. 6, edited by L. Berkowitz, 203-34. New York: Academic Press.

Ross, L. 1977. The intuitive psychologist and his shortcomings. In *Advances in experimental social psychology* Vol. 10, edited by L. Berkowitz. New York: Academic Press.

Rotter, J. B. 1980. Interpersonal trust, trustworthiness, and gullibility. *American Psychologist* 35:1-7.

Solomon, L. 1960. The influence of some types of power relationships and game strategies upon the development of interpersonal trust. *Journal of Abnormal and Social Psychology* 61: 223-30.

[5]
Solving Social Dilemmas
A REVIEW

DAVID M. MESSICK

MARILYNN B. BREWER

David M. Messick received his Ph.D. in Social Psychology from the University of North Carolina at Chapel Hill. His research has focused on a number of aspects of decision making, especially for situations of social interdependence. He is currently Professor and Chair of the Psychology Department at the University of California, Santa Barbara.

Marilynn B. Brewer is currently professor of psychology and Director of the Institute for Social Science Research at the University of California at Los Angeles, where she moved after nine years on the psychology faculty at University of California, Santa Barbara. Her primary research interests include the study of social stereotypes and intergroup relations.

Garrett Hardin analyzed the parable, "The Tragedy of the Commons," in his very important article (1968). The parable describes a situation in which a number of herdsmen graze their herds on a common pasturage. Each herdsman is aware that it is to his benefit to increase the size of his herd because, while each of his animals represents potential profit to him, the cost of grazing the animal, measured as the damage done to the common pasturage, is shared by

AUTHORS' NOTE: We want to thank Julian Edney, Sam Komorita, Rod Kramer, Charles Plott, Dean Pruitt, Phillip Shaver, Wolfgang Stroebe, and Henk Wilke for their many useful and interesting comments on the penultimate version of this review. Time and space limitations prevented us from incorporating as many of their ideas as we wished.

all of the herdsmen. Responding to this incentive, each herdsman rationally decides to increase his herd size and, as this happens, the quality of the commons deteriorates. The carrying capacity of the commons is exceeded and as the process continues, which it is likely to do because no individual herdsman will find it beneficial to unilaterally reduce the size of his herd, it approaches its tragic conclusion, the collapse of the commons and the ultimate destruction of the herds that grazed on it.

Hardin's parable is a story about a form of social interdependence in which the collective consequence of reasonable individual choices is disaster. Scientists in a variety of disciplines have read lessons from this parable that pertain to population control (Baden, 1977), political organization (Orbell & Wilson, 1978), the economics of public goods (Olson, 1965; Samuelson, 1954), and the arrangement of reinforcement contingencies (Platt, 1973). Economists, political scientists, sociologists, and biologists, as well as social psychologists, have seen issues in this simple tale that are of central importance in their respective disciplines. Excellent books by Cross and Guyer (1980), Schelling (1978), and Hardin and Baden (1977) describe a wide range of social phenomena to which the tragedy of the commons relates. Arrow's (1963) important book is also relevant. Reviews highlighting psychological dimensions of the problem have been written by Dawes (1980), Dawes and Orbell (1981), Edney and Harper (1978), Edney (1980, 1981), and Stroebe and Frey (1982).

This review will be organized into four sections. In the first we will propose a classification of social (and individual) traps or dilemmas. In the second section we will briefly review the research paradigms that have been used to study experimentally the various types of social dilemmas. The third section is the review of research findings, the heart of the chapter. We conclude by offering some advice on the difference between more and less fruitful research in this area.

SOCIAL TRAPS

Cross and Guyer (1980) and Platt (1973) view the tragedy of the commons as a special type of *social trap*. Social traps are peculiar arrangements of rewards and punishments in which behaviors that are gratifying for the individual in the short term, imply long-term punishments for the individual and for others as well. We are lured into the trap by our short-term self-interest, ignoring the long-term collective costs; the trap is sprung when the future collective costs must be paid. A *social fence* or *countertrap* exists when the short-term aversive consequences of an act deter us from performing the act and when the act would produce long-term positive benefits both to ourselves and to others if performed. The immediate, personal negatives prevent us from providing long-term positives.

There are three distinctions that we believe to be essential in Cross and Guyer's (1980) discussion of social traps. The first is the distinction between social traps and fences that is outlined in the preceding paragraph. The second distinction is whether the trap (or fence) is a one-person situation or a situation, such as the tragedy of the commons, in which more than one person is involved. The final distinction concerns the importance of the temporal disjunction between the positive and negative consequences. In some cases, the essence of the trap is that the negative consequence of a behavior is delayed while the positive consequence is immediate; in other situations, the trap can be sprung with no delay whatsoever.

These three distinctions lead to the three-dimensional classification of social traps that is presented in Table 1.1. While our focus in this article is on social dilemmas, the four prototypical collective traps on the right of Table 1.1, it will be useful as a contrast to examine briefly one-person or individual traps.

Individual Traps

The first of these (cell 1 in the table) is the rather common one in which we do things for immediate positive gain, but which are likely to cause disagreeable future outcomes. The sweetness of a banana split is immediate; the fatness it causes comes later. The pleasure of smoking tobacco is immediate; the increased rate of heart disease and lung cancer is the bill that must be paid down the road. Hangovers follow binges, although medication that produces nausea when combined with alcohol tends to move the aversive properties of alcohol ingestion forward in time to make them more nearly coincident with the positive "buzz" that alcohol produces. This type of treatment shifts the trap from the first to the third cell in Table 1.1.

There are many traps in which we do things for a positive consequence but confront immediate negative outcomes (cell 3). Reckless driving can be thrilling but it can also be harmful, and the harm will be immediate. Individual no-delay traps have a self-eliminating quality if the behaviors have sufficiently unpleasant consequences. Time delay traps, on the other hand, do not have this property. By the time the smoker gets lung cancer (that is to say, experiences the negative consequence), it is too late. Hangovers, which are not as delayed as lung cancer, still may not follow the act of drinking closely enough to significantly influence its frequency. So, while nondelay traps have a built-in corrective, delayed traps have less.

TABLE 1.1
A Three-Dimensional Classification of Social Traps

| | Individual | | Collective | |
	Delay	No Delay	Delay	No Delay
Trap	1	3	5	7
Fence	2	4	6	8

Fences (cells 2 and 4) refer to situations in which a behavior is avoided, which if it had not been, could have produced positive future outcomes. Students who avoid studying do not score as high as they could on later exams, and people who avoid the dentist must eventually see him, often at a greater cost of dollars and pain than if they had seen him regularly. A university faculty member may forgo a future promotion by failing to face the aversive job of writing up research results.

Not all fences have delayed consequences. Fear often deters us from doing things that, if done, would have immediate positive consequences. Many people will never savor the delicacy of snails or of caviar because the idea of eating such things is revolting to them. Many young people never discover the joy of reading because they believe that it will be boring. When we do not go skiing with friends because we think it will be too hard or when we stay away from an entertaining play because we think it will be dull, we're being controlled by fences. Phobias, of course, are the Great Walls of individual fences.

Individual fences are rendered even more difficult to solve than individual traps because if the behavior does not occur, there is no opportunity to learn of the positive consequences. Fences, therefore, even undelayed ones, tend to have a self-perpetuating rather than a self-correcting quality.

Collective Traps

Collective traps are defined somewhat differently from one-person traps. Implicit in the notion of traps and counter-traps is the principle that a behavior or choice has at least two different consequences, one positive and one negative. In time-delay or temporal traps, these consequences are differentially distributed through time; in nondelay traps these two consequencs are differentially attended to. In *collective traps,* the positive and negative consequences are differentially distributed across members of a group. In traps, in contrast to fences, an individual has an inducement to take an action that results in a positive consequence for him or her but which also has negative consequences for others. This arrangement is reversed in collective fences; the individual is deterred from taking an action that would be personally costly but that would be beneficial to others.

We need to narrow our focus at this point because there are many situations having these characteristics that we will ignore in this review. It is necessary to distinguish between symmetric and asymmetric situations. In symmetric situations, we do not distinguish among the participants; the incentive structure is identical for each of them, as in the tragedy of the commons. In asymmetric situations, the participants have different preferences or incentive structures. If one person gags because of another's cigar smoke, the two clearly do not have identical preferences, although this situation would qualify as a collective trap in that the behavior one person finds rewarding, another finds repulsive. These asymmetric situations are called *externality traps* by Cross and Guyer (1980).

Symmetric collective traps or *social dilemas* are characterized by the existence of identical incentive structures for all participants and by the fact that when the participants all respond to their individual incentives, disregarding the social consequences, all the participants are worse off than if they ignored their individual incentives. The consequence of each herdsman increasing the size of his herd is that these same herdsmen are made worse off. Thus, the two essential qualities of social dilemmas are that (1) each person has an individually rational choice that, when made by all members of the group, (2) provides a poorer outcome than that which the members would have received if no members made the rational choice.

Social dilemmas, like one-person traps, can have immediate or delayed outcomes, and they can be traps or fences. A social dilemma trap is a situation, like the tragedy of the commons, in which the individually rational choice is to do something, which, when done by all, leads to individual and collective disaster. A collective fence, however, is characterized by an incentive not to do something which, when not done by any, or when done by too few people, results in a poorer state of affairs than if everyone had done it. Cross and Guyer (1980) give an example of such a situation when they describe the thinking of a prototypical citizen considering whether to shovel the snow from his or her sidewalk after a blizzard. All the citizens realize that if they alone shoveled the snow from their sidewalks, the situation would not be improved since their neighbors' sidewalks would still be unnavigable. As a result, none of the residents shovel their snow and all of them remain trapped (literally) in their houses. The consequences of not shoveling (and of shoveling) are pretty much immediate, making this an example of a no-delay collective fence (cell 8 in Table 1.1).

The problem of public goods, long noted in the literature of economics (e.g., Samuelson, 1954; Olson, 1965), is a classic collective fence.[1] The problem is this: If a good is going to be made available to anyone who chooses to use it, then what incentive does one have to pay to establish the good? The answer generally given is that the incentive is too weak for the good to be provided (Brubaker, 1975) or for it to be provided at an optimal level (Samuelson, 1954). Public television is a public good: If a community has public television, anyone can enjoy the benefit without paying the cost. If public television depended exclusively on voluntary donations, it would have failed long ago. Why should we pay for public TV? Unlike films in theaters, we don't need to pay to enjoy. The success of a local station, moreover, will not depend on one person's donation. Although we would prefer to have public TV and lose the donation than to have the donation and lose public TV, the cost isn't worth it. However, when everyone decides that the cost is not worth it, we obtain our less preferred outcome of keeping our money and losing the station. This is not the consequence of a single person's decision, but the consequence of a multitude of such decisions. The fact that the collective consequence would be remote in time, a delayed consequence, further blurs the connection between our individual choices and the collective outcome. Those who enjoy the public good without paying the cost are referred to as *free riders*. Stroebe and Frey (1982) have reviewed a number of studies from economics and psychology bearing on free riding and the provision of public goods.

In collective traps the collective problems arise from what people do, not from what they fail to do. The traffic jams that we endure at 7:30 a.m. and 5:30 p.m. arise because we (and thousands like us) like to arrive at our offices at 8:00 a.m. and to leave around 5:00 p.m. Unlike the consequences in the tragedy of the commons, the results of our choice of departure times are immediate and maddeningly predictable. We may squander fossil fuels by driving alone rather than car pooling, or by driving faster rather than slower, or by maintaining our homes too hot in winter or too cold in summer, without worrying

about long-term effects. We may even ignore the shorter-term consequence of having to pay our fuel and electricity bills in a month or so.
As we collectively ignore these costs, we collectively overuse the
resource and collectively pave the way for disasters that none of us
caused individually. Collective traps with delayed consequences
(cell 5, Table 1.1) and especially collective fences with delayed
outcomes (cell 6) seem to present the most difficult cf all dilemmas to
solve because the connections between our individual choices and the
consequences of these choices are not only diffused through time,
they are also diffused by the choices of others.

RESEARCH PARADIGMS

The three and one-half dimensional classification of social traps
that we have presented (fences versus traps, delayed versus immediate
consequences, individual versus collective situations, and symmetric
versus asymmetric collective situations) not only helps one to understand the diversity of situations that have entrapping qualities, it also
draws our attention to important variables that differentiate laboratory
research paradigms that have been used to study solutions to these
traps. Here we will describe some of the paradigms that have been
used to study collective traps.

N-Person Prisoners Dilemma

Certainly the earliest (Hoggatt, 1959; Rapoport, Chammah, Dwyer,
& Gyr, 1962; Bixenstine, Levitt, & Wilson, 1966) and the most
frequently used research paradigm that has been used to study social
dilemmas is the N-person prisoner's dilemma (NPD). In the NPD,
each member of a group is permitted to make one of, typically, two
choices, either a "defecting" or a "cooperative" choice. The defecting
choice is the individually optimal choice for each subject to make
because that choice provides the subject a higher payoff than the
cooperative choice regardless of the choices of the other members of
the group. The defecting choice also has the property that it reduces
the payoffs to all the other group members. Moreover, it reduces the
others' payoffs enough so that if all group members make the defecting
choice, they all get lower payoffs than if they all make the cooperative
choice. The basic dependent variable in NPDs is the frequency or
proportion of cooperative responses. The two-person prisoner's
dilemma (PD) was the research instrument used in an avalanche of
experiments over a couple of decades (Pruitt & Kimmel, 1977). The
essential characteristics of the two-person PD are (1) that each

individual has a dominating choice, that is, a choice that provides a higher payoff than the other choice no matter what the other person chooses, and (2) that when both persons choose the dominating strategy both are worse off than when both choose the dominated or irrational strategy.

Dawes (1980) has noted that the two-person version of the PD differs from the N-person version in three ways that tend to make the two-person version less representative of the social situations that we intend to model with the paradigm than the N-person one. First, the cost of choosing the dominating or defecting strategy is born by the one other player and is spread out across several or many others. Second, when one chooses to defect in a two-person group, the other knows that one did. Anonymity is impossible, which is not the case in larger groups. Finally, each person in a two-person group has control over the outcome to the other; by choosing the dominating, defecting choice one punishes the other, and by making the cooperative choice one rewards the other. This direct linkage between one's behavior and another's outcomes is not characteristic of real-world collective dilemmas.

NPD games are no-delay collective traps. Each person has an incentive to make the defecting choice, and if everyone does so, everyone is worse off than if no one made it. The payoffs are immediate. While the trap does not depend on the temporal distribution of rewards, many investigators have their subjects play the same game over a series of trials which adds a temporal dimension to the paradigm (for example, Kelley & Grzelak, 1972; Caldwell, 1976). When subjects are allowed to make the same choice on a series of trials, they can gain information about the behavior of others, but the entrapping quality of the situation does not depend on the repetition of response.

Replenishable Resource Traps

A number of studies have been conducted using a paradigm in which the consequences of a choice are distributed through time (for example, Brechner, 1977; Cass & Edney, 1978; Edney & Harper, 1978; Jorgenson & Papciak, 1981; Messick, Wilke, Brewer, Kramer, Zemke, & Lui, 1983). In studies of this type, a group of subjects share a common pool of resources. The subjects have individual responses that allow them to extract or to harvest resources from the pool. It is to the subjects' individual advantage to harvest and accumulate as much of the resource as possible. The resource pool in this paradigm is not a constant size. As resources are used, the pool can replenish itself according to some predetermined replenishment schedule although, typically, there is a maximum that the pool cannot exceed. Optimal use of the resource generally consists of keeping the pool level close to its maximum and harvesting, in any period, only as much as will be replenished in that period. Overuse of the pool in a period will provide an individual or group an immediate gain, but the long-term consequence will be depletion of the pool and the subsequent inability to make harvests at a later time.

Resource replenishment dilemmas add a level of complexity not found in the NPD paradigm in that, unlike the NPD, each trial in a sequence is not like all others. The level of the pool at a given time will depend on the collective harvest decisions that have been made previously. Consequently, one's decisions must take account not only of the current pool level but also of the level of the pool in the future.

With resource dilemmas, the major dependent variables are the rate at which the resource is harvested and, in some cases, the time it takes before the pool is depleted.

It is appropriate to point out here that one major difference between resource dilemmas and the NPD paradigm, in addition to the importance of delay, is that, in the former it is possible to have a one-person "group" whereas the smallest number of persons for whom the NPD can be defined is two. Thus, efforts to contrast individual to group behavior (Cass & Edney, 1978; Messick & McClelland, 1983) are possible within this paradigm but not in the NPD paradigm.

Public Goods Provision

Whereas there is a reasonable amount of methodological similarity in various efforts to study collective traps, no single paradigm like the NPD or the renewable resource paradigm has emerged for studying public goods provision. One reason there is so little paradigmatic homogeneity in experimental studies of public good provision may be that the studies have been done in a variety of academic disciplines. Studies have been reported by economists (Bohm, 1972; Issac, McCue, & Plott, 1982), sociologists (Marwell & Ames, 1979), and by political scientists and social psychologists (Van de Kragt, Orbell, & Dawes, 1982). The methodological and disciplinary diversity would be a benefit if the results of this variety of paradigms led to a common conceptual consensus. Unfortunately, this has not proven to be the case.

We will briefly describe a few of the experiments that have been done on public goods provision to illustrate the diversity of tasks that have been used. In all these cases, the consequences of the group decisions are immediate or, if delayed, the delay is not an essential part of the trap.

All the tasks that have been used to study public goods have the following features in common: Each member of a group can make a contribution of money, tokens, or effort to a shared good, the benefits of which, if any, are distributed equally to all members regardless of the members' contributions. The magnitude of the benefits generally increases with the total group contribution but, sometimes, the optimal level of contribution is less than the maximal level. Thus, it is possible for groups to contribute too little, as could be expected, since one can enjoy one's share of the benefits without contributing for them, or too much.

Perhaps the simplest of tasks of this kind was used by Van de Kragt and associates (1982). In their studies, every member of a group would receive a monetary reward of $10 if some subsect of a specified size volunteered to pay $5. If fewer than that number volunteered, no bonus would be provided to anyone. Subjects made their choices anonymously, the results were announced, and the subjects were paid accordingly. As in the NPD, the subjects' choice here is binary: to join the contributing set or not to join it.If more than the minimal number of subjects contribute, then the group is paying too much for the bonus. If too few contribute, the group does not obtain the bonus.

A completely different task was used in a study by Sweeney (1973), who had his subjects ride stationary exercise bicycles attached to an electrical generator. There were six subjects in a group, each of whose generator was purportedly attached to a common light. The subjects were told that all subjects in the group would be given experimental credit for their participation if the group light stayed "brightly illuminated" for at least 10 minutes. In this study, the public good was experimental credit and the cost was the effort required to ride the exercycle.

The last experimental approach to the public goods problem that we will mention was used by Marwell and Ames (1979), who contacted high-school age people by telephone. People who agreed to participate were given a number of tokens that could be invested in a private or a public option. The private option converted each token to 1¢, which the subject could keep. The rate of conversion of tokens invested in the public exchange depended on how many tokens had been invested in this exchange. If there were more than 200 per group member, then the public exchange paid off at a better rate than the private option. The dependent variable in this study was, of course, the number of tokens invested in the public exchange. A similar task was used in a laboratory setting by Issac and associates (1982).

Delayed Fences

We found only two experiments in which the benefit derived from investing in a public good is delayed in time and in which the group goal is not to provide a public good, but to maintain one that exists.

These two studies, by Rubenstein, Watzke, Doktor, and Dana (1975) and Watzke, Dana, Dokter, and Rubenstein (1972) used identical tasks in which, on each of a series of trials, each subject in a group of five was dealt seven cards from a deck containing fifty. Some of the cards were red and some were blue. If a person received five or more blue cards, that person won four units (exchangeable for money); if the hand contained four or fewer blue cards, the person lost a unit. Clearly, the more blue cards in the deck, the better everyone's chance of winning. At the end of each trial, when the subjects returned their cards to the experimenter-dealer, one blue card was automatically replaced by a red one unless the subject took some action. The subject could prevent the replacement by paying a cost of two units and the subject could have a red card replaced by a blue one at a cost of four units. Thus, subjects could pay to maintain or improve the quality of their common resource for future trials.

This type of situation appears to be a rather common one, despite the lack of experimental research simulating it. The financing of public radio and television stations, the maintenance of volunteer groups, and contributing to organizations like the Red Cross or the American Cancer Society are examples. The characteristics of these situations are that one pays a personal cost to contribute to a good that one will have access to regardless of whether one contributes or not. Moreover, the individual benefit that derives from the individual contribution is small relative to the contribution, although everyone would prefer to have the good than not to have it.

The maintenance of a public good is in many ways analogous to the renewable resource paradigm. There is a common pool that periodically pays each group member some amount that is a positive function of the pool size; the larger the pool, the larger the benefit. The pool size decreases as the payoffs are made and if the pool is not replenished by donations from the group members, it will collapse. The cost and payoff parameters have to be arranged so that the total group payoff per unit donation is larger than the unit donation, but that the per person payoff is smaller than the unit donation. In this way each member is better off if all donate a unit than if none donate anything, but it is not to any single group member's benefit to make the donation.

It would be very interesting to see if the dynamics of maintaining a public good are similar to the dynamics of using renewable resources.

ALTERNATIVE APPROACHES TO SOLVING SOCIAL DILEMMAS

In discussing solutions to social dilemmas, it is convenient to distinguish between solutions that derive from independent changes in individual behavior, on the one hand, and solutions that come about through coordinated, organized group action on the other. The distinction between individual and structural solutions can be illustrated by considering the responses that were made in California to the droughts of 1976 and 1977. First, citizens were urged to initiate a variety of water conservation efforts that included flushing toilets less often, watering vegetation less often, driving a dirtier car than one might choose, and so on. The appeals for individual conservation were successful, resulting in a per capita reduction of water consumption of about 30 percent in the Santa Barbara area (Maki, Hoffman, & Berk, 1978). The total demand for water in a water jurisdiction depends not only on the per capita consumption rate but also on the total number of individual users. A reduction in per capita use would help alleviate the shortage only if the total number of consumers did not increase in proportion to the per capita reduction. But how does one control the number of users? In two water districts in the Santa Barbara, California, region, this was done by placing a moratorium on new water connections. Clearly this action is not one that can be taken by a single consumer. It is a policy that can be instituted by a regulatory agency, like a water district board of directors, but it is not something that is under the control of each citizen. Citizens can express approval or disapproval of such policies by their votes in elections for water board directors, but the moratorium itself is a structural, not an individual, solution.

In this section we will review some research bearing on factors that facilitate individual solutions to social dilemmas. In the next section we will review some research on structural factors.

Solving Social Dilemmas Through Influence on Individual Choice

In an experiment involving an N-person prisoner's dilemma paradigm, Dawes, McTavish, and Shaklee (1977) examined the effect of *communication* among group members prior to decision making on the choices that were made. They found that when groups had the opportunity to discuss the dilemma in advance, individuals in those groups made significantly fewer defecting choices (i.e., more cooperative choices) than individuals in groups with no prior discussion. Brechner (1977) and Edney and Harper (1978a, 1978b) also found that open communication among group members increased the probability that individuals would sacrifice self-interest in the resource conservation dilemma. The implications of this finding are limited, however, in that for many real-world dilemmas, such direct communication among group members is not an available solution to the problem. Most social dilemmas involve large collectivities that are extended in time and space, offering little or no opportunity for group members to communicate or negotiate a solution to the choice problem.

Although communcation per se may not be a viable solution for large-scale social dilemmas, it is possible to analyze why communication among group members alters choice behavior and then to consider alternative ways to produce these same effects. Our review of the literture suggests that communication increases the probability that individuals will make cooperative choices in at least four different ways. First, discussing the dilemma provides information on what choices others in the group say they are willing to make, thus establishing group norms and introducing conformity pressures in favor of collective choices. Second, talking about their decisions may cause group membrs to believe that others are committed to making cooperative choices; enhanced trust in turn reduces the perceived risk involved in making the cooperative choice oneself. Third, discussion provides an opportunity for the use of moral suasion among group members and for the communication of relevant social values that support collective goals. Finally, discussion of a common problem may create a sense of group identity and cohesion that increases the probability that individuals will take the group interest into account when making their own decisions. (In this regard it is of interest to note that Dawes and associates' experiment included another condition in which groups were allowed to engage in discussion but restricted to a topic irrelevant to the choice. Under these conditions, communication did not enhance cooperation. Apparently simply getting acquainted with other group members is not sufficient to create the group bond engendered by mutual recognition of a common problem.) Each of these four factors in isolation has been found to influence cooperative choices in a variety of social dilemma paradigms.

Information about others' choices. Dawes and associates (1977) also found a positive relationship between individuals' *perceptions* of how many group members would cooperate and their own cooperative choice. Subjects who cooperated predicted that a larger number of other group members also chose cooperatively than did subjects who defected, and subjects in groups that communicated about the dilemma predicted more cooperation than subjects in groups that did not communicate.

In the Dawes and associates experiment, choices were made anonymously and only once. When a multitrial NPD or a resource dilemma situation is used, the effects of feedback about how other group members actually do behave (rather than just beliefs about how they behave) can be studied. As Messick and associates (1983) point out, knowledge about others' behavior can have potentially conflicting effects on individual choice decisions. For instance, learning that other group members are behaving cooperatively (making a cooperative choice in the NPD, restraining their harvest in a resource dilemma, or contributing to the public good) introduces normative conformity pressures to behave cooperatively, but it also relieves some pressure on the individual to be cooperative because one's own cooperative choice is less essential to the collective welfare (if others do it, I don't need to). Similarly, information that other group members are making selfish or defecting choices leads to conformity in favor of self-interest but also enhances the need for individual restraint in the collective interest. Hence, feedback about others' behavior can create conflict between tendencies to conform and tendencies toward individual or collective rationality.

Apparently both factors are operative in dilemma situations where others' past behavior is known. Sweeney (1973), in a simulation involving contributing effort toward a public good, found that if subjects perceived that they could make an *effective* contribution to the group goal, they tended to contribute even though few others were contributing. However, if they perceived their own contribution would be *ineffective* they contributed slightly more if they were given information that many others were contributing than if they were given information that few others were. Jerdee and Rosen (1974) found that, in the absence of communication, introducing a confederate who made a defecting (cost-cutting) bid in a simulated business game increased defecting choices by other players. Also Messick and associates (1983) found that subjects given false feedback that other group members were overutilizing the resource pool in a replenishable resource trap tended, on the average, to increase their own harvests across trials, whereas subjects given feedback that other members were *consistently* underutilizing the pool tended to maintain moderate harvests across trials.

Trust in other group members. An individual may be concerned about the collective welfare but only willing to act cooperatively if others in the group do so also. In large-scale dilemma situations, unilateral exercise of personal restraint in the interest of collective welfare is futile unless a substantial number of others behave similarly, and unilateral self-sacrifice puts the individual at risk of being a "sucker" while others free ride. Thus, the decision to behave cooperatively often rests on *trust* that others will do likewise. Much prior research on the relationship between trust and cooperation in dilemma situations assumes that interpersonal trust develops from a sequence of interactions that reveal or disclose the motives and intentions of other individuals (for example, Boyle & Bonacich, 1970). In many dilemmas, however, individuals must respond without knowledge of who the others in the collectivity are or what their past behavior has been. Choosing to cooperate in such situations requires a kind of "depersonalized trust" (Brewer, 1981) that operates in the absence of any prior history of interaction among interdependent others. Such depersonalized trust could exist, for instance, in a relatively homogeneous social group where individuals presume that they share common values, attitudes, and goals.

Some research evidence exists showing that an individual's prior beliefs about the trustworthiness of others in a collective dilemma situation influences personal choices made in such settings. Kelley and Stahelski (1970) demonstrated that cooperators and competitors maintain different views about the social motives and intentions of others that influence their own behavior and their interpretations of others' behavior in PD-type games. Utilizing the replenishable resource paradigm, Messick and associates (1983) found that subjects' prior beliefs about others' willingness to exercise restraint influenced their own harvesting decisions. In the face of feedback that the resource pool was being overutilized, those who expressed initial low trust that others could be counted on to restrain their harvest tended to increase their own harvest across trials as the pool became depleted; in contrast, those who indicated high initial trust tended to *decrease* their own harvest across trials in an effort to preserve the resource pool.

While trust may develop from generalized beliefs about the motivations of others, depersonalized trust can also be enhanced by confidence that noncooperators in a group will be sanctioned in some way, a principle that is exlored in Bates's (1979) clever analysis of order-preserving institutions in tribal societies. Caldwell (1976) found that the availability of a mechanism whereby the group could penalize defectors significantly increased cooperative choices in the NPD situation. In a sociological analysis of the NPD, Bonacich (1972) has suggested that the development of group *norms* serves a similar function, simultaneously providing a set of expectations about how other group members are likely to behave and creating an implicit threat that violations of the norms will be punished. In a series of experiments involving five-person interacting groups (Bonacich, 1972, 1976) he found that the content of communication among group members tends to focus on the normative requirement of cooperative choices and expressions of how angry the group would be toward a noncooperator. Under such open communication conditions, the rate of cooperative responding was very high (93-94%) even in the face of high monetary incentives to defect.

Normative control and trust in others' choices is also enhanced if individual decisions are personally identifiable. Studies comparing private with public choice conditions in the NPD (Bixentine et al., 1966; Fox & Guyer, 1978) generally obtain higher rates of cooperation when choices are disclosed publicly. Similarly, in a resource dilemma situation involving no opportunity for communication, Jorgenson and Papciak (1981) found that conditions of high identifiability (name tags and feedback on individual choices) produced more conservation of the resource pool than did conditions of low identifiability.

Social values and responsibility. Apart from trust in others or fear of sanctions for noncooperation, individuals may choose to respond cooperatively because of the value that they place on behavior that serves the collective welfare above self-interest. In a thoughtful review of the commons problem, Edney (1980) suggests that the dilemma should be thought of primarily as "a conflict of human values" (p. 141) rather than purely an issue of rationality. One purpose of educating individuals about the nature of social dilemmas is to make salient the need for social responsibility in individual actions. In a study involving a "carpooling" simulation, Stern (1976) found that "education" in the form of detailed information about long-term consequences of actions increased cooperative decisions and extended the preservation of a resource pool. Dawes and Orbell (1981) report on two experiments in which a one-trial NPD decision was preceded by a lengthy "sermon" from the experimenter in which the choice dilemma was portrayed in terms of moral issues involving ethics, group benefit, and exploitation. The effect of such moralizing was to raise the rates of cooperative choices to levels equivalent to those obtained in groups permitted to communicate about the dilemma among themselves.

Individual differences in social values prove to be highly related to their choices in social dilemma situations. In an extension of Kuhlman and Marshello's (1975) research on social motives, Liebrand (1982) found that subjects with a cooperative value orientation (i.e., a preference for maximizing *joint* outcomes) consistently showed more personal restraint in a resource conservation dilemma than subjects with competitive (maximize relative gain) or individualistic (maximizing own gain) orientations.

Apart from pre-existing individual differences in social values, the value attached to cooperative responding may be enhanced by increasing feelings of *personal responsibility* for collective outcomes (Fleishman, 1980). Sweeney (1973), for instance, found that subjects' willingness to contribute effort toward a group goal was greatest when feedback indicated that their contribution was effective in achieving the collective goal. In small groups, provision of public good is enhanced by knowledge that each individual contribution constitutes a substantial proportion of the total and that one individual's failure to contribute may spoil the whole group's outcomes (Olson, 1965; Stroebe & Frey, 1982). In larger groups the sense of responsibility may be more diffused and perceptions of individual efficacy attenuated (Fleishman, 1980).

Social responsibility may also be affected by perceptions of the seriousness of the collective problem. In a resource dilemma situation, Jorgenson and Papciak (1981) found that clear feedback indicating that pool size was being depleted produced more restraint in harvest size than the absence of such feedback, particularly when individuals could be identified. And in a real-world conservation setting, Talarowski (1982) found that householders who believed that a drought-caused water shortage was immediate and severe conserved more than those who did not believe that the drought had produced a serious shortage.

Ingroup identity. Brewer (1979, 1981; and Edney, 1980) have suggested that cooperative solutions to social dilemmas may be facilitated by exploiting the constructive social ties and affiliative bonds arising from social group identity. The sense of membership in a common group or social category probably enhances all of the factors discussed above that influence individuals' willingness to exercise personal restraint in the interests of collective welfare. In the first place, conformity pressures are greater in cohesive groups, so cooperative modeling should have more impact when awareness of group membership is high. In addition, research on ethnocentrism and ingroup bias (Brewer, 1979; Levine & Campbell, 1972) indicates that members of an ingroup tend to perceive other ingroup members in generally favorable terms, particularly as being *trustworthy, honest* and *cooperative.* Such attributions are likely to induce a willingness to trust the motives and intentions of other group members even in the absence of explicit controls on their behavior.

Awareness of group membership also enhances the effectiveness of normative pressures to cooperate by increasing the probability that noncooperators will be subjected to negative sanctions. In addition, inclusion in a social unit reduces psychological distance among group members and makes it less likely that individuals will make sharp distinctions between own and others' welfare, thereby increasing the weight given to collective outcomes in individual decision making. Common membership in a social category is one basis for arousal of what Hornstein (1972) calls "promotive tension," whereby one individual's goal orientation becomes coordinated to another's goal attainment. Effects of category membership are enhanced when group members perceive that they are subject to some common fate (Campbell, 1958; Rabbie & Horwitz, 1969). Thus, the recognition that a collective dilemma exists may contribute to group identity and enhance the probability of cooperative solutions.

Group identification may also increase the perceived effectiveness of individual actions. In any large-scale social dilemma, the behavior of isolated individuals has imperceptible effects on the collective welfare even though the accumulated effects of those behaviors is great. When individuals feel, however, that their actions are *representative* of some larger social entity, the *perceived* impact of those actions is magnified and the individuals' sense of personal responsibility for collective outcomes enhanced. Behaviors that are symbolic at the individual level are quite real in their impact at the group level.

The effects of salient social category membership on individual behavior in simulated social dilemmas has been studied in a series of experiments by Kramer and Brewer (1983). In these studies, instructions that emphasize common category identity of the collective as a whole, or experiences of common fate, tend to increase subjects' willingness to exercise personal restraint in a resource dilemma under conditions of rapid depletion of the resource pool. When collective identity is absent or undermined, on the other hand, subjects tend to increase their individual harvests across trials as the common pool becomes depleted.

Although enhanced group identification seems to have potentially powerful effects on individual decision making, these effects may be somewhat ethereal or unpredictable. Group boundaries can be both arbitrary and unstable, creating inconsistencies in group definition and loyalties, and the presence of overlapping or subordinate group identities can introduce competitive as well as cooperative orientations (compare Komorita & Lapworth, 1982a). Thus, attempts to solve social dilemmas through influences on individual choice may have to be combined with institutional changes that support such efforts (Buckley, Burns, & Meeker, 1974). Some of the structural changes that can alter the nature of the commons dilemma are reviewed below.

Solving Social Dilemmas
Through Structural Changes

Structural solutions to social dilemmas either eliminate or alter the pattern of incentives that characterize social dilemmas. Real world examples of structural solutions are easy to find. Charging water consumers for the water they use is a structural solution since it qualitatively changes the incentives for use. Linaweaver, Geyer and Wolff (1967) have estimated that metering water, as opposed to flat rate billing, reduced consumption by nearly 35%. Increasing the cost of water, also a structural change, should reduce consumption (Turnovsky, 1969; Pope, Stepp, & Lytle, 1975) although at the risk of incurring political opposition from consumers.

In the arena of public goods, the *closed shop* is a structural solution to the problem of free riding in labor unions. To prevent nonunion employees from enjoying the benefits provided by the union while not paying the membership fee, the closed shop concept simply requires all employees to join the union as a condition of employment. In California as well as other states, school districts in which teachers are represented by a union may assess a *union fee* on teachers who choose not to join the union. Unlike the closed shop, teachers are not required to join the union, but they are required to pay a fee, in lieu of union dues, to contribute to the benefits provided by the union and to eliminate the incentive to ride free.

The access to common resources, as in the tragedy of the commons, has often been eliminated in order to solve a social dilemma. The overuse that so frequently results from free access has led to the replacement of free access by a variety of allocation schemes that include paying for access (similar to water metering); the establishment of limits or quotas, as in hunting or fishing; turning access to the commons over to a superordinate authority, as several European nations have done in establishing state-owned oil companies; and simply turning the commons into private property. This last solution characterized the transformation of the American West from open ranges for cattle to private ranches. A similar "privatization" has occurred with regard to national fishing rights. After having extended its fishing rights from 4 to 12 miles in 1958, and from 12 to 50 miles in 1973, tiny Iceland extended them from 50 to 200 miles in 1976. At issue were the cod banks that were being depleted by overfishing by several other European countries. In rapid succession, most other coastal nations extended their economic territorial zones to 200 miles also.

While structural or institutional solutions to social dilemmas have been the focus of many investigations by nonpsychologists (e.g., Ostrom & Ostrom, 1977; Orbell & Wilson, 1978; Olson, 1965), social psychologists have been relatively mute on the topic. In this section we will review several types of structural solutions to social dilemmas with the intent of identifying important research questions in addition to describing empirical findings.

Payoff structures. The one type of structural change that has been widely investigated experimentally is the effect of the payoff structure. Because the payoff structures differ in the four different paradigms that we have identified, it will be convenient to review briefly the findings from the different paradigms separately.

In N-person PD's and other nondelay traps, changing the payoff structure generally tends to influence behavior as common sense would lead one to expect. Kelley and Grzelak (1972), using a PD with groups of 13 or 14 subjects, found that more subjects made the defecting choice the greater the incentive for defection and the less the benefit for others provided by the cooperative choice. Bonacich, Shure, Kahan, and Meeker (1976) also report data consistent with these conclusions. The provision of an option to penalize individuals who defect has also been shown by Caldwell (1976) to increase cooperation. Komorita and Lapworth (1982b) show that adding a third choice to a two-choice NPD can reduce the frequency of cooperative responses.

Probably the most systematic study of the effects of payoff structures on cooperative choice in NPD's has been reported by Komorita, Sweeney, and Kravitz (1980). The results of this study, which was an effort to evaluate a theory proposed by Komorita (1976), provided substantial support for the hypotheses that the propensity to choose cooperatively (1) decreases with increases in the incentive to defect and (2) increases as the benefits provided to others by the cooperative choice increase. Thus, cooperative choice can be seen, at least in part, as a resolution of the desire to increase personal gain and to provide benefits to other members of the group.

With no-delay social fences, the public goods paradigm, there have been no such systematic explorations of payoff structures as those described above. Issac and associates (1982) found that members of a group who gained less from a public good than other group members paid less for the provision of the good than the members who gained more. In a similar vein, Marwell and Ames (1979) found that groups were most likely to invest in a public good if the group was small and if it contained an individual who received more from the public good than the cost of its provision. (Such an individual is not in a true social dilemma, of course, since the individual merely exchanges a smaller for a larger amount of money.)

Alfano and Marwell (1980) report an intriguing finding having to do with the nature of the public good. Some goods, like pay increases resulting from the establishment of a union, are continuous or divisible. One can get a little or a lot or amounts in between. Other types of goods, however, like a public park or a community hospital, are relatively nondivisible and discontinuous; either they are created or not. In order to see if there is any difference in people's willingness to pay for divisible as opposed to nondivisible public goods, Alfano and Marwell (1980) allowed dormitory residents to contribute 225 tokens to either a public or a private good. For half of the groups, the public good was divisible, that is, each subject was paid his or her share of the public good in dollars. For the other half, the public good was nondivisible. the total amount of money available to the group would be the same as with the divisible good, but the group had to spend the money on a group project. Individuals got nothing.

Alfano and Marwell found that nearly twice as many tokens were spent on the public good when it was nondivisible than when it was divisible. This may reflect an increased sense of group membership created by the nondivisible (that is, group) good as compared to the individual payoffs, or it may reflect a perception that the group outcome is more valuable than the sum of its components. In any case, this is an intriguing result that needs to be replicated and better understood.

In social traps and fences involving delayed consequences, the level of the resource pool is an important component of the payoff structure. A number of studies indicate that subjects exercise self-restraint when such restraint is necessary to increase the size or quality of the resource pool (Cass & Edney, 1978; Jorgenson & Papciak, 1981; Messick, 1983; Messick & McClelland, 1983;

Rubenstein et al., 1975; and Watzke et al., (1972). The only study that did not find such an effect (Messick et al., 1983) was one in which subjects' choices had no effect on the pool size and in which the pool was perceived to be dropping because of the overuse of the pool by other group members. When the pool is seen to drop because the replenishment rate is low, subjects reduce their harvests considerably, although not to optimal levels (Messick, 1983).

Minimal contributing sets. We earlier reviewed a number of possible consequences of open communication among the members of a group. An additional consequence that we did not mention at that time is that groups that can communicate are able to find solutions requiring coordinated actions by the members that would be difficult or impossible for groups lacking communication to arrange. A study by van de Kragt and associates (1982) nicely illustrates how communication can facilitate one type of coordinated solution to a small-scale public goods problem.

Subjects in this study served in seven-person groups and each of the seven persons received a $10 benefit if some specified number of members volunteered to contribute $5.00 toward it. Van de Kragt and associates (1982) found that all of the ten groups that could discuss the problem got the benefit provided and seven of them did so with the minimal (optimal) number of contributors. Groups that could not discuss the problem managed to optimally provide the bonus only 30% (10 or 34 groups) of the time, and 35% (12 of 34) of the groups failed to get the $10 benefit provided at all because too few members volunteered to contribute toward it.

The discussion clearly improved the groups' performance and did so because the groups used the discussion to designate a *minimal contributing set* of members, the subset who would contribute their $5 to obtain the benefit. Group members got included in the minimal contributing set either through volunteering or as the result of a lottery. Once designated as members of the set, all subjects contributed.

The establishment of minimal contributing sets eliminates the symmetry among members. Each member under this solution is assigned a role as a contributor, who will net $5, or as a noncontributor, who will gain $10, if all members fulfill their roles. The group will have achieved the public good and it will have done so for the minimum possible price.

Van de Kragt and associates (1982) point out that the establishment of minimal contributing sets alters the perceived incentive structure so as to encourage the group members to fulfill their roles. If a designated contributor believes that the others will execute their roles, then the contributor will surely execute his or hers because the outcome will depend exclusively on the contributor's choice, and that choice will be whether to contribute $5 to get $10 in return or to keep the $5. If others can be depended on to follow their role prescriptions, then it is in the contributor's best interest to contribute. Since this is true for the other contributors as well, surely they can be depended on to make their contributions.

Privatization of resources. The conversion of commonly owned resources into privately owned resources represents a structural solution to certain types of social dilemmas that raises many profound issues. The general question that we are concerned with is do we behave differently in dealing with privately rather than commonly owned resources and what are the implications of these differences for solutions to social dilemmas?

We should point out here that this question is meaningless in some of the paradigms that we have described. The comparison of the use of privately owned versus commonly owned resources will necessarily involve a comparion of one person's performance with the performance of a group and the prisoner's dilemma, for example, as well as some of the public goods paradigms simply cannot be defined for a single person. The resource management paradigm, however, is suitable for studying this issue and it has been so used in several studies.

Cass and Edney (1978) report an experiment using the replenishable resource paradigm in which they varied both the visibility of the resource level and whether subjects in groups of four could harvest from any of twelve separate subpools or whether each subject had access only to three subpools assigned exclusively to that subject. Both of these variables influenced the subjects' harvest decisions. Subjects were closest to optimal (they were told what the optimal strategy was) when they had private pools and when they could see the pool levels. Visible resources without private pools produced the next best performance, followed by private pools and no visibility. As might be expected, the worst performance was found when subjects had no private pools and no visibility.

Messick and McClelland (1983) report a study that reaches a similar conclusion about privatization. Using a different resource replenishment task, these researchers varied the size of the group that had access to a resource while covarying the size of the resource pool to keep the per person level of the initial (and maximum) pool constant. Thus six-person groups began with 60 units, three person groups began with 30 units, and individuals had 10 resource units in their private pools. On each cycle, the pool replenished itself by increasing its level by one-third so long as the pool size did not exceed the maximum. The experiment lasted for 50 cycles or until the pool level dropped to zero.

The results of this experiment were straightforward. Individuals maintained their private pools for an average of nearly 31 cycles. The corresponding means for groups of three and six, respectively, were 10.7 and 9.7. Resources used in common with others were depleted much more quickly than privately controlled resources. Both Messick and McClelland (1983) and Cass and Edney (1978) found that group use differs from individual use in the very early stages of the experiment, with initial harvests being much larger from commonly used resource pools than from individually used ones. The reasons for this initial difference are not yet clear.

While privatization of resources may seem an appealing solution to some social dilemmas, it may often have serious drawbacks. How does one privatize air, for instance? If a resource is going to be privatized, who gets to share in the resource? All citizens? Citizens of a city? A county? A state? A nation? (If the state of California had a coastline of 4000 miles and that coastal property was to be divided equally among the state's 22 million residents, each resident would receive about one foot of coastal property. Hardly enough to build a cottage on.) Is the resource to be sold to the highest bidder, thereby assuring that wealthy citizens control the resource? Or should it be allotted to citizens who can prove that they can use the resource wisely? Privatization may solve social dilemmas but it may create other social problems.

Reducing group size. A number of authors have hypothesized that social dilemmas will be harder to solve the larger the number of group members (Komorita, 1976; Messick, 1973; Olson, 1965). The experiments on privatization, reducing the group to a single member, are consistent with this hypothesis. A number of other experiments that do not use individuals versus groups have also found that cooperation or self-restraint decreases as group size increases (Fox & Guyer, 1978; Hamburger, Guyer, & Fox, 1975; Kahan, 1972; Komorita & Lapworth, 1982a; Marwell & Schmidt, 1972). Thus, reducing group size, where feasible, would seem a viable means of solving social dilemmas.

The reasons why people are more cooperative in smaller rather than larger groups are not as clear, however. Bonacich and associates

(1976) suggest that it is because the payoffs change as group size increases, and they present some data to support their claim. Marwell and Schmidt (1972) propose that people cooperate only when others do and that larger groups will be more likely than smaller ones to contain one or more noncooperators. Olson (1965) and Messick (1973) point out that the larger the group, the less important any single person's behavior will be and the less the impact it will have on the group outcome. Stroebe and Frey (1982) suggest that the public goods problem is closely related to altruistic intervention in emergencies where people are less likely to be helpful in larger than in smaller groups (Latané & Darley, 1979; Morgan 1978). Whatever the ultimate answers, group size is an important structural variable the effects of which need further study.

Establishing a superordinate authority. Both Hardin (1968) and Cross and Guyer (1980) suggest the establishment of a superordinate authority as a solution to the tragedy of the commons or to social traps. One way in which this might be done is through an election in which one person is elected to have exclusive authority to harvest a resource for the entire group and to allocate the harvest to the group members. In studies reported by Messick and associates (1983) and by Messick (1983) just such an approach was taken. In these experiments, subjects were given false feedback about the harvest of five others in a replenishable resource task. After 10 cycles with this task, the subjects were asked a series of questions before beginning a new session. One of the questions that they were asked was whether they wanted to proceed in the second session as they had in the first, with each of the six group members making an individual harvest decision, or whether they would prefer to elect one of the group members as leader and have that person make a harvest for the entire group and allocate the harvest to the individual members.

The results of these two studies were in complete agreement. When subjects thought that others were overusing the resource, causing the pool to drop, 60% to 70% of them favored changing the system and electing a leader. However, when the resource was not being overused, most subjects preferred not to change the decision structure but to continue as they had previously. These experiments tested the additional hypothesis that subjects would prefer to change the decision structure if there were large differences in the amounts harvested by the group members. The studies reported by Messick (1983) and Messick and associates (1983) found no support for the hypothesis that large inequalities in harvest would promote tendencies to change the decision structure. A very similar study reported by Rutte and

Wilke (1983) did find support for the idea, however. It has not yet been determined whether the difference between the findings of Messick (1983) and Messick and associates (1983) and Rutte and Wilke (1983) reflects a cultural difference—the first two of these studies were conducted in the United States with American university students while the last was conducted in Holland with Dutch university students—or a difference in experimental detail. There is some evidence that the former may be the case. Dutch students seemed to be more sensitive to the differences among the harvests of the others than American students.

FUTURE RESEARCH:
PROMISES AND PERILS

The general question that we want to address in this concluding section is the question of what social psychologists can contribute through laboratory experimentation to our understanding of how social dilemmas can be solved. Our answer to this question is that our contribution can be maximized through theory-guided research that illuminates the basic psychological processes involved in these situations. The experimental research that we have reviewed here is at least in part an intellectual descendant of two-person PD research, a research endeavor more memorable for its volume than for its important discoveries. With the history of that line of research in mind we will presume to offer some suggestions for new research that we hope will avoid sterility and enhance the quality of the contributions that social psychologists can make.

Purposes of Laboratory Research

Laboratory research is uniquely suited to testing hypotheses about fundamental casual processes. The questions addressed in social psychological laboratory experiments are generally of two types: Those investigating basic psychological processes or those studying the structural or environmental factors that influence behavior in specific contexts. Examples of the latter sort are, Does the decision whether or not to join a labor union depend on group size? What factors affect how much money people send to their local public television station? How do people respond to deteriorating environmental quality? What factors influence whether people do or do not conserve resources or recycle wastes? Examples of questions about basic psychological processes might be: How are decisions influenced by beliefs about others and vice versa? How do attributions affect choices? How do group boundaries get formed and how do they influence behavior? Good laboratory experiments will either enhance our knowledge of basic psychological processes or of the influences on behavior in some important social setting. Excellent research does both.

In order for laboratory experiments to be useful in answering questions about extra laboratory behavior, the laboratory situations must simulate the important features of the nonlaboratory situation, thus enhancing the probability that generalizations characterizing behavior in the laboratory will also characterize behavior outside of the laboratory. The laboratory can then be used to study behavior in situations that would be impractical, impossible, or unethical to create in the real world. No one would want to create a serious drought just to be able to study people's responses to it. For purposes of generalization, if it is possible to study behavior in its natural ecology, then all things being equal, it is preferable to do so. If that cannot be done, the laboratory situations should be carefully created to simulate the important aspects of the natural ecology.

If a laboratory experiment is intended primarily to examine some basic psychological process, then there is less need for the experimental situation to simulate a natural environment. In fact, the unsurpassed virtue of the laboratory experiment is precisely that situations can be created in the laboratory that will not occur outside, situations that allow one to pull apart normally confounded variables or to create stimulus configurations that can elicit informative responses. The guide in designing experiments of this type ought to be theory.

Our position is that the best experiments on social dilemmas are likely to be those that strike a compromise between being good simulations and posing important basic questions, a compromise in which a research question which could shed light on behavior in social dilemmas is derived from basic theory and tested in a thoughtfully designed laboratory simulation. Sometimes sacrifices in the realism of the simulation may be called for in order to get clean answers to conceptual questions. There is no inherent harm in this so long as experimenters remain aware of the fact that the experimental situation, in and of itself, is of no interest and that the goal of doing experiments is not to develop a theory of behavior in one narrow laboratory task. The laboratory experiment derives its value from its ability to shed light on basic processs or to study influences on behavior in simulated natural environments. The relative fruitlessness of two-person game research may be attributed in large measure to the fact that experimenters seem to have forgotten this crucial fact. The two-person, two-choice game isn't a realistic simulation of any important natural situations that we can think of, and only a few of the experiments dealt with basic psychological processes.

Laboratory simulations of social dilemmas provide rich settings for testing theories about basic cognitive, motivational, and social processes while at the same time enhancing our understanding of social psychological dimensions of important social problems. Some of the basic issues this research has contributed to, issues that are by no means resolved, are summarized as illustrative examples.

Beliefs about others. Dawes and associates (1977) found a positive correlation between people's choices in an NPD and what they expected others to do. Cooperators tended to expect others to cooperate while defectors tended to expect defection. The direction of causation, however, is unclear. Dawes and associates (1977) presented additional data that suggest that the choice one makes influences one's predictions about others behavior as much as vice versa. Messé and Sivacek (1979) present further evidence supporting this interpretation and further try to differentiate a self-justification motive from the general "false consensus effect" described by Ross, Green, and House (1977). There is more to be known about how our own decisions influence our beliefs about others as well as the effects our beliefs have on our future choices.

Value tradeoffs. Our review of the research on payoff structures led to the conclusion that behavior in social dilemma situations reflects a resolution of some sort of trade-off between the costs that socially responsible behavior impose on us and the benefits that such behavior will produce for the other members of the group. Yet there is much that we do not know about how this trade-off gets made. Messick (1974) showed that the public goods social dilemma disappears if people place even a relatively small weight on the group good in their utility functions, a principle that might explain the high level of contribution found by Alfano and Marwell (1980). What are needed are empirical studies, perhaps in the context of the framework offered by MacCrimmon and Messick (1976), that will elucidate the principles governing the trade-offs between our own and others' outcomes.

Personal efficacy. A principle that is central to the analyses of Messick (1973), Olson (1965), and Stroebe and Frey (1982) is that people will be more likely to behave responsibly if their behavior may make a difference than if it does not make a difference. Sweeney's (1973) results support this principle as do the findings of van de Kragt and associates (1982). However, if people only make group-oriented choices when they are likely to make a difference, how do we explain why people vote in national elections or send $25 to local public television stations? Do they exaggerate the importance of their contribution (Ross & Sicoly, 1979) or does the sense of efficacy derive from something beyond the impact of a single behavior?

Ingroup bias. Brewer (1979) has reviewed the literature indicating that people tend to overevaluate and overreward others who are viewed as members of the same group. Komorita and Lapworth (1982) report two studies suggesting that group categorization processes are important in determining peoples' choices in NPD's. How such ingroup or outgroup biases would be aroused in social dilemmas and what their consequences would be are questions that are only beginning to be answered (Kramer & Brewer, 1983).

Guidelines for Future Research

The list above illustrates the kinds of theoretical issues that can be fruitfully studied within the social dilemma paradigm. We conclude by posing three questions that experimenters might do well to ask themselves in evaluating potential experiments in this area. The goal of these questions is to encourage researchers to assess the importance of a study before doing it and to assess its importance in terms of the extent to which the experiment (1) elucidates basic psychological or social psychological processes and in so doing, (2) helps clarify how people respond to social dilemmas.

The first question is this: Can the research question be addressed in any of the four types of social dilemmas that we have discussed? If so, it is more likely to produce findings of general interest than if not. For example, one can ask about the effect of making cooperative behavior more costly in all of the paradigms. Such questions are transparadigmatic. However, questions about the effects of changes in a parameter characterizing only one of the paradigms may not have counterparts in the other paradigms. Unless there are sound theoretical reasons for asking paradigm-specific questions, such questions are not likely to be of broad general interest.

The next question is: Does the experiment get at some basic psychological process that operates outside of the dilemma context? Perhaps a more concrete way to pose the question is to ask if there are people who do not care about social dilemma research but who would still be interested in the results of the study nevertheless. If so, the study is more likely to contribute to broad theoretical concerns than if not. The finding of the positive correlation between peoples' choices and their predictions of what others will do (Dawes et al., 1977) is an excellent example of such a result.

The final question bears on the external generalizability of the experiment: Would a policy maker in government or business find the result of the experiment useful or of interest? If so, the experiment is more likely to be of some practical importance than if not.

We suspect that only rarely would one expect "yes" responses to all three questions. However, if one cannot confidently expect a "yes" response to any of them, one might do well to think further before proceeding with an experiment. There are more experiments that can be done than are worth doing and it is as important as it is tricky to determine which are which.

NOTE

1. There is a sizable economic literature on the public goods problem that we lack space to review. Readers interested in this work should consult Issac, McCue, & Plott (1982), Plott (1983), or Smith (1979) for entrees to this work.

REFERENCES

Alfano, G., & Marwell, G. Experiments on the provision of public goods by groups III: Non-divisibility and free riding in "real" groups. *Social Psychology Quarterly*, 1980, *43*, 300-309.

Arrow, K. J. *Social choice and individual values.* New York: John Wiley, 1963.

Baden, J. Population, ethnicity, and public goods: The logic of interest-group strategy. In G. Hardin & J. Baden (Eds.), *Managing the commons.* San Francisco: W. H. Freeman, 1977.

Bates, R. H. The preservation of order in stateless societies: A reinterpretation of Evans-Pritchard's *The Nuer. Frontiers of Economics,* 1979, 1-13.

Bixentine, V. E., Levitte, C. A., & Wilson, K. V. Collaboration among six persons in a prisoner's dilemma game. *Journal of Conflict Resolution,* 1966, *10,* 488-496.

Bohm, P. Estimating the demand for public goods: An experiment. *European Economic Review,* 1972, *3,* 111-130.

Bonacich, P. Norms and cohesion as adaptive responses to political conflict: An experimental study. *Sociometry,* 1972, *35,* 357-375.

Bonacich, P. Secrecy and solidarity. *Sociometry*, 1976, *39*, 200-208.

Bonacich, P., Shure, G. H., Kahan, J. P., & Meeker, R. J. Cooperation and group size in the n-person prisoners' dilemma. *Journal of Conflict Resolution*, 1976, *20*, 687-706.

Boyle, R., & Bonacich, P. The development of trust and mistrust in mixed-motive games. *Sociometry*, 1970, *33*, 123-239.

Brechner, K. C. An experimental analysis of social traps. *Journal of Experimental Social Psychology*, 1977, *13*, 552-564.

Brewer, M. B. In-group bias in the minimal intergroup situation: A cognitive-motivational analysis. *Psychological Bulletin*, 1979, *86*, 307-324.

Brewer, M. B. Ethnocentrism and its role in interpersonal trust. In M. Brewer & B. Collins (Eds.) *Scientific inquiry and the social sciences*. San Francisco: Jossey-Bass, 1981.

Brubaker, E. R. Free rider, free revelation, or golden rule? *Journal of Law and Economics*, 1975, *18*, 147-161.

Buckley, W., Burns, T., & Meeker, L. D. Structural resolutions of collective action problems. *Behavioral Science*, 1974, *19*, 277-297.

Caldwell. M. D. Communication and sex effects in a five-person prisoner's dilemma game. *Journal of Personality and Social Psychology*, 1976, *33*, 273-280.

Campbell, D. T. Common fate, similarity, and other indices of aggregates of persons as social entities. *Behavioral Science*, 1958, *3*, 14-25.

Cass, R. C., & Edney, J. J. The commons dilemma: A simulation testing resource visibility and territorial division. *Human Ecology*, 1978, *6*, 371-386.

Cross, J. G., & Guyer, M. J. *Social traps*. Ann Arbor: University of Michigan Press, 1980.

Dawes, R. M. Social dilemmas. *Annual Review of Psychology*, 1980, *31*,, 169-193.

Dawes, R. M., McTavish, J., & Shaklee, H. Behavior, communication, and assumptions about other people's behavior in a commons dilemma situation. *Journal of Personality and Social Psychology*, 1977, *35*, 1-11.

Dawes, R. M., & Orbell, J. Social dilemmas. In G. Stephenson & J. Davis (Eds.), *Progress in applied social psychology (Vol. 1)*. Chichester: John Wiley Ltd., 1981.

Edney, J. J. The commons problem: alternative perspectives. *American Psychologist*, 1980, *35*, 131-150.

Edney, J. J. Paradoxes on the commons: Scarcity and the problem of equality. *Journal of Community Psychology*, 1981, *9*, 3-34.

Edney, J. J., & Harper, C. S. The commons dilemma: A review of contributions from psychology. *Environmental Management*, 1978, *2*, 491-507. (a)

Edney, J. J., & Harper, C. S. Heroism in a resource crisis: A simulation study. *Environmental Management*, 1978, *2*, 523-527. (b)

Fleishman, J. A. Collective action as helping behavior: Effects of responsiblility diffusion on contributions to a public good. *Journal of Personality and Social Psychology*, 1980, *38*, 629-637.

Fox, J., & Guyer, M. "Public" choice and cooperation in n-person prisoner's dilemma. *Journal of Conflict Resolution*, 1978, *22*, 469-481.

Hamburger, H., Guyer, M., & Fox, J. Group size and cooperation. *Journal of Conflict Resolution*, 1975, *19*, 503-531.

Hardin, G. The tragedy of the commons. *Science*, 1968, *162*, 1243-1248.

Hardin, G., & Baden, J. (Eds). *Managing the commons*. San Francisco: W. H. Freeman, 1977.

Hoggatt, A. C. An experimental business game. *Behavioral Science*, 1959, *4*, 192-203.

Hornstein, H. A. Promotive tension: The basis of prosocial behavior from a Lewinian perspective. *Journal of Social Issues*, 1972, *28* (3), 191-218.

Issac, R. M., McCue, R. F., & Plott, C. R. Public goods provision in an experimental environment. *Social Science Working Paper*, 482, California Institute of Technology, 1982.

Jerdee, T. H., & Rosen, B. Effects of opportunity to communicate and visibility of individual decisions on behavior in the common interest. *Journal of Applied Psychology*, 1974, *59*, 712-716.

Jorgenson, D. O., & Papciak, A. S. The effects of communication, resource feedback, and identifiability on behavior in a simulated commons. *Journal of Experimental Social Psychology*, 1981, *17*, 373-385.

Kahan, J. P. Noninteraction in an anonymous three-person prisoner's dilemma game. *Behavioral Science*, 1973, *18*, 124-127.

Kelley, H. H., & Grzelak, J. Conflict between individual and common interest in an N-person relationship. *Journal of Personality and Social Psychology*, 1972, *21*, 190-197.

Kelley, H. H., & Stahelski, A. J. Social interaction basis of cooperators' and competitors' beliefs about others. *Journal of Personality and Social Psychology*, 1970, *16*, 66-91.

Komorita, S. S. A model of the N-person dilemma-type game. *Journal of Experimental Social Psychology*, 1976, *12*, 357-373.

Komorita, S. A., & Lapworth, C. W. Cooperative choice among individuals versus groups in an N-person dilemma situation. *Journal of Personality and Social Psychology*, 1982, *42*, 487-496. (a)

Komorita, S. S., & Lapworth, C. W. Alternative choices in social dilemmas. *Journal of Conflict Resolution*, 1982, *26*, 692-708. (b)

Komorita, S. S., Sweeney, J., & Kravitz, D. A. Cooperative choice in the n-person dilemma situation. *Journal of Personality and Social Psychology*, 1980, *38*, 504-516.

Kramer, R. D., & Brewer, M. B. *Group identity effects on resource conservation decisions in a simulated commons dilemma.* Unpublished manuscript, 1983.

Kuhlman, D. M., & Marshello, A. Individual differences in game motivation as moderators of preprogrammed strategic effects in prisoner's dilemma. *Journal of Personality and Social Psychology*, 1975, *32*, 922-931.

Latané, B. & Darley, J. M. *The unresponsive bystander: Why doesn't he help?* New York: Appleton-Century-Crofts, 1970.

Levine, R. A., & Campbell, D. T. *Ethnocentrism: Theories of conflict, ethnic attitudes and group behavior.* New York: John Wiley, 1972.

Liebrand, B. G. *Interpersonal differences in social dilemmas: a game theoretic approach.* Unpublished dissertation, University of Groningen, 1982.

Linaweaver, F. P., Geyer, J. C., & Wolff, J. P. Summary report on the residential water use project. *Journal of the American Water Works Association*, 1967, *59*, 267-282.

MacCrimmon, K. R., & Messick, D. M. A framework for social motives. *Behavioral Science*, 1976, *21*, 86-100.

Maki, J. E., Hoffman, D. M., & Berk, R. A. A time series analysis of the impact of a water conservation campaign. *Evaluation Quarterly*, 1978, *2*, 107-118.

Marwell, G., & Ames, E. Experiments on the provision of public goods I: Resources, interest, group size, and the free rider problem. *American Journal of Sociology*, 1979, *84*, 1335-1360.

Marwell, G., & Ames, R. E. Experiments on the provision of public goods II: Provision points, stakes, experience and the free rider problem. *American Journal of Sociology,* 1980, *85,* 926-937.

Marwell, G., & Schmidt, D. R. Cooperation in a three-person prisoner's dilemma. *Journal of Personality and Social Psychology,* 1972, *31,* 376-383.

Messé, L. A. & Sivacek, J. M. Predictions of others' responses in a mixed-motive game: Self-justification or false consensus? *Journal of Personality and Social Psychology,* 1979, *37,* 602-607.

Messick, D. M. To join or not to join: An approach to the unionization decision. *Organizational Behavior and Human Performance,* 1973, *10,* 145-156.

Messick, D. M. When a little "group interest" goes a long way: A note on social motives and union joining. *Organizational Behavior and Human Performance,* 1974, *12,* 331-334.

Messick, D. M. Solving social dilemmas: Individual and collective approaches. Unpublished paper, 1983.

Messick, D. M. & McClelland, C. L. Social traps and temporal traps. *Personality and Social Psychology Bulletin,* 1983, 9: 105-110.

Messick, D. M., Wilke, H., Brewer, M. B., Kramer, R. M., Zemke, P. E., & Lui, L. Individual adaptations and structural change as solutions to social dilemmas. *Journal of Personality and Social Psychology,* 1983, *44,* 294-309.

Morgan, C. J. Bystander intervention: Experimental test of a formal model. *Journal of Personality and Social Psychology,* 1978, *36,* 43-55.

Olson, M. *The logic of collective action.* Cambridge, MA: Harvard University Press, 1965.

Orbell, J. M., & Wilson, L. A. Institutional solutions to the N-person prisoner's dilemma. *American Political Science Review,* 1978, *72,* 411-421.

Ostrom, V., & Ostrom, E. A theory for institutional analysis of commons problems. In G. Hardin & J. Baden (Eds.), *Managing the commons.* San Francisco: W.H. Freeman, 1977.

Platt, J. Social Traps. *American Psychologist,* 1973, *28,* 641-651.

Plott, C. R. Externalities and corrective policies in experimental markets. *Economic Journal,* 1983.

Pope, R. M., Jr., Stepp, J. M., & Lytle, J. S. Effects of price change on the domestic use of water over time. *Clemson University: WRRI Report, 56,* 1975.

Pruitt, D. G., & Kimmel, M. J. Twenty years of experimental gaming: Critique, synthesis and suggestions for the future. *Annual Review of Psychology,* 1977, *28,* 363-392.

Rabbie, J. M., & Horwitz, M. Arousal of ingroup-outgroup bias by a chance win or lose. *Journal of Personality and Social Psychology,* 1969, *13,* 269-277.

Rapoport, A., Chammah, A., Dwyer, J., & Gyr, J. Three-person non-zero-sum negotiable games. *Behavioral Science,* 1962, *7,* 38-58.

Ross, L., Green, D. & House, P. The "false consensus effect:" An egocentric bias in social perception and attribution processes. *Journal of Experimental Social Psychology,* 1977, *13,* 279-301.

Ross, M., & Sicoly, F. Egocentric biases in availability and attribution. *Journal of Personality and Social Psychology,* 1979, *37,* 322-336.

Rubenstein, F. D., Watzke, G., Doktor, R. H., & Dana, J. The effects of two incentive schemes upon the conservation of a shared resource by five person groups. *Organizational Behavior and Human Performance,* 1975, *13,* 330-338.

Rutte, C. G., & Wilke, H.A.M. Role change in a social dilemma situation. Unpublished manuscript, 1983.

Samuelson, P. A. The pure theory of public expenditure. *Review of Economics and Statistics,* 1954, *36,* 387-390.

Schelling, T. C. *Micromotives and macrobehavior.* New York: Norton, 1978.

Smith, V. L. Incentive compatible experimental processes for the provision of public goods. In V. L. Smith (Ed.), *Research in experimental economics.* Greenwich, CT: JAI Press, 1979.

Stern, P. C. Effects of incentives and education on resource conservation decisions in a simulated commons dilemma. *Journal of Peronality and Social Psychology,* 1976, *34,* 1285-1292.

Stroebe, W., & Frey, B. S. Self-interest and collective action: The economics and psychology of public goods. *British Journal of Social Psychology,* 1982, *21,* 121-137.

Sweeney, J. W. An experimental investigation of the free-rider problem. *Social Science Research,* 1973, 227-292.

Talarowski, F. S. *Attitudes toward and perceptions of water conservation in a Southern California Community.* Unpublished dissertation, University of California, Santa Barbara, 1982.

Turnovsky, S. J. The demand for water: Some empirical evidence on consumers' response to a commodity uncertain in supply. *Water Resources Research,* 1969, *5,* 350-361.

van de Kragt, A., Orbell, J. M., & Dawes, R. M. The minimal contributing set as a solution to public good problems. Paper presented at the annual meeting of the American Psychological Association, Washington, DC, 1982.

Watzke. G. E., Dana. J. M., Doktor. R. H., & Rubenstein, F. D. An experimental study of individual vs. group interest. *Acta Sociologica,* 1972, *15,* 366-370.

The Volunteer Dilemma

J. Keith Murnighan
University of British Columbia
Jae Wook Kim
A. Richard Metzger
University of Illinois at Urbana–Champaign

This paper uses evolutionary, social psychological, organizational, and game theoretic literatures as frames to explore the dilemma of the choice to volunteer. Although one's group may benefit from voluntary action, volunteers typically incur more costs than others, even when their actions are successful. The four experiments presented here addressed when and why people volunteer in fictitious financial scenarios that varied group size, the number of volunteers required, the payoffs to volunteers and nonvolunteers, and the need to work more or for smaller outcomes than others. The results suggest that, in general, undergraduates, M.B.A.s, and executives volunteered most often when personal benefits were high. Executives also focused on issues related to self-interest when they were questioned about voluntary action in the workplace. The discussion raises issues about voluntary action in situations in which people interact at a distance and speculates about implications for the dynamics and antecedents of altruistic action.•

A group of penguins is standing on an ice floe. They haven't eaten for some time and they're getting restless, pushing toward the edge of the floe and peering into the water. They know there are fish in the water, but there may also be a hungry killer whale or a leopard seal, too. So they hover by the edge of the ice—until one is pushed in.

Independent groups of small birds and ground squirrels are feeding in an open field. Each occasionally glances up, checking for predators. If one is seen, they must sound the alarm to avoid being easy prey. By calling out, however, an individual may draw the predator's special attention. It turns out that ground squirrels are more likely to call out an alarm when kin are near. The birds do better and exercise what appears to be an optimal solution: Whoever calls out the alarm gets to fly in the middle of the flock as they try to escape from the predator.

A group of soldiers, at rest in their trench, hear and see an enemy grenade drop among them. Whoever covers the grenade will protect his colleagues but will die in the process. While most of the group hesitates, one soldier leaps on the grenade just before it goes off.

All three stories describe the life-and-death decisions that can characterize the volunteer dilemma. While most volunteers face less serious risk, costs are normally part of volunteering. Voluntary action is nevertheless an everyday essential for effective organizational action. Voluntary organizations, by definition, could not exist without volunteers. More generally, in the private and public sector, voluntary action is needed to complete the work of task forces, special interest groups, and, from a broad perspective, all informal organizational action (Katz, 1964). The choice to volunteer, however, is usually an individual dilemma: Although group benefits may increase if someone volunteers to contribute and achieve a goal, volunteers themselves typically incur increased costs. They can choose either of the two horns of the dilemma: They can volunteer to do more and gain less than the rest of the group, or they can hope that someone else will volunteer, knowing that if no one does, their group will not receive the benefits volunteering could produce. This paper presents four basic

•

We would like to thank Greg Oldham and Madan Pillutla for their constructive comments on an early version of this manuscript, Associate Editor Robert Sutton, Herbert Simon, and two anonymous reviewers for their particularly perceptive reactions and suggestions, and Linda Pike for her faultless editing.

experiments that begin to address when and why people choose to volunteer. Evolutionary, social psychological, organizational, and game theoretic literatures contribute to the conceptualization of the volunteer dilemma developed here. In the process, they present a clear argument that volunteering is a general organizational phenomenon. They also raise the question of whether, and to what extent, altruism plays a part in volunteering.

Evolutionary and Social Psychological Perspectives

In his seminal work on the evolution of reciprocal altruism, Trivers (1971) noted that, in all human cultures, people share food, implements, and knowledge and help the sick, the wounded, the young, the old, and each other in times of danger. Most human beings seem to understand that the economics of reciprocal altruism—combining the small costs to a giver with great benefits to a receiver and then returning the favor—can establish a system of long-run mutual benefit. Quid pro quo is expected, although reciprocity may only be accomplished over some time.

Both cooperation and reciprocal altruism include either an explicit or implicit assumption that the exchange will be balanced and fair (de Waal and Luttrell, 1988): In long-term relationships, both parties may expect that everything will even out in the end. The length of the relationship depends on whether expectations continue to be met by both or all the parties. The key difference between systems of reciprocal altruism and volunteering is that a voluntary act rarely includes strong expectations of reciprocity or the monitoring mechanisms needed to assure it. Rather, volunteering may depend on emotional, moral, or empathic feelings that are typically associated with altruism (e.g., Hoffman, 1981). In his review of voluntary action research, for instance, Smith (1983: 23) defined volunteering as behavior that has more market value to the recipient than it does to the volunteer, that is primarily "motivated by the expectation of psychic benefits," and that is neither biosocially determined, economically necessitated, nor sociopolitically compelled. For Smith, volunteers freely choose their voluntary acts without expecting a complete quid pro quo. In this definition, in which volunteering is essentially altruistic, although not necessarily in an evolutionary sense, the direct effects of an altruistic act reduce an individual's potential progeny.

Until Simon's (1990) recent article, an evolutionary perspective suggested that altruism without the expectation of direct or delayed reciprocation is effective only when the altruistic action is taken toward one's close kin (Hamilton, 1964). Unreciprocated altruism (i.e., random altruism) is viewed as ineffective (Trivers, 1971), as net fitness (i.e., number of likely progeny) drops with no reciprocal increment. Krebs and Miller (1985) noted, for instance, that Darwinian notions of altruism require that one enhances the net fitness of another at some net cost to one's own fitness and that altruism, therefore, may not be evolutionarily supportable (e.g., Campbell, 1983). This suggested that "pure" altruism, which is enacted with no clear expectation of reciprocation, was an evolutionary anomaly and that only

Volunteer Dilemma

weak altruism that included some expectation of reciprocity could be evolutionarily supportable. Berkowitz and Daniels (1964), however, documented that people often help one another without expectations of specific acts of reciprocity from the aided person but, rather, with expectations of generalized reciprocity. This may be best exemplified by the statement we often heard to justify volunteering in our experiments: "What goes around comes around." In particular, volunteers rarely demand completely balanced reciprocity from everyone in their group, although they may hope for personal returns from their efforts.

Frank (1988), Hoffman (1981), and Schwartz (1977) argued that pure altruism exists, even in the face of little support for its existence in rational models of human behavior. They focused on the importance of sympathy, empathy, and moral obligation, respectively, and argued that these emotions may be natural and possibly instinctive reactions to seeing others in distress. Thus, individuals who realize that they alone see someone in danger often respond almost automatically to help. Batson (1987) and his colleagues have supported this logic and have presented an impressive set of experiments showing that stronger feelings of empathy lead to a greater likelihood of altruistic behavior, even when a potential altruist can easily escape the situation and the responsibility it may engender (e.g., Batson et al., 1983). In addition, Batson et al. (1988) have shown that several egoistic interpretations of the empathy-altruism linkage have less explanatory power than the simple notion that empathy can evoke altruism. As will become clear later, our four experiments provide an opportunity to determine whether volunteering, an activity that may include some element of altruism, occurs in the absence of empathy.

Simon's (1990) contribution to the altruism debate is a rational model that shows how altruism, strictly defined as foregoing progeny, can thrive. He argued that our inability to conscientiously evaluate whether behaviors reduce our net fitness in the short run and our ability to learn "proper behaviors," including altruism, can ultimately be collectively advantageous, as long as society's altruistic demands are not excessive. Voluntary action, then, is one of the altruistic behaviors that people may learn. In the context of this research, where voluntary or nonvoluntary acts are expected to affect wealth rather than progeny, we can assess some of the limits of the learning of this proper behavior.

The Organizational Approach to Volunteering

Two distinct organizational literatures address volunteering. Voluntary action research investigates completely voluntary organizations and obvious cases of voluntary action, such as donating blood. Although the research in this area has been somewhat unsystematic and often anecdotal, several conceptual contributions are noteworthy. The second area concerns prosocial and organizational citizenship behaviors.

Voluntary action research is often directed toward identifying (1) an altruistic personality and (2) the situational contingencies that might stimulate voluntary action. Thus, Allen and Rushton (1983) reviewed the personality characteristics of community mental health volunteers and concluded that they are abnormally empathic and emotionally stable, have strong internal moral standards, positive mental attitudes and positive self-esteem, exhibit strong self-efficacy, and see themselves as being more pleasant than others. Schwartz (1977), by contrast, claimed that no systematic data support the notion of a generalized altruistic personality.

Research on voluntary organizations has put only secondary emphasis on altruism. Results suggest that people volunteer to (1) improve their skills and make themselves more employable (Stinson and Stam, 1976); (2) stimulate social interactions that may develop into friendships (e.g., Sharp, 1978); (3) put themselves in position for employment when it becomes available; or (4) obtain other self-oriented benefits (Gluck, 1975). In addition, Kessler's (1975) research indicates that, rather than citing altruistic motives as most important, blood donors indicate that they donate more due to habit and the inability to answer the question, "Why not?"

Smith (1983: 25) summarized this literature forcefully: "Volunteers are not generally altruistic although they like to think of themselves as altruistic." He suggested that appeals to altruism are not effective mechanisms for developing and maintaining voluntary action. Instead, volunteering seems "to be directly and positively associated with the ratio of benefits to costs." He went on, saying that "volunteers are not angelic humanitarians in any sense. They are human beings, engaging in unpaid, uncoerced activities for various kinds of tangible and intangible incentives" (Smith, 1983: 25). Kessler's (1975) data on blood donors support this logic. Among occupational groups that donated most frequently in organized blood drives, postal workers gave the most and, surprisingly, social workers the least. Both got a day off work. But their differential donations were explained by the fact that, while the letter carriers' mail was delivered by someone else, social workers' tasks simply accumulated, awaiting their return. The voluntary action research literature, then, is quite pessimistic about the presence of altruistic motives in purely voluntary situations. Nevertheless, volunteering in most organizational settings may involve more than just altruistic motives. In particular, perceptions that volunteering is expected or that it may contribute to personal promotions may combine with altruistic dispositions to augment organizational volunteering.

Recent writing (e.g., Brief and Motowidlo, 1986; Organ, 1988) on prosocial behavior and organizational citizenship behavior takes a different approach. Brief and Motowidlo (1986) explicitly included volunteering as one of several forms of prosocial behavior. Organ's (1988: 4) definition of organizational citizenship behavior as "individual behavior that is discretionary, not directly or explicitly recognized by the formal reward system, and that in the aggregate promotes the effective functioning of the organization" is exactly what we would refer to as organizational volunteering. The empirical study of prosocial and organizational citizenship behavior, however, has significantly trailed conceptual discussions. No data, for instance, exist to test Organ and Konovsky's (1989) hypothesis that trust in

Volunteer Dilemma

the long-term fairness of the organization might determine whether diffuse, unspecified social exchange—rather than explicit economic exchange—might characterize the , employment relationship. Recent research (e.g., Organ and Konovsky, 1989; George and Bettenhausen, 1990) has identified several job-related factors that are correlated with prosocial and organizational citizenship behavior, but we have no hard evidence on the causal dynamics that might encourage specific individual actions.

The Game Theoretic Approach to Volunteering

The prisoners' dilemma (Tucker, 1950), which has been used as a basic building block in theories of evolution (Axelrod and Hamilton, 1981), agency (Jensen and Meckling, 1976), and social dilemmas (Dawes, 1980), arises because short-run individualistic strategies that are economically rational result, if everyone chooses individualistically, in a deficient equilibrium that everyone prefers less than other outcomes. Although similar in many ways, the volunteer dilemma, outlined in Table 1, does not qualify as a prisoner's dilemma, because one specific set of conditions makes volunteering rational. The volunteer dilemma establishes three choice contingencies (Rapoport, 1987): (1) Not enough people have volunteered and one additional volunteer won't help; (2) one more volunteer will lead to success for the group; and (3) enough people have already volunteered. For the first and third cases, not volunteering is both efficient and beneficial, individually and collectively, because it saves unnecessary expenditures. Only in the second case is volunteering rational, efficient, and beneficial—for all group members and for the volunteer. The dilemma results when people have incomplete information and don't know which contingency they are facing.

Communication among group members solves the information problem and the volunteer dilemma. For instance, van der Kragt, Orbell, and Dawes' (1983) public-goods experiment, where three or five of seven group members needed to contribute their $5 endowments for all group members to receive a $10 reward, showed that groups that could communicate before making their choices solved the problem easily: All 12 groups contributed enough, and 10 of the 12 contributed exactly enough. Some groups drew lots to see which group members would contribute; others depended on volunteers. Rapoport (1985, 1987) noted that public-goods games of this kind generate the possibility for both fear and greed: Contributors may fear that they will lose their contribution if too few others contribute; noncontributors may be tempted by greed, since their outcomes exceed contributors' unless the group is one contributor short. Both fear and greed encourage noncontribution; either can explain why some groups do not contribute enough. Research separating the effects of fear and greed (Dawes et al., 1986; Rapoport and Eshed-Levy, 1989) suggests that, while both drive noncontributions, greed predominates. Our hypotheses for the effects of the different payoff schemes in this research derive from the predictions of game theoretic and other rational models and from results from voluntary action research that people will be more attracted by high than by low payoffs:

Hypothesis 1: The proportion of volunteers will drop as volunteers' payoffs drop.

Hypothesis 2: The proportion of volunteers will drop as nonvolunteers' payoffs increase.

No public-goods experiments have studied volunteering directly. Diekmann's (1985, 1986) studies of the volunteer dilemma concentrated on the effects of group size. As we did in our research, he investigated the no-loss volunteer dilemma, outlined in Table 1, which removes fear as a motive by allowing volunteers whose contributions were insufficient to attain the group goal to retain their contributions. Greed, however, remains: Nonvolunteers gain more than volunteers when the group contributes enough.

Diekmann's theoretical and empirical results supported the hypothesis that most game theoretic and social psychological models (e.g., diffusion of responsibility) would predict: The proportion of volunteers in a group dropped as group size increased. This finding is identical to Latane and Darley's (1970) bystander effect: As they and others observed in a variety of creative studies, people are more likely to help someone in distress if they think that they are the only one who can help. As people perceive that others can help, they become less likely to assist a potential victim. Thus, we expected results similar to Diekmann's for group size:

Hypothesis 3: The proportion of volunteers will drop as group size increases.

Table 1

An Individual's Payoffs in the General and the No-loss Volunteer Dilemmas

Choice	$m - 2$ volunteers or fewer	$m - 1$ volunteers	m volunteers
General volunteer dilemma			
Volunteer	$-e$	$r - e$	$r - e$
Do not volunteer	0	0	r
No-loss volunteer dilemma			
Volunteer	0	$r - e$	$r - e$
Do not volunteer	0	0	r

Note: m = volunteers necessary to achieve the public good; r = bonus payoff if enough people volunteer; e = the cost of volunteering; $r > e > 0$.

Our first experiment acted as a starting point to investigate the volunteer dilemma and test our three hypotheses. We designed a replication and extension of Diekmann's work by including a more diverse array of group sizes and payoffs in a relatively large factorial design. Our subsequent experiments proceeded incrementally, adding structural variables to increase the scope of the investigation. All considered whether altruistic reactions might surface in volunteering situations when no obvious reasons for feelings of empathy existed.

Volunteer Dilemma

Experiment 1 gave respondents a chance to win "free" money: Not generating a volunteer did not lead to losses, only to a lack of potential gain. In addition, no one was asked to exert any effort to attain these potential winnings. Nevertheless, they faced a potentially perplexing choice: They could volunteer and win a small amount or they could choose not to volunteer and possibly win a larger amount. The social context was minimized by describing the other actors as strangers who would not be seen again. Thus, there was little basis for empathy or other psychic motivators for altruistic action. Instead, the situation was blatantly economic, leading to real-world parallels in impersonal, possibly ultracompetitive interactions. Thus, volunteering choices could be attributed either to the payoff structure or to strong personal dispositions.

METHODS

All four experiments shared a common methodology. All participants were students enrolled in management classes at the University of Illinois at Urbana-Champaign. They responded to a series of volunteer dilemmas as part of a classroom exercise (with one exception, as noted). All potential monetary payoffs described in the scenarios were fictitious. Participants nevertheless reported a high degree of involvement in the task. They were asked to treat each scenario as if it were the only situation like this that they would ever encounter. Everyone made his or her decisions independently.

Each experiment used a mixed hybrid factorial design with participants responding to a randomly sampled subset of the many possible scenarios. Since participants never responded to the same set of scenarios in the same order (this makes the design a mixed hybrid), a repeated-measures analysis was not possible. More conservative between-subjects analyses, which sacrificed some of the advantages of repeated measures, were used.

Because the dependent variable was categorical (volunteering or nonvolunteering), the data were analyzed with the CATMOD (categorical data modeling) procedure (Agresti, 1990). CATMOD treats the responses as generalized logits of the marginal probabilities of the dependent variable. The result is a chi-square test. Additional analyses, using normal analysis of variance, however, yielded similar results.

EXPERIMENT 1

Participants were 106 first-year M.B.A. students in four classes. They received packets of ten scenarios that asked them to imagine that they were in a waiting room with a group of strangers when someone approached them with a proposition. The person offered to pay many of them a high amount (e.g., $10,000) if at least one of the group would accept a lower dollar amount (e.g., $1000). If at least one person was willing to take the smaller amount, everyone would receive what they asked for. Otherwise (i.e., if everyone asked for the high amount), everyone would receive nothing. The following is an example of the scenarios:

You are in a waiting room with 99 strangers. A distinguished-looking individual comes up to you and says "I would be willing to pay many of you $200 if at least one of you is willing to accept $2. You may not talk about it or communicate with each other in any way. If, at least one of you chooses $2, all of you will get what you asked for. If all of you ask for $200, none of you will get anything." If you were in this situation, what would you choose: $2 or $200?

The scenarios spanned a wide range of situational contingencies. Group sizes (GS) were 2, 5, 10, 25, and 100; payoffs for volunteers were small or large (VPAY = $2 or $1000); and payoffs for nonvolunteers (NVPAY) were small, moderate, or large. When VPAY was $2, NVPAY was $4, $20, or $200; when VPAY was $1000, NVPAY was $2000, $10,000, or $100,000. The five group sizes were crossed with the six payoff sets, resulting in 30 scenarios. Each packet contained a random sample of 10 from this set, randomly ordered.

Results and Discussion

Analysis of the results of Experiment 1 assessed the effects of group size (5 levels), VPAY (2 levels), and NVPAY (3 levels) on the frequency of choices to volunteer in a between-subjects CATMOD ANOVA. Table 2 shows the means and frequencies. All three main effects were significant ($\chi^2 \geq 46.48$, $p < .001$ in each case); no interactions were significant. As group size increased, the proportion of volunteers dropped. As VPAY increased from $2 to $1,000, the proportion of volunteers increased, from 28 to 50 percent. Changes in NVPAY from twice as much as VPAY to ten and to 100 times VPAY led to monotonic decreases in the volunteering rate, from 53 to 35 to 29 percent. Each independent variable had consistent effects across all levels of the other variables.

Table 2

Percentages of Volunteers in Groups in Which Only One Volunteer Was Needed—Experiment 1

Group size	Volunteer/nonvolunteer payoffs						Mean
	$2/$4	$2/$20	$2/$200	$1K/$2K	$1K/$10/K	$1K/$100K	
2	69	42	26	84	79	59	60
5	29	37	23	70	55	53	45
10	53	12	29	70	41	38	41
25	26	9	6	44	34	26	25
100	29	18	6	50	24	26	25
Mean	41	24	18	64	46	40	39
Mean (volunteer payoff)		28			50		

Note: Frequencies in each cell range from 33 to 38. Total frequencies for group sizes range from 202 to 212; for payoffs, from 174 to 186. Overall, there were 1,053 responses.

The three hypotheses, that people would react to group size and to the monetary payoffs as a rational model would predict, were clearly supported. In particular, the data suggest that the payoff structure had potent effects. The proportion of volunteers in each condition, however, was considerably larger than the proportion required, especially when VPAY was $1000. For instance, when group size was

Volunteer Dilemma

100 and the nonvolunteer payoff was $2000, 50 percent of the respondents volunteered—when only 1 of 100 was required. Thus, in the aggregate, people were tremendously inefficient. Many respondents noted that they were risk averse: They were quite happy with $1000, and they could assure themselves of this by volunteering. Several also claimed that they were altruistic. Though fewer people volunteered as the payoffs for nonvolunteering increased (to $10,000 and $100,000), volunteers were still much more frequent than the situation required. But as NVPAY increased, more people appeared ready to take rather than avert the risk. The fact that inefficiencies continued, and actually increased monetarily, again leaves open the possibility of some element of altruistic action.

These results can be interpreted as resulting from a complex mix of motivations, including greed, risk aversion, and altruism. Since it is hard to imagine that people were motivated by a desire to avoid inefficiencies, the excess volunteering, from an optimal model's perspective, suggests risk aversion and altruism as causal factors. And the effects of greed are clear, as volunteering dropped when the nonvolunteers' payoffs increased.

Another motivation for volunteering in this experiment could have been to reduce uncertainty: By volunteering, people determined their own outcomes. Not volunteering, by contrast, preserves uncertainty, since someone else must volunteer for a person to receive a payoff. Experiment 2 was designed to increase the uncertainty associated with volunteering. By increasing the required number of volunteers, volunteering no longer removed uncertainty: Volunteers always needed others, sometimes many others, to volunteer as well. Experiment 2 also expanded our study's domain by increasing the number of required volunteers from 1 through 80 percent of the group's size, across the different group sizes.

The public-goods experiment cited earlier (Dawes et al., 1986) suggests that requiring more volunteers should increase the number of volunteers. Since no strong theory exists in this area, we have no reason to expect that this effect will systematically vary within different group sizes. Thus, we predict:

Hypothesis 4: For any group size, increasing the required number of volunteers will lead to an increase in the number of volunteers.

Several theoretical models provide the basis for suggestions that requiring more volunteers may have different effects *across* the different group sizes: All imply that the proportion of volunteers will dwindle when group size increases, even when the required number of volunteers also increases. First, larger groups may reduce social identity and lead to feelings of anomie, fatalism, and little motivation to volunteer. Larger groups may also accentuate feelings of reactance if people feel that a requirement for many volunteers restricts their freedom (Brehm, 1966). And finally, research on group dynamics and negotiation (e.g., Komorita, 1974) suggests that larger groups have more difficulties coalescing. If people perceive this as well, they may be less reluctant to volunteer in larger groups, even with an increase in the number of volunteers required.

By contrast, research suggests that small groups, even with minimal interaction, may quickly define themselves as part of an in-group (Tajfel, 1982). For small groups, people may be able to generate their own identification with each other and they may perceive a greater likelihood of achieving the number of volunteers required (e.g., 4 out of 5 may be easier to achieve than 80 out of 100). All of this reasoning suggests that the negative effects of group size will surpass the positive effects of increasing the required number of volunteers when groups get large. This leads to a new hypothesis:

Hypothesis 5: As group size increases, the positive effects of increasing the required number of volunteers will have increasingly smaller effects. Particularly for large groups, volunteers will increase at a decreasing rate.

This hypothesis does not specify what constitutes small and large groups. With respect to altruistic tendencies, we might expect that people so inclined will be less affected by reactance, since they tend to volunteer anyway. Thus, economic inefficiencies due to too many volunteers will suggest the presence of altruism more strongly than in the first study, since risk aversion cannot be so easily assuaged without removing uncertainty.

EXPERIMENT 2

Participants in this study were 193 undergraduate students enrolled in six sections of an introductory management course. Each student responded to twelve scenarios that duplicated those in Experiment 1, except that the required number of volunteers (VRQ) ranged widely, from 1 to 80 percent of the group. In addition, to test whether people's responses were independent of order, we categorized scenarios that were ordered first, second, and third as Block 1, fourth through sixth as Block 2, etc., and compared whether responses to identical scenarios in different blocks led to different responses.

To ensure comparability across group sizes (of 5, 10, 25, and 100), scenarios included VRQs of 20, 40, 60, and 80 percent for each group size. Additional scenarios were also included for some group sizes: For GS = 5, VRQs were 1, 2, 3, and 4; for GS = 10, VRQs were 1, 2, 4, 5, 6, and 8; for GS = 25, VRQs were 1, 2, 5, 10, 15, and 20; and for GS = 100, VRQs were 1, 2, 5, 10, 20, 40, 60, and 80. Twenty-four GS-VRQ combinations and the six payoff schemes ($2/$4, $2/$20, $2/$200, $1000/$2000, $1000/$10,000, $1000/$100,000) were crossed to create 144 different scenarios. Each packet contained (1) two scenarios with GS = 5; (2) three scenarios with GS = 10; (3) three scenarios with GS = 25; and (4) four scenarios with GS = 100. Each of the six possible dollar payoffs was represented twice in each packet. No two scenarios in a packet had the same VRQ for any group size. Except for these constraints, scenarios were randomly assigned to packets and randomly ordered.

Volunteer Dilemma

Results and Discussion

The most comprehensive analysis crossed five factors: group size (4 levels), volunteer payoffs (2), nonvolunteer payoffs (3), the number of volunteers required (VRQ: 20, 40, 60, or 80 percent of the group size), and blocks (1 through 4) for the twelve scenarios. The block factor led to no significant main or interaction effects, suggesting that order did not seriously affect people's responses; subsequent analyses pooled over blocks. When group size was large (e.g., 100), other VRQs were also possible (e.g., 1, 2, 5, and 10 percent). Thus, separate analyses were also conducted for larger group sizes. The results were consistent with those of Experiment 1 for the single-volunteer cases. They were also consistent in the separate analyses within the different group sizes: All main effects were significant ($\chi^2 \geq$ 12.98, $p < .05$ in each case).

Table 3

Percentages of Volunteers in Groups in Which Multiple Volunteers Were Needed—Experiment 2

Percentage of group required to volunteer (VRQ)	Group size				
	5	10	25	100	Mean
1	—	—	—	22	22
2	—	—	—	18	18
4	—	—	23	—	23
5	—	—	—	28	28
8	—	—	30	—	30
10	—	33	—	35	34
20	44	41	31	48	41
40	44	49	53	.55	50
50	—	56	—	—	56
60	66	61	58	56	60·
80	80	69	63	65	69
Mean	58	52	43	41	48

Note: Frequencies in each cell range from 86 to 101. Total frequencies for group sizes range from 384 to 763; for percentages of the group required to volunteer, from 86 to 387. Overall, there were 2,289 responses.

As shown in Table 3 and Figure 1, for each group size, and overall, as VRQ increased, so did the number of volunteers, supporting hypothesis 4. The increase in volunteering was monotonic and consistent, with one minor exception (2 volunteers required in a group of 100). Increases in the rate of volunteering did not, however, increase as rapidly as the rate of volunteers required. For larger groups, the percentage of volunteers exceeded the percentage required only until VRQ exceeded 50 percent of the group. Then groups moved from inefficiency (too many volunteers) to insufficiency (not enough volunteers).

The results depicted in Figure 1 indicate that for groups of size 5, increases in volunteers followed increases in the required number of volunteers very closely: As 2, 3, and 4 members of the group were required to participate, 44, 66, and 80 percent of the participants indicated that they would volunteer. With each successively larger group, however, the volunteering rate increased at a more and more severely decreasing rate, as hypothesized.

Figure 1. The relationship of volunteering rates to the number of volunteers required in groups of different sizes.

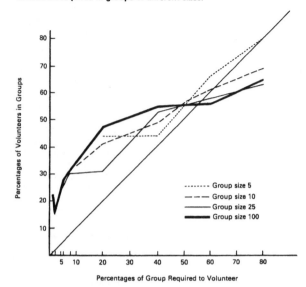

Most conditions led to more volunteers than were required. This again suggests that altruistic tendencies may be reflected in the data, while risk aversion is a less likely explanation, because volunteering no longer removes uncertainty. But these tendencies are less evident as group size and VRQ both increased.

The insufficient volunteering in larger groups with 60 or 80 percent VRQs may have resulted from reactance or defeatism, that is, to either their freedom being threatened or to pessimism at their chances of getting enough volunteers. Either case might lead someone to choose the higher payoff for nonvolunteering, on the one hand with defiance, on the other with resignation (that it doesn't matter anyway). Beneath the simple economic reactions, then, the progression of volunteering situations we have studied admit the possibility of a variety of motivations that shift from altruism and risk aversion to egoism and greed to reactance and pessimism.

Experiments 3 and 4 were designed to bring these motivations closer to the surface. By adding the concept of work, i.e., requiring volunteers either to work more than nonvolunteers for the same (fictitious) financial payoff or to receive less pay for the same amount of work, altruism and egoism may become more active, with egoism reflected in motives like deservingness.

The two conditions in which volunteers worked were the *same-pay* condition, in which everyone (volunteers who did work and nonvolunteers who did not) received the same pay if enough volunteers worked, and the *different-pay* condition, in which volunteers and nonvolunteers both worked the

Volunteer Dilemma

same amount of time, but volunteers earned less than nonvolunteers (who had agreed to work only for a higher payoff) if enough people volunteered.

A strictly rational model would suggest that adding work to both volunteer and nonvolunteer choices would lead to volunteering rates that are identical to those in the nonwork scenarios of Experiments 1 and 2. Theories of equity and deservingness (e.g., Adams, 1965), however, suggest that the addition of work will reduce volunteering rates. Now people must not only volunteer, they must also work, either more than nonvolunteers or for less pay. In this experiment, people who volunteer do so to attain undercompensation, a condition equity theory indicates people will avoid. As some people in the first two experiments noted, they were happy to volunteer for free money, but they would be damned if they would volunteer to work more or earn less than someone else. Essentially, having to volunteer *and* work, without commensurate benefits, was expected to be particularly distasteful. This fits the notion that nonvolunteers are perceived as the greedy out-group by volunteers and that the distance between them grows when the in-group is asked to exert efforts on the out-group's behalf. These reactions also fit the voluntary action literature's view of volunteers, who come across as serving their own interests rather than being altruistic. We thus propose,

Hypothesis 6: Adding work requirements will reduce volunteering rates.

Altruistic tendencies should again blunt this disinclination to volunteer. In particular, situations in which volunteers are required to work for minuscule pay provide an opportunity to observe particularly altruistic volunteering. Table 4 gives an overview of the progression of the experimental designs for the four experiments.

EXPERIMENT 3

Participants were 57 M.B.A. students in two class sections. Two types of work situations, same and different pay, were represented by six scenarios in each packet (except for six packets that contained six nonwork scenarios). The following is an abbreviated example of one of the same-pay scenarios:

You are one of a group of 100, all strangers, who work alone in their homes for a company that hires people to work independently. Your boss needs at least 60 of you to work on an additional task that would take 16 hours this weekend. As compensation, he would pay everyone $200 if at least 60 of you were willing to do the work. If at least 60 of you choose to do the work, everyone would receive $200, whether they worked or not. At least 60 people must be willing to work for $200 for everyone to get paid. Would you work or not? (Note: You have plenty of time and the ability to do the work, which is not at all objectionable. This offer does not obligate you in any way, and your employer is totally reliable.)

Pay and work time took ten values: $2 for 5 minutes or 1 hour; $20 for 5 minutes or 1 hour; $200 for 1 or 16 hours; $1000 for 16 or 160 hours; and $100,000 for 160 or 1000 hours.

In the different-pay scenarios, participants could work for a high dollar amount, a low dollar amount, or not at all. We

Table 4

Progression of Experimental Designs from Experiments 1 to 4

#1	Participants: Volunteers required: Group sizes:	M.B.A. students 1 2, 5, 10, 25, 100
	Volunteer payoffs: (Nonvolunteer payoffs):	$2 $1,000 ($4, $20, $200) ($1K, $10K, $100K)
#2	Participants: *Volunteers required:* Group sizes:	Undergraduates 1–80% of group size 2, 5, 10, 25, 100
	Volunteer payoffs: (Nonvolunteer payoffs):	$2 $1,000 ($4, $20, $200) ($1K, $10K, $100K)
#3	Participants: Volunteers required: Group sizes:	M.B.A. students 1–80% of group size 2, 5, 10, 25, 100
	Same-pay payoffs: *(Work times):*	$2 (5 min.; 1 hr.) $20 (5 min.; 1 hr.) $200 (1 hr.; 16 hrs.) $1,000 (16; 160 hrs.) $100,000 (160; 1000 hrs.)
	Different-pay: *Volunteer payoffs/* *Nonvolunteer payoffs:* *(Work times):*	$2/$4 (5 min.; 1 hr.) $2/$20 (5 min.; 1 hr.) $2/$200 (1 hr.) $1000/$2000 (1; 16; 40 hrs.) $1000/$100K (16; 40 hrs.)
#4	*Participants:* Volunteers required Group sizes:	Executive M.B.A. students 1–80% of group size 2, 5, 10, 25, 100
	Same-pay payoffs:	$20 (5 min.; 1 hr.; 8 hrs.)
	(Work times):	$200 (5 min.; 1 hr.; 8 hr.) $1000 (40; 1000 hrs.) $100,000 (8; 40; 1000 hrs.)
	Different pay: Volunteer-payoffs/ Nonvolunteer payoffs: (Work times):	$2/$20 (5 min.; 1 hr.) $2/$200 (5 min.; 1 hr.) $1000/$2000 (16; 40 hrs.) $1000/$100K (16; 40 hrs.)

Note: Entries in italics are the major additions to each experiment.

---

operationally defined working for the high amount as nonvolunteering. If enough others volunteered to work for the low dollar amount, nonvolunteers would work and get the high amount. People who volunteered to work for the low dollar amount were operationally defined as volunteers. If enough people volunteered, volunteers would work and get the low amount. People who chose not to work did not get paid. If not enough people volunteered to work for the low dollar amount, no one would work or get paid.

There were 10 pay and work-time combinations: $2 (VPAY) or $4 (NVPAY) for 5 minutes or 1 hour; $2 or $20 for 5 minutes or 1 hour; $2 or $200 for 1 hour; $1000 or $2000 for 1, 16, or 40 hours; $1000 or $100,000 for 16 or 40 hours. GSs and VRQs ranged over the same values as in Experiment 2.

Volunteer Dilemma

Results and Discussion

The same-pay and the different-pay work scenarios were analyzed separately. Analyses only included those conditions with sizable cell sizes ($N \geq 10$); the same- and different-pay conditions each yielded only one significant effect, for payoffs, $\chi^2 (9) = 19.90$, $p < .02$. Tables 5 and 6 show the frequencies of volunteers and nonvolunteers. Both suggest that dollars per hour is a strong driving force in these volunteering choices.

Table 5

Percentages of Volunteers for Payoff Schemes When Pay was the Same for Volunteers Who Worked and Nonvolunteers Who Did Not—Experiments 3 and 4

Pay/work time	Pay per hr.	Experiment 3	Experiment 4
$2/5 min.	$24/hr.	61 (31)	–
$2/1 hr.	$2/hr.	11 (27)	–
$20/5 min.	$240/hr.	90 (31)	87 (83)
$20/1 hr.	$20/hr.	81 (31)	42 (159)
$20/8 hrs.	$2.50/hr.	–	13 (78)
$200/5 min.	$2400/hr.	–	94 (68)
$200/1 hr.	$200/hr.	85 (33)	87 (149)
$200/8 hrs.	$25/hr.	–	73 (88)
$200/16 hrs.	$12.50/hr.	59 (32)	–
$1K/16 hrs.	$62.50/hr.	97 (30)	–
$1K/40 hrs.	$25/hr.	–	60 (163)
$1K/160 hrs.	$6.25/hr.	29 (31)	–
$1K/1000 hrs.	$1/hr.	–	13 (68)
$100K/8 hrs.	$12,500/hr	–	100 (72)
$100K/40 hrs.	$2500/hr.	–	99 (157)
$100K/160 hrs.	$625/hr.	85 (27)	–
$100K/1000 hrs.	$100/hr.	86 (37)	91 (68)
Mean		69 (310)	70 (1153)

Note: Frequencies of total respondents are shown in parentheses. Total frequencies exceed the number of respondents, since many participants responded to several scenarios with the same pay and work time (although they varied in group size and/or the number of volunteers required).

In the same-pay condition, the lowest pay ($2 per hour) led to 3 of 27 people volunteering. In the different-pay condition, very low pay led all but one or two people either to volunteer only for high pay or not work. This suggests the presence of very little altruism. By contrast, pay exceeding $100 per hour in the same-pay conditions led to volunteering rates that peaked at less than 100 percent (although at $62.50 per hour, all but one respondent volunteered). High pay for both volunteers and nonvolunteers in the different-pay conditions led to few people choosing not to work. As before, most people seem to have responded from self-interest.

Due to a proliferation of scenarios and a shortage of respondents, Experiment 3 suffered from small cell sizes that were insufficient for testing hypothesis 6. All three experiments suffered from the problems associated with student respondents, although many of the students did have work experience. Experiment 4 was designed to alleviate both problems. It expanded the population of

Table 6

Percentages of Volunteers, Nonvolunteers, and Nonworkers For Different-pay Scenarios —Experiments 3 and 4

VPAY/NVPAY/Time to work (VPAY per hr./NVPAY per hr.)	Experiment 3				Experiment 4			
	Vols	Nvols	Nwrkrs	N	Vols	Nvols	Nwrkrs	N
$2/$4/5 min. ($24/$48)	39	48	12	(33)	–	–	–	
$2/$4/1 hr. ($2/$4)	3	25	72	(32)	–	–	–	
$2/$20/5 min. ($24/$240)	25	56	19	(32)	24	62	14	(253)
$2/$20/1 hr. ($2/$20)	0	68	32	(34)	5	39	56	(241)
$2/$200/5 min. ($24/$2400)	–	–	–		16	75	9	(217)
$2/$200/1 hr. ($2/$200)	5	76	19	(37)	3	83	14	(205)
$1K/$2K/1 hr. ($1000/$2000)	76	21	3	(29)	–	–	–	
$1K/$2K/16 hrs. ($62.50/$125)	66	29	6	(35)	55	40	4	(253)
$1K/$2K/40 hrs. ($25/$50)	48	45	6	(31)	37	50	13	(242)
$1K/$100K/16 hrs. ($62.50/$6250)	27	61	12	(33)	30	68	2	(216)
$1K/$100K/40 hrs. ($25/($2500)	15	82	3	(33)	13	77	10	(204)
Mean (total frequencies)	30	52	19	(329)	24	61	16	(1831)

Note: Total frequencies are in parentheses. Vols, Nvols, and Nwrkrs refer to the proportion of people who chose to work for the low payoff amount, the high payoff amount, and not to work. Total frequencies exceed the number of respondents, since many participants responded to several scenarios.

respondents from undergraduate and M.B.A. students to full-time business executives. In addition, to take advantage of their greater experience, this study began to explore the executives' descriptions of and reactions to volunteering in their own organizations.

EXPERIMENT 4

Participants were 41 students in one executive M.B.A. class. Most had been out of college for at least 10 years, and all were employed full time in central Illinois. Each executive responded to two packets, one in class and one at home. The in-class packets consisted of two free-money scenarios, four same-pay scenarios, and four different-pay scenarios, with each type followed by a short questionnaire. The homework packets consisted of the same scenario types in a different format, allowing as many as 16 responses per page. Each page of nonwork scenarios, for instance, asked for responses to all the possible VRQs for a specified group size and for two low/high dollar pairs. Thus, for GS = 5 and VPAY/NVPAY of $2/$4 and $2/$200, respondents recorded eight decisions in a 2 × 4 grid, all on one page, combining the two payoff schemes and the four possible VRQs (1, 2, 3, and 4). The homework packets contained two pages of nonwork scenarios, four of same-pay work scenarios, and

Volunteer Dilemma

four of different-pay work scenarios, with each type followed by a short questionnaire. A more general questionnaire on volunteering at their normal workplace completed the task.

Results and Discussion

The first analyses assessed whether the different formats (class versus home) had any effect: Responses to identical questions in the different formats led to no significant t-tests (p-values generally exceeded .25), so they were combined for the overall analyses. The analyses of same-pay included payoff schemes (11 levels; see Table 5), group size (5, 10, 25, 100), and VRQ (20, 40, 60, 80 percent of group size) in a variety of overlapping analyses (due to some empty cells in the overall design).[1] The main effects for payoffs were the only consistently significant result ($x^2 > 29.75$, $p < .001$). Means for the payoff schemes are shown in Table 5.

The effects for GS and VRQ were significant in the analyses of variance but were less frequently significant in CATMOD. Several of the CATMOD analyses of VRQ led to significant results, similar to those for nonwork scenarios; CATMOD analyses of GS led to no significant effects.

The analysis of the different-pay scenarios included payoff schemes (8 levels; see Table 6) by GS (4) by VRQ (4); it yielded significant main effects for VRQ [x^2 (6) = 20.05, $p < .005$] and payoffs [x^2(6) = 285.69, $p < .001$] and a significant group size by payoffs interaction [x^2(42) = 77.05, $p < .001$].[2] The payoff-scheme main effect (see Table 6) indicates that nonworking was most frequent and volunteering was least frequent when NVPAY per hour was lowest; volunteering was most frequent when VPAY per hour was highest ($1000 for 16 hours work—$62.50 per hour); volunteering was rare for low VPAY per hour. The effect for VRQ indicates that people volunteered more when 80 percent were needed (44 percent, versus 20 percent when only one was required). Thus, requiring many volunteers in the work scenarios led to far fewer volunteers than in the comparable nonwork scenarios in Experiments 1 and 2.

The interaction (see Table 7) shows that when GS was large (25 or 100) and VPAY was high ($1000), volunteering was relatively frequent (33 to 64 percent), except for 40 hours of work time combined with NVPAY of $100,000. Not surprisingly, NVPAY of $100,000 led to many volunteering to work only for this high payoff (53 to 79 percent). Many people volunteered when GS was small (5 or 10), VPAY per hour was high ($1000 for 16 hours—$62.50/hour), and NVPAY was relatively low ($2000); fewer volunteered when GS was small (5 or 10) and VPAY per hour was lower ($1000 for 40 hours—$25/hour). When volunteers only received $2 for 1 hour, volunteering rates were very low (0 to 12 percent); they increased somewhat when VPAY was $2 for 5 minutes. Nonworking rates were highest when NVPAY was low ($20 per hour), ranging from 37 to 88 percent. These results suggest that pay per hour may be the primary causal factor in volunteering choices in this study and that some variations occur across group sizes.

1
The analyses included in the same-pay condition were: (1) GS (5, 10) × VRQ (20, 40, 60, 80 percent) × pay per hour ($20/8 hrs., $200/8 hrs., $2000/40 hrs., $100,000/40 hrs.); (2) GS (5, 25, 100) × VRQ (20, 40, 60, 80 percent) for $20/1 hr.; (3) GS (5, 10, 25) × VRQ (20, 40, 60, 80 percent) × pay per hour ($2000/40 hrs., $100,000/40 hrs.); (4) GS (5, 25) × VRQ (20, 40, 60, 80 percent) × pay per hour ($20/1 hr., $2000/40 hrs., $100,000/40 hrs.); (5) GS (5, 100) × VRQ (20, 40, 60, 80 percent) × pay per hour ($20/1 hr., $200/8 hrs., $200/5 min.); (6) GS (25, 100) × VRQ (20, 40, 60, 80 percent) × pay per hour ($20/1 hr., $200/1 hr.); (7) GS (25, 100) × VRQ (20, 40, 60, 80 percent) for $100,000/8 hrs.

2
This interaction should be interpreted cautiously, as the distributions within each cell in the interaction are based on unequal frequencies in the other conditions. Although a close inspection of the data suggests that these unequal frequencies did not lead to systematic differences within the cells of the interaction, caution is still in order.

Table 7

Percentages of Volunteers, Nonvolunteers, and Nonworkers in the Interaction of Payoff Schemes and Group Size for Different-pay Scenarios—Experiment 4

VPAY/NVPAY/Time to work (VPAY per hr./NVPAY per hr.)	Group size			
	5 V-NV-NW	10 V-NV-NW	25 V-NV-NW	100 V-NV-NW
$2/$20/5 min. ($24/$240)	12-78-10	22-54-24	22-71-6	50-44-6
$2/$20/1 hr. ($2/$20)	6-34-59	12-31-57	0-12-88	7-56-37
$2/$200/5 min. ($24/$2400)	10-90-0	17-61-22	25-75-0	18-82-0
$2/$200/1 hr. ($2/$200)	4-92-4	11-67-22	0-89-11	0-86-14
$1K/$2K/16 hrs. ($62.50/$125)	74-24-2	73-23-5	65-33-3	51-44-5
$1K/$2K/40 hrs. ($25/$50)	27-69-4	37-45-18	59-39-2	49-32-20
$1K/$100K/16 hrs. ($62.50/$6250)	47-53-0	22-78-0	47-53-0	33-56-11
$1K/$100K/40 hrs. ($25/$2500)	11-72-17	14-79-7	28-72-0	11-69-19
Mean	26-63-11	26-53-21	31-55-14	28-57-15

Note: The columns labeled V-NV-NW refer to the proportions of people who chose to work for the low payoff amount, for the high payoff amount, or chose not to work. Frequencies in each cell range from 25 to 50. Total frequencies for group sizes range from 283 to 323.

Volunteering in work versus nonwork situations.
Hypothesis 6, that the addition of work would reduce volunteering rates, could be tested by comparing reactions to the nonwork and different-pay scenarios when the payoff schemes were identical. The different-pay scenarios added both a specified amount of time to complete the work and the possibility of not working. To make comparisons, responses to work only for the high payoff or to not work were combined and operationalized as nonvolunteering.

The analyses included four payoff schemes: VPAY/NVPAY of $2/$20; $2/$200; $1000/$2000; and $1000/$100,000. In the work scenarios, the time allotted for work was either short or long and varied for low- and high-payoff schemes. The short and long times for the low-payoff pairs ($2/$20 and $2/$200) were 5 minutes and 1 hour; for the high payoffs ($1,000/$2,000 and $1,000/$100,000), they were 16 and 40 hours. The analysis included GS (5, 10, 25, and 100) by VPAY ($2 or $1000) by NVPAY ($20 or $200, and $2,000 or $100,000) by work time (short, long, or no work) by VRQ (20, 40, 60, and 80 percent). Analyses of the entire sample, or just the executives in Experiment 4, which provided the bulk of the data, were very similar; only the executives' data are reported here.

Given the results already reported, we expected significant effects for work time, since more people volunteered when payoffs were identical and time was shorter. The most revealing elements of this analysis, then, were whether people chose volunteering more in the nonwork scenarios than in either of the work scenarios (i.e., short and long work times).

Volunteer Dilemma

Table 8

Percentages of Volunteers for the Interaction of Work Time, Group Size, and Volunteer Payoffs for Nonwork and Different-pay Scenarios

Group size	Volunteer payoffs					
	$2 Work time			$1,000 Work time		
	None	Short	Long	None	Short	Long
5	40	11	5	63	62	22
10	35	20	11	53	49	28
25	28	24	0	59	55	41
100	28	35	3	**68**	40	32

Note: Figures in darker type indicate conditions in which people volunteered significantly more in the nonwork scenarios than in either of the work scenarios.

The results showed significant effects for work time, as expected, as well as for VRQ, VPAY, and NVPAY (in each case $\chi^2 > 29.80$, $p < .001$). The only significant interactions included work time, GS, and VPAY [$\chi^2(6) = 15.22$, $p < .02$]. Post hoc tests of the three-way interaction, presented in Table 8, indicated that nonwork volunteering significantly exceeded volunteering in both work scenarios for the low volunteer payoffs ($2) when groups were small (5 or 10) and for the high volunteer payoffs ($1,000) when the groups were largest (100). Volunteering when no work was involved also exceeded volunteering in work situations in four other conditions, but not significantly. In the remaining condition, nonwork volunteering more closely approximated work volunteering when time was short. A second analysis that combined the two work-time conditions and compared them with the nonwork conditions led to large, significant differences in all four group sizes and both payoff levels. Thus, these data provide considerable support for hypothesis 6.

GENERAL DISCUSSION

This research began with the idea of systematically investigating the underlying dynamics of the volunteer dilemma. Three samples of people reacted to a number of variables in work and nonwork volunteer dilemmas. To obtain the quantity and variety of responses we desired, our measures necessarily assessed people's expressed intentions to volunteer rather than actual volunteering choices. In addition, we only investigated socially isolated situations in which respondents faced a potential gain: The risk of losses and the dynamics of complicated social interactions were not included. The results of these four experiments were nevertheless consistent and clear.

Experiment 1 replicated and extended Diekmann's (1985) results: Fewer people volunteered as group size increased; increasing volunteers' payoffs increased the number of volunteers; and increasing nonvolunteers' payoffs increased the number of nonvolunteers. Experiment 2 replicated these effects, supported the prediction that the number of volunteers increased as the number required increased, and found that when multiple volunteers were required, the number of volunteers increased at a decreasing rate as group size increased. Experiments 3 and 4 documented the strong effects of work payoffs, with few volunteers surfacing in work situations when pay per hour was low. Finally, comparisons of work and nonwork scenarios indicated that people tended to volunteer less when work was involved. All of the results support the predictions derived from instrumental models of voluntary action.

Certainly the notion that work should be rewarded commensurate with effort is not new (March and Simon, 1958). Neither is the idea that higher rewards are more tolerable than lower rewards (Adams, 1965). But even in the nonwork scenarios, people seemed to focus more on their own outcomes than others'. People said they would volunteer *if* their financial rewards were good or it didn't take too much time, or both. These findings are systematic and consistent: They suggest that instrumental issues (money or work time) are critical in determining voluntary action. In this context, it appears that greed dominated altruism.

The postexperimental responses of the executives in Experiment 4 also support this instrumental interpretation. In their open-ended responses to questions probing the reason for their choices, executives tended to provide instrumental reasons, for instance, "The low dollar amount (i.e., VPAY) was important if it was worth my time"; "I paid attention to the really high dollar payoffs" (i.e., NVPAY); and "Work hours are critical because they determine your rate of pay." In addition, when they were asked to identify the key influences in their decisions, almost everyone mentioned money. Only 3 of 32 respondents did not mention money in the nonwork scenarios; only 1 of 32 did not mention it in the different-pay scenarios; and everyone mentioned money in the same-pay scenarios. Two or three respondents mentioned "helping others" as one of their key influences.

Questions about volunteering at their own workplace also led to instrumental responses, although the challenge of the task and time constraints were also mentioned frequently. A strong majority (approximately 85 percent) indicated that they had seen volunteers in their organization "do better in the company because they volunteered." Almost all of the executives who held supervisory positions rewarded their subordinates' voluntary action. At the same time, at least one executive viewed the altruistic and instrumental aspects of volunteering paradoxically: "Volunteering should come naturally but should be reinforced."

The open-ended reflections of the executives come close to fitting Smith's (1983) conclusion about pure altruism in organizations, i.e., that it does not exist. The data from Experiments 1 through 4 are not so extreme, since at least some volunteering surfaced for most of the lowest payoffs. For most participants in this research, however, instrumentality and greed seemed to surface when the payoffs made these motivations worthwhile. Results are similar in other bargaining contexts in which recent research has also eliminated the potentially biasing effects of relationships and context. Studies of ultimatum bargaining, for instance, have found little evidence that ultimatum

Volunteer Dilemma

offerers are motivated by feelings of fairness (e.g., Pillutla and Murnighan, 1993). Instead, most offerers in these studies acted self-interestedly and strategically, especially when they could take personal benefit from an information advantage. Similarly, research on bargaining in veto games (in which one individual, the veto player, was a required member of any coalition) found that separating the five members of a bargaining group and making their interactions anonymous led to extremely high payoffs for the veto players, averaging 90 percent or more of the possible payoffs (Murnighan and Szwajkowski, 1979). Bargaining face-to-face in the same veto games led to a significant reduction in the veto players' payoffs (Murnighan, 1985).

Like the current results, these findings suggest that people who are given little contact with others will have little concern for them and will exhibit considerable concern for themselves. The presence of social isolation, then, seems to relieve people of any social conscience. Strangely enough, this resonates with Piaget's (1974) concept of object permanence in children: Just as young children apparently lose any idea of an object's existence when it is out of sight, so, too, do many participants in these studies seem to lose any feelings of social responsibility when other people are out of sight. A small number, however, seem to have learned the proper altruistic behavior of volunteering, in Simon's (1990) terms. They represent the minority who volunteered at almost every opportunity. Thus, although the altruism glass may not be half full, it also does not appear to be completely empty. More directly, some people can be depended upon to volunteer, even when they have little or no contact with the people they help.

Although the lack of either interpersonal relationships or other contextual factors might not be expected to inspire much sympathy, empathy, or moral obligation (as required by Frank, 1988, Hoffman, 1981, and Schwartz, 1977, respectively) or much altruism, these results provoke but certainly do not answer questions about the frailty of altruistic action. Kessler's (1975) research presents at least one alternative for some of the pessimism that these results suggest. He studied on-call blood donors, who could be summoned any time of the day or night to give blood, and found that they often said that they made up stories about the people who received their blood but whom they never saw. One donor reported visualizing a young girl and a family who loved her; in the fantasy, she needed a transfusion to keep fighting leukemia. This suggests that participants in experiments like ours might be shocked back into social responsibility with suitable cognitive interventions. Regan and Totten's (1975) manipulation of asking people to adopt an empathic attitude, for instance, would be one method for achieving altruistic actions without social contact. The discouraging part of this hypothesis, of course, is that such suggestions are needed to begin with.

Taking a literal, organizational perspective, these data suggest that, in the long run, prosocial behavior and organizational citizenship may depend on salient organizational or personal rewards. The literature on voluntary organizations (also somewhat pessimistic) provides several clues to the character these forces might take. First, people in a variety of organizations might volunteer to improve the chances that they will be employed, possibly in a more fulfilling position (Stinson and Stam, 1976). Thus, an astute supervisor might use the same technique used by the United States Armed Forces to entice recruits: "Learn a skill—join the Army." Second, the notion that volunteering can stimulate social interactions (Sharp, 1978) suggests that requests for voluntary action should be plural rather than singular. Third, voluntary action can be connected to getting ahead in a company, either formally or by implication. As indicated by the executives in Experiment 4, companies seem to understand this general notion already and typically do reward voluntary action.

This begs the question, of course, of whether voluntary action is possible in the absence of instrumental rewards. In Simon's (1990) terms, how can people be convinced that altruistic, voluntary action is proper behavior? Drawing insights from the notion that altruism is most beneficial when it is directed toward close kin, we might speculate that the current trend toward divisionalization, making interacting work units smaller and more cohesive, and the sincere use of transformational leadership (House, 1977; Bass, 1985), with its dependence on the inspiration of superordinate goals, can achieve kin-like connections among unrelated people, making altruistic, voluntary acts normal. Similarly, people may be more likely to volunteer when their identification with the organization is salient to them (Kramer, 1993). In addition, Loewenstein, Thompson, and Bazerman (1989) have shown that positive interpersonal relationships can contribute to individuals attaining social utility from others' outcomes. Thus, when people feel positively toward each other, their own self-interests —determined in part by the outcomes of positively evaluated others—can contribute to voluntary action.

At the other extreme, organizations to which these data may be most pertinent and applicable are those where individualism, even to the state of isolation, predominates. Thus, the ultracompetitive atmosphere of many Wall Street firms during the proliferation of insider trading (Stewart, 1991) may be one example of egoistic, nonvoluntary interaction at its outer limits. The prospects portended by such an analogy provide little confidence that volunteering will surface in such environments. Alternatively, collectivist cultures, whether domestically or internationally, are those in which voluntary action may be proper behavior and in which social contacts may not need to be visible for altruistic acts to occur. Certainly, strong social bonds make visualizations of others easier, providing a firmer impetus for volunteering. Opening the door to research on contextual and interpersonal factors could lead to the notion that people are not as greedy as they might otherwise seem and that expecting them to contribute to the greater good should not necessarily be a faint hope.

Volunteer Dilemma

REFERENCES

Adams, J. Stacy
1965 "Inequity in social exchange." In L. Berkowitz (ed.), Advances in Experimental Social Psychology, 2: 267–299. New York: Academic Press.

Agresti, Alan
1990 Categorical Data Analysis. New York: Wiley.

Allen, Natalie J., and J. Philippe Rushton
1983 "Personality characteristics of community mental health volunteers: A review." Journal of Voluntary Action Research, 12: 36–49.

Axelrod, Robert, and William D. Hamilton
1981 "The evolution of cooperation." Science, 211: 1390–1396.

Bass, Bernard M.
1985 Leadership and Performance beyond Expectations. New York: Free Press.

Batson, C. Daniel
1987 "Prosocial motivation: Is it ever altruistic?" In L. Berkowitz (ed.), Advances in Experimental Social Psychology, 20: 65–122. New York: Academic Press.

Batson, C. Daniel, K. O'Quin, J. Fultz, M. Vanderplas, and Alice Isen
1983 "Self-reported distress and empathy and egoistic versus altruistic motivation for helping." Journal of Personality and Social Psychology, 45: 706–718.

Batson, C. D., J. L. Dyck, J. R. Brandt, J. D. Batson, A. L. Powell, M. R. McMaster, and C. Griffitt
1988 "Five studies testing two new egoistic alternatives to the empathy-altruistic hypothesis." Journal of Personality and Social Psychology, 55: 52–77.

Berkowitz, Leonard, and L. R. Daniels
1964 "Affecting the salience of the social responsibility norm: Effects of past help on the response to dependency relationships." Journal of Abnormal and Social Psychology, 68: 275–281.

Brehm, Jack W.
1966 A Theory of Psychological Reactance. New York: Academic Press.

Brief, Arthur R., and Stephen J. Motowidlo
1986 "Prosocial organizational behaviors." Academy of Management Review, 11: 710–725.

Campbell, Donald T.
1983 "The two distinct routes beyond kin selection to ultrasociality: Implications for the humanities and social sciences." In D. L. Bridgeman (ed.), The Nature of Prosocial Behavior: 126–147. New York: Academic Press.

Dawes, Robyn M.
1980 "Social dilemmas." In Mark R. Rosenzweig and Lyman W. Porter (eds.), Annual Review of Psychology, 31: 169–193. Palo Alto, CA: Annual Reviews.

Dawes, Robyn M., John Orbell, Randy Simmons, and Alphons van der Kragt
1986 "Organizing groups for collective action." American Political Science Review, 80: 1171–1185.

Diekmann, Andreas
1985 "Volunteer's dilemma." Journal of Conflict Resolution, 29: 605–610.
1986 "Volunteer's dilemma: A social trap without a dominant strategy and some empirical results." In A. Diekmann and P. Mitter (eds.), Paradoxical Effects of Social Behavior: Essays in Honor of Anatol Rapoport: 97–103. Heidelberg: Physica-Verlag.

Frank, Robert H.
1988 Passions within Reason: The Strategic Role of the Emotions. New York: W.W. Norton.

George, Jennifer M., and Kenneth Bettenhausen
1990 "Understanding prosocial behavior, sales performance, and turnover: A group-level analysis in a service context." Journal of Applied Psychology, 75: 698–711.

Gluck, Peter R.
1975 "An exchange theory of incentives of urban political party organization." Journal of Voluntary Action Research, 4: 104–115.

Hamilton, William D.
1964 "The general evolution of social behavior." Journal of Theoretical Biology, 7: 1–32.

Hoffman, Martin L.
1981 "Is altruism part of human nature?" Journal of Personality and Social Psychology, 40: 121–137.

House, Robert J.
1977 "A 1976 theory of charismatic leadership." In J. G. Hunt and L. L. Larson (eds.), Leadership: The Cutting Edge: 189–207. Carbondale, IL: Southern Illinois University Press.

Jensen, M. C., and W. H. Meckling
1976 "Theory of the firm: Managerial behavior, agency costs, and ownership structure." Journal of Financial Economics, 3: 305–360.

Katz, Daniel
1964 "The motivational basis of organizational behavior." Behavioral Science, 9: 131–146.

Kessler, Ronald C.
1975 "A descriptive model of emergency on-call blood donation." Journal of Voluntary Action Research, 4: 159–171.

Komorita, Samuel S.
1974 "A weighted probability model of coalition formation." Psychological Review, 81: 242–256.

Kramer, Roderick M.
1993 "Cooperation and organizational identification." In J. K. Murnighan (ed.), Social Psychology in Organizations: Advances in Theory and Research: 244–268. Englewood Cliffs, NJ: Prentice Hall.

Krebs, Dennis L., and Dale T. Miller
1985 "Altruism and aggression." In G. Lindzey and E. Aronson (eds.), The Handbook of Social Psychology, 3rd ed., 2: 1–71. Reading, MA: Addison-Wesley.

Latane, Bibb, and John M. Darley
1970 The Unresponsive Bystander: Why Doesn't He Help? New York: Appleton-Century-Crofts.

Loewenstein, George, Leigh Thompson, and Max H. Bazerman
1989 "Social utility and decision making in interpersonal contexts." Journal of Personality and Social Psychology, 57: 426–441.

March, James G., and Herbert A. Simon
1958 Organizations. New York: Wiley.

Murnighan, J. Keith
1985 "Coalitions in decision-making groups: Organizational analogs." Organizational Behavior and Human Decision Processes, 35: 1–26.

Murnighan, J. Keith, and Eugene Szwajkowski
1979 "Coalition bargaining in four games that include a veto player." Journal of Personality and Social Psychology, 37: 1933–1946.

Organ, Dennis W.
1988 Organizational Citizenship Behavior: The Good Soldier Syndrome. Lexington, MA: Lexington Books.

Organ, Dennis W., and Mary Konovsky
1989 "Cognitive versus affective determinants of organizational citizenship behavior." Journal of Applied Psychology, 74: 157–164.

Piaget, Jean
1974 Understanding Causality. New York: Norton.

Pillutla, Madan, and J. Keith Murnighan
1993 "Fairness and ultimatum bargaining." Working paper, Faculty of Commerce, University of British Columbia.

Rapoport, Amnon
1985 "Provision of public goods and the MCS experimental paradigm." American Political Science Review, 79: 148–155.

1987 "Research paradigms and expected utility models for the provision of step-level public goods." Psychological Review, 94: 74–83.

Rapoport, Amnon, and D. Eshed-Levy
1989 "Provision of step-level public goods: Effects of greed and fear of being gypped." Organizational Behavior and Human Performance, 44: 325–344.

Regan, Dennis T., and J. Totten
1975 "Empathy and attribution: Turning observers into actors." Journal of Personality and Social Psychology, 32: 850–856.

Schwartz, S. H.
1977 "Normative influences on altruism." In L. Berkowitz (ed.), Advances in Experimental Social Psychology, 10: 221–279. New York: Academic Press.

Sharp, Elaine B.
1978 "Citizen organizations in policing issues and crime prevention: Incentives for participation." Journal of Voluntary Action Research, 7: 45–58.

Simon, Herbert A.
1990 "A mechanism for social selection and successful altruism." Science, 250: 1665–1668.

Smith, David Horton
1983 "Altruism, volunteers, and volunteerism." Journal of Voluntary Action Research, 12: 21–36.

Stewart, James B.
1991 Den of Thieves. New York: Simon and Schuster.

Stinson, Thomas F., and Jerome M. Stam
1976 "Toward an economic model of voluntarism: The case of participation in local government." Journal of Voluntary Action Research, 5: 52–60.

Tajfel, Henri
1982 Social Identity and Intergroup Relations. Cambridge: Cambridge University Press.

Trivers, Robert L.
1971 "The evolution of reciprocal altruism." Quarterly Review of Biology, 46: 35–57.

Tucker, A. W.
1950 "A two-person dilemma." Unpublished manuscript, Department of Mathematics, Stanford University.

van der Kragt, Alphons J. C., John M. Orbell, and Robyn M. Dawes
1983 "The minimal contributing set as a solution to public goods problems." American Political Science Review, 77: 112–122.

de Waal, Frans B. M., and Lesleigh M. Luttrell
1988 "Mechanisms of social reciprocity in three primate species: Symmetrical relationship characteristics or cognition?" Ethology and Sociobiology, 9: 101–118.

[7]

JOURNAL OF EXPERIMENTAL SOCIAL PSYCHOLOGY 27, 379–391 (1991)

Resource Dilemmas and Discount Rates in Decision Making Groups

ELIZABETH A. MANNIX

Center for Decision Research, University of Chicago

Received February 2, 1990

In an exercise which simulates the organization as a resource dilemma, discount rates were manipulated to examine their impact on coalition formation and group outcomes. Subjects played a 15-round resource allocation game. They had the option of forming coalitions, which decreased the size of the resource pool, or practicing collective resource allocation, which increased it. Groups with a high discount rate used resource distribution strategies (coalition formation) that resulted in lower individual as well as group outcomes. Groups in the low discount condition adopted collective strategies that increased the size of their resource pool over time. Implications for small group decision making in organizations are discussed. © 1991 Academic Press, Inc.

Social dilemmas have been a topic of research since Hardin's (1968) classic article on "The Tragedy of the Commons." Social dilemmas examine group decision making in a mixed-motive context. They can be characterized as *N*-person prisoner's dilemmas in which each individual receives a higher payoff for a socially defecting choice than for a cooperative choice, yet all individuals have a higher payoff if all cooperate than if all defect (Hardin, 1968; Cross & Guyer, 1980; Schelling, 1978; Brewer & Kramer, 1986; Dawes, 1988). Common examples of social dilemmas often include environmental resource pools, such as water supplies, fossil fuels, or fisheries, that are self-generating at some specified rate and that must be conserved or they will be permanently destroyed. In these situations, often called social traps (Platt, 1973), the individually rational choice is to take as much of the resource as possible. However,

This research was supported by a grant from the Dispute Resolution Research Center, Kellogg Graduate School of Business, Northwestern University. The author thanks George Loewenstein, Max Bazerman, David Messick, and three anonymous reviewers for their helpful comments on an earlier draft of this manuscript. Address correspondence and reprint requests to the author at the Center for Decision Research, University of Chicago, Graduate School of Business, 1101 E. 58th Street, Chicago, IL 60637.

this choice is detrimental to the group as a whole, and if all individuals do make such a choice, they risk eliminating the resource.

In making the choice whether to reduce their own consumption or to take as much of the resource as possible immediately, individuals make a choice between helping oneself or helping the group (Kramer, 1990). Certainly, however, it is important to recognize that helping the group can result in a long-term advantage for the individual group members as well. When a social trap has consequences over time, a temporal trap exists (Platt, 1973; Messick and McClelland, 1983). The difficulty of temporal traps is that one must not only delay one's gratification and trust that the future decisions of the other group members will be cooperative, but also see the connection between one's present choice and the future choices of others. The combination of these requirements can result in little apparent incentive for individuals to make decisions with long-term rather than short-term benefits.

One setting that can readily be viewed in social dilemma terms is an organization. Organizations might be described as large resource pools consisting of funding, personnel, access to information, office space, skill, etc. (Mannix, 1989; Kramer, 1990). Decisions regarding the distribution of these resources are often made by groups (social traps) and have short- as well as long-term consequences (temporal traps). When organizational resources are limited and organization members are rewarded based on the success of their particular groups or divisions, intraorganizational conflict results. Because most organization members do not have the authority or the power to take the resources they desire alone, coalitions form to resolve conflict and distribute resources. In social dilemma terms, this coalition formation can be conceived of as coordinated "defection" on the part of a subset of organization members.

Several different definitions of a coalition have been proposed by researchers in many fields. One that applies well to the organizational setting was suggested by Murnighan and Brass (1990, p. 3) and will be adopted here: "A coalition is defined as any subset of a group that pools its resources or unites as a single voice to determine a decision for the entire group." Early research on coalitions focused primarily on who coalesces with whom and how the resources are distributed (Luce and Raiffa, 1957; Caplow, 1956; Chertkoff, 1967; Gamson, 1961). Later, social psychologists moved to broaden the issues addressed by coalition researchers, recognizing some of the contributions of political scientists by including factors such as justice norms and ideological issues in coalition theories (Komorita & Hamilton, 1984; Komorita & Kravitz, 1983; Miller & Crandall, 1980; Miller & Komorita, 1986; Murnighan, 1986).

In the organizations area several theorists have focused on the benefits accrued by the coalition members and the potential benefits to the organization by coalition activity (March & Simon, 1958; Cyert & March,

1963; Thompson, 1967; Pfeffer, 1981; Mintzberg, 1983). These discussions tend to view coalition formation either as a positive activity or without any qualitative evaluation. Indeed, it may be that some coalition activity brings high outcomes to coalition members in addition to bringing benefit to the organization (Pfeffer, 1981). However, assuming that most organization members are motivated to maximize their own gain,[1] this is only one side of this activity. It is also possible under different circumstances that decisions made by coalitions will result in inefficient outcomes when viewed from the perspective of the organization as a whole.

Although defection in prisoner and social dilemmas has previously been conceptualized as an individual activity, I would like to suggest that coalitions may also be viewed as a type of defection at the group level, where some organization members obtain short-term gains and other organization members are left without resources. Individuals or groups outside the winning coalition may be less effective or may suffer reduced productivity without the necessary resources. Eventually, the viability of the organization as a whole could be affected. These negative results may be most likely in organizations with scarce resources and strong competition between divisions or profit centers and that make decisions with little intervening superordinate authority.

DISCOUNT RATES AND INTERTEMPORAL CHOICE

What circumstances are more likely to lead to groups making resource allocation decisions through coalition formation? One answer may be found by looking at the temporal nature of the group decision process. As mentioned above, one of the interesting features of social dilemmas is that they are often complicated by time (Platt, 1973; Messick and McClelland, 1983). Temporal traps involve the opposition between short- and long-term consequences (Messick and McClelland, 1983). At the individual level, many of the choices people make everyday are between an unpleasant behavior now that will result in a positive future outcome and a pleasant behavior now that will result in a negative future outcome. An economist recognized this phenomenon at the turn of the century as he noted that people often sharply discount the future (Jevons, 1871/1911). Since that time, economists have used the discounted utility model and the concept of discount rates to describe choices made over time. However, there are a number of "anomalies" of intertemporal

---

[1] It might be noted that in some group situations individuals will not be motivated to maximize their own gain, but rather to see their fellow group members benefit or to distribute resources based on need. Clark and Mills (1979) note this as a distinction between communal and exchange relationships. It is assumed that people in organizations are involved in relationships based on social exchange, and these are the types of relationships that are examined in this research.

382   ELIZABETH A. MANNIX

choice that the discounted utility model is incapable of explaining (Loewenstein and Prelec, 1989; Strotz, 1956; Ainslie, 1975). Even in areas where
the discounted utility model is adequate, it is not helpful in explaining
why people make intertemporal choices; its function is only to summarize
how they make those choices. Ideas from social and cognitive psychology
have recently been incorporated into some of the economic work on
intertemporal choice, adding to the explanations of why people make the
choices that they do (Loewenstein, 1986; Schelling, 1984).

Researchers have found that in making choices across time individuals
will often choose an immediate, although smaller, reward over a delayed
but more valuable reward (Ainslie, 1975). In the organizational setting,
an added problem is the collective consequences of such intertemporal
choices. That is, temporal traps are often social traps as well, posing a
conflict between the individual and the group outcome. Individual actions
that have a delayed negative effect for the individual as well as for the
group are particularly interesting and difficult social dilemmas to solve
(Messick and Brewer, 1983). In a resource dilemma that occurs across
time, individuals have several issues to focus on: their own immediate
outcomes, their outcomes in the future, their outcomes compared to the
outcomes of other group members, the size of the resource pool now,
and the size of the resource pool in the future. The nature of a social
dilemma implies that these issues are interdependent. However, individuals have cognitive limitations and they may simplify the task before them,
choosing strategies that will result in higher immediate gains, regardless
of the consequences that those strategies might have for the future or for
the group.

People have cognitive limitations which make their performance in
complex situations less than optimal. When discount rates are high it may
be difficult for people to tell when the discounting is so high that it is
actually more advantageous to defect rather than cooperate. As Axelrod
(1984) has noted, when discount rates increase the probability that a
defecting strategy is optimal also increases. Calculating when defecting
outperforms cooperating is a difficult task, even under conditions of complete information. Therefore, it may be simpler to treat every decision
as though it were the *last* decision. That is, as if the future did not exist.
An additional complication occurs when conditions do not provide complete information, as when there are other individuals involved, whose
choice behavior is uncertain. In these instances, correct calculations are
likely to be impossible. Solving the problem of maximizing short- and
long-term gain at the individual as well as the group level is a highly
complex task. As a result, group members in resource dilemma situations
may choose stategies such as coalition formation which give them resources
without delay, even if such strategies diminish the future of the resource
pool. Therefore, the central hypothesis of this study is that groups with

a high discount rate will be more likely to form coalitions and distribute funding to a subset of group members, resulting in lower group outcomes, than groups that have a low discount rate.

METHOD

Subjects, task, and procedures. Subjects were 150 male and female Master of Management students at the Kellogg Graduate School of Management at Northwestern University who participated in this experiment as part of a classroom exercise. The experimental design manipulated discount rate as a between-subjects variable. Subjects participated in mixed-gender groups of five, resulting in fifteen groups in each of two cells (high discounting (12%) vs low discounting (2%)). Upon arrival to the laboratory, subjects were instructed that they would be involved in a group negotiation task and were given background and role playing instructions. After reading the instructions subjects were asked to answer a brief questionnaire which ensured that the instructions were clear and served as a manipulation check. After all subjects had answered the questionnaire correctly the experimenter explained the task and subjects were permitted to ask questions. Subjects were randomly assigned to groups of five and sent into separate rooms.

The subjects were told that they were one of five vice presidents in Zephyr, Inc. Zephyr was described as a small industrial company operating under a decentralized structure with five primary divisions, labeled A, B, C, D, and E. The subjects were told that each division acted as its own profit center, competing against the others for company resources and rewards. Subjects were told that money had been made available for research and promotion projects to occur jointly between the divisions. The divisions were encouraged to work together on these projects, and money would be allocated only to projects involving *three, four, or five* divisions. The vice presidents themselves were to decide how the funding was to be divided. In accordance with the social exchange view of organizations (Clark and Mills, 1979), subjects were told that their goal was to gain as much R&D funding for their own division as possible over all the rounds of play. They were instructed that they would play up to 20 "rounds" of this exercise. Subjects actually played only 15 rounds to minimize end-game effects.

The social dilemma aspect of this game was represented by the amount of funding that was available for each round. The resource pool varied depending on how many divisions were included in the funded group. The exercise began with a $60,000 funding pool. In round one, each group had $60,000 to divide. How much money they would have to divide in round 2 (i.e., the size of the resource pool) depended on how many group members received funding in round one. If the group allocated funding to three of the five group members in round 1, then the resource pool for the following round would decrease by 4% to $57,600. This is the amount that the group would have to allocate in round 2. If the group allocated funding to four of the five members in round 1, then the resource pool for round 2 would decrease by 2% to $58,800. However, if the group allocated funding to all five members in round 1, the resource pool would be increased by 3% for round 2 to $61,300. The funding for round 3 was then calculated using the amount that had been available in round 2 as a base. Subjects were given complete information on the effects their resource distributions would have on the size of the resource pool.

Each group had a neutral group facilitator to assist them in the decision making process. The procedure was designed to allow no verbal communication. The facilitator managed the voting procedure and did all the computational work. At the beginning of each round the group facilitator selected a "proposal/voting form" from a stack of forms visible to the subjects. Each form had the divisions listed at the top in a random order. One proposal form was used for each round. For each round, the division listed first on the proposal form was designated as the first "proposer" for that round, and that individual was given the

384   ELIZABETH A. MANNIX

TABLE 1
PROTOTYPICAL EXPERIMENTAL RESULTS

	Cumulative group total (equal division)	Individual total for coalition members
Stable three-way coalition—2%	$607,731	$202,577
Stable three-way coalition—12%	$355,761	$118,587
Stable four-way coalition—2%	$524,403	$174,801
Stable four-way coalition—12%	$388,676	$097,169
Stable five-way coalition—2%	$961,775	$192,355
Stable five-way coalition—12%	$494,210	$098,842

proposal form, which only he or she could see. He or she proposed a funding allocation for that round by checking off the divisions he or she wanted to include on the proposal form. Below each included division the proposer was instructed to write a percentage indicating the proposed funding for that division.

When the proposal was completed the proposer handed the form to the group facilitator. The facilitator read off the proposal and called for a simultaneous vote from the divisions included in the proposal. Only the divisions included in a proposal were permitted to vote, and the proposer was required to vote yes. A proposal became binding if all divisions that were included in that proposal voted yes. If the proposal was *not* accepted, the group facilitator gave the proposal form to the next division listed on the proposal form, who made another proposal. Subjects were permitted to go through the proposal cycle no more than twice, resulting in a maximum of ten proposals per round. If no acceptable proposal was found, all the divisions received zero funding, and the money remained unused for that round.

If a proposal was accepted the facilitator announced which divisions had received funding and how much funding was allocated to each division. The facilitator then announced the amount of funding available for the following round and began the next round. Each round began with a new proposal form, which had a different ordering of divisions listed at the top. After the last round subjects completed a 12-item questionnaire which included questions on strategies, influence, power, and satisfaction. Each question was on a 5-point Likert-type scale.

Experimental manipulations. The discount rate was either high (12%) or low (2%). Subjects were told that the industrial chemical market that Zephyr participated in was becoming increasingly high tech, having to cope with a shorter product life and intense competition. Because the money being divided was for the research and promotion of new products, money obtained early in the exercise was worth more than money obtained in the future. To represent the decreasing value of money over time, a compounded rate of either 2% (low) or 12% (high) was deducted from each funding pool, beginning in round 2. In the task instructions a chart was given that showed the multiplier that would be applied to the resource pool in each round.

Subjects were told that the amount they earned in each round would be expressed in "round 1 dollars." In each round the number of dollars earned was multiplied by the appropriate amount to adjust that round's earnings to round 1 dollars. Subjects were told that their objective was to maximize the number of round 1 dollars earned across the total number of rounds. For example, in the 2% discount condition, $10,000 earned in round 1

TABLE 2

MEAN NUMBER OF GROUP MEMBERS RECEIVING
FUNDING BY DISCOUNT RATE AND ROUND

	Discount rate	
	Low	High
Round block 1	4.60	4.09
Round block 2	4.54	3.81
Round block 3	4.29	3.64

would be worth $10,000 in round 1 dollars, but only $9220 in round 5. Similarly, in the 12% discount condition $10,000 earned in round 5 would be worth $6,000 in round 1 dollars.

Table 1 shows six "idealized" funding scenarios, based on the change in the resource pool size given and the applicable discount rate. If group members are able to distribute funding to all five group members on all rounds the group outcome will be at its highest. Any divergence from this must lower the group outcome, but individual group members may increase their own outcomes at the group's expense. However, because there are several allocation decisions, and the group members are highly interdependent, high individual gain is not assured by coalition formation unless a group member is included in all or many of the coalitions formed.

RESULTS

Thirty groups playing 15 rounds of this exercise resulted in 450 total funding allocation decisions. The central hypothesis predicted that high discount groups would be more likely than low discount groups to distribute funding to a subset of group members, and hence would have poorer group performance. The mean number of coalitions formed in each of the experimental conditions was computed. A t test was conducted which compared the number of these distributions in low versus high discount groups. The results indicated that groups with a low discount rate did have fewer coalitional agreements ($M = 4.13$) than high discount groups ($M = 8.93$), $t(28) = 3.68$, $p < .001$.

The above analysis, however, does not include the possible impact of round on coalition size. Therefore, data from the 15 rounds was collapsed across blocks of five to indicate early, middle, and late rounds. The data was then subjected to a 2 (discount rate) × 3 (round block) analysis of variance (ANOVA), with repeated measures on the second factor. The analysis revealed a significant effect for round, such that over time the number of group members included in the funding allocation decreased, $F(2, 56) = 5.22$, $p < .01$. Of greater interest is the significant effect of discount rate on the number of people receiving funding in each round, $F(1, 28) = 13.76$, $p < .001$, indicating that high discount rate groups included significantly fewer people in their funding allocations than low

386   ELIZABETH A. MANNIX

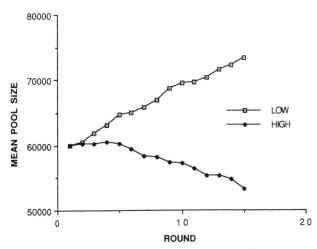

FIG. 1.   Change in resource pool size in low and high discount rate groups.

discount rate groups. The interaction was not significant, $F < 1$. The means are shown in Table 2.

To compare group outcomes across the two discount conditions, non-discounted group outcomes were computed. These sums were simply the outcomes that each group would have received if there had been no devaluing of future dollars. As a result of forming more coalitions, high discount groups had significantly lower group outcomes ($M = \$867,173.2$) than low discount groups ($M = \$1,003,182.27$) $t(28) = 3.29, p < .005$.

Another way to measure the performance of high and low discount rate groups is to measure the change in the size of the resource pool available to them over the 15 rounds. The 15 rounds were again collapsed to form three blocks of five rounds each and nondiscounted dollars were used for comparability. A 2×3 ANOVA was conducted using discount rate as a between-groups factor and round blocks as a within-groups factor. The effect of discount rate was significant, $F(1, 28) = 10.80, p < .005$, as was the interaction between discount rate and round blocks, $F(2, 56) = 10.64, p < .001$. The main effect of round block was not significant, $F < 1$. These results indicate that low discount rate groups were able to increase the size of the resource pool, while high discount rate groups decreased the pool size over time. Figure 1 illustrates the mean size of the resource pool by round in each of the two conditions.

Of additional interest is the pattern of proposals and voting within each round. There may be more disagreement in the high discount rate groups than in the low discount rate groups regarding how to manage the resource pool. That is, while some players might recognize the benefits of building the resource pool, other players are likely to be unwilling to delay acquiring resources. As a first test, the average number of proposals used by groups within each round was calculated. If there was more disagreement in the high discount rate groups, they might need more proposals to reach consensus. An ANOVA was conducted on the data with discount rate as a between-groups factor and round blocks as a within-groups factor. The number of proposals did not differ significantly in high ($M = 1.29$) versus low discount rate groups ($M = 1.47$), $F < 1$.

The above result might indicate a similar amount of disagreement (or agreement) in the two conditions. However, it may be that a greater number of people voted "no" on each proposal in the high discount rate condition than in the low discount rate condition. This would indicate less agreement on how the resource pool should be divided and possibly more conflict over short- versus long-term gain. To test this the number of group members actually voting no within each round was calculated. The data was subjected to a 2 (discount rate) $\times$ 3 (round blocks) ANOVA, with repeated measures on the second factor. Only the effect of discount rate was significant, indicating that group members in the high discount rate condition did vote no significantly more times per round ($M = 2.64$) than group members in the low discount rate condition ($M = 1.28$), $F(1, 28) = 5.44$, $p < .05$.

Following the experiment subjects completed a questionnaire. A multivariate analysis of variance (MANOVA) indicated significant differences in the perceptions of individual and group behavior by low and high discounted groups, $F(12, 122) = 9.79$, $p < .0001$. Six of the 12 questions resulted in significant univariate analyses. Individuals in the high discount condition were more likely than individuals in the low discount condition to report that the discount rate greatly reduced the value of future dollars, $F(1, 133) = 59.23$, $p < .0001$; that their group was very competitive and group members cared only about their own outcomes, $F(1, 133) = 9.97$, $p < .005$; that group members retaliated against other group members who had omitted them from a funding distribution, $F(1, 133) = 12.14$, $p < .001$; that they tried to maximize their funding relative to the other members of the group, $F(1, 133) = 6.65$, $p < .01$; and that they did *not* try to maximize the funding of the group as a whole, $F(1, 133) = 20.98$, $p < .0001$. In addition, subjects in the high discount condition reported that they found it more difficult than subjects in the low discount condition to form large coalitions than small ones, $F(1, 133) = 10.81$, $p < .005$. Remaining univariate tests were not significant, all $Fs < 1$.

DISCUSSION

The results suggest that a highly devalued future may be disruptive to groups making decisions within the context of a resource dilemma. Individuals in groups with a higher discount rate used resource distribution strategies (coalition formation) that resulted in lower individual as well

388   ELIZABETH A. MANNIX

as group outcomes. High discount groups also significantly reduced the resource pool over time, while the low discount groups were able to significantly increase the size of the resource pool, resulting in higher cumulative outcomes. These results support the proposition that members of groups with highly discounted futures will focus more on immediate, individual outcomes than on their cumulative or group outcomes.

The questionnaire results offer some insights as to the effects of high discounting on each individual's perceptions and beliefs. Individuals in high discount rate groups reported that they perceived more competitive and retaliatory behavior in their groups than individuals in low discount groups. In addition, individuals in the high discount condition reported that they tried to maximize their funding relative to the other members of the group and they did not try to maximize the funding of the group as a whole. This indicates that even if a group member in the high discount condition started the task in cooperative mode, that mode was likely to change, if only for defensive reasons. Not only did these individuals not care about the outcomes of the group or of other group members, they actually perceived the task to have winners and losers. They tried to "beat" the scores of other group members, even when the task was explicitly intraorganizational. These results imply that individuals in contexts with a highly devalued future may operate with completely different interpretations of the task before them than individuals with relatively low discounting.

Why the high discount rate resulted in this increased competitiveness cannot be fully explained by this initial study; however, some mechanisms might be proposed. The first explanation was discussed earlier; that is, participants in the high discount condition may have viewed the future as having so little value that they actually treated each round as though it was the last. In other words, the discounting may have approximated an end-game effect, mimicking a single round game. After all, most of the time we are rewarded for immediate outcomes, not over the long term. The relationship between discounting and end-game effects is an interesting one that should be tested by comparing similar studies using discounting with those using either single-trial or shortened trial games.

A second factor may be the effect of anchoring, such that individuals judge their outcomes based on previously selected anchors (Tversky and Kahneman, 1973). In calculating their potential outcomes it may be difficult for players to see how much the funding actually affects the value of dollars. In the high discount condition individuals saw their outcomes rapidly decrease from their early outcomes. Group members may have been highly disturbed by the difference caused by the discounting and thus shifted to a more short term, and hence, competitive orientation, forming coalitions to improve their immediate outcomes. Even individuals who begin the task with a cooperative orientation might switch to coalition formation and short-term gains in the face of severe discounting.

Finally, discounting may not only affect the value of dollars involved, but also the value of relationships. Some group members may have begun the task with intentions to behave cooperatively and increase the resource pool, but were thwarted by the perceived intentions and actual behaviors of other group members. One defector in a high discount condition may generate more fear and defensive behavior than the same defector in a more stable environment. In addition, the uncertainty of each player's future behavior may make it less likely that group members will find "loyalty" important. Both the effect of anchoring and the effect of relationships might have been further explored through more extensive questionnaires. For example, how accurately could subjects predict their own outcomes, or the outcomes of their fellow group members? What predictions would subjects make regarding the proposal and voting behavior of group members, and how do they interpret the specific behavior that actually occurs (e.g., Why was I left out of the proposal?)?

Outside of the laboratory many factors blur our perception of the future's value, and the results of this study may be diluted. For example, we rarely have the value of discounted dollars calculated for us so clearly. Without such complete and salient information, the impact of even very high discount rates may be diluted. For example, would high inflation (high discount rates) result in less cooperative behavior? Inflation might act in a way similar to scarce resources; as money is worth less we have fewer goods and services available to us. We use credit more, increasing our short-term gain, but costing us more in the long term. Cooperative behavior in several areas is likely to be reduced as people are less willing to contribute to charities and other public goods. Competitive behavior might be further increased by the salience of the inflation rate, how often it was a media topic, or how often one's paycheck was insufficient to purchase the same items one could buy before inflation. In addition, the recognition that others were behaving noncooperatively might increase the discount rate's effect.

Communication is also a topic to consider in this context. In situations where the future is highly discounted one of the ways to improve cooperation may be through communication and the building of long-term relationships. That is, one way to deal with future uncertainty is to make it more certain though side payments or trust building, neither of which were permitted in this study. However, allowing communication might also have given individuals in the high discount groups the ability to form a stable three-way coalition through all 15 rounds, something no group was ever able to do. Thus, in some contexts, verbal communication might have resulted in only a more organized depletion of the resource pool. This remains an empirical question and the subject of future research.

It is important to end by reaffirming that coalitional activity is not detrimental to all types of organizations. The argument presented in this paper is meant to point out that there are instances when coalitions might have damaging effects, something not much addressed previously. The test of whether coalitions are detrimental or not may have as much to do with the larger context as with the goals of the coalition members. In some instances cooperatively motivated coalition members may serve to maintain and build resource pools rather than destroy them. Indeed, energetic and benevolent coalitions may benefit sluggish or poorly motivated group members.

REFERENCES

Ainslie, G. (1975). Specious reward: A behavioral theory of impulsiveness and impulse control. *Psychological Bulletin,* **82,** 463–496.

Axelrod, R. (1984). *The evolution of cooperation.* New York: Basic Books.

Brewer, M., & Kramer, R. (1986). Choice behavior in social dilemmas: Effects of social identity, group size, and decision framing. *Journal of Personality and Social Psychology,* **50,** 543–549.

Caplow, T. A. (1956). A theory of coalitions in the triad. *American Sociological Review,* **21,** 489–493.

Chertkoff, J. M. (1967). A revision of Caplow's coalition theory. *Journal of Experimental Social Psychology,* **3,** 172–177.

Clark, M. S., & Mills, J. (1979). Interpersonal attraction in exchange and communal relationships. *Journal of Personality and Social Psychology,* **37,** 12–24.

Cross, J. G., & Guyer, M. J. (1980). *Social traps.* Ann Arbor: Univ. of Michigan Press.

Cyert, R., & March, J. (1963). *A behavioral theory of the firm.* Englewood Cliffs, NJ: Prentice–Hall.

Dawes, R. (1988). *Rational choice in an uncertain world,* New York: Harcourt Brace Jovanovich.

Gamson, W. (1961). A theory of coalition formation. *American Sociological Review,* **26,** 373–382.

Hardin, G. (1968). The tragedy of the commons. *Science,* **162,** 1243–1248.

Jevons, W. S. (1871/1911). *The theory of political economy.* London: Macmillan & Co.

Komorita, S. S., and Hamilton, T. P. (1984). Power and equity in coalition bargaining. In *Research in the sociology of organizations* (Vol. 3). Greenwich, CT: Jai Press.

Komorita, S. S., & Kravitz, D. (1983). Coalition formation: A social psychological approach. In P. B. Paulus (Ed.), *Psychology of group influence.* Hillsdale, NJ: Erlbaum.

Kramer, R. (1990). Multi-party negotiation and the "Tragedy of the Commons" in Organizations: Social psychological aspects of strategic choice. In R. Lewicki, B. Sheppard, & M. Bazerman (Eds.), *Research on negotiation in organizations* (Vol. 3), Greenwich, CT: Jai Press.

Loewenstein, G. (1986). *The economics of intertemporal choice: A critical history.* Working paper, University of Chicago.

Loewenstein, G., & Prelec, D. (1989). *Anomalies of intertemporal choice: Evidence and interpretation.* Working paper, University of Chicago, Center for Decision Research.

Luce, R. D., & Raiffa, H. (1957). *Games and decision: Introduction and critical survey.* New York: Wiley.

Mannix, E. A. (1989). *Coalitions in the organizational context: A social dilemmas perspective.* Unpublished doctoral dissertation, University of Chicago.

March, J. G., & Simon, H. A. (1958). *Organizations.* New York: Wiley.

Messick, D. M., & Brewer, M. B. (1983). Solving social dilemmas: A review. In L. Wheeler (Ed.), *Review of personality and social psychology.* Beverly Hills, CA: Sage Publications.

RESOURCE DILEMMAS   391

Messick, D. M., & McClelland, C. L. (1983). Social traps and temporal traps. *Personality and Social Psychology Bulletin,* **9,** 105–110.

Miller, C., & Crandall, R. (1980). Experimental research on the social psychology of bargaining and coalition formation. In P. Paulus (Ed.), *Psychology of group influence.* Hillsdale, NJ: Erlbaum.

Miller, C., & Komorita, S. (1986). Coalition formation in organizations: What laboratory studies do and do not tell us. In R. Lewicki, B. Sheppard, & M. Bazerman (Eds.), *Research on negotiation in organizations* (Vol. 2). Greenwich, CT: Jai Press.

Mintzberg, H. (1983). *Power in and around organizations.* Englewood Cliffs, NJ: Prentice–Hall.

Murnighan, K. (1986). Organizational coalitions: Structural contingencies and the formation process. In R. Lewicki, B. Sheppard, & M. Bazerman (Eds.), *Research on negotiation in organizations* (Vol. 1). Greenwich, CT: Jai Press.

Murnighan, K., & Brass, D. (1990). Intraorganizational coalitions. In R. Lewicki, B. Sheppard, & M. Bazerman (Eds.), *Research on negotiation in organizations* (Vol. 3), Conn.: Greenwich, CT: Jai Press.

Pfeffer, J. (1981). *Power in organizations.* Boston: Pitman.

Platt, J. (1973). Social traps. *American Psychologist,* **28,** 641–651.

Schelling, T. C. (1978). *Micromotives and macrobehavior.* New York: Norton.

Schelling, T. (1984). Self command in practice, in policy, and in a theory of rational choice. *American Economic Review,* **74,** 1–11.

Strotz, R. H. (1956). Myopia and inconsistency in dynamic utility maximization. *Review of Economic Studies,* **23,** 166–180.

Thompson, J. (1967). *Organizations in action.* New York: McGraw–Hill.

Tversky, A., & Kahneman, D. (1973). Availability: A heuristic for judging frequency and probability. *Cognitive Psychology,* **5,** 207–232.

[8]

Journal of Personality and Social Psychology
1997, Vol. 72, No. 4, 810-825

The Claiming Effect: Why Players Are More Generous in Social Dilemmas Than in Ultimatum Games

Richard P. Larrick and Sally Blount
University of Chicago

The term *procedural frames* is introduced and defined as different representations of structurally equivalent allocation processes. Study 1 compared 2 well-known games, sequential social dilemmas and ultimatum bargaining, that share the same structure: Player 1 creates an allocation of a resource and Player 2 decides whether to allow it or deny it. Study 1 found that Player 1 made more favorable allocations and Player 2 accepted more unfavorable allocations in a social dilemma frame than in an equivalent ultimatum bargaining frame. Study 2 revealed the critical determinant was whether Player 2 had to respond to an allocation by accepting or rejecting it (as in the ultimatum game) or by making a claim (as in the social dilemma). Two additional studies explored how these actions are perceived. The inconsistency of behavior across procedural frames raises methodological concerns but illuminates construal processes that guide allocation.

Two of the most-studied paradigms in mixed-motive research have been *social dilemmas* and *ultimatum bargaining games* (Komorita & Parks, 1995). These allocation procedures differ substantially in how the actions of participants are described. In ultimatum bargaining games, players propose a division of a common resource and accept or reject the proposal; in social dilemmas, players make a claim from a common resource. However, versions of these games have been developed that are structurally equivalent but that appear to induce different rates of cooperation. Players appear to be more generous in sequential social dilemmas than in ultimatum bargaining games. The following research tests the existence of the social dilemma–ultimatum bargaining framing effect. The findings offer insight into a specific bias in bargaining, which we call the *claiming effect*, as well as the more general role that the subjective interpretation of action plays in allocation decisions.

Procedural Frames in Mixed-Motive Interaction

The identification of framing effects has a long history in the study of mixed-motive interaction. Schelling (1960) provided some early examples of how preference changes under different representations of similar tacit bargaining games. More recently, framing effects from the judgment and decision-making literature (Tversky & Kahneman, 1981) have been applied to negotiation decisions (Neale & Bazerman, 1991; Schurr, 1987). For example, Bazerman, Magliozzi, and Neale (1985; Neale & Bazerman, 1985) predicted that bargainers would be more willing to make concessions when their outcomes were defined in terms of net profit (a gain frame) than in terms of reduction in gross profit (a loss frame), because of the asymmetry of losses and foregone gains (Tversky & Kahneman, 1991). Their results supported this prediction and demonstrated that outcome-framing effects generalize to the process of bargaining.

A second type of framing effect that occurs in mixed-motive interaction is produced by differences in procedural frames. We define *procedural frames* as different ways of describing actions (as opposed to outcomes) in structurally equivalent allocation procedures. Although the concept is related to previous analyses of procedural differences (Lind & Tyler, 1988), it is intended to be more restrictive: *Procedural frames* refer to different representations of structurally equivalent allocation procedures (Fagley, 1993). The best known example of a procedural frame is the difference between *commons* dilemmas and *public goods* dilemmas (Brewer & Kramer, 1986; Fleishman, 1988; McCusker & Carnevale, 1995; Rutte, Wilke, & Messick, 1987). In commons dilemmas, participants take from a common resource, whereas in public goods dilemmas, participants contribute to a common resource. Brewer and Kramer (1986) argued that "despite differences in the way the two collective problems are studied . . . the basic structures of the decision faced by individuals in both cases are equivalent" (p. 543). If participants were influenced only by the structure of a procedure, there would be no difference between the dilemmas. However, the descriptions of the actions invite different interpretations of out-

We contributed equally to this research. Some findings reported in Study 1 were initially reviewed in Larrick and Blount (1995). This research was supported by funding from the University of Chicago Graduate School of Business and from the William S. Fishman research fellowship, 1995–1996.

We would like to thank Linda Babcock, Colin Camerer, David Messick, and Michael Morris for helpful comments during the development of this research. We also thank the participants at the University of Chicago Behavioral Science Workshop and at the following conferences: the conference on Negotiation in its Social Context, Stanford University, May 1993; the 6th International Conference on Social Dilemmas, Netherlands Institute for Advanced Study in the Humanities and Social Sciences, June 1995; and the annual meeting of the Economic Science Association Conference, Tucson, Arizona, October 1995.

Correspondence concerning this article should be addressed to Richard P. Larrick or Sally Blount, Graduate School of Business, University of Chicago, 1101 East 58th Street, Chicago, Illinois 60637. Electronic mail may be sent via the Internet to rick.larrick@gsb.uchicago.edu or sally.blount@gsb.uchicago.edu.

comes: *Taking* suggests receiving a gain, and *giving* suggests suffering a loss. Because passing up a gain is not as painful as incurring an equivalent loss (Tversky & Kahneman, 1991), cooperation is harder to achieve in commons dilemmas than in public goods dilemmas. Brewer and Kramer (1986) equated the dilemma structures by comparing participants who could take up to 25 points from the common pool with participants who first received 25 points from the common pool and then could give up to 25 points back. As predicted, taking led to more cooperation than giving back. Thus, Brewer and Kramer (1986) demonstrated the importance of procedural frames: Different ways of describing actions in equivalent allocation structures can influence participants' interpretation of outcomes and thereby modify their decisions to cooperate.

Why are procedural framing effects such as the commons dilemma–public goods dilemma difference important? For economists, they undermine the assumption that decision makers' preferences are invariant to task description (Roth, 1994), and for social psychologists, they raise a note of caution about generalizing across paradigms (Brewer & Kramer, 1986). More important, they confirm the central role that construals play in allocation decisions and offer insight into important social psychological variables. As Allison, Beggan, and Midgley (1996) recently argued, interpretation plays a critical role in how participants behave in social dilemmas. They proposed that the metaphors evoked by an allocation task, such as "game," "arms race," "family," "communistic society," and "chaos," convey expectations, norms, and beliefs that influence behavior (Allison et al., 1996). A classic illustration is Eiser and Bhavnani's (1974) finding that cooperation rates are higher when a prisoner's dilemma is described as an international negotiation rather than economic bargaining. In a similar vein, linguistic research has shown that different descriptions of an action can affect how perceivers interpret causality in interpersonal interactions (Brown & Fish, 1983; Hoffman & Tchir, 1990; Kanouse, 1972; Semin & Marsman, 1994). Semantic differences may influence interpersonal behavior by evoking different understandings of responsibility and blame for an outcome. Thus, when procedural frames are discovered, they can help identify the metaphorical (Allison et al., 1996) and semantic (Semin & Marsman, 1994) features that influence allocation preferences (Schelling, 1960). In the following research, we explore the behavioral and psychological effects of procedural frames derived from two popular paradigms in mixed-motive research: ultimatum bargaining games and sequential social dilemmas.

Ultimatum Bargaining Games and Sequential Social Dilemmas

Two paradigms have dominated the field of mixed-motive research (Komorita & Parks, 1995). The social dilemma paradigm (Dawes, 1980) has been a popular method, for over 20 years, of studying the trade-off between personal and collective outcomes. More recently, the ultimatum bargaining paradigm (Camerer & Thaler, 1995; Guth, Schmittberger, & Schwarze, 1982) has generated a great deal of research on the trade-off between personal and comparative outcomes. In the past decade, these paradigms have been used or discussed in more than 100 and 30 articles, respectively (based on a search of major psy-

chology and economics journals). Although research on the two games has been abundant, it has also been relatively isolated: Social psychologists have been more likely to study social dilemmas, whereas experimental economists have been more likely to study ultimatum games (Komorita & Parks, 1995). This difference largely reflects the research goals and questions particular to each field.

The ultimatum bargaining game was designed by economists to test the theoretical assumption that utility maximization can be equated with maximizing personal monetary payoffs (Guth et al., 1982). In the ultimatum bargaining game, two participants are asked to divide a fixed amount of money. One participant is given the role of proposing a division (Player 1), and the other is given the role of accepting or rejecting the proposal (Player 2). If Player 2 accepts the division, both participants receive the proposed amount; if Player 2 rejects it, neither receives anything. Following from the assumption that people seek to maximize personal payoffs, the equilibrium analysis predicts that Player 1 should offer Player 2 the smallest possible positive amount and keep the remainder. Further, Player 2 should accept this offer because it is greater than the alternative of zero. Research has consistently shown, however, that these predictions fail because participants are motivated by concerns about fairness in comparative payoffs. Participants in the Player 1 position usually offer the other participant more than a trivial amount, often an equal division (Camerer & Thaler, 1995; Guth & Tietz, 1990). And participants in the Player 2 position who receive unfavorable offers frequently reject them, preferring to get nothing at all (Camerer & Thaler, 1995; Guth & Tietz, 1990).

The social dilemma paradigm was originally inspired by Hardin's (1968, p. 1243) "tragedy of the commons" and was designed to test individual-allocation decisions when maintaining a group resource conflicts with maximizing individual gain (Dawes, 1980; Messick & Brewer, 1983). Social dilemmas are simulated in the laboratory by having a group of participants claim resources from a joint, replenishable pool. In the typical study, participants make a series of simultaneous, anonymous claims from the pool. Other versions examine the effect of sequential claims and one-round play (Budescu, Rapoport, & Suleiman, 1992; Budescu, Suleiman, & Rapoport, 1995; Erev & Rapoport, 1990; Rapoport, Budescu, & Suleiman, 1993). Cooperation is measured as the degree to which individuals reduce their own consumption to increase the group resource. Research typically shows that groups have difficulty maintaining sustainable levels of the common resource.

Perhaps because these games have different research traditions, structurally equivalent versions have been developed that appear to yield surprisingly different results: Players appear to be more generous in sequential social dilemmas than ultimatum games. Budescu et al. (1992) studied a version of the social dilemma in which two-person groups were asked to share a common resource pool. Each member made a claim from the pool, and if the total of the claims did not exceed the pool, both members were granted their request; otherwise, each received nothing. In some conditions, claims were made sequentially, so that Player 2 made a claim knowing the amount of Player 1's claim. From a game-theoretic perspective, this one-round version of a social dilemma is equivalent to the traditional ultimatum game: Player 1's claim implicitly creates a division, and

Player 2 can accept it by claiming an amount less than or equal to the remainder or reject it by claiming more than the remainder (Larrick & Blount, 1995; see Blount & Larrick, 1997a, for a more extensive discussion of the game-theoretic equivalence of these games). In keeping with ultimatum game results, Budescu et al. (1992) found that Player 1 tended to claim more than Player 2. However, social dilemma players in both roles appeared to be more generous than their ultimatum game counterparts. In a typical ultimatum bargaining game, 50% of the participants in the Player 1 role take more than an equal share of the pool for themselves, and 40% of the participants in the Player 2 role are unwilling to accept an amount smaller than one fourth of the pool (e.g., Blount, 1995). By contrast, Budescu et al. (1992) found in a sample of 40 participants that only 35% in the Player 1 role took more than an equal share of the pool and that 89% in the Player 2 role who were offered an amount smaller than one fourth of the pool were willing to accept it (D. Budescu, personal communication, December 1995).

A high rate of cooperation in sequential social dilemmas was also found by Messick and Allison (1987) in a study of six-player, sequential social dilemmas. Participants were asked to make claims from a pool of 24 points (in which each point was potentially worth $.50). An equal distribution of the points would be 4 to each player. Although the dilemma was presented as a six-player game, all participants were assigned the role of Player 6 and were presented with unequal claims by the first five players that left them with 3, 2, 1, or 0 points. Ninety percent of all participants claimed an amount equal to or less than the remaining points, thereby letting all players receive their claims. Most dramatically, 73% of the participants who were left 0 claimed 0! Player 2 participants in ultimatum bargaining games rarely, if ever, are willing to accept nothing.

Defining Cooperation in Ultimatum Bargaining Games and Sequential Social Dilemmas

In the following studies, we measured cooperation in terms of the distributive generosity of players' decisions. Specifically, we focused on the effect that players' decisions had on the relative distribution of a common pool between themselves and others. Our specific measures were the average outcomes allocated to Player 2 by Player 1—offering higher average amounts was considered more generous—and the average minimum outcomes accepted by Player 2—accepting lower average amounts was considered more generous. Both of these actions are cooperative in the sense that they make a completed transaction more likely to occur, thereby maximizing joint outcome (Kelley & Thibaut, 1978; McClintock, 1972; Messick & McClintock, 1968). However, in most mixed-motive games, it is difficult to infer actual motivations because of confounded behavioral choices (see Bornstein et al., 1983 for a complete analysis of social motivations in unilateral allocation decisions). For example, because generous concessions facilitate completing a transaction in fixed-sum bargaining, they may be motivated by cooperation (the desire to improve the collective outcome), but they could also arise from altruism (the desire to improve the other party's outcome) or individualism (the desire to improve the expected value of one's own outcome). Hence, we restrict our use of the terms *cooperation* and *generosity* to the distributive

consequence of a behavior and leave the question of motivation for the discussion.

In addition to these measures, we examined decisions about two extreme allocations that come closer to revealing motivation: how often Player 2 was willing to let Player 1 take all of the pool (Messick & Allison, 1987) and how often Player 1 decided to make an equal or better allocation to Player 2 (Allison & Messick, 1990). In the first case, the willingness of Player 2 to take an allocation of $0 is noteworthy because it represents an indifference point for personal monetary payoffs (Messick & Allison, 1987). Is Player 2 willing to maximize the joint outcome (and Player 1's outcome) when his or her own payoff remains constant? The willingness to accept a zero allocation shows a concern for the other (or the collective) independent of the self; the willingness to reject demonstrates a desire to punish the other. Similarly, the willingness of Player 1 to make an equal allocation is significant because it represents a balance between concern for self and other. In contrast, making an unequal allocation is more competitive because it increases Player 1's payoff at the expense of Player 2 (Allison & Messick, 1990). Unfortunately, an equal allocation can also be motivated by strategic considerations (i.e., attempting to increase the probability of completing a deal by taking into account Player 2's likely response), so it is not possible to attribute as generous an intent to Player 1's equal allocation as it is to Player 2's acceptance of a zero allocation.[1]

Study 1

Both ultimatum bargaining games and two-person sequential social dilemmas depict the same underlying allocation procedure: The first player creates a division, and the second player can agree to it or veto it. In the ultimatum frame, this is described as Player 1 proposing a division and Player 2 deciding to accept or reject it. In the social dilemma frame, it is described as Player 1 making a claim and Player 2, knowing the remainder, also making a claim. Previous findings indicate that these frames induce different levels of cooperation. However, because these results came from studies conducted by different researchers, a variety of methodological differences, such as participant populations and instructions, might have contributed to apparent differences. Study 1 addressed this problem by holding all of these factors constant. Thus, if the difference in generosity between games remained, it could be attributed only to differences between procedural frames.

Method

Participants

One hundred five masters of business administration (MBA) students at Northwestern University and the University of Chicago participated

---

[1] Although Bornstein et al. (1983) were concerned with unilateral decisions in minimal group studies and not with interdependent decisions in strategic games, their analysis provides a framework for identifying the specific social motivations underlying each player's decision. For Player 2, the zero allocation represented a choice between maximizing joint gain but favoring the other group and minimizing the difference in gain. Player 1's decision about making an equal allocation represented a choice between minimizing the difference in gain and maximizing relative own gain.

in the study as part of a class exercise. One third of the participants were randomly selected for payment. Their exact payments were calculated from the responses they gave on the questionnaire and were made in a subsequent class period.

Design

Participants read and answered a Resource Allocation Exercise questionnaire. Two versions were distributed randomly. One version was phrased in terms of a sequential social dilemma, and the other was phrased in terms of an ultimatum game. On completion, the questionnaires were collected, and a short debriefing was conducted.

To conserve sample size, all participants provided decisions as both Player 1 and Player 2 in the same questionnaire. For the Player 1 decision, participants made an allocation, and for the Player 2 decision, participants responded to all possible Player 1 allocations. Their questionnaires were then randomly paired outside of class, with 1 participant randomly assigned to the Player 1 role and 1 to the Player 2 role. Player 1's allocation (e.g., "$6.00 for Player 1 and $1.00 for Player 2") was compared with Player 2's response (e.g., accept) for that allocation, and each player was paid on the basis of the outcome.

Materials

The instructions informed participants of the following:

> You will be randomly paired with a student in another section to participate in a resource-allocation task. In this task, there will be a potential pool of $7.00 made available by the experimenter. Each student in the pair will be randomly assigned to the role of either Player 1 or Player 2.

The description of Player 1's and Player 2's actions varied by condition. In the ultimatum game condition, participants were told the following:

> Player 1 will be asked to propose a division of $7.00 between the 2 players, such as $X for Player 1 and $7 − X for Player 2. Then, Player 2 will be asked whether he or she accepts or rejects this proposal. If Player 2 accepts the proposal, each player will get the amount Player 1 proposed. If Player 2 rejects the proposal, neither student will receive any money.

In the social dilemma condition, participants were told the following:

> Player 1 will be asked to state a claim for some portion of $7.00, such as $X. Then, knowing $X, Player 2 will be asked to state his or her claim for some portion of $7.00, let's say $Y. If the total of the two claims ($X + $Y) is equal to or less than $7.00, each player will get the amount he or she claimed. If the total is more than $7.00, neither student will receive any money.

After reading the instructions, participants were presented with two sets of questions that elicited their decisions as Player 1 and Player 2. The order of the decisions was counterbalanced across questionnaires. Participants were told that if they were selected for payment, they would be randomly assigned to one of the two player roles, and their answer for that role would be matched with the response of a randomly selected partner in the opposing role.[2]

Dependent Measures

Decision as Player 1. Participants were told, "If the random assignment process assigns you to the Player 1 role, we will use your answer to this question to determine your outcome from the exercise." In the ultimatum game condition, participants were asked, "If you are assigned to the Player 1 role, what amount of money between $0.00 and $7.00 would you offer to Player 2?" Participants answered the question by stating the amount they would propose to keep for themselves and the amount they would propose to give to Player 2. In the social dilemma condition, participants were asked, "If you are assigned to the Player 1 role, how much of the $7.00 would you claim?" which they answered by stating the amount they would claim for themselves and the amount that would be available for Player 2. (They were asked to make responses that were multiples of $.50 and totaled to $7.00.)

Decision as Player 2. Participants were told, "If the random assignment process assigns you to the Player 2 role, we will use your answer to this question to determine your outcome from the exercise." Participants' decisions as Player 2 were elicited by presenting them with every possible Player 1/Player 2 allocation, starting at $7.00/$0.00 and decreasing by $0.50 to $0.00/$7.00. In the ultimatum game condition, the first allocation was phrased as "If Player 1 proposes $7.00 for Player 1, $0.00 for Player 2," to which participants responded by checking "accept" or "reject." In the social dilemma condition, the first allocation was phrased as "If Player 1 claims $7.00 for Player 1, which leaves $0.00," to which participants responded by stating how much they would claim for themselves.

To analyze the Player 2 decision, each participant's responses were coded as a single value: the smallest outcome that the participant accepted as Player 2 (i.e., the minimum acceptable outcome). In the ultimatum game condition, this amount was the smallest offer for which the participant marked "accept." In the social dilemma condition, this amount was the smallest remainder left by Player 1 for which the participant did not claim more than the remainder.

Results and Discussion

There were no effects of response order on participants' Player 1 and Player 2 decisions ($Fs < 1.0$, $ps > .30$), so this variable was omitted from subsequent analyses. As predicted, participants given the social dilemma frame accepted lower outcomes as Player 2 than did participants given the ultimatum frame. The average minimum outcome that participants allowed as Player 2 was significantly lower in the social dilemma condition ($M = \$1.31$) than in the ultimatum game condition ($M = \$1.90$), $t(104) = 2.28$, $p < .05$.[3] In addition, Figure 1 shows that the game manipulation had a significant effect on how participants responded to the $7.00/$0.00 allocation. Thirty percent of the participants (16 of 54) in the social dilemma condition claimed $0.00 (thereby allowing it), compared with only 2% (1 of 51) in the ultimatum game condition who accepted this allocation, $\chi^2(1, N = 105) = 12.63$, $p < .001$ (after Yates's correction for continuity).

The difference in the amounts that Player 1s allocated to Player 2s was in the predicted direction ($M = \$2.72$ in the social dilemma condition vs. $M = \$2.48$ in the ultimatum game condition) but was not significant, $t(104) = 1.24$, ns. However, the game manipulation did have a marginally significant effect

---

[2] In Studies 2 through 4, all participants were selected for payment.
[3] Both the outcomes accepted as Player 2 and the offers made as Player 1 are not normally distributed, which violates an assumption made in parametric tests such as t tests and analysis of variance. However, we report parametric test results because skewness and kurtosis have very little effect on the Type I error rate (Stevens, 1990). Extreme kurtosis (e.g., a uniform or bimodal distribution) does significantly increase the Type II error rate (i.e., failing to detect a true difference in means).

on the frequency with which participants made the equal allocation of $3.50/$3.50. As may be seen in Figure 2, 56% of the
participants (31 of 54) in the social dilemma condition left
$3.50 or more to Player 2, whereas only 37% (19 of 51) in the
ultimatum condition offered that amount, $\chi^2(1, N = 105) =$
3.50, $p = .06$ (after Yates's correction for continuity).

The results of Study 1 provided initial support for the existence of the social dilemma–ultimatum game framing effect.
Participants given the social dilemma frame were significantly
more likely to accept zero allocations as Player 2 than were
participants given the ultimatum frame. And there was a marginally significant trend for participants in the social dilemma frame
to make more equal allocations as Player 1 than participants in
the ultimatum frame, which was tested again in a subsequent
study. The findings indicate that how bargainers' actions are
described influences their decisions to cooperate. Study 2 was
designed to test the relative importance of these actions.

Study 2

Why do participants cooperate more when a two-party sequential allocation procedure is framed as a social dilemma
rather than an ultimatum game? The principal remaining differences between the frames are the descriptions of each players'
action: Player 1 divides the resource in ultimatum games but
claims an amount in social dilemmas, and Player 2 accepts or
rejects an offer in ultimatum games but claims an amount in
social dilemmas. One salient difference between these actions
is how confrontational they seem to be. First, consider Player
1's action. Proposing a division implies more control over Player
2's outcome than merely claiming an amount because the divi-

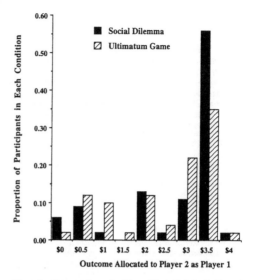

Figure 2. Outcome allocated to Player 2 by participants in Player 1
role for each condition.

sion explicitly names Player 2's outcome, whereas claiming
does not. And for Player 2, accepting or rejecting a proposal is
a very direct, evaluative response, whereas making a claim is a
more independent, nonevaluative response.

Unfortunately, Study 1 cannot distinguish the relative contributions of each players' actions because the games confounded
them. To eliminate this confound, Study 2 systematically manipulated the form of each player's action. The ultimatum game
and social dilemma descriptions of Player 1's action (divide vs.
claim) and Player 2's action (accept or reject vs. claim) were
crossed in a full factorial design. This made it possible to test the
importance of each form of action. For example, one possible
explanation for the difference in Player 2's behavior in social
dilemmas and ultimatum games is that the games elicit different
norms of distributive fairness. Perhaps making a claim creates
the appearance that Player 1 got to the resource first, and the
norm "first come, first served" entitles Player 1 to take as much
of the resource as desired. Proposing a division, on the other
hand, requires that Player 1 give some consideration to both
parties' outcomes, which makes a fairness norm of equal split
more appropriate.[4] The entitlement explanation would be supported if Player 2 responded differently to the two forms of
Player 1's action. In addition, the factorial design provided a
test for the presence of possible interactions. For example, a
second explanation for the high rate of cooperation in social
dilemmas is the similarity between the players' actions (Brown,
1965). Because both players make a claim, they may feel more

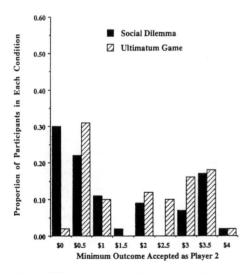

Figure 1. Minimum outcome accepted by participants in Player 2 role
for each condition.

---

[4] We thank David Messick for suggesting this explanation.

similar and equal than do players in ultimatum games. The similarity explanation predicts that the cell in which Player 1 and Player 2 both make claims should produce a disproportionately higher rate of cooperation than the other three cells.

Finally, a measure was included to address a possible artifactual explanation for Player 2's compliance with the $7.00/$0.00 allocation. Perhaps participants in the social dilemma condition claimed $0 because they incorrectly believed that they could not claim more than the remaining amount. A subset of participants was presented with an additional question to test their understanding of the rules.

Method

Participants

Two hundred nineteen MBA students at the University of Chicago participated in the study as part of a class exercise. All participants were paid on the basis of their decisions.

Design and Materials

The instructions and procedure were identical to those used in Study 1, except that the descriptions of the Player 1 actions (dividing vs. claiming) and Player 2 actions (accepting or rejecting vs. claiming) were independently manipulated in a 2 × 2 between-participant factorial design shown in Table 1. As in Study 1, all participants provided decisions as both Player 1 and Player 2.

Dependent Measures

Decisions as Player 1 and Player 2. The response formats used in Study 1 were repeated in Study 2. As in Study 1, participants were told that their answers would be matched with those of another player to determine their outcome for the exercise. For the Player 2 decision, they were presented with every possible Player 1/Player 2 allocation, starting at $7.00/$0.00 and decreasing by $0.50 to $0.00/$7.00. Participants answered using the format that corresponded to their condition (marking

"accept" or "reject" or filling in an amount claimed). For the Player 1 decision, they responded either by dividing (i.e., filling in the amounts that they allocated to themselves and to Player 2) or by claiming (i.e., filling in the amount that they claimed for themselves and the amount that was available for Player 2). Because Study 1 found that decision order was not a significant factor, Study 2 presented all participants with the Player 2 decision first.

Comprehension check. A final question was added to a subsample of 27 questionnaires in the Player 2 claiming conditions, to verify that participants had understood the instructions correctly. After making their decisions, participants in the Player 2 claiming condition were shown a $7.00/$0.00 allocation to which another participant had responded by claiming $1.00. They were asked whether this response was allowed by the rules and to describe the consequences.

Results

The average minimum outcome that participants accepted as Player 2 is given in Table 2. A two-factor analysis of variance (ANOVA) revealed a significant main effect for the form of the Player 2 action, such that claiming ($M = 1.49) led to a lower outcome being allowed than did accepting or rejecting ($M = 2.01), $F(1, 215) = 6.87$, $p < .01$. The form of the Player 1 action (dividing vs. claiming) and the interaction were not significant ($Fs < 1.4$, $ps > .20$). The percentage of participants who allowed the $7.00/$0.00 allocation is reported in Table 3. Because the analysis involved two dichotomous independent variables and a dichotomous dependent variable, we conducted a log-linear analysis, which tested changes in goodness of fit when each effect was removed from a saturated model. A large reduction in goodness of fit would indicate that a term was a significant predictor of the dependent variable. The analysis revealed that the form of the Player 2 action was a significant predictor, $\chi^2_{change}(1, N = 219) = 13.92$, $p < .001$. As may be seen in Table 3, participants instructed to make a claim as Player 2 were more likely to allow the $7.00/$0.00 allocation (30%) than were participants instructed to accept or reject (10%).

Table 1

Instructions in 2 × 2 Factorial Design Crossing Player 1's Actions and Player 2's Actions

Description of Player 1's action	Description of Player 2's action	
	Accepting or rejecting	*Claiming*
Dividing	"Player 1 will be asked to propose a division of the $7.00 between the two players, such as $X for Player 1 and $7 − X for Player 2. Then, knowing the proposal, **Player 2 will be asked whether he or she accepts or rejects Player 1's proposal. If Player 2 accepts the proposal, player 1 will receive $X, and Player 2 will receive $7 − X. If Player 2 rejects the proposal,** neither student will receive any money."	"Player 1 will be asked to propose a division of the $7.00 between the two players, such as $X for Player 1 and $7 − X for Player 2. Then, knowing the proposal, *Player 2 will be asked to state a claim for some portion of the $7.00, let's say $Y. If the total of the two amounts ($X + $Y) is equal to or less than $7.00, each player will get the amount he or she claimed. If the total is more than $7.00, neither student will receive any money.*"
CLAIMING	"PLAYER 1 WILL BE ASKED TO STATE A CLAIM FOR SOME PORTION OF THE $7.00, SUCH AS $X. THEN KNOWING $X, **Player 2 will be asked whether he or she accepts or rejects Player 1's claim. If Player 2 accepts the claim, Player 1 will receive $X, and Player 2 will receive $7 − X. If Player 2 rejects the claim, neither** student will receive any money."	"PLAYER 1 WILL BE ASKED TO STATE A CLAIM FOR SOME PORTION OF THE $7.00, SUCH AS $X. THEN, KNOWING $X, *Player 2 will be asked to state a claim for some portion of the $7.00, let's say $Y. If the total of the two claims ($X + $Y) is equal to or less than $7.00, each player will get the amount he or she claimed. If the total is more than $7.00, neither student will receive any money.*"

Note. To facilitate comparisons, phrases with identical wording have been placed in identical font. Exceptions are underlined. Actual instructions were presented in uniform font.

Table 2
Average Minimum Acceptable Outcome as Player 2

Description of Player 1's action	Description of Player 2's action				
	Accepting or rejecting		Claiming		
	M (SD)	n	M (SD)	n	M
Dividing	$2.06 ($1.50)	60	$1.66 ($1.52)	63	$1.85
Claiming	$1.95 ($1.43)	50	$1.26 ($1.47)	46	$1.62
M	$2.01		$1.49		

Table 4
Percentage of Participants in Each Cell Offering a $3.50/$3.50 or Better Allocation as Player 1

Description of Player 1's action	Description of Player 2's action				Overall percentage
	Accepting or rejecting		Claiming		
	Percentage	n	Percentage	n	
Dividing	48%	60	57%	63	53%
Claiming	34%	50	57%	46	45%
Overall percentage	42%		57%		

Neither the main effect for the form of the Player 1 action ($p > .10$) nor the interaction ($p > .90$) was statistically significant.

The independent variables did not significantly affect the average amount that participants allocated to Player 2 as Player 1 ($ps > .10$). However, the proportion of participants who made an equal or better allocation to Player 2 did differ by condition. The log-linear analysis revealed that the form of the Player 2 action was a significant predictor of Player 1's allocation, χ^2_{change} (1, $N = 219$) = 4.85, $p < .05$. As may be seen in Table 4, participants were more likely to make the equal allocation as Player 1 when instructions described Player 2's action as claiming (57%) than as accepting or rejecting (42%). There was no significant effect for the form of the Player 1 action or for the interaction ($ps > .20$).

After their Player 1 and Player 2 decisions, 27 participants in the Player 2 claiming condition were shown a $7.00/$0.00 allocation to which another participant had responded by claiming $1.00. They were asked whether this response was permitted by the rules, and all but 1 (4%) correctly reported that it was. This finding indicates that Player 2's high rate of compliance was not an artifact of misunderstanding. Additional evidence against the artifactual explanation comes from a study by Blount and Larrick (1997a) in which participants in the Player 2 claiming condition marked their decisions about the $7.00/0.00 allocation by placing a check next to "I will claim $0" or "I will claim more than $0." This format made it obvious that the game permitted claiming more than the remainder; nevertheless, the

results replicated the finding that participants allowed the $7.00/ $0.00 allocation more often in the claiming condition (28%) than in the accept-or-reject condition (6%).

Discussion

The results of Study 2 showed that describing Player 1's action as the more confrontational "proposing a division" or the more neutral "making a claim" did not significantly affect cooperation. Thus, the explanation that the fairness norm "first come, first served" entitled Player 1 to claim $7.00 cannot explain Player 2's compliance, because when Player 2 was given the option to reject it, they did. (An additional study by Blount & Larrick, 1997b, verified that the two games do not differ in the extent to which they evoke an equality vs. first come, first served fairness norm.) In addition, the similarity between Player 1's and Player 2's actions in the social dilemma cell did not produce a disproportionately higher rate of cooperation. Differences in cooperation were mainly attributable to the form of Player 2's action: Participants were more likely to allow the $7.00/$0.00 allocation as Player 2 and more likely to make the $3.50/$3.50 allocation as Player 1 when Player 2's response was described as claiming rather than as accepting or rejecting. Study 3 was designed to measure differences in how claiming and accepting or rejecting are construed.

Study 3

Study 2 demonstrated that the form of Player 2's action was an important explanation for differences in cooperation. What is the difference between the more confrontational "accept or reject" and the more neutral "claim?" Two aspects of these responses appear to be important. First, the decision to accept or reject is a reaction to Player 1's behavior, whereas the decision to claim an amount is a relatively independent action. Reactions differ from actions in the causal attributions they elicit: Reactions are attributed to objects, whereas actions are attributed to subjects (Semin & Marsman, 1994). Second, the decision to accept or reject asks for a direct evaluation of Player 1's behavior and provides a clear means of expressing it, whereas the decision to claim an amount does not ask for a direct evaluation and provides only an indirect means of expressing approval or disapproval. We believe that these differences affect how participants in each role perceive their decisions. Study 3 was

Table 3
Percentage of Participants in Each Cell Allowing the $7.00/$0.00 Allocation as Player 2

Description of Player 1's action	Description of Player 2's action				Overall percentage
	Accepting or rejecting		Claiming		
	Percentage	n	Percentage	n	
Dividing	8%	60	24%	63	16%
Claiming	12%	50	37%	46	24%
Overall percentage	10%		30%		

designed to examine the effect these differences have on Player 2's interpretation of actions toward Player 1. Study 4 returns to the issue of how these differences might influence Player 1's decision.

Consider how Player 2 might think about rejecting a $7.00 claim made by Player 1. Because rejecting it is merely a reaction to Player 1's behavior (Semin & Marsman, 1994), Player 2 can blame Player 1 for any harm that results. Moreover, there is no ambiguity about the meaning of Player 2's decision—"reject" is a clear protest to Player 1's behavior. The comparable decision of claiming an amount greater than $0, however, may create more troubling attributions in the mind of Player 2. In this case, Player 2's decision is independent of Player 1's decision (Semin & Marsman, 1994), and Player 2 may feel more responsibility for inflicting harm on Player 1 (Ritov & Baron, 1990; Spranca, Minsk, & Baron, 1991). In addition, the meaning of Player 2's decision is ambiguous: Claiming more than $0 could be a protest, but it could also be interpreted as stupidity or greed. It is these differences in perceptions, we believe, that deter some participants, who would otherwise be willing to "reject" a $7.00/$0.00 allocation, from claiming more than $0.

Study 3 was designed to provide a preliminary test of the perceptions evoked by rejecting and claiming. After reading a description of the game, participants were asked how likely they would be to deny a $7.00/$0.00 allocation if they were Player 2. Then they were asked to report the thoughts that they had while making their likelihood decision. They responded to a set of adjectives that distinguished between favorable and unfavorable self-attributions: *selfish, wasteful, and vindictive* versus *rational, fair, and reasonable*. By having participants rate their agreement with these and similar adjectives, Study 3 was able to test whether perceptions varied for the different Player 2 actions.

In addition, Study 3 was designed to eliminate a potential confound in the instructions in Studies 1 and 2. In these studies, the description of Player 2's action as claiming or as accepting or rejecting was followed by different explanations for the consequences of Player 2's decision. Participants in the claiming condition were told, "If the total of the two claims ($X + $Y) is equal to or less than $7.00, each player will get the amount he or she claimed. If the total is more than $7.00, neither student will receive any money." Participants in the accept-or-reject condition were told, "If Player 2 accepts the claim, Player 1 will receive $X, and Player 2 will receive $7 − X. If Player 2 rejects the claim, neither student will receive any money." The problem with these descriptions is that they emphasize different aspects of Player 2's decision: The claiming description emphasizes the players' joint action with Player 1, whereas the accept-or-reject description emphasizes Player 2's individual action. Thus, the high rate of cooperation in the claiming condition could have been due to the perception of a common fate created by the emphasis on joint action (Campbell, 1958). To eliminate this possible confound, a new version of the claiming condition was included in Study 3, in which Player 2's individual action was emphasized. If behavior and perceptions were found to be the same in both claiming conditions, it would show that it is the act of claiming itself, and not whether it appears to be a joint or individual action, that influences participants' decisions to cooperate.

Method

Participants

One hundred eighty-nine MBA students at the University of Chicago participated in the study as part of a class exercise. As in Study 2, all participants were paid on the basis of their decisions.

Design and Materials

The instructions were the same as those used in Study 2, except that the form of Player 1's action was not manipulated (Player 1's action was always described as "claiming") and an additional Player 2 condition was included. The form of Player 1's action was held constant because Study 2 revealed that it did not have a significant effect on the rate of cooperation. The description of Player 2's action was manipulated in a three-level, one-factor, between-participant design. Two of these conditions replicated the claiming and accept-or-reject descriptions in Study 2 (see the bottom row of Table 1). A third condition consisted of an alternative description of claiming that eliminated the confound present in Studies 1 and 2. The new claiming condition was identical to the previous claiming condition except that the phrase used to describe the consequences of Player 2's action was shifted from a joint focus ("If the total of the two claims ($X + $Y) is equal to or less than $7.00, each player will get the amount he or she claimed. If the total is more than $7.00, neither student will receive any money") to an individual focus ("If Player 2's claim ($Y) is equal to or less than the remainder ($7 − X), each player will get the amount he or she claimed. If Player 2's claim is more than the remainder, neither student will receive any money"), to make it parallel to the focus of the accept-or-reject condition. We refer to the new claiming condition as *individual* focus and the original claiming condition as *joint* focus. As in Studies 1 and 2, participants provided decisions as both Player 1 and Player 2.

Dependent Measures

Perceptions of denying a $7.00–$0.00 allocation. After reading the description of the game, but before making their actual Player 1 and Player 2 decisions, participants answered a series of questions about how they would respond to a $7.00/$0.00 allocation as Player 2. First, they were told to imagine that they had been assigned to the role of Player 2. In the claiming conditions, they were asked, "If Player 1 claims $7.00, which leaves $0, how likely would you be to claim more than $0?" In the accept or reject condition, they were asked, "If Player 1 claims $7.00, which leaves $0, how likely would you be to reject the claim?" Participants responded on a 9-point scale ranging from *very unlikely* (1) to *very likely* (9). Participants were then asked, "As you made your decision about the question above, to what extent did you have the following thoughts?" The subsequent adjectives were preceded by the stem "Claiming more than $0 would be . . ." or "Rejecting the claim would be . . ." matched to condition. The adjectives that followed were *wasteful, self-centered, fair, rational, vindictive, reasonable, incompetent, selfish,* and *justifiable.* The adjectives were rated on a 9-point scale, ranging from *strongly disagree* (1) to *strongly agree* (9).

Decisions as Player 1 and Player 2. The response formats used in Studies 1 and 2 were repeated in Study 3. As in the previous studies, participants were told that their answers would be matched with those of another player to determine their outcome for the exercise. As in Study 2, all participants made the Player 2 decision first. For the Player 2 decision, they were presented with every possible Player 1/Player 2 allocation, starting at $7.00/$0.00 and decreasing by $0.50 to $0.00/$7.00. Participants answered using the format that corresponded to their condition (checking "accept" or "reject" or filling in an amount claimed). For the Player 1 decision, they always responded by filling in the amount that they claimed and the amount that was available for Player 2.

Results

Perceptions of Denying a $7.00/$0.00 Allocation

A one-factor ANOVA revealed that the form of Player 2's action significantly affected participants' responses to the question, "If Player 1 claims $7.00, which leaves $0, how likely would you be to claim more than $0 [reject the claim]?" $F(2, 186) = 12.12, p < .001$. Participants in the accept or reject condition expressed a higher likelihood ($M = 8.00$) than did participants in the two claiming conditions (joint-focus $M = 5.38$ and individual-focus $M = 6.00$). Planned comparisons confirmed that the two claiming conditions were not significantly different from each other, $t(186) = 1.12, p > .25$, but were significantly less than the accept-or-reject condition, $t(186) = -4.78, p < .001$.

Participants were then asked, "As you made your decision about the question above, to what extent did you have the following thoughts?" They rated a series of adjectives on a 9-point scale that ranged from *strongly disagree* (1) to *strongly agree* (9). The means for their agreement ratings are presented in Table 5. A two-factor ANOVA was performed, which included one 3-level between-participant factor (form of Player 2's action) and one 9-level within-participant factor (adjective). (For analysis, coding for *wasteful, self-centered, vindictive, incompetent,* and *selfish* was reversed, so that higher scores on all nine adjectives indicated a favorable perception of denying the $7.00/$0.00 allocation.) The ANOVA found an unsurprising main effect for adjective, $F(8, 175) = 13.34, p < .001$, which indicated that strength of endorsement varied across the items, and found no interaction between adjective and the form of Player 2's action ($F = 1.0, p = .30$). As predicted, the form of the Player 2 action significantly affected perceptions of denying the $7.00/$0.00 allocation, $F(2, 182) = 12.79, p < .001$. The planned comparisons reported in Table 5 show that there was no differ-

ence between the two claiming conditions in participants' endorsement of adjectives but that the two claiming conditions did differ significantly from the accept-or-reject condition. Specifically, participants in the accept-or-reject condition thought that denying the $7.00/$0.00 allocation was less wasteful, vindictive, incompetent, and selfish and more fair, rational, reasonable, and justifiable than did participants in the claiming conditions.

Note that there were several adjectives for which the conditions produced different rates of neutral responses. Participants in the claiming conditions (joint focus and individual focus) gave the neutral response more frequently than did participants in the accept-or-reject condition for the adjectives *fair* (29% and 28% vs. 8%), $\chi^2(1, N = 185) = 10.11, p < .01$, and *rational* (20% and 20% vs. 3%), $\chi^2(1, N = 185) = 9.68, p < .01$, and less frequently for the adjective *vindictive* (14% and 8% vs. 29%), $\chi^2(1, N = 185) = 9.74, p < .01$.

A drawback of using a postdecision self-report technique is that although generally valid (Ericsson & Simon, 1993), it can invite some degree of postdecision justification. To address this problem, we conducted additional analyses that controlled for participants' initial likelihood judgment about denying the $7.00/$0.00 allocation. We performed a 2 (accept or reject vs. claiming) × 9 (adjective) analysis of covariance (ANCOVA), which included the likelihood judgment as a covariate. (A test of the covariate regression coefficients revealed no difference between conditions [$p > .20$], thereby satisfying the ANCOVA requirement of homogeneous slopes.) As with the original analysis, there was a main effect for adjective, $F(8, 176) = 11.84, p < .001$. And, as expected, the initial likelihood judgment was a highly significant predictor of participants' perceptions, with those disposed to deny the $7.00/$0.00 allocation seeing it as a more favorable action to take, $F(1, 182) = 126.85, p < .001$. The difference in the form of Player 2's response, however, was still an important predictor of aggregate perceptions, with "claiming more than $0" judged less favorably than "rejecting a claim of $0," $F(1, 182) = 6.41, p < .01$. Univariate tests revealed that three specific perceptions—*rational, vindictive,*

Table 5

Participants' Average Degree of Agreement That an Adjective Described Their Thoughts About Denying a $7.00/$0.00 Allocation as Player 2

Adjective	Form of Player 2's action			Planned comparison 1 vs. 2 & 3 *t* statistic	Planned comparison 2 vs. 3 *t* statistic
	Accepting or rejecting *M (SD)*	Claiming (joint focus) *M (SD)*	Claiming (individual focus) *M (SD)*		
Wasteful	3.68 (2.83)	5.45 (3.06)	4.98 (3.07)	−3.32***	0.88
Self-centered	4.45 (3.00)	5.17 (3.02)	5.18 (2.71)	−1.60	−0.01
Fair	6.47 (2.84)	5.71 (2.62)	5.45 (2.45)	2.15*	0.55
Rational	6.91 (2.80)	4.78 (2.93)	5.10 (2.79)	4.47***	−0.63
Vindictive	4.29 (2.62)	5.97 (2.91)	6.23 (2.95)	−4.11***	−0.52
Reasonable	7.13 (2.57)	5.52 (2.72)	5.98 (2.52)	3.40***	−0.98
Incompetent	2.31 (2.18)	3.67 (2.89)	3.73 (2.52)	−3.52***	−0.13
Selfish	3.76 (2.83)	5.38 (2.94)	5.30 (2.73)	−3.59***	0.17
Justifiable	7.73 (1.91)	5.87 (2.71)	6.42 (2.44)	4.30***	−1.27

Note. All adjectives were rated on a 9-point scale, ranging from 1 (*strongly disagree*) to 9 (*strongly agree*). For all planned comparisons, *df* = 182.
* *p* < .05.   *** *p* < .001.

and *selfish*—remained significantly different across the Player 2 conditions, even after participants' initial decision was controlled, $Fs(1, 182) > 3.80$, $p < .05$. Thus, even if one makes the conservative assumption that the relationship between perceptions and initial decision is entirely the result of postdecision justification, claiming and accepting or rejecting still evoke significantly different perceptions.

Decisions as Player 1 and Player 2

The average minimum outcome that participants allowed as Player 2 was significantly affected by the form of Player 2's action, $F(2, 186) = 8.89$, $p < .001$. Participants who responded by claiming (either with joint-focus or individual-focus instructions) accepted a lower outcome ($Ms = \$1.13$ and $\$1.42$, respectively) than did participants who responded by accepting or rejecting ($M = \$2.15$). Planned comparisons confirmed that the means for the two claiming conditions were not significantly different from each other, $t(186) = 1.15$, $p > .25$, but were significantly less than the accept-or-reject condition, $t(186) = 4.05$, $p < .001$. The proportion of participants who, as Player 2, allowed the $\$7.00/\$0.00$ allocation was also significantly affected by the form of Player 2's action, $\chi^2(2, N = 189) = 21.35$, $p < .001$. Participants who responded by claiming allowed the $\$7.00/\$0.00$ allocation more frequently (45% for joint-focus and 39% for individual-focus instructions) than did participants who responded by accepting or rejecting (10%), $\chi^2(1, N = 189) = 19.22$, $p < .001$ (after Yates's correction for continuity).

The average amount that participants allocated to Player 2 as Player 1 was also significantly affected by the form of Player 2's action, $F(2, 185) = 3.21$, $p < .05$. Participants allocated more to Player 2 as Player 1 when Player 2's action was described as claiming (joint-focus $M = \$3.10$, and individual-focus $M = \$3.22$) than as accepting or rejecting ($M = \$2.81$). Planned comparisons confirmed that the means for the two claiming conditions were not significantly different from each other, $t(185) = .75$, $p > .45$, but were significantly higher than the accept-or-reject condition, $t(185) = 2.43$, $p < .02$. The proportion of participants who made an equal or better allocation to Player 2 as Player 1 also differed by condition, $\chi^2(2, N = 189) = 10.49$, $p < .01$. Participants were more likely to make the $\$3.50/\$3.50$ allocation as Player 1 when instructions described the Player 2 action as claiming (73% in both the joint-focus and individual-focus conditions) than as accepting or rejecting (49%), $\chi^2(1, N = 189) = 9.45$, $p < .01$ (after Yates's correction for continuity).

Discussion

Study 3 replicated the main finding of Study 2. When Player 2's action was described as claiming rather than as accepting or rejecting, participants were more likely to allow a $\$7.00/\$0.00$ allocation as Player 2 and to make a $\$3.50/\$3.50$ allocation as Player 1. Moreover, this difference was equally strong when claiming was described as a joint action or as an individual action. Study 3 also showed that participants' thoughts about denying a $\$7.00/\$0.00$ allocation varied with the description of Player 2's action. Participants who responded by rejecting the

allocation felt that it was a fairer and less selfish decision than did participants who responded by claiming more than $0. We believe that two factors, attributions of responsibility and the clarity of evaluation, underlie the different perceptions of these actions. First, Player 2 is reluctant to inflict harm on Player 1 when the response is independent because, as an "act of commission," it increases a sense of moral responsibility (Ritov & Baron, 1990; Spranca et al., 1991). Second, Player 2 is reluctant to inflict harm when the response allows only an ambiguous protest and is open to many interpretations. The consequence is that rejecting Player 1's $7.00 claim seems to be an evaluation of Player 1's greed and is perceived as fair and rational but claiming more than $0 seems to be an expression of Player 2's greed and is perceived by Player 2 as selfish and wasteful, if done deliberately, or incompetent, if done by mistake.

Study 4

Three studies have shown that the description of Player 2's action consistently affects the decisions made by participants as Player 2. Perhaps even more surprisingly, they have shown that the description of Player 2's action consistently affects the decisions made by participants as Player 1. Player 1 is more likely to make an equal allocation when Player 2 responds by claiming than by accepting or rejecting. Study 4 was designed to explore some possible explanations for Player 1's behavior.

Two very different motivations can give rise to offering an equal allocation. One is an intrinsic desire to be fair. The other is a desire to maximize expected payoff in the face of strategic uncertainty. An old debate in the ultimatum game literature illustrates this point well. Originally, Player 1's fair offers were interpreted as demonstrating that Player 1 had a taste for fairness. With time, however, researchers demonstrated that many participants in the Player 1 role had little intrinsic interest in fairness but, instead, were acting strategically, anticipating that Player 2 might have a taste for fairness (Forsythe, Horowitz, Savin, & Sefton, 1994; Kahneman, Knetsch, & Thaler, 1986). Many participants made an equal allocation simply to play it safe against fair-minded opponents.

We believe that self-interested caution, not a desire for fairness, may be the main explanation for Player 1's generosity toward Player 2s who claim. Because claiming is done relatively independently of Player 1's decision, Player 1 may think that a variety of factors, such as willfulness or incompetence, could lead Player 2 to claim more than the remainder. The action of accepting or rejecting, on the other hand, is dependent on Player 1's allocation. It presents a simple decision to go along or to retaliate. Thus, Player 1 may have more confidence that Player 2 will accept a given allocation than that Player 2 will answer that allocation with the right claim.

To distinguish whether equal allocations were motivated by self-interest or an intrinsic desire to be fair, Study 4 included measures of Player 1's expectations about Player 2's likely responses. If Player 1 were to correctly recognize that 30% of participants in the Player 2 claiming condition would allow a $\$7.00/\$0.00$ allocation and that 80% would allow $\$4.50/\$2.50$, then making an offer of $\$3.50/\$3.50$ would be very altruistic: Player 1 would be sacrificing some personal payoff to be fair to Player 2. On the other hand, if Player 1 were to expect most participants in the Player 2 claiming condition to hold firm at an equal allocation, then offering $3.50/$3.50 would be a (misinformed) strategic decision.

Study 4 was also designed to address a potential methodological concern about Studies 1 through 3. In all three studies, participants were asked to describe a strategy for both the Player 1 and Player 2 roles. It is possible that playing both roles could have biased decisions in some systematic way (although we believe it could not have caused the differences in behavior found between games). For example, all participants in Studies 2 and 3 answered the Player 2 decision before the Player 1 decision. It is possible that making the Player 2 decision informed their decision as Player 1, most likely leading to greater caution. A more complicated consequence of playing both roles is that it may have induced participants to devise a metastrategy for the two roles. For example, perhaps participants struck a balance in aggressiveness by being highly aggressive in one role but unaggressive in the other. This option of mixing risk could produce more risky aggregate behavior than would be found if participants were assigned to one role alone. To address this methodological concern, Study 4 was designed to test the initial social dilemma—ultimatum bargaining framing effect when participants are assigned to a role at the outset of the task.

Method

Participants

Participants were 304 MBA students at the University of Chicago who completed the task as part of a class exercise. As in Studies 2 and 3, all participants were paid on the basis of their decisions.

Procedure and Materials

The materials used were the same as the Study 1 social dilemma and ultimatum bargaining game descriptions, with the exception that participants were assigned to a specific role (Player 1 or Player 2) in the third sentence of the instructions. For example, participants who were assigned to the Player 1 role in the ultimatum game were told the following:

> In this exercise, you will be randomly paired with another student to participate in a resource allocation task. In this task, there is a potential pool of $7.00, and there are two roles, Player 1 and Player 2. You have been randomly assigned to the Player 1 role. As Player 1, you will be asked to propose a division of $7.00 between the two players, such as X for Player 1 and $7 - X$ for Player 2.

The remaining instructions and questions were identical to the Study 1 versions, except that participants were asked only the questions corresponding to their assigned role.

A subset of Player 1 participants were asked to provide expectations about the proportion of Player 2 participants who would allow various allocations. Participants in the ultimatum game (social dilemma) condition were told the following:

> Imagine that a hypothetical Player 1 is making an offer [claim] that could be matched with any of 100 potential Player 2s' responses. For each possible Player 1 offer [claim] listed below (a through e), provide your estimate of how many Player 2s are likely to (1) accept it [claim equal to or less than what's left] or (2) reject it

[claim more]. For each possible offer [claim], the values you assign in spaces (1) and (2) should total 100.

Five Player 1 allocations followed. In the ultimatum game condition, the precise wording for the first allocation was, "If Player 1 were to propose: (a) $7.00 for Player 1, $0.00 for Player 2." Underneath the heading, "How many Player 2s out of 100 do you think would . . ." were two columns, "(1) ____ accept it? + (2) ____ reject it? = 100," which forced participants to provide estimates summing to 100. The social dilemma condition questions had the same format, although the wording was changed to "If Player 1 were to claim: (a) $7.00 for Player 1, which leaves $0.00" and "(1) ____ claim $0.00? + (2) ____ claim more? = 100." The remaining four allocations were: $6.50/$0.50, $5.50/$1.50, $4.50/$2.50, and $3.50/$3.50. Half of the participants in each condition answered the expectation questions before making their own allocation, and half answered them after.

Results and Discussion

Player 1 and Player 2 Decisions

The effect of game description found in Study 1 was replicated in Study 4. As in Study 1, participants in the Player 2 role accepted lower outcomes in the social dilemma condition than in the ultimatum game condition. Forty percent (31 of 78) of the Player 2 participants in the social dilemma condition allowed the $7.00/$0.00 allocation, compared with only 16% (14 of 86) in the ultimatum game condition, $\chi^2(1, N = 164) = 10.16, p < .001$ (after Yates's correction for continuity). The average minimum outcome allowed by participants in the social dilemma condition ($M = \$1.19$) was lower than the outcome accepted by participants in the ultimatum game condition ($M = \$1.58$), although this effect was only marginally significant, $F(1, 163) = 3.22, p < .08$.

The decisions of participants in the Player 1 role confirmed the marginal effect found in Study 1. Seventy-five percent of the Player 1 participants (51 of 68) in the social dilemma condition allocated $3.50 or more to Player 2, compared with only 51% (37 of 72) in the ultimatum condition offering that amount, $\chi^2(1, N = 140) = 7.37, p < .01$ (after Yates's correction for continuity). The difference in the average amount that participants allocated to Player 2 was in the predicted direction ($M = \$3.17$ in the social dilemma condition vs. $M = \$2.93$ in the ultimatum game condition) but, as in Study 1, was not significant, $F(1, 139) = 1.96, p = .16$.

Player 1 Expectations

Seventy-three participants assigned to the Player 1 role were asked to provide estimates of the number of 100 Player 2s who would allow or deny a series of five allocations. We conducted a 2 × 2 × 5 ANOVA, with game (social dilemma vs. ultimatum game) and order (expectations elicited before vs. after the allocation decision) as between-participant factors and level of allocation (five levels) as a within-participant factor. There were no significant order effects or interactions (all $Fs < 1.2$, $ps > .30$), and there was an unsurprising level-of-allocation effect, such that more equal allocations were predicted to be more acceptable, $F(1, 69) = 200, p < .001$. As can be seen in Table 6, there was a main effect of game, such that Player 1 participants in the social dilemma condition were more pessimistic

Table 6
Player 1's Mean Estimate of Number of 100 Player 2s Who Would Allow Each Allocation

	Allocation (Player 1/Player 2)				
	\$7.00/\$0.00	\$6.50/\$0.50	\$5.50/\$1.50	\$4.50/\$2.50	\$3.50/\$3.50
Game	*M (SD)*	*M (SD)*	*M (SD)*	*M (SD)*	*M (SD)*
Social dilemma ($n = 35$)	1.0 (2.3)	9.1 (19.0)	15.1 (22.2)	26.3 (26.5)	68.4 (24.9)
Ultimatum game ($n = 38$)	0.2 (0.6)	14.5 (29.3)	27.3 (30.7)	40.0 (32.6)	86.3 (20.6)

than participants in the ultimatum condition, about the acceptability of most allocations, $F(1, 69) = 5.68, p < .02$. A significant Level of Allocation $\times$ Game interaction, $F(4, 276) = 3.09$, $p < .02$, revealed that the game effect was much stronger for the \$3.50/\$3.50 allocation, univariate $F(1, 69) = 10.94, p < .001$, than for the other allocations, univariate $Fs(1, 69) < 3.8$, $ps < .06$. The strong game effect for the \$3.50/\$3.50 allocation appears to have been due to decreased variance in the dependent variable, because many participants predicted that nearly all 100 Player 2s would accept the allocation. The tendency to report such high levels of confidence differed significantly by game: In the ultimatum condition, 71% of Player 1 participants believed that at least 90 of 100 Player 2s would accept the equal allocation, whereas in the social dilemma condition, only 36% of Player 1 participants were so confident, $\chi^2(1, N = 73) = 7.74, p < .01$ (after Yates's continuity correction).

Discussion

Study 4 confirmed that the framing effects found in Studies 1 through 3 were robust to decision-elicitation procedures. Specifically, the initial social dilemma–ultimatum game framing effect found in Study 1 was not diminished when participants were assigned to a specific player role. The magnitudes of the framing effects in Study 4 were virtually identical to those found in Studies 1 through 3. In Studies 1 through 4, the percentage of Player 2 participants allowing the \$7.00/\$0.00 allocation in the claiming versus accept-or-reject conditions were 30% vs. 2%, 30% vs. 10%, 43% vs. 10%, and 40% vs. 16%. In those same conditions, the percentage of Player 1 participants making the \$3.50/\$3.50 allocation were 56% vs. 37%, 57% vs. 42%, 73% vs. 49%, and 75% vs. 51%. Although the Study 4 responses were somewhat more generous than those in Studies 1 and 2 (perhaps reflecting less risk taking or greater concern for the opponent), they were of similar generosity to those of Study 3, providing little evidence that playing two roles significantly altered behavior.

Study 4 also provided insight about why Player 1 participants are more likely to make an equal allocation when Player 2 claims rather than accepts or rejects. Player 1 participants were relatively pessimistic about Player 2 making a cooperative counterclaim, even in response to the equal allocation. Their tendency, therefore, to offer the equal allocation appears to be a strategic decision motivated by self-interest. We believe that the open-ended claiming response creates the perception of independence.

Player 1 may believe that Player 2, out of pride or stupidity, could make an aggressive claim regardless of the amount that is left. By contrast, the close-ended accept or reject response creates the appearance of dependence on Player 1's initial allocation. Accurately or not, Player 1 may feel that Player 2's behavior will be more predictable and compliant.

General Discussion

We began this article with the observation that structurally equivalent versions of two-party social dilemmas and ultimatum bargaining games were being studied with different results. Through the studies reported here, we verified the existence of this procedural framing effect and showed that a subtle difference in how an action is framed can produce a large and consistent change in allocation preferences. Study 1 confirmed that participants in a sequential social dilemma behaved more generously than did participants in an equivalent ultimatum game. In particular, participants were more likely to accept a \$7.00/\$0.00 allocation as Player 2 and to offer a \$3.50/\$3.50 allocation as Player 1. Study 2 revealed that the procedural framing effect was primarily due to the form of Player 2's action. Participants were more generous when Player 2's action was described as claiming than when it was described as accepting or rejecting. Study 3 showed that claiming and accepting or rejecting evoked different interpretations of fairness and selfishness in denying a \$7.00/\$0.00 allocation. We argued that claiming more than \$0 is a more independent and ambiguous action than rejecting a claim of \$7.00, which makes Player 2 in the claiming condition more reluctant to inflict harm on their Player 1 partner. The results confirmed that participants felt that claiming more than \$0 was more selfish and less fair than rejecting a claim of \$7.00. Finally, Study 4 revealed that Player 1 participants had different expectations about Player 2's rate of compliance in ultimatum games and social dilemmas. Nearly 90% of Player 2s were expected to accept an equal allocation, compared with only 70% expected to claim \$3.50 or less. The tendency for Player 1 to offer equal allocations to Player 2s who claim appears to be a strategic rather than generous act.

The Source of Bias: Rejecting or Claiming?

The studies reported here have shown that social dilemma frames and ultimatum frames lead to different bargaining decisions, even though they both describe the same two-party, sequential allocation procedure. Could participants, through reflection, recognize the deeper structure in these games and show consistent preferences across frames? If so, then their subsequent enlightened preferences can serve as a benchmark for interpreting the direction of bias. For example, it is possible that both frames induce a bias (in opposite directions) or that one frame alone accounts for the discrepancy. A study that we conducted on perceptions of procedural fairness in ultimatum games and social dilemmas seems to provide a benchmark (Blount & Larrick, 1997b). In this study, participants read the same game descriptions used in Study 1 and then answered 11 procedural fairness questions (Tyler, 1994), before making their decisions as Player 1 and Player 2. These questions asked about dimensions of control, such as, "Who has more control over the allocation process?" and "Who has more control over the allocation outcome?" (which were answered on a 21-point scale, with the anchors *Player 1 has complete control* and *Player 2 has complete control*), and relationship, such as "Do Player 1 and Player 2 have similar or conflicting interests?" (which was answered on a 21-point scale, with the anchors *their interests are highly similar* and *their interests are highly conflicting*).

Perceptions of power and similarity did not differ between the two game conditions. For example, participants in both conditions believed that Player 1 had more control over the process (ultimatum game $M = 6.6$ and social dilemma $M = 5.4$, ns) and that Player 2 had more control over the outcome (ultimatum game $M = 14.67$ and social dilemma $M = 14.61$, ns). Having perceived the same structure underlying the two games, participants in both conditions no longer behaved differently. Not surprisingly, the $7.00/$0.00 allocation was accepted by just 3% of the ultimatum game participants (1 of 34). Quite surprisingly, however, the typical 30% to 40% rate of acceptance among social dilemma participants dropped to only 7% (2 of 30). This dramatic shift in cooperation suggests that it is the act of claiming that ordinarily induces a bias, specifically, a bias to comply. The more basic frame in these two-party, sequential allocation procedures appears to be the ultimatum frame.

Player 1's Strategic Failure When Player 2 Claims

Study 4 revealed that Player 1's expectations in the ultimatum game condition were reasonably accurate. Player 1 participants correctly predicted that almost no Player 2s would accept a $7.00/$0.00 allocation, that half would accept a $4.50/$2.50 allocation, and that about 90% would accept a $3.50/$3.50 allocation. The modal Player 1 allocation of $3.50/$3.50 turned out to be a wise one. It was the allocation that had the highest expected value (EV: $3.43), given the actual distribution of Player 2 responses, exceeding the next best allocation ($6.50/$0.50) by $0.20; deviating from it only slightly ($4.00/$3.00) was quite costly in terms of EV ($3.12).

By comparison, the Player 1 expectations in the social dilemma condition were strikingly inaccurate. Player 1 participants believed that almost no Player 2s would allow a $7.00/$0.00 allocation, and that only 30% would allow a $4.50/$2.50 allocation, and that only 70% would allow a $3.50/$3.50 allocation, whereas the true percentages were roughly 30%, 80%, and 100%, respectively. Their modal allocation of $3.50/$3.50 yielded a high EV ($3.50) but was not as good as four other

allocations: $6.50/$0.50 (EV = $3.64), $6.00/$1.00 (EV = $3.60), $5.00/$2.00 (EV = $3.70), and $4.50/$2.50 (EV = $3.60). Expected value ignores attitudes about risk, but assuming that decision makers could tolerate a minimum amount of risk, such as a three in four chance of success, the $5.00/$2.00 and $4.50/$2.50 allocations were still more advantageous than an equal allocation.

All four studies showed that when Player 2 claims, Player 1 has an opportunity to exploit Player 2's generosity but does not take it. How deep is the failure to recognize the opportunity? One means for testing this failure is to see whether experience reduces it. For example, Harrison and McCabe (1992) had participants alternate playing the role of Player 1 and Player 2 in a variant of the ultimatum game. They found rapid learning: Having once been Player 2, participants moved away from making an equal allocation to an allocation that barely exceeded Player 2's minimum. This is consistent with a well-established finding in the social judgment literature that people use their own attitudes and behavior to predict the attitudes and behavior of others (Marks & Miller, 1987). Some have argued that this tendency produces egocentric overgeneralizations about others, or a "false-consensus effect" (Ross, Greene, & House, 1977), whereas others have argued that it is a reasonable strategy when dealing with limited information and may actually be underused (Dawes, 1989, 1990).

The methods used in Studies 1 through 3 allowed us to examine whether our participants generalized from their experience as Player 2. In all three studies, participants made decisions as both Player 1 and Player 2. In some conditions of Study 1 and in all conditions of Studies 2 and 3, participants made their Player 2 decision first. Participants in the Player 2 claiming conditions therefore knew their own willingness to allow unfavorable allocations before they made their decision as Player 1, and participants in the Player 2 accept-or-reject conditions knew their own tendencies to be firm. Did they use the knowledge about their own behavior to generalize (or overgeneralize) to the behavior of other players?

To explore whether experience with the Player 2 role affected decisions as Player 1, we calculated two measures of association between Player 1 and Player 2 responses: the percentage of participants who gave identical responses in both roles and the Pearson product-or-moment correlation coefficients between their responses. The identical response variable measured the percentage of participants who allocated to Player 2 as Player 1 an amount equal to their own minimum as Player 2. The Pearson correlation measured the relative correspondence between these variables (i.e., not whether they were identical, but whether they were linearly related). These measures were calculated for the claiming conditions and accept-or-reject conditions in the three studies reported here, as well as for three similar studies reported elsewhere. The measures of association reported in Table 7 indicate that with the exception of Study 2, decisions as Player 1 and Player 2 tended to correspond more closely in the accept-or-reject conditions than in the claiming conditions. Statistical tests performed on the pooled data found that participants in the claiming conditions gave significantly fewer identical responses (28%) than did participants in the accept-or-reject conditions (42%), $\chi(1, N = 730) = 14.08$, $p < .001$. And the correlation coefficients calculated for the

Table 7

Measures of Association Between Participants' Responses as Player 1 and as Player 2

| | Form of Player 2 action | | | | | |
| | Claiming | | | Accepting or rejecting | | |
Study	Identical response	r	n	Identical response	r	n
Study 1	25%	.29	36	35%	.46**	34
Study 2	35%	.17	109	38%	.17	110
Study 3	19%	.17*	126	40%	.59***	62
Blount & Larrick (1997a)	26%	.22*	80	46%	.30	33
Blount & Larrick (1997b; Study 1)	36%	.11	39	51%	.70***	37
Blount & Larrick (1997b; Study 2)	43%	.36*	30	50%	.79***	34
Pooled data	28%	.18***	420	42%	.40***	310

Note. All measures are within-participant comparisons of the amount a participant allocated to Player 2 as Player 1 and the minimum amount allowed as Player 2. Identical response is the percentage of participants who allocated to Player 2 (as Player 1) the same amount that they themselves allowed as Player 2. *r* is the Pearson product–moment correlation between these amounts. Study 1 data included only those conditions in which participants made their Player 2 decisions before their Player 1 decisions. See the reference section for more information on additional studies.
* $p < .05$. ** $p < .01$. *** $p < .001$.

pooled data were significantly different from each other at $p = .001$ (using Fisher's *r*-to-*z* transformation).[5]

The tendency to generalize from one's behavior is weaker after making a claim than after deciding to accept or reject. Once again, this is consistent with the notion that the independence of claiming makes Player 2's behavior less predictable than accepting or rejecting. A second factor that might underlie the difference is that accepting or rejecting is evaluative and draws more attention to fairness. (Recall that in Study 3, there was a good deal of consensus that rejecting a \$7.00/\$0.00 allocation was fair, whereas there was a significant proportion of neutral feelings about the fairness of claiming more than \$0.) Fairness judgments are notoriously egocentric: Bargainers tend to make self-serving fairness judgments and then assume that informed, reasonable observers would reach the same conclusion (Babcock, Loewenstein, Issacharoff, & Camerer, 1995; Thompson & Loewenstein, 1992). The accept-or-reject response, therefore, may lead to more egocentric generalization because it evokes fairness judgments more strongly than claiming does.

It would be interesting in subsequent studies to examine the salience of fairness in each game and to test whether it mediates generalizing to others from one's own behavior. More generally, these simple, well-controlled games would be a useful context for testing what moderates whether people generalize too much (Ross et al.'s, 1977, "false consensus") or too little (Dawes's, 1990, version of "false uniqueness") from their own behavior. The findings could inform both experimental economic research on learning and social psychological research on the egocentricity of judgments.

The Claiming Effect

Framing Player 2's response in a sequential allocation as claiming an amount rather than as accepting or rejecting Player 1's allocation has four behavioral consequences. First, it makes Player 2 more inclined to allow highly unfavorable allocations, such as the \$7.00/\$0.00 allocation we have studied. Second, it deters Player 1 from making unequal allocations. Third, these two effects in combination increase the percentage of transactions that are completed. For example, if all possible pairs of Player 1 allocations and Player 2 decisions were matched in Study 1 (using the frequency distributions in Figures 1 and 2), there would be an 85% completion rate when Player 2 claims (in the social dilemma frame), compared with a 70% completion rate when Player 2 accepts or rejects (in the ultimatum bargaining frame). This same pattern was replicated in the other three studies. The fourth consequence of Player 2's claiming is that it reduces participants' willingness to generalize from their own decision as Player 2 to the allocation they make as Player 1 (as shown in Table 7).

The claiming effect, like the commons dilemma–public goods dilemma effect, illustrates the importance of construal processes in bargainers' decisions (Allison et al., 1996). In addition, it extends the concept of procedural frames to more social psychological factors. Whereas the commons dilemma–

[5] There was no difference in variance between the claiming and accept–reject conditions for either the Player 1 decision (respective *SD*s = 1.08 vs. 1.17), $F(417, 307) = 1.17, p > .10$, or the Player 2 decision (respective *SD*s = 1.45 vs. 1.37), $F(417, 307) = 1.12, p > .30$, and the direction of difference was opposite for the two decisions, which indicated that the difference in correlation between the two conditions was not an artifact of restricted range. Regression analyses that included dummy variables for individual studies yielded standardized regression coefficients (part correlations) of the same magnitude as the Pearson correlation coefficients found for the pooled data ($\beta = .19$ for claiming and $\beta = .40$ for accept–reject). An interaction test for the difference in slope was significant, $t(721) = 3.47, p < .001$.

824   LARRICK AND BLOUNT

public goods dilemma effect is produced by the asymmetry of gains and losses, the claiming effect occurs because of changes in perceptions of control and responsibility. Naturally, there are many other influences of procedural description on behavior that need to be explored. We believe that procedural framing effects can be useful tools in future research for identifying new linguistic (Semin & Marsman, 1994) and metaphorical (Allison et al., 1996; Bazerman & Carroll, 1987) features that influence bargaining and allocation behavior.

The claiming effect also has implications for research on sequential social dilemmas and ultimatum bargaining games. In their recent review of mixed-motive interaction, Komorita and Parks (1995) recommended these games as useful paradigms for studying basic social psychological aspects of bargaining, such as judgments of fairness. In addition, they noted that the games' similarities offer the possibility of using research in one paradigm to inform the other (Komorita & Parks, 1995). We believe that such comparisons would be extremely valuable, and that they can be made as long as potential limitations are recognized. For example, it appears that the findings on learning in the ultimatum game literature (e.g., Harrison & McCabe, 1992) may not generalize well to the sequential social dilemma literature. In addition, the "taste for fairness" explanations that have dominated the ultimatum game literature may be less relevant to sequential social dilemmas, for which fairness judgments appear to be less important. Naturally, these speculations are based on preliminary findings, and future research is needed to uncover the range of psychological differences that distinguish these games.

We close by considering some possible implications of procedural framing effects in everyday allocations. The existence of procedural frames suggests that more powerful parties could exploit weaker parties by manipulating procedural descriptions (see Lind and Tyler's, 1988, discussion of "false consciousness"). For example, bargainers (or institutions) who can successfully frame an allocation process as a social dilemma rather than an ultimatum game will have an advantage over other participants. And, in fact, many real-world resource dilemmas seem to be framed this way. For many scarce resources, society's Player 1s make a claim, and Player 2s—new arrivals and new generations—have nothing left from which to make a counterclaim. Framed in this way, Player 2 may be reluctant to block Player 1's claim because doing so requires an act of commission: Attempting to take more than what is left. A different frame, such as the decision to accept or reject, is likely to increase Player 2's willingness to challenge unfavorable allocations even if it jeopardizes joint outcome. A practical implication is that protest leaders and bargainers may find it more politically effective to frame their response as rejecting unfair allocations than making a selfish counterclaim.

References

Allison, S. T., Beggan, J. K., & Midgley, E. H. (1996). The quest for "similar instances" and "simultaneous possibilities": Metaphors in social dilemma research. *Journal of Personality and Social Psychology, 71*, 479–497.

Allison, S. T., & Messick, D. M. (1990). Social decision heuristics in the use of shared resources. *Journal of Behavioral Decision Making, 3*, 195–204.

Babcock, L., Loewenstein, G., Issacharoff, S., & Camerer, C. (1995). Biased judgments of fairness in bargaining. *American Economic Review, 85*, 1337–1343.

Bazerman, M. H., & Carroll, J. S. (1987). Negotiator cognition. In B. Staw & L. Cummings (Eds.), *Research in organizational behavior* (Vol. 9, pp. 247–288). Greenwich, CT: JAI Press.

Bazerman, M. H., Magliozzi, T., & Neale, M. A. (1985). Integrative bargaining in a competitive market. *Organizational Behavior and Human Decision Processes, 35*, 294–313.

Blount, S. (1995). When social outcomes aren't fair: The effect of causal attributions on preferences. *Organizational Behavior and Human Decision Processes, 63*, 131–144.

Blount, S., & Larrick, R. P. (1997a). *The claiming effect in ultimatum games.* Unpublished manuscript, University of Chicago.

Blount, S., & Larrick, R. P. (1997b). *Guided by fairness: Distributive and procedural fairness judgments explain ultimatum bargaining behavior.* Unpublished manuscript, University of Chicago.

Bornstein, G., Crum, L., Wittenbraker, J., Harring, K., Insko, C. A., & Thibaut, J. W. (1983). On the measurement of social orientations in the minimal group paradigm. *European Journal of Social Psychology, 13*, 321–350.

Brewer, M. B., & Kramer, R. M. (1986). Choice behavior in social dilemmas: Effects of social identity, group size, and decision framing. *Journal of Personality and Social Psychology, 50*, 543–549.

Brown, R. (1965). *Social psychology.* New York: Free Press.

Brown, R., & Fish, D. (1983). The psychological causality implicit in language. *Cognition, 14*, 237–273.

Budescu, D. V., Rapoport, A., & Suleiman, R. (1992). Simultaneous vs. sequential requests in resource dilemmas with incomplete information. *Acta Psychologica, 80*, 297–310.

Budescu, D. V., Suleiman, R., & Rapoport, A. (1995). Positional and group size effects in resource dilemmas with uncertain resources. *Organizational Behavior and Human Decision Processes, 61*, 225–238.

Camerer, C., & Thaler, R. H. (1995). Ultimatums, dictators and manners. *Journal of Economic Perspectives, 9*, 209–219.

Campbell, D. T. (1958). Common fate, similarity, and other indices of the status of aggregates of persons as social entities. *Behavioral Science, 3*, 14–25.

Dawes, R. M. (1980). Social dilemmas. *Annual Review of Psychology, 31*, 169–193.

Dawes, R. M. (1989). Statistical criteria for establishing a truly false consensus effect. *Journal of Experimental Social Psychology, 25*, 1–17.

Dawes, R. M. (1990). The potential nonfalsity of the false consensus effect. In R. M. Hogarth (Ed.), *Insights in decision making* (pp. 179–199). Chicago: University of Chicago Press.

Eiser, J. R., & Bhavnani, K. (1974). The effect of situational meaning on the behavior of subjects in the Prisoner's Dilemma Game. *European Journal of Social Psychology, 4*, 93–97.

Erev, I., & Rapoport, A. (1990). Provision of step-level public goods: The sequential contribution mechanism. *Journal of Conflict Resolution, 34*, 401–425.

Ericsson, K. A., & Simon, H. A. (1993). *Protocol analysis: Verbal reports as data.* Cambridge, MA: MIT Press.

Fagley, N. S. (1993). A note concerning reflection effects versus framing effects. *Psychological Bulletin, 113*, 451–452.

Fleishman, J. A. (1988). The effects of decision framing and others' behavior on cooperation in a social dilemma. *Journal of Conflict Resolution, 32*, 162–180.

Forsythe, R., Horowitz, J., Savin, N., & Sefton, M. (1994). Fairness in simple bargaining experiments. *Games and Economic Behavior, 6*, 347–369.

Guth, W., Schmittberger, R., & Schwarze, B. (1982). An experimental analysis of ultimatum bargaining. *Journal of Economic Behavior and Organization, 3,* 367–388.

Guth, W., & Tietz, R. (1990). Ultimatum bargaining behavior: A survey and comparison of experimental results. *Journal of Economic Psychology, 11,* 417–449.

Hardin, G. (1968). The tragedy of the commons. *Science, 162,* 1243–1248.

Harrison, G. W., & McCabe, K. A. (1992). Testing noncooperative bargaining theory in experiments. *Research in Experimental Economics, 5,* 137–169.

Hoffman, C., & Tchir, M. A. (1990). Interpersonal verbs and dispositional adjectives: The psychology of causality embodied in language. *Journal of Personality and Social Psychology, 58,* 765–778.

Kahneman, D., Knetsch, J., & Thaler, R. H. (1986). Fairness and the assumption of economics. *Journal of Business, 59,* S285–S300.

Kanouse, D. E. (1972). Language, labelling, and attribution. In E. E. Jones, D. E. Kanouse, H. H. Kelley, R. E. Nisbett, S. Valins, & B. Weiner (Eds.), *Attribution: Perceiving the causes of behavior* (pp. 121–135). New York: General Learning Press.

Kelley, H. H., & Thibaut, J. W. (1978). *Interpersonal relations.* New York: John Wiley.

Komorita, S. S., & Parks, C. D. (1995). Interpersonal relations: Mixed-motive interaction. *Annual Review of Psychology, 46,* 183–207.

Larrick, R. P., & Blount, S. (1995). Social context in tacit bargaining games: Consequences for perceptions of affinity and cooperative behavior. In R. M. Kramer & D. M. Messick (Eds.), *Negotiation as a social process* (pp. 268–284). Thousand Oaks, CA: Sage.

Lind, E. A., & Tyler. T. R. (1988). *The social psychology of procedural justice.* New York: Plenum.

Marks, G., & Miller, N. (1987). Ten years of research on the false consensus effect: An empirical and theoretical overview. *Psychological Bulletin, 102,* 72–90.

McClintock, C. G. (1972). Social motivation: A set of propositions. *Behavioral Science. 17,* 438–454.

McCusker. C., & Carnevale, P. J. (1995). Framing in resource dilemmas: Loss aversion and the moderating effects of sanctions. *Organizational Behavior and Human Decision Processes, 61,* 190–201.

Messick, D. M., & Allison, S. T. (1987). Accepting unfairness: Outcomes and attributions. *Representative Research in Social Psychology, 17,* 39–50.

Messick, D. M., & Brewer, M. B. (1983). Solving social dilemmas: A review. In L. Wheeler & P. Shaver (Eds.), *Review of personality and social psychology* (Vol. 4, pp. 11–44). Beverly Hills, CA: Sage.

Messick, D. M., & McClintock, C. G. (1968). Motivational basis of choice in experimental games. *Journal of Experimental Social Psychology, 4,* 1–25.

Neale, M. A., & Bazerman, M. H. (1985). The effects of framing and negotiator overconfidence on bargainer behavior. *Academy of Management Journal, 28,* 34–49.

Neale, M. A., & Bazerman, M. H. (1991). *Cognition and rationality in negotiation.* New York: Free Press.

Rapoport, A., Budescu, D. V., & Suleiman, R. (1993). Sequential requests from randomly distributed shared resources. *Journal of Mathematical Psychology, 37,* 241–265.

Ritov, I., & Baron, J. (1990). Reluctance to vaccinate: Omission bias and ambiguity. *Journal of Behavioral Decision Making, 3,* 263–277.

Ross, L., Greene, D., & House, P. (1977). The "false consensus effect": An egocentric bias in social perception and attribution processes. *Journal of Experimental Social Psychology, 13,* 279–301.

Roth, A. E. (1994). Bargaining. In J. Kagel & A. E. Roth (Eds.), *Handbook of experimental economics* (pp. 253–348). Princeton, NJ: Princeton University Press.

Rutte, C. G., Wilke, H. A., & Messick, D. M. (1987). The effects of framing social dilemmas as give-some or take-some games. *British Journal of Social Psychology, 26,* 102–108.

Schelling, T. C. (1960). *The strategy of conflict.* Cambridge, MA: Harvard University Press.

Schurr, P. H. (1987). Effects of gain and loss decision frames on risky purchase negotiations. *Journal of Applied Psychology, 72,* 351–358.

Semin, G. R., & Marsman, G. (1994). "Multiple inference-inviting properties" of interpersonal verbs: Event instigation, dispositional inference, and implicit causality. *Journal of Personality and Social Psychology, 67,* 836–849.

Spranca, M., Minsk, E., & Baron, J. (1991). Omission and commission in judgment and choice. *Journal of Experimental Social Psychology, 27,* 76–105.

Stevens, J. (1990). *Intermediate statistics: A modern approach.* Hillsdale, NJ: Erlbaum.

Thompson, L. L., & Loewenstein, G. (1992). Egocentric perceptions of fairness and interpersonal conflict. *Organizational Behavior and Human Decision Processes, 51,* 176–197.

Tversky, A., & Kahneman, D. (1981). The framing of decisions and the psychology of choice. *Science, 211,* 453–458.

Tversky, A., & Kahneman, D. (1991). Loss aversion in riskless choice: A reference dependent model. *Quarterly Journal of Economics, 106,* 1039–1061.

Tyler, T. R. (1994). Psychological models of the justice motive: Antecedents of distributive and procedural justice. *Journal of Personality and Social Psychology, 67,* 850–863.

Received October 30, 1996
Revision received November 22, 1996
Accepted November 22, 1996 ∎

INTERNATIONAL JOURNAL OF PSYCHOLOGY, 2000, *35* (2), 111–116

Social Dilemmas

Robyn M. Dawes
*Carnegie-Mellon University,
Pittsburgh, USA*

David M. Messick
*Northwestern University,
Evanston, USA*

In social dilemma situations, each individual always receives a higher payoff for defecting than for cooperating, but all are better off if all cooperate than if all defect. Often, however, people in social dilemmas attend more to the group's payoffs than to their own, either automatically or to behave "appropriately." But whereas social identity elicits cooperative behaviour in dilemmas, it is generally only for the benefit of an "in-group." Dilemmas between groups (requiring self-sacrificial behaviour within) are often the most extreme. Consequently, the framing and manipulation of group identity is critical to cooperation rate as demonstrated by careful laboratory experimentation.

Dans les situations de dilemme social, il est plus rentable pour chaque individu de démissionner que de coopérer, mais tous s'en trouvent mieux si tous coopèrent que s'ils démissionnent. Cependant, les personnes aux prises avec des dilemmes sociaux considèrent davantage les retombées pour le groupe que pour elles-mêmes, de façon automatique ou pour se comporter de façon correcte. Bien que l'identification sociale favorise le comportement coopératif en situation de dilemme, cela ne vaut que pour le groupe d'appartenance. Les dilemmes entre groupes (qui requièrent le sacrifice de soi à l'intérieur du groupe) sont souvent les plus extrêmes. Des expériences en laboratoire montrent que l'encadrement et la manipulation de l'identification au groupe affectent fortement le taux de coopération.

Social dilemmas are situations in which each member of a group has a clear and unambiguous incentive to make a choice that—when made by all members—provides poorer outcomes for all than they would have received if none had made the choice. Thus, by doing what seems individually reasonable and rational, people end up doing less well than they would have done if they had acted unreasonably or irrationally. This paradoxical possibility has emerged in many contexts and it has been widely discussed in psychology (Dawes, 1980; Komorita & Parks, 1997; Messick & Brewer, 1983) and almost all the other social sciences. For example, the recent address of the President of the American Political Science Association (Ostrom, 1998) dealt with precisely this problem, which is called the "collective action problem" in that discipline.

Examples of social dilemmas include the problems associated with the provision of public goods. For example, my contribution to my local public television station will be too small to make a difference in the ultimate success or failure of the station. Therefore, it is pointless for me to make a contribution even though I would prefer to have the station and pay the contribution than to save the contribution and lose the station. (Note that I am *not* asked to pay for public television "what it's worth" to me; in fact, most requests for such donations are for considerably less; the problem arises because any contribution at all is pointless from a purely egoistic perspective.) When all of the viewers of the station understand the problem and reach the egoistically rational conclusion, however, they will decide not to pay their contributions, the station will go bankrupt, and we will all lose the station even though we all would have preferred to make our contributions and keep it.

Another example may be found in a common business situation. All the departments of a corporation have been told to cut their costs. Costs, however, are of two types: those incurred to do the work of the department and those incurred to help other departments. Each department head realizes that the sensible costs to cut are those that involve supporting other departments. Cutting those costs improves the bottom line of the head's department no matter what reduction in efficiency results from the withdrawal of support from other departments, whereas cutting costs associated with the work of the department would directly reduce its efficiency. So each department cuts back on the aid it gives to other departments. Thus, if the total support each department received from all the others was greater than the cost savings, the net result is that each department is worse off than before the cost cutting.

Requests for reprints should be addressed to Robyn M. Dawes, Department of Social and Decision Sciences, Pittsburgh, PA 15213, USA (Tel: +1 412 268 2055; Fax: +1 412 268 6938; E-mail: rd1b@andrew.cmu.edu).

This article was written while the first author was the Olof Palme Visiting Professor at Göteborg and Stockholm Universities, Sweden. The visiting professorship is financially supported by the Swedish Council for Research in the Humanities and Social Sciences.

A few more examples should suffice. Imagine that you and a group of seven casual acquaintances are having a dinner out. You all agree in advance of the meal to share the cost of the meal equally. As you examine the menu and the wine list you see a number of options that are very tempting but also that are very expensive. You realize that if you order an expensive main course and an expensive bottle of wine you will only have to pay one eighth of the cost yourself with the additional seven eighths being distributed equally among the others. This cost sharing obviously presents an opportunity for you to enjoy yourself without having to pay the full cost. When every person at the table reasons in the same manner, however, all are collectively and individually stunned by the bill. It is far more than any one of you would have guessed. This example does not represent a problem for a society or for a corporation. However, the analogous problem of medical insurance is such a problem. People who pay medical insurance premiums are free to select the most expensive care they can and they all are shocked by the bill (next year's premiums). You invest in a fishing boat and license and then want to take the largest catch that you can. You are then shocked when the fishery is seriously reduced in size, because after all you personally were responsible for only a minute fraction of this reduction.

A PSYCHOLOGICAL ANALYSIS OF SOCIAL DILEMMAS

We have illustrated what a social dilemma is with examples. The examples also permit us to discuss the ways in which social dilemmas can be solved and to highlight the challenges to psychological theories of decision making in these troublesome situations. In the case of the public good, one strategy that has been employed is to create a moral sense of duty to support it—for instance, the public television station that one watches. The attempt is to reframe the decision as doing one's duty rather than making a difference—again, in the wellbeing of the station watched. The injection of a moral element changes the calculation from "Will I make a difference" to "I must pay for the benefit I get."

In our organizational example, it is unrealistic to think that department managers will voluntarily reduce their own performance in order to benefit other departments. Therefore, the solution to this problem must arise from leadership at the upper levels of the organization. The type of changes that are predictable must be avoided by regulations, constraints, or other rules that make it difficult for departments to shift costs from themselves to others in the organization. Cost shifting is not the same as cost reduction.

The final illustration, the shared meal and its more serious counterparts, requires yet another approach. Here there is no hierarchy, as in the organizational example, that can be relied upon to solve the problem.

With the shared meal, all the diners need to be aware of the temptation that they have and there need to be mutually agreed-upon limits to constrain the diners. Alternatively, the rule needs to be changed so that everyone pays for what they ordered. The latter arrangement creates responsibility in that all know that they will pay for what they order. Such voluntary arrangements may be difficult to arrange in some cases. With the medical insurance, the insurance company may recognize the risk and insist on a principle of co-payments for medical services. This is a step in the direction of paying for one's own meal, but it allows part of the "meal" to be shared and part of it to be paid for by the one who ordered it. The fishing version is more difficult. To make those harvesting the fish pay for some of the costs of the catch would require some sort of taxation to deter the unbridled exploitation of the fishery. Taxation, however, leads to tax avoidance or evasion. But those who harvest the fish would have no incentive to report their catches accurately or at all, especially if they were particularly successful, which simultaneously means particularly successful—compared to others at least—in contributing to the problem of a subsequently reduced yield. Voluntary self-restraint would be punished as those with less of that personal quality would thrive while those with more would suffer. Conscience, as Hardin (1968) noted, would be self-eliminating.

How is it possible to create a psychological theory to explain decision making in such complex and varied situations? The theory must be flexible enough to be applicable to a wide variety of contexts, and it must also be concrete enough to make predictions whose validity can be assessed. In particular, it must predict which factors will enhance or diminish the rate of choices favouring ego versus choices favouring the group, and in which situations. One such theory is that of March (1994). March's theory stresses the importance of three factors. The first is the perception of appropriateness, that is, the answer to the question, "What kind of situation is this?" In our first example, it is precisely this feature that public television campaigns try to exploit. They want to induce their viewers to see the situation as one in which the viewer is consuming an entertainment good and incurring the duty to pay for it. The second part of March's theory raises the question of the identity of the decision-maker. "What kind of person am I?" is the question that is asked here. To be an ambitious department manager in the second of our examples implies dealing with cost-cutting requirements precisely as we suggested. In the case of our shared meal, if we see ourselves as part of a social group we may resist the temptation to order expensive fare because we would not want our colleagues to pay for it either. But if we are just hungry individuals, we may very well go ahead and order up the good stuff. The final element of March's conceptualization deals with the role of rules. He proposes that in many cases when we know who we are and what kind of a situation we are in, what is to be done is more or less given, dictated by normative rules of what is appropriate for people like us to do in situations like this. If I am a responsible person and I am indebted to the public television station, I write out a cheque. If I am an effective manager and the situation calls for cost cutting, I cut services to other departments. March's emphasis on rules is particularly important in situations that evoke ethical or moral considerations because in these domains obeying the relevant rules is the essence of morality and character.

GROUP IDENTITY

Messick (1999) has developed March's framework for application to experimental research environments. One implication of this perspective is the recognition that relatively minor changes in the social environment can induce major changes in decision making because these minor changes can change the perceived appropriateness of a situation. One variable that has been shown to make such a difference is whether the decision maker sees herself as an individual or as a part of a group.

To study how this variable relates to behaviour in social dilemma situations, we ask three questions: (1) When do we form groups? (2) When do people identify themselves with their group as opposed to an individualistic identification? and (3) What is the effect of such identification on social dilemma behaviour? We must note before considering these questions that the simple formation of a group, or identification of people within it as group members, does not necessarily imply cooperative behaviour.

First consider natural groups—such as "my country right or wrong," or "just the two of us against the world." Note that such natural groups are defined in terms of boundaries that *simultaneously* delineate a set of members as belonging to the group and differentiate these members from members of other groups, however "fuzzily" these boundaries may be drawn. Thus, whereas it is possible to define integers without reference to fractions, decimals, irrational numbers, and transcendental ones, we really cannot define a social group without differentiating those people who belong to it from other people who do not. When we ourselves are part of a group, theorists generally refer to the member comprising it as a "in-group," whereas those outside it are often referred to as the "out-group." This differentiation does not necessarily imply hostility between in-group and out-group, although it often does exist. Moreover, group boundaries are not just occasionally fuzzy and malleable but can define both superordinate and subordinate groups as subsets or supersets of others. Thus, the heads of corporation departments discussed earlier might identify with the department or with the corporation itself (or have some mix of group identities or varying group identities depending upon the circumstances), and

their behaviour may be affected by such identifications. In fact, as we shall see, identification with a specific as opposed to a superordinate group containing the specific one may have profound consequences.

Observing the types of natural groups described earlier, social psychologists have been quite interested in finding out how important the distinction between groups must be in order to affect behaviour. Clearly, when countries are at war, identification as a citizen of one or another country is extraordinarily important, as in other circumstances is identification as an Albanian or Serbian resident of Kosovo, a Catholic or Protestant citizen of Northern Ireland, or a Hutu or Tutsi in Rwanda. But social psychologists have asked whether is it necessary to have such striking differences and profound consequences for group members in order to elicit behaviour that is associated with group identity. Primarily from experimentation and secondarily from acute observation, the answer is no. In fact, it is easy both to create groups and group identification—and to elicit the behaviours associated with such identification—on a very *minimal* basis, as in the story from the *Cat in the Hat* where people consider themselves inferior or superior either because they do or do not have stars pasted on their stomachs, or much earlier in *Gulliver's Travels* where Jonathan Swift created a fantasy war between those who break their soft-boiled eggs on the small side versus those who break them on the large side. Bertrand Russell has also written short stories based on the same theme—that people are capable of creating group identities and intergroup hostilities on totally silly bases.

The people who are most identified with research on creating in-group identification and out-group hostility on the most minimal of possible bases are Tajfel and Turner (1986; Turner, Hogg, Oakes, Reicher, & Wetherell, 1987). Brewer and Miller (1996) and Hogg and Abrams (1988) review this work. They interpret the existence of minimal groups in slightly different ways, but concur that it can be established with (distressing) ease. The general finding has been that simply by creating groups on the basis of aesthetic preference or even on the basis of an arbitrary feedback that each person is an "overestimator of dots" or a "underestimator of dots" (after making a quick judgement of how many there are in a display flashed on the wall), people act more favourably toward their in-group than toward the out-group. The standard manipulation has been the distribution of money or "points" to others who are identified only on the basis of their group membership.

What implications do such studies have for the effect of group identity on social dilemma behaviour? It turns out that—as might be predicted—people tend to cooperate with other members of their own group (however minimally it is constructed) and defect when interacting with members of other groups, even when group membership is determined on an explicitly *random basis*.

GROUP CONFLICTS

Insko (e.g. Insko, Schopler, Hoyle, Dardis, & Graetz, 1990) pioneered work on "individual-group discontinuity" in choice in social dilemma situations. When people act as individuals who are interacting with other individuals, they are far more cooperative than when they form groups that interact with other groups. Although this differentiation can be ascribed sometimes to fear and (more often) to greed—where group members reinforce each other for taking a greedy stance—other research has indicated that often the "discontinuity" is between co-operative behaviour toward the in-group and defecting behaviour toward the out-group, combined with a sense of mistrust or hostility. That is, people will make self-sacrificial choices when the benefits go to members of their own group, but not when the benefits go to members of an out-group. In both situations people are functioning as group members. Thus, the discontinuity found is not just between individual behaviour versus group behaviour, but rather a function of the type of group identification that can be achieved.

The importance of the type identification is well illustrated in a series of studies by Orbell, van de Kragt, and Dawes (1988). Participants, about two thirds University of Oregon students and one third from the town of Eugene, Oregon, arrive at the experiment in groups of 14. They are separated into two groups of seven on a clearly random basis, by themselves drawing white or blue poker chips from a bookbag; to emphasize the randomness to which these two subgroups of seven are constructed, participants are encouraged to examine the bookbag before the draws are made and are required to shake it. Then the two groups of seven go to two different rooms.

The game that presents a social dilemma structure is very simple. Each participant is given a "stake" of 6 dollars. If the participant chooses to "give the 6 dollars to the group," it becomes 12 dollars—with 2 dollars going to each of the other six members. Each participant receives the benefit of any other participants' "give-away" choice independent of whether she or he chooses to keep the 6 dollars or gives it away. Thus, each participant has a 6 dollar dominating strategy to keep the money, while if all keep rather than give it away, all receive 6 dollars when all could have received 12 dollars; moreover, each giveaway choice results in an increase of total wealth of 6 dollars; thus, this "give-away game" presents participants with a uniform social dilemma situation (see Dawes, 1975).

The critical manipulation was whether give-away choices led to the distribution of 12 dollars to the other participants in one's own room or to comparable participants in the other room. For example, the give-away decision of participant A would go to participant B, C . . . G in the same room or in a different room. We also manipulated whether or not participants could talk. The results were clear cut. When participants were not allowed to talk to each other, it didn't matter whether the bonus for giving away the money went to one's own group or to the group in the other room. Approximately 38% of the participants gave the money away; when, however, they could talk, there was a striking difference. Approximately 79% of them gave away the money when it went to those in their own room with whom they were communicating, but only about 30% when the money went to people in the other room. Discussions ranged from "wouldn't it be wonderful if we all kept our money and they all gave their money to us," to "the right thing to do is give the money away." The former type of argument prevailed over the latter. Moreover, as reported in Caporael, Dawes, Orbell, and van de Kragt (1989), people who gave away the money in the absence of communication tended to state that they did so because it was "the right thing to do," whereas those who gave it away after discussion gave it away "to benefit the group."

The observed type of instant hostility between groups to everyone's detriment can also be found in the work of Bornstein (e.g. 1992). He sets up competing group social dilemmas in which each individual faces a social dilemma *within* his or her own group, while there is a simultaneous social dilemma that exists between groups. He does so by constructing a group competition between two groups, in which the one with more self-sacrificing individuals receives greater benefit than the one with fewer, very much like the logical structure of a war between two countries. Here, we give a schematic example. Suppose that a group of 10 people is randomly divided into 2 groups of 5, each member of each group is given a 10 dollar stake that can be given to his or her own group, and the members of the group who achieve the greater number of give-away choices all receive 20 dollars. But there is a 3 dollar compensation for all group members if the two groups tie, that is, if an equal number of each of the two groups gives the 10 dollars to their group. What happens when the group members can talk within their own groups but intergroup communication is prohibited? Almost invariably, all members of groups in experiments similar to this give away their money to their own group. Thus, in the situation outlined, all would end up receiving 3 dollars, whereas all would have received 13 dollars (their original 10 dollars plus 3 dollars for the tie) if the experimenter "gave a war and nobody came." Bornstein has many variations on this general paradigm, all leading to the same conclusions. Although there are many other variables that lie beyond the scope of this paper that affect the actual rate of giving away the money to one's own group, the dismal conclusion remains. Even though the groups are randomly constructed, subjects have a vigorous tendency to support their own groups, to the detriment to both the other group and ultimately themselves and their own group members. Bornstein (personal communication, 1996) believes that he is observing the initiation of a war in miniature. When group members are able to discuss the problem, they reinforce the belief that they are all committed to helping the group, and that they possess the solidarity necessary for their group to predominate. At the same time they believe that at least some of the members of the other group (whom they cannot observe) will be sufficiently "weak" so that they will not support their own in-group. Psychological characteristics of self-sacrifice and commitment are believed to exist to a much greater extent in people observed than in people unobserved—even though both observed and unobserved people are drawn randomly from the exact same population.

A SOLUTION

The Bornstein "two group social dilemma" situation pitted group against group, where self-sacrificial behaviour benefited one's own group, to the detriment of the collectivity. The Orbell et al. (1988) work was often conceptualized by the subjects themselves as group against group ("wouldn't it be wonderful if they all gave their money to us, and we all kept our money"), but there was no uniform payment to either group, and self-sacrificial behaviour benefited the other group. Is it possible that in a two group situation the juxtaposition of groups can lead to cooperative behaviour for the in-group that does not simultaneously hurt the out-group? The answer is yes. Kramer and Brewer (1986) presented six subjects with a "depleting resource" social dilemma (the details of which are not important to this summary). In one condition, they achieve subgroup identity of three participants (e.g. A, B, and C) as opposed to the remaining three (D, E, and F) through a "common fate" manipulation in which the three people in the subgroup formed were told that their payoffs were determined by a single coin toss. What happened then was that when (phony) feedback indicated that other members of one's own subgroup were harvesting the commons too rapidly (so that it was being depleted), participants attempted to "compensate" by harvesting less. However, when the participants who were depleting the resource too rapidly were those identified as members of the other group, participants actually increased their harvesting—consistent with the philosophy that "we might as well take what we can get while we can still get it." Note that here, using restraint to balance defection on the part of one's own group members benefits people in the other group as well as in one's own group. Thus, it is not necessary to have a conflict between groups in order to get cooperative in-group behaviour as a result of juxtaposing two groups.

This finding raises the question of whether a large group can withstand fractionation into subgroups. The answer is yes, but only under certain circumstances. In the Orbell et al. work, the experimenters created a variation on the 2 group problem by allowing all 14 subjects to talk to each other prior to random division into 2 separate groups meeting in separate rooms. Here, there were 3 possible payoffs. Twenty-one dollars could be given to the group in the other room (with 3 dollars going to each member) or 12 dollars could be given to the other members in one's own group (with 2 dollars going to each other member) or 5 dollars could be kept. The result was that many commitments were made in the 14-person superordinate group at the beginning to give away the 21 dollars. People would unilaterally promise to do so or would make additional commitments of the form "I am willing to do it if others are." When *all* subjects in the 14-person group, at one point or other, made either a conditional or unconditional commitment, 84% subsequently gave away the 21 dollars. However, when at least one person made no such commitment— either by outright refusal or by saying nothing—the rate of giving away the 21 dollars was only 58%. That was a striking difference. Even more striking, however, was the finding that in those groups that did not achieve the "solidarity" of all making a commitment at one point or other, there was absolutely no relationship at the individual level between having made such a commitment and giving the 21 dollars away, or between hearing the number of others who had made such a commitment at giving the 21 dollars away—which after division implied that there was no correlation across groups between the number of people who made the commitment and the number who gave the 21 dollars away. This step-level result was not expected, and it raised questions that are not yet answered about the importance of unanimity and solidarity and commitment and how these factors interact to create cooperative behaviour within groups when there is temptation to renege on any commitments made. The empirical finding was that commitments were functional in the presence of unanimity, but not otherwise. As Atiyah (1981) points out, promises and commitments are binding only in the presence of reciprocal promises and commitments. Perhaps the participants in the Orbell et al. work are treating the *entire* remainder of the group as equivalent to a single person who must reciprocate if promises are to be kept. Failure on the part of a few people to do so could then become functionally equivalent to shilly-shallying about a commitment on the part of a single individual.

Of course, correlation does not imply causation. So it could be that the apparent effectiveness of the commitments simply reflected the unanimity, or it could be that such commitments are only functional *given* unanimity, an argument subsequently made by Baker (1998). The current research does not provide an answer to these questions.

IMPLICATIONS

From an applied perspective the implication about group identity is clear. It can be a two-edged sword in achieving cooperation. When it is clearly a parochial matter (as in wars between two countries or in Bornstein's manufactured two group dilemma), it can encourage local cooperation and global defection. However, when a superordinate group identity can be achieved, it can lead to cooperation between groups, at least in the presence of personal commitments. It may, thus, not have been a coincidence that (Tom Finholt, personal communication, 1987) United States foreign policy became noticeably more aggressive in South America after the invention of the telegraph, where negotiators could establish an instant link back to Washington—a link that may well have reinforced the identity as a representative of the United States, rather than as a member of a group of people trying to negotiate a solution to a difficult problem. Nor is the agreement achieved in the early Salt Talks between the US and the USSR negotiators during their famous "walk in the woods" surprising in light of these findings. When the two negotiators were together without any cues about their identities as representatives of the United States or the Soviet Union, they actually reached a solution (a solution that was promptly vetoed by the central authority of *both* sides). If we wish negotiators to be cooperative, we must do whatever we can to enhance their identity as negotiators dealing with a particular problem, rather than their identity of a representative or a particular group that is in conflict with another group. To hope, in contrast, for a super-superordinate identity as a "human being" is just too optimistic.

REFERENCES

Atiyah, P. (1981). *Promises, morals and law.* New York: Oxford University Press.

Baker, C.M. (1998). *Cooperation as the norm: Social dilemmas and the role of social norms in promoting cooperation.* Unpublished paper, Carnegie Mellon University.

Bornstein, G. (1992). The free-rider problem in intergroup conflicts over step-level and continuous public goods. *Journal of Personality and Social Psychology, 62,* 597–606.

Brewer, M.B., & Miller, N. (1996). *Intergroup relations.* Ann Arbor, MI: Brooks Cole.

Caporael, L.R., Dawes, R.M., Orbell, J.M., & van de Kragt, A.J.C. (1989). Selfishness examined: Cooperation in the absence of egoistic incentives. *Behavioral and Brain Sciences, 12,* 683–739.

Dawes, R.M. (1975). Formal models of dilemmas in social decision-making. In M.F. Kaplan & S. Schwartz (Eds.), *Human judgement and decision processes: Formal and mathematical approaches* (pp. 87–106). New York: Academic Press.

Dawes, R.M. (1980). Social dilemmas. *Annual Review of Psychology, 31,* 169–193.

Hardin, G. (1968). The tragedy of the commons. *Science, 162,* 1243–1248.

Hogg, M.A., & Abrams, D. (1988). *Social identifications: A social psychology of intergroup relations and group processes.* London: Routledge.

Insko, C.A., Schopler, J., Hoyle, R.H., Dardis, G.J., & Graetz, K.A. (1990). Individual–group discontinuity as a function of fear and greed. *Journal of Personality and Social Psychology, 58,* 68–79.

Komorita, S.S., & Parks, C.D. (1997). *Social dilemmas.* Boulder, CO: Westview.

Kramer, R.M., & Brewer, M.B. (1986). Social group identity and the emergence of cooperation in resource conservation dilemmas. In H. Wilke, D. Messick, & C. Rutte (Eds.), *Experimental social dilemmas* (pp. 177–203). Frankfurt am Main, Germany: Verlag Peter Lang.

March, J.G. (1994). *A primer on decision making.* New York: Free Press.

Messick, D.M. (1999). Alternative logics for decision making in social situations. *Journal of Economic Behavior and Organization, 39,* 11–28.

Messick, D.M., & Brewer, M.B. (1983). Solving social dilemmas: A review. *Review of Personality and Social Psychology, 4,* 11–44.

Orbell, J.M., van de Kragt, A.J.C., & Dawes, R.M. (1988). Explaining discussion-induced cooperation. *Journal of Personality and Social Psychology, 54,* 811–819.

Ostrom, E. (1998). A behavioural approach to the rational choice theory of collective action. *American Political Science Review, 92,* 1–22.

Tajfel, H., & Turner, J.C. (1986). The social identity theory of intergroup behaviour. In S. Worchel & W. Austin (Eds.), *Psychology of intergroup relations* (pp. 7–24). Chicago: Nelson-Hall.

Turner, J.C., Hogg, M., Oakes, P., Reicher, S., & Wetherell, M. (1987). *Rediscovering the social group: A self-categorization theory.* Oxford: Basil Blackwell.

Part II
Third-Party Intervention

[10]

SPLITTING-THE-DIFFERENCE
IN INTEREST ARBITRATION

HENRY S. FARBER*

This study develops two models of the behavior of interest arbitrators in
which the arbitrator has some exogenous notion of an equitable settlement
and yet is also influenced to some extent by the positions of the parties. The
author argues that it is the arbitrator's notion of an equitable outcome that
determines the positions of the parties, and empirical evidence suggesting
that the arbitrator merely splits the difference is misleading. In fact, the parties are likely to position themselves around the expected arbitration award,
suggesting that the expected arbitration outcome shapes the parties' bargaining positions rather than the reverse. There is nevertheless some truth to the
notion that an arbitrator who is sensitive to the demands of the parties can
chill bargaining. The author therefore proposes that the arbitration award be
made independent of actual negotiating positions through a closed-offer
mechanism.

THE major criticism of conventional interest arbitration is that the arbitrator tends to "split the difference" between the final positions of the parties.[1] Critics argue that this tendency induces the parties to bring extreme positions into arbitration, resulting in a chilling of bargaining and excessive reliance on the arbitration procedure. It is argued here that the arbitrator's behavior cannot be explained as simply splitting the difference, because each party would then have the incentive to enter arbitration with a position as extreme as possible and such behavior by the parties is not generally observed. It follows that the behavior of the arbitrator must be more complex than the critics assume.

Recent work by Farber and Katz suggests that it is the uncertainty surrounding the arbitration award that drives the negotiation process.[2] This uncertainty imposes

*The author is an associate professor in the Depart-
ment of Economics at Massachusetts Institute of
Technology. Support for this research was provided by
the National Science Foundation and useful comments
by participants in workshops at Cornell University,
Rensselaer Polytechnic Institute, and the University of
Western Ontario.

[1]See Carl M. Stevens, "Is Compulsory Arbitration
Compatible with Bargaining?" *Industrial Relations*,
Vol. 5, No. 1 (February 1966), pp. 38–52; Peter Feuille,
"Final Offer Arbitration and the Chilling Effect,"
Industrial Relations, Vol. 14, No. 3 (October 1975),
pp. 302–10; and Charles Feigenbaum, "Final Offer
Arbitration: Better Theory than Practice," *Industrial
Relations*, Vol. 14, No. 3 (October 1975), pp. 311–17.

[2]Henry S. Farber and Harry C. Katz, "Interest Arbitration, Outcomes, and the Incentive to Bargain,"
Industrial and Labor Relations Review, Vol. 33, No. 1
(October 1979), pp. 55–63. The assumption that
positive direct costs of arbitration (such as time and
attorney's fees) are negligible, made by Farber and
Katz, is retained in this analysis.

Industrial and Labor Relations Review, Vol. 35, No. 1 (October 1981). © 1981 by Cornell University.
0019-7939/81/3501-0070$01.00

SPLITTING-THE-DIFFERENCE ANALYZED 71

costs on the risk-averse parties, which give them the incentive to reach a negotiated settlement. Their model differs sharply from the split-the-difference school, however, in the sense that in their model the parties' positions have no effect on the arbitrator or the arbitration award. The arbitrator merely imposes what he or she considers to be an equitable settlement on the basis of exogenous criteria.

In this study two models of arbitrator behavior are developed in which the arbitrator has some exogenous notion of an equitable settlement and yet is also influenced to a certain extent by the positions of the parties. This would seem to be a more realistic representation of arbitrator behavior, and it has some important implications for the arbitration process.

In the first model, the arbitrator attempts to find an equitable compromise between the positions of the parties. The important feature of this model is that, while the arbitration outcome will look like a split-the-difference decision, the parties will actually take final positions that are located symmetrically around the arbitrator's notion of the equitable outcome. Thus, it is the expected arbitration outcome which determines the bargaining positions rather than the reverse.

In the second model, the arbitrator does not necessarily desire to fashion a compromise between the final positions of the parties, but he or she does impose a settlement that is some mix of the arbitrator's notion of the equitable award and the positions of the parties. In this model the uncertainty concerning the arbitrator's notion of the fair award is crucial, and it is shown again that it is the expected arbitration outcome that determines the bargaining positions of the parties rather than the reverse. It is also demonstrated that in the face of increased uncertainty concerning the arbitrator's notion of the equitable award, the parties will modify their positions to increase the weight that the arbitrator puts on the relatively certain positions of the parties. Finally, it is concluded that the size of the contract zone of potential settlements that both parties prefer to arbitration is reduced if the arbitrator does consider the positions

of the parties in the fashioning of the award. Thus, there is some truth to the notion that an arbitrator who is sensitive to the demands of the parties will chill bargaining.[3]

Throughout the analysis it will be assumed that the parties are expected utility maximizers and that bargaining takes place over the division of some unidimensional "pie" of fixed size.[4] Each party is assumed to have a well-defined cardinal utility function that orders the various splits of the pie.[5] The definition of an uncertain situation that is used below is one in which the precise outcome is unknown but the parties form well-defined expectations of the probability distribution of the various possible outcomes.[6]

---

[3]The size of the contract zone in the case in which the parties have identical expectations about the potential arbitration award is a measure of the total costs that the arbitration procedure imposes on the parties if it is utilized. If these costs are large it will be less likely that differences in expectations about the potential arbitration award will eliminate the contract zone and result in a failure to reach a negotiated settlement. In addition, a more costly arbitration procedure will be less likely to be used as a device by one party or the other to shift the blame for an unfavorable settlement to some outside party. Thus, the size of the contract zone in the case in which the parties have identical expectations about the arbitration award is one indicator of the ability of an arbitration procedure to encourage negotiated settlements. See Henry S. Farber, "An Analysis of Final-Offer Arbitration," *Journal of Conflict Resolution*, Vol. 24, No. 4 (December 1980), pp. 683–705 and Henry S. Farber, "Does Final-Offer Arbitration Encourage Bargaining," *Proceedings of the Thirty-Third Annual Winter Meeting of the Industrial Relations Research Association, 1980*, pp. 219–26, for more detailed discussions of these issues.

[4]Vincent Crawford, "Compulsory Arbitration and Negotiated Settlements," *Journal of Political Economy*, Vol. 87 (February 1979), pp. 131–60, analyzes arbitration schemes in situations that include disagreement over a number of distinct issues. This raises some interesting questions of the *ex post* Pareto efficiency of arbitrated awards.

[5]See R. Duncan Luce and Howard Raiffa, *Games and Decisions* (New York: John Wiley and Sons, 1957) for a more detailed exposition of this utility framework.

[6]This contrasts with a framework that draws a distinction between situations in which the agents have knowledge of a probability distribution of outcome (called risk) and situations in which the probabilities of outcomes are completely unknown or are not meaningful (called uncertainty). See Luce and Raiffa, *Games and Decisions* and James G. March and

Equitable Compromise

Suppose the arbitrator attempts to fashion an award that is an equitable compromise between the last offers of the parties. More formally, let

(1) $\qquad y_f = \alpha\, y_A + [1 - \alpha\,]y_B$

where y_A and y_B are the shares for party A that are yielded by the last positions of parties A and B, respectively. The shares yielded to party B are $1 - y_A$ and $1 - y_B$, respectively. The share y_f is the award to party A of the arbitrator, and it is a weighted average of the last offers of the parties. The parameter α defines the nature of the compromise and $0 \le \alpha \le 1$.

If the arbitrator always splits the difference by some constant fraction α, then each party will have the incentive to make its offer as extreme as possible. To demonstrate this formally let the utility of party A from the arbitration be $U_A(y_f)$ and note that party A has control over y_A. Differentiating $U_A(y_f)$ with respect to y_A yields the result that $\frac{\partial U_A}{\partial y_A} = \alpha\, U_A'(y_f)$, which is greater than zero for all values of y_A and y_B assuming positive marginal utility. Thus, A will demand all of the pie ($y_A = 1$). Analogously B will demand all of the pie ($1 - y_B = 1$ or $y_B = 0$) and the outcome will be extreme positions and an arbitration award of α to party A.

This model is unrealistic because there is no incentive for the parties to moderate their positions. The arbitrator is assumed to split the difference and the parties cannot alter that fact by modifying their positions. A more reasonable analysis would assume that the arbitrator has some exogenously derived notion of an equitable award to party A (y_e), which is used to some extent in fashioning the compromise. A natural way for y_e to enter the arbitration process is for the relative weight given to y_A and y_B (α and $[1 - \alpha]$ respectively) by the arbitrator to be a function of the reasonableness of the positions of the parties relative to y_e. More formally, let $\alpha = g(y_e - \frac{y_A + y_B}{2})$ where g is a mon-

Herbert A Simon, *Organizations* (New York: John Wiley and Sons, 1959), pp. 136–42.

otonically increasing function and $g(0) = 1/2$. Intuitively, this implies that if the average offer is exactly what the arbitrator feels is equitable, then $\alpha = 1/2$ and the award will be an equal split of the difference. The award will also be the arbitrator's notion of the equitable outcome, of course. If the average offer is greater than (less than) the equitable award, then α will be less than (greater than) $1/2$. In other words, the arbitrator attempts to offset what he or she considers a bias in the average offer by not splitting the difference equally: if one of the offers is high, the arbitrator will skew the compromise toward the lower offer and vice versa.

Given this model of arbitrator behavior, the optimal set of final positions for the parties can be derived. A natural definition of the equilibrium pair of final positions for this problem is that of a Nash equilibrium. Given that the parties are manipulating their respective offers so as to maximize their respective expected utilities, the Nash equilibrium pair of offers is the pair that has the property that neither party can achieve a higher expected utility by changing its offer.[7] Analytically, party A sets its last offer (y_A) so as to maximize its expected utility conditional on party B's last offer (y_B). Party B sets its last offer in an analogous fashion. The pair of final offers that simultaneously satisfies both these conditional maximization problems is the Nash equilibrium.

Assume for the moment that the parties know with certainty what the arbitrator thinks is fair (y_e). In this case parties A and B set their final positions so as to maximize $U_A(y_f)$ and $U_B(1 - y_f)$, respectively. The first-order conditions for maxima of these functions are

---

[7]See J.F. Nash, Jr., "Equilibrium States in N-Person Games," *Proceedings of the National Academy of Sciences of the U.S.A.*, Vol. 36 (1950), pp. 48–49.

If either party is attempting to do anything other than maximize its expected utility from the current arbitration, then this analysis is incorrect. For instance, one party may try to sabotage the long-run viability of the procedure by submitting very extreme offers because it feels that whatever dispute settlement mechanism would replace arbitration would make the party sufficiently well off to offset the loss of current utility due to the extreme offer.

(2) $\dfrac{\partial U_A}{\partial y_A} = U_A'(y_f)\,\dfrac{\partial y_f}{\partial y_A} = 0,$ and

(3) $\dfrac{\partial U_B}{\partial y_B} = -U_B'(1-y_f)\,\dfrac{\partial y_f}{\partial y_B} = 0,$

where these are two equations in the two unknowns (y_A and y_B). Using the definition of y_f in Equation 1, noting that $\alpha = g(y_e - \dfrac{y_A + y_B}{2})$, and rearranging terms yields

(4) $0 = \alpha - \dfrac{1}{2}\,[y_A - y_B]g'(y_e - \dfrac{y_A + y_B}{2}),$ and

(5) $0 = (1 - \alpha) -$

$\dfrac{1}{2}\,[y_A - y_B]g'(y_e - \dfrac{y_A + y_B}{2}\,).$

It is clear from these equations that $\alpha = (1 - \alpha) = 1/2$, which implies that the average final position is equal to the arbitrator's notion of the equitable outcome $\dfrac{(y_A + y_B)}{2} = y_e$.[8] Implicit in this equilibrium is the notion that if either party makes its offer more extreme, then the loss in the weight attached to its offer will offset any gain from the change in its offer.

This result has a very important implication for understanding the outcomes of bargaining under arbitration. It suggests that to all outward appearances the arbitrator can be described as splitting the difference between the parties equally, but that is *not* what he or she is doing in this model. In fact the causality is precisely the opposite. The parties are positioning themselves symmetrically around the arbitrator's preferred position.

Noting that $\alpha = 1/2$ and substituting into Equation 4 yields the result that

(6) $y_A - y_B = \dfrac{1}{g'(0)},$

which is the equation determining the difference between the final positions of the parties. The quantity $g'(0)$ represents how sharply the arbitrator is affected by devia-

tion from y_e of the average position of the parties. If the arbitrator is very sensitive to the position of the parties, then the parties' positions will tend to converge to y_e. If, on the other hand, the arbitrator is not sensitive to the positions of the parties, then the final offers will tend to diverge, as was pointed out in prior discussion.

A missing element from this discussion concerns the costs of arbitration. If, as Farber and Katz suggest, the major costs of arbitration come from uncertainty about y_e, then how uncertainty would affect this analysis needs to be considered.[9] While the role of uncertainty in the equitable compromise model will not be analyzed formally, uncertainty is given a central role in the model of equitable settlement (as opposed to compromise) that is developed in the next section.[10]

Equitable Settlement

One drawback to the equitable compromise model is that it forced the arbitrator to impose a settlement that was some sort of compromise between the positions of the parties. A more realistic model would have the arbitrator exercising more discretion in fashioning an award when the parties' offers are far apart while having the arbitrator be more heavily influenced by the positions of the parties when they are close together. In particular, the arbitration award might be a weighted average of the arbitrator's notion of an equitable settlement and the average position of the parties, where the weight on the parties' position is an inverse function of the difference between the final positions of the parties. The intuition behind this formulation is that the arbitrator will feel more constrained by the parties' positions when they are near agreement than when they are not.

To formalize this argument, let y_e represent the arbitrator's notion of an equitable award and let y_A and y_B represent the final

---

[8]This symmetric outcome is formally a result of the specification that y_A and y_B have identical effects on α.

[9]Farber and Katz, "Interest Arbitration, Outcomes, and the Incentive to Bargain."

[10]The equitable compromise model was analyzed in the case in which there is uncertainty about y_e, and the results are qualitatively identical to those derived in the next section for the equitable settlement model.

positions of the parties. The arbitration award (y_f) can be represented as

$$(7) \quad y_f = [1 - \gamma]y_e + \gamma \left[\frac{y_A + y_B}{2}\right]$$

where γ represents the weight the arbitrator puts on the positions of the parties. The quantity γ is specified to be a function of $y_A - y_B$. This is $\gamma = h(y_A - y_B)$ where $0 \leq \gamma \leq 1$, $h' < 0$, and $h(0) = 1$. Intuitively, as the parties' final positions diverge, the arbitrator pays progressively less attention to the obvious compromise solution ($\frac{y_A + y_B}{2}$) and more attention to his or her own preference (y_e). In the case in which the parties are close to agreement, γ is close to 1 and the arbitrator exercises little discretion.

As with the equitable compromise model the parties can affect the arbitration outcome by manipulating their final positions. Thus, it is necessary to derive the equilibrium pair of final positions the parties will reach. The same Nash equilibrium concept that was used above can be used here. In the absence of uncertainty concerning y_e, Equations 2 and 3 represent the first-order conditions for maxima of U_A and U_B, respectively. However, now y_f is defined by Equation 7 rather than by Equation 1. Using the definitions of y_f and γ, differentiating, and rearranging terms yields

$$(8) \quad 0 = \frac{\gamma}{2} + \left[\frac{y_A + y_B}{2} - y_e\right]h'(y_A - y_B), \text{ and}$$

$$(9) \quad 0 = \frac{\gamma}{2} - \left[\frac{y_A + y_B}{2} - y_e\right]h'(y_A - y_B).$$

These are the first-order conditions that determine the Nash equilibrium pair of final positions. Manipulation of these equations yields the result that $\frac{y_A + y_B}{2} = y_e$, which implies that $y_f = y_e$. In other words, the parties set their final offers so that the average is equal to the arbitrator's notion of the equitable award. This makes the actual arbitration award equal to y_e, and once again it appears as if the arbitrator is splitting the difference when according to this model the parties' offers are determined by the arbitrator's preferences.

A second conclusion that can be drawn from Equations 8 and 9 is that the arbitrator will put no weight on the offers of the party in equilibrium ($\gamma = 0$). This suggests that the final positions diverge to their limits and that $y_A - y_B$ approaches unity. This is not consistent with the evidence, and it suggests that an important element is missing from the model. It is necessary at this point to introduce uncertainty concerning what the arbitrator thinks is equitable.

To introduce uncertainty concerning y_e into the model, note that the parties are attempting to maximize their expected utilities. These are:

$$(10) \quad E(U_A) = {_0}\!\int^1 U_A(y_f)f(y_e)dy_e, \quad \text{and}$$

$$(11) \quad E(U_B) = {_0}\!\int^1 U_B(1 - y_f)f(y_e)dy_e$$

where $f(y_e)$ is the prior probability density function of the parties on y_e. Note that y_f as defined in Equation 7 is a function of y_e so that the expected utilities are rather complex. In order to demonstrate some of the properties of this model of arbitration, the model will be worked out in terms of particular parameterizations of the utility functions and the probability density function on y_e. In particular, let $U_A(y) = 1 - exp(-\delta_A y)$ and $U_B(1 - y) = 1 - exp(-\delta_B[1 - y])$ where these utility functions exhibit constant absolute risk aversion and the parameters δ_A and δ_B are the absolute risk aversions of the parties.[11]

It is further assumed that y_e is distributed normally with mean $\bar{y}_e$ and variance σ^2. This distribution has probability mass outside of the unit interval so that it is not strictly correct for the pie-splitting problem. If the variance is small enough and the mean is near the center of the interval, however, then the mass outside the 0-1 range will be small and the distortion will be minimal. Since y_f is the linear function of y_e defined in Equation 7, y_f is distributed normally with mean $\bar{y}_f = (1 - \gamma)\bar{y}_e + \gamma\left(\frac{y_A + y_B}{2}\right)$

---

[11]For an arbitrary utility function $U(x)$, absolute risk aversion is defined as $\delta(x) = -\dfrac{U''(x)}{U'(x)}$. See John W. Pratt, "Risk Aversion in the Small and in the Large," *Econometrica*, Vol. 32 (January-April 1964), pp. 122–36 for a discussion of the concept of risk aversion.

and variance $(1 - \gamma)^2 \sigma^2$. Finally, assume that the weight the arbitrator puts on the positions of the parties (γ) is defined by

(12) $\gamma = exp(- \lambda [y_A - y_B])$

where λ is a parameter that determines how quickly γ falls as the positions of the parties diverge. Note that if the offers of the parties are identical, then $\gamma = 1$.

Using the specifications of the utility functions and the distribution of y_f and the Laplace transform of a normally distributed random variable, the expected utilities are approximately

(13) $E(U_A) = 1 - exp \left\{ - \delta_A \bar{y}_f \right.$

$\left. + \frac{1}{2} \sigma^2 [1 - \gamma]^2 \delta_A^2 \right\},$ and

(14) $E(U_B) = 1 - exp \left\{ - \delta_B [1 - \bar{y}_f] \right.$

$\left. + \frac{1}{2} \sigma^2 [1 - \gamma]^2 \delta_B^2 \right\}.$

Differentiating these expressions for $E(U_A)$ and $E(U_B)$ with respect to y_A and y_B, respectively, using the definition of γ in Equation 12 and the definition of $\bar{y}_f$, noting that $\frac{\partial \gamma}{\partial y_A} = - \frac{\partial \gamma}{\partial y_B} = - \lambda \gamma$, setting the results equal to zero, and rearranging terms yields

(15) $0 = \left\{ \bar{y}_e - \frac{y_A + y_B}{2} - \sigma^2 [1 - \gamma] \delta_A \right\} \lambda + \frac{1}{2},$

and

(16) $0 = \left\{ - \bar{y}_e + \frac{y_A + y_B}{2} - \sigma^2 [1 - \gamma] \delta_B \right\} \lambda + \frac{1}{2}.$

These two equations define the Nash equilibrium pair of final positions.

Subtraction of Equation 15 from Equation 16 yields the result that

(17) $\frac{y_A + y_B}{2} = \bar{y}_e - \frac{1}{2} \sigma^2 [1 - \gamma] [\delta_A - \delta_B],$

which suggests that the average last position is skewed against the more risk-averse party relative to y_e. In addition, substituting into Equation 7 yields the result that

(18) $\bar{y}_f = \bar{y}_e - \frac{1}{2} \sigma^2 \gamma [1 - \gamma] [\delta_A - \delta_B],$

which suggests that the average arbitration

award is also skewed against the more risk-averse party. This is because the more risk-averse party takes a final position that is closer to the mean of the distribution of what the arbitrator thinks is fair than the less risk-averse party in order to reduce the disutility of a bad outcome on y_e.

Addition of Equations 15 and 16 yields the result that

(19) $\gamma = 1 - \dfrac{1}{\lambda \sigma^2 [\delta_A + \delta_B]},$

which implicitly defines $y_A - y_B$ through the definition of γ in Equation 12. Thus, the difference between the final offers is an inverse function of (and the weight the arbitrator puts on the position of the parties (γ) is a direct function of) the uncertainty concerning y_e (σ^2), the total risk aversion ($\delta_A + \delta_B$), and the rate of decay of the weight the arbitrator puts on the parties' positions (λ).

Given the concern that dependence of the arbitration award on the positions of the parties may chill bargaining, it is instructive to derive the contract zone of potential negotiated settlements that are preferred by both parties to arbitration.[12] The lower limit (y_L) is derived by finding the share that yields party A the same level of utility as A's expected utility from arbitration. This is derived from $U_A(y_L) = E(U_A)$. Similarly, the upper limit (y_U) is derived from $U_B(1 - y_U) = E(U_B)$. Party A will be willing to accept any offer greater than y_L rather than arbitrate, and party B will be willing to yield any demand less than y_U rather than arbitrate. The size of this contract zone is[13]

(20)
$CZ = y_U - y_L = \frac{1}{2} \sigma^2 [1 - \gamma]^2 [\delta_A + \delta_B].$

The important result is that the size of the contract zone is inversely related to the weight the arbitrator puts on the positions of the parties. In the limiting case where the arbitrator puts no weight on the posi-

[12]See note 3.

[13]The limits of the contract zone are

$y_L = \bar{y}_f - \frac{1}{2} \sigma^2 [1 - \gamma]^2 \delta_A$ and

$y_U = \bar{y}_f + \frac{1}{2} \sigma^2 [1 - \gamma]^2 \delta_B.$

tions of the parties ($\gamma = 0$ by definition), $CZ = \frac{1}{2} \sigma^2 [\delta_A + \delta_B]$, which is clearly larger than the contract zone in the case in which the arbitrator is sensitive to the parties. This suggests that there may indeed be some chilling of bargaining when the parties are aware that they can alter the arbitration award.

There may be another more fundamental reason why this type of arbitrator behavior may chill bargaining. Since y_A and y_B are the actual bargaining positions of the parties and the optimal positions for getting the most out of the arbitrator are such that $y_A > y_B$, it may be true that the parties will be reluctant to concede from these positions in an attempt to reach agreement. This is because they may fear getting caught with inferior positions for arbitration if agreement is not reached.[14] A potential remedy is to modify the arbitration process so that pre-arbitration bargaining positions are irrelevant to the arbitration decision.[15] Under such a closed-offer system, the parties would be prohibited from using any offers or counteroffers made during negotiations by either party as evidence in the arbitration hearing. Hence, the parties would have less reluctance to concede during negotiations because they would not fear damage to their prospects in arbitration.

Some insight into the role of uncertainty can be gained by substituting from Equation 19 for $1 - \gamma$ into Equation 20, which yields

$$(21) \qquad CZ = \frac{1}{2\sigma^2 \lambda^2 [\delta_A + \delta_B]}.$$

This is surprising because it implies that as the uncertainty (or the level of risk aversion)

rises, the size of the contract zone shrinks. The explanation is that in the face of increased uncertainty the parties act to reduce its impact by increasing γ. This shifts the weight of the arbitrator's decision from the uncertain value of y_e to the relatively certain positions of the parties. In the other direction, as the uncertainty falls, γ will decrease resulting in an increase in size of the contract zone until $y_A - y_B = 1$ after which further decreases in σ^2 will reduce the size of the contract zone.

The center of the contract zone (CCZ), which can represent the location of negotiated settlements, is[16]

$$(22) \qquad CCZ = \frac{y_U + y_L}{2} = \overline{y}_j -$$

$$\frac{1}{4} \sigma^2 [1 - \gamma]^2 [\delta_A - \delta_B]$$

$$= \overline{y}_e - \frac{1}{4} \sigma^2 [1 - \gamma]^2 [\delta_A - \delta_B].$$

It is clear that the center of the contract zone is skewed against the more risk-averse party both relative to the average arbitration award and to the mean of the prior distribution on y_e. However, the degree of skewness is smaller in the case in which the parties can influence the arbitration outcome ($\gamma > 0$) than in the case in which the arbitrator is not influenced by the parties ($\gamma = 0$) by definition.

Summary and Conclusions

The major conclusion to be drawn from this analysis is that it is not reasonable to model arbitrator behavior as a mechanical splitting of the difference without reference to some exogenous notion of an equitable award. Even when the arbitrator does consider the positions of the parties, the arbi-

---

[14]Final-offer arbitration (FOA) schemes are not subject to this criticism to the same degree as conventional arbitration schemes because in most FOA schemes the official final offers are distinct from the last bargaining positions of the parties. See Farber, "An Analysis of Final-Offer Arbitration," for a detailed analysis of FOA.

[15]For similar reasons Hoyt N. Wheeler, "Closed-Offer: An Alternative to Final-Offer Selection," *Industrial Relations*, Vol. 16, No. 3 (October 1977), pp. 298–305, has argued for precisely this modification.

---

[16]The determination of exactly what point within the contract zone the parties will agree on is beyond the scope of this study. The center was selected simply to summarize the location of the potential negotiated settlements. These results must be interpreted with caution because it may be true that the proportion of the contract zone that a party is able to capture in negotiations is a function of its risk aversion relative to the risk aversion of the other party.

SPLITTING-THE-DIFFERENCE ANALYZED   77

trator's notion of the equitable award is central in that it determines the positions of the parties rather than the reverse.

Another important implication of the analysis is that consideration of the positions of the parties by the arbitrator may chill bargaining for at least two reasons. First, the fact that the parties must consider how their concessions in bargaining will affect a possible arbitration award will reduce their willingness to concede. This suggests that a better procedure would be to ensure that the arbitration award is independent of the actual bargaining positions of the parties. One mechanism for doing this would be through use of a closed-offer arbitration procedure to allow the arbitrator to see only a special pair of final positions that the parties have formulated expressly for this purpose. The positions taken during bargaining would then be free to indicate true concessionary behavior unadulterated by any consideration of how they might affect the arbitration award.

The second reason why consideration of the positions of the parties by the arbitrator may chill bargaining is signalled by the fact that the size of the contract zone of potential negotiated settlements shrinks when the parties can influence the arbitration award. This is because the parties can mitigate the risk of the arbitrator having an unfavorable notion of an equitable award by moving their positions to put a smaller weight on the arbitrator's uncertain notion of the equitable award.[17]

In conclusion, the models developed here suggest that any arbitration procedure must rely on the arbitrator's exogenous notion of an equitable outcome. This notion will define negotiated settlements as well as arbitrated settlements even when the arbitrator is influenced by the positions of the parties. Empirical evidence that suggests that the arbitrator is merely splitting the difference may be misleading, as the true causal chain is likely to be that the parties have positioned themselves around the arbitration award.

---

[17]Final-offer arbitration is subject to this same phenomenon because the parties can mitigate the risk by submitting less extreme final offers. See Farber, "An Analysis of Final-Offer Arbitration."

[11]

NORMS OF DISTRIBUTIVE JUSTICE IN INTEREST ARBITRATION

MAX H. BAZERMAN*

This study uses a simulation methodology to analyze the use of three alternative norms of distributive justice by arbitrators in conventional interest arbitration. Sixty-nine experienced arbitrators each provided decisions in 25 hypothetical wage cases in which seven factors, such as the inflation rate and the ability to pay, were systematically varied. Individually, most arbitrators were very consistent in the weights they gave to these seven factors in their decisions across cases, but arbitrators differed significantly among themselves in the weight assigned each factor. Also, arbitrators' subjective assessments of their weighting policies often differed from their actual weighting practices. The most common norm followed by these arbitrators was "anchored equity": maintaining the status quo by adjusting the present wage by the average negotiated increase in the industry.

THIS paper presents a methodology and a set of empirical results that provide insight into the decision-making criteria arbitrators employ in labor disputes. The results also show the relationship of these specific criteria to more abstract norms of administering distributive justice, thereby suggesting how arbitration can work in resolving other kinds of disputes as well.

*The author is Associate Professor of Organizational Behavior at Northwestern University. Much of the work on this paper was completed while the author was on the faculty at the Massachusetts Institute of Technology. He thanks Elizabeth Lepkowski and Joel Adler for their excellent assistance in collecting and analyzing data. He also thanks for their insightful comments Thomas Kochan, Beber Helburn, John Carroll, James Dean, Henry Farber, Harry Katz, Robert McKersie, Margaret Neale, Gerald Rose, and the participants in the MIT Industrial Relations Workshop. This work was supported by a National Science Foundation grant.

Although arbitrators have in the past readily described how they decide cases, very little is known objectively about their actual decision processes. This gap in our knowledge inhibits the training of new arbitrators and also makes it difficult to predict how the use of arbitration will affect the outcomes of disputes over, for example, divorce, consumer affairs, and managerial decisions.

To develop a basis for such predictions or generalizations, this paper constructs a typology of norms of dispensing distributive justice that are generalizable to many types of conflict and yet specific enough to allow their use in a simulation of arbitrator decision making. The simulation employed here—an analysis of the decisions of 69 arbitrators in a set of 25 hypothetical wage disputes—identifies the relative importance of the three norms in arbitrators' resolution of labor-management disputes. The

Industrial and Labor Relations Review, Vol. 38, No. 4 (July 1985). © 1985 by Cornell University.
0019-7939/85/3804 $01.00

implications of these findings for the extension of arbitration to other dispute settings are then discussed.

Research Questions

Most recent studies of interest arbitration have analyzed the impact of alternative arbitration methods on negotiator behavior. The most important issue in this literature has concerned the extent to which conventional arbitration chills negotiation and whether some form of final-offer arbitration performs better in that respect.[1] The development of more effective methods of arbitration is an important and interesting problem, and indeed one aim of the present study is to examine the extent to which interest arbitrators split the difference between the parties' final offers in conventional arbitration.[2]

Most recent research has largely ignored, however, an equally important aspect of the arbitration process—the decision processes of arbitrators.[3] What evidence, for example, is most important to arbitrators? Is there consistency in the awards of a particular arbitrator, or across arbitrators, in the criteria that are important in award determination? The relevant literature does not address those critical questions, which are the primary focus of this study. To the extent that awards differ across arbitrators for reasons other than the facts of the cases, an added source of variation exists—the arbitration process.

Those questions raise, in turn, a more basic question, "What is a good judicial decision?" The principles that should govern the allocation of constrained resources, which is the arbitrator's task, have been a subject of debate among philosophers for centuries. Bird has noted, for example, that the classical utilitarian philosophers—Bentham, Mill, and Sidgwick—defined the purpose of social justice as the distribution of resources to achieve "the greatest satisfaction for the greatest number."[4] Keeley, however, has criticized this definition because it is difficult to translate into a measurable construct; because of the questionable validity of interpersonal comparisons of satisfaction among competing parties; because of the difficulty in assuring implementation of the stated goals; and because of the vague connection between aggregate social utility and system stability.[5] Each of Keeley's criticisms of the utilitarian position is relevant to the problem of defining social justice in the context of arbitration.

In addition, the classical philosophic principles of distributive justice deal with distribution among individuals, whereas the arbitration process distributes goods between the coalitions of union and management. Although the classical position may question the form of modern organizations, this paper examines the arbitrator's task given these organizations. With these criticisms in mind, this paper will explore how the problem of distributive justice is resolved in interest arbitration by specifying three alternative norms of dispensing distributive justice; by proposing a unique methodology for testing the reliance of arbitrators on the three norms; and by discussing the generalizability of those norms to models of distributive justice in other forms of conflict resolution by neutrals.

Elkouri and Elkouri's discussion of the arbitrator's function suggests that the best arbitrated resolution is one that is simultaneously equitable and completely acceptable to both parties, while also maximizing

[1]Carl M. Stevens, "Is Compulsory Arbitration Compatible with Bargaining?" *Industrial Relations*, Vol. 5, No. 2 (February 1966), pp. 38–50.

[2]This question is also examined by Max H. Bazerman and Henry S. Farber ("Arbitrator Decision Making: When Are Final Offers Important?", forthcoming in *Industrial and Labor Relations Review*) in their analysis of aggregate patterns of arbitrator judgment. Both papers use the same data base, but the present study is distinct in its focus on the variation that exists across arbitrators.

[3]There are a few important exceptions. See, for example, Orley Ashenfelter and David Bloom, "Models of Arbitration Behavior: Theory and Evidence," *American Economic Review*, Vol. 74, No. 1 (March 1984), pp. 111–24. Again, this paper investigates the general patterns of arbitrator behavior, whereas the present study examines the variation among arbitrators.

[4]Otto A. Bird, *The Idea of Justice* (New York: Praeger, 1967), pp. 118–60.

[5]Michael Keeley, "A Social-Justice Approach to Organizational Evaluation," *Administrative Science Quarterly*, Vol. 23, No. 1 (June 1978), pp. 272–92.

560   INDUSTRIAL AND LABOR RELATIONS REVIEW

the outcomes valued by both parties.[6] A bit of reflection suggests that this task is at best formidable and at worst impossible. These goals may not be simultaneously achievable and in some cases may be directly conflicting. What criteria do arbitrators actually use in making decisions? The three alternative norms of distributive justice delineated below suggest possible answers to this question.

Alternative Distributive Justice Norms

Absolute equity. The most commonly accepted norm in arbitration might be labeled "absolute equity." The absolute-equity principle follows from the social-psychological position of Deutsch, who suggests that in cooperative relations in which economic productivity is a primary objective, equity in an absolute sense should be the dominant principle of distributive justice.[7] The absolute-equity norm also underlies libertarian theories of justice, which argue that individuals are entitled to the resources that a free market provides.[8] Singer further argues that deviating from an equitable distribution reduces the incentives offered by a free market.[9]

In the context of collective bargaining, the absolute-equity norm closely approximates (and for our purposes will be measured by) the criteria of inflationary pressures on employees; the financial condition of the firm; and comparisons to similar firms. In essence, absolute equity requires that the contract terms should be determined according to an *absolute* comparison to those of comparable firms. With respect to wages, for example, this principle holds that, within certain constraints concerning the needs of employees and the

firm, wages in the firm in arbitration should match the actual wage levels in comparison firms, as opposed to matching only the rate of wage adjustments in comparison firms. Consistent with this logic, Kochan et al. found that comparison to the absolute wages of similar employees is the criterion that one group of interest arbitrators in New York State believed was most important in their decisions.[10]

Equality. In contrast to the arguments in favor of the absolute-equity principle, Rawls's egalitarian theory of justice holds that resources should be distributed equally except in those cases in which an unequal distribution would actually work to everyone's advantage.[11] This principle of equality, however, addresses the distribution of all resources (not just disputed resources) and the distribution of resources among all individuals (not coalitions) in a society. In this paper, the definition of the equality norm will be limited to the degree to which arbitrators equally divide *disputed resources* between the *defined coalitions* (union and management) in the dispute, that is, the extent to which they split the difference between the parties' final positions.

Starke and Notz provide moderately convincing evidence that arbitrators and students acting as arbitrators tend to split the difference in conventional arbitration,[12] but their anlaysis is based on the awards made in only a single case. In addition, Farber argues that a more accurate description of the process may be that the parties, in determining their final offers, position themselves around the expected arbitration award.[13]

Anchored equity. In addition to the philosophical tenets of absolute equity and

[6]Frank Elkouri and Edna A. Elkouri, *How Arbitration Works*, 3d ed. (Washington, D.C.: Bureau of National Affairs, 1976), pp. 53–56.

[7]Morton Deutsch, "Equity, Equality, and Need: What Determines Which Value Will Be Used as the Basis of Distributive Justice?" *Journal of Social Issues*, Vol. 31, No. 3 (1975), pp. 137–49.

[8]Robert Nozick, *Anarchy, State and Utopia* (New York: Basic Books, 1974), pp. 149–275.

[9]Peter Singer, "Rights and the Market," in John Arthur and William H. Shaw, eds., *Justice and Economic Distribution* (Englewood Cliffs, N.J.: Prentice-Hall, 1978), pp. 207–21.

[10]Thomas A. Kochan, Mordehai Mironi, Ronald G. Ehrenberg, Jean Baderschneider, and Todd Jick, *Dispute Resolution Under Factfinding and Arbitration: An Empirical Evaluation* (New York: American Arbitration Association, 1979), pp. 105–107.

[11]John Rawls, *A Theory of Justice* (Cambridge, Mass.: Harvard University Press, 1971).

[12]Frederick A. Starke and William W. Notz, "Pre- and Post-Intervention Effects of Conventional vs. Final Offer Arbitration," *Academy of Management Journal*, Vol. 24, No. 4 (December 1981), pp. 832–50.

[13]Henry S. Farber, "Splitting-the-Difference in Interest Arbitration," *Industrial and Labor Relations Review*, Vol. 35, No. 3 (October 1981), pp. 70–77.

equality, a third means of achieving distributive justice can be derived from the work of Kahneman and Tversky.[14] They suggest that humans have a systematic tendency to make judgments by selecting an "anchor" and making only minor adjustments from that anchor. In the arbitration context, this implies that decisions will be made by making adjustments from the natural anchor—the status quo. This maintenance of the status quo is evidenced by arbitrators who, in making decisions, think in terms of adjusting the *present wage* by the average *percent increase* in comparable firms.[15] When the present wage is higher or lower than that in comparison firms, following the anchored equity norm will result in ,awards distinctly different from those following the absolute equity norm. Indeed, choosing between anchored equity and absolute equity may be a common task arbitrators face in resolving conflicts in labor-management relations and in other settings.

The anchored-equity norm implies that the previous labor contract is a factor in the arbitrator's judgment, and the use of a percent-increase criterion means that the award will be influenced by previously existing conditions. This norm is consistent with the World War II Labor Board's decisional strategy, which explicitly gave great weight to maintaining the position of the firm and workers in their industry wage structures.[16] In addition, the anchored-equity norm is consistent with the stabilization goals for arbitration espoused by Taylor.[17] Extended use of arbitration under this stabilizing norm, however, would result in well-paid employees tending to stay well paid, while poorly paid employees stay poorly paid. Thus, absolute inequities in previous contracts are likely to remain to

the extent that arbitrators think in terms of matching percent adjustments rather than the actual wages in comparison firms.

The key distinction between the absolute-equity and anchored-equity norms is that absolute equity takes into account what the appropriate wage should be independent of the currently existing wage, whereas anchored equity accounts for what the appropriate percentage adjustment should be to the present wage. Arbitrators who follow the anchored-equity norm assume that there is a reason for present conditions, and they include that assumption in their judgments. Arbitrators who act on the basis of absolute equity view each situation as a clean slate and ignore the historical precedent of the present wage.

In addition to confusion over the norms that arbitrators actually engage in, there is diverse opinion about what arbitrators should do. Although the labor arbitration literature commonly subscribes to the concept of equity, it is less clear in distinguishing between absolute and anchored equity. And many scholars argue that the tendency to compromise (equality) is normal and appropriate behavior.[18]

Testing for the Alternative Norms

To test arbitrators' pursuit of the three norms of administering distributive justice, this study asked participating arbitrators to make quantitative award decisions that were then included in a regression analysis.[19] Their awards in a large number of cases were then categorized by a set of criterion factors, which in turn took on a number of values. If there are a sufficient number of cases in which the arbitrator makes an award and if each case is described by the same set of factors, a regression equation can be developed for the arbitrator that objectively describes his or her idiosyncratic model for arriving at arbitration

[14]See, for example, Amos Tversky and Daniel Kahneman, "Judgment Under Uncertainty: Heuristics and Biases," *Science*, Vol. 185, No. 4157 (September 1974), pp. 1124–31.

[15]These conclusions are based on a pretest of the experimental materials with practicing arbitrators. In fact, the idea for this norm of the status quo emerged from this pretesting process.

[16]Kochan et al., *Dispute Resolution*, pp. 1–2.

[17]George W. Taylor, "Voluntarism, Tripartitism and Stabilization," *The Termination Report of the National War Labor Board*, Vol. 1 (Washington, D.C.: GPO, 1945), pp. 178–82.

[18]C. M. Stevens, "Is Compulsory Arbitration Compatible with Bargaining?" *Industrial Relations*, Vol. 5, No. 1 (February 1966), pp. 38–50.

[19]See Paul Slovic and Sarah Lichtenstein, "Comparison of Bayesian and Regression Approaches to the Study of Information Processing in Judgment," *Organizational Behavior and Human Performance*, Vol. 6, No. 6 (November 1971), pp. 649–744.

awards. This methodological procedure, referred to as "policy capturing," has previously been used to investigate promotion policy, performance appraisal, and job choice.[20] Although many scholars have attempted to develop more complex representations of judgment, previous research has documented that the basic linear regression provides a robust representation of actual decision processes.[21]

While policy-capturing research has demonstrated its power in describing expert and nonexpert judgment, it has also shown that only moderate agreement typically exists between the objective weights used by raters (the weights they actually put on alternative factors) and the subjective weights (the weights raters think they put on alternative factors).[22] Further, subjective weights tend to underestimate the objective importance of major factors in decision making and overestimate the objective importance of minor factors.[23] Following this reasoning, we predict that arbitrators will perceive a more equal rating across factors than an objective analysis would indicate.

This study examines the three norms described above as contributors to the award decisions of arbitrators. In addition, the objective weights that arbitrators use will be compared to the subjective weights that they think they use. Also investigated here is the consistency of the objective weights across arbitrators.

Method

Subjects

Case simulations were mailed to the entire membership of the National Academy of Arbitrators (NAA) and the participants of a regional meeting of the American Arbitration Association (AAA) (N = 584), yielding 69 usable responses (61 from the members of the NAA and eight from members of the AAA, with 67 being men and two, women). The mean age of the respondents was 60 years. Based on self-reported data, the mean number of interest-arbitration cases that had been heard by the response group was 31, while the mean number of total arbitration cases heard by the response group was 989.

To compare this sample to the broader population of arbitrators, these data can be compared to those collected by Helburn and Rodgers, who obtained 286 responses from members of the NAA to a survey that required far less time from participants than this one.[24] Respondents in their sample had an average age of 60.5, which coincides with the expectations of individuals consulted by the author who are knowledgeable about this organization. The mean number of interest-arbitration cases heard by their respondents was 13.1, and the mean number of total arbitration cases was 295.3. Thus, the mean age of respondents in the present study is very similar to that of the larger sample, and their arbitration experience is significantly greater.

The low response rate is indicative of the problems facing the researcher investigating the decision processes involved in interest arbitration. To create a valid study, it was necessary to obtain a sample with substantial relevant experience. Yet, based on preliminary discussions with arbitrators and researchers, a number of problems were anticipated. First, the task requested of the arbitrators—to decide on a wage award in 25 hypothetical cases—required a considerable amount of time, a valuable commodity to successful arbitrators. Second, since the ratio of interest-arbitration to

[20]Steven A. Stumpf and Manuel London, "Capturing Rater Policies in Evaluating Candidates for Promotion," *Academy of Management Journal*, Vol. 24, No. 4 (December 1981), pp. 752–66; Sheldon Zedeck, "An Information Processing Model and Approach in the Study of Motivation," *Organizational Behavior and Human Performance*, Vol. 18, No. 1 (February 1977), pp. 47–77; and Daniel C. Feldman and Hugh J. Arnold, "Position Choice: Comparing the Importance of Organizational and Job Factors," *Journal of Applied Psychology*, Vol. 63, No. 6 (December 1978), pp. 706–710.

[21]Stumpf and London, "Capturing Rater Policies."

[22]Richard L. Cook and Thomas R. Stewart, "A Comparison of Seven Methods for Obtaining Subjective Descriptions of Judgmental Policy," *Organizational Behavior and Human Performance*, Vol. 13, No. 1 (February 1975), pp. 31–45.

[23]Slovic and Lichtenstein, "Comparison of Bayesian and Regression Approaches."

[24]From the author's personal correspondence with Professors Beber Helburn and Robert Rodgers of the University of Texas, Austin, Texas, 1983.

grievance-arbitration cases is quite low, individuals with little interest-arbitration experience were expected to decline participation in the study. Since those who did participate had much experience in interest arbitration, this expectation was confirmed. Third, and probably most important, preliminary discussions with arbitrators underscored the fact that many arbitrators do not believe that their decision-making behavior can be modeled or described by simulated cases. Vividly depicting this concern is the following correspondence with the author from an arbitrator who chose not to participate in the study:

... You are on an illusory quest: Other arbitrators may respond to your questionnaire; but in the end you will have nothing but trumpery and a collation of responses which will leave you still asking how arbitrators decide cases. ... Telling you how I would decide in the scenarios provided would really tell you nothing of any value in respect of what moves arbitrators to decide as they do. As well ask a youth why he is infatuated with that particular girl when her sterling virtues are not that apparent. As well ask my grandmother how and why she picked a particular "mushmellon" from a stall of "mushmellons." Judgment, taste, experience, and a lot of other things too numerous to mention are factors in the decisions.

In short, the decision to use the most experienced sample available for this study was intentional and made with the expectation of the considerable resistance and the low response rate that were obtained. These methodological trade-offs are critical ones that must be recognized in doing research of this kind.

Procedure

Each arbitrator was asked to judge 25 hypothetical interest-arbitration cases in which the only issue remaining unresolved was wages. Each was asked to specify the wage rate he or she would award in each case under conventional arbitration procedures.

The Cases

Each of the 25 hypothetical cases was described in a paragraph in terms of seven decisional criteria, such as the inflation rate or the current wage. For each criterion,

there were five possible amounts. The total set of 25 cases had five cases for each of the five levels of each criterion.

The simulations were set in the private sector, despite the fact that most experience in the United States with interest arbitration has been in the public sector. This choice was made for a number of reasons, the most important of which was that the private sector allowed greater diversity in the presentation of the 25 scenarios and thus created obvious experimental benefits over the use of public sector cases. In addition, interest arbitration was developed in the private sector, and its use in private sector labor relations has received attention from many who advocate its extension to other uses.

In order to maintain parallelism among the cases, while also providing necessary diversity, 25 industries were selected that in 1981 had average national wages that, after slight adjustments, formed a systematic pattern ranging in multiples of 5 percent from .4 to 1.6 times $8.66, where $8.66 was the mean of all 25 actual national average wages. This procedure allowed the wages awarded by arbitrators to be standardized to the $8.66 norm by multiplying the amount given in the award by the product $8.66 divided by the national wage.[25]

As noted, seven criteria were chosen for this study to represent the three norms of administering distributive justice discussed earlier: absolute equity; equality; and anchored equity. Three criteria[26] measured the *absolute-equity* norm: (1) *the inflation rate* was specified as 7, 9, 11, 13, or 15 percent;[27] (2) *the financial health of the firm*

---

[25] This procedure necessitates the exclusion of the national average wage from subsequent analyses. It did, however, allow for the manipulation of the variables as multiples of the national wage. The procedure is further described below.

[26] Other equity criteria exist, such as industry wage comparisons, but the number of factors investigated had to be limited to experimental purposes.

[27] In any experimental study of the importance of alternative criteria and norms, results are crucially dependent on the choice of levels for the independent variables. In this study, the levels chosen were based on extensive pretesting with practicing arbitrators. Thus, although the selection of levels may not be the best possible, every attempt was made to select face-valid levels within the constraints of the methodology.

was specified as terrible, poor, fair, good, or excellent; and (3) *the average wage in the local area* for similarly qualified employees was specified as the average national wage in the focal company's industry times 87, 94, 101, 108, or 115 percent.

Two criteria measured the *equality* norm:[28] (4) *management's final offer* was specified as the average national wage in the focal company's industry times 104, 105.5, 107, 108.5, or 110 percent; and (5) *the union's final offer* was specified as the average national wage in the focal company's industry times 111.5, 113, 114.5, 116, or 117.5 percent. Finally, two criteria measured the *anchored-equity* norm: (6) *the present wage* in the focal company was specified as the average national wage in the company's industry times either 96.5, 98, 99.5, 101, or 102.5 percent; and (7) *the average wage increase in other union contracts in the focal company's industry* was specified as 6, 8, 10, 12, or 14 percent.

Orthogonality (a correlation of 0.0) between all possible criteria was the guiding principle in the creation of 25 sample cases out of the 78,125 (5^7) possible cases.[29] Although orthogonality may not best approximate the natural state of these variables, it is easier to interpret the importance of alternative factors when there is no intercorrelation.[30]

The following is one of the 25 simulated cases:

In a town with 102,000 people,[31] workers with similar skills and backgrounds to the employees of this radio and broadcasting company were paid $8.31 per hour, while the national wage for this industry was $8.23 per hour. The financial outlook for this company is fair in light of the 11 percent inflation rate. The present average wage for this company's union is $8.44 per hour. Contract negotiations have reached an impasse. Both sides, however, have agreed to submit final offers to you, the arbitrator, and to be bound by your decision for a period of one year. Comparable pay increases from collective bargaining agreements in the industry are running about 8 percent this year. Management's final offer is $8.56 (a 1.4 percent increase), while the union's final offer is $9.55 (a 13.2 percent increase).

After the arbitrators rendered their awards in the 25 cases,[32] they assigned subjective weights to the seven criteria, plus an eighth category for "other considerations." The specific task required that the arbitrator allocate 100 points to the eight factors according to their relative importance in their award. Some of the comparisons that follow necessitate having the seven independent criteria (rather than the eight categories) add up to 100. To obtain this property, the weights of the seven independent criteria were adjusted by dividing the weight of each of the seven by the sum of the weights of all seven. The resulting seven adjusted subjective weights add up to 100. This procedure, previously used by Hoffman and by Zedeck and Kafry,[33] is easily understood and insures that subjective impressions are translated into numerical form without interpretation by the researcher.

---

[28]A different definition of equality could be based on the resistance points, rather than final offers, of the two parties. That definition, in turn, would result in a different definition of the point of equality if the parties' final offers are not equidistant from their resistance point. Also, final offers are easy to measure, whereas no satisfactory procedure exists for measuring resistance points.

[29]The group of 25 cases used in this study is only one of many possible sets of cases that would create perfect orthogonality between all seven criteria. Although care was taken to identify cases that would exhibit perfect orthogonality, the selection of this particular set over other orthogonal sets was arbitrary. More details on how this procedure is implemented are available from the author.

[30]Sheldon Zedeck and Dita Kafry, "Capturing Rater Policies for Processing Evaluation Data," *Organizational Behavior and Human Performance*, Vol. 18, No. 2 (April 1977), pp. 269–94.

[31]The size of the city or town had no systematic effect on the wages awarded. Moreover, this variable was not meant to measure any of the three norms of administering distributive justice.

[32]The cases were presented to each arbitrator in the same sequence, but this sequence was chosen randomly with respect to the criteria that were manipulated. In retrospect, a better approach would have been to present the cases to the arbitrators in different sequences in order to control for any effect that the order might have on the awards.

[33]Paul J. Hoffman, "The Paramorphic Representation of Clinical Judgment," *Psychological Bulletin*, Vol. 57, No. 2 (March 1960), pp. 116–31; and Zedeck and Kafry, "Capturing Rater Policies."

The Arbitrators

The arbitrators were then asked to provide data on their gender, age, the number of interest-arbitration cases they had heard, the number of total arbitration cases heard, their primary occupation (full-time arbitrator, professor, attorney with nonlabor practice, union advocate or attorney, management advocate or attorney, or other), and the fields in which they had received a graduate degree (law, economics, industrial relations, business, other, or none). Finally, arbitrators could give their names and addresses if they wished to receive a copy of the results. Anonymity was guaranteed; they returned their responses to the author in unmarked business-reply envelopes.

Analyses

A multiple-regression equation was computed for each arbitrator. The squared multiple correlation, R^2, indicates the consistency of the arbitrator's judgment across the 25 cases. Given the orthogonality of the seven independent criteria, zero-order correlations between each of the criteria and the wage award could be used to index the importance of each criterion for each arbitrator's overall wage judgments. To allow comparisons of weights among arbitrators and of objective to subjective weights, another index, relative weights, was developed to represent the relative importance of each criterion. This index represents the objective, implicit weights used by arbitrators.

Relative weights (RW) are computed as follows:[34]

$$RW_{is} = B_{is}r_{is}/R_s^2,$$

where RW_{is} is the relative weight of the ith criterion for the sth arbitrator; B_{is} is the beta weight of the ith criterion; r_{is} is the zero-order correlation between the ith factor and wage determination; and R_s^2 is the squared multiple correlation for the sth arbitrator. Since the sum of the relative weights is 1.0, Hoffman's index describes the relative contribution of the seven criteria as a proportion of the *predictable* linear variation. These relative contributions can then be compared to assess the explanatory power of each of the three norms of administering distributive justice. Multiplication of the relative weights by 100 permits a direct comparison between these objective weights and the subjective weights obtained from the 100-point allocation procedure.[35] Finally, the relative weights can be compared, averaged, clustered, or treated in other ways as new data, with the arbitrator treated as the unit of analysis.

Results

Table 1 presents the relative objective weights of each of the seven independent criteria for a sample of the 69 arbitrators. For example, 44.4 percent of the predictable variation in the awards of arbitrator A that can be explained by the seven manipulated criteria was accounted for by a single criterion: the financial health of the firm. Although relative weights are by definition positive, if the associated beta was negative (an unusual occurrence), it is so noted in the table. The column averages represent the average relative weights associated with each of the seven criteria. In general, one or two criteria accounted for the majority of the predictable variation for each arbitrator. Among all 69 arbitrators, the two most heavily weighted relative weights for each arbitrator (for example, for arbitrator A, the financial health of the firm and the present wage), on average, explained 72.4 percent of the predicted variation.

The R^2 associated with each arbitrator is also noted in Table 1, as well as the average R^2 across arbitrators. R^2 measures the degree to which an arbitrator's judgment can be consistently predicted by the seven linear criteria. These results show the participating arbitrators to be very consistent in making awards. Across all 69 arbitrators, the average R^2 was equal to .693; that is, the linear equation based on their judgments explained, on average, 69.3 percent of the variation in their award behavior.

---

[34]Hoffman, ibid.

[35] Zedeck and Kafry, "Capturing Rater Policies."

Table 1. Relative Weights[a] (and Simple Correlations[b]) for Each of the Independent Criteria, by Representative Arbitrator.[c]

Arbitrator	Inflation Rate	Financial Health of the Firm	Average Local Wage	Management's Final Offer	Union's Final Offer	Average Collective Bargaining Increase	Present Wage	R^2
A	0.0 (.00)	44.4[d] (.50)	0.0 (.00)	1.3 (.09)	2.8 (.13)	15.0 (.29)	36.4 (.45)	.5609
B	2.3 (.14)	40.8 (.59)	0.2 (.04)	2.9 (.16)	0.6 (.07)	4.8 (.20)	48.4 (.64)	.8486
C	0.7 (.07)	51.4 (.63)	5.5 (.21)	12.9 (.31)	4.6 (.19)	3.6 (.17)	21.3 (.40)	.7665
D	0.6[d] (−.06)	0.2 (.03)	45.4 (.53)	43.0 (.52)	1.7 (.10)	3.3 (.14)	5.8 (.19)	.6268
E	9.1[d] (−.23)	1.6 (.09)	37.5 (.46)	22.3 (.36)	1.5 (.09)	10.3 (.24)	17.7 (.32)	.5683
F	2.3 (.13)	22.9 (.42)	20.4 (.39)	25.4 (.44)	1.5[d] (−.11)	2.0 (.12)	25.5 (.44)	.7557
G	0.4[d] (−.06)	0.6 (.07)	0.0 (0.0)	0.0 (0.0)	0.3[d] (−.05)	66.9 (.74)	31.8 (.51)	.8123
H	0.2[d] (−.04)	0.1 (.03)	0.2* (−.04)	0.0 (0.0)	0.7[d] (−.08)	62.2 (.78)	37.1 (.60)	.9809
I	0.0 (0.0)	6.7 (.23)	0.0 (0.0)	6.1 (.22)	3.1 (.16)	58.7 (.69)	25.5 (.46)	.8202
Mean Across All 69 Arbitrators	4.0	20.6	7.4	12.7	3.7	21.2	30.5	.693

[a] Relative weights have been multiplied by 100 and can be read as a percent; e.g., for Arbitrator A, 44.4 percent of the explainable variation in the award is accounted for by the financial health of the firm.

[b] Zero-order correlations between the independent factor and the wage award.

[c] The results for all 69 arbitrators could not be included due to space limitations but are available from the author.

[d] Denotes that the relative weight is based on a negative regression coefficient.

The R^2 values ranged from a high of 1.00 to a low of .2018. Differences in the R^2 values were not significantly related to any of the demographic data collected.

Examination of the mean objective relative weights in Table 2 for the seven criteria shows that three criteria accounted for 72.3 percent of the explainable variation in award determination. Specifically, the present wage (30.5 percent), the average collective bargaining percent increase in the industry (21.2 percent), and the financial health of the firm (20.6 percent) were the salient factors, in the aggregate, to explain the judgments of arbitrators. This result suggests that the first two factors, which anchor judgments near the terms of the previous labor contract, are the most important bases for arbitrator judgment (accounting for 51.7 percent of the explainable variation). Further, arbitrators focused on the firm's ability to pay as the most important absolute-equity consideration. The other absolute-equity indicators and the final offers of union and management, in the aggregate, contributed little to the explainable variation in the judgments of this group of arbitrators.

Table 2 also compares the average objective weights (from Table 1) to the average

Table 2. Average Relative Objective and Relative Subjective Weights. (standard deviations in parentheses)

Criterion†	Objective		Subjective	
1. Inflation Rate	4.0	(7.1)	15.4	(9.3)
2. Financial Health	20.6	(16.8)	22.4	(15.9)
3. Average Local Wage	7.4	(13.9)	9.5	(7.3)
4. Management's Final Offer	12.7	(13.9)	8.9	(7.6)
5. Union's Final Offer	3.7	(5.2)	10.5	(7.6)
6. Average Collective Bargaining Increase	21.2	(18.3)	16.0	(14.5)
7. Present Wage	30.5	(17.7)	17.2	(11.1)
Total	100.1		99.9	

†The average relative objective and relative subjective weights differ at the .001 level for the first, fifth, sixth, and seventh criteria. The differences between the weights for the other three factors were not significant at the .05 level.

subjective weights that the arbitrators believe that they had used in making their awards. The data indicate the arbitrators believed that they used a more equal weighting policy than an objective analysis of their decisions suggests. Although the seven objective weights varied from 3.7 percent to 30.5 percent (range = 26.9 percent), the subjective weights varied only from 8.9 percent to 22.4 percent (range = 13.5 percent). This finding suggests that arbitrators claim that they are using a very complex decision process, but their actual decisions are often explainable in terms of a relatively small number of criteria.

This difference between objective and subjective weights is confirmed by comparing these weights for each of the seven independent criteria using univariate t-tests. The differences between objective and subjective weights were significant (p < .001) for four of the seven factors. As predicted, the most important objective factors (the present wage and the average bargained increase) were viewed as significantly less important by the subjective procedure, while the least important objective factors (the union's final offer and the inflation rate) were seen as significantly more important by the subjective procedure.

An important caveat in interpreting the mean relative weights is that the standard deviations associated with these means are large. Table 1 allows an examination of the decision-making norms of each of the sample arbitrators. In order to aggregate these results to describe the strategies of different groups of arbitrators, cluster analysis[36] was used to identify empirically three distinct clusters of arbitration practices based on the seven relative weights. Cluster analysis empirically groups individuals to maximize the similarity within each cluster, while simultaneously minimizing the similarity between clusters. Cluster A comprised 25 arbitrators (represented by arbitrators A, B, and C in Table 1), cluster B comprised of 14 arbitrators (arbitrators D, E, and F in Table 1), and cluster C comprised 30 arbitrators (arbitrators G, H, and

[36]Michael R. Anderberg, *Cluster Analysis for Applications* (New York: Academic Press, 1973).

Table 3. Cluster Mean Relative Weights.
(standard deviations in parentheses)

	Cluster					
Criterion†	A (N = 25)		B (N = 14)		C (N = 30)	
1. Inflation Rate	2.0	(2.8)	5.0	¦(9.4)	5.0	(8.3)
2. Financial Health	37.5	(13.0)	10.7	(10.9)	10.9	(8.5)
3. Average Local Wage	3.1	(3.4)	23.3	(17.2)	3.6	(4.1)
4. Management's Final Offer	13.0	(10.8)	25.4	(20.7)	6.4	(6.8)
5. Union's Final Offer	3.2	(4.4)	6.0	(6.4)	3.1	(5.0)
6. Average Collective Bargaining Increase	14.8	(9.5)	10.7	(10.8)	31.3	(21.9)
7. Present Wage	26.0	(13.5)	18.7	(13.7)	39.6	(18.2)
Total	99.6		99.8		99.9	

†Differences exist in the means of the three clusters for the second, third, fourth, sixth, and seventh criteria at the .001 level. The differences between means for the other two factors were not significant at the .05 level.

1 in Table 1). Table 3 displays the mean relative weights for each cluster.

Cluster A arbitrators weighted the financial health of the firm and the present wage most heavily in their awards; their cluster is therefore termed "organizational information." These two factors combine to account for 63.5 percent of the explainable variation in the judgment of cluster A arbitrators. Arbitrators in cluster B, termed "mixed model," weighted the present wage, the average local wage, and management's final offer most heavily. Characteristic of this group was their more equal weighting across the seven criteria. This group of arbitrators is most representative of the more complex model that arbitrators claim they use in giving subjective weights. Arbitrators in Cluster C, termed "anchored equity," weighted the present wage and the average collective bargaining increase in the industry most heavily. These two factors accounted for 70.9 percent of the explainable variation in the judgment of cluster C arbitrators.

To determine the significance and strength of the cluster differences, separate between-cluster ANOVAs and paired-cluster comparisons were conducted for each criterion. With the exception of the inflation rate and the union's final-offer, strong differences emerge between clusters on all of the remaining variables. Cluster A weighted the financial health of the firm significantly more heavily (p <

.001) than either of the other two clusters; cluster B weighted the average local wage and management's final offer significantly more heavily (p < .001) than the other two clusters; and cluster C weighted the average collective bargaining increase in the industry significantly more heavily (p < .001) than the other two clusters. And finally, cluster C gave the present wage significantly more weight than did cluster A (p < .001), while cluster A gave this criterion significantly more weight than cluster B did (p < .05). The clusters did not differ significantly on the basis of any of the demographic data collected.

Discussion

This study examined how arbitrators make judgments based on a variety of independent criteria to determine distributive justice in interest-arbitration cases. One result of the analysis showed that each arbitrator's judgment is, on average, very consistent across cases. Despite this consistency, the data also suggest that arbitrators do not have an accurate view of the decisional norms they follow. They tend to believe that they use more factors than the objective data suggest, and they tend to discount the critical role that one or two primary criteria play in their decision making.

Although this sample of arbitrators was extremely consistent in their own decisions, they greatly differed among one another.

Three distinct clusters of norms emerged from the data analysis. Cluster A based their judgments primarily on organizational information, that is, information that was obtainable from the firm as opposed to information about conditions external to the firm. Cluster B exhibited mixed norms in their awards. This group appeared to adjust the present wage according to local comparisons, while at the same time trying to award a wage consistently above management's final offer. Cluster C, the largest, exhibited an unexpectedly high amount of anchoring in their judgments. This group seemed simply to adjust the present wage in the firm by the average percent increase in the firm's industry.

In addition, the results strongly suggest that, for the most part, the final offers of the two parties do not play an important role in arbitrators' decision processes.[37] That finding does not mean that arbitrators primarily follow absolute-equity norms; rather, they are strongly influenced by the status quo. In each of the three clusters of arbitration polices, the present wage surfaced as an important criterion in wage determination; in fact, it was the only factor to be of major importance in all three clusters. This result suggests that many arbitrators focus on determining the equitable percent increase in wages, not on determining an equitable absolute wage. That norm tends to maintain rather than correct absolute inequities in the pay structure.

The finding that arbitrators are affected strongly by the anchored-equity norm suggests that conventional arbitration tends to produce a real wage rate very similar to that in the previous contract. Interestingly, although this study refutes the common criticism that conventional arbitration leads arbitrators to split the difference, which in turn leads to the chilling effect, the results pose another criticism of conventional arbitration. Specifically, if arbitrators follow an anchored-equity norm of distributive justice, conventional arbitration may inhibit

either party, or both, from correcting conditions that are inequitable when judged by some absolute standard. This criticism is particularly potent under economic conditions in which the definition of equality is changing faster than an anchored-equity norm can make corresponding adjustments. Alternatives such as final-offer arbitration may provide a better system for responding to change and setting new standards.

This study addresses a very different set of questions from those in the existing literature on arbitration, which has mainly tried to describe subjectively the complexity of the entire arbitration process. Instead, this analysis has objectively identified only a small piece of this process: the values underlying arbitrators' decision making. Future research should integrate the richness of previous research with the control and objectivity of this study. Furthermore, control and objectivity should be generalized to the study of grievance arbitration, final-offer arbitration, tripartite arbitration, and the arbitration of disputes outside the labor-management domain, such as divorce and consumer problems.

In interpreting the results of this study, care should be taken in generalizing the mean relative weights observed in the simulation to actual arbitration and other forms of judicial decision making. Nevertheless, the study does provide evidence of three norms of administering distributive justice that can be examined and measured in other third-party contexts; it demonstrates that neutrals are likely to exhibit wide variation in their norms of decision making; it suggests that Kahneman and Tversky's anchored-equity norm is also applicable to judicial decision making; and it introduces a valid methodology for studying third-party decision processes.

This analysis also raises a number of questions for the institution of arbitration and other uses of third-party intervention. Is it acceptable that widespread differences exist in norms of dispensing distributive justice? Is it acceptable for arbitrators to concentrate on the equitable percent increase in wages rather than on an equitable level of wages? What norms are most

---

[37]Somewhat similarly, Bazerman and Farber, in "Arbitrator Decision Making," find that arbitrators split the difference when, and only when, the two parties are already close to agreement.

and least desirable? And finally, what structural changes could be made in the training and certification of neutrals that would create the desired shifts, if any, in the decision-making norms used by neutrals?

Finally, this paper suggests a methodology for training new arbitrators, for identifying the decision-making norms followed by arbitrators, and for examining the impact of a variety of structural changes, such as the form of arbitration, on arbitrators' decisions. It is therefore not necessary to implement a legislative change before having a chance to predict the impact of that change. Low-cost simulation using experienced arbitrators as subjects may provide a wealth of information on the potential impact of a change on the decisions of arbitrators.

[12]

Sloan Management Review   Fall 1985   39

Analyzing the Decision-Making Processes of Third Parties

Max H. Bazerman
Henry S. Farber

Northwestern University
Massachusetts Institute of Technology

In this article, the authors raise a key question that has dominated the arbitration literature, "Can arbitration be taught, or is it simply an art form?" Through their analysis of how arbitrators actually make decisions, they reveal a number of findings: (1) arbitrators tend to make decisions that maintain the status quo; (2) arbitrators put greater weight on the offers of the parties when the parties' final positions are very close to agreement; (3) there is wide variation in the awards made by a homogeneous group of experienced arbitrators even when all the arbitrators are given the same facts; and (4) arbitrators do not have a very good idea of how they make decisions. They then discuss these findings in terms of their applicability to managers who may assume a third-party role in the decision-making process. Ed.

The importance of negotiation to managerial behavior has been recognized recently in both the academic and professional literatures.[1] In this article we argue that the study of third-party intervention is also an important and overlooked topic relevant to managers. Anytime two or more parties within one organization or in different organizations jointly make decisions and do not have the same preferences, they are negotiating. In addition, anytime the parties in the negotiation can bring in a third party (e.g., their manager), the decision processes of a third party become an important ingredient to the dispute. For example, the manager making a budgetary decision when choices must be made between conflicting interests in the organization is acting as a third party; the executive who must choose between two divisions concerning their mutual desire to enter the same market is acting as a third party; the judge making a decision between two corporations is acting as a third party; the president of the United States making a decision over a budget dispute between two branches of the government is acting in the role of a third party.[2]

The central role of third-party decision making has been recognized in an impressive array of managerial contexts, ranging from labor/management relations to budgetary decisions to the daily activities involved in managerial behavior.[3] Recent research has explored the effect of alternative forms of third-party intervention (e.g., arbitration versus mediation) and alternative methods of conflict resolution that can be used by a manager in a third-party role.[4] However, very little work has been done on the decision processes employed by third parties in making actual decisions. The central question that we address is: "What basis do third

parties use in deciding between the claims of the parties in the dispute?"

Conventional Arbitration

Our study limits the empirical analysis to one form of third-party intervention — conventional arbitration. Under conventional arbitration, if the parties do not reach agreement on their own, they are compelled to accept the decision of a mutually agreed upon third party. Thus, anytime a manager renders a final decision on a dispute between two subordinates, he/she is acting in the role of arbitrator under conventional arbitration. However, without knowing more about the actual decision processes of third-party experts, important barriers will remain in training new professional arbitrators, in training managers as third-party decision makers, and in analyzing how arbitration affects the negotiation process. While the empirical analysis is based on the decisions of labor relations arbitrators, we believe that important insights are provided on decision norms relevant to third-party decisions in a variety of organizational contexts.

Fisher and Ury argued that dispute intervention is a "growth industry."[5] Wall and Schiller documented the overloads that exist in the court system and proposed alternative third-party mechanisms for dealing with disputes outside the courts.[6] Rubin called for greater attention to the training of third-party skills.[7] These scholars argue for the need to train additional arbitrators and managers in third-party skills. This leads to the question of what form of training is appropriate. What is it that we can tell arbitrators and managers about third-party decision making?

Ample evidence suggests that third-party intervention is a valid topic for research by

Max H. Bazerman is Associate Professor at the Kellogg Graduate School of Management of Northwestern University. Dr. Bazerman holds the B.S. degree from the University of Pennsylvania and the M.S.O.B. and Ph.D. degrees from Carnegie-Mellon University. He (with Henry S. Farber) is the recipient of the Edwin E. Ghiselli Award for Research Design from the American Psychological Association and a grant from the Sloan School of Management's 1990s Project to study negotiating transactions in the service sector. Dr. Bazerman is on the editorial board of the *Academy of Management Journal* and the *Journal of Occupational Behavior* and a contributing reviewer to many leading journals. He is the author of *Negotiating in Organizations* and the forthcoming *Judgment in Managerial Decision Making*, as well as articles appearing in such journals as *Journal of Occupational Behavior*, *Academy of Management Journal*, and *Journal of Applied Psychology*.

social scientists, yet the training of arbitrators is viewed as an art form, and scientific answers to the above questions have not been forthcoming.[8] Students, therefore, are given minimal scientific guidance and are encouraged to learn the process through observation of the practice of arbitration — often in the form of an apprenticeship. Although we believe that the study of the intuitions of arbitrators is important, we also believe that the science of arbitration is equally important, despite the fact that it has been overlooked.

How to Learn from Arbitrator Decision Making

A number of benefits can be gained from heeding our findings of how professional arbitrators arrive at decisions.

1. Examine Objective Decision Processes of Arbitrators

Arbitrators have provided accounts of how they make decisions.[9] Unfortunately, much evidence exists to support the arguments that arbitrators are not very good at explaining how they make decisions,[10] although they have unwarranted confidence in their fallible explanations of their decision processes.[11] Still, by examining the objective (actual) decision processes of arbitrators, we learn to: (1) understand important determinants of their decision processes; (2) evaluate the accuracy of subjective reports of third-party decision processes; and (3) develop a better understanding of how negotiators would bargain if they acted rationally and fully understood the arbitration system that was in effect.

2. Provide Feedback and Training

Just as any feedback helps an individual learn, feedback on how one actually arbitrates provides information that may influence the arbitrator's subsequent decisions. In addition, a fair question from the student of arbitration is: "What factors really affect your decision?" We provide evidence

demonstrating that the factual answer from most arbitrators is, "I don't know." In contrast, our methodology begins to answer the student's question.

3. Identify How Arbitrators Make Decisions

The willingness of negotiators to make concessions depends on what they expect to receive if they do not reach agreement. If arbitration is invoked when the parties fail to agree, negotiator behavior will be affected by the expected behavior of the arbitrator.[12] In earlier studies, we have shown that negotiator judgment is systematically distorted in ways that reduce the parties' likelihood of reaching agreement.[13] Part of this distortion is based on divergent and optimistic expectations between the parties concerning the likely behavior of a third party.[14] Therefore, if we can identify how arbitrators actually make decisions, we will be able to train negotiators in ways that will improve their ability to predict arbitration awards and their likelihood of reaching mutually agreeable resolutions.

Five Key Questions

By focusing on a number of central questions that are relevant for understanding the behavior of third parties, we highlight many of the important debates that exist in the arbitration literature.

1. What factors are most important in the decision processes of arbitrators? Elkouri and Elkouri suggest that the optimal arbitrated resolution would be one that is (1) equitable, (2) completely acceptable to both parties, and (3) efficient in the sense that no alternative solution exists that makes at least one party better off without making the other party worse off.[15] Unfortunately, creating such an award is a formidable task at best and impossible at worst. These goals may not be simultaneously achievable and in some cases may be directly conflicting. More concretely, two specific norms have typically dominated the discussion of factors af-

Sloan Management Review　　　　　　　　Fall 1985　　　　　　　41

Henry S. Farber is Associate Professor in the Department of Economics at M.I.T. Dr. Farber holds the B.S. degree from Rensselaer Polytechnic Institute, the M.S. degree from Cornell University, and the Ph.D. degree from Princeton University. He is currently Research Associate at the National Bureau of Economics, a Member of the Visiting Committee, Department of Economics, Princeton University, and Associate Editor of the *Quarterly Journal of Economics*. Dr. Farber has written widely on many aspects of the economics of labor unions. His articles have appeared in such journals as *American Economic Review*, *Journal of Political Economy*, *Econometrics*, and *Industrial and Labor Relations Review*.

fecting the decisions of arbitrators — equity and equality. The most commonly accepted norm is equity. The equity position suggests that decisions should be based on a set of comparable standards. This is consistent with the social psychological position of Deutsch, who suggests that in cooperative relations in which economic productivity is a primary objective, equity should be the dominant norm by which agreements are reached.[16] While our society may argue in favor of the equity principle, Starke and Notz posit that actual arbitrators tend to follow a norm of equality by splitting the difference between the last offers of the parties under conventional arbitration (where the arbitrator is free to impose any settlement).[17] We provide empirical evidence regarding the extent to which arbitrators actually split the difference.

Our research also explores a third norm, which has not been recognized in the literature on dispute resolution by third parties — that is, how arbitrators administer distributive justice. This norm is derived from the decision research of Tversky and Kahneman, who suggest that individuals have a systematic tendency to make judgments by selecting an anchor (e.g., last year's contract) and making only minor adjustments from that anchor.[18] This maintenance of the status quo is consistent with arbitrators who suggest that they think in terms of (1) percent increases to the present wage and (2) comparisons to percent increases of contracts of comparable firms in making awards. Many arbitrators would argue that using the present wage as an anchor is typically "fair." However, in cases where the present wage is inequitable, the anchoring will tend to maintain the inequity that existed in the previous contract.

2. When do arbitrators split the difference between the offers of the parties? It has been suggested that arbitrators tend to split the difference between the last offers of the parties in conventional arbitration.[19] Farber argues that arbitrators fashion awards based both on external factors (e.g., comparable

wages, inflation, financial condition of the firm) and on the last offers where the relative weight of the offers depends on their quality.[20] Consider two dimensions of the quality of the offers. The first is the average of the offers (the split-the-difference solution). It may be the case that this coincides relatively closely with what the arbitrator thinks is reasonable based on the external factors. In this case there is no real distinction between splitting the difference and making an award based on the external factors. However, if the average of the offers is far from what the arbitrator thinks is reasonable, then the arbitrator may deviate from the split-the-difference solution. The second is how near the parties are to agreement (the difference between the last offers). It may be the case that when the parties are near agreement, the arbitrator perceives little discretion in making an award. On the other hand, when the parties are far from agreement, the arbitrator may not perceive the offers as conveying important information and may ignore them in determining the appropriate award. Thus, this question examines the possibility that there are systematic determinants of when the arbitrators split the difference.

3. Does arbitrator behavior cause a "chilling effect" in negotiation? While the use of conventional arbitration has been increasing, critics have suggested that it might have a number of negative effects on the negotiation process.[21] The most important of these is that the arbitrator may "split the difference," which can encourage negotiators to avoid concessions.[22] Such a "chilling effect" would occur to the extent that the disputing parties will attempt to take advantage of the arbitrator's split-the-difference behavior by maintaining a polar position. The chilling effect is viewed as a major limitation in the use of conventional arbitration as a third-party dispute mechanism. Our central concern is to determine the extent to which concern over the chilling effect has any basis in the actual behavior of arbitrators. If substantial splitting-the-difference behavior is found, then there may be cause for concern

that conventional arbitration does chill bargaining. On the other hand, if no splitting-the-difference behavior is found, then it is reasonable to conclude that the actual behavior of arbitrators is not responsible for a chilling of bargaining. However, false beliefs by negotiators could still lead to a chilling effect.

Note that the observation that arbitration awards in actual cases generally are consistent with a split-the-difference rule for arbitrator behavior is not sufficient evidence to conclude that arbitrators, in fact, split the difference. This is because the offers of the parties are subject to manipulation by the parties, and they are likely to reflect the parties' expectations regarding the likely decision of the arbitrator.[23] In other words, the (expected) arbitration award may exert a strong influence on the offers rather than the offers exerting a strong influence on the award. We will present evidence regarding the relationship between the offers and the arbitration award that is not subject to this sort of ambiguous interpretation.

4. Is there consistency across the decisions of professional arbitrators? One justification for the existence of the institution of arbitration is that it is a judicial system for the "fair" resolution of disputes. This would imply that there is consistency across arbitrators in the criteria they use to make decisions so that the outcome does not arbitrarily depend on the identity of the arbitrator in a particular case.

Another justification for the existence of arbitration (or any other dispute settlement mechanism) is that it supplies an incentive for the parties to reach agreement on their own by imposing costs on the parties in the event they fail to agree. Farber and Katz argue that arbitration imposes costs primarily on the basis of uncertainty regarding what the arbitration award will be.[24] To the extent that there is consistency across arbitrators in the criteria they use to make awards, there will be less uncertainty than in the case where arbitrators differ greatly and the parties are uncertain as to the identity of the arbitrator in a particular case.

The two justifications for arbitration outlined here require opposite degrees of consistency. On grounds of fairness, the arbitrators ought to be consistent. In order to create uncertainty, the arbitrators ought to be inconsistent. Clearly, it is important to determine how much consistency there is across arbitrators in order to determine the balance that has been struck between these competing goals for arbitration. We will present evidence regarding the degree of consistency that exists across professional arbitrators.

5. Do arbitrators know what they do? Arbitrators have readily expressed their subjective views about the decision processes of arbitrators. However, the behavioral decision theory literature repeatedly shows only moderate agreement between the objective decision processes of decision makers and their subjective reports of their decision processes.[25] In addition, research suggests that decision makers claim more complicated models with more factors being important than objective analyses dictate. That is, it is common for a variety of experts to claim a greater degree of required sophistication than what actually exists. Thus, the decision talents of arbitrators may be more trainable than is suggested by the "art form" perspective of arbitration that many arbitrators hold.

Rationale for a Simulation Methodology

Some authors (e.g., Ashenfelter and Bloom) have attempted to understand how arbitrators make decisions by modeling the decisions of arbitrators in actual cases.[26] While these studies are very useful, we believe that data based on actual cases have serious limitations for specifying the factors that influence arbitrator judgment. These limitations exist since the facts of the case (those variables that we define as representing the equity and anchoring norms) are likely to affect the parties' offers. Thus, in evaluating the impact of the offers of the parties on an arbitrator's decisions, the researcher cannot distinguish between a direct effect of the offers and a statistical artifact created by the offers being correlated with other relevant information that is not measured explicitly by the researcher.

The simulation approach that we take, where arbitrators are asked to decide carefully designed hypothetical cases, is not susceptible to this criticism because the facts available to the arbitrator are strictly controlled and they are all observed by the researcher. Thus, any correlation between the offers and the arbitration award can be attributed to a direct effect of the offers on the award. We gathered data from sixty-nine practicing arbitrators (members of the National Academy of Arbitrators and the participants of a regional meeting of the American Arbitration Association) who were asked to decide the same set of twenty-five hypothetical cases. The mean number of actual interest arbitration cases previously heard by the response group was 31, while the mean number of total number of arbitration cases heard by the response group was 989. In each case, arbitrators were asked to provide the wage that would be awarded under a conventional arbitration scheme.

In addition to using a unique approach, our research attempts to answer different questions from past research. Most of the existing literature tried to describe subjectively the complexity of the entire arbitration process. This study uses an objective procedure to identify only a small piece of this process — how arbitrators integrate the factors they deem relevant in fashioning an award. Future research should integrate the richness of past research with the strengths of the current research. Further, the sort of approach used in the current research could be used to examine grievance arbitration, final offer arbitration, tripartite arbitration, and arbitration outside the labor-management domain (e.g., divorce, managerial behavior, etc.).

A Hypothetical Study: The Wage Structure

Each of the twenty-five hypothetical cases was described by a precisely controlled set of information regarding seven orthogonally manipulated factors. Three factors represented issues associated with an *equity norm* of distributive justice and were related to economic considerations:

— The inflation rate was stated to be either 7%, 9%, 11%, 13%, or 15%;

— The financial health of the firm was stated to be either terrible, poor, fair, good, or excellent; and

— The average local wage for similarly qualified employees was stated to be equal to the average national wage in the industry (which was provided to the arbitrator) times either 87%, 94%, 101%, 108%, or 115%.

Two factors represented issues associated with an *equality norm* of distributive justice:

— Management's final offer was stated to be equal to the average national wage in the industry times either 104%, 105.5%, 107%, 108.5%, or 110%; and

— The union's final offer was stated to be equal to the average national wage in the industry times either 111.5%, 113%, 114.5%, 116%, or 117.5%.

Finally, two factors represented issues that are argued to represent an *anchoring norm* of distributive justice:

— The present wage was stated to be equal to the average national wage times either 96.5%, 98%, 99.5%, 101%, or 102.5%; and

— The average wage increase of other contracts in the industry was stated to be 6%, 8%, 10%, 12%, or 14%.

The cases were created such that each of the independent variables had a correlation of zero with each of the other independent variables. Multivariate analyses for each arbitrator and for the aggregate of all arbitrators were run to determine answers to the five central questions specified earlier.[27]

Table 1   **Average Relative Importance of the Seven Manipulated Factors**

Variable	Relative Importance Weights
Inflation Rate	4.0
Financial Health of the Firm	20.6
Average Local Wage	7.4
Management's Final Offer	12.7
Union's Final Offer	3.7
Average Arbitrated Increase in the Industry	21.2
Present Wage	30.5
Total	99.9

Note: The summation of the seven factors to 100 (99.9) is artificially created to increase our ability to compare the relative importance of the seven factors. A more detailed description of this procedure is provided in M.H Bazerman, "Norms of Distributive Justice in Interest Arbitration," *Industrial and Labor Relations Review*, in press.

Answers to the Five Key Questions

1. Important Factors in Arbitrator Decision Making

The arbitration literature has been concerned about whether decisions are affected by an equity or an equality norm. Overall, our results suggest that the final offers of the parties, for most arbitrators, play only a very small role in their decision processes. However, our study did not suggest that arbitrators use equity norms exclusively. While the equity norms were found to be important, arbitrators were found to be strongly affected by the status quo — the anchoring norm. Arbitrators were highly affected by the present wage. More specifically, the results imply that many arbitrators determine the equitable percent increase, rather than the equitable wage. Arbitrators do not correct past inequities in the structure of pay; rather, they maintain existing inequities. These conclusions are based on the data in Table 1, which shows the average percent of variation accounted for (out of the total variation

explained by regression analysis for each of the sixty-nine arbitrators) in the decisions of the arbitrators by each of the seven manipulated factors. At one level, this suggests that arbitrators follow a very conservative strategy that in some situations might appear to be unjust. However, arbitrators are quick to defend their choice by arguing that the existing wage structure represents a stable and workable situation that the parties themselves would be unlikely to alter on their own. The use of the anchoring norm is also consistent with the World War II Labor Board's strategy of explicitly deciding to give great weight to maintaining the position of the firm and workers in their industry wage structure.

Regardless of one's evaluation of this strategy, the use of the strategy suggests that conventional arbitration will lead to a wage structure that is very similar to the status quo. Interestingly, while these results refute the common criticism that conventional arbitration leads arbitrators to split the difference, it raises the alternative criticism that arbitrators are primarily following an anchoring norm that may prevent an industry from responding adequately (even through negotiation) to large changes in the economic environment.

2. When Do Arbitrators Consider the Offers of the Parties?

While arbitrators are not primarily motivated by a split-the-difference rule, the results suggest that some attention is paid to the offers of the parties. Our findings show that the tendency of arbitrators to split the difference depends significantly on the degree of difference between the parties' final positions. Arbitrators rely more heavily on the offers in the case when the parties are near agreement. One explanation for this may be that where the parties are near agreement (offers are close together), the arbitrator realizes that any award far from the offers is not likely to be acceptable to the parties or workable in practice. On the other hand, when the parties are not near agreement (offers are far apart), there is no clear consensus

Sloan Management Review   Fall 1985   45

between the parties as to what is acceptable or workable. In this case the arbitrator has more discretion.

3. Does Arbitrator Behavior Cause a Chilling Effect?

The finding that the weight the arbitrator puts on the offers of the parties in making awards is affected by the quality of the offers suggests that there are limits to the degree to which the parties can manipulate the arbitration award by manipulating their offers. (This is true for both interpretations outlined above.) For example, if the union's offer is extreme (high), then a further increase may lead the arbitrator to ignore the offers of the parties or skew the "split" toward the management offer. Thus, the simple reasoning behind the "chilling effect" can be rejected. It does not make sense to assume that the arbitrator will simply split the difference. Nor does it make sense to assume that negotiators follow this false logic to the extreme and make unreasonable offers.

These findings suggest that the argument for the chilling effect makes sense within a limited range — under which the arbitrator is paying attention to the offers of the parties and not skewing the "split." Thus, the argument that negotiators stay extremely far apart in expectation of the arbitrator's compromise is based on a misunderstanding of the role that the offers play in arbitrator decision making. The evidence noted above, that it appears that arbitration awards split the difference between the offers, could be interpreted in light of our results as the reverse: the parties formulate their offers on the basis of the expected arbitration award.[28]

4. Is There Consistency across Arbitrators?

Each of the above sections addressed questions regarding general patterns across our group of experienced arbitrators. This section addresses the question of whether arbitrators follow a common strategy of dispute resolution. The answer is "no." Large differences were found across arbitrators concerning wage awards — even though all

arbitrators examined the exact same data. In addition, considerable evidence suggests that *substantial* differences exist among arbitrators concerning which factors arbitrators weighted most heavily across the twenty-five cases. These differences were observed in the relatively sterile confines of controlled simulated cases. It is expected that the complexities of actual cases would further differentiate how arbitrators deal with the complex task of integrating the various pieces of information that affect an arbitrator's judgment.

When labor relations scholars discuss the determinants of an arbitration award, they often identify the various factors involved in the case. This study suggests that differences between arbitrators may be important determinants of how cases are decided, even within an apparently homogeneous group of arbitrators. These differences (which are tracked by many organizations) may be manifested not only in a bias toward union or management but also in how arbitrators weight factors involved in the decision. This raises a host of questions concerning whether the training of arbitrators should create stronger norms regarding the importance of varying factors or whether uncertainty due to the arbitrator is a healthy ingredient in the arbitration process.[29]

5. Do Arbitrators Know What They Do?

Our research *objectively* assessed the weights that each arbitrator attached to each manipulated factor. In addition, we asked each arbitrator to report *subjectively* the weight that he or she attached to each factor. The agreement between these weights assesses the degree to which arbitrators "know what they do." The data suggest that most arbitrators do *not* have an accurate view of their decision policies. They tend to think that they use more factors than the objective analysis suggests. Further, arbitrators tend to deemphasize the critical role that one or two primary factors play in their judgment. Thus, arbitrators tend to describe a more complicated decision than their actions dictate.

How to Interpret the Findings

The use of the simulation methodology has provided a number of unique advantages. However, it also raises potential limitations of the study — especially concerning the issue of generalization. Are the results relevant to actual arbitration cases in the labor-management area? Are the results relevant to third-party decisions of managers? The former question was critically discussed in a confidential communication that we received from a nonparticipating member of the targeted sample of arbitrators:

> You are on an illusory quest! Other arbitrators may respond to your questionnaire, but in the end you will have nothing but trumpery and a collation of responses which will leave you still asking how arbitrators decide cases. . . . Telling you how I would decide in the scenarios provided would really tell you nothing of any value in respect of what moves arbitrators to decide as they do. As well, ask a youth why he is infatuated with that particular girl when her sterling virtues are not that apparent. As well, ask my grandmother how and why she picked a particular "mushmellon" from a stall of "mushmellons." Judgment, taste, experience, and a lot of other things too numerous to mention are factors in the decisions.

This expressive arbitrator clearly argues that the work reported cannot capture the arbitration process. But is this correct? We think not. Simply because arbitrators cannot articulate what it is they do, does not mean that they do not act in a consistent fashion that can be uncovered through a careful examination of their decisions. Our analysis uncovered strong and persistent relationships between arbitration awards and the specific factors that were manipulated in the simulations. If the arbitrator quoted here was correct, then we would not be likely to find the sort of strong relationships that we, in fact, find. It is predicted that many of the results (the maintenance of the status quo, the inconsistency across arbitrators, etc.) would generalize to actual cases. Equally important, as we earlier argued, is the fact that actual cases cannot be used for an exploration of some of these questions due to the confounding of the offers with unobserved facts.

What the Results Mean to Managers

It is also important to address the degree to which the current research can be assumed to generalize to managerial decision making. If these results fully generalize to the third-party decisions, a number of new findings would be available to the managerial community. Such generalizations would imply that managers (1) tend to maintain the status quo in their dispute resolution efforts; (2) pay attention to conflicting subordinate positions only when they are already close to agreement; (3) have wide variation in their third-party decision policies (even within a specific organization); and (4) have little idea of the policies that govern their choices. While caution should be exercised in over-generalizing the specific results of our work, our results certainly identify a set of issues worthy of managerial thought. Managers would be well advised to at least consider whether the results of our arbitrators are relevant to describing their third-party decisions and the third-party decisions of other managers in their organization.

In addition to providing these speculative conclusions concerning managerial third-party decision making, this study also has important implications for the training of managers as third parties. We no longer need to treat third-party intervention as an art form. We can develop managerial simulations that allow us to examine how experienced managers make decisions between conflicting subordinates. We can use the systematic analyses illustrated in this article to give managers feedback as to how they actually make decisions, which may be contradictory to how they think that they make decisions. And we can highlight some of the common patterns of decisions that may not be in the best interest of the organization. For example, maintaining the status quo, a common finding in our study, is a strategy of questionable validity for managers under changing environmental conditions. Only by systematically understanding what managers and other parties actually do can we identify important observations worthy of managerial attention.

Sloan Management Review Fall 1985 47

This article was written while Dr. Farber was a fellow at the Center for Advanced Study in the Behavioral Sciences. He received support for his research from the National Science Foundation under Grants Nos. SES–8207703 and BNS 76–22943 and from the Sloan Foundation as an Alfred P. Sloan Research Fellow. Dr. Bazerman received support for his research from the National Science Foundation under Grant No. BNS 81–07331.

Conclusion

This study examined a number of questions concerning the decision processes of arbitrators. In addition, it offers a very different approach for understanding third-party intervention. We argue not that this is the right research approach, but that this research approach complements previous work that has sought to explain the arbitration process. Further, this research raises a number of critical questions concerning third-party intervention. Is it acceptable that experts arrive at very different decisions given an identical set of facts? If not, what can be done to change this? Is it acceptable that managers may think in terms of an appropriate adjustment to previous practices, rather than in terms of the optimal resolution in an absolute sense? Are there norms of distributive justice that are not acceptable for managers to follow? How does the understanding of third-party decision making affect the behavior of negotiators? And finally, what do the answers to these questions suggest for the training of new arbitrators and the training of managers in their role as third party?

References

1
H. Mintzberg, "The Manager's Job: Fact and Folklore," *Harvard Business Review*, July–August 1975, pp. 49–61;
R. Fisher and W. Ury, *Getting to Yes* (Boston, MA: Houghton-Mifflin, 1981);
H. Raiffa, *The Art and Science of Negotiation* (Cambridge, MA: Harvard University Press, 1982);
M.H. Bazerman and R.J. Lewicki, eds., *Negotiating in Organizations* (Beverly Hills, CA: Sage Publications, 1983).

2
W.W. Notz, F.A. Starke, and J. Atwell, "The Manager as Arbitrator: Conflicts over Scarce Resources," in *Negotiating in Organizations*, ed. M.H. Bazerman and R.J. Lewicki (Beverly Hills, CA: Sage Publications, 1983).

3
H.S. Farber and H.C. Katz, "Interest Arbitration, Outcomes, and the Incentive to Bargain," *Industrial and Labor Relations Review* 33 (1979): 55–63;
J.Z. Rubin, "The Use of Third Parties in Organizations: A Critical Response," in *Negotiating in Organizations*, ed. M.H. Bazerman and R.J. Lewicki (Beverly Hills, CA: Sage Publications, 1983);
Notz, Starke, and Atwell (1983).

4
J. Brett and S. Goldberg, "Mediator-Advisers: A New Third Party Role," in *Negotiating in Organizations*, ed. M.H. Bazerman and R.J. Lewicki (Beverly Hills, CA: Sage Publications, 1983);
M.H. Bazerman and M.A. Neale, "Heuristics in Negotiation: Limitations to Dispute Resolution Effectiveness," in *Negotiating in Organizations*, ed.
M.H. Bazerman and R.J. Lewicki (Beverly Hills, CA: Sage Publications, 1983);
B.H. Sheppard, "Managers as Inquisitors: Some Lessons from the Law," in *Negotiating in Organizations*, ed. M.H. Bazerman and R.J. Lewicki (Beverly Hills, CA: Sage Publications, 1983).

5
Fisher and Ury (1981).

6
J.A. Wall and L.F. Schiller, "The Judge Off the Bench: A Mediator in Civil Settlement Negotiation," in *Negotiating in Organizations*, ed. M.H. Bazerman and R.J. Lewicki (Beverly Hills, CA: Sage Publications, 1983).

7
Rubin (1983).

8
D. Pruitt and J.Z. Rubin, *Social Conflict: Escalation, Impasse, and Resolution* (Reading, MA: Addison-Wesley, 1985);
Raiffa (1982).

9
C.B. Donn, "Games Final Offer Arbitrators Might Play," *Industrial Relations* 16 (1977): 306–314;
G. Swimmer, "Final Position Arbitration and Intertemporal Compromise: The University of Alberta Compromise," *Relations Industrielles* 30 (1975): 533–536;
M. Ryder, "The Impact of Applicability on the Arbitrator," *Academy of Arbitrators* 21 (1968): 94–108.

10
S. Zedeck and D. Kafry, "Capturing Rater Policies for Processing Evaluation Data," *Organizational Behavior and Human Performance* 18 (1977): 269–294.

11
B. Fischhoff. "Debiasing," in *Judgment under Uncertainty: Heuristics and Biases*, ed. D. Kahneman, P. Slovic, and A. Tversky (New York: Cambridge University Press, 1981).

12
Farber and Katz (1979);
H.S. Farber, "An Analysis of Final-Offer Arbitration," *Journal of Conflict Resolution* 5 (1980): 683–705;
H.S. Farber, "Splitting-the-Difference in Interest Arbitration," *Industrial and Labor Relations Review* 35 (1981): 70–77.

13
Bazerman and Neale (1983);
M.H. Bazerman, "Negotiator Judgment: A Critical Look at the Rationality Assumption," *American Behavioral Scientist* 27 (1983): 211–228.

14
M.H. Bazerman and M.A. Neale. "Improving Negotiation Effectiveness under Final Offer Arbitration: The Role of Selection and Training," *Journal of Applied Psychology* 67 (1982): 543–548.

15
F. Elkouri and E.A. Elkouri, *How Arbitration Works*, 3rd ed. (Washington, DC: Washington Bureau of National Affairs, 1976).

16
M. Deutsch, "Equity, Equality, and Need: What Determines Which Value Will Be Used as the Basis of Distributive Justice?" *Journal of Social Issues* 31 (1975): 137–149;
F.A. Starke and W.W. Notz, "Pre- and Post-Intervention Effects of Conventional vs. Final Offer Arbitration," *Academy of Management Journal* 24 (1981): 832–850;
A. Tversky and D. Kahneman, "Judgment under Uncertainty: Heuristics and Biases," *Science* 29 (1974): 176–184.

17
Starke and Notz (1981).

18
Tversky and Kahneman (1974).

19
C.M. Stevens, "Is Compulsory Arbitration Compatible with Bargaining?" *Industrial Relations* 5 (1966): 38–50;

P. Feuille, "Final Offer Arbitration and the Chilling Effect," *Industrial Relations* 14 (1975): 302–310;
C. Feigenbaum, "Final Offer Arbitration: Better Theory Than Practice," *Industrial Relations* 14 (1975): 311–317.

20
Farber (1981).

21
T.A. Kochan, "Collective Bargaining and Organizational Behavior Research," in *Research in Organizational Behavior*, Vol. 2, ed. B.M. Staw and L.L. Cummings (Greenwich, CT: JAI Press, 1980).

22
Stevens (1966).

23
Farber (1981).

24
Farber and Katz (1979).

25
R.L. Cook and T.R. Stewart, "A Comparison of Seven Methods for Obtaining Subjective Descriptions of Judgmental Policy," *Organizational Behavior and Human Performance* 13 (1975): 31–45.

26
O. Ashenfelter and D.E. Bloom, "Models of Arbitrator Behavior: Theory and Evidence," *American Economic Review* 74 (1984): 111–124.

27
For more details on the methodology, analytical procedures, and detailed estimates, see:
M.H. Bazerman, "Norms of Distributive Justice in Interest Arbitration," *Industrial and Labor Relations Review*, in press;
M.H. Bazerman and H.S. Farber, "Arbitrator Decision Making: When Are Final Offers Important?" *Industrial and Labor Relations Review*, in press.

28
Farber (1981).

29
Farber and Katz (1979).

[13]

ORGANIZATIONAL BEHAVIOR AND HUMAN PERFORMANCE 34, 97–111 (1984)

The Effects of Negotiation and Arbitration Cost Salience on Bargainer Behavior: The Role of the Arbitrator and Constituency on Negotiator Judgment

MARGARET A. NEALE

University of Arizona

Recent literature reports a reliance on third-party intervention procedures in contract negotiation. This study suggests that the relative evaluation of the costs related to arbitration (such as the uncertainty and expense of arbitration), and the costs related to negotiation (such as loss of face or perceived incompetency) provide a partial explanation for the increasing frequency of the negotiator's use of arbitration procedures rather than reaching a negotiated settlement. The relative salience of negotiation-related costs (high and low) and the relative salience of arbitration-related costs (high and low) were manipulated in a 2 × 2 design, involving 147 subjects negotiating a five-issue contract. The results were consistent with the hypothesized relationships. Implications of the results of this study for improving the understanding of and control over negotiator behavior are discussed.

In the area of bargaining and negotiation, there seems to be a reliance on neutral third-party intervention to settle controversial issues (Berry, 1982; Burger, 1982; Feuille, 1975; Kochan & Baderschneider, 1978; Thomas & Schmidt, 1976; Wheeler, 1975). This finding is in opposition to typical bargaining model predictions which suggest that if negotiators were rational utility maximizers, all negotiations would end in resolution at the point that maximizes the product of the utilities of each participant (Nash, 1950; Zeuthan, 1930) or when a positive contract zone—a set of outcomes which would be preferred over the imposition of a strike—exists (Walton & McKersie, 1965). However, negotiators often fail to reach agreement even when positive contract zones exist (Walton & McKersie, 1965).

This position suggests, and observation confirms that economic models do not fully account for negotiator behavior. With few exceptions (Bazerman & Neale, 1982; Neale & Bazerman, 1983), the literature has not

This research was supported by Grant SS-48-82-05 from the Social Science Research Council. Correspondance and requests for reprints should be directed to Margaret A. Neale, Department of Management and Policy, College of Business and Public Administration, University of Arizona, Tucson, AZ 85721. The author particularly thanks Max Bazerman, Greg Northcraft, Gerrit Wolf, and two anonymous reviewers for their helpful comments on earlier drafts.

98   MARGARET A. NEALE

specified the ways in which negotiators make decisions concerning out-come alternatives. The purpose of this paper is to explore systematic ways in which negotiators emphasize a personal cost/benefit analysis over an organizational cost/benefit analysis by resorting to third-party impasse resolution procedures rather than reaching a negotiated settlement. More specifically, this paper attempts to explain the negotiator's tendency to invoke arbitration even when the costs associated with arbitration exceed the greatest potential the party can expect to gain or when the negotiator can do no better objectively in the arbitral outcome than the opponent's final offer.

Costs and Benefits of Arbitration and Negotiation

While the reliance on third-party intervention techniques applies to mediation, factfinding, and arbitration, it has particularly intriguing implications in the more constraining form of interest arbitration procedures.[1] In the realm of collective bargaining, arbitration as an alternative to the strike exists in both the public and private sectors. Because most legally organized public sector employees are legislatively denied the right to strike, arbitration often serves as the substitute (i.e., compulsory arbitration). In the private sector, parties may agree in advance to arbitrate differences in the terms of subsequent agreements (i.e., voluntary arbitration) (Elkouri & Elkouri, 1979). Regardless of its compulsory or voluntary nature, arbitration provides an impartial third party to decide a final, binding outcome to the dispute within the constraints of the form of arbitration used. In either compulsory or voluntary arbitration, it is typically viewed as an alternative to the strike which preserves the balance of power between management and labor (Anderson, 1980).

Theoretically, in order for arbitration to be effective in promoting negotiated settlements, it must exact a price for its use in much the same way that a strike penalizes both the company (through lost production) and the employees (through lost wages). The existence of a strike potential creates a contract zone within which any settlement is preferred to taking the strike. Arbitration, because of its potential costs, must also create a contract zone as does the potential for a strike. The costs, in part, associated with arbitration consist of (1) the increased uncertainty of the outcome because of the third party, (2) the fees and expenses of the arbitrator, (3) the additional time and expense incurred by the parties, and (4) the lower quality of arbitrated outcomes (Crawford, 1979).

---

[1] Arbitration in disputes of the basic terms and conditions of employment is "interest arbitration." Arbitration of disputes involving the interpretation or application of laws, agreements, or customary practices is termed "rights arbitration" (Elkouri & Elkouri, 1979). For the purpose of this study, arbitration refers solely to interest arbitration.

COST SALIENCE AND NEGOTIATOR BEHAVIOR   99

One of the basic assumptions of arbitration is that its costs are critical in its effectiveness as an impasse resolution procedure. It must serve as a deterrent to impasse and be rarely invoked (Farber & Katz, 1979; Feuille, 1975). Thus, a critical issue in the effectiveness of arbitration is to determine how negotiators evaluate the costs of invoking arbitration relative to the costs of reaching a negotiated settlement.

Although arbitration is usually described in terms of its costs, there are aspects of the arbitration procedure which may make resorting to arbitration more attractive. Probably the primary benefit of arbitration, specifically, and third-party intervention, generally, is that its use transfers the responsibility of the outcome to the third party and away from the two negotiating parties. The negotiator is usually representing a diverse group of individuals (in the case of collective bargaining, the union membership or the company) whose goals and expectations are not easily reducible to one particular demand package. Thus, the negotiator is faced with a set of expectations and evaluations by each member of his/her constituency as to what a successful outcome would be. Optimizing outcomes across such a diverse set of demands, in this case, is likely to increase the attractiveness of arbitration by removing such an impossible task from the shoulders of the negotiator. Relatedly, negotiators have used the threat of arbitration to gain sufficient freedom to continue the negotiation without the burden of close scrutiny by the constituency.

A negotiated settlement is typically conceptualized in terms of benefits rather than costs. The benefits can most easily be described in terms of the negotiator control over the outcome. Negotiated settlements are generally perceived as being superior to settlements produced by third parties because of their (1) certainty (each negotiator knows in advance to what it is s/he is agreeing), (2) increased sense of control over and responsibility for the outcome, and (3) the increased quality of the negotiated contract in comparison to one fashioned by a third party (Crawford, 1979; Stevens, 1966; Wheeler, 1978).

The costs of negotiation are those primarily associated with the participant's evaluation by the constituency or an opponent. Particularly important in this evaluation are the costs associated with the "bargainers' dilemma" (Podell & Knapp, 1969). That is, negotiators are perceived as weak if concessions are made, but concessions are necessary if a negotiated settlement is to be obtained. Associated with the evaluation by constituency of the negotiator's concessionary behavior is the concern with the imposition of sanctions. Constituency-imposed, objective sanctions could typically include loss of position or refusal by the constituency to ratify the tentative contract. Less obvious, but more pervasive, are those subjective costs relating to the perception of competency of the negotiator by his/her constituency and/or opponents. These more ambig-

100   MARGARET A. NEALE

uous costs of negotiation become particularly vivid to the individual who is less likely to negotiate a package which meets the expectations of his/ her constituency (or is seen by the opponent as incompetent).

These subjective cost evaluations may seriously affect how the negotiator assesses his/her options, particularly when the costs of arbitration are assessed on an organizational basis while those of negotiation are assessed on a personal basis. That is, the costs of arbitration are typically paid by the organization while the costs of poor negotiation, by the negotiator. Thus, prior to impasse, this negotiator may be primarily concerned with the immediate, personal costs of failing to secure a contract which is sufficiently attractive to his/her constituency. The need of the negotiator to appear competent may so strongly dominate the negotiator's attention as to reduce the current valuation of any future costs of impasse resolution procedures to relative insignificance. That is, it may lead the negotiator to ignore a realistic cost/benefit evaluation of the situation, which might evaluate the costs to the individual and the organization in a quite different manner.

Outcome Salience and the Cost/Benefit Evaluation

The salience or vividness of costs associated with negotiation and arbitration may provide some insight into the behaviors of negotiators. Tversky and Kahneman (1973) suggest that the inappropriate use of certain simplifying decision strategies or judgmental heuristics are responsible, in large measure, for observed deviations from rationality in human decision making. Of particular interest here is the judgmental strategy known as the availability heuristic—the ease of retrieval from memory, imagination, or perception of a particular event's occurrence (Tversky & Kahneman, 1973). Of the three explanations for the misapplication of this heuristic (bias because of ease of retrievability, of search effectiveness, or of illusory correlation), the bias because of ease of retrievability is directly related to the issue of salience and vividness of the information. In its correct application, the availability heuristic provides the following rule: events that are recalled easily are more frequently occurring than less easily recalled events. However, when information is particularly vivid or salient to an individual, it is also more easily retrieved from memory, independent of frequencies. Thus, because this particular heuristic links ease of retrievability and frequency of occurrence, information which is highly salient to the individual will be perceived as more frequent or likely to occur. The vividness of personal costs associated with negotiation such as loss of face or perceived incompetence is likely to be greater than the vividness of organizational costs associated with arbitration. Nisbett and Ross (1980) provide support for this asymmetrical cost assessmer.c in suggesting that the vividness depends upon the extent to which the information is emotionally interesting or concrete and image producing.

From this explanation, it is expected that the comparative salience of these two costs for the negotiator will systematically affect negotiator behavior. For example, if the negotiator's constituency is quite adamant in their demands for increased paid vacation days and the opposing negotiator is unwilling to meet this demand completely, then the negotiator is predicted to be more likely to invoke arbitration rather than accept an opponent's less than complete capitulation. As the negotiator's goal is to maximize expected utility (the *organization's* expected utility) for the final contract, the pressure by different members of the constituency to maximize their particular goals (which may be inconsistent with organizational goal maximization) may seriously influence the appraisal of the expected utility of a particular, potential settlement. This may result in a nonrational choice of outcomes. The costs of arbitration can be affected, for example, by arbitrator behavior. The less information there is about the arbitrator or the arbitration process, the greater the uncertainty as to the arbitral outcome. Were the costs of arbitration to be made particularly salient to the negotiator, s/he is expected to deviate in the direction of choosing a negotiated settlement when the objective assessment of the situation would indicate arbitration.

Based upon this perspective, the behavior of the negotiator should reflect his/her evaluation of the outcome-related costs. That is, negotiators to whom the arbitration costs are more vivid should behave in a more concessionary manner. Because of this concessionary tendency, they should also experience greater success in reaching a negotiated settlement. Further, because negotiated contracts are usually superior to contracts developed by a neutral third party (Crawford, 1979; Elkouri & Elkouri, 1979), the outcome should be a contract of greater perceived value than that obtained through the intervention of a third party. Negotiators who value highly the benefits of arbitration should reflect this choice in their behavior. They would be expected to demonstrate less concessionary behavior resulting in a greater incidence of impasse. Further, because a third party determines the outcome in case of impasse, the overall level of perceived outcome success in terms of the value of the contract should not be so great.

HYPOTHESES

From this discussion, a number of specific predictions can be made concerning the effect of the differential salience of negotiation- and arbitration-related costs on negotiator behavior. Formally stated, the following hypotheses are proposed.

102   MARGARET A. NEALE

    I. Negotiators to whom negotiating costs are highly salient will behave in a less concessionary manner and secure less successful outcomes than will negotiators to whom the costs of negotiation are less salient.

   II. Negotiators to whom the costs of arbitration are highly salient will behave in a more concessionary manner and secure more successful outcomes than will negotiators with less salient arbitration costs.

METHODS

Subjects were 147 undergraduate students (67 females and 80 males) enrolled in an introductory personnel course at the College of Business Administration at the University of Texas. They were told they were participating in a study of bargaining behavior.

A 2 × 2 factorial design was employed. Factor A was the salience of negotiation costs while Factor B was the salience of arbitration costs. Because of the nature of the manipulations, confederates were used extensively. The subjects were assigned to the management negotiating team. The other two team members of each management negotiating team were confederates as was the union negotiator. There were eight confederates (four males and four females) who participated in the research. The confederates were rotated through the role of the union negotiator and the management team member. Prior to the negotiation, the confederates participated in 2 weeks of training to ensure their negotiating strategies were consistent. While in the management team role, regardless of condition, they were given the same "target" aspiration level. Of course, this only represented a target because the third member of the team—the subject—would also have input. The union confederates, who were blind to the experimental condition of their opponents, were trained to conduct their negotiations based upon the reciprocity norm (Esser & Komorita, 1975). They matched the concessions of their opponents to the break-even point of the contract, based upon their net benefits. If their opponents did not agree to a settlement prior to or including the break-even point, the negotiations would cease and arbitration would be invoked.

Once the management negotiating team was present, they were asked to draw lots to choose a member to be the primary negotiator. The subject was always chosen as the primary negotiator while the confederates composed the team. All three members of each team received an information packet consistent with their assigned role and condition in the simulation. The bargaining situation was a revision (Grigsby & Bigoness, 1982) of Campbell's (1960) bargaining simulation. Participants were told they would be negotiating a five-issue contract in face-to-face bargaining with the primary negotiator of the union negotiating team. The five issues were hospital and medical plan, night shift differential, wages, vacation pay, and paid sick days. Each issue was presented with a scale of possible settlement points and participants were instructed to make their bids conform to those points. The net benefits (the value of that particular settlement point for the represented organization) for the company and the union were asymmetric to each other to prevent the negotiators from dividing the issues in the middle in lieu of actual bargaining. Further, the issue of vacation pay was more important to the union and night shift differential was more important to the company.

The differential salience of the costs of negotiation was manipulated prior to the development of the management team goals through the constituency's (team's) control of the reward structure of the primary negotiator. In the low-salience condition, the primary negotiator received a predetermined amount ($5) of money, regardless of his/her performance. In the high-salience condition, the primary negotiator received monetary compensation after the contract was determined ranging from $0 to $10 based upon the evaluation of his/her performance by the remaining team members (the confederates). The confederates evaluated the subjects such that the average dollar value of the compensation ($5) across subjects was equal to the reward of $5 of the low-salience condition which was not contingent upon behavior. The subjects were unaware of this constraint.

In order to manipulate the salience of arbitration costs, the management team in the high-salience condition had the costs and inherent uncertainty of arbitration carefully explained to them and engaged in a discussion of the relation of these costs to their behavior. The major points in this explanation included (1) the degree of uncertainty introduced into the process by the third party and the loss of control over the outcome, (2) the fees charged by the arbitrator which were to be split by the parties, (3) the time required by the negotiating team and related personnel to participate in the arbitral process, and (4) the lowered quality of the final contract which was related to the loss of control over the outcome. Subjects in the low-salience condition were informed of the costs of arbitration and were given the same dollar costs (fees) as those in the high-salience condition, but they were not involved in a subsequent discussion of the costs.

After the induction, the three management team members agreed on what the final contract would resemble in terms of particular settlement points. Then the primary management negotiator and the (same sex) union negotiator (confederate) were paired in a separate room to begin their negotiations. The primary negotiators were aware that their "team" members were observing their behavior through a one-way mirror. Only in the high-salience condition was there any mention of formal evaluations being conducted based upon these observations. All dyads were aware that if they did not reach agreement on all five issues, the current contract indicated that the unresolved issues would be submitted to final offer arbitration.

During the negotiation phase, subjects and confederates were observed to be quite involved in the actual bargaining process. Findings of previous work with this simulation (without monetary incentives) consistently showed high subject involvement with and commitment to the assigned role and task by a large majority of the participants. At the end of the 20-min interaction, participants who had not reached resolution were asked to submit a final offer to the arbitrator. The arbitrator was a decision rule. The choice of offers was made in favor of the party that evidenced the greater rate of concessions. Neither the subject nor the confederate were aware of the arbitrator's decision rule. Upon receiving the arbitrator's award, they completed a short questionnaire which assessed the arbitration manipulation. Dyads who reached agreement were asked to provide a signed copy of the final contract and complete a short manipulation-check questionnaire.

The hypotheses concerned the prediction of concessionary process and successful outcomes. The dependent construct of concessionary process was a combination of (1) the number of issues resolved and (2) the concessionary rate. The concessionary rate was the dollar difference between the negotiator's original position on the five issues and the sum of the net benefits for all five issues in the final offer position (or contract, if resolution occurred). Based upon the information available in this simulation, the original position of all participants, regardless of condition, was identical. Number of issues resolved were those issues agreed upon (0–5) during the 20-min negotiating session. The successful outcome construct was a combination of (1) bargaining outcome and (2) contract success. Bargaining outcome was whether the negotiation ended in resolution or impasse. Contract success was the sum of the net benefit for each of the five issues in the final contract, regardless of how the outcome was determined.

RESULTS

Correlations of the variables which compose the dependent constructs confirmed the expected relationship. A correlation of .66 was observed between bargaining outcome and contract success. A correlation coefficient of .76 was observed between number of issues resolved and concessionary rate. The two variables for each construct were then standardized with a mean of 0 and a standard deviation of 1 and combined. The resulting concessionary process construct had a mean of 0 and a standard deviation of 1.8. The outcome construct had a mean of 0 and a

TABLE 1
ANOVA SOURCE TABLE

	df	MS	F ratio	Significance
Process				
NEG	1	43.86	13.87	.001
ARB	1	13.49	4.27	.05
NEG × ARB	1	3.30	1.04	NS
Error	143	3.16		
Outcome				
NEG	1	21.61	6.71	.05
ARB	1	1.40	.44	NS
NEG × ARB	1	.49	.15	NS
Error	143	3.21		

standard deviation of 1.9. The remaining analyses were conducted using these constructs. An initial analysis of variance was conducted to determine specific effects of the gender of the bargaining dyad and particular confederates. In no case did these variables have a significant influence on the negotiation as measured by the dependent variables. From the questionnaire data, a manipulation check on the arbitration condition (the extent to which arbitration was viewed as a costly and uncertain option) was significant in its influence on the participant's behavior [$F(1,146) = 5.07, p < .001$].

A multivariate analysis of variance (MANOVA) was performed on the dependent constructs by the main effects of the relative salience of negotiation costs (NEG) and the relative salience of arbitration costs (ARB). The Wilks lambda criteria proved significant for both NEG [$F(2,143) = 6.5, p < .005$] and ARB [$F(2,143) = 3.01, p < .05$].

The overall source table for the analyses appears in Table 1. There were no significant interaction effects. The manipulation of the relative salience of negotiation costs affected both the concessionary process construct and the successful outcome construct. As was predicted, individuals in the low-salience NEG condition exhibited more consessionary process relative to those in the high-salience NEG condition [$F(1,144) = 13.9, p < .005; .509 (SD = 1.7)$ versus $-.533 (SD = 1.9)$]. Table 2 presents the means and standard deviations for each condition. Secondly, the relative salience of the negotiation costs exerted significant influence on the successful outcome construct in the predicted direction [$F(1,144) = 6.75, p < .01$]. That is, negotiators in the low-salience NEG condition were more likely to experience more successful outcomes than were negotiators in the high-salience condition [$.357 (1.7)$ versus $.413 (1.9)$]. Consistent with the hypotheses, the relative salience of arbitration costs (ARB) significantly affected the concessionary process construct in the bargaining sim-

106   MARGARET A. NEALE

TABLE 2
MEANS AND STANDARD DEVIATIONS

Main effect means (SD)

Process	
NEG	
High	− .533 (1.9)
Low	.509 (1.7)
ARB	
High	.302 (1.6)
Low	− .328 (1.9)
Outcome	
NEG	
High	− .413 (1.9)
Low	.357 (1.7)
ARB	
High	.130 (1.7)
Low	− .243 (1.8)

Interaction means (SD)

Arbitration salience	Negotiation salience	
	High	Low
High	− .067 (1.7)* − .271 (1.8)**	.674 (1.5)* .401 (1.7)**
Low	− 1.000 (2.0)* − .555 (1.9)**	.344 (1.8)* .312 (1.8)**

* Process means.
** Outcome means.

ulation [$F(1,144) = 4.26$, $p < .05$]. That is, when negotiators were in the low-salience ARB condition, they demonstrated less concessionary process behavior than did negotiators to whom the salience or arbitration was high [− .328 (1.9) versus .302 (1.6)]. While the effect of relative salience of arbitrated costs on the successful outcome construct did not reach significance [$F(1,144) = .44$, (NS)], the means were in the predicted direction.

DISCUSSION

The general pattern of results provides support for the theoretical position that the relative salience of negotiation-related and/or arbitration-related costs affects negotiator behavior. When negotiation-related costs are high, the negotiator will demonstrate behavior which suggests a reduced willingness to concede. This unwillingness to compromise negotiating position is probably instituted to preserve the integrity of constituency demands and results in a situation that is conducive to impasse

COST SALIENCE AND NEGOTIATOR BEHAVIOR   107

TABLE 3
PERCENTAGE OF NEGOTIATED SETTLEMENTS BY CONDITION

Salience of arbitration costs	Salience of negotiation costs	
	High	Low
High	50.0%	74.4%
Low	39.5%	67.5%

and the use of arbitration. Further, when the negotiation-related costs are highly salient, this unwillingness to compromise during the negotiation process may extend into the development of the final offers submitted to the arbitrator. Then, this lack of compromise on the part of the negotiator would affect the arbitrator's choice, especially when the arbitrator was a decision rule (as in this case) which chose the more concessionary final offer. What is clear is that the final outcomes of negotiators in this condition were adversely affected by the salience of negotiation-related costs. They were less likely to reach a settlement and the resulting arbitrated outcomes were of lesser value.

The relative salience of arbitration costs (increasing the uncertainty of the outcome, dollar, and time costs of the arbitrator, and quality of the outcome) affected how the participants bargained. In general, negotiators to whom the costs of arbitration were highly salient behaved in a manner which had a positive effect on the negotiation process. This is, negotiators in this condition were more concessionary in their behavior. When the salience of arbitration costs were low, negotiators were less likely to concede and resolved fewer issues in the negotiation session.

While these findings indicate considerable support for the hypotheses, the effect of the relative salience of arbitration costs on the successful outcome construct did not reach significance, although the means were in the predicted direction. The most likely explanation for this lack of significance is in examining the differential probabilities of these two groups to reach a negotiated settlement under conditions of final offer arbitration (see Table 3). Previous research with this particular simulation under final offer by package arbitration (Neale & Bazerman, 1983) indicated that the base rate of agreement under this form of arbitration was approximately 67%. In this experiment, the condition which most closely approximates the previous study was that of the low-salience negotiation-related costs/low-salience arbitration-related costs. The percentage of those negotiating teams which reached agreement under this condition was 68. This represents a relatively high resolution rate with no manipulation. Altering the relative salience of arbitration-related costs such that they become vivid to the negotiator while keeping the salience of negotiation costs low produced a resolution rate of 74%. The outcome from this set of conditions represents the highest rate of both predicted and actual negotiated settlements. The lack of significant differences between outcomes means for the high- and low-salience ARB condition may be the result of a "ceiling" effect on the likelihood of reaching agreement. While it is theoretically possible for each negotiating dyad to reach agreement, constraints on the parties—particularly that of time and individual negotiating style—make this an unlikely outcome. Thus, it seems reasonable to suspect the lack of significance may be partly the result of the existence of a ceiling effect as the differences in the means are in the predicted directions. However, in examining the differences in the two most extreme conditions (high arbitration-related costs, low negotiation-related costs and low arbitration-related costs, high negotiation-related costs), there is an increase in resolution rate of almost 35%. Future studies might use conventional arbitration as the procedure used when parties fail to reach agreement as it results in approximately equal resolution and impasse rates (Neale & Bazerman, 1983).

The results concerning the relative salience of negotiation versus arbitration costs are consistent with others (Bartunek, Benton, & Keys, 1975; Brown, 1970; Brown & Garland, 1971; Frey & Adams, 1972) that suggest constituency demands—the costs associated with negotiation— are an extremely potent source of influence on negotiator behavior. That is, when negotiators are held accountable by their constituencies, they exhibit lower rates of compromise and fewer deviations from initial positions as well as taking longer to reach agreement than do negotiators not held so accountable. Further, constituency-related costs strongly dominate the arbitration-related costs as the former are considerably more vivid and direct in their relationship to the negotiator. Thus, the reliance of negotiators on third-party impasse procedures (Feuille, 1977; Wheeler, 1975) may, from this perspective, stem from the increasingly strident demands of constituencies which lead the negotiators to discount the uncertainty and related costs of arbitration.

This line of reasoning lends support to the contention that the primary role of third-party intervention procedures (or threat of such intervention) may be to allow the negotiators to compromise and then attribute this behavior to the third party (Rubin, 1980). This view suggests that third-party intervention at impasse may be conceptualized by the negotiator, not in terms of increasing the uncertainty with which s/he must cope, but as a means of allowing him/her both to compromise and to displace the responsibility for that behavior to the third party. From this perspective, the more accountable the negotiator is to his/her constituency, the greater the likelihood that third-party intervention will be instituted.

The findings of this investigation provide a partial explanation of the tendency for negotiators to choose the risky option of arbitration. The study suggests that negotiators may have somewhat different goals concerning negotiated settlements than researchers have often suggested (Crawford, 1979; Nash, 1950; Zeuthan, 1930). Maximizing the economic value of the negotiation may be a goal of the negotiator, but this research suggests some qualification of this goal is needed. The negotiators may maximize the economic value of the negotiation through resolution, given that the economic value of the outcome is sufficient to meet the constituency's minimum requirements. If these are not met, then it seems that the negotiator's course would be to reduce the costs s/he must pay by invoking arbitration, in spite of the lowered quality of the contract (Crawford, 1979) or the introduction of uncertainty (Farber & Katz, 1979).

Further, it seems that the strength of the effect of constituency-based costs in reducing the negotiator's willingness to behave in a concessionary manner is instrumental in increasing the reliance on third-party procedures. If negotiators wish to improve the overall quality of their contracts, then the deleterious aspects of an overriding commitment to the constituency's position must somehow be reduced. Perhaps as Nisbett and Ross (1980) suggest, if individuals are made aware of the effect of the inappropriate use of certain heuristics or informational shortcuts, they will be less likely to use them in inappropriate situations. In this particular case, the availability heuristic (Tversky & Kahneman, 1973) suggests that which is most easily remembered is most frequent in its occurrence. Thus, if negotiators were cognizant that information which is most vivid to the individual (such as costs associated with the negotiator not meeting the demands of his/her constituency) is likely to be easily remembered and perceived as a very probable event, then the negotiators may be able to approximate with greater accuracy the probability that this event would occur. This would require the negotiator to discount his/her initial assessment of the event's probability of occurrence. While this procedure may result in a more objective evaluation of the choice of outcomes, recent work by Staw and Ross (1978) suggest those who are committed to and follow a chosen course of action are perceived as better leaders. An interesting variant of this experiment would be to assess a constituency's evaluation of negotiator behavior. An important concern to the negotiator is whether s/he will be rated more highly by the constituency if s/he perserveres to arbitration rather than reaching a negotiated outcome.

While not within the scope of this experiment, the results of the differential valuation of negotiation- and arbitration-related costs may explain the observed number of negotiated settlements which occur after arbitration has been invoked but prior to the issuance of the award (Feuille, 1975). Once impasse is declared and arbitration is invoked, the costs associated with negotiation (loss of face or perceived incompetency) are no longer so salient as the responsibility for the outcome has been

110   MARGARET A. NEALE

transferred to the arbitrator. Simultaneously, the costs associated with arbitration have become salient to both parties such that they may be willing to reevaluate their final positions prior to invoking arbitration and continue unofficial negotiations. Further compromise during the arbitration phase of the process may result in the development of a contract which is preferrable over the uncertainty of the outcome inherent in arbitration to the participants. Because the constraints of the "bargainers' dilemma" (Podell & Knapp, 1969) surrounding concessionary behavior no longer exist, concessionary behavior to circumvent the control of the arbitrator by reaching agreement prior to the issuance of an arbitral award may be perceived by the constituency as exceptional strategy and skill.

These findings suggest some interesting applications of this research to real world negotiations and third-party interventions as well as new avenues for research. Based upon this work, it seems that the relative salience of negotiation-related and arbitration-related costs plays an important role in the behavior of negotiators. Thus, it is critical that organizations (such as the company, the union, or other disputing entities) acknowledge the impact of the represented group in influencing negotiator strategy and behavior. If resolution of the conflict is of primary importance, then serious consideration should be given to reducing the influence of the constituency or utilizing a nonbinding third-party procedure to facilitate concessionary behavior.

Future research in this area might well address the actual motives of the negotiators in their evaluation of outcome choices (impasse or resolution). That is, does the choice of invoking impasse in a negotiation result from a defensive response of the negotiator in order to save face and appear competent (defensive distortion) or is the choice the result of a perception by the negotiator, however erroneous, that the constituency would receive a more favorable decision if a third party influenced the outcome (motivated misperception). Information about the negotiator's motives/perceptions could greatly increase our understanding of and control over negotiator behavior.

REFERENCES

Anderson, J. (1980). The impact of arbitration: A methodological assessment. *Industrial Relations, 20,* 129–148.

Bartunek, J., Benton, A., & Keys, C. (1975). Third party intervention and the bargaining behavior of group representatives. *Journal of conflict Resolution, 1975,* 532–557.

Bazerman, M. H., & Neale, M. A. (1982). Improving negotiator effectiveness under final offer arbitration: The role of selection and training. *Journal of Applied Psychology, 67,* 543–548.

Berry, L. (1982, July 14). Negotiating a divorce: Mediators helping couples avoiding courtroom wars. *Austin-American Statesman.*

Brown, B. (1970). Face saving following experimentally induced embarrassment. *Journal of Experimental Social Psychology, 6,* 255–271.

Brown, B., & Garland, H. (1971). The effects of incompetency, audience acquaintanceship, and anticipated evaluative feedback on face saving behavior. *Journal of Experimental Social Psychology,* **1,** 490–520.

Burger, W. E. (1982). Isn't there a better way? *American Bar Association Journal,* **68,** 274–277.

Campbell, R. (1960). *Originally in group productivity: III. Partisan commitment and productive independence in a collective bargaining situation,* Columbus: Ohio State Univ. Research Foundation.

Crawford, V. (1979). On compulsory arbitration schemes. *Journal of Political Economy,* **87,** 131–159

Elkouri, F., & Elkouri, E. (1979). *How arbitration works.* Washington, D.C.: Bureau of National Affairs.

Esser, J., & Komorita, S. (1975). Reciprocity and concession making in bargaining. *Journal of Personality and Social Psychology,* **31,** 864–872.

Farber, H., & Katz, H. (1979). Interest arbitration, outcomes, and the incentive to bargain. *Industrial and Labor Relations Review,* **33,** 55–63.

Feuille, P. (1975). Final offer arbitration and the chilling effect. *Industrial Relations,* **14,** 302–310.

Feuille, P. (1977). Final offer arbitration and negotiating incentives. *Arbitration Journal,* **32,** 203–220.

Frey, R., & Adams, J. (1972). The negotiator's dilemma: Simultaneous ingroup and outgroup conflict. *Journal of Experimental Social Psychology,* **8,** 331–346.

Grisby, D., & Bigoness, W. (1982). The effects of third party intervention on preintervention bargaining behavior. *Journal of Applied Psychology,* **67,** 549–554.

Kochan, T., & Baderschneider, J. (1978). Dependence on impasse procedures: Police and firefighters in New York State. *Industrial and Labor Relations Review* **31,** 431–440.

Nash, J. (1950). The bargaining problem. *Econometrica,* **18,** 155–162.

Neale, M., & Baxerman, M. (1982). The effect of perspective taking ability under alternate forms of arbitration on the negotiating process. *Industrial and Labor Relations Review,* **36,** 378–388.

Nisbett, R., & Ross, L. (1980). Human inference: *Strategies and shortcomings of social judgment,* Englewood Cliffs, NJ: Prentice–Hall.

Podell, J., & Knapp, W. (1969). The effects of mediation on the perceived firmness of the opponent. *Journal of Conflict Resolution,* **13,** 511–520.

Rubin, J. (1980). Experimental research on third party intervention in conflict: Toward some generalizations. *Psychological Bulletin,* **87,** 379–391.

Staw, B., & Ross, J. (1978). Commitment to a policy decision: A multi-theoretical perspective. *Administrative Science Quarterly,* **23,** 40–64.

Stevens, C. (1966). Is compulsory arbitration compatible with bargaining? *Industrial Relations,* **5,** 38–50.

Thomas, K., & Schmidt, W. (1976). A survey of managerial interests with respect to conflict. *Academy of Management Journal,* **19,** 315–318.

Tversky, A., & Kahneman, D. (1973). Availability: A heuristic for judging frequency and probability. *Cognitive Psychology,* **5,** 207–232.

Walton, R., & McKersie, R. (1965). *A behavioral theory of negotiation,* New York: McGraw–Hill.

Wheeler, H. (1975). Compulsory arbitration: A narcotic effect? *Industrial Relations,* **14,** 117–120.

Wheeler, H. (1978). How compulsory arbitration affects comprise activity. *Industrial Relations,* **17,** 80–84.

Zeuthan, F. (1930). *Problems or monopoly and economic welfare,* London: Routledge.

RECEIVED: April 1, 1983.

[14]

✧✧✧

Three Approaches to Resolving Disputes

Interests, Rights, and Power

It started with a pair of stolen boots. Miners usually leave their work clothes in baskets that they hoist to the ceiling of the bathhouse between work shifts. One night a miner discovered that his boots were gone.[1] He couldn't work without boots. Angry, he went to the shift boss and complained: "Goddammit, someone stole my boots! It ain't fair! Why should I lose a shift's pay and the price of a pair of boots because the company can't protect the property?"

"Hard luck!" the shift boss responded. "The company isn't responsible for personal property left on company premises. Read the mine regulations!"

The miner grumbled to himself, "I'll show them! If I can't work this shift, neither will anyone else!" He convinced a few buddies to walk out with him and, in union solidarity, all the others followed.

The superintendent of the mine told us later that he had replaced stolen boots for miners and that the shift boss should have done the same. "If the shift boss had said to the miner, 'I'll buy you a new pair and loan you some meanwhile,' we wouldn't have had a strike." The superintendent believed that his way of resolving the dispute was better than

3

4   **Getting Disputes Resolved**

the shift boss's or the miner's. Was he right and, if so, why? In what ways are some dispute resolution procedures better than others?

In this chapter, we discuss three ways to resolve a dispute: reconciling the interests of the parties, determining who is right, and determining who is more powerful. We analyze the costs of disputing in terms of transaction costs, satisfaction with outcomes, effect on the relationship, and recurrence of disputes. We argue that, in general, reconciling interests costs less and yields more satisfactory results than determining who is right, which in turn costs less and satisfies more than determining who is more powerful. The goal of dispute systems design, therefore, is a system in which most disputes are resolved by reconciling interests.

Three Ways to Resolve Disputes

The Boots Dispute Dissected

A dispute begins when one person (or organization) makes a claim or demand on another who rejects it.[2] The claim may arise from a perceived injury or from a need or aspiration.[3] When the miner complained to the shift boss about the stolen boots, he was making a claim that the company should take responsibility and remedy his perceived injury. The shift boss's rejection of the claim turned it into a dispute. To resolve a dispute means to turn opposed positions—the claim and its rejection—into a single outcome.[4] The resolution of the boots dispute might have been a negotiated agreement, an arbitrator's ruling, or a decision by the miner to drop his claim or by the company to grant it.

In a dispute, people have certain interests at stake. Moreover, certain relevant standards or rights exist as guideposts toward a fair outcome. In addition, a certain balance of power exists between the parties. Interests, rights, and power then are three basic elements of any dispute. In resolving a dispute, the parties may choose to focus their attention on one or more of these basic factors. They may seek to (1) reconcile

Three Approaches to Resolving Disputes   **5**

their underlying interests, (2) determine who is right, and/or (3) determine who is more powerful.

When he pressed his claim that the company should do something about his stolen boots, the miner focused on rights—"Why should I lose a shift's pay and the price of a pair of boots because the company can't protect the property?" When the shift boss responded by referring to mine regulations, he followed the miner's lead and continued to focus on who was right. The miner, frustrated in his attempt to win what he saw as justice, provoked a walkout—changing the focus to power. "I'll show them!" In other words, he would show the company how much power he and his fellow coal miners had—how dependent the company was on them for the production of coal.

The mine superintendent thought the focus should have been on interests. The miner had an interest in boots and a shift's pay, and the company had an interest in the miner working his assigned shift. Although rights were involved (there was a question of fairness) and power was involved (the miner had the power to cause a strike), the superintendent's emphasis was on each side's interests. He would have approached the stolen boots situation as a joint problem that the company could help solve.

Reconciling Interests

Interests are needs, desires, concerns, fears—the things one cares about or wants. They underlie people's positions—the tangible items they *say* they want. A husband and wife quarrel about whether to spend money for a new car. The husband's underlying interest may not be the money or the car but the desire to impress his friends; the wife's interest may be transportation. The director of sales for an electronics company gets into a dispute with the director of manufacturing over the number of TV models to produce. The director of sales wants to produce more models. Her interest is in selling TV sets; more models mean more choice for consumers and hence increased sales. The director of manufacturing

6   **Getting Disputes Resolved**

wants to produce fewer models. His interest is in decreasing manufacturing costs; more models mean higher costs.

Reconciling such interests is not easy. It involves probing for deep-seated concerns, devising creative solutions, and making trade-offs and concessions where interests are opposed.[5] The most common procedure for doing this is *negotiation,* the act of back-and-forth communication intended to reach agreement. (A procedure is a pattern of interactive behavior directed toward resolving a dispute.) Another interests-based procedure is *mediation,* in which a third party assists the disputants in reaching agreement.

By no means do all negotiations (or mediations) focus on reconciling interests. Some negotiations focus on determining who is right, such as when two lawyers argue about whose case has the greater merit. Other negotiations focus on determining who is more powerful, such as when quarreling neighbors or nations exchange threats and counterthreats. Often negotiations involve a mix of all three—some attempts to satisfy interests, some discussion of rights, and some references to relative power. Negotiations that focus primarily on interests we call "interests-based," in contrast to "rights-based" and "power-based" negotiations. Another term for interests-based negotiation is *problem-solving negotiation,* so called because it involves treating a dispute as a mutual problem to be solved by the parties.

Before disputants can effectively begin the process of reconciling interests, they may need to vent their emotions. Rarely are emotions absent from disputes. Emotions often generate disputes, and disputes, in turn, often generate emotions. Frustration underlay the miner's initial outburst to the shift boss; anger at the shift boss's response spurred him to provoke the strike.

Expressing underlying emotions can be instrumental in negotiating a resolution. Particularly in interpersonal disputes, hostility may diminish significantly if the aggrieved party vents her anger, resentment, and frustration in front of the blamed party, and the blamed party acknowledges the validity of such emotions or, going one step further, offers an

Three Approaches to Resolving Disputes   **7**

apology.[6] With hostility reduced, resolving the dispute on the basis of interests becomes easier. Expressions of emotion have a special place in certain kinds of interests-based negotiation and mediation.

Determining Who Is Right

Another way to resolve disputes is to rely on some independent standard with perceived legitimacy or fairness to determine who is right. As a shorthand for such independent standards, we use the term *rights*. Some rights are formalized in law or contract. Other rights are socially accepted standards of behavior, such as reciprocity, precedent, equality, and seniority.[7] In the boots dispute, for example, while the miner had no contractual right to new boots, he felt that standards of fairness called for the company to replace personal property stolen from its premises.

Rights are rarely clear. There are often different—and sometimes contradictory—standards that apply. Reaching agreement on rights, where the outcome will determine who gets what, can often be exceedingly difficult, frequently leading the parties to turn to a third party to determine who is right. The prototypical rights procedure is adjudication, in which disputants present evidence and arguments to a neutral third party who has the power to hand down a binding decision. (In mediation, by contrast, the third party does not have the power to decide the dispute.) Public adjudication is provided by courts and administrative agencies. Private adjudication is provided by arbitrators.[8]

Determining Who Is More Powerful

A third way to resolve a dispute is on the basis of power. We define power, somewhat narrowly, as the ability to coerce someone to do something he would not otherwise do. Exercising power typically means imposing costs on the other side or threatening to do so. In striking, the miners exercised power by imposing economic costs on the company. The

8   **Getting Disputes Resolved**

exercise of power takes two common forms: acts of aggression, such as sabotage or physical attack, and withholding the benefits that derive from a relationship, as when employees withhold their labor in a strike.

In relationships of mutual dependence, such as between labor and management or within an organization or a family, the question of who is more powerful turns on who is less dependent on the other.[9] If a company needs the employees' work more than employees need the company's pay, the company is more dependent and hence less powerful. How dependent one is turns on how satisfactory the alternatives are for satisfying one's interests. The better the alternative, the less dependent one is. If it is easier for the company to replace striking employees than it is for striking employees to find new jobs, the company is less dependent and thereby more powerful. In addition to strikes, power procedures include behaviors that range from insults and ridicule to beatings and warfare. All have in common the intent to coerce the other side to settle on terms more satisfactory to the wielder of power. Power procedures are of two types: power-based negotiation, typified by an exchange of threats, and power contests, in which the parties take actions to determine who will prevail.

Determining who is the more powerful party without a decisive and potentially destructive power contest is difficult because power is ultimately a matter of perceptions. Despite objective indicators of power, such as financial resources, parties' perceptions of their own and each other's power often do not coincide. Moreover, each side's perception of the other's power may fail to take into account the possibility that the other will invest greater resources in the contest than expected out of fear that a change in the perceived distribution of power will affect the outcomes of future disputes.

Interrelationship Among Interests, Rights, and Power

The relationship among interests, rights, and power can be pictured as a circle within a circle within a circle (as

Three Approaches to Resolving Disputes 9

Figure 1. Interrelationships Among Interests, Rights, and Power.

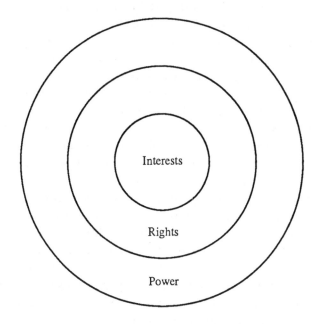

Interests

Rights

Power

in Figure 1). The innermost circle represents interests; the middle, rights; and the outer, power. The reconciliation of interests takes place within the context of the parties' rights and power. The likely outcome of a dispute if taken to court or to a strike, for instance, helps define the bargaining range within which a resolution can be found. Similarly, the determination of rights takes place within the context of power. One party, for instance, may win a judgment in court, but unless the judgment can be enforced, the dispute will continue. Thus, in the process of resolving a dispute, the focus may shift from interests to rights to power and back again.

Lumping It and Avoidance

Not all disputes end with a resolution. Often one or more parties simply decide to withdraw from the dispute. Withdrawal takes two forms. One party may decide to "lump

10   **Getting Disputes Resolved**

it,'' dropping her claim or giving in to the other's claim because she believes pursuing the dispute is not in her interest, or because she concludes she does not have the power to resolve it to her satisfaction. The miner would have been lumping his claim if he had said to himself, "I strongly disagree with management's decision not to reimburse me for my boots, but I'm not going to do anything about it." A second form of withdrawal is avoidance. One party (or both) may decide to withdraw from the relationship, or at least to curtail it significantly.[10] Examples of avoidance include quitting the organization, divorce, leaving the neighborhood, and staying out of the other person's way.

Both avoidance and lumping it may occur in conjunction with particular dispute resolution procedures. Many power contests involve threatening avoidance—such as threatening divorce—or actually engaging in it temporarily to impose costs on the other side—such as in a strike or breaking off of diplomatic relations. Many power contests end with the loser lumping her claim or her objection to the other's claim. Others end with the loser engaging in avoidance: leaving or keeping her distance from the winner. Similarly, much negotiation ends with one side deciding to lump it instead of pursuing the claim. Or, rather than take a dispute to court or engage in coercive actions, one party (or both) may decide to break off the relationship altogether. This is common in social contexts where the disputant perceives satisfactory alternatives to the relationship.

Lumping it and avoidance may also occur before a claim has been made, thus forestalling a dispute. Faced with the problem of stolen boots, the miner might have decided to lump it and not make a claim for the boots. More drastically, in a fit of exasperation, he might have walked off the job and never returned.

Which Approach Is "Best"?

When the mine superintendent described the boots dispute to us, he expressed a preference for how to resolve dis-

Three Approaches to Resolving Disputes   **11**

putes. In our language, he was saying that on the whole it was better to try to reconcile interests than to focus on who was right or who was more powerful. But what does "better" mean? And in what sense, if any, was he correct in believing that focusing attention on interests is better?

What "Better" Means: Four Possible Criteria

The different approaches to the resolution of disputes— interests, rights, and power—generate different costs and benefits. We focus on four criteria in comparing them: transaction costs, satisfaction with outcomes, effect on the relationship, and recurrence of disputes.[11]

Transaction Costs. For the mine superintendent, "better" meant resolving disputes without strikes. More generally, he wanted to minimize the costs of disputing—what may be called the transaction costs. The most obvious costs of striking were economic. The management payroll and the overhead costs had to be met while the mine stood idle. Sometimes strikes led to violence and the destruction of company property. The miners, too, incurred costs—lost wages. Then there were the lost opportunities for the company: a series of strikes could lead to the loss of a valuable sales contract. In a family argument, the costs would include the frustrating hours spent disputing, the frayed nerves and tension headaches, and the missed opportunities to do more enjoyable or useful tasks. All dispute resolution procedures carry transaction costs: the time, money, and emotional energy expended in disputing; the resources consumed and destroyed; and the opportunities lost.[12]

Satisfaction with Outcomes. Another way to evaluate different approaches to dispute resolution is by the parties' mutual satisfaction with the result. The outcome of the strike could not have been wholly satisfactory to the miner—he did not receive new boots—but he did succeed in venting his frustration and taking his revenge. A disputant's satisfaction depends largely on how much the resolution fulfills the interests that led her to make or reject the claim in the first place.

12   **Getting Disputes Resolved**

Satisfaction may also depend on whether the disputant believes that the resolution is fair. Even if an agreement does not wholly fulfill her interests, a disputant may draw some satisfaction from the resolution's fairness.

Satisfaction depends not only on the perceived fairness of the resolution, but also on the perceived fairness of the dispute resolution procedure. Judgments about fairness turn on several factors: how much opportunity a disputant had to express himself; whether he had control over accepting or rejecting the settlement; how much he was able to participate in shaping the settlement; and whether he believes that the third party, if there was one, acted fairly.[13]

Effect on the Relationship. A third criterion is the long-term effect on the parties' relationship. The approach taken to resolve a dispute may affect the parties' ability to work together on a day-to-day basis. Constant quarrels with threats of divorce may seriously weaken a marriage. In contrast, marital counseling in which the disputing partners learn to focus on interests in order to resolve disputes may strengthen a marriage.

Recurrence. The final criterion is whether a particular approach produces durable resolutions. The simplest form of recurrence is when a resolution fails to stick. For example, a dispute between father and teenage son over curfew appears resolved but breaks out again and again. A subtler form of recurrence takes place when a resolution is reached in a particular dispute, but the resolution fails to prevent the same dispute from arising between one of the disputants and someone else, or conceivably between two different parties in the same community. For instance, a man guilty of sexually harassing an employee reaches an agreement with his victim that is satisfactory to her, but he continues to harass other women employees. Or he stops, but other men continue to harass women employees in the same organization.

The Relationship Among the Four Criteria. These four different criteria are interrelated. Dissatisfaction with outcomes may produce strain on the relationship, which contributes to the recurrence of disputes, which in turn increases

Three Approaches to Resolving Disputes 13

transaction costs. Because the different costs typically increase and decrease together, it is convenient to refer to all four together as the costs of disputing. When we refer to a particular approach as "high-cost" or "low-cost," we mean not just transaction costs but also dissatisfaction with outcomes, strain on the relationship, and recurrence of disputes.

Sometimes one cost can be reduced only by increasing another, particularly in the short term. If father and son sit down to discuss their conflicting interests concerning curfew, the short-term transaction costs in terms of time and energy may be high. Still, these costs may be more than offset by the benefits of a successful negotiation—an improved relationship and the cessation of curfew violations.

Which Approach Is Least Costly?

Now that we have defined "better" in terms of the four types of costs, the question remains whether the mine superintendent was right in supposing that focusing on interests is better. A second question is also important: when an interests-based approach fails, is it less costly to focus on rights or on power?

Interests Versus Rights or Power. A focus on interests can resolve the problem underlying the dispute more effectively than can a focus on rights or power. An example is a grievance filed against a mine foreman for doing work that contractually only a miner is authorized to do. Often the real problem is something else—a miner who feels unfairly assigned to an unpleasant task may file a grievance only to strike back at his foreman. Clearly, focusing on what the contract says about foremen working will not deal with this underlying problem. Nor will striking to protest foremen working. But if the foreman and miner can negotiate about the miner's future work tasks, the dispute may be resolved to the satisfaction of both.

Just as an interests-based approach can help uncover hidden problems, it can help the parties identify which issues are of greater concern to one than to the other. By trading off issues of lesser concern for those of greater concern, both

14   **Getting Disputes Resolved**

parties can gain from the resolution of the dispute.[14] Consider, for example, a union and employer negotiating over two issues: additional vacation time and flexibility of work assignments. Although the union does not like the idea of assignment flexibility, its clear priority is additional vacation. Although the employer does not like the idea of additional vacation, he cares more about gaining flexibility in assigning work. An agreement that gives the union the vacation days it seeks and the employer flexibility in making work assignments would likely be satisfactory to both. Such joint gain is more likely to be realized if the parties focus on each side's interests. Focusing on who is right, as in litigation, or on who is more powerful, as in a strike, usually leaves at least one party perceiving itself as the loser.

Reconciling interests thus tends to generate a higher level of mutual satisfaction with outcomes than determining rights or power.[15] If the parties are more satisfied, their relationship benefits, and the dispute is less likely to recur. Determining who is right or who is more powerful, with the emphasis on winning and losing, typically makes the relationship more adversarial and strained. Moreover, the loser frequently does not give up, but appeals to a higher court or plots revenge. To be sure, reconciling interests can sometimes take a long time, especially when there are many parties to the dispute. Generally, however, these costs pale in comparison with the transaction costs of rights and power contests such as trials, hostile corporate takeovers, or wars.

In sum, focusing on interests, compared to focusing on rights or power, tends to produce higher satisfaction with outcomes, better working relationships and less recurrence, and may also incur lower transaction costs. As a rough generalization, then, an interests approach is less costly than a rights or power approach.

Rights Versus Power. Although determining who is right or who is more powerful can strain the relationship, deferring to a fair standard usually takes less of a toll than giving in to a threat. In a dispute between a father and teenager over curfew, a discussion of independent standards such

Three Approaches to Resolving Disputes   **15**

as the curfews of other teenagers is likely to strain the relationship less than an exchange of threats.

Determining rights or power frequently becomes a contest—a competition among the parties to determine who will prevail. They may compete with words to persuade a third-party decision maker of the merits of their case, as in adjudication; or they may compete with actions intended to show the other who is more powerful, as in a proxy fight. Rights contests differ from power contests chiefly in their transaction costs. A power contest typically costs more in resources consumed and opportunities lost. Strikes cost more than arbitration. Violence costs more than litigation. The high transaction costs stem not only from the efforts invested in the fight but also from the destruction of each side's resources. Destroying the opposition may be the very object of a power contest. Moreover, power contests often create new injuries and new disputes along with anger, distrust, and a desire for revenge. Power contests, then, typically damage the relationship more and lead to greater recurrence of disputes than do rights contests. In general, a rights approach is less costly than a power approach.

Proposition

To sum up, we argue that, in general, reconciling interests is less costly than determining who is right, which in turn is less costly than determining who is more powerful. This proposition does not mean that focusing on interests is invariably better than focusing on rights and power, but simply means that it tends to result in lower transaction costs, greater satisfaction with outcomes, less strain on the relationship, and less recurrence of disputes.

Focusing on Interests Is Not Enough

Despite these general advantages, resolving *all* disputes by reconciling interests alone is neither possible nor desirable. It is useful to consider why.

16   **Getting Disputes Resolved**

When Determining Rights or Power Is Necessary

In some instances, interests-based negotiation cannot occur unless rights or power procedures are first employed to bring a recalcitrant party to the negotiating table. An environmental group, for example, may file a lawsuit against a developer to bring about a negotiation. A community group may organize a demonstration on the steps of the town hall to get the mayor to discuss its interests in improving garbage collection service.

In other disputes, the parties cannot reach agreement on the basis of interests because their perceptions of who is right or who is more powerful are so different that they cannot establish a range in which to negotiate. A rights procedure may be needed to clarify the rights boundary within which a negotiated resolution can be sought. If a discharged employee and her employer (as well as their lawyers) have very different estimations about whether a court would award damages to the employee, it will be difficult for them to negotiate a settlement. Nonbinding arbitration may clarify the parties' rights and allow them to negotiate a resolution.

Just as uncertainty about the rights of the parties will sometimes make negotiation difficult, so too will uncertainty about their relative power. When one party in an ongoing relationship wants to demonstrate that the balance of power has shifted in its favor, it may find that only a power contest will adequately make the point. It is a truism among labor relations practitioners that a conflict-ridden union-management relationship often settles down after a lengthy strike. The strike reduces uncertainty about the relative power of the parties that had made each party unwilling to concede. Such long-term benefits sometimes justify the high transaction costs of a power contest.

In some disputes, the interests are so opposed that agreement is not possible. Focusing on interests cannot resolve a dispute between a right-to-life group and an abortion clinic over whether the clinic will continue to exist. Resolution will likely be possible only through a rights contest, such

Three Approaches to Resolving Disputes   **17**

as a trial, or a power contest, such as a demonstration or a legislative battle.

When Are Rights or Power Procedures Desirable?

Although reconciling interests is generally less costly than determining rights, only adjudication can authoritatively resolve questions of public importance. If the 1954 Supreme Court case, *Brown* v. *Board of Education* (347 U.S. 483), outlawing racial segregation in public schools, had been resolved by negotiation rather than by adjudication, the immediate result might have been the same—the black plaintiff would have attended an all-white Topeka, Kansas public school. The societal impact, however, would have been far less significant. As it was, *Brown* laid the groundwork for the elimination of racial segregation in all of American public life. In at least some cases, then, rights-based court procedures are preferable, from a societal perspective, to resolution through interests-based negotiation.[16]

Some people assert that a powerful party is ill-advised to focus on interests when dealing regularly with a weaker party. But even if one party is more powerful, the costs of imposing one's will can be high. Threats must be backed up with actions from time to time. The weaker party may fail to fully comply with a resolution based on power, thus requiring the more powerful party to engage in expensive policing. The weaker party may also take revenge—in small ways, perhaps, but nonetheless a nuisance. And revenge may be quite costly to the more powerful if the power balance ever shifts, as it can quite unexpectedly, or if the weaker party's cooperation is ever needed in another domain. Thus, for a more powerful party, a focus on interests, within the bounds set by power, may be more desirable than would appear at first glance.

Low-Cost Ways to Determine Rights and Power

Because focusing on rights and power plays an important role in effective dispute resolution, differentiating rights

18 **Getting Disputes Resolved**

and power procedures on the basis of costs is useful. We distinguish three types of rights and power procedures: negotiation, low-cost contests, and high-cost contests. Rights-based negotiation is typically less costly than a rights contest such as court or arbitration. Similarly, power-based negotiation, marked by threats, typically costs less than a power contest in which those threats are carried out.

Different kinds of contests incur different costs. If arbitration dispenses with procedures typical of a court trial (extensive discovery, procedural motions, and lengthy briefs), it can be much cheaper than going to court. In a fight, shouting is less costly than physical assault. A strike in which workers refuse only overtime work is less costly than a full strike.

The Goal:
An Interests-Oriented Dispute Resolution System

Not all disputes can be—or should be—resolved by reconciling interests. Rights and power procedures can sometimes accomplish what interests-based procedures cannot. The problem is that rights and power procedures are often used where they are not necessary. A procedure that should be the last resort too often becomes the first resort. The goal, then, is a dispute resolution system that looks like the pyramid on the right in Figure 2: most disputes are resolved through reconciling interests, some through determining who is right, and the fewest through determining who is more powerful. By contrast, a distressed dispute resolution system would look like the inverted pyramid on the left in Figure 2. Comparatively few disputes are resolved through reconciling interests, while many are resolved through determining rights and power. The challenge for the systems designer is to turn the pyramid right side up. It is to design a system that promotes the reconciling of interests but that also provides low-cost ways to determine rights or power for those disputes that cannot or should not be resolved by focusing on interests alone. The chapters that follow discuss how a designer might go about creating such a system.

Three Approaches to Resolving Disputes 19

**Figure 2. Moving from a Distressed to an Effective
Dispute Resolution System.**

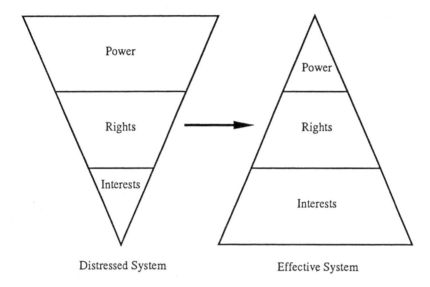

Distressed System   Effective System

❖❖

Notes

Chapter One

1. In order to steer between the Scylla of sexist language and the Charybdis of awkward writing, we have chosen to alternate the use of masculine and feminine pronouns.

177

2. This definition is taken from Felstiner, W.L.F., Abel, R. L., and Sarat, A. "The Emergence and Transformation of Disputes: Naming, Blaming, Claiming." *Law and Society Review*, 1980-81, *15*, 631-654. The article contains an interesting discussion of disputes and how they emerge.

3. See Felstiner, W.L.F., Abel, R. L., and Sarat, A. "The Emergence and Transformation of Disputes: Naming, Blaming, Claiming." *Law and Society Review*, 1980-81, *15*, 631-654.

4. In speaking of resolving disputes, rather than processing, managing, or handling disputes, we do not suggest that resolution will necessarily bring an end to the fundamental conflict underlying the dispute. Nor do we mean that a dispute once resolved will stay resolved. Indeed, one of our criteria for contrasting approaches to dispute resolution is the frequency with which disputes recur after they appear to have been resolved. See Merry, S. E., "Disputing Without Culture." *Harvard Law Review*, 1987, *100*, 2057-2073; Sarat, A. "The 'New Formalism' in Disputing and Dispute Processing." *Law and Society Review*, 1988, *21*, 695-715.

5. For an extensive discussion of interests-based negotiation, see Fisher, R., and Ury, W. L. *Getting to Yes*. Boston: Houghton Mifflin, 1981. See also Lax, D. A., and Sebenius, J. K. *The Manager as a Negotiator*. New York: Free Press, 1986.

6. Goldberg, S. B., and Sander, F.E.A. "Saying You're Sorry." *Negotiation Journal*, 1987, *3*, 221-224.

7. We recognize that in defining rights to include both legal entitlements and generally accepted standards of fairness, we are stretching that term beyond its commonly understood meaning. Our reason for doing so is that a procedure that uses either legal entitlements or generally accepted standards of fairness as a basis for dispute resolution will focus on the disputants' entitlements under normative standards, rather than on their underlying interests. This is true of adjudication, which deals with legal rights; it is equally true of rights-based negotiation, which may deal with either legal rights or generally accepted standards. Since, as we shall show, procedures that focus on normative standards are more costly than

Notes   **179**

those that focus on interests, and since our central concern is with cutting costs as well as realizing benefits, we find it useful to cluster together legal rights and other normative standards, as well as procedures based on either.

8. A court procedure may determine not only who is right but also who is more powerful, since behind a court decision lies the coercive power of the state. Legal rights have power behind them. Still, we consider adjudication a rights procedure, since its overt focus is determining who is right, not who is more powerful. Even though rights, particularly legal rights, do provide power, a procedure that focuses on rights as a means of dispute resolution is less costly than a procedure that focuses on power. A rights-based contest, such as adjudication, which focuses on which disputant ought to prevail under normative standards, will be less costly than a power-based strike, boycott, or war, which focuses on which disputant can hurt the other more. Similarly, a negotiation that focuses on normative criteria for dispute resolution will be less costly than a negotiation that focuses on the disputants' relative capacity to injure each other. Hence, from our cost perspective, it is appropriate to distinguish procedures that focus on rights from those that focus on power.

9. Emerson, R. M. "Power-Dependence Relations." *American Sociological Review*, 1962, *27*, 31–41.

10. Hirschman, A. O. *Exit, Voice, and Loyalty: Responses to Declines in Firms, Organizations and States*. Cambridge, Mass.: Harvard University Press, 1970. Exit corresponds with avoidance, loyalty with lumping it. Voice, as we shall discuss later, is most likely to be realized in interests-based procedures such as problem-solving negotiation and mediation.

11. A fifth evaluative criterion is procedural justice, which is perceived satisfaction with the fairness of a dispute resolution procedure. Research has shown that disputants prefer third-party procedures that provide opportunities for outcome control and voice. See Lind, E. A., and Tyler, T. R. *The Social Psychology of Procedural Justice*. New York: Plenum, 1988; Brett, J. M. "Commentary on Procedural Justice Papers." In R. J. Lewicki, B. H. Sheppard, and M. H. Bazer-

180   **Notes**

man (eds.), *Research on Negotiations in Organizations.* Greenwich, Conn.: JAI Press, 1986, 81–90.

We do not include procedural justice as a separate evaluation criterion for two reasons. First, unlike transaction costs, satisfaction with outcome, effect on the relationship, and recurrence, procedural justice is meaningful only at the level of a single procedure for a single dispute. It neither generalizes across the multiple procedures that may be used in the resolution of a single dispute nor generalizes across disputes to construct a systems-level cost. The other costs will do both. For example, it is possible to measure the disputants' satisfaction with the outcome of a dispute, regardless of how many different procedures were used to resolve that dispute. Likewise, it is possible to measure satisfaction with outcomes in a system that handles many disputes by asking many disputants about their feelings. Second, while procedural justice and distributive justice (satisfaction with fairness of outcomes) are distinct concepts, they are typically highly correlated. See Lind, E. A., and Tyler, T. R. *The Social Psychology of Procedural Justice.* New York: Plenum, 1988.

12. Williamson, O. E. "Transaction Cost Economics: The Governance of Contractual Relations." *Journal of Law and Economics,* 1979, *22*, 233–261; Brett, J. M., and Rognes, J. K. "Intergroup Relations in Organizations." In P. S. Goodman and Associates, *Designing Effective Work Groups.* San Francisco: Jossey-Bass, 1986, 202–236.

13. For a summary of the evidence of a relationship between procedural and distributive justice—that is, satisfaction with process and with outcome—see Lind, E. A., and Tyler, T. R. *The Social Psychology of Procedural Justice.* New York: Plenum, 1988. Lind and Tyler also summarize the evidence showing a relationship between voice and satisfaction with the process. For evidence of the effect of participation in shaping the ultimate resolution beyond simply being able to accept or reject a third party's advice, see Brett, J. M., and Shapiro, D. L. "Procedural Justice: A Test of Competing Theories and Implications for Managerial Decision Making," unpublished manuscript.

Notes   **181**

14. Lax, D. A., and Sebenius, J. K. *The Manager as Negotiator.* New York: Free Press, 1986.

15. The empirical research supporting this statement compares mediation to arbitration or adjudication. Claimants prefer mediation to arbitration in a variety of settings: labor-management (Brett, J. M., and Goldberg, S. B. "Grievance Mediation in the Coal Industry: A Field Experiment." *Industrial and Labor Relations Review,* 1983, *37,* 49-69), small claims disputes (McEwen, C. A., and Maiman, R. J. "Small Claims Mediation in Maine: An Empirical Assessment." *Maine Law Review,* 1981, *33,* 237-268), and divorce (Pearson, J. "An Evaluation of Alternatives to Court Adjudication." *Justice System Journal,* 1982, 7, 420-444).

16. Some commentators argue that court procedures are always preferable to a negotiated settlement when issues of public importance are involved in a dispute (see, for example, Fiss, O. M. "Against Settlement." *Yale Law Journal,* 1984, *93,* 1073-1090), and all agree that disputants should not be pressured into the settlement of such disputes. The extent to which parties should be encouraged to resolve disputes affecting a public interest is, however, not at all clear. See Edwards, H. T. "Alternative Dispute Resolution: Panacea or Anathema?" *Harvard Law Review,* 1986, *99,* 668-684.

Part III
Multi-Party Competitive Contexts

[15]

Psychological Bulletin
1978, Vol. 85, No. 5, 1130–1153

Models of Coalition Behavior: Game Theoretic, Social Psychological, and Political Perspectives

J. Keith Murnighan
Organizational Behavior Group
Department of Business Administration
University of Illinois at Urbana-Champaign

This article reviews three classes of game theoretic solution concepts (solutions, subsolutions, and the core; bargaining set models; and the Shapley value), four social psychological models of coalition formation (minimum resource theory, minimum power theory, bargaining theory, and the weighted probability model), and three sets of political coalition models (minimum size, minimum range, and policy distance minimization). The research that has been conducted on characteristic function games, on experimental coalition situations involving more than three players, and on coalition governments is summarized and the models are evaluated. The advantages of collaboration among the three areas are discussed.

Formal theory concerning coalition behavior has been studied by game theorists since 1944 (von Neumann & Morgenstern), by social psychologists since 1956 (Caplow), and by political scientists since 1962 (Riker). The three areas have adopted different philosophical approaches and have made limited progress in their relatively independent pursuits of knowledge. Game theorists have developed elaborate and elegant mathematics but have paid little attention to the applicability of their results to human behavior. Social psychologists have collected a large amount of data on three-person groups but have only recently expanded their descriptive models in attempts to predict bargaining behavior in larger, more complicated conflict situations. Political scientists have attempted to explain the dynamics of coalition governments but are hindered in their theoretical testing by an emphasis on "postdiction" rather than prediction. This article summarizes selected portions of the research and

theory from the three areas and attempts to locate the common ground among them. A concerted effort bridging the areas holds promise for breakthroughs that each field alone might find unattainable.

This article limits its review to aspects of the three areas that are most similar and therefore have the greatest collaborative potential. Extensive reviews of the game theory literature have been done by Luce and Raiffa (1957) and An. Rapoport (1970). Reviews of earlier social psychological research have been done by Chertkoff (1970) and Stryker (1972). The political science perspective is exemplified in books by Groennings, Kelley, and Leiserson (1970) and DeSwaan (1973). Present coverage of game theoretic models is restricted to characteristic function models of cooperative games; coverage of social psychological models is restricted to those that make a priori predictions for either the formation of or the payoffs to certain coalitions; treatment of political models is restricted to those that attempt to explain the conscious formation of observable coalitions (E. W. Kelley, 1968). These restrictions preclude discussion of models of partition function games (Thrall & Lucas, 1963), political studies of roll call votes (e.g., Hinckley, 1972), and other inferred coalitions.

The author would like to thank Jerome M. Chertkoff and Alvin E. Roth for their helpful commentary on an earlier version of this article.

Requests for reprints should be sent to J. Keith Murnighan, Organizational Behavior Group, Department of Business Administration, University of Illinois, Urbana, Illinois 61801.

Game Theoretic Models

A major distinction in the study of *n*-person games is made between cooperative and noncooperative games. Cooperative games are those in which the players have the opportunity to communicate with one another and to form binding agreements. Noncooperative games do not permit binding agreements and may even forbid communications. Thus, for example, the usual form of the Prisoner's Dilemma game is noncooperative. Cooperative games generally presuppose bargaining or interaction among the players as the process that determines the players' payoffs.

In describing models of cooperative games, almost no assumptions concerning the underlying dispositions of the players are made, with one notable exception. As with the social psychological models, players are assumed to be rational in that they attempt to maximize their outcomes. The game theoretic models, then, instead of making assumptions about the actors in the game, focus primarily on game characteristics, emphasizing the generality of their approach to many different games. The characteristic function of a game specifies a value or payoff to each possible coalition, including one-person coalitions. For instance, a three-person game with outcomes of 1 for each two- or three-person coalition and 0 for all one-person coalitions would have the following characteristic function:

$$v(A) = v(B) = v(C) = 0, \quad v(AB) = v(AC)$$
$$= v(BC) = v(ABC) = 1,$$

where $v(\ )$ indicates the value or payoff to a coalition, and A, B, and C are actors or parties in the game.

The characteristic function, then, emphasizes the payoffs that coalitions receive: Coalitions are differentiated on the basis of the payoffs they can obtain.

Solutions and Subsolutions

Von Neumann and Morgenstern's (1944) presentation of *n*-person conflict situations led them to the question of what outcomes might be considered stable. They introduced the notions of *imputation* and *domination*. An imputation is a payoff configuration that satisfies conditions of individual rationality (i.e., a party will not accept a payoff from a coalition that is less than the payoff it can receive playing alone) and Pareto optimality (i.e., a payoff will not be considered if another payoff increases the outcomes of at least one of the included parties while not reducing the payoffs of any of the other included parties). Domination refers to a relationship between potential imputations: For a game with characteristic function v, an imputation $y = (y_1, \ldots, y_n)$ that specifies a payoff for each of the n players dominates an imputation $x = (x_1, x_2, \ldots, x_n)$ with respect to a nonempty coalition Q when the following conditions are met:

$$v(Q) \geq \sum_{i \in Q} y_i, \tag{1}$$

$$y_i > x_i \text{ for every } i \text{ in Q.} \tag{2}$$

In other words, every player in the coalition Q prefers y to x, and the value of the coalition is enough for each player in Q to receive the payoff at y.

An example of a set of imputations from the game mentioned above would be

$$(\tfrac{1}{2}, \tfrac{1}{2}, 0), \quad (\tfrac{1}{2}, 0, \tfrac{1}{2}), \quad (0, \tfrac{1}{2}, \tfrac{1}{2}),$$

where the imputations refer to payoffs to (A, B, C) when the AB coalition has formed, the AC coalition has formed, and the BC coalition has formed, respectively. An alternative imputation, $(\tfrac{3}{4}, 0, \tfrac{1}{4})$, dominates the first member of the above set of imputations. In other words, Players A and C receive greater payoffs in this imputation than they did in the first, and they have the power to enforce the new imputation if they wish. Notice also that the third imputation in the above set dominates this alternative imputation. A series of imputations where one imputation succeeds and dominates the previous imputation could result in an endless string of dominations. However, von Neumann and Morgenstern (1944) noted that certain sets of imputations do promote at least a fragile form of stability. (For instance, consider the situation where you are Player A and Player C offers you $\tfrac{3}{4}$. If you realize that Player B can then retaliate with the third imputation in the above set, you may be content to stay at a point where you receive $\frac{1}{2}$.) They worked from two assumptions: Any solution set should contain imputations that (a) do not dominate each other and (b) dominate any imputation outside the set. The example above, where the set of imputations gives a payoff of $\frac{1}{2}$ to each member of a coalition but does not specify which coalition will form, satisfied both assumptions. Thus it is a von Neumann-Morgenstern solution set. It is not, however, the only solution set for this game. Other solutions all take the form where one player receives a fixed payoff and the other two players bargain over what remains. Such *discriminatory solutions* consist of all outcomes where one player receives a fixed amount, $d \leq \frac{1}{2}$, and the other players' payoffs sum to $(1 - d)$. For most n-person games, there are large numbers of solution sets. In addition, as with other game theoretic models, not only are the outcomes for particular coalitions not unique, there is also little attempt to determine which coalition or coalitions might form most frequently.

An additional problem with von Neumann and Morgenstern's concept of solution sets is the fact that they do not exist for every n-person characteristic function game. Lucas (Note 1) found an example of a 10-person game that does not have a solution. Its complexity precludes including it here.

Roth (1976) recently reported a modification of the concept of solutions, called subsolutions. The concept of subsolutions relaxes the condition that states that any imputation outside the solution set is dominated by a member in the set to state that any imputation outside the subsolution set that dominates a member of the set is in turn dominated by another member of the set. In this way, only imputations that threaten members of the set need to be dominated by another member of the set. This modification removes the problem of the general existence of solution sets but does not change the non-uniqueness of the solution or the indeterminacy of particular coalitions.

A solution is always a subsolution; however, a set of payoffs may be a subsolution without being a solution. Solutions and subsolutions, although different theoretically, can appear strikingly similar in the outcomes

that are expected for a particular game. In the following game, however, there is a clear difference between them:

$$v(A) = v(B) = v(C) = v(BC) = 0,$$
$$v(AB) = v(AC) = v(ABC) = 1.$$

One solution for this game is the set of points of the form $[p, (1 - p)/2, (1 - p)/2]$, where p varies from 1 to 0. Subsolutions in this game also include sets of outcomes where Player A obtains payoffs no smaller than some constant $c > 0$. Thus, a subsolution may result when Player A is unwilling to be totally excluded from a share of the payoff. Solutions, on the other hand, all include the possibility of a zero payoff for Player A.

There is another solution concept that has the advantage of yielding fewer predictions for games where it is not empty. The core consists of the imputations in a game that are undominated. In the game just discussed, the core consists of a single payoff, $(1, 0, 0)$, where A obtains the entire payoff. This does not necessarily imply that Players B and C will accept a payoff of zero in a coalition with Player A; rather, it implies that if Player A can induce B and C to compete for his favors, the payoffs will move toward $(1, 0, 0)$. For this example, the core is an extreme point; in other games, the core is not so extreme. For instance, when $v(i) = 0$, $v(ij) = \frac{1}{2}$, $v(ijk) = 1$, the core consists of the set of all outcomes (x_1, x_2, x_3) such that the sum of any two players' payoffs is greater than or equal to $\frac{1}{2}$ (i.e., $x_i + x_j \geq \frac{1}{2}$, $i \neq j$) and $x_1 + x_2 + x_3 = 1$. Due to the fact that the core is the set of outcomes that are not dominated by any other outcome, it is a compelling solution for game theorists and is one that is a subset of most of the other game theoretic solution concepts (including solutions and subsolutions). The core of a game, however, may be empty.[1]

Bargaining Set Models

Another approach to n-person characteristic function games is that of the bargaining set

---

[1] The core is empty in the first characteristic function game discussed in this article, where $v(i) = 0$, $v(ij) = v(ijk) = 1$, because no outcome or set of outcomes is undominated.

(Aumann & Maschler, 1964). As with solutions, the bargaining set assumes individual rationality; it does not, however, assume Pareto optimality. Rather, the bargaining set is based on the concepts of objections and counterobjections. The bargaining set resembles the core (which it contains) and is always nonempty. The use of an example makes an explanation of the theory much easier. Consider the following characteristic function game:

$$v(i) = 0, \quad v(AB) = 70, \quad v(AC) = 60,$$
$$v(BC) = 50, \quad v(ABC) = 75,$$

where i refers to individual players, A, B, and C. Suppose that Players A and C are negotiating to divide the 60 points that they can obtain, with A proposing that he receive 45 points, and C, 15 points. Player C can raise an *objection* to A by saying that he can form a coalition with Player B, giving Player B 20 points (which is more than he would receive if A and C formed a coalition) and obtaining 30 points for himself. Given this objection, however, A can raise a *counterobjection*, saying that he can retain his original 45 points in a coalition with B and give B 25 points (which is more than C is offering him in his objection).

In this example, one member of a potential coalition may attempt to increase his or her payoffs by using alternative coalitions as a threat. In general, an objection of Player i against Player j proposes an alternative coalition Q, such that i is included in Q, j is excluded from Q, and the members of Coalition Q receive larger payoffs than they did previously. A counterobjection also proposes an alternative coalition, say, R, where Player j obtains at least as much as j did in the original coalition with Player i and where other members of R do at least as well or better than they did in Q. The bargaining set, then, consists of those payoff configurations where a valid counterobjection can be raised for any possible objection. (For a particular game, generation of the bargaining set can be quite involved; see Maschler, 1966). Thus, a fragile state of stability, similar in nature to the solution concept of von Neumann and Morgenstern (1944), is proposed.

For the last characteristic function game

mentioned above, the bargaining set contains the following payoff configurations:

$$(40, 30, 0), \quad (40, 0, 20), \quad (0, 30, 20).$$

(It also contains elements for the grand coalition; however, different forms of the bargaining set specify different outcomes for the grand coalition.) Several relationships among the members of the bargaining set are interesting to note. In this example, as in other examples where $v(i) = 0$, $v(ABC) \leq [\Sigma v(ij)]/2$, and $v(ij) =$ some positive integer, the payoff configurations in the bargaining set, regardless of the final coalition structure, specify constant payoffs to the players when they are included in the winning coalition. Such games are called *quota games*, because quotas, ω_i, can be assigned to each player such that

$$v(ij) = \omega_i + \omega_j,$$

where

$$i, j = A, B, C, \quad \text{and} \quad i \neq j.$$

For quota games, the bargaining set predicts that each player should receive his or her quota, irrespective of the coalition that forms. However, as with the other models that have been discussed, the bargaining set does not specify which of the possible coalitions might form most frequently. For games that are more complicated than quota games, the bargaining set does not predict a specific payoff for each of the included players but instead predicts a range of outcomes for each player. For instance, consider the following characteristic function:

$$v(i) = v(BC) = v(BD) = v(CD) = 0,$$
$$v(Aj) = v(Ajk) = v(BCD) = 72,$$

where $i =$ any player (A, B, C, or D), and j and $k =$ any player except A. In this Apex game, Player A is denoted the Apex player because he needs only one partner to form a winning coalition and can only be excluded by a coalition of all the other players. The bargaining set includes payoff configurations for the two-person coalitions such that $36 \leq x_A \leq 54$ and $18 \leq x_j \leq 36$, where x_A refers to the Apex player's payoff and x_j refers to A's coalition partner's payoff.

Two additional models, both of which are

related to the bargaining set, have been proposed in order to make more specific predictions for most games. The kernel (Davis & Maschler, 1965) for the game above specifies equal outcomes for Player A and A's partner. The rationale for this outcome is that when two or more potential coalition members trade objections and counterobjections, one player may, in a sense, outweigh another if the excess payoff he or she can receive from an alternative coalition exceeds the excess payoff the potential coalition partner can receive in the alternative coalition he or she proposes. Thus, an equilibrium state may occur when neither player outweighs the other, that is, when the excess each can obtain from alternative coalitions is equal. For three-person quota games, the kernel and the bargaining set are identical. For more complicated games, the kernel is included in the bargaining set. In this last example, the kernel is the set of points $x_A = 36$, $x_j = 36$.

Another variation of the bargaining set, the competitive bargaining set (Horowitz, 1973), predicts the opposite endpoint of the bargaining set's range of predictions in this game. The competitive bargaining set assumes that players not included in the originally considered coalition will not sit by passively, waiting for one member of this coalition to make an objection, but will make proposals themselves. Thus, a strong objection that a member of a potential coalition can make would be what Horowitz called a "multi-threat," that is, an objection that says that a player can obtain higher payoffs in any alternative coalition. The set of outcomes in the competitive bargaining set, then, consists of those payoff configurations where a "counter-multithreat" can be raised for any multi-threat. For the example above, the competitive bargaining set specifies outcomes of 54 For Player A and 18 for A's partner.

The Shapley Value

Shapley (1953) approached n-person games from an entirely different perspective by attempting to make an a priori evaluation of the game for each of the players. To do so, Shapley stated three axioms that any value function should have (see Shapley, 1953, for a formal statement of the axioms). He then proved that a function satisfying these axioms existed and that it was unique. The resulting function can be interpreted by assuming that (a) the coalition of all the players forms in a random order, adding one player at a time; (b) each player receives the marginal payoff that accrues to the coalition when he or she joins; and (c) each ordering of the all-player coalitions is equally likely. The Shapley value for Player i, then, equals $\sum_j P_j x_{ij}$, where P_j refers to the probability of one order of formation and x_{ij} refers to the marginal payoff (i.e., the additional payoff realized by the coalition when Player i has joined) assigned to Player i, in that order. Roth (1977a, 1977b) has recently shown that for players who are risk neutral with respect to both ordinary risk (i.e., they evaluate uncertain payoffs by using expected values) and strategic risk (i.e., they evaluate themselves as average bargainers; see Roth, 1977a, for a formal definition of *average*), such a value is equivalent to the expected utility for playing a game. Thus, the Shapley value can be considered as a measure of the value of playing a particular position in a game.

For the quota game mentioned earlier in this article, where $v(i) = 0$, $v(AB) = 70$, $v(AC) = 60$, $v(BC) = 50$, and $v(ABC) = 75$, the Shapley value for players (A, B, C) is (30, 25, 20). The model does not predict the payoffs to the members of particular coalitions; rather, it predicts overall payoffs. Thus, Player A should average a payoff of 30 for each of the total number of plays of this game.

The Shapley value has been interpreted as a measure of a player's pivotal power in the sense that it assigns a value to each of the players depending on when their presence in a coalition is pivotal (i.e., when their presence increases the total payoff to the coalition). The Shapley value has also been used as the basis for a social psychological model of coalition formation, minimum power theory (Gamson, 1964). An assumption that players will divide the payoffs they receive from particular coalitions in proportion to the pivotal power they contribute to that coalition allows minimum power theory to predict that the winning coalition or coalitions that require the least total pivotal power will form most frequently. This model is discussed further below with the other social psychological models. It is worth mentioning, however, that minimum power theory is the only model that draws from both game theory and social psychology in formulating predictions.

Social Psychological Models

While the game theoretic models have focused on the different payoffs that coalitions can obtain, the social psychological models have focused on the differing amounts of resources that players can bring to coalitions. This emphasis originated with the first social psychological model of coalition behavior (Caplow, 1956) and has allowed the models to predict, in most cases, not only how coalition members will divide the payoff they receive but also what coalition will form. Although this result is an advantage relative to the game theoretic models, the social psychological models not only lack the generality of the game theoretic models, they also tend to disregard what the optimal strategies might be in particular coalition situations. This reflects the descriptive philosophy underlying the social psychological models, compared with the normative philosophy underlying the game theoretic models.

Caplow's Model

Caplow's (1956) model was the first social psychological theory of coalition formation. Caplow stated that players will attempt to control as many other players as possible. In Caplow's terms, all members of a coalition control players outside the coalition, and within the coalition, the member or members with the most resources control the other coalition members. Resources are important, then, to determine which coalitions have a majority and which players are controlled within a coalition.

Caplow listed six types of coalitions that differed in the relationship among the players' resources. Two types gave one player dictatorial power; the remaining four types, for Players A, B, and C, were (a) $A = B = C$; (b) $A > B, B = C, A < (B + C)$; (c) $A >$

$B > C$, $A < (B + C)$; and (d) $A < B$, $B = C$. The model then made predictions on the basis of each player's attempt to maximize control over the others. For instance, in the second type above, consider Player B's point of view. In an AB coalition, B controls C but is controlled within the coalition by A. In the BC coalition, on the other hand, B and C are equal in the coalition and both control A. This increases B's control relative to the AB coalition; it similarly increases C's control relative to the AC coalition. Thus the model predicts the BC coalition in games of this type. The model does not predict, however, what the payoff distribution will be. In addition, it is restricted to three-person coalition situations.

Caplow (1959) qualified his predictions by stating that control is important only in *continuous* coalition situations. In episodic situations, where rewards are obtained in periodic, predetermined conditions, control is not as important as is sharing in the payoffs. Given an episodic situation, then, Caplow's model predicts that, except for situations where a dictator exists, any coalition should form, and the best prediction for the reward division is an equal split. Caplow (1959) also stated that if the conflict situation is a terminal one, where all the players fight until only one remains, coalitions will only form when two of the players have equal resources; they will coalesce and terminate the existence of the third player while continuing to exist themselves in what might be called a state of uneasy détente.

Most of the data on coalitions in the triad have been collected on the Type 3 game: The results indicate that the BC coalition is most frequent. Because Caplow's original model predicted either the AC or the BC coalition in this type of game, Chertkoff (1967) proposed a revised version of the model. Chertkoff noted that an assumption of reciprocated choice would allow the Caplow model to make accurate predictions of the BC coalition in Type 3 games. Caplow's original analysis stated that in this coalition type, C is indifferent between either the AC or the BC coalitions (in each, he controls one player and is controlled by one). Likewise, Player A is indifferent between the AB and the AC coalitions (he controls both players in each). Player B, however, prefers the BC coalition (where he controls two players). Thus B will always, according to the theory, choose Player C as his coalition partner. Chertkoff noted that if one assumes that reciprocal choices are necessary to form a coalition, and one multiplies the proportions of individual choices to determine the proportion of reciprocal choices, the BC coalition should occur 50% of the time, the AC coalition should occur 25% of the time, and no reciprocal choices should occur the remaining 25% of the time. If the players are allowed to make new choices when no coalition forms, the BC coalition should result twice as often, overall, as the AC coalition. For the other triad types, this additional assumption results in no change in the model's predictions. This change improves the predictions of Caplow's model for many of the data that have been reported.

Minimum Resource Theory

Gamson (1961a) proposed his minimum resource theory to predict not only what coalition might be expected to form in a coalition situation but also what payoffs the members of that coalition might receive. Gamson assumed that the players would attempt to maximize their payoffs (an assumption that is common to almost all coalition theories) and that they would expect their payoffs to be determined by the parity norm, that is, each player's payoffs would be directly proportional to the resources he or she contributed to the coalition. For instance, in a coalition situation where Players A, B, and C had resources (votes) of 4, 3, and 2, respectively, Players B and C would expect to divide the payoff such that B received 60% and C received 40%. The two assumptions lead to the prediction that the coalition with the least amount of resources necessary to form a majority will form and that the coalition members will divide the payoff according to the parity norm. Such coalitions will maximize the coalition members' individual rewards because no allotments will be necessary for resources in excess of the minimum necessary.

Gamson's minimum resource theory makes predictions that are identical to those made by Chertkoff's revision of Caplow's models in the six types of triads, and it also makes predictions for the payoff division. In addition, the theory applies to any *n*-person ($n \geq 3$) coalition situation where the players are assigned resources.

Gamson's use of an equitylike principle (i.e., the proportion of a player's inputs are expected to be equal to the proportion of his or her outcomes) is also the underlying assumption in minimum power theory (mentioned above). Instead of using resources as a measure of a person's inputs, minimum power theory uses pivotal power as a measure of a person's contributions. For example, in the 4-3-2 game mentioned above, each player is pivotal twice; if the payoff is constant to all majority coalitions, all three players are equal in pivotal power. Minimum power theory, then, predicts that AB, AC, and BC are equally likely and that the payoff division in each case should be 50–50. Thus, although the two models make quite different predictions in a number of situations, their underlying philosophy is quite similar.

Bargaining Theory

Komorita and Chertkoff's (1973) bargaining theory represents a radical departure from earlier models of coalition formation. Unlike the other models, bargaining theory predicts that for most games, the players' rewards will change over time. (The other models make only static predictions.) The predictions are based on the use of alternative coalitions as threats during coalition bargaining. For instance, if Players A and C are bargaining over the rewards they will receive from an AC coalition in the 4-3-2 game, both A and C will use the possibility of forming a coalition with B as a threat. Thus, bargaining theory utilizes some of the underlying logic of bargaining set theory. It also utilizes one of the assumptions of minimum resource theory, namely, that players will use the parity norm in determining their expected rewards. However, bargaining theory also considers the possibility that the players may use an *equality norm*, that is, all players divide the payoff equally. In fact, the prediction for the initial trial is that the players will expect their rewards to be midway between the predictions of the parity norm and those of the equality norm. The coalition that maximizes the player's rewards, given such expectations, is predicted to form. On subsequent trials, the model predicts that the players will use their maximum expectation from alternative coalitions, whether that is determined by the parity norm or the equality norm, as a threat in their negotiations. The predictions for payoff divisions at the asymptotic trial are derived by assuming that each player's reward will be proportional to his or her maximum expectation in alternative coalitions. The model predicts that as the trials progress, the players will form coalitions that minimize their temptation to defect. This temptation to defect is smallest in the coalition that minimizes the discrepancy between the predicted asymptotic reward and the players' maximum expectation from alternative coalitions. Because larger coalitions present more players with temptations to defect, bargaining theory typically predicts that coalitions with few members will be most frequent (like the weighted probability model below).

In the 4-3-2 game, the predictions for the initial trial are that the BC coalition will form and will divide the payoff so that B receives 55% and C receives 45% (which is midway between equality, 50%–50%, and parity, 60%–40%). On the asymptotic trial, however, bargaining theory predicts that in the BC coalition, B will receive 50% and C will receive 50%. Both players' maximum expectations in alternative coalitions (i.e., AB and AC) are 50%, as determined by the equality norm. Their threats are equal, and therefore, the theory's predictions are for an equal payoff division. (Predictions for AB and AC on the asymptotic trial are 53%–47%, rounded off.) In addition, B's and C's predicted payoffs equal their maximum expectations in alternative coalitions, reducing their temptation to defect to zero. Thus, the BC coalition is predicted to form; Coalitions AB and AC are not predicted to form because temptation to defect is greater than zero for each of the players.

Bargaining theory, then, makes differential predictions for the most frequent coalition and its members' payoffs over trials on the basis of the quality of the players' alternatives. It does not, however, specify when the asymptotic trial will occur. It also does not make predictions for situations when maximum expectations cannot be determined, that is, when resources are not assigned to the players.

The Weighted Probability Model

Komorita (1974) also proposed the weighted probability model to account, at least in part, for the preponderance of coalitions where the number of members was as small as possible. In coalition situations that include more than three players, either two- or three-person coalitions can often attain a majority. Smaller coalitions are expected to occur more frequently than larger coalitions because a large coalition may not only be "more difficult to form but may also be more difficult to maintain" (Komorita, 1974, p. 243). The weighted probability model assumes that individuals will attempt to maximize their rewards, that minimum winning coalitions will form, and that the probability of a coalition forming is an inverse function of size:

$$P(C_j) = \frac{w_j}{\Sigma w_j},$$

where $P(C_j)$ is the probability that Coalition j will form, and $w_j = 1/(n_j - 1)$, the weight that indicates the difficulty in forming Coalition j as a function of n_j, the number of players included in it. Thus, in a game where 4 two-person and 1 four-person coalitions constitute the set of minimum winning coalitions, the probability of one of the two-person coalitions equals 1 divided by $4\frac{1}{3}$. The theory presently assumes that

$$P_i = \Sigma P(C_j), \quad i \, \epsilon \, C_j,$$

where P_i is the probability that Player i will be included in the winning coalition, C_j, and where the summation is over all minimum winning coalitions that include Player i. Thus, a player who is included in each of the two-person coalitions but not the four-person coalition in the example above will have a probability of inclusion of 4 divided by $4\frac{1}{3}$. The model then assumes that the players' rewards are proportional to their probability of inclusion (a notion that, like minimum resource and minimum power theories, is an equitylike principle):

$$R_{ij} = \frac{P_i}{\Sigma P_k}, k \, \epsilon \, C_j,$$

where R_{ij} equals Player i's expected reward in coalition C_j and where the summation is over all the members of C. Finally, in the event that two or more coalitions of equal size present an individual with the same expected reward, the model assumes that he or she will choose the coalition where the players have equal or relatively equal resources.

The model's predictions can be interpreted by noting that resources are instrumental only in determining the minimum winning coalitions and that the minimum winning coalition or coalitions with the fewest number of players should form. Unlike bargaining theory, determination of the predicted rewards depends on the quantity and size rather than the quality of one's alternatives. A player with twice as many alternatives of equal size as another player will be predicted to receive a payoff that is twice the size of the other player's.

For instance, in a game like the one discussed above, where a majority of 28 votes is needed for a winning coalition and where Players A, B, C, D, and E have 24, 9, 8, 7, and 6 votes, Player A has 4 two-person alternatives, and Players B, C, D, and E have 1 two-person and 1 four-person alternative. Because four-person coalitions have a weight, w_j, that is one third the weight of a two-person coalition, $P_A = 4$, and $P_B = P_C = P_D = P_E = 1\frac{1}{3}$. Thus, the model predicts that Player A should receive three times as much of the payoff as B, C, D, or E (i.e., 75%–25%). In addition, although Players B, C, D, and E differ in the amount of resources at their disposal, the number of alternative coalitions they can form is equal, and therefore their predicted payoffs are equal.

The weighted probability model has an advantage over the other social psychological models because (a) it does not depend on the allotment of resources to the players, thus making it applicable to games where resources are not specified, and (b) it makes exact predictions for the probabilities of the different coalitions. Its applications are restricted, however, to simple majority games, where the prize to a winning coalition is constant and where it takes a majority to win.

Political Models

The game theoretic and social psychological models have focused on the immediate results of the coalition process: formation of a coalition and the division of a payoff among its members. The political perspective brings an additional consideration into the modeling of coalition behavior, the expectation of policies that a coalition will attempt to implement following its formation. Thus, the political point of view emphasizes long-run rather than short-run considerations. One indication of this perspective is the frequent use of a coalition's duration as a primary dependent variable in theoretical tests.

The political literature on coalition behavior is rich in descriptive detail. Unfortunately, investigations into the similarities between the formation and functioning of coalitions within different countries and theoretical models of such behaviors and processes has lagged behind the developments in game theory and social psychology, possibly because of an emphasis on the case study approach. It should be noted, however, that in marked contrast with social psychological investigations, the political literature has frequently utilized the political implications derived from game theory.

Riker's Size Principle

Riker's (1962) theory of political coalitions was the first formal model of coalition behavior in political science. It remains the field's most prominent and most frequently tested model. In deriving a prediction for the size of political coalitions, Riker made several assumptions: (a) Actors are rational (i.e., they prefer winning to losing). (b) The game is zero sum (i.e., the sum of the payoffs to all the players equals zero). (c) Players have perfect information (i.e., they know the present condition and every possible move that any player can make). (d) Side payments are allowed (i.e., the coalition members can divide their mutual payoff). (e) Winning coalitions are the only entities that have value (i.e., blocking and losing coalitions do not have positive values). (f) Members of the winning coalition receive positive payoffs. (g) Coalitions have the ability to add or drop members. The first four assumptions are typical of game theoretic models; the last three are politically relevant. Riker's result, given the seven assumptions, is that minimum winning coalitions will form, that is, removal of a single member of the coalition would render it no longer winning. In political coalitions, where each vote is equal (i.e., the game is symmetric), this result is identical to the prediction of Gamson's minimum resource theory: A minimum winning coalition controls the smallest amount of resources necessary to realize success. Thus the notion of minimizing either a coalition's resources or the number of its members has been identified by two independently derived models, giving the two models a measure of concurrent validity.

Riker's assumptions, especially when they are applied to actual political situations, are quite stringent. He recognized this potential objection and proposed a revised size principle that relaxed the assumption of perfect information: "In social situations similar to *n*-person games with side-payments, participants create coalitions just as large as they believe will ensure winning and no larger" (Riker, 1962, p. 47). With very poor information, then, a coalition might conceivably grow to a size that would significantly differ from that of a minimum winning coalition.

Koehler (1972) has also relaxed Riker's assumption of the game being zero sum and has shown that minimum winning coalitions should occur in nonzero-sum games (which are more analogous to most real political situations). A more significant variant of Riker's model has been proposed by Leiserson (1968). Working from the perspective of von Neumann-Morgenstern (1944) solutions, Leiserson proposed a *bargaining proposition* whereby the number of parties rather than the number of players in a coalition is predicted to be as small as possible. Thus, if three moderately sized parties are sufficient to form a coalition but one large party and one moderately sized party are also sufficient, Leiserson's bargaining proposition predicts that the two-party coalition will form. This formulation is very similar to Komorita's weighted probability model.

A final variant of Riker's model has recently been proposed by Dodd (1974). Like Leiserson, Dodd has focused on parties rather than individuals as coalition members. In a model designed for multiparty parliaments, Dodd predicted that minimum winning coalitions will form, where minimum winning coalitions are defined as those that are no longer winning with the removal of any party rather than any actor. Thus, in the example above of Leiserson's predictions, the model predicts either the two- or the three-party coalition.

The Minimum Range – Conflict of Interest Model

Three authors (Axelrod, 1970; Leiserson, 1966; Rosenthal, 1970) have proposed models that are based on the intuitive notion that parties with similar ideologies will be the most likely coalition partners. If one assumes that political parties can be placed on a unidimensional ideological scale [2] (e.g., from liberal to conservative), coalitions that minimize ideological range should form.

These models, then, explicitly reject the "strange bedfellows" notion that parties with markedly different policy positions will form an alliance in their mutual interest. Instead, they predict that all coalition members will be adjacent to at least one other coalition member on the ideological scale. Thus, in a country where seven parties (A, B, C, D, E, F, and G) are placed in alphabetical order on the ideological scale, a coalition including Parties A, C, and F will not be predicted to form, even if its combined membership is sufficient to win. Instead, coalitions such as ABC, CDE,

---

[2] Leiserson (1966) has shown that this approach can be generalized to ideological spaces of several dimensions.

and DEFG will be predicted to form. Coalitions with extra, unnecessary parties are not assumed to form: For instance, if coalitions ABC and ABCD both include a sufficient number of members to form a majority, ABC is predicted, and ABCD is not. Like Dodd's (1974) model, there is no preference given, however, to minimizing the number of parties in the coalition. Should coalitions AB and BCDE be sufficient to win and small enough so that a loss of one party renders them no longer winning, then Leiserson's (1966) original minimum range theory predicts that either of them might form.

Rosenthal (1970) proposed a similar, more formal model. He posited that parties are either preferred or not preferred as coalition partners and that coalitions will only form among preferred parties. Rosenthal's model assumes that coalitions form by adding one actor at a time and that parties that are richly interconnected with one another (i.e., each prefers all of the others as a coalition partner) but are not interconnected with other parties will be the most likely coalition partners. This model does not assume a single, unidimensional ideological scale but proposes that bilateral bargaining occurs prior to the formation of a majority coalition and that the relationships between pairs of parties rather than among the entire set of parties is of predominant importance.

Axelrod's (1970) conflict of interest model makes the same predictions as do the other two minimum range models. The rationale for the predictions, however, is based on minimizing conflict of interest. *Minimally connected winning coalitions* are defined in exactly the same way that minimum range coalitions are defined and are based on the notion that such coalitions will result in the least conflict of interest among coalition members. Even though it makes intuitive sense that conflict will be reduced to a minimum in small connected coalitions, the notion of a minimization of the number of parties within the coalition is not included to reduce conflict further within the coalition.

The fact that this consideration is not incorporated in the conflict of interest model raises the possibility that the models were derived from the available data (i.e., past

coalition governments) and that their subsequent tests are merely tautological exercises, that is, evaluating a model on the same data that were used to formulate the model. This notion applies to each of the political models reviewed here: All of them are involved more in "postdiction" than in prediction. The results of future coalition governments, which change only too slowly for new theoretical tests, are necessary before the validity of the models can be adequately ascertained.

Needless to say, minimum range theory makes markedly different predictions from those made by the size principle, its variants, or Leiserson's (1968) bargaining principle. Axelrod (1970) offered a simple example. Given four parties (A, B, C, D) with the following respective numbers of seats in the legislature (14, 3, 12, 2) and the parties arranged along the ideological scale in alphabetical order, the models make the following predictions: (a) The size principle predicts the coalition with the smallest number of seats necessary to win. Since 16 of the total of 31 are needed to win, only AD is predicted. (b) Leiserson's bargaining principle predicts that the smallest number of parties will form a winning coalition. Since no party can win alone, two-party coalitions will be favored. They are AB, AC, and AD. (c) Dodd's multiparty parliamentary model predicts AB, AC, AD, and BCD. (d) Minimum range theory focuses on connected coalitions with no extraneous parties: It predicts AB or BCD. DeSwaan (1973) has pointed out that Leiserson's (1966) minimum range model is somewhat ambiguous in that it may also include coalitions that skip one of the parties along the ideological scale. For instance, the range of Coalitions WXZ and WXYZ are the same (they span from Party W to Party Z); if both have sufficient resources to obtain a majority, both may be predicted. Although Leiserson (1966) was not clear on this point, Axelrod (1970) excluded from the predicted set coalitions such as WXZ. This version of minimum range theory has been called "closed" minimum range theory (DeSwaan, 1973) and is differentiated below from a more encompassing set of predictions that includes coalitions such as WXZ.

The Policy Distance Minimization Model

The size principle and its variants assume that actors in coalition situations wish to maximize their hold on offices within the government. The minimum range models assume, at least implicitly, that the similarity of the resultant government's policies to one's own position is also desired. DeSwaan (1970, 1973) proposed a policy distance minimization model whereby involvement in the determination of a government's policies is a party's primary goal. Thus, because acquisition of government offices or cabinet posts is of secondary importance, larger than minimum winning coalitions (where the actors are parties rather than individuals) are possible.

In presenting the model, DeSwaan made several strong assumptions. He assumed that parties can be placed on a single, unidimensional ideological scale or, in the event that several scales are necessary, that the relative weight of each of the dimensions is known. An additional assumption states that within each party, individual's policy preferences are symmetric around the first preference of the median individual in that party. In other words, the first preferences of the members of the party will be arranged around the median individual's first preference such that the distance between the first preference of the nth member to the right of median and the median individual's first preference is identical to the comparable distance for the first preference of the nth member to the left.

DeSwaan continued with an assumption that governmental policies are determined by majority rule and that the most likely policies will coincide with the most preferred policies of the median individual within the coalition. In addition, all players are assumed to expect this outcome and all have complete information concerning the other parties' resources, ideological preferences, and strategies.

The predictions of the model, when coalitions of the whole are excluded, are that parties will attempt to become the central party within the coalition government. Thus, parties to one's left on the ideological scale, for instance, will be valued when one is to

the left of the median of a potential coalition: Adding parties in this fashion will increase the centrality of one's own position, even at the cost of increasing the size of the coalition beyond the minimum required.

Like Riker's (1962) size principle, De-Swaan's model is based on a highly restrictive set of assumptions. Given the complexities of the political arena, strict fulfillment of the assumptions is not expected, but neither is fulfillment necessary. This article has focused on the predictive capability of the different models, and thus their validity is based not on the accuracy of their assumptions but on the accuracy of their predictions. In addition, like Riker's model, the policy distance minimization model has been derived rather than merely proposed. Thus, it is also similar to the game theoretic models in its formal treatment of coalition behavior.

Several problems, however, remain in De-Swaan's model. Including larger than minimum winning coalitions expands the predicted set and reduces the possibility of disconfirmation. Also, as with the minimum range model, the placement of parties on an ordinal ideological scale ignores differences in distance between parties. For instance, two adjacent parties on the scale may espouse highly disparate ideologies and may be in the predicted set. Such coalitions, however, are very unlikely, and the minimum range model's predictions, then, include more coalitions than are necessary.

Unlike the game theoretic and social psychological models, political theories have undergone rather intense scrutiny. Riker's (1962) notion of minimizing the size of winning coalitions has been frequently criticized. Butterworth (1971), for instance, has proposed that rational players might form larger than minimum winning coalitions: An individual who may be excluded from a minimum winning coalition will be motivated to bribe his or her way into the winning coalition, thus making it larger than the minimum necessary to win. In an expanded debate, Butterworth (1974) and Shepsle (1974a, 1974b) concluded that, should a minimum winning coalition form, it will be inherently unstable. Frohlich (1975) has also shown that in an essential symmetric zero-sum game, restrictive conditions are necessary before minimum winning coalitions might be expected. Thus, they may be both unlikely and, as was originally posited by Riker (1962), unstable.

In addition, Taylor (1972) has pointed out that each of the current models focuses on a single criterion (e.g., minimum size, fewest parties, postcoalition policy distance, etc.) that, when minimized, is proposed to explain the formation of governmental coalitions. Taylor pointed out that it is difficult to imagine that all coalition members in all countries will be motivated by the same criteria in forming coalition governments. He has also shown that unless every party in a country uses those same criteria for the formation of a government and applies the criteria in the same order, single-criterion models will hold little explanatory value. It remains, however, for empirical tests to show whether these models hold any predictive value.

Other Models

Four other models are not seriously discussed because their predictions are more limited than those of the models that have been presented.

One game theoretic model, which is not discussed at length here, is the pure bargaining problem considered by Nash (1953). A pure bargaining problem consists of a set of feasible outcomes, any one of which can be achieved only if the players reach unanimous agreement. If unanimous agreement is not reached, then a prespecified disagreement outcome results. In games of this type, every player possesses a veto over any possible agreement, so the only coalition that can act effectively is the coalition of all the players.

Nash proposed a set of axioms that a solution to this bargaining problem should obey. He showed that there is a unique solution satisfying these axioms: It selects the feasible agreement that maximizes the product of the gains made by the players. Like the Shapley value, Nash's solution can be interpreted as a risk-neutral utility function for playing a game (Roth, 1978).

A social psychological model, anticompetitive theory (Gamson, 1964), makes predictions based almost entirely on the sex of the players. As a result of the data from several studies, Vinacke (1971) has concluded that females in coalition situations tend to exhibit accommodative behavior: They tend to form larger than minimum winning coalitions, they tend to split payoffs equally regardless of their power position, they tend to make proposals that are not in their own interests, etc. Males, on the other hand, have tended to exhibit exploitative behavior, showing a strong drive to win and playing very competitively. (It should be noted that the generality of these tendencies has been questioned by Caplow, 1968, and Stryker, 1972.) The anticompetitive model predicts sex differences in coalition behavior but makes few specific predictions concerning which coalition will form and how the coalition members will apportion the rewards.

Laing and Morrison (1973, 1974) have proposed a model whereby players attempt to form coalitions to improve or at least maintain their relative position in the system. One variant assumes that players focus on their rank in the system; the other assumes that players focus on the interval between themselves and other players above or below them in status (which is operationalized by accumulated payoff). Like the game theoretic models, each version of Laing and Morrison's model makes predictions that can be supported by a variety of outcomes. In addition, the model makes predictions only after the results of previous bargaining are known. Future predictions are dependent on the results of prior bargaining rather than the original nature of the game being played. This is both a strength and a weakness: The ubiquitous changes in real coalition situations are reflected by this approach; problems of analysis and long-range prediction, however, are particularly troublesome.

Brams and his colleagues (Brams, 1972; Brams & Garriga-Pico, 1975; Brams & Heilman, 1974; Brams & Riker, 1972) have presented several normative political models concerning the optimal times of joining one of two "protocoalitions," that is, coalitions that do not control a majority. The models depend on the individual's motivation to increase the probability of the protocoalition becoming the majority coalition, on the individual's motivation to maximize his portion of the benefits from the coalition, on the individual's motivation to join the coalition as an individual or with other individuals, and so forth. At present, the complexity of the models and the difficulties inherent in measuring critical variables reduce the potential for empirical testing of the models; indeed, they have not been tested to date. Thus, these models are not pursued further in this presentation.

Empirical Findings

With the exception of several political scientists, researchers studying coalition behavior have rarely considered more than one of the three approaches in a single study. Rather, independent empirical investigations have predominated within each area. The research is briefly summarized below as it relates to each area.

Experiments in Game Theory

Kalisch, Milnor, Nash, and Nering (1954) conducted the first experimental studies in game theory. Their results, however, may have been particular to the individuals in their limited sample (eight people). In addition, most of the games they investigated were played only once. Similar limitations hamper the interpretation of studies by Maschler (Note 2) and Selten and Schuster (1968). Riker's (1967, 1971) studies can also be questioned because the experimenters discussed the session in such detail that one solution set had a special significance for the players; that most of them arrived at it is not surprising.

Buckley and Westen conducted two studies (Buckley & Westen, 1973; Westen & Buckley, 1974) that investigated four- and five-person games with constant payoffs to majority coalitions. The most frequent outcomes were majority coalitions that divided the payoff equally. Reanalysis (Buckley & Westen, 1976) led to a slight superiority for the kernel and the bargaining set over von Neumann and Morgenstern's (1944) solutions in these games. Lieberman (1971) reported similar findings for three-person games.

Lieberman (1962) presented the results of the first experimental investigation of quota games. The three-person zero-sum quota game he studied yielded quotas of 6, 4, and 2 for Players A, B, and C: Coalitions AB and BC were most frequent, and equal divisions of the payoff again predominated.

Am. Rapoport and his colleagues have used a computerized procedure in a series of experiments (Horowitz & Rapoport, 1974; Kahan & Rapoport, 1974, 1977; Medlin, 1976; Am. Rapoport & Kahan, 1976). All of the studies have focused on the predictions of the bargaining set (or subsets of the bargaining set) for quota games.

Four of the five studies investigated the same set of five games, where A, B, and C's quotas were (60, 35, 30), (60, 55, 30), (51, 44, 37), (63, 43, 23), and (76, 42, 8). The first study (Kahan & Rapoport, 1974) in the series studied the effects of public or secret offers in these games: AB coalitions were more frequent than AC or BC coalitions, and the players' overall payoffs were quite close to their quotas, supporting the bargaining set. Effects due to games indicated that Player A received more than his quota in the second and third games, where the BC coalitions were most frequent. In the other games, BC coalitions were relatively infrequent, and Player A received somewhat less than a quota payoff.

Medlin (1976) and Am. Rapoport and Kahan (1976) investigated the effects of a range of values taken by the grand coalition (i.e., ABC) for the same five games. The grand coalition formed frequently when it was possible, and it became more frequent as its payoff increased. Am. Rapoport and Kahan also found a difference in games: AB rather than ABC coalitions were most frequent in Game 5. Medlin (1976), however, found no differences in the frequency of the grand coalition over games.

Kahan and Rapoport (1977) investigated differences in one-person values and found that when one-person values were symmetric to the players' quotas, the data were similar to findings (Kahan & Rapoport, 1974) when the one-person values were zero. In the inversely symmetric conditions, however, AB coalitions were very frequent, even when the grand coalition was possible. Player C, who had a relatively high one-person value but a low quota, was often content to take his one-person value. Player A, on the other hand, who had a relatively low one-person value but a high quota, was eager to enter a coalition and tended to receive payoffs that were lower than his quota. Thus, the results in this condition did not support the bargaining set predictions. The authors presented what they called a "quota-value model," one that borrows both from the bargaining set and the Shapley value, to explain their results. The model does explain the results in both the symmetric and the inversely symmetric conditions better than the other models considered do. However, it has not been tested on additional data and is not considered in depth here.

Finally, Horowitz and Rapoport (1974) investigated four- and five-person Apex games and manipulated (a) the order for the presentation of offers, with the Apex player either first or last, and (b) the value of the Apex coalition (for half of the groups it was 1.5 times larger than the payoff for the coalition of all other players). The kernel and the competitive bargaining set models make different predictions in these games, and thus this study was able to contrast them empirically. The bargaining set for these games is defined by a range of outcomes from the kernel to the competitive bargaining set.

The results indicated that the Apex coalition occurred in 45 of 48 plays, with significantly higher payoffs for the Apex player when he made his offers first rather than last. Most important, the payoffs to the players were within the bargaining set and were considerably closer to the competitive bargaining set's predictions than to the kernel's.

Two studies of a different nature (Murnighan & Roth, 1977, 1978) investigated the effects of information and communication availability on the behavior of a monopolist in three-person and large-group games where winning coalitions received a constant payoff. The results in 3-person groups indicated that the monopolist's mean payoffs ranged from 56.5% to 76.7%; in groups ranging from 7 to 12 players, the monopolists' mean payoffs ranged from 77.6% to 97.3%. Both

studies suggested that the monopolists' payoffs increased over trials in the conditions where communications were not allowed. In addition, the data suggest that communication opportunities and group size interacted to affect a monopolist's payoffs: With small groups (i.e., 3, 7, or 8 players), communication opportunities seemed to limit the monopolist's payoffs; with larger groups (i.e., between 9 and 12 players), communication opportunities did not inhibit an increase in the monopolist's payoffs over trials. A last result indicated that with the groups of 7 or more players, the monopolist was able to obtain payoffs that were as large as his demands, irrespective of communication opportunities. In the communication conditions, however, the monopolist's demands were relatively low, suggesting that the opportunity for the non-monopolists to communicate led to cautious play by the monopolists.

The game used in these studies, where one player was a monopolist, resulted in identical predictions for the weighted probability model and minimum power theory. Each model predicts that the monopolist's payoff should be $100 - 100/n$, where n equals the number of players in the group. The predictions were supported in the three-person groups and received some support, when communication opportunities were available, in the large-group study.

The data were also compared with the game theoretic concept of the core, which in these games subsumes the predictions of all of the forms of the bargaining set and indicates that the monopolist will receive the entire payoff. Although this extreme prediction was not strictly supported in either study, the increases in the monopolist's payoffs over trials in the no-communication conditions suggest that in both studies, the bargaining was moving toward the core. In addition, in the large-group study, the monopolist received 99% or more of the payoff in a majority of the agreements in the no-communication groups.

In summary, results from experiments using characteristic function games generally support the predictions of the bargaining set, although this support has not been universal. The core received some support in games with a monopolist, but only when communication opportunities were restricted. Due to their nonuniqueness, solutions and subsolutions have not been adequately tested. The only model that appears to have little empirical value is the kernel.

Social Psychological Research

Empirical research on coalition behavior by social psychologists has primarily focused on interactions in triads. Caplow's (1956) early impetus and the convenience of studying the smallest possible group size have probably contributed to this emphasis. In particular, triads whose resources are distributed so that $A > B > C$ and $A < (B + C)$ have received the most attention. This may be due to Vinacke and Arkoff's (1957) results: They found that the 3-2 coalition was most frequent in the 4-3-2 game and thus did not support Caplow's original theory (which predicted either the 4-2 or the 3-2 coalition).

From a game-theoretic perspective the studies on triads are somewhat limited in their generalizability. Triads can produce at most three distinct game types: (a) one in which any two players can win, that is, each player is equal (but may differ from other players in the number of votes he or she controls); (b) one in which one player has veto power and must be included in every coalition, although he or she cannot win alone; and (c) one in which one player is a dictator and can win by playing alone. Almost all of the studies on the triad have investigated the first of these three situations; many (cf. Chertkoff, 1970; Stryker, 1972) have found that the two players with the fewest resources are most likely to form coalitions. Thus the conclusion that "strength is weakness" has been frequent. This conclusion, however, may be an artifact of three-person games of this type: The player who controls the most resources in these games has *conditional power*, that is, power only if the other members of the group do not form a coalition. In Vinacke and Arkoff's (1957) paradigm, for instance, the player with four votes in the 4-3-2 game will win if the other players do not form a coalition. Vinacke and Arkoff reported that no coalition formed on approximately 2% of the

trials. Thus it is almost certain that a coalition will form, and the advantage gained by having conditional power is illusory. Thus the perception of conditional power is detrimental to the "strong" player.

The three-person studies, then, generally show that coalitions with the least number of resources will form. H. H. Kelley and Arrowood (1960), however, reported that after several trials with each player playing in the same position, coalitions between the two players with the smallest number of resources are no more frequent than the other coalitions. Thus, even the stability of the strength-is-weakness conclusion is questionable.

Because of the possibility of limited generalizability of the three-person studies, the present article focuses on research conducted on larger groups ($n \geq 4$). Games with larger groups have particular advantages in that they can model a greater diversity of conflict situations. Table 1 summarizes the tests of the models' predictions in such studies.

Willis (1962) and Shears (1967) conducted the first social psychological studies of tetrads. Two-person coalitions were most frequent, tending to support the more recent models. In addition, the data for payoff division in Shears's study seem to support the predictions of the weighted probability model, compared with the minimum resource, minimum power, and bargaining theories. However, the data were collected prior to the presentation of the theories, and thus support for a theory may be confounded with the use of the data in constructing the theory. These two early studies do support the conclusion that coalitions will form with the smallest number of players more frequently than will larger coalitions. This explicitly supports the weighted probability model and implicitly supports bargaining theory.

Chertkoff (1971) investigated the possibility that the formation of small coalitions could have been due to a procedural artifact. Three-person coalitions form in two steps: In the first step a two-person coalition must form; in the second step, a third coalition member is added. Thus, three-person coalitions may be less frequent due to procedural difficulties rather than to factors inherent in the game or the other manipulations. Chert-

Table 1
Positive and Negative Empirical Support for Four Coalition Models for Frequency and Payoff Predictions

		Model							
		Minimum resource		Minimum power		Bargaining		Weighted probability	
Study	Game	+	−	+	−	+	−	+	−
Willis (1962)	5-3-3-2	F[b]		F[ab]		F, P[ab]		F, P[ab]	
	4-4-3-2	F[b]		F[ab]		F, P[ab]		F, P[ab]	
Shears (1967)	3-1-1-1	F, P[b]		P[b]	F[b]	F, P[ab]		F, P[ab]	
	4-2-2-1		F, P[b]	F, P[b]		P[ab]		F, P[ab]	
Chertkoff (1971)	8-(3-3)-3			F, P		F, P[a]			F, P[ab]
	8-3-3-3		F, P	F, P		F, P[a]		F, P[ab]	
Komorita & Meek	8-4-3-2		F, P	F, P		F, P[a]		F, P[a]	
(Note 3)	8-3-3-3		F, P	F, P		F, P[a]		F, P[a]	
Komorita & Moore (1976)	10-9-8-3	F	P	F, P		F, P		F, P	
Michener, Fleishman, & Vaske (1976)	8 Apex		F, P	F, P		F, P		F, P[b]	
	8 veto	P	F	P	F	F	P	F[b]	P[b]
Murnighan, Komorita, & Szwajkowski (1977)	8-3-3-3		F, P	F, P		F, P		F	P
	8-7-1-1		F, P	F, P			P	F	P
	8-7-7-7	F	P	F, P		F, P		F	P
Gamson (1961b)	25-25-17-17-17	F,P[b]		F, P		F, P[ab]			F, P[ab]
Murnighan (in press)	10-9-8-7-5		F, P	P[b]		F[b]	P	F	P
	15-14-10-8-5	F	P	F, P[b]		F	P	F	P
	10-7-5-3-2	P	F	F, P[b]		F, P		F	P
	24-9-8-7-6		F, P	P[b]		F[b]		F, P	

Note. This table is meant to be a summary of the primary research findings in the cited studies. The data within each study are not as clear-cut as the table implies: Most studies found mixed support for the models. Games without entries could not be clearly evaluated. F = frequency; P = payoff.
[a] Research reported prior to presentation of the model.
[b] Evaluations made by the present author rather than by the study's author or authors.

koff investigated three games, each played for one trial: 80-60-30, 80-(30-30)-30, and 80-30-30-30. A comparison of the last two games showed that the (30-30)-30 coalition was considerably more frequent than the 30-30-30 coalition, indicating that procedural effects may have influenced the earlier results.

Komorita and Meek (Note 3) revised the earlier coalition formation procedures to allow three-person coalitions to form in a single step. Player X could make an offer for an XYZ coalition by sending the same three-person proposal to both Y and Z. If both accepted, the XYZ coalition formed. Komorita and Meek again found that in both games studied, two-person coalitions were significantly more frequent than three-person coalitions. In addition, the frequencies of the different two-person coalitions in the 8-4-3-2 game were not significantly different from one another.

Komorita and Moore (1976) reported the first study to test the two recent models after they were proposed. The models' predictions in the 10-9-8-3 game they studied are: (a) Minimum resource theory—9-8-3 coalition with payoffs of (45-40-15); (b) Bargaining theory—9-8-3, (36-34-30); and (c) Minimum power theory and the weighted probability model—any coalition, (33-33-33). The results indicated that 9-8-3 was most frequent for male and female groups, and 10-9-8 was fairly frequent for females. The players' outcomes changed over trials: Player 10's outcomes decreased over trials, and Player 3's outcomes increased over trials. All players' outcomes tended to approach equality as the trials progressed, suggesting increasing support over time for the minimum power theory and the weighted probability model. The results for males supported the theories more than did the results for females. Vinacke's notion (1971) of anticompetitiveness in females, then, was also supported by this study.

Murnighan, Komorita, and Szwajkowski (1977) studied tetrads in three different games and manipulated the reference groups of the players to investigate some of the underlying motivations of the players with respect to their instructions. The players' reference groups were either the players they were bargaining with or players in other groups who were playing in the same position as themselves. Results indicated that there was greater competition and more support for each of the theories when players had reference groups of other similar players. This result reinforces Komorita and Moore's (1976) findings for females: It appears that the theories' predictions receive the most support when the players are competitively motivated. Departures from this condition (due to sex or reference groups) reduce predictability and generalizability.

Michener, Fleishman, and Vaske (1976) tested the predictions of bargaining theory, minimum resource theory, and minimum power theory in 16 four-person games, 8 of which included a veto player. Bargaining theory's inappropriateness in making predictions for veto games is apparent in the data on coalition members' outcomes. Minimum power theory made significantly better predictions in this case than did either bargaining theory or minimum resource theory. Because bargaining theory is based on the notion of threats, and nonveto players cannot threaten the veto player with the potential formation of a coalition excluding him or her, the model is not amenable to predictions in veto games and is not strictly appropriate in such situations. Thus, although one might apply a theory to situations that it was not originally intended to model, in this case the limits of bargaining theory appear to be games that include a veto player.

Three studies have been conducted on larger groups. Gamson (1961b) investigated five-person groups in three different games.

Only one of the games is easily interpretable; results supported minimum resource theory's prediction of the 17-17-17 coalition. In addition, choice of a friend over a stranger as one's coalition partner was only somewhat more likely than the reverse and varied over conditions.

Vinacke (1971) conducted a study with male and female groups and varied the number of players for each of five games. The results in the two games that were appropriate for differentiating among the current models neither supported nor rejected any of them. As in some of the earlier studies, sex differences were apparent. Females tended to display accommodative behavior; males tended to display exploitative behavior. This was particularly evident in the dictatorship and monopolist games: Female dictators and monopolists did not push for higher payoffs. Instead, they often included unnecessary players in the coalitions and demanded relatively low payoffs for themselves.

Murnighan (in press) studied the coalition behavior of five players in each of four games. Resources (i.e., votes) were assigned to players to reflect each of the four possible strategic distributions that are possible in five-person games where each player is realistically involved in the play and no player holds veto or dictatorial power (von Neumann & Morgenstern, 1944): (a) $A > (B = C = D = E)$, (b) $A > (B = C) > (D = E)$, (c) $(A = B) > (C = D = E)$, and (d) $A = B = C = D = E$.

In addition to tests of the social psychological models (see Table 1), the overall payoffs of the players were compared with the Shapley value, which received some support. In addition, the results suggested an explanation for the strength-is-weakness phenomenon so frequently encountered in three-person research. Players with identical strategic positions (as determined by their Shapley value) but different resources evidenced the strength-is-weakness phenomenon; players with different strategic positions supported a strength-is-strength interpretation (i.e., more powerful positions received higher payoffs than did less powerful positions). The underlying reason for the strength-is-weakness effect appears to be relatively high subjective proba-

1148   J. KEITH MURNIGHAN

Table 2
Empirical Tests of the Size Principle

Study	Country	Time period	Support	Prevalent coalition size
Merkl (1970)	West Germany	1946–1954	No	Larger than minimum
Peterson (1970)	Brazil	1947–1965	Some	Larger than minimum
Rosenthal (1970)	France	1951–1956	Some	Minimum winning or less
Browne (1971)	Many	1945–1970	No	Minimum number of parties
DeSwaan (1973)	Many	1918–1940 1945–1972	No	Closed minimum range
Dodd (1974)	Many	1918–1940 1945–1972	No	Minimum number of parties
Nachmias (1974)	Israel	1949–1970	No	Larger than minimum

bilities assigned to the acceptance of one's offer by players with the least amount of resources, given identical strategic positions.

In summary, the social psychological research on coalition behavior in situations with four or more players (see Table 1) has typically found that if two-person coalitions are possible, they will be more frequent than three-person coalitions. Minimum resource theory and minimum power theory have received relatively little support. The weighted probability model has been supported, primarily in predicting the frequency of coalition formations. Bargaining theory has received substantial support, with instances of nonsupport in specific conditions (e.g., with female players, noncompetitive reference groups, and in veto games). Any evaluation of the accuracy of the models is, however, bound by the criteria selected. The prediction failures that both the weighted probability model and bargaining theory have experienced suggest that refinement of the models' assumptions (e.g., Chertkoff & Esser, 1977) is appropriate.

Political Research

Riker's (1962) size principle has been repeatedly tested in a number of settings. In his original presentation, Riker focused on evidence from "overwhelming majorities," coalitions that include all or almost all of a country's parties. Overwhelming majorities often form immediately after wartime; explanations for this phenomenon center around the country's desire to ignore differences and move effectively toward a unified state. Riker (1962) has shown that, as predicted, overwhelming majorities are quickly disbanded or reduced and that political systems in this situation move toward coalitions of minimum size.

Subsequent research has tested the size principle in several multiparty parliamentary governments (see Table 2). In only two cases, however, has there been any support for minimum winning coalitions.[3] Instead of coalitions of minimum size (i.e., 50% of the parliamentary seats plus one), the most prevalent coalitions are larger than minimum winning. Nachmias (1974) proposed a model to account for these results. He posited that in countries where one large party is dominant (but does not have a majority), coalitions will tend to be large: The dominant party will have little to lose by allowing extra parties into the coalition and may be able to obtain greater acceptance of its proposed policies. Thus this proposal supports, at least tangentially, the tenets of DeSwaan's (1973) model.

Although all the studies in Table 2 did not test for the formation of minimum-party coalitions, as was proposed by Leiserson (1968), two of the studies reported that they were most frequent. Dodd's (1974) study is particularly noteworthy: It included 17

---

[3] This does not include studies of "coalitions" that are based on roll call votes. This presentation has excluded such studies (e.g., Hinckley, 1972; Koehler, 1972; Pomper, 1970) because they focus on behavior that may be merely coincidental rather than coalitional (e.g., E. W. Kelley, 1968).

countries, considered coalition behavior from 1918 through 1972, and found not only that coalition governments with a minimum number of parties were most frequent but that they were also more durable than either larger or smaller coalition governments. Thus Leiserson's (1968) bargaining proposal received strong support in this study, as it did in his original evaluation of the proposal. As indicated in Table 2, the bargaining proposal received additional support from Browne's (1971) study. The countries and times studied by Browne, however, were almost all included in Dodd's sample. (The only exception was Israel, 1945–1970.) Thus, the two tests are not independent.

Neither Dodd (1974) nor Browne (1971) considered the ideologies of the parties within the countries in their studies. DeSwaan (1973) studied nine countries and used expert opinion to place parties on a left–right (liberal–conservative) ideological scale. As with the other recent tests, the accuracy of the models was determined by correcting for the number of predictions it made. DeSwaan (1973) found little or no support for models that do not consider party ideology (i.e., minimum size and minimum party models), found support for only one rather ad hoc version of his policy distance minimization model, and found the most support for the minimum range models, in particular the closed minimum range model. Thus, Leiserson's (1966), Axelrod's (1970), and to some degree, Rosenthal's (1970) models all were supported independently of their own investigations. Of the different versions of the policy distance minimization model, DeSwaan found support for a version of the model that predicted closed (i.e., connected) coalitions, thus adding further support for the predictability of closed, or connected, coalitions.

Research on coalition governments has also on occasion addressed game-theoretic and social psychological predictions. Leiserson (1968) and Browne (1971), for instance, found that the coalitions that were included in von Neumann and Morgenstern's (1944) solution set were quite frequent. Strong support was not found for the model, however, due to the larger number of coalitions within the predicted set. Another study, by Browne

and Franklin (1973), however, yielded strong support for Gamson's (1961a) assumption of the parity norm. Their results from 13 countries showed that the distribution of ministerial seats awarded to a party within the government was correlated .93 with the number of parliamentary seats the party held. Thus, payoffs were proportional to resources. The deviation from a perfect correlation appeared to be due, at least in part, to somewhat overproportionate payoffs to relatively small parties, especially within small coalitions. The overwhelming determinant of ministerial appointments, however, appeared to be a party's hold on parliamentary seats.

In summarizing and evaluating the empirical research on political coalitions, it is important to note that very few of the tests compared the predictions of several theories simultaneously. Instead, a single model was often compared with the data. DeSwaan's (1973) study, then, is noteworthy, for it compared 13 different models (some were proposed on an ad hoc basis as logical extensions of models that had been more formally presented). The fact that the minimum size and minimum party models received virtually no support, especially when paired with the results summarized in several of the studies in Table 2, seriously weakens the proposition that size is the primary criterion for the formation of political coalitions. Instead, it appears that the ideologies of one's coalition partners are extremely important and that strange bedfellows are indeed rare in coalition governments.

Conclusions

This review has covered the three areas of research on coalition behavior with little reference to work that has considered more than a single area. This treatment reflects the current state of this field of inquiry: Little overlap currently exists. Indeed, in considering which models have been the most accurate predictors of coalition bargaining, each area would have to be treated separately. The closed minimum-range model appears to explain most accurately the formation of coalition governments; bargaining theory appears to have an edge over the weighted probability model in accurately predicting the outcomes of resource-distribution games; and various models are applicable, depending on the conditions, in differential-payoff games. How can any of these models be applied to real coalition situations, such as decision-making groups (Cartwright, 1971), family interactions (Caplow, 1968), international negotiations, or organizational interactions?

Before answering this question, the impact of the variables central to each area might be evaluated when all of them are operative, that is, when payoffs, resources, and ideological similarity may vary. Each of the current research paradigms could incorporate these variables into theoretical tests. (Political scientists' focus on fixed-payoff coalition governments may hamper some of their efforts.) In addition, researchers in each area might consider testing as many models as possible, regardless of their origin, whenever theoretical tests are appropriate. The optimal situation would be a series of studies that manipulated or measured payoff differences, resource distributions, and ideological similarity in a variety of situations, potentially incorporating other important variables such as communication opportunities and sex of the players. Research that investigated the effects of two of the three central variables would also be a significant contribution. At this point, questions concerning the relative importance of each of these variables, questions that are crucial to understanding the dynamics of coalition behavior, cannot be answered.

In addition, further research integrating the determinants of coalition formation, following Michener, Lawler, and their colleagues (Lawler, 1975a, 1975b; Michener & Lawler, 1971, 1975; Michener & Lyons, 1972; Michener & Zeller, 1972), with the consequences of coalition formation would help to complete an overall picture of coalition processes.

In summary, three areas have made relatively independent sets of investigations on coalitions and coalition behavior. Each has adopted a separate outlook and can contribute useful perspectives concerning the processes and outcomes of coalition bargaining. Game theory's emphasis on a coalition's payoffs, social psychology's emphasis on a player's resources, and political science's emphasis on ideological similarity have resulted in impressive findings within each area. Collaboration among the three areas appears not only possible but appropriate for further advances in the study of coalition behavior.

Reference Notes

1. Lucas, W. F. *A game with no solution* (Publication RM-5518-PR). Santa Monica, Calif.: Rand Publications, 1967.

2. Maschler, M. *Playing an n-person game, an experiment* (Econometric Research Memorandum 73). Princeton, N.J.: Princeton University, 1965.

3. Komorita, S. S., & Meek, D. *Some preliminary tests of a bargaining theory of coalition formation.* Unpublished manuscript, Indiana University, 1972.

References

Aumann, R. J., & Maschler, M. The bargaining set for cooperative games. In M. Dresher, L. S. Shapley, & A. W. Tucker (Eds.), *Advances in game theory*. Princeton, N.J.: Princeton University Press, 1964.

Axelrod, R. *Conflict of interest.* Chicago: Markham, 1970.

Brams, S. J. A cost/benefit analysis of coalition formation in voting bodies. In R. G. Niemi & H. F. Weisberg (Eds.), *Probability models of collective decision making*. Columbus, Ohio: Merrill, 1972.

Brams, S. J., & Garriga-Pico, J. E. Deadlocks and bandwagons in coalition formation: The $\frac{1}{2}$ and $\frac{2}{3}$ rules. *American Behavioral Scientist*, 1975, *18*, 34–58.

Brams, S. J., & Heilman, J. C. When to join a coalition and with how many others depends on what you expect the outcome to be. *Public Choice*, 1974, *17*, 11–25.

Brams, S. J., & Riker, W. H. Models of coalition formation in voting bodies. In J. F. Herndon & J. L. Bernd (Eds.), *Mathematical applications in political science* (Vol. 4). Charlottesville: University of Virginia Press, 1972.

Browne, E. C. Testing theories of coalition formation in the European context. *Comparative Political Studies*, 1971, *3*, 391–412.

Browne, E. C., & Franklin, M. N. Aspects of coalition payoffs in European parliamentary democracies. *American Political Science Review*, 1973, *67*, 453–469.

Buckley, J. J., & Westen, T. E. The symmetric solution to a five-person constant-sum game as a description of experimental game outcomes. *Journal of Conflict Resolution*, 1973, *17*, 703–721.

Buckley, J. J., & Westen, T. E. Bargaining set theory and majority rule. *Journal of Conflict Resolution*, 1976, *20*, 481–495.

MODELS OF COALITION   1151

Butterworth, R. L. A research note on the size of winning coalitions. *American Political Science Review,* 1971, *65,* 741–745.

Butterworth, R. L. Comment on Shepsle's "On the size of winning coalitions." *American Political Science Review,* 1974, *68,* 519–521.

Caplow, T. A theory of coalitions in the triad. *American Sociological Review,* 1956, *21,* 489–493.

Caplow, T. Further development of a theory of coalitions in the triad. *American Journal of Sociology,* 1959, *64,* 488–493.

Caplow, T. *Two against one.* Englewood Cliffs, N.J.: Prentice-Hall, 1968.

Cartwright, D. Risk taking by individuals and groups: An assessment of research employing choice dilemmas. *Journal of Personality and Social Psychology,* 1971, *20,* 361–378.

Chertkoff, J. M. A revision of Caplow's coalition theory. *Journal of Experimental Social Psychology,* 1967, *3,* 172–177.

Chertkoff, J. M. Sociopsychological theories and research on coalition formation. In S. Groennings, E. W. Kelley, & M. Leiserson (Eds.), *The study of coalition behavior.* New York: Holt, Rinehart & Winston, 1970.

Chertkoff, J. M. Coalition formation as a function of differences in resources. *Journal of Conflict Resolution,* 1971, *15,* 371–383.

Chertkoff, J. M., & Esser, J. K. A test of three theories of coalition formation when agreements can be short-term or long-term. *Journal of Personality and Social Psychology,* 1977, *35,* 237–249.

Davis, M., & Maschler, M. The kernel of a cooperative game. *Naval Research Logistics Quarterly,* 1965, *12,* 223–259.

DeSwaan, A. An empirical model of coalition formation as an *n*-person game of policy distance minimization. In S. Groennings, E. W. Kelley, & M. Leiserson (Eds.), *The study of coalition behavior.* New York: Holt, Rinehart & Winston, 1970.

DeSwaan, A. *Coalition theories and cabinet formations.* San Francisco: Jossey-Bass, 1973.

Dodd, L. C. Party coalitions in multiparty parliaments: A game-theoretic analysis. *American Political Science Review,* 1974, *68,* 1093–1117.

French, J. R. P., & Raven, B. The bases of social power. In D. Cartwright (Ed.), *Studies in social power.* Ann Arbor, Mich.: Institute for Social Research, 1959.

Frohlich, N. The instability of minimum winning coalitions. *American Political Science Review,* 1975, *69,* 943–946.

Gamson, W. A. A theory of coalition formation. *American Sociological Review,* 1961, *26,* 373–382. (a)

Gamson, W. A. An experimental test of a theory of coalition formation. *American Sociological Review,* 1961, *26,* 565–573. (b)

Gamson, W. A. Experimental studies of coalition formation. In L. Berkowitz (Ed.), *Advances in experimental social psychology* (Vol. 1). New York: Academic Press, 1964.

Groennings, S., Kelley, E. W., & Leiserson, M. *The*

study of coalition behavior. New York: Holt, Rinehart & Winston, 1970.

Hinckley, B. Coalitions in Congress: Size and ideological distance. *Midwest Journal of Political Science,* 1972, *16,* 197–207.

Horowitz, A. D. The competitive bargaining set for cooperative *n*-person games. *Journal of Mathematical Psychology,* 1973, *10,* 265–289.

Horowitz, A. D., & Rapoport, Am. Test of the kernel and two bargaining set models in four- and five-person games. In An. Rapoport (Ed.), *Game theory as a theory of conflict resolution.* Dordrecht, The Netherlands: Reidel, 1974.

Kahan, J. P., & Rapoport, Am. Test of the bargaining set and kernel models in three-person games. In An. Rapoport (Ed.), *Game theory as a theory of conflict resolution.* Dordrecht, The Netherlands: Reidel, 1974.

Kahan, J. P., & Rapoport, Am. When you don't need to join: The effects of guaranteed payoffs on bargaining in three-person cooperative games. *Theory and Decision,* 1977, *8,* 97–126.

Kalisch, G., Milnor, J. W., Nash, J., & Nering, E. D. Some experimental *n*-person games. In R. M. Thrall, C. H. Coombs, & R. L. Davis (Eds.), *Decision processes.* New York: Wiley, 1954.

Kelley, E. W. Techniques of studying coalition formation. *Midwest Journal of Political Science,* 1968, *12,* 62–75.

Kelley, H. H., & Arrowood, A. J. Coalitions in the triad: Critique and experiment. *Sociometry,* 1960, *23,* 231–244.

Koehler, D. H. The legislative process and the minimal winning coalition. In R. G. Niemi & H. F. Weisberg (Eds.), *Probability models of collective decision making.* Columbus, Ohio: Merrill, 1972.

Komorita, S. S. A weighted probability model of coalition formation. *Psychological Review,* 1974, *81,* 242–256.

Komorita, S. S., & Chertkoff, J. M. A bargaining theory of coalition formation. *Psychological Review,* 1973, *80,* 149–162.

Komorita, S. S., & Moore, D. Theories and processes of coalition formation. *Journal of Personality and Social Psychology,* 1976, *33,* 371–381.

Laing, J. D., & Morrison, R. J. Coalitions and payoffs in three-person sequential games. *Journal of Mathematical Sociology,* 1973, *3,* 3–25.

Laing, J. D., & Morrison, R. J. Sequential games of status. *Behavioral Science,* 1974, *19,* 177–196.

Lawler, E. J. An experimental study of factors affecting the mobilization of revolutionary coalitions. *Sociometry,* 1975, *38,* 163–179. (a)

Lawler, E. J. The impact of status differences on coalitional agreements. *Journal of Conflict Resolution,* 1975, *19,* 271–285. (b)

Leiserson, M. *Coalitions in politics.* Unpublished doctoral dissertation, Yale University, 1966.

Leiserson, M. Factions and coalitions in one-party Japan: An interpretation based on the theory of games. *American Political Science Review,* 1968, *62,* 770–787.

Lieberman, B. Experimental studies   of conflict in

1152   J. KEITH MURNIGHAN

two-person and three-person games. In J. Criswell, H. Solomon, & P. Suppes (Eds.), *Mathematical models in small group processes*. Stanford, Calif.: Stanford University Press, 1962.

Lieberman, B. Coalition formation and change. In B. Lieberman (Ed.), *Social choice*. New York: Gordon & Breach, 1971.

Luce, R. D., & Raiffa, H. *Games and decisions*. New York: Wiley, 1957.

Maschler, M. The inequalities that determine the bargaining set. *Israel Journal of Mathematics*, 1966, *4*, 127–134.

Medlin, S. M. Effects of grand coalition payoffs on coalition formation in three-person games. *Behavioral Science*, 1976, *21*, 48–61.

Merkl, P. H. Coalition politics in West Germany. In S. Groennings, E. W. Kelley, & M. Leiserson (Eds.), *The study of coalition behavior*. New York: Holt, Rinehart & Winston, 1970.

Michener, H. A., Fleishman, J. A., & Vaske, J. J. A test of the bargaining theory of coalition formation in four-person groups. *Journal of Personality and Social Psychology*, 1976, *34*, 1114–1126.

Michener, H. A., & Lawler, E. J. Revolutionary coalition strength and collective failure as determinants of status reallocation. *Journal of Experimental Social Psychology*, 1971, *7*, 448–460.

Michener, H. A., & Lawler, E. J. Endorsement of formal leaders: An integrative model. *Journal of Personality and Social Psychology*, 1975, *31*, 216–223.

Michener, H. A., & Lyons, M. Perceived support and upward mobility as determinants of revolutionary coalition behavior. *Journal of Experimental Social Psychology*, 1972, *8*, 180–195.

Michener, H. A., & Zeller, R. A. The effects of coalition strength on the formation of contractual norms. *Sociometry*, 1972, *35*, 290–304.

Murnighan, J. K. Strength and weakness in four coalition situations. *Behavioral Science*, in press.

Murnighan, J. K., Komorita, S. S., & Szwajkowski, E. Theories of coalition formation and the effects of reference groups. *Journal of Experimental Social Psychology*, 1977, *13*, 166–181.

Murnighan, J. K., & Roth, A. E. The effects of communication and information availability in an experimental study of a three-person game. *Management Science*, 1977, *23*, 1336–1348.

Murnighan, J. K., & Roth, A. E. Large group bargaining in a characteristic function game. *Journal of Conflict Resolution*, 1978, *22*, 299–317.

Nachmias, D. Coalition politics in Israel. *Comparative Political Studies*, 1974, *7*, 316–333.

Nash, J. Two-person cooperative games. *Econometrica*, 1953, *21*, 128–140.

Peterson, P. Coalition formation in local elections in the station of Sao Paulo, Brazil. In S. Groennings, E. W. Kelley, & M. Leiserson (Eds.), *The study of coalition behavior*. New York: Holt, Rinehart & Winston, 1970.

Pomper, G. M. Conflict and coalitions at the Constitutional Convention. In S. Groennings, E. W.

Kelley, & M. Leiserson (Eds.), *The study of coalition behavior*. New York: Holt, Rinehart & Winston, 1970.

Rapoport, Am., & Kahan, J. P. When three is not always two against one: Coalitions in experimental three-person games. *Journal of Experimental Social Psychology*, 1976, *12*, 253–273.

Rapoport, An. *N-person game theory*. Ann Arbor: University of Michigan Press, 1970.

Riker, W. H. *The theory of political coalitions*. New Haven, Conn.: Yale University Press, 1962.

Riker, W. H. Bargaining in a three-person game. *American Political Science Review*, 1967, *61*, 91–102.

Riker, W. H. An experimental examination of formal and informal rules of a three-person game. In B. Lieberman (Ed.), *Social choice*. New York: Gordon & Breach, 1971.

Rosenthal, H. Size of coalition and electoral outcomes in the Fourth French Republic. In S. Groennings, E. W. Kelley, & M. Leiserson (Eds.), *The study of coalition behavior*. New York: Holt, Rinehart & Winston, 1970.

Roth, A. E. Subsolutions and the supercore of cooperative games. *Mathematics of Operations Research*, 1976, *1*, 43–49.

Roth, A. E. Bargaining ability, the utility of playing a game, and models of coalition formation. *Journal of Mathematical Psychology*, 1977, *16*, 153–160. (a)

Roth, A. E. The Shapley value as a von Neumann-Morgenstern utility. *Econometrica*, 1977, *45*, 657–664. (b)

Roth, A. E. The Nash solution and the utility of bargaining. *Econometrica*, 1978, *46*, 587–594.

Selten, R., & Schuster, K. G. Psychological variables and coalition forming behavior. In K. Borch & J. Mossin (Eds.), *Risk and uncertainty*. London: Macmillan, 1968.

Shapley, L. S. A value for *n*-person games. In H. W. Kuhn & A. W. Tucker (Eds.), *Contributions to the theory of games* (Vol. 2). Princeton, N.J.: Princeton University Press, 1953.

Shears, L. M. Patterns of coalition formation in two games played by male tetrads. *Behavioral Science*, 1967, *12*, 130–137.

Shepsle, K. A. On the size of winning coalitions. *American Political Science Review*, 1974, *68*, 509–519 (a)

Shepsle, K. A. Minimum winning coalitions reconsidered: A rejoinder to Butterworth's "Comment." *American Political Science Review*, 1974, *68*, 522–524. (b)

Stryker, S. Coalition formation. In C. G. McClintock (Ed.), *Experimental social psychology*. New York: Macmillan, 1972.

Taylor, M. On the theory of governmental coalition formation. *British Journal of Political Science*, 1972, *2*, 361–386.

Thrall, R. M., & Lucas, W. F. *N*-person games in partition function form. *Naval Research Logistics Quarterly*, 1963, *10*, 281–298.

Vinacke, W. E. Negotiations and decisions in a

politics game. In B. Lieberman (Ed.), *Social choice*. New York: Gordon & Breach, 1971.

Vinacke, W. E., & Arkoff, A. An experimental study of coalitions in the triad. *American Sociological Review*, 1957, *22*, 406–414.

von Neumann, J., & Morgenstern, O. *Theory of games and economic behavior*. Princeton, N.J.: Princeton University Press, 1944.

Westen, T. E., & Buckley, J. J. Toward an explanation of experimentally obtained outcomes to a simple, majority rule game. *Journal of Conflict Resolution*, 1974, *18*, 198–236.

Willis, R. H. Coalitions in the tetrad. *Sociometry*, 1962, *25*, 358–376.

Received July 25, 1977 ∎

[16]

I Won the Auction
But Don't Want the Prize

MAX H. BAZERMAN
Sloan School of Management, MIT

WILLIAM F. SAMUELSON
Boston University School of Management

The "winner's curse" occurs in competitive situations when a successful buyer finds that he or she has paid too much for a commodity of uncertain value. This study provides an experimental demonstration of the winner's curse, and identifies factors that affect the existence and magnitude of this bidding abnormality. In an auction setting, two factors are shown to affect the incidence and magnitude of the winner's curse: (1) the degree of uncertainty concerning the value of the item up for bid and (2) the number of competing bidders. Increasing either factor will increase the range of value estimates and bids, making it more likely that the winning bidder will overestimate the true value of the commodity and thus overbid.

A number of researchers have suggested that the winner of a sealed-bid auction will often lose—that is, the object acquired will be worth less than the price paid. The winning bidder has fallen prey to the "winner's curse." This idea has been suggested theoretically (Case, 1979; Oren and Williams, 1975; Rothkopf, 1980; Winkler and Brooks, 1980) and has been applied to bidding on oil leases (Capen et al., 1971), stock market investments (Miller, 1977), and baseball players (Cassing and

------

AUTHOR'S NOTE: We thank Elizabeth Lepkowski for data collection and data analysis assistance. This article benefited from comments from Terry Connelly and seminars presented at Carnegie-Mellon University, the University of Texas at Austin, and Boston University, and was supported in part by National Science Foundation Grant #BNS-8107331 and a grant from Boston University School of Management.

JOURNAL OF CONFLICT RESOLUTION, Vol. 27 No. 4, December 1983 618-634
© 1983 Sage Publications, Inc.

Douglas, 1980). The rationale for this overbidding is that (1) while the average bidder may accurately estimate the value of the commodity up for sale in an auction, some bidders will underestimate this value and others will overestimate it, (2) the bidder who most greatly overestimates the value of the commodity will typically win the auction and (3) the amount of overestimation will often be greater than the difference between the winning bidder's estimate of the value of the commodity and his or her bid. Thus the winner of a competitive auction should expect to find that the commodity acquired is worth substantially less than his or her prior estimate of its value. While the theory and applicability of this effect have been noted, the winner's curse has not been subjected to rigorous empirical investigation, and the conditions under which this effect is likely to occur have not been documented.

To begin the discussion, consider the following scenarios:

> You are a major oil company bidding against a dozen other companies for an off-shore oil lease. None of the bidding firms has good information on the actual value of the lease. Your bid is the highest, and you win the lease. Should you be pleased?

> You are a major conglomerate considering an acquisition. Many other firms are also considering this acquisition. The actual value of the target firm is highly uncertain. After six firms submit competing offers, your bid is the highest. Your offer is accepted, and you obtain the acquisition. Have you been successful?

> You are the owner of a baseball team. A sometimes great, sometimes terrible pitcher has declared free agency. Like most teams, you are in need of good pitching. In the free agency draft, 10 teams (including yours) appear interested in the player. After negotiating with each team, the player accepts your offer. Is it time to celebrate?

In each of these scenarios, the casual observer would note that you have won the competition. Moreover, you have obtained a commodity at a price that your best estimate suggests is a good value—otherwise you would not have made the offer. However, the following reasoning may raise some doubts. Perhaps the sole reason you were the highest bidder is the fact that you have significantly overestimated the actual value of the commodity. If this is the case, you may have fallen prey to the winner's curse.

Why does the winner's curse occur? With help of a few minor assumptions, Figure 1 graphically demonstrates the logic of the effect in an auction context. As depicted, the bidders' value estimates are normally distributed with a mean equal to the actual value of the commodity. In turn, the distribution of bids is determined by a leftward

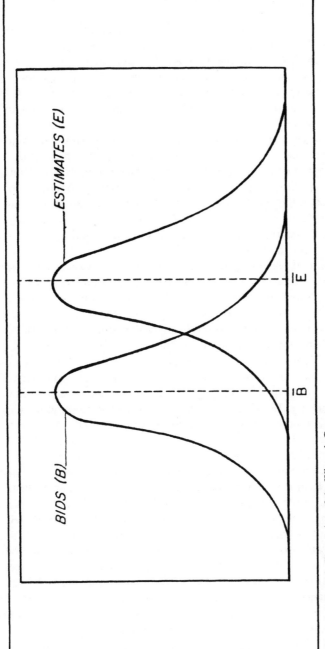

Figure 1: Graphic Illustration of the Winner's Curse

Variables: E = estimates; B = bid; D = (amount of disounting) =E − B.

Assumptions: (1) True Value ≈ E; (2) True Value will be equal for all bidders.

shift of the distribution of estimates—that is, on the average, bidders discount their estimates in making their bids. As Figure 1 shows, a winning bid drawn from the right tail of the bid distribution may exceed the actual value of the good. Likewise, when the winner's margin of overestimation exceeds the discount in making a bid, he or she will overpay for the item acquired. Why does the individual fall prey to the winner's curse? We argue that the answer lies in the exclusion of a relevant piece of information from the decision processes of the bidders. If an individual assumes that his or her bid will win the auction, this piece of data should indicate that the bidder has probably overestimated the value of the commodity in comparison to other competitors. When the correct inference is drawn, the bidder should revise the estimate of the true value of the item downward and lower the bid accordingly. By failing to take this inference into account, the winning bidder risks paying too much for the "prize."

This line of reasoning presupposes an objective value assessment— that is, the winner's curse is measured as the difference between the individual's bid and the objective (though unknown) value of the commodity. However, it is important to recognize that the individual may place a purely subjective value on the commodity.[1] For instance, it is possible for the individual to overbid for the commodity, be aware of the overbid, and yet experience no regret. This can occur when winning has some psychological utility in itself, or when the commodity has personal or intrinsic value (e.g., a painting). Conversely, a winning bidder may pay less than the value of the commodity yet experience a subjective winner's curse. For example, an individual who aspires to obtain the item at 85% of its objective worth will be dissatisfied if he obtains it at 92% of its worth.

The psychological literature suggests that the first case is more likely to occur than the second. Specifically, cognitive consistency theorists (Aronson, 1968; Festinger, 1957; Wicklund and Brehm, 1976) would predict that a bidder who has objectively overpaid for an item is likely to exaggerate its true value in order to rationalize his or her bid. Such attempts at dissonance reduction are likely if the acquired commodity does not have a clearly specified value, since this allows more degrees of freedom in the interpretation of value. While it is important to recognize the difference between the objective and subjective interpretations, our central theme concerns the existence of an objective winner's curse (using commodities that have clear objective values).

1. We are indebted to an anonymous referee for pointing out this key issue.

The key remaining question is this: How does one identify conditions under which the winner's curse is likely to occur? This article identifies two factors affecting the likelihood and magnitude of the winner's curse. The first factor is the degree of uncertainty concerning the value of the item up for bid. The greater the uncertainty about this value, the greater the variance of bidder values estimates. For example, if a $1 bill is auctioned off, there will be no uncertainty about the value of the item, and no variance in bidder estimates would be predicted. Excluding deviant bidding behavior and unusual auction rules (e.g., see Shubik, 1971), bids in excess of $1 would never occur. In contrast, if a jar with 100 pennies (this number unknown to the subjects) is auctioned, there will be far more uncertainty about the value of the item and greater variance in estimates, introducing the possibility of the winner's curse. The same point can be made graphically. Increasing the spread of estimates and bids in Figure 1 makes it much more likely that a winning bid, lying in the right tail of the bid distribution, will exceed the actual value of the item for sale.

When submitting a bid, the individual cannot use the actual variance of estimates and bids as a measure of commodity uncertainty since they cannot be observed. Instead, each bidder has only a personal assessment of the uncertainty surrounding the value of the commodity to rely on. In the experiment, personal uncertainty is measured by the range size of each individual's stated 90% confidence interval. The aggregate uncertainty of a given commodity is calculated as the average of these personal range sizes over all individuals. An initial question, then, is whether aggregate commodity uncertainty—while normatively relevant—is a useful indicator of the actual (and unobservable to the bidders) variance in estimates and bids.

A second question is whether or not the typical bidder recognizes this uncertainty and takes it into account when making a bid. We shall take as our starting point the following "null" hypothesis: The typical individual's bid depends only on that individual's value estimate and note on the perceived uncertainty concerning the item's value. A competing hypothesis is that for a given initial value estimate, greater value uncertainty lowers bids. This may occur for two reasons. The bidder may recognize this as the correct normative response in accordance with the argument above. Alternatively, a risk-averse bidder may assess a lower certainty equivalent amount for the item when its value is more uncertain and bid lower according. Under the null hypothesis, failure to discount bids in response to greater uncertainty will increase the likelihood and magnitude of the winner's curse. (Of course, the same result may occur under the competing hypothesis if discounting, though present, is insufficient to counteract the upward bias in the winning bid caused by the increased uncertainty in estimates.)

A second factor affecting the existence and magnitude of the winner's curse is the size of the bidding population. As the number of bidders increase, so will the range of estimates and bids. For example, if the bidding group size is 4, the likelihood of finding someone in the extreme right tail of the estimate curve (Figure 1) is far less than if the size of the bidding group is 26. This suggests that subjects, in environments where the winner's curse is likely, should increase their discounting as the bidding group size increases to counteract the greater likelihood of the winning bidder overbidding. Specifically, the individual should engage in the simple train of thought:

> If mine proves to be the winning bid, what can I conclude about the commodity's true value relative to my estimate and bid? The appropriate inference is that in all likelihood I've overestimated the true value. Furthermore, the implied margin of overestimation increases with the number of competing bidders, and I should lower my bid accordingly."[2]

In contrast, we predict that subjects will fail to increase their discounts as the number of competitors increases, for two reasons. First, they will fail to understand the inference to be drawn from the fact that their bid is the highest and will overlook the relevance of bidding group size as it influences the winners' curse. Second, bidders commonly reason as follows: "I will have to bid closer to the real value (my estimate) if I am going to win [so to speak] the auction with so many bidders." As a descriptive matter, it is difficult to say which effect—the tendency toward discounting (the normatively appropriate response) or toward increased bids—is stronger. As an initial attack on the issue, we adopt the null hypothesis that bids are insensitive to the number of competitors.

2. This discounting is necessary regardless of the a priori likelihood that the individual will win the auction. For instance, it is less likely that the individual will win against a large number of bidders; nonetheless he or she should discount appropriately and increase his or her discount as the number of bidders increases. What the result depends on is reasonable enough bidding behavior on the parts of the other bidders so the individual can infer that if he or she wins, his or her estimate will have an upward bias (the more so the greater the number of competitors). The experimental results amply confirm that the subject bids depend closely on estimates; therefore, supporting the inference that a winning bid means a high estimate.

Together, the null hypotheses concerning bidding behavior imply our main testable result: With the failure of bidding adjustments by subjects, the magnitude of the winner's curse will increase with increases in commodity uncertainty and the number of bidders.Capan, Clapp, and Campbell (1971) and Case (1979) previously suggested that the winner of a competitive auction will commonly pay more than the actual value of the acquired commodity. Their studies, however, did not attempt controlled experimentation to the conditions that lead to the existence of the winner's curse. Following the logic above, our experiment examines the following hypothesized effects:

(1) The winner of a sealed-bid auction of a highly uncertain commodity with a large number of bidders will typically pay more than the value of the commodity.
(2) As the aggregate uncertainty surrounding the commodity increases, so too the variance of bids.
(3) Individual bids depend on value estimates only; they do not depend on (a) the amount of uncertainty surrounding the item for sale, or (b) the number of bidders competing for the item.
(4) The likelihood and magnitude of the winner's curse will increase as (a) the uncertainty surrounding the commodity increases, and (b) the size of the bidding population increases.

METHOD

SUBJECTS

Subjects were M.B.A. students (N = 419) in 12 microeconomics classes at Boston University (class sizes varying from 34 to 54). The experiment as an introduction to "decision making under uncertainy" and provided data for this research.

PROCEDURE

Each class participated in four sealed-bid auctions, bidding on a different commodity in each of the auctions. Unknown to the subjects, all commodities had a value of $8.00 (e.g., 800 pennies, 160 nickels, 200 large paper clips assigned a value of four cents, and 400 small paper clips assigned a value of two cents. Subjects were told that the highest bidder would pay his or her bid and receive the defined value of the auctioned commodity in return. For example, if the highest bid was $7.00, the individual bidding would receive a net payment of $8.00 – $7.00 (or $1.00). Thus subjects bid on the value of the commodity, not the commodity itself. In addition to their bids, subjects provided their best estimate of the value of each of the commodities and placed 90% confidence bounds around these estimates. To promote the best possible estimates, a $2.00 prize was given for the closest estimate to the true value in each auction. All information on one auction was completed before the next auction began, and no feedback was provided until all parts of the experiment were completed.

EXPERIMENTAL DESIGN

The analysis focused on two independent variables—commodity uncertainty and size of the bidding population—as separate factors affecting the magnitude of winning bids. For each item, commodity uncertainty was defined as the mean of the 90% confidence range sizes across subjects. Bidding size was manipulated by telling each subject, on a personal information sheet, the number of bidders in his or her auction group. Further, it was stressed that the subject was competing only against those bidders and not the whole class. The auction group sizes used where 4, 6, 8, 10, 12, 14, 16, 18, 20, 22, 24, and 26. All subjects in a class were given identical information on group size for each auction. Thus 48 observations were obtained through the participation of 12 classes in four auctions, for four different commodities, with four different bidding sizes in effect. In addition, a Latin Squares Design was used to eliminate any order effects or covariation between the two independent variables. The complete experimental design is displayed in Table 1.

ANALYSES

For each auction, we calculated the average value of the winning bid (AWB). Instead of assigning particular subjects to auction groups, we determined the highest bidder for each of the total possible combinations of auction groups that could be drawn from the total number of students in the class. Obviously a very large number of possible combinations existed for each of the 48 auctions. We then averaged the values

TABLE 1
Experimental Design

Class	Auction 1		Auction 2		Auction 3		Auction 4		Class Size
	Commodity	AGS	Commodity	AGS	Commodity	AGS	Commodity	AGS	
1	P	4	2¢	10	N	16	4¢	22	24
2	N	18	2¢	24	P	6	4¢	12	28
3	N	8	4¢	14	P	20	2¢	26	31
4	2¢	16	P	22	4¢	4	N	10	35
5	2¢	6	N	12	4¢	18	P	24	54
6	4¢	20	N	26	2¢	8	P	14	33
7	N	22	4¢	16	P	10	2¢	4	34
8	P	12	4¢	6	N	24	2¢	18	35
9	2¢	14	P	8	4¢	26	N	20	28
10	4¢	10	N	4	2¢	22	P	16	49
11	4¢	24	P	18	2¢	12	N	6	32
12	P	26	2¢	20	N	14	4¢	8	36

AGS = auction group size.
P = 800 pennies
N = 160 nickels
2¢ = 400 small paper clips (valued at 2¢ per clip)
4¢ = 200 large paper clips (valued at 4¢ per clip)

of the high bids over all possible auctions group combinations. Formally, the AWB is defined as:

$$AWB = \sum_{I=1}^{N} P_i B_i.$$

Where

$$P_i = [K/N-i+1][1 - \sum_{j=1}^{i-1} P_j],$$
$$\text{for } 1 \leq i \leq N-K+1,$$

and

$$Pi = 0, \quad \text{for } N-K=1 < i \leq N.$$

Here, N is the number of students in the class, K is the number of bidders in the auction group, B_i is the value of the ith highest bid in class, and P_i is the probability that the ith highest bidder in the class will appear in and be the highest bidder in an auction group drawn at random (i.e., with all possible auction groups equally likely). The degree and severity of the winner's curse is indicated by the average magnitude of overpayment—the difference between the actual value of the commodity and the average bid.

RESULTS

PRELIMINARY ANALYSES

The effect depicted in Figure 1 assumes that the mean estimate of the value of a commodity will be approximately equal to the true value of that commodity. If estimates are lower on the average than the true value, any test of the winner's curse would be conservative since the tail of the distribution of bids is actually compared to the true value—not to the mean of the distribution of estimates. In fact, across the four commodities, the average value estimate was $5.13 ($2.87 below the true value). This underestimation should reduce the likelihood and magnitude of the winner's curse across all auction groups. We assume that the underestimation observed is specific to our task and does not represent a generalizable estimation bias.

Hypothesis 1. The mean AWB for the 48 auctions was $10.01, with a standard deviation of $5.48. Thus the average auction resulted in a loss of $2.01 to the winning bidder. Twelve auctions had AWBs under $7.00, 10 had AWBs between $7.00 and $8.00, 3 had AWBs between $8.00 and $9.00, and 23 auctions resulted in AWBs over $9.00. Thus strong support for the winner's curse occurred despite significant underestimation of value. Had the subjects been unbiased in their estimates (i.e., had the true value been $5.13), the average loss would have been $4.88.

Hypothesis 2. The measure of aggregate commodity uncertainty (the mean 90% confidence range size across all 419 subjects) took on the following values for the four commodities: two cent pieces, $5.20; pennies, $5.40; nickels, $6.02; and four-cent pieces, $6.58. While commodity uncertainty affected the variance of bids in the predicted direction, the effect was far from precise. The relationship is specified by the following raw score regression equation (N = 48):

$$SDB = -2.0 + .83 \ UNC + \epsilon \qquad [1]$$
$$(p = .152)$$
$$R^2 = .14 \qquad F = 7.6$$

where SDB denotes the standard deviation of bids in each auction and UNC denotes aggregate commodity uncertainty. For this equation, the standardized regression weight is .15.

Hypothesis 3. To test the effects of commodity uncertainty and the number of competitors on bidding behavior, we estimated the following regression equation (N = 48):

$$BID = -.002 + .41 \ EST + .025 \ UNC - .009 \ K + \epsilon, \qquad [2]$$
$$(p < .001) \quad (ns) \qquad (ns)$$
$$R^2 = .58 \qquad F = 19.98$$

where BID denotes the mean bid for each of the 48 auctions, EST the mean value estimate, UNC the aggregate commodity uncertainty, and K the number of bidders. Neither UNC nor K significantly affected the value of the mean bid. The equation indicates, however, that the mean bid was about 41% of the mean estimate and that the independent variables (primarily the mean estimate) explain a surprising amount of the variation (58%) of bids across auctions. For this equation, the standardized regression weights are .58, .02, and –.08 for EST, UNC, and K, respectively. Table 2 provides simple correlations among the four variables in the equation.

Like equation 1, equation 2 uses the auction groups as the unit of analysis. A similar result occurs when individual bids are examined. Consider the following raw score regression, which uses each bid as an observation (N = 1676):

$$BID_i = 1.31 + .53\ EST_i - .03\ UNC_i - .009\ K + \epsilon,$$

$$(p < .001)\ (p < .001)\qquad (ns)$$

$$R^2 = .45\quad F = 463.0$$

where the subscripts i denote individual bids, estimates, and uncertainty, respectively. Note that the effect of UNC_i is significant and in the anticipated direction, but the size of the effect is very small. When other things are equal, a dollar increase in the individual's 90% confidence range reduces his or her bid by only three cents. The standardized regression weights for this equation are .69, –.12, and –.02 for EST, UNC, and K, respectively.

Hypothesis 4. Finally, to test the relationship between the average winning bid, commodity uncertainty, and the number of bidders, the following regression equation was estimated:

$$AWB = -13.64 + 3.61\ UNC + .18\ K + \epsilon. \qquad [4]$$

$$(P < .001)\quad (p < .005)$$

$$R^2 = .182,\ F = 5.018$$

The standardized regression weights for this equation are .36 and .23 for UNC and K, respectively.

A close inspection of the auction data reveals that AWB is sensitive to idiosyncratic bidding behavior (i.e., a handful of grossly inflated bids). For this reason the explanatory power of equation 4 is limited. In all, it explains only about 18% of the variation in AWB. Moreover, the

TABLE 2
Pearson Correlations

	Mean Value Estimate	Commodity Uncertainty	Number of Bidders
Average winning bid	.445**	.362**	.227*
Number of bidders	.109	.00	
Commodity uncertainty	.744**		

* p < .005; ** p < .001.

coefficient magnitudes should be taken to be no more than suggestive of the relative effects of the twin factors on the winner's curse. With these in mind, a number of rough conclusions can be drawn. First, the equation indicates that commodity uncertainty has the greater influence on the average winning bid. For instance, pegging UNC and K at their mean values ($5.80 and 15 respectively), one estimates AWB to be $10.00. A 20% increase in UNC (from $5.80 to $7.00) results in a 43% increase in AWB (from $10 to $14.30). In turn, a 20% increase in the number of bidders (from 15 to 18) increases AWB by only 5%. Second, by setting AWB equal to $8.00, one can determine the values of UNC and K at which the winner's curse is first predicted to occur. For instance, when two-cent pieces are up for bid (UNC = $5.20), the AWB first is expected to exceed $8.00 when the number of bidders (K) is 13. By contrast, when four-cent pieces, the most uncertain commodity, are auctioned, the winner's curse is predicted to occur with as few as 4 bidders (in which case AWB = $10.83). Finally, equation 4 can be used to indicate the correct bidding response to changes in UNC and K. For instance, suppose that all competitiors adjust their bids according to

$$\Delta \text{BID}_i = -3.61 \, \Delta \text{UNC} - .18 \, \Delta \text{K}. \qquad [5]$$

Individuals lower their bids $3.61 for each dollar increase in UNC and 18¢ for each additional bidder. With this adjustment, the AWB will remain constant across all auction conditions, eliminating the increased incidence of the winner's curse as UNC and/or K increase. Thus the estimated coefficients in equation 4 specify the size of the necessary adjustment by the population of bidders.

DISCUSSION

These results generally support the findings of Capen et al. (1971) and Case (1979) on the frequency of the winner's curse in an auction context. However, the current results find a great deal of variation in the existence and magnitude of this effect. Furthermore, two explanatory variables—commodity uncertainty and the size of the bidding population—have theoretically and empirically been shown to account for much of this variation. The explanation for these effects is that subjects fail to draw the appropriate inference under uncertainty and to adjust their bids sufficiently in light of this inference. The evidence suggests that subjects employ naive bidding strategies, basing bids upon unconditional value estimates and disregarding relevant information such as the uncertainty surrounding the commodity and number of bidders. The correct normative bidding behavior is more subtle. All participants should base their bids on the expected value of the commodity if their bid is the highest. Assuming reasonable bidding behavior by competitors, a participant can infer that he or she was the highest bidder because he or she had the most optimistic value estimate. If it is presumed that one bidder's information is neither better nor worse (though possibly different) than another's, then pooling all the individual assessments (taking a simple average if they are independent and unbiased) provides the best estimate of the item's value. Clearly the highest bidder's estimate (and the accompanying bid) will be upwardly biased. This bias increases with an increase in the uncertainty surrounding the commodity and/or an increase in the number of bidders, since either effect leads to a greater range of estimates and bids. The evidence strongly indicates that individuals fail to undertake this necessary inference and to adjust their bids accordingly. Thus while individuals recognize that uncertainty exists, they do not take this into account sufficiently when formulating their bidding strategies (equations 2 and 3). Nor do they adjust their bids with changes in the number of competitors. In the absence of bidding adjustment, one would expect the frequency and magnitude of the winner's curse to depend directly on the uncertainty surrounding the value of the commodity and on the number of competing bidders. This hypothesis was confirmed by the experimental evidence (equation 4).

While we join with other analysts (e.g., Wilson, 1977) in arguing that individuals should recognize the winner's curse and pursue appropriate normative bidding strategies, our data strongly suggest that untrained subjects fail to do so in predictable ways. By identifying the twin factors that contribute to overbidding, our study suggests appropriate remedies. For instance, a superficial analysis of the winner's curse would recommend staying away from auctions altogether. Our findings, in contrast, suggest that it is possible to determine a profitable bidding strategy by incorporating information on the number of bidders and commodity uncertainty (equation 5).

The subtlety of this inferential task raises additional questions concerning the sources of individual judgmental biases. For instance, if informed of the competing bids, would a winning bidder stick by a previous price offer or withdraw it if given the chance? What if the subject were shown the other competitors' value estimates—or, more suggestively, the mean of the competing estimates? Even in these "full information" cases, many winning bidders, overconfident of their estimated values, might be expected to stick by their bids. Indeed, it is interesting to speculate as to how many winning bidders, given full information about competing bids and estimates, would jump at the chance to obtain the item at a discount price equal to the highest competing bid. Even at this lower price, the purchaser falls prey to the winner's curse, suffering a small average loss on the transaction. A final experimental modification would allow syndicates (two or more individuals acting as a team) to submit bids. One would expect a group bid, based on a (presumably better) pooled-value estimate, to be less susceptible to inferential bias and to the winner's curse. The form of training that can lead to optimal improvement in bidding judgments is a topic for further investigation.

APPLICATIONS

In competitive procurements, it is commonly held that the contract winner may be simply the most optimistic firm (the one that most grossly underestimates program costs) rather than the most efficient. In bidding for off-shore oil tracts, a common belief is that the winner often pays too much for the lease. However, evidence bearing on the importance of the winner's curse in these contexts is sketchy at best. Frequent cost overruns in procurement stem partially from cost misestimates (the winner's curse) but are frequently due to poor contract incentives for the winning firm to seek cost economies. Estimates in the 1970s suggested that the U.S. government had received approximately the full monetary value for off-shore tracts sold. In aggregate, tract winners may not have been cursed, but perhaps the greater surprise is that oil companies have failed to earn excessive profits! The industry has not obtained the bargains that might have been expected.

The winner's curse plays a part in a variety of other bidding settings, from the free agent market in major league baseball to the practice of blind bidding for film exhibition rights. Teams that compete for baseball superstars should recognize that a player's past performance is a highly uncertain predictor of future performance. In line with the experimental results presented above, one would expect high-variance ball players sought by numerous major league teams would prove to be the most overpaid (vis-à-vis their actual performance). Frequently exhibitors must bid for movie rights before a given film has been seen or even completed. Favored by distributors, this practice of blind bidding has been resisted by exhibitors and banned in several states. Exhibitors complain of paying too much for films that prove to be flops. It appears that exhibitors may fall prey to the winner's curse, and, for this reason, that distributors have a positive incentive to keep the bidding blind.

The increase in the number of corporate takeovers in the 1980s has provided evidence that acquiring companies often pay too much for what they get. As many as one-third of all acquisitions prove to be failures, and an additional one-third fail to live up to expectations (Wall Street Journal, 1981). Our analysis suggests that potential acquirers should temper their optimism by recognizing that successfully acquired companies are likely to be worth far less than the expected value estimated by the acquirer. Indeed, an acquirer is in the greatest danger of falling prey to the winner's curse during a bidding war over a takeover candidate. Some of the largest and most publicized takeover contests— for example, Dupont's winning bid for Conoco against the competition of Mobil and Seagram—have resulted in purchase premiums more than 50% above market prices. The success or failure of these acquisitions remains to be seen.

This experiment demonstrates the presence of nonrational judgment in the domain of competitive bidding. In terms of the judgment literature, we suggest that more attention be given to competitive situations—the context in which most judgments take place. In terms of the bidding literature, we suggest that more attention be given to both descriptive models and controlled experimentation. Normative theory provides an anchor from which we can record judgmental deficiencies but is seldom, by itself, able to describe actual judgments. Future research in these directions should result in a better understanding of competitive judgments through the integration of descriptive models, normative theory, and actual problems.

This article introduces a new set of questions to the literature on conflict resolution. When multiple parties engage in negotiation and competitive bidding, how can an individual avoid a transaction in which he or she pays more than the agreement is worth? We offer a simple starting point for decision makers in conflict situations: Determine if new information would be available if you assumed you were going to "win" the competition. Often recognition of this information can keep a competitor from falling prey to the winner's curse. Future research should elaborate on determinants of the likelihood and magnitude of the winner's curse and extend our results to a variety of conflict domains.

REFERENCES

ARONSON, E. (1968) "Dissonance theory: Progress and problems," in R. Abelson et al. (eds.) Theories of Cognitive Consistency. Chicago: Rand McNally.

CAPEN, E. C., R. V. CLAPP, and W. M. CAMPBELL (1971) "Competitive bidding in high risk situations." J. of Petroleum Technology 23: 641-653.

CASE, J. H. (1979) Economics and the Competitive Process. New York: New York Univ. Press.

CASSING, J. and R. W. DOUGLAS (1980) "Implication of the auction mechanism in baseball's free agent draft." Southern J. of Economics 47: 110-121.

FESTINGER, L. (1957) A Theory of Cognitive Dissonance. Stanford, CA: Stanford Univ. Press.

MILLER, E. M. (1977) "Risk, uncertainty, and divergence of opinion." J. of Finance 32: 1151-1168.

OREN, M. E. and A. C. WILLIAMS (1975) "On competitive bidding." Operations Research 23: 1072-1079.

ROTHKOPF, M. H. (1980) "On multiplicative bidding strategies." Operations Research 28: 570-575.

SHUBIK, M. (1971) "The dollar auction game: a paradox in noncooperative behavior and escalation." J. of Conflict Resolution 15: 109-111.

Wall Street Journal (1981) "To win a bidding war doesn't insure success of merged companies." September 1: 1.

WICKLUND, R. A. and J. W. BREHM (1976) Perspectives on Cognitive Dissonance. Hillsdale, NJ: Lawrence Erlbaum.

WILSON, R. (1977) "A bidding model of perfect competition." Rev. of Econ. Studies 4: 511-518.

WINKLER, R. L. and D. G. BROOKS (1980) "Competitive bidding with dependent value estimates." Operations Research 28: 603-613.

The Winner's Curse and Public Information in Common Value Auctions

By JOHN H. KAGEL AND DAN LEVIN*

Experienced bidders show sensitivity to the strategic considerations underlying common value auctions, but not to item valuation considerations. Auctions with large numbers of bidders (6-7) produce more aggressive bidding than with small numbers (3-4), resulting in negative profits, the winner's curse. Providing public information about the value of the item increases seller revenue in the absence of a winner's curse, but produces the contrary result in its presence.

Common value auctions constitute a market setting in which participants may be particularly susceptible to judgment failures that affect market outcomes. In a common value auction, the value of the auctioned item is the same to all bidders. What makes the auction interesting is that bidders are unaware of the value of the item at the time the bids are placed. Mineral lease auctions, particularly the federal government's outer continental shelf (OCS) oil lease auctions, are common value auctions. There is a common value element to most auctions. Bidders for an oil painting may purchase for their own pleasure, a private value element, but they may also bid for investment and eventual resale, reflecting an uncertain common value element.

Judgmental failures in common value auctions are known as the "winner's curse." Assume that all bidders obtain unbiased estimates of an item's value and that bids are an increasing function of these estimates. The high bidder then tends to be the one with the most optimistic estimate of the item's value. Unless this adverse-selection problem is accounted for in the bidding process, it will result in winning bids that produce below normal or even negative profits. The systematic failure to account for this adverse selection problem is referred to as the "winner's curse."

Oil companies claim they fell prey to the winner's curse in early OCS lease sales (E. C. Capen, R. V. Clapp, and W. M. Campbell, 1971; John Lorenz and E. L. Dougherty, 1983; and references cited therein). Similar claims have been made in auctions for book publication rights (John Dessauer, 1981) in professional baseball's free agency market (James Cassing and Richard Douglas, 1980) and in corporate takeover battles (Richard Roll, 1986). Economists typically treat such claims with caution as they imply that bidders repeatedly err, in violation of basic notions of economic rationality. This caution is justified given the inherent problems in interpreting field data, self-serving motives of many of the claimants, and the general absence of conventional statistical tests documenting these claims. However, common value auction experiments using financially motivated, but inexperienced, subjects demonstrate a strong

*Department of Economics, University of Houston-University Park, Houston, TX 77004. Financial support was received from the Information Science and Technology Division and the Economics Division of NSF; the Energy Laboratory and the Center for Public Policy of the University of Houston-University Park. Ray Battalio, Don Meyer, and Carl Kogut ran auction series 1 and 2; Ron Harstad and Doug Dyer assisted in series 3–8. Doug Dyer and Susan Garvin provided valuable research assistance. This paper has benefited from discussions with Badi Baltagi, Ron Harstad, Mark Issac, Asbjord Moseidjord, Jim Smith, and Philip Sorensen, the comments of Daniel Friedman, Robert Wilson, two referees, and participants in seminars at the University of Houston, Texas A&M University and the University of Indiana. An earlier version of this paper was presented at the 1985 Winter Econometric Society meetings. We alone are responsible for errors and omissions.

and nearly ubiquitous winner's curse which continues to significantly depress profits after as many as 15–20 auction periods (Kagel et al., 1986).

It is one thing to find that inexperienced bidders commit a winner's curse. It is another to find that experienced bidders do the same. Here we report the results of common value auction experiments with experienced subjects, survivors of one or more initial series of experiments. With continued experience, bidders' judgment improve. In auctions involving a limited number of competitors (3–4 bidders), average profits are consistently positive and closer to the Nash equilibrium bidding outcome than to the winner's curse hypothesis: behavior consistent with traditional notions of the effects of repeated exposure to market conditions, in conjunction with profit incentives and survival pressures. However, learning is situationally specific as bids are found to be an increasing function of the number of rivals faced, in clear violation of risk-neutral Nash equilibrium bidding theory under our design. This contributes to a reemergence of the winner's curse, with bankruptcies and negative profits, in auctions with large numbers (6–7) of bidders.

Just as Nash equilibrium bidding theory predicts, experimental manipulations providing public information reducing uncertainty about item value reliably result in higher winning bids and increased seller's revenues in the absence of a winner's curse. However, in the presence of a winner's curse, this same public information generates lower average winning bids and reduced seller's revenues. The differential response to public information conditional on the presence or absence of a winner's curse has practical implications which have largely gone unrecognized in the literature.

The paper is organized as follows. Section I describes the structure of the experiments. Section II characterizes the Nash equilibrium bidding strategies for the auction, provides a formal definition of the winner's curse, and states the research hypotheses that guided our investigations. The results of the experiments are reported and discussed in Section III. Section IV extends the analysis

to field settings where our experimental results help explain a puzzling outcome of OCS lease sales: namely, that public information reducing item uncertainty increased bidder's profits, just as observed in our laboratory experiments in the presence of a winner's curse. A concluding section summarizes our research results and poses questions for further research.

I. Structure of the Auctions

A. *Basic Auction Structure*

Subjects were recruited for two-hour sessions consisting of a series of auction periods. In each auction period, a single unit of a commodity was sold to the high bidder at the high-bid price, with bidders submitting sealed bids for the item (a first-price, sealed-bid procedure). The high bidder earned profits equal to the value of the item less the amount bid; other bidders earned zero profits for that auction period.

In each auction period, the value of the item, x_0, was drawn randomly from a uniform distribution on the interval $[\underline{x}, \bar{x}]$. Subjects submitted bids without knowing the value of x_0. Private information signals, x_i, were distributed prior to bidding. The x_i were randomly drawn from a uniform distribution centered on x_0 with upper bound $x_0 + \varepsilon$ and lower bound $x_0 - \varepsilon$. As such, the x_i constitute unbiased estimates of the value of x_0 (or could be used to compute unbiased estimates in conjunction with the endpoint values $\underline{x}, \bar{x}$). Given x_i, ε, and the endpoint values, each bidder could compute an upper and lower bound on the value of x_0; these were $\min \{ x_i + \varepsilon, \bar{x} \}$ and $\max \{ x_i - \varepsilon, \underline{x} \}$, respectively. The bounds associated with a given x_i were computed and reported along with the x_i.

The distribution underlying the signal values, the value of ε, and the interval $[\underline{x}, \bar{x}]$ were common knowledge. The value of ε varied across auctions (see Table 1). All changes in ε were announced and posted. With signal values drawn independently relative to x_0, they satisfy the criteria of strict positive affiliation (Paul Milgrom and Robert Weber, 1982) which, roughly speak-

896   THE AMERICAN ECONOMIC REVIEW   DECEMBER 1986

TABLE 1—EXPERIMENTAL CONDITIONS[a]

Auction Series	Subject Population (no. starting exp.)	Market Period	ε	$\underline{x}$	$\bar{x}$	Public Information[b] (market periods)	Number Active Bidders (market periods)	Experience
1	Texas A&M Undergraduates (5)	1–18	$12	$15	$100	Random signal (10–18)	5(1–18)	First-price common value
2	Texas A&M Undergraduates (4)	1–18	$12	$15	$100	Random signal (10–18)	4(1–18)	First-price common value
3	U. Houston Graduate/Senior Undergraduates (7)	1–8 9–17,24–25 18–23	$12 $18 $30	$25	$225	Low signal (12–25)	7(1–4) 6(5–6) 5(7–11) 4(12–25)	Second-price common value, some first-price common value
4	U. Houston Graduate/Senior Undergraduates (8)	1–6 7–14 15–25	$12 $18 $30	$25	$225	Low signal (8–25)	7(1–10) 6(11–25)	Second-price common value, some first-price common value
5	U. Houston Graduate/Senior Undergraduates (9)	1–9 10–15,24–26 16–23	$12 $18 $30	$25	$225	Low signal (7–26)	7(1–26) 7(1–26)	First and Second-price common value
6	U. Houston Graduate/Senior Undergraduates (4)	1–5 6–16,28–31 17–21 22–27	$12 $18 $24 $30	$25	$225	Low signal (9–31)	4(1–11) 4(1–11) 3(12–31)	First and Second-price common value
7	U. Houston Graduate/Senior Undergraduates (6)	1–5 6–13,26–32 33–37 14–25	$12 $18 $24 $30	$25	$225	Low signal (9–32)	4(1–19) 6(20–37)	First and Second-price common value
8	U. Houston Graduate/Senior Undergraduates (7)	1–6 7–16 17–23	$12 $18 $30	$30	$500	None	4(1–23)[c] 7(10–23)	First-price common value, some private value

[a] Starting balances were $8 in experiments 1 and 2, $10 in all others.

[b] Profits were earned in markets with both public and private information in experiments 1 and 2; in only one market in experiments 3–8. The market paying profits was determined by a coin flip in experiments 3–8.

[c] Period 10 on involved a bidding in two markets with 4 subjects bidding first in a "small" market and all 7 subjects bidding in a "large" market.

ing, requires that large values for a given signal make it more likely that rivals signal values, and x_0, are large rather than small.

Bids were restricted to be nonnegative and rounded to the nearest penny. After all bids were collected, they were posted on the blackboard in descending order next to the corresponding signal values, x_0 was announced, subjects' profits were calculated, and balances were updated.[1] Earnings of the

high bidder were also announced, but his/her identity was not. The x_0 values and the associated signal values were all determined randomly strictly according to the process described to the subjects.

To cover the possibility of losses, subjects were given starting balances of $8.00 in auction series 1–2, and $10.00 in series 3–8. Profits and losses were added to this balance. If a subject's balance went negative, he was no longer permitted to bid; he was paid the $4.00 participation fee and free to leave the experiment. The auction survivors were paid their end of experiment

[1] In auction series 1 and 2, the top three bids were posted, and the signal values underlying the bids were not revealed.

balance in cash, along with their participation fee.[2]

Given the information structure and uncertainty inherent in common value auctions, negative profits will occasionally be
realized even if the market immediately locks
into the risk-neutral Nash equilibrium outcome. The starting capital balance served to
account for this possibility, and to impose
clear opportunity costs on overly aggressive
bidding. Balances were set so that: (i) subjects could commit at least one gross bidding
error, learn from their mistake, and still have
a large enough balance to actively participate in the auctions, and (ii) conservative
bidders who were shut out from winning by
overly aggressive counterparts would earn a
reasonable return for participating.

B. Auctions with Public Information

Approximately one-third of the way
through auction series 1–7, we introduced
bidding in two separate auction markets
simultaneously. Bidding in the first auction
market continued as before under private
information conditions. After these bids were
collected, but before they were posted, we
introduced a public information signal and
asked subjects to bid again. (Subjects retained their original private information signals; no new private information signals were
distributed.) We employed two types of public information signals. In series 1 and 2, we
randomly drew an additional signal, x_i, from
the interval $[x_0 - \varepsilon, x_0 + \varepsilon]$, and posted it. In
series 3–7, the lowest of the private informa-
tion signals distributed, x_L, was posted. Bidders were always accurately informed of
whether the public information signal was
random or the lowest private information
signal.

Profits were paid (or losses incurred) in
only one of the two auction markets, determined on the basis of a coin flip after all

bids were collected.[3] Subjects were told that
they were under no obligation to submit the
same or different bids in the two markets,
but should bid in a way they thought would
"maximize profits." All bids from both
markets were posted along with the corresponding private information signals.

The dual market bidding procedure, involving the same set of bidders with the
same item value and the same set of private
information signals, has the advantage of
directly controlling for between subject variability and extraneous variability resulting
from variations in item value and private
information signals. Some critics have mistakenly concluded that the procedure involves a "portfolio" problem so that the
optimal bid in one market affects bids in the
other market. This conclusion is unwarranted, however. There is no way that bids
in the private information market can be
used to hedge bids in the public information
market any more than bids in the private
information market in period t can be used
to hedge bids in the private information
market in period $t + 1$. In analyzing each
member of a set of auctions, $t = 1, 2, ..., T$,
as a single-shot auction (which we do below),
we are assuming that the utility function is
intertemporally separable in profits from the
auction, $U = \sum_{t=1}^{T} u(\Pi_t)$. Similarly we are assuming separability in bidding between the
dual markets. The breakdown of the separability assumption in either case (for example, $U = u(\sum_{t=1}^{T} \Pi_t)$) has comparable implications, namely no effect in the case of
risk-neutral bidders, while risk-averse bidders will tend to be less risk averse than
under separable preferences, as they can rely
on the law of large numbers to smooth the
variance in profits across auctions.

Of course, it is another matter entirely
whether bidders actually bid as if their preferences are separable between the dual
markets or over time. Experiments 1 and 2
explicitly tested for separability, holding ε
constant throughout and having a relatively

[2] Series 1 and 2 had a $3 participation fee. Many
subjects in series 3–7 had signed a contract to participate in 3 different auction series, for which they were
paid a single participation fee of $25 at the end of the
last series.

[3] Once again, series 1 and 2 involved an exception to
these procedures as profits and losses were computed
and paid in both the public and private information
markets.

large number of private information auctions (9) before introducing dual markets. Regression analysis using dummy variables showed no systematic response to bids in the private information market under the dual market procedure.[4] Similar tests, conducted in a related series of first-price auctions, showed no systematic effects in going from private information markets only to dual markets with public information, and from dual markets to markets with public information only (Kagel, Ronald Harstad, and Levin, 1986). Bid patterns over time are presented in reporting our results.

C. *Varying Numbers of Bidders*

A number of tactics were employed to study the effects of varying the number of bidders. Auction series 1–6 used a between-groups design with different series having different numbers of active bidders. In pursuit of this objective, series 4 and 5 had more subjects than active bidders, in order to control for bankruptcies, with a simple rotation rule to determine which subjects would be active in any given auction period.[5] Variations in the number of active bidders in these series (see the eighth column in Table 1) resulted from bankruptcies.

Auction series 7 and 8 involved planned variations in the number of active bidders. Series 7 employed a crossover design, starting with 4 active bidders rotating among a set of 6 total bidders. In auction period 20, the rotation procedure ceased, and all 6 bid-

ders were active in the remaining auction periods. Auction series 8 employed a within-subjects design, starting out with 4 active bidders rotating between 7 total bidders. In auction period 10, dual market bidding procedures similar to those used to study the effects of public information were introduced; only numbers of active bidders varied between markets.[6] We refer to the different market sizes here as series 7 and 8 small, and 7 and 8 large. Auction series 3 involved a large unplanned variation in number of active bidders due to bankruptcies in early auction periods. Our analysis distinguishes between these early auction periods with 5 or more active bidders (series 3 large), and the later periods with 4 active bidders (series 3 small), as market outcomes were distinctly different between the two situations.

D. *The Experience Factor*

All auctions employed experienced subjects. In series 1 and 2, all subjects had been in one earlier first-price common value auction series using similar design parameters (see Kagel et al., 1986, auction series 4–6). These earlier auctions all began with 6 active bidders, but as a result of bankruptcies ended with 3–5 bidders. Recruitment into these experiments was restricted to subjects who had not gone bankrupt in the initial auction series.

Auction series 3–8 are numbered in chronological order as they involved a common core of subjects, recruited in varying combinations, in the different series. Thirteen of the 15 bidders in series 3 and 4 had participated in an earlier series of second-price

---

[4]The bid function had the form $b_{it} = \alpha_0 + \alpha_1 x_{it} + \alpha_2 Y_{it}$ as suggested by equation (2), where α_i were constants to be estimated (ε was constant in these auctions). The function was fit to individual subject data for signals in the interval (1), and a dummy variable added to account for simultaneous bidding in two auctions. Combining independent *t*-tests on the dummy variable coefficient using the *z* statistic suggested in Ben Winer (1971, p. 50), we were unable to identify any systematic effects associated with simultaneous bidding ($z = -.124$).

[5]For example, with 9 subjects and 7 active bidders, in period 1, subjects 1–7 were active; in period 2, subjects 2–8 were active, etc. Inactive subjects received signals and bid, but these bids were discarded (the latter was common knowledge).

[6]Using a single set of private information signals and a single true value, x_0, 4 subjects first bid in a small market. Then, before these bids were opened, all 7 subjects bid in a large market. The 4 subjects in the small market continued to be determined through rotation, and bids only counted in one of the two markets using a coin flip rule. Raymond Battalio, Carl Kogut, and Donald Meyer (1983) report tests of the separability assumption underlying the dual market technique in private value auctions with varying numbers of bidders. They found no systematic biases associated with the dual market technique.

common value auction experiments with similar design parameters. (The distinguishing characteristic of these second-price auctions was that the high bidders earned the item and paid the second-highest bid price.) Most of these subjects had been in two or more second-price series, at least one of which involved 6–7 active bidders throughout. The two remaining subjects had been in a first-price common value series involving 5–6 active bidders throughout (Kagel et al., 1986, auction series 11). Seven of the 9 subjects in series 5 were recruited from series 3 and 4, with the remaining 2 having extensive second-price experience. All 6 bidders in series 7 had been in both auction series 3 and 5, or 4 and 5. Three of the 4 bidders in series 6 had been in series 4, with the fourth bidder having been in series 3 and 5. Series 8 was conducted several months after the others and involved 3 veterans of series 7, 2 from series 6, and 2 bidders with experience in first-price auctions with positively affiliated private values (Kagel, Harstad, and Levin). Several subjects in this series had gone bankrupt in their initial common value auction series, but were included provided the bankruptcy occurred after a fair number of auction periods (15 or more periods was the rule of thumb employed).[7] Subjects were recruited into later series in this sequence without regard to performance earlier in the sequence.

II. Theoretical Considerations

A. *Private Information Conditions*

1. *The Nash Equilibrium*. The most common equilibrium bidding model in the economic's literature is that of a noncooperative Nash equilibrium with risk-neutral bidders (hereafter RNNE). Robert Wilson (1977) was the first to develop a Nash equilibrium solution for first-price common value auctions, while

Milgrom and Weber provide some significant extensions and generalization of the Wilson model.

We restrict our analysis in the text to signals in the interval

$$(1) \qquad \underline{x} + \varepsilon \le x_i \le \bar{x} - \varepsilon.$$

The optimal bid function in this interval is, of course, affected by the bid function in the interval $x_i < \underline{x} + \varepsilon$, which in turn is affected by the added information associated with the end-point value, $\underline{x}$.[8] Assuming risk neutrality on bidder's part, the Nash equilibrium bid function for signals in (1) is

$$(2) \qquad b(x_i) = x_i - \varepsilon + Y,$$

where $Y = [2\varepsilon/(N+1)]\exp[-(N/2\varepsilon)(x_i - (\underline{x} + \varepsilon))]$ and N stands for the number of active bidders in the market. Y contains a negative exponential, and diminishes rapidly as x_i moves beyond $\underline{x} + \varepsilon$.

Under (2), expected profits for the high bidder are

$$(3) \qquad E[\Pi|W] = 2\varepsilon/(N+1) - Y.$$

In addition, the model predicts that the high signal holder always wins the auction. This follows directly from the assumption that all bidders use the same bid function, the only

---

[7] In a private value auction, bidders know their value for the item with certainty, but only the distribution of their rivals' values. Under the first-price rule, the high bidder wins the item and earns profits equal to his private value less the bid price; others earn zero profits.

[8] For $x_i < \underline{x} + \varepsilon$, the RNNE bid function is

$$b(x_i) = \underline{x} + (x_i + \varepsilon - \underline{x})/(N+1)$$

and yields zero expected profits. This equilibrium bid function is obtained from Wilson (1977) under the initial condition $b(x_i) = \underline{x}$ for $x_i = \underline{x} - \varepsilon$. The initial condition for the bid function in (2) exploits continuity in the bid function at the junction point $x_i = \underline{x} + \varepsilon$. For $x_i > \bar{x} - \varepsilon$, the optimal bid function defies analytic solution. For observations in this interval, we employ the bid function (2) in comparing performance with the RNNE model. This tends to overstate the RNNE bid, hence underestimate the discrepancy between actual and predicted bids. Since the bias is small, and favors the null hypothesis, correcting for it will not change the conclusions reached. These bid functions are explicitly derived in Kagel et al. (1984).

difference being their private information, x_i, regarding the value of the item.[9]

Accounting for risk aversion on bidder's part complicates the model's predictions, as equilibrium bids can lie to either side of the RNNE prediction, depending upon the form of the utility function and the degree of risk aversion assumed. We do not pursue these extensions here, as they appear secondary to understanding the experiments' outcomes.[10] Note that under the RNNE there is no winner's curse as bidders fully account for the adverse-selection problem in determining their bids. The RNNE bidding model provides a convenient benchmark against which to compare the experiments' outcomes.

2. *Judgmental Failures: The Winner's Curse.* In common value auctions, bidders usually win the item when they have the highest, or one of the highest, estimates of value. Under these conditions an unbiased estimate of value, $E[x_0|x_i]$, is biased as

$$E[x_0|x_i] > E[x_0|X_i = x_1] \quad \text{for } N > 1$$

where $E[x_0|X_i = x_1]$ is the expected value conditional on having the highest private information signal. Assuming that the highest signal holder always wins the auction and risk neutrality, or risk aversion, bids in excess of $E[x_0|X_i = x_1]$ will insure negative profits on average, and can only result from failure to recognize the adverse-selection problem inherent in winning the auction. Since we have no reason to assume risk

loving, and the highest signal holder usually wins the auction, bids in excess of $E[x_0|X_i = x_1]$ will be attributed to such judgmental failures, and will be referred to as the winner's curse.[11]

For signal values in the interval (1),

$$(4) \quad E[x_0|x_i] = x_i;$$

$$(5) \quad E[x_0|X_i = x_1] = x_i - \varepsilon(N-1)/(N+1).$$

Avoiding the winner's curse requires considerable discounting of bids relative to signal values.[12] Further, the size of the discount is an increasing function of both N and ε.

In first-price sealed-bid auctions, strategic considerations generally dictate discounting of bids relative to the expected value of the item. Strategic discounting results strictly from known dispersion in rivals' values. It is informative to compare the bid function (2), and the size of the discount in (5), with strategic discounting based on the dispersion in the x_i values. Suppose that bidders completely ignore the adverse-selection problem inherent in the auction, employing (4) to compute the expected value of the item: they act as if they are in an auction with positively affiliated private values, where the x_i represents the value of the item to bidder i, and values are independently distributed over the interval (1). Under risk neutrality, the bid function here is[13]

$$(6) \quad b^s(x_i) = x_i - (2\varepsilon/N) + (Y/N),$$

---

[9] The model can be generalized to account for both private value and common value elements (see Wilson, 1981, for example). In this case, the high signal holder does not always win the item, even assuming identical bidding strategies. Undoubtedly, actual auction sales, even OCS lease sales, contain both private and common value elements. Developments in Section III suggest that the Nash equilibrium model must be generalized to account for individual differences in risk attitudes and/or information-processing capacities, as well as simple random errors on bidder's part. Developing and testing such a model lies beyond the scope of the present paper.

[10] Milgrom and Weber, section 8, and Steven Matthews (1986) develop some results for risk-averse bidders.

[11] Results from private value auction experiments generally support an assumption of risk neutrality or risk aversion (James Cox, Bruce Roberson, and Vernon Smith, 1982; Kagel, Harstad, and Levin).

[12] The size of the discount seems remarkably large, particularly for larger N's. To get an idea of the adverse-selection bias involved here, compared to alternative distributions, we normalize it in terms of the standard error of the underlying distribution. For x_i in (1) the standard error of the uniform distributions is $\sigma = 2\varepsilon/\sqrt{12}$. From (5), knowing that your estimate is the maximum of N such estimates, means that it is biased upwards by the amount $\sqrt{12}(N-1)\sigma/2(N+1)$. For $N = 2$–8, the resulting bias is quite similar to what would be found if the x_i were normally distributed around x_0.

[13] Kagel, Harstad, and Levin experimentally investigate first-price sealed bid auctions with positively affili-

where the expression Y is the same as in (2) above.

Comparing equation (5) with (6) shows that strategic discounting produces a winner's curse whenever $N > 3$. Further, strategic considerations (6), item valuation considerations (5), and the RNNE bid function (2) all call for greater discounting of bids relative to signal values with increases in ε.[14] Since evidence from private value auctions shows bidders to be sensitive to the strategic considerations inherent in these auctions (James Cox, et al.; our 1985 paper), we expect bidders to be sensitive to variations in ε.

However, with increasing numbers of bidders, equations (2), (5), and (6) give conflicting directions. Differentiation of (6) shows that strategic considerations require higher bids in the presence of more rivals as signal values are more congested. Item valuation considerations as expressed in (5) require less aggressive bidding as the adverse-selection problem becomes more severe. The net effect of these two forces, expressed in the RNNE bid function, is for bids to remain constant or decrease in the presence of more rivals.[15] This conflict between item valuation and strategic considerations suggests that structural variations in numbers of bidders is critical to determining whether experienced bidders learn to avoid the winner's curse in small groups out of a trial and error survival process that is situationally specific, as opposed to "understanding" the adverse-selection problem as it applies to new situations. If the survival process results in

generalized learning (one interpretation of optimality via survival arguments in economics), behavior in both large and small groups should show comparable deviations from the RNNE reference point.[16] However, in the absence of generalized learning, behavior is likely to be markedly different, to the extent that the winner's curse, having been largely or entirely eliminated in small groups, will reemerge with increases in group size.

B. Effects of Public Information

1. *The Nash Equilibrium.* Extensions of the common value auction model show that public information reducing item valuation uncertainty will increase average seller's revenues (reduce bidder's profits) under the RNNE (Milgrom and Weber). This holds even though public information signals of the sort employed here, x_p, will on average lie below the maximum private information signal, x_1. The economic forces at work here are roughly as follows: On average,

$$E[x_0 | X_i = x_1] = E[x_0 | X_i = x_1, X_p]$$

for the bidder actually holding the highest private information signal, x_1. (All symmetric, noncooperative Nash equilibria involve agents bidding as if $x_i = x_1$, since their bid only "counts" when this presumption is satisfied.) However, due to the affiliation of the signal values, for bidders whose private information signals $x_i < x_1$, the public information signal will, *ex post*, raise the average expected value of the item. This will induce an upward revision of these bids, which in

---

ated private values, where private values were generated using exactly the same procedures generating the x_i values here. Equation (6) corresponds to the bid function developed there. Note, these private value experiments show bids commonly in excess of (6) with $N = 6$.

[14] In addition, an increase in ε increases the variance associated with the naive expectation (4). Thus to the extent that bidders are generally risk averse and bid more cautiously in the face of increased risk, but are poor Bayesians so that they continue to employ the naive expectation (4), they will respond correctly (at least directionally) to changing ε.

[15] Differentiation of (2) with respect to N shows the Y term to require lower bids in the presence of more rivals.

[16] An earlier reader of this paper argued that optimality by survival arguments implied "correct" responses under all possible states of the world, as survivors had experienced all relevant states and had learned to adapt to them. While acknowledging the validity of this interpretation, it seems to rob the survival argument of empirical content as: 1) the survival process would never be complete as real economies are repeatedly subject to changing conditions and changes in the set of agents, and 2) there would be no role left for economic theory in terms of understanding behavioral processes or in predicting responses to novel economic conditions.

turn puts pressure on the bidder with the highest private information signal, x_1, to bid more out of strategic considerations.

As an experimental device, the use of the low private information signal, x_L, as the public information signal has several advantages. First, the RNNE bid function with public information is readily solved analytically with x_L. Second, x_L provides a substantial amount of information concerning the location of x_0, and the signal values rivals are likely to have. For signals in the interval (1),

$$(7) \quad E\big[x_0 | X_i = x_1, X_p = x_L\big] = (x_L + x_i)/2$$

provides a sufficient statistic for the value of x_0 given the set of private information signals distributed, under the presumption that $x_i = x_1$. From (7), it is clear that announcing x_L should reduce the average spread in beliefs about the underlying value of the item between any two bidders by one-half. Under private information conditions, a similar reduction in beliefs would require halving ε, as this halves the average spread between any two private information signals (as well as the spread in expected values under (5)). Thus, announcing x_L induces strong competitive pressures on the high bidder and translates into relatively large increases in seller's revenues, or reduced bidder's profits (see equation (9) below), while still maintaining an interesting auction.

The RNNE bid function with, public information, x_L, and private information signals in the interval (1) is[17]

$$(8) \quad b(x_i, x_L) = x_L + \left[\frac{N-2}{N-1}\right]$$

$$\times \left[\frac{x_i + x_L}{2} - x_L\right]$$

$$= \frac{N}{2(N-1)} x_L + \frac{(N-2)}{2(N-1)} x_i.$$

[17]For x_i in the interval (1), the RNNE equilibrium bid function is obtained under the initial condition that $b(x_L) = x_L$. Note that ε is not explicitly represented in (8). However, the average difference $(x_i + x_L)/2 - x_L$ depends directly on ε.

Expected profits are substantially diluted, being

$$(9) \quad E[\Pi | W, X_L] = \varepsilon/(N+1).$$

This is a little more than one-half of the expected profits under private information conditions (3).

With risk aversion we cannot unambiguously determine whether public information will increase or decrease average seller's revenues (Milgrom and Weber). The impact depends upon the particular form of the utility function assumed, the degree of risk aversion displayed, and the extent to which public information dilutes private information differences. Nevertheless, we would anticipate that under most plausible scenarios, the relatively large dilution of private information differentials inherent in releasing x_L, would cause seller's revenues to increase, or at least not to decrease.

2. Judgmental Failures: The Winner's Curse.
The judgmental error underlying the winner's curse consists of the high bidder's systematic overestimation of the item's value. To the extent that the magnitude of these judgmental errors decreases as the uncertainty concerning the value of the item decreases, public information will result in a downward revision in the most optimistic bidder's valuation of the item. This introduces a potentially powerful offset to any strategic forces tending to raise bids.[18] This effect is well illustrated through extending the notion of strategic discounting to auctions with public information, and comparing the resultant discount function with (6).

[18]Note that unbiased random errors, even if they do not result in high bids in excess of $E[x_0|X_i = x_1]$, will *not* cancel out here in terms of their effects on seller's revenues. This results from the auction selection mechanism whereby market outcomes overrepresent bids with upward biases, resulting in average bids in excess of the RNNE. Consequently, if public information reduces the magnitude of these item valuation errors, public information will still result in a downward revision of the market price, which offsets the strategic forces promoting increased revenues. High bids in excess of $E[x_0|X_i = x_1]$ can constitute an extreme form of these errors and/or a systematic tendency, on at least some bidder's part, to overestimate the item's value.

Under strategic discounting, we continue to assume that bidders employ naive expectations to determine the value of the item, to the point that they ignore the positional information inherent in announcing x_L, and act as if they are in a private value auction. For x_i and x_L in the interval (1), a naive expectation of x_0 is the same as (7):

$$(10) \quad E[x_0|x_i, x_L] = (x_i + x_L)/2.$$

Consequently, under risk neutrality, the strategic discount function and the RNNE bid function (8) coincide here. Note that this follows directly from the fact that the naive (10) and sophisticated expectations (7) coincide. In markets with private information, the two bid functions differ as the expectations differ.

Comparing (6) with (8), $b^s(x_i) > b(x_i, x_L)$ on average for all $N \geq 3$. In auctions where bidders employ naive expectations, but strategic discounting, announcing x_L will result in *reductions* in average seller's revenues (increases in average bidder's profits) with 3 or more bidders. Finally, given that previous experimental studies indicate sensitivity to the strategic implications inherent in auction markets, and the coincidence of the strategic bid function with the RNNE bid function, the RNNE model should provide a fairly good predictor of market performance with x_L announced, irrespective of its predictive adequacy in comparable markets with private information only.

C. Summary of Research Questions of Primary Interest

We conclude this section by summarizing the research questions of primary interest in the form of hypotheses to be tested.

HYPOTHESIS 1: *Under private information conditions market outcomes for experienced bidders are observationally indistinguishable from the RNNE as (i) the high signal holder usually wins the auction, and (ii) prices do not deviate substantially or systematically from the RNNE prediction.*

HYPOTHESIS 2: *Announcing x_L, the lowest private information signal, raises average*

seller's revenues by the average amount predicted under the RNNE model.

HYPOTHESIS 3: *Under private information conditions, experienced bidders avoid the winner's curse as average profits are closer to the RNNE level than the zero/negative profits predicted under the winner's curse.*

HYPOTHESIS 4: *Public information raises average seller's revenue.*

HYPOTHESIS 5: *Hypotheses 3 and 4 apply uniformly to experiments with small and large numbers of bidders.*

HYPOTHESIS 6: *Bidders are sensitive to the strategic implications of the auctions so that when the strategic discounting model and the RNNE model coincide, the RNNE model provides a reasonable characterization of the data.*

Hypotheses 1 and 2 involve strong predictions, which if satisfied would imply satisfaction of all the other hypotheses as well. Hypotheses 3–5 involve weaker predictions which may be satisfied even though Hypotheses 1 and 2, strictly interpreted, fail. Nevertheless confirmation of these weaker predictions would indicate that the RNNE model provided a reasonable "ballpark" characterization of behavior in general: that for experienced bidders, at least, the repeated nature of market decision processes in conjunction with survival pressures and profit opportunities, eliminate the judgmental failures underlying the winner's curse. Further, conditional on the confirmation of Hypotheses 3–5, one of the key policy implications of the theory, the revenue-enhancing effects of public information, would be reasonably accurate as well.

Finally, Hypothesis 6 captures the notion that bidders in private value auction experiments have been shown to be sensitive to the strategic implications inherent in these auctions. Hence, we would expect the RNNE model to perform well here when its predictions coincide with strategic discounting. If Hypothesis 6 is satisfied, but Hypotheses 1–5 are not, we have indirect evidence that it is the judgmental errors underlying the

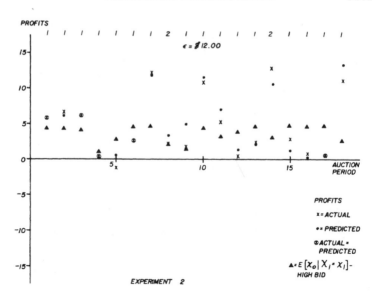

FIGURE 1

winner's curse that are responsible for the breakdown in the model's performance.

III. Experimental Results

A. *Bidding Patterns with Private Information*

Figures 1–5 provide representative data for market outcomes over time. The rank of the high bidder's signal value is shown at the top of each figure: 1 for the highest signal value, 2 for the second highest, etc. Closed triangles show the difference between $E[x_0|X_i = x_1]$ for the high bidder and the high bid. A negative (positive) value here indicates that the high bid exceeded (fell below) $E[x_0|X_i = x_1]$, implying negative (positive) expected profits should the high signal holder win the auction. Cross marks show actual profits earned, with closed circles showing profits predicted under the RNNE: cross marks below (above) closed circles indicate that the actual bid exceeded (was less than) the RNNE prediction and by how much. Eyeballing the data, there appears to be little systematic variation in bids over

time, within a given auction series, independent of variations in N and ε.

Table 2 provides summary statistics of auction outcomes.[19] Columns 4–6 show, respectively, actual profits earned, profits predicted under the RNNE, and profits earned as a percentage of the RNNE prediction. For comparative purposes, column 3 shows profits predicted under the strategic discounting formulation (profits predicted using the bid function 6, assuming that the highest signal holder always won the auction). The last two columns report the average frequency with which the high signal holder won the item, and the frequency with which the high bid exceeded $E[x_0|X_i = x_1]$.

---

[19]Our computations include all auctions under dual market procedures, regardless of whether bidders actually made profits (or losses) as a consequence of our coin flip procedure. Since the coin flip was made after bids from both markets had been accepted, its outcome should not affect decisions. Experiments involving experienced, as opposed to super-experienced, subjects had one or more dry runs with no money at stake. These auction periods are *not* included in the analysis.

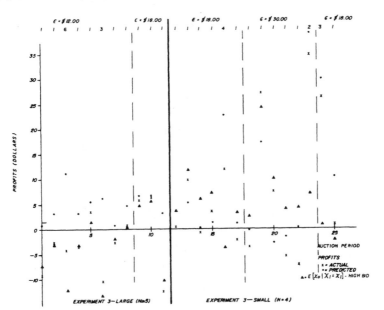

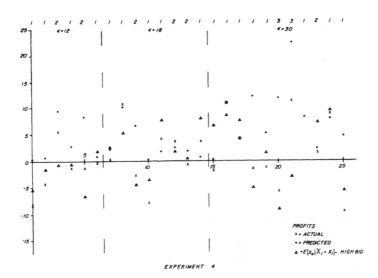

FIGURE 2

FIGURE 3

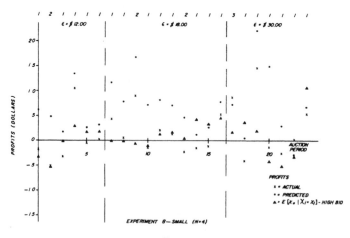

FIGURE 4

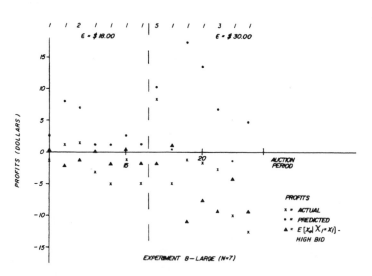

FIGURE 5

The auction series were ordered by the number of active bidders, beginning with the small group experiments, as we kept drawing the same conclusion: there were substantial differences in the ability of the RNNE bidding model to provide a ballpark characterization of the data in auctions involving small numbers (3–4) of bidders compared to those with large numbers (6–7) of bidders. In auction series that began with small numbers of bidders, one can observe bankruptcies (series 6) and some bidding in excess of $E[x_0|X_i = x_1]$. There was at least one large group series where average profits were positive and bidding was generally below $E[x_0|X_i = x_1]$ (series 7 large). However, the

TABLE 2— PROFITS AND BIDDING BY EXPERIMENT AND NUMBER OF ACTIVE BIDDERS:
PRIVATE INFORMATION CONDITIONS (Profits measured in dollars)

Auction Series (No. of Periods)	No. of Active Bidders	Average Profits with Strategic Discounting (standard error of mean)	Average Actual Profits (t-statistic)[a]	Average Profits Under RNNE (standard error of mean)	Profits as a Percentage of RNNE Prediction	Percentage of Auctions Won by High Signal Holder	Percentage of High Bids $b_1 > E[x_0 \mid X_i = x_1]$
6 (31)	3–4	3.25 (1.51)	3.73 (2.70)[b]	9.51 (1.70)	39.2	67.7	22.6
2 (18)	4	−.75 (1.07)	4.61 (4.35)[c]	4.99 (1.03)	92.6	88.9	0.0
3 small (14)	4	−3.82 (2.40)	7.53 (2.07)	6.51 (2.65)	115.7	78.6	14.3
7 small (19)	4	−.12 (1.56)	5.83 (3.35)[c]	8.56 (2.07)	68.1	63.2	10.5
8 small (23)	4	−2.24 (1.05)	1.70 (1.56)	6.38 (1.21)	26.6	84.6	39.1
1 (18)	5	−1.90 (.85)	2.89 (3.14)[c]	5.19 (.86)	55.7	72.2	27.8
3 large (11)	5–7	−5.19 (.55)	−2.92 (−1.49)	3.65 (.62)	−80.5	81.8	63.6
7 large (18)	6	−10.11 (.96)	1.89 (1.67)	4.70 (1.03)	40.2	72.2	22.2
4 (25)	6–7	−10.03 (1.05)	−.23 (−.15)	4.78 (.92)	−4.8	69.2	46.2
5 (26)	7	−8.07 (1.04)	−.41 (−.44)	5.25 (1.03)	−7.8	42.3	65.4
8 large (14)	7	−11.04 (1.35)	−2.74 (−2.04)	5.03 (1.40)	−54.8	78.6	71.4

[a] Tests null hypothesis that mean is different from 0.0.
[b] Significant at 5 percent level, 2-tailed t-test.
[c] Significant at 1 percent level, 2-tailed t-test.

general pattern was one of positive average profits in small groups which, while well below the RNNE criteria, were clearly closer to the RNNE prediction than the zero/ negative profit levels of the winner's curse: profits averaged across experiments with 3–4 bidders were $4.68 per auction period, about 65.1 percent of the RNNE models prediction of $7.19 per auction period.[20] In contrast, auctions involving 6–7 bidders had average

[20]Averages reported here and elsewhere in the text are simple, unweighted averages across experiments, unless noted otherwise. All RNNE profit calculations are exact, based on the bid function in (2) and fn. 8.

actual profits of −$.88 per auction period. While this is substantially better than profits predicted under strategic discounting, −$8.89, indicating considerable adjustment to the adverse-selection problem, these adjustments were far from complete, as profit levels were negative, closer to the winner's curse prediction than the RNNE prediction of $4.68 per auction period. Further, comparing large and small group auctions, actual profits decreased substantially more than profit opportunities as measured by the RNNE criteria. The latter profit criteria dropped by $2.51 per auction period, while actual profits fell by $5.56. Thus, in going from small to large groups, profit perfor-

908   THE AMERICAN ECONOMIC REVIEW   DECEMBER 1986

TABLE 3—PROFITS AND BIDDING UNDER VARYING LEVELS OF ε
(All profits in dollars)

No. of Bidders	ε	Average Profits with Strategic Discounting (standard error of mean)	Average Actual Profits (t-statistics)[a]	Average Profits Under RNNE[b] (standard error of mean)	Profits as a Percentage of the RNNE Prediction
3–4	12	−1.24 (.69)	2.60 (1.74)	4.52 (1.44)	57.5
	18	−.24 (1.03)	3.98 (3.71)[d]	7.20 (1.05)	55.4
	24/30	.60 (1.94)	6.75 (3.33)[d]	11.22 (2.06)	60.2
6–7	12	−3.68 (.54)	−1.86 (−2.21)[c]	3.46 (.56)	−53.8
	18	−8.51 (.52)	−.95 (−1.00)	3.19 (.51)	−29.8
	24/30	−12.31 (.89)	.60 (.51)	7.12 (.94)	8.4

[a] Tests null hypothesis that mean is different from 0.0.
[b] Based on sample of signal values drawn.
[c] Significant at 5 percent level, 2-tailed t-test.
[d] Significant at 1 percent level, 2-tailed t-test.

mance deteriorated above and beyond that predicted under the RNNE.

In both small and large groups, the bidder with the high private information signal generally won. Averaging across auction series, the percentages were 76.6 and 68.8 percent for small and large groups, respectively. Thus, the adverse-selection mechanism hypothesized to underly the winner's curse was present for both group sizes. The high bid, b_1, was below $E[x_0|X_i = x_1]$ in 82.7 percent of all auctions involving small number of bidders, but was below this value in only 46.2 percent of those auctions involving large numbers. The judgmental errors underlying the winner's curse were largely absent in small groups, but were quite prevalent in larger groups.[21]

Table 3 shows the relationship between profits and ε where the averages are computed over auction periods. We continue to distinguish between auctions involving small (3–4) and large (6–7) numbers of bidders, and pool the data for $\varepsilon = 24$ and $\varepsilon = 30$ as there were relatively few observations at $\varepsilon = 24$. In auctions involving small numbers of bidders, actual profits increased with increases in ε and constituted a relatively stable fraction of the profits predicted under the RNNE. With large numbers of bidders (6–7), average losses decreased with increases in ε, with positive average profits earned at $\varepsilon = 24$–30. Reduced losses with ε increasing implies that bids were reduced proportionately more relative to signal values. A stable proportionate discount in terms of ε would have resulted in larger absolute dollar losses as ε increased.[22] Instead, sub-

[21] The adverse-selection discount identifying the winner's curse fails to account for the high signal holder not always winning the item. Bidders should have been responsive to this and used a smaller adverse-selection discount based on actual frequencies with which different ranked signal holders won. Since over 90 percent of all auctions were won by the first- or second-highest signal holder, $E[x_0|X_i = x_2]$ serves as a reasonable *upper* bound on the relevant discount. Using this mea-

sure, less than 1 percent of all small group auctions had a winner's curse, while 28.7 percent of all large group auctions did. Our conclusion regarding the differential frequency of the winner's curse in large and small groups is unaffected, although the overall frequency is reduced substantially.

[22] Recall that $E[x_0|X_i = x_1]$ is decreasing in ε.

jects took advantage of the increased profit opportunities inherent in the increased value of ε.

We used multiple regression analysis to summarize and quantify the influences on bidding in the private value auctions. Using an error components model, and restricting our analysis to signal values in the interval (1), Table 4 shows the results of two alternative bid function specifications.[23] The first regression involves a generalized version of the bid function (2), allowing for a nonzero intercept and including numbers of bidders as a right-hand side variable. Under this specification, both the intercept coefficient and the coefficient associated with the variable Y in (2) were not significantly different from zero. The second regression drops these two terms. Under both specifications, the x_i critically influences bids with an estimated coefficient value close to 1.0, as implied under the RNNE bid function and under strategic bidding. Further, bidders were clearly sensitive to changes in ε, so that we can soundly reject any naive bidding models which postulate a constant, fixed discount relative to x_i. On the other hand, the coefficient on ε is significantly below unity, and this contradicts the RNNE bid function. These results parallel those from private value auctions, where increases in the distribution of underlying values resulted in lower bids, but these bids were not reduced as much as predicted under the risk neutrality hypothesis (Kagel, Harstad, and Levin). Fi-

TABLE 4—ERROR COMPONENTS ESTIMATES OF BID FUNCTION IN PRIVATE INFORMATION MARKETS[a]

$$b(x_i) = -4.30 + 1.00x_i - .73\varepsilon$$
$$\qquad (3.36) \quad (.002) \quad (.03)$$
$$\qquad\qquad + .70N - .02Y \qquad R^2 = .99$$
$$\qquad\qquad (.16) \quad (.14) \qquad \sigma_\eta = 4.94$$

$$b(x_i) = 1.00x_i - .74\varepsilon + .65N \qquad R^2 = .99$$
$$\qquad (.002) \quad (.03) \quad (.15) \qquad \sigma_\eta = 4.94$$

[a] Standard errors are shown in parentheses.

nally, the aggressive forces associated with increased numbers of bidders win out over the item valuation influences, as we find a statistically significant, positive coefficient associated with N under both specifications. The increased aggressiveness of individual bids with increases in N is in direct contradiction to the predictions of the RNNE bidding model. It adds to the dilution of bidders profits associated with increased N predicted under the RNNE, with the net result a persistent winner's curse with $N = 6$ or 7.

Learning patterns over time are not explored in detail here. The interested reader should consult Kagel et al. (1986) where individual learning patterns of inexperienced bidders are analyzed. The data reported there show considerable learning on survivors part, as most start out bidding in excess of $E[x_0 | X_i = x_1]$. Comparing the results here with end-of-experiment performance for these inexperienced bidders shows continued learning as well: averaging over the last 5 periods of 5 auction series of 3–4 inexperienced bidders shows 28 percent of all high bids in excess of $E[x_0 | X_i = x_1]$ (compared to 17.3 percent here) with profits averaging 27.5 percent of the RNNE prediction (compared to 65.1 percent here).[24] It is important to note, however, that the learning resulting in the strong performance of the RNNE model in small groups appears to be situationally

[23] An error components specification was employed, with error term

$$\eta_{it} = u_i + v_{it} \qquad i = 1, \ldots, N; \quad t = 1, \ldots, T;$$

where u_i is a subject-specific error term, assumed constant subject across auction series, and v_{it} is an auction period error term. Standard assumptions were employed: $u_i \sim (0, \sigma_u^2)$ and $v_{it} \sim (0, \sigma_v^2)$ where u_{it} and v_{it} are independent among each other and among themselves. Badi Baltagi's (1986) weighted least squares computational procedure was used to invert the variance-covariance matrix. A fixed-effects error specification generated similar coefficient estimates and standard errors. Permitting the u_i to vary with subject participation in different auction series yields similar estimates except for the variable N, which increases in value with no loss in statistical significance.

[24] There are no large group end-of-experiment data from the inexperienced subject experiments to compare with the results reported here, as bankruptcies precluded keeping groups of 6–7 bidders intact for very long.

TABLE 5–EFFECTS OF PUBLIC INFORMATION ON SELLER'S REVENUES
(All revenue figures in dollars)

Acution Series (No. of Periods)	No. of Active Bidders	Average Change in Revenues		
		Actual (t-statistic)[a]	Predicted (standard error of mean)	
			RNNE Model	Strategic Discounting
6	3–4	4.38	7.62	1.38
(23)		$(2.71)^{b}$	(1.54)	(1.41)
3 small	4	−2.71	3.83	−6.51
(14)		(−.99)	(2.05)	(1.58)
7 small	4	6.58	7.46	−3.46
(11)		$(2.79)^{b}$	(1.74)	(1.52)
7 large	6	.22	1.64	−13.16
(18)		(.15)	(.87)	(1.26)
4	6–7	−3.20	1.25	−15.75
(18)		(−1.36)	(.82)	(1.07)
5	7	−2.40	2.43	−12.34
(20		(−1.83)	(.86)	(1.30)

[a] Tests null hypothesis that mean is 0.0.
[b] Significant at 5 percent level, 2-tailed t-test.

specific, and does not provide the "understanding" to respond appropriately to increased numbers of rivals (see Table 4), or to avoid the winner's curse in large group auctions.

B. Effects of Public Information on Seller's Revenues

Table 5 shows the actual effects of announcing x_L on average revenues and the predicted effects under both the RNNE and the strategic discounting models. As in Table 2, we have ordered the results by number of active bidders.

Averaging across the 3 auction series with small numbers of bidders, x_L raises revenues an average of $2.75 per auction period. Pooling auction periods, a t-test shows this to be statistically significant ($t = 2.41$, $p < .02$, 1-tailed test), although well below the RNNE prediction of a $6.30 increase in revenues. Public information reduced revenues in series 3, the auction series which came closest to the RNNE model's predictions under private information conditions. Nevertheless, this seems like an anomaly rather than the norm, since under all other conditions where the

winner's curse was weak or nonexistent, as it was in series 6 and series 7 small and large, revealing the low information signal, x_L, raised seller's revenues (also see the discussion that follows).

Averaging across auctions with large numbers of bidders, public information *reduced* seller's revenues $1.79 per auction period. A t-test based on pooled observations indicates that this decrease is statistically significant ($t = -1.48$, $p < .08$, 1-tailed test). While the reduced revenues are well below the predictions of the strategic discounting model, they are opposite in sign and magnitude to the RNNE model which calls for a $1.78 *increase* in revenue.

A within-auction series analysis reinforces the importance of the winner's curse in determining whether public information raises or lowers revenues. The first two columns of Table 6 show the effects of announcing x_L conditional on the presence or absence of a winner's curse in large group auctions, for those auction periods where the RNNE model predicts an increase. A *chi*-square test shows the winner's curse to significantly affect the validity of the RNNE model's prediction ($\chi^2 = 4.25$, $p < .05$). The third

TABLE 6—EFFECTS OF THE WINNER'S CURSE ON REVENUE RAISING EFFECTS
OF PUBLIC INFORMATION[a]

| | Number of Periods in Auction | | |
| | Large Numbers (6–7) | | Small Numbers[b] (3–4) |
Change in Seller's Revenues	Winner's Curse	No Winner's Curse	No Winner's Curse
Increase	6	12	29
Decrease	11	5	10

[a]Auction market periods where RNNE predicted an increase in seller's revenues. Winner's curse defined in terms of high bid in private information market in excess of $E[x_0|X_i = x_1]$.

[b]Winner's curse present in 3 auction periods where RNNE predicts increase in seller's revenues. Hence omitted.

column of the table shows the effects on revenue in the absence of a winner's curse in the small group auctions. The pattern here is much the same as found in auctions with 6–7 bidders in the absence of a winner's curse ($\chi^2 = .086$).[25]

In the two auction series where public information consisted of posting an additional, randomly drawn, private information signal, public information raised revenues $.27 per auction (an average increase of −$.80 in experiment 1 and $1.33 in experiment 2). Note that neither of these series exhibited significant traces of the winner's curse under private information conditions. In contrast, in an earlier series of experiments involving inexperienced subjects, revealing a random public information signal consistently *reduced* revenues, in this case by an average of $2.95 per auction (Kagel et al., 1984). In 2 of these 4 auction series, average profits were negative under private information conditions, while in 3 of the 4, the high bid exceeded $E[x_0|X_i = x_1]$ in 40 percent or more of the auctions. These results serve to reinforce the hypothesis that an absence of a winner's curse is a necessary condition for public information to raise average revenues.

Table 7 reports market outcomes relative to the RNNE model's predictions with x_L announced. Average actual profits were positive in all experiments. While there is considerable variation in profits relative to the RNNE model's predictions across auction series (especially series 3 and 6), on average profits were only slightly less than predicted ($3.20 actual vs. $3.41 predicted). Further, unlike private information conditions, there were no systematic differences in realized profits relative to predictions as the number of active bidders varied. These results, at the market level at least, are consistent with our earlier suggestion that the RNNE model would provide a more accurate characterization of performance with x_L announced, compared with private information conditions.

More detailed analysis of the data, however, shows that more is at work here than simple strategic discounting with all bidders employing identical bid functions. With x_L announced, there is almost a complete breakdown of the prediction that the bidder with the highest private information signal wins the auction. In these experiments the high private information signal holder won only 29.5 percent of all auctions. This is only modestly above what one would expect if chance factors alone determined whether the high private signal holder won, an expected frequency of 21.8 percent.

---

[25]Results similar to these have been found in a companion series of 6 second-price common value auction experiments.

TABLE 7—PROFITS AND BIDDING WITH PUBLIC INFORMATION (x_L)
(All profits in dollars)

Auction Series (No. of Periods)	No. of Bidders	Average Actual Profits (t-statistic)[a]	Average Profits Under RNNE (standard error of mean)	Profits as a Percentage of RNNE Prediction	Percent of Auctions Won by High Signal Holder
6 (23)	3–4	.15 (.08)	2.96 (1.60)	5.1	30.4
3 small (14)	4	10.24 (3.33)[c]	2.68 (2.03)	382.0	21.4
7 small (11)	4	2.07 (.86)	4.54 (2.00)	45.6	18.2
7 large (18)	6	1.67 (1.56)	3.06 (.62)	54.6	27.8
4 (18)	6–7	3.43 (2.24)[b]	4.14 (1.04)	82.9	44.4
5 (20)	7	1.64 (1.62)	3.06 (.86)	53.6	35.0

[a] Tests null hypothesis that mean is 0.0.
[b] Significant at 5 percent level, 2-tailed t-test.
[c] Significant at 1 percent level, 2-tailed t-test.

Detailed examination of the data shows a handful of bidders (20.0 percent) winning a disproportionately large number (57.7 percent) of the auctions with x_L announced. This handful of bidders did quite well as a group, earning average profits of $2.79 per auction period won, as compared to $2.89 for all other bidders. A distinguishing characteristic of these bidders is that they were relatively more aggressive than their rivals under private information conditions (ranking bids as a fraction of signal values consistently placed them in the top half of all bidders). The increased aggressiveness of this handful of bidders in the public information markets (they won only 15.1 percent of all private information auctions in which they did not have the highest private information signal, compared to 54.7 percent of the corresponding public information auctions) is directly attributable to the sharp reduction in beliefs about the underlying value of item inherent in announcing x_L. This reduction in the effective dispersion of information concerning x_0 permitted differences in risk attitudes and information processing capacities to play an increased role in the outcomes of auctions with public information.[26]

Table 8 reports the results of statistical estimates of individual bid functions with x_L announced. Recall from (8) that the parameters associated with the variables x_L and x_i are a function of the number of bidders present. The specifications in Table 8 employ different slope coefficients for these variables in small group ($N = 3–4$) and large group ($N = 6–7$) cases. With $N = 3–4$, the estimated slope coefficients for public and private information, are close to the theoretical bid function prediction (with $N = 4$, these are .67 and .33 for public and private information, respectively). With $N = 6–7$, more weight is attached to public rather than

[26] However, these bidders were unable to overcome the inherent disadvantage of holding only public information, as their average profits did not deviate significantly from zero in cases where they held the low private information signal.

TABLE 8—ERROR COMPONENTS ESTIMATES OF BID FUNCTION IN MARKETS
WITH x_L ANNOUNCED

$$b(x_i, x_L) = - \underset{(6.2)}{.95} + \underset{(.05)}{.24x_i} - \underset{(.06)}{.07x_i^*} + \underset{(.05)}{.72x_L} + \underset{(.06)}{.12x_L^*} + \underset{(.07)}{.14\varepsilon} + \underset{(.70)}{.08N} \qquad \begin{array}{l} R^2 = .98 \\ \sigma_\eta = 7.39 \end{array}$$

$$b(x_i, x_L) = \underset{(.05)}{.24x_i} - \underset{(.05)}{.07x_i^*} + \underset{(.05)}{.72x_L} + \underset{(.06)}{.12x_L^*} + \underset{(.06)}{.14\varepsilon} \qquad \begin{array}{l} R^2 = .98 \\ \sigma_\eta = 7.37 \end{array}$$

Note: $x_i^* = x_i$ if $N = 6$ or 7, $x_i^* = 0$ otherwise; $x_L^* = x_L$ if $N = 6$ or 7, $x_L^* = 0$ otherwise.
[a]Standard errors are shown in parentheses.

private information, in contrast to the theoretical bid function prediction (with $N = 7$, predicted weights are .58 and .42, respectively). Further, ε has a modest positive, statistically significant, effect on bids, contrary to the predictions of both the RNNE and strategic discounting models, in which x_L and x_i capture all the information necessary (recall equation (8)).

C. *Summary of Experimental Outcomes of Primary Interest*

The data permit us to reach clear conclusions regarding the research hypotheses of primary interest specified in Section II, subsection 3. With respect to Hypotheses 1 and 2, we reject the strong form of the RNNE bidding model, irrespective of the number of rivals in the market or whether the market involves private or public information. Bidding consistently exceeded the RNNE prediction in private information markets, was highly variable relative to the RNNE reference point in markets with public information, and x_L failed to raise revenues by the predicted amount, even in markets without a winner's curse. The weak form of the RNNE model consistently outperformed the winner's curse and the strategic discounting model in markets with small numbers of rivals, consistent with Hypotheses 3 and 4. However this ballpark characterization of the data failed on both counts in markets with large numbers of rivals, leading us to reject Hypothesis 5. Finally, bidders were sensitive to the strategic implications of the auctions, responding correctly to variations in ε and coming close, on average, to the

RNNE model's prediction with x_L announced. This confirms Hypothesis 6, which in turn suggests that the rejection of Hypotheses 1–5, particularly the rejection of Hypothesis 5, follows from the judgmental errors underlying the winner's curse.

IV. Towards Generalizability: But Is This How the Real World Operates?

A common criticism of experimental research in economics is that behavior in the laboratory is unlikely to be representative of field behavior. This criticism increases, as well it should, with the degree to which laboratory behavior deviates from accepted economic theory and common understanding of what constitutes "rational" economic behavior. Critics argue that auction market subjects, MBA students and senior undergraduates, are inherently less sophisticated, and clearly less experienced, than executives in the relevant industry, that experimental subjects do not have as much time to think and respond to events as industry executives, and that they lack the assistance of expert advisors that many industries have, to cite some of the prominent criticisms we have encountered. One can rebut these arguments on grounds that the experimental designs drastically simplify the decision-making structure, thereby obviating the need for expert advisors and reducing time requirements to make sensible decisions. Further, experimental subjects receive substantially more feedback, with shorter delays, regarding the outcomes of their decisions, so that the feedback loops that promote learning and adjustment over time are substantially stronger for experimental sub-jects compared to industry executives. (This is particularly true in the case of OCS lease sales where executives know that returns on investment will only be revealed years after bids have been accepted, and the responsible parties might well be in different positions within the company, or moved to a rival firm.)

Logical arguments can only go so far in debates of this sort. The question posed here is, what do the relevant data outside the laboratory look like compared to laboratory-generated data? Is the same model capable of organizing behavior in both settings? Do the field data obviously contradict the laboratory data?

The remainder of this section examines these issues in the context of the U.S. government's outer continental shelf lease sales. Note that our objective here is not to definitively test between competing explana-tions using field data. If we thought the field data had this kind of potential, there would be no need to resort to laboratory experi-ments in the first place (see Vernon Smith, 1982, and Charles Plott, 1982, for general discussions of the problems involved in using field data to test between models of market behavior and the advantages of laboratory experiments). Rather, our objective is to show that a reasonable analysis of the available data does not falsify the hypothesis that similar economic processes are at work in both settings. If this can be done, the burden of proof rests on those who would argue that the results don't generalize to demonstrate that their arguments are correct.

The concept of a winner's curse arose from petroleum geologists analysis of OCS bidding patterns and industry based calcula-tion of rates of return from winning lease sales (Capen et al.; Lorenz and Dougherty). In a more recent analysis, Walter Mead, Asbjorn Moseidjord, and Philip Sorensen (1983) found after-tax rates of return on all OCS leases in the Gulf of Mexico issued from 1954 to 1969 to be less than average returns on equity for U.S. manufacturing corporations. Mead et al. view lease pur-chases as high risk investments and con-clude that "... they (lessees) have historically received no risk premium and may have paid too much for the right to explore for and produce oil and gas on federal offshore lands" (1983, pp. 42–43).[27] In light of the effects of public information on bidder's profits reported here, a second element of Mead et al.'s (1983) calculations, namely rate of return *differentials* between drainage and wildcat leases, provides important cor-roborating evidence for the argument that lessees probably paid "too much" in these early OCS lease sales. The remainder of this section details this argument.[28]

A wildcat lease involves a tract for which there are no drilling data available that would indicate potential productivity. When a hy-drocarbon reservoir has been located on a wildcat tract that is expected to extend into adjacent unleased acreage, the adjacent tract is defined by the U.S. Geological Service (USGS) as a drainage tract. Considerably more information is available regarding the economic potential of drainage than wildcat tracts. This information has both public and private components. An important public information component is that drainage tracts are unlikely to be dry, thereby signifi-cantly reducing the uncertainty (relative to wildcat tracts) that hydrocarbons will be found. However, developers of the wildcat tract (called neighbors) are likely to have superior private information relative to non-neighbors regarding the quantity of oil likely

---

[27] There is some argument as to whether investors require risk premiums for investing in oil and gas leases. A number of writers suggest that risk-averse bidders would require a premium relative to investing in alter-native activities. Others, one of our referees included, argue that large oil companies with access to capital markets and having a diversified portfolio of leases would not be expected to earn risk premiums.

[28] Our analysis is not concerned with absolute rates of return, or absolute present discounted value calcula-tions, for OCS sales compared to other industries. Rather, we are concerned exclusively with *differences* in rate of return between drainage and wildcat leases. Differential rate calculations within an industry, by the same research team, should be relatively more robust to the empirical problems encountered in obtaining such measure than comparisons across industries by different research groups.

to be found, oil pressures, and other significant seismic information.[29]

If the information available on drainage leases were purely public, it should, according to Nash equilibrium bidding theory, raise average seller's revenues, hence reducing bidder's profits (recall Section II).[30] If the information were purely private, under Nash equilibrium bidding theory it would increase the rate of return for insiders (neighbors) relative to outsiders (nonneighbors), *and* reduce the average rate of return for nonneighbors below what would be earned in the absence of insider information (Wilson, 1975a, b; M. Weverbergh, 1979). If the added information on drainage leases contains both public and private information elements, rates of return for neighbors should be greater than for nonneighbors, but with nonneighbor returns definitely less than in the absence of the additional information (both the public and private information components push in this direction for nonneighbors).

What Mead et al. found were higher rates of return on drainage compared to wildcat leases for *both* neighbors (88.6 percent higher) *and* nonneighbors (56.2 percent higher). Further, nonneighbors won 43.2 percent of all drainage leases. While the higher rate of return for neighbors compared with nonneighbors can be explained by the presence of insider information (the explanation Mead et al. offer, 1983, 1984), the substantially higher rates of return for nonneighbors remains puzzling within the context of Nash equilibrium bidding theory. However, the higher rate of return for *both* neighbors and

nonneighbors on drainage leases is perfectly consistent with our experimental findings, given the existence of a winner's curse in bidding on wildcat leases. According to this explanation, the additional information available from neighbor tracts served to correct for the overly optimistic estimate of lease value recorded in the average winning bids on wildcat tracts, thereby raising average profits for both neighbors and nonneighbors alike. In this respect, the OCS lease data parallel our experimental results with public information in the presence of a winner's curse.

What alternative explanations are available to explain *both* nonneighbors and neighbors rates of return being higher on drainage leases? Mead et al. suggest two alternatives. First, one might argue that the lower rate of return on wildcat leases reflects the option value of the private information consequent on discovering hydrocarbons. The higher rate of return of neighbors over nonneighbors on the drainage leases certainly suggests that neighbors had valuable proprietary information, the prospect of which would depress the value of the wildcat leases. However, returns to this proprietary information were far from certain to be realized, while the differential overall rate of return on leases in the Gulf, counting wildcats alone vs. counting wildcats plus drainage leases, was small, amounting to 7 percent of the wildcat rate of return (Mead et al., 1983). Thus the revealed value of the option is small and is unlikely to fully account for the depressed rate of return on wildcats relative to nonneighbors. Second, one can argue that the existence of insider information (and its common knowledge) scared off nonneighbors so that they did not bid, or bid very little, relative to lease value. Consequently, when nonneighbors won, since they bid quite low, they obtained higher rates of return as well. However, the frequency with which nonneighbors won drainage leases seems inconsistent with this argument.[31] To be sure,

[29] Only drainage leases have neighbors, namely those responsible for the development of the neighboring wildcat tract.

[30] All leases had the same royalty rate and were allocated on the basis of a first-price cash bonus bid. Drainage leases were spread throughout the Gulf so that each lease is likely to represent an independent pool of oil (Asbjorn Moseidjord, personal communication). The revenue-raising (profit-reducing) effects of public information in the RNNE model are expectations based on samples of independent observations (Milgrom and Weber). Hence, the drainage lease sample satisfies the assumptions of the model.

[31] Under Nash equilibrium bidding theory, it is not perfectly clear what ought to happen to the frequency

the average number of bids on drainage leases was less than on wildcats (2.88 vs. 3.33), but the data suggest only a modest 6.4 percent decline in the rate of return in going from leases with 2 bids to leases with 3–4 bids (Mead et al., 1983; 1984).[32]

Note that we do not dispute Mead et al.'s (1984) argument that neighbors had proprietary information leading to higher rates of return on drainage leases than wildcats, or on drainage leases relative to nonneighbors. What we are claiming is that this proprietary information does not fully account for the substantially higher rates of return on drainage leases over wildcat leases for *both* neighbors and nonneighbors alike. Rather this element of the data is more readily explained by the public information component of the drainage lease designation, in conjunction with a winner's curse on wildcat leases. This explanation has the virtue of parsimony and consistency with the experimental results reported here.[33]

Our analysis of field data has been limited to 1954–69, prior to the publication of Capen et al.'s article alerting the industry to the presence of a winner's curse, and suggesting ways to avoid it. Many would argue that adjustments in bidding in the 1970's, partly in response to Capen et al.'s article and related publications, has eliminated the winner's curse in OCS lease sales, although opinions are not unanimous on the subject (see Lorenz and Dougherty, for example). We know of no rate-of-return studies on drainage vs. wildcat leases for the 1970's similar to Mead et al.'s for the 1960's that might help resolve the issue. We do know that at times there are significant discrepancies between cognitive understanding of the "right" thing to do and actual behavior. For mineral rights auctions, this involves firms recognizing and admitting that their geologists' estimates of value (and their economists' estimates of future price) have a significant error component, and that in the absence of insider information are unlikely to be better (on average) than their rivals. Such an admission is no small matter when paying substantial salaries to these professionals. As such we reserve judgment for the moment on the issue of a continuing winner's curse in OCS sales. Even assuming elimination of a winner's curse in more recent OCS lease sales does not affect our argument here, however: the available data outside the laboratory are consistent with data inside it

---

with which the informationally disadvantaged will win auctions. We suspect that this depends critically on the underlying distributions of item value and private information signals, and the nature of the insider information. However, all formal Nash equilibrium bidding models developed to date have the less informed earning lower profits than under symmetric information conditions (Wilson, 1975a,b; Weverbergh).

[32] Numbers of bidders in field environments is endogenous, depending in part on perceived lease value, rather than exogenous, as commonly treated in the auction market literature (and as one can arrange for in the laboratory). As such it is far from clear why, in theory, rates of return should vary systematically with numbers of bidders in field environments, unless again we postulate the existence of a winner's curse that is exaggerated with increased numbers of bidders.

[33] Drainage tracts have sharply reduced exploration costs as there are substantially fewer dry holes drilled per lease than on wildcats. Further, there are reduced production costs as a consequence of existing investments on neighbor leases and possibilities of joint production. In efforts to reconcile Mead et al.'s (1983) estimates of higher rates of return on drainage leases with their own estimates that prior drilling raised seller's revenues in the Gulf, Jeffrey Leitzinger and Joseph Stiglitz (1984) argue that developers capture at least some of the rent associated with reduced production costs on drainage leases. No explanation is offered for how this can plausibly account for the full differential rate of return between wildcat and drainage leases. Nor

why, since these savings are public knowledge and contain a strong common value element, traditional motions of rent capture in competitive markets should fail. (Reduced production costs are in large measure available to both neighbors and nonneighbors as a consequence of the federal government's ability to force unitization, and the strong effects of these enforcement powers on voluntary unitization of tracts; see Gary Liebcap and Steven Wiggins, 1985.) An alternative explanation is that Mead et al.'s rate of return estimates are incorrect. However, there are equally strong, if not stronger, reasons to suppose that Leitzinger and Stiglitz's estimates of information externalities, which are based on the size of the bonus bid on drainage compared with wildcat leases, are highly exaggerated, as the public information component associated with the drainage lease designation is systematically biased towards raising the expected value of these leases.

in the absence of extensive efforts to alert bidders to the presence of a winner's curse.

V. Conclusions

Our experiments provide an empirical example of a market where individual judgment errors significantly alter market outcomes. Bidders in common value auctions, as in other auctions, are sensitive to the strategic opportunities inherent in the auction process. However, when strategic considerations and adverse-selection forces resulting from uncertainty about the value of the item conflict, behavior fails to conform, in important ways, with the requirements of Nash equilibrium bidding strategies.

Although we reject the general applicability of Nash equilibrium bidding models, market outcomes come closer to the risk-neutral Nash equilibrium model's predictions than to the winner's curse in auctions with small numbers (3–4) of bidders. In addition, there is considerable adjustment to the adverse-selection problem with large numbers (6–7) of bidders. However, these adjustments are far from complete, as profit levels are consistently negative, in conformity with the winner's curse. The existence of a winner's curse in large groups, in conjunction with the positive effect of the number of bidders on the size of individual bids, indicates that avoidance of the winner's curse in small groups is specific to the situation, and does not carry over to auctions with larger numbers of bidders. Bidders have learned to avoid the winner's curse in small groups out of a trial and error survival process, as opposed to "understanding" the adverse-selection problem as it applies to new situations.

Accounting for judgmental errors in these markets has some practical policy implications in terms of whether sellers choose to obtain and release information narrowing down the value of the auctioned item. In the absence of judgmental errors, this information clearly enhances seller's revenues, as Nash equilibrium bidding theory predicts. In the presence of judgmental errors, however, such information will almost surely reduce average revenues, a factor ignored to date in the literature.

Given sufficient experience and feedback regarding the outcomes of their decisions, we have no doubt that our experimental subjects, as well as most bidders in "real world" settings, would eventually learn to avoid the winner's curse in any particular set of circumstances. The winner's curse is a disequilibrium phenomenon that will correct itself given sufficient time and the right kind of information feedback.[34] Clearly the attenuation of the feedback loop between a decision and determining the outcomes of that decision, as is commonly the case in outer continental shelf lease sales and a number of other settings, serves to perpetuate the phenomena. Further, comparative evaluations of management performance in terms of money "left on the table" (the difference between the high bid and the second high bid) can do little to arrest the problem since the winner's curse is ubiquitous and applies fairly uniformly across individuals at early stages of the learning process (Kagel et al., 1986). Finally, to the extent that market participants feel that they have an inside edge, and better judgmental abilities than their rivals, the winner's curse is bound to be difficult to eliminate.

Apart from the important task of replicating our experiments, a number of interesting research questions remain to be explored. Since avoidance of the winner's curse involves a learning process, exactly what mechanisms, if any, insure market memory of past mistakes? To what extent do new entrants learn from experience compared to learning from observation or formal education? Do inexperienced bidders learn more quickly in markets dominated by experienced bidders? What are the dynamics of markets characterized by continual entry of new "suckers" who must learn from personal experience, and do we observe these dynamics in field environments?

---

[34]Auction series 7 large clearly indicates this as it involved super-experienced subjects all of whom had been in at least two previous large group series.

INSTRUCTIONS

This is an experiment in the economics of market decision making. The National Science Foundation has provided funds for conducting this research. The instructions are simple, and if you follow them carefully and make good decisions you may earn a CONSIDERABLE AMOUNT OF MONEY which will be PAID TO YOU IN CASH at the end of the experiment.

1. In this experiment we will create a market in which you will act as buyers of a fictitious commodity in a sequence of trading periods. A single unit of the commodity will be auctioned off in each trading period. There will be several trading periods.

2. Your task is to submit written bids for the commodity in competition with other buyers. The precise value of the commodity at the time you make your bids will be unknown to you. Instead, each of you will receive information as to the value of the item which you should find useful in determining your bid. The process of determining the value of the commodity and the information you will receive will be described in Sections 6 and 7 below.

3. The high bidder gets the item and makes a profit equal to the difference between the value of the commodity and the amount they bid. That is,

$$(\text{VALUE OF ITEM}) - (\text{HIGHEST BID}) = \text{PROFITS}$$

for the high bidder. If this difference is negative, it represents a loss.

If you do not make the high bid on the item, you will earn zero profits. In this case, you neither gain nor lose money from bidding on the item.

4. You will be given a starting capital credit balance of $10.00. Any profit earned by you in the experiment will be added to this sum, and any losses incurred will be subtracted from this sum. The net balance of these transactions will be calculated and paid to you in CASH at the end of the experiment.

The starting capital credit balance, and whatever subsequent profits you earn, permit you to suffer losses in one auction to be recouped in part or in total in later auctions. However, should your net balance at any time during the experiment drop to zero (or less), you will no longer be permitted to participate. Instead we will give you your participation fee and you'll be free to leave the auction.

You *are* permitted to bid in excess of your capital credit balance in any given period.

5. During each trading period you will be bidding in a market in which *all* the other participants are also bidding. After all bids have been handed in they will be posted on the blackboard. We will circle the high bid and note the second high bid, and post the value of the item. We will also indicate whether a profit or loss was earned by the high bidder.

6. The value of the auctioned commodity (V^*) will be assigned randomly and will lie between $25.00 and $225.00 inclusively. For each auction, *any value* within this interval has an *equally likely chance* of being drawn. The value of the item can never be less than

$25.00 or more than $225.00. The V^* values are determined randomly and independently from auction to auction. As such a high V^* in one period tells you nothing about the likely value in the next period— whether it will be high or low. It doesn't even preclude drawing the same V^* value in later periods.

7. Private Information Signals:

Although you do not know the precise value of the item in any particular trading period, you will receive information which will narrow down the range of possible values. This will consist of a private information signal which is selected randomly from an interval whose lower bound is V^* minus epsilon (ε), and whose upper bound is V^* plus epsilon. *Any value* within this interval has an *equally likely* chance of being drawn and being assigned to one of you as your private information signal. You will always know what the value of epsilon is.

For example, suppose that the value of the auctioned item is $128.16 and that epsilon is $6.00. Then each of you will receive a private information signal which will consist of a randomly drawn number that will be between $122.16 ($V^* - \varepsilon = \$128.16 - \$6.00$) and $134.16 ($V^* + \varepsilon = \$128.16 + \$6.00$). Any number in this interval has an equally likely chance of being drawn.

The line diagram below shows what's going on in this example.

The data below show the entire set of signals the computer generated for our sample bag. (Note we've ordered these signal values from lowest to highest.)

$V^* = \$128.16$; $\varepsilon = \$6.00$. Signal values: $122.57
124.14
124.68
126.76
128.84
129.51
129.96
129.98
132.07

You will note that some signal values were above the value of the auctioned item, and some were below the value of the item. Over a sufficiently long series of auctions, the differences between your private information signal and the value of the item will average out to zero (or very close to it). For any given auction, however, your private information signal can be above or below the value of the item. That's the nature of the random selection process generating the signals.

You will also note that V^* must always be greater than or equal to your signal value $- \varepsilon$. The computer calculates this for you and notes it. Further, V^* must always be less than or equal to your sample value $+ \varepsilon$. The computer calculates this for you and notes it.

Finally, you may receive a signal value below $25.00 (or above $225.00). There is nothing strange about this, it just indicates V^* is close to $25.00 (or $225.00) relative to the size of epsilon.

8. Your signal values are strictly private information and are not to be revealed to anyone else prior to opening the bids.

You will be told the value of ε prior to bidding and it will be posted on the blackboard. However, you will not be told the value of V^* until after the bids have been posted. Finally we will post all of the signal values drawn along with the bids.

9. No one may bid less than $0.00 for the item. Nor may anyone bid more than their signal value $+ \varepsilon$. Any bid in between these two values is acceptable.

Bids must be rounded to the nearest penny to be accepted.

In case of ties for the high bid, we will flip a coin to determine who will earn the item.

10. You are not to reveal your bids, or profits, nor are you to speak to any other subject while the experiment is in progress.

11. As promised, everyone will receive $4 irrespective of their earnings for participating in the experiment.

Let's summarize the main points: (1) High bidder earns the item and earns a profit = value of item − high bid price. (2) Profits will be added to your starting balance of $10.00, losses subtracted from it. Your balance at the end of experiment will be paid in cash. If balance turns negative you're no longer allowed to bid. (3) Your private information signal is randomly drawn from the interval $V^* - \varepsilon, V^* + \varepsilon$. The value of the item can never be more than your signal value $+ \varepsilon$, or less than your signal value $- \varepsilon$. (4) The value of the item will always be between $25.00 and $225.00.

Are there any questions?

ADDITIONAL INSTRUCTIONS: PERIODS WITH PUBLIC INFORMATION

1. From now on bidding will be done twice during each trading period, once under each of two different information conditions. First, you will bid on the basis of your private information signals, just as you have been doing. After these bids have been made and collected, but before they are opened, you will be provided with additional information (to be described shortly) concerning the value of the item *and be asked to bid again on the commodity.* This additional information will be posted on the blackboard for everyone to see and will be referred to as a public information signal.

2. The public information signal will consist of posting on the blackboard the *lowest* of the private information signals any of you received. Note we will not reveal the bid of the player with the lowest information signal, just the signal value.

3. Note that V^* does *not* change between auctions. Your private information signals do *not* change between auctions either. However, what the public information signal does do is provide *everyone* with additional information about the possible value of V^*.

4. After both sets of bids have been collected they will be opened and the bids posted in each market and

the high bid noted. We will also post the value of the item and compute profits and/or losses in the two markets as before:

PROFITS = (VALUE OF ITEM) − (HIGH BID PRICE).

Finally, to speed things up a bit we will no longer post all of the signal values drawn along with the bids.

5. However, we will only actually pay profits (or hold you accountable for losses) in one of the two markets. We will flip a coin to decide which market to pay off in. Heads we pay off in the market with private information values only, tails we pay off in the market with private and public information.

6. There is no obligation to make the same bid, or to bid differently in the two markets. This is strictly up to you to decide what to do in terms of what you think will generate the greatest profits.

Are there any questions?

REFERENCES

Baltagi, Badi H., "Pooling Cross-Sections with Unequal Time-Series Lengths," *Economics Letters,* 1986, *18,* 133–36.

Battalio, Raymond C., Kogut, Carl and Meyer, Donald J., "Individual and Market Bidding Behavior in a Vickery First Price Auction: Varying Market Size and Information," paper presented at Econometric Society Winter Meetings, 1983.

Capen, E. C., Clapp, R. V. and Campbell, W. M., "Competitive Bidding in High-Risk Situations," *Journal of Petroleum Technology,* June 1971, *23,* 641–53.

Cassing, James and Douglas, Richard W., "Implications of the Auction Mechanism in Baseball's Free Agent Draft," *Southern Economic Journal,* July 1980, *47,* 110–21.

Cox, James C., Roberson, Bruce and Smith, Vernon L., "Theory and Behavior of Single Object Auctions," in V. L. Smith, ed., *Research in Experimental Economics,* Vol. 2, Greenwich: JAI Press, 1982.

Dessauer, John P., *Book Publishing,* New York: Bowker, 1981.

Kagel, John H. et al., "First-Price, Sealed-Bid, Common Value Auctions: Some Initial Experimental Results," Center for Public Policy Discussion Paper 84–1, University of Houston, 1984.

———, "First Price Common Value Auctions: Bidder Behavior and the 'Winner's Curse'," mimeo., University of Houston, 1986.

Kagel, John H., Harstad, Ronald M. and Levin, Dan, "Information Impact and Allocation Rules in Auctions with Affiliated Private Values: A Laboratory Study," mimeo., University of Houston, 1986.

_____ and Levin, Dan, "Individual Bidder Behavior in First-Price Private Value Auctions," *Economics Letters*, 1985, *19*, 125–28.

Leitzinger, Jeffrey J. and Stiglitz, Joseph E., "Information Externalities in Oil and Gas Leasing," *Contemporary Policy Issues*, March 1984, *5*, 44–57.

Libecap, Gary D. and Wiggins, Steven N., "The Influence of Private Failure on Regulation: The Case of Oil Field Unitization," *Journal of Political Economy*, August 1985, *93*, 690–714.

Lorenz, John and Dougherty, E. L., "Bonus Bidding and Bottom Lines: Federal Offshore Oil and Gas," SPE 12024, 58th Annual Fall Technical Conference, October 1983.

Matthews, Steven A., "Comparing Auctions for Risk Averse Buyers: A Buyer's Point of View," *Econometrica*, forthcoming 1986.

Mead, Walter, J., Moseidjord, Asbjorn and Sorensen, Philip E., "The Rate of Return Earned by Leases Under Cash Bonus Bidding in OCS Oil and Gas Leases," *Energy Journal*, October 1983, *4*, 37–52.

_____, _____, and _____, "Competitive Bidding Under Asymmetrical Information: Behavior and Performance in Gulf of Mexico Drainage Lease Sales, 1959–

1969," *Review of Economics and Statistics*, August 1984, *66*, 505–08.

Milgrom, Paul R. and Weber, Robert J., "A Theory of Auctions and Competitive Bidding," *Econometrica*, September 1982, *50*, 1089–122.

Plott, Charles R., "Industrial Organization Theory and Experimental Economics," *Journal of Economic Literature*, December 1982, *20*, 1485–527.

Roll, Richard, "The Hubris Hypothesis of Corporate Takeovers," *Journal of Business*, April 1986, *59*, 197–216.

Smith, Vernon L., "Microeconomic Systems as an Experimental Science," *American Economic Review*, December 1982, *72*, 923–55.

Weverbergh, M., "Competitive Bidding With Asymmetric Information Reanalyzed," *Management Science*, March 1979, *25*, 291–94.

Wilson, Robert, (1975a) "Comment on David Hughart, Informational Assymetry, Bidding Strategies and the Marketing of Offshore Petroleum Leases," mimeo., Stanford University, 1975.

_____, (1975b) "On the Incentive for Information Acquistion in Competitive Bidding with Asymmetrical Information," mimeo., Stanford University, 1975.

_____, "A Bidding Model of Perfect Competition," *Review of Economic Studies*, October 1977, *44*, 511–18.

_____, "The Basic Model of Competitive Bidding," mimeo., Stanford University, 1981.

Winer, Ben J., *Statistical Principles in Experimental Design*, 2nd ed., New York: McGraw-Hill, 1971.

[18]

THE MORE THE MERRIER?
SOCIAL PSYCHOLOGICAL ASPECTS OF
MULTIPARTY NEGOTIATIONS IN ORGANIZATIONS

Roderick M. Kramer

Contemporary views of organizations have often stressed the conflictual nature of intraorganizational relations (Boulding, 1972; Katz & Kahn, 1978; Pfeffer & Salancik, 1977). Organizational conflict has been regarded as an almost inevitable consequence of the interdependence among different individuals and groups with respect to the diverse tasks they are trying to accomplish, the heterogeneous goals they are pursuing, and the limited but essential resources for which they may be competing. Negotiation is one of the central mechanisms used to resolve such conflicts (Kochan & Verma, 1983). Indeed, organizations have been characterized as *negotiated* social orders (Strauss, 1978).

Given their obvious importance in organizations, it is not surprising that organizational researchers have become increasingly interested in negotiation processes (e.g., Bazerman & Lewicki, 1983; Lewicki & Litterer, 1985; Lewicki, Sheppard, & Bazerman, 1986). Although there has been a great deal of research on negotiations, much of it has focused on two-party or *dyadic* negotiation processes (Greenhalgh, 1987a; Northcraft & Neale, this volume). In contrast, the study of *multiparty* negotiations (negotiations involving more than two parties) has received comparatively little attention from researchers. The lack

Research on Negotiation in Organizations, Volume 3.
Handbook of Negotiation Research, pages 307-332.
Copyright © 1991 by JAI Press Inc.
All rights of reproduction in any form reserved.
ISBN: 1-55938-249-X.

of attention to multiparty negotiations is evident when surveying recent reviews of negotiation research: If they mention multiparty negotiations at all, it is only to acknowledge their greater complexity and affirm the need for more research (Bazerman, 1986; Bazerman, Mannix, & Thompson, 1988, and Raiffa, 1982 are notable exceptions).

The shortage of research on this topic is unfortunate, because negotiations often involve more than two parties. For example, negotiations in organizations can involve individuals from many different groups or subunits in an organization, either as direct participants in a negotiation process, or indirectly as constituents who may affect and be affected by its outcome. Thus, the problem of multiparty interaction represents an important level of complexity common to organizational negotiations, even if it is not characteristic of our theories regarding them.

The primary purpose of this paper is to address this gap in the literature. The paper has two goals. One goal is to provide an overview of multiparty negotiations. Given the shortage of research on this topic, such an overview seems warranted. The first part of the paper thus examines some of the general characteristics of multiparty negotiations in organizations. Several questions are addressed. First, what are some of the distinctive types of multiparty negotiations commonly observed in organizational settings? Second, what are the important dimensions along which these different types of negotiation vary? Third, how are multiparty negotiations different from dyadic negotiations?

One of the main conclusions that will emerge from the analysis presented is that multiparty negotiations differ from dyadic negotiations in primarily three ways. First, in terms of their greater "size" (i.e., the number of parties involved in the negotiation process). Second, in terms of their greater complexity. Third, in terms of the greater degree of social differentiation or heterogeneity between the parties involved in them. In recognition of these important differences, the second major goal of the paper is to examine how these three factors affect the process and outcome of a multiparty negotiation. This topic occupies the second half of the paper.

In addressing these issues, this paper adopts a social psychological perspective. According to this perspective, a multiparty negotiation process can be conceptualized in terms of the interaction among multiple individuals who are interdependent not only with respect to the specific outcomes they are negotiating, but also interdependent *socially* in terms of their formal and informal relationships with other individuals or groups in the organization. Because of this social interdependence, negotiators can best be characterized as *social* information processors and decision makers whose behavior is influenced by a variety of interpersonal, intragroup, and intergroup processes. These processes, in turn, are shaped by the particular organizational context or setting within which they are embedded.

In approaching multiparty negotiations from a social psychological perspective, this paper treats the individual negotiator as the appropriate unit of analysis. Negotiation behavior is viewed as the product of individual perceptions, cognitions, and motivations. In this respect, the approach adopted here differs from other approaches which have been taken toward understanding multiparty negotiations. For example, sociological conceptions have generally afforded greater emphasis to macro-level or structural determinants of negotiation behavior (e.g., Baldridge, 1971; Strauss, 1978), while economic conceptions (e.g., Baldwin & Clark, 1987) have tended to minimize psychological assumptions by treating negotiators as rational actors.[1]

The paper is organized as follows. First, I describe some common types of multiparty negotiations found in organizations, and identify several prominent dimensions along which they vary. Second, I discuss some of the major differences between dyadic and multiparty negotiations. I next consider some of the implications of these differences for understanding negotiation processes and outcomes. Finally, I conclude the chapter by suggesting some implications of a social psychological perspective on multiparty negotiations and offering some recommendations for future research.

NATURE AND CHARACTERISTICS OF MULTIPARTY NEGOTIATIONS

Because there has been relatively little research on multiparty negotiations in organizations, it might be useful to begin by identifying some common examples or types of such negotiations. One prevalent type of multiparty negotiation involves "common pool dependencies" (Miles, 1980). Common pool situations occur when individuals or groups in an organization are interdependent with respect to some valuable but limited pool of resources. The common resource pool may be divisible, in which case it may be possible to satisfy to varying degrees the different parties' interests, or it may be indivisible, so that the satisfaction of one party's interests effectively precludes satisfying those of the others. An example of a divisible resource is a "pool" of budgetary resources that must be allocated among various individuals or subunits in an organization. Examples of indivisible resources are a highly coveted office space or a senior position in an organization.

A distinction can also be drawn between common pools that are centrally versus collectively managed. In the case of centrally managed resource pools, a centralized decision maker has the power to decide how resources will be allocated. For example, in many universities, a department chair allocates resources such as salary, research funds, and lab space among the various faculty members in the department. Each faculty member individually and independently negotiates with the department chair. Thus, each is

interdependent with the others in so far as they are all competing for their
share of the available resources, but they may have little opportunity to directly
influence one another or negotiate among themselves (apart from covert
attempts to coordinate their actions or collude). Many competitive bidding
situations that arise in organizations have similar features (see, e.g., Bazerman
& Samuelson, 1983; Shubik, 1971).

In the case of negotiations where there is no central allocator, the parties
must explicitly negotiate among themselves, more or less as equals, in order
to collectively decide how the resources available to them will be divided. The
annual negotiations by the members of the Joint Chiefs of Staff regarding how
defense allocations will be distributed among the military services is one
example which has been widely studied (Kanter, 1975).

Collective bargaining and third-party intervention are two other common
forms of multiparty negotiation observed in organizations. Collective
bargaining can involve as few as two individuals each representing different
constituencies in the organization, or can involve multiple teams of negotiators
and even outside groups or agencies. Thus, these negotiations can be quite
complex. Third-party interventions typically involve two or more disputants
and a third-party intervenor. These negotiations can also be quite complex,
because the third party can assume many different roles in such situations,
ranging from a mediatior who assists the parties in discovering a resolution
of their conflict to an arbitrator who imposes a solution on them. Third parties
may work with the disputants as they meet face-to-face, or may act as a buffer
relaying messages and offers to the parties who remain isolated from one
another. Because extensive literatures on both collective bargaining (see, e.g.,
Kochan & Katz, 1988) and third-party interventions (see, e.g., Rubin, 1986;
Sheppard, 1984) already exist, these topics will not be addressed in detail here.

It should be noted that there are many other organizational phenomena that
involve multiple parties that might not be construed as negotiations *per se* but
in which negotiation processes play a central role. For example, during the Cuban
Missile Crisis, the members of the EXCOMM (President Kennedy's group of
advisors) were sharply divided over whether to use military versus diplomatic
actions to remove Soviet missiles from Cuba. The process by which they resolved
this disagreement has been extensively studied, but almost exclusively from the
standpoint of decision-making paradigms (Allison, 1971; Janis, 1983). A
negotiation paradigm provides a powerful alternative approach to analyzing such
group phenomena (see Bazerman, Mannix, & Thompson, 1988).

Although the few examples I have offered here do not exhaust the range
and variety of multiparty negotiations that may be encountered in
organizations, they may be regarded as fairly prototypical. In this respect, they
are useful in suggesting some representative dimensions along which such
negotiations vary. The major dimensions along which multiparty negotiations
differ may be characterized in terms of: (1) the number of parties involved and

the nature of their role in the negotiation; (2) the outcome being sought and the processes used to obtain that outcome; and (3) the level of social differentiation among the parties.[2]

Number of Parties and Role. The most conspicuous dimension along which multiparty negotiations differ is the number of parties who are involved in the negotiation. I refer to this dimension as the size of the negotiation. Defining the "size" of a negotiation is somewhat problematic because the nature of the parties' involvement or role can vary substantially across negotiations. Negotiators may be *principals*, acting on their own behalf, or they may be acting as *agents* representing others. They may participate directly in the negotiation itself or be constituents who try to affect its outcome by influencing the agents who represent them. Here, the term size refers to the number of parties who are directly involved in the negotiation process.[3]

Process and Outcome Related Variables. Multiparty negotiations can also be distinguished with respect to the outcomes the parties are seeking, and the processes used to achieve those outcomes. In some negotiations, consensus or unanimity among the parties is the desired outcome. In negotiating a new strategic plan for a corporation, for example, it may be essential for all of the parties to agree with the final agreement. In other negotiations, agreement by a subset of the parties (e.g., a simple majority) may be sufficient.

The particular outcome that is being sought can influence the processes that may be used during negotiation. For example, when agreement by a simple majority is sufficient, relatively simple decision procedures such as voting may be used. When consensus is desired, however, the parties may prefer to use more elaborate procedures such as collaborative problem solving and brainstorming in order to discover solutions that satisfy all of the parties and increase their commitment to the final agreement.

Multiparty negotiations can also differ in terms of whether they entail primarily explicit versus tacit bargaining processes or some mixture of the two. In explicit negotiation, the parties "openly" communicate their aspirations, preferences, and constraints, and inquire into those of the other party (Greenhalgh, 1987a). Much of the behavior we commonly associate with negotiations, such as the exchange of proposals and counterproposals, are forms of explicit bargaining. However, negotiation behavior can be tacit as well (Schelling, 1960; Strauss, 1978). Tacit bargaining behavior includes covert unilateral initiatives negotiators take to achieve such goals as preempting others, promoting coalitions and/or minimizing overt conflict. Tacit behavior also includes various forms of indirect expression of motives through nonverbal cues and signals (Greenhalgh, 1987a). Tacit bargaining is likely to be used when communication is incomplete, perceived to be impossible or, for some other reason, problematic (Schelling, 1960).

Because of their inherent complexity, most multiparty negotiations involve a mixture of both explicit and tacit bargaining. For example, during the Cuban Missile Crisis, the United States and Soviet Union, and Cuba and the Soviet Union were engaged in explicit negotiations regarding the conditions under which Soviet Missiles would be removed from Cuba. However, in addition to the formal exchange of proposals and counterproposals, each side employed tacit maneuvers, such as strategically positioning its military forces. These maneuvers were used to demonstrate resolve and signal commitment to various implicit deadlines and points of confrontation (e.g., announcement of the quarantine perimeter enabled the United States to indicate both a point at which confrontation would occur, as well as when it would occur, since the speed of the Soviet ships racing toward it were known to both parties). As is argued in more detail below, tacit bargaining processes may play an especially important role in multiparty negotiations.

Level of Social Differentiation. Social differentiation refers to the number of distinct social categories in a group of interdependent individuals. The level of actual social differentiation or heterogeneity in a multiparty negotiation may be low or high, depending on the number of organizational and social categories the negotiators represent. For example, the parties involved in a negotiation may all be from the same group (e.g., a negotiation among the members of the Board of Directors of a corporation) or from two or more different groups (e.g., a negotiation involving production, marketing, and sales personnel).

The parties may be similar or different along social and demographic variables, such as gender, race, and educational background. For example, the members of a labor negotiating team may be primarily black, female, and have only a high school education on average, whereas the management team with which they are negotiating may be composed primarily of white, male college graduates with MBAs. These social categorical distinctions, when correlated with organizationally-defined group boundaries which are relevant to a negotiation, can become highly salient to negotiators. This last point is important because, as is discussed in more detail below, it is the perceived rather than actual social differentiation among a group of negotiators that most strongly affects their behavior.

DIFFERENCES BETWEEN DYADIC AND MULTIPARTY NEGOTIATIONS

As noted earlier, there has been a great deal of research on dyadic-level negotiation processes. It might be worthwhile, therefore, to consider some of the differences between dyadic and multiparty negotiations. A systematic examination of such differences may be useful in understanding whether there are unique or "emergent" features of multiparty negotiations which merit special attention. This section describes a number of differences between dyadic and multiparty negotiations. These differences reflect both quantitative as well as qualitative differences between dyadic and multiparty negotiations. (Note: At this point, I simply describe these differences; their consequences will be elaborated on in subsequent sections).

Perhaps the single most important difference between dyadic and multiparty negotiations is the greater complexity of the latter. This complexity can assume several forms, including informational complexity, computational complexity, social complexity, procedural complexity, and strategic complexity. Each of these different forms of complexity will be discussed in turn here.

Informational and Computational Complexity. Along with the increased number of parties in a multiparty negotiation, there will usually be an increase in the number of issues at stake as well. As a result, the volume of information that each negotiator must possess can be very large. As Midgaard and Underdal (1977, p. 332) observed, "One of the most fundamental consequences of increasing the number of parties is that the negotiation situation tends to become less lucid, more complex, and therefore, in some respects, more demanding. As size increases, there will be more values, interests, and perceptions to be integrated or accommodated." The proliferation of parties and issues increases the "bargaining space" or set of logically possible agreements. This makes multiparty negotiations computationally more complex than dyadic negotiations.

Social Complexity. In addition to their greater informational and computational complexity, multiparty negotiations are also characterized by greater social complexity than dyadic negotiators. Social complexity is manifested in several ways. First, in the case of multiparty negotiations who are all members of a single group, group dynamics may play an important role in shaping the process and outcome of the negotiation (Bazerman, Mannix, & Thompson, 1988). For example, processes such as social comparison, social influence, conformity, cohesiveness, and leadership may exert considerable influence on negotiators' behavior. Similarly, pathological group dynamics such as groupthink (Janis, 1983) and escalation of commitment (Bazerman, Giuliano, & Appelman, 1984) may affect the dynamics of their negotiation. Groups in which there is excessive concern about maintaining high espirit de corps or avoiding conflict may tend to settle on relatively inferior compromises, rather than engage in energetic problemsolving and confrontation in order to explore solutions that might improve their joint outcomes. In negotiations involving only two parties, in contrast, such factors may have less impact (Bazerman, Mannix, & Thompson, 1988).

In the case of negotiations involving parties representing more than two groups, interaction processes associated with intergroup dynamics, including stereotyping, categorization, discrimination, and so forth may play an important role in shaping negotiation processes (Morley & Stephenson, 1977).

Procedural Complexity. Multiparty negotiations also entail greater procedural complexity compared to dyadic negotiations. All of the processes characteristic of a negotiation—the exchange of information about interests and needs, attempts to integrate proposals, and so forth—become more difficult as the number of parties increases. For this reason, it has generally been regarded as axiomatic that the greater the number of parties, the longer a negotiation process can take (Sebenius, 1983). Because of this complexity, formalized procedures such as voting, "rules of order," and norms may be more heavily utilized in multiparty compared to dyadic negotiations (Bazerman, Mannix, & Thompson, 1988; Raiffa, 1982).

Strategic Complexity. In dyadic negotiations, each party commonly exerts some degree of "fate control" (Kelley, 1979) over the other. By refusing to reach agreement or threatening to "walk," both parties in a dyadic negotiation can stall or even permanently stalemate a negotiation. In multiparty negotiations, this is often not possible, because the remaining parties can elect to form coalitions, make side agreements, or otherwise overrule the noncooperative party. Thus, the addition of parties introduces fundamental changes in the strategic complexity of a negotiation. In this section, I describe some of the forms such strategic complexity assumes.

The problem of strategic complexity is illustrated by considering the effects of negotiators' strategic choices on the process and/or outcome of a multiparty negotiation. Negotiation can be construed as a form of social influence in which one party is trying to influence another. This influence is exerted through the use of specific types of behavior (e.g., threats or promises). Thus, from the standpoint of the individual negotiator, the negotiation process consists of a series of *strategic choices* regarding which behaviors to use to achieve one's goals (Pruitt & Rubin, 1986).

In the case of dyadic negotiations, the problem of strategic choice is relatively simple. Negotiators can tailor their behavior very precisely to preempt, match or counter those of the person with whom they are negotiating. Through the use of strategies such as "tit-for-tat" (Axelrod, 1984) and GRIT (Lindskold, 1978), they can try to develop a specific kind of relationship with that person. For example, they can begin a negotiation by unilaterally revealing important information in order to signal their trust in the other party or their willingness to cooperate with them. If that behavior does not produce the desired result (e.g., if it is not reciprocated by the other party), they can adjust their behavior accordingly.

The problem of strategic choice becomes considerably more complicated in multiparty contexts because behaviors directed at one party may be observable by (and therefore affect) others with whom the negotiator must subsequently interact. The effects of the observability of behavior on the negotiation process are complex, but two possibilities merit special consideration. First, behaviors that might be quite effective when negotiating with only one other party may be problematic when multiple parties are involved. For example, a negotiator might prefer to use a noncooperative strategy against a particularly hostile or competitive adversary. However, to the extent that this behavior is observable by other parties with whom she will subsequently negotiate, she may be concerned that her behavior will be misconstrued (e.g., that it will be misattributed to a competitive orientation or motive on her part, rather than correctly attributed to a defensive motive). To guard against this possibility, she may act more cooperatively than she might otherwise.

Observability can produce exactly the opposite response as well. In the case of highly competitive multiparty negotiations, in which negotiators fear exploitation by others, they may engage in noncooperative behaviors in order to demonstrate their firmness or resolve. Thus, even though they might prefer cooperating with a given person, they may defer doing so in order to establish a reputation for toughness that may prove beneficial later. This logic is similar to what game theorists have called the "demonstration effect" (Wilson, 1989) and what Smith (1988) referred to more colloquially as "porcupine power." Porcupine power may be particularly useful in negotiation situations where the costs of misplaced trust are high or when it is important to deter competitive individuals. As both of these examples illustrate, negotiators in a multiparty situation need to worry not only about the direct effects of their behavior on the particular person with whom they happen to be interacting at the moment, but also the *collateral* affects of that behavior on others with whom they might have to negotiate subsequently.

As the number of parties involved in a negotiation increases, negotiators may experience increasingly severe *role conflict* or *role strain* (Kahn & Wolfe, 1964; Kressel, 1981). Role conflict and role strain in negotiations have most often been discussed with respect to the effects of constituents on a negotiator's behavior. For example, Kressel (1981, p. 227) observed that "negotiators may be pressured by their constituents into presenting the constituents' demands vehemently and without backing down, while their opposite numbers across the bargaining table may expect these same negotiators to adhere to norms of moderation and compromise." Similar role strain may be associated with trying to interact with multiple negotiation parties. There may be no single, consistent set of behaviors that a negotiator can use that will be effective with all of the parties with whom he or she must interact.

The strategic complexity inherent in multiparty negotiations is greater than dyadic negotiations for another reason as well. As Sebenius (1983) pointed out, negotiators may *intentionally* manipulate the size and complexity of a negotiation in search of strategic benefits or advantages. For example, negotiators can use the addition or subtraction of parties to a negotiation to advance their positions or undermine those of other parties. Negotiators can add parties who will act as allies to increase their power in the bargaining situation. They may add parties to spread risks. Finally, they may add parties in order to worsen the consequences of not reaching an agreement for another party.

Multiparty negotiations are also more complex than dyadic negotiations because, as the number of parties increases, the number of possible alliances or coalitions increases as well. As Caplow (1968) showed, the addition of even one person to a dyadic relationship introduces enormous complexity in terms of the greater number of possible strategic relationships among the parties. Through the formation of coalitions, the power relations among the parties may be fundamentally changed, as may the patterns of communication, resource exchange, and so on. (see, e.g., Murnighan, 1978; 1986). All of these factors can radically alter the process and outcome of a negotiation.

These are only some of the ways in which multiparty negotiations differ from dyadic negotiations. These differences primarily reflect the greater size, complexity, and level of social differentiation characteristic of negotiations involving more than two parties. One way of further thinking about the unique or emergent properties of multiparty negotiations, then, is to examine how size, complexity, and differentiation affect a negotiation. In the following sections, I examine this issue. I focus particular attention on how these three factors adversely influence the process and outcome of a negotiation. Specifically, I attempt to illustrate how size, complexity, and differentiation affect the way in which negotiators process information, the expectations they have prior to negotiation, and the behaviors they use during negotiation.

CONSEQUENCES OF COMPLEXITY, SIZE AND DIFFERENTIATION

Negotiations can be analyzed with respect to a number of different criteria pertaining to both their outcomes and the processes used in achieving those outcomes. One way of evaluating the outcome of a negotiation is in terms of whether the agreement that is reached by the parties is *pareto-optimal* (Raiffa, 1982). In pareto-optimal agreements, the parties have achieved the maximum joint gains that are possible. Thus, none of the parties can improve its position unless another does worse. Empirical studies have shown that the agreements negotiators reach are often pareto-*inferior* in so far as "gains to trade" are still available at the conclusion of a negotiation (Bazerman, Magliozzi, & Neale,1985; Thompson & Hastie, 1988). This issue of the pareto-optimality of an agreement, it should be emphasized, is not merely an academic matter, of interest only to game theorists or economists. On the contrary, pareto-inferior agreements may be enormously costly, both to the parties involved in a negotiation as well as the organization as a whole. Thus, it is important to understand the conditions under which agreements fall short of pareto-optimality.

In addition to evaluating negotiations in terms of their outcomes, it is also useful to consider the nature of the processes used by negotiators to reach those outcomes, and the efficiency of those processes. In fact, Raiffa (1982) rather colorfully characterized the negotiation process as a "dance," the efficiency of which could be judged in terms of whether or not the successive offers by the parties were *pareto-improving* (i.e., moved them closer to pareto-optimality). Accordingly, in the analysis that follows, I examine how complexity, size and differentiation affect the efficiency of a negotiation, the nature of the processes used during negotiation, and the optimality of outcomes obtained.

Effects of Informational Complexity

As the number of negotiators increases, the amount of information that each must process also increases. If the amount of information is too great, negotiators may experience *information overload*. Evidence of how information overload affects a negotiation was provided by Morley (1982), in an analysis of the multilateral negotiations at the Paris Peace Conference of 1919. According to Morley (1982), information overload adversely affected the ability of the parties to prepare adequately for their negotiations. Because of the larger number of parties and issues involved in these negotiations, they did not have sufficient time to study relevant documents or collect needed information.

In addition to interfering with their efforts to prepare for the negotiation, Morley reported that information overload impaired negotiators' ability to recognize when concessions had even been made. Individual concessions, he argued, became "embedded in a mass of detail" and were therefore lost (p. 395). Winham (1977), using a simulated multilateral negotiation, found a similar pattern of results, concluding that "more than half the time the participants failed to agree on the *nature* of concessions or failed to agree *when* concessions were made to them" (p. 359, emphases added).

Increases in the amount of information that must be processed can also affect *how* that information is processed. When processing demands are high, negotiators may have a tendency to rely on judgmental heuristics (Tversky & Kahneman, 1974) which facilitate rapid processing and evaluation of information. Although the use of such heuristics reduces the "cognitive" burden on decision makers, it can also diminish the quality of their decision-making process (Bazerman, Mannix, & Thompson, 1988). For example, information that happens to be more available in memory (Tversky & Kahneman, 1974) or more salient to negotiators (Neale, 1984) may be overweighted during decision making.

Informational complexity can also lead to higher levels of *uncertainty* regarding other parties' positions or interests (Midgaard & Underdal, 1977; Walton & McKersie, 1965; Winham, 1977). Because of the volume of information that has to be processed, there is less opportunity for negotiators to probe and validate alternative hypotheses regarding the interests or needs of the other parties. As Winham (1977) noted, complexity not only affects negotiators' capacity to learn what their opponents' strategies are, it also "increases the ambiguity of information available to them and makes that information subject to more varying interpretations" (p. 351).

When uncertainty and ambiguity are high, negotiators may be less able to discover clear guidelines for action. To resolve this uncertainty, they may try to find similarities between the negotiation in which they are currently involved in and past situations with which they are familiar. As a result, analogies with salient historical examples may exert a disproportionate influence on how they interpret or construe the present situation (Neustadt & May, 1986). When contemplating how to deal with the Soviet Union during the Berlin Crisis, for example, President Kennedy compared the dilemma he faced to the dilemma Chamberlain confronted when trying to decide whether to negotiate with Hitler. Kennedy was determined to avoid the mistake Chamberlian had made in being overly conciliatory toward and trusting of Hitler.

Such comparisons suggest the importance of individuals' knowledge base and memory when negotiating. As Bazerman and Carroll (1987) observed, negotiators use their preexisting knowledge bases to make "educated guesses . . . . instead of analyzing the elements [of a situation] *de novo* from first principles. Thus, we tend to appreciate the power of analogy, such as when Afghanistan is called a "Vietnam" for the Soviets. *It seems much easier to reason comparatively from representative cases based on our existing knowledge structures than to reason absolutely"* (p. 268, emphasis added). Although sometimes useful, invoking such analogies may distort interpretation of the current situation, causing decision makers to overemphasize points of similarity at the expense of less obvious dissimilarities. As a result, they may overestimate the likelihood that the present situation will unfold in the same way as the previous one, or overlook opportunities for alternative resolutions.

As noted earlier, the large number of parties and issues involved in a multiparty negotiation may make it extremely difficult for negotiators to develop an adequate cognitive representation of the situation (Axelrod, 1974). Memory capacity constraints and limits to negotiators' "cognitive complexity" (Tetlock, 1983) may limit their ability to develop sufficiently complex representations of the interdependent relationships among all of the various parties' positions and interests. If we make realistic allowances for the fact that negotiators' positions and interests will *change* over time, moreover, the enormity of the problem of maintaining "updated" cognitive representations over the course of a protracted negotiation becomes even more evident. As a result, negotiators may act on the basis of serious misperceptions or misunderstandings of the underlying interests or positions of the other parties (Morley, 1982; Midgaard & Underdal, 1977). This can interfere with their ability to locate integrative potential in the negotiation (Bazerman, Mannix, & Thompson, 1988).

Of course, the complexity of a multiparty negotiation increases not only the cognitive burden on negotiators; it also increases the physical and psychological stress placed on them. The effects of such stress on a negotiator's performance have been described in many first-hand accounts (e.g., Carter, 1985; Kennedy, 1969). In describing Henry Kissinger's involvement in the Middle East negotiations, Kressel (1981) has illustrated how "the necessity of constantly shuttling among Israel, Egypt, Syria, Saudi Arabia, and Jordan—each with its different *dramatis personae* and somewhat different issues" complicated Kissinger's task (p. 229).

Stress has been found to have a variety of effects on negotiations, including producing greater hostility among negotiators, leading them to adopt tougher bargaining strategies, and resulting in less optimal outcomes (Hopmann & Walcott, 1977). Stress can impair the quality of decision making during negotiation as well (Janis, 1989). Under high levels of stress, negotiators may avoid or deny unpleasant trade-offs and fall back on well-learned but inappropriate responses.

Effects of Procedural Complexity

As observed above, all of the procedures involved in a negotiation—exchanging information, integrating proposals, and others—become more complex as the number of parties increases. To reduce procedural complexity, negotiators may employ various *social heuristics* (Allison & Messick, 1987). Social heuristics consist of relatively simple, normatively acceptable decision rules, such as "divide equally," which negotiators can use to facilitate agreement. Although the results produced by using such heuristics may not always be optimal from the standpoint of maximizing the outcomes of either the individual parties or the organization as a whole, they provide simple, quick, and mutually acceptable solutions.

In a similar way, negotiators may use "focal point solutions" and tacit bargaining to avoid confrontation or prevent escalation of conflict in a negotiation (Schelling, 1960). For example, when negotiating the division of a large sales territory, the parties involved may decide to use certain obvious landmarks such as prominent buildings or geographic landmarks as focal points for the demarcation of their individual territories. The division of territory implied by such landmarks may be acceptable to the parties not because of any compelling economic criteria, but because they are relatively easy to identify and therefore provide a basis for agreement and avoiding further conflict.

The efficacy of such solutions is derived from the "intrinsic magnetism of particular outcomes, especially those that enjoy prominence, uniqueness, simplicity, precedent, or some rationale that makes them qualitatively differentiable from the continuum of possible outcomes" (Schelling, 1960, p. 70). Such "focal point" solutions may be especially likely to be used when the costs of extended bargaining are perceived to be high or when no other mutually acceptable criteria for settlement of a dispute are available, conditions which may be more likely to obtain as the number of parties involved in a negotiation increases.

Effects of Size

Up to this point, I have examined how various types of complexity affect negotiations. I turn now to consideration of how the number of parties involved in a negotiation influence negotiation processes.[4] In discussing this issue, it is useful to introduce a distinction between cooperative and noncooperative negotiation processes.

A variety of generic terms have been used to describe the behavior of negotiators. Many researchers (e.g., Lewicki & Litterer, 1985; Walton & McKersie, 1965) have found useful the distinction between *integrative* versus *distributive* behaviors. Pruitt (1983) distinguished between *contentious behaviors* that further the interests of one party at the expense of others, and *integrative* or *problem-solving behaviors* that further their joint interests. Lax and Sebenius (1986) categorized negotiation behavior in terms of *value creating* versus *value claiming* behaviors. Finally, Deutsch (1973, 1985) emphasized the distinction between *cooperative* and *competitive* bargaining behaviors.

For the purposes of the present analysis, Deutsch's general characterization of a cooperative process is particularly useful. Cooperative behavior, according to Deutsch (1985), "leads to the defining of conflicting interests as a mutual problem to be solved by collaborative effort. It facilitates the recognition of the legitimacy of each other's interests and of the necessity of searching for a solution that is responsive to the needs of all" (p. 255-256).

In the last few years, there has been a great deal of research on the conditions under which cooperation in multi-person situations is likely to emerge (see, e.g., Kerr, 1983; Kramer & Brewer, 1986; Messick & Brewer, 1983). I argue below that this research has implications for understanding why a negotiation process might become *less* cooperative as the number of parties increases. In the discussion presented below, attention is focused on two such factors: (1) individuals' perceptions of the efficacy of their actions; and (2) their expectations regarding whether others will reciprocate their efforts to cooperate. The main thrust of the argument is that, as the number of parties involved in a negotiation increases, perceived efficacy and expectations of reciprocity tend to decrease. Consequently, individuals may be more likely to engage in what has been called "aversive competition" (Kuhlman, Camac, & Cunha, 1986) or "defensive noncooperation" (Kramer, forthcoming), a form of defensively motivated noncooperative behavior that is aimed at protecting one's self against exploitation.

The general hypothesis that the level of cooperation among a "group" of interdependent decision makers will decrease as the size of the group increases was first proposed by Olson (1965). Since then, it has received empirical support from a number of studies (See Brewer & Kramer, 1986 for an overview). Among the reasons that have been advanced to explain the deleterious effects of group size on cooperation are decreases in the incentives associated with cooperating in larger groups (Olson, 1965), motivational losses (Kerr, 1983; Kerr & Brunn, 1983), deindividuation (Hamburger, Guyer, & Fox, 1975), social loafing or diffusion of responsibility (Messick & McClelland, 1983) and lower perceived efficacy and/or control over outcomes (Kerr, 1989).

As implied by much of the earlier discussion of the effects of size and complexity on information processing, achieving cooperative outcomes can require a great deal of effort on the part of negotiators: In order to reach agreement, they must exchange information regarding their interests, explore alternative agreements that further their joint interests, and decide what behaviors to use in trying to induce the other parties to cooperate. Thus, the "transaction costs" associated with cooperative bargaining can be high in multiparty negotiations.

Negotiators' willingness to incur such costs may depend on their perceptions of the efficacy of their actions and/or control over the process and outcome of the negotiation. In order to *initiate* a cooperative process, for example, they may have to believe that their efforts to induce others to cooperate are likely to be successful (Lindskold, 1978; Pruitt & Kimmel, 1967).

Previous research has shown that individuals are less likely to initiate a course of action when they perceive low control over their situation (Langer, 1975; Seligman, 1975) or have a low sense of self-efficacy (Bandura, 1986). In a recent paper, Kerr (1989) argued that individuals' perceived self-efficacy with respect to solving a social dilemma decreases as the number of individuals involved in the dilemma increases. As a result, the level of cooperation declines, because each individual reasons that his or her actions make little difference on the final outcome of the dilemma. Kerr proposed further that cooperation depends not only on individuals' perceptions of personal efficacy (i.e., whether or not they think their own actions make a difference) but also their perceptions of *collective* efficacy (i.e., whether they believe the group as a whole can solve its problem through cooperation).

One of the important conclusions that emerged from this study is that, under some conditions, individuals will presume that both personal and collective efficacy decrease with group size even in situations where in fact they do not. Kerr characterized this as an "illusion of efficacy" and suggested that it may reflect a general bias "leading people to see large-group dilemmas, in which self-efficacy is already objectively low, as even worse than they actually are" (p. 309). Because personal and collective efficacy often are objectively lower in larger groups, according to Kerr, individuals overgeneralize the impact of group size to situations where the relationship doesn't hold.

The results of research on the effects of group size on cooperation suggests that as the number of parties involved in a multiparty negotiation increases, individual negotiators may perceive *relatively* less control over the negotiation process or its outcome compared to negotiators in dyadic situations. Lower perceived control may lead them to underestimate the prospects for cooperation to develop among them.

Effects of Social Differentiation

Research has found that the level of social differentiation among decision makers influences how cooperative they are when interacting with each other (Kramer & Brewer, 1986). Specifically, as the level of social differentiation in a group increases, the level of cooperation tends to decrease (Komorita & Lapworth, 1982; Kramer & Brewer, 1984). There are several psychological processes that may explain this relationship between social differentiation and cooperation.

Social Categorization Effects

A substantial number of studies have shown that placing objects into distinctive categories can affect how observers perceive and evaluate members of those categories. For example, research by Tajfel and his associates (Tajfel, 1969; Tajfel & Wilkes, 1963) demonstrated that individuals tend to overestimate similarity among members of a common category, while overestimating differences between members from different categories. These categorization effects have been observed with respect to both nonsocial and social objects. For example, even assigning individuals to temporary and completely arbitrary groups has been found to be sufficient to induce perceptions of "ingroup" versus "outgroup" membership (Brewer, 1979).

This research also suggests that "ingroup" members tend to perceive and evaluate other ingroup members in relatively positive terms compared to outgroup members. In particular, outgroup members are perceived as less friendly, less cooperative, and less trustworthy compared to other ingroup members (Brewer & Silver, 1978). Ingroup members expect outgroup members to be more competitive compared to ingroup members (Kramer, 1989b). Finally, ingroup members tend to perceive outgroup members as more responsive to relatively coercive rather than conciliatory influence tactics compared to ingroup members (Rothbart & Hallmark, 1988).

The effects of social categorization on social judgment and behavior have two important implications. First, with respect to negotiations involving cross-category (intergroup) interactions, social categorization may lead negotiators to overestimate the differences between their interests and positions and those of the other group. Consequently, they may underestimate the potential for agreement or fail to detect areas of mutual interest. Negotiations involving within-category (intragroup) interactions, in contrast, may result in negotiators overestimating similarity between their own positions and those of other members of their group. This may lead them to misperceive others' true interests and thereby interfere with integrative bargaining.

Expectations of Reciprocity

In discussing the conditions that facilitate integrative bargaining, Lewicki and Litterer (1985) noted that negotiators must create a free flow of information and be willing to reveal their true objectives The process of *unilaterally* revealing information, however, is risky because such actions can be exploited by other parties or interpreted as a sign of weakness or gullibility. Thus, before negotiators may be willing to engage in such behavior, they may need to have some expectation that their actions will be reciprocated, or, at the very least, reassurance that they will not be exploited. Recent experiments have found evidence of just such a relationship between individuals' expectations of reciprocity and their willingness to cooperate with others (Messick, Wilke, Brewer, Kramer, Zemke-English, & Lui, 1983; Pruitt & Kimmel, 1967).

In reviewing the literature on ingroup bias and ethnocentrism in social perception, Brewer (1981) proposed that expectations of reciprocity may be correlated with social categories. She suggested that "within a social category the probability of reciprocity is presumed, a priori, to be high while *between categories it is presumed to be low or subject to individual negotiation*" (p. 356, emphases added).

Low expectations of reciprocity can affect negotiation behavior in at least two ways. First, when expectations of reciprocity are low, individuals may be less likely to communicate openly or initiate other forms of integrative bargaining. For example, one technique that helps parties achieve integrative outcomes is logrolling. In logrolling, the parties agree to "trade off" on two issues, each of which is more important to one party than the other (Lewicki & Litterer, 1985). If their expectations of reciprocity are low, negotiators may perceive little incentive to proposing such trade-offs or trusting the other person to live up to his or her side of a bargain. Low expectations of reciprocity can also cause negotiators to adopt relatively short-term perspectives on their relationships with others. Specifically, they may be less willing to engage in cooperative strategies such as GRIT (Lindskold, 1978), which are intended to build trust and cooperation, but which are predicated on longer-term interactions.

Social Competition

In organizational settings, comparative outcomes are often of greater significance than absolute outcomes. For example, the *proportion* of the annual budget that an individual or group manages to win control over as a result of a negotiation may be much more important than the absolute amount of resources they end up with. For this reason, social comparisons may be especially important to organizational actors when they are evaluating how well they have done in a negotiation or the fairness of its outcome.

There is evidence that individuals engage in social comparison not only to obtain information that is useful for evaluating their performance, but also to enhance their feelings of positive self-esteem or superiority relative to others in similar situations (Wood, 1989). In the case of highly differentiated groups, such "motivated" social comparisons may involve not only interpersonal but also *intergroup* comparisons (Turner, 1975). Negotiators with different organizational or group identities may engage in what Tajfel and Turner (1986) have called "social competition" in order to promote positive distinctiveness between their own group and these other groups. As Taylor and Moghaddam (1987) have argued, "individuals wish to belong to groups that compare favorably with, and are distinct from, other groups and that lead to positive evaluations for themselves" (p. 78). Thus, when negotiating, they may be more concerned with maximizing their *relative* gain over others rather than trying to discover ways to further their joint gains. This may lead them to adopt competitive rather than cooperative orientations toward other groups.

Intergroup Anxiety

The term "intergroup anxiety" (Stephan & Stephan, 1985) refers to the tension or discomfort that many individuals experience when interacting with members of different groups. Intergroup anxiety has been attributed to individuals' anticipation of negative consequences associated with intergroup contact. For example, individuals may fear not being in control or feeling awkward when dealing with members of other groups. Second, they may fear being taken advantage of or being evaluated negatively by the other group. Finally, they may fear negative evaluations by members of their own group (e.g., they may fear rejection or scorn if they appear too conciliatory or weak in their dealings with other groups).

The more heterogeneous or dissimilar the individuals involved in a multiparty negotiation, the greater the degree of intergroup anxiety they may experience. Intergroup anxiety can have two affects on negotiations. First, it may lead individuals to approach their interactions with others with negative expectations. These negative expectations can produce self-confirming interactions (Cooper & Fazio, 1986). Intergroup anxiety can also lead the parties to avoid contact or communication with each other. To the extent that this happens, they may be less likely to develop accurate perceptions of their interests and less likely to discover integrative solutions.

IMPLICATIONS AND RECOMMENDATIONS FOR FUTURE RESEARCH

This paper has accomplished several goals. First, it has identified some of the common types of multiparty negotiations found in organizations, and articulated major dimensions along which such negotiations vary. Second, it has described a number of differences between dyadic and multiparty negotiations. These differences suggest that considerable caution must be used when trying to generalize the results of research on dyadic negotiation to multiparty situations. Theories and models of multiparty negotiations, if they are to do justice to the phenomena, may have to differ in certain fundamental ways from those used to describe dyadic bargaining problems.

What might such differences look like? In a recent assessment, Carroll and Payne (this volume) observed that negotiation research has generally taken one of four approaches:

1. a normative approach, based on rational models of bargaining;
2. a structural approach, focusing on the "macro" determinants of bargaining behavior;
3. a psychological approach focused largely on individual differences; and
4. a cognitive or information processing approach.

Each of these approaches has made important contributions to our understanding of negotiation processes.

However, each of these four perspectives has tended to minimize or ignore the impact of social processes on negotiations. The analysis presented in this paper suggests that social processes are both more complex and assume greater causal significance in multiparty negotiations compared to dyadic negotiations. Consequently, the development of adequate models and theories about such negotiations would seem to require a fifth perspective that is explicitly more social psychological in emphasis. A social psychological perspective would draw attention to the fact that organizational negotiations do not occur in a vacuum, but are embedded in a complex network of intra-and intergroup relations.

This paper has provided only an outline, rather than a detailed picture, of what such a perspective might look like. In recognition of this fact, and given that so little empirical work has been done on multiparty negotiations, it may be appropriate to conclude by offering some recommendations for future research. There are at least three streams of research which may prove particularly promising in further developing a social psychological perspective on multiparty negotiations. First, there is a great deal of research currently being done on the role of cognitive and social perception processes in dyadic negotiations (see, e.g., Bazerman & Neale, 1983; Carroll, Bazerman, & Maury, 1988; Carroll & Payne, this volume; Thompson & Hastie, 1988). Extension of this research to the multiparty level of analysis could be very useful. Such an extension would examine how negotiators' perceptions and cognitions change as a function of increasing size, complexity, and differentiation.

A second stream of research which may prove useful in this regard is the social psychological literature on intergroup processes (see Brewer & Kramer, 1985 and Messick & Mackie, 1989 for recent reviews). As this paper has tried to suggest, there are conceptual insights and empirical results in this literature that have direct relevance to understanding multiparty negotiations in organizations. However, much of this research has had little impact on negotiation theorists. As Messick and Mackie (1989) have cogently observed, "It strikes us as curious that the immense literature on conflict management, a literature large enough to support two scholarly journals—*The Journal of Conflict Resolution* and *The Negotiation Journal*—remains by and large apart from the literature on intergroup relations and *vice versa*. An inspection of the reference lists of [recently published texts] . . . . reveals very little common content" (p. 69). An integration of these two heretofore independent streams of research might prove valuable.

There is also a need for more research on the *dynamics* of multiparty negotiations. We know very little about the temporal characteristics and interactive processes associated with multiparty negotiation. The handful of empirical studies which are available in the social psychological literature have generally used only outcome measures as dependent variables; process measures, for the most part, have been ignored (Morley & Stephenson, 1977 is an exception to this generalization). To address this gap in the literature, recent theory and research on the dynamics of conflict may be quite useful. Pruitt and Rubin (1986), for example, have presented a rich theory regarding conflict escalation, stalemate, and deescalation. Their analysis of "transformations" and "structural changes" associated with the escalation of conflict could be used to develop theory regarding why cooperation levels might decline over time in multiparty situations.

The complexity of multiparty negotiation processes raises a methodological question as to how such processes might best be studied. Many of the questions raised in this paper would seem to be amenable to investigation using conventional social psychological methods, such as laboratory experiments. However, a caveat is in order here: although laboratory experiments may be useful, it is important to consider their limitations as well. Many of the elements of organizational settings that contribute to the complexity of multiparty negotiations are perforce excluded from or, at the very least, extremely difficult to capture in a laboratory experiment. For example, the long-term interdependencies and social relationships among organizational actors are missing from such experiments. In fact, as Greenhalgh (1987b) has argued, such relationships have usually been systematically eliminated from these experiments. As a result, the impact of the social and organizational contexts within which negotiations occur has been minimized or ignored. Therefore, use of other methodologies, including field experiments and grounded theory may be essential for the development of theory regarding multiparty negotiations.

ACKNOWLEDGMENTS

The author is very grateful to Max Bazerman, Blair Sheppard, Roy Lewicki, Robin Pinkley, and Elizabeth Mannix for their many helpful comments. Shellee Wiedemeier deserves special thanks for her nimble fingerwork and editorial contribution to this paper. I thank Stephanie Woerner for doing a wonderful job helping me locate relevant literature. I am also grateful to Jon Bendor and Dave Baron for their suggestions.

NOTES

1.   Because of space constraints, I have not attempted to review the nonsocial psychological literature on multiparty negotiation in organizations. In preparing this paper, I found that this literature is rather widely dispersed across a number of social science disciplines, with little cross-disciplinary citation. This makes location of such material difficult. Therefore, it may be helpful to provide a short "bibliographic" overview of some of this other literature. Discussions of multiparty negotiations at the international level can be found in Winham (1987) and Zartman (1974). Many economists, political scientists, and game theorists have approached the problem of multiparty negotiation from the perspective of cooperative and noncooperative game theory (see, e.g., Baron and Ferejohn, 1987; Colman, 1982; Ordeshook, 1986; Sutton, 1986). There is a literature on the sociology of multiparty negotiations (see Strauss, 1978 for an overview). There are literatures on topics closely related to multiparty negotiation, such as strategic voting (Raiffa, 1982), social dilemmas (Messick & Brewer, 1983), problems of collective action (Olson, 1965), competitive markets (e.g., Bazerman, Magliozzi, & Neale, 1985; Rapoport & Kahan, 1984) and

oligopolistic competition (Wilson, 1989). These literatures provide conceptual insights into how parties in multiperson contexts behave when trying to resolve conflict.

2. There are, of course, many other dimensions along which such negotiations vary, including the structure of the task (e.g., whether it is a simultaneous versus sequential negotiation), the nature of the outcome interdependence (e.g., whether it is zero-sum versus mixed-motive), the physical setting (e.g., whether the negotiators are face to face or communicate via the exchange of written proposals). Because these features of a negotiation are not unique to multiparty negotiations, I do not consider them in detail here.

3. The literature on the effects of constituents on the negotiation process is not reviewed here because many excellent discussions are available (See, e.g., Carnevale, Pruitt, & Britton, 1979; Greenhalgh, 1987a; Lewicki & Litterer, 1985).

4. Much of this analysis depends on the results of research on multiparty phenomena other than negotiations (e.g., social dilemmas). Although I regard the propositions offered below to be reasonable extrapolations from this research, they should be regarded as speculative in so far as they have not been subjected to empirical evaluation within a negotiation context per se.

REFERENCES

Allison, G. T. (1971). *Essence of decision: Explaining the Cuban missile crisis*. New York: Little-Brown.

Allison, S., & Messick, D. M. (1987). *Social decision heuristics in the use of shared resources*. Unpublished manuscript.

Axelrod, R. (1974). Decision for neoimperialism: The deliberations of the British Eastern Committee in 1918. In R. Axelrod (Ed.), *Structure of decision*. Princeton, NJ: Princeton University Press.

_____ (1984). *The evolution of cooperation*. New York: Basic Books.

Baldridge, J. V. (1971). *Power and conflict in the university*. New York: John Wiley.

Baldwin, R. E., & Clarke, R. N. (1987). Game-modeling multilateral trade negotiations. *Journal of Policy Modeling, 9*, 257-284.

Bandura, A. (1986). Self-efficacy mechanisms in human agency. *American Psychologist, 37*, 122-147.

Baron, D. P., & Ferejohn, J. A. (1987). *Bargaining in legislatures* (Research Paper No. 936). Graduate School of Business, Stanford University.

Bazerman, M. H. (1986). *Judgment in managerial decision making*. New York: John Wiley.

Bazerman, M. H., & Carroll, J. S. (1987). Negotiator cognition. *Research in Organizational Behavior* (Vol. 9, pp. 247-288). Greenwich, CT: JAI Press Inc.

Bazerman, M. H., Giuliano, T., & Appelman, A. (1984). Escalation in individual and group decision making. *Organizational behavior and human performance, 33*, 141-152.

Bazerman, M. H., & Lewicki, R. J. (1983). *Negotiating in organizations*. Beverly Hills, CA: Sage.

Bazerman, M. H., Magliozzi, T., and Neale, M. A. (1985). Integrative bargaining in a competitive market. *Organizational behavior and human performance, 34*, 294-313.

Bazerman, M. H., Mannix, E. A., & Thompson, L. L. (1988). Groups as mixed-motive negotiations. In E. J. Lawler & B. Markovsky (Eds.), *Advances in groups processes: Theory and research* (Vol. 5). Greenwich, CT: JAI Press.

Bazerman, M. H., & Neale, M. A. (1983). Heuristics in negotiation: Limitations to dispute resolution effectiveness. In M. H. Bazerman & R. J. Lewicki (Eds.), *Negotiating in organizations*. Beverly Hills, CA: Sage.

Bazerman, M. H., & Samuelson, W. F. (1983). I won the auction but don't want the prize. *Journal of Conflict Resolution, 27*, 618-634.

Berkovitch, J. (1984). Problems and approaches in the study of bargaining and negotiation. *Political Science, 36,* 125-143.

Boulding, K. E. (1972). The organization as a party to conflict. In J. M. Thomas & W. G. Bennis (Eds.), *Management of change and conflict.* New York: Penguin.

Brewer, M. B. (1979). In-group bias in the minimal intergroup situation: A cognitive-motivational analysis. *Psychological Bulletin, 86,* 307-324.

_____. (1981). Ethnocentrism and its role in interpersonal trust. In M. B. Brewer & B. E. Collins (Eds.), *Scientific inquiry and the social sciences.* New York: Jossey-Bass.

Brewer, M. B., & Kramer, R. M. (1985). The Psychology of Intergroup attitudes and behavior. *Annual Review of Psychology, 36,* 219-243.

_____. (1986). Choice behavior in social dilemmas: Effects of social identity, group size, and decision framing. *Journal of Personality and Social Psychology, 50,* 543-549.

Brewer, M. B., & Silver, M. (1978). Ingroup bias as a function of task characteristics. *European Journal of Social Psychology, 8,* 393-400.

Caplow, T. (1968). *Two against one: Coalitions in triads.* Englewood Cliffs, NJ: Prentice-Hall.

Carnevale, P. J., Pruitt, D. G., & Britton, S. D. (1979). Looking tough: The negotiator under constituent surveillance. *Personality and Social Psychology Bulletin* 118-121.

Carroll, J. S., Bazerman, M. H., & Maury, R. (1988). Negotiator cognitions: A descriptive approach to negotiators' understanding of their opponents. *Organizational Behavior and Human Decision Processes, 41,* 352-270.

Carroll, J. S., & Payne, J. (1989, April). *An information-processing approach to two-party negotiations.* Paper presented at fourth annual Conference on Research on Negotiations in Organizations, Northwestern University.

Carter, J. (1985). *The blood of Abraham.* Boston: Houghton Mifflin.

Colman, A. M., (1982). *Game theory and experimental games: The study of strategic interaction.* Oxford: Pergamon Press.

Cooper, J., & Fazio, R. H. (1986). The formation and persistence of attitudes that support intergroup conflict. In S. Worchel & W. G. Austin (Eds.), *Psychology of intergroup relations.* Chicago: Nelson-Hall.

Deutsch, M. (1973). *The resolution of conflict: Constructive and destructive processes* New Haven, CT: Yale University Press.

_____. (1985). *Distributive justice: A social psychological perspective.* New Haven, CT: Yale University Press.

Greenhalgh, L. (1987a). Interpersonal conflicts in organizations. In C. L. Cooper & I. T. Robertson (Eds.), *International Review of Industrial and Organizational Psychology.* New York: Wiley.

_____. (1987b). Relationships in negotiations. *Negotiation Journal,* 235-243.

Hamburger, H., Guyer, M., & Fox, J. (1975). Group size and cooperation. *Journal of Conflict Resolution, 19,* 503-531.

Hogg, M. A., & Abrams, D. (1988). *Social identifications: A social psychology of intergroup relations and group processes.* London: Routledge.

Hopmann, P. T., & Walcott, C. (1977). The impact of external stresses and tensions on negotiations. In Druckman, D. (Ed.), *Negotiations: Social-psychological perspective.* Beverly Hills, CA: Sage.

Janis, I. L. (1983). *Groupthink* (2nd ed.). Boston: Houghton Mifflin.

_____. (1989). *Crucial decisions: Leadership in policymaking and crisis management.* New York: Free Press.

Kahn, R. L., & Wolfe, D. (1964). Role conflict in organizations. In R. L. Kahn & E. Boulding (Eds.), *Power and conflict in organizations.* New York: Basic.

Kanter, A. (1975). *Defense politics: A budgetary perspective.* Chicago: The University of Chicago Press.

Katz, D., & Kahn, R. L. (1978). *The social psychology of organizations.* (2nd ed.). New York: Wiley.

Kelly, H. H. (1979). *Personal relationships.* Hillsdale, NJ: Erlbaum.

Kennedy, R. F. (1969). *Thirteen days: A memoir of the Cuban missile crisis.* New York: Mentor Books.

Kerr, N. L. (1983). Motivational losses in small groups: A social dilemma analysis. *Journal of Personality and Social Psychology, 45,* 819-828.

_____ (1989). Illusions of efficacy: The effects of group size on perceived efficacy in social dilemmas. *Journal of Experimental Social Psychology, 25,* 287-313.

Kerr, N. L., & Bruun, S. (1983). The dispensability of member effort and group motivation losses: Free rider effects. *Journal of Personality and Social Psychology, 44,* 78-94.

Kochan, T. A., & Katz, H. C. (1988). *Collective bargaining and industrial relations.* Homewood, IL: Irwin.

Kochan, T. A., & Verma, A. (1983). Negotiations in organizations: Blending industrial relations and organizational behavior approaches. In M. H. Bazerman & R. J. Lewicki, *Negotiating in organizations.* Beverly Hills, CA: Sage.

Komorita, S. S., & Lapworth, C. (1982). Cooperative choice among individuals versus groups in an n-person dilemma situation. *Journal of Personality and Social Psychology, 42,* 487-496.

Kramer, R. M. (1989a). *Getting while the getting is good: Defensive noncooperation in a nasty social dilemma.* Unpublished manuscript.

_____ (forthcoming). When the going gets tough: The effects of resource scarcity on group cooperation and conflict. In E. Lawler & B. Markovsky (Eds.), *Advances in group processes.* Greenwich, CT: JAI Press.

_____ (1989b). Windows of vulnerability or cognitive illusions? Cognitive processes and the nuclear arms race. *Journal of Experimental Social Psychology, 25,* 79-100.

Kramer, R. M., & Brewer, M. B. (1984). Effects of group identity on resource use in a simulated commons dilemma. *Journal of Personality and Social Psychology, 46,* 1044-1057.

_____ (1986). Social group identity and the emergence of cooperation in resource conservation dilemmas. In H. Wilke, C. Rutte, & D. M. Messick (Eds.), *Experimental studies of social dilemmas.* Frankfurt, Germany: Peter Lang.

Kressel, K. (1981). Kissinger in the Middle East: An exploratory analysis of role strain in international mediation. In J. Z. Rubin (Ed.), *Dynamics of third party intervention: Kissinger in the Middle East.* New York: Praeger.

Kuhlman, D. M., Camac, C., & Cunha, D. (1986). Individual differences in social orientation. In H. Wilke, C. Rutte, & D. M. Messick (Eds.), *Experimental studies of social dilemmas.* Frankfurt, Germany: Peter Lang.

Langer, E. J. (1975). The illusion of control. *Journal of Personality and Social Psychology, 32,* 311-328.

Lax, D. A., & Sebenius, J. K. (1986). *The manager as negotiator: Bargaining for cooperation and competitive gain.* New York: Free Press.

Lewicki, R. J., & Litterer, J. A. (1985). *Negotiation.* Homewood, IL: Irwin.

Lewicki, R. J., Sheppard, B. H., & Bazerman, M. H. (1986). *Research on negotiations in organizations.* Greenwich, CT: JAI Press.

Lindskold, S. (1978). Trust development, the GRIT proposal, and the effects of conciliatory acts on conflict and cooperation. *Psychological Bulletin, 85,* 772-793.

Messick, D. M., & Brewer, M. B. (1983). Solving social dilemmas: A review. In L. Wheeler (Ed.), *Review of Personality and Social Psychology.* Beverly Hills, CA: Sage.

Messick, D. M., & Mackie, D. (1989). Intergroup relations. *Annual Review of Psychology, 40,* 45-81.

Messick, D. M., & McClelland, C. (1983). Social traps and temporal traps. *Personality and Social Psychology Bulletin, 9,* 105-110.

Messick, D. M., Wilke, H., Brewer, M. B., Kramer, R. M., Zemke-english, P., & Lui, L. (1983). Individual adaptations and structural change as solutions to social dilemmas. *Journal of Personality and Social Psychology, 44*, 294-309.

Midgaard, K., & Underdal, A. (1977). Multiparty conferences. In Druckman, D. (Ed.), *Negotiations: Social psychological perspectives*. Beverly Hills: Sage.

Miles, R. H. (1980). *Macro organizational behavior*. Santa Monica, CA: Goodyear.

Morley, I. E., (1982). Preparation for negotiation: Conflict, commitment, and choice. In H. Brandstatter, J. H. Davis, & G. Stocker-Kreichgauer (Eds.), *Group decision making*. New York: Academic Press.

Morley, I. E., & Stephenson, G., (1977). *The social psychology of bargaining*. London: Allen & Unwin.

Murnighan, J. K. (1978). Models of coalition behavior: Game theoretic, social psychological, and political perspectives. *Psychological Bulletin, 85*, 1130-1153.

_____ (1986). Organizational coalitions: Structural contingencies and the formation process. In R. J. Lewicki, B. H. Sheppard, & M. H. Bazerman (Eds.), *Research on negotiation in organizations* (Vol. 1). Greenwich, CT: JAI Press.

Neale, M. A. (1984). The effect of negotiation and arbitration cost salience on bargainer behavior: The role of arbitrator and constituency in negotiator judgment. *Organizational behavior and human performance, 34*, 97-111.

Neustadt, R. E., & May, E. R. (1986) *Thinking in time: The uses of history for decision makers*. New York: The Free Press.

Olson, M. (1965). *The logic of collective action*. Cambridge, MA: Harvard University Press.

Ordeshook, P. C., (1986). *Game theory and political theory*. Cambridge: Cambridge University Press.

Pfeffer, J., & Salancik, G. R. (1977). Organization design: The case for a coalitional model of organizations. *Organizational Dynamics*, 15-29.

Pruitt, D. G. (1983). Achieving integrative agreements. In M. H. Bazerman & R. J. Lewicki (Eds.), *Negotiating in organizations*. Beverly Hills, CA: Sage.

Pruitt, D. G., & Kimmel, M. J. (1967). Twenty years of experimental gaming: Critique, synthesis, and suggestions for the future. *Annual Review of Psychology, 28*, 363-392.

Pruitt, D. G., & Rubin, J. Z. (1986). *Social conflict: Escalation, stalemate, and settlement*. New York: Random House.

Rapoport, A., & Kahan, J. P., (1984). Coalition formation in a five-person market game. *Management Science, 30*, 326-333.

Raiffa, H. (1982). *The art and science of negotiation*. Cambridge, MA: Harvard University Press.

Rothbart, M., & Hallmark, W. (1988). Ingroup-outgroup differences in the perceived efficacy of coercion and conciliation in resolving social conflict. *Journal of Personality and Social Psychology, 55*, 248-257.

Rubin, J. Z. (1986). *Dynamics of third party intervention: Kissinger in the Middle East*. New York: Praeger.

Rubin, J. Z., & Brown, B. R., (1975). *The social psychology of bargaining and negotiation*. New York: Academic Press.

Schelling, T. C. (1960). *The strategy of conflict*. Cambridge, MA: Oxford University Press.

Sebenius, J. K. (1983). Negotiation arithmetic: Adding and subtracting issues and parties. *International Organization, 37*, 1-34.

Seligman, M. E. P. (1975). *Helplessness: On depression, development, and death*. San Francisco: Freeman.

Sheppard, B. H. (1984). Third party conflict intervention: A procedural framework. In B. M. Staw & L. L. Cummings (Eds.), *Research in Organization behavior* (Vol. 6). Greenwich, CT: JAI Press.

Shubik, M. (1971). The dollar auction game: A paradox in noncooperation behavior and escalation. *Journal of Conflict Resolution, 15*, 109-111.

Smith, H. (1988). *The power game*. New York: Random House.

Stephan, W. G., & Stephan, C. W. (1985). Intergroup anxiety. *Journal of Social Issues, 41*, 157-175.

Strauss, A. (1978). *Negotiations: Varieties, contexts, processes and social order*. San Francisco: Jossey-Bass.

Sutton, J. (1986). Non-cooperative bargaining theory: An introduction. *Review of Economics Studies. 53*, 709-724.

Tajfel, H. (1969). Cognitive aspects of prejudice. *Journal of Social Issues, 25*, 79-97.

Tajfel, H., & Turner, J. C. (1986). The social identity theory of intergroup behavior. In S. Worchel & W. G. Austin (Eds.), *Psychology of intergroup relations*. Chicago: Nelson-Hall.

Tajfel, H., & Wilkes, A. (1963). Classification and qualitative judgment. *British Journal of Social Psychology, 54*, 101-114.

Taylor, D. M., & Moghaddam, F. M. (1987). *Theories of intergroup relations*. New York: Praeger.

Tetlock, P. E. (1983). Policy makers' images of international conflict. *Journal of Social Issues, 39*, 67-86.

Thompson, L., & Hastie, R. (1988). Judgment tasks and biases in negotiation. In B. H. Sheppard, M. H. Bazerman and R. J. Lewicki (Eds.), *Research in negotiation in organizations* (Vol. 2). Greenwich, CT: JAI Press.

Turner, J. C. (1975). Social comparison and social identity. Some comparisons for intergroup behavior. *European Journal of Social Psychology, 5*, 5-34.

Tversky, A., & Kahneman, D. (1974). Judgment under uncertainty: Heuristics and biases. *Science, 185*, 1124-1131.

Walton, R., & McKersie, R. (1965). *A behavioral theory of negotiation*. New York: McGraw-Hill.

Wilson, R. (1989). Deterrence in oligopolistic competition. In P. C. Stern, R. Axelrod, R. Jervis, & R. Radner (Eds.), *Perspectives on deterrence*. Oxford: Oxford University Press.

Winham, G. R. (1977). Complexity in international negotiation. In Druckman, D. (Ed.), *Negotiations: Social psychological perspectives*. Beverly Hills, CA: Sage.

——————— (1987). Multilateral economic negotiation. *Negotiation Journal*, 175-189.

Wood, J. V. (in press). Contemporary theory concerning social comparisons of personal attributes. *Psychological Bulletin*.

Zartman, I. W. (1974). The political analysis of negotiations. *World Politics, 26*, 385-399.

[19]

Jumping the Gun:
Imperfections and Institutions Related to the Timing
of Market Transactions

By Alvin E. Roth and Xiaolin Xing*

This paper concerns the difficulties associated with establishing a time at which a market will operate. We first describe the experience of several dozen markets and submarkets, from entry-level professional labor markets in the United States, Canada, England, and Japan, to the (American) market for postseason college football bowls. The difficulties these markets have experienced in coordinating the timing of transactions have been decisive in determining how they are organized today. The paper develops a framework in which to address the timing of transactions and the tendency observed in many of these markets for transactions to become earlier and earlier. (JEL D40, C78, J44, N30)

The timing of transactions is a little-studied feature of markets, but one which plays a large role in their ability to function. Because transactions involve at least two parties, their timing involves coordination, and much of the benefit of a market has to do with bringing together many buyers and sellers at the same time, so that they can consider a wide range of possible transactions. In many of the markets discussed in this paper, from markets for new lawyers and doctors to the market for postseason college football bowls, efforts to coordinate and control the timing of transactions have played a decisive role in shaping how each market is organized. In many cases, problems concerned with the timing of transactions led to potentially large losses of efficiency.[1]

Table 1 lists a selection of markets that have experienced, and in some cases continue to experience, serious problems associated with the timing of transactions. (These markets will each be discussed in more detail in the body of the paper, where Table 1's notations about "stages" will be explained.) In virtually all of these markets, the problems originate with the incentives that some market participants have to try to "jump the gun," and arrange transactions just a little earlier than their competitors. In most of these markets, substantial resources

*Roth: Department of Economics, University of Pittsburgh, Pittsburgh, PA 15217; Xing: Department of Economics, University of Pittsburgh, and Department of Economics and Statistics, National University of Singapore. In the course of investigating so many markets, we have incurred many intellectual debts, both to participants in those markets, who have taken the time to guide our investigation and to colleagues who have offered advice. For their help, we thank Max Bazerman, Dean Billick, Jim Boster, Ed Bozik, William Brubaker, Michael Carifio, Sue Campbell, August Colenbrander, Dave DeJong, Steve Gaulin, Steven Hatchell, Stanley Hollander, Eric Johnson, Ulrich Kamecke, John Kelly, Kazutoshi Koshiro, Alex Kozinski, Allan Lichter, Howard Marvel, Barry McGee, Ivan Mensh, Tim Messer, Louis Oberdorfer, Jack Ochs, Masahiro Okuno-Fujiwara, Donald Parsons, Elliott Peranson, Mark Perlman, Bob Perloff, Richard Randlett, Reuben Slesinger, Jamienne Studley, August Swanson, John Swofford, Larry Summers, Hiromi Tojima, Spyros Vassilakis, Gerald Zaltman, Bill Zame, and Carl Zimet. This work has also been partially supported by grants from the National Science Foundation and the Alfred P. Sloan Foundation. We also thank the four anonymous referees who made the effort to consider a paper of such unusual length and content.

[1] In contrast to transactions, which involve *coordination* of timing, relatively more attention has been paid to the timing of investments, as in patent races (see e.g., the survey by Jennifer Reinganum [1989]), in which there are long-lasting benefits to being first. The establishment of retail outlets and new product introductions may sometimes fall into this category as well.

TABLE 1—A SELECTION OF MARKETS WITH TIMING PROBLEMS

Market	Organization	Stage
Postseason college football bowls	National Collegiate Athletic Association (NCAA)	1 and 3
Entry-level legal labor markets:		
Federal court clerkships	Judicial conferences	2, 1
American law firms	National Association for Law Placement (NALP)	1
Canadian articling positions	Articling Student Matching Program	
Toronto		4
Vancouver		3 or 4
Alberta (Calgary and Edmonton)		3
Entry-level business school markets		
New MBA's		1 (occasionally)
New marketing professors		1
Other entry-level labor markets:		
Japanese university graduates	Ministry of Labor; Nikkeiren	2
Clinical psychology internships	Association of Psychology Internship Centers	2
Dental residencies (three specialties and two general programs)	Postdoctoral Dental Matching Program	3
Optometry residencies	Optometric Residency Matching Services	1 and 3
Other two-sided matching:		
Fraternity rush		1
Sorority rush	National Panhellenic Conference	3
Entry-level medical labor markets:		
American first-year postgraduate (PGY1) positions	National Resident Matching Program (NRMP)	3
Canadian first-year positions	Canadian Intern and Resident Matching Service	3
U.K. regional markets for preregistration positions:	Regional health authorities	
Edinburgh		3
Cardiff		3
Birmingham		4, 1
Newcastle		4, 1
Sheffield		3 or 4, 1
Cambridge		3
London Hospital		3
American specialty residencies:		4
Neurosurgery	Neurological Surgery Matching Program	
Ophthalmology	Ophthalmology Matching Program	3
Otolaryngology	Otolaryngology Matching Program	3
Neurology	Neurology Matching Program	3
Urology	AUA Residency Matching Program	3
Radiation Oncology	Radiation Oncology Matching Program	1 and 3
Other specialties[a]	NRMP	3 and 4
Advanced speciality positions:		
12 (primarily surgical) specialities[b]	Specialties Matching Services	3
Three medical subspecialties[c]	Medical Specialties Matching Program	3
Four ophthalmology subspecialties	Ophthalmology Fellowship Match	3
Plastic surgery	Plastic Surgery Matching program	3

[a]Anesthesiology, emergency medicine, orthopedics, physical medicine, psychiatry, and diagnostic radiology.
[b]Colon/rectal surgery, dermatology, emergency medicine, foot/ankle surgery, hand surgery, ophthalmic plastic and reconstructive surgery, pediatric emergency medicine, pediatric orthopedics, pediatric surgery, reproductive endocrinology, sports medicine, and vascular surgery.
[c]Cardiovascular disease, gastroenterology, and pulmonary disease.

have been devoted to control these timing problems. Many of the market organizations listed in Table 1 have been created solely for the purpose of controlling the timing of transactions (while in other cases this function has been undertaken by existing organizations).

Most of the markets mentioned in Table 1 are entry-level labor markets for professionals. Timing problems are particularly easy to identify in these markets, because while employment contracts can be signed at any time, employment itself typically begins only following the attainment of the necessary professional qualifications, such as graduation from medical, law, or business school, or university. In many of these markets, the date at which contracts were signed crept earlier and earlier from year to year, until in several cases contracts came to be signed as much as two years in advance of the date at which employment would begin. This unraveling of appointment dates often occurred despite the vigorous efforts of market participants to halt it due to the costs it imposed (costs of having to hire in anticipation of uncertain future need, costs of potential mismatches caused by the uncertainty of employees' qualifications before they had completed their training, and the increased costs of search and loss of liquidity as the variance in times of appointment increased). In many cases the process was halted or reversed only by the introduction of new procedures and forms of organization.

That similar phenomena can be observed in markets other than labor markets will be shown by examining the market for postseason college football bowl games. It is possible to focus clearly on questions about timing in this market also, because bowl games are played only following the conclusion of the regular college football season, but arrangements between teams and bowls may be made well before the end of the season. The costs of making arrangements long before the end of the season arise from the uncertainty concerning which will be the most highly regarded teams at the end of the season, and the consequent difficulty of arranging matches that will draw the largest television audiences by pitting against each

other teams with a claim to be the best. Yet the National Collegiate Athletic Association, despite the considerable enforcement power at its disposal, has been unable to enforce a date before which bowl bids may not be made. It recently gave up the attempt, prompting a significant reorganization of the market.

Because problems of timing may be easier to detect early in the history of markets, before they have been resolved, we also briefly examine the regulations governing medieval markets, typically weekly markets for ordinary commodities. The benefits that these markets provided depended to a large extent on the ability of buyers and sellers to coordinate on a time and a place for the market, and the laws governing the establishment and conduct of markets seem to reflect this. (In contrast to the markets in Table 1, we rely for descriptions of these and the other markets in Table 3 on secondary sources, and we observe only institutions in place, not the evolution of the market that led to their adoption.)

Indirectly, one of the larger themes of this paper is that markets may require a good deal of organization. This runs counter to the view implicit in much of the economic literature, which is that markets are largely self-organizing, in contrast to firms, whose more complex structure arises in response to market failures. The markets studied in this paper exhibit a good deal of complex structure themselves, which also arises in response to market failure.

That being the case, it is natural to ask why many markets—including many entry-level professional labor markets—appear *not* to experience the timing problems that are the subject of this paper, and why they manage to function well without any of the institutions which characterize the markets in Tables 1 and 3. Why does the entry-level market for new economics professors, for example, behave differently from the markets for American law-school graduates, or for graduates of elite Japanese universities? And why do some academic labor markets (e.g., in mathematics, chemistry, and biology) seem to be moving in the direction of later, rather than earlier appointments? This will be discussed in Section V.

The present paper builds on the work reported in Roth (1984, 1986), Roth (1990, 1991), and Susan Mongell and Roth (1991), which studied the centralized market-clearing mechanisms adopted in the market for first-year postgraduate positions for American doctors, in seven regional markets for British doctors, and in the recruitment process of American sororities, respectively. Only some of these centralized procedures succeeded in halting the unraveling of transaction dates. The analysis in these earlier papers focused on whether or not the outcome produced by the matching mechanism was *unstable* in the sense that some firm and worker who were not matched to each other would each prefer to be so matched. This analysis organized a lot of the observed market behavior, but because it employs static models it could address only indirectly the causes of unraveling over time.

The larger set of markets examined in the present paper, which includes additional markets that have adopted centralized procedures as well as markets that have not, allows a broader investigation of hypotheses about the causes, costs, and cures of unraveling transaction dates. We will propose formal models which for the first time directly address the causes of unraveling in environments in which timing decisions are explicit and when information may evolve over time. We will see that unraveling can occur in markets in which prices can adjust freely (such as the market for new associates in large law firms), as well as in those in which they cannot (such as the market for judicial clerkships in federal courts), and that associated with this unraveling is the potential for inefficient market outcomes.

In order to facilitate the description and comparison of the many markets in Table 1, Section I of this paper will describe common features observed in the evolution of these markets over time, divided into four stages. Section II will then provide the background to the present investigation, by briefly reviewing the American and British medical markets. Those observations demonstrate the importance of unstable matchings as a contributor to unraveling of transaction dates.

Section III will describe some of the particular features of each of the new markets considered in this paper. It is a long section, containing an unusual amount of descriptive material, which we feel is necessary to establish our claims that many markets experience the timing problems we describe. By looking carefully at a relatively large collection of markets, our intention is to establish that these timing problems play an important and persistent role in a wide variety of settings, and that they can usefully be organized around the four stages proposed in Section I. Section III concludes with a brief discussion of several markets whose histories we have not investigated, but which have also developed institutions related to timing. These include medieval markets, entry-level markets for professional athletes, marriage in a variety of cultures, and postdoctoral positions in academia. The descriptive material in Section III provides the motivation for the formal models in Section IV, which demonstrate that unraveling may have more than one cause. In addition to the static instabilities studied in Roth (1984, 1991), we show that the way information about agents evolves over time may be a cause of intertemporal instabilities which lead to unraveling, as may be the market power which accrues to agents as a result of the heterogeneity of the market. Section V concludes with a discussion, including a discussion of possible empirical tests of some of the predictions generated by the models.

I. Unraveling in a Prototypical Market

Each of the dozen nonmedical and several dozen or so medical markets and submarkets in Table 1[2] have evolved over time in ways that share many elements of a common pattern, with several fairly distinct stages. Despite the diversity among these markets, there are so many common ele-

---

[2] Precisely how many markets are represented in Table 1 depends on an assessment of how distinct the markets are in the different medical specialties, and for the different dental residencies. The relatively small overlap among these specialty markets is discussed in Subsection III-C.

ments in the timing problems they have encountered that it will greatly facilitate their description and comparison to begin with the somewhat idealized description of a four-stage process as experienced by a prototypical market. For convenience, we will refer to the participants in this proto-typical market as if it were an entry-level professional labor market.

Stage 1 begins when the market comes into being (e.g., when a few hospitals begin offering internships, or when federal court clerkships are created by legislation) and the relatively few transactions are made without overt timing problems. By the middle of stage 1 the market has grown, and some appointments are being made rather early, with some participants finding that they do not have as wide a range of choices as they would like: students have to decide whether to accept early job offers or take a chance and wait for better jobs, and some employers find that not all of the students they are interested in are available by the time they get around to making offers. The trade journals start to be full of exhortations urging employers to wait until the traditional time to make offers, or at least not to make them any earlier next year than this year. Toward the end of stage 1, the rate of unraveling accelerates, until sometimes quite suddenly offers are being made so early that there are serious difficulties in distinguishing among the candidates. There is no uniform time for offers to be made nor is there a customary duration for them to be left open, so participants find themselves facing unnaturally thin markets, and on both sides of the market a variety of strategic behaviors emerge, many of which are regarded as unethical practices. Various organizations concerned with the market may have proposed guidelines intended to regulate it, without notable success. As stage 1 ends, influential market participants are engaged in a vigorous debate about what can and should be done. From beginning to end, stage 1 may have covered a period of more than 50 years, or fewer than 10.

In *stage 2*, either an existing market organization or a new one created for the purpose attempts to establish a uniform date before which offers should not be made,

and often an earlier date before which interviews should not be conducted, and a later date (or time) before which candidates who have received offers should not be required to respond. Sometimes this is hardly successful at all, with many market participants ignoring or circumventing the rules, and with those who obey them quickly finding that this puts them at a disadvantage. Even when uniform dates are successfully established and maintained, the market often experiences a great deal of congestion and chaotic behavior, as the deadline for accepting or rejecting offers grows near. A firm is eager to know whether its offers will be accepted, in time so that if it has unfilled positions it may approach its most preferred alternative candidates before they have had to accept any offers they have received; and candidates who have received offers, but not from their first-choice firm, are intent upon waiting until the last allowable moment before accepting any offer, in the hope of receiving a better one. Particularly if, as often seems to be the case, some fraction of candidates hold on to multiple offers as the final deadline approaches, this means that just before the deadline expires many transactions still remain to be made. Firms whose first-choice candidates reject them may now find that their next dozen candidates have already accepted offers, and candidates may receive preferred offers moments after making a verbal commitment to accept an earlier offer. In some markets such verbal commitments are virtually always honored, and in others they are sometimes reneged on. In either event, in the aftermath, many firms and candidates have just missed making connections they would have preferred. The result is that the following year witnesses a resurgence of strategic behaviors designed to avoid being caught short at the end of the market. Often new rules are formulated to prohibit the more brazen of these, and new adaptations are made. While some markets have persisted for many seasons in this fashion, systems of formalized dates are often abandoned, with the market either reverting to stage 1, or moving on to stage 3.

Stage 3 begins when centralized market-clearing procedures are instituted, either on a voluntary basis or with an attempt to compel participation and prevent transactions from being made other than through the centralized procedures. Participants normally make initial contacts with each other and arrange interviews in a decentralized way but then participate in the centralized procedure instead of making offers to one another directly. In some markets the centralized procedure is scheduled to move back the date at which appointments are made (i.e., to reverse prior unraveling), while in other markets it serves simply to halt further unraveling. We observe at least three distinct classes of centralized procedures. The first class of procedures comprises the "matchmaker" mechanisms employed in many entry-level health-care labor markets and in the entry-level market for Canadian lawyers in Toronto, Vancouver, and Alberta. Under these procedures, firms submit rank-order lists of students, and students submit rank-order lists of firms; and the centralized mechanism then produces a matching of students with firms. The second class of procedures comprises the "draft" mechanisms employed in many entry-level labor markets for professional athletes (see Table 3). Under these procedures, teams take turns choosing students from a pool of eligible candidates, one student at a time, until every team has had a choice, after which the process begins again. Typically the rule for determining the order in which teams make choices is designed to promote balance among teams in the same league. The final class of procedures, of which we know in detail only the example of the market for college football bowls, is a system of overlapping contracts between and among teams and consortia of teams (conferences), on the one hand, and the business enterprises which promote the games (bowls) and, most recently, consortia of bowls on the other. Centralized mechanisms are not always successful, and so stage 3 sometimes ends with the abandonment of the mechanism and the reversion to stage 1. There are many examples of mechanisms which have proved quite long-lasting, however, and for many of these markets stage 3 may be the final stage in the market's evolution. However some of these markets go on to stage 4.

In *stage 4*, with centralized procedures in place, unraveling begins (or continues) in the period before the mechanism is employed, as firms and students attempt to gather information about one another or gain advantage over their competitors before participating in the market-clearing procedure. The markets in which we have observed this kind of unraveling employ matchmaking mechanisms, and the unraveling has often taken the form of recruiting students for summer internships (or in the case of some medical specialties for "audition electives"), which amount to extensive interviewing opportunities in which the student spends a period of weeks or even months at the firm. Because of the length of time involved, students can interview in this way at only a very small number of firms (often only one), and firms can interview only a few students in this way. Because the percentage of new employees hired by each firm who were previously summer interns there sometimes becomes quite high, these internships can become a way of moving the recruiting process before the centralized matching mechanism, and the process of recruiting summer interns may start to resemble the stage-1 unraveling discussed above. (In some cases, these early recruiting activities may have predated the establishment of the centralized mechanism; i.e., they may be remnants of stage-1 unraveling that persist even after the establishment of centralized procedures.) However such unraveling prior to the central market-clearing mechanism does not eliminate all its benefits. A matchmaking mechanism still ensures, for example, that a desirable firm which ultimately wishes to fill five new positions can do so. This contrasts with the situation which existed in stage 1, when employment offers were made in a decentralized way, when it might have been that such a firm would have had to make ten offers to have a good chance of filling five positions, and it might have ended up in any given year with fewer than five new employees, or more.

Figure 1 summarizes this discussion and shows both the stages and the paths we have observed between them. Table 1 lists next to each market the most recently ob-

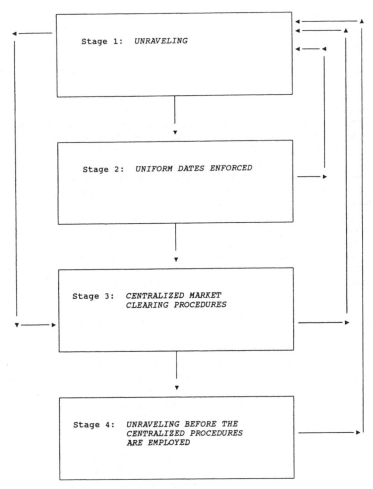

FIGURE 1. STAGES AND TRANSITIONS OBSERVED IN THE MARKETS OF TABLE 1

served stage, and if this stage has been reached from a higher stage, then that is shown also (e.g., the "2,1" next to Federal court clerkships indicates that a uniform offer date [stage 2] was tried and abandoned, and that the market has reverted to stage 1). Stages 1 and 2 are not always perfectly distinct, since the guidelines that are often formulated at the end of stage 1 can resemble more formal attempts to control dates of appointment, particularly when both are unsuccessful. Similarly, stages 3 and 4 are not always perfectly distinct.

We now turn to the description of the particular markets, beginning with an account of the medical markets studied in Roth (1984, 1991).

II. Background: American and British Doctors

A. *First-Year Postgraduate Positions for American Doctors*

The entry-level labor market for new American physicians is perhaps the classic case of transition from stage 1 to stage 2 to stage 3. Since it has been described in Roth (1984), only a brief description is given here.

Appointment dates unraveled from about the turn of the century until 1945, so that by 1944 medical students were arranging their postgraduate employment as interns two years in advance of graduation. Starting in 1945 a regime of uniform dates and times was introduced, and it was enforced with the help of an apparently successful refusal by medical schools to provide information about students prior to a specified date. This succeeded in reversing the unraveling, and appointment dates were first moved back into the junior year, and then into the senior year of medical school. However, in 1945 the period specified for offers to remain open was ten days, and this interval shrunk rapidly, so that by 1949 a 12-hour period was rejected as too long, and no minimum duration at all was specified. The congestion in the market, with its collateral missed opportunities and hasty agreements which were later sometimes not honored, led to the adoption, in 1952, of a (voluntary) centralized market-clearing procedure of the matchmaker variety. It was shown in Roth (1984) that this procedure is a stable matching mechanism, which is to say it always produces a matching that is stable with respect to the preference orderings submitted by the hospitals and students.[3]

With modifications to meet the changing market, this procedure remains in use today, and it serves to fill most of the approximately 20,000 first-year positions which become available each year. The recent evolution of the market, which has grown to include a variety of specialty residencies and positions for physicians beyond the first year after medical-school graduation, will be discussed later. First we turn to the similar experience of the entry-level markets in each region of Britain's National Health Service. Here too we will be brief, as these markets are studied in detail in Roth (1991).

B. Regional Markets for Preregistration Positions in the United Kingdom

Following graduation from medical school in the United Kingdom, a doctor must complete a year of preregistration experience before becoming fully eligible to practice. Each region of the National Health Service organizes its own market for preregistration house officers, with an average size of about 200 positions annually.

In the mid-1960's, dates of appointment in these markets had unraveled to well over a year before graduation from medical school. Uniform appointment dates had apparently been attempted in some regions, without success. A Royal Commission on Medical Education (1965–1968) studied the problem, noted that it had been solved by a centralized matchmaking mechanism in the United States, and recommended that regional markets establish their own matchmaking mechanisms (in which participation was compulsory). Because the details of the mechanism used in the United States were not then thought to be important (either in the United Kingdom or the United States), each of the regions was left to develop its own mechanism. Because some of the resulting matchmaking mechanisms failed to halt unraveling while others succeeded, the experience of these markets thus provides a natural experiment for examining the role of the mechanism itself.

Roth (1991) showed that the mechanisms adopted in two of the successful regions, Edinburgh and Cardiff, were stable match-

[3]The question of whether the resulting matching is also stable with respect to the true preferences is more complicated. It is not a dominant strategy for all participants to state their true preferences, but equilibrium misrepresentation of preferences also yields matchings that are stable with respect to the true preferences, although there are unstable equilibria as well in markets with many-to-one matching (see Roth and Marilda Sotomayor, 1990 [theorems 4.4, 4.16, 5.14, and 5.18]). Ulrich Kamecke (1992) considers how an entry-level market organized in this way may interact with the market for senior physicians. The Canadian and American entry-level markets also interact, with Canadian students able to participate both in the U.S. market and in the Canadian Intern and Resident Matching Service, which is organized separately from, but coordinated with, the U.S. market.

ing mechanisms.[4] These mechanisms halted unraveling, and they are still in use. In contrast, matchmaker mechanisms implemented in Birmingham, Newcastle, and Sheffield (and in Edinburgh from 1967 to 1969) failed to halt unraveling and were subsequently abandoned. Because of the way in which they frequently produced unstable matchings, they gave participants the incentive to make under-the-table agreements well in advance of the formal procedure, which was subsequently used only in a pro forma way. By the time these mechanisms were abandoned, up to 80 percent of positions were prearranged (and formalized through the mechanism with submitted rank-order lists containing only a single, prearranged choice), which worked to the great disadvantage of those who participated without prearrangement (see Roth, 1991).

A final class of mechanisms, employed in the two smallest markets studied (for students at the Cambridge and London Hospital medical schools), each used linear-programming matchmaker mechanisms that may produce unstable matchings. However both of these mechanisms have controlled unraveling and are still in use. Roth (1991) speculated that the success of these potentially unstable mechanisms may be due in part to the fact that the participants in both of these small (approximately 100-position) markets have ongoing relationships with one another, and in part to the difficulty of using the linear-programming mechanisms in a pro forma way to effect a prearranged match. We will suggest another possibility in our discussion of Example 2 in Subsection IV-B.

We turn next to the new markets considered in this paper. Since these descriptions are necessarily selective, we will concentrate on providing good examples for each of

stages 1–4. These examples also suggest that unraveling may be due to causes other than instability. With this in mind, we pay particular attention to the way information about candidates' qualifications develops over time and to the way in which attempts to halt or reverse unraveling are sensitive to the degree of participation they elicit from key players.

III. A Selection of Markets with Timing Problems

In discussing the markets in Table 1, we will spend the most time in discussing those chosen as examples of stages 1 and 2. This is partly because stage-3 markets have been discussed at length in Roth (1984, 1990, 1991), but also because stages 1 and 2 exemplify the problems faced by all of these markets. All the markets have experienced stage 1, and the difficulties experienced by some of the markets in establishing uniform times (stage 2) also illuminate the difficulties of establishing and maintaining more centralized (stage-3) institutions.

A. *Examples of Stage 1: Unraveling*

To illustrate stage-1 unraveling, we will discuss two legal markets (the market for Federal court clerkships and the market for new associate positions in large law firms) as well as the market for postseason college football bowls. We will also briefly discuss the markets for new MBA graduates of American business schools and for new professors of marketing in business schools. We pay particular attention to the way information evolves over time in these markets, and this will play a big role in the formal models of Section IV.

Our discussion of both entry-level legal markets will concentrate on a period from the mid-1970's through the 1980's. To give some perspective on the size of the larger market of which these two submarkets are a part, note that the number of new graduates from ABA-accredited law schools grew in this period from just under 29,000 in 1974 to just over 36,000 by 1990 (National Association for Law Placement, 1988a, 1991).

---

[4]Questions of stability have to be reformulated in these markets in terms of preferences over pairs of positions because students require two positions, one in medicine and one in surgery.

1. *Federal Court Clerkships.*—Perhaps the most prestigious position that a new law-school graduate can take is as a law clerk for a distinguished federal judge. Obtaining such a position is a big step up on the career path of a young lawyer. And having a talented and compatible staff of clerks is a major component of judges' productivity. So it is not surprising that this market has exhibited fierce competition and generated a good deal of strategic behavior among the participants.[5]

The market for judicial clerkships dates from 1886, for Supreme Court Justices, but did not begin to approach its present size until Congress authorized the hiring of clerks for U.S. circuit (appeals) judges in 1930, and for U.S. district court judges in 1936. Presently Justices may hire four law clerks, circuit judges three, and district judges two (Alvin Rubin and Laura Bartell, 1989). The number of judges has grown over the years, and today there are about 2,200 clerkships for U.S. circuit and district court judges, in 13 federal circuit courts (the Federal, District of Columbia, and First through Eleventh circuits),[6] and 94 district courts. It is the market for these positions that has experienced the most unraveling.[7]

Salary for these positions is fixed, and not subject to negotiation between judges and

candidates. However the desirability of and competition for particular clerkships vary. Circuit courts are generally regarded as more prestigious than district courts, and among the circuits, the District of Columbia circuit is widely regarded as the most prestigious. Also, individual judges on a given court have different reputations, concerning both how they work with their clerks and the degree to which they take an interest in a clerk's future career advancement (a special case being that some judges have a reputation as "feeders" of clerks to the Supreme Court).

Accounts of the market for clerkships from the 1950's indicate that it was a leisurely process in those days, with jobs being arranged at the end of the third year of law school, just as the student graduated and became available to occupy the position. Gradually the dates at which appointments were arranged became earlier, in a process that has accelerated over the last decade. In recent years, appointments have come to be made over a year in advance, to students in the middle of their second year of law school. Many judges make offers to second-year students in February and March, around the time that elections are held for the editorial boards of law reviews (which give a good early indicator of who are regarded as the most promising students); and some judges now make offers in January.

Aside from the unraveling of the appointment dates themselves, the process by which offers are actually made and received has also evolved, and (some) judges and (some) students have adopted what are regarded as "sharp" practices. On the judges' side the most notable of these are variations on "short fuse" or "exploding offers." (While the term "exploding offer" used to be applied to an offer which would be withdrawn if it were not accepted in some very short time, such as an hour, today the term seems to refer to offers in which no time at all is given, i.e., to offers which must be accepted during the telephone conversation in which they are delivered.) Some students play a form of "answering-machine tag" in which they try to buy time to contact other judges

---

[5]Alex Kozinski (1991 p. 1707) of the Ninth Circuit of the U.S. Court of Appeals writes:

This is the market that determines the career paths of some of the country's smartest and most promising young lawyers; it would be astounding if it were conducted with the gentility of a minuet. We are, after all, training courtroom gladiators not ballroom dancers.

[6]The circuit courts average about 12 judges each (with the largest being the Ninth Circuit in the West, the smallest the First Circuit in New England, and most other courts being very close to the average). Patricia Wald (1990 p. 152) writes that in the circuit courts "it is not unusual for a judge to receive 300–400 clerk applications, most from top-drawer candidates."

[7]The Supreme Court, which hires 37 clerks (four for each Justice plus one for the court itself) now largely draws from the pool of clerks of other Federal courts rather than from the pool of new graduates. There are also clerkships for other Federal courts than those we consider (e.g., Claims, Tax, International Trade, Military Appeals, Veterans Appeals) as well as some state and local courts.

to whom they have applied by making themselves unavailable to respond immediately to an offer.[8]

Both the unraveling of appointment dates and the spread of the associated strategic behavior have given rise to repeated attempts to reform the market. However these attempts have themselves generated some controversy. Judges on opposing sides of this issue have explained themselves (cf. Wald, 1990; Kozinski, 1991), which gives an unusual window on this market.[9] Wald, in the D.C. circuit, has been an active proponent of reform of the market, while Kozinski, in the Ninth circuit, is an opponent of the plans that have so far been considered. However both agree on the costs which unraveling imposes. Kozinski (1991 p. 1710) summarizes these succinctly as follows:

> To be sure, we would all prefer to know *precisely* how a particular student will do during the full six semesters he spends in law school. If a decision could magically be delayed until after graduation, we would have all of an applicant's grades as well as the potential input of a large battery of law school professors. Also, we could be better informed about the student's performance in various ex-

tracurricular activities. Did she do an excellent job as a law review editor? Did she publish and, if so, what does the product look like? Did he compete in moot court and, if so, how high did he place?...All of these would be mighty helpful hints when picking clerks.

Motivated by such concerns, a number of unsuccessful attempts were made to control the unraveling of appointment dates. Wald (1990 p. 156) summarizes them as follows:

> Since the early 1980s there have been sporadic attempts to establish ground rules. The Judicial Conference of the United States established an ad hoc committee in 1982 that recommended a schedule for beginning interviews in September of the candidates' third year but set no fixed, enforceable time within which to make offers. Many judges abided by the recommended guideline but a substantial number did not. Because of the consequent tensions, the effort was abandoned. In successive years, judges in several circuits agreed to deadlines on offers in April or July, but again, many judges were unwilling to accept these constraints.
>
> Throughout the eighties there were, alternatively, open-season years (judges were free to make an offer at any time) and years in which many (but not all) judges in many (but not all) circuits agreed to hold to a specified deadline.

As the decade drew to a close, an attempt was made to establish more broadly uniform dates for offers to be made, and a uniform time that these offers should be left open. Wald (1990 pp. 157–58) summarizes these most recent attempts as follows:

> In 1989...a group of judges, including several circuit chiefs, undertook a campaign to have the Judicial Councils, the governing bodies for the circuits, adopt deadlines for clerkship offers. Recognizing that it was unlikely such a directive could be enforced against an errant judge, it was still hoped that a policy directive from the

---

[8] In this market (unlike some we consider) it is apparently rare for a student who has accepted an exploding offer over the phone to renege subsequently when a preferred offer arrives. (It may be that the benefit of having even the most distinguished federal judge as a mentor is largely dissipated if there is another federal judge—with lifetime tenure—who will regard a young lawyer as dishonest or unethical.) However Kozinski (1991 p. 1728) writes "Incidents where law clerks wriggle out of commitments with judges are more common than one would guess. They are usually predicated on some changed circumstances but sometimes reflect merely a change of heart. Even under the best of circumstances, it is an extremely delicate matter and the judge's reaction might well turn on whether he relied on the clerk's commitment in turning away other qualified applications."

[9] This controversy has also generated a number of stories in the popular press, some of which have in turn raised concerns among judges about the public image of the judiciary (see e.g., David Margolick, 1989; Saundra Torry, 1991).

Councils would carry more weight than an informal agreement of judges. In the spring of 1989, the District of Columbia Judicial Council passed the following Resolution:

'Commencing in 1990, the D.C. Circuit Council is committed to the practice that no job offers, tentative or final, shall be made to law clerk applicants before May 1st of the applicant's second year.'

...In the end, the D.C., Federal, First, Second, Third, Fourth, Sixth, Eighth, Tenth, and a majority of judges on the Ninth adopted some form of limiting resolution. The Fifth, Seventh, and Eleventh declined. There were two variations in the resolutions: some, but not all, contained a provision that the offers remain open for twenty-four hours; some made compliance with the May 1st deadline contingent upon the concurrence of all other circuits; some agreed unilaterally.

As Mayday approached, complying judges grew increasingly anxious; efforts to get agreement on a twenty-four-hour waiting period for acceptances failed...By consensus, a one-hour waiting period was fixed.

Wald goes on to say (p. 159):

What actually happened on May 1? A few judges weakened at the end and made calls ahead of the deadline. This, in turn, provoked the students to call other judges they preferred before the noon deadline, so there was a destabilizing flurry of predeadline transactions. But the major complaint was the frenzy with which offers had to be made and accepted. Those judges who gave their choices time to reflect found themselves severely disadvantaged.... By 12:15 virtually all of the bidding in the D.C. Circuit was over. Between 12:00 and 12:15, judges were making offers on one line as calls came in on a second from frantic applicants trying to learn if they were to get an offer before they responded to the offer of another judge.

Wald and colleagues from the First, Second, and Third circuits subsequently conducted a survey of the U.S. circuit judges to better assess the outcome. Fifty-two of the 65 judges replying answered yes to the question "Prior to May 1 noon EDT, did any applicants that you sought for interviews already have a clerkship?" In a memo reporting the survey results to all U.S. District and Circuit Court judges, James Oakes et al. (1991) write that they are notifying the American Association of Law Schools that:

there are no guideposts in place for 1991...[and]...if they are concerned about the acceleration of the law clerk hiring process, they will have to do something about it themselves.

Wald concluded her 1990 article with a discussion of the "medical model." After describing the centralized market-clearing mechanisms used in the market for first-year medical graduates, she suggested that a centralized procedure adapted to the specific needs of judges be considered as a solution to the problem of unraveling appointment dates in the law-clerk market.

Kozinski (1991 p. 1719), in discussing why he opposes any move toward either a centralized market-clearing system or a system of uniform dates, writes:

...not all clerkships are created equal. Geography plays a role. Judges on the east coast enjoy the advantage of proximity to many of the country's best law schools. Prestige counts. Some circuits, the D.C. Circuit in particular, tend to draw a disproportionate share of the nation's top applicants. Seniority matters. Judges with many years on the bench naturally have an advantage over upstarts like me who have to work hard at achieving a national reputation. The problem with many reform proposals is that they tend to reinforce these patterns by decreasing the means by which less-favored clerkships can compete for desirable applicants.

He goes on to note that a common feature of uniform-date procedures, whether centralized or decentralized is that:

> such plans eliminate a very important bargaining tool for judges competing for the most gifted clerkship candidates—the ability to make offers early and entice applicants into ending the anxiety and uncertainty by accepting early.

We will return to this point in Example 1 in Section IV.

In closing, we note that the unraveling of appointment dates has proved resistant to the efforts of the law schools as well as the judicial conferences. Kozinski (1991 p. 1725) notes, for example, that:

> At some schools, the placement office insists on collecting the letters of recommendation so that all may be sent at a 'proper date.' Streetwise students avoid this pitfall by asking their recommenders to send letters directly to the judges.

The incentives for professors in accommodating students in this way, he notes, is that there is considerable value to professors (e.g., in attracting good research assistants) in maintaining a reputation of being a "feeder" to good clerkships.

Thus in the market for judicial clerkships, attempts to halt or reverse the unraveling of appointment dates by establishing a uniform date for appointments have so far failed. We turn next to the other "elite" market for new law-school graduates, the market for positions in the largest law firms. In contrast to the market for clerkships, in this market salaries play a large role.

2. *American Law Firms.*—The highest starting salaries paid to new law graduates are paid to those who enter the largest law firms (with over 250 attorneys), and the larger the law firm, the higher is the salary distribution. In 1990, about 12 percent of new law graduates whose first jobs were in law firms took positions in the largest firms, which for our purposes are those with over

250 attorneys.[10] The very highest salaries of all are paid by the largest New York firms, which in 1990 paid a median starting salary to new graduates of $83,000. The competitiveness of this market is reflected in the fact that the interquartile range (25th–75th percentiles) of these salaries was only $1,000 (National Association for Law Placement, 1991 p. 52). This is a market that has also seen "salary wars" that resulted in large jumps from year to year: in 1968 the starting salaries at the largest Wall Street firms jumped 58 percent, from $9,500 to $15,000, and in 1986 25 percent, from an average of $49,573 in 1985 to $61,203 in 1986.[11]

However, competition in this market has not been confined to wages. The market has also experienced serious unraveling, in many ways parallel to that experienced in the judicial clerkship market, but with important differences as well. In particular, much of the unraveling has come in the recruitment and hiring of students for summer positions as "summer associates." Because many firms fill the majority of their new hiring needs by hiring students who have been their summer associates, the competition to recruit and hire the most promising summer associates has become a proxy for

---

[10] The 1990 salary survey (National Association for Law Placement, 1991) classifies the largest firms in two categories: 251–500 attorneys and over 501 attorneys. However, the salary distributions for firms in these two categories are virtually identical. The survey reports (p. 16) that in 1990 the national median starting salary was $30,000 for firms with no more than 10 attorneys, $40,000 for those with 11–25 attorneys, $45,000 for 26–50 attorneys, $53,000 for 51–100, $60,000 for 101–250, and $70,000 for firms with 251 or more attorneys.

[11] The figure of $15,000 from 1968 (which is before the earliest National Association for Law Placement [NALP] salary survey) was the starting salary at Cravath, Swaine & Moore, which was quickly matched by other New York firms (see Sidney Zion, 1968). For the 1986 figure see NALP (1988 pp. xxii, 201). Note that the size of the largest firms has also changed in this period: in the 1986 salary survey, the largest category of firms is 100 or more attorneys. For a discussion of some determinants of legal salaries, see Richard Freeman (1975) and Ronald Ehrenberg (1989).

entry-level hiring.[12] And the hiring dates of both full-time and summer associates has unraveled.

Briefly, in the 1950's and 1960's relatively few law schools even had formal placement offices to arrange on-campus interviews, and law students largely found their own post-graduation employment, around the time of their graduation.[13] By the early 1970's, on-campus recruitment was common, and summer associate positions for second-year students began to be common as well. By the late 1970's, even first-year students were being offered summer associate positions, and by the middle of the 1980's the unraveling of recruiting had proceeded to such an extent that some students were being offered summer associate positions before they had matriculated at law school.[14] Thus a large part of the hiring of law students was based on recruiting that took place long before their law-school record was complete.

In an attempt to regulate the market, the National Association for Law Placement (NALP), formed in 1971, issued regulations to govern recruitment by law firms. The revisions these regulations underwent are illuminating, because they speak of the pressures the rules were under from law firms and law students prepared to obey the letter of the law while contravening its spirit. For example, in 1987 the NALP's Recruitment Practices Committee proposed revisions, which were adopted in 1988, of its "General Standards for the Timing of Offers and Acceptances." Figure 2 reproduces parts of the 1988 regulations (NALP, 1988b) as they appeared in a memo (LaNell D. Black and Jerrie Hawley, 1988), showing new additions underlined and deletions crossed out, in order to make the changes clear.

Black and Hawley (1988) provide some explanations of the proximate causes of these rule changes. They note that terms such as "should" and "may" have been replaced by "shall," to disabuse those who thought that these guidelines were intended only as suggestions. They note that paragraph 1 is a response to short-fuse and exploding offers.[15] Regarding paragraph 2, they note that there is particular concern about the deepest unraveling (i.e., that connected with first-year students) but that this

---

[12]A survey of 1982 summer associates by the National Association for Law Placement found that 90 percent of those working at the largest (more than 100 attorneys) New York firms received offers of permanent employment, and that across the country such firms filled just over 60 percent of their new hiring with students who had been 1982 summer associates or had just completed judicial clerkships (Daniel Wise, 1983). (There is some ambiguity in these numbers, because some but not all of the students who had just completed judicial clerkships will have been summer associates at the firms which they join after their clerkships.) A 1987 survey (see Wise, 1987) reported on 32 New York firms of which 18 filled over 50 percent of their hiring with returning 1986 summer associates. (Again, the numbers are probably too low, since, for example the prestigious firm of Cravath, Swaine & Moore, which employed 44 summer associates, and made offers to all of them, had only 13 return the following year [29.5 percent], while 25 [57 percent] accepted judicial clerkships and may have returned after completing them.

[13]Harvard University was an exception and formed a placement office after World War II. John Ferrick (1984 p. 24) notes that "It handled arrangements for large Wall Street firms to conduct interviews with upper-class students." He further notes that in the next decade "a small handful of other institutions" began to help arrange on-campus interviews and that by 1984 every accredited law school had a placement service, with the bulk of these having been established in the early 1970's.

[14]We are indebted to Jaime Studley, then the Executive Director of the National Association for Law Placement, for this latter observation (pers. comm., 7

September 1988). See also Mark Rust (1986) and the National Association for Law Placement's "General Standards for the Timing of Offers and Acceptances" discussed next. In some schools the schedule of on-campus recruiting had moved to before the start of the school year. For example, Rust (1986 p. 23) quotes an administrator at Columbia as follows: "We have four hundred employers here in the last week of August, and we schedule eleven thousand interviews. The overwhelming bulk of those interviews are over by the first day of class."

[15]"This provision was drafted so that no students would be pressured into 'on the spot' decisions—a common problem for first year students in particular" (Black and Hawley, 1988).

"1~~2~~. All offers to law students <u>shall</u> ~~should~~ remain open for at least two weeks after the date made. <u>This provision shall be construed for students covered by paragraphs 3 and 4 below so that the later response date is applied.</u>

"2~~3~~. Prospective employers <u>shall</u> ~~should~~ not <u>initiate contact with, interview, or make offers to</u> ~~begin recruiting or schedule interviews with~~ first semester <u>first year</u> students before ~~November 15 and should not make offers to such students until after~~ December 15. <u>First semester first year students shall not initiate contact with prospective employers before December 1.</u>

"3~~1~~. Prospective employers offering positions <u>prior to October 1</u> to second and third year students ~~prior to October 1 to students~~ employed by them during the preceding summer <u>shall</u> ~~should~~ leave those offers open until at least November 15, provided the student reaffirms his/her interest in the offer within 30 days of the date of the offer letter...

"4. Prospective employers offering positions in the fall to other students who were not employed by them during the preceding summer <u>shall</u> ~~should~~ leave their offers open until at least December 15, provided the student reaffirms his/her interest...

"6~~5~~. ...After October 1, a law student <u>shall</u> ~~may~~ not hold open more than four offers of employment simultaneously<u>, including offers received as a result of previous summer employment</u>. For each offer received that places a student over the limit, the student <u>shall</u> ~~must~~, within one week of receipt of the excess offer, reject an offer. <u>It is recommended that employers provide copies of offer letters to the students' placement directors to assist them in monitoring this standard.</u>

"8~~7~~. Violations of these standards should be reported to the student's Placement Director.

"9~~8~~. A law school may deny use of its placement facilities to students and employers who fail to adhere to these principles and standards for law placement and recruitment activities."

FIGURE 2. REVISIONS OF THE NALP "GENERAL STANDARDS FOR THE TIMING OF OFFERS AND ACCEPTANCES"

has proved difficult to control.[16] Paragraph 6 responds to frequent employer complaints about "offer hoarding" by students (see e.g., Timothy Corcoran, 1986).

Regarding the enforcement of these regulations, which is relegated to the law schools in paragraphs 6, 8, and 9, Black and Hawley (1988) note that "It is recognized that not all law schools have adequate resources at this time to ensure total student compliance." Indeed, the regulations seem to have proved difficult to enforce. For one thing, these regulations were met almost immediately with lawyerly changes in strategy. For example, some law firms began to give offers which met the letter of paragraphs 1, 3, and 4 by remaining open for the required period, but which structured the compensation so that the offer was competitive because it included a "signing bonus" which could only be collected if the offer was accepted much more promptly (Studley, pers. comm., 7 September 1988).

The recession of the early 1990's has cast some of this unraveling in a new light. In 1991 there were firms which, at the last moment, withdrew offers which had been accepted more than a year in advance of when employment was to begin (Ken Myers, 1991). That is to say, they laid off associates

---

[16]"The questions surrounding recruiting of first year students engendered the most discussion and the widest divergence of opinion. There are many people who would like to remove first year students from the placement/recruitment process altogether but the reality is that most first year students do not want to be excluded and simply set out independently to find employment...and many employers would feel disadvantaged in this competitive environment if they were not allowed to pursue first year students....

"Please note the additional sentence in this provision which sets forth the *earliest* date first semester first year students may contact employers...this should cut down on the amount of correspondence with first semester students (many of whom begin writing employers as early as August)..." (Black and Hawley, 1988).

An unrevised regulation, in the NALP's accompanying "Principles of Law Schools" is that "Law Schools should not offer placement services to first semester students prior to November 1 (Black and Hawley, 1988). Recall in this context the similar experience of law schools in the judicial clerkship market.

who had not yet reported for their first day of work. This underlines one of the costs of the unraveling of appointment dates. On the other hand, early indications are that the percentage of new hires in the largest firms who were former summer associates may be quite high for the class of 1991, and so the incentives for students to compete for these positions remains.

Thus in the market for new associates, particularly new associates in the largest law firms, attempts to halt the unraveling of recruiting and of appointment dates have been unsuccessful, as have attempts to establish uniform dates (however early) for recruiting and hiring. Thus the problems of unraveling are not confined to markets in which salaries cannot be easily adjusted to help clear the market.

We turn next to a very different sort of market which has experienced very similar problems, and for which the manner in which information develops over time is particularly clear.

3. Postseason College Football Bowls.— The market for postseason college football games is one in which the evolution of information over time is both regular and public. Each week throughout the fall, college football teams play each other. Each Monday or Tuesday, newspapers all over the country publish widely followed polls distributed by the Associated Press (AP) and the United Press International (UPI), ranking the top 25 teams (out of just over a hundred "Division 1A" schools). (The AP polls sportswriters, while the UPI polls college coaches.) After the conclusion of the regular season, selected teams meet each other in postseason games, called bowls, which are played in late December and early January, with a concentration of the most lucrative bowls on New Year's Day, a national holiday which offers access to a potentially large television audience.

The National Collegiate Athletic Association (NCAA) tried for a number of years to prevent unraveling of the dates at which bowls and teams finalized agreements about which teams would play in which bowls. However it gave up in failure following the

1990–1991 football season. This in turn has prompted a rapid reorganization of the market. Consequently, we concentrate here on the period 1989 through the beginning of 1992, which covers three seasons.

The bowls themselves are independent businesses, each of which controls a stadium and makes contracts with a television network and possibly with a corporate sponsor. In the 1989–1990 season there were 18 postseason bowls, with a combined payout to participating teams of just under $59 million (see Football Bowl Association, 1990). In the 1990–1991 season a new bowl, sponsored by the Blockbuster Video corporation, entered the market, making a total of 19 bowls.[17] The most lucrative of these bowls is the Rose Bowl (which in 1989–1990 paid $6.6 million to each team). However the Rose Bowl is a "closed" bowl: it has a long-term contract with the Big Ten and Pacific-10 football conferences, and each year the champions of those two conferences play each other in the Rose Bowl (and the conferences share the bowl revenues of their champions). Thus the Rose Bowl is not involved in the unraveling of transaction dates.

But none of the other bowls with payoffs per team of over $1 million is in the same situation.[18] In the 1989–1990 season the Fiesta Bowl was an "open" bowl, which is to say that it needed to find two teams to play on January 1. The other top bowls

were all "semi-closed," which means that they each had a contract with one football conference, whose champion would be one of the teams to play, and that the bowl would therefore need to find one additional team to play on New Year's Day.[19] The available pool from which these additional teams come consists of teams that are not in any football conferences ("independents") or are in conferences but are not contractually tied to any bowl.

Because the attractiveness of the product —the bowl game—depends on the attractiveness of the teams, there is consequently great competition among the top bowls to sign up the most attractive teams. A big component of the attractiveness of a team is its ranking at the end of the regular season, and its potential, following the bowl games, to be regarded as the putative "national champion."[20] Of course, the earlier in the regular season that semi-closed and open bowls reach agreement with particular teams in the available pool, the harder it is to predict what their ranking will be at the end of the season. On the other side of the

---

[17]These are the All American Bowl, Blockbuster Bowl, California Raisin Bowl, Domino's Pizza Copper Bowl, Eagle Aloha Bowl, Federal Express Orange Bowl, Florida Citrus Bowl, Freedom Bowl, Hall of Fame Bowl, John Hancock Bowl, Liberty Bowl, Mazda Gator Bowl, Mobil Cotton Bowl, Peach Bowl, Poulan/Weed Eater Independence Bowl, Rose Bowl, Sea World Holiday Bowl, Sunkist Fiesta Bowl, and USF&G Sugar Bowl.

[18]The other bowls with over $1 million payoffs per team in the 1989–1990 season are the Orange ($4.2 million per team), Sugar ($3.3 million), Cotton ($2.9 million), Fiesta ($2.5 million), Citrus ($1.2 million), Gator ($1.2 million), and Holiday ($1.0 million). Except for the Holiday Bowl, all of these play on January 1, as does the Hall of Fame Bowl ($.94 million). (see Football Bowl Association [1990] for payoffs, and NCAA [1990] for dates.)

[19]The champion of the Big Eight conference plays in the Orange Bowl, the Southeastern conference champion plays in the Sugar Bowl, the Southwest Conference champion plays in the Cotton Bowl, and the Atlantic Coast Conference champion plays in the Citrus bowl (with some escape clauses in case the ACC champion is ranked highly enough in the UPI poll to be a contender for the "national championship"—about which, see footnote 20.

[20]Following the bowl games, the AP (sportswriters' poll) and UPI (coaches' poll) publish final team rankings for the year, and a team which is ranked number 1 in both polls is widely regarded as the national champion. Although there is a very high correlation between the AP and UPI rankings throughout the year, the fact that the top-ranked team only rarely plays the second-ranked team in a postseason bowl makes the determination of the best team problematic. Factors other than rankings which also play a role in making teams attractive to bowls are the ticket-sales potential (which depends on the loyalty of the fans and their proximity to the bowl), television drawing power (which has to do with success in previous years as well as the current year) and the conference with which the team may be associated. For teams that do not have a shot at the national championship, these other factors are of increased importance. (The coaches' poll is now sponsored by USA Today-CNN.)

VOL. 84 NO. 4   *ROTH AND XING: JUMPING THE GUN*   1009

market, the earlier a team signs with a semi-closed or open bowl, the harder it is to predict the ranking of its competition on New Year's Day.

For this and related reasons, the NCAA attempted to control the date at which bowl agreements were signed. It did this by specifying a date (colloquially called "Pick-Em Day") before which such agreements were forbidden. In particular, in the 1989–1990 and 1990–1991 seasons, the NCAA regulations specified that bowls may not offer and teams may not accept "a formal invitation" "from August 1 to:

(a) The conclusion of [the team's] football game on the Saturday after the third Tuesday in November, or
(b) Six P.M. local time on the same date, whichever is earlier." [NCAA, 1989 pp. 6–7; 1990 pp. 7–8]

That is, the NCAA attempted to delay agreements until a date that was itself well before the end of the regular season, since most teams would still have two games remaining after Pick-Em Day. Serious penalties were specified for violations of this rule, including a one-year suspension of postseason bowl eligibility for both bowls and teams. Despite the fact that the NCAA has enforced comparable penalties on teams for violations of player recruiting (see Subsection III-E), these penalties were not enforced in the matter of bowl agreements, and the regulations failed to stop the unraveling of transaction dates.

To get a sense of what was going on, consider the 1990–1991 season. (This was the straw that broke the camel's back, so to speak, since after this season the NCAA abandoned attempts to control the date of transactions.) Table 2 shows how the AP (writers' poll) rankings of teams evolved over time, for the teams which played in postseason bowls. (Houston, Florida, and Oklahoma, highly ranked teams—numbers 9, 11, and 20 at the end of the regular season—had been declared ineligible for postseason play by the NCAA, and are therefore not represented in the table.) The rankings are given for each Tuesday through

the season, as well as the postseason rankings which followed the completion of the bowl games. Note that the rankings may vary widely from the beginning of the season to the end, as in the case of Auburn, which was ranked as number 3 in September but had dropped out of the rankings by the end of the regular season.

Pick-Em Day in 1990 was Saturday, November 24, and the most widely publicized agreements reached before that time were reached at least 13 days earlier. Notre Dame, an independent (and always a television favorite), had begun the season as the number-1 ranked team and had recovered from an early loss to regain that position by early November. In the meantime, Colorado had overcome an early season loss and a draw to become the number 4 team in the AP rankings (and number 3 in the UPI ranking). When Colorado beat Oklahoma State to clinch the Big Eight championship, they were assured a berth in the Orange Bowl and a rise in the rankings to number 2. The next day, on Sunday November 11, 13 days before Pick-Em Day, an agreement was announced between the Orange Bowl and Notre Dame that was widely reported in the news (see e.g., Malcolm Moran, 1990). At the time the agreement was reported, this meant that the currently first- and second-ranked teams would meet in the Orange Bowl. Announced the same day was Virginia's acceptance of a bid from the Sugar Bowl to play the still to be determined Southeastern Conference champion.[21] Following the Orange Bowl agreement, the University of Miami agreed to play in the Cotton Bowl against the still to be determined Southwest Conference champion. At this point, Notre Dame, Virginia, and Miami each still had four games remaining in the regular season.

---

[21]This came after Virginia decided to decline an offer from the Fiesta Bowl because of the controversy surrounding the failure of a referendum the previous Tuesday to make an Arizona state holiday in honor of Martin Luther King, Jr. (the Fiesta Bowl is played in Tempe, Arizona).

TABLE 2—1990 COLLEGE FOOTBALL BOWL GAMES: RATINGS

Legal bid date (6:00 P.M. Saturday, November 24) — under 11/27, 11/20.
Notre Dame to Orange Bowl, Virginia to Sugar Bowl, Miami to Cotton Bowl → at 11/13.

Bowl	Matches	Postgame	12/4	11/27	11/20	11/13	11/6	10/30	10/23	10/16	10/9	10/2	9/25	9/18
Rose	Washington (Pacific-10)	5	8	9	9	10	2	7	7	13	17	17	12	21
	Iowa (Big Ten)	18	17	18	13	13	6	13	15	22	25	—	—	—
Orange	Notre Dame (Independent)	6	5	7	7	1	1	2	3	6	8	1	1	1
	Colorado (Big Eight)	1	1	1	1	2	4	9	10	14	14	12	20	20
Sugar	Virginia (Atlantic Coast)	23	—	—	17	8	11	1	1	1	2	4	7	10
	Tennessee (Southeastern)	8	10	12	14	14	9	11	11	3	5	6	5	6
Cotton	Miami (Independent)	3	4	3	2	3	5	8	8	2	3	9	10	9
	Texas (Southwest)	12	3	5	6	7	14	14	13	19	—	—	—	22
Fiesta	Louisville (Independent)	14	18	17	20	20	22	25	—	—	—	—	—	—
	Alabama (Southeastern)	—	25	—	—	—	—	—	—	—	—	—	—	—
Citrus	Nebraska (Big Eight)	24	19	19	10	11	13	3	4	4	7	8	8	8
	Georgia Tech (Atlantic Coast)	2	2	2	3	4	7	16	16	11	18	23	—	—
Gator	Michigan (Big Ten)	7	12	13	15	16	19	20	20	10	1	3	6	7
	Mississippi (Southeastern)	21	15	15	21	15	16	17	17	18	24	—	—	—
Hall of Fame	Clemson (Atlantic Coast)	9	14	14	16	17	18	18	19	22	15	16	19	17
	Illinois (Big Ten)	25	16	16	22	22	17	5	5	8	11	13	14	15
Holiday	Texas A&M (Southwest)	15	—	—	—	—	—	—	—	25	20	19	11	12
	Brigham Young (Western)	22	13	4	4	5	8	10	9	12	13	11	4	4

Ratings (writers' poll)

Notes on the date columns: the *Legal bid date* was 6:00 P.M. Saturday, November 24 (column 11/27). The assignments "Notre Dame to Orange Bowl, Virginia to Sugar Bowl, Miami to Cotton Bowl" occurred at column 11/13.

Bowl	Matches	Postgame	12/4	11/27	11/20	11/13	11/6	10/30	10/23	10/16	10/9	10/2	9/25	9/18
Liberty	Ohio State (Big Ten)	—	24	25	19	21	—	—	—	—	—	20	15	16
	Air Force (Western)	—	—	—	—	—	—	—	—	—	—	—	—	—
John Hancock	Southern California (Pacific-10)	20	21	21	18	19	23	21	21	15	16	15	18	5
	Michigan State (Big Ten)	16	22	23	24	23	24	—	—	24	22	18	22	24
Peach	Indiana (Big Ten)	19	—	20	23	24	—	—	—	20	—	—	—	—
	Auburn (Southeastern)	—	23	24	25	25	15	4	2	5	6	5	3	3
All-American	North Carolina State (Atlantic Coast)	—	—	—	—	—	—	—	—	—	—	—	—	—
	Southern Mississippi (Independent)	—	—	—	—	—	—	—	—	—	—	—	—	—
Aloha	Syracuse (Independent)	—	—	—	—	—	—	—	—	—	—	—	—	—
	Arizona (Pacific-10)	—	—	—	—	—	25	23	23	21	21	25	16	18
Copper	California (Pacific-10)	—	—	—	—	—	—	—	—	—	—	—	—	—
	Wyoming (Western)	—	—	—	—	—	—	19	18	—	23	—	—	—
Freedom	Oregon (Pacific-10)	—	—	—	—	—	20	22	25	—	19	22	—	—
	Colorado State (Western)	—	—	—	—	—	—	—	—	—	—	—	—	—
Independence	Maryland (Atlantic Coast)	—	—	—	—	—	—	—	—	—	—	—	—	—
	Louisiana Tech (Independent)	—	—	—	—	—	—	—	—	—	—	—	—	—
California	San Jose State (Big West)	—	—	—	—	—	—	—	—	—	—	—	—	—
	Central Michigan (Mid-American)	—	—	—	—	—	—	—	—	—	—	—	—	—
Blockbuster	Penn State (Independent)	11	7	10	11	18	21	24	—	—	—	—	—	—
	Florida State (Independent)	4	6	8	8	9	12	12	12	7	10	2	2	2

These agreements were able to elude NCAA penalties because they were "unofficial" and "informal." At the same time, although they were presumably legally unenforceable, the fact that the same bowls and teams are involved with one another year after year apparently makes it quite rare for such agreements to be broken.[22]

Shortly after these agreements, Notre Dame lost a game and finished the regular season ranked number 5. Virginia, which had lost only one game prior to its agreement with the Sugar Bowl, lost two games subsequently, and finished the regular season unranked in the AP poll (and ranked number 23 in the UPI poll). By the end of the regular season it was clear that no bowl would have the number-1 and number-2 teams (Colorado and Georgia Tech, respectively), and indeed when the bowl games were over there was no consensus national champion: Colorado was ranked number 1 in the AP poll, and Georgia Tech was atop the UPI poll.[23]

Faced with a persistent and public inability to enforce Pick-Em Day, the NCAA abandoned the attempt (and began to consider some kind of centralized matching procedure).[24] The Football Bowl Association (FBA) responded with an attempt to enforce a Pick-Em Day of its own (to be November 17 in 1991) and voted to levy a fine of $250,000 on any member who violated this understanding.[25]

However the FBA was no more successful than the NCAA, and following the 1991–1992 season, *Sports Illustrated* summarized the situation as follows (William of North Carolina) explained this decision in a letter (to Roth, 15 March 1991) as follows:

The decision was made to eliminate from the NCAA Bylaws legislation that prohibits an institution from tying into a bowl before a particular date because the particular piece of legislation was being largely ignored and, most importantly, could not be enforced. In recent years, the NCAA has worked toward eliminating rules that were unenforceable, and the membership overwhelmingly felt that this was one of those rules. The bowl association has on its own decided to implement its controls, and there will continue to be a selection date, although it will not be an NCAA violation if an institution does not adhere to that date.... Whether or not this will improve the situation, of course, remains to be seen. If this does not work, our committee is looking at the possibility of instituting a draft whereby teams would be ranked and given a drafting order, and the teams would be allowed to pick the bowl they would like to attend, or the bowls would be ranked in a particular drafting order and they would be allowed to draft teams into their bowl. Either of these would take place on a pre-determined date.

[25]Steven Hatchell, chair of the executive committee of the Football Bowl Association (and Executive Director of the Orange Bowl) wrote about the situation in a letter (to Roth, 25 February 1991) as follows:

There have been obvious violations of the selection date process in recent years. While many of the bowls do not issue the "formal" invitation until that Saturday in late November, they have informally put the entire deal together. The earliest date many bowls have made agreements was in late October. This past year, many of the bowl pairings were known by the first weekend in November.

While all bowls have been accused of moving too early in this process, the problem seems to have increased with the recent influx of new bowl games. There are currently 19 postseason bowls, which has forced many of the smaller bowls to choose matchups as early as possible to avoid being left completely out of the picture....

[At the NCAA Convention last month] the Football Bowl Association decided that some action must be taken. We voted unanimously to maintain the selection date at its current time frame in late November and impose a $250,000 fine to any bowl that violates the deadline. It was our belief that the combination of the bowls' trust in each other and the public embarrassment that a fine would bring to the bowl and its title sponsor would be enough to withstand the temptation.

---

[22]Because of the substantial penalties for breaking NCAA rules, there are no public accounts of the details of these informal agreements. However in confidential discussions with participants in this market, great confidence was expressed in the reliability of such agreements, once made. This is not to say that these agreements are never broken, and we heard of at least one occasion in which a university broke an unofficial agreement with a major bowl and was ostracized by the bowl (and perhaps by some other bowls, although this is less clear) for several years thereafter.

[23]The best matchup turned out to be in the Cotton Bowl, which at the end of the regular season had the number 3 and 4 teams in both polls. The fact that many teams had made early arrangements worked to the advantage of the new Blockbuster Bowl, which had not been in a position to attract highly ranked teams early in the year. It hosted Florida State and Penn State, each of which had lost two games early in the season and were not highly ranked in early November, but which were the number 6 and 7 teams at the end of the regular season.

[24]John Swofford, chair of the Postseason Football Subcommittee (and Athletic director at the University

Reed, 1991 p. 128):

> Although the Football Bowl Association did a lot of blustering, saying that bowls that committed to teams prematurely could be fined as much as $250,000, the feeling now is that so many bowls broke the agreement, the FBA would make itself even more of a joke—if that's possible—by launching an investigation.

The 1991–1992 bowls also failed to produce a matchup of the top two teams and again ended without producing a consensus national champion (the AP chose Miami, while the UPI chose Washington).

Aside from the size of the television audiences which matchups of top-ranked teams would draw, the FBA has reason to be concerned that the failure to produce a national champion is an invitation for entry into their market. In 1992 the Home Shopping Network proposed to the NCAA a $33 million package for a bowl to be held January 18, between the two top-ranked teams. Although this proposal has not advanced, the threat is clear.

In the meantime, teams and bowls were reorganizing themselves to meet the evolving market conditions. A new football conference, the Big East, was formed (including Miami as its most prominent team).[26] This new conference, together with four other conferences (Atlantic Coast, Big Eight, Southeastern, and Southwest) and Notre Dame joined in a consortium with the Orange, Sugar, Cotton, and Fiesta bowls, whose object is to reverse the unraveling of transaction dates and to increase the chance of a bowl game between the two highest-ranked teams.[27] To this end, the consortium agreement specifies a somewhat complicated procedure by which teams will be matched to bowls, based on their rankings at the end of the regular season.[28] Before the agreement was concluded, the Blockbuster Bowl weighed in with an offer to become a closed bowl with the champions of the Big East and ACC, but this was rejected. After the consortium agreement was made, and long before the start of the 1992–1993 season, the Blockbuster Bowl announced (on May 20, 1992) an agreement that Penn State (one of the few remaining independent teams, but due to join the Big Ten Conference in 1993) would play in its game on January 1, 1993. The Blockbuster's chair, Charlie Frankel, was quoted in *The New York Times* (21 May 1992, p. B7) "We've just set a new precedent for pick-'em day."[29]

This market is thus in considerable flux. Having failed in repeated attempts to enforce a uniform date for transactions, large parts of the market are moving to increasingly centralized procedures (i.e., involving more teams and bowls), while other parts of the market are unraveling further.

4. *Business-School Markets: New MBA's and Marketing Professors.*—We conclude the examples of unraveling with a brief mention

---

[26] The Big East teams are Boston University, Miami, Pittsburgh, Rutgers, Syracuse, Temple, Virginia Tech, and West Virginia.

[27] The goals and form of the consortium evolved out of complex multilateral negotiations, with the initial impetus being the desire of the new Big East conference to assure its champion of a postseason bowl. The Big East and ACC together approached the Orange, Sugar, and Cotton Bowls, and Notre Dame and the Fiesta Bowl became involved in the course of the negotiations.

[28] If the top two teams are from the Big East, ACC, or Notre Dame, they will play each other in the Fiesta Bowl. Otherwise the bowl whose host team (under the preexisting semi-closed bowl agreements) is the highest ranked will get the highest ranked of the Big East, ACC, or Notre Dame teams, and the remaining teams will be allocated in order of rankings. As of this writing some details (such as the current status of the semi-closed bowl agreements) seem still to be under discussion.

[29] At the end of the 1992–1993 regular season, the consortium did indeed produce a match between the number-1 and number-2 ranked teams (Miami and Alabama, respectively) in the Sugar Bowl, and the victor, Alabama, was subsequently ranked number 1 in both the writers' and coaches' polls. The Blockbuster Bowl did not fare as well as in the previous year, however: although Penn State was considered a contender for the national championship when it accepted the Blockbuster offer before the season began, it entered the Blockbuster Bowl ranked number 21 at the end of the season, where it played (and lost to) 13th-ranked Stanford.

of two markets which depart from the pattern of the markets discussed above in that the unraveling they have experienced seems to be regarded as being of manageable proportions. Therefore, in these markets, no market-wide efforts have been made to reverse it. Our point in concluding the discussion of stage-1 unraveling with these markets is to avoid giving the impression that unraveling necessarily leads to market reorganization.

The top MBA graduates from the most prestigious business schools have for some years been regarded as attractive recruits for a variety of businesses. The most aggressive firms (e.g., consulting firms in the 1970's, and investment banking firms in the 1980's) have periodically engaged in early offers with short fuses. (Margaret Neale and Max Bazerman [1991 p. 123] also describe a variation on exploding offers in which the offered salary goes down for every day that the candidate delays accepting.) Although we are not aware of any attempt to organize a market-wide response to such practices, the deans of particular business schools whose students are the subjects of such offers have sometimes responded with threats to deny the offending firms easy access to their graduates, typically by denying them on-campus recruiting facilities. There seems to be little evidence or consensus on how effective such sanctions have proved to be.

The situation in marketing is that the major job market for new business-school professors of marketing is organized around the summer meetings of the American Marketing Association. The market thus occurs a little over a year in advance of the date for which the positions are to be filled. This was not always the case: in the 1950's the American Marketing Association still held its market-oriented meeting at the Allied Social Sciences meetings between Christmas and New Year's Day. The change to the earlier meeting means that graduate students are often interviewed and hired before having begun their dissertation work (and there is a consequent problem when the time comes for tenure evaluation). The marketing historian Stanley Hollander summarizes the situation in a letter (to Roth, 8 April 1991) as follows:

When I received my doctorate in February of 1954, the schools at which I interviewed wanted to read my dissertation. Today, most of us are hiring new entrants at the ABD level. Our practice here [at Michigan State University's Graduate School of Business] is to make appointments at the visiting assistant level until the degree is obtained, in good part to avoid the start of the tenure clock.

Thus the unraveling in this market has involved not only the time at which new marketing professors are recruited, but also the point in their careers at which they assume their new responsibilities. However, as in the MBA market, we are not aware of any market-wide response to the unraveling of the market.

Having now looked at markets whose unraveling has promoted active attempts to control it and at markets whose unraveling has been regarded much more casually, we turn to markets which have enjoyed at least a measure of success at controlling the unraveling of appointment dates.

B. *Examples of Stage 2: Enforcement of Uniform Dates*

We have already seen some of the difficulties encountered by markets that attempt to halt unraveling by enforcing a regime of uniform dates—in the markets for Federal Court clerkships and postseason college football bowls. In both of those markets, the attempts to enforce uniform dates never really met with any success at all and were abandoned. In this section, we consider two markets in which systems of uniform dates and times have been employed for many years.

The first of these is the market for new humanities and social-science graduates of elite Japanese universities.[30] Repeated at-

---

[30]Preeminent among these elite universities is the University of Tokyo, but the group of universities whose graduates are the targets of the competitive recruiting practices to be described also probably includes, to different degrees, Hitotsubashi, Hokkaido, Keio, Kobe, Kyoto, Kyushu, Nagoya, Osaka, Tohoku, Tokyo Insti-

tempts have been made to enforce uniform dates before which positions should not be advertised, students should not be recommended, applicants should not be interviewed, and offers should not be made. Periodically, these attempts have broken down. However the formalities of observing at least some of these dates have often been observed, with the breakdowns coming in a variety of informal arrangements, including some unusual strategic behavior unique to this market (as far as we know).

The second market to be considered in this section is the market for clinical psychology interns in the United States. That market has employed a system of uniform dates and times since the early 1970's, although it has faced continuous problems.

1. *Japanese University Graduates.*—We will concentrate on the years 1970 through 1990, a period for which we have contemporaneous accounts.[31] However, the unraveling of the market, and even attempts to halt the unraveling through the establishment of uniform times for recruiting, apparently go back much further.[32]

The 1970's were marked by a series of agreements between firms (through various employers' federations such as Nikkeiren [The Japan Federation of Employers' Associations]), university organizations (such as the Association of National Universities),

and government ministries (including the Ministry of Education, and later the Labor Ministry) concerning dates at which various recruiting activities could be undertaken. These agreements failed in two ways. First, some of their clauses, such as those which prohibited firms from giving employment exams or from having students make visits to companies before certain dates, were largely ignored. Others, such as those which prohibited firms from making formal offers of employment before a certain date, were circumvented through informal guarantees of employment, known as *naitei*. As a result, employment decisions for university graduates unraveled despite these agreements. The popular name for this unraveling is *aota-gai*, which translates as "harvesting rice while it is still green." In what follows, keep in mind that the Japanese academic year begins in April and ends in March.

In 1970, amidst concern that the universities might be disrupted in June in connection with the renewal of the U.S.–Japan security treaty, *Asahi Shimbun* (22 April 1970, morning edition, p. 14) reported that *aota-gai* was being replaced by *sanae-gai*—"harvesting rice while it is newly planted." Despite an agreement that companies would not begin recruiting before June 1 (for technical graduates, and July 1 for others), the story reported that large banks had already held their employment exams, and the chairman of the employment committee of the Union of Private Universities was quoted as saying that there were cases of *naitei* to juniors in the middle of February. The situation was apparently not improved by an adjustment of the dates in 1972 which prohibited the beginning of recruitment only until May 1 of the junior year.

In 1975, a new attempt to reverse unraveling was initiated, in which companies were to invite students for on-site interviews only after October 1 of the senior year, and were not to hold employment exams until November 1. When this too failed to halt the unraveling, a 1979 agreement specified that a committee including the Labor Ministry would monitor compliance, and firms which violated the agreement would, after a

---

tute of Technology, and Waseda. (Engineering graduates are apparently hired in a somewhat different way, which appears to involve long-term relationships between some companies and some professors.)

[31]Our published sources are from the *Japan Economic Journal* and the *Japan Times*, which are both in English, and from *Asahi Shimbun* and *Nihon Keizai Shimbun*. We are grateful to Ms Hiromi Tojima of the University of Tokyo for translations of these latter accounts from Japanese into English.

[32]A retrospective story in the *Nihon Keizai Shimbun* (12 October 1984, evening edition, p. 3) says "The history of the agreement goes back to 1953. It was a time of job shortages, and students came to start their job-hunting activities early. At a meeting for solving the problem, seven universities, 28 business organizations, and some ministries concerned agreed that universities should not begin to recommend seniors to companies until October 1."

warning, be publicly named. This had the effect of increasingly driving the recruiting "underground" (so that company visits were arranged informally, through the "old boy" network of alumni from a given university), but it did not halt the unraveling. In 1981 the Labor Ministry announced that starting in 1982 it would no longer monitor the agreement, since it had no effective way of enforcing it.[33]

Throughout the 1980's, attempts were made first to maintain the "ten-eleven" (October-November) dates and, after 1986, an earlier schedule that allowed contacts in August and offers in October. These attempts were without notable success. The offering of *naitai* continued, particularly as the disadvantages of trying to abide by the official dates while others did not became apparent.[34] There were increasing reports that companies would essentially try to kidnap those applicants to whom they had offered *naitai*, to prevent them from interviewing at other companies. (Notice the close strategic relationship of this tactic to the exploding offers observed in the markets for American lawyers.) In 1988 the Nikkeiren established a telephone line to which students could appeal if they found themselves in this situation.[35] Summarizing

the history of these "gentlemen's agreements," the *Japan Economic Journal* wrote (17 March 1990, p. 1) "there is an even greater shortage of gentlemen corporate recruiters than university graduates."

Thus, over a period of more than 20 years, attempts to set dates for the recruiting of new university graduates and for the signing of formal contracts has not effectively controlled the dates at which de facto recruiting, through informal channels, takes place.

We turn next to a market in which the control of transaction dates has been more successful, although certainly not without many problems.

2. *Clinical Psychology Internships.*—Clinical psychologists are employed as interns prior to completing their doctoral training. The first internships seem to have been established in the early part of this century and to have become a regular part of professional development in the 1930's and 1940's.[36] In recent years the market has involved just over 2,000 internships each year, offered at about 500 sites (Philip Laughlin and John Worley, 1991 p. 434; Carl Zimet, pers. comm. [letter to Roth, 21 June 1991]) (see also Bernhard Blom et al., 1990a p. 20).

The timing problems experienced by this market were a sufficient cause of concern by the 1960's that a new organization, the As-

---

[33] The *Nihon Keizai Shimbun* (27 November 1981, morning edition, p. 1) has a story covering the Labor Ministry announcement and reviewing the history of the various failed "gentlemen's agreements" about recruiting. Note the parallel between the Labor Ministry's decision and the decision of the NCAA no longer to try to enforce a date for college bowl transactions.

[34] The *Japan Economic Journal* (5 October 1985, p. 4) summarizes the situation by saying "no parties to the agreement are keeping their word," and notes that "*Aota-gai* is a situation in which the honest are made fools of."

[35] The following description (in a year when first contacts were prohibited before August 20) is from the *Japan Times* (8 July 1989):

Many companies, after offering *naitei*, also resort to "*kosoku*," or physical restraint, in order to prevent the students from having contact with other companies.... In order to help these students, Nikkeiren last year established a telephone line at its Employment and Education Policy Department to listen to their complaints. Nikkeiren had to issue warnings to some of the companies to "release" the students. They received 530 calls from students and 157 companies were re-

ported to have resorted to detaining students.... This year, the hotline was set up on April 17, about 10 weeks earlier than last year. Nikkeiren Chairman Eiji Suzuki said last week that it has already received 108 calls.

In some of the cases, students were told to report to companies on July 1 and July 2. "July 2 is the day for the state examination for public officials" [a Nikkeiren] spokesman said. "It is quite possible that companies were trying to prevent the students from taking that exam."...

Nikkeiren's 1984 survey, which covers most major companies, shows that 88.4 percent of them think the agreement on recruiting graduates should be continued, although 87.7 percent admitted that they did not abide by it.

[36] Philip Laughlin and John Worley (1991) identify what may have been the first internship, in 1908, and discuss the emergence of an accreditation process in the 1930's and 1940's.

sociation of Psychology Internship Centers (APIC) was founded in 1968 specifically to combat it. James Stedman (1989) reports that, in 1972, APIC proposed a system of uniform dates of appointment which was adopted for the 1973 recruiting season. Subject to many modifications and periodic reevaluations, the system remains in use today.[37] Starting in the 1970's, APIC began to distribute a newsletter, which provides a record of the virtually continuous difficulties which the system of uniform dates and times has experienced, and of the modifications considered (and occasionally adopted) to ameliorate these.

One set of modifications involved the period for which offers were required to remain open. In 1976 this period was reduced from five days to three, and in 1978 from three days to one. The Uniform Notification Plan for most of the 1980's specified that offers are to be made no earlier than 8:00 A.M. Central Standard Time of the second Monday in February, and that offers must be accepted or rejected by noon the next day.[38]

This system of uniform times has generated complaints about several kinds of behavior. The first of these concerns simple violations of the rules, involving offers made before the legal time or demands for a response before the legal time. For example, surveys conducted by Michael Carifio et al. (1987) and Carifio and William Grace (1992a,b) find that between 10 percent and 25 percent of applicants surveyed report being made an offer before uniform selection day. (One attempt to deal with this was made in 1988, when under an "Early Acceptance" plan, offers before the second Monday in February were legalized under the condition that replies not be demanded until the usual time, but this plan was abandoned after one year.) A related complaint is that applicants are subjected to a great deal of informal pressure both to indicate in advance whether they will accept an offer and to reply before the deadline.[39]

Still a third class of complaints concerns congestion in the final hours of the system. Some of this simply involves the difficulty of transacting a good deal of business in a

---

[37]About the early, undocumented history of this organization, Stedman (1989 p. 35) remarks: "All three of these founding fathers [of APIC] were very clear about one historical fact, namely that APIC was organized primarily to deal with a lack of regularity in the intern selection process. Ivan Mensh said students of the late '60s complained about deals being made between internship sites and certain select students."

Ronald Fox (1990) recalls that "Obtaining agreement for a Uniform Notification date was difficult, but most people agreed that some order needed to be brought to the chaos created by every program setting dates as it pleased.... Some of our major problems with a uniform date were in large cities with several internship programs which competed with each other for students. Each was afraid to agree to an honor system which might leave them 'holding the bag' when notification date arrived."

In 1992 APIC changed its name to the Association of Psychology Postdoctoral and Internship Centers (APPIC), reflecting the growth of postdoctoral as well as predoctoral internships. To avoid confusion we will refer to the organization as APIC, the name it operated under throughout the period we discuss.

[38]The formal rules of the present Uniform Notification Procedure were first adopted for the 1979–1980 season (although, as will be discussed, some modifications were adopted in 1988, and subsequently dis-

carded). The relevant rules read as follows (Stedman, 1989 pp. 37–38):

2. Accepted applicants are to be notified no earlier than 8:00 A.M. Central Standard time (CST) of the second Monday in February. Those applicants must respond no later than 12:00 CST the following day.
3. Alternate applicants accepted between 8:00 A.M. Monday and 12:00 noon on Tuesday may be asked to respond by Tuesday noon CST but not earlier.
4. Applicants accepted after Tuesday noon should be prepared to make a relatively quick decision, on the assumption that they have already considered any earlier offers....
6. Applicants who are being thought of as alternates for the center's first choices may be notified of their alternate status but not before 8:00 A.M. CST on the second Monday in February.
7. Once a center's positions are filled, all remaining applicants should be so notified.

In 1991 these rules were again modified. Among other changes, the interval specified in rules 2–4 was reduced from 16 hours to 7 hours. See Roth and Xing (1994) for a discussion of the implications of changes in the time during which offers remain open.

[39]Just as the discussion of legal markets by lawyers often focuses on the precise wording of rules, clinical psychologists frequently discuss the *affective* responses to these practices, such as how stressful and anxiety-provoking they are.

short time and in accordance with the guidelines.[40] However there are also numerous reports of particular behavior which concentrates transactions very late in the specified period. This includes the holding of multiple offers by candidates (rather than the prompt rejection of all but one) and the practice of internship centers telling many candidates that they are highly ranked alternates (with the consequence that they do not accept offers already received until the last moments before noon on Tuesday).[41]

An interesting feature of the history of this market is that, motivated by the success of the centralized market-clearing system used by medical graduates, there have been proposals virtually throughout the history of the uniform notification plan that the psychologists too should move to a centralized matching mechanism (see e.g., Ivan Mensh and Orgel, 1978; Association of Psychology Internship Centers, 1981, 1985; Briggs, 1984).[42] None of these proposals got beyond the proposal stage until the 1990–1991 recruiting season, when a trial run of a centralized matching procedure was conducted, for information purposes, alongside the usual procedure, by which transactions were actually made (see Blom and Sanford Pederson (1988, 1989; Blom et al., 1989, 1990a,b). However, following problems in the way this trial run was conducted, the computerized system was rejected by the

APIC membership. Thus, with all its troubles, the Uniform Notification Procedure remains in place.

We turn next to some markets which have adopted centralized market-clearing procedures.

C. *Examples of Stage 3: Centralized Market-Clearing Procedures*

Just as familiarity with the American medical market permitted regional markets in Britain to move (in some cases directly) from unraveling to centralized market-clearing, the medical model was familiar in other health-care professions as well. We next consider two nonmedical health-care markets that turned to the medical model of centralized matching to solve their timing problems.

1. *Other Health-Care Markets: Dentistry and Optometry.*—A 1984 survey of residency program directors in the dental specialty of oral and maxillofacial surgery (OMS) revealed that just over 70 percent of them "had experienced the late withdrawal of an applicant who had initially accepted a firm offer" (John Kelly, 1985a p. 1). This was after unsuccessful attempts had been made to adopt a system of uniform dates.[43] Shortly thereafter, a decision was made to adopt a centralized market-clearing process, and National Matching Services Inc., the firm which runs the medical match for the National Resident Matching Program, was commissioned to run a similarly organized dental match.

---

[40] For example David Briggs (1984 p. 11) reports that filling four positions from 44 applications involved more than 100 completed phone calls and another 100 attempted calls.

[41] Guidelines to encourage students to formulate their preferences ahead of time and quickly reject all but the most preferred offer have been proposed from time to time without notable success (see e.g., Cynthia Belar and Sidney Orgel, 1980 p. 674; Grace, 1985 p. 480). It is obviously to the advantage of an internship center to have as many as possible of its acceptable candidates available until the last minute, in case it should be rejected by its more preferred candidates.

[42] The Association of Psychology Internship Centers (1985) reference involved the solicitation of detailed cost estimates from Eliott Peranson, currently of National Matching Services Inc., which operates the medical match on behalf of the National Resident Matching Program.

[43] Responses were received from 70 of the 99 non-military residency programs, covering 140 out of a possible 195 positions (with the largest program offering four positions). A parallel survey of residents elicited responses from 190 of the residents. An interesting difference between the two surveys is that only three program directors reported making offers before November 3, but 39 residents reported *receiving* offers before November 3. Kelly (1985b p. 3) remarks "This discrepancy in reporting points graphically to the problem or deficiency of our present system [of uniform dates], that of a major breach of ethical, honest behavior."

This match, which is now called the Post-doctoral Dental Matching Program, was sufficiently successful so that it has grown in the ensuing years to include other dental specialties. In addition to OMS the match for 1992–1993 included pediatric and peri-odontal residencies, as well as residencies in general practice (mostly in hospitals), and advanced education in general dentistry (mostly in dental schools). Together these made for a market of 1,204 positions. How-ever, although the match is organized so that applicants may apply to any combina-tion of programs, the submarkets are largely distinct: of 1,837 applicants for 1992–1993 positions, 1,527 (83 percent) applied to only one kind of program. Of the 993 applicants who ranked one of the three specialty pro-grams, only 70 (7 percent) had ranked an-other kind of program first (National Matching Services, 1992).

In optometry,[44] the success of centralized matching is not yet clear. Residencies in optometry first became available in the mid-1970's, to provide opportunities for spe-cialty training, and as part of a movement for optometrists to become more involved in primary care (instead of merely diagnosis and vision correction). Only a small number of residency positions are available, and most of these are affiliated with Depart-ment of Veterans Affairs (VA) health-care facilities (where a one-year residency gives two years of seniority for those who obtain a position at a VA facility). In 1990 the Amer-ican Optometric Association accredited 40 residency programs at VA facilities and an-other dozen at schools of optometry and other sites.

The National Association of VA Op-tometrists (NAVAO) organized and oper-ated a centralized match in 1986. However, while the majority of VA programs partici-pate in the NAVAO match, by 1990 it had attracted only one school-based residency program to participate, so that a substantial portion of the market continues to operate in a decentralized way. This places some participating programs at a disadvantage in competing with nonparticipating programs. The rates of participation thus appear to be in flux, and it is too early to predict the outcome. (We will see a similar situation when we discuss the market for radiation oncology residencies, and the effect of par-ticipation rates will be discussed in Section V in connection with Examples 4 and 5 and Theorem 2.) In 1991 NAVAO handed over control of the matching service to an inde-pendent organization newly created for the purpose, Optometric Residency Matching Services, Inc., in an effort to encourage the inclusion of the non-VA residency programs (but as of 1992 only two such programs had chosen to participate). Another problem facing this match is that students have sometimes reneged on their match agree-ment and taken a nonresidency position (rather than a different residency).

We turn next to some centralized match-ing procedures which have halted further unraveling in the markets in which they operate, but which are scheduled so that the matches that are made through them still occur quite early by the historical stan-dards of those markets.

2. *Fraternities and Sororities.*—Fraterni-ties and sororities are social organizations for undergraduate men and women widely found on the campuses of American col-leges and universities. In the 1800's, only seniors were admitted to membership, but competition for desirable members caused an unraveling of dates at which members were recruited. (This unraveling, or "rush-ing," entered the language as the name still used for fraternity and sorority membership drives today.) By the turn of the century, recruitment dates had unraveled through the four years of college, and (at least in some regions of the country) into the preparatory schools from which particular colleges traditionally drew their students. In 1928 the National Panhellenic Conference, the umbrella organization of sororities, adopted a centralized matching procedure, called the Preferential Bidding System, which effectively deferred recruiting until

---

[44] This description is primarily based on conversa-tion and correspondence with Tim Messer.

students had actually arrived on campus as freshmen. However no similar centralized system was adopted by fraternities (see Mongell and Roth [1991] and the references quoted there).

In the intervening years, the demographic makeup and geographic mobility of college students has changed sufficiently so that recruitment before college admission has become increasingly impractical. Today both sorority and fraternity recruitment begin at roughly the same time—as soon as students arrive on campus—even though only the sororities use a centralized mechanism. Thus this is a case in which the continued use of a centralized mechanism no longer appears to have a major impact on the time at which recruitment takes place. Note however that the benefits of sorority and fraternity membership can also begin as soon as students are admitted to membership, since today it is common for sororities and fraternities to own houses in which their members live, and membership becomes a focus of social life throughout the four years of college.

Thus, unlike the professional labor markets we consider, the early recruiting of contemporary fraternities and sororities does not involve agreeing to transactions long before they will be consummated.[45] We turn next to consider some medical labor markets in which centralized mechanisms are used to make transactions long before the start of employment.

3. *Medical Specialties.*—As medical practice has become more specialized, entry-level positions have also, and first-year generalist internships have been replaced by more specialized first-year residencies.[46]

However, medical specialization requires clinical experience considerably past the first postgraduate year, and while the unraveling in appointment dates for first-year postgraduate (PGY1) positions had been successfully reversed by the introduction of centralized matching, unraveling for more advanced residencies continued. To deal with this unraveling, beginning in 1978 and gathering steam throughout the 1980's, many specialties successfully introduced centralized matching for their advanced residencies and fellowships (i.e., for positions which begin 2–6 years after graduation from medical school). Unlike the centralized match for PGY1 positions, the matches for these more advanced positions often take place substantially in advance of the beginning of employment. In fact, a number of matches for PGY2 and PGY3 positions take place before the match for PGY1 positions.

In 1978, a centralized match was introduced for second-year postgraduate positions in ophthalmology.[47] This match is independent of and takes place before the National Resident Matching Program (NRMP) match for PGY1 positions. Since then, other matches which operate independently and take place before the NRMP

---

[45] In this regard, an interesting account of various of the institutions that have been used to allocate housing to Harvard undergraduates is given by Susan Collins and Kala Krishna (1993).

[46] Reflecting this change, the matching program for first-year medical graduates was called the National Intern Matching Program prior to 1968 when it was renamed the National Intern and Resident Matching Program, and in 1978 it took its current name, the National Resident Matching Program, following the demise of the first-year rotating internship.

[47] August Colenbrander, who organized that match, writes (letter to Roth, 19 February 1991): "For twelve years before that, the desirability of a match had been discussed, but people did not dare enter into one for fear that some program directors would not 'play by the rules.' The running joke was: 'Father you need to get me into Medical School, I was just offered an Ophthalmology residency.'" Colenbrander has subsequently become the coordinator for the PGY2 and three matches in neurological surgery, otolaryngology, and neurology, for the PGY4–6 matches in plastic surgery, and fellowships in four ophthalmology subspecialties (retina, cornea, glaucoma, and pediatrics). Based on the publicly available description of the matching algorithm used in these matches, it appears to be a stable matching mechanism, at least for uncomplicated matches. Because of the complexity of these markets, and the occurrence of special cases (e.g., the matching of married couples [see Roth, 1984]), we are not in a position to assert that the algorithms always produce stable matchings. However, for the purposes of this paper, it seems justified to count both these matching algorithms, and the NRMP specialty matches (to be described shortly) as stable mechanisms.

have been established for PGY2 positions in neurological surgery, for PGY2 and PGY3 positions in otolaryngology, and for PGY3 positions in urology. In these matches, medical-school seniors obtain their second- and third-year employment from 18 to 30 months before they will begin work, and also *before* they will be matched to their PGY1 positions.

Part of the reason for this may have to do with the fact that students need particular preparation to take different advanced positions, and advanced knowledge of admission to a specialty with limited entry can guide this preparation. But the timing also seems to reflect competition among specialties. For example, dermatologists initially attempted to schedule an independent match for advanced positions during the PGY1 year instead of during the senior year of medical school but had to abandon this initial attempt in view of the timing of other matches (Colenbrander, pers. comm. [letter to Roth, 24 March 1991]).[48] In contrast, the somewhat less competitive specialty of neurology (cf. Colenbrander, 1989) runs a two-tier match, with only some PGY2 positions being filled by medical-school seniors 18 months in advance, and the rest being filled by first-year residents, only six months in advance.

In the 1980's, the NRMP also began to include PGY2 positions in its match, so that medical-school seniors could match *simultaneously* to their PGY1 and their PGY2 positions.[49] The specialties offering a substantial percentage of their PGY2 positions through the NRMP are anesthesiology, emergency medicine, orthopedics, physical medicine, psychiatry, and diagnostic radiology (see National Resident Matching Service, 1990; Allen Lichter, 1992). While these specialty submarkets allow students to apply to more than one specialty, in practice this seems to be rare: in 1990, 82 percent of seniors participating in the match applied to only one

kind of specialty program (National Resident Matching Program, 1990 p. 9).[50] Similarly, the NRMP has sponsored separate matches by a dozen advanced specialties, under its Specialties Matching Services, and a common match for three advanced medical subspecialties under the Medical Specialties Matching Program.[51] Despite their common match (in which applicants can apply to more than one kind of program), even the markets for the three medical subspecialties are quite distinct: out of 2,029 applicants in the 1991 match, 1,933 (95 percent) applied to programs in only one subspecialty (National Resident Matching Program, 1991b table 5). Part of the reason for how separate these specialty markets are may have to do with the process of preparing for each match, which in some cases begins long before the match itself. We will speak about aspects of this shortly, when we discuss examples of stage-4 unraveling.

It should be noted that not all specialty matches were successful on their first attempt. In the 1960's, independent specialty matches were attempted and subsequently abandoned in psychiatry, radiology, orthopedic surgery, and pediatrics (see Lichter, 1992 p. 1148). It is illuminating therefore to consider the case of radiation oncology, which is currently in the process of trying to organize a match.

---

[48] Dermatology now runs such a match as part of the Specialties Matching Service of the NRMP.

[49] For each PGY2 position, a student may submit a supplemental preference list of PGY1 positions.

[50] Arrangements can also be made for students who wish to participate in more than one of the four PGY2 specialty matches run by Colenbrander (letter to Roth, 5 March 1991), although here too this seems to be the exception.

[51] The specialty matches run separately under the Specialties Matching Services are colon/rectal surgery, dermatology, emergency medicine, foot/ankle surgery, hand surgery, ophthalmic plastic and reconstructive surgery, pediatric emergency medicine, pediatric orthopedics, pediatric surgery, reproductive endocrinology, sports medicine, and vascular surgery (see National Residents Matching Program, 1991a). The internal-medicine subspecialties run under the Medical Specialties Matching Program are cardiovascular disease, gastroenterology, and pulmonary disease (see National Resident Matching Program, 1991b). The exact make-up of these programs changes from year to year.

Lichter (1992) reports that, in 1989, the first year of the radiation-oncology match, out of approximately 150 positions, only 120 were included in the match (and apparently some of the most competitive positions were not), and "a significant number of candidates withdrew to occupy the 30–35 residency slots that were offered outside the match" (p. 1151).[52] He notes that additional programs withdrew in the second year of the match and that a larger number of candidates withdrew after entering the match to accept these positions. As Lichter notes (p. 1149):

> When there are far more applicants than there are training positions, the temptation for an applicant to take a residency position offered outside the match is nearly overwhelming. Since non-match programs are not bound by a uniform acceptance date, such programs often preempt the match process by making offers days or weeks in advance of the match deadline. If sufficient numbers of applicants are removed from the match process due to this unfair competition, the specialty match inevitably collapses. This threatens to happen currently in Radiation Oncology.

Thus in radiation oncology, as in optometry, participation in the match is still in flux.[53] In Section V we will consider why the percentage of participants may be so important.

With the proliferation of advanced positions, medicine starts to give us a picture of unraveling not only in entry-level labor markets, but throughout the initial decade of increasingly specialized career paths. The many medical specialty markets exhibit sur-prisingly little overlap, in terms of how many applicants for one kind of specialty also apply for positions in other specialties that may be available through the same match. The process of unraveling that has brought the different submarkets to the point where they wish to participate in a centralized match has occurred fairly separately as well, with different specialties joining at different times, often after experimenting with attempts at a uniform appointment date.[54,55]

However, as we have begun to note, the establishment of centralized matching mechanisms—even stable mechanisms—does not necessarily end such unraveling. We turn now to consider this phenomenon in more detail.

D. *Examples of Stage 4: Unraveling Before a Centralized Mechanism*

It would be surprising, given the intensity of strategic behavior that we have observed in markets in stage 1 or stage 2, if all efforts to gain competitive advantage ended when markets established centralized market-clearing procedures, even if the mechanisms involved are stable. Some of the most widely reported practices, such as the efforts of employers to extract from students pledges to rank them first, may or may not involve an actual unraveling of the dates at which

---

[52]The match was held in December 1989. Prior to 1989, offers had customarily been extended to medical-school seniors in October and November (see Lichter, 1991 p. 1150). Compare this to the January and February match dates for the other specialties.

[53]For the 1993 match, radiation oncology participated in the NRMP match, with six programs offering 10 first-year positions and 60 programs offering 129 second-year positions.

[54]That is not to say, of course, that there is not interaction between different specialty markets, particularly for the relatively junior (PGY2 and PGY3) positions. A medical-school senior who participates in one of the pre-NRMP matches (e.g., in ophthalmology) and fails to obtain a position goes on to pursue another specialty through the NRMP. However, many of the other most competitive specialties are already foreclosed to such a student. An interesting question which is far beyond the scope of the present study is how the relative timing of entry into different specialties—and the early timing of all of the most competitive of them—influences the pattern of physician choice of specialties, including primary-care specialties.

[55]For some of the earliest discussions about matching in the different specialties, which shed light on their history and prehistory, see José Barchilon and Ward Darley (1968), Philip Calcagno (1968), Frederick Malkinson (1969), Sherman Coleman and Darley (1971), John Tucker et al. (1978), and Ferris Hall (1981).

decisions are made. We will concentrate here on practices which clearly do, and in which substantial resources are expended well in advance of the start of the centralized match.

Because of the long and varied experience that medical markets have had with stable matching mechanisms, they are a natural source of examples, and we will also consider the market for new graduates of Canadian law schools.

1. *Medical Markets.*—The Association of American Medical Colleges (AAMC) gathers information through an annual Graduation Questionnaire to which around 75 percent of graduating medical-school seniors reply (see e.g., Association of American Medical Colleges, 1990a). They also conduct an annual forum on problems in the transition from medical school to residency (see e.g., Association of American Medical Colleges, 1991b), which provides input from program directors as well. These sources provide evidence of some unraveling before the centralized match for both the least competitive and the most competitive positions.

At the least competitive end, the most common kind of PGY1 positions are in internal medicine, and these medical residents perform much of hospitals' day-to-day work, so it is a matter of concern to those hospitals that fail to fill all of their positions. Hospitals that fail to fill their positions in the match are left to try to fill them after the match with unmatched students, who are often graduates of foreign medical schools.[56] It appears that some of the hospitals that regularly fail to fill all their positions have begun to recruit foreign medical graduates *before* the match.[57]

At the most competitive end of the market, several specialties (orthopedic surgery and neurosurgery prominent among them) have begun to suggest to applicants that they must take part in *audition electives* if they wish to be seriously considered as candidates for residencies. An audition elective, typically taken early in the senior year of medical school, before the centralized match, is an on-site clinical experience of several weeks' duration. Thus it is not feasible for a student to audition at more than a very few programs away from his own institution. Nevertheless, in the 1991 survey, 36 percent of students planning to take a residency in orthopedic surgery, and 28 percent of students planning to take one in neurosurgery reported that they had taken *two or more* electives in that specialty at an institution *other* than their own (Association of American Medical Colleges, 1991a table 5). Over 80 percent of the students interested in those two specialties reported that they had been told by one or more programs that they were more likely to be selected if they took an audition elective in the specialty at that institution (Association of American Medical Colleges, 1991a table 4). These figures represent an increase for both specialties over the previous year (Association of American Medical Colleges, 1990b).

Note that, to the extent that programs indeed favor students who have had successful audition electives with them over students with whom they are acquainted only through ordinary interviews, the increase in audition electives means that the matching decisions are being made well before the match. Because students can take very few audition electives, their choices among certain specialties, and among programs in those specialties, are also being made increasingly early. At the same time, programs can use audition electives to inter-

---

[56] In 1990 and 1991, for example, just under 7 percent of U.S. students, but approximately 40 percent of graduates of foreign medical schools, were unmatched by the NRMP (National Resident Matching Program, 1991a).

[57] Because some foreign students who make arrangements before the match presumably do not enter the match at all, it has so far proved difficult to estimate the magnitude of this phenomenon. But see Associa-

tion of American Medical Colleges (1991b p. 8) for a brief discussion of the withdrawal of foreign students *after* the match. See also the discussion of the apparently growing use of financial incentives in this connection (Association of American Medical Colleges, 1991b pp. 10–11).

view only relatively few students, and these must be chosen even earlier during medical school than the schedule of the match would suggest. Thus, programs are faced with selecting which students to accept for audition electives on the basis of even less information than would be available at the time of the match.

A similar unraveling is at work in the market for Canadian lawyers, which we consider next.

2. *Canadian Lawyers.*—Canadian lawyers must serve an "articling" year following their graduation from law school, before admission to the bar. As in many of the markets we have discussed, where a lawyer serves his articling position has an important effect on his subsequent career, particularly as a very high percentage of articling positions at the most prestigious firms result in offers of permanent employment at the same firm.[58] The center of the market for Ontario lawyers is in Toronto, while the market in British Columbia centers on Vancouver. We will concentrate on the larger, Toronto market.

Appointment dates began to unravel in the 1970's, eventually moving back before the completion of the second year of law school. The Ontario Law Society proposed guidelines for a system of uniform dates for offers and acceptances, but this proved less than satisfactory, and in 1986 in Toronto (and in 1987 in Vancouver) a centralized matching procedure was introduced.[59]

However, in recent years, there has also been a growth among major firms of pro-grams to employ students in the summer following their second year of law school. Barry McGee at the Toronto law firm of Blake, Cassels & Graydon writes (letter to Roth, 25 March 1991) that "the vast majority of summer students return to the same firm to article," and that

> Students now feel virtually compelled to obtain a summer job in Toronto after their second year in law school and as a result, a substantial portion of the articling hiring process has now been placed on the shoulders of the summer program. Students are being hired for summer positions halfway through their second year in law school.... Everyone recognizes that this is a back-door method of obtaining an articling position.

Thus this market has come to resemble the American law-firm market, even though a centralized matching system is in place. The centralized match nevertheless continues to offer substantial advantages, even to firms that arrange much of their articling hiring in advance through summer studentships. McGee goes on to say:

> The major advantage [the matching system] has for law firms is that the firm can be assured that it will not end up hiring more students than it wanted to hire. Prior to implementation of the match, that was often a problem. Our firm generally made twice as many offers as we had positions available, and there was always a prospect that we would end up with many more [articling] students than we wished to hire.

Thus we see a tendency toward unraveling even in markets which have instituted pre-dominantly stable matching procedures.[60,61]

---

[58] In one major Toronto firm the "hire back" rate has been in the range of 60–70 percent.

[59] In both cases, the technical support for the match is provided by National Matching Services, Inc., the firm which supports the medical matches run by the NRMP, and the basic design of the match is a stable matching mechanism. The Vancouver and Toronto markets are largely separate. In 1991, there were 691 students applying for 556 positions in Toronto, and 237 students applying for 150 positions in Vancouver, with only 23 students who applied for positions in both cities (National Matching Services, 1991a, b). In 1993 Alberta (Calgary and Edmonton) implemented an articling student matching program, with a match to take place in July (Elliott Peranson, pers. comm. [letter to Roth, 13 January 1993]).

[60] However the unraveling seems to be less severe than the stage-1 unraveling observed in the American law-firm market. In the Canadian market, only the larger firms have summer programs, and the number of summer positions is typically no more than half of the number of articling positions which are ultimately filled (Peranson, pers. comm. [14 August 1992]).

[61] In the legal recession of the early 1990's, when firms are hiring fewer students and many students are

Before concluding the descriptive portion of this paper, and to further place the phenomena we describe in context, we consider several other markets in which timing seems to be important, including some academic labor markets in which the trend is toward later, rather than earlier, appointment dates.

E. *Other Markets with Institutions Related to Timing*

1. *Athletes and Osteopaths.*—Table 3 lists several markets with institutions having to do with market timing. The most closely connected to the markets already studied are the markets for athletes. Athletes are highly trained professionals whose talents are uncertain when they are young and are revealed more fully as they grow older. For athletes, physical age as well as professional training may play a large role in the resolution of uncertainty, since athletes in many sports are recruited before they have reached their physical maturity in terms of size, speed, and strength. In several American professional sports, teams acquire the services of new professional athletes through centralized drafts. However, the age at which athletes are predominantly drafted varies, with hockey and baseball drafting substantial numbers of players as they graduate from high school (and then continuing to train them in minor leagues), while basketball and football draft primarily college athletes (with college athletic teams serving

as substitutes for minor-league training). While college teams do not participate in any centralized market-clearing mechanisms, there are uniform dates before which agreements with high-school athletes cannot be finalized, with fairly strict enforcement by the NCAA.[62]

Of course athletic drafts serve other functions than control of timing, since they are also used to create the possibility of balance among teams which compete with each other. Nonetheless, the age and educational status at which athletes are eligible to enter a draft are issues that come under periodic challenge, which suggests that timing issues are of considerable importance.[63]

One aspect of athletic drafts worth mentioning is that they do not produce stable outcomes, nor do they need to, since the rules under which leagues operate do not allow a team to hire a player drafted by another team. (However, in the case of athletes who can play a second sport, or who

---

having trouble finding positions, the Toronto market is beginning to experience a limited amount of both earlier and later unraveling. Some firms are opting out of the match to make early offers to good students, and in response their competitors feel pressure to make early offers also. (This seems to have happened with firms engaging primarily in family law and in criminal litigation.) At the same time, a few small firms which have been unsuccessful in competing for the best students have decided to do their recruiting six or seven months *after* the match, so that they can avoid the expense of interviewing students who are not very interested in them, and so that they interview at a time when they will also have more information about how many articling students they will need.

[62] Nearly all Division 1A schools have agreed to abide by the rules associated with what is called the National Letter of Intent. Each year there is a date (typically in the first two weeks of February) and time (specified to the minute) before which high-school athletes cannot commit to attend a given school, by signing a National Letter of Intent. Because the letter is signed before a student's grades and standardized exam scores may be available, the school (which also signs the letter) commits itself to offer an athletic scholarship contingent on the student being eligible for academic admission. The penalty for failing to honor the commitment is that the student loses a year of eligibility to play college sports.

[63] In 1992, Major League Baseball instituted a change in its draft rules which, if it survives challenges in arbitration and the courts, will increase the percentage of players who become professionals directly out of high school. Under prior rules, a team which drafted a high-school player lost its rights to him if he went to college instead of turning pro, and he had to be re-drafted when he graduated from college. High-school players who did not receive attractive offers after being drafted could thus get a second chance, four years later, by going to college. College players are more mature: in the 1992 draft, all but seven of the 28 first-round draft choices were college players (see Bill Koenig and Deron Snyder, 1992). Under the recently changed rules, however (see e.g., Murray Chass, 1992), a team which drafts a high-school player retains the rights to his services for five years.

TABLE 3—OTHER MARKETS WITH INSTITUTIONS
RELATED TO TIMING

Market	Institution
American professional sports	
Basketball	draft
Football	draft
Hockey	draft plus minor leagues
Baseball	draft plus minor leagues
College sports	uniform signing dates
Osteopathic internships	matchmaker mechanism
Marriage	minimum legal age laws, matchmaking, "bespoke" institutions
Academic job markets in mathematics, biology, chemistry	postdoctoral positions
Medieval and modern commodity markets	uniform timing (e.g., laws against "forestalling")

have been drafted out of high school and have the option of going to college, instabilities are sometimes resolved by the threat to do so.)

A similar measure of compulsory power seems to be available in the match which places osteopathic interns. In that market, the match is conducted by the same organization that accredits schools and practitioners. The algorithm used is both unstable and easy to manipulate, but the level of control in that market seems adequate to prevent a breakdown of the matching procedures.[64]

2. *Marriage.*—A class of transactions in which unraveling is not at all uncommon is

---

[64] See Helen Baker and Janice Wachtler (1991 table 2) for the low incidence of match violations. Osteopaths use a priority matching algorithm which first seeks to make 1-A matches, then 2-A, then 1-B, and so forth (where students rank programs 1,2,3... and programs rank students A,B,C...). This procedure obviously makes students very sensitive about listing a second choice, which they might be matched to (as a 2-A match) and thus miss a chance at their first choice (as a 1-B match). In response to this, the rules of the match specify that "Students are not permitted to list any...programs...more than once, or to leave intervening blank lines (i.e., listing programs only on the first and third lines) in an attempt to subvert the matching algorithm" (American Osteopathic Association, 1992 p. 5).

in the arrangement of marriages. While in many modern societies the age at marriage seems to be getting later (see e.g., Ted Bergstrom and Mark Bagnoli, 1993), in developing countries it is not so unusual to find marriages arranged quite early, particularly for women. In some countries (India is one), minimum-age laws have proved difficult to enforce (see e.g., Geeta Ramaseshan, 1992), and at various times and places formal and informal matchmaking arrangements have emerged. In searching for a striking example of unraveling, we considered places where child marriages occur, and even primitive societies in which unborn children may be betrothed (contingent on their gender). However, the most striking example we have encountered involves a stone-age aboriginal people of Australia, the Arunta. Because the Arunta are polygynous, there is a relative shortage of women. Baldwin Spencer and F. J. Gillen (1927) describe "the most usual method of obtaining a wife" (p. 469) among the Arunta with the following example:

> A ... man and a ... woman ... had a daughter.... About the same time a ... man and a ... woman had a son born.... The two fathers consulted, and the result was that the little girl was made *Tualcha mura* to the infant boy. The latter is the prospective husband of the prospective daughter *of the ... girl*" (p. 471 [final emphasis added]).

That is, the infant girl is to be the *mother-in-law* of the infant boy. The arrangements for marriage are made by the father of the infant boy on behalf of his son, with the father of the infant girl on behalf of one of his granddaughters by his infant daughter. Thus in this society marriages are transacted more than a generation in advance of when they can be consummated.

We turn next to a collection of markets in which the time of transactions seems to be getting later, rather than earlier.

3. *Academic Markets for Mathematicians, Biologists, and Chemists.*—Rather than occupying conventional academic appoint-

ments upon completing the Ph.D., in many scientific fields it is becoming common for graduates first to obtain postdoctoral appointments—sometimes more than one—before being considered for assistant-professor positions, particularly at the most competitive universities. The National Science Foundation conducts surveys of new Ph.D.'s which contain data on the numbers going directly into conventional academic positions versus those going into postdoctoral appointments. Because the survey does not distinguish between academic appointments at research universities and others, the figures give only an imprecise picture, but they reflect a general trend that is quite clear in mathematics, biology, and chemistry. In each case, the ratio of postdoctoral positions to academic positions has climbed from 1970 to 1990. In mathematics, the ratio of postdoctoral appointments to academic appointments grew in that period from 0.08 to 0.5, in chemistry from 2.08 to 9.16, and in biology from 1.51 to 8.85 (tabulations made from table 15 of National Science Foundation [1991]).[65]

In biology and chemistry, postdocs in large labs play a role rather similar to medical interns and residents (in that they are essential for the running of the lab). There is some possibility that unraveling in these markets is beginning to go in both directions: on the one hand, more years as a postdoc are required to be competitive for tenure-track positions at top schools, while on the other hand, initial postdoctoral appointments may be made earlier and earlier in the graduate-student career.

Needless to say, it is easier to evaluate the academic promise of a new Ph.D. with two additional years as a postdoc than of a new Ph.D. In the concluding discussion, we will suggest that this tendency toward later appointment dates is a reflection of the same forces that, under different conditions

of supply and demand, cause unraveling to earlier appointment dates.[66]

For our final examples, we look to markets which operate periodically (e.g., every day or every week). In these markets timing is also important, even though it becomes harder to specify precisely what is meant by making a transaction early (since any transaction made when the market is closed is earlier than the next market but later than the previous market).

4. Medieval and Modern Commodity Markets.—Although we have so far concentrated on labor markets, similar phenomena may occur in markets generally, and in commodity markets in particular. One opportunity to look for evidence is before markets become well established and, as always, in the rules and regulations which govern markets. For example, reporting on various markets from the 13th to 16th centuries in England, Louis Salzman (1931 p. 75) reports that town bylaws often "contained clauses against 'forestalling,' that is to say, intercepting goods before they reach the open market." He goes on to say (p. 76):

> Thus at Norwich no one might forestall provisions by buying, or paying 'earnest money' for them before the Cathedral bell had rung for the mass of the Blessed Virgin; at Berwick-on-Tweed no one was to buy salmon between sunset and sunrise, or wool and hides except at the market-cross between 9 and 12; and at Salisbury persons bringing victuals into the city were not to sell them before broad day.

What is at issue here seems to be the market itself, which attracts buyers and sellers only insofar as there is a reasonable prospect that there will be a good supply of both at

---

[65]See Ehrenberg (1991) for a much fuller discussion of these data, and the difficulties in interpreting them. He notes (table 7.9) that the majority of U.S. citizens and permanent residents who take postdocs go on to academic appointments.

[66]Transactions also have a tendency to occur quite late in environments in which negotiations about terms are conducted under a deadline (see Roth et al., 1988), but it seems likely that the causes of this phenomenon are different than those studied here.

the appointed time and place.[67] In particular, the appropriate time for a market is when many buyers and sellers are gathered, and if many trades are transacted early, the market may become so diffuse as to no longer attract many participants.[68,69]

Of course the ability of market organizers to restrict the timing of transactions depends on the legal environment. In 1906 the Chicago Board of Trade instituted a regulation prohibiting members from transacting for grain in transit, after the close of the market, at any price other than the closing market bid. (That is, they did not prohibit transactions, but prohibited new bids in private transactions after the market close.) In 1913 the District Court for the Northern District of Illinois found this to be an illegal practice, in violation of the Sherman Act. However in 1918 the Supreme Court reversed this decision, holding that the regulation was a legitimate measure to establish an orderly market.[70]

A more contemporary example may be the situation which followed the collapse of the command economy in the former Soviet Union. In 1990, as the restructuring of the economy opened up new avenues of trade, there were widespread reports that shops were empty and that consumers were obtaining goods through privileged channels (e.g., at work, before goods reached shops). For example, *The New York Times* (24 November 1991, section 3, p. 1) reports that Polaroid's joint venture in the Soviet Union

> has had to hire a person just to make deals with collective farms for eggs, meat, and other essentials for its workers. Otherwise, many employees would have to skip work to forage for such things.

The more such early private deals are done, the less there is in the shops, and the longer shoppers who need to go to the shops must stand in line, and the more incentive there is for firms to try to make deals directly with suppliers. Thus, there was a tendency to unravel along the distribution chain.

IV. A Modeling Framework

We have seen considerable variety in the behavior of markets which experience unraveling of transaction times. This section seeks to place this variety into a common framework. However, we will not be proposing that all unraveling results from exactly the same cause. Instead, we consider several reasons why some participants have an incentive to try to change the timing of transactions. Since there are only two direc-

---

[67] In Pittsburgh until a few years ago, the farmers' market which runs on Tuesday and Thursday afternoons in Highland Park used to begin only after the firing of a starter's gun, but this practice was discontinued because it was felt that some of the customers objected to guns. However, the farmers maintain pressure on each other not to begin selling before the appointed time.

[68] Unraveling of a market of this fashion can take place in space as well as in time. For example, Salzman also reports (1931 p. 132) that under medieval laws markets could be prevented from being established too near to an existing market, and also, for markets on rivers, nearer to the sea:

> Besides injury through mere proximity, and anticipation in time, there might be damage due to interception of traffic.... Such interception was more usual in the case of water-borne traffic. In 1233 Eve de Braose complained that Richard Fitz-Stephen had raised a market at Dartmouth to the injury of hers at Totnes, as ships which ought to come to Totnes were stopped at Dartmouth and paid customs there. No decision was reached, and eight years later Eve's husband, William de Cantelupe, brought a similar suit against Richard's son Gilbert. The latter pleaded that his market was on Wednesday and that at Totnes on Saturday; but the jury said that the market at Dartmouth was to the injury of Totnes, because Dartmouth lies between it and the sea, so that ships touched there and paid toll instead of going to Totnes; and also that cattle and sheep which used to be taken to Totnes market were now sold at Dartmouth; the market at Dartmouth was therefore disallowed.

[69] In suggesting that laws controlling the timing of transactions contributed to the growth of exchange and commerce, we are following in a tradition of explaining other medieval legal and economic institutions in this way, as in the work of Douglass North (1990) and Avner Greif (1993), for example.

[70] *Board of Trade of City of Chicago* v. *United States*, Supreme Court of the United States, 1918, 246 U.S. 231, 38 S. Ct. 242, 62 L. Ed. 683 (see also Richard Posner and Frank Easterbrook, 1981 pp. 172–77). We are indebted to an anonymous referee for this citation.

tions (earlier and later) in which the time of transactions can be changed, different reasons sometimes change the timing in the same direction. The essential condition for unraveling is that some firms have an incentive to make early offers to workers who have an incentive to accept them.

The models we will explore are descendents of the "marriage model" proposed by David Gale and Lloyd Shapley (1962), and the "assignment model" proposed by Shapley and Martin Shubik (1972), which differ in that money may be transferred freely in the latter, but not in the former. Both of these models are "two-sided" matching models in the sense of Roth and Sotomayor (1990), in that every agent belongs to one of two disjoint sets representing, for example, firms and workers, or buyers and sellers.[71] However, where those models are static, we will consider situations in which choices are made over time; and where those models are deterministic, here we allow for uncertainty which resolves itself over time.

For simplicity, we consider situations in which there may be some "final" period T (e.g., the end of the regular college football season, or law-school graduation) after which uncertainty can no longer be resolved before transactions must be made. It is also possible to make transactions at earlier times, $T-1$, $T-2$, and so forth. At these earlier times, agents on both sides of the market may have only probabilistic informa-

tion about the state that will prevail at time T. In the examples we look at here, we keep things simple by supposing that the uncertainty is only about the qualifications and relative standings of the workers (e.g., the law students, or the college teams) and that the properties of the firms are known throughout. Both the preferences of firms for workers and the preferences of workers for firms may depend on how the uncertainty is resolved (e.g., not only may firms prefer to employ certain kinds of workers, but a student's preferences over firms will depend on his own characteristics and qualifications at time T). Thus, in signing contracts before time T for employment after time T, both firms and workers face uncertainty (e.g., a firm may not know how it will evaluate a particular student in comparison to others before final semester grades are in, and a law student may not know if he will wish to pursue a career as a litigator until after he has participated in moot court).

In this context, there is a potential for transaction times to unravel whenever it is not an equilibrium for all contracts (for employment following time T) to be signed at time T. We will discuss three related reasons—all involving pairwise instabilities —why transactions may have a tendency to move from time T to $T-1$ (or from any time t to $t-1$).

The first of these has to do with instabilities at time T. Suppose that the institutional arrangements at time T are such that, if all parties wait to make their transactions at that time, an unstable matching will result (i.e., if there will be pairs of agents, not matched to each other, who would prefer to be so matched). If the uncertainty at time $T-1$ is sufficiently small compared to the cost of being mismatched, then such agents have an incentive to make their transactions early to avoid the unstable institutions at time T (e.g., the congestion in the last moments of a uniform timing regime, or an unstable centralized market-clearing mechanism). Unraveling of this sort was observed clearly in Roth (1991).

A different reason for unraveling, which exists even if there are institutional arrange-

---

[71] Two-sidedness is natural when we consider labor markets—see Vincent Crawford (1991) for a clear discussion of some of the modeling issues. It is a little less natural when we consider the market for college football bowls, since in that market transactions involve *three* sides: two teams and the bowl. But except for the Fiesta Bowl, the most competitive bowls are of the semi-closed variety, so in the short term this market is two-sided in the period we consider, since each semi-closed bowl needs to attract only one team. Similarly, commodity markets need not be two-sided in the long term, since a buyer may turn into a seller, but it is not a bad approximation for the short term, particularly for medieval markets since many transactions by middlemen were made illegal (by laws against "regrating" and "engrossing" [see e.g., Robert Palgrave, 1910]), so that participants were either buyers or sellers of a given commodity, but not both.

ments which will lead to a *stable* matching at time T, is that some participants may prefer to arrange their transactions before some uncertainties are resolved. By moving early, they may force other participants to move early also. The result of this process can be *ex ante* as well as *ex post* Pareto inefficient.

A third reason for unraveling has to do with the attraction of being on the market when the competition for one's services will be stiff. Even if there are institutional arrangements which will lead to a stable matching at time T, it may be that the expected success of worker w in obtaining a position if everyone waits until time T depends on the competition for his services that will exist then. So if certain firms are planning to fill their positions before time T, even if these are firms that would not normally succeed in hiring worker w at time T, it may be in w's interest to accept an earlier offer.

In contrast to the models in Roth (1984, 1991) and Mongell and Roth (1991), it is not our goal here to model in detail the strategic choices facing agents in one of the particular markets. Instead, we hope to help explain the common phenomena observed in many markets (with different detailed strategic environments). Consequently we focus on simple examples. Since unraveling due to instability at time T is a phenomenon identified in Roth (1984, 1991), we concentrate on the two new potential causes of unraveling identified here: the evolving uncertainty and the exercise of market power.

A. Dynamic Models with Fixed Wages and Negotiated Wages

1. *The Marriage and Assignment Models.* —We begin by introducing the static matching models on which we will build. The basic marriage model consists of two disjoint sets of players (e.g., firms and workers) $F = (f_1, f_2, \ldots, f_n)$ and $W = (w_1, w_2, \ldots, w_m)$. An outcome is a matching between firms and workers (which may leave some firms and workers unmatched). Agents have preferences over agents on the other side of the

market (and over the possibility of being unmatched), and they prefer one matching to another if and only if they are matched to a preferred partner. (The wages associated with each job description may be thought of as fixed, and reflected in the preferences of the workers.) A matching is unstable if some agent would prefer to remain single (unmatched) rather than be matched to his partner at that matching, or if some pair of agents, not matched to each other, would each prefer the other to the partners they are matched with.

Formally, a *matching* is a one-to-one correspondence μ from the set $F \cup W$ onto itself of order two [i.e., $\mu^2(x) = x$] such that if $\mu(f) \neq f$ then $\mu(f)$ is in W and if $\mu(w) \neq w$ then $\mu(w)$ is in F. The interpretation is that, if for any agent a $\mu(a) = a$, then a is unmatched; otherwise a is matched to $\mu(a)$, who must be an agent on the other side of the market (i.e., firms are matched to workers, and vice versa). Each firm f has preferences which can be represented by an expected utility function u_f defined on $W \cup \{f\}$, and each worker w has an expected utility v_w defined on $F \cup \{w\}$. A matching μ is *unstable* if some agent a prefers a to $\mu(a)$, or if for some pair (f, w), f prefers w to $\mu(f)$ and w prefers f to $\mu(w)$. A matching is *stable* if it is not unstable. Gale and Shapley (1962) showed that the set of stable matchings is always nonempty. Furthermore, when no agent is indifferent between any two mates, there exists for each side of the market (F and W) a stable matching that is optimal for that side, in the sense that no agent on that side of the market prefers any other stable matching.

The basic assignment model also consists of two disjoint sets of players $F = (f_1, f_2, \ldots, f_n)$ and $W = (w_1, w_2, \ldots, w_m)$, and (in addition) an $n \times m$ matrix $Y = \{Y_{ij}\}$ for $i = 1, \ldots, n$ and $j = 1, \ldots, m$, where $Y_{ij} \geq 0$ is firm f_i's income from employing worker w_j. A matching μ (as above) yields a total income, $Y(\mu)$, equal to the sum over all matched firms f_i of the quantities Y_{ij} such that $\mu(f_i) = w_j$. An outcome of the model consists of a matching μ together with a nonnegative $n + m$ vector of payoffs (π, s)

$= (\pi_1, \ldots, \pi_n; s_1, \ldots, s_m)$ such that $\pi_1 + \cdots + \pi_n + s_1 + \cdots + s_m = Y(\mu)$. The interpretation is that workers can take only one job, firms have only one position, and unmatched firms and workers produce zero. Workers and firms are risk-neutral income maximizers, so that their utilities over outcomes $[\mu, (\pi, s)]$ are the same as their payoffs at those outcomes.

An outcome $[\mu, (\pi, s)]$ is *stable* if for all firms f_i and workers w_j, $\pi_i + s_j \geq Y_{ij}$. (If this constraint were not satisfied for some i and j, then the outcome would be unstable with respect to f_i and w_j, since f_i could afford to offer w_j a salary $t > s_j$ such that $Y_{ij} - t > \pi_i$, so both f_i and w_j would prefer to be matched to each other at salary t than to accept the terms of the outcome $[\mu, (\pi, s)]$.) If $[\mu, (\pi, s)]$ is a stable outcome, we will refer to μ as a stable matching and to (π, s) as a stable payoff vector, and say (π, s) is compatible with μ. Note that at a stable outcome, if $\mu(f_i) = w_j$, then $\pi_i + s_j = Y_{ij}$, so although sidepayments between agents not matched to each other are feasible, they do not occur at stable outcomes.

Shapley and Shubik (1972) showed that the set of stable outcomes is always nonempty and that a stable matching must be an "optimal assignment" that maximizes the sum of the payoffs to the firms and workers over the set of all matchings. They further showed that every optimal assignment is a stable matching, and every stable payoff vector is compatible with every optimal assignment. Thus the payoff vector is what distinguishes different stable outcomes (as far as the utility of the players is concerned). For almost every assignment matrix the stable matching is unique.[72] Shapley and Shubik showed that there always exists a firm-optimal stable payoff vector at which every firm's profit is as high as at any other stable outcome, and every worker's salary is as low as at any other stable outcome. (There is also a worker-optimal stable payoff vector, and when this is different from the firm-optimal stable payoff vector there is a continuum of stable outcomes.)

When institutional arrangements produce matches that are unstable with respect to some pair or pairs of agents, then those agents have an incentive to transact with one another early, to avoid the instability. This is the kind of unraveling that was observed by Roth (1991) in Birmingham and Newcastle. However this kind of unraveling does not explain the transitions from stable market-clearing mechanisms to the stage-4 unraveling observed in markets such as those for Canadian lawyers or neurosurgeons, nor does it explain the failure of stable stage-3 mechanisms to displace unraveling in various markets, particularly in those markets that have unsuccessfully attempted to adopt stable mechanisms. In what follows, we show that instability is neither necessary nor sufficient to cause unraveling.

2. *The Multiperiod Models.*—Agents may become matched to one another at times T or $T - 1$. At time $T - 1$ there may be uncertainty about the attributes that each worker will have at time T. The most convenient way to model this uncertainty will be to say that a worker w at time T is an agent with certain attributes, but that at time $T - 1$, before the attributes are known, the workers can be identified only as members of the set of agents $A = \{a_1, \ldots, a_m\}$, and that associated with each agent a_j is a probability distribution P_j over possible attributes. It will be sufficient for our purposes here to suppose that the attributes are something like class rank at time T, and that the probability distributions P_j are probability vectors $P_j = (p_{j1}, \ldots, p_{jm})$ with p_{jk} being the probability that agent a_j will become worker w_k at time T. (So the matrix $P = \{p_{ij}\}$ specifies the uncertain transition from the set A of time-$(T - 1)$ agents to the set W of time-T agents.)

In the fixed-wage model (based on the marriage model), the utility of firm f who matches with agent a_j at time $T - 1$ is the expected utility $u_f(a_j) = p_{j1}u_f(w_1) + \cdots + p_{jm}u_f(w_m)$. Similarly, the expected utility (for employment after time T) of

---

[72] That is, when we view an assignment matrix as a point in Euclidean $n \times m$ space, the set at which the optimal assignment is not unique has measure zero.

agent a_j who matches with firm f at time $T-1$ may depend on the resolution of the uncertainty. One extreme case is when agent a_j's utility does not depend at all on his attributes, so that his expected utility function is the same at time $T-1$ and T. Another extreme case is when agent a_j's utility depends entirely on his attributes, that is, when his utility is a simple expected utility $v_j = p_{j1}v_1(f) + \cdots + p_{jm}v_m(f)$.

In the negotiated-wage model (based on the assignment model), if at time $T-1$ firm f_i offers a salary s to worker a_j and the offer is accepted, then a_j receives a utility of s for certain, while firm f_i's expected utility is the expected value $p_{j1}(Y_{i1} - s) + \cdots + p_{jm}(Y_{im} - s)$.

At time $T-1$, each firm may either choose to wait until period T or offer to match to any one worker. (An offer in the fixed-wage model consists of the choice of some agent a_j, while in the negotiated-wage model it consists of an agent a_j and a salary s.) Each firm makes this decision without knowing the decision of other firms, and any offers are delivered simultaneously. Any worker who has not received an offer has no actions to take at time $T-1$, while any worker who has received offers may accept at most one. A worker who accepts an offer and the firm f whose offer is accepted leave the market at time $T-1$ and are matched to one another. All other workers and firms remain on the market.

For our present purpose we may model, without loss of generality, the matching at time T as a revelation mechanism. In the fixed-wage model, firms still on the market at the beginning of time T know only that any offer they made at $T-1$ was rejected, and workers still on the market know only which firms approached them at time $T-1$ and were rejected. Based on this information (and the parameters $\mathbf{M}$, which become common knowledge at time T when the uncertainty about workers is resolved), each agent who was not matched at time $T-1$ submits an ordinal preference list of acceptable partners to the revelation mechanism, which produces a match. For any marriage model $\mathbf{M}$, this defines a two-stage strategic game, $\mathbf{G} = G(\mathbf{M}, \mathbf{P}; T, T-1)$, and the one-

stage game $\mathbf{G}' = G'(\mathbf{M}; T)$ which would occur if no firms made proposals at time $T-1$.

In the negotiated-wage model, firms and workers still on the market at time T are also matched by a revelation mechanism. Any firm f_i still on the market (knowing only that any offer it made at $T-1$ was rejected) must state a vector $(Y_{i1}, \ldots, Y_{im})$ of incomes for each worker. In addition, it will be convenient to assume that a firm will not make an offer at time T to a worker who has rejected its offer at $T-1$.[73] We model this by supposing that, if f_i has made an offer to agent a_j and was rejected at $T-1$, and a_j is now worker w_k, the revelation mechanism will compute the time-T match with $Y_{ik} = -1$ (so that w_k is unacceptable to f_i, who would prefer to remain unmatched and receive 0). The revelation mechanism matches the firms and workers remaining at time T according to the firm-optimal stable outcome for the agents still on the market, according to the stated matrix $\mathbf{Y}'$ as modified to take into account offers made at $T-1$. In the one-period game played by those remaining at time T, the workers have no strategic choices, and it is a dominant strategy for the firms to state their true values (see Roth and Sotomayor, 1990 theorem 8.16).

B. Uncertainty and Transaction Times

THEOREM 1: *Both in the fixed and negotiated wage models, instability of the outcome at time T is neither a necessary nor a suffi-*

---

[73]This has the effect of "perfecting" the equilibrium we examine. There are other, more complicated ways to model this without altering the rules of the game, for example, by putting into the model a small amount of incomplete information that would not change any agent's actions at equilibrium but would cause a firm to update unfavorably its priors about a worker who deviated from equilibrium by rejecting an equilibrium offer at time $T-1$, so that after such a rejection the firm would prefer not to be matched to that worker. The reason perfection is an issue is that there is always a trivial, imperfect equilibrium at which every worker plans to reject any early offer and no firm makes any early offers.

cient condition for unraveling to occur at a perfect equilibrium.

We will prove Theorem 1 for the fixed-wage model; for the negotiated-wage model nonnecessity will follow from Theorem 3, and the proof of nonsufficiency is similar to the proof given via Example 2. To prove that instability at time T is not necessary for there to be unraveling we will suppose that the game G' produces stable matchings at all of its equilibria in undominated strategies,[74] and we will show that there may nevertheless be no equilibria of G at which all agents wait until time T to be matched.

Example 1: Unraveling Despite Stability at time T. — Let the set of firms be $F = \{f_1, f_2, f_3\}$ and the set of workers at time T be $W = \{w_1, w_2, w_3\}$. All firms have the same preferences, given by $u_{f1} = u_{f2} = u_{f3} = u$ such that the utility of being unmatched is 0, and

$$u(w_1) = 4 \quad u(w_2) = 2 \quad u(w_3) = 1.$$

All workers have the same preferences, given by $v_{w1} = v_{w2} = v_{w3} = v$ such that the utility of being unmatched is 0, and

$$v(f_1) = 10 \quad v(f_2) = 9 \quad v(f_3) = 1.$$

In the marriage market M which arises if no agents are yet matched at time T, there is a unique stable matching μ which matches firm i to worker i, that is, $\mu = [(f_1, w_1), (f_2, w_2), (f_3, w_3)]$.

Agents who are not matched before time T will participate in the stable matching mechanism G' which produces the firm-optimal stable match in terms of the stated preferences. Because there is a unique stable matching at time T, all equilibria in undominated strategies of the game $G'(M, T)$ produce the outcome μ (since it is a dominant strategy in this case for all agents to state their true preferences [see Roth and Sotomayor, 1990 theorem 4.7]).

[74] The mechanisms which produce the optimal stable matching for one side of the market have this property; see theorem 4.16 in Roth and Sotomayor (1990).

At time $T - 1$ the agents are identified as $\{a_1, a_2, a_3\}$, and the probabilities p_{jk} that a_j will become w_k at time T are given by

$$p_{11} = \tfrac{2}{3} \quad p_{12} = \tfrac{1}{6} \quad p_{13} = \tfrac{1}{6}$$

$$p_{21} = \tfrac{1}{6} \quad p_{22} = \tfrac{2}{3} \quad p_{23} = \tfrac{1}{6}$$

$$p_{31} = \tfrac{1}{6} \quad p_{32} = \tfrac{1}{6} \quad p_{33} = \tfrac{2}{3}.$$

This defines the two-stage game $G = G(M, P; T, T-1)$, about which we can say the following.

PROPOSITION 1: *Instability at time T is not a necessary condition for unraveling. In the game G of Example 1, there is no perfect equilibrium at which all agents are matched at time T. There is a perfect equilibrium at which all agents are matched at time $T - 1$.*

PROOF:

Let σ be an $(n + m)$-tuple of strategies at which no matches occur at time $T - 1$, and suppose that σ is a perfect equilibrium. Then the players must use undominated strategies at time T, and so σ produces the unique stable matching μ, which gives f_2 an expected utility of 2. Therefore, f_2 would prefer to match with worker a_1 (or even a_2) at time $T - 1$, since his expected utility from matching to a_1 at $T - 1$ is $(\tfrac{2}{3})4 + (\tfrac{1}{6})2 + (\tfrac{1}{6})1 = 19/6 > 2$. Worker a_1 would have a higher expected utility if matched to f_2 at $T - 1$, since then he would lock in a utility of 9, instead of an expected utility of $(\tfrac{2}{3})10 + (\tfrac{1}{6})9 + (\tfrac{1}{6})1 = 50/6 < 9$. Thus, the assumption that σ is an equilibrium means that a_1 does not receive an offer from f_2 (or f_1) at $T - 1$. But the assumption that σ is perfect implies that a_1 cannot plan to reject the offer if f_2 deviates from σ by making an offer to a_1 at $T - 1$. So σ cannot be a perfect equilibrium.

For the last statement in the proposition, consider the strategy $(n + m)$-tuple at which each f_i makes an offer to a_i at $T - 1$, each a_j accepts the best offer (i.e., offer from the lowest-indexed firm) he receives from f_i with $i \le j$, and every player plans to submit his true preferences at time T in case he is still in the market. This is a perfect equilibrium at which all matches are made at time $T-1$.[75] This concludes the proof of the proposition.

Note that we can interpret Example 1 along the lines of Kozinski's concern that uniform appointment dates would "eliminate a very important bargaining tool for judges competing for the most gifted clerkship candidates...." Suppose f_2 is a judge with a clerkship that is a little less desirable than that offered by f_1, but substantially more desirable than others that may be available. Then the example shows why f_2 may be unwilling to wait until law students have been in school long enough so that their records may be confidently compared, since by doing so he will always lose the best candidate to f_1. Clearly, judges f_1 and f_2 have different interests in the matter; and even though f_1 would prefer that all judges hire their clerks at time T, if f_2 goes early, f_1 prefers to go early also.[76]

We next show that unraveling need not occur even if matchings at time T will be *unstable.*

Example 2: No Unraveling Despite Instability at Time T.—Let everything be as in Example 1, except that $u_{f_1}(w_2) = 11/3$, and the matching mechanism $\mathbf{G}'$ will produce the matching $\mu' = [(f_1,w_2),(f_2,w_1),(f_3,w_3)]$ if all agents remain unmatched at time T. (All other utilities, and the probability matrix $\mathbf{P}$ remain as in Example 1.) That is, $\mathbf{G}'$ is a matching mechanism that ignores the stated preferences of the players but matches workers to firms on the basis of workers' identifiable attributes. Thus the strategies of the players in the two-stage game involve only their choices at time $T-1$. Note that the matching μ' is unstable with respect to firm f_1 and worker w_1, both of whom would prefer to be matched to each other at time T.

Despite this, f_1 has no incentive to approach agent a_1 at time $T-1$ (even though a_1 would respond positively), since his expected utility from matching with a_1 at $T-1$ is only $(\frac{2}{3})4 + (\frac{1}{6})(\frac{11}{3}) + (\frac{1}{6})1 = 3.4$, which is less than the utility of $\frac{11}{3}$ that f_1 obtains by waiting until time T. Of course, f_2 has no incentive to go early if no one else does (since he matches with w_1 by waiting until T), and although f_3 would like to go early, no worker will accept his offer at $T-1$ (even if he could credibly commit to be unavailable at time T) since even worker a_3, with the poorest prospects, would prefer to wait and take the chance that he will be the first- or second-ranked worker at time T. Thus, even though waiting until time T produces an unstable matching, it is a (perfect) equilibrium for all agents to match at time T.

Recalling our earlier discussion of the centralized market-clearing procedures used in the Cambridge and London Hospital medical schools, Example 2 suggests an additional factor which could contribute to the survival of these unstable mechanisms. Given the potential costs of unraveling, even the unstable centralized procedures employed in those two markets, which prevent unraveling, may be preferable to the decentralized procedures they replaced, which did not. The next result shows that the costs of unraveling may be borne by all of the agents.

THEOREM 2: *Unraveling may be ex ante as well as ex post inefficient, in both the fixed-wage and negotiated-wage models.*

For the negotiated-wage model, the result follows from Theorem 3. The proof for the fixed-wage model is given in the Appendix,

---

[75] The argument that the equilibrium is perfect needs to establish that there is a set of vanishingly small mistakes ("trembles") for which it is optimal for the least desirable firm's offer to be accepted at time $T-1$. If the chance that f_3 will mistakenly leave agent a_3 off its list of acceptable matches at time T is larger than the probability that one of the other agents will mistakenly fail to offer or accept a match at time $T-1$, then it is optimal for a_3 to accept f_3's offer at $T-1$.

[76] If f_2 hires student a_1 at time $T-1$, then if f_1 nevertheless waits until time T his expected utility is no more than $(\frac{1}{3})4 + (\frac{2}{3})2 = \frac{16}{6}$, but if he makes an offer to a_1 himself at time $T-1$, a_1 will accept, and f_1's expected utility would be $\frac{19}{6}$.

by considering Example A1. The essential feature of that example is that workers' utilities for different firms depend on their type at time T (e.g., how students feel about litigation firms depends on how good they turn out to be at litigation), so early matches have a chance of being mismatches.

We turn next to a different cause of unraveling.

C. *Market Power and Transaction Times*

In the two-period game $\mathbf{G} = G(\mathbf{F}, \mathbf{W}, \mathbf{Y}, \mathbf{P})$, if $\mathbf{P}$ is positive (i.e., if $p_{jk} > 0$ for all j and k) then (except on a set of measure zero) there is a positive "social cost" in arranging matches at time $T - 1$, which can be measured by the difference between the expected total income of the participants at the optimal assignment and at the match which occurs. Nevertheless, we will see that, even if a stable (and efficient) match is assured if all agents wait until time T, there is a strong tendency toward unraveling.

To see why, let $[\boldsymbol{\mu}, (\boldsymbol{\pi}, \underline{\mathbf{s}})]$ be the firm-optimal stable outcome of the one-period (time-T) assignment game $(\mathbf{F}, \mathbf{W}, \mathbf{Y})$ (i.e., $\underline{\mathbf{s}}$ is the lowest vector of salaries compatible with a stable outcome. The reason the salary $\underline{s}_j > 0$ of a worker w_j matched to firm f_i cannot be lower without producing instability is that there is some other firm f_k who would prefer to be matched to w_j if $\underline{s}_j$ were any lower (i.e., $\pi_k + \underline{s}_j = Y_{kj}$. If exactly one such firm f_k supports w_j's salary at the firm-optimal stable outcome, call f_k the *principal competitor* of firm f_i. (If the reason $\underline{s}_j$ cannot be lowered is that it equals 0, or if there are two other firms who would prefer w_j at any salary lower than $\underline{s}_j$, then f_i does not have a principal competitor. A principal competitor has to be a single firm which is keeping up the price of some worker.)[77]

For any probability matrix $\mathbf{P}$, we will say that the uncertainty is less than ε if for every agent a_j there is some k for which $1 - p_{jk} < \varepsilon$. If the uncertainty about workers' attributes resolves itself in a continuous way, we may expect that the uncertainty can be made arbitrarily small by making the periods short (i.e., by making time $T - 1$ close to time T). However, if uncertainty resolves itself in a discrete way (e.g., when exams are taken), this may not be possible. Although in Theorem 3 we speak of "sufficiently small" uncertainty, examples can be constructed in which the results go through when the uncertainty is quite large.

THEOREM 3: *Let $(\mathbf{F}, \mathbf{W}, \mathbf{Y})$ be an assignment game in which time-T matches are made at the firm-optimal stable outcome, and in which at least one firm f_k is a principal competitor. Then there exists an $\varepsilon > 0$ such that for all positive $\mathbf{P}$ with uncertainty less than ε, there is no perfect equilibrium of the game $\mathbf{G} = G(\mathbf{F}, \mathbf{W}, \mathbf{Y}, \mathbf{P})$ at which all matches are made at time T.*

PROOF:

Let $[\boldsymbol{\mu}, (\boldsymbol{\pi}, \underline{\mathbf{s}})]$ be the firm-optimal stable outcome of the assignment game $(\mathbf{F}, \mathbf{W}, \mathbf{Y})$, with $\mu(f_i) = w_j$, and f_k the principal competitor of f_i. Let σ be an $(n + m)$-tuple of strategies such that no matches are made until time T. If σ is an equilibrium then it must be that no offers were made at time $T - 1$ and rejected, because any firm f_i which makes a rejected offer at $T - 1$ could have done better by withholding the offer and preserving the possibility of being

---

[77]Note that the set of matrices $\mathbf{Y}$ for which there is at least one principal competitor is a set of positive measure, since there is an open set around such a matrix (viewed as a point in Euclidean $n \times m$ space) in which principal competitors are preserved. However the set of matrices for which there are no principal

competitors also has positive measure (although it is not open). Consider, for example, a square matrix in which the diagonal elements are all strictly greater than 1, and the off-diagonal elements are all strictly less than 1. The firm-optimal stable outcome has each f_i matched to w_i at a salary of 0, and there is an open set around this matrix at which this is also true. Thus, no firm has a principal competitor, on a set of positive measure. Xing (1992) considers a class of games in which firms are strictly ordered by their efficiency, and every firm except the most efficient firm is the principal competitor of the next most efficient firm.

matched to any worker at time T. Therefore, no early offers are made at σ, which
implies that if, contrary to the theorem, σ is
a perfect equilibrium, then the outcome at
time T must be $[\mu(\pi, s)]$.

It will be simplest to continue the argument for the case of no uncertainty (i.e., the
case such that for every agent a_j there is
some k for which $p_{jk} = 1$), and then observe
that the argument goes through for positive
matrices $\mathbf{P}$ when the uncertainty is sufficiently small. To this end, suppose now that
f_k were to deviate from σ by making an
offer to w_j at $T - 1$ (since there is no uncertainty, w_j can be identified at time $T - 1$),
and suppose that w_j were to reject this
offer. Then at time T the matrix of incomes
$\mathbf{Y}'$ would differ from $\mathbf{Y}$ in that $Y'_{kj} < Y_{kj}$.
The matching μ would continue to be an
optimal assignment for the new matrix (since
$\mu(f_k) \neq w_j$), so the only difference for w_j
would be that $s'_j < s_j$, because f_k was the
principal competitor determining the value
of s_j. Thus for any salary t with $s'_j < t < s_j$,
$Y_{kj} - t > \pi_k$. If σ is a perfect equilibrium,
w_j cannot plan to reject such an offer of t
from f_k at time $T - 1$, and it would therefore be profitable for f_k to make such an
offer. Therefore, σ is not a perfect equilibrium, and there is no perfect equilibrium at
which all matches are made at time T. To
see that the argument goes through when $\mathbf{P}$
is a positive probability matrix with sufficiently small uncertainty, note that all inequalities in the argument are strict and
would be preserved for sufficiently small
uncertainty. All that would change is that,
at time $T - 1$, f_k would make the early offer
to that agent a_q such that p_{qj} was near 1.
This completes the proof.

Theorem 3 shows that unraveling is not
an isolated phenomenon. It also underlines
the manner in which this kind of unraveling
is related to the heterogeneity of the market, since if firms and workers are largely
homogeneous, there will not in general be
any principal competitors. Thus we might
expect to see this kind of unraveling in
high-end professional labor markets rather
than in markets in which labor is a commodity. As noted above, perfect equilibrium

matching under the conditions of Theorem
3 is inefficient. That is, we can state the
following corollary.

COROLLARY: *For games as in Theorem
3, in which there is at least one principal
competitor, if the probability matrix* $\mathbf{P}$ *is positive, perfect equilibria are ex ante inefficient
(except on a set of measure zero) if the uncertainty is sufficiently small.*

V. Discussion

Having seen how unraveling occurs in a
number of markets, and having considered
some models which suggest explanations for
that unraveling, it may help put things in
perspective to consider why some markets
do *not* unravel. Consider the market for
new assistant professors of economics at
research universities. Like many of the markets discussed in Sections II and III, this is
an entry-level market for professionals. But
in this market, most transactions are not
completed until students have made substantial progress on their Ph.D. disserta-
tions and have good prospects of completing the Ph.D. before beginning their
employment in the next academic year. Why
don't academic departments of economics
"jump the gun" and hire their new assistant
professors several years before they complete their Ph.D.'s?[78]

The models we have considered suggest
that unraveling may be impeded if the uncertainty associated with hiring early is relatively large compared to the possible bene-

[78]Richard Carson and Peter Navarro (1988) provide
a nice description of the recent job market for beginning academic economists and note that a relatively
small amount of unraveling occurs in what they call the
"preemptive market." This largely occurs in the
semester before the job-market meetings at the end of
the calendar year. In the late 1960's, when new Ph.D.'s
in economics were in relatively short supply, there were
also schools which made exploding offers. For example,
in January 1970, Ohio State University was authorized
to fill six positions, and it made offers to 11 candidates,
saying that the offer would remain open only until the
first six acceptances were received (Howard Marvel
and Don Parsons, pers. comm., 1 October 1992).

fits. If it is very difficult to evaluate the research potential of an economics graduate student before a substantial part of the dissertation has been completed, as seems to be the case, the risk of hiring a poor student (as in Example 2) may prevent economics departments from attempting to make very early hires.

Note that, at research universities, the entry-level job markets in different disciplines frequently share many features (e.g., letters of reference, large professional meetings, and on-campus interviews). If these institutions tend to produce stable matchings, the reason new marketing assistant professors are today recruited well before they complete the Ph.D., while new economics assistant professors are recruited around the time at which they complete the Ph.D. and new mathematics assistant professors are recruited after postdoctoral positions, may have to do with the different balance of supply and demand in those markets.[79] However, the empirical investigation of this hypothesis may involve more than a straightforward comparison of the ratio of new Ph.D.'s to academic positions to see whether this is lowest for marketing and highest for mathematics, since not all students may have a high likelihood of being eligible for jobs in research departments, and since there are markets other than academia for new Ph.D.'s.

Another factor which may contribute to the relatively limited unraveling of the beginning market for academic economists (and even academic marketers) is that in academic markets, unlike many of the nonacademic markets considered here, it is practical to hire late as well as early. That is, a department which finds that it cannot get the new Ph.D.'s it wants can try to enter the market later instead of earlier, and hire at the associate or full-professor level. However, for most of the markets in which we have observed unraveling, this is not a practical alternative.

This is clearest when a perishable commodity like postseason college football bowl games is involved, but it is also the case in many of the professional labor markets discussed. For some of these markets, like the market for medical interns or federal court clerks, the nature of the position makes it attractive to the best junior candidates, but unattractive to candidates of similar quality later in their careers. In the market for new graduates of Japanese universities, the firms most involved in the unraveling of the market appear to be those that primarily offer lifetime employment, and so they also have little opportunity to hire senior candidates away from their competitors. For law firms, the problem of adverse selection presents itself: because the quality of an associate lawyer's work may be largely invisible outside of his firm, a firm that attempts to hire associates away from a competitor is faced with the likelihood that the competitor firm would make attractive counteroffers only to the best of its associates, so that the raiding firm would attract only the worst.[80] (In contrast, adverse selection is much less of a problem when raiding a competing academic department's associate professors, since the quality of their work can be judged from their published articles.) It may be possible to develop quantitative tests of the effect of the availability of senior candidates on unraveling in the market for junior candidates by considering markets for professional athletes such as baseball players, in which changes in the rules of free-agency have changed the availability of senior candidates.[81]

---

[79] For example, in a market with a fixed number n of firms and a variable number m of workers, it is easy to construct models with the following property: as m increases, the ability to identify with sufficiently high probability which will be the n most desirable workers decreases. Then sufficiently large m will cause recruiting to occur at time T.

[80] This problem of adverse selection is modeled by Xing (1992).

[81] If the availability of established players as free agents has influenced the costs that teams are willing to bear in competing for very young athletes, it might be possible to detect this both in the age at which the average ballplayer becomes professional and in the expenditures on minor-league teams.

The fact that unraveling may be quite inefficient suggests one reason why so much effort has been expended to halt or reverse it in the markets discussed in Sections II and III. In that context, it is worth considering what advice we can tentatively offer at this point. To date we have not observed any markets that have adopted a centralized market-clearing procedure that produces stable outcomes and then subsequently abandoned it after achieving high levels of initial participation. While the models explored in this paper suggest that this is a possibility that may yet be observed, the success of stable mechanisms where they have been adopted suggests that the stress on the market produced by the various kinds of instabilities may be cumulative, so that removing one kind of instability may go a long way to help coordinate transaction times. However, the argument used to prove Theorem 3 suggests why, in a market in which transaction times have already unraveled, it may not be a simple matter to reverse the unraveling by instituting a stable matching mechanism at some later time T.

The fact that workers have incentives to be matched when there is substantial competition for their services means that, as long as a substantial percentage of firms do not wait until time T, there will be incentives for workers to enter the market early also. Thus in markets such as radiation oncology and optometry, in which initial rates of participation in a stable mechanism are not high, the ultimate success of even a stable mechanism may be in doubt. Both the models and the experience of the many markets that have attempted to halt unraveling suggest that a cautious plan of attack would be to attempt to introduce a stable matching mechanism initially at an early time, when a substantial percentage of transactions are already taking place, and then to move the time at which the mechanism operates later only after it has attracted a high rate of participation. For markets in which a stable mechanism offers the possibility of an equilibrium at which transactions are made relatively late, this kind of gradual approach may increase the

likelihood of a successful transition from an inefficient early equilibrium to a more efficient late one. Of course, as shown by Example 1, there may be markets for which even a stable mechanism is insufficient to produce a late equilibrium.

In conclusion, the evolution of unraveling in the markets studied by Roth (1984, 1991) and Mongell and Roth (1991) was associated with the existence of worker–firm pairs which created instability in the final matchings. The present paper seeks to make two contributions. The first is to establish empirically, by considering a wider selection of markets, that unraveling of transaction times is a much more general phenomenon than had previously been evident. The second is to identify additional causes of unraveling (and of changes in the timing of transactions in either direction). We do not claim that these are the only causes of unraveling. On the contrary, unraveling seems to occur in a sufficiently wide range of markets so that it is likely that there are many causes. The additional causes we have identified have also involved pairwise instabilities (i.e., they can be studied at the level of specific worker–firm pairs), and this "pairwiseness" provides the common theoretical thread between the intertemporal instabilities introduced in this paper and the static instabilities of the classical two-sided matching models. We have also shown that unraveling may result in inefficiency. Whether the unraveling observed in any particular market is inefficient is of course a difficult empirical question. Indeed, one of the main contributions of this paper should be that it raises a host of empirical questions related to the timing of transactions.

At the most general level, this paper is about the organization and evolution of market institutions related to the timing of transactions. There is a sense in which the existence of an orderly market is a public good, and given the difficulties inherent in providing public goods, it should therefore not be so surprising that establishing a uniform time for a market may often present difficulties. For many of the markets discussed, the difficulties associated with coordinating the timing of transactions have been decisive in determining how the markets have come to be organized.

APPENDIX

Example A1: Inefficient Outcomes Caused by Early Appointments. —For simplicity in this example, we will incorporate into the rules of the game the commonly observed behavioral phenomenon that a firm which has made an offer to a particular student and been rejected will not subsequently make an offer to the same student (recall footnote 73).

Let the set of firms be $F = \{f_1, f_2, f_3\}$ and the set of workers (graduating students) at time T be $W = \{w_1, w_2, w_3\}$. Firms' utilities u_f and workers' utilities v_w are given by

$$u_{f_1}(w_1) = 10 \quad u_{f_1}(w_2) = 5 \quad u_{f_1}(w_3) = 2$$

$$u_{f_2}(w_1) = 10 \quad u_{f_2}(w_2) = 7 \quad u_{f_2}(w_3) = 2$$

$$u_{f_3}(w_1) = 2 \quad u_{f_3}(w_2) = 10 \quad u_{f_3}(w_3) = 7$$

$$v_{w_1}(f_1) = 10.5 \quad v_{w_1}(f_2) = 10 \quad v_{w_1}(f_3) = 9$$

$$v_{w_2}(f_1) = 10.5 \quad v_{w_2}(f_2) = 10 \quad v_{w_2}(f_3) = 8$$

$$v_{w_3}(f_1) = 8 \quad v_{w_3}(f_2) = 9.4 \quad v_{w_3}(f_3) = 9.$$

An unmatched player's utility is zero.

In the marriage market M which arises if no agents have made offers before time T, there is a unique stable matching μ which matches firm i to worker i, that is, $\mu = [(f_1, w_1), (f_2, w_2), (f_3, w_3)]$. The payoffs at time T are:

$$u_{f_1}(w_1) = 10 \quad u_{f_2}(w_2) = 7 \quad u_{f_3}(w_3) = 7$$

and

$$v_{w_1}(f_1) = 10.5 \quad v_{w_2}(f_2) = 10 \quad v_{w_3}(f_3) = 9.$$

As in Example 1, agents who are not matched before time T will participate in the stable matching mechanism G' which produces the firm-optimal stable match in terms of the stated preferences. Because there is a unique stable matching at time T,

all equilibria in undominated strategies of the game $G'(M, T)$ produce the outcome μ. Recall however that if a firm has been rejected by a student at time $T - 1$ it may not be matched to that student at time T: this can be modeled by supposing that in this case the mechanism treats the firm's utility for being matched with that student as -1.

At time $T - 1$ the students are identified as $A = \{a_1, a_2, a_3\}$, and the probabilities p_{jk} that a_j will become w_k at time T are given by

$$p_{11} = 0.6 \quad p_{12} = 0.2 \quad p_{13} = 0.2$$

$$p_{21} = 0.2 \quad p_{22} = 0.6 \quad p_{23} = 0.2$$

$$p_{31} = 0.2 \quad p_{32} = 0.2 \quad p_{33} = 0.6.$$

If firm f_i matches with student a_j at time $T - 1$, then their utilities are their expected utilities at time T, which in both cases involve the uncertainty about a_j's attributes at time T. In the case of the firm, this uncertainty is about which w_k will turn out to have been hired, while in the case of the student, the uncertainty is about what his preferences will be at time T (e.g., a student knows that if his qualifications turn out to be those which make him w_3 then he has little chance of promotion at firm f_1). So, for example, the expected utility of firm f_1 when matched to student a_1 at time $T - 1$ is

$$Eu_{f_1}(a_1)$$

$$= p_{11}u_{f_1}(w_1) + p_{12}u_{f_1}(w_2) + p_{13}u_{f_1}(w_3)$$

$$= 0.6(10) + 0.2(5) + 0.2(2) = 7.4$$

and the expected utility of student a_1 when matched to firm f_1 at $T - 1$ is

$$Ev_{a_1}(f_1)$$

$$= p_{11}v_{w_1}(f_1) + p_{12}v_{w_2}(f_1) + p_{13}v_{w_3}(f_1)$$

$$= 0.6(10.5) + 0.2(10.5) + 0.2(8) = 10.$$

If no offers are made at time $T - 1$, then at a perfect equilibrium the outcome will be $\mu = [(f_1, w_1), (f_2, w_2), (f_3, w_2)]$ at time T, and the expected utility of the agents at time $T-1$ will be $Eu_{f_i}(\mu) = u_{f_i}(\mu(f_i)) = u_{f_i}(w_i)$, and $Ev_{a_j}(\mu) = p_{j1}v_{w_1}(f_1) + p_{j2}v_{w_2}(f_2) + p_{j3}v_{w_3}(f_3)$, so the expected-utility vector for the firms is $Eu_F(\mu) = (10, 7, 7)$ and for the students $Ev_A(\mu) = (10.1, 9.9, 9.5)$.

We can now say the following about the two-stage game $G = G(M, P; T, T-1)$.

PROPOSITION A1: *Unraveling may be Pareto inefficient. In the game* G *of Example A1, there is no perfect equilibrium at which all agents are matched at time T. There is a perfect equilibrium at which all agents are matched at time $T-1$, and this equilibrium is ex ante Pareto inefficient: all agents would prefer that all matches be delayed until time T.*

PROOF:

Let σ be an equilibrium $(n+m)$-tuple of strategies at which no matches occur at time $T-1$. Then at σ no firm has made an offer at time $T-1$ (since a firm which had made a rejected offer would have done better to preserve all its options until time T). If (in contradiction to the second statement of the proposition) σ is a perfect equilibrium, then the players must use undominated strategies at time T, and so σ produces the unique stable matching μ, which gives f_2 an expected utility of 7. Therefore, f_2 would prefer to match with worker a_1 at time $T-1$, since $Eu_{f_2}(a_1) = 7.8$.

Suppose f_2 deviates from σ by making an offer to a_1 at $T-1$ but a_1 rejects it. Then, by assumption, at time T student a_1 cannot match with f_2. So a_1's expected utility after rejecting f_2's offer is $p_{11}v_{w_1}(f_1) + p_{12}v_{w_2}(f_3) + p_{13}v_{w_3}(f_3) = 0.6(10.5) + 0.2(8) + 0.2(9) = 9.7$, which is less than $Ev_{a_1}(f_2) = 9.88$. Since σ is a perfect equilibrium, this implies that a_1 would have accepted f_2's offer if it had been made, which in turn implies that σ is not an equilibrium (since f_2 would have done better by making an offer to a_1).

For the last statement in the proposition, consider the strategy $(n+m)$-tuple τ at which each f_i makes an offer to a_i at $T-1$,

each a_j accepts the best offer (i.e., the offer from the lowest-indexed firm) he receives from f_i with $i \le j$, and every player plans to submit his true preferences at time T in case he is still on the market. It is easy to verify that this is a perfect equilibrium at which all matches are made at time $T-1$, and each f_i is matched to a_i. Thus the expected utilities for the firms at this equilibrium are given by $Eu_{f_i}(\tau) = Eu_{f_i}(a_i)$, so the vector of firms' expected utilities is $Eu_F(\tau) = (7.4, 6.6, 6.6)$. The expected utilities for the students are given by $Ev_{a_j}(\tau) = Ev_{a_j}(f_j)$, so the vector of students' expected utilities is $Ev_A(\tau) = (10, 9.88, 8.8)$. Since $Eu_F(\tau) < Eu_F(\mu)$ and $Ev_A(\tau) < Ev_A(\mu)$, all firms and workers would be better off if no offers were made at time $T-1$, and instead the matching μ were made at time T.

REFERENCES

American Osteopathic Association. *The 1992 intern training program directory*. Chicago: American Osteopathic Association, 1992.

Association of American Medical Colleges. *1990 Graduation questionnaire results: All schools summary*. Washington, DC: Association of American Medical Colleges, 1990a.

_____. "Experiences of 1990 Graduates in Obtaining a Residency." Mimeo, Association of American Medical Colleges, Washington, DC, 1990b.

_____. "Experiences of 1991 Graduates in Obtaining a Residency." Mimeo, Association of American Medical Colleges, Washington, DC, 1991a.

_____. "Proceedings of the 1990 AAMC Forum on the Transition from Medical School to Residency." Mimeo, Association of American Medical Colleges, Washington, DC, 1991b.

Association of Psychology Internship Centers. "Results of Survey Dealing with a Computerized Matching Program for Internship Selection." *APIC Newsletter*, 10 April 1981, 6(2), p. 10.

_____. "Internal Selection Procedures: Briggs' Proposal." *APIC Newsletter*, 12–18 October 1985, 11(1), pp. 12–18.

Baker, Helen H. and Wachtler, Janice. "Osteopathic Graduate Medical Education." *Journal of the American Osteopathic Association*, November 1991, *91*(11), pp. 1128–40.

Barchilon, José and Darley, Ward. "National Psychiatric Residency Matching Program." *Journal of Medical Education*, September 1966, *41*(9), part 1, pp. 884–88.

Belar, Cynthia D. and Orgel, Sidney A. "Survival Guide for Internal Applicants." *Professional Psychology*, August 1980, *11*(4), pp. 672–75.

Bergstrom, Ted and Bagnoli, Mark. "Courtship as a Waiting Game." *Journal of Political Economy*, February 1993, *101*(1), pp. 185–202.

Black, LaNell D. and Hawley, Jerrie. Unpublished memorandum (distributed as NALP Bulletin), National Association for Law Placement, Washington, DC, 21 March 1988.

Blom, Bernhard E. and Pederson, Sanford L. "Procedural Aspects of Piloting an APIC Computerized Internal Matching Program." *APIC Newsletter*, Fall 1988, *13*(2), pp. 34–42.

_____. "Comments, Questions and Responses on Computer Matching: Part II." *APIC Newsletter*, Spring 1989, *14*(1), pp. 40–45.

Blom, Bernhard E.; Pederson, Sanford L. and Klepac, Robert K. "From the Computer Matching Committee." *APIC Newsletter*, Spring 1989, *14*(1), pp. 35–39.

_____. "The Computerized Internship Matching Pilot Study: Further Results, Cautions and Excuses." *APIC Newsletter*, Spring 1990a, *15*(1), pp. 20–22.

_____. "The Computerized Internship Matching Pilot Study: Concerns, Questions and Answers." *APIC Newsletter*, Spring 1990b, *15*(1), pp. 23–26.

Briggs, David W. "Proposal for a Centralized Computer Internship Matching System." *APIC Newsletter*, April 1984, *9*(2), pp. 11–16.

Calcagno, Philip L. "National Pediatric Residency Matching Program." *American Journal of Diseases of Children*, November 1968, *116*(5), pp. 534–36.

Carifio, Michael S.; Buckner, Kathryn E. and

Grace, William C. "APIC Guidelines: Are They Really That Helpful?" *Professional Psychology: Research and Practice*, August 1987, *18*(4), pp. 407–9.

Carifio, Michael S. and Grace, William C. "Ignored Data on the Development of Psychology Internships." *American Psychologist*, March 1992a, *47*(3), p. 428.

_____. "Ethics and Internship Training: A Mixed Picture?" Mimeo, National Institute on Drug Abuse, 1992b.

Carson, Richard and Navarro, Peter. "A Seller's (and Buyer's) Guide to the Job Market for Beginning Academic Economists." *Journal of Economic Perspectives*, Spring 1988, *2*(2), pp. 137–48.

Chass, Murray. "For '92 Draft Picks, Owners Have Lengthened the Leash." *New York Times*, 2 June 1992, p. B10.

Coleman, Sherman S. and Darley, Ward. "Matching Plan for Orthopaedic Surgery." *Clinical Orthopaedics and Related Research*, March–April 1971, (75), pp. 117–24.

Colenbrander, August. "Ophthalmology, Otolaryngology, Neurology, and Neurological Surgery Matching Programs: Comparative Statistics for the PGY-2 Matches." Mimeo, P.O. Box 7999, San Francisco, CA, 1989.

Collins, Susan M. and Krishna, Kala. "The Harvard Housing Lottery: Rationality and Reform." Working Paper, Brookings Institution, Washington, DC, 1993.

Corcoran, C. Timothy, III. "A Law Firm's View of Student Abuses." *National Law Journal*, 31 March 1986, p. 14.

Crawford, Vincent P. "Comparative Statics in Matching Markets." *Journal of Economic Theory*, August 1991, *54*(2), pp. 389–400.

Ehrenberg, Ronald G. "An Economic Analysis of the Market for Law School Students." *Journal of Legal Education*, Supplement 1989, *39*(5), pp. 627–54.

_____. "Academic Labor Supply," in Charles Clotfelter, Ronald Ehrenberg, Malcolm Getz, and John Siegfried, eds., *Economic challenges in higher education*. Chicago: University of Chicago Press, 1991, pp. 141–258.

Feerick, John D. "Job Placement Services Needed in Law Schools." *National Law*

Journal, 31 December 1984, p. 24.

Football Bowl Association. "Football Bowl Association 1990–1991." Brochure (available from Federal Express Orange Bowl, 601 Brickell Key Drive, Suite 206, Miami, FL 33131), 1990.

Fox, Ronald E. "The History of the APIC Selection Process: A Personal Prequel." *APIC Newsletter*, Spring 1990, *15*(1), pp. 27–28.

Freeman, Richard B. "Legal 'Cobwebs': A Recursive Model of the Market for New Lawyers." *Review of Economics and Statistics*, May 1975, *57*(2), pp. 171–79.

Gale, David and Shapley, Lloyd. "College Admissions and the Stability of Marriage." *American Mathematical Monthly*, January 1962, *69*(1), pp. 9–15.

Grace, William C. "Evaluating a Prospective Clinical Internship: Tips for the Applicant." *Professional Psychology: Research and Practice*, August 1985, *16*(4), pp. 475–80.

Greif, Avner. "Contract Enforceability and Economic Institutions in Early Trade: The Maghribi Traders' Coalition." *American Economic Review*, June 1993, *83*(3), pp. 525–48.

Hall, Ferris M. "Resident Matching Programs in Radiology." *AJR, American Journal of Roentgenology*, September 1981, *137*, pp. 631–32.

Kamecke, Ulrich. "Limited Competition in a Centralized Matching Market." Mimeo, University of Bonn, 1992.

Kelley, John P. "Summary of Matching in Program Surveys." Mimeo, Massachusetts General Hospital, 1985a.

_____. Untitled presentation to dental residency program directors. Mimeo, Massachusetts General Hospital, 1985b.

Koenig, Bill and Snyder, Deron. "Top Picks Are Filled with Big-Time Hopes." *USA Today Baseball Weekly*, 3–9 June 1992, *2*, p. 23.

Kozinski, Alex. "Confessions of a Bad Apple." *Yale Law Journal*, April 1991, *100*(6), pp. 1707–30.

Laughlin, Philip R. and Worley, John L. "Roles of the American Psychological Association and the Veterans Administration in the Development of Internships in Psychology." *American Psychologist*, April 1991, *46*(4), pp. 430–36.

Lichter, Allen S. "The Residency Match in Radiation Oncology." *International Journal of Radiation Oncology, Biology, and Physics*, 1992, *22*(5), pp. 1147–54.

Malkinson, Frederick D. "National Residency Matching Program for Dermatology." *Archives of Dermatology*, March 1969, *99*, pp. 350–53.

Margolick, David. "Annual Race for Clerks Becomes a Mad Dash, with Judicial Decorum Left in the Dust." *New York Times*, 17 March 1989, p. 24.

Mensh, Ivan N. and Orgel, Sidney A. "National Intern and Resident Matching Program." *APIC Newsletter*, April 1978, *3*(2), pp. 10–11.

Mongell, Susan and Roth, Alvin E. "Sorority Rush as a Two-Sided Matching Mechanism." *American Economic Review*, June 1991, *81*(3), pp. 441–64.

Moran, Malcolm. "Colorado vs. Notre Dame in Orange Bowl." *New York Times*, 12 November 1990, p. B10.

Myers, Ken. "Latest on the Recession Front: Firms Rescind Offers to Students." *National Law Journal*, 24 June 1991, p. 2.

National Association for Law Placement. *Class of 1986 employment report and salary survey*, Jane E. Thieberger, ed. Washington, DC: National Association for Law Placement, 1988a.

_____. *Principles and standards for law placement and recruitment activities, as adopted June 10, 1988*. Washington, DC: National Association for Law Placement, 1988b.

_____. *Class of 1990 employment report and salary survey*. Washington, DC: National Association for Law Placement, 1991.

National Collegiate Athletic Association. *1989–90 NCAA postseason football handbook*. Mission, KS: National College Athletic Association, 1989.

_____. *1990–91 NCAA postseason football handbook*. Overland Park, KS: National College Athletic Association, 1990.

National Matching Services. "Articling Student Matching Program for the 1992–1993 Articling Term (Ontario)." Mimeo, National Matching Services, Toronto, 1991a.

_____. "Matching Program for 1992–1993 Articling Positions in Vancouver." Mimeo, National Matching Services, Toronto, 1991b.

_____. "Postdoctoral Dental Matching Program: Summary Results of the Matching Program for 1992–1993 Positions." Mimeo, National Matching Services, Toronto, 1992.

National Resident Matching Program. *NRMP data*. Evanston, IL: National Resident Matching Program, April 1990.

_____. *NRMP data*. Evanston, IL: National Resident Matching Program, April 1991a.

_____. *MSMP data*. Evanston, IL: National Resident Matching Program, June 1991b.

National Science Foundation. *Science and engineering doctorates: 1960–90*. Washington, DC: National Science Foundation, 1991.

Neale, Margaret A. and Bazerman, Max H. *Cognition and rationality in negotiation*. New York: Free Press, 1991.

North, Douglass C. *Institutions, institutional change, and economic performance*. Cambridge, Cambridge University Press, 1990.

Oakes, James L.; Wald, Patricia M.; Breyer, Stephen and Becker, Edward R. "Timing of Law Clerk Selection." Unpublished memorandum, United States Court of Appeals, 9 January 1991.

Palgrave, Robert Harry Inglis. "Forestallers and Regrators," in R. H. I. Palgrave, ed., *Dictionary of political economy*, Vol. 2. London: Macmillan, 1910, pp. 107–8; republished, Detroit: Gale Research, 1976.

Posner, Richard A. and Easterbrook, Frank H. *Antitrust cases, economic notes, and other materials*. St. Paul, MN: West, 1981.

Ramaseshan, Geeta. "Child Marriages in India." *CWAS Newsletter* (Asian Studies Program, University of Pittsburgh), Spring 1992, *10*(3), pp. 2–4.

Reed, William F. "Bowl Race Disgrace." *Sports Illustrated*, 25 November 1991, *75*, p. 128.

Reinganum, Jennifer F. "The Timing of Innovation: Research, Development, and Diffusion," in Richard Schmalensee and Robert Willig, eds., *Handbook of indus-*

trial organization. New York: North-Holland, 1989, pp. 849–908.

Roth, Alvin E. "The Evolution of the Labor Market for Medical Interns and Residents: A Case Study in Game Theory." *Journal of Political Economy*, December 1984, *92*(6), pp. 991–1016.

_____. "On the Allocation of Residents to Rural Hospitals: A General Property of Two-Sided Matching Markets." *Econometrica*, March 1986, *54*(2), pp. 425–27.

_____. "New Physicians: A Natural Experiment in Market Organization." *Science*, 14 December 1990, *250*, pp. 1524–28.

_____. "A Natural Experiment in the Organization of Entry-Level Labor Markets: Regional Markets for New Physicians and Surgeons in the United Kingdom." *American Economic Review*, June 1991, *81*(3), 415–40.

Roth, Alvin E.; Murnighan, J. Keith and Schoumaker, Françoise. "The Deadline Effect in Bargaining: Some Experimental Evidence." *American Economic Review*, September 1988, *78*(4), pp. 806–23.

Roth, Alvin E. and Sotomayor, Marilda A. Oliveira. *Two-sided matching: A study in game-theoretic modeling and analysis*. Cambridge: Cambridge University Press, 1990.

Roth, Alvin E. and Xing, Xiaolin. "Turnaround Time and Bottlenecks in Market Clearing: A Comparative Analysis of Labor Market Institutions." Unpublished manuscript, University of Pittsburgh, 1994.

Rubin, Alvin B. and Bartell, Laura B. *Law clerk handbook: A handbook for law clerks to federal judges*. Washington DC: Federal Judicial Center, 1989.

Rust, Mark E. "Flyback Frenzy." *Student Lawyer*, November 1986, *15*(3), pp. 20–25.

Salzman, Louis Francis. *English trade in the middle ages*. Oxford: Clarendon, 1931.

Shapley, Lloyd S. and Shubik, Martin. "The Assignment Game I: The Core." *International Journal of Game Theory*, 1972, *1*(1), pp. 111–30.

Spencer, Sir Baldwin and Gillen, F. J. *The Arunta: A study of a stone age people*. London: Macmillan, 1927; reprinted, Oosterhout, Netherlands: Anthropological Publications, 1966.

Stedman, James M. "The History of the APIC Selection Process." *APIC Newsletter*, Fall 1989, *14*(2), pp. 35–43.

Torry, Saundra. "Annual Chase for Clerks Begins as Judges Throw Out Reforms." *Washington Post*, 28 January 1991, p. 5.

Tucker, John; Cantrell, Robert; Smith, Raymond; Jafek, Bruce; Shumrick, Donald; Cummings, Charles and Parkin, James. "*Resolved:* All Otolaryngology Programs Should Participate in the Residency Matching Program." *Archives of Otolaryngology*, November 1978, *104*(11), pp. 627–35.

Wald, Patricia M. "Selecting Law Clerks." *Michigan Law Review*, October 1990, *89*(1), pp. 152–63.

Wise, Daniel. "Four of Five Summer Associates Stay with Firms in City." *New York Law Journal*, 7 October 1983, pp. 1, 6.

_____. "For Summer Law Associates There Is No Lack of Job Offers." *New York Law Journal*, 17 July 1987, pp. 1, 3.

Xing, Xiaolin. "Unraveling of Appointment Dates in Entry-Level Labor Markets." Ph.D. dissertation, Department of Economics, University of Pittsburgh, 1992.

Zion, Sidney E. "New Lawyers to Find Salary Market Bullish." *New York Times*, 15 February 1968, p. 45.

[20]

ORGANIZATIONAL BEHAVIOR AND HUMAN DECISION PROCESSES 50, 1–23 (1991)

Power Balance and the Rationality of Outcomes in Matching Markets

HARRIS SONDAK* AND MAX H. BAZERMAN†

*Fuqua School of Business, Duke University and †J. L. Kellogg Graduate School of Management, Northwestern University

Negotiated outcomes in market contexts where unique goods are offered include the matching of buyers and sellers and the terms of dyadic agreements. In a laboratory simulation of the MBA job market, subjects played the roles of job candidates or corporate recruiters. Subjects found jobs or hired employees and agreed to the terms of their employment contracts. The balance of power between the sides of the market was manipulated by 1) increasing the longevity of employment offers, or 2) improving the alternatives to agreement of recruiters. The results suggest that the quality of negotiated agreements between dyad members increased by unequal power. At the market level of analysis, the results suggest that exploding offers lower the quality of matching outcomes. These results are discussed in terms of their implications for competitive practices in matching markets. © 1991 Academic Press, Inc.

Negotiations often occur in market contexts where many people carry out transactions simultaneously. In these situations the opportunities and outcomes available to one negotiator often depend on the opportunities and choices of many other market participants. Various factors systematically affect the likelihood that an individual will achieve a desired outcome in market contexts. One important influence on a negotiator's power is the quality of his or her alternatives (Raiffa, 1982; McAlister, Bazerman, & Fader, 1986). If buyers can choose among many sellers, for example, they have more power than when there are few sellers in the market, while if sellers offer their goods to many alternative buyers, they are relatively powerful. This research investigates the effects of power balance on negotiator behavior in market contexts and suggests factors that affect the quality of negotiated agreements in these contexts.

In commodity markets it makes little difference who transacts with whom because the goods that one participant has to offer are indistinguishable from those of a competitor. In commodity markets what mat-

The authors thank Dawn Iacobucci, Margaret Neale, Robin Pinkley, Kathleen Valley, the members of the Negotiation Seminar Series at Northwestern University, and two anonymous reviewers, for their helpful comments on an earlier draft of this paper. This research was supported by grants from the Dispute Resolution Research Center at Northwestern University and the National Institute for Dispute Resolution. Send requests for reprints to: Prof. Harris Sondak, Fuqua School of Business, Duke University, Durham, NC 27706.

2   SONDAK AND BAZERMAN

ters is price, and price is determined by relative supply and demand. In other markets, the differences in the goods they offer clearly distinguish one buyer or seller from another and lead participants to prefer to transact with some individuals on the opposite side of the market rather than others (Gale & Shapley, 1962; Roth & Sotomayor, 1990). A matching problem exists in these markets concerning who should transact with whom.

Labor markets are an important example of markets where matching makes a difference. Firms and employees have characteristics that make some assignments more preferred than others, and members of both sides in labor markets are concerned with finding a good match. Poor matching solutions have been suggested as one cause of high rates of employee turnover, especially in the first year of employment (Baysinger & Mobley, 1983; Mortensen, 1988). Other examples of markets with a matching problem are marriage, sorority pledges, and real estate markets (Kelso & Crawford, 1982; Mongell & Roth, 1991). Many of these matching markets are negotiation contexts that most individuals enter only a few times in their lives. We use the term *quasi-markets* to refer to those markets that contain a matching problem and in which many individuals carry out infrequent transactions.

Rationality for a matching problem is a market-level construct and is defined as market stability (Gale & Shapley, 1962; Diamond & Maskin, 1979, 1982; Roth & Sotomayor, 1990; Mortensen, 1988). Matching solutions are stable when no pair of participants on opposite sides of the market prefer each other to the parties with whom they are currently matched (Gale & Shapley, 1962; Roth, 1982). When a matching solution is unstable, dissatisfied parties are able to form mutually preferred matches by abandoning their commitments after the market has closed. Stable solutions are equilibrium solutions so that no party has an incentive to behave otherwise provided that no one else behaves otherwise. They are Pareto efficient in the sense that no matched pair in the market can do better without making another pair worse off.

A case study by Roth (1984) of the job market for graduating medical students provides evidence that the matching solutions in that market were unstable through the 1940's, at high cost to many participants. A centralized matching clearinghouse, the National Resident Matching Program, was instituted in the early 1950's that uses a computerized algorithm to assign students to hospitals according to the stated preferences of the participants on both sides of the market. This algorithm identifies stable matching solutions (Gale & Shapley, 1962; Roth, 1984).

Harrison and McCabe (1990) investigated the impact of information completeness and market complexity on the strategic choices made by laboratory subjects in a market with a matching problem. Their general finding was that while subjects can behave optimally in a simple market environment when they have very good information about the preferences of the other participants and the matching algorithm, the more complex the market and the less complete the information, the further their outcomes deviate from rationality.

Matching is often only one of the issues to be negotiated in quasi-markets. Other issues, however, are often encompassed by matching to some degree. That is, depending on the particular market context, the various issues involved in the transaction may be decided by the assignment of buyer and seller (Gale, 1984; Rubinstein & Wolinsky, 1985). Residency positions offered to graduating medical students by hospitals, for example, are offered with location, salary, job duties, and the duration of the contract all specified in advance by the hospitals (Roth, 1984). Thus a medical student's preference for one position over another reflects his or her preference not just for the hospital itself but includes the various terms of the offered positions. In other markets, participants must not only find appropriate matches, but also must negotiate many of the terms of their particular agreements. In the market for graduating MBA students, for example, salary, starting date, location, and initial duties often are negotiated (Mannix & Bazerman, 1988).

At the dyadic level of analysis, each particular agreement should be integrative so that the interests of the two parties are reconciled to create high joint gain (Pruitt, 1981, 1983). An agreement is fully integrative, or Pareto efficient for a dyad, when no alternative agreement exists for that pair of negotiators that would be preferred by both individuals, or that one would prefer and to which the other would be indifferent (Raiffa, 1982).[1]

Sondak and Bazerman (1989) investigated the ability of participants in quasi-markets to match themselves while simultaneoulsy negotiating the terms of agreement. A laboratory simulation of the MBA labor market was used to compare subjects' actual performance to that predicted by rational models for matching and negotiation. Their major finding was

---

[1] Integrativeness is sometimes defined as Pareto efficiency and sometimes as maximized joint benefit (e.g., Raiffa, 1982 and Pruitt, 1983, respectively). While the point at which total joint gains are maximized is Pareto efficient, not all Pareto efficient points maximize total joint gains. Lax and Sebenius (1987) argue that using total joint outcome as a measure of integrativeness confounds notions of efficiency and equity because a particular distribution is sometimes thereby indicated. What makes Pareto efficiency an attractive definition of integrativeness, however, is that at any Pareto efficient point both negotiators cannot simultaneously profit, and thus there is no incentive to the negotiators to "integrate" their interests any further. Tripp and Sondak (in press) suggest that different empirical findings will result from using Pareto efficiency rather than joint profit as the definition of integrativeness under two conditions: 1) if there is no strictly distributive issue and 2) when differences in distribution can be expected across experimental conditions.

4   SONDAK AND BAZERMAN

that subjects consistently fail to achieve stable matching solutions at the market level, and that subjects tend to form dyadic agreements that leave a significant amount of the available resources unallocated.

The present study extends the line of research reviewed above by manipulating the balance of power between the two sides of a quasi-market. Individuals' outcomes in markets depend on the actions of many other individuals, and interdependence is an important aspect of power (cf. Emerson, 1964). Understanding the factors that affect these interdependencies is therefore important for understanding the behavior of negotiators in market contexts. The next section introduces research hypotheses about the effects of two different power manipulations on the distribution of benefit, the integrativeness of dyadic agreements, and the quality of matching solutions in quasi-markets.

Balance of Power: Alternatives and Reservation Prices

According to Raiffa's prescriptive model of negotiations, a negotiator's reservation price or bottom line should depend on how well he or she can expect to do elsewhere if the current negotiation ends in impasse (Raiffa, 1982). The relationship between alternatives and current negotiations is an important issue for negotiating in markets because alternatives are quite salient in these contexts. That an alternative is available at all suggests that the negotiation may be taking place within a market: unless a negotiator is going to do without whatever is at issue, the existence of alternatives implies that he or she can choose among various suppliers.

There are at least two ways that a negotiator's alternatives can be improved in market contexts. First, a negotiator can locate alternative trading partners within the market. Second, a negotiator may have an alternative that is not readily available to other market participants.

A negotiator's ability to locate desirable alternative partners in market contexts may depend on the length of time he or she has before having to respond to a previous offer. In labor markets, for example, some firms tend to limit the life of their offers of employment. Some short-lived offers "explode" by progressively decreasing in value and are used by firms to put pressure on job candidates to respond quickly. While they allow firms flexibility in filling open positions, exploding offers decrease the opportunity for candidates to compare one offer with another. Long-lived offers, compared to short-lived offers, are likely to increase the bargaining power of job candidates relative to firms because the longer-lived an offer, the longer it remains a viable alternative. Long-lived offers allow candidates more time to negotiate with multiple firms and thus to gather information about alternative positions before having to respond.

There are many ways that a negotiator may have an alternative that is not readily available to other market participants. A graduating MBA student may, for example, have the opportunity to work for a friend of the family who is not actively recruiting on the market. Conversely, a firm may have access to a potential recruit who is not actively on the job market.

If the reservation prices of many members of one side of a market are shifted through either of the means suggested above, the average transaction price in the market is likely to move in the direction of that shift for two reasons. First, Raiffa's prescriptive analysis suggests that shifting the reservation prices of the members of one side of the market will require the negotiators on the other side of the market to change their price, if they want to conclude an agreement (Raiffa, 1982). Second, Nash's analysis (1950) predicts that the midpoint of the range between two negotiators' resistance points is a likely transaction price in a symmetric game and with one end of the bargaining range having shifted, the midpoint would be similarly moved.

Summarizing the above arguments about alternatives to agreement, the following hypothesis is suggested:

Hypothesis 1: If the quality of alternatives available to members of one side of a quasi-market is increased, that side of the market will gain a larger share of the resources available in the market.

Balance of Power and Integrative Outcomes

When the alternatives available to opposing negotiators are unequally attractive, a power imbalance exists between the negotiators. The party with better alternatives can threaten to walk away from the present negotiation unless his or her outcome exceeds the benefit available elsewhere. In addition to affecting the distribution of resources between sides of a market as suggested above, the relative quality of alternatives available to the two sides of a market may affect the efficiency of dyadic agreements.

The effects of unequal bargaining power on negotiators' ability to create integrative agreements have been tested empirically, but with inconsistent results. McAlister, Bazerman, and Fader (1986) hypothesized that unequal power would lead negotiators to focus their attention on the distribution of resources, distracting them from finding solutions that maximized joint gains. Power in their study was operationalized as economic supply and demand and was manipulated by varying the number of buyers or sellers in a laboratory simulation of a market as well as the maximum number of transactions participants were allowed to complete. McAlister *et al.*'s findings were that equal power led to higher joint gain than did unequal power. Roloff and Dailey (1988), however, found that when the two parties to a negotiation had equally attractive alternatives to

6   SONDAK AND BAZERMAN

an agreement with each other, their joint outcomes were less than when
their alternatives were unequal or when they had no explicit alternatives.
Roloff and Dailey argued that negotiators with equally attractive alternatives may focus their attention on those alternatives. Negotiators would
then not have the high aspirations for the current negotiation that can lead
to finding joint gains. When the quality of alternatives is asymmetrical,
however, the disadvantaged party will search for an integrative outcome
because unless the pool of available resources is made sufficiently large,
either the party with a good alternative will abandon the current negotiation, or the disadvantaged party will be unable to receive an acceptable
amount.

Drawing on the empirical finding of McAlister, Bazerman, and Fader
(1986) on the one hand, and Roloff and Dailey (1988) on the other hand,
the following competing hypotheses are suggested:

> *Hypothesis 2a:* Dyads in which negotiators have *equal* power are
> more likely to form integrative agreements than dyads in which ne-
> gotiators have unequal power.

> *Hypothesis 2b:* Dyads in which negotiators have *unequal* power are
> more likely to form integrative agreements than dyads in which ne-
> gotiators have equal power.

Longevity of Offers and the Quality of Matching Solutions

In addition to being one method of improving the alternatives available
to negotiators on one side of a market, increasing the longevity of offers
may have a second effect on negotiated outcomes in quasi-markets. Long-
lived offers are likely to improve the quality of the matching solutions in
quasi-markets, to the potential benefit of both sides of the market.

Providing job candidates with additional time to compare offers allows
both sides of the market to have choices that can improve the matching
solution.[2] Rather than being faced with a sequence of yes/no choices,
candidates would be able to choose between better and worse offers;
firms select among the various candidates in the market when extending
offers. Increasing the life of offers in labor markets thus transforms the
task from one in which job candidates are trying to find any acceptable
match to one in which they, like firms, are trying to find a good match.
Better matching solutions seem likely when both sides of a market are
attempting to improve on current possibilities, rather than when one side
is just trying to find any match.

Allowing negotiators in quasi-markets to compare offers should lead to

---

[2] This is true only within limits. At a certain point, firms would be incapacitated by very
long-lived offers.

a better matching solution because better information would then be available in the market before matches were finalized. The stability of matching solutions depends on integrating the set of preferences among the participants in a market since unstable matches occur when pairs can form matches mutually preferred to their current assignments (Roth, 1982). Based on game-theoretic analysis, Mortensen (1988) argues that individuals in matching markets may create unstable matching solutions because of the high cost of gaining information about match quality. Allowing job candidates to hold offers for a longer time decreases their opportunity cost of searching for better alternatives because, with long-lived offers, assignments can be considered while participants attempt to improve on them.

Thus two distinct effects can be expected from increasing the life of offers. First, as discussed above, the power effects of long-lived offers can be expected to favor job candidates. This effect was the subject of Hypothesis 1. Second, increasing the length of offers increases the quality of information available to market participants and should improve the matching solutions that result. Based on Mortensen (1988) and Roth's (1982) analysis, the following hypothesis is therefore suggested:

> *Hypothesis 3:* When offers extended in quasi-markets are long-lived, the quality of the matching solution will be higher than when offers are short-lived.

METHOD

Subjects

Two hundred eighty-eight students from the J. L. Kellogg Graduate School of Management at Northwestern University participated in 12 runs of a job market simulation as a class exercise.

Procedures

The procedures used in this study were based on those reported in Sondak and Bazerman (1989). Twenty-four students participated in each run of the simulation. Sixteen students played the roles of graduating MBA students seeking jobs while the remaining eight students played corporate recruiters; students were assigned at random to a role. Six markets were assigned to each of the two conditions, Candidate Biased or Recruiter Biased. The markets were randomly assigned to conditions, except that the assignment of markets balanced the classes of particular instructors between conditions.

Subjects were given instructions that stated that the exercise was a job market simulation and that four issues were of importance to them for the purposes of the simulation: 1) quality of match, 2) salary, 3) starting date,

8   SONDAK AND BAZERMAN

and 4) control of job assignment. Included in the instructions was a profit
schedule that indicated subjects' preferences for these issues and their
possible scores (examples of these profit schedules are shown in Tables
1a and 1b). The subjects' task was to maximize their outcomes as represented by their total scores across the four issues. Candidates sought the
best job they could get, while recruiters sought to hire the two best possible candidates.

Scores were expressed in dollars of value for each of the issues. For

TABLE 1a
SCHEDULE FOR RECRUITER A

| | Quality of candidate |
Candidate	Dollar Equivalent in Salary
16	7500
7	7000
9	6500
12	6000
5	5500
3	5000
11	4500
8	4000
14	3500
2	3000
1	2500
6	2000
13	1500
4	1000
15	500
10	0

Salary
$35,000 to $50,000 (round $1000's)
You will be scored in terms of salary less than $50,000

| | Starting date |
Date	Dollar Equivalent in Salary
July 1	2000
August 1	1000
September 1	0

Control of job assignment	
Control	Dollar equivalent in salary
Firm (Firm assigns division & project)	4000
Shared (Candidate chooses division but firm assigns project)	2000
Candidate (candidate chooses division & project)	0

matching, each subject was assigned a unique and randomly generated rank ordering of all members of the opposite side of the market. An agreement with a higher ranked match was worth more than an agreement with one that was lower ranked. For the other three issues, all recruiters had identical preferences, as did all candidates. Salary could range between $40,000 and $50,000 with recruiters seeking to pay a low salary, and candidates seeking a high salary. Salary was scored as amount above $40,000 for candidates and below $50,000 for recruiters.

Starting date and control of job assignment were issues that could be logrolled to create high joint gain (Pruitt, 1983). Integrative potential was available from these two issues because while job candidates preferred to start late in the season and wished to control their job assignment and recruiters preferred the reverse on each issue, the relative importance of the issues to the two sides was opposite. Because there were three levels

TABLE 1b
SCHEDULE FOR CANDIDATE #1

Quality of firm	
Firm	Dollar Equivalent in Salary
E	7000
H	6000
D	5000
C	4000
G	3000
A	2000
B	1000
F	0

Salary
$40,000 to $55,000 (round $1000's)
You will be scored in terms of salary greater than $40,000

Starting date	
Date	Dollar Equivalent in Salary
July 1	0
August 1	2000
September 1	4000

Control of job assignment	
Control	Dollar equivalent in salary
Firm (Firm assigns division & project)	0
Shared (Candidate chooses division but firm assigns project)	1000
Candidate (candidate chooses division & project)	2000

10   SONDAK AND BAZERMAN

each for starting date and job assignment, nine possible agreements were possible. Table 2 shows these nine agreements and their worth to the candidate and recruiter. Four of the combinations were clearly less than fully integrative because of the existence of alternative agreements that would increase benefit to both the candidate and recruiter. These four combinations were July/Shared Control, July/Candidate Control, August/ Shared Control, and August/Candidate Control. The other five agreements would all seem to be equally Pareto efficient because no joint gains are apparent from any of them. However, because salary was negotiable in this exercise, September/Firm Control was in fact the only fully integrative agreement. Each increase of $1000 in benefit to his or her opponent on starting date and control of job assignment cost a negotiator $2000. He or she could have given up the same value to the opponent in salary for just $1000. For example, the agreement of August/Firm Control and a salary of $45,000 would give the candidate $2000 and the firm $5000 from starting date and job assignment and $5000 each from salary, for a total value to the candidate of $7000 and $10,000 to the recruiter. Agreeing to September/Firm Control and a salary of $44,000, however, would give each negotiator $4000 from starting date and job assignment, and would give the candidate $4000 from salary, for a total of $8000, and would still give the recruiter a total of $10,000.

Job candidates were seated together in a large central room, each at a work station. Each recruiter had his or her own office. The two sides of the market could communicate both in face-to-face interviews that took place in the recruiters' offices and by notes that were passed by research assistants. Periods for letter writing lasted 10 min and alternated with two

TABLE 2
POSSIBLE AGREEMENTS ON STARTING DATE AND CONTROL OF JOB ASSIGNMENT

Starting date	Control of job assignment	Value[a]		Score[b]
		Candidate	Recruiter	
July	Firm	0	6	4
July	Shared	1	4	6
July	Candidate	2	2	8
August	Firm	2	5	2
August	Shared	3	3	4
August	Candidate	4	1	6
September	Firm	4	4	0
September	Shared	5	2	2
September	Candidate	6	0	4

[a] Value is expressed in thousands of dollars.

[b] Integrativeness scores were assigned to both candidate and recruiter; the lower the score, the more Pareto efficient the agreement.

5-min periods for interviews. There were ten periods in all and the exercise took 1 h 40 min.

Quality of alternatives. In the Candidate Biased condition, both candidates and recruiters were instructed that they had alternative opportunities outside the present market worth $5000. Thus, if candidates failed to be hired in the simulation, they would score $5000; recruiters would score $5000 for each unfilled position. These amounts also represent the value of the alternatives to agreement available to market participants in Sondak and Bazerman (1989).

In the Recruiter Biased condition, candidates' alternatives continued to be worth $5000, but recruiters were told that the employees whom they could hire from outside the market would each be worth $11,500. This amount was intended to raise recruiters' expectations and demands without being so high as to create too many impasses. This amount represents the 25th percentile of recruiters' scores in Sondak and Bazerman (1989). That is, 25% of the agreements from the earlier study yielded less than $11,500 to the recruiter involved.

Longevity of offers. In the Recruiter Biased condition, as in the markets reported in Sondak and Bazerman (1989), the life of all job offers was restricted to one period so that offers expired at the end of the period in which they were extended. Under these rules, recruiters were allowed to extend only that number of offers for which they currently had open positions. The longevity of offers was manipulated in the Candidate Biased condition by extending the minimum life of all offers to three periods, or until the end of period 9, whichever was longer.[3] Recruiters in the Candidate Biased condition were allowed to extend one more offer than they had open positions; recruiters were penalized, however, for hiring more than their quota of new employees. Recruiters were told that the penalty for each employee they hired beyond their quota of two would be $20,000. This penalty was severe enough that it was quite unlikely that hiring extra employees would be profitable. The maximum score obtainable by a recruiter, if he or she managed to obtain his or her highest level on every issue, was $23,500 for each of his or her open positions; the highest score actually obtained by a recruiter for a single position in Sondak and Bazerman (1989) was $18,000. Extending an extra offer allowed recruiters flexibility while they waited for a response to or the expiration of a previously extended offer, but since recruiters could not renege on offers, this was a risky strategy. Although subjects on both sides of the market in the Candidate Biased condition began with outside alternatives worth $5000, because candidates could hold offers for three

---

[3] Period 10 was reserved as a final chance for the market to clear.

periods, the quality of their alternatives within the market could change across time.

After the rules of the market were explained, the simulation began. When a candidate accepted a job with a recruiter, a contract was completed and signed by both parties. The contracts showed the terms of agreement and the period during which the agreement was extended and completed. After signing a contract, a candidate was out of the market; recruiters were out when they had filled their quota and, in the Candidate Biased condition, when any additional outstanding offers had expired.

ANALYSIS

Optimality of Results within Conditions

The quality of dyadic agreements was measured by an index of "integrativeness." The nine possible agreements were scored according to how well they represented the integrative trade-off of starting date and job assignment. The range for these scores was from 0 to 8, with 0 representing a fully integrative agreement, 4 representing a compromise incorporating the middle level of each issue, and 8 representing an anti-integrative agreement that gives each party his or her preferred level on the issue of *least* importance. The scores associated with each possible agreement on these issues are shown in Table 2. A *t*-test was run for each condition comparing the actual scores for integrativeness with the score that would result were every agreement to have been fully integrative.

At the market level, if at least one match was unstable because a pair of participants preferred to match with each other than with their assignments when the market ended, the market failed to reach a stable matching solution. The distance from stability was measured in two ways. The first method was to count the number of candidates who preferred firms other than those with which they were matched that also preferred them.[4] A *t*-test was run for each condition to compare the number of candidates per market who could successfully replace their matches to that of the fully stable matching solution.

The second way of measuring a market's distance from stability was to calculate its "matching efficiency." To assess the matching efficiency of a market, the scores actually achieved by participants were compared to two hypothetical scores. Subjects' actual matching scores were compared to the scores they would receive if they were matched according to the algorithm used to create stable matching solutions in the market for grad-

---

[4] The number of matches that firms could successfully replace equals the number of candidates who can successfully "jump ship." Thus this measure can be counted from either point of view.

uating medical students.[5] Subjects' actual matching scores were also compared to the scores they could expect to receive if they were matched at random. The distance between the scores generated by the optimal matching solution and the expected value of random matches was the possible improvement over the expected value of random matches achievable in the experimental markets. Matching efficiency was the percentage of this possible improvement realized by each run of the market. The matching efficiency of the markets in the two conditions was compared to that of the fully efficient model by *t*-tests.

Tests of Hypotheses

Distribution of benefit. Hypothesis 1 suggests that the side of the market that has its alternatives improved will profit from those improvements at the expense of the other side. The proportion of the total benefit produced in each of the twelve market simulations that was gained by candidates was calculated by dividing the sum of the candidates' scores by the total benefit gained by all market participants. Hypothesis 1 predicts that this proportion will be greater in the Candidate Biased condition than in the Recruiter Biased condition. To test this hypothesis, the proportion of the total benefit allocated to candidates was compared across conditions by *t*-tests.

Comparing the resuts from the Candidate Biased condition with those of the Recruiter Biased condition will not, however, distinguish the effects of the two different power manipulations used in this study (increased longevity of offers and higher reservation prices for recruiters). Comparing both conditions to the findings from the six runs of the simulation reported in Sondak and Bazerman (1989), however, will demonstrate the independent effects of the manipulations because the previous set of markets were intermediate to those reported here. In Sondak and Bazerman (1989), offers exploded in one period as in the Recruiter Biased condition, while each side had an alternative worth $5000 as in the Candidate Biased condition. Hypothesis 1 suggests that the benefit to candidates in the Candidate Biased condition should be greater than it was in the six runs of the market reported in Sondak and Bazerman (1989), while

---

[5] For many matching problems, multiple stable solutions exist. Roth (1985) has shown that among the possible stable solutions, all members of one side of the market prefer one solution, and all members of the opposite side prefer another solution. In addition, the solution that is best from the point of view of the members of one side of the market is worst from the opposite point of view. The algorithm that matches medical students to the hospitals that hire them produces the hospital-optimal match. The candidate-optimal solution for the market simulation produces greater total collective benefit and thus was used as the optimal solution in the measure of matching efficiency.

14   SONDAK AND BAZERMAN

the benefit to candidates in the Recruiter Biased condition should be less. These differences were assessed by *t*-tests.

The subjects in both the present study and in the study reported by Sondak and Bazerman (1989) were management students at the J. L. Kellogg Graduate School of Management at Northwestern University. While the subject population was the same in both studies, the samples were distinct: no subject participated more than once. Comparing across studies may present potential difficulties. Environmental conditions that could affect the outcomes of the studies, for example, may have changed. Comparing across studies assumes that such differences did not have important effects.

Dyadic negotiating. The competing Hypotheses 2a and 2b suggest that the balance of power will affect the quality of the dyadic agreements. Neither McAlister *et al.* (1986) nor Roloff and Dailey (1988) made predictions comparing the quality of agreements across two different unequal power conditions. To test these hypotheses, therefore, the results for the present runs of the simulation were compared to those from Sondak and Bazerman (1989), where the power was relatively equal. Thus, Hypothesis 2a would suggest that the results from Sondak and Bazerman (1989) can be expected to be *superior* to those in both the Candidate Biased condition and the Recruiter Biased condition, while according to Hypothesis 2b, the earlier results will be *inferior* to those in both conditions. Since the two methods of shifting the balance of power were expected to produce the same result, a planned comparison was used to test the difference in integrativeness between the earlier results and the combined results from the two Biased conditions. Additionally, a χ^2 test was used to test for differences between the number of dyads that incorporated the fully integrative trade-off into their agreements in Sondak and Bazerman (1989) and the number of dyads that did so in each Biased condition.

Matching. Hypothesis 3 suggests that the matching solution will be better when offers are long-lived rather than short-lived. The results produced by subjects in the Candidate Biased condition were thus expected to be superior to those from the Recruiter Biased condition. It was again helpful to compare the present results with those from Sondak and Bazerman (1989). In both the Recruiter Biased condition and the simulations reported in Sondak and Bazerman (1989), offers lived for only one period; only in the Candidate Biased condition was the life of offers extended to three periods. Thus the matching solutions in the Candidate Biased condition should be superior both to those of the Recruiter Biased condition and those from Sondak and Bazerman (1989); additionally, the latter two sets of results should not differ from each other. The mean number of candidates per market who could successfully jump ship was compared across conditions by planned comparisons, as was the mean matching efficiency per market.

RESULTS

Optimality of Results

The results within both the Candidate Biased condition and the Recruiter Biased condition support the finding from Sondak and Bazerman (1989) that participants in quasi-markets fail to achieve optimal results at both dyadic and market levels of analysis. For dyadic negotiation, the integrativeness of the agreements in both the Candidate Biased condition and the Recruiter Biased condition was significantly below the optimal level. The results for dyadic negotiating, from both the Candidate and Recruiter Biased conditions were significantly worse than those produced by the optimal model ($t = -10.04$, $df = 95$, $p < .001$, and $t = -9.45$, $df = 95$, $p < .001$, respectively). The mean level of integrativeness in the Candidate Biased condition was 1.92 ($SD = 1.89$), and in the Recruiter Biased condition, 1.94 ($SD = 1.99$); under the optimal model, all dyads would score 0.

At the market level of analysis, no matching solution produced in the simulations was fully stable. In the Candidate Biased condition 7.8 of the 16 candidates on average ($SD = 1.94$) could find preferred matches that preferred them. In the Recruiter Biased condition, the mean number of candidates who could successfully jump ship was 7.0 of 16 ($SD = 1.41$). Under a stable matching solution, though every individual may not be matched with his or her first choice, no candidate could find a preferred match that also preferred him or her. The differences between actual and optimal results were statistically significant in both conditions (Candidate Biased: $t = 9.89$, $df = 5$, $p < .001$; Recruiter Biased: $t = 12.12$, $df = 5$, $p < .001$). In addition, the matching efficiency in both the Candidate Biased condition and the Recruiter Biased condition was significantly below that of the optimal model. The mean matching efficiency in the Candidate Biased condition was .880 ($SD = .086$), and in the Recruiter Biased condition was .808 ($SD = .085$); the optimal model produces fully efficient solutions. The differences between actual and optimal results for matching efficiency were significant in both conditions (Candidate Biased: $t = -3.40$, $df = 5$, $p < .02$; Recruiter Biased: $t = -5.54$, $df = 5$, $p < .01$).

Tests of Hypotheses

Distribution of benefit. The results for the proportion of total benefit gained by candidates in each condition supported Hypothesis 1. In the

16   SONDAK AND BAZERMAN

Candidate Biased condition, the mean proportion of the total benefit produced in the market simulations that was gained by the candidates was .57 (SD = .04), while in the Recruiter Biased condition, the mean proportion gained by candidates was .48 (SD = .01). This difference across conditions in the mean benefit gained by the two sides was statistically significant (t = 4.29, df = 10, p < .01). Comparing these results with those from Sondak and Bazerman (1989) indicates that both power manipulations tended to have the predicted effects. In the six earlier runs of the market simulation, the mean proportion of the total benefit gained by candidates was .52 (SD = .03). This proportion differed from the proportion of the total benefit that was gained by candidates both in the Candidate Biased condition (t = −2.40, df = 10, p < .05), and in the Recruiter Biased condition (t = 2.22, df = 10, p < .06).

Dyadic negotiating. The mean levels of integrativeness in both Biased conditions were higher than that of the runs reported in Sondak and Bazerman (1989), consistent with Hypothesis 2b. The mean scores on the integrativeness scale are shown in Table 3; a lower score represents a more integrative agreement. The planned comparison between the present results and the results from Sondak and Bazerman (1989), however, indicated that these differences were not statistically significant (t = −1.45, df = 285, *ns*).

Also consistent with Hypothesis 2b, the percentage of agreements that were fully integrative were higher in the two biased conditions. These frequencies are also shown in Table 3. The χ^2 test of independence indicated that the experimental treatment of a dyad did affect the likelihood that the dyad would reach a fully integrative agreement (χ^2 = 6.89, df = 2, p < .05). Partitioning the χ^2 indicated that the frequency of fully integrative agreements in Sondak and Bazerman (1989) differed from the frequency of fully integrative agreements in the Recruiter Biased condition at the .05 level, though not from that of the Candidate Biased condition. As expected, the frequencies across the two biased conditions did not differ significantly.

TABLE 3
QUALITY OF DYADIC NEGOTIATING

	Candidate Biased condition	Recruiter Biased condition	Sondak & Bazerman (1989)
Mean integrativeness	1.92	1.94	2.27
Standard deviation	1.89	1.99	1.80
Number of dyads incorporating the fully integrative trade-off	37/96	42/96	25/96

Matching. There was little difference in the number of candidates who could jump ship across conditions, contrary to Hypothesis 3. The mean number of candidates per market in each condition who could find preferred matches that preferred them is shown in Table 4. These frequencies did not differ significantly between the Candidate Biased and Recruiter Biased conditions ($t = -.85$, $df = 10$, ns). Because increasing the longevity of offers was expected to increase matching stability, the results from the Candidate Biased condition were compared with the combined results from the Recruiter Biased condition and Sondak and Bazerman (1989). The planned comparisons of the number of candidates who could jump ship were not statistically significant ($t = 1.39$, $df = 15$, ns).

The pattern of results for matching efficiency, however, suggests some support for Hypothesis 3. The mean matching efficiency per market in each condition is also shown in Table 4. The matching efficiency across the two Biased conditions did not differ significantly ($t = 1.45$, $df = 10$, ns). However, the planned comparison of matching efficiency for the Candidate Biased condition with the combined results of the Recruiter Biased condition and the simulations reported in Sondak and Bazerman (1989) was marginally significant ($t = 1.82$, $df = 15$, $p < .09$); the matching efficiency in the latter two conditions did not differ ($t = -.52$, $df = 10$, ns).

DISCUSSION

The results of this study reinforce the suggestion made by Sondak and Bazerman (1989) that negotiator performance in quasi-markets consistently fails to reach optimal levels. The results also suggest two factors that may influence the quality of negotiation in quasi-markets.

Comparing the results of the market simulations with optimal models of dyadic negotiation and matching indicates that important amounts of resources were lost to market participants at both levels of analysis. The mean level of integrativeness in the twelve market simulations reported

TABLE 4
QUALITY OF MATCHING SOLUTIONS

	Candidate Biased condition	Recruiter Biased condition	Sondak & Bazerman (1989)
Mean number of candidates who could jump ship per market	7.8	7.0	6.5
Standard deviation	1.94	1.41	1.22
Mean matching efficiency per market	.880	.808	.779
Standard deviation	.086	.085	.114

18   SONDAK AND BAZERMAN

here was about 1.9, on a scale where compromises were scored as 4 and fully integrative trade-offs were scored as 0. These results indicate that subjects incorporated into their agreements only about half the possible gain from logrolling their interests. This aggregate gain in integrativeness mostly resulted from about 40% of the dyads fully logrolling their interests. Many dyads failed to take advantage of the integrative potential in this task. If 60% of the dyads in real labor markets were to fail to integrate their interests fully, a great amount of benefit could be lost. Fully integrative agreements are valuable because they may be the only way that an agreement is possible, they are more likely to be stable, they tend to strengthen the relationship between the negotiators, and they are more likely to contribute to the welfare of the community in which they occur (Pruitt, 1981).

The results for matching efficiency indicate that market participants were overlooking another important source of benefit. Matching efficiency averaged about 85% for the twelve runs of the market. That is, market participants lost about 15% of the gain available in the market from matching according to their preferences rather than at random. Matching is an important issue to firms and students as shown by the attention given to "fit" through selection procedures and by the use of executive placement agencies. On average more than 7/16 of the matches in the experimental markets reported here were unstable so that individuals could find preferred matches who also preferred them. The turnover in personnel in real labor markets can, in part, be attributed to mismatches (Mortensen, 1988). If nearly half of the matches in the real MBA labor market are unstable in this sense, the turnover is likely to be extensive and costly indeed. The stability and levels of efficiency of the matching solutions in the simulated markets reported here in fact seem likely to exceed those of real labor markets since real markets are more complex matching contexts. Harrison and McCabe (1990) found that the more complex the market, the further matching outcomes deviate from rationality.

The difference in the distribution of benefit between the two Biased conditions was not large in terms of percentages: In the Candidate Biased condition, candidates were awarded 57% of the total benefit while in the Recruiter Biased condition, candidates received 48% of the benefit. However, in terms of real dollar amounts, such a difference may represent a large amount of money. For example, just at the J. L. Kellogg Graduate School of Management, more than 400 graduating management students found jobs in 1989 with an average salary of more than $51,000 (Office of Career Development and Placement, J. L. Kellogg Graduate School of Management, 1989). If the salaries paid to the students can be considered an estimate of the benefit available to market participants, then more than

$20 million was available for distribution in this small segment of the MBA job market. Nine percent of this amount is about $1.8 million dollars, or $4500 per student.

The results for dyadic negotiating offer some support for the Roloff and Dailey (1988) hypothesis that having alternatives of unequal attractiveness encourages integrative agreements. Although the manipulation of alternatives had no effect on the extent to which agreements in the aggregate were integrative, unequal power compared to the procedure in Sondak and Bazerman (1989) did tend to increase the number of dyads who included the fully integrative trade-off in their agreements. That the number of fully integrative agreements tended to be lower in Sondak and Bazerman (1989) than when negotiators had asymmetric alternatives suggests that negotiators in Sondak and Bazerman (1989) used the issues that could be logrolled to distribute benefit to a greater extent than did negotiators in the two Biased conditions. In the Biased conditions, negotiators were more likely to use these issues exclusively to create benefit. Using the issues that had integrative potential to distribute benefit was a wasteful practice in this exercise. It may be that in the unequal power conditions negotiators perceived resources to be more scarce, requiring them to utilize all the available benefit, thus encouraging the fully integrative trade-off.

At the market level of analysis, the number of candidates at the close of the market who could find firms they preferred that preferred them did not differ significantly across conditions. Two explanations for these results are possible. First, the longevity of offers may really have no effect on the instability of matching solutions. Second, it may be that with their limited information about others' preferences, it is impossible for subjects to create a stable matching solution in the 1 h 40 min duration of this exercise. The result that matching efficiency tended to be highest when the offers were long-lived suggests, however, that subjects may in fact be able to improve their matches when offers are longer-lived. While instabilities existed in all conditions, the higher mean matching efficiency score in the Candidate Biased condition suggests that the matches that could be abandoned when offers were long-lived were superior to those that could be abandoned with short-lived offers. Thus the results for matching efficiency give some support to the suggestion that the use of exploding offers is a practice that decreases the benefit of the matching solution available to the entire market.

One limitation of this study is the single integrative aspect of the experimental task. Various different ways of forming integrative agreements have been described (e.g., Pruitt, 1983), and this study allows only one technique of increasing joint gain at the dyadic level. While both McAlister *et al.* (1986) and Roloff and Dailey (1988) use similar logrolling tasks

20   SONDAK AND BAZERMAN

to test their hypotheses, the generalizability of their and our findings should be tested with other kinds of integrative problems.

A difficulty with conducting research on experimental markets is that market-level variables are very expensive to test in terms of numbers of subjects. In order to study negotiation in these contexts, however, it is important to include market-level variables even if market-level results, and the conclusions drawn from them, have to be provisional because of low statistical power. It would have been possible to increase the statistical power of the analyses while maintaining the same total number of subjects by decreasing the number of subjects per market simulation and increasing the number of markets. However, in matching problems like the one modeled in the simulations reported here, decreasing the size of the market simplifies the task faced by participants. If there were only one firm and one job candidate in the market, to take an extreme example, the matching solution would be obvious. It is not clear at what point the task becomes complex enough not to be trivial, while still making the most efficient use of subjects.

Placement offices in management schools tend to discourage the use of exploding offers, but many firms in various industries use them anyway. The use of exploding offers is not limited to the market for management students, of course; in labor markets where employers are competing intensely for job candidates, exploding offers may appear attractive to firms hoping to increase their flexibility in pursuing highly valued candidates. The results of this study suggest that industries that encourage poor matching solutions by extending short-lived offers will have to pay the cost of less-than-optimal matching solutions. Since this cost is borne by all firms in the industry, including those firms that do not extend offers that explode quickly, a social dilemma may exist in these markets. If every firm refrains from using exploding offers the overall benefit available to all firms from the matching solution may increase, though it may be, or may appear to the individual firms to be, in the interest of each firm to extend exploding offers. Firms may believe that whether or not other firms in the market extend exploding offers, their own advantage in driving hard bargains may compensate them for the inefficiencies in matching that result and affect everyone. Of course, a social dilemma exists only if the advantages for dyadic bargaining outweigh the costs of inefficient matches for each firm, regardless of the actions of the other firms.

Situations that involve the preferences of many individuals are social choice problems. Rational solutions to social choice problems often are difficult to specify because of the logical problems in aggregating the preferences of many individuals (cf. Sen, 1970). For the matching problem in quasi-markets there is a reasonable answer to the question of who is best matched with whom: stable matching solutions are always possible

(Roth, 1982). These solutions are attractive social choice options because they are nondictatorial in that they take account of the preferences of every participant, and they do not waste resources because they are Pareto efficient.

If stable solutions are accepted as desirable it must be decided which of the stable solutions should be implemented. Explicitly including issues that can be negotiated separately from the assignment of individuals can help resolve this problem since one side can be compensated with gains on these issues for accepting a matching solution that favors the other side. The exercise reported here, for example, allows salary to be negotiated independently and can be used to compensate firms for accepting the candidate-optimal matching solution.

As Roth (1982) points out, matching markets can be either decentralized, as is the market for graduating management students, or they can be institutionalized, as is the market for medical residents. Achieving stable solutions is likely to be difficult in decentralized markets because the complexity of the matching problem places great demands on negotiators. Despite the likelihood that they will profit from a centralized matching procedure, many people may prefer to take their chances with the less structured market. A dislike of highly structured social choice mechanisms might be similar to resistance to the use of linear decision models for individual choices (cf. Dawes, 1988).

Dawes (1979) explicitly addresses linear decision models as social choice mechanisms. Linear models have consistently been shown to produce superior results to global, expert judgments in predicting uncertain events. Personnel selection and the diagnosis of psychological or physical disease are examples of contexts in which linear models could be used effectively; the selection of bullets to be used by the Denver Police Department is an example of a social decision procedure that was facilitated by using linear models (Dawes, 1979).

People do not like to use linear decision models, despite their well-reported superiority. Dawes (1979; 1989) suggests that people tend to reject the use of linear models because they are overconfident of their own judgments; because the times when intuitive judgment succeeds or when statistically based decisions fail are particularly salient; because they wish the world to be more controllable and predictable than it is so they reject models with explicitly low predictive power, ironically in favor of methods which, though they pretend to be deterministic, have even lower predictive ability; or because they resist the idea of ''reducing'' people to numerical scores.

The purpose of the algorithm used by the National Resident Matching Program is not prediction, except in the sense of predicting the stability of the matching solution. However, it, like linear decision models, mechan-

22　　　　　　　　　SONDAK AND BAZERMAN

ically combines input to determine outcomes and as such removes control from the individuals in the market. The benefits people seek in matching contexts are often very important to them; people often want enduring relationships for marriage and employment, for example. It may be that perceived control over outcomes is important enough in these contexts that individuals would be willing to sacrifice efficiency for control.

While it is important to understand dyadic negotiation processes, negotiation researchers should look beyond the dyad. Whenever a negotiator has alternative sources of the goods he or she seeks, a market context is implied. Negotiators' decision making within a dyadic situation is likely to be influenced by the question: "Is this the right person for me to be negotiating with?" Our results suggest that such market effects should not be neglected.

REFERENCES

Baysinger, B. D., & Mobley, W. H. (1983). Employee turnover: Individual and organizational analysis. In K. Rowland & G. Ferris (Eds.), *Research in personnel and human resources management,* (Vol. 1). Greenwich, CT: JAI Press.

Dawes, R. M. (1979). The robust beauty of improper linear models in decision making. *American Psychologist,* 34, 571–582.

Dawes, R. M. (1988). *Rational choice in an uncertain world.* San Diego: Harcourt Brace Jovanovich.

Diamond, P., & Maskin, E. (1979). An equilibrium analysis of search and breach of contract, I: Steady states. *Bell Journal of Economics,* 10, 282–316.

Diamond, P., & Maskin, E. (1982). An equilibrium analysis of search and breach of contract, II: A non-steady state example. *Journal of Economic Theory,* 25, 165–195.

Emerson, R. M. (1964). Power-dependence relations: Two experiments. *Sociometry,* 27, 282–298.

Gale, D. (1984). Equilibrium in a discrete exchange economy with money. *International Journal of Game Theory,* 13, 61–64.

Gale, D., & Shapley, L. (1962). College admissions and the stability of marriage. *American Mathematical Monthly,* 69, 9–15.

Harrison, G. W., & McCabe, K. A. (1990). Stability and preference distortion in resource matching: An experimental study of the marriage market. Unpublished manuscript, University of South Carolina, Department of Economics.

Kelso, A. S. Jr., & Crawford, V. P. (1982). Job matching, coalition formation, and gross substitutes. *Econometrica,* 50, 1483–1504.

Lax, D. A., & Sebenius, J. K. (1987). Measuring the degree of joint gains achieved by negotiators. Unpublished manuscript, Harvard University, Harvard Business School.

Mannix, E. M., & Bazerman, M. H. (1988, October). Negotiations in a market context: Limitations on rationality. Paper presented at TIMS/ORSA, Denver, CO.

McAlister, L., Bazerman, M. H., & Fader, P. (1986). Power and goal setting in channel negotiations. *Journal of Marketing Research,* 23, 228–236.

Mongell, S. J., & Roth, A. E. (1991). Sorority rush as a two-sided matching mechanism. *American Economic Review,* 81, 441–464.

Mortensen, D. T. (1988). Matching: Finding a partner for life or otherwise. *American Journal of Sociology,* 94, S215–S240.

Office of Career Development and Placement, J. L. Kellogg Graduate School of Management. (1989). *1989 Placement Report*. Northwestern University.

Pruitt, D. G. (1981). *Negotiation Behavior*. New York: Academic Press.

Pruitt, D. G. (1983). Achieving integrative agreements. In M. H. Bazerman & R. H. Lewicki (Eds.), *Negotiating in organizations*. Beverly Hills: Sage.

Raiffa, H. (1982). *The art and science of negotiation*. Cambridge, MA: Belknap.

Roloff, M. E., & Dailey, W. O. (1988). The effects of alternatives to reaching agreement on the development of integrative solutions to problems: The debilitating side effects of shared BATNA. Unpublished manuscript, Northwestern University.

Roth, A. E. (1982). The economics of matching: Stability and incentives. *Mathematics of Operations Research, 7*, 617–628.

Roth, A. E. (1984). The evolution of the labor market for medical interns and residents: A case study in game theory. *Journal of Political Economy, 92*, 991–1016.

Roth, A. E. (1985). Conflict and coincidence of interest in job matching: Some new results and open questions. *Mathematics of Operation Research, 10*, 379–389.

Roth, A. E., & Sotomayor, M. A. O. (1990). *Two sided matching: A study in game-theoretic modelling and analysis*. Cambridge: Cambridge University Press.

Rubinstein, A., & Wolinsky, A. (1985). Equilibrium in a market with sequential bargaining. *Econometrica, 53*, 1133–1150.

Sen, A. (1970). *Collective choice and social welfare*. Amsterdam: North-Holland.

Sondak, H., & Bazerman, M. H. (1989). Matching and negotiation processes in quasi-markets. *Organizational Behavior and Human Decision Processes, 44*, 261–280.

Tripp, T. M., & Sondak, H. An evaluation of dependent variables in experimental negotiation studies: Impasse rates and Pareto efficiency. In press, *Org. Behavior and Human Decision Processes*.

Received: May 26, 1989

[21]

Organizational Behavior and Human Decision Processes
Vol. 80, No. 3, December, pp. 252–283, 1999
Article ID obhd.1999.2861, available online at http://www.idealibrary.com on IDE▲L®

The Negotiation Matching Process: Relationships and Partner Selection

Ann E. Tenbrunsel

College of Business Administration, University of Notre Dame

Kimberly A. Wade-Benzoni

Stern School of Business, New York University

Joseph Moag

J. L. Kellogg Graduate School of Management, Northwestern University

and

Max H. Bazerman

*J. L. Kellogg Graduate School of Management, Northwestern University;
and Harvard Business School, Harvard University*

We present 3 studies that examine the process of partner selection in negotiations and the influence that relationships may have on the partner-selection decision. In Study 1, we present a simulated matching market experiment in which we compare the matching process when relationships can influence the partner-selection decision with the matching process when relationships cannot influence this decision. We find that when relationships are not allowed to influence the matching process, there are more economically optimal agreements, a larger market surplus, and more search activity. In Study 2, a simulation of a naturally occurring market selection process provides additional quantitative support for the findings from Study 1 and offers qualitative data on the reasoning process behind partner selection, including

This paper benefited from comments from Dan Ilgen, Keith Murnighan, Al Roth, Harris Sondak, Brian Uzzi, and three anonymous reviewers. Support for this paper was provided by the Dispute Resolution Research Center at Northwestern University.

Address and correspondence and reprint requests to Ann E. Tenbrunsel, College of Business Administration, University of Notre Dame, Notre Dame, IN 46556-0399.

252

the social factors that are influential in this decision. Study 3
utilizes a repeated trial experimental simulation to offer further
support for the negative relationship between relationships and
economic outcomes and to suggest that the relative power of
the negotiators influences the extent to which relationships help
versus hurt individual profitability. Implications of these findings are discussed.   © 1999 Academic Press

A critical issue facing employees and employers, buyers and suppliers, and
joint venture partners is the selection of a negotiation partner. Yet, the vast
majority of studies in the existing negotiation literature have structured the
partner-selection process by preselecting negotiation partners. The exclusion
of the actual partner-selection process in negotiation research could be limiting,
as research shows that substantial economic suboptimality exists as the result
of selection mismatches (Roth & Sotomayor, 1990; Sondak & Bazerman, 1991).
We investigate the impact that relationships have in producing this economic
suboptimality and potential reasons—including the consideration of social outcomes and a lack of awareness of the economic costs—why individuals rely on
relationships to find a negotiation partner.

Ample research suggests that matching markets—markets in which individuals must locate a partner—produce less than optimal outcomes. Roth (1984;
Roth & Sotomayor, 1990), for instance, documented the complexity and difficulty associated with the matching process in the job market for graduating
medical students. Roth and Xing (1994) suggest that other markets share
some of the same matching problems, including the markets for federal court
clerkships, new marketing professors, clinical psychology internships, dental
residencies, college football bowls, and sorority and fraternity rush. Similarly,
the markets for marriages, MBA graduates, real estate, and joint venture
partnerships have been cited as examples of markets with matching difficulties
(Mongell & Roth, 1991; Mortensen, 1994; Neale & Bazerman, 1991; Roth &
Xing, 1994). Experimentally, Sondak and Bazerman (1989, 1991) have shown
that economically optimal outcomes are also unlikely in simulated matching
markets.

As these examples illustrate, the process of matching in general, and of
finding the best match in particular, is a very difficult task, producing less
than optimal consequences (Mortensen, 1994). One way to evaluate matching
outcomes at the market level is to determine the degree of economic rationality
that is obtained. "Rationality" is defined as market stability (Roth & Sotomayor,
1990) which occurs when every match results in an outcome that equals or
exceeds the outcome from any other potential match (Mortensen, 1994). In this
sense, markets are completely rational when no pair of participants on opposite
sides of the market will be economically better off with each other than they
are with the parties to whom they are currently matched (Gale & Shapley,
1962; Roth, 1982). Thus, rational markets optimize matches by avoiding the
possibilities of gains from switching partners.

We conducted three studies that examine the partner-selection process and the role that relationships may play in the matching decision. In our first study, we investigate the assertion that relationships may negatively influence economic outcomes, including market and individual profitability. Study 2 provides additional support for this finding but identifies several reasons individuals may accept this economic loss, including a consideration of social outcomes and a lack of awareness of the economic costs. Study 3 also provides support for the basic hypothesis that relationships can decrease economic outcomes but investigates one contingent factor—the power of the negotiator—that determines when relying on relationships during the partner-selection process is economically beneficial versus detrimental.

The Benefits of Relationships

Most models of economic behavior assume that the behavior of rational, self-interested individuals is minimally affected by social relations (Granovetter, 1985), so that, in a matching context, individuals seek out an optimal exchange, regardless of the other party's identity. Researchers (Baker, 1990; Ben-Porath, 1980; Greenhalgh, 1987; Podolny, 1993, 1994; Powell, 1990) and numerous examples to the contrary challenge this assumption. Coleman (1988) argues that the assumption that relationships have no influence "flies in the face of empirical reality: persons' actions are shaped, redirected, constrained by the social context." Baker (1994) asserts that "relationships are a fundamental human need." Similarly, Burt (1982) contends that actors exist and evaluate alternatives within a social context. From a matching perspective, it has been posited that groups recruit mostly through social contacts (McPherson, Popielarz, & Drobnic, 1992). Indeed, German companies contemplating the selection of partners for interfirm cooperative research and development have been found to place extra emphasis on personal contacts above and beyond technical expertise (Brockhoff, Gupta, & Rotering, 1991). Similarly, relationships are argued to heavily impact the corporation–investment banking interface (Baker, 1990) as well as the construction, publishing, and film industries (Powell, 1990).

Individuals rely on relationships in matching decisions for many reasons. Personal relations have been argued to reduce opportunism (Baker, 1990) and the moral hazard problem (Ben-Porath, 1980) and to increase cooperation in prisoner's dilemma games (Granovetter, 1985), the integrative quality of bargaining agreements (Valley, Neale, & Mannix, 1995), and the effectiveness of problem solving created by asymmetric information (Valley, Moag, & Bazerman, 1998). Baker (1994) suggests that the relationship-oriented strategy employed by Mark Twain Bancshares has boosted performance: he argues that their decentralized boards of directors, which are composed of members drawn from the local business community, have promoted strong ties with customers, which in turn has resulted in a growth in assets, earnings, and return on equity.

People use personal contacts in matching situations partially because they are a basis for trust and information in an uncertain world (Ben-Porath, 1980; Lawler & Yoon, 1996; Podolny, 1994; Powell, 1990). When actors are faced with uncertainty, they turn to others whom they know and trust (Galaskiewicz,

1985; Podolny, 1994). The trustworthiness characteristic of personal relations makes transactions possible that, absent of this trust, would not occur (Coleman, 1988). Trust facilitates transactions because people believe that better information comes from dealing with someone they have known in the past (Granovetter, 1985): such information is seen as more unique (Coleman, 1988), representing knowledge that the actor may not be able to get otherwise (Baker, 1994). Thus, a positive reputation and beneficial past dealings with a person can act as proxies for trust and reliability.

In addition to reducing uncertainty, relying on personal relations can also be a direct response to cognitive limitations. While economic models assume that actors are hyperrational with unlimited information-processing and analytical faculties, in reality individuals are subject to bounded rationality (March & Simon, 1958). As a result, people develop informal mechanisms to simplify their interactions with others, such as dealing with individuals they know. A reliance on those that are close or familiar can ease the difficulty of identifying sources of data and decrease the number of interactions required in the search for data (Valley, 1992). Indeed, the accessibility of an information source has been found to be related to the frequency of its use (O'Reilly, 1982) and to the quantity of information provided to the actor from that source (Smeltzer, Van Hook, & Hutt, 1991).

The Hidden Costs of Relationships

Many researchers have argued, however, that the reliance on relationships can become a double-edged sword, beneficial for facilitating certain transactions but detrimental for others (Coleman, 1988). For example, Coleman asserts that while strong relationships help to establish effective norms that facilitate interactions, one's attention can be focused toward certain objectives but away from other, perhaps equally important, goals. One important goal that may be de-emphasized is one's own economic interests. Relationships can become such a dominant influence that the economic interests of the focal actor take on secondary importance. Geertz (1963) asserts that strong ties may result in businesses focusing more on the relationship and helping related individuals than on developing the economic enterprise. Similarly, Granovetter (1992) suggests that while relationships can increase trust, they can also turn a successful business into a relief agency; thus, ultimate success may depend on building trust from relations without incurring their costs.

Fry, Firestone, and Williams (1983) were among the first to empirically explore the negative influence of relationships in negotiations. In a study comparing dating couples and mixed-dyad stranger couples, they predicted that prior involvement with one's negotiation partner would decrease the ability to find mutually beneficial outcomes. They found that while dating couples exchanged more truthful information and used pressure tactics less frequently, they also had lower aspirations and generated fewer offers, which blocked the discovery of high joint outcomes. Fry et al. suggest that despite added benefits from increased information exchange, the relationship itself can be problematic if the need to preserve affectional ties results in the avoidance of conflict, thereby producing more "accessible" but less mutually satisfactory outcomes. The focus on preserving the relationship may lead to an aversion to conflict, including avoiding a discussion of differing interests, which in turn reduces the likelihood that mutually beneficial outcomes will be discovered.

We suggest that relationships may also reduce economic outcomes in the matching process: when strong ties are allowed to influence the matching process (relationship-accessible markets), there will be a decrease in the number of economically optimal matches—or matches that maximize aggregate surplus[1]—that are formed in comparison to when strong ties are not allowed to influence this process (relationship-inaccessible markets). Thus, we posit that market rationality, in the form of economically optimal matches, is inversely related to relationship influence in the matching process. More specifically, we predict the following:

HYPOTHESIS 1. There will be fewer economically optimal matches in relationship-accessible markets than in relationship-inaccessible markets.

We therefore agree with Coleman (1988) that social relationships may be so powerful that they facilitate certain actions but constrain others. In particular, a reliance on relationships is likely to limit the amount of information that market participants seek to obtain. Granovetter's (1973) discussion of strong and weak ties suggests that weak ties may contribute valuable information to the focal actor. Interactions with weak ties expose individuals to knowledge beyond that which comes from one's friendship circle; thus, these interactions are likely to provide more diverse information than interactions between strong ties (McPherson et al., 1992; Smeltzer et al., 1991). In this way, then, weak ties are likely to carry information that is not provided by strong ties. Although strong ties may provide more in-depth information about a given transaction, they may limit the breadth of information by decreasing the number of people (information sources) that one seeks out. Strong ties, and their accompanying time demands, reduce opportunities for keeping weaker ties active, which in turn decreases the diversity of information available about the market and the probability of finding an economically optimal match. This logic resonates with Burt (1982), who suggests that social ties may reduce the number of exchanges that one has with other ties in a market by decreasing the likelihood of transactions between actors not connected by such ties. Social networks have been argued to serve as access constraints that limit the number of contacts in which one engages (Podolny, 1993) and to restrict the amount of information available to participants (Baker, 1990). Thus, we predict the following:

HYPOTHESIS 2. Individuals will engage in less search for a potential partner in relationship-accessible markets than in relationship-inaccessible markets.

Strong ties should also affect the allocation of match resources. Lerner (1974),

---

[1] See Mortensen (1994) for a discussion of optimal market structures and the relationship to aggregate surplus.

for instance, suggests that harmonious relationships display more equal distributions while relationships among less well acquainted individuals exhibit more equitable distributions. Greenberg (1983) discovered that the more individuals liked each other and the better friends they were, the more likely they were to divide a restaurant check evenly. Sondak, Neale, and Pinkley (1997) also found that relationships increased the prevalence of equality as a distribution norm in negotiations. We therefore predict the following:

HYPOTHESIS 3. Relationship-accessible markets will have more agreements based on equality than relationship-inaccessible markets.

Drawing on economic and sociological perspectives, we thus predict that the influence of strong ties on partner selection in a matching market has effects at the market, match, and individual level. To investigate our predictions, we utilize two methodologies. In Studies 1 and 3, experimental manipulation that compares markets in which relationships cannot influence the matching process (relationship-inaccessible markets) with markets in which relationships can influence the matching process (relationship-accessible markets) is used to directly test the influence of relationships on the matching process. In Study 2, a naturally occurring partner-selection process is emulated to provide qualitative insight in the partner-selection decision.

STUDY 1

Methods

Tests of the hypotheses involved comparing outcomes in relationship-accessible markets with outcomes in relationship-inaccessible markets. In each type of market, participants had to find a negotiation partner and negotiate a deal. To manipulate whether or not relationships could influence the matching process, either participants knew the identity of one of their potential match partners and this potential partner was a relatively strong tie (relationship-accessible) or they did not know the identity of any of their potential match partners (relationship-inaccessible). Dependent variables were collected from the negotiation forms and questionnaires (described below) that were used in the negotiation process.

The design utilized a residential real estate simulation. Each market consisted of three buyers (A, B, C) who were looking to buy a house and three sellers (A, B, C) who were looking to sell their house. There were eight markets in this study, four relationship-accessible markets and four relationship-inaccessible markets. Forty-eight graduate business students participated in the study as part of a negotiations class.

Participants were seated in an auditorium, buyers on one side and sellers on the other, although at this point they were unaware of their roles. Participants first received general information on the nature of the simulation, including a description of a typical market. Participants were also told that all negotiations would be conducted via written forms that would be collected and delivered to targets they designated. Participants were informed that their goal was to obtain as much surplus profit as possible, which was equivalent to the sale price minus the reservation price for the seller and the reservation price minus the sale price for the buyer. (The reservation price was described to the sellers as the lowest price for which they were willing to sell their house; the reservation price was described to the buyers as the highest price they were willing to pay to buy a particular house.)

Participants then received role information indicating whether they were Buyer A, B, or C or Seller A, B, or C. At this point they were not informed what market they were in. The role information of the buyers and sellers included descriptions of the three houses that were on the market and their list prices. The buyers' role information included their preferences and reservation prices for each of the listed houses. Buyer A was informed that he/she preferred Seller A's house (their first choice) over Seller B's house (their second choice), which was preferred over Seller C's house (their third choice). Similarly, Buyer B was informed that he/she preferred Seller B's house over Seller C's house, which was preferred over Seller A's house. Buyer C was informed that he/she preferred Seller C's house over Seller A's house, which was preferred over Seller B's house.

Buyers' preferences translated to different reservation prices, or maximum prices, that they were willing to pay: Buyers were willing to pay as much as $400,000 for their first choice, $395,000 for their second choice, and $390,000 for their third choice. For example, Buyer A was informed that he/she would pay up to $400,000 for Seller A's house, $395,000 for Seller B's house, and $390,000 for Seller C's house. The role information for the sellers indicated that they did not have preferences for buyers; rather, they simply wanted to sell their house for as high a price as possible, provided that the price exceeded $360,000 (their reservation price). The difference between the reservation prices of the buyer and the seller reflected the joint surplus that was available to the partners to divide. If a buyer matched with his/her first choice, the joint surplus available to the partners was equal to $40,000, or the reservation price of the buyer ($400,000) minus the reservation price of the seller ($360,000). Likewise, if a buyer matched with his/her second choice, the match produced $35,000 in joint surplus ($395,000 − $360,000), whereas a match with the buyer's third choice produced a joint surplus of $30,000 ($390,000 − $360,000).

After reading their role information, participants were told that they would have an opportunity to meet with someone on the opposite side of the market prior to the negotiation. Thus, a buyer would have an opportunity to meet with a seller and vice versa. Participants were told that they could share information and discuss strategies but they could not create a binding agreement. Participants were informed of their meeting partner's role. That is, they were told with which buyer (A, B, or C) or which seller (A, B, or C) they would be meeting. They were not told, however, which market their meeting partner would be in; in fact, they were explicitly informed that they would not know at this point whether or not their meeting partner would be in their market.

Unbeknownst to the participants, everyone met with a relatively strong tie.

Two weeks prior to the simulation, all participants had completed a questionnaire assessing their ties with everyone else in the class. Specifically, participants were asked to rate each person in the class in terms of how much time they spent with that person outside of class. Ratings were conducted on a 7-point scale, with a 1 indicating that the participant spent no time with this person outside of class and a 7 indicating that the participant spent a significant amount of time with this person outside of class. The average strength of the tie in the classroom was 1.47 (with 78.8% = 1, 9.9% = 2, 4.2% = 3, 3.1% = 4, 1.5% = 5, 1.4% = 6, and 1.1% = 7). Meeting pairs were arranged to maximize the strength of the ties. The average strength of the tie of the meeting pairs was 4.25 (with 4.2% = 1, 12.5% = 2, 20.8% = 3, 20.8% = 4, 16.7% = 5, 8.3% = 6, and 16.7% = 7).

Following a 10-min meeting with their "friend," participants returned to their seat and received their market assignment and general negotiation rules. Their market-assignment information sheet identified the market in which they would participate and informed them whether their meeting partner was in their market. For example, buyers were provided with the following information: "You are in market X. The seller that you just met with is/is not in your market."

Participants were then provided with final negotiation rules. These rules informed the participants that they were allowed to communicate only with those on the opposite side of the market. Thus, buyers could communicate only with sellers and sellers could communicate only with buyers. Furthermore, only two types of forms—communication forms and offer forms—could be used in the negotiation process. Both types of forms contained a space to designate which person the form should be given to (i.e., Seller A, B, or C) and which person the form was from (i.e., Buyer A, B, or C). Communication forms were used to exchange any type of information desired by the sender. Participants were told that they could exchange as many communication forms at a time, to as many different potential partners, as they wished. Offer forms, which included only a space for offer price, were used to make an explicit offer by either a buyer or a seller. The offer forms had an expiration limit of 3 min; thus, if the offer was not responded to during this time period, the offer would be considered null and void. Participants were told that they could send only one offer form at a time and that they could not reveal their personal identity (i.e., name, negotiator number) on any of the forms. Forms were collected by six individuals not involved in the class. These forms were taken to the back of the room, sorted, and then hand-delivered by another individual so that participants could not track to whom their forms were going.

Participants were given 35 min to find a partner. During the simulation, the matches that were formed were identified (without the price of the transaction) in the front of the room so that the remaining market participants knew which participants were still active. In addition, the instructor kept a record of the time remaining in front of the room. Following the exercise, participants completed a postnegotiation questionnaire.

The eight markets were identical, with one exception. In the four relationship-accessible markets, the participant's meeting partner was in his/her market. Thus, the participant knew the identity, and had met with, one of the participants on the other side of the market. The identities of the two other participants on the other side of the market remained unknown. In the four relationship-inaccessible markets, the participant's meeting partner was not in his/her market. Thus, in these markets, the identities of all three participants on the other side of the market were unknown (although these participants could be strong ties, the participant did not know whether they were). In this way, relationships could not influence the matching process because the identity of the market participants was eliminated. For example, a buyer in the relationship-inaccessible market did not know the identity of the sellers; thus, while strong ties between this buyer and the potential sellers may have existed, the ability of the relationship to influence the matching process was eliminated. In the relationship-accessible markets, a participant did know the identity of one of the participants on the other side of the market and thus his/her relationship with this person could have impacted the partner-selection process.

The hypotheses for this study include dependent variables related to economically optimal agreements, search activity, and equal agreements. Consistent with Mortensen (1994), optimal agreements maximize market profit surplus. As described earlier, market profit surplus is highest with A–A, B–B, and C–C matches; other combinations of matches are economically suboptimal. Search activity was measured by the number of forms (communication, offer, and total) that a given market participant sent. Equal agreements were defined as those in which the joint profit was divided equally between the two market participants (i.e., each participant received the same amount of profit). In addition, individuals were asked to rate how happy they were with their outcome on a scale from 1 to 6 (with 1 = very unhappy and 6 = very happy).

Results

To test Hypothesis 1, the number of optimal agreements in each market was calculated (see Table 1). A chi-square test revealed that there was a significant difference in the number of optimal agreements across markets, so that there were more optimal agreements in the relationship-inaccessible markets than in the relationship-accessible markets ($\chi^2(1) = 6.31$, $p < .05$, $\eta^2 = .26$). Also supporting this hypothesis, joint profit was significantly higher ($F(1, 22) =$

TABLE 1

Number of Optimal Matches: Study 1

	Market	
	Relationship-inaccessible	Relationship-accessible
# of optimal matches	12	7
# of suboptimal matches	0	5

6.60, $p < .05$, $\eta^2 = .23$) in the relationship-inaccessible markets (joint profit = \$40,000) than in the relationship-accessible markets (joint profit = \$37,500). Additional analysis revealed that happiness was significantly related to the optimality of the match, so that participants were significantly more happy ($F(1, 46) = 3.94$, $p < .05$, $\eta^2 = .08$) in optimal matches (happy = 4.3) than in suboptimal matches (happy = 3.6). There was no indication, however, that happiness with the outcome, was significantly related to whether or not participants matched with a friend ($F(1, 46) = 2.70$, ns).

An examination of the influence of relationship restrictions on search activity revealed that market participants engaged in more search in the relationship-inaccessible markets than in the relationship-accessible markets, supporting Hypothesis 2. There were significantly more communication ($F(1, 46) = 3.97$, $p < .05$, $\eta^2 = .08$), offer ($F(1, 46) = 21.19$, $p < .0001$, $\eta^2 = .32$), and total forms (communication + offer; ($F(1, 46) = 18.40$, $p < .0001$, $\eta^2 = .29$) exchanged in the relationship-inaccessible markets than in the relationship-accessible markets (see Table 2).

The third hypothesis, which predicted an influence of relationship restriction on the number of equal agreements, was marginally supported. In the relationship-accessible markets, 25% of the agreements reflected an equal division of the surplus profit, whereas in the relationship-inaccessible markets, 0% of the agreements reflected an equal division. This difference, in the predicted direction, was marginally significant ($\chi^2(1) = 3.43$, $p < .06$, $\eta^2 = .14$).

Discussion

In support of the hypotheses, restricting the influence of strong ties on the matching process increased the number of economically optimal agreements, match profitability, and the amount of search activity in which participants engaged. Furthermore, analysis suggested that individuals were less happy when they were in a suboptimal match than when they were in an optimal match. The results also provided weak support for the influence of relationships on the division of resources, implying that restricting the ability of relationships to influence the matching process reduces the number of equal agreements.

A search to understand the relationship between economic outcomes, search activity, and participants' satisfaction with outcomes can take at least two possible directions. One of those directions focuses on the role that decision biases may play in assessing the cost and benefits of various matching partners.

TABLE 2

Number of Forms Exchanged: Study 1

Market	Number of forms exchanged		
	Communication	Offer	Total
Relationship-inaccessible	6.5	6.0	12.5
Relationship-accessible	5.0	3.2	8.2

It may be that individuals are simply unaware of the economic implications of strong tie matches and thus do not realize that matching with friends reduces their search and produces more economically suboptimal agreements.

Yet another explanation focuses on the role that social forces play in influencing the matching decision. The study presented here was relatively one-sided, focused on the economic aspects of the matching process. Missing is another, equally important, aspect: the social costs and benefits of matching with friends. While individuals may incur an economic cost when they match with friends, social benefits (i.e., preservation of the relationship, trust, enjoyment) may outweigh economic costs, making a strong tie match the preferred matching strategy and thus reducing the need to engage in search activity. Conversely, social costs and obligations of not matching with a friend (i.e., potential of retaliation, damage to the relationship) may be so high that individuals do not pursue economically rational strategies (including engaging in search activity) in fear of incurring these social costs, even if this results in a lower economic outcome and potentially less satisfaction with this outcome.

To further understand the role of strong ties in the matching process it is necessary to examine the potential viability of these forces. While it is not possible to compare the strength of these forces in a laboratory setting, it is possible to gain insight into the role that biases and social forces may play in the matching decision. Gaining this insight was the motivation for our second study.

STUDY 2

The first study provided quantitative data on the influence that strong ties may have on the matching process, offering insight into the economic effects of relationships on the partner-selection decision. To better understand these outcomes, we wanted to gain a qualitative understanding of how these decisions are made. Specifically, we were interested in gaining perspective on the reasoning process of an individual faced with the decision of whom to select as a negotiation partner. What are individuals looking for in a negotiation partner that may lend itself to matching with a strong tie? What advantages are strong ties perceived to have? What may help explain the economic suboptimality of matching with strong ties?

The purpose of our second study is therefore twofold. First, we wanted to replicate the most important results from the first study by further investigating the relationship between strong ties and economic outcomes and between strong ties and search activity. Second, we also wanted to help make sense of this data by exploring answers to the above questions. To accomplish this, the second study more closely simulates a naturally occurring matching process by allowing individuals to freely choose their matching partner.

Methods

Fifty-four masters of business administration students participated in the study as part of a class exercise. These students participated in the real estate simulation described in Study 1. In this study, there were nine real estate markets, each with three buyers (A, B, C) and three sellers (A, B, C). Students were randomly assigned to participate in one of these markets. The general information provided to the participants on the market structure and on their role (including their preferences and reservation prices) was exactly the same as that described in Study 1.

Unlike in Study 1, however, there were no prearranged meetings with a strong tie and participants could identify and verbally communicate with each other. Upon reading the instructions, participants were provided with information on the identities of the other market participants. The six participants making up a market (three buyers and three sellers) then met in a designated room and were given 30 min to find a partner and negotiate a deal. Participants could structure the market however they wished but buyers could not talk to buyers and sellers could not talk to sellers. They were told that their goal was to maximize their individual surplus as defined by their role and that they could use whatever strategies they felt would help them achieve this. Upon completing a deal, participants filled out a summary sheet indicating the nature of their deal. While not allowing for a causal test of the influence of friendships, the structure of this study allowed for insight into a naturally occurring partner-selection process.

To provide this insight, participants completed both a pre- and a postnegotiation questionnaire. The prenegotiation questionnaire was completed after participants had read their general and role-specific information and were given information as to the identities of the market participants but before they participated in the market negotiation. This questionnaire asked participants to rate the importance of four criteria—final price, prior relationship, trust, and quality of information exchanged—in the selection of a partner by dividing up 100 points among the four factors and to describe their reasons for these ratings. In addition, participants indicated how much time they spent with each of the potential partners outside of class on the same 7-point scale described in Study 1 (with 1 = no time and 7 = significant portion of time). The postnegotiation questionnaire was distributed after the market simulation was completed. The questionnaire asked participants to describe their negotiation experience, including their reasons for selecting their negotiation partner, the advantages and disadvantages of each potential partner, and the number of different partners with whom they negotiated.

Results

Results supported the findings from Study 1 that strong ties produce economically suboptimal agreements and reduce joint surplus. Data suggested that the "tie profile" of one's potential partners was related to market and match profitability, where tie profile is defined as the tie strength of one's potential partners. This profile was measured in two ways: the "high tie," measured as the strongest tie of one's potential partners, and the "aggregate ties" of one's potential partners, defined by the sum of the ties of the potential partners.[2] Correlational data revealed that both high tie and aggregate ties were negatively related to the probability of obtaining an economically optimal agreement ($r(26) = -.33, p < .05$, and $r(25) = -.34, p < .05$, respectively) and to the joint surplus obtained by a given match ($r(26) = -.39, p < .05$, and $r(25) = -.39, p < .05$, respectively). The data suggest that having potential partners who are strong ties, either because of one partner who is a very good friend or because of several partners who are strong acquaintances, reduces the economic value of the resulting agreements. Also in support of the first study, the data suggest that tie profile was negatively correlated with the number of potential partners with whom one spoke ($r(52) = -.30, p < .05$, and $r(50) = -0.36$, $p < .01$; high tie and aggregate tie, respectively), as was the focal negotiator's tie rating of his/her partner ($r(50) = -.43, p < .01$) and the partner's tie rating of the focal negotiator ($r(50) = -.39, p < .01$). Furthermore, search activity and outcomes were positively related. Specifically, the number of potential partners with whom one spoke was positively correlated with the probability of an optimal match ($r(26) = .33, p < .05$), so that speaking with one partner resulted in an average joint surplus of $32,500 and 0% optimal agreements, speaking with two partners resulted in an average joint surplus of $36,578 and 53% optimal agreements, and speaking with all three partners resulted in an average joint surplus of $37,968 and 75% optimal agreements.

Why, then, would negotiators match with friends, if the result is less than economically optimal? The data suggest several possible, potentially additive, reasons. First, negotiators' utility function may include social factors, so that their definition of "optimal" is different from the more traditional, economic definition. Second, the presence of strong ties may change the strategies of negotiators, reducing their goals and aspirations. Third, negotiators may fall prey to biased perceptions of relationships and may not be aware of the potential costs that can be incurred by matching with a strong tie. Analyses suggest that all three of these reasons may be at work.

One of the reasons that negotiators may match with strong ties, despite their economic costs, is that noneconomic criteria influence the choice of a negotiation partner. An examination of the criteria that were important in the selection of a partner supports this assertion. The division of 100 points between the four criteria revealed an average of 57 points for price, 19 for trust, 17 for quality of information, and 10 for prior relationship. Thus, while price was important, noneconomic factors, such as trust and quality of information, were also important in the context represented in this study. Qualitative data lend additional insight into these ratings. When participants were asked to describe what they were looking for in a potential partner, fairness, honesty, trust, and a smooth interaction were frequently mentioned themes. One common theme among these comments was a desire for fairness, represented by comments

---

[2] Aggregate ties could potentially range from 3 (a rating of 1 for each potential partner) to 21 (a rating of 7 for each potential partner). In this study, the range was from 3 to 16, with an average of 6.3.

that indicated that participants were looking for "fairness," "a willingness to work towards an equitable agreement," "a fair transaction," and "fairness for both sides." Criteria such as "honesty of the seller," "an honest representation of house," and "trust" suggested that honesty and trust are also important. Factors such as flexibility, ease of communication, and willingness to negotiate signify that criteria that make the negotiation process easier are a third type of noneconomic criteria that may influence the matching process, with references to "willingness to negotiate," "willingness," "ability to communicate information," "ability to listen," "flexibility of the seller," and "ease of negotiation" supporting this assertion. Thus, in addition to maximizing economic criteria, negotiators appear to be looking for a partner that will simplify the negotiation process. This is perhaps best exemplified by one individual who commented that "prior relationship, trust, etc., may make the process go more smoothly."

An examination of postnegotiation comments concerning the advantages of matching with each of the three potential partners suggests that strong ties may be correlated with these criteria. As represented by the following comments, participants listing the advantages of matching with their strongest ties focused primarily on the central themes of fairness, honesty, trust, and information sharing: "he was willing to compromise, he seemed more honest"; "honesty and desire to sell"; "he seemed up front and honest, attitude, likeness, forthright nature, integrity"; "was the most forthright in sharing information"; "he was open and honest about other offers and seemed to share information"; "I felt that the discussion was honest"; "we put off discussing price as long as possible [while I] discussed my concerns"; and "I trusted [the buyer] genuinely." Strong ties appeared to provide a level of comfort, with the advantages of matching with the strongest tie including "I was most comfortable with the discussion" and "we came to an agreement that felt good."

In addition to providing noneconomic benefits, strong ties may also influence the negotiation by changing the negotiation strategies that are employed. In particular, ties that generate strong affect may influence negotiators' goals, so that they alter their minimum price based on the relationship: "I would [change] the price for a friend." Data also suggest that the influence of relationships on reservation prices and search activity may be related, so that negotiators, in an attempt to reduce search costs, make attractive offers to strong ties that are close to their bottom line: "Because he is a close friend, I offered him my minimum price right away—it would have been a very quick and easy negotiation if it had been accepted."

Results also indicate, however, that negotiators may not be aware of the influence that strong ties have in the matching process. While, as asserted above, trust and relationship were important criteria that negotiators looked for in a potential partner, price was the most important criterion. Furthermore, the importance of price as a criterion was not related to the tie profile of one's potential partner ($r(51) = .00$, *ns*, and $r(53) = -.08$ *ns*; aggregate ties and high tie, respectively), even though actual outcomes were related to the profile. Thus, while having a strong tie profile reduces the economic value of the outcomes, there is no evidence that individuals with strong ties value these economic outcomes any less than individuals without strong ties.

Negotiators also do not seem to be aware of the impact of strong ties on search activity. When asked to rate the extent of their search relative to those of others in the market, 19% of participants rated their search as less than average, 66% as average, and 15% as above average. However, this perception of one's search activity was not related to the aggregate ties of one's potential partner ($r(50) = -.10$, *ns*), to the focal negotiator's tie rating of his/her partner ($r(50) = .02$, *ns*), or to the partner's tie rating of the focal negotiator ($r(48) = .15$, *ns*), even though actual search activity was negatively related to these measures. Thus, despite the fact that strong ties do limit search, there is no indication that participants are aware of this relationship.

Discussion

The second study provides additional support for the findings from Study 1, suggesting that when relationships can influence the matching process, match optimality and search activity are reduced. These data also imply, however, that economic concerns are only part of the matching decision. Strong tie matches may be preferred, despite their economic costs, because they provide social benefits, such as making the negotiation proceed smoother and engendering feelings of trust, fairness, and honesty. While the weights assigned to these various forces cannot be extrapolated to other contexts, the results do suggest that social forces can be an important component in the matching decision. These social factors may in turn influence negotiators' strategies. In addition to reducing search, strong ties may influence the pattern of concessions, so that negotiators "cut to the chase" with friends by making a reasonable opening offer. In congruence with Fry et al. (1983), it may be that affective ties temper aspiration and reservation prices. Negotiation research on reservation prices (White & Neale, 1994) would propose that this influence may be rational if the cost of finding a new partner (i.e., transaction costs as well as the cost to the existing relationship for even engaging in search activity) is higher for strong versus weak ties.

Before assessing whether a reliance on relationships during the matching process is rational, however, it is necessary to determine whether negotiators are aware of their influence and weigh the advantages and disadvantages accordingly, or whether they are unaware of this influence and thus hold biased perceptions of strong ties. The data lend support to the latter hypothesis. There was no evidence that those with strong ties valued economic outcomes any less, and yet they ended up in matches characterized by lower surpluses. Thus, negotiators may fully intend to maximize economic outcomes but be unaware that strong ties prevent them from doing so. Furthermore, there is no indication that individuals are aware that having strong ties reduces their search activity. While it is not possible to assess to what extent this lack of awareness extends to other contexts, it is suggestive of one potentially valid explanation for the negative relationship between strong tie matches and economic outcomes.

STUDY 3

The first two studies demonstrated that relying on relationships to find a negotiation partner can produce economic costs but provide social benefits that are noneconomic in nature. Given the repeated finding that strong ties can reduce economic outcomes, we believe that it is important to further investigate factors that may impact this relationship and potentially change its direction. We argue that power is one of those factors. More specifically, we investigate the possibility that relationships may have a differential impact on economic outcomes, depending on the relative power of the individual negotiator.

We utilize the notion of a multiplicative matching market to directly examine the impact of power in the partner-selection process. A multiplicative market is based on the assumption that match profitability is a multiplicative function of the resources of the two parties. In this type of market, partnerships generate more profit than a simple sum of the resources of the two players. Potential partners can vary in terms of their power, or the extent to which they bring more or less resources to a match, which in turn influences the resulting profitability of a given match. Coalition theory is useful in understanding this notion of power as it relates to partner selection in these types of markets. In this literature, resources are defined to be those goods which can produce benefit when they are used in combination with other goods (Murnighan & Vollrath, 1984). The more resources one possesses, the more the joint benefit that is produced in a multiplicative matching market. Thus, one measure of power is the amount of resources one possesses relative to other parties.

Given the definition of economically optimal matches as those that produce the maximum market surplus (Mortensen, 1994), a multiplicative market is most profitable (has the most surplus) when high-power players and low-power players match with like-powered players. Suboptimal high-low power matches, on the other hand, produce less overall market profit and less aggregate-level individual profit. For example, if a matching market had two buyers—"A" (worth 2) and "B" (worth 4)—and two sellers—"A" (worth 2) and "B" (worth 4)—the market would be most profitable with an A–A and a B–B match (market profitability = $[(2 \times 2) + (4 \times 4) = 20]$) than with two A–B matches (market profitability = $[(2 \times 4) + (4 \times 2) = 16]$).

Optimal high-high or low-low power matches as defined from a market-level perspective, however, have different implications for high- versus low-power players, so that optimal from a market perspective may not be optimal from an individual perspective. The more resources a potential partner provides, the more profit a given partnership produces, meaning that it is in the best interests of all parties to match with a high-power player who can provide these resources. Consider the perspective of a low-power player. A low-power player has two potential match partners: a high-power player (a market suboptimal match) and a low-power player (a market optimal match). Matching with a high-power player provides more joint venture profit than matching with a low-power player; thus for the low-power player there is more profit to divide in a market suboptimal match (a low–high match) than in a market optimal match (a low–low match). The reverse is true for the high-power player: the joint profit is higher if he/she matches with a market optimal match (a high-power player) than if he/she matches with a market suboptimal match (a low-power player). Thus, for the high-power player, there is more profit to divide in a market optimal match than in a market suboptimal match. It is easy to see that a market suboptimal high–low match limits the opportunity available to the more powerful party but helps the less powerful one. Thus, as suggested by Hypothesis 1, to the extent that matches are created based on relationship concerns, economically suboptimal matches are more likely, resulting in relatively lower payoffs for high-power parties and relatively higher payoffs for low-power parties.

Hypothesis 3, which predicts that strong-tie matches will tend to have more equal agreements, also suggests that strong ties will adversely affect high-power players' outcomes. An equality distribution norm, which was argued to be more prevalent in markets characterized by strong ties, ignores the inputs of each partner, reducing the relative outcome of the more powerful partner and increasing the relative outcome of the less powerful player. Thus, Hypotheses 1 and 3 both suggest that strong-tie matches will hurt high-power players and help low-power players because they will produce more economically suboptimal matches (Hypothesis 1) and more equal agreements (Hypothesis 3), which will have detrimental effects on the high-power players but a beneficial impact on the low-power players. We therefore predict that power and market restrictions will interact to influence individual profitability so that:

HYPOTHESIS 4. High-power players will be less profitable, and low-power players more profitable, in relationship-accessible markets than in relationship-inaccessible markets.

Relationships should also have a differential impact on profitability over time. Mortensen (1994) suggests that the quality of a market's matches improves with age since the matching process is one of finding the right "fit" through trial and error processes which requires time and experience in the market. Relationships, however, may impede this process by increasing the likelihood that partners will stay with their current match partner (McPherson et al., 1992).[3] For strong ties, the process is cyclical: matches increase the strength of strong ties, which in turn strengthen and stabilize the match (Valley, 1992). In this way, relationships with others can create inertial tendencies in the market and constrain one's ability to adapt (Podolny, 1993; Powell, 1990). Webster and Wind (1972) observe that buyers must often be jolted out of a pattern of placing repeat orders with the same supplier; thus, strong ties can serve as competitive barriers that are hard to break (Baker, 1994). In contrast,

---

[3] The retention introduced by strong-tie matches increases the "stickiness" of the market rather than increasing market stability as defined from a market rationality perspective: high-power players in strong-tie matches with low-power players stay with their partner because of the tie, even though they would be more profitable if they were matched with another high-power player. While stable from a match-level perspective, these types of matches are not "stable" from a rational market perspective, which defines a stable structure as one in which the aggregate surplus from a match is greater than or equal to the surplus from matches not in the market structure.

weak ties are quickly broken as individuals find and establish better matches (McPherson et al., 1992).

Thus, as participants have more opportunity to create transactions, those with strong ties are likely to stay matched with their transaction partners. In contrast, negotiators not tied to a specific transaction partner through a strong tie are likely to continue to search for a better transaction partner. In most markets, negotiators improve their effectiveness through increased experience (Bazerman, Magliozzi, & Neale, 1985; Smith, 1982). Strong ties serve as a barrier to the learning-through-experience process. This barrier helps the low-power players who can stay in the market suboptimal but personally profitable low–high matches. However, the barrier hurts the high-power players, as it reduces the likelihood that they will switch to the market optimal and person-ally profitable high–high matches. Hence, the strength of the relationship predicted in Hypothesis 4 is posited to increase over time, creating the following three-way interaction:

HYPOTHESIS 5. Strong ties, power, and time will interact so that over time, high-power players will experience a greater profit deficit and low-power players a greater profit surplus in the relationship-accessible market as compared to the relationship-inaccessible market.

Methods

Forty-eight masters of business students enrolled in a decision-making class participated in the study, which involved a joint venture exercise between U.S. manufacturers of video games and Japanese marketing firms. Participants were randomly assigned to one of two markets, a relationship-inaccessible market or a relationship-accessible market, and to one of two roles, manufac-turer or marketer. Participants were placed into two separate rooms corres-ponding to the two markets. In each market, there were 12 U.S. manufacturers and 12 Japanese marketers. Participants were initially divided by role so that all manufacturers were on one side of the room and all marketers were on another. Participants were asked to list on a form the four people on the other side of the room that they knew the best; thus, manufacturers in a given market were asked to list four marketers that they knew the best within their market and marketers were asked to list four manufacturers that they knew the best within their market. The forms were collected from the students.

Participants were then provided with background knowledge about the exer-cise and their specific role information. Hoping to expand their sales by market-ing their products in Japan, the participants were told that U.S. manufacturers saw a joint venture with a Japanese marketing firm as an entry into the restricted distribution channels and as a way to gain expertise in the Japanese consumer market. The Japanese marketers were looking to expand their U.S. client base and thus were hoping to capitalize on the success of U.S. video games. In addition to information about the company, the role information contained a number that reflected the participant's power. (This number system was adapted from a game developed by Al Roth and Keith Murnighan; see Murnighan, 1992.) Participants were told that this number was confidential;

other market participants did not have access to it in their role information. To operationalize differences in power, participants in each role were randomly assigned to either a high or a low number. Manufacturers with high power were assigned a number of 1900, 2000, or 2100; manufacturers with low power were assigned a number of 900, 1000, or 1100. Marketers with high power were assigned a number of 900, 1000, or 1100 and marketers with low power were assigned a number of 400, 500, or 600. (Changing the scale of points for manufacturers and marketers and avoiding the use of identical numbers for all high- or low-power parties within a role limited the transparency of the simulation.) Participants were told that the profit for a particular joint venture between a marketer and a manufacturer would be determined by multiplying the marketer's number by the manufacturer's number. This profit structure was created to match the multiplicative assumption discussed previously and to create a strong incentive to find the best partner possible.

The participant's task was twofold: (a) find a partner and form a joint venture and (b) agree with the partner on how to divide the profit resulting from the joint venture. Participants could discuss anything they wished. They were instructed that they could reveal their number if they desired, but that they did not have to do so. All participants were told that their goal was to maximize their profitability.

Participants were given 15 min to find a partner. Participants had nametags that indicated their company name and their role (manufacturer or marketer). Participants were told they could move freely about the room to discuss potential agreements. Upon reaching an agreement, joint venture partners were asked to complete a summary form that listed their company's name, their number, the profit from the joint venture, and the division of the profit between the two partners. If participants did not reach an agreement before the time limit was reached, their outcome was zero (the worst possible outcome).

To test for the influence of experience, two 15-min rounds were conducted. All parties stayed in the same market for the two rounds. Individuals were assigned the same role and the same number for both rounds. The use of two rounds allowed for repeated tests of Hypotheses 1, 3, and 4 and a test of Hypothesis 5.

The two markets were run identically except for two differences. To manipulate restrictions on matching with strong ties in Round 1, participants in the relationship-inaccessible market had to adhere to a "no strong ties" rule in which they were not allowed to form a joint venture with any of the four names that they had listed on their form as those they knew the best. In Round 2, participants in the relationship-inaccessible market were not allowed to form a joint venture with any of the four names on the list nor were they allowed to form a joint venture with their partner from Round 1. These restrictions were not placed on participants in the relationship-accessible market.

Our predictions focus on the influence of strong ties on the number of optimal matches (those that maximize profit surplus, Mortensen, 1994), number of equal agreements, and individual profitability. To determine the number of economically optimal agreements, the number of high–high matches and low–

low matches was counted. Equality of agreements was measured by counting the number of agreements that split the profit equally among the two participants. Individual profitability refers to the amount of profit that each joint venture partner received from his/her particular match. This information was obtained from the summary form that partners completed that indicated the profit of their joint venture and the allocation of that profit to each partner.

Results

Across both markets and both rounds, all parties created joint ventures. A statistical summary of the main variables in this study is provided in Table 3. To test Hypothesis 1, the number of optimal matches in each market in each round was computed (see Table 4). A chi-square test revealed that, overall, there were significantly more optimal matches in the relationship-inaccessible market than in the relationship-accessible market ($\chi^2(1) = 5.5$, $p < .05$, $\eta^2 = .11$). Although the data are in the predicted direction, there was not a significant difference in the number of optimal matches across markets for Round 1 ($\chi^2(1) = 0.69$, ns). However, in Round 2, consistent with the expectations suggested in Hypothesis 1, a significant chi-square test documented more optimal matches in the relationship-inaccessible market than in the relationship-accessible market ($\chi^2(1) = 8.00$, $p < .005$, $\eta^2 = .33$). While in both markets there were more optimal matches in Round 2 than in Round 1, indicating that learning did occur, overall there were more optimal matches in the relationship-inaccessible than in the relationship-accessible markets.

An examination of Hypothesis 3 indicated that, in Round 1, the relationship-inaccessible market had 4 agreements (out of 12) that split the profit equally and the relationship-accessible market had 6 (out of 12). In Round 2, there were 5 agreements (out of 12) in the relationship-inaccessible market and 6 (out of 12) in the relationship-accessible market that split the profit equally. While these results are in the predicted direction for both rounds, neither difference approached significance.

The following regression equations were used to test Hypothesis 4:

$$\text{Individual Profit–Round 1} = B_0 + B_1(\text{Market}) + B_2(\text{Power})$$
$$+ B_3(\text{Role}) + B_4(\text{Market*Power}) + e$$
$$\text{Individual Profit–Round 2} = B_0 + B_1(\text{Market}) + B_2(\text{Power})$$
$$+ B_3(\text{Role}) + B_4(\text{Market*Power}) + e$$

The dependent variables, Individual Profit–Round 1 and Individual Profit–Round 2, refer to the dollar profit that a participant received as a result of the joint venture in Rounds 1 and 2, respectively. The first independent variable, Market, is a dichotomous variable that takes on a value of 1 when the participant was in the relationship-inaccessible market and a value of 0 when the participant was in the relationship-accessible market. The second and third

272   TENBRUNSEL ET AL.

TABLE 3
Descriptive Statistics and Correlations: Study 3

Variable[a]	Mean	SD	1	2	3	4	5	6	7	8
1. Market	0.50	0.51								
2. Power	0.50	0.51	.00							
3. Role	0.50	0.51	.00	.00						
4. Indiv. Profit (Rd 1)	0.56M	0.30M	.03	.60***	.26					
5. Indiv. Profit (Rd 2)	0.60M	0.37M	.07	.79***	.18	.67***				
6. Efficient (Rd 1)	1.42	0.50	.17	.00	.00	−.02/.29	.00/.01			
7. Efficient (Rd 2)	1.75	0.44	.58**	.00	.00	.01/.12	.14/.21	.10/.10		
8. Joint Profit (Rd 1)	1.11M	0.54M	.04/.04	.57**/.67***	.00/.00	.91***/.98***	.57**/.64***	.19/.19	.04/.05	
9. Joint Profit (Rd 2)	1.20M	0.70M	.07/.07	.83***/.84***	.00/.00	.68***/.59**	.96***/.98***	−.01/−.07	.19/.18	.58**/.58**

[a] Correlations indicated by a "/" provide the correlation for the marketing subsample followed by the correlation for the manufacturer subsample. Dichotomous dependent variables (6, 7) are coded on a 1–2 scale, with 1 indicating inefficient agreements and 2 indicating efficient agreements.

** $p < .01$.

*** $p < .001$.

TABLE 4

Number of Optimal Matches: Study 3

	Market	
	Relationship-inaccessible	Relationship-accessible
Round 1		
# of optimal matches	6	4
# of suboptimal matches	6	8
Round 2		
# of optimal matches	12	6
# of suboptimal matches	0	6

independent variables, Power and Role, were included as control variables that independently influenced individual profitability. Power is a dichotomous variable that reflects whether the participant had a high or a low number within his/her role; this variable takes on a value of 1 when the participant had a high number and a value of 0 when the participant had a low number. Role is a dichotomous variable that indicates whether the participant was a manufacturer or marketer; this variable takes on a value of 1 when the participant was the manufacturer and a value of 0 when the participant was a marketer. The fourth independent variable, Market*Power, is a measure of a two-way interaction of Market and Power which was created to test Hypothesis 4. This variable takes on a value of 1 when Market equals Power (i.e., a participant with a high number in the relationship-inaccessible market or a participant with a low number in the relationship-accessible market) and a value of 0 when Market does not equal Power (i.e., a participant with a low number in the relationship-inaccessible market or a participant with a high number in the relationship-accessible market).

The results of the regression equations are shown in Table 5 and graphically displayed in Fig. 1. While both rounds exhibit similar patterns, the interaction is not significant for Round 1 but is significant and positive for the second round, as predicted by Hypothesis 4. In the second round, the addition of the Market*Power interaction led to a significant R^2 change (F-change (1, 43) = 6.97, $p < .01$), increasing the R^2 from 0.67 to 0.71. A look at the combined results from both rounds suggests that this interaction results from high-power parties obtaining a higher profit when they are restricted from using strong ties (mean = \$.896M) than when they are not restricted (mean = \$.731M), while low-power parties obtain lower profit when they are restricted from using strong ties (mean = \$.295M) than when they are not restricted (mean = \$.388M). As anticipated, power and role were also significant predictors of Round 1 and Round 2 profitability. A regression analysis was also run to test Hypothesis 5, which formalizes the relative influence of Hypothesis 4's two-way interaction over time. The following regression equation was used:

TABLE 5

Regression Analysis for Hypothesis 4: Study 3

Independent variable	B	β	t	$<p$
Dependent Variable: Individual Profit–Round 1				
Market	20,833	.04	0.31	ns
Power	356,250	.60	5.28	0.001***
Role	158,167	.26	2.35	0.05*
Market*Power	98,583	.17	1.46	ns
Constant	239,333		3.17	0.01**
	R^2		0.45	
	$F = 8.91, p < .001***$			
Dependent Variable: Individual Profit–Round 2				
Market	50,417	.07	0.84	ns
Power	587,542	.79	9.75	0.001***
Role	133,490	.18	2.22	0.05*
Market*Power	159,125	.22	2.64	0.01**
Constant	133,672		1.98	0.05*
	R^2		0.71	
	$F = 26.90, p < .001***$			

* $p < .05$.
** $p < .01$.
*** $p < .001$.

$$\text{Individual Profit} = B_0 + B_1(\text{Market}) + B_2(\text{Power}) + B_3(\text{Role}) + B_4(\text{Round})$$
$$+ B_5(\text{Market*Power}) + B_6(\text{Market*Power*Round})$$

The dependent variable, Individual Profit, is equivalent to Individual Profit–Round 1 in the first round and Individual Profit–Round 2 in the second round. The first three independent variables, Market, Power, and Role, and the Market*Power interaction are described above. The fourth independent variable, Round, takes on a value of 1 in Round 1 and a value of 2 in Round 2. The fifth independent variable, Market*Power*Round, is a three-way interaction between Market, Power, and Round. This variable takes on a value of 2 when Market equals Power in Round 2 (i.e., a participant with a high number in the relationship-inaccessible market or a participant with a low number in the relationship-accessible market in Round 2), a value of 1 when Market equals Power in Round 1 (i.e., a participant with a high number in the relationship-inaccessible market or a participant with a low number in the relationship-accessible market in Round 1), and a value of 0 when Market does not equal Power in Round 1 or Round 2 (i.e., a participant with a low number in the relationship-inaccessible market or a participant with a high number in the relationship-accessible market in either Round 1 or Round 2). While the three-way interaction is not significant ($t = 0.20$, ns), the data are in the predicted

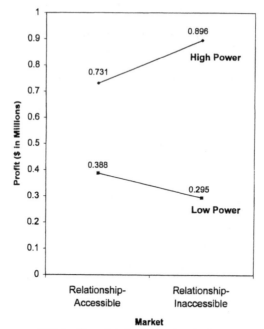

FIG. 1. Power*Market interaction: Study 3.

direction. More specifically, the profit deficit realized by high-power participants and the profit surplus realized by low-power players in the relationship-
accessible market as compared to the relationship-inaccessible market grow
over time: high-power players experience a greater profit deficit in the relationship-accessible market as compared to the relationship-inaccessible market in
Round 2 ($.209M) than in Round 1 ($.119M), and low-power players experience
a greater profit surplus in the relationship-accessible market as compared
to the relationship-inaccessible market in Round 2 ($.109M) than in Round
1 ($.078M).

Discussion

Providing additional support for the findings from Studies 1 and 2, the results
suggest that strong ties can negatively influence market profitability. From a
market-level perspective, restricting the formation of matches to those involving strangers or weak acquaintances resulted in more economically optimal
matches. Restrictions on joint venture partnerships did not significantly decrease the number of agreements that used equality as the distribution; however, the results were in the predicted direction. From an individual perspective,
participants who had a higher profit potential (high-power parties) were more
profitable in markets that did not permit matches between strong-tie relationships than in markets that did allow such formations. Conversely, individuals
who had a lower profit potential (low-power parties) were more profitable in

markets that did permit formations between strong-tie relationships than in those that did not. Thus, from a purely economic perspective, matching with strong ties is an economically beneficial strategy for low-power participants but can be economically detrimental for high-power participants. As discussed previously, however, these economic outcomes must be considered along with social outcomes that are accrued from strong tie matches.

The interpretation and applicability of these results should consider several limitations imposed by the study. One potential limitation is that participants in the relationship-accessible market had more potential partners available to them than did participants in the relationship-inaccessible market (a participant had 12 participants available to him/her in Round 1 and Round 2 in the relationship-accessible market versus 8 [Round 1] or 7 [Round 2] in the relationship-inaccessible market). We believe that this difference, however, provides a more conservative test of our hypotheses. An economic perspective would suggest that the imposition of a restriction that decreases the options available to an individual would decrease performance. Our results suggest the opposite: the imposition of a no-friends restriction actually improved the economic performance of the market and the performance of high-power players, despite the fact that they had fewer potential partners from whom to choose. This inconsistency can perhaps be best explained from a sociological standpoint. The addition of the market-level constraint can be seen as removing another constraint, that is, the normative constraint that compels individuals to match with friends even when it is not in their best economic interest to do so. As Burt (1982) suggests, social structure can constrain actors' ability to take action. Thus, market-level constraints that reduce the force of this social constraint may increase the profitability of the market and of high-power market participants.

This study also utilized a different type of market structure—a multiplicative market—than that used in the first two studies. We felt that this type of market is characteristic of many "real-world" markets. Joint ventures, for example, are formed to obtain the synergistic benefits that result from the interaction between two parties. Using the context of this study, one firm may have a good product while the other firm has the ability to market the product; however, if one firm brings no benefit, and thus has no value, the other party cannot compensate. The type of relationship embodied by this example is characteristic of a multiplicative relationship. While we argue that the multiplicative assumption does characterize many markets, we also recognize that in other markets, such as those studied in Studies 1 and 2, the assumption does not apply.

This study also differs from the first two studied in that the strength of the tie between potential match partners was not measured. Rather, individuals in the relationship-inaccessible markets were prevented from matching with their four strongest ties, independent of the strength of the tie. One may argue that this limits our findings, as the manipulation was not very strong for participants who either had more than four strong ties or did not have any strong ties at all. We believe that this limitation increases the conservative nature of our test as it reduces the potential effect of our manipulation. More-over, we also believe that this measure of strong ties accurately reflects individual differences in strong ties in the real world. The number and strength of strong ties vary from individual to individual and across different contexts. Long-time participants in a given market would most likely have a greater number of strong ties and those ties would be of greater strength than those of a newcomer in that same market. However, we argue that it is not only the absolute strength of the tie that influences market and individual profitability but also the relative strength of a given tie for a given participant. Individuals are drawn to their strongest tie, regardless of the absolute level of the strength of that tie. As an illustration, imagine that you are a member of a university's organizational behavior faculty and attend two different functions at the school: one that involves all of the marketing and organizational behavior department faculty and one that involves one representative from each department in the university. At the first function, you may interact very little with the marketing faculty because you have stronger ties in the organizational behavior department, but at the second function, as the marketing representative may be your strongest tie relative to the rest of the ties, you will probably interact a substantial amount. Thus, it is not only the absolute strength of the tie that is important in forming a match but also the strength of the tie relative to other possible ties.

CONCLUSION

These studies imply that relationships can affect the economic and social outcomes involved in the matching process. Results suggest that strong tie matches negatively affect market efficiency, match profitability, and the individual profitability of high-power players, but positively influence the individual profitability of low-power players; furthermore, the data imply that relationships are positively associated with social outcomes that are an important consideration in the partner-selection decision. In doing so, these findings both provide support for theoretical propositions relating to the role of relationships in negotiations and offer an enhanced and more integrated perspective. First, this paper provides one of the first examinations of the partner-selection process, which has been noticeably absent from the negotiation literature. As such, we find that the matching process is affected by social relations, which is congruent with those who have argued that our decisions are made, not in a vacuum, but as part of a larger social context (Baker, 1990; Ben-Porath, 1980; Burt, 1982; Coleman, 1988; Granovetter, 1985; Greenhalgh, 1987; Podolny, 1993, 1994; Powell, 1990).

The results also provide support for those who have asserted that relationships can have a negative impact on economic outcomes (Coleman, 1988; Galaskiewicz, 1985; Granovetter, 1985, 1992), not only in the intranegotiation process (cf. Fry et al., 1983) but also in the internegotiation process that occurs during the search for a negotiation partner. Markets in which matches between strong ties were unrestricted achieved lower market and individual profitability as compared to markets in which such matches were restricted. However, the findings also identify one contingent factor—the power of the negotiator—that can impact the relationship between strong-tie matches and individual profitability, so that strong-tie matches are economically beneficial to low-power players but economically detrimental to high-power players.

These findings clarify and elaborate on a pattern described by Roth and Xing (1997). In their work, they note that when interviews precede a centralized match process, the parties often use the interview process to create a relationship, which decreases the efficiency of the matching mechanism. As the parties implicitly (or explicitly, often in violation of the rules of the market) discuss their commitments to each other, they do so at the expense of the overall market.

The data offer several reasons as to why individuals may still prefer to match with strong ties, despite their economic costs. First, there may be certain situations where the direction of this finding is reversed and strong tie matches are actually economically profitable. The empirical evidence presented in this paper suggested that strong ties do reduce search, supporting the assertion that relationships reduce transaction costs (Powell, 1990), but also demonstrating that this search activity was negatively related to economic outcomes. In these studies, however, search costs were essentially nonexistent and thus profitability was determined solely by the value of the outcome that a particular match generated. However, in other situations where this assumption does not hold true, matching with strong ties may in fact be a profitable strategy if search costs are a large component of net profitability. On the other hand, the relatively small differences between suboptimal and optimal agreements, particularly in Study 1, meant that search activity was not as influential in determining final profitability as it might be in other situations where this difference is larger. When there is a greater difference between suboptimal and optimal matches, the negative relationship between strong ties and search activity would have even more of an impact on economic profitability. Thus, while the data from these studies suggest that matching with strong ties puts one at an economic disadvantage, accurately assessing the economic impact of this matching strategy involves a consideration of the actual search costs and the differences between suboptimal and optimal matches that are particular to a given context.

More important, the data suggest that a "relationship heuristic" may be pursued, despite its economic costs, because individuals' utility functions include both economic and social components. This investigation provided a perspective as to what factors may be important to the individual in process selection, revealing that individuals place a value on criteria other than profitability, such as fairness, trust, exchange of information, and ease of transaction. Furthermore, strong ties are seen as more likely to provide these social benefits. Therefore, while strong tie matches may produce economic disadvantages, these must be weighed against the accompanying social benefits.

Finally, the data offered the possibility that individuals may incur the economic costs of matching with a strong tie because they hold biased assumptions about the associated net benefits and costs. Individuals appeared to be unaware of the negative relationship between strong tie matches, search activity, and economic outcomes. Thus, the economic suboptimality that strong ties generate may be accepted by individuals because biased perceptions disguise the hidden costs of such relationships.

An interpretation of the results from these studies should take into account their general limitations. In addition to the limitations noted in the Discussion sections, one potential limitation that applies to all studies is the lack of economic incentive for participants. In Studies 1 and 3, however, the impact of this limitation is reduced because it is constant across both conditions. Furthermore, while the set of potential partners was finite and identifiable, thus enhancing the ability to identify optimal partners, participants did not have full information about the market structure (i.e., they were unaware of the reservation prices of others in Studies 1 and 2, unaware of profit potential in Study 3), which may have counteracted this effect. Again, these conditions were constant across our manipulations in Studies 1 and 3, limiting a potential confounding effect, but not necessarily addressing concerns related to generalizability to situations in which these conditions are different. We do believe, however, that most "real" market participants do not operate with full knowledge of the market. As Mortensen (1994) states, finding the ideal match partner involves time and effort because market participants are not aware of the true quality of potential matches. Finally, and perhaps most important, the studies did not allow for a comparison of the relative strength of economic and social forces or an investigation of how these forces vary across contexts, which also limits the generalizability of the findings.

We agree with Mortensen (1994) that expanding our knowledge of matching markets is a "fruitful research paradigm." Future attention should be directed toward addressing the noted limitations and expanding on the theoretical ideas and empirical findings that were offered in this paper. While this paper provided insight into the influence of strong ties on the matching process, answering the question "should individuals match with strong ties?" requires more research that draws on the ideas generated by these results. First, more research is needed to investigate both the social benefits and costs that accrue from strong tie matches. From a social benefit perspective, it is important to identify other social advantages, such as trust, that are derived from such matches, including the long-term implications of such advantages. In addition to the social benefits that are accrued from relying on relationships in the matching process, the investigation into social outcomes needs to be expanded to include the costs of not matching with strong ties. For example, what impact (i.e., betrayal, deception, reputation, retribution) does the pursuit of an "economically rational" strategy have on the relationship? How does engaging in a full search socially and economically impact the participant, in both the short and the long term?

Once both the economic and social implications of strong tie matches are more clearly understood, it is important that research be directed toward understanding when the trade-off between these two forces make such matches advantageous versus disadvantageous. This understanding will come from investigating how economic and social costs and benefits vary across markets, relationship types, and firm characteristics. This type of research might indicate that relying on relationships to find a partner is a useful strategy when individuals and/or firms possess relatively low amounts of power, search costs are high, trust and exchange of information are strong determinants of reaching an optimal agreement, and the impact of reaching an agreement extends over long periods of time (see Ben-Porath, 1980). Identifying market environments that match these conditions will be useful in ascertaining situations where this type of strategy would be appropriate. For example, strong ties, because they reduce search time, may be beneficial in markets characterized by high opportunity costs, increased turnover, or lengthy selection processes. Similarly, in markets in which there is a great deal of uncertainty, perhaps due to the young age of the market (Podolny, 1994), infrequent transactions, low barriers to entry, or complex structures, the ability to trust one's partner may be the largest determinant of success. Conversely, when one possesses a large amount of power and a great deal of knowledge about the market structure and in markets in which there is strong continuity among market participants and relatively low search costs, the strong-tie matching heuristic may result in suboptimal outcomes.

Research on the scripts that are evoked by various contexts would also be useful in investigating the benefits and costs of strong tie matches. Different contexts—which may vary in terms of their linguistic cues, power differences, temporal features, etc. (Messick, 1999)—may generate different scripts, or rules of appropriate behavior; in turn, these scripts impact judgments of appropriate behavior and expectations of others (Abelson, 1976; Forgas, 1982; Messick, 1999; Robinson, Keltner, Ward, & Ross, 1995). Drawing on this research, it may be that such scripts influence the social costs and benefits derived from strong tie matches by influencing the extent to which such matches are appropriate and/or expected (i.e., in some contexts, it may be completely standard that individuals pick the best "economic" match and incur few social costs but in other contexts, such as those manipulated in these studies, violating the relationship may have very serious social implications). Investigating the relationship between scripts and strong tie matches should provide further insight into the interplay between economic and social forces in various contexts.

We also believe that further examining the partner-selection process from a psychological perspective would strengthen our knowledge of matching markets, and the advice we can provide about the partner selection process. Sondak (1990) has documented that students and firms show little interest in using a matching algorithm in the MBA job market context even though empirical evidence suggests that this would improve the outcomes for the vast majority of participants. Unrestricted and decentralized matching procedures provide participants with control in deciding with whom to discuss possible agreements, whether to extend or accept offers, and with whom to sign a contract (Sondak, 1990). While a centralized matching procedure that restricts the influence of relationship ties would reduce the individual's control, it could increase the aggregate profitability of the players. However, we speculate that if we had asked our participants in the relationship-accessible markets if they would like to add a market restriction barring the use of strong ties, the proposal would have been overwhelmingly rejected, partially because of the misperceptions that individuals may have about such ties that do not allow for an accurate assessment of the costs and benefits. There are several possible explanations for these perceptions. First, from a cognitive perspective, the upsides of relationships are more vivid than their downsides; that is, people can easily imagine how a relationship will help them, but fail to consider the loss of potential economic benefits that result from ignoring their weak ties. In addition, they do not think about how the strong relationships of other parties will distort the market and reduce the potential partners that are available to them. From a motivational perspective, individuals are motivated to think that their relationships are superior. Taylor and Brown (1988) have argued that people create a variety of biased interpretations about the world in order to help them feel good about themselves; specifically, people have illusions of superiority, optimism, and control. Consistent with this view, we argue that people are motivated to believe that their relationships are stronger than the relationships of others, and that they can obtain the benefits of relationships more readily than other people can. The joint effects of the vividness of one's relationships and the belief in the superiority of these relationships may account for the preference to use strong ties despite their costs. Future research that further assesses the accuracy of the perceptions that individuals hold about strong tie matches will allow for a determination of whether such perceptions are biased and whether these biases influence the likelihood that an individual will find the appropriate match.

Finally, we believe that these studies have theoretical implications for the negotiations literature. The last decade has witnessed a proliferation of interest in the topic of negotiation and, more recently, in the impact of relationships on the negotiation process and outcomes. While the negotiation literature has made great advances, a void exists; virtually all negotiation research has focused on the dyad once it has been established, ignoring the fact that each party might have selected a different negotiation partner. Our results illustrate that partner selection can have a substantial impact on one's outcome, suggesting that the choice of a matching partner may be as important as the negotiation within that match. We hope our research enhances the negotiation literature by using both economic and sociological perspectives to address the implications of relationships in the selection of a negotiation partner. Given the results of these studies, we think that it is important for negotiation researchers to turn some of their attention to the process of partner selection and, in doing so, to draw from all disciplines that will help shed light on this topic.

REFERENCES

Abelson, R. P. (1976). Script processing in attitude formation and decision making. In J. Carroll & J. Payne (Eds.), *Cognition and social behavior.* Hillsdale, NJ: Erlbaum

Baker, W. E. (1990). Market networks and corporate behavior. *American Journal of Sociology*, **96**, 589–625.

Baker, W. E. (1994). *Networking smart*. New York: McGraw–Hill.

Bazerman, M. H., Magliozzi, T., & Neale, M. A. (1985). The acquisition of an integrative response in a competitive market. *Organizational Behavior and Human Performance*, **34**, 294–313.

Ben-Porath, Y. (1980). The F-connection: Families, friends, and firms and the organization of exchange. *Population and Development Review*, **6**, 1–30.

Brockhoff, K., Gupta, A. K., & Rotering, C. (1991). Inter-firm R&D co-operations in German. *Technovation*, **11**, 219–228.

Burt, R. S. (1982). *Toward a structural theory of action*. New York: Academic Press.

Coleman, J. S. (1988). Social capital in the creation of human capital. *American Journal of Sociology*, **94**, S95–S120.

Forgas, J. P. (1982). Episode cognition: Internal representations of interaction routines. *Advances in Experimental Social Psychology*, **15**, 59–101.

Fry, W. R., Firestone, I. J., & Williams, D. L. (1983). Negotiation process and outcome of stranger dyads and dating couples: Do lovers lose? *Basic and Applied Social Psychology*, **4**, 1–16.

Galaskiewicz, J. (1985). *Social organization of an urban grants economy: A study of business philanthropy and nonprofit organizations*. Orlando, FL: Academic Press.

Gale, D., & Shapley, L. (1962). College admissions and the stability of marriage. *American Mathematical Monthly*, **69**, 9–15.

Geertz, C. (1963). *Peddlers and princes*. Chicago: Univ. of Chicago Press.

Granovetter, M. (1973). The strength of weak ties. *American Journal of Sociology*, **78**, 1360–1379.

Granovetter, M. (1985). Economic action and social structure: The problem of embeddedness. *American Journal of Sociology*, **91**, 481–510.

Granovetter, M. (1992). Economic institutions as social constructions: A framework for analysis. *Acta Sociologica*, **35**, 3–11.

Greenberg, J. (1983). Equity and equality as clues to the relationship between exchange participants. *European Journal of Social Psychology*, **13**, 195–196.

Greenhalgh, L. (1987). Relationships in negotiations. *Negotiation Journal*, **3**, 235–243.

Lawler, E. J., & Yoon, J. (1996). Commitment in exchange relations: A test of a theory of relational cohesion. *American Sociological Review*, **61**, 89–108.

Lerner, J. J. (1974). Social psychology of justice and interpersonal attraction. In T. Huston (Ed.), *Foundations of interpersonal attraction*. New York: Academic Press.

March, J. G., & Simon, H. A. (1958). *Organizations*. New York: Wiley.

McPherson, J. M., Popielarz, P. A., & Drobnic, S. (1992). Social networks and organizational dynamics. *American Sociological Review*, **5**, 153–170.

Messick, D. M. (1999). Alternative logics for decision making in social settings. *Journal of Economic Behavior and Organization*, **38**, 11–28.

Mongell, S. J., & Roth, A. E. (1991). Sorority rush as a two-sided matching mechanism. *American Economic Review*, **81**, 441–464.

Mortensen, D. T. (1994). Matching: Finding a partner for life or otherwise. *American Journal of Sociology*, **9**, S215–S240.

Murnighan, J. K. (1992). *Bargaining games*. New York: Morrow.

Murnighan, J. K., & Vollrath, D. A. (1984). Hierarchies, coalitions and organizations. *Research in the Sociology of Organizations*, **3**, 157–187.

Neale, M. A., & Bazerman, M. H. (1991). *Cognition and rationality in negotiation*. New York: Free Press.

O'Reilly, C. A. (1982). Variations in decision makers' use of information sources: The impact of quality and accessibility of information. *Academy of Management Journal*, **2**, 756–771.

Podolny, J. M. (1993). A status-based model of market competition. *American Journal of Sociology,* **98,** 829–872.

Podolny, J. M. (1994). Market uncertainty and the social character of economic exchange. *Administrative Science Quarterly,* **39,** 458–483.

Powell, W. W. (1990). Neither market nor hierarchy: Network forms of organization. *Research in Organization Behavior,* **12,** 295–336.

Robinson, R. J., Keltner, D., Ward, A., & Ross, L. (1995). Actual versus assumed differences inconstrual: "Naive realism" in intergroup perception and conflict. *Journal of Personality and Social Psychology,* **68,** 404–417.

Roth, A. E. (1982). The economics of matching: Stability and incentives. *Mathematics of Operations Research,* **7,** 617–628.

Roth, A. E. (1984). The evolution of the labor market for medical interns and residents: A case study in game theory. *Journal of Political Economy,* **92,** 991–1016

Roth, A. E., & Sotomayor, M. A. O. (1990). *Two-sided matching: A study in game-theoretic modeling and analysis.* Cambridge, MA: Cambridge Univ. Press.

Roth, A. E., & Xing, X. (1994). Jumping the gun: Imperfections and institutions related to the timing of market transactions. *American Economic Review,* **84,** 992–1044.

Roth, A. E., & Xing, X. (1997). Turnaround time and bottlenecks in market clearing: Decentralized matching in the market for clinical psychologists. *Journal of Political Economy,* **105,** 284–329.

Smeltzer, L. R., Van Hook, B. L., & Hutt, R. W. (1991). Analysis of the use of advisors as information sources in venture startups. *Journal of Small Business Management,* **29,** 10–20.

Smith, V. L. (1982). Microeconomic systems as an experimental science. *American Economic Review,* **72,** 923–955.

Sondak, H. (1990). *Centralized and decentralized matching procedures: A behavioral approach to social choice.* Unpublished doctoral dissertation, Northwestern University, Evanston, IL.

Sondak, H., & Bazerman, M. H. (1989). Matching and negotiation processes in quasi-markets. *Organizational Behavior and Human Decision Processes,* **44,** 261–280.

Sondak, H., & Bazerman, M. H. (1991). Power balance and the rationality of outcomes in matching markets. *Organizational Behavior and Human Decision Processes,* **5,** 1–23.

Sondak, H., Neale, M. A., & Pinkley, R. L. (1997). *Relationship input and resource constraints: Determinants of distributive justice in individual preferences and negotiated agreements.* Working Paper, University of Utah.

Taylor, S. E., & Brown, J. D. (1988). Illusion and well-being: A social psychological perspective. *Psychological Bulletin,* **103,** 193–210.

Valley, K. L. (1992). *Relationships and resources: A network exploration of allocation decisions.* Unpublished doctoral dissertation, Northwestern University, Evanston, IL.

Valley, K. L., Moag, J., & Bazerman, M. H. (1998). Relationships as the solution to the winner's curse. *Journal of Economic Behavior in Organizations,* **34,** 211–238.

Valley, K. L., Neale, M. A., & Mannix, E. A. (1995). Friends, lovers, colleagues, strangers: The effects of relationships on the process and outcome of negotiation. In R. J. Bies, R. J. Lewicki, & B. H. Sheppard (Eds.), *Research on negotiations in organizations.* Greenwich, CT: JAI Press.

Webster, F., & Wind, Y. (1972). *Organizational buying behavior.* Englewood Cliffs, NJ: Prentice Hall.

White, S. B., & Neale, M. A. (1994). The role of negotiator aspirations and settlement expectancies on bargaining outcomes. *Organizational Behavior and Human Decision Processes,* **57,** 303–317.

Received June 26, 1998

[22]

Econometrica, Vol. 70, No. 4 (July, 2002), 1341–1378

THE ECONOMIST AS ENGINEER: GAME THEORY, EXPERIMENTATION, AND COMPUTATION AS TOOLS FOR DESIGN ECONOMICS[1]

By Alvin E. Roth[2]

Economists have lately been called upon not only to analyze markets, but to design them. Market design involves a responsibility for detail, a need to deal with all of a market's complications, not just its principle features. Designers therefore cannot work only with the simple conceptual models used for theoretical insights into the general working of markets. Instead, market design calls for an engineering approach. Drawing primarily on the design of the entry level labor market for American doctors (the National Resident Matching Program), and of the auctions of radio spectrum conducted by the Federal Communications Commission, this paper makes the case that experimental and computational economics are natural complements to game theory in the work of design. The paper also argues that some of the challenges facing both markets involve dealing with related kinds of complementarities, and that this suggests an agenda for future theoretical research.

Keywords: Market design, game theory, experimental economics, computational economics.

1. INTRODUCTION: DESIGN ECONOMICS

The economic environment evolves, but it is also designed. Entrepreneurs and managers, legislators and regulators, lawyers and judges, all get involved in the design of economic institutions. But in the 1990's, economists, particularly game theorists, started to take a very substantial role in design, especially in the design of markets. These developments suggest the shape of an emerging discipline of *design economics*, the part of economics intended to further the design and maintenance of markets and other economic institutions.[3]

---

[1] This paper is dedicated to Bob Wilson, the Dean of Design.

[2] Fisher-Schultz Lecture. This paper has a checkered history. Versions of it were delivered as the Leatherbee Lecture at the Harvard Business School on April 21, 1999, as the Fisher-Schultz Lecture at the European meeting of the Econometric Society in Santiago de Compostela, on August 31, 1999, and as the Pazner Lecture at the University of Tel Aviv, on February 29, 2000. I have also struggled with some of these issues in my Clarendon Lectures at Oxford in April 1998, in Roth and Sotomayor (1990), Roth (1991), Roth and Peranson (1999), Roth (2000), and in the market design sections of my webpage at *http://www.economics.harvard.edu/~aroth/alroth.html*, and in the class on market design I co-taught with Paul Milgrom at Harvard in the Spring of 2001. This paper has benefited from the many helpful comments I received on those earlier occasions, and from sympathetic readings by my colleagues and the editor and referees.

[3] Economists have also become involved in the design of economic environments such as incentive systems within firms, negotiating platforms, contracts, etc., but in the present article I shall draw my examples from market design.

Game theory, the part of economics that studies the "rules of the game," provides a framework with which to address design. But design involves a responsibility for detail; this creates a need to deal with complications. Dealing with complications requires not only careful attention to the institutional details of a particular market, it also requires new tools, to supplement the traditional analytical toolbox of the theorist. The first thesis of this paper is that, *in the service of design, experimental and computational economics are natural complements to game theory.*

Another kind of challenge is professional rather than technical, and has to do with whether and how it will become customary to report design efforts in the economics literature. The recent prominence of economists in design arose from several events, external to the profession, that created a need for designs of unusual markets. Not only did this give economists a chance to employ what we know, it gave us a chance to learn practical lessons about design. Whether economists will often be in a position to give highly practical advice on design depends in part on whether we report what we learn, and what we do, in sufficient detail to allow scientific knowledge about design to accumulate. The second theme of the present paper is that, for this purpose, *we need to foster a still unfamiliar kind of design literature in economics, whose focus will be different than traditional game theory and theoretical mechanism design.*[4]

If the literature of design economics does mature in this way, it will also help shape and enrich the underlying economic theory. The third goal of the present paper will be to show how *recent work on design has posed some new questions for economic theory, and started to suggest some answers.*

To see how these issues hang together, it may help to consider briefly the relationship between physics and engineering, and between biology, medicine, and surgery.

Consider the design of suspension bridges. The simple theoretical model in which the only force is gravity, and beams are perfectly rigid, is elegant and general. But bridge design also concerns metallurgy and soil mechanics, and the sideways forces of water and wind. Many questions concerning these complications can't be answered analytically, but must be explored using physical or computational models. These complications, and how they interact with the parts of the physics captured by the simple model, are the domain of the engineering literature. Engineering is often less elegant than the simple underlying physics, but it allows bridges designed on the same basic model to be built longer and stronger over time, as the complexities and how to deal with them become better understood.

---

[4] In this connection, Baldwin and Bhattacharyya (1991), speaking of the 1984 auction of Conrail's assets and of asset sales in general, write "the literature has yet to explain the diverse methods of sale we observe, and provides little guidance in choosing among alternatives. Furthermore, those who actually make the selection almost never discuss the experience, and thus, from a practical standpoint, we know very little about why one method is chosen over another." (For connections between engineering design and the design of the firms and industries that produce them, see Baldwin and Clark (2000).)

It was not a foregone conclusion that bridge building would have a scientific component; the earliest bridges were no doubt built without much formal analysis, and experience was accumulated only insofar as it could be passed from builder to apprentice, or learned from observation. But the close relationship of physics and engineering goes back at least as far as Archimedes.

Surgery and its relation to medicine and biology provide a more cautionary tale. The famous oath that Hippocrates formulated for physicians in the fifth century BC includes a specific prohibition against doing surgery. Two millennia later, in medieval Europe, surgery was still not considered the province of medical specialists. In England, responsibility for surgery was vested in the Worshipful Company of Barbers, which underwent a number of changes over the centuries and was not fully separated from surgery until 1745.[5] This was not an unreasonable assignment of responsibilities, as barbering required expertise in keeping blades sharp and in stanching the flow of blood, both also essential for surgery. But the modern connections between surgery and medicine, and between medicine and biology, have certainly improved the quality of the surgery, and also of medicine and biology.

The analogy to market design in the age of the internet should be clear. As marketplaces proliferate on the web, a great deal of market design is going to be done by computer programmers, among others, since they possess some of the essential expertise. Economists will have an opportunity to learn a lot from the markets that result, just as we will learn from our own work designing unusual markets. But if we want this knowledge to accumulate, if we want market design to be better informed and more reliable in the future, we need to promote a scientific literature of design economics. Today this literature is in its infancy. My guess is that if we nurture it to maturity, its relation with current economics will be something like the relationship of engineering and physics, or of medicine and biology.

1.1. *Design in the 1990's:*[6]

The 1990's were a formative decade for design economics because economists were presented with opportunities to take responsibility for the design of detailed

---

[5] As of this writing, the headquarters of the barbers' organization in London is still called Barber-Surgeons' Hall. For a brief history, see "The history of the company," at http://www.barberscompany. org/.

[6] Economists' interest in market design long predates the 90's; one has only to think of Vickery's 1961 article on auctions, or Gale and Shapley's 1962 article on matching mechanisms. The study of auctions blossomed into a substantial theoretical literature, including discussions of the design of revenue maximizing auctions under simple assumptions, and an empirically oriented literature studying the outcomes of particular auctions. (Notable early theoretical papers are Myerson (1981), Milgrom and Weber (1982b), Maskin and Riley (1984), Bulow and Roberts (1989); see Wilson (1992) for a broad overview of the auction literature.) The study of matching mechanisms also produced a substantial theoretical literature, accompanied by empirically oriented papers studying the evolution of labor markets, beginning with a study of the market for American physicians (Roth (1984)). (See Roth and Sotomayor (1990) for an overview of much of the theory, and Roth and Xing (1994) for a discussion

rules for complex markets, and their suggestions were quickly implemented in large, operating markets. This in turn produced an opportunity to evaluate the new designs. Two notable design efforts were:
- the design of labor clearinghouses such as the one through which American doctors get their first jobs; and
- the design of auctions through which the U.S. Federal Communications Commission sells the rights to transmit on different parts of the radio spectrum.

The importance of good design is nowhere better illustrated than in a third set of markets in which economists have played a role, but in which politicians and regulators also continue to be deeply involved, namely markets for electric power. (See Wilson (2002) for an account of the most detailed design work.) Economists participated in the design of only parts of these markets, while other parts remained subject to regulation. An unworkable hybrid resulted in California, where utility companies were brought to the verge of bankruptcy by the rising prices in the unregulated wholesale market, which far exceeded the regulated prices at which electricity could be sold to consumers.

While these markets are very different from each other, their design efforts had some striking similarities that distinguish them from more conventional work in economics.[7]

On a technical level, each of these markets presented designers with the problem of dealing with goods that could be *complements* for one another, not just substitutes. In labor markets, how desirable a particular job is for one member of a two-career couple may depend on how good a job the other member of the couple can get in the same city. Similar complementarities arise when employers have preferences over groups of workers. In spectrum auctions, a given bandwidth of spectrum may be more valuable to a company if the company can also

---

of the evolution of labor markets and other matching processes.) Mechanism design in general, in the spirit laid out in Hurwicz (1973) has become a recognized subject in the theoretical literature, and even boasts a specialized journal, the *Review of Economic Design*. The strategic issues associated with motivating market participants to reveal privately held information have been explored from a design orientation, as in the work of Groves and Ledyard (1977) on mechanisms to promote the efficient provision of public goods (see Green and Laffont (1979) for an early overview). And the interest in design is not only theoretical; experimenters have explored alternative designs in simple settings, often motivated by general concerns like public goods provision (see Ledyard (1995) for a survey), or by forms of market organization such as auctions (see Kagel (1995)), and sometimes by particular allocation problems, arising e.g. from airports or space stations (e.g. Rassenti, Smith, and Bulfin (1982), Grether, Isaac, and Plott (1981), and Ledyard, Porter, and Wessen (2000), JEE). All of this helped lay the groundwork for the assumption of design responsibilities that took place in the 90's.

[7] A wider ranging essay might also include the design of the large scale privatizations of state assets that began in Eastern Europe and the former Soviet Union following the fall of the Berlin Wall in November 1989, although I am not sure to what extent economists played direct roles in the designs of the various privatization plans. One of the most interestingly designed privatizations was the (then) Czechoslovak privatization in 1992, meant to identify prices (in terms of vouchers issued to all citizens) at which the market would clear, via a multi-round auction in which prices for over- and under-demanded firms were readjusted from round to round. The results of that auction have been studied in several papers; see, e.g., Svejnar and Singer (1994), Filer and Hanousek (1999), and Gupta, Ham, and Svejnar (2000). See also the admirable discussion of creating markets for macroeconomic risks in Shiller (1993).

obtain geographically contiguous licenses, so that it can offer a broader area of service, or if it can win licenses for adjacent radio frequencies, so that it can transmit more data. And in electricity markets, power generation is quite distinct from power transmission, but both must be consumed together. And power can be generated more cheaply from an already operating generator than from a cold start, so there are complementarities over time, and between power generation and various "ancillary services" like reserve capacity needed to keep the transmission network operating. These complementarities play a strong role in the resulting market designs.

Aside from technical issues, these design efforts also shared some features that seem to be characteristic of the context in which markets are designed. First, design is often required to be *fast*. In each of these three cases, only about a year elapsed between the commissioning of a new market design and its delivery. Second, design need not be an entirely *a priori* craft; much can be learned from the *history* of related markets, and sometimes there is an opportunity and a need to tinker with new designs, based on early experience. Finally, at least some of the work of design reflects the fact that the adoption of a design is at least partly a *political* process.

In what follows, I will attempt to develop these themes. I will do so in particular in connection with the (re)design of the entry level labor market for American doctors. That design effort, which I led, is the focus of this paper. It was able to profitably employ theory, historical observation, experimentation, and computation. Section 3 will then consider, briefly, the design of the FCC auctions, emphasizing the points of similarity in the work of design. The most recent FCC designs, of auctions in which bids can be made for packages of items, are closely related to some of the issues that arise in the design of labor market matching mechanisms. Section 4 concludes with an overview, and an exhortation.

2. THE ENTRY-LEVEL LABOR MARKET FOR AMERICAN DOCTORS

The entry-level position for an American doctor is called a residency (and was formerly called an internship). A good residency substantially influences the career path of a young physician, and residents provide much of the labor force of hospitals, so this is an important market for both doctors and hospitals. In the 1940's, the fierce competition for people and positions led to a kind of market failure (to be described below) that turns out to also have occurred in quite a few entry-level professional labor markets (Roth and Xing (1994)). This market failure was resolved in the early 1950's by the organization of a very successful clearinghouse to facilitate the matching of doctors to residency programs (Roth (1984)). Today this clearinghouse is called the National Resident Matching Program (NRMP).

Over the years, the medical profession underwent profound changes, some of them with important consequences for the medical labor market. In the Fall of 1995, amidst a crisis of confidence in the market, I was retained by the Board of Directors of the NRMP to direct the design of a new clearinghouse algorithm for the medical match. This design, reported in detail in Roth and Peranson (1999) was completed in 1996, and adopted in 1997 as the new NRMP algorithm. Since then, over 20,000 doctors a year have been matched to entry level positions in the general medical labor market using the new algorithm, as well as a smaller number of more senior positions in about thirty medical specialty labor markets also organized by the NRMP.

The Roth-Peranson design has also been adopted by entry level labor markets in other professions since its adoption by American physicians. (Other markets that have adopted it to date are, in the United States, Postdoctoral Dental Residencies, Osteopathic Internships, Osteopathic Orthopedic Surgery Residencies, Pharmacy Practice Residencies, and Clinical Psychology Internships,[8] and, in Canada, Articling Positions with Law Firms in Ontario, Articling Positions with Law Firms in Alberta, and Medical Residencies.)[9]

To understand the design problem, we need to understand the kinds of market failure that sometimes lead to the adoption of clearinghouses, and the manner in which clearinghouses themselves succeed and fail. For this it will help to start with a brief history of the American medical market.

2.1. *A Brief History of the Market*

The medical internship, as it was then called, came into being around 1900, and soon became the entry level position for American physicians. The labor market for such positions was decentralized, with students typically seeking positions around the time they graduated from medical school. But competition among hospitals for good students gradually led to earlier and earlier dates of appointment, despite repeated attempts to halt the process. By the 1940's students were being appointed to jobs two full years before graduation from medical school, i.e. hiring was two years before the start of employment. This meant that students were being hired before much information about their medical school performance was available to potential employers, and before students themselves had much exposure to clinical medicine to help them decide on their own career preferences.[10]

A serious attempt to reform the market and eliminate this source of inefficiency in matching was made in 1945, when the medical schools banded together and agreed to embargo student transcripts and letters of reference until an agreed date. This effectively controlled the unravelling of appointment dates, and as this became clear, the dates at which contracts were to be signed was moved back into the senior year of medical school.

But new problems developed between the time offers were issued and the deadline before which they had to be accepted. Briefly, students who had been

[8] See Roth and Xing (1997) for a description of the clinical psychology market in the years when it operated as a telephone market, before it adopted a centralized match.

[9] A related mechanism is now used to match new Reform rabbis to their first congregation (Bodin and Pankin (1999)).

[10] This kind of unraveling of transaction dates is a common problem; for descriptions of it in some contemporary markets see Avery, Jolls, Posner, and Roth (2001) on the market for appellate court law clerks, and Avery, Fairbanks, and Zeckhauser (2001) on early admissions to college.

offered a job at one hospital, but told that they were on the waiting list for a job that they preferred, wished to wait as long as possible before accepting or rejecting the offer they were holding. This meant that waiting lists did not progress very fast, and that there were lots of last minute decisions, with decisions made in haste often regretted and sometimes not honored.

After several years of unsuccessful tinkering with the rules governing offers and deadlines, the chaotic recontracting that was being experienced became intolerable. It was decided to organize a centralized clearinghouse, modeled on regional clearinghouses that already existed in Philadelphia and Boston.[11] Students and internship programs would arrange interviews in a decentralized way, as before, but instead of engaging in a chaotic process of exploding offers, acceptances, and rejections, students would submit a rank order list of the jobs for which they had interviewed, and employers (internship directors) would submit a rank order list of the students they had interviewed. An algorithm would be devised to process the lists submitted in this way and produce a recommended matching of students to hospitals.

After a brief trial of an algorithm that was replaced because it had unacceptable incentive properties, an algorithm was adopted that proved very successful. Starting in 1951, and lasting into the 1970's, over 95% of positions were filled through the match. Small changes were made in the clearinghouse rules from time to time. There was some dropoff in this percentage in the 1970's, most interestingly among the growing number of married couples, graduating together from medical school, who wished to find two positions in the same city. When I first studied the market (see Roth (1984)) there had been an attempt to accommodate married couples that had been largely unsuccessful. But a subsequent further change of rules allowing couples to rank pairs of positions successfully attracted couples to once again participate in the match.

In the mid 1990's, the market experienced a serious crisis of confidence. (The various national medical student organizations issued resolutions, and eventually Ralph Nader's organization Public Citizen got involved.) There was a great deal of talk about whether the market served students' interests, and whether students would be well advised to "game the system" or even to circumvent the market entirely. It was in this context that I was asked to direct the design of a new algorithm, and to compare different ways of organizing the match.

Now, if an economist is going to act as a doctor to a medical market, he can do worse than to consult medical authorities on the standard of care. Hippocrates' [circa 400BC] advice on this subject applies to design economists too:

> "The physician must be able to tell the antecedents, know the present, and foretell the future—must mediate these things, and have two special objects in view with regard to disease, namely, to do good or to do no harm."

---

[11] I am indebted to Dr. Cody Webb for bringing these regional clearinghouses to my attention. For Philadelphia, see Hatfield (1935). For Boston, see Mullin and Stalnaker (1952), who suggest (p. 200) that elements of the national clearinghouse may have been taken directly from the Boston plan.

For the medical marketplace, this means that before replacing a clearinghouse that had effectively halted the coordination failures that preceded its introduction in the 1950's, it is important to know what causes clearinghouses to be successful. Fortunately, this can be addressed empirically, as there are both successful and unsuccessful clearinghouses in various labor markets. To discuss these, we will first need a simple theoretical model. We start with a somewhat *too* simple model—think of this as the simple model of a bridge with perfectly rigid beams—and then we'll complicate it as needed when we talk about the complications of the medical market.

2.2. *A (Too) Simple Model of Matching*[12]

There are disjoint sets of firms and workers, $F = \{f_1, \ldots, f_n\}$ and $W = \{w_1, \ldots, w_p\}$. (I will refer interchangeably to firms and workers, and to hospitals and students, or applicants, when speaking of the medical market.) Each worker seeks one job, and each firm f_i seeks (up to) q_i workers. A matching is a subset of $F \times W$, i.e. a set of matched pairs, such that any worker appears in no more than one pair, and any firm f_i appears in no more than q_i pairs. A matching is identified with a correspondence $\mu: F \cup W \to F \cup W$ such that $\mu(w) = f$ and $w \in \mu(f)$ if and only if (f, w) is a matched pair; and if no matched pair contains w, then $\mu(w) = w$ (i.e. if a worker is not matched to a firm, then she is matched to herself).[13]

Each agent has complete and transitive preferences over the "acceptable" agents on the other side of the market, i.e. over those that it prefers rather than remaining unmatched (or leaving a position empty) and waiting for the less desirable post-match market, called "the scramble."[14] The preferences of firms and workers will be given as lists of the acceptable agents on the other side of the market. For example, the preferences of a worker w_i are given by $P(w_i) = f_2, f_4, \ldots$, indicating that she prefers firm f_2 to f_4 [$f_2 >_{wi} f_4$], etc.

Because firms may be matched to groups of workers, firm f_i's preference list $P(f_i) = w_i, w_j, \ldots w_k$ of acceptable workers does not fully define it's preferences over groups of workers it might employ. For this simple model, it is enough to specify that a firm's preferences for groups are "responsive" to their preferences over individual workers (Roth (1985)), in the sense that, for any set of workers $S \subset W$ with $|S| < q_i$, and any workers w and w' in W/S, $S \cup w >_{f_i} S \cup w'$ if and only if $w >_{f_i} w'$, and $S \cup w >_{f_i} S$ if and only if w is acceptable to f_i. That is, if

---

[12] This is essentially the model of Gale and Shapley (1962), as extended in Roth (1985) for the case when firms employ multiple workers and hence have preferences over groups of workers.

[13] It is more usual to define a matching directly in terms of the correspondence, but it was easier to describe the couples algorithm using this formulation, adapted from Blum, Roth, and Rothblum (1997).

[14] By modeling workers' preferences as over firms rather than over positions, we are taking all positions offered by the same firm to be identical or (in practice) treating the different positions that might be offered by a firm as being offered by different sub-firms. Also, wages and other personal terms are set prior to the match, and are reflected in the preferences.

a firm prefers worker w to w', this means that the firm would always prefer to add w instead of w', to any group of other workers, and always prefers to add an acceptable worker when a space is available.

A matching μ is *blocked by an individual* k if $\mu(k)$ is unacceptable to k, and it is *blocked by a pair of agents* (f, w) if they each prefer each other to their mates at μ, i.e. if

$$[w >_f w' \text{ for some } w' \text{ in } \mu(f) \text{ or } w \text{ is acceptable to } f \text{ and } |\mu(f)| < q_f],$$

and

$$f >_w \mu(w).$$

A matching x is *stable* if it isn't blocked by any individual or pair of agents. When preferences are responsive, the set of stable matchings equals the core (defined by weak domination) of the game whose rules are that any worker and firm may be matched, if and only if they both agree.

Gale and Shapley (1962) showed that the set of stable matchings in this simple model is never empty, by observing that algorithms like the one below always produce a stable outcome. For our present purpose, the algorithm should be read as a way to process preference lists that workers and firms have submitted to a centralized clearinghouse. But the steps of the algorithm are written as if workers and firms were going through a decentralized process of application and eventual acceptance or rejection. This should help make clear why algorithms of this sort have been independently invented over the years in a number of markets. (It was shown in Roth (1984) that the algorithm adopted for the medical match in 1951 is equivalent to an algorithm like the one below, but with offers of positions being initiated by the hospitals rather than applications for positions being initiated by the students.)

Deferred Acceptance Algorithm, with workers applying (roughly the Gale-Shapley (1962) version):

1.a. Each worker applies to his or her first choice firm.

1.b. Each firm f (with q_f positions) rejects any unacceptable applications and, if more than q_f acceptable applications are received, "holds" the q_f most preferred, and rejects the rest.

$$\vdots$$

k.a. Any worker whose application was rejected at step $k-1$ makes a new application to its most preferred acceptable firm that hasn't yet rejected it (i.e. to which it hasn't yet applied).

k.b. Each firm f holds its (up to) q_f most preferred acceptable applications to date, and rejects the rest.

STOP when no further applications are made, and match each firm to the applicants whose offers it is holding.

Call the matching that results from this worker-proposing algorithm μ_W. To see that it is stable, note first that no unacceptable matches are even temporarily held,

1350   ALVIN E. ROTH

so the only possible cause of instability would be a blocking pair. But suppose worker w prefers firm f to her outcome $\mu_W(w)$. Then she must have applied to firm f before the final step of the algorithm, and been rejected. Hence firm f does not prefer worker w to (any of) its workers, and so (w, f) is not a blocking pair.

This proves the first of the following theorems, all of which apply to the simple market modeled above. We will see that the theoretical picture changes when we consider the complexities of the medical market.

Theorems Concerning Simple Matching Markets

THEOREM 1: *The set of stable matchings is always nonempty (Gale and Shapley (1962)).*

THEOREM 2: *The deferred acceptance algorithm with workers proposing produces a "worker optimal" stable match, that matches each worker to the most preferred firm to which she can be matched at a stable matching. The parallel "firm proposing" algorithm produces a "firm optimal" stable matching that gives to each firm f_i the (up to) q_i most preferred workers to which it can be matched at a stable matching. The optimal stable matching for one side of the market is the least preferred stable matching for the other side (Gale and Shapley (1962); Roth and Sotomayor (1989)).*

THEOREM 3: *The same applicants are matched and the same positions are filled at every stable matching. Furthermore, a firm that does not fill all its positions at some stable matching will be matched to the same applicants at every stable matching (McVitie and Wilson (1970); Roth (1984, 1986)).*

THEOREM 4: *When the worker proposing algorithm is used, but not when the firm proposing algorithm is used, it is a dominant strategy for each worker to state her true preferences. (There exists no algorithm that always produces a stable matching in terms of the stated preferences and that makes it a dominant strategy for all agents to state their true preferences.) Furthermore, when the firm proposing algorithm is used, the only applicants who can do better than to submit their true preferences are those who would have received a different match from the applicant proposing algorithm (Roth (1982, 1985), Roth and Sotomayor (1990)).*

2.3. The Importance of Stability

The theoretical motivation for concentrating on the set of stable outcomes is that, if the market outcome is unstable, there is an agent or pair of agents who have the incentive to circumvent the match. Even in a large market, it is not hard to ascertain if an outcome is unstable, because the market can do a lot of parallel processing. Consider a worker, for example, who has received an offer

TABLE I

STABLE AND UNSTABLE (CENTRALIZED) MECHANISMS

Market	Stable	Still in use (halted unraveling)
American medical markets		
NRMP	yes	yes (new design in '98)
Medical Specialties	yes	yes (about 30 markets)
British Regional Medical Markets		
Edinburgh ('69)	yes	yes
Cardiff	yes	yes
Birmingham	no	no
Edinburgh ('67)	no	no
Newcastle	no	no
Sheffield	no	no
Cambridge	no	yes
London Hospital	no	yes
Other healthcare markets		
Dental Residencies	yes	yes
Osteopaths (<'94)	no	no
Osteopaths (≥'94)	yes	yes
Pharmacists	yes	yes
Other markets and matching processes		
Canadian Lawyers	yes	yes (except in British Columbia since 1996)
Sororities	yes (at equilibrium)	yes

from her third choice firm. She only needs to make two phone calls to find out if she is part of a blocking pair.

The empirical evidence offers a good deal of support to this intuition. Table I lists a number of markets that have at one point in their history adopted centralized clearinghouses (see Roth (1990, 1991), Roth and Xing (1994, 1997), and Mongell and Roth (1991)). In addition, it indicates whether they produce matchings that are stable with respect to the submitted preferences. (The question of whether they are stable with respect to the actual preferences will be discussed below.) The table further lists whether these clearinghouses were successful (at halting unraveling) and are still in use, or whether they have failed and were abandoned.

The table suggests that producing a stable matching is an important criterion for a successful clearinghouse. Stable mechanisms have mostly (but not always) succeeded, and unstable mechanisms have mostly (but not always) failed. The situation is complicated by the many differences among the markets in the table other than the stability or instability of their clearinghouse algorithm. The set of markets that come closest to providing a crisp comparison are the different regional markets for new physicians and surgeons in Britain (Roth (1990, 1991)). Of these, the two that employ stable mechanisms have succeeded, while all but two of those that do not employ stable mechanisms have failed. But even here, there are differences between the markets—e.g. differences between Newcastle and Edinburgh—other than the organization of their clearinghouses. It could therefore be possible that the success of a stable clearinghouse in Edinburgh and the failure of an unstable one in Newcastle were for reasons other than how these clearinghouses were designed.

2.3.1. *Experimental Evidence*

Laboratory experiments can help clarify the impact of different clearinghouse designs. In a controlled environment, we can examine the effect of different matching algorithms while holding everything else constant. In this spirit, Kagel and Roth (2000) report an experiment that compares the stable, deferred acceptance market mechanisms used in Edinburgh and Cardiff with the kind of unstable, "priority matching" mechanism used in Birmingham, Newcastle, and Sheffield. Unver (2000b, c) reports a follow-up experiment that additionally compares these two classes of algorithms with the linear programming based algorithms used in Cambridge and at the London Hospital.

The successful algorithms adopted first in Edinburgh (in 1969) and then in Cardiff are essentially firm-proposing deferred acceptance algorithms. An alternative kind of algorithm that was widely tried in England proper (in Birmingham, Newcastle, and Sheffield), but always soon abandoned, defined a "priority" for each firm-worker pair as a function of their mutual rankings. Such an algorithm matches all priority 1 couples and removes them from the market, then repeats for priority 2 matches, priority 3 matches, etc. For example, in Newcastle, the priorities for firm-worker rankings were organized by the *product* of the rankings, (initially) as follows: 1-1, 2-1, 1-2, 1-3, 3-1, 4-1, 2-2, 1-4, 5-1... That is, the first priority is to match firms and workers who each list one another as their first choice, the second priority is to match a firm and worker such that the firm gets its second choice while the worker gets his first choice, etc.

This can produce unstable matchings—e.g. if a desirable firm and worker rank each other fourth, they will have such a low priority ($4 \times 4 = 16$) that if they fail to match to one of their first three choices, it is unlikely that they will match to each other. (E.g. the firm might match to its fifteenth choice worker, if that worker has ranked it first.)

The Kagel and Roth experiment created a simple laboratory environment in which subjects would initially gain experience with a decentralized matching market with sufficient competition and congestion to promote unraveling of appointments.[15] The subjects would have the opportunity to make early matches, but at a cost. Once subjects had time to adapt to this market, one of the two centralized matching mechanisms would be made available for those subjects who did not make early matches. The only difference between the two conditions of the experiment was that one employed the priority matching algorithm used unsuccessfully in Newcastle, and the other the stable matching algorithm used successfully in Edinburgh. The idea was not to reproduce the Edinburgh and Newcastle

---

[15] The role of congestion was clearly seen in the unusually fast, but nevertheless congested telephone market operated by clinical psychologists, prior to their adoption of a centralized clearinghouse (Roth and Xing (1997)).

markets, but rather to see whether the algorithms employed in those labor clearinghouses had the same effect in a simple environment in which any difference could be unambiguously interpreted as being due to the algorithm.

Each experimental market consisted of 12 subjects, half of whom were assigned the role of firms and half of workers. Subjects were paid according to with whom they matched, and when (with payoffs for a successful match ranging from $4 to $16 per market). Each matching market consisted of three periods, called (in order) periods −2, −1, and 0, to denote that the profit to a worker or firm from any match was reduced by $2 if the match was made in period −2, by $1 if the match was made in period −1, and by $0 if the match was made in (the final) period 0. A firm or worker who had not matched by the end of period 0 earned nothing.

In each matching market, firms could hire one worker, and likewise each worker could accept only one job. Firms were restricted to one offer in each period. Workers who received multiple offers in any period could accept at most one. Contracts were binding; a firm whose offer was accepted, and a worker who accepted an offer could not make other matches in a later period.

Each experimental session began with 10 consecutive decentralized matching markets. After the tenth decentralized matching market it was announced that, in each subsequent market, periods −2 and −1 would proceed as before, but henceforth period 0 would employ a centralized matching algorithm. For the centralized matching algorithm, subjects were instructed that if they were not matched prior to round 0, they were to "submit a rank order list of their possible matches, and the centralized matching mechanism (which is a computer program) will determine the final matching, based on the submitted rank order lists." In each experimental session we then conducted an additional 15 matching markets, with periods −2 and −1 employing the same decentralized procedures described above, but with one of the two centralized matching algorithms in place in period 0. Half of the experimental sessions employed the stable, Edinburgh algorithm, and half employed the unstable priority matching algorithm used in Newcastle.

An experiment like this yields a rich set of data, but for our present purposes, one figure, of aggregate behavior, will suffice. Figure 1 shows the average costs paid by all subjects in a given market for making early matches, over time. (If all 12 subjects made matches at period −2 this cost would be $24, if all matched at period −1 it would be $12, while if no subjects made early matches this cost would be 0.) The figure shows that after the subjects have gained some experience with the decentralized market, there is a good deal of actual early matching (reflecting a great deal of attempted early matching; the realized cost is around $8 in periods 6–10.) In periods 11–15, i.e. the first 5 periods after a centralized clearinghouse has been introduced, the amount of early matching is about the same for both mechanisms. But by periods 21–25, the Newcastle algorithm has not reduced early contracts, while the stable algorithm has. Thus the experimental results qualitatively reproduce the field results, under conditions in which

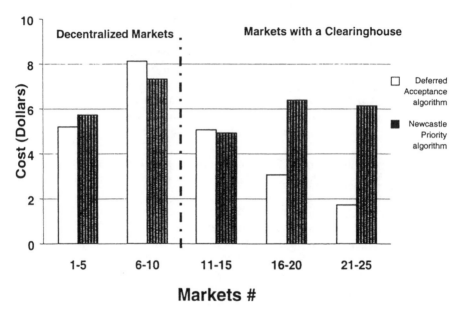

FIGURE 1.— Average costs of early markets, over time. In the first ten markets, #1–10, only the decentralized matching technology is available, and the participants match early, despite the cost. Starting with Market 11, and continuing through market 25, participants who wait until the last market period can use a centralized matching mechanism. In one cell of the experiment this was a stable, deferred acceptance algorithm of the kind used in Edinburgh, and in the other it was the unstable priority algorithm used in Newcastle. With the stable mechanism, costs of going early fell over time, indicating that more matches were being made at the efficient time.

the differences in outcomes can be unambiguously attributed to the matching algorithms. This adds confidence that the differences observed in the field are also due to the different clearinghouse designs (and not to some other difference between Edinburgh and Newcastle).[16]

[16] The subsequent experiment by Unver (2000b, c) adds support to the hypothesis that the long life of the linear programming mechanisms used at the London Hospital and in Cambridge has less to do with desirable features of those algorithms than with special features of those markets (these are the two smallest markets, and each involves only the graduates of a single medical school and jobs in the associated teaching hospital (Roth (1991)). In Unver's experiments, the linear programming mechanism performed no better than the priority matching mechanism when the mechanisms were employed in otherwise identical markets. Unver goes on to reproduce the main laboratory observations in a computational comparison of the mechanisms, in which each of the experimental conditions are played by genetic algorithms rather than by human subjects. This further clarifies the manner in which the mechanisms differ in the rewards they give to different strategies. And the comparisons with a prior computational study of these markets (Unver (2000a)) are illuminating in that they suggest that some kinds of strategic behavior come more naturally than others to human subjects; that

TOOLS FOR DESIGN ECONOMICS   1355

2.4. *Complications in the American Medical Market*

As the above discussion suggests, there is ample evidence that stability of the outcome is a critical element of clearinghouse design. The evidence proved sufficiently compelling to the various stakeholders in the American medical market so that the design discussion was always framed in terms of what kinds of stable matching mechanisms would perform best from various points of view. But this turns out to be a deceptively simple question, because the complications of the medical market radically change the theoretical properties of any matching mechanism. To state the matter starkly, none of the conclusions of Theorems 1–4 apply to the medical match, not even that a stable matching always exists. Under the conditions that actually prevail in the match, counterexamples can be constructed to all the conclusions of Theorems 1–4.[17]

What makes the NRMP different from a simple market is that it has complications of two kinds: complications that cause two positions to be linked to one another, and complications that involve the preferences of employers for variable numbers of workers. In the first category are *couples*, who need a pair of positions, and individual applicants who also need two positions, because they match to positions for second year graduates, and then need to find a prerequisite first year position. In the second category are requests by residency programs to have an even or an odd number of matches, and reversions of unfilled positions from one residency program to another, typically in the same hospital.[18]

For the present discussion, I will concentrate on the implications for design of the fact that there are couples in the market. In the 1990's there were somewhat more than 20,000 applicants for residencies participating in the match each year, and of these approximately 1,000 were in couples, seeking two jobs together. Table II gives statistics for the five years used most heavily for computational experiments during the design.

In the early 1980's, there were already couples in the market, and attempts had been made to modify the clearinghouse to accommodate them. However these attempts had not met with much success; many couples circumvented the match and made arrangements with hospitals on their own. It will help clarify the design problem to briefly consider that earlier attempt.

Prior to 1983, couples participating in the match (after being certified by their dean as a legitimate couple) were required to specify one of their members as the "leading member." They would then submit a rank ordering of positions for each

---

study showed that when genetic algorithms are allowed to operate on a wide strategy set, they might learn to manipulate the unstable mechanisms more thoroughly than the human subjects in the experiment did.

[17] Except of course the impossibility result in the second sentence of Theorem 4.

[18] This situation arises when the director of a program for second year graduates, e.g. in neurology, who require first year training, e.g. in internal medicine, makes an arrangement with the internal medicine director that the neurology residents will spend their first year with the other first year medicine residents. So internal medicine will now seek to hire fewer residents than it would otherwise. However, if the neurology program doesn't fill as many positions as anticipated, these empty positions have to be "reverted" to the medicine program, so that it will have the residents it needs.

TABLE II

NUMBER OF APPLICANTS, AND COUPLES BY YEAR

Year:	1987	1993	1994	1995	1996
Number of applicants submitting preference lists	20071	20916	22353	22937	24749
Number of applicants participating as part of a couple (i.e. twice the number of couples)	694	854	892	998	1008

member of the couple; i.e. a couple submitted two preference lists. The leading member was then matched to a position in the usual way, the preference list of the other member of the couple was edited to remove distant positions, and the second member was then matched if possible to a position in the same vicinity as the leading member. The algorithm applied to these lists was essentially a hospital proposing deferred acceptance algorithm, and so the resulting outcome was stable with respect to the individual lists submitted. That is, the resulting matching had no instabilities with respect to the individual worker-firm pairs. However it is easy to see why such an outcome would often in fact have an instability involving a couple and perhaps two employers, once we recognize that instabilities involving couples may look slightly different than those involving single workers.

Consider a couple whose first choice is to have two particular jobs in, say, Boston, and whose second choice is to have two particular jobs in New York. The leading member might be matched to his or her first choice job in Boston, while the other member might be matched to some undesirable job in Boston. Since the fundamental law of marriage is that you can't be happier than your spouse, an instability could now exist. If their preferred New York residency programs ranked them higher than students matched to positions in those programs, the couple, on calling the hospitals in New York, would find those hospitals glad to have them. (The students originally matched to those New York positions might be told that, due to an unexpected budget shortfall, their positions no longer existed.)

To make this precise, we can augment our simple model to accommodate couples who have preferences over pairs of positions, and can submit a rank order list that reflects this.

2.4.1. *A More Complex Market: Matching with Couples*

This model is the same as the simple model above, except the set of workers is replaced by a set of applicants that includes both individuals and couples.

Denote the set of applicants by $A = A1 \cup C$, where $A1$ is the set of (single) applicants who seek no more than one position, and C is the set of couples. A member of C is a couple $\{a_i, a_j\}$ such that a_i is in the set $A2$ (e.g. of husbands) and a_j is in the set $A3$, and the sets of applicants $A1$, $A2$, and $A3$ together make up the entire population of individual applicants, denoted $A' = A1 \cup A2 \cup A3$.

The reason for denoting the set of applicants both as A and as A' is that from the point of view of the firms, the members of a couple $c = \{a_i, a_j\}$ are two distinct applicants who seek distinct positions (typically in different residency programs), while from the point of view of the couple they are one agent with a single preference ordering of pairs of positions. That is, each couple $c = \{a_i, a_j\}$ in C has preferences over ordered pairs of positions, i.e. an ordered list of elements of $F \times F$. The first element of this list is some (r_i, r_j) in $F \times F$ which is the couples' first choice pair of residency programs for a_i and a_j respectively, and so forth. Applicants in the set $A1$ have preferences over residency programs, and residency programs (firms) have preferences over the individuals in A', just as in the simple model. A matching is a set of pairs in $F \times A'$.

Each single applicant, each couple, and each residency program submits to the centralized clearinghouse a Rank Order List (ROL) that is their stated preference ordering of acceptable alternatives.

As in the simple model, a matching μ is blocked by a single applicant (in the set $A1$), or by a residency program, if μ matches that agent to some individual or residency program not on its ROL. A matching is blocked by an individual couple (a_i, a_j) if they are matched to a pair (r_i, r_j) not on their ROL. No individual or couple blocks a matching at which he or it is unmatched.

A residency program r and a single applicant a in $A1$ together block a matching μ precisely as in the simple market, if they are not matched to one another and would both prefer to be.

A couple $c = (a_1, a_2)$ in A and residency programs r_1 and r_2 in F block a matching μ if the couple prefers (r_1, r_2) to $\mu(c)$, and if either r_1 and r_2 each would prefer to be matched to the corresponding member of the couple, or if one of them would prefer, and the other already is matched to the corresponding couple member. That is, c and (r_1, r_2) block μ if:

1. $(r_1, r_2) >_c \mu(c)$; and if either
2. $\{(a_1 \notin \mu(r_1)$, and $a_1 >_{r_1} a_i$ for some $a_i \in \mu(r_1)$ or a_1 is acceptable to r_1 and $|\mu(r_1)| < q_1\}$ and either $a_2 \in \mu(r_2)$ or $\{(a_2 \notin \mu(r_2), a_2 >_{r_2} a_j$ for some $a_j \in \mu(r_2)$ or a_2 is acceptable to r_2 and $|\mu(r_2)| < q_2\}$

or

3. $\{a_2 \notin \mu(r_2)$, and $a_2 >_{r_2} a_j$ for some $a_j \in \mu(r_2)$ or a_2 is acceptable to r_2 and $|\mu(r_2)| < q_2\}$ and $a_1 \in \mu(r_1)$.

A matching is *stable* if it is not blocked by any individual agent or by a pair of agents consisting of an individual and a residency program, or by a couple together with one or two residency programs.

It isn't hard to see why the presence of couples will cause design problems. Consider the deferred acceptance algorithm discussed above for the market without couples. It is a "one pass" algorithm: in the worker proposing version, each worker moves down her preference list only once. The reason this produces a stable matching is that no firm ever regrets any rejections it issues, since it only does so when it has a better worker in hand. So there is never a need for a worker to reapply to a firm that has already rejected her.

1358   ALVIN E. ROTH

Now consider the case in which some pair of workers is applying for positions as a couple (a, b), by submitting a preference list of pairs of firms, and suppose that at some point in the algorithm their applications are being held by the pair of firms (f, g), and that, in order to hold b's application, firm g had to reject some other worker c. Suppose at the next step of the algorithm, firm f, holding a's application, gets an offer it prefers, and rejects worker a. Suppose further that couple (a, b)'s next choice, after positions at firms f and g, is positions at two other firms f' and g'. Then in order to move down the couple's preference list, worker b has to be *withdrawn* from firm g. This creates a potential instability involving firm g (which now regrets having rejected worker c), and worker c. So an algorithm like the deferred acceptance procedure will no longer be able to operate in one pass through worker c's preferences, since to do so would miss this kind of instability.

This is not a difficulty linked to a particular kind of algorithm. In Roth (1984) I showed that, when couples are present, the set of stable matchings may be empty, and hence no algorithm can be guaranteed to converge to stability. Parenthetically, the difference between the treatment in that paper and in the design problem illustrates what I mean when I say that design carries a responsibility for detail. In Roth (1984) I found it sufficient to note that allowing couples to submit preference lists over pairs of positions would improve the chance of reaching a stable outcome, but that this might not completely solve the problem because stable matchings might sometimes not exist. While that was a reasonable observation to make as a disinterested observer, as a designer I had to think about an algorithm that will perform well, even in the absence of a theorem establishing that it will always produce a stable matching.

It seemed likely that no "one pass" algorithm would be feasible, and that therefore any algorithm would need to check for and resolve instabilities that might be present at intermediate stages. With this in mind, we took as the basis for the conceptual design of the new algorithm the class of algorithms explored in Roth and Vande Vate (1990), which, starting from any matching, seek to resolve instabilities one at a time. That paper showed how, in a simple market, instabilities could be sequenced in such a way that the process would always converge to a stable matching. The idea is that, starting from an unstable matching, a new matching can be created by "satisfying" one of its blocking pairs (f, w); i.e. creating a new matching in which f and w are matched with one another, perhaps leaving a worker previously matched to f unmatched, and a position previously occupied by w vacant.[19]

When the algorithm starts, all positions are empty, and the algorithm begins, like the applicant-proposing deferred acceptance algorithm, by satisfying blocking pairs involving unmatched applicants. Then, as potential instabilities develop due to the presence of couples, these are resolved one at a time. Each step of the algorithm begins by selecting an applicant, either an individual or a couple, and

---

[19] The paper was motivated by the observation by Knuth (1976) that the process of satisfying a sequence of blocking pairs could sometimes cycle, and return to matchings already considered.

letting that applicant start at the top of the applicant's preference list, and work down until the most preferred firm or firms willing to hold the application is reached. Applicants who are displaced in this process continue working their way down their preference lists, and when this causes a member of a couple to be withdrawn from a residency program, that residency program is put on the "hospital stack" to be checked later for potential instabilities. It is this process that causes the algorithm to take more than one pass through some applicants' preferences, as applicants who form blocking pairs with a hospital will be put back on the "applicant stack" to be considered again, starting with their most preferred programs. Throughout, the algorithm is applicant-proposing in the sense that, whenever there are multiple blocking pairs involving the same applicant, the blocking pair that is satisfied next is the one most preferred by the applicant.

In a simple market, without couples, the order in which applicants are placed in (and hence drawn from) the applicant stack can be shown not to matter, because the algorithm would produce the applicant-optimal stable matching no matter in what order the applicants were processed. However the order can matter when couples are present. Consequently, we performed computational experiments before making sequencing choices. These computational experiments focused on two issues:

• Do sequencing differences cause substantial or predictable changes in the match result (e.g., do applicants or programs selected first do better or worse than their counterparts selected later)?

• Does the sequence of processing affect the likelihood that an algorithm will produce a stable matching?

Computational experiments to test the effect of sequencing were conducted using data from three NRMP matches: 1993, 1994, and 1995. The results were that sequencing effects existed, but were unsystematic, and on the order of 1 in 10,000 matches. In the majority of years and algorithm sequences examined, the match was unaffected by changes in sequencing of algorithm operations, and in the majority of the remaining cases only 2 applicants received different matches. However sequencing decisions did influence the speed of convergence to a stable matching. Because sequencing decisions had no systematic effect on outcomes, it was decided to design the algorithm to promote rapid convergence to stability.

Based on these computational experiments, the applicant proposing algorithm for the NRMP was designed so that all single applicants are admitted to the algorithm for processing before any couples are admitted. This reduces the number of times that the algorithm encounters cycles and produced the fastest convergence.

Of course in examples for which no stable matching exists, like that of Roth (1984), no procedure for detecting and resolving cycles will produce a stable matching. But one result of the computational experiments conducted during the design of the algorithm is that the procedure never failed to converge to a stable matching. So there is reason to believe that the incidence of examples with no stable matchings may be rare.

TABLE III

COMPUTATIONAL EXPLORATION OF THE DIFFERENCE BETWEEN HOSPITAL AND
APPLICANT PROPOSING ALGORITHMS

Applicants	1987	1993	1994	1995	1996
Number of Applicants Affected	20	16	20	14	21
Applicant Proposing Result Preferred	12	16	11	14	12
Program Proposing Result Preferred	8	0	9	0	9
New Matched	0	0	0	0	1
New Unmatched	1	0	0	0	0

2.4.2. *Comparison of the Applicant and Program Proposing Algorithms*

Once alternative worker-proposing and firm-proposing algorithms could be compared, it was possible to examine the scope for (designer) discretion in choosing a stable matching. Unexpectedly, it turned out that this scope is very limited. The requirement that a matching be stable determines 99.9% of the matches; only one applicant in a thousand is affected by the choice of algorithm. Table III illustrates this on the data from the same matches shown in Table II. Recall that in each of those matches, there were more than 20,000 applicants. But as Table III shows, only about 20 applicants a year would have received different jobs from an applicant proposing algorithm than from a hospital proposing algorithm.

The table confirms that some of the properties of the set of stable matches are different in fact as well as in theory when couples and the other complications of the medical market are present. In a simple match, without couples or other complications, all of the applicants would have preferred the applicant proposing match, and no applicants who were matched or unmatched at the outcome of one algorithm would change employment status at the outcome of the other.[20]

On the other hand, Table III also illustrates the very small magnitude at which these differences from the simple model are exhibited. Of the more than 100,000 applicants involved in the data from which Table III is drawn, only two who were unmatched at one stable matching were matched at another. (Note also that even this tiny difference is unsystematic; it doesn't suggest that one or the other of the algorithms produces a higher level of employment.)

If this were a simple market, the small number of applicants whose matching is changed when we switch from hospitals proposing to applicants proposing would imply that there was also little room for strategic behavior when it

---

[20] Table III reflects results from the actual market, not the simplified market with couples as its only complication. It is easiest to see why the welfare comparisons from the simple model do not carry over to the medical market by considering the case of an individual who needs two jobs, e.g. a second year job in his desired specialty and a first year job that provides the necessary preparation. If he does better in the applicant proposing algorithm because of an improvement in his specialty position, he now requires a corresponding first year position, from which he displaces another applicant, who consequently does worse.

comes time to state rank order lists. Theorem 4 doesn't guarantee that this will be the case in the complex market. However the method of proof of Theorem 4 allowed a set of computational experiments on the submitted preference lists to be designed that would determine an upper bound on the number of applicants who could potentially have profited from changing their preference lists, based on the preferences submitted in previous years. *Under the assumption that the preference lists submitted in previous years represent the true preferences*, these computational experiments confirmed that the numbers of applicants who could have potentially profited by submitting different (shorter) preference lists are almost the same as those in Table III. Similarly, the number of residency programs that could potentially profit by changing their preferences or their stated capacities (cf. Sonmez (1997)) is comparably small (see Roth and Peranson (1999) for the design and results of these computational experiments).

However the assumption that the submitted preference lists are a good proxy for the true preferences needs careful investigation. If instead of reflecting the true preferences, the submitted preferences instead reflect misrepresentations of the preferences induced by experience with the existing clearinghouse, then it could be that a new algorithm would over time elicit quite different preferences, and affect many more applicants than the above calculations suggest. To state the competing hypotheses starkly, it could be that the set of stable matchings is small because the market is large, or it could be that the set of stable matchings is in fact large, but appears small because participants have successfully gamed the system. (At equilibrium, the set of stable matchings would appear to be small in terms of the submitted preferences.) Some further computation was required to resolve this issue.

Roth and Peranson report a set of theoretical computations on simple matching models with randomly generated preferences, to determine how the size of the market influences the size of the set of stable matchings, measured by how many applicants receive different matches at different stable matchings. For these computations we considered markets with no match complications, so that Theorems 1–4 apply. In particular, firm and worker optimal stable matches exist, and we can compute the number of applicants who receive different matches at different stable matchings by simply counting the applicants who receive different matches at the optimal stable matchings for each side. (The proof is simple: if an applicant's best and worst stable matching are the same, then he is matched to the same firm at every stable matching.)

When preferences are highly correlated, the set of stable matchings is small regardless of the size of the market. But when preferences are uncorrelated, the core quickly grows quite large, if as the market grows large, the number of firms on an applicant's preference list grows correspondingly large. (By the time there are 500 firms and workers, over 90% of workers receive different matches at different stable matchings). However, in the medical market, applicants and residency programs only list one another on their preferences if they have completed an interview, and so no applicant has a very long list of programs (and the vast majority have fewer than 15 programs on their submitted preference list). When

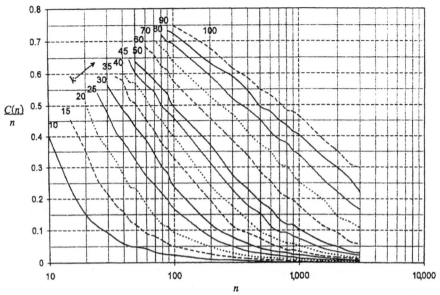

FIGURE 2.— Small core of large markets, with k fixed as n grows. $C(n)/n$ is the proportion of workers who receive different matches at different stable matchings, in a simple market with n workers and n firms, when each worker applies to k firms, each firm ranks all workers who apply, and preferences are uncorrelated (from Roth and Peranson (1999)). Note that for any fixed k, the set of stable matchings grows small as n grows large.

this restriction is added, the set of stable matchings shrinks rapidly as the size of the market grows, and essentially reproduces the results obtained in the computational investigation of the medical market (see Figure 2). In these computations, there is no question what are the true preferences, and the fact that the set of stable matchings is small confirms that there are effectively no opportunities for firms or applicants to profitably manipulate their preferences. That is, in the simulations, we know the true preferences, and we see that the opportunities for profitable strategic misrepresentation are as small as they are in the field data.

The fact that only one in a thousand applicants in the match could even potentially profit from misrepresenting his or her preferences, together with the fact that no one can tell if they are in this tenth of a percent of the population, and that those who are not can only hurt themselves by misrepresenting their preferences, makes it easy to advise applicants that the incentives for straightforward reporting of rank order lists are clear.

Another observation from the matches we have analyzed is that we have never yet observed in the field data a year in which no stable matching could be found. This is despite the fact that, when couples and other complementarities exist, the set of stable matchings can be empty. It appears that, when the percentage of couples is not too high, as the market becomes large and the set of stable matchings becomes small, it also becomes less likely to be empty. Preliminary computational simulations support this conjecture, but at the moment it remains a conjecture.

The computational results suggest an agenda for theoretical work quite different than might have been expected to follow from the prior theory. We cannot hope to find, say, restrictions on agents' preferences that will be met in the market and will allow us to generalize the conclusions of Theorems 1–4. The conclusions of those theorems don't in fact generalize to the medical market. But the conclusions of the theorems are in some sense close to being correct; the number of individual firms and workers for whom the conclusions are violated is small. The computational results suggest that there may be theorems that explain why it becomes increasingly unlikely that the set of stable matchings will be either large or empty, as the market grows large.

The availability of computation meant that the design effort could proceed without waiting for theoretical resolution of outstanding problems. Computation was used in several quite different ways in the course of the design and evaluation of the new medical labor market. We relied on computation in three places:

- Computational experiments were used in the algorithm design.
- Computational explorations of the data from previous years were used to study the effect of different algorithms.
- Theoretical computation, on simple markets to which existing theoretical results apply, was used to understand the effect of market size.

Before moving on, a word is in order about the political context in which this new design was adopted as the matching algorithm for the American medical match. The crisis of confidence that sparked the initial demand for a new market design also led to a heightened sensitivity about the conduct of the design effort. Early in the process I fielded visits from the American Medical Students Association, as well as numerous conference calls with members of the board of directors of the National Resident Matching Program, whose members represent a variety of institutional and student interests. While I worked on the design, I maintained a web page on which I posted my interim reports.

My status was that of an outside expert hired to design a new algorithm that would be able to handle all the match complications, and to evaluate the scope for favoring one side of the market over the other (i.e. applicants and residency programs) while achieving a stable matching. The responsibility for deciding whether to adopt the new design was retained by the NRMP, in consultation with its various constituencies. Once my design and evaluation were complete, I conferred at length with the various interested parties (including travelling to present the results to representatives of the various organizations of residency directors). Although it was widely anticipated that the results of the study would provoke bitter disagreement, the fact that the set of stable matchings proved to be so small was widely understood to mean that making the match as favorable as possible to applicants would not create any systematic problems for any segment of residency programs. Consequently my reports were received without provoking much controversy, and the NRMP board voted in May of 1997 to adopt the new algorithm for the match starting in 1998. The first few years of operation of the new match design seem to have been extremely smooth, and while many issues related to the medical labor market continue to be of lively concern, the organization of the match no longer appears to be a source of significant controversy.[21]

We turn next to consider briefly an ongoing design process that is embedded in a much more formal political process.

3. THE FCC SPECTRUM AUCTIONS[22]

In 1993 the US Congress amended the Communications Act of 1934 to direct the Federal Communications Commission (FCC) to design and conduct auctions to efficiently allocate radio spectrum licenses. The first auction was held in July of 1994. In the interim, the FCC hired John McMillan (then of UCSD) to advise their staff, and instituted a series of hearings at which the major potential bidders could offer proposals and comments on auction design. Many of the interested parties also hired game theorists to help formulate their proposals.

How spectrum licenses were previously allocated in the U.S. didn't give much guidance, since spectrum had been given away free for most of the 20th century. Until 1981, spectrum licenses were allocated through a political process called "comparative hearings." After 1981, licenses were allocated by lottery. Both procedures led to lots of rent-seeking behavior and bureaucratic complications, and to very substantial delays.

However, spectrum licenses had been auctioned overseas, and the experience of these related markets taught some important lessons. In Australia, satellite-television licenses had been sold in a sealed-bid, first-price auction with rules that merely specified that, if the winning bid were withdrawn after the auction,

---

[21] Because design involves detail, I have chosen to tell one story in depth rather than many without detail, but I can't resist putting in some pointers to the elegant theoretical and experimental work on matching individuals with indivisible objects such as student housing in Abdulkadiroglu and Sonmez (1998, 1999, 2000), Balinski and Sonmez (1999), and Chen and Sonmez (2002). That work builds on the observation by Shapley and Scarf (1974) that in a simple "housing market" model of allocation of indivisible goods there is a nonempty core reachable by an algorithm of "top trading cycles" proposed by David Gale, which yields a unique allocation when preferences are strict (Roth and Postlewaite (1977)), and that the mechanism that chooses this allocation is strategy proof (Roth (1982b)). Note also the practical work of designing decentralized web-based job matching services such as reported in Nakamura, Percy, Davenport, Fraser, and Piper (1998). In this latter context, note that complementarities will be endemic to job markets, since they arise, e.g., even from budget constraints (Mongell and Roth (1986)). For a contemporary problem in labor market design, see the study of the market for law clerks for the US Circuit Courts of appeals in Avery, Jolls, Posner, and Roth (2001), and for some experimental tests of proposed design solutions see Haruvy, Roth, and Unver (2002).

[22] Detailed accounts of some of the events reviewed in this section can be found in FCC (1997, 2000) and on the FCC auction website at *http://www.fcc.gov/wtb/auctions/Welcome.html*, in Cramton (1995), McAfee and McMillan (1996), McMillan (1994), and Milgrom (2000). I concentrate here on a few issues, and ignore others, such as the mandate to design the auctions in a way that made special provisions for certain affirmative action concerns (on which see Ayres and Cramton (1996)).

the next highest bid would become the winning bid. This procedure was gamed in spectacular fashion by a newcomer to the industry. After the auction closed, it was found that not only had this bidder submitted the highest bid, but it had also submitted the next highest bid, and the next, and the next. By withdrawing each high bid in turn, it eventually purchased the two licenses up for auction at massively lower prices than its initially winning bids (McMillan (1994)). With this experience in mind, the withdrawal rules adopted by the FCC required up-front deposits by bidders wishing to participate in the auction, and established that a high bidder who withdrew his bid would be liable for the difference between the withdrawn winning bid and the actual selling price.

Much of the discussion of auction design focused on the questions of how to promote efficient allocation, by eliciting bidding that would reveal the value of the licenses to the bidders, and allocate licenses where they were most valued. Because a spectrum license for new communication services has a large but uncertain value, one hazard facing bidders, called the "winner's curse," is that a bidder who overestimates the value of the license is more likely to submit the winning bid, and runs the risk of bidding more than the license will prove to be worth. Knowing that other bidders have comparable estimates would reduce the chance that the bidder's own estimate was mistaken. Not knowing how much other users think the license is worth, therefore, means that each bidder has to treat his own estimate with great caution. In a sealed bid auction, this would mean that a bidder would be wise to bid substantially less than his estimated value for the license.[23]

To allow bidders to get a sense of what the other bidders think the licenses are worth ("price discovery"), it was decided not to have a sealed bid auction, but to let bidders observe each others' bids in a multi-round ascending bid auction. It was further decided that this should be a first price auction, in which the winning bidders pay the full price they have bid.[24]

A chief concern was how to deal with the potential complementarities that might influence bidders' valuations of groups of licenses. To be concrete, suppose

---

[23] Our current understanding of the winner's curse is itself a case study of the interaction between field data, theory, and experimental economics. It was discussed in the context of auctions for drilling rights for oil (Capen, Clapp, and Cambell (1971)), it was modelled theoretically in "common value" auctions in which agents understand the danger and how to discount appropriately (cf. Wilson (1969), Milgrom and Weber (1982a, b), Klemperer (1998)) and it has been studied experimentally in the laboratory where profit-making behavior is sometimes learned only slowly and painfully (cf. Kagel and Levin (1986, 1999)).

[24] McMillan (1994) writes that based on the experience of a spectrum auction in New Zealand, it was judged politically unwise to have a second price auction that would be subject to the criticism that the government was selling licenses to firms at a price less than what it knew they were willing to pay. Bidders too may be reluctant to reveal their true reservation prices as freely as they might do in truly isolated second price auctions (cf. Rothkopf, Tiesberg, and Kahn (1990)), so that not all the potential advantages of second price auctions may be realizable in practice. However, for a generalization of second price auctions to multiple goods, see the patent by Ausubel (2000). (The fact that auction methods are now patented speaks volumes about the changing nature of the design business.)

a bidder values licenses A and B at 100 (million) each if he can get both, but otherwise only at 50 each. How should they be auctioned so that if their highest value is achieved only if they are owned together, the bidder can afford to bid aggressively on them, without too much risk that he will win only one of them, but pay more than it is worth on its own?

Some complementarities could be dealt with by appropriate definition of the licenses themselves. For example, the first auction, in 1994, was for Narrowband Personal Communication Services (PCS), two-way paging services in which a central transmitter relays a message to a personal device, which can then transmit a return message. The central transmitter is powerful, and can transmit on a noisy frequency, but the personal device is low powered, and must transmit on a quiet frequency. So efficient use of this technology calls for the pairing of two complementary frequencies. Rather than rely on the auction to aggregate efficient pairs, the Narrowband PCS licenses were each defined to be for an appropriate pair of frequencies. That is, from the outset, the rights that were being auctioned were for a complementary pair of frequencies (see Cramton (1995)).[25]

However not all potential complementarities can be clearly defined by the technology, and so a major design question was how to structure the auction to allow bidders to take into account any important complementarities in their valuations. The idea of auctioning spectrum licenses one at a time was rejected for this reason, as was the idea of simultaneously beginning separate auctions for many licenses, but letting each one end independently, when no bidder wished to raise his bid on that license. Instead, in proposals put forward by Preston McAfee of the University of Texas (representing Airtouch Communications) and by Paul Milgrom and Bob Wilson of Stanford (representing Pacific Bell), it was suggested that all the licenses being sold at a given time be auctioned simultaneously, and that none of the auctions should end until they all did. That is, in this proposal, which was ultimately adopted, the market for every license would remain open until no bidder wished to raise his bid on any license. (The impact of the academic commentators, especially Milgrom and Wilson, on all aspects of the FCC design, is evident in the FCC documents, for example the Notice of Proposed Rulemaking (FCC, 1993) and the Final Report and Order (FCC, 1994). At the same time, the tremendously detailed rules needed in order to produce a working auction, and to guard against foreseeable contingencies, represent many person-months of work by the FCC staff.)

There was concern that the auction rules should not give bidders an incentive to avoid making serious bids until the end, in an effort to benefit from the information contained in other bidders' bids, without revealing any of their own.

---

[25] Of course no auction design can prevent the winners' curse in an auction involving a new technology like paging, for which there are wildly different forecasts. One of the licenses I have followed was won at the auction in 1994 by KDM Messaging/ATT for $80,000,000, but was sold to TSR Wireless for $20,000,000 in 1999, and after TSR declared Chapter 7 bankruptcy in December 2000, this license was sold at the liquidation auction for $3,585,266 (*In re* TSR Wireless, LLC, Nos. 00-41857 & 0041858 (Bankr. D. N.J. Mar. 28, 2001) at [4]). (Of course, a sharp price decline is not itself a proof that the winner's curse was the cause.)

This would inhibit the price discovery that the multi-round design is intended to promote, and might also simply make the auctions long and cumbersome.

To prevent bidders from concealing their intentions by delaying their bids, the spectrum auctions imposed an *activity rule*, proposed by Milgrom and Wilson. Under this rule, bidders had to maintain their eligibility to bid on a given volume of licenses (measured in population of the area covered) by being the high bidder, or by raising their bids by specified minimum percentages, on a sufficient volume of licenses. Bidders who did not remain active in this way on a sufficient volume of licenses would see their eligibility decline to reflect the volume of licenses they were actively bidding on. That is, this activity rule specified that a bidder who did not remain active would not be able to suddenly become active on a high volume of licenses late in the auction.

As of this writing more than two dozen spectrum auctions have been run under a simultaneous, multiple round auction design, with numerous small modifications made along the way based on early experience.[26] Overall, these auctions appear to be working smoothly, and they have raised many billions of dollars of revenue.

The largest design change to date is presently scheduled to be implemented in the 2002 auction of 700 MHz spectrum licenses suitable for high speed internet access. Instead of requiring bidders to submit bids for individual licenses, and to assemble the packages they want by bidding simultaneously on multiple licenses, the new rules allow bidders to explicitly bid for *packages* of licenses. This is meant to solve the "exposure problem" of simultaneous bidding, in which bidders with strong complementarities are exposed to the risk of winning only part of the package they are trying to assemble, and of having bid more for that part than it is worth to them on its own. Under package bidding, a bidder will either win the whole package or none of it.

To determine the winning bids, when bidders bid on different packages of their own devising, the auction has to determine the revenue-maximizing set of packages. This will make the auction more complicated in the sense that a bid for a particular package that is not part of the revenue maximizing set of packages when it is made, may later become part of the revenue maximizing set, as higher bids for other packages come in.

---

[26] One of the more difficult problems encountered to date has to do with who owns the license if, after submitting a winning bid, a firm files for bankruptcy. In the C block broadband PCS auction, the rules allowed generous installment payment plans, "which led to all the major bidders defaulting and declaring bankruptcy" (Cramton (2000)). The FCC no longer allows such payment plans, but resolving the bankruptcies, and putting this spectrum to use may depend on further legislation or on rulings from the bankruptcy court. Making collusion difficult has also been a concern. In early auctions, bidders signaled their intentions using the last digits of their (six digit) bids to communicate (three digit) license identification numbers. (See Cramton and Schwartz (2000) for some detailed examples in which threats were communicated in this way.) In 1997 the FCC changed the bidding format, and allowed only bids in preset increments, to prevent this. Bid withdrawals were also used for signaling in early auctions, and these too have been limited. See the FCC's anticollusion page at *www.fcc.gov/wtb/auctions/collusio/collusio.html*.

Interestingly, discussion of package bidding began even prior to the first auction in 1994, because of concern that complementarities might be of great importance.[27] Two kinds of potential difficulties with package bidding loomed large in these discussions. The first class of anticipated difficulties concerned combinatorial properties of such an auction. Because of the large number of possible packages (there are $2^n - 1$ subsets of n licenses), it might not be possible to run a package bidding auction properly, either because of the computational difficulty of computing the revenue maximizing set of packages, or because of difficulty in eliciting and presenting the bids in a way that would make the progress of the auction easily comprehensible to the bidders.

A second class of difficulties concerned the incentives that bidders might face in a package bidding auction. With so many potential packages to bid on, activity rules might lose their force, and bidders who wished to delay revealing the packages they were interested in and the prices they were willing to pay might be able to maintain apparent activity by "parking" their bids on packages unlikely to be part of the winning set of packages.

Also, package bidding can create a free-rider problem among small regional bidders in a way that gives an artificial advantage to large bidders who want packages providing comprehensive national coverage. Consider the problem facing a regional firm interested in a single license. Its bid will be part of the revenue maximizing set of packages only if its bid, together with those of the other regional bidders, sum to more than the bid on the national package comprising licenses in all the regions. But this means that the success of the regional bids depends mostly on the bids of the other regional bidders—there is little incentive for each regional bidder to bid aggressively. (And, since each winning bidder must pay the full amount of the winning bid, there is ample incentive to stick with a low bid and hope that the other regional bidders will raise their bids enough to raise the sum of the regional bids above the bid for the national package.) Consequently, a large bidder who seeks to win a package of national scope may not have to bid aggressively, and may win the national package even in the case that the regional licenses have a higher value separately. In the auction design discussion, this came to be known as the "threshold problem," in the sense that the national bid establishes a threshold that the sum of the regional bids must surpass.[28]

---

[27] In fact, discussion of package bidding preceded the discussion of spectrum licenses entirely, having come up in connection with other complementarities. Rassenti, Smith, and Bulfin (1982) report an experiment showing that efficiencies can be realized by allowing package bidding in an environment in which complementarities were motivated by the need of airlines for complementary takeoff and landing slots. (See also the experiments of Grether, Isaac, and Plott (1981), who report experiments with a nonauction mechanism for allocating packages of airline slots by committee decision.) For early theoretical discussions of package bidding, see Vickrey (1961) and Bernheim and Whinston (1986), and, in a two-sided matching context in which firms bid for groups of workers, Kelso and Crawford (1982).

[28] A more careful historian than I will have to see if the economists lined up on each side of the package bidding question were representing firms with predictable interests in the matter. (In addition, designers can have professional incentives to see their designs adopted, and these needn't always be perfectly aligned with their client's interests.) But politics is part of design, and we're going to have to learn to deal with the politics *of* design.

Each of these questions raised by the complementarities in the market eluded analytical solutions, but lent themselves to computational and experimental exploration. Computational studies were conducted to understand how difficult it would be to compute a winning set of bids from a set of submitted package bids. While the worst case scenarios make it computationally intractable to compute the winning set of bids, when most bidders bid on only small subsets of packages the average problem is not hard, and can be solved with commercial integer programming packages (see, e.g., Kelly and Steinberg (2000), Rothkopf, Pekec, and Harstad (1998), or see deVries and Vohra (2000) for an overview).

Ease of use, and threshold problems, were addressed at least in principle by experiments (cf. Cybernomics (2000), Plott (1997), Ledyard, Porter, and Rangel (1997)). Because the package bidding mechanisms being considered are all novel, there isn't a source of field data that would be informative for design. So, unlike in the design of the medical match, the role of experiments here wasn't to complement field data, but to add an empirical component to the discussion in the absence of field data. In addition, the impetus for package bidding was motivated by the strong sense that complementarities existed, but without any data or models to predict their distributions. So experiments were constructed not to test specific hypotheses related to the spectrum market, but rather as "proof of concept" demonstrations that package bidding could achieve efficiencies that might be missed in single item auctions. (Plott (1997) describes the role that experiments played at various parts in the FCC's process of soliciting comments and advice.) The experiments show that package bidding can indeed achieve some of the hoped for efficiencies in simple environments. While the implications of these results for the proposed spectrum auctions remained a subject of lively controversy among the potential bidders and their advisors, experiments provided an empirical dimension to the debate.

The Cybernomics experiment compared the simultaneous ascending auction to a package bidding auction under various configurations of values. In the experiment, as complementarities became more important in bidder valuations of packages, the efficiency of the simultaneous ascending auction diminished, while the package bidding auction was largely unaffected. The package bidding auctions also took many more rounds to complete. Partly motivated by this latter observation, Ausubel and Milgrom (2001) analyzed the performance of a simple package bidding auction in which bidders are assumed to bid "straightforwardly," in the sense that at each round they make whatever is the minimum allowable bid at that time on the package that would maximize their profits at current prices.

They observe that when bidders bid straightforwardly, the auction operates as a deferred acceptance algorithm, with results quite similar to those found in the matching literature. In particular they deduce some analogs to the matching results in Theorems 1, 2, and 4, discussed earlier. The outcome of the package bidding auction they analyze with straightforward bidding will be the point in the core that is optimal for the buyers (i.e., it minimizes seller revenue), and if goods are substitutes, straightforward bidding will be a dominant strategy for buyers.

As in the case of matching theory, complementarities and budget constraints can create complications.[29]

Following a conference on combinatorial bidding held in May, 2000, at which a wide range of views were solicited, the FCC (2000, 2001) rules for package bidding strike a cautious compromise.[30] Based largely on a proposal by Milgrom (2000), the auction allows bidders to formulate bids for no more than a dozen packages. The idea is to reduce the combinatorial complexity, as well as the opportunities to evade the activity rules by making early bids on less valuable packages. It is worth noting the similar ways in which complementarities were addressed in the spectrum auctions and in the labor market clearinghouse designs. As in the package bidding auctions, the complementarities involving couples on the job market were addressed by allowing the couples to submit "package bids" for pairs of jobs.[31]

Overall, looking at the FCC auction design process from 1993 to the present, we see an ongoing design discussion in which decisions were made, then modified and revisited in light both of experience and of further discussion. While the FCC retained design responsibility, and FCC staff made the final design decisions, and hammered out the detailed procedures, the FCC solicited and implemented suggestions from economists at every stage of the process.[32] By and large, the FCC has mostly chosen to gradually adapt its initial design, rather than to make

---

[29] Ausubel and Milgrom thus establish a close parallel between the auction and matching literatures, with some of the closest points of contact in the matching literature being the "package bidding" by firms for groups of workers in Kelso and Crawford (1982) and Roth and Sotomayor (1990, Chapters 5 and 6), and Mongell and Roth (1986) (regarding budget constraints).

[30] The conference papers are available on the FCC website at *http://www.fcc.gov/wtb/auctions/combin/papers.html.*

[31] Other complementarities in the medical match, not discussed in detail here, were addressed similarly. Applicants needing a second year position and a complementary first year position were invited to submit "supplementary lists" of first year positions for each such second year position, and the supplementary list was activated only when a second year position was obtained. In this way applicants needing two jobs could express their preferences for a package consisting of a pair of positions.

[32] The broad participation by economists in the design discussion is made clear in the FCC call for comments (2000). Footnote 3 reads:

"The progress the Bureau has made in designing and testing a combinatorial bidding system has been made possible only by the extraordinary work done by a number of people. The procedures we are proposing are based largely on a paper presented by Stanford University Professor Paul R. Milgrom at the Conference on Combinatorial Bidding jointly sponsored by the Federal Communications Commission, the Stanford Institute for Economic Policy Research, and the National Science Foundation, that took place on May 5–7, 2000 at the Aspen Institute's Wye River Conference Center. Paul R. Milgrom, FCC-SIEPR-NSF, Wye Woods Conference: Lessons plus a Simple Proposal (May 2000). This paper builds on ideas from many of the people who attended the conference. Some of the proposals we are considering are also importantly based on the reports by Professor Charles R. Plott of the California Institute of Technology, Charles River Associates Incorporated, Market Design, Inc., and Computerized Market Systems, Inc. that were produced pursuant to contract with the FCC, and the Cybernomics, Inc. reports by Jeffrey Banks, David Porter, Stephen Rassenti, and Vernon Smith that weres also written pursuant to contract with the FCC. In addition, Professor John Ledyard of the California Institute of Technology has rendered invaluable assistance. These papers and reports, as well as the other papers presented at the conference, can be found at the Commission's website on the conference, http://conbin.fcc.gov."

radical changes. It was in this spirit that the FCC adopted the Milgrom proposal of limiting bidders to bid on no more than 12 packages of licenses. (It seems likely that this limit will be lifted in future auctions as more confidence develops in the design and operation of combinatorial auctions).

Aside from presenting economists with an opportunity to think about these design issues, the completed auctions will present an opportunity to investigate the magnitudes of some of the effects that have played a role in the design debate, including the magnitude of the complementarities between licenses. The rather different experiences of various European spectrum auctions (see Klemperer (2002b)) also present fertile grounds for further investigation.[33]

A little further afield, the growing number of auctions on the internet provide a new opportunity to investigate the effects of different auction designs. Some of the concerns that occupied the designers of spectrum auctions, such as the need for rules to promote price discovery by preventing bidders from withholding their bids until the end, can be investigated by comparing different rules used for ending internet auctions. With this in mind, Roth and Ockenfels (2001) compare bidding behavior on eBay and Amazon. Auctions conducted by eBay have a fixed deadline for ending the auction, while Amazon auctions, which have otherwise similar rules, cannot close until both the scheduled end time has been reached *and* ten minutes have passed with no bidding. This difference in rules has a dramatic effect on the distribution of bids over time, with bids on eBay concentrated very near the end, while bids on Amazon are not. In terms of price discovery, early bids are less informative about final selling price on eBay than on Amazon. Of course there are other differences between the markets found on eBay and

---

[33] Different concerns may influence the design of related auctions, as in the recent work by Ken Binmore and Paul Klemperer on spectrum auctions in the UK. A prime concern in the U.K. market had to do with making sure that there were more licenses for sale than incumbent broadcasters, to encourage competition by newcomers. Binmore and Klemperer (2002) report that initially, the plan was to auction four licenses, and there were already four incumbent firms. It was feared that an ascending auction on the American model would allow the incumbents to collusively divide up the market, without facing much competition from new entrants, who would be deterred from bidding aggressively by a well justified fear of the winner's curse. To ameliorate these concerns, a hybrid auction was considered whose final stage would be a sealed bid auction, and experiments on this hybrid appeared promising. However the government finally was persuaded to auction an additional license, and an ascending auction on the American model was adopted, with the licenses themselves defined in a way intended to make new entrants competitive. The auction was successful in that it raised unprecedented revenue. In Germany, in contrast, the auctions were criticized by economists for their design on the grounds that new entrants might be deterred: see Jehiel and Moldovanu (2001) and Klemperer (2002a). However these auctions raised even more revenue than the English auctions (although less per capita). See Grimm, Riedel, and Wolfstetter (2001) and Wolfstetter (2001) for a different take on the German auctions. See Klemperer (2002b) for a discussion of all the European 3G spectrum auctions, most of which employed an ascending design, but many of which had disappointing results. In general, the European spectrum auctions have made clear that, quite apart from the details of auction design, the outcome depends on some of the underlying industrial organization. For example, several European auctions have been preceded by mergers of potential bidders. And to the extent that a single European market for telecommunications will emerge, it will have been affected not merely by the individual spectrum auctions conducted by national governments, but by how these auctions and their outcomes interact.

Amazon, and so this is an issue that also repays study in the controlled conditions of the laboratory. Ariely, Ockenfels, and Roth (2001) show that the difference in rules for ending the auction has the same effect in the lab as in the field. And in the laboratory, this difference in ending rules is the only difference between the auctions studied, since the same goods are sold under both rules, and (the same number of) bidders are randomly assigned to each kind of auction, rather than self selecting themselves between auctions, as in the field data. That is, here too experiments and field studies work in harness to show that in eBay-style auctions with fixed deadlines, many bidders reserve much of their activity to the closing seconds of the auction, in contrast to auctions that are automatically extended when late bids arrive.[34]

4. CONCLUDING REMARKS

When I was asked in 1995 to redesign the labor market clearinghouse for American physicians, I had to confront the fact that none of the available theory—e.g. none of the theorems in my book on the subject (Roth and Sotomayor (1990))—could be directly applied to the complex market. All the theorems were about simpler, static models, in which there were no complementarities. Like Theorems 1–4 in this paper, the theorems all took the form "in a simple model, the following things always happen." The only theoretical parts of the book that applied directly to the medical market were the *counterexamples*—and they all warned that, in more complicated markets, problems could sometimes arise. What was missing in the theory, but needed in design, was a sense of magnitudes; how often those problems would arise, and how big their consequences would be.

It turned out that the simple theory offered a surprisingly good guide to the design, and approximated the properties of the large, complex markets fairly well. Field and laboratory data showed that the static idea of stability went a long way towards predicting which kinds of clearinghouse could halt the dynamics of unraveling. And computation showed that many of the departures from the simple theory were small, and that some of the most severe problems that the counterexamples anticipated, such as the possibility that no stable matching would exist, were rare in large markets. Computation also revealed that large markets could achieve even nicer incentive properties than anticipated by the simple theory. That is, by unanticipated good luck, some of the knotty problems posed by couples, and other complementarities, could be solved without losing the most attractive design options that the simple theory suggested.

When I speak of unanticipated good luck, I mean that these computational and experimental results, while suggested by the theory of simple matching markets, are not explained by that theory. These results point to a need for new theory, to

---

[34] Here too the empirical observations motivate new theory: cf. Ockenfels and Roth (2001). In between field studies and laboratory experiments are field experiments in which some controlled variation is introduced into a natural, uncontrolled population. See, e.g., Lucking-Reilly (1999), who has been a pioneer in using field experiments to study internet auctions, by auctioning the same goods by different auction rules.

explain and further explore the behavior of large labor markets with couples and linked jobs. We also need new theory to explore the dynamics of market failures like unraveling, and their cures. Also, some of the nice properties of the medical market turn out to be related to the fact that each applicant interviews for only a small fraction of the jobs on the market (recall Figure 2). This seems likely to be an important variable, not only for this market. As electronic communication increases (standardized application forms, tele-conferencing, etc.) it may well be that the fraction of jobs to which an applicant can apply, and exchange meaningful information, will increase, in many markets. The results discussed here suggest that this may have important consequences, but we will need better theory than we have today to know what to expect.

Some of these same, general design themes also emerged in the design of the radio spectrum auctions. The simple theory there was somewhat less tightly connected to the final design decisions. McAfee and McMillan (1996) summarize the early role of theory in various aspects of the debate, and conclude as follows:

> "A lesson from this experience of theorists in policy-making is that the real value of the theory is in developing intuition. The role of theory, in any policy application, is to show how people behave in various circumstances, and to identify the trade-offs involved in altering those circumstances. What the theorists found to be the most useful in designing the auction and advising the bidders was not complicated models that try to capture a lot of reality at the cost of relying on special functional forms. Such theorizing fails to develop intuition, as it confounds the effects of the functional forms with the essential elements of the model. A focused model that isolates a particular effect and assumes few or no special functional forms is more helpful in building understanding" (p. 172).

Here, too, computation and experimentation played a role in filling the gaps between theory and design, particularly in connection with the forthcoming auctions that allow package bidding. The simple theory organized the discussion, and the design effort has opened the door on a whole new realm of auction theory that needs to be developed. Early indications are that there are further formal connections that can be profitably made between the auction and matching literatures.

Some of this theory is starting to make inroads on the question of how complementarities make market design difficult. Milgrom (2000) shows, in an auction context, that the real threat to the existence of equilibria is associated with goods that are complements to some bidders but not to others. This is also characteristic of the kinds of complementarities found in labor markets with couples—the positions that a couple regards as complements are not typically regarded as complements by others in the labor force.

The largest lesson in all this is that design is important because markets don't always grow like weeds—some of them are hothouse orchids. Time and place have to be established, related goods need to be assembled, or related markets linked so that complementarities can be handled, incentive problems have to be overcome, etc. If game theory is going to be as important a part of design economics as it is a part of economic theory, we'll have to develop tools not just to develop conceptual insights from simple models, but also to understand how

1374   ALVIN E. ROTH

to deal with these complications of real markets. These complications come in two kinds:

• complications in the strategic environment, and consequently in the possible outcomes, and the strategies available to the players; and

• complications in the behavior of real economic agents (who may not be the simple maximizers we are accustomed to studying in formal game theory, even in simple environments).

Computational methods will help us analyze games that may be too complex to solve analytically. Laboratory experiments will help inform us about how people will behave when confronted with these environments, both when they are inexperienced and as they gain experience. We'll need to learn from further experience how and when these tools can best be employed in different kinds of design efforts. And, since design involves anticipating how people will behave in novel environments, these concerns will make us want to deepen our understanding of *learning* in strategic environments. Successful designs must not only perform well in the long term, they must not crash and burn in the short term, and so models of learning with the ability to predict behavior in new environments will be a valuable addition to the designer's toolbox, alongside the more familiar, equilibrium analyses of long term behavior.[35]

In closing, we can start to see the shape of the economics of design. A decade ago, as part of its centenary celebrations, the *Economic Journal* asked a number of economists to write an essay about what the next hundred years might bring in various areas of economics. The last paragraph of my essay (Roth (1991)), read as follows:

> "... in the long term, the real test of our success will be not merely how well we understand the general principles that govern economic interactions, but how well we can bring this knowledge to bear on practical questions of microeconomic engineering... Just as chemical engineers are called upon not merely to understand the principles that govern chemical plants, but to design them, and just as physicians aim not merely to understand the biological causes of disease, but their treatment and prevention, a measure of the success of microeconomics will be the extent to which it becomes the source of practical advice, solidly grounded in well tested theory, on designing the institutions through which we interact with one another."

A decade makes a difference. The steps we have taken make the difficulties in constructing an engineering science of design economics even more apparent. But there are grounds to feel optimistic that, in the matter of design, game theory and experimental and computational economics can be harnessed together for the work at hand.

Dept. of Economics, Harvard University, Littauer Center, Cambridge, MA 02138-3001, U.S.A.; al_roth@harvard.edu; http://www.economics.harvard.edu/~aroth/alroth.html

Manuscript received February, 2001; final revision received August, 2001.

[35] See, e.g., Roth and Erev (1995) and Erev and Roth (1998) for one train of thought in that direction.

REFERENCES

ABDULKADIROGLU, A., AND T. SONMEZ (1998): "Random Serial Dictatorship and the Core from Random Endowments in House Allocation Problems," *Econometrica*, 66, 689–701.

———— (1999): "House Allocation with Existing Tenants," *Journal of Economic Theory*, 88, 233–260.

———— (2000): "School Choice: A Solution to the Student Assignment Problem," Mimeo, Columbia University.

ARIELY, D., A. OCKENFELS, AND A. E. ROTH (2001): "An Experimental Analysis of Late-Bidding in Internet Auctions," in preparation, Harvard University.

AUSUBEL, L. M. (2000): "System and Method for an Efficient Dynamic Auction for Multiple Objects," U.S. Patent Number 6,026,383, issued 15 Feb 2000.

AUSUBEL, L. M., AND P. MILGROM (2001): "Ascending Auctions with Package Bidding," Working Paper, University of Maryland.

AVERY, C., A. FAIRBANKS, AND R. ZECKHAUSER (2001): "What Worms for the Early Bird? Early Admissions at Selective Colleges," Working Paper, Harvard University.

AVERY, C., C. JOLLS, R. POSNER, AND A. E. ROTH (2001): "The Market for Federal Judicial Law Clerks," *University of Chicago Law Review*, 68, 793–902.

AYRES, I., AND P. CRAMTON (1996): "Deficit Reduction Through Diversity: How Affirmative Action at the FCC Increased Auction Competition," *Stanford Law Review*, 48, 761–815.

BALDWIN, C. Y., AND S. BHATTACHARYYA (1991): "Choosing the Method of Sale: A Clinical Study of Conrail," *Journal of Financial Economics*, 30, 69–98.

BALDWIN, C. Y., AND K. B. CLARK (2000): *Design Rules: The Power of Modularity*, Volume 1. Cambridge, MA: MIT Press.

BALINSKI, M., AND T. SONMEZ (1999): "A Tale of Two Mechanisms: Stubent Placement," *Journal of Economic Theory*, 84, 73–94.

BERNHEIM, B. D., AND M. WHINSTON (1986): "Menu Auctions, Resource Allocation and Economic Influence," *Quarterly Journal of Economics*, 101, 1–31.

BINMORE, K., and P. KLEMPERER (2002): "The Biggest Auction Ever: The Sale of the British 3G Telecom Licenses," *Economic Journal*, forthcoming.

BLUM, Y., A. E. ROTH, AND U. G. ROTHBLUM (1997): "Vacancy Chains and Equilibration in Senior-Level Labor Markets," *Journal of Economic Theory*, 76, 362–411.

BODIN, L., AND (RABBI) A. PANKEN (1999): "High Tech for a Higher Authority: The Placement of Graduating Rabbis From Hebrew Union College–Jewish Institute of Religion," Working Paper, Hebrew Union College–Jewish Institute of Religion.

BULOW, J., AND J. ROBERTS (1989): "The Simple Economics of Optimal Auctions," *Journal of Political Economy*, 97, 1060–1090.

CAPEN, E. C., R. V. CLAPP, AND W. M. CAMBELL (1971): "Competitive Bidding in High-Risk Situations," *Journal of Petroleum Technology*, 23, 641–653.

CHEN, Y., AND T. SONMEZ (2002): "Improving Efficiency of On-Campus Housing: An Experimental Study," *American Economic Review*, forthcoming.

CRAMTON, P. (1995): "Money Out of Thin Air: The Nationwide Narrowband PCS Auction," *Journal of Economics and Management Strategy*, 4, 267–343.

———— (2000): "Lessons from the United States Spectrum Auctions," Prepared Testimony before the United States Senate Budget Committee, 10 February.

CYBERNOMICS (2000): "An Experimental Comparison of the Simultaneous Multi-Round Auction and the CRA Combinatorial Auction," paper presented at the FCC Combinatorial Auction Conference, May 5–7, 2000.

DE VRIES, S., AND R. VOHRA (2000): "Combinatorial Auctions: A Survey," Working Paper, Northwestern University.

EREV, I., AND A. E. ROTH (1998): "Predicting How People Play Games: Reinforcement Learning in Experimental Games with Unique, Mixed Strategy Equilibria," *American Economic Review*, 88, 848–881.

FEDERAL COMMUNICATIONS COMMISSION (1997): "The FCC Report to Congress on Spectrum Auctions," October 9, FCC 97-353.

1376   ALVIN E. ROTH

—— (2000): "Auction of Licenses in the 747-762 and 777-792 MHZ Bands Scheduled for September 6, 2000: Comment Sought on Modifying the Simultaneous Multiple Round Auction Design to Allow Combinatorial (Package) Bidding," Public Notice DA00-1075, May 18.

—— (2001): "Auction of Licenses in the 747-762 and 777-792 MHZ Bands Scheduled for March 6, 2001: Modifications to the Calculation for Determining Minimum Acceptable Bids and the Provisions Concerning 'Last and Best Bids' and other Procedural Issues," Public Notice DA 01-12, January 5.

FILER, R. K., AND J. HANOUSEK (1999): "Informational Content of Prices Set Using Excess Demand: The Natural Experiment of Czech Voucher Privatization," Mimeo, CERGE, Charles University.

GALE, D., AND L. SHAPLEY (1962): "College Admissions and the Stability of Marriage," *American Mathematical Monthly*, 69, 9–15.

GREEN, J. R., AND J.-J. LAFFONT (1979): *Incentives in Public Decision-Making*. Amsterdam: North-Holland.

GRETHER, D. M., M. R. ISAAC, AND C. R. PLOTT (1981): "The Allocation of Landing Rights by Unanimity among Competitors," *American Economic Review*, 71, 166–171.

GRIMM, V., F. RIEDEL, AND E. WOLFSTETTER (2001): "Low Price Equilibrium in Multi-Unit Auctions: The GSM Spectrum Auction in Germany," Working Paper, Humboldt University (Berlin).

GROVES, T., AND J. O. LEDYARD (1977): "Optimal Allocation of Public Goods: A Solution to the Free Rider Problem," *Econometrica*, 45, 783–809.

GUPTA, N., J. C. HAM, AND J. SVEJNAR (2000): "Priorities and Sequencing in Privatization: Theory and Evidence from the Czech Republic," Mimeo, William Davidson Institute, University of Michigan.

HARUVY, E., A. E. ROTH, AND U. UNVER (2002): "The Dynamics of Law Clerk Matching: An Experimental and Computational Investigation of Some Proposed Market Designs," Working Paper, Harvard Business School.

HATFIELD, J. N. (1935): "How Philadelphia Hospitals Appoint Interns," National Hospital Forum, February (2 pages, unnumbered).

HIPPOCRATES (approx. 400 B.C.): Of The Epidemics, Book I, Section II, Translated by Francis Adams.

HURWICZ, L. (1973): "The Design of Mechanisms for Resource Allocation," Richard T. Ely Lecture, *The American Economic Review*, Papers and Proceedings of the Eighty-fifth Annual Meeting of the American Economic Association, 63, 1–30.

JEHIEL, P., AND B. MOLDOVANU (2001): "The European UMTS/IMT-2000 License Auctions," Mimeo, University of Mannheim.

KAGEL, J. H. (1995): "Auctions: A Survey of Experimental Research," in *Handbook of Experimental Economics*, ed. by J. Kagel and A. Roth. Princeton: Princeton University Press, 501–585.

KAGEL, J. H., AND D. LEVIN (1986): "The Winner's Curse and Public Information in Common Value Auctions," *American Economic Review*, 76, 894–920.

—— (1999): "Common Value Auctions with Insider Information," *Econometrica*, 67, 1219–1238.

KAGEL, J. H., AND A. E. ROTH (2000): "The Dynamics of Reorganization in Matching Markets: A Laboratory Experiment Motivated by a Natural Experiment," *Quarterly Journal of Economics*, 115, 201–235.

KELLY, F., AND R. STEINBERG (2000): "A Combinatorial Auction with Multiple Winners for Universal Service," *Management Science*, 46, 586–596.

KELSO, A. S., JR., AND V. P. CRAWFORD (1982): "Job Matching, Coalition Formation, and Gross Substitutes," *Econometrica*, 50, 1483–1504.

KLEMPERER, P. (1998): "Auctions with Almost Common Values: The Wallet Game and Its Applications," *European Economic Review*, 42, 757–769.

—— (2000): "Why Every Economist Should Learn Some Auction Theory," in *Advances in Economics and Econometrics: Invited Lecture to 8th World Congress of the Econometric Society*, ed. by M. Dewatripont, L. Hansen, and S. Turnovsky. Cambridge: Cambridge University Press.

—— (2002a): "What Really Matters in Auction Design," *Journal of Economic Perspectives*, 16, 169–190.

—— (2002b): "How Not to Run Auctions: The European 3G Telecom Auctions," *European Economic Review*, forthcoming.

KNUTH, D. E. (1976): *Marriages Stables*. Montreal: Les Presses de l'Universite de Montreal.

LEDYARD, J. O. (1995): "Public Goods: A Survey of Experimental Research," in *The Handbook of Experimental Economics*, ed. by John H. Kagel and Alvin E. Roth. Princeton: Princeton University Press.

LEDYARD, J. O., D. PORTER, AND A. RANGEL (1997): "Experiments Testing Multi Object Allocation Mechanisms," *Journal of Economics and Management Strategy*, 6, 639–675.

LEDYARD, J., D. PORTER, AND R. WESSEN (2000): "A Market Based Mechanism for Allocating Space Shuttle Secondary Payload Priority," *Experimental Economics*, 2, 173–195.

LUCKING-REILLY, D. (1999): "Using Field Experiments to Test Equivalence Between Auction Formats: Magic on the Internet," *American Economic Review*, 89, 1063–1080.

MASKIN, E., AND J. RILEY (1984): "Optimal Auctions with Risk Averse Buyers," *Econometrica*, 52, 1473–1518.

MCAFEE, R. P., AND J. MCMILLAN (1996): "Analyzing the Airwaves Auction," *Journal of Economic Perspectives*, 10, 159–175.

MCMILLAN, J. (1994): "Selling Spectrum Rights," *Journal of Economic Perspectives*, 8, 145–162.

MCVITIE, D. G., AND L. B. WILSON (1970): "Stable Marriage Assignments for Unequal Sets," *BIT*, 10, 295–309.

MILGROM, P. (2000): "Putting Auction Theory to Work: The Simultaneous Ascending Auction," *Journal of Political Economy*, 108, 245–272.

MILGROM, P., AND R. WEBER (1982a): "The Value of Information in a Sealed-Bid Auction," *Journal of Mathematical Economics*, 10, 105–114.

——— (1982b): "A Theory of Auctions and Competitive Bidding," *Econometrica*, 50, 1089–1122.

MONGELL, S. J., AND A. E. ROTH (1986): "A Note on Job Matching with Budget Constraints," *Economics Letters*, 21, 135–138.

——— (1991): "Sorority Rush as a Two-Sided Matching Mechanism," *American Economic Review*, 81, 441–464.

MULLIN, F. J., AND J. M. STALNAKER (1952): "The Matching Plan for Internship Placement: A Report of the First Year's Experience," *Journal of Medical Education*, 27, 193–200.

MYERSON, R. B. (1981): "Optimal Auction Design," *Mathematics of Operations Research*, 6, 58–63.

NAKAMURA, A., M. PERCY, P. DAVENPORT, R. FRASER, AND M. PIPER (1998): "The Genesis of CareerOwl: The Story of How SSHRC Funded University Research Led to an On-line Electronic Hiring Hall for Canadian Post Secondary Students and Alumni," *http://www.careerowl.ca/papers/TheGenesisofCareerOwl11.pdf*, accessed 6/28/00.

OCKENFELS, A., AND A. E. ROTH (2001): "Late-Bidding in Second-Price Internet Auctions: Theory and Evidence," Working Paper, Harvard University.

PLOTT, C. R. (1997): "Laboratory Experimental Testbeds: Application to the PCS Auction," *Journal of Economics and Management Strategy*, 6, 605–638.

RASSENTI, S. J., V. L. SMITH, AND R. L. BULFIN (1982): "A Combinatorial Auction Mechanism for Airport Time Slot Allocation," *Rand Journal of Economics*, 13, 402–417.

ROTH, A. E. (1982a): "The Economics of Matching: Stability and Incentives," *Mathematics of Operations Research*, 7, 617–628.

——— (1982b): "Incentive Compatibility in a Market with Indivisible Goods," *Economics Letters*, 9, 127–132.

——— (1984): "The Evolution of the Labor Market for Medical Interns and Residents: A Case Study in Game Theory," *Journal of Political Economy*, 92, 991–1016.

——— (1985): "The College Admissions Problem is not Equivalent to the Marriage Problem," *Journal of Economic Theory*, 36, 277–288.

——— (1986): "On the Allocation of Residents to Rural Hospitals: A General Property of Two-Sided Matching Markets," *Econometrica*, 54, 425–427.

——— (1990): "New Physicians: A Natural Experiment in Market Organization," *Science*, 250, 1524–1528.

——— (1991): "A Natural Experiment in the Organization of Entry Level Labor Markets: Regional Markets for New Physicians and Surgeons in the U.K.," *American Economic Review*, 81, 415–440.

—— (1996): "The NRMP as a Labor Market," *Journal of the American Medical Association*, 275, 1054–1056.

—— (2000): "Game Theory as a Tool for Market Design," in *Game Practice: Contributions from Applied Game Theory*, ed. by Fioravante Patrone, Ignacio García-Jurado, and Stef Tijs. Dordrecht, The Netherlands: Kluwer, 7–18.

ROTH, A. E., AND I. EREV (1995): "Learning in Extensive-Form Games: Experimental Data and Simple Dynamic Models in the Intermediate Term," *Games and Economic Behavior*, 8, 164–212.

ROTH, A. E., AND A. OCKENFELS (2001): "Last-Minute Bidding and the Rules for Ending Second-Price Auctions: Evidence from eBay and Amazon Auctions on the Internet," *American Economic Review*, forthcoming.

ROTH, A. E., AND E. PERANSON (1997): "The Effects of the Change in the NRMP Matching Algorithm," *Journal of the American Medical Association*, 278, 729–732.

—— (1999): "The Redesign of the Matching Market for American Physicians: Some Engineering Aspects of Economic Design," *American Economic Review*, 89, 748–780.

ROTH, A. E., AND ANDREW POSTLEWAITE (1977): "Weak Versus Strong Domination in a Market With Indivisible Goods," *Journal of Mathematical Economics*, 4, 131–137.

ROTH, A. E., AND M. SOTOMAYOR (1989): "The College Admissions Problem Revisited," *Econometrica*, 57, 559–570.

—— (1990): *Two-Sided Matching: A Study in Game-Theoretic Modeling and Analysis*, Econometric Society Monograph Series. Cambridge: Cambridge University Press.

ROTH, A. E., AND JOHN H. VANDE VATE (1990): "Random Paths to Stability in Two-Sided Matching," *Econometrica*, 58, 1475–1480.

ROTH, A. E., AND X. XING (1994): "Jumping the Gun: Imperfections and Institutions Related to the Timing of Market Transactions," *American Economic Review*, 84, 992–1044.

—— (1997): "Turnaround Time and Bottlenecks in Market Clearing: Decentralized Matching in the Market for Clinical Psychologists," *Journal of Political Economy*, 105, 284–329.

ROTHKOPF, M. H., A. PEKEC, AND R. HARSTAD (1998): "Computationally Manageable Combinatorial Auctions," *Management Science*, 44, 1131–1147.

ROTHKOPF, M. H., T. J. TEISBERG, AND E. P. KAHN (1990): "Why Are Vickrey Auctions Rare?" *Journal of Political Economy*, 98, 94–109.

SHAPLEY, L., AND H. SCARF (1974): "On Cores and Indivisibility," *Journal of Mathematical Economics*, 1, 23–28.

SHILLER, R. J. (1993): *Macro Markets: Creating Institutions for Managing Society's Largest Economic Risks*, Clarendon Lectures in Economics. Oxford: Oxford University Press.

SONMEZ, T. (1997): "Manipulation via Capacities in Two-Sided Matching Markets," *Journal of Economic Theory*, 77, 197–204.

SVEJNAR, J., AND M. SINGER (1994): "Using Vouchers to Privatize an Economy: The Czech and Slovak Case," *Economics of Transition*, 2, 43–69.

UNVER, M. U. (2000a): "Backward Unraveling over Time: The Evolution of Strategic Behavior in the Entry-Level British Medical Labor Markets," *Journal of Economic Dynamics and Control*, forthcoming.

—— (2000b): "Computational and Experimental Analyses of Two-Sided Matching Markets," Ph.D. Thesis, University of Pittsburgh.

—— (2000c): "On the Survival of Some Unstable Two-sided Matching Mechanisms: A Laboratory Investigation," Mimeo, University of Pittsburgh.

VICKREY, W. (1961): "Counterspeculation, Auctions and Competitive Sealed Tenders," *Journal of Finance*, 16, 8–37.

WILSON, R. B. (1969): "Competitive Bidding with Disparate Information," *Management Science*, 15, 446–448.

—— (1992): "Strategic Analysis of Auctions," in *Handbook of Game Theory*, ed. by R. J. Aumann and S. Hart. Amsterdam: North Holland, 228–279.

—— (2002): "Architecture of Power Markets," *Econometrica*, 70, 1299–1340.

WOLFSTETTER, E. (2001): "The Swiss UMTS Spectrum Auction Flop: Bad Luck or Bad Design?" Working Paper, Humboldt University (Berlin).

Part IV
Learning and Debiasing

[23]

The Robust Beauty of Improper Linear Models in Decision Making

ROBYN M. DAWES *University of Oregon*

ABSTRACT: *Proper linear models are those in which predictor variables are given weights in such a way that the resulting linear composite optimally predicts some criterion of interest; examples of proper linear models are standard regression analysis, discriminant function analysis, and ridge regression analysis. Research summarized in Paul Meehl's book on clinical versus statistical prediction—and a plethora of research stimulated in part by that book—all indicates that when a numerical criterion variable (e.g., graduate grade point average) is to be predicted from numerical predictor variables, proper linear models outperform clinical intuition. Improper linear models are those in which the weights of the predictor variables are obtained by some nonoptimal method; for example, they may be obtained on the basis of intuition, derived from simulating a clinical judge's predictions, or set to be equal. This article presents evidence that even such improper linear models are superior to clinical intuition when predicting a numerical criterion from numerical predictors. In fact, unit (i.e., equal) weighting is quite robust for making such predictions. The article discusses, in some detail, the application of unit weights to decide what bullet the Denver Police Department should use. Finally, the article considers commonly raised technical, psychological, and ethical resistances to using linear models to make important social decisions and presents arguments that could weaken these resistances.*

Paul Meehl's (1954) book *Clinical Versus Statistical Prediction: A Theoretical Analysis and a Review of the Evidence* appeared 25 years ago. It reviewed studies indicating that the prediction of numerical criterion variables of psychological interest (e.g., faculty ratings of graduate students who had just obtained a PhD) from numerical predictor variables (e.g., scores on the Graduate Record Examination, grade point averages, ratings of letters of recommendation) is better done by a proper linear model than by the clinical intuition of people presumably skilled in such prediction. The point of this article is to review evidence that even improper linear models may be superior to clinical predictions.

A *proper linear model* is one in which the weights given to the predictor variables are chosen in such a way as to optimize the relationship between the prediction and the criterion. Simple regression analysis is the most common example of a proper linear model; the predictor variables are weighted in such a way as to maximize the correlation between the subsequent weighted composite and the actual criterion. Discriminant function analysis is another example of a proper linear model; weights are given to the predictor variables in such a way that the resulting linear composites maximize the discrepancy between two or more groups. Ridge regression analysis, another example (Darlington, 1978; Marquardt & Snee, 1975), attempts to assign weights in such a way that the linear composites correlate maximally with the criterion of interest in a new set of data.

Thus, there are many types of proper linear models and they have been used in a variety of contexts. One example (Dawes, 1971) was presented in this Journal; it involved the prediction of faculty ratings of graduate students. All gradu-

---

Work on this article was started at the University of Oregon and Decision Research, Inc., Eugene, Oregon; it was completed while I was a James McKeen Cattell Sabbatical Fellow at the Psychology Department at the University of Michigan and at the Research Center for Group Dynamics at the Institute for Social Research there. I thank all these institutions for their assistance, and I especially thank my friends at them who helped.

This article is based in part on invited talks given at the American Psychological Association (August 1977), the University of Washington (February 1978), the Aachen Technological Institute (June 1978), the University of Groeningen (June 1978), the University of Amsterdam (June 1978), the Institute for Social Research at the University of Michigan (September 1978), Miami University, Oxford, Ohio (November 1978), and the University of Chicago School of Business (January 1979). I received valuable feedback from most of the audiences.

Requests for reprints should be sent to Robyn M. Dawes, Department of Psychology, University of Oregon, Eugene, Oregon 97403.

ate students at the University of Oregon's Psychology Department who had been admitted between the fall of 1964 and the fall of 1967—and who had not dropped out of the program for non-academic reasons (e.g., psychosis or marriage)— were rated by the faculty in the spring of 1969; faculty members rated only students whom they felt comfortable rating. The following rating scale was used: 5, outstanding; 4, above average; 3, average; 2, below average; 1, dropped out of the program in academic difficulty. Such overall ratings constitute a psychologically interesting criterion because the subjective impressions of faculty members are the main determinants of the job (if any) a student obtains after leaving graduate school. A total of 111 students were in the sample; the number of faculty members rating each of these students ranged from 1 to 20, with the mean number being 5.67 and the median being 5. The ratings were reliable. (To determine the reliability, the ratings were subjected to a one-way analysis of variance in which each student being rated was regarded as a treatment. The resulting between-treatments variance ratio (η^2) was .67, and it was significant beyond the .001 level.) These faculty ratings were predicted from a proper linear model based on the student's Graduate Record Examination (GRE) score, the student's undergraduate grade point average (GPA), and a measure of the selectivity of the student's undergraduate institution.[1] The cross-validated multiple correlation between the faculty ratings and predictor variables was .38. Congruent with Meehl's results, the correlation of these latter faculty ratings with the average rating of the people on the admissions committee who selected the students was .19;[2] that is, it accounted for one fourth as much variance. This example is typical of those found in psychological research in this area in that (a) the correlation with the model's predictions is higher than the correlation with clinical prediction, but (b) both correlations are low. These characteristics often lead psychologists to interpret the findings as meaning that while the low correlation of the model indicates that linear modeling is deficient as a method, the even lower correlation of the judges indicates only that the wrong judges were used.

An *improper linear model* is one in which the weights are chosen by some nonoptimal method. They may be chosen to be equal, they may be chosen on the basis of the intuition of the person making the prediction, or they may be chosen at

random. Nevertheless, improper models may have great utility. When, for example, the standardized GREs, GPAs, and selectivity indices in the previous example were weighted equally, the resulting linear composite correlated .48 with later faculty rating. Not only is the correlation of this linear composite higher than that with the clinical judgment of the admissions committee (.19), it is also higher than that obtained upon cross-validating the weights obtained from half the sample.

An example of an improper model that might be of somewhat more interest—at least to the general public—was motivated by a physician who was on a panel with me concerning predictive systems. Afterward, at the bar with his wife and me, he said that my paper might be of some interest to my colleagues, but success in graduate school in psychology was not of much general interest: "Could you, for example, use one of your improper linear models to predict how well my wife and I get along together?" he asked. I realized that I could—or might. At that time, the Psychology Department at the University of Oregon was engaged in sex research, most of which was behavioristically oriented. So the subjects of this research monitored when they made love, when they had fights, when they had social engagements (e.g., with in-laws), and so on. These subjects also made subjective ratings about how happy they were in their marital or coupled situation. I immediately thought of an improper linear model to predict self-ratings of marital happiness: rate of lovemaking minus rate of fighting. My colleague John Howard had collected just such data on couples when he was an undergraduate at the University of Missouri—Kansas City, where he worked with Alexander (1971). After establishing the intercouple reliability of judgments of lovemaking and fighting, Alexander had one partner from each of 42 couples monitor these events. She allowed us to analyze her data, with the following results: "In the thirty happily married

---

[1] This index was based on Cass and Birnbaum's (1968) rating of selectivity given at the end of their book *Comparative Guide to American Colleges*. The verbal categories of selectivity were given numerical values according to the following rule: most selective, 6; highly selective, 5; very selective (+), 4; very selective, 3; selective, 2; not mentioned, 1.

[2] Unfortunately, only 23 of the 111 students could be used in this comparison because the rating scale the admissions committee used changed slightly from year to year.

couples (as reported by the monitoring partner) only two argued more often than they had intercourse. All twelve of the unhappily married couples argued more often" (Howard & Dawes, 1976, p. 478). We then replicated this finding at the University of Oregon, where 27 monitors rated happiness on a 7-point scale, from "very unhappy" to "very happy," with a neutral midpoint. The correlation of rate of lovemaking minus rate of arguments with these ratings of marital happiness was .40 ($p < .05$); neither variable alone was significant. The findings were replicated in Missouri by D. D. Edwards and Edwards (1977) and in Texas by Thornton (1977), who found a correlation of .81 ($p < .01$) between the sex–argument difference and self-rating of marital happiness among 28 new couples. (The reason for this much higher correlation might be that Thornton obtained the ratings of marital happiness after, rather than before, the subjects monitored their lovemaking and fighting; in fact, one subject decided to get a divorce after realizing that she was fighting more than loving; Thornton, Note 1.) The conclusion is that if we love more than we hate, we are happy; if we hate more than we love, we are miserable. This conclusion is not very profound, psychologically or statistically. The point is that this very crude improper linear model predicts a very important variable: judgments about marital happiness.

The bulk (in fact, all) of the literature since the publication of Meehl's (1954) book supports his generalization about proper models versus intuitive clinical judgment. Sawyer (1966) reviewed a plethora of these studies, and some of these studies were quite extensive (cf. Goldberg, 1965). Some 10 years after his book was published, Meehl (1965) was able to conclude, however, that there was only a single example showing clinical judgment to be superior, and this conclusion was immediately disputed by Goldberg (1968) on the grounds that even the one example did not show such superiority. Holt (1970) criticized details of several studies, and he even suggested that prediction as opposed to understanding may not be a very important part of clinical judgment. But a search of the literature fails to reveal any studies in which clinical judgment has been shown to be superior to statistical prediction when both are based on the same codable input variables. And though most nonpositivists would agree that understanding is not synonymous with prediction, few would agree that it doesn't entail some ability to predict.

Why? Because people—especially the experts in a field—are much better at selecting and coding information than they are at integrating it.

But people *are* important. The statistical model may integrate the information in an optimal manner, but it is always the individual (judge, clinician, subjects) who chooses variables. Moreover, it is the human judge who knows the directional relationship between the predictor variables and the criterion of interest, or who can code the variables in such a way that they have clear directional relationships. And it is in precisely the situation where the predictor variables are good and where they have a conditionally monotone relationship with the criterion that proper linear models work well.[3]

The linear model cannot replace the expert in deciding such things as "what to look for," but it is precisely this knowledge of what to look for in reaching the decision that is the special expertise people have. Even in as complicated a judgment as making a chess move, it is the ability to code the board in an appropriate way to "see" the proper moves that distinguishes the grand master from the expert from the novice (deGroot, 1965; Simon & Chase, 1973). It is not in the ability to integrate information that people excel (Slovic, Note 2). Again, the chess grand master considers no more moves than does the expert; he just knows which ones to look at. The distinction between knowing what to look for and the ability to integrate information is perhaps best illustrated in a study by Einhorn (1972). Expert doctors coded biopsies of patients with Hodgkin's disease and then made an overall rating of the severity of the process. The overall rating did not predict survival time of the 193 patients, all of whom

---

[3] Relationships are conditionally monotone when variables can be scaled in such a way that higher values on each predict higher values on the criterion. This condition is the combination of two more fundamental measurement conditions: (a) independence (the relationship between each variable and the criterion is independent of the values on the remaining variables) and (b) monotonicity (the ordinal relationship is one that is monotone). (See Krantz, 1972; Krantz, Luce, Suppes, & Tversky, 1971). The true relationships need not be linear for linear models to work; they must merely be approximated by linear models. It is not true that "in order to compute a correlation coefficient between two variables the relationship between them must be linear" (advice found in one introductory statistics text). In the first place, it is always possible to compute something.

died. (The correlations of rating with survival time were all virtually 0, some in the wrong direction.) The variables that the doctors coded did, however, predict survival time when they were used in a multiple regression model.

In summary, proper linear models work for a very simple reason. People are good at picking out the right predictor variables and at coding them in such a way that they have a conditionally monotone relationship with the criterion. People are bad at integrating information from diverse and incomparable sources. Proper linear models are good at such integration when the predictions have a conditionally monotone relationship to the criterion.

Consider, for example, the problem of comparing one graduate applicant with GRE scores of 750 and an undergraduate GPA of 3.3 with another with GRE scores of 680 and an undergraduate GPA of 3.7. Most judges would agree that these indicators of aptitude and previous accomplishment should be combined in some compensatory fashion, but the question is how to compensate. Many judges attempting this feat have little knowledge of the distributional characteristics of GREs and GPAs, and most have no knowledge of studies indicating their validity as predictors of graduate success. Moreover, these numbers are inherently incomparable without such knowledge, GREs running from 500 to 800 for viable applicants, and GPAs from 3.0 to 4.0. Is it any wonder that a statistical weighting scheme does better than a human judge in these circumstances?

Suppose now that it is not possible to construct a proper linear model in some situation. One reason we may not be able to do so is that our sample size is inadequate. In multiple regression, for example, b weights are notoriously unstable; the ratio of observations to predictors should be as high as 15 or 20 to 1 before b weights, which are the optimal weights, do better on cross-validation than do simple unit weights. Schmidt (1971), Goldberg (1972), and Claudy (1972) have demonstrated this need empirically through computer simulation, and Einhorn and Hogarth (1975) and Srinivisan (Note 3) have attacked the problem analytically. The general solution depends on a number of parameters such as the multiple correlation in the population and the covariance pattern between predictor variables. But the applied implication is clear. Standard regression analysis cannot be used in situations where there is not a "decent" ratio of observations to predictors.

Another situation in which proper linear models cannot be used is that in which there are no measurable criterion variables. We might, nevertheless, have some idea about what the important predictor variables would be and the direction they would bear to the criterion *if* we were able to measure the criterion. For example, when deciding which students to admit to graduate school, we would like to predict some future long-term variable that might be termed "professional self-actualization." We have some idea what we mean by this concept, but no good, precise definition as yet. (Even if we had one, it would be impossible to conduct the study using records from current students, because that variable could not be assessed until at least 20 years after the students had completed their doctoral work.) We do, however, know that in all probability this criterion is positively related to intelligence, to past accomplishments, and to ability to snow one's colleagues. In our applicant's files, GRE scores assess the first variable; undergraduate GPA, the second; and letters of recommendation, the third. Might we not, then, wish to form some sort of linear combination of these variables in order to assess our applicants' potentials? Given that we cannot perform a standard regression analysis, is there nothing to do other than fall back on unaided intuitive integration of these variables when we assess our applicants?

One possible way of building an improper linear model is through the use of *bootstrapping* (Dawes & Corrigan, 1974; Goldberg, 1970). The process is to build a proper linear model of an expert's judgments about an outcome criterion and then to use that linear model in place of the judge. That such linear models can be accurate in predicting experts' judgments has been pointed out in the psychological literature by Hammond (1955) and Hoffman (1960). (This work was anticipated by 32 years by the late Henry Wallace, Vice-President under Roosevelt, in a 1923 agricultural article suggesting the use of linear models to analyze "what is on the corn judge's mind.") In his influential article, Hoffman termed the use of linear models a *paramorphic* representation of judges, by which he meant that the judges' psychological processes did not involve computing an implicit or explicit weighted average of input variables, but that it could be simulated by such a weighting. Paramorphic representations have been extremely successful (for reviews see Dawes & Corrigan, 1974; Slovic & Lichtenstein, 1971) in contexts in which predictor variables have conditionally monotone relationships to criterion variables.

The bootstrapping models make use of the weights derived from the judges; because these weights are not derived from the relationship between the predictor and criterion variables themselves, the resulting linear models are improper. Yet these paramorphic representations consistently do better than the judges from which they were derived (at least when the evaluation of goodness is in terms of the correlation between predicted and actual values).

Bootstrapping has turned out to be pervasive. For example, in a study conducted by Wiggins and Kohen (1971), psychology graduate students at the University of Illinois were presented with 10 background, aptitude, and personality measures describing other (real) Illinois graduate students in psychology and were asked to predict these students' first-year graduate GPAs. Linear models of every one of the University of Illinois judges did a better job than did the judges themselves in predicting actual grade point averages. This result was replicated in a study conducted in conjunction with Wiggins, Gregory, and Diller (cited in Dawes & Corrigan, 1974). Goldberg (1970) demonstrated it for 26 of 29 clinical psychology judges predicting psychiatric diagnosis of neurosis or psychosis from Minnesota Multiphasic Personality Inventory (MMPI) profiles, and Dawes (1971) found it in the evaluation of graduate applicants at the University of Oregon. The one published exception to the success of bootstrapping of which I am aware was a study conducted by Libby (1976). He asked 16 loan officers from relatively small banks (located in Champaign–Urbana, Illinois, with assets between $3 million and $56 million) and 27 loan officers from large banks (located in Philadelphia, with assets between $.6 billion and $4.4 billion) to judge which 30 of 60 firms would go bankrupt within three years after their financial statements. The loan officers requested five financial ratios on which to base their judgments (e.g., the ratio of present assets to total assets). On the average, the loan officers correctly categorized 44.4 businesses (74%) as either solvent or future bankruptcies, but on the average, the paramorphic representations of the loan officers could correctly classify only 43.3 (72%). This difference turned out to be statistically significant, and Libby concluded that he had an example of a situation where bootstrapping did not work—perhaps because his

judges were highly skilled experts attempting to predict a highly reliable criterion. Goldberg (1976), however, noted that many of the ratios had highly skewed distributions, and he reanalyzed Libby's data, normalizing the ratios before building models of the loan officers. Libby found 77% of his officers to be superior to their paramorphic representations, but Goldberg, using his rescaled predictor variables, found the opposite; 72% of the models were superior to the judges from whom they were derived.[4]

Why does bootstrapping work? Bowman (1963), Goldberg (1970), and Dawes (1971) all maintained that its success arises from the fact that a linear model distills underlying policy (in the implicit weights) from otherwise variable behavior (e.g., judgments affected by context effects or extraneous variables).

Belief in the efficacy of bootstrapping was based on the comparison of the validity of the linear model of the judge with the validity of his or her judgments themselves. This is only one of two logically possible comparisons. The other is the validity of the linear model of the judge versus the validity of linear models in general; that is, to demonstrate that bootstrapping works because the linear model catches the essence of the judge's valid expertise while eliminating unreliability, it is necessary to demonstrate that the weights obtained from an analysis of the judge's behavior are superior to those that might be obtained in other ways, for example, randomly. Because both the model of the judge and the model obtained randomly are perfectly reliable, a comparison of the random model with the judge's model permits an evaluation of the judge's underlying linear representation, or *policy*. If the random model does equally well, the judge would not be "following valid principles but following them poorly" (Dawes, 1971, p. 182), at least not principles any more valid than any others that weight variables in the appropriate direction.

Table 1 presents five studies summarized by Dawes and Corrigan (1974) in which validities

---

[4] It should be pointed out that a proper linear model does better than either loan officers or their paramorphic representations. Using the same task, Beaver (1966) and Deacon (1972) found that linear models predicted with about 78% accuracy on cross-validation. But I can't resist pointing out that the simplest possible improper model of them all does best. The ratio of assets to liabilities (!) correctly categorizes 48 (80%) of the cases studied by Libby.

TABLE 1

Correlations Between Predictions and Criterion Values

Example	Average validity of judge	Average validity of judge model	Average validity of random model	Validity of equal weighting model	Cross-validity of regression analysis	Validity of optimal linear model
Prediction of neurosis vs. psychosis	.28	.31	.30	.34	.46	.46
Illinois students' predictions of GPA	.33	.50	.51	.60	.57	.69
Oregon students' predictions of GPA	.37	.43	.51	.60	.57	.69
Prediction of later faculty ratings at Oregon	.19	.25	.39	.48	.38	.54
Yntema & Torgerson's (1961) experiment	.84	.89	.84	.97	—	.97

Note. GPA = grade point average.

(i.e., correlations) obtained by various methods were compared. In the first study, a pool of 861 psychiatric patients took the MMPI in various hospitals; they were later categorized as neurotic or psychotic on the basis of more extensive information. The MMPI profiles consist of 11 scores, each of which represents the degree to which the respondent answers questions in a manner similar to patients suffering from a well-defined form of psychopathology. A set of 11 scores is thus associated with each patient, and the problem is to predict whether a later diagnosis will be psychosis (coded 1) or neurosis (coded 0). Twenty-nine clinical psychologists "of varying experience and training" (Goldberg, 1970, p. 425) were asked to make this prediction on an 11-step forced-normal distribution. The second two studies concerned 90 first-year graduate students in the Psychology Department of the University of Illinois who were evaluated on 10 variables that are predictive of academic success. These variables included aptitude test scores, college GPA, various peer ratings (e.g., extraversion), and various self-ratings (e.g., conscientiousness). A first-year GPA was computed for all these students. The problem was to predict the GPA from the 10 variables. In the second study this prediction was made by 80 (other) graduate students at the University of Illinois (Wiggins & Kohen, 1971), and in the third study this prediction was made by 41 graduate students at the University of Oregon. The details of the fourth study have already been covered; it is the one concerned with the prediction of later faculty ratings at Oregon. The final study (Yntema & Torgerson, 1961) was one in which experimenters assigned values to ellipses presented to the subjects, on the basis of figures' size, eccentricity, and grayness. The formula used was $ij + kj + ik$, where i, j, and k refer to values on the three dimensions just mentioned. Subjects

in this experiment were asked to estimate the value of each ellipse and were presented with outcome feedback at the end of each trial. The problem was to predict the true (i.e., experimenter-assigned) value of each ellipse on the basis of its size, eccentricity, and grayness.

The first column of Table 1 presents the average validity of the judges in these studies, and the second presents the average validity of the paramorphic model of these judges. In all cases, bootstrapping worked. But then what Corrigan and I constructed were *random linear models*, that is, models in which weights were randomly chosen except for sign and were then applied to standardized variables.[5]

The sign of each variable was determined on an a priori basis so that it would have a positive relationship to the criterion. Then a normal deviate was selected at random from a normal distribution with unit variance, and the absolute value of this deviate was used as a weight for the variable. Ten thousand such models were constructed for each example. (Dawes & Corrigan, 1974, p. 102)

On the average, these random linear models perform about as well as the paramorphic models of the judges; these averages are presented in the third column of the table. Equal-weighting models, presented in the fourth column, do even better. (There is a mathematical reason why equal-weighting models must outperform the average random model.[6]) Finally, the last two columns present

---

[5] Unfortunately, Dawes and Corrigan did not spell out in detail that these variables must first be standardized and that the result is a standardized dependent variable. Equal or random weighting of incomparable variables— for example, GRE score and GPA—without prior standardization would be nonsensical.

[6] Consider a set of standardized variables S_1, X_2, X_m, each of which is positively correlated with a standardized variable Y. The correlation of the average of the Xs with the Y is equal to the correlation of the sum of the

the cross-validated validity of the standard regression model and the validity of the optimal linear model.

Essentially the same results were obtained when the weights were selected from a rectangular distribution. Why? Because linear models are robust over deviations from optimal weighting. In other words, the bootstrapping finding, at least in these studies, has simply been a reaffirmation of the earlier finding that proper linear models are superior to human judgments—the weights derived from the judges' behavior being sufficiently close to the optimal weights that the outputs of the models are highly similar. The solution to the problem of obtaining optimal weights is one that —in terms of von Winterfeldt and Edwards (Note 4)—has a "flat maximum." Weights that are near to optimal level produce almost the same output as do optimal beta weights. Because the expert judge knows at least something about the direction of the variables, his or her judgments yield weights that are nearly optimal (but note that in all cases equal weighting is superior to models based on judges' behavior).

The fact that different linear composites correlate highly with each other was first pointed out 40 years ago by Wilks (1938). He considered only situations in which there was positive correlation between predictors. This result seems to hold generally as long as these intercorrelations are not negative; for example, the correlation between $X + 2Y$ and $2X + Y$ is .80 when X and Y are uncorrelated. The ways in which outputs are relatively insensitive to changes in coefficients (provided changes in sign are not involved) have been investigated most recently by Green (1977),

---

Xs with Y. The covariance of this sum with Y is equal to

$$\left(\frac{1}{n}\right) \sum_i y_i(x_{i1} + x_{i2} \ldots + x_{im})$$

$$= \left(\frac{1}{n}\right) \sum y_i x_{i1} + \left(\frac{1}{n}\right) \sum y_i x_{i2} \ldots + \left(\frac{1}{n}\right) \sum_i y_i x_{im}$$

$$= r_1 + r_2 \ldots + r_m \text{ (the sum of the correlations).}$$

The variance of y is 1, and the variance of the sum of the Xs is $M + M(M - 1)\bar{r}$, where $\bar{r}$ is the average intercorrelation between the Xs. Hence, the correlation of the average of the Xs with Y is $(\Sigma r_i)/(M + M(M - 1)\bar{r})^{\frac{1}{2}}$; this is greater than $(\Sigma r_i)/(M + M^2 - M)^{\frac{1}{2}} = $ average r_i. Because each of the random models is positively correlated with the criterion, the correlation of their average, which is the unit-weighted model, is higher than the average of the correlations.

Wainer (1976), Wainer and Thissen (1976), W. M. Edwards (1978), and Gardiner and Edwards (1975).

Dawes and Corrigan (1974, p. 105) concluded that "the whole trick is to know what variables to look at and then know how to add." That principle is well illustrated in the following study, conducted since the Dawes and Corrigan article was published. In it, Hammond and Adelman (1976) both investigated and influenced the decision about what type of bullet should be used by the Denver City Police, a decision having much more obvious social impact than most of those discussed above. To quote Hammond and Adelman (1976):

> In 1974, the Denver Police Department (DPD), as well as other police departments throughout the country, decided to change its handgun ammunition. The principle reason offered by the police was that the conventional round-nosed bullet provided insufficient "stopping effectiveness" (that is, the ability to incapacitate and thus to prevent the person shot from firing back at a police officer or others). The DPD chief recommended (as did other police chiefs) the conventional bullet be replaced by a hollow-point bullet. Such bullets, it was contended, flattened on impact, thus decreasing penetration, increasing stopping effectiveness, and decreasing ricochet potential. The suggested change was challenged by the American Civil Liberties Union, minority groups, and others. Opponents of the change claimed that the new bullets were nothing more than outlawed "dum-dum" bullets, that they created far more injury than the round-nosed bullet, and should, therefore, be barred from use. As is customary, judgments on this matter were formed privately and then defended publicly with enthusiasm and tenacity, and the usual public hearings were held. Both sides turned to ballistics experts for scientific information and support. (p. 392)

The disputants focused on evaluating the merits of specific bullets—confounding the physical effect of the bullets with the implications for social policy; that is, rather than separating questions of what it is the bullet should accomplish (the social policy question) from questions concerning ballistic characteristics of specific bullets, advocates merely argued for one bullet or another. Thus, as Hammond and Adelman pointed out, social policymakers inadvertently adopted the role of (poor) ballistics experts, and vice versa. What Hammond and Adelman did was to discover the important policy dimensions from the policymakers, and then they had the ballistics experts rate the bullets with respect to these dimensions. These dimensions turned out to be stopping effectiveness (the probability that someone hit in the torso could not return fire), probability of serious injury, and probability of harm to bystanders. When the ballistics experts rated the bullets with respect to these dimensions, it turned out that the last two were almost perfectly confounded, but they were not perfectly confounded with the first. Bullets do not vary along a single dimension that confounds effectiveness with lethalness. The probability of serious injury or harm to bystanders is highly related to the penetration of the bullet, whereas the probability of the bullet's effectively stopping someone from returning fire is highly related to the width of the entry wound. Since policymakers could not agree about the weights given to the three dimensions, Hammond and Adelman suggested that they be weighted equally. Combining the equal weights with the (independent) judgments of the ballistics experts, Hammond and Adelman discovered a bullet that "has greater stopping effectiveness and is less apt to cause injury (and is less apt to threaten bystanders) than the standard bullet then in use by the DPD" (Hammond & Adelman, 1976, p. 395). The bullet was also less apt to cause injury than was the bullet previously recommended by the DPD. That bullet was "accepted by the City Council and all other parties concerned, and is now being used by the DPD" (Hammond & Adelman, 1976, p. 395).[7] Once again, "the whole trick is to decide what variables to look at and then know how to add" (Dawes & Corrigan, 1974, p. 105).

So why don't people do it more often? I know of four universities (University of Illinois; New York University; University of Oregon; University of California, Santa Barbara—there may be more) that use a linear model for applicant selection, but even these use it as an initial screening device and substitute clinical judgment for the final selection of those above a cut score. Goldberg's (1965) actuarial formula for diagnosing neurosis or psychosis from MMPI profiles has proven superior to clinical judges attempting the same task (no one to my or Goldberg's knowledge has ever produced a judge who does better), yet my one experience with its use (at the Ann Arbor Veterans Administration Hospital) was that it was discontinued on the grounds that it made obvious errors (an interesting reason, discussed at length below). In 1970, I suggested that our fellowship committee at the University of Oregon apportion cutbacks of National Science Foundation and National Defense Education Act fellowships to departments on the basis of a quasi-linear point system based on explicitly defined indices,

departmental merit, and need; I was told "you can't systemize human judgment." It was only six months later, after our committee realized the political and ethical impossibility of cutting back fellowships on the basis of intuitive judgment, that such a system was adopted. And so on.

In the past three years, I have written and talked about the utility (and in my view, ethical superiority) of using linear models in socially important decisions. Many of the same objections have been raised repeatedly by different readers and audiences. I would like to conclude this article by cataloging these objections and answering them.

Objections to Using Linear Models

These objections may be placed in three broad categories: technical, psychological, and ethical. Each category is discussed in turn.

TECHNICAL

The most common technical objection is to the use of the correlation coefficient; for example, Remus and Jenicke (1978) wrote:

> It is clear that Dawes and Corrigan's choice of the correlation coefficient to establish the utility of random and unit rules is inappropriate [*sic*, inappropriate for what?]. A criterion function is also needed in the experiments cited by Dawes and Corrigan. Surely there is a cost function for misclassifying neurotics and psychotics or refusing qualified students admissions to graduate school while admitting marginal students. (p. 221)

Consider the graduate admission problem first. Most schools have k slots and N applicants. The problem is to get the best k (who are in turn willing to accept the school) out of N. What better way is there than to have an appropriate rank? None. Remus and Jenicke write as if the problem were not one of comparative choice but of absolute choice. Most social choices, however, involve selecting the better or best from a set of alternatives: the students that will be better, the bullet that will be best, a possible airport site that will be superior, and so on. The correlation

---

[7] It should be pointed out that there were only eight bullets on the *Pareto frontier*; that is, there were only eight that were not inferior to some particular other bullet in both stopping effectiveness and probability of harm (or inferior on one of the variables and equal on the other). Consequently, any weighting rule whatsoever would have chosen one of these eight.

coefficient, because it reflects ranks so well, is clearly appropriate for evaluating such choices.

The neurosis–psychosis problem is more subtle and even less supportive of their argument. "Surely," they state, "there is a cost function," but they don't specify any candidates. The implication is clear: If they could find it, clinical judgment would be found to be superior to linear models. Why? In the absence of such a discovery on their part, the argument amounts to nothing at all. But this argument from a vacuum can be very compelling to people (for example, to losing generals and losing football coaches, who know that "surely" their plans would work "if"—when the plans are in fact doomed to failure no matter what).

A second related technical objection is to the comparison of average correlation coefficients of judges with those of linear models. Perhaps by averaging, the performance of some really outstanding judges is obscured. The data indicate otherwise. In the Goldberg (1970) study, for example, only 5 of 29 trained clinicians were better than the unit-weighted model, and none did better than the proper one. In the Wiggins and Kohen (1971) study, no judges were better than the unit-weighted model, and we replicated that effect at Oregon. In the Libby (1976) study, only 9 of 43 judges did better than the ratio of assets to liabilities at predicting bankruptcies (3 did equally well). While it is then conceded that clinicians should be able to predict diagnosis of neurosis or psychosis, that graduate students should be able to predict graduate success, and that bank loan officers should be able to predict bankruptcies, the possibility is raised that perhaps the experts used in the studies weren't the right ones. This again is arguing from a vacuum: If other experts were used, then the results would be different. And once again no such experts are produced, and once again the appropriate response is to ask for a reason why these hypothetical other people should be any different. (As one university vice-president told me, "Your research only proves that you used poor judges; we could surely do better by getting better judges"—apparently not from the psychology department.)

A final technical objection concerns the nature of the criterion variables. They are admittedly short-term and unprofound (e.g., GPAs, diagnoses); otherwise, most studies would be infeasible. The question is then raised of whether the findings would be different if a truly long-range

important criterion were to be predicted. The answer is that of course the findings *could* be different, but we have no reason to suppose that they *would* be different. First, the distant future is in general less predictable than the immediate future, for the simple reason that more unforeseen, extraneous, or self-augmenting factors influence individual outcomes. (Note that we are not discussing aggregate outcomes, such as an unusually cold winter in the Midwest in general spread out over three months.) Since, then, clinical prediction is poorer than linear to begin with, the hypothesis would hold only if linear prediction got much worse over time than did clinical prediction. There is no a priori reason to believe that this differential deterioration in prediction would occur, and none has ever been suggested to me. There is certainly no evidence. Once again, the objection consists of an argument from a vacuum.

Particularly compelling is the fact that people who argue that different criteria or judges or variables or time frames would produce different results have had 25 years in which to produce examples, and they have failed to do so.

PSYCHOLOGICAL

One psychological resistance to using linear models lies in our selective memory about clinical prediction. Our belief in such prediction is reinforced by the availability (Tversky & Kahneman, 1974) of instances of successful clinical prediction—especially those that are exceptions to some formula: "I knew someone once with . . . who . . . ." (e.g., "I knew of someone with a tested IQ of only 130 who got an advanced degree in psychology.") As Nisbett, Borgida, Crandall, and Reed (1976) showed, such single instances often have greater impact on judgment than do much more valid statistical compilations based on many instances. (A good prophylactic for clinical psychologists basing resistance to actuarial prediction on such instances would be to keep careful records of their own predictions about their own patients—prospective records not subject to hindsight. Such records could make all instances of successful and unsuccessful prediction equally available for impact; in addition, they could serve for another clinical versus statistical study using the best possible judge —the clinician himself or herself.)

Moreover, an illusion of good judgment may be reinforced due to selection (Einhorn & Hogarth, 1978) in those situations in which the prediction

of a positive or negative outcome has a self-fulfilling effect. For example, admissions officers
who judge that a candidate is particularly qualified for a graduate program may feel that their
judgment is exonerated when that candidate does
well, even though the candidate's success is in
large part due to the positive effects of the program. (In contrast, a linear model of selection
is evaluated by seeing how well it predicts performance *within* the set of applicants selected.)
Or a waiter who believes that particular people
at the table are poor tippers may be less attentive
than usual and receive a smaller tip, thereby having his clinical judgment exonerated.[8]

A second psychological resistance to the use of
linear models stems from their "proven" low validity. Here, there is an implicit (as opposed to
explicit) argument from a vacuum because neither
changes in evaluation procedures, nor in judges, nor
in criteria, are proposed. Rather, the unstated
assumption is that these criteria of psychological
interest are in fact highly predictable, so it follows that if one method of prediction (a linear
model) doesn't work too well, another might do
better (reasonable), which is then translated into
the belief that another *will* do better (which is
not a reasonable inference)—once it is found.
This resistance is best expressed by a dean considering the graduate admissions who wrote, "The
correlation of the linear composite with future
faculty ratings is only .4, whereas that of the
admissions committee's judgment correlates .2.
Twice nothing is nothing." In 1976, I answered
as follows (Dawes, 1976, pp. 6–7):

In response, I can only point out that 16% of the variance
is better than 4% of the variance. To me, however, the
fascinating part of this argument is the implicit assumption that that other 84% of the variance is predictable
and that we can somehow predict it.
Now what are we dealing with? We are dealing with
personality and intellectual characteristics of [uniformly
bright] people who are about 20 years old. . . . Why are
we so convinced that this prediction can be made at all?
Surely, it is not necessary to read *Ecclesiastes* every night
to understand the role of chance. . . . Moreover, there
are clearly positive feedback effects in professional development that exaggerate threshold phenomena. For
example, once people are considered sufficiently "outstanding" that they are invited to outstanding institutions,
they have outstanding colleagues with whom to interact
—and excellence is exacerbated. This same problem
occurs for those who do not quite reach such a threshold
level. Not only do all these factors mitigate against
successful long-range prediction, but studies of the success
of such prediction are necessarily limited to those accepted,
with the incumbent problems of restriction of range and
a negative covariance structure between predictors (Dawes,
1975).

Finally, there are all sorts of nonintellectual
factors in professional success that could not possibly be evaluated before admission to graduate
school, for example, success at forming a satisfying or inspiring libidinal relationship, not yet evident genetic tendencies to drug or alcohol addic-
tion, the misfortune to join a research group that
"blows up," and so on, and so forth.

Intellectually, I find it somewhat remarkable
that we are able to predict even 16% of the
variance. But I believe that my own emotional
response is indicative of those of my colleagues
who simply assume that the future is more predictable. *I want it to be predictable, especially
when the aspect of it that I want to predict is
important to me.* This desire, I suggest, translates itself into an implicit assumption that the
future is in fact highly predictable, and it would
then logically follow that if something is not a
very good predictor, something else might do better (although it is never correct to argue that it
necessarily will).

Statistical prediction, because it includes the
specification (usually a low correlation coefficient)
of exactly how poorly we can predict, bluntly
strikes us with the fact that life is not all that
predictable. Unsystematic clinical prediction (or
"postdiction"), in contrast, allows us the com-
forting illusion that life is in fact predictable and
that we can predict it.

ETHICAL

When I was at the Los Angeles Renaissance Fair
last summer, I overhead a young woman complain
that it was "horribly unfair" that she had been
rejected by the Psychology Department at the
University of California, Santa Barbara, on the
basis of mere numbers, without even an interview.
"How can they possibly tell what I'm like?"
The answer is that they can't. Nor could they
with an interview (Kelly, 1954). Nevertheless,
many people maintain that making a crucial social
choice without an interview is dehumanizing. I
think that the question of whether people are
treated in a fair manner has more to do with the
question of whether or not they have been de-
humanized than does the question of whether
the treatment is face to face. (Some of the worst
doctors spend a great deal of time conversing with

---

[8] This example was provided by Einhorn (Note 5).

their patients, read no medical journals, order few or no tests, and grieve at the funerals.) A GPA represents $3\frac{1}{2}$ years of behavior on the part of the applicant. (Surely, not all the professors are biased against his or her particular form of creativity.) The GRE is a more carefully devised test. Do we really believe that we can do a better or a fairer job by a 10-minute folder evaluation or a half-hour interview than is done by these two mere numbers? Such cognitive conceit (Dawes, 1976, p. 7) is unethical, especially given the fact of no evidence whatsoever indicating that we do a better job than does the linear equation. (And even making exceptions must be done with extreme care if it is to be ethical, for if we admit someone with a low linear score on the basis that he or she has some special talent, we are automatically rejecting someone with a higher score, who might well have had an equally impressive talent had we taken the trouble to evaluate it.)

No matter how much we would like to see this or that aspect of one or another of the studies reviewed in this article changed, no matter how psychologically uncompelling or distasteful we may find their results to be, no matter how ethically uncomfortable we may feel at "reducing people to mere numbers," the fact remains that our clients are people who deserve to be treated in the best manner possible. If that means—as it appears at present—that selection, diagnosis, and prognosis should be based on nothing more than the addition of a few numbers representing values on important attributes, so be it. To do otherwise is cheating the people we serve.

REFERENCE NOTES

1. Thornton, B. Personal communication, 1977.
2. Slovic, P. Limitations of the mind of man: Implications for decision making in the nuclear age. In H. J. Otway (Ed.), *Risk vs. benefit: Solution or dream?* (Report LA 4860-MS). Los Alamos, N.M.: Los Alamos Scientific Laboratory, 1972. [Also available as *Oregon Research Institute Bulletin,* 1971, *11*(17).]
3. Srinivisan, V. *A theoretical comparison of the predictive power of the multiple regression and equal weighting procedures* (Research Paper No. 347). Stanford, Calif.: Stanford University, Graduate School of Business, February 1977.
4. von Winterfeldt, D., & Edwards, W. *Costs and payoffs in perceptual research.* Unpublished manuscript, University of Michigan, Engineering Psychology Laboratory, 1973.
5. Einhorn, H. J. Personal communication, January 1979.

REFERENCES

Alexander, S. A. H. *Sex, arguments, and social engagements in marital and premarital relations.* Unpublished master's thesis, University of Missouri—Kansas City, 1971.

Beaver, W. H. Financial ratios as predictors of failure. In *Empirical research in accounting: Selected studies.* Chicago: University of Chicago, Graduate School of Business, Institute of Professional Accounting, 1966.

Bowman, E. H. Consistency and optimality in managerial decision making. *Management Science,* 1963, *9,* 310–321.

Cass, J., & Birnbaum, M. *Comparative guide to American colleges.* New York: Harper & Row, 1968.

Claudy, J. G. A comparison of five variable weighting procedures. *Educational and Psychological Measurement,* 1972, *32,* 311–322.

Darlington, R. B. Reduced-variance regression. *Psychological Bulletin,* 1978, *85,* 1238–1255.

Dawes, R. M. A case study of graduate admissions: Application of three principles of human decision making. *American Psychologist,* 1971, *26,* 180–188.

Dawes, R. M. Graduate admissions criteria and future success. *Science,* 1975, *187,* 721–723.

Dawes, R. M. Shallow psychology. In J. Carroll & J. Payne (Eds.), *Cognition and social behavior.* Hillsdale, N.J.: Erlbaum, 1976.

Dawes, R. M., & Corrigan, B. Linear models in decision making. *Psychological Bulletin,* 1974, *81,* 95–106.

Deacon, E. B. A discriminant analysis of predictors of business failure. *Journal of Accounting Research,* 1972, *10,* 167–179.

deGroot, A. D. *Het denken van den schaker* [*Thought and choice in chess*]. The Hague, The Netherlands: Mouton, 1965.

Edwards, D. D., & Edwards, J. S. Marriage: Direct and continuous measurement. *Bulletin of the Psychonomic Society,* 1977, *10,* 187–188.

Edwards, W. M. Technology for director dubious: Evaluation and decision in public contexts. In K. R. Hammond (Ed.), *Judgement and decision in public policy formation.* Boulder, Colo.: Westview Press, 1978.

Einhorn, H. J. Expert measurement and mechanical combination. *Organizational Behavior and Human Performance,* 1972, *7,* 86–106.

Einhorn, H. J., & Hogarth, R. M. Unit weighting schemas for decision making. *Organizational Behavior and Human Performance,* 1975, *13,* 171–192.

Einhorn, H. J., & Hogarth, R. M. Confidence in judgment: Persistence of the illusion of validity. *Psychological Review,* 1978, *85,* 395–416.

Gardiner, P. C., & Edwards, W. Public values: Multiattribute-utility measurement for social decision making. In M. F. Kaplan & S. Schwartz (Eds.), *Human judgment and decision processes.* New York: Academic Press, 1975.

Goldberg, L. R. Diagnosticians vs. diagnostic signs: The diagnosis of psychosis vs. neurosis from the MMPI. *Psychological Monographs,* 1965, *79*(9, Whole No. 602).

Goldberg, L. R. Seer over sign: The first "good" example? *Journal of Experimental Research in Personality,* 1968, *3,* 168–171.

Goldberg, L. R. Man versus model of man: A rationale, plus some evidence for a method of improving on clinical inferences. *Psychological Bulletin,* 1970, *73,* 422–432.

Goldberg, L. R. Parameters of personality inventory construction and utilization: A comparison of prediction strategies and tactics. *Multivariate Behavioral Research Monographs*, 1972, No. 72-2.

Goldberg, L. R. Man versus model of man: Just how conflicting is that evidence? *Organizational Behavior and Human Performance*, 1976, *16*, 13–22.

Green, B. F., Jr. Parameter sensitivity in multivariate methods. *Multivariate Behavioral Research*, 1977, *3*, 263.

Hammond, K. R. Probabilistic functioning and the clinical method. *Psychological Review*, 1955, *62*, 255–262.

Hammond, K. R., & Adelman, L. Science, values, and human judgment. *Science*, 1976, *194*, 389–396.

Hoffman, P. J. The paramorphic representation of clinical judgment. *Psychological Bulletin*, 1960, *57*, 116–131.

Holt, R. R. Yet another look at clinical and statistical prediction. *American Psychologist*, 1970, *25*, 337–339.

Howard, J. W., & Dawes, R. M. Linear prediction of marital happiness. *Personality and Social Psychology Bulletin*, 1976, *2*, 478–480.

Kelly, L. Evaluation of the interview as a selection technique. In *Proceedings of the 1953 Invitational Conference on Testing Problems*. Princeton, N.J.: Educational Testing Service, 1954.

Krantz, D. H. Measurement structures and psychological laws. *Science*, 1972, *175*, 1427–1435.

Krantz, D. H., Luce, R. D., Suppes, P., & Tversky, A. *Foundations of measurement* (Vol. 1). New York: Academic Press, 1971.

Libby, R. Man versus model of man: Some conflicting evidence. *Organizational Behavior and Human Performance*, 1976, *16*, 1–12.

Marquardt, D. W., & Snee, R. D. Ridge regression in practice. *American Statistician*, 1975, *29*, 3–19.

Meehl, P. E. *Clinical versus statistical prediction: A theoretical analysis and a review of the evidence.* Minneapolis: University of Minnesota Press, 1954.

Meehl, P. E. Seer over sign: The first good example. *Journal of Experimental Research in Personality*, 1965, *1*, 27–32.

Nisbett, R. E., Borgida, E., Crandall, R., & Reed, H. Popular induction: Information is not necessarily nor-mative. In J. Carrol & J. Payne (Eds.), *Cognition and social behavior*. Hillsdale, N.J.: Erlbaum, 1976.

Remus, W. E., & Jenicke, L. O. Unit and random linear models in decision making. *Multivariate Behavioral Research*, 1978, *13*, 215–221.

Sawyer, J. Measurement *and* prediction, clinical *and* statistical. *Psychological Bulletin*, 1966, *66*, 178–200.

Schmidt, F. L. The relative efficiency of regression and simple unit predictor weights in applied differential psychology. *Educational and Psychological Measurement*, 1971, *31*, 699–714.

Simon, H. A., & Chase, W. G. Skill in chess. *American Scientist*, 1973, *61*, 394–403.

Slovic, P., & Lichtenstein, S. Comparison of Bayesian and regression approaches to the study of information processing in judgment. *Organizational Behavior and Human Performance*, 1971, *6*, 649–744.

Thornton, B. Linear prediction of marital happiness: A replication. *Personality and Social Psychology Bulletin*, 1977, *3*, 674–676.

Tversky, A., & Kahneman, D. Judgment under uncertainty: Heuristics and biases. *Science*, 1974, *184*, 1124–1131.

Wainer, H. Estimating coefficients in linear models: It don't make no nevermind. *Psychological Bulletin*, 1976, *83*, 312–317.

Wainer, H., & Thissen, D. Three steps toward robust regression. *Psychometrika*, 1976, *41*, 9–34.

Wallace, H. A. What is in the corn judge's mind? *Journal of the American Society of Agronomy*, 1923, *15*, 300–304.

Wiggins, N., & Kohen, E. S. Man vs. model of man revisited: The forecasting of graduate school success. *Journal of Personality and Social Psychology*, 1971, *19*, 100–106.

Wilks, S. S. Weighting systems for linear functions of correlated variables when there is no dependent variable. *Psychometrika*, 1938, *8*, 23–40.

Yntema, D. B., & Torgerson, W. S. Man–computer cooperation in decisions requiring common sense. *IRE Transactions of the Professional Group on Human Factors in Electronics*, 1961, *2*(1), 20–26.

[24]

EXPERIENCE, EXPERTISE, AND DECISION BIAS IN NEGOTIATION:

THE ROLE OF STRATEGIC CONCEPTUALIZATION

Margaret A. Neale and Gregory B. Northcraft

Over the last two decades, many aspects of negotiation have been the focus of research efforts, including: individual differences in bargaining behavior (e.g., Rubin & Brown, 1975), structural characteristics of negotiation exchanges (e.g., Lewicki & Litterer, 1985), and negotiation strategies and tactics (e.g., Pruitt, 1983; Fisher & Ury, 1981). In general these research efforts have sought to identify the determinants of negotiation outcomes, and to develop recommendations for improving the effectiveness of bargaining behaviors.

The upswing of research interest in behavioral aspects of decision making in the last decade (e.g., Kahneman, Slovic, & Tversky, 1982; Einhorn & Hogarth, 1978) has generated a new stream of research in bargaining and negotiation: research which analyzes bargaining and negotiation as a behavioral decision-making process (Raiffa, 1982; Neale & Bazerman, 1985a). The purpose of this paper is to evaluate four major claims about the role of decision making in negotiation and to present a model of negotiator expertise which integrates the evaluations of the four claims.

The recent research in behavioral decision making has shown that individual decision makers (and negotiators) are subject to the biasing effects of inappropriately applied cognitive heuristics. There is, however, an increasingly

Research on Negotiation in Organizations, Volume 2, pages 55-75.
ISBN: 0-89232-639-5

vocal controversy concerning the validity of these findings. Some researchers contend that the systematic distortions of decision making observed in laboratory experiments are a function of the stimulus-impoverished setting, the absence of feedback, and the use of student subjects (Christensen-Szalanski & Beach, 1982; Hogarth, 1981; Berkeley & Humphrey, 1982). The implication of this contention is that decision makers in the "real world" will make decisions that are relatively free of bias—that "real world" experience will have cured decision makers of the inappropriate use of cognitive heuristics. Unfortunately, research has not shown experience alone to be an effective safeguard against bias. For experience to have a corrective effect, it must provide negotiators feedback that is timely, diagnostic, and organized (Thaler, 1986). Negotiation expertise, then, only can be expected to develop after negotiators have acquired the ability to gather and organize timely and diagnostic feedback. How negotiators acquire this ability to gather and organize feedback is the focus of this paper.

The four claims to be considered in this paper are:

Claim #1:   The findings of individual decision-making research explain a great deal of the poor outcomes obtained by negotiators.

Claim #2:   While the findings of individual decision-making research may explain problems encountered by *novice* negotiators, experience should immunize negotiators against continued use of biased decision-making heuristics.

Claim #3:   Experience alone isn't a great "teacher": problems with learning-from-experience lead negotiators to persist in making inappropriate use of cognitive heuristics.

Claim #4:   Bargaining expertise will produce outcomes that are bias free only after negotiators have acquired cognitive schemas that outline effective methods of learning from negotiation experience.

This paper evaluates the first three claims in order to provide a foundation for evaluating the fourth claim. The first three claims summarize past research efforts as they relate to understanding negotiation as a decision-making process. Evaluation of the fourth claim offers new insights into the origins, limitations, and controversies surrounding the development of bargaining expertise.

CLAIM #1:   NEGOTIATION
AND DECISION HEURISTICS

Negotiation represents a special case of decision making. Like group decision making, negotiation always involves multiple parties—usually dyads—

representing their own or constituencies' interests. However, unlike many other kinds of decision-making process, the focal decision-making goals of the parties involved are apparently incompatible. This makes negotiation a dynamic process; apparent goal incompatibility forces the decisions made by the parties to be inter-dependent (Bazerman, 1986). Thus, the outcomes of a negotiation are based only partially upon the deliberations of a particular participant. The way in which that individual processes information and implements strategies directly influences both the behavior of his or her fellow negotiator(s) and the tenor of subsequent interactions and exchanges between the two parties.

This focus on negotiations as dyadic, interdependent decision behavior has given rise to a series of studies which complement the findings of individual decision-making research. In particular, these studies have examined the impact of individual cognitive heuristics on negotiated decisions. Cognitive heuristics are "rules of thumb" which are used as shortcuts in the thinking process (Kahneman & Tversky, 1972). They are rules which, when appropriately applied, result in more efficient cognitive processing. When inappropriately applied, these cognitive shortcuts systematically bias decision outcomes.

Recent research on the role of cognitive heuristics in negotiation has sought to clarify the role of these individual heuristics in the dyadic, interdependent exchange of negotiation. A variety of heuristics have been identified which systematically distort the negotiation process and potentially bias negotiation outcomes. Four of these cognitive heuristics are framing, anchoring-and-adjustment, availability, and overconfidence.

Framing

The notion of framing comes from prospect theory (Kahneman & Tversky, 1979). Framing has to do with situational determinants of risk-preferences and the effects of these risk-preferences on decision behavior. Prospect theory suggests that decision makers are risk-averse when choosing between certain gains and the risk of larger or no gains, but are risk-seeking when choosing between certain losses and the risk of larger or no losses. (For a more detailed discussion of framing, see Tversky & Kahneman, 1981). Framing studies have shown that given the same objective situation, the way a decision is worded or presented (i.e., whether outcomes are "framed" in terms of perspective gains or prospective losses) will influence risk-preference and thereby affect decision behavior (e.g., Northcraft & Neale, 1986). Most recently, roles have been shown to be a source of the cognitive frames that decision makers bring to situations (Neale, Huber, & Northcraft, 1987).

In a negotiation, the risk-averse course of action is to yield enough concessions to insure a negotiated settlement; the risk-seeking course of action is to hold out for a better offer, greater concessions, etc., and risk the possibility of no settlement or the possibility of an unfavorable judgment by an arbitrator. A variety of studies (Bazerman, Magliozzi, & Neale, 1985; Neale & Bazerman, 1985b; Neale & Northcraft, 1986; Neale, Huber, & Northcraft, 1987) consistently have demonstrated that negotiators who are positively framed (e.g., focused on the potential profits of transactions) complete more transactions than negotiators who are negatively framed (e.g., focused on the potential expenses of transactions). Negatively framed negotiators, on the other hand, complete individual transactions of greater value. These findings are consistent with the contention that positive framing leads to risk-aversion. Positively-framed negotiators therefore are more willing to make concessions in order to complete transactions, but at the cost of less average value per transaction.

Anchoring-and-Adjustment

Anchoring-and-adjustment is a cognitive process by which judgments of value are influenced and biased. Slovic and Lichtenstein (1971) found that (1) an arbitrarily chosen reference point (anchor) significantly influenced judgments and (2) judgments were insufficiently adjusted away from the reference point toward the true value of the object of estimation. The insufficient adjustment of the judgment away from the anchor provides the source of bias. In a demonstration of this effect, Tversky and Kahneman (1974) had subjects estimate the percentage of African countries in the United Nations. Each subject was given a reference point for making the estimate (a number between 1 and 100) by the spinning of a "wheel of fortune." Subjects first had to decide whether their "wheel of fortune" number was higher or lower than the correct percentage and then had to give their best estimate of the correct percentage. Despite the fact that the reference point each subject was provided obviously had nothing to do with the estimation task, the reference point each subject was provided obviously had nothing to do with the estimation task, the reference point significantly influenced estimates. The median estimate of subjects given a reference point of 10 was 25%, while the median estimate of subjects given a reference point of 65 was 45%. Financial incentives for accuracy did nothing to diminish anchoring of the estimates.

The anchoring-and-adjustment bias intrudes in the negotiation process in several ways. First, anchoring-and-adjustment provides a partial explanation for the importance of initial offers in bargaining. Rubin and Brown (1975) note that "early moves" are critical in determining the psychological context in which a negotiation occurs, and research has shown that bargaining outcomes are influenced more by initial offers than subsequent concession rate (Liebert, Smith, Hall, & Keiffer, 1968). Bargaining often occurs when two parties differ in their opinions of the appropriate exchange rate for an item (for instance, a piece of property). An initial offer serves to "anchor" subsequent estimates by both negotiators of the item's value (i.e., exchange rate). Thus, "tough-to-soft" (Chertkoff & Conley, 1967) and "door-in-the-face" (Coker, Neale, & Northcraft, 1987) bargaining strategies are both successful in negotiations because they take advantage of the anchoring effects of tough initial offers.

Anchoring-and-adjustment also provide an explanation for the effectiveness of goal-setting (Huber & Neale, 1986) and limit-setting (Neale & Bazerman, 1985c) in negotiation. Just as does an initial offer, the goal or limit acts as a cognitive anchor, driving a negotiator's perception of where the negotiation should be heading. In fact, the anchoring-and-adjustment effects of goal- and limit-setting may render them useful techniques for insulating negotiators against the anchoring effects of initial offers. Goals and limits will anchor estimates of resource value *before* initial offers by another party have a chance to do so.

Availability

The ideally rational decision maker, when assessing possible courses of action, should be able to call forth all past experiences and present information relevant to assessing the probable consequences of each alternative. Unfortunately, not all of a decision maker's past experiences are equally likely to have been coded in long-term memory, nor are all coded experiences equally likely to be recalled when needed to make a decision. Further, not all present information is equally likely to come to a decision maker's attention. Consequently, the availability (Tversky & Kahneman, 1973) of information—both from the past and the present—can play a significant role in decision behavior.

Research on information availability has focused on two judgmental tasks: construction and recall. Construction has to do with understanding behavior in the present by constructing causal explanations (i.e., assessing the importance of probable causes). Colorful, dynamic, concrete, and otherwise vivid or distinctive stimuli disproportionately attract attention and consequently disproportionately influence decision makers' deliberations (Taylor, 1981). For instance, opportunity costs are much less concrete than out-of-pocket costs and therefore much less likely to be adequately taken into account in financial decisions (Northcraft & Neale, 1986).

Further, personal perspective renders some information more available (Wicklund, 1975). For instance, when a decision maker constructs explanations for the behaviors of another individual, that individual is a central perceptual stimuli; in constructing explanations for his or her own behaviors, the decision maker himself or herself perceptually is nowhere to be seen. This gives rise to a fundamental attribution error (Ross, 1981) in which decision makers routinely are more likely to attribute the behaviors of others to personal characteristics but see their own behaviors as reactions to environmental stimuli.

Recall has to do with the availability of past experiences in memory. Not surprisingly, the attention-attracting capabilities of experiences influence the probability that those experiences will either be stored or recalled from memory and therefore available for decision-making purposes. Perhaps more surprising is the fact that ease of retrieval is used as an inferential cue by decision makers to estimate an event's future probability of occurence (Tversky & Kahneman, 1973). Apparently decision makers implicitly assume that ease of retrieval from memory is a direct reflection of frequency of occurrence in the past, and thereby the probability of future occurrence. Thus, particularly vivid past experiences will be seen as extremely likely to reoccur simply because those experiences come to mind so easily.

While research on the effects of availability on bargaining behavior is sparse, recall and construction biases both may be relevant to the negotiation context. In a laboratory study of bargaining, Neale (1984) found that manipulating the availability of personal and organizational costs produced systematic changes in negotiator behavior. When personal costs of settlement were made particularly salient or vivid, negotiators were less likely to settle; when third-party intervention costs for the organization were highlighted, negotiators facilitated settlements. The fundamental attribution error will lead a negotiator to see his or her own behavior as much more responsive to the contingencies of the negotiation context.

Overconfidence

Despite the growing literature documenting instances and sources of decision bias, evidence suggests that decision makers have unwarranted confidence in their fallible judgments (Einhorn, 1980). Researchers have studied confidence levels in a variety of ways. (For a review, see Lichenstein, Fischhoff, & Phillips, 1982). Generally, research has shown that probabilities assigned to uncertain events (such as winners of horse races or correctness of an answer to a general knowledge question) are unjustifiably high, with 89% confidence intervals covering as little as 60% of true values (Alpert & Raiffa, 1982).

Laboratory research also has demonstrated overconfidence in the context of negotiations. Bazerman and Neale (1982) found that when negotiators under final offer arbitration were asked to estimate the likelihood that the arbitrator would accept their final offer, all negotiators as a group responded that there was, on average, a 67.8% probability that their offer would be accepted. While any *one* offer submittd under final offer arbitration might have a 67% probability of being accepted, with two sides to every negotiation, the mean level of confidence across all negotiators should be 50%. Thus, negotiators were overconfident that the offers they were proposing to the arbitrator would be accepted. Further, Neale and Bazerman (1985b) found that negotiator overconfidence decreased negotiators' willingness to make concessions, since they misjudged the amount of concessions necessary to reach resolution. Thus, overconfidence led to lower resolution rates and less successful outcomes.

Given the breadth and consistency of findings demonstrating the influence of cognitive heuristics on bargaining processes and outcomes, one might have expected these findings to be quickly incorporated into models of negotiation behavior. However, some researchers and practitioners have been hesitant to accept these findings—primarily because most of the research has been conducted with student samples within the confines of laboratory evironments. The external validity of these findings thus is an important concern to researchers and therefore the topic of the second claim examined in this paper.

CLAIM #2: THE ROLE OF EXPERIENCE

Taken together, the results of these various studies make a strong case for the contention that cognitive heuristics have a systematic and predictable influence on negotiator behavior. However, there are two grounds for questioning (or at least qualifying) the importance of these findings. Most research on the role of cognitive heuristics in negotiation (as well as virtually all of the initial research identifying cognitive heuristics) has been conducted in laboratory settings. These studies have examined student subjects negotiating or making other decisions in task domains (e.g., real estate, international health policy, appliance wholesaling) with which the subjects are unfamiliar (see Northcraft & Neale, 1984). Thus, one might suspect that the behavior of professional negotiators making (for them) familiar and *routine* bargaining and negotiation decisions would *not* be accurately characterized by the literature on decision bias. Susceptibility to judgmental bias may disappear as experience accumulates and task familiarity grows.

The ability of experience to eliminate or attenuate decision bias lies in the potential of performance feedback to diagnose and correct inappropriate uses of decision heuristics. Hogarth (1981) has allowed that dismissing the research on cognitive heuristics because of its laboratory origins would be naive. However, he also cautions that decision-making researchers have not paid sufficient attention to the "continuous, adaptive nature of the judgmental processes used to cope with a complex, changing environment" (Hogarth, 1981, p. 198). Researchers have tended to focus instead on the discrete processes of choice and prediction, isolated from the corrective potential of environmental feedback. Thus, laboratory demonstrations of the biasing effects of cognitive heuristics may grossly underrepresent their real world adaptiveness in the presence of appropriately corrective environmental feedback. By a process roughly captured in Figure 1, trial-and-error learning from experience should cause inappropriate heuristic use to be "selected out" of a negotiator's decision-making repertoire. These concerns were echoed in Berkeley and Humphrey's

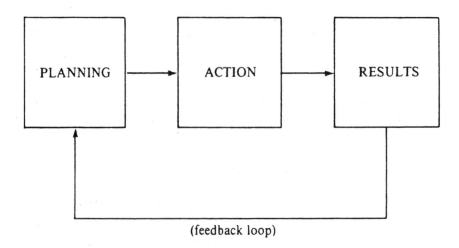

Figure 1.

(1982) claim that the importance of decision bias demonstrated in the laboratory is premised on the assumption that subjects have accepted the small (and relatively stimulus-impoverished) world of the laboratory as a "naturalized" reflection of the real world in which they make decisions.

The bottom line of this external validity concern is that the literature on decision bias from the inappropriate use of cognitive heuristics may paint an overly pessimistic picture of negotiator judgment *potential*. Naturally, cognitive heuristics represent a trade-off between process costs and outcome optimally. Decision-making procedures whose quality exceeds task demands (Hogarth, 1981) or the competence of the competition (Einhorn, 1980) not only are unnecessary but also constitute a waste of resources on decision process. After all, it is not always necessary or important to reach the pareto-optimal boundary in a negotiation. The additional costs in time, cognitive processing, and other resources may prove much more dear than the advantage in a negotiated outcome they can buy. In some instances, then, the use of cognitive shortcuts and the bargaining behaviors they produce may be quite appropriate. On the other hand, one certainly would assume that where the demands for decision quality are high (for instance, where large sums of money depend upon the quality of negotiated decisions), trial-and-error learning will have disposed of cognitively biased negotiating procedures in favor of more environmentally-adaptive responses. This purported ability of trial-and-error learning to correct decision bias is the focus of Claim #3.

CLAIM #3:   THE FUTILITY OF FEEDBACK?

As noted above, Hogarth (1981) has suggested that the poor performance of negotiators demonstrated in the cognitive bias literature may arise because of the methodology used to study judgment and choice in the laboratory. In the artificial confines of the laboratory, negotiation decisions are examined as a discrete and static process; in the "real world," negotiation decision making is more on-going, continuous, and dynamic. Negotiators make decisions, experience consequences, and (one would hope) learn from results to make better or different subsequent decisions. The key feature which distinguishes these two settings (the laboratory and the "real world") is feedback.

Feedback is critical to trail-and-error learning in its generating, modifying, maintaining, or encouraging the abandonment of various hypotheses (Hogarth, 1981). Without feedback as to specific performance, the decision maker has little opportunity—or reason—to alter his/her behavior (Landy & Farr, 1982). However, feedback, as with many other processes, can facilitate or inhibit learning as a function of its specificity (Earley, 1987), credibility (Northcraft & Earley, 1989) diagnosticity, accuracy (Cummings, Schwab, & Rosen, 1971), and timeliness (Einhorn, 1980). If feedback is ambiguous, nondiagnostic, misleading, or just poorly managed, it cannot be corrective and may even reinforce inappropriate behavior (Einhorn & Hogarth, 1978). While feedback has not been a focus of negotiation research, psychological researchers have identified three "barriers" which prevent decision makers from "learning" from feedback: (1) lack of search for and use of disconfirming feedback, (2) incorrect interpretation of the causes of outcomes, and (3) the use of unaided memory for coding, storing, and retrieving outcome information (Einhorn, 1980; Einhorn & Hogarth, 1978).

Search

Decision makers often become psychologically invested in the decisions they make (see Staw, 1976), and this investment can influence a decision maker's receptivity to feedback about a previous choice. Psychological investment may lead a decision maker to see feedback about a belief or prior decision in a much more positive light than others would see it (Hastorf & Cantril, 1954). Research suggests that the distortion of feedback by psychological investment is more a function of subliminal direction of attention and consequent distortion of evidence availability then nonveridical perception (Miller & Ross, 1975; Lord, Ross, & Lepper, 1979). Further, evidence availability may be biased even without any intrusions of the decision maker's motivations. For instance, co-workers are more likely to bring favorable than unfavorable news to a decision maker's attention (Rosen & Tesser, 1970), thus providing the decision maker greater access to positive then negative feedback.

64   MARGARET A. NEALE and GREGORY B. NORTHCRAFT

Interpretation

Even if a decision maker correctly perceives a negative outcome resulting from a previous decision, that negative feedback only will serve a corrective function if its causes are correctly identified. Whether negative feedback dictates a change in strategy is highly dependent upon the source to which the negative consequences are attributed (Kelley, 1972). Unfortunately, attribution of causality often is more a matter of opinion than fact, and as such may be subject to bias. For instance, if the decision maker feels his or her self-image is on the line, he or she may find positive interpretations more compelling or easier to believe, and may find it easy to assimilate potentially-negative feedback into a "doing OK" causal schema that downplays the negative features of an outcome in favor of its positive ones (Nisbett & Ross, 1980). Further, friends of a decision maker are (by virture of being friends) likely to share the decision maker's assumptions and perspectives and, therefore, find plausible and support the decision maker's self-serving attributions and assimilations.

Distortions in the interpretation of feedback can occur even in the absence of protective motivations. Simple expectations provide the decision maker a perceptual set that drives the perception and interpretation of feedback, and thereby distorts the process of learning from experience (O'Reilly, Northcraft, & Sabers, 1989).

Practical Constraints

In addition to psychological limitations on the use of corrective feedback, there also are several practical constraints. Einhorn and Hogarth (1978) report that decision makers have a great deal of difficulty determining what type of feedback is necessary to determine the accuracy of a previous choice. Both experienced managers and professional statisticians had a very difficult time choosing feedback which could validate their claims. While there is some evidence that scientific training will improve a decision maker's skill in choosing particular forms of feedback (particularly disconfirming evidence), a majority of analytically sophisticated subjects made the same errors as did the less analytically sophisticated subjects.

Another practical roadblock to the use of feedback is that often the results of all possible outcomes cannot be observed. Usually the selection of one alternative or the implementation of one set of behaviors precludes the decision maker from "knowing" the results had other alternatives been selected. Negotiators, for instance, must choose to make concessions or "hold out" during a negotiation. The results of the chosen course of action necessarily are less diagnostic and corrective if they cannot be compared to and contrasted with the results that would have obtained from the course of action *not* taken.

CLAIM #4:   BEYOND EXPERIENCE

It seems apparent that the attainment of corrective feedback from experience may be problematic for negotiators. And in support of this conclusion, research has found that experience often does not help and may even bias an individual's judgments and performance (Einhorn & Hogarth, 1978; Bushyhead & Christensen-Szalanski, 1981).

On the other hand, several studies have demonstrated that experience with a task improves judgments concerning that task (Phelps & Shanteau, 1978; Slovic, 1969; Christensen-Szalanski & Beach, 1982). This is not surprising, of course. Cognitive processing should be susceptible to change through trial-and-error. This is, after all, the essence of *learning*: trying, failing, and trying again in a different way, failing again, and so on. The two important questions are: (1) under what circumstances does experience in a task provide sufficient learning for the individual to know the "ins-and-outs" of the task, and (2) under what circumstances does experienece only lead to an endless progression of as-yet-unconfirmed (and possibly grossly incorrect) speculations?

The answers to these questions may lie in a better understanding of what it means to have learned from experience—what it means to be an expert. While very little work has focused specifically on expertise in negotiation, consideration of the work on expertise in judgment and decision making nevertheless may provide valuable insights into expertise in "negotiation-as-decision-making."

Expertise implies so extensive a background and training in an area that the error-adjustment and hypotheses-testing phases of learning are complete, or significantly reduced in new circumstances. A variety of definitions have been offered to distinguish experts from amateurs. Boulding (1958) reports that expertise implies skill (i.e., the ability to produce good outcomes consistently) in a specific task or domain of tasks. Einhorn (1974) suggests that expertise is a consensual process based upon a core of knowledge with which experts should (1) cluster variables in similar ways, (2) have high inter-expert reliability, and (3) combine and weight information similarly.

Both views seem important, but misleading. Einhorn's definition ignores the importance of being able to produce good outcomes. After all, expertise must be more than just being able to "talk a good game." Boulding's criterion, on the other hand, focuses expertise almost entirely on outcome quality. While trial-and-error learning will reinforce effective behaviors, the behaviors it reinforces may be effective only under the limited circumstances of the experienced trials and errors. As Fiske (1961) has observed, a hallmark of expertise is the ability of the expert to *adjust* his or her skills to be adaptive and successful (i.e., continue to produce good outcomes) even in the face of *new* environmental demands. Thus, expertise implies more than situation-specific skill—it implies the capacity to generalize or transfer skill *beyond* the limited circumstances under which trial-and-error learning has occurred. Expertise means having a strategy for accomplishing the task which is sufficiently general or abstract to transfer to different tasks and settings.

The transferability of skill, in turn, implies a causal understanding of the task well beyond knowing simply which behaviors are effective. It implies knowing *why* effective behaviors are effective. This is consistent with Einhorn's (1974) comment on experts' consenual task understanding, which suggests experts have internalized a common causal representation of the task. Thus, the foundation of expertise is more than having an effective strategy. An expert must possess a conceptualization of the task which explains why a particular strategy is effective. The expert must have a *strategic conceptualization* of the task.

A strategic conceptualization differs from other cognitive representations of tasks in terms of completeness. Conceptual schemas (Taylor & Crocker, 1981) identify features of situations that are important, and may include information about how these features relate to other. For instance, a schema for a negotiation might include information about bids, counter-offers, and cues about when bids and counter-offers are appropriate. Schemas also might include information about which features to monitor for feedback. Scripts, on the other hand, summarize "a coherent sequence of events expected by the individual, involving him either as participant or observer" (Abelson, 1976, p. 33). Scripts are often well-learned behavior patterns (task strategies) that produce good outcomes under very specific circumstance. The existence of an effective script, however, does not imply effective transferability to other situations. Schemas summarize what features of a situation are important and how these variables are related to each other, while scripts summarize how the features can be manipulated to produce good outcomes. While a strategic conceptualization would certainly include script and schema information, the expertise in a strategic conceptualization lies in knowledge about *why* the features identified in the schema are the important features and *why* the pattern of behaviors prescribed by the script is effective.

The practical significance of a strategic conceptualization, as depicted in Figure 2, should be obvious. Dawes and Corrigan (1974) note that expertise (particularly in prediction tasks) means knowing which environmental cues need to be monitored and which can be ignored. Even in a simple task, this is no mean feat. As William James has suggested, to the novice a given task must appear as something of a "big blooming buzzing confusion" (1979, p. 32) of innumerable potential cues. How does the decision maker know to which potential sources of feedback to attend? The schematic elements of a strategic conceptualization define some environmental parameters as critical and others, as irrelevant. Similarly, during "trial-and-error" phases of effective strategy acquisition, the decision maker is faced with an infinite number of possible hypotheses to test. The strategic conceptualization limits the universe of

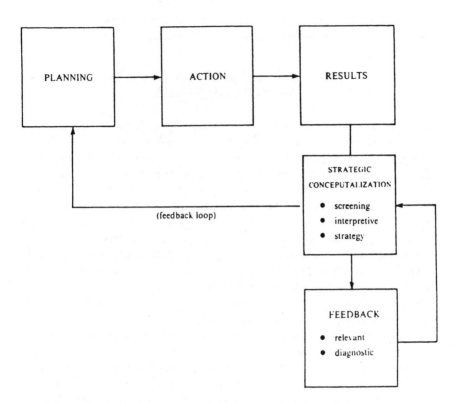

Figure 2.

possibilities from which the decision maker must sample, allowing feedback to work its wonders more efficiently. This is consistent with the findings of Johnson, Duran, Hassebrock, Moller, Prietula, Feltovick, and Swanson (1981) that experts make decisions by classifying situations as tasks with which they are familiar and then applying previously-successful solutions to the tasks-at-hand. The strategic conceptualization provides the basis for classifying situations *and* supplies the previously-successful solution to apply.

Significantly, the schematic elements of strategic conceptualizations provide a form of perceptual set mentioned earlier in the discussion of experience. In the earlier discussion, it was noted that perceptual sets can interfere with appropriate "trial-and-error" learning by leading to distorted search, interpretation, and memory of potentially-diagnostic feedback. The flip side of this concern is that perceptual sets also are *necessary* to "trial-and-error" learning—first by limiting the set of strategic hypotheses to test and second by dictating which environmental cues to monitor to confirm or reject strategy candidates. The right perceptual set (i.e., an effective strategic conceptualization) is what makes feedback diagnostic, and is what makes an expert an expert. The wrong perceptual set interferes with trial-and-error learning.

STRATEGIC CONCEPTUALIZATION AND DECISION BIAS

The claim being made here is that high quality negotiation outcomes can occur in one of three ways: (1) a negotiator *randomly* may happen upon an effective strategy, without even knowing what he or she has done correctly (e.g., ritual or superstitious behavior); (2) a negotiator may acquire a strategic conceptualization of the negotiation situation which summarizes which strategies are effective and why effective negotiation strategies work and ineffective ones do not. While the outcomes of these three possibilities might be indistinguishable on an individual outcome basis, success from experience is preferable to chance success as it is stable over time. As long as circumstances do not change, a negotiator who has learned an effective strategy will continue to be successful. Of course, understanding why effective negotiating strategies are effective means having an appropriate strategic conceptualization of the negotiation process. That knowledge results in success not only over time but also over different circumstances, including previously unencountered ones! Thus, strategic conceptualization is the foundation of expertise. Two important questions remain, however. First, is this concept—the strategic conceptualization—useful for explaining the development and acquisition of negotiation expertise? Second, what is the role of strategic conceptualizations in immunizing negotiators from decision bias?

Two recent comparisons of expert and amateur negotiators have addressed these two concerns directly. These two studies were designed to examine the influence of two previously discussed decision biases (anchoring-and-adjustment and framing) on expert decision makers. In both studies, experts were individuals who had sufficiently extensive backgrounds in an area of negotiation that "the error phase of trial-and-error learning certainly would be complete" (Northcraft & Neale, 1984, p. 1). The difficulty with this definition is that it does not distinguish between those individuals who have developed an appropriate strategic conceptualization of their negotiations and those who have only considerable experience. However, there was an important distinction between these two studies. The first study involved a *novel* negotiating task. As noted earlier, superior performance in a novel setting occurs as a function of an appropriate strategic conceptualization which can be transferred or generalized to new situations. Thus, superior performance in this study implied the existence of an appropriate strategic conceptualization. The second study did not involve a novel task, but did use a means for eliciting directly negotiators' strategic conceptualization of the task.

In the first study (Neale & Northcraft, 1986), two samples of negotiators—experts and amateurs—participated in separate runs of a competitive three-issue market simulation develop by Bazerman et al. (1985). A key feature of the simulation is the potential for negotiators to trade off gains on two issues (rather than "splitting the difference"). This creates the potential for integrative agreements of high joint benefit and makes it easy to identify attempts by negotiators to be integrative. The expert sample in the study consisted of eighty professional corporate real estate negotiators with an average of 10.5 years of experience negotiating transactions who reported spending an average of 32% of their workday in actual negotiations. One hundred and seventy-eight undergraduate and graduate business students composed the amateur sample.

The results of this study identified important differences among these groups of negotiators in novel tasks. First, experts and amateur negotiators did not differ in their susceptibility to the framing bias. However, experts and amateurs did differ in their performance. Experts were significantly more integrative (i.e., were able to achieve agreements of greater joint benefit) than were amateurs. In fact, while both experts and amateur negotiators became more integrative over time, the initial agreements negotiated by the amateurs tended not to utilize the integrative potential of the task; even the initial contracts of the experts, on the other hand, exceeded the joint benefit potential of purely distributive approaches to the negotiation. Apparently the experts were able to recognize quickly the negotiation situation as one with integrative potential and utilize this to achieve both greater personal and joint benefits.

This result may reflect the value of strategically conceptualizing the negotiating process. It seems a common expectation among naive negotiators that bargaining is primarily a distributive process (Bazerman & Neale, 1982). Thus, negotiating becomes a mechanism by which disputing parties divide a pool of resources. The results of these expectations are that bargaining outcomes resemble compromise solutions. Alternatively, expert negotiators seem to be able to recognize situations in which integrative appoaches to negotiation offer the possibility of greater joint benefits.

These results are intriguing in that while there were important differences between experts and amateurs in terms of outcome effectiveness, there were no differences in terms of susceptibility to decision bias. In this study, the strategic conceptualization of negotiation as having both integrative and distributive potential fostered superior outcomes in a novel task. However, the presence of this performance-enhancing strategic conceptualization in no way decreased the experts' susceptibility to the framing bias.

The second study (Northcraft & Neale, 1987) examined the anchoring-and-adjustment bias in the information rich, real-world setting of residential real estate sales. Real estate agents and brokers who had been in the real estate sales business for an average of 8 years and completed, on average, 16.2

transactions per year composed the expert sample. Undergraduate business students composed the amateur sample.

Participants in this study received ten pages of information about a house they were asked to evaluate, as well as being given the opportunity to examine the property and surrounding area in detail. Subjects then were asked to provide estimates of the value of the property. These estimates were consistent with subjects—*both* amateurs and experts—using an anchoring-and-adjustment heuristic in making their value judgments. Of all the information provided to subjects, only one item varied: the listing price. Yet this one item significantly biased the subjects' estimates of the property's value.

Differences, however, did exist among amatuers and experts. While estimates of both samples were significantly biased by listing prices, amateur subjects appeared more aware of the role that listing price was playing in their decision making process. In the checklist and descriptions of the expert sample, experts flatly denied their use of listing price as a consideration in the valuing of the property. In fact, experts when queried provided a rich and substantial strategic conceptualization for property valuation. Yet, their judgments were statistically indistinguishable from those of the amateurs.

The results of the second study may be particulary enlightening. In the first study, experts were susceptible to decision bias, but negotiated superior outcomes. In the second study, the experts' recitation of a highly developed (and apparently appropriate) strategic conceptualization notwithstanding, they were, again, highly susceptible to the decision bias (i.e., anchoring-and-adjustment in this case) and also *failed* to produce superior outcomes. The failure of real estate agents' strategic conceptutalization of the valuation task can be traced to the impossibility of getting appropriately diagnostic feedback for the task. Because there is no objective "market value" of property against which to compare judgments, real estate agents may have a good sense of what they are supposed to be doing, but no idea if, in fact, they are doing it. Thus, possession of an appropriate strategic conceptualization apparently does not automatically insulate decision makers from decision bias. In the absence of properly diagnostic feedback it may not even guarantee superior performance.

While in neither of these studies did the possession of an appropriate strategic conceptualization ameliorate decision bias, there are important distinctions between the two studies which may be suggestive. In the study of novel-task negotiating, there was no reason to suspect that an appropriate strategic conceptualization of the task (i.e., including awareness of integrative potential) would prevent decision bias. The notion of integrative potential awareness is compatible with framing effects.

The judgments of real-estate agents are a somewhat different matter. The strategic conceptualization they described using in the judgment of property value included: (1) identification of a variety of factors and (2) a specific weighting scheme for integrating the information provided in the factors. While the absence of diagnostic feedback renders the point moot in this case, it is important to realize that this approach to real estate value judgments *is fundamentally incompatible* with anchoring-and-adjustment. In fact, the strategic conceptualiztion detailed by the real estate agent subjects accurately could be described as one specifically designed to preclude the possibility of decision bias in the judgment task.

This suggests that the avoidance of decision bias by experts might be tied to the extent to which the strategic conceptualiztion for a negotiation task includes procedures that *specifically* address the causes of decision bias. In turn, this implies that the ultimate success of strategic conceptualizations in preventing decision bias by experts should be revealed by the successes of direct attempts to prevent decision bias—attempts where the strategic conceptualization provided deals *primarily* with the prevention of decision bias.

Unfortunately, the growing literature on attempts to "debias" decision makers does not paint an optimistic picture. Attempts to cure decision bias through extensive training have met with only limited success at best. (For a review, see Fischhoff, 1982). Alpert and Raiffa (1982) used feedback linked with conceptual discussion about the potential for bias in trying to cure overconfidence. They found that the probability for judgmental error with their subjects "fell from a shocking 41% to a depressing 23% (Alpert & Raiffa, 1982, p. 304). Adams and Adams (1958) also found modest improvement in susceptibility to bias after training, but Choo (1976) found almost none. Not surprisingly, *quantity* of training is not the critical variable in differentiating between successful and unsuccessful debaising efforts. While Lichtenstein and Fischhoff (1980) found appreciable improvement in judgment after ten sessions of extensive training, they noted that virtually all gains in judgment quality occurred following the first training session. Providing a good strategic conceptualization of the root cause of decision bias and lots of practice with feedback seems to be a key to debiasing efforts—but not so key that it guarantees success.

CONCLUSION

The picture now seems almost complete. Experience (through trial-and-error learning) can lead to superior negotiator perfomance. However, the truly adaptive superior performance of expertise comes from having an appropriate strategic conceptualization of the negotiation process—a cognitive causal schema of negotiation that guides both performance and feedback interpretation.

Interestingly, the attainment of expert negotiator performance via strategic conceptualization and feedback does not necessarily imply *unbiased* performance. Even attempts to prevent decision bias directly (by supplying negotiators or decision makers with bias-incompatible strategic conceptualization) have met only with limited success. This suggests that cognitive heuristics may operate preconsciously—beyond the reach of cognitive corrective strategies.

If cognitive bias in negotiation is preconscious, amelioration of bias will depend upon the identification of non-cognitive aids to decision making. For instance, worksheets have been used successfully to overcome availability effects (Northcraft & Neale, 1986). The development of computerized decision aids as a means of compensating for decision bias seems particularly promising in this vein. The most sophisticated approach to the avoidance of decision bias via decision aids is the use of expert systems (Gorry & Krumland, 1983). An expert system is a programmed computational algorithm used to generate a decision. The appropriate considerations (inputs) for the decision are programmed in along with a weighting and valuing scheme for integrating the inputs, and a series of decision rules. The a priori specification of the decision process prevents transitory cognitive precesses (such as availability or anchoring-and-adjustment) from having an effect. Further, pre-decisional specification of the computational algorithm opens the process to public scrutiny. This means that faulty assumptions and incorrect computational strategies in the expert system program are likely to be exposed and corrected. The expert system then can provide a comparison for decisions made by human information processors.

Whether expert systems (or decisions aids of other sorts) hold any promise for decreasing bias in negotiation behavior remains an issue to be settled by future research. So, too, is the subtle question of where appropriate strategic conceptualization originate and how they come to be acquired. For now suffice it to say that given the apparent inevitability of decision bias, even experts can hope only to be better decision makers and negotiators—not infallible ones.

REFERENCES

Abelson, R.P. (1976). Script processing in attitude formation and decision-making. In J.S. Carroll & J.W. Payne (Eds.). *Cognition and social behavior*. Hillsdale, NJ: Erlbaum.

Adams, P.A., & Adams, J.K. (1958). Training in confidence judgments. *American Journal of Psychology, 41*, 747-751.

Alpert, M., & Raiffa, H. (1982). A progress report on the training of probability assessors. In D. Kahneman, P. Slovic, & A. Tversky (Eds.), *Judgment under uncertainty* (pp. 294-305). Cambridge: Cambridge University Press.

Bazerman, M.H. (1986). *Judgment in managerial decision making*. New York: John Wiley and Sons.

Bazerman, M.H., Magliozzi, T., & Neale, M.A. (1985). Integrative bargaining in a competitive market. *Organizational Behavior and Human Decision Processes, 35*, 294-313.

Bazerman, M.H., & Neale, M.A. (1982). Improving negotiator judgment: The role of selection and training. *Journal of Applied Psychology, 67*, 543-548.

Berkeley, D., & Humphrey, P. (1982). Structuring decision problems and the "bias heuristic." *Acta Psychologia, 50,* 201-252.

Boulding, K.E. (1958). *The skills of the economist.* Cleveland: Howard Allen.

Bushyhead, J., & Christensen-Szalanski, J.J.J. (1981). Feedback and the illusion of validity in a medical clinic. *Medical Decision Making, 1,* 115-123.

Chertkoff, J.M., & Conley, M. (1967). Opening offer and frequency of concession as a bargaining strategy. *Journal of Personality and Social Psychology, 7,* 181-185.

Choo, G.T. (1976). *Training and generalization in assessing group probabilities for discrete events* (Tech. Report 76-5). Uxbridge, England: Brunel Institute of Organizational and Social Studies.

Christensen-Szalanski, J.J.J., & Beach, L. (1982). Experience and the baserate fallacy. *Organizational Behavior and Human Performance, 29,* 270-278.

Coker, D.A., Neale, M.A., & Northcraft, G.B. (1987). *Structural and individual influence on the process and outcome of negotiation* (Working paper). Tucson: University of Arizona.

Cummings, L.L., Schwab, D.P., & Rosen, M. (1971). Performance and knowledge of results as determinants of goal setting. *Journal of Applied Psychology, 55,* 526-530.

Dawes, R.M., & Corrigan, B. (1974). Linear models in decision making. *Psychological Bulletin, 81,* 95-106.

Earley, P.C. (1988). Computer generated feedback in the subscription-processing industry. *Organizational Behavior and Human Decision Processes, 41,* 50-64.

Einhorn, H.J. (1974). Expert judgment: Some necessary conditions and an example. *Journal of Applied Psychology, 59,* 562-571.

Einhorn, H.J. (1980). Overconfidence in judgment. *New Directions for Methodology of Social and Behavioral Science, 4,* 1-16.

Einhorn, H.J., & Hogarth, R.M. (1978). Confidence in judgment: Persistence of the illusion of validity. *Psychological Review, 85,* 395-416.

Fischhoff, B. (1982). Debiasing. In D. Kahneman, P. Slovic, & A. Tversky (Eds.), *Judgment under uncertainty: Heuristics and biases.* Cambridge: Cambridge University Press.

Fisher, R., & Ury, W. (1981). *Getting to yes.* Boston: Houghton-Mifflin.

Fiske, D.W. (1961). The inherent variability of behavior. In D.W. Fiske & S.R. Maddi (Eds.), *Functions of work experience.* Homewood, IL: Dorsey Press.

Gorry, G.A., & Krumland, R.B. (1983). Artificial intelligence and decision support systems. In J. Bennett (Ed.), *Building decision support systems* (pp. 205-220). Reading, MA: Addison-Wesley.

Hastorf, A.H., & Cantril, H. (1954) They saw a game: A case study. *Journal of Abnormal and Social Psychology, 49,* 129-134.

Hogarth, R.M. (1981). Beyond discrete biases: Functional and dysfunctional aspects of judgmental heuristics. *Psychological Bulletin, 90,* 197-217.

Huber, V.L. & Neale, M.A. (1986). Effects of cognitive heuristics and goals on negotiator performance and subsequent goal setting. *Organizational Behavior and Human Decision Processes, 38,* 342-365.

James, W. (1979). *Some problems of philosophy.* Cambridge, MA: Harvard University Press.

Johnson, P.E., Duran, A.S., Hassebrock, F., Moller, J., Prietula, M., Feltovick, P.J., & Swanson, D.B. (1981). Expertise and error in diagnostic reasoning. *Cognitive Science, 5,* 235-283.

Kahneman, D., & Slovic, P., & Tversky, A. (1982). *Judgment under uncertainty: Heuristics and biases.* Cambridge: Cambridge University Press.

Kahneman, D., & Tversky, A. (1972). Subjective probability: A judgment of representativeness. *Cognitive Psychology, 3,* 430-454.

Kahneman, D., & Tversky, A. (1979). Prospect theory: An analysis of decisions under risk. *Economntrica, 47,* 263-291.

Kelley, H.H. (1972). Attribution in social interaction. In E.E. Jones, D.E. Kanouse, H.H. Kelly, R.E. Nisbett, S. Valins, & B Weiner (Eds.), *Attribution: Perceiving the causes of behavior.* Morristown, NJ: General Learning Press.

Landy, F.J., & Farr, J.L. (1982). *The measurement of work performance.* New York: Academic Press.

Lewicki, R.J., & Litterer, J. (1985). *Negotiation.* Homewood, IL: R.D. Irwin.

Litchenstein, S., & Fischhoff, B. (1980). Training for calibration. *Organizational Behavior and Human Performance, 26,* 149-171.

Lichenstein, S., Fischhoff, B., & Phillips, L.D. (1982). Calibration of probabilties: The state of the art to 1980. In D. Kahneman, P. Slovic, & A. Tversky (Eds.), *Judgment under uncertainty: Heuristics and biases.* Cambridge: Cambridge University Press.

Leibert, R.M., Smith, W.P., Hall, J.H., & Keiffer, M. (1968). The effects of information and magnitude of initial offer on interpersonal negotiation. *Journal of Experimental Psychology, 4,* 431-441.

Lord, C., Ross, L., & Lepper, M.R. (1979). Biased assimilation and attitude polarization: The effects of prior theories on subsequently considered evidence. *Journal of Personality and Social Psychology, 37,* 2098-2019.

Miller, D.T., & Ross, L. (1975). Self-serving biases in the attribution of causality: Fact or fiction? *Psychological Bulletin, 82,* 213-225.

Neale, M.A. (1984). The effect of negotiation and arbitration cost salience on bargaining behavior: The role of arbitrator and constituency in negotiator judgment. *Organizational Behavior and Human Performance, 36,* 97-111.

Neale, M.A., & Bazerman, M.H. (1985a). Perspectives for understanding negotiation: Viewing negotiation as a judgmental process. *Journal of Conflict Resolution, 29,* 33-35.

Neale, M.A., & Bazerman, M.H. (1985b). The effect of framing and negotiator overconfidence on bargainer behavior. *Academy of Management Journal, 28,* 34-49.

Neale, M.A., & Bazerman, M.H. (1985c). When will externally set goals improve negotiator behavior? A look at integrative behavior in a competitive market. *Journal of Occupational Behavior, 6,* 19-32.

Neale, M.A., Huber, V.L., & Northcraft, G.B. (1987). The framing of negotiation: Contextual versus task frame. *Organizational Behavior and Human Decision Processes, 39,* 228-241.

Neale, M.A., & Northcraft, G.B. (1986). Experts, amateurs, and refrigerators: Comparing expert and amateur decision making on a novel task. *Organizational Behavior and Human Decision Process, 38,* 305-317.

Nisbett, R.E., & Ross, L. (1980). *Human inference: Strategies and shortcomings of social judgment.* Englewood Cliff, NJ: Prentice-Hall.

Northcraft, G.B., & Earley, P.C. (1989). Technology, credibility, and feedback use. *Organizational Behavior and Human Decision Processes, 44,* 83-96.

Northcraft, G.B., & Neale, M.A. (1986). Opportunity costs and the framing of resource allocation decisions. *Organizational Behavior and Human Decision Processes, 37,* 28-38.

Northcraft, G.B., & Neale, M.A. (1987). Experts, amateurs, and real estate: An anchoring-and-adjustment perspective on property pricing decisions. *Organizational Behavior and Human Decision Processes, 39,* 84-97.

Northcraft, G.B., & Neale, M.A. (1984). *Experts versus amateurs: The role of expertise in human information processing and decision behavior.* Grant proposal funded by the National Science Foundation, Information Sciences and Technology Division.

O'Reilly, C.S., Northcraft, G.B., & Sabers, D. (1989). The confirmation bias in special education eligibility decisions. *School Psychology Review, 18*(1), 126-135.

Phelps, R., & Shanteau, J. (1978). Livestock judges: How much information can an expert use? *Organizational Behavior and Human Performance, 21,* 209-218.

Pruitt, D.G. (1983). Integrative agreements: Nature and antecedents. In M.H. Bazerman & R.J. Lewicki (Eds.), *Negotiating in organizations*. Beverly Hills, CA: Sage.

Raiffa, H. (1982). *The art and science of negotiation*. Cambridge, MA: Harvard Press.

Rosen, S., & Tesser, A. (1970). On the reluctance to communicate undesirable information: The MUM effect. *Sociology, 33*, 253-263.

Ross, M. (1981). Self-centered biases in attributions of responsibility: Antecedents and consequences. In E.T. Higgins, C.P. Herman, & M.P. Zanna (Eds.), *Social cognition: The Ontario symposium on personality and social psychology* (Vol. 1). Hillsdale, NJ: Erlbaum.

Rubin, J.Z., & Brown, B.R. (1975). *The social psychology of bargaining and negotiation*. New York: Academic Press.

Slovic, P. (1969). Analyzing the expert judge: A descriptive study of a stock-broker's decision processes. *Journal of Applied Psychology, 53*, 255-263.

Slovic, P., & Lichtenstein, S. (1971). Comparison of Bayesian and regression approaches to the study of information processing in judgment. *Organizational Behavior and Human Performance, 6*, 649-744.

Staw, B.M. (1976). Knee-deep in the big muddy: A study of escalating commitment to a chosen course of action. *Organizational Behavior and Human Performance, 16*, 27-44.

Taylor, S.E. (1981). The availability bias in social perception and interaction. In D. Kahneman, P. Slovic, & A. Tversky (Eds.), *Judgment under uncertainty: Heuristics and biases*. Cambridge: Cambridge University Press.

Taylor, S.E., & Crocker, J. (1981). Schematic bases of social information processing. In E.T. Higgins, C.P. Herman, & M.P. Zanna (Eds.), *Social cognition: The Ontario syposium on personality and social psychology* (Vol. 1). Hillsdale, NJ: Erlbaum.

Thaler, R.H. (1986). The psychology conference handbook: Comments on Simon, on Einhorn and Hogarth, and on Tversky and Kahneman. *Journal of Business, 59*, S279-S284.

Tversky, A., & Kahneman, D. (1973). Judgment under uncertainty: Heuristics and biases. *Science, 185*, 1124-1131.

Tversky, A., & Kahneman, D. (1974). Availabilty: A heuristic for judging frequency and probabilty. *Cognitive Psychology, 5*, 207-232.

Tversky, A., & Kahneman, D. (1981). The framing of decisions and the psychology of choice. *Science, 211*, 453-458.

Wicklund, R.A. (1975). Objective self-awareness. In L. Berkowitz (Ed.), *Advances in experimental social psychology* (Vol. 9). New York: Academic Press.

[25]

ORGANIZATIONAL BEHAVIOR AND HUMAN DECISION PROCESSES **48**, 1–22 (1991)

An Evaluation of Learning in the Bilateral Winner's Curse

SHERYL B. BALL

School of Management, Boston University

MAX H. BAZERMAN

Kellogg Graduate School of Management, Northwestern University

AND

JOHN S. CARROLL

Sloan School of Management, Massachusetts Institute of Technology

Recent research on bilateral bargaining behavior under uncertainty has found that, under asymmetric information, negotiators develop inferior bidding strategies because they fail to incorporate valuable information about the decisions of their opponents. This results in negative profits, or the "winner's curse." The present study provided subjects multiple opportunities for feedback as well as experience in both negotiation roles. Neither learning opportunity eliminates the winner's curse. © 1990 Academic Press, Inc.

The dominant perspective of economic theories of negotiation has been built around the cornerstone of rationality (Coase, 1960; Hoffman & Spitzer, 1982; Fudenberg & Tirole, 1981; Tracy, 1986). In contrast, substantial evidence suggests that individual decison makers (Kahneman & Tversky, 1979) and, more specifically, negotiators (Bazerman & Carroll, 1987) deviate from rationality in systematically predictable ways. One well-substantiated finding is that individuals tend to ignore valuable information about the decisions of their opponents in bilateral negotiations, and fall victim to the winner's curse (Samuelson & Bazerman, 1985; Carroll, Bazerman, & Maury, 1988). In contrast, experimental economic studies show that many market deviations disappear with even a small amount of feedback (Plott, 1982). However, these results exist at the market level. No evidence exists to show whether individual deviations

This research was supported by NSF Grant SES-8596029 and the Dispute Resolution Research Center at Northwestern University. The authors benefited from discussions at seminars on the paper at the University of Texas, Harvard, University of Chicago, MIT, Berkeley, Stanford, and Northwestern.

Address requests for reprints to Dr. Sheryl Ball at the Department of Finance and Economics, School of Management, Boston University, Boston, MA 02215.

from rationality in negotiation also disappear with a reasonable amount of experience and feedback. This paper examines whether the tendency to ignore the decisions of the opponent negotiator (and the resulting winner's curse) is eliminated through experience, feedback, and reversing roles or whether this deviation from rationality is resistant to the learning opportunities that negotiators experience.

Although economic theories of negotiation assume rationality, research shows that negotiators may fail to reach efficient agreements because (1) they are overconfident in their assessment of what they will get out of the negotiation (Neale & Bazerman, 1983; Farber, 1981; Thompson & Hastie, 1990), (2) they feel committed to a previous course of action and escalate their commitment in order to justify their current position in the conflict (Staw, 1976, 1981), and/or (3) the outcomes are "framed" as losses rather than gains (Bazerman, Magliozzi, & Neale, 1985). This orientation is implicitly acknowledged in Raiffa's (1982) argument that we need to develop prescriptions for negotiators that incorporate the actual decision processes of opponents, rather than assuming fully rational opponents in the game theoretic tradition.

This paper focuses on one specific bias that is especially important in competitive situations: negotiators fail to consider the informational content of their opponent's actions. Samuelson and Bazerman (1985) found that under asymmetric information negotiators systematically deviate from normative behavior and, consequently, fall prey to the "winner's curse": they consistently (and voluntarily) enter into loss-making purchases. Their analysis relied on the following class of example:

> One firm (the acquirer) is considering making an offer to buy out another firm (the target). The complication is that the acquirer is uncertain about the ultimate value of the firm. Though it has reason to believe that the target will be worth more under its management than under present ownership, the acquirer (even after making its best estimates) does not know that target's ultimate value. Target management, on the other hand, has an accurate estimate of value and so shares none of the acquirer's uncertainty. In these circumstances what final price offer should the acquirer make for the target?

Two important features characterize this class of example. First, the fact that the company is more valuable to the acquirer than to the target means that ex post there is a value at which both sides can profit from a transaction. Second, one side has much better information than the other and will selectively accept any offer that is made. Selective acceptance is a key property in Akerlof's (1970) fascinating description of the "market for lemons" that inspired research on the winner's curse. The existence of selective acceptance *should* also put the less well-informed party on guard:

> If the target takes our offer, are we going to acquire a lemon? After all, the target is more likely to sell a poor company than a good one. What does their acceptance tell me? It tells me that the value of the firm comes from the pessimistic part of the a priori distribution.

This tendency to ignore information that is available by considering the decisions of opponent negotiators is consistent with research on the winner's curse in an auction content. Research has shown that "winning bidders" often find that they have overpaid for the acquired commodities (Kagel & Levin, 1986; Capen, Clapp, & Campbell, 1971; Cassing & Douglas, 1980; Roll, 1986). This occurs because the highest bid is likely to be from an individual with one of the more optimistic estimates of the commodity's value. If this adverse selection problem is not accounted for by the bidders, winning bids will frequently result in negative returns. Bazerman and Samuelson (1983) and Kagel and Levin (1986) have shown that this adverse selection process increases with the number of bidders and the uncertainty of the value of the commodity. However, bidder judgment fails to incorporate the relevance of adverse selection or the mediating influences of the number of bidders and commodity uncertainty.

It has been argued (e.g., Smith, 1982) that observed failures of rational models are attributable to the cost of thinking and will thus be eliminated by proper incentives. Tversky and Kahneman (1986), however, document many failures of incentives to correct systematic deviations from rationality. More relevant to the current problem, research has shown that individuals fail to avoid the winner's curse even when they were paid for good performance, when their intellectual reputations were at stake, when they were given hints, and when unusually analytical subjects were used (Samuelson & Bazerman, 1985; Carroll et al., 1988).

It has also been argued that individuals in the real world (in comparison to individuals in one-shot judgmental tasks) will correct their judgments by learning from feedback regarding past decisions. This view is represented by Kagel and Levin (1986) in their analysis of the winner's curse in an auction context:

> Given sufficient experience and feedback regarding the outcomes of their decisions, we have no doubt that our experimental subjects, as well as most bidders in "real world" settings, would eventually learn to avoid the winner's curse in any particular set of circumstances. The winner's curse is a disequilibrium phenomenon that will correct itself given sufficient time and the right kind of information feedback. (p. 917)

In fact, Kagel and Levin (1986) do show a reduction in the winner's curse in the auction context as *the market* learns over time. Some of this learning is through the disappearance of the most aggressive bidders from the market. Additional learning occurs through the observation of consistent losses being suffered by winners in the auction.

There can be little disagreement that we do learn many things through our life experiences. However, the case regarding judgmental distortions is less clear. Tversky and Kahneman (1986) have argued that basic judgmental biases are unlikely to be corrected in the real world because learning requires accurate and immediate feedback which is rarely available because:

> (i) outcomes are commonly delayed and not easily attributable to a particular action; (ii) variability in the environment degrades the reliability of feedback. . . ; (iii) there is often no information about what the outcome would have been if another decision had been taken; and (iv) most important decisions are unique and therefore provide little opportunity for learning (see Einhorn and Hogarth, 1978) . . . any claim that a particular error will be eliminated by experience must be supported by demonstrating that the conditions for effective learning are satisfied. (pp. 274–275)

The empirical portion of this paper consists of two studies. The first study offers a strong test of the ability of subjects to learn to incorporate the decisions of others into their decisions. Since Carroll *et al.* (1988) documented the resilience of the winner's curse in bilateral negotiations, we attempted to incorporate the best possible conditions to facilitate learning. The variability of the environment (Tversky and Kahneman's second explanation for the difficulty of learning) is part of the winner's curse phenomenon. However, the other three difficulties (i, iii, and iv above) can be experimentally eliminated. Thus, this research addresses whether or not the ability to consider the informational signal contained in decisions of others in a bilateral negotiation problem can be learned in a highly favorable environment. Clearly, the experimental economics literature would expect learning in a reasonable amount of time (e.g., Kagel & Levin, 1986). However, an extreme position of the deviation from rationality literature would argue that learning would be very difficult under even highly favorable circumstances. Tversky and Kahneman have offered a more moderate position that accepts the potential for learning under the best of circumstances. The second study increases the subjects opportunity to learn by adding more experience than provided in the first study and exposes subjects experientially to the same problem from the perspective of the other party (the target).

EXPERIMENT 1

Methods

The experimental task was a modified version of one of the three examples used by Samuelson and Bazerman (1985), shown in Appendix 1. This task is based on an example presented in Akerlof (1970). In this problem, potential acquirers only know that the company is equally likely to be worth any value between $0 and $100 and that, whatever its value, it is worth 50% more to the acquirer than to the target owner. The target owner knows the exact value and will accept any bid at or above that value. What should the acquirer bid?

The most common response (90 of 123 subjects) found by Samuelson and Bazerman (1985) was in the $50–$75 range. The simple (naive) logic that accounts for this result can be exemplified as follows:

> The value of the firm is uncertain, but its expected value to the target is $50/share. The expected value of the firm to me is $75/share. Thus, I can make a reasonable profit by offering some price slightly in excess of $50/share. I offer $60/share (or $51/share).

This logic would be rational if the target was also uninformed about the value of the firm. However, an informed target will only accept an offer if it is profitable, which a subject can assess through the appropriate conditional logic or through the use of a simple example:

> Suppose that I make an offer of $60/share. If it is accepted, then the firm must be worth between $0 and $60/share. The average value of the firm to the target when my offer is accepted is $30/share, and $45/share to me. My profit has the expected value of $45–$60, or −$15/share when my offer is accepted. The conclusion is that the expected value of the investment is −25% making the optimal bid $0.

The first experiment was designed to incorporate the best possible conditions to facilitate learning. Subjects were given the same task as in Samuelson and Bazerman (1985), modified to allow subjects the opportunity to make their choices *with feedback* on 20 consecutive trials. Notice that in the Samuelson and Bazerman (1985) study, subjects actually had a one-third chance of making money if their non-zero bid was accepted. Subjects in the present study had the same chance of making money in any trial; however, an approximation of the likelihood of making money over the course of the experiment by bidding the same positive value on all trials is only 1.4%.

Sixty-nine first year Masters of Management students at Northwestern University's Kellogg Graduate School of Management were recruited from introductory decision science classes. Twenty-one of these subjects were in a protocol condition that is explained below.

All subjects were told that they would be participating in a study of how people make investment decisions under uncertainty and that they would be paid for their participation based on how well they performed. In addition, this exercise served as part of an introduction to probability theory. The subjects were given as much time as they needed to complete the task and results were discussed in class after the experiment was completed (with personalized feedback). The actual experiments took place in a computer lab.

Subjects were given a set of instructions (Appendix 1) and time to read them. After any questions were answered, two aspects of the problem

6   BALL, BAZERMAN, AND CARROLL

were stressed: First, it was emphasized that there would be 20 chances to acquire the company but that the values of the companies in each year were independent. The meaning of "independence" in a statistical sense was briefly discussed (Appendix 2). Second, it was noted that, as indicated in the instructions, acquiring the company was a neutral event and that the only measure of performance was the value of a subject's assets at the end of the experiment.

At this point, the computers were turned on. Each subject was sitting at a personal computer that was programmed to receive a subject's bid, generate a random number for the target value, determine whether the bid was accepted, calculate any change in assets, and display the results to the subject.

Each subject started the experiment with $600 in assets which they were told was worth one cent on the dollar to them at the end of the experiment. Every time a subject entered a bid, the computer displayed the "true" value of the company, whether the bid was accepted, and how much money had been won or lost. The "current value of assets" was reported and the subject was told what trial had been completed.

Results

"Learning" was defined as bidding 0 for the company from any particular trial until the end of the experiment.[1] We found that, in the first experiment, 7% ($n = 5$) learned during the course of the experiment. There were no other marginal learners. This percentage is equivalent to previous studies with this task (Samuelson & Bazerman, 1985; Carroll *et al.*, 1988). None of these subjects bid correctly from the first trial; the average trial in which those five subjects learned (began to bid $0 or $1) was Trial 8.

The mean of reported bids in all trials was 52.61, which is consistent with other experiments done with this task (Samuelson & Bazerman, 1985; Carroll *et al.*, 1988). Furthermore, the means across the 20 trials did

---

[1] In the first experiment one subject leveled off at $1 and this was defined as learning despite the small negative expected return that this offers because the subject indicated that he had not understood that 0 was an acceptable bid. In subsequent experiments subjects were told that if they did not consider the odds to be in their favor that they would bid 0 and not risk losing any money. Therefore, $1 was no longer considered to be evidence of learning.

In the first part of the second experiment one subject bid 0 in Trials 19 and 20 and was not classified as a learner. This is because he had previously bid 0 and then returned to a positive bidding strategy and in the second part of the experiment he returned to a positive bidding strategy. Bidding 0 twice was thus not seen as evidence of learning, only as repeatedly trying a 0 bidding strategy.

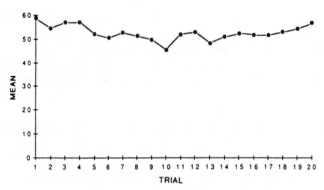

FIG. 1. Mean bids across trials for subjects in Experiment 1.

Trial	Mean	SD	Min	Max	% in $50–$75 range
1	58.61	27.80	0	130	58
2	55.21	25.67	0	115	54
3	57.00	28.29	1	150	52
4	57.06	25.92	1	130	57
5	51.99	24.81	1	100	55
6	50.25	24.52	0	100	46
7	52.55	24.32	0	100	41
8	51.14	27.03	0	125	43
9	49.64	22.94	0	110	42
10	45.37	24.46	0	100	43
11	51.81	29.22	0	125	43
12	52.87	27.15	0	100	48
13	48.23	29.01	0	150	33
14	50.86	29.64	0	150	45
15	52.35	31.85	0	150	48
16	51.62	29.03	0	150	39
17	51.67	29.17	0	110	36
18	53.10	31.20	0	130	41
19	54.52	30.66	0	150	41
20	56.99	33.83	0	150	43

not differ dramatically suggesting that the bidding strategies themselves did not change. Figure 1 shows the mean bid for each trial.[2]

One interesting change in bidding behavior is a drop in the number of subjects making bids in the $50–$75 range (the range where most of the bids in the one-shot problem occurred). This is probably because feedback was giving subjects information to consider other than the facts presented in the instructions, thus leading them away from the naive analysis presented above.

[2] Aggregate data from Experiment 1 are quadratic; however, analysis of individual subjects' bids over time show a multitude of bidding patterns. This suggests that the quadratic nature of the aggregate data is not important.

8   BALL, BAZERMAN, AND CARROLL

Some attempts were made to predict which subjects would learn. If the problem itself was too mathematically complex, then subjects who were more skilled in mathematics would outperform the others. All students participating in the experiment had recently completed a unit on the uniform probability distribution in their quantitative methods class.

The classes from which subjects were drawn were divided into three levels, according to student's quantitative ability. We drew students only from the most and least quantitative classes. Fifty-five percent of subjects tested were from classes where students had very quantitative backgrounds (e.g., engineering) and 45% were from nonquantitative backgrounds (e.g., English). Three of 38 students from the highly quantitative sections learned compared to 2 of 31 students from the nonquantitative sections (no significant difference).[3]

We mention above that one specific bias which hinders negotiators' abilities to reach efficient outcomes is that negotiators tend to ignore information about what their opponent knows in order to simplify the negotiation problem they are facing. An attempt was made to find subjects who were more apt to consider the thoughts of others by administering a perspective-taking ability survey to all subjects at the conclusion of the experiment (Neale & Bazerman, 1983). The rationale was that the people who considered the thoughts of others better would be less likely to disregard their opponent's information when they attempted to simplify this task. Scores on this survey, however, were not found to be a significant predictor of who would learn.

Protocol Analysis

In order to understand why most subjects failed to learn in this experiment, 21 of the 69 subjects were randomly selected and asked to "think aloud" during their deliberations, to provide verbal protocols of their thought processes. Although verbal protocol collection has been criticized as disruptive and inaccurate (Nisbitt & Wilson, 1977), Russo, Johnson, and Stephens (1986) found that protocol collecting might actually improve subjects' performance in a task similar to ours. Carroll *et al.* (1988) found no significant difference between their study using verbal protocols and one in which verbal protocols were not collected. We also found no significant difference in either the mean reported bid ($t = .203$, ns) or the proportion of subjects who learned ($t = .227$, ns) between the sample where protocols were collected and the one where they were not collected.

Verbal protocols were collected by having subjects complete the same

---

[3] We acknowledge that the small number of learners gives this test little power; however, we find no evidence to support the claim that the problem is mathematically complex.

experiment as the other subjects with the following exception. Before they were given the instructions they were told:

> We are interested in studying not only what decisions people make, but also how they arrive at these decisions. Speak all of your thoughts out loud and we will tape record them. Everything that goes through your head is equally important, even if you said it once before.

The tape recorder was then turned on and the subjects were given their directions. If a subject forgot to keep talking, the experimenter would remind them to think aloud.

Subjects' protocols were transcribed, divided into statements each representing a single thought or idea, and categorized using a coding scheme developed for this study. Many of these codes were taken from Carroll *et al.* (1988). Others that were specifically relevant to a repeated trial "Acquiring a Company" problem were added. The results of the analysis are reported in Appendix 3. Codes are sorted into three categories (Naive, Good, Neutral) according to whether they represented good or bad reasoning in solving this problem. Since there were only two learners who provided protocols, any conclusions about patterns of thought in subjects who learned should be considered preliminary. In addition, the lack of learners among this group limits the analyses that can be conducted. Rather, the results of the protocol analysis are presented as anecdotal evidence that may help clarify the lack of rational behavior described earlier.

It is not surprising that learners differ from nonlearners. A clear example of this is that both of the learners and none of the nonlearners developed a generalized hypothetical argument (code 11). An example of a generalized hypothetical argument is "For any bid I make, no matter what the magnitude, there are two-thirds as many values of the company where I will lose as there are where I will win." This finding parallels that of Carroll *et al.* (1988). This suggests that it is not a matter of bidding for fun, but a failure to analyze the problem which caused the nonlearners to continue to bid. In fact, the only subject who mentioned bidding for fun was one of the learners.

Many subjects started out by looking at the problem very analytically and coming up with a "best bid," which they would then submit for a few periods. The negative results which they received quickly convinced them that they had taken the wrong approach and they began to modify their bids in response to feedback.

> Well, I'm going to say that they didn't do super well, but they did about average, which would given them 50, so . . . I'm going to say 75 (Year 1). The company is unwilling to accept your bid (Year 2). This year is totally independent of what they were valued last year so it shouldn't be affected so I'm going to say 75 again because I think that's the best strategy . . . (Year 7). Now I'm in the hole because I was too aggressive. . . . I don't want to be put in a position where I'm losing any more money . . . so I'm going to bid 50 this time.

10   BALL, BAZERMAN, AND CARROLL

Some subjects assumed that they did not have enough information to analyze the problem and chose a strategy of relying on feedback ex ante: "There's nothing to do except guess for the first one" or "Since there is no information at all about the best way to do this, I can probably find a pattern." Sixty-three percent of the nonlearners made a guessing or gambling assumption (code N3) at some time during the experiment: "That's how I win money in Vegas—gut feel." Many realized from the feedback that there was something wrong with the system they were using to come up with bids but were unable to find a more successful way of analyzing the problem. At least one subject correctly remarked that the odds were better in Las Vegas.

Many subjects tried to formulate strategies based on how much money they had left (code N5, 56%). Some of these subjects decided that since they were running out of time or money that they should bid more to recoup losses (Thaler, 1980), and others reasoned in the opposite way. In order to test the extent to which these end-period effects were preventing subjects from learning, we replicated this study. The following are changes from the original design: (1) Subjects were not told how many chances they would have to acquire the company. (2) Verbal emphasis was put on the fact that zero was an acceptable bid. (3) Subjects were undergraduate students from the University of Arizona who had experience in other economics experiments. In a group of 30 subjects, 10% learned. We conclude that end-period effects did not significantly affect behavior.

As noted above, when compared with experiments where subjects were given only one trial at this problem, we report a similar percentage of correct answers. Although feedback permitted more familiarity with the problem, the feedback also generated barriers to learning the correct response. The tendency, for example, for nonlearners to focus on using past values of company T to attempt to forecast future values shows that they were distracted from thinking about the facts of the problem once they had feedback to think about.

The feedback that subjects saw was often misinterpreted. Because subjects did not lose every time their bids were accepted, many began to believe that some bids they were submitting were winning bids. They thus concluded that they had found the "solution" to the puzzle: "It worked the first time, I'm not making a decision again."

Information was often misanalyzed, despite the training that subjects were receiving in probability. An example of this is that despite written and verbal emphasis on the statistical independence of trials some subjects began to ignore this information when other strategies failed them: "Ok, here we've got four high numbers in a row, and the law of averages would tell me that the next one is going to be low." We do not see this as a failure of our experimental design, but rather as a partial explanation of why the winner's curse phenomenon is so persistent. These patterns are consistent with discussions of the gambler's fallacy in the behavioral decision theory literature (Tversky & Kahneman, 1974).

Some subjects clearly interpreted the feedback in the correct way and still continued to bid. One subject undertook a guessing strategy after reasoning:

> "The pure object of this game is to frustrate the hell out of me. Because no matter which direction I take I can only lose or break even."

The sentiment, if not the observation, was echoed by most of the non-learners in both samples. The protocol analysis suggests that feedback does not help in solving non-market winner's curse problems. For, unlike markets where feedback gives subjects information about *what* they are doing wrong, our feedback can merely show subjects that they are doing *something* wrong. Since the probabilistic nature of the problem makes even this information a very noisy signal about subjects' performance, subjects reach many incorrect conclusions about how to interpret the feedback and adjust their bidding strategies.

EXPERIMENT 2

The results of the first experiment showed an extreme lack of learning. The second experiment was designed to explore whether any viable way to improve subject performance on this task exists or whether further evidence exists for the resiliance of our tendency to ignore the cognitions of others.

Methods

The second experiment was designed specifically to test whether additional experience and/or experience in the other's (the target's) role would improve subjects' performance in the acquirer role. Forty-four subjects from Northwestern University and the University of Arizona were recruited to participate in the "role reversal" condition of this experiment, which lasted 2 days.[4] The first day was considered a "training session" and was held 4 days to 1 week before the second session. In the first session, subjects were told that they would be participating in two roles, both as the buyer (the acquirer) and as seller (the target) in a negotiation.

The instructions were a modified version of those used in the first experiment, but were more general and did not emphasize the buyer role to the subject. After reading these general instructions, subjects were asked to complete the task used in the first experiment. Then, the computer's instructions explained to subjects that they would now act as the target in the same negotiation task. Subjects were told the value of the

---

[4] Tests were conducted to determine whether there were any identifiable subject pool effects. No significant differences were found.

12   BALL, BAZERMAN, AND CARROLL

company that they were trying to sell in that period and then given an offer and asked to accept or reject the offer (in 20 new trials). (The random values and bids were taken from a representative subject's experience from Experiment 1.) At the end of each period, the computer calculated their earnings that period, their total earnings, and the period earnings and total earnings of their imaginary opponent. This training was intended to improve the subject's rationality in the role of acquirer by increasing their understanding of the likely decisions of the seller. On the second day, subjects were asked to again act in the role of the uninformed party using the same computer simulation as in Experiment 1.

A second group of 34 subjects from Northwestern University and the University of Arizona participated in the "extended trial" condition of this experiment. These subjects did everything as the "role reversal" subjects, except they were not given a chance to act as the target. This was done as a control group for the second experiment and to determine whether extended trials over 2 days, without reversing roles, would be sufficient to facilitate learning.

Results

The first part of the second experiment showed learning by 9% (4 of 44) and 6% (2 of 34) of the subjects in the "role reversal" and "extended trial" conditions, respectively. The mean bids across trials for these two groups of subjects are shown in Figs. 2 and 4. These results are not significantly different from results in the first experiment nor from previous research.

The data from the "role reversal" subjects in the portion of the experiment where they played the role of the target were not surprising. Thirteen of the 422 acceptances (3%) were unprofitable.[5] This is most likely an experimental effect due to the fact that the computer program did not require subjects to confirm their acceptance of the offer. Thus, hitting a wrong key was interpreted as an acceptance.

In 31 of 458 rejections (7%), subjects could have earned money had they accepted. However, in 18 of these 31 cases, the rejected bids had earnings of $7 (translates to 7 cents in actual payment to subjects) or less. Subjects may have mistakenly believed that they could increase future offers by turning down offers which yielded low profits, thus increasing total earnings. On the other hand, since no subject rejected a profitable bid in the last 10 trials, earlier incorrect rejections could be the result of initially misunderstanding the task. Thus, it can be assumed that all subjects understood the target's role by the end of their 20 trials in that role.

---

[5] Six of these 13 errors were from the same subject, who may have misunderstood the task.

LEARNING IN THE BILATERAL WINNER'S CURSE   13

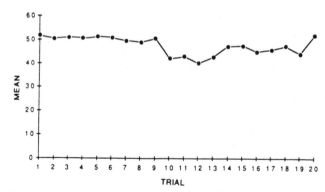

FIG. 2. Mean bids across trials for "role reversal" subjects in part 1 of Experiment 2.

Trial	Mean	SD	Min	Max	% in $50–$75 range
1	51.66	29.56	0	101	57
2	50.47	23.17	0	100	48
3	51.05	21.00	0	100	59
4	50.55	24.15	0	120	48
5	51.30	21.52	0	100	57
6	50.55	22.06	0	100	59
7	49.34	22.02	0	86	52
8	48.75	24.12	0	110	49
9	50.34	25.69	0	100	48
10	41.93	22.33	0	75	46
11	42.84	21.77	0	75	43
12	39.98	23.01	0	75	32
13	42.59	24.43	0	100	46
14	47.07	27.34	0	150	50
15	47.41	27.83	0	120	48
16	44.88	29.81	0	150	34
17	45.77	26.54	0	100	36
18	47.20	25.77	0	100	41
19	44.00	28.23	0	100	34
20	51.91	32.53	0	101	43

When the subjects in the "role reversal" condition were called back to repeat the winner's curse task, the percentage of learners jumped from 9% (4 of 44) to 37% (15 of 41).[6] This is a significant improvement in learning ($z = 7.13$). The mean bids across trials for the "role reversal" subjects in the second part of the experiment are shown in Fig. 3. In addition, the mean bid over 20 trials of the *nonlearners* changed from $51.30 to $33.80, suggesting that, although they had not learned to avoid bids with negative expected values, they did learn to lower the

---

[6] Three of the original 44 subjects from the first session of the second experiment failed to return for the second session. Since they were all nonlearners it seems plausible that this is due to frustration with the task. Earnings for the first session were lower than the mean for 2 of the 3 subjects but were higher than the earnings of other subjects who did return.

14   BALL, BAZERMAN, AND CARROLL

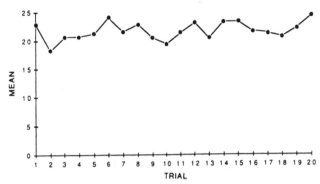

FIG. 3. Mean bids across trials for "role reversal" subjects in part 2 of Experiment 2.

Trial	Mean	SD	Min	Max	% in $50–$75 range
1	22.85	25.51	0	79	20
2	18.29	18.70	0	62	10
3	20.68	19.03	0	62	10
4	20.65	20.12	0	64	10
5	21.20	21.77	0	90	2
6	24.10	24.01	0	90	15
7	21.59	22.33	0	80	7
8	22.87	21.40	0	62	15
9	20.46	19.53	0	68	10
10	19.34	19.27	0	70	5
11	21.41	22.37	0	70	12
12	23.22	25.59	0	90	10
13	20.51	24.38	0	92	12
14	23.34	25.24	0	92	17
15	23.39	24.54	0	80	20
16	21.68	25.03	0	80	10
17	21.37	24.25	0	80	10
18	20.76	23.90	0	90	7
19	22.29	26.47	0	90	17
20	24.41	32.70	0	126	17

chance that they would lose money in any period. It is interesting to note that this learning took place between the 20th and 21st trials, not between the 21st and 40th trials (Figs. 2 and 3).

When the subjects in the "extended trial" condition were called back to repeat the winner's curse task, the percentage of learners jumped from 6 to 12% (4 of 34). Based on a one-sided test we cannot reject the hypothesis of no difference from the result in experiment 1 at the 10% level. The mean bids across trials for the "extended trial" subjects in the second part of the experiment are shown in Fig. 5. In addition, the mean bid of nonlearners dropped from $50.13 to $33.66, again suggesting that experience teaches subjects to decrease their per period risk although subjects did not learn to eliminate it (Figs. 4 and 5).

LEARNING IN THE BILATERAL WINNER'S CURSE   15

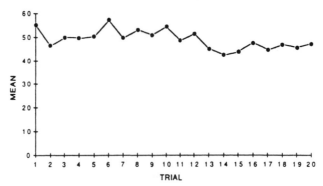

FIG. 4. Mean bids across trials for "extended trial" subjects in part 1 of Experiment 2.

Trial	Mean	SD	Min	Max	% in $50–$75 range
1	55.20	22.03	4	100	62
2	46.41	29.99	4	100	50
3	49.88	24.02	4	100	41
4	49.44	21.37	0	100	53
5	50.02	18.73	9	100	53
6	56.94	21.31	4	90	56
7	49.47	20.48	15	99	47
8	52.97	22.88	20	125	53
9	50.68	25.25	0	100	44
10	51.48	26.93	0	124	41
11	48.32	26.95	0	101	38
12	51.21	22.91	0	100	47
13	44.91	21.29	0	100	44
14	42.26	19.39	0	76	44
15	43.74	21.64	0	75	47
16	47.44	23.33	0	100	44
17	44.41	21.11	0	101	50
18	46.85	29.79	0	150	35
19	45.68	23.44	0	75	50
20	47.41	24.49	0	100	50

The data from the second experiment show that more experience in this market does not eliminate the winner's curse. At best it causes marginal learning where subjects bid less aggressively. In addition, experience in both roles in the market does not eliminate the winner's curse. It does, however, help a significant number of subjects to learn.

DISCUSSION AND CONCLUSIONS

The emerging characterization of decision-making in competitive situations is not a positive one. Bazerman and Carroll (1987) specified a wide variety of deficiencies in judgment in competitive situations. However, their work tended to be limited to one-shot decisions. Hope existed that

16   BALL, BAZERMAN, AND CARROLL

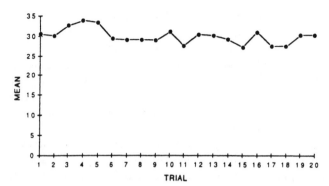

FIG. 5. Mean bids across trials for "extended trial" subjects in part 2 of Experiment 2.

Trial	Mean	SD	Min	Max	% in $50–$75 range
1	30.44	17.11	0	60	24
2	30.06	18.93	0	60	27
3	32.62	19.15	0	75	24
4	33.76	22.90	0	100	24
5	33.09	24.49	0	100	18
6	29.00	18.46	0	75	18
7	28.79	17.97	0	65	15
8	28.79	18.86	0	70	21
9	28.50	18.56	0	65	21
10	30.65	19.51	0	65	29
11	27.11	17.24	0	65	18
12	29.94	20.40	0	70	15
13	29.56	20.61	0	65	21
14	28.56	21.68	0	88	12
15	26.65	18.79	0	75	15
16	30.38	22.58	0	100	15
17	26.97	18.46	0	75	15
18	26.94	17.39	0	50	24
19	29.76	19.86	0	65	18
20	29.65	20.62	0	65	27

experience would provide the feedback opportunities for learning to take place. This hope was consistent with Hogarth's (1981) criticism of the bias literature for focusing on static, one-shot decision tasks. Experiment 1 provided the best feedback that we could design and appropriate incentives to guarantee the motivation of the subjects, yet the results are no different from those found in the one-shot experiments.

With 20 trials to gain experience, feedback after each trial, and decreasing asset balances, why did subjects continue to make positive bids? To answer this question, it is useful to consider the two earlier studies of the bilateral winner's curse. Samuelson and Bazerman (1985) identified the tendency to make bids with negative returns, presumably because subjects ignored the importance of conditional information that is revealed when the opponent accepts their offer. Subjects were posited to be assuming that their opponent's decisions would be based on their own expected value. When Carroll *et al.* (1988) replicated this effect and collected verbal protocols on a one-shot version of a bilateral winner's curse game, they found that subjects made a variety of simplifying assumptions to ease their decision task, both those posited by Samuelson and Bazerman and other unexpected simplifications. A wide variety of assumptions in subjects' decision-making distracted them from the necessary normative logic to analyze this problem effectively. In the current multitrial version, the subject has even more opportunity for distraction. We saw the same simplified strategies that were exhibited in previous studies. In addition, we saw subjects frequently try to figure out a pattern across the trials (e.g., a string of high-valued companies or a low-valued company being followed by a high-valued company). This occurred despite the fact that the subjects were told, and at some level believed, that the true values of the companies across trials were independent. The results suggest that subjects, in attempting to deal with a variety of data, were distracted by false cues that inappropriately attracted much of their attention. The many trials that provide an opportunity for experience also provide additional distractions from the necessary normative logic.

Yet, it is still surprising that the extra opportunities for learning did not overpower these problems. Plott and Sunder (1985) show that subjects in a securities market can learn to consider the informational content of their opponent's actions. Kagel and Levin (1986) found significantly more "learning" in their study of the winner's curse in an auction context. In addition, their optimism quoted at the beginning of this paper clarifies their view that subjects would learn to avoid the winner's curse in any specific context with a reasonable amount of feedback. While one can argue that the results would change with more trials and higher incentives, there is no limit to the use of this speculation. The fact remains that our subjects failed to learn in an environment that has led virtually all audiences exposed to this experiment to predict learning within 20 trials.

We argue that a fundamental problem with learning the correct response in our bilateral winner's curse task, and in real-world bilateral winner's curse tasks, is the inherent variability in the feedback. Tversky and Kahneman (1986) noted that variability in real-world environments degrades the quality of feedback. In our task, the subject wins money one-third of the time that the target accepts the offer. This positive feedback can keep a bidder bidding in the absence of the appropriate normative logic. In contrast, in Kagel and Levin's auctions, the frequency of winning is far rarer, leading to the lesson "you can't win at this game." Thus, there is no evidence that Kagel and Levin's subjects are any better at obtaining a strategic conceptualization of the situation (Neale and Northcraft, 1990), only that "you can't win at this game if you make aggressive bids." Furthermore, some of the learning observed in their markets results not because subjects began to understand the market, but because the most aggressive and least rational individuals are likely to go bankrupt and be forced to leave the market because of their prior losses.

This raises a fundamental issue of what is being learned in multitrial games. One would like to think that subjects are learning rational behavior in some generalizable form. However, an alternative is that they learn the right answer without necessarily learning the correct logic. If everyone loses in a specific game, it is easy to "learn" not to play that game. This would leave the decisionmaker ill-equipped if the environment changes or if the decisionmaker changes to a different decision task. Dyer, Kagel, and Levin (1987) studied a group of construction managers who routinely participated in low-bid auctions. In a series of low-bid auctions they found that the managers did no better than student subjects. That managers were presumably able to avoid the winner's curse in business shows that they had learned the strategy without understanding why the strategy works. Kagel and Levin (1986) reach a similar conclusion about their subjects who did learn. Learning the correct response in noisier environments may be beyond the capabilities of most individuals. Brehmer (1980) found that learning cue–outcome relationships is much more difficult under uncertainty.

One criticism of this experiment is its artificiality. The buyer has very poor information. The seller has perfect information. The transaction occurs in an artificial take-it-or-leave-it final offer form. No face-to-face negotiation is allowed. While we make no claim about the realism of the task, we believe that this artificial task is useful for understanding the nature of the underlying decisions of the subjects. Obviously, the real world rarely offers the opportunity to collect repeated trials on the same decisionmaker in an environment where a rational decision can be identified. Thus, the artificiality is needed.

Despite the artificiality of the experimental task, it is easy to see the applicability of the central decision bias in this paper to many real-world contexts. Consider the following situations:

> You are in a foreign land. You see a ruby in a marketplace. You know a little about gems and assess the value of this gem at $5000. You offer the merchant $1000. He grabs your money and hands you the stone. How do you feel?

> You accept a new faculty position in a new city. You know very little about the real estate market in this city. You spend a weekend looking at the housing market. You make an offer, and it is immediately accepted. Did you make a good purchase?

In both situations, you obtain information by the acceptance of your offer. Most individuals do not consider this potential information in formulating their offer. What do you know once your offer is accepted? Perhaps that the value of the commodity was in the tail of the distribution of your assessment of that commodity. The seller is most likely to accept your offer when his or her confidential information suggests that your assessment of the true value is higher than reality. Obviously, this logic applies to any situation with asymmetric information, including acquisitions where the target knows more about the target than the acquirer can expect to know.

The limited results of the role-switching experiment provides mild laboratory support for a real-world phenomenon. It shows that experience in each role in a decision-making situation can allow people to make better decisions. This happens not because role-switching allows people to decrease the amount of uncertainty in the environment, but because it helps people focus on their adversary's decisions. This focus takes the form of both realizing the importance of their adversary's decisions, but also of understanding how their adversary makes decisions. Thus, it aids people in becoming more rational in a game-theoretic sense.

In conclusion, this study attempts to add to our knowledge of the winner's curse and to clarify the seriousness of this problem for individual decisionmakers and for economic theory. The results suggest a more resistant strain of irrational decision-making than expected by economic theory, or even by critics of economic theory (Tversky and Kahneman, 1986). We need to improve our models of decision-making to develop a viable descriptive theory of negotiator behavior.

APPENDIX 1

Acquiring a Company

In the following exercise you will represent Company A (the acquirer), which is currently considering acquiring Company T (the target) by means of a tender offer. You plan to tender in cash for 100% of the Company T's shares but are unsure of how high a price to offer. The main complication is this: the value of Company T depends directly on the outcome of a major oil exploration project it is currently undertaking. Indeed the very viability of Company T depends on the exploration outcome. If the project fails, the company under current management will be worth nothing—$0/share. But if the project succeeds, the value of the company under current management could be as high as $100/share. All share values between $0 and $100 are considered equally likely. By all estimates, the company will be worth considerably more in the hands of Company A than under current management. In fact, whatever the ultimate value under current management, *the company will be worth 50% more under the management of Company A than under Company T*. If the project fails, the company is worth $0 per share under either management. If the exploration project generates a $50/share value under current management, the value under Company A is $75/share. Similarly, a $100/share value under Company T implies a $150/share value under Company A, and so on.

The board of directors of Company A has asked you to determine the price they should offer for Company T's shares. This offer must be made *now*, *before* the outcome of the drilling project is known. From all indications, Company T would be happy to be acquired by Company A, *provided it is at a profitable price*. (Bids equal to or greater than the value of the firm under current management will be accepted.) Moreover, Company T wishes to avoid, at all cost, the potential of a takeover bid by any other firm. You expect Company T to delay a decision on your bid until the results of the project are in, then accept or reject your offer before the news of the drilling results reaches the press.

Thus, *you (Company A) will not know the results of the exploration project when submitting your price offer, but Company T will know the results when deciding whether or not to accept your offer. In addition, Company T is expected to accept any offer by Company A that is greater than or equal to the (per share) value of the company under current management.*

As the representative of Company A, you are deliberating over price offers in the range of $0/share (this is tantamount to making no offer at all) to $150/share. Your bid should be expressed in even dollar amounts. You will have a chance to bid on a company similar to Company T every year for the next 20 years.

Company A's assets are currently worth $600. You will have 20 chances to bid on Company T in order to increase the amount of Company A's (and thus your) assets. If in any year you bid less than the value of the company under current management your bid will be rejected and your assets will neither increase nor decrease. If you bid more than this value than your bid will be accepted and your assets will change by the difference between the value under Company A's management and your bid.

You are being paid on a performance basis at the rate of 1 cent on the dollar. This means that if you end up with $600 in assets at the end of the experiment you will be paid $6. Likewise, if you end up with $800 in assets at the end of the experiment you will be paid $8. Notice that acquiring the company is a neutral event—your performance will be judged only on the value of your assets at the end of this exercise.

You may refer back to these instructions at any time during exercise. Feel free to mark on them—they are yours to keep.

Please formulate your first period bid before turning on the computer.

APPENDIX 2
Verbal Instructions

There are two things which I would like to stress before you begin the experiment.

First, the instructions tell you that "you will have a chance to bid on a company similar to Company T every year for the next 20 years." By this we mean 20 chances to bid for different and independent companies. The true value of each company is equally likely to be any value between 0 and 100. The values of the 20 companies are randomly determined by the computer and are statistically independent. This means that knowing the value of the company or companies in any previous year or years gives you *no* information about what the value will be this year. This means, for example, that if you observe a high value one year you *should not* believe either that there is a trend for companies to have high values, nor that "the law of averages" will cause the value in the next year to be low.

Second, the instructions tell you "acquiring the company is a neutral event—your performance will be judged only on the value of your assets at the end of the experiment." This means that you should not care about the number of companies that you acquire for any reason other than the fact that acquiring a company will either increase or decrease the value of your assets.

APPENDIX 3
Protocol Analysis

Protocol code/category		Learners (N = 2)	Nonlearners (N = 19)
Naive			
1	Assume value of company	0	2
4	Bad hypothetical	0	12

N1	Improper understanding of probability	0	7
N2	Time specific risk attitude	0	6
N3	Guessing/Gambling assumption	0	12
N4	Naive reaction to feedback	0	3
N5	Naive reaction to level of assets	0	11
Good			
6	Dealer knows more	0	2
7	Don't have to buy	2	1
10	Specific hypothetical	2	3
11	Generalized hypothetical	2	0
N6	Proper understanding of probability	1	3
Neutral			
12	50% more to me	0	7
13	Maximize value to me	1	3
16	Median range value	0	10
N8	No reaction to feedback	2	5
N9	Take practice tries	1	2

Note. Numbered codes were taken from Carroll et al. (in press). Codes beginning with "N" were added to capture statements specific to many trial experiments with this negotiation problem.

REFERENCES

Akerlof, G. (August 1970). The market for lemons: Qualitative uncertainty and the market mechanism. *Quarterly Journal of Economics,* 488–500.

Bazerman, M. H., and Carroll, J. S. (1987). Negotiator cognition. In L. L. Cummings & B. M. Staw (Eds.), *Research in organizational behavior* (Vol. IX). Greenwich, CT: JAI Press.

Bazerman, M. H., Magliozzi, T., & Neale, M. A. (1985). The acquisition of an integrative response in a competitive market. *Organizational Behavior and Human Performance,* 34, 294–313.

Bazerman, M. H. and Samuelson, W. F. (1983). "I Won the Auction but don't want the Prize." *Journal of Conflict Resolution,* Vol 27, No. 4, 618–634.

Brehmer, B. (1980). In one word: Not from experience. *Acta Psychologica,* 45, 223–241.

Capen, E. C., Clapp, R. V., & Campbell, W. M. (1971). Competitive bidding in high risk situations. *Journal of Petroleum Technology,* 23, 641–653.

Carroll, J. S., Bazerman, M. H., & Maury, R. (1988). Negotiator cognition: A descriptive approach to negotiators understanding of their opponents. *Organizational Behavior and Human Decision Processes,* 41, 352–370.

Cassing, J., & Douglas, R. W. (July 1980). Implications of the auction mechanism in baseball's free agent draft. *Southern Economic Journal,* 47, 110–121.

Coase, R. (October 1960). The problem of social cost. *Journal of Law and Economics,* 3, 1–44.

Dyer, D., Kagel, J. H., & Levin, D. (1987). *The winner's curse in low price auctions.* Unpublished manuscript, University of Houston.

22   BALL, BAZERMAN, AND CARROLL

Farber, H. S. (April 1981). Splitting-the-difference in interest arbitration. *Industrial and Labor Relations Review*, 35, 70–77.

Fundenberg, D., & Tirole, J. (November 1981). Sequential bargaining with incomplete information. *Review of Economic Studies*, 50, 221–248.

Hoffman, E., & Spitzer, M. L. (April 1982). The Coase theorem: some experimental evidence. *Journal of Law and Economics*, 25, 73–98.

Hogarth, R. H. (1981). *Judgment and choice: The psychology of decision*. New York: Wiley.

Kagel, J. H., & Levin, D. (1986). The winner's curse and public information in common value auctions. *American Economic Review*, 76, 894–920.

Kahneman, D., & Tversky, A. (1979). Prospect theory: An analysis of decision under risk. *Econometrica*, 47, 263–291.

Neale, M. A., & Bazerman, M. H. (1983). The effect of perspective taking ability under alternative forms of arbitration on the negotiation process. *Industrial and Labor Relations Review*, 33, 378–388.

Neale, M. A., & Northcraft, G. B. (1990). Experience, expertise, and decision bias in negotiation: The role of strategic conceptualization. In B. H. Sheppard, M. H. Bazerman, & R. J. Lewicki (Eds.), *Research in negotiations in organizations* (Vol. 2). Greenwich, CT: JAI Press.

Nisbitt, R. E., & Wilson, T. D. (1977). Telling more than we can know: Verbal reports on mental processes. *Psychological Review*, 84, 231–259.

Plott, C. R. (1982). Industrial organization theory and experimental economics. *Journal of Economic Literature*, 20, 1485–1527.

Plott, C. R., & Sunder, S. (1985). Efficiency of experimental markets with insider information: An application of rational-expectations models. *Journal of Political Economy*, 90, 663–698.

Raiffa, H. (1982). *The art and science of negotiation*. Cambridge, MA: Harvard Univ. Press.

Roll, R. (April 1986). The Hubris hypothesis of corporate takeovers. *Journal of Business*, 59, 197–216.

Russo, J. E., Johnson, E. J., & Stephens, D. L. (1986). *The validity of verbal protocols*. Working paper.

Samuelson, W. F., & Bazerman, M. H. (1985). Negotiation under the winner's curse. In V. Smith (Ed.), *Research in experimental economics* (Vol. III). Greenwich, CT: JAI Press.

Smith, V. (December 1982). Microeconomic systems as an experimental science. *American Economic Review*, 72, 923–955.

Staw, B. M. (1976). Knee-deep in the big muddy: A study of escalating commitment to a chosen course of action. *Organizational Behavior and Human Performance*, 16, 27–44.

Staw, B. M. (1981). The escalation of commitment of a course of action. *Academy of Management Review*, 6, 577–587.

Thaler, R. (1980). Toward a positive theory of consumer choice. *Journal of Economic Behavior and Organization*, 1, 39–60.

Thompson, L. L., & Hastie, R. (1990). Negotiator's perceptions of the negotiation process. In B. H. Sheppard, M. H. Bazerman, & R. J. Lewicki (Eds.), *Research in negotiation in organizations* (Vol. 2). Greenwich, CT: JAI Press.

Tracy, J. S. (January 1986). *An empirical test of an asymmetric information model of strikes*. Mimeo.

Tversky, A., & Kahneman, D. (1974). Judgment under uncertainty: Heuristics and biases. *Science*, 185, 1124–1131.

Tversky, A., & Kahneman, D. (October 1986). Rational choice and the framing of decisions. *The Journal of Business*, 59, 251–284.

RECEIVED: February 10, 1988

[26]

Timid Choices and Bold Forecasts:
A Cognitive Perspective on Risk Taking

Daniel Kahneman • Dan Lovallo

Department of Psychology, University of California, Berkeley, California 94720
Walter A. Haas School of Business Administration, University of California, Berkeley, California 94720

D ecision makers have a strong tendency to consider problems as unique. They isolate the current choice from future opportunities and neglect the statistics of the past in evaluating current plans. Overly cautious attitudes to risk result from a failure to appreciate the effects of statistical aggregation in mitigating relative risk. Overly optimistic forecasts result from the adoption of an inside view of the problem, which anchors predictions on plans and scenarios. The conflicting biases are documented in psychological research. Possible implications for decision making in organizations are examined.
(*Decision Making; Risk; Forecasting; Managerial Cognition*)

The thesis of this essay is that decision makers are excessively prone to treat problems as unique, neglecting both the statistics of the past and the multiple opportunities of the future. In part as a result, they are susceptible to two biases, which we label isolation errors: their forecasts of future outcomes are often anchored on plans and scenarios of success rather than on past results, and are therefore overly optimistic; their evaluations of single risky prospects neglect the possibilities of pooling risks and are therefore overly timid. We argue that the balance of the two isolation errors affects the risk-taking propensities of individuals and organizations.

The cognitive analysis of risk taking that we sketch differs from the standard rational model of economics and also from managers' view of their own activities. The rational model describes business decisions as choices among gambles with financial outcomes, and assumes that managers' judgments of the odds are Bayesian, and that their choices maximize expected utility. In this model, uncontrollable risks are acknowledged and accepted because they are compensated by chances of gain. As March and Shapira (1987) reported in a well-known essay, managers reject this interpretation of their role, preferring to view risk as a challenge to be overcome by the exercise of skill and choice as a commitment to a goal. Although managers do not deny the possibility of failure, their idealized self-image is not a gambler but a prudent and determined agent, who is in control of both people and events.

The cognitive analysis accepts choice between gambles as a model of decision making, but does not adopt rationality as a maintained hypothesis. The gambling metaphor is apt because the consequences of most decisions are uncertain, and because each option could in principle be described as a probability distribution over outcomes. However, rather than suppose that decision makers are Bayesian forecasters and optimal gamblers, we shall describe them as subject to the conflicting biases of unjustified optimism and unreasonable risk aversion. It is the optimistic denial of uncontrollable uncertainty that accounts for managers' views of themselves as prudent risk takers, and for their rejection of gambling as a model of what they do.

Our essay develops this analysis of forecasting and choice and explores its implications for organizational decisions. The target domain for applications includes choices about potentially attractive options that decision makers consider significant and to which they are willing to devote forecasting and planning resources. Examples may be capital investment projects, new products, or acquisitions. For reasons that will become obvious, our

0025-1909/93/3901/0017$01.25
Copyright © 1993, The Institute of Management Sciences

critique of excessive risk aversion is most likely to apply to decisions of intermediate size: large enough to matter for the organization, but not so large as to be truly unique, or potentially fatal. Of course, such decisions could be perceived as both unique and potentially fatal by the executive who makes them. Two other restrictions on the present treatment should be mentioned at the outset. First, we do not deal with decisions that the organization explicitly treats as routinely repeated. Opportunities for learning and for statistical aggregation exist when closely similar problems are frequently encountered, especially if the outcomes of decisions are quickly known and provide unequivocal feedback; competent management will ensure that these opportunities are exploited. Second, we do not deal with decisions made under severely adverse conditions, when all options are undesirable. These are situations in which high-risk gambles are often preferred to the acceptance of sure losses (Kahneman and Tversky 1979a), and in which commitments often escalate and sunk costs dominate decisions (Staw and Ross 1989). We restrict the treatment to choices among options that can be considered attractive, although risky. For this class of projects we predict that there will be a general tendency to underestimate actual risks, and a general reluctance to accept significant risks once they are acknowledged.

Timid Choices

We begin by reviewing three hypotheses about individual preferences for risky prospects.

Risk Aversion. The first hypothesis is a commonplace: most people are generally risk averse, normally preferring a sure thing to a gamble of equal expected value, and a gamble of low variance over a riskier prospect. There are two important exceptions to risk aversion. First, many people are willing to pay more for lottery tickets than their expected value. Second, studies of individual choice have shown that managers, like other people, are risk-seeking in the domain of losses (Bateman and Zeithaml 1989, Fishburn and Kochenberger 1979, Laughhunn et al. 1980).[1] Except for these

cases, and for the behavior of addictive gamblers, risk aversion is prevalent in choices between favorable prospects with known probabilities. This result has been confirmed in numerous studies, including some in which the subjects were executives (MacCrimmon and Wehrung 1986, Swalm 1966).[2]

The standard interpretation of risk aversion is decreasing marginal utility of gains. Prospect theory (Kahneman and Tversky 1979a; Tversky and Kahneman 1986, 1992) introduced two other causes: the certainty effect and loss aversion. The certainty effect is a sharp discrepancy between the weights that are attached to sure gains and to highly probable gains in the evaluation of prospects. In a recent study of preferences for gambles the decision weight for a probability of 0.95 was approximately 0.80 (Tversky and Kahneman 1992). Loss aversion refers to the observation that losses and disadvantages are weighted more than gains and advantages. Loss aversion affects decision making in numerous ways, in riskless as well as in risky contexts. It favors inaction over action and the status quo over any alternatives, because the disadvantages of these alternatives are evaluated as losses and are therefore weighted more than their advantages (Kahneman et al. 1991, Samuelson and Zeckhauser 1988, Tversky and Kahneman 1991). Loss aversion strongly favors the avoidance of risks. The coefficient of loss aversion was estimated as about 2 in the Tversky-Kahneman experiment, and coefficients in the range of 2 to 2.5 have been observed in several studies, with both risky and riskless prospects (for reviews, see Kahneman, Knetsch and Thaler 1991; Tversky and Kahneman 1991).

Near-Proportionality. A second important generalization about risk attitudes is that, to a good first approximation, people are proportionately risk averse: cash equivalents for gambles of increasing size are (not quite) proportional to the stakes. Readers may find it instructive to work out their cash equivalent for a 0.50 chance to win $100, then $1,000, and up to $100,000. Most readers will find that their cash equivalent increases by a factor of less than 1,000 over that range, but most will also find that the factor is more than 700. Exact

---

[1] Observed correlations between accounting variability and mean return have also been interpreted as evidence of risk-seeking by unsuccessful firms (Bowman 1982, Fiegenbaum 1990, Fiegenbaum and Thomas 1988), but this interpretation is controversial (Ruefli 1990).

[2] A possible exception is a study by Wehrung (1989), which reported risk-neutral preferences for favorable prospects in a sample of executives in oil companies.

proportionality for wholly positive prospects would imply that value is a power function, $u(x) = x^a$, where x is the amount of gain (Keeney and Raiffa 1976). In a recent study of preferences for gambles (Tversky and Kahneman 1992), a power function provided a good approximation to the data over almost two orders of magnitude, and the deviations were systematic: cash equivalents increased slightly more slowly than prizes.

Much earlier, Swalm (1966) had compared executives whose planning horizons, defined as twice the maximum amount they might recommend be spent in one year, ranged from $50,000 to $24,000,000. He measured their utility functions by testing the acceptability of mixed gambles, and observed that the functions of managers at different levels were quite similar when expressed relative to their planning horizons. The point on which we focus in this article is that there is almost as much risk aversion when stakes are small as when they are large. This is unreasonable on two grounds: (i) small gambles do not raise issues of survival or ruin, which provide a rationale for aversion to large risks; (ii) small gambles are usually more common, offering more opportunities for the risk-reducing effects of statistical aggregation.

Narrow Decision Frames. The third generalization is that people tend to consider decision problems one at a time, often isolating the current problem from other choices that may be pending, as well as from future opportunities to make similar decisions. The following example (from Tversky and Kahneman 1986) illustrates an extreme form of narrow framing:

> Imagine that you face the following pair of concurrent decisions. First examine both decisions, then indicate the options you prefer.
>
> Decision (i) Choose between:
> (A) a sure gain of $240 (84%)
> (B) 25% chance to gain $1000 and 75% chance to gain nothing (16%)
>
> Decision (ii) Choose between:
> (C) a sure loss of $750 (13%)
> (D) 75% chance to lose $1000 and 25% chance to lose nothing (87%)

The percentage of respondents choosing each option is shown in parentheses. As many readers may have discovered for themselves, the suggestion that the two problems should be considered concurrently has no ef-

fect on preferences, which exhibit the common pattern of risk aversion when options are favorable, and risk seeking when options are aversive. Most respondents prefer the conjunction of options A & D over other combinations of options. These preferences are intuitively compelling, and there is no obvious reason to suspect that they could lead to trouble. However, simple arithmetic shows that the conjunction of preferred options A & D is dominated by the conjunction of rejected options B & C. The combined options are as follows:

> A & D: 25% chance to win $240 and 75% chance to lose $760,
> B & C: 25% chance to win $250 and 75% chance to lose $750.

A decision maker who is risk averse in some situations and risk seeking in others ends up paying a premium to avoid some risks and a premium to obtain others. Because the outcomes are ultimately combined, these payments may be unsound. For a more realistic example, consider two divisions of a company that face separate decision problems.[3] One is in bad posture and faces a choice between a sure loss and a high probability of a larger loss; the other division faces a favorable choice. The natural bent of intuition will favor a risk-seeking solution for one and a risk-averse choice for the other, but the conjunction could be poor policy. The overall interests of the company are better served by aggregating the problems than by segregating them, and by a policy that is generally more risk-neutral than intuitive preferences.

People often express different preferences when considering a single play or multiple plays of the same gamble. In a well-known problem devised by Samuelson (1963), many respondents state that they would reject a single play of a gamble in which they have equal chances to win $200 or to lose $100, but would accept multiple plays of that gamble, especially when the compound distribution of outcomes is made explicit (Redelmeier and Tversky 1992). The question of whether this pattern of preferences is consistent with utility theory, and with particular utility functions for wealth has been discussed on several occasions (e.g., Lopes 1981, Tversky and Bar-Hillel 1983). The argument that emerges from these discussions can be summarized as "If you wish to obey the axioms of utility

---

[3] We are endebted to Amos Tversky for this example.

theory and would accept multiple plays, then it is logically inconsistent for you to turn down a single play". We focus on another observation: the near-certainty that the individual who is now offered a single play of the Samuelson gamble is not really facing her last opportunity to accept or reject a gamble of positive expected value. This suggests a slightly different argument: "If you would accept multiple plays, then you should accept the single one that is offered now, because it is very probable that other bets of the same kind will be offered to you later". A frame that includes future opportunities reduces the difference between the two versions of Samuelson's problem, because a rational individual who is offered a single gamble will adopt a policy for $m + 1$ such gambles, where m is the number of similar opportunities expected within the planning horizon. Will people spontaneously adopt such a broad frame? A plausible hypothesis, supported by the evidence for narrow framing in concurrent decisions and by the pattern of answers to Samuelson's problems, is that expectations about risky opportunities of the future are simply ignored when decisions are made.

It is generally recognized that a broad view of decision problems is an essential requirement of rational decision making. There are several ways of broadening the decision frame. Thus, decision analysts commonly prescribe that concurrent choices should be aggregated before a decision is made, and that outcomes should be evaluated in terms of final assets (wealth), rather than in terms of the gains and losses associated with each move. The recommended practice is to include estimates of future earnings in the assessment of wealth. Although this point has attracted little attention in the decision literature, the wealth of an agent or organization therefore includes future risky choices, and depends on the decisions that the decision maker anticipates making when these choices arise.[4] The decision frame should be broadened to include these uncertainties: neglect of future risky opportunities will lead to decisions that are not optimal, as evaluated by the agent's own utility function. As we show next, the costs of neglecting future

---

[4] Two agents that have the same current holdings and face the same series of risky choices do not have the same wealth if they have different attitudes to risk and expect to make different decisions. For formal discussions of choice in the presence of unresolved uncertainty, see Kreps (1988) and Spence and Zeckhauser (1972).

opportunities are especially severe when options are evaluated in terms of gains and losses, which is what people usually do.

The Costs of Isolation

The present section explores some consequences of incorporating future choice opportunities into current decisions. We start from an idealized utility function which explains people's proportional risk preferences for single gambles. We then compute the preferences that this function implies when the horizon expands to include a portfolio of gambles.

Consider an individual who evaluates outcomes as gains and losses, and who maximizes expected utility in these terms. This decision maker is risk-averse in the domain of gains, risk-seeking in the domain of losses, loss-averse, and her risky choices exhibit perfect proportionality. She is indifferent between a 0.50 chance to win $1,000 and a sure gain of $300 (also between 0.50 chance to win $10,000 and $3,000 for sure) and she is also indifferent between the status quo and a gamble that offers equal chances to win $250 or to lose $100. The aversion to risk exhibited by this individual is above the median of respondents in laboratory studies, but well within the range of observed values. For the sake of simple exposition we ignore all probability distortions and attribute the risk preferences of the individual entirely to the shape of her utility function for gains and losses. The preferences we have assumed imply that the individual's utility for gains is described by a power function with an exponent of 0.575 and that the function in the domain of losses is the mirror image of the function for gains, after expansion of the X-axis by a factor of 2.5 (Tversky and Kahneman 1991). The illustrative function was chosen to highlight our main conclusion: with proportional risk attitudes, even the most extreme risk aversion on individual problems quickly vanishes when gambles are considered part of a portfolio.

The power utility function is decreasingly risk averse, and the decrease is quite rapid. Thus, a proportionately risk averse individual who values a 0.50 chance to win $100 at $30 will value a gamble that offers equal chances to win either $1,000 or $1,100 at $1,049. This preference is intuitively acceptable, indicating again that the power function is a good description of the utility of outcomes for single gambles considered in isolation. The power function fits the psychophysical relation of subjective magnitude to physical magnitude in many other contexts (Stevens 1975).

To appreciate the effects of even modest aggregation with this utility function, assume that the individual owns three independent gambles:

> one gamble with a 0.50 chance to win $500,
> two gambles, each with a 0.50 chance to win $250.

Simple arithmetic yields the compound gamble:

> 0.125 chance to win $1,000, and 0.25 to win $750, $500, and $250.

If this individual applies the correct probabilities to her utility function, this portfolio will be worth $433 to her. This should be her minimum selling price if she owns the gamble, her cash equivalent if she has to choose between the portfolio of gambles and cash. In contrast, the sum of the cash equivalents of the gambles considered one at a time is only $300. The certainty premium the individual would pay has dropped from 40% to 13% of expected value. By the individual's own utility function, the cost of considering these gambles in isolation is 27% of their expected value, surely more than any rational decision maker should be willing to pay for whatever mental economy this isolation achieves.

The power of aggregation to overcome loss aversion is equally impressive. As already noted, our decision maker is indifferent between accepting or rejecting a gamble that offers a 0.50 chance to win $250 and a 0.50 chance to lose $100. However, she would value the opportunity to play two of these gambles at $45, and six gambles at $304. Note that the average incremental value of adding the third to the sixth gamble is $65, quite close to the EV of $75, although each gamble is worth nothing on its own.

Finally, we note that decisions about single gambles will no longer appear risk-proportional when gambles are evaluated in the context of a portfolio, even if the utility function has that property. Suppose the individual now owns a set of eleven gambles:

> one gamble with a 0.50 chance to win $1,000,
> ten gambles, each with a 0.50 chances to win $100.

The expected value of the set is $1,000. If the gambles were considered one at a time, the sum of their cash

equivalents would be only $600. With proper aggregation, however, the selling price for the package should be $934. Now suppose the decision maker considers trading only one of the gambles. After selling a gamble for an amount X, she retains a reduced compound gamble in which the constant X is added to each outcome. The decision maker, of course, will only sell if the value of the new gamble is at least equal to the value of the original portfolio. The computed selling price for the larger gamble is $440, and the selling price for one of the smaller gambles is $49. Note that the premium given up to avoid the risk is 12% of expected value for the large gamble, but only 2% for the small one. A rational decision maker who applies a proportionately risk averse utility function to aggregate outcomes will set cash equivalents closer to risk neutrality for small gambles than for large ones.

As these elementary examples illustrate, the common attitude of strong (and proportional) aversion to risk and to losses entails a risk policy that quickly approaches neutrality as the portfolio is extended.[5] Because possibilities of aggregation over future decisions always exist for an ongoing concern, and because the chances for aggregation are likely to be inversely correlated with the size of the problem, the near-proportionality of risk attitudes for gambles of varying sizes is logically incoherent, and the extreme risk aversion observed for prospects that are small relative to assets is unreasonable. To rationalize observed preferences one must assume that the decision maker approaches each choice problem as if it were her last—there seems to be no relevant tomorrow. It is somewhat surprising that the debate on the rationality of risky decisions has focused almost exclusively on the curiosities of the Allais and Ellsberg paradoxes, instead of on simpler observations,

---

[5] The conclusions of the present section do not critically depend on the assumption of expected utility theory, that the decision maker weights outcomes by their probabilities. All the calculations reported above were repeated using cumulative prospect theory (Tversky and Kahneman 1992) with plausible parameters ($a = 0.73$; $b = c = 0.6$ and a loss aversion coefficient of 2.5). Because extreme outcomes are assigned greater weight in prospect theory than in the expected utility model, the mitigation of risk aversion as the portfolio expands is somewhat slower. Additionally, the risk seeking that prospect theory predicts for single low-probability positive gambles is replaced by risk aversion for repeated gambles.

such as the extraordinary myopia implied by extreme and nearly proportional risk aversion.

Risk Taking in Organizations: Implications and Speculations

The preceding sections discussed evidence that people, when faced with explicitly probabilistic prospects in experimental situations, tend to frame their decision problem narrowly, have near-proportional risk attitudes, and are as a consequence excessively risk averse in small decisions, where they ignore the effects of aggregation. Extending these ideas to business decisions is necessarily speculative, because the attitudes to risk that are implicit in such decisions are not easily measured. One way to approach this problem is by asking whether the organizational context in which many business decisions are made is more likely to enhance or to inhibit risk aversion, narrow framing and near-proportionality. We examine this question in the present section.

Risk Aversion. There is little reason to believe that the factors that produce risk aversion in the personal evaluation of explicit gambles are neutralized in the context of managerial decisions. For example, attempts to measure the utility that executives attach to gains and losses of their firm suggest that the principle of decreasing marginal values applies to these outcomes (MacCrimmon and Wehrung 1986, Swalm 1966). The underweighting of probable gains in comparisons with sure ones, known as the certainty effect, is also unlikely to vanish in managerial decisions. The experimental evidence indicates that the certainty effect is not eliminated when probabilities are vague or ambiguous, as they are in most real-life situations, and the effect may even be enhanced (Curley et al. 1986, Hogarth and Einhorn 1990). We suspect that the effect may become even stronger when a choice becomes a subject of debate, as is commonly the case in managerial decisions: the rhetoric of prudent decision making favors the certainty effect, because an argument that rests on mere probability is always open to doubt.

Perhaps the most important cause of risk aversion is loss aversion, the discrepancy between the weights that are attached to losses and to gains in evaluating prospects. Loss aversion is not mitigated when decisions are made in an organizational context. On the contrary, the asymmetry between credit and blame may enhance the

asymmetry between gains and losses in the decision maker's utilities. The evidence indicates that the pressures of accountability and personal responsibility increase the status quo bias and other manifestations of loss aversion. Decision makers become more risk averse when they expect their choices to be reviewed by others (Tetlock and Boettger 1991) and they are extremely reluctant to accept responsibility for even a small increase in the probability of a disaster (Viscusi et al. 1987). Swalm (1966) noted that managers appear to have an excessive aversion to any outcome that could yield a net loss, citing the example of a manager in a firm described as "an industrial giant", who would decline to pursue a project that has a 50–50 chance of either making for his company a gain of \$300,000 or losing \$60,000. Swalm hypothesized that the steep slopes of utility functions in the domain of losses may be due to control procedures that bias managers against choices that might lead to losses. This interpretation seems appropriate since "several respondents stated quite clearly that they were aware that their choices were not in the best interests of the company, but that they felt them to be in their own best interests as aspiring executives."

We conclude that the forces that produce risk aversion in experimental studies of individual choice may be even stronger in the managerial context. Note, however, that we do not claim that an objective observer would describe managerial decisions as generally risk averse. The second part of this essay will argue that decisions are often based on optimistic assessments of the chances of success, and are therefore objectively riskier than the decision makers perceive them to be. Our hypotheses about risk in managerial decisions are: (i) in a generally favorable context, the threshold for accepting risk will be high, and acceptable options will be *subjectively* perceived as carrying low risk, (ii) for problems viewed in isolation the willingness to take risks is likely to be approximately constant for decisions that vary greatly in size, and (iii) decisions will be narrowly framed even when they could be viewed as instances of a category of similar decisions. As a consequence, we predict (iv) an imbalance in the risks that the organization accepts in large and in small problems, such that relative risk aversion is lower for the aggregate of small decisions than for the aggregate of large decisions. These hypotheses are restricted to essentially favorable situations,

22

which often yield risk aversion in laboratory studies. We specifically exclude situations in which risk seeking is common, such as choices between essentially negative options, or choices that involve small chances of large gain.

Narrow Framing. We have suggested that people tend to make decisions one at a time, and in particular that they are prone to neglect the relevance of future decision opportunities. For both individuals and organizations, the adoption of a broader frame and of a consistent risk policy depends on two conditions: (i) an ability to group together problems that are superficially different; (ii) an appropriate procedure for evaluating outcomes and the quality of performance.

A consistent risk policy can only be maintained if the recurrent problems to which the policy applies are recognized as such. This is sometimes easy: competent organizations will identify obvious recurring questions—for example, whether or not to purchase insurance for a company vehicle—and will adopt policies for such questions. The task is more complex when each decision problem has many unique features, as might be the case for acquisitions or new product development. The explicit adoption of a broad frame will then require the use of an abstract language that highlights the important common dimensions of diverse decision problems. Formal decision analysis provides such a language, in which outcomes are expressed in money and uncertainty is quantified as probability. Other abstract languages could be used for the same purpose. As practitioners of decision analysis well know, however, the use of an abstract language conflicts with a natural tendency to describe each problem in its own terms. Abstraction necessarily involves a loss of subtlety and specificity, and the summary descriptions that permit projects to be compared almost always appear superficial and inadequate.

From the point of the individual executive who faces a succession of decisions, the maintenance of a broad decision frame also depends on how her performance will be evaluated, and on the frequency of performance reviews. For a schematic illustration, assume that reviews occur at predictable points in the sequence of decisions and outcomes, and that the executive's outcomes are determined by the *value* of the firm's outcomes since the last review. Suppose the evaluation

function is identical to the utility function introduced in the preceding numerical examples: the credit for gaining 2.5 units and the blame for losing 1 unit just cancel out. With this utility function, a single gamble that offers equal probabilities to win 2 units or to lose 1 unit will not be acceptable if performance is evaluated on that gamble by itself. The decision will not change even if the manager knows that there will be a second opportunity to play the same gamble. However, if the evaluation of outcomes and the assignment of credit and blame can be deferred until the gamble has been played twice, the probability that the review will be negative drops from 0.50 to 0.25 and the compound gamble will be accepted. As this example illustrates, reducing the frequency of evaluations can mitigate the inhibiting effects of loss aversion on risk taking, as well as other manifestations of myopic discounting.

The attitude that "you win a few and you lose a few" could be recommended as an antidote to narrow framing, because it suggests that the outcomes of a set of separable decisions should be aggregated before evaluation. However, the implied tolerance for "losing a few" may conflict with other managerial imperatives, including the setting of high standards and the maintenance of tight supervision. By the same token, of course, narrow framing and excessive risk aversion may be unintended consequences of excessive insistence on measurable short-term successes. A plausible hypothesis is that the adoption of a broad frame of evaluation is most natural when the expected rate of success is low for each attempt, as in drilling for oil or in pharmaceutical development.[6] The procedures of performance evaluation that have evolved in these industries could provide a useful model for other attempts to maintain consistent risk policies.

Near Proportionality of Risk Attitudes. Many executives in a hierarchical organization have two distinct decision tasks: they make risky choices on behalf of the organization, and they supervise several subordinates who also make decisions. For analytical purposes, the options chosen by subordinates can be treated as independent (or imperfectly correlated) gambles, which usually involve smaller stakes than the decisions made personally by the superior. A problem of risk aggre-

[6] We owe this hypothesis to Richard Thaler.

gation inevitably arises, and we conjecture that solving it efficiently may be quite difficult.

To begin, ignore the supervisory function and assume that all decisions are made independently, with narrow framing. If all decision makers apply the same nearly-proportional risk attitudes (as suggested by Swalm 1966), an unbalanced set of choices will be made: The aggregate of the subordinates' decisions will be more risk averse than the supervisor's own decisions on larger problems—which in turn are more risk averse than her global utility for the portfolio, rationally evaluated. As we saw in an earlier section, the costs of such inconsistencies in risk attitudes can be quite high.

Clearly, one of the goals of the executive should be to avoid the potential inefficiency, by applying a consistent policy to risky choices and to those she supervises—and the consistent policy is *not* one of proportional risk aversion. As was seen earlier, a rational executive who considers a portfolio consisting of one large gamble (which she chose herself) and ten smaller gambles (presumably chosen by subordinates) should be considerably more risk averse in valuing the large gamble than in valuing any one of the smaller gambles. The counter-intuitive implication of this analysis is that, in a generally favorable context, an executive should encourage subordinates to adopt a higher level of risk-acceptance than the level with which she feels comfortable. This is necessary to overcome the costly effects of the (probable) insensitivity of her intuitive preferences to recurrence and aggregation. We suspect that many executives will resist this recommendation, which contradicts the common belief that accepting risks is both the duty and the prerogative of higher management.

For several reasons, narrow framing and near-proportionality could be difficult to avoid in a hierarchical organization. First, many decisions are both unique and large at the level at which they are initially made. The usual aversion to risk is likely to prevail in such decisions, even if from the point of view of the firm they could be categorized as recurrent and moderately small. Second, it appears unfair for a supervisor to urge acceptance of a risk that a subordinate is inclined to reject—especially because the consequences of failure are likely to be more severe for the subordinate.

In summary, we have drawn on three psychological principles to derive the prediction that the risk attitudes that govern decisions of different sizes may not be coherent. The analysis suggests that there may be too much aversion to risk in problems of small or moderate size. However, the conclusion that greater risk taking should be encouraged could be premature at this point, because of the suspicion that agents' view of prospects may be systematically biased in an optimistic direction. The combination of a risk-neutral attitude and an optimistic bias could be worse than the combination of unreasonable risk aversion and unjustified optimism. As the next sections show, there is good reason to believe that such a dilemma indeed exists.

Bold Forecasts

Our review of research on individual risk attitudes suggests that the substantial degree of risk to which individuals and organizations willingly expose themselves is unlikely to reflect true acceptance of these risks. The alternative is that people and organizations often expose themselves to risk because they misjudge the odds. We next consider some of the mechanisms that produce the 'bold forecasts' that enable cautious decision makers to take large risks.

Inside and Outside Views

We introduce this discussion by a true story, which illustrates an important cognitive quirk that tends to produce extreme optimism in planning.

> In 1976 one of us (Daniel Kahneman) was involved in a project designed to develop a curriculum for the study of judgment and decision making under uncertainty for high schools in Israel. The project was conducted by a small team of academics and teachers. When the team had been in operation for about a year, with some significant achievements already to its credit, the discussion at one of the team meetings turned to the question of how long the project would take. To make the debate more useful, I asked everyone to indicate on a slip of paper their best estimate of the number of months that would be needed to bring the project to a well-defined stage of completion: a complete draft ready for submission to the Ministry of Education. The estimates, including my own, ranged from 18 to 30 months. At this point I had the idea of turning to one of our members, a distinguished expert in curriculum development, asking him a question phrased about as follows: "We are surely not the only team to have tried to develop a curriculum where none existed before. Please try to recall as many such cases as you can. Think of them as they were in a

stage comparable to ours at present. How long did it take them, from that point, to complete their projects?" After a long silence, something much like the following answer was given, with obvious signs of discomfort: "First, I should say that not all teams that I can think of in a comparable stage ever did complete their task. About 40% of them eventually gave up. Of the remaining, I cannot think of any that was completed in less than seven years, nor of any that took more than ten". In response to a further question, he answered: "No, I cannot think of any relevant factor that distinguishes us favorably from the teams I have been thinking about. Indeed, my impression is that we are slightly below average in terms of our resources and potential".

This story illustrates several of the themes that will be developed in this section.

Two distinct modes of forecasting were applied to the same problem in this incident. The *inside view* of the problem is the one that all participants in the meeting spontaneously adopted. An inside view forecast is generated by focusing on the case at hand, by considering the plan and the obstacles to its completion, by constructing scenarios of future progress, and by extrapolating current trends. The *outside view* is the one that the curriculum expert was encouraged to adopt. It essentially ignores the details of the case at hand, and involves no attempt at detailed forecasting of the future history of the project. Instead, it focuses on the statistics of a class of cases chosen to be similar in relevant respects to the present one. The case at hand is also compared to other members of the class, in an attempt to assess its position in the distribution of outcomes for the class (Kahneman and Tversky 1979b). The distinction between inside and outside views in forecasting is closely related to the distinction drawn earlier between narrow and broad framing of decision problems. The critical question in both contexts is whether a particular problem of forecast or decision is treated as unique, or as an instance of an ensemble of similar problems.

The application of the outside view was particularly simple in this example, because the relevant class for the problem was easy to find and to define. Other cases are more ambiguous. What class should be considered, for example, when a firm considers the probable costs of an investment in a new technology in an unfamiliar domain? Is it the class of ventures in new technologies in the recent history of this firm, or the class of developments most similar to the proposed one, carried out

in other firms? Neither is perfect, and the recommendation would be to try both (Kahneman and Tversky 1979b). It may also be necessary to choose units of measurement that permit comparisons. The ratio of actual spending to planned expenditure is an example of a convenient unit that permits meaningful comparisons across diverse projects.

The inside and outside views draw on different sources of information, and apply different rules to its use. An inside view forecast draws on knowledge of the specifics of the case, the details of the plan that exists, some ideas about likely obstacles and how they might be overcome. In an extreme form, the inside view involves an attempt to sketch a representative scenario that captures the essential elements of the history of the future. In contrast, the outside view is essentially statistical and comparative, and involves no attempt to divine future history at any level of detail.

It should be obvious that when both methods are applied with equal intelligence and skill, the outside view is much more likely to yield a realistic estimate. In general, the future of a long and complex undertaking is simply not foreseeable in detail. The ensemble of possible future histories cannot be defined. Even if this could be done, the ensemble would in most cases be huge, and the probability of any particular scenario negligible.[7] Although some scenarios are more likely or plausible than others, it is a serious error to assume that the outcomes of the most likely scenarios are also the most likely, and that outcomes for which no plausible scenarios come to mind are impossible. In particular, the scenario of flawless execution of the current plan may be much more probable a priori than any scenario for a specific sequence of events that would cause the project to take four times longer than planned. Nevertheless, the less favorable outcome could be more likely overall, because there are so many different ways for things to go wrong. The main advantage of the outside approach to forecasting is that it avoids the snares of scenario thinking (Dawes 1988). The outside view provides some protection against forecasts that are not

[7] For the purposes of this exposition we assume that probabilities exist as a fact about the world. Readers who find this position shocking should transpose the formulation to a more complex one, according to their philosophical taste.

KAHNEMAN AND LOVALLO
Choices and Forecasts

even in the ballpark of reasonable possibilities. It is a conservative approach, which will fail to predict extreme and exceptional events, but will do well with common ones. Furthermore, giving up the attempt to predict extraordinary events is not a great sacrifice when uncertainty is high, because the only way to score 'hits' on such events is to predict large numbers of other extraordinary events that do not materialize.

This discussion of the statistical merits of the outside view sets the stage for our main observation, which is psychological: the inside view is overwhelmingly preferred in intuitive forecasting. The natural way to think about a problem is to bring to bear all one knows about it, with special attention to its unique features. The intellectual detour into the statistics of related cases is seldom chosen spontaneously. Indeed, the relevance of the outside view is sometimes explicitly denied: physicians and lawyers often argue against the application of statistical reasoning to particular cases. In these instances, the preference for the inside view almost bears a moral character. The inside view is valued as a serious attempt to come to grips with the complexities of the unique case at hand, and the outside view is rejected for relying on crude analogy from superficially similar instances. This attitude can be costly in the coin of predictive accuracy.

Three other features of the curriculum story should be mentioned. First, the example illustrates the general rule that consensus on a forecast is not necessarily an indication of its validity: a shared deficiency of reasoning will also yield consensus. Second, we note that the initial intuitive assessment of our curriculum expert was similar to that of other members of the team. This illustrates a more general observation: statistical knowledge that is known to the forecaster will not necessarily be used, or indeed retrieved, when a forecast is made by the inside approach. The literature on the impact of the base rates of outcomes on intuitive predictions supports this conclusion. Many studies have dealt with the task of predicting the profession or the training of an individual on the basis of some personal information and relevant statistical knowledge. For example, most people have some knowledge of the relative sizes of different departments, and could use that knowledge in guessing the field of a student seen at a graduating ceremony. The experimental evidence indicates that base-rate in-

formation that is explicitly mentioned in the problem has some effect on predictions, though usually not as much as it should have (Griffin and Tversky 1992, Lynch and Ofir 1989: for an alternative view see Gigerenzer et al. 1988). When only personal information is explicitly offered, relevant statistical information that is known to the respondent is largely ignored (Kahneman and Tversky 1973, Tversky and Kahneman 1983).

The sequel to the story illustrates a third general observation: facing the facts can be intolerably demoralizing. The participants in the meeting had professional expertise in the logic of forecasting, and none even ventured to question the relevance of the forecast implied by our expert's statistics: an even chance of failure, and a completion time of seven to ten years in case of success. Neither of these outcomes was an acceptable basis for continuing the project, but no one was willing to draw the embarrassing conclusion that it should be scrapped. So, the forecast was quietly dropped from active debate, along with any pretense of long-term planning, and the project went on along its predictably unforeseeable path to eventual completion some eight years later.

The contrast between the inside and outside views has been confirmed in systematic research. One relevant set of studies was concerned with the phenomenon of overconfidence. There is massive evidence for the conclusion that people are generally overconfident in their assignments of probability to their beliefs. Overconfidence is measured by recording the proportion of cases in which statements to which an individual assigned a probability p were actually true. In many studies this proportion has been found to be far lower than p (see Lichtenstein et al. 1982; for a more recent discussion and some instructive exceptions see Griffin and Tversky 1992). Overconfidence is often assessed by presenting general information questions in a multiple-choice format, where the participant chooses the most likely answer and assigns a probability to it. A typical result is that respondents are only correct on about 80% of cases when they describe themselves as "99% sure." People are overconfident in evaluating the accuracy of their beliefs one at a time. It is interesting, however, that there is no evidence of overconfidence bias when respondents are asked after the session to estimate the number of questions for which they picked the correct answer. These global estimates are accurate, or some-what pessimistic (Gigerenzer et al. 1991, Griffin and Tversky 1992). It is evident that people's assessments of their overall accuracy does not control their confidence in particular beliefs. Academics are familiar with a related example: finishing our papers almost always takes us longer than we expected. We all know this and often say so. Why then do we continue to make the same error? Here again, the outside view does not inform judgments of particular cases.

In a compelling example of the contrast between inside and outside views, Cooper et al. (1988) interviewed new entrepreneurs about their chances of success, and also elicited from them estimates of the base rate of success for enterprises of the same kind. Self-assessed chances of success were uncorrelated to objective predictors of success such as college education, prior supervisory experience and initial capital. They were also wildly off the mark on average. Over 80% of entrepreneurs perceived their chances of success as 70% or better. Fully one-third of them described their success as certain. On the other hand, the mean chance of success that these entrepreneurs attributed to a business like theirs was 59%. Even this estimate is optimistic, though it is closer to the truth: the five-year survival rate for new firms is around 33% (Dun and Bradstreet 1967).

The inside view does not invariably yield optimistic forecasts. Many parents of rebellious teenagers cannot imagine how their offspring would ever become a reasonable adult, and are consequently more worried than they should be, since they also know that almost all teenagers do eventually grow up. The general point is that the inside view is susceptible to the fallacies of scenario thinking and to anchoring of estimates on present values or on extrapolations of current trends. The inside view burdens the worried parents with statistically unjustified premonitions of doom. To decision makers with a goal and a plan, the same way of thinking offers absurdly optimistic forecasts.

The cognitive mechanism we have discussed is not the only source of optimistic errors. Unrealistic optimism also has deep motivational roots (Tiger 1979). A recent literature review (Taylor and Brown 1988) listed three main forms of a pervasive optimistic bias: (i) unrealistically positive self-evaluations, (ii) unrealistic optimism about future events and plans, and (iii) an illusion

of control. Thus, for almost every positive trait—including safe driving, a sense of humor, and managerial risk taking (MacCrimmon and Wehrung 1986)—there is a large majority of individuals who believe themselves to be above the median. People also exaggerate their control over events, and the importance of the skills and resources they possess in ensuring desirable outcomes. Most of us underestimate the likelihood of hazards affecting us personally, and entertain the unlikely belief that Taylor and Brown summarize as "The future will be great, especially for me."

Organizational Optimism

There is no reason to believe that entrepreneurs and executives are immune to optimistic bias. The prevalence of delusions of control among managers has been recognized by many authors (among others, Duhaime and Schwenk 1985, March and Shapira 1987, Salancik and Meindl 1984). As we noted earlier, managers commonly view risk as a challenge to be overcome, and believe that risk can be modified by "managerial wisdom and skill" (Donaldson and Lorsch 1983). The common refusal of managers to refuse risk estimates provided to them as "given" (Shapira 1986) is a clear illustration of illusion of control.

Do organizations provide effective controls against the optimistic bias of individual executives? Are organizational decisions founded on impartial and unbiased forecasts of consequences? In answering these questions, we must again distinguish problems that are treated as recurrent, such as forecasts of the sales of existing product lines, from others that are considered unique. We have no reason to doubt the ability of organizations to impose forecasting discipline and to reduce or eliminate obvious biases in recurrent problems. As in the case of risk, however, all significant forecasting problems have features that make them appear unique. It is in these unique problems that biases of judgment and choice are most likely to have their effects, for organizations as well as for individuals. We next discuss some likely causes of optimistic bias in organizational judgments, some observations of this bias, and the costs and benefits of unrealistic optimism.

Causes. Forecasts often develop as part of a case that is made by an individual or group that already has, or is developing a vested interest in the plan, in a context of competition for the control of organizational resources. The debate is often adversarial. The only projects that have a good chance of surviving in this competition are those for which highly favorable outcomes are forecast, and this produces a powerful incentive for would-be promoters to present optimistic numbers. The statistical logic that produces the winner's curse in other contexts (Capen, Clapp and Campbell 1971; Bazerman and Samuelson 1983; Kagel and Levin 1986) applies here as well: the winning project is more likely than others to be associated with optimistic errors (Harrison and March 1984). This is an effect of regression to the mean. Thus, the student who did best in an initial test is also the one for whom the most regression is expected on a subsequent test. Similarly, the projects that are forecast to have the highest returns are the ones most likely to fall short of expectations.

Officially adopted forecasts are also likely to be biased by their secondary functions as demands, commands and commitments (Lowe and Shaw 1968, Lawler and Rhode 1976, Lawler 1986, Larkey and Smith 1984). A forecast readily becomes a target, which induces loss aversion for performance that does not match expectations, and can also induce satisficing indolence when the target is exceeded. The obvious advantages of setting high goals is an incentive for higher management to adopt and disseminate optimistic assessments of future accomplishments—and possibly to deceive themselves in the process.

In his analysis of "groupthink," Janis (1982) identified other factors that favor organizational optimism. Pessimism about what the organization can do is readily interpreted as disloyalty, and consistent bearers of bad news tend to be shunned. Bad news can be demoralizing. When pessimistic opinions are suppressed in this manner, exchanges of views will fail to perform a critical function. The optimistic biases of individual group members can become mutually reinforcing, as unrealistic views are validated by group approval.

The conclusion of this sketchy analysis is that there is little reason to believe organizations will avoid the optimistic bias—except perhaps when the problems are considered recurrent and subjected to statistical quality control. On the contrary, there are reasons to suspect that many significant decisions made in organizations are guided by unrealistic forecasts of their consequences.

Observations. The optimistic bias of capital investment projects is a familiar fact of life: the typical project finishes late, comes in over budget when it is finally completed, and fails to achieve its initial goals. Grossly optimistic errors appear to be especially likely if the project involves new technology or otherwise places the firm in unfamiliar territory. A Rand Corporation study on pioneer process plants in the energy field demonstrates the magnitude of the problem (Merrow et al. 1981). Almost all project construction costs exceeded initial estimates by over 20%. The norm was for actual construction costs to more than double first estimates. These conclusions are corroborated by PIMS data on start-up ventures in a wide range of industries (cited by Davis 1985). More than 80% of the projects studied fell short of planned market share.

In an interesting discussion of the causes of failure in capital investment projects, Arnold (1986) states:

> Most companies support large capital expenditure programs with a worst case analysis that examines the projects' loss potential. But the worst case forecast is almost always too optimistic. . . . When managers look at the downside they generally describe a mildly pessimistic future rather than the worst possible future.

As an antidote against rosy predictions Arnold recommends staying power analysis, a method used by lenders to determine if organizations under severe strain can make payments. In effect, the advice is for managers to adopt an outside view of their own problem.

Mergers and acquisitions provide another illustration of optimism and of illusions of control. On average, bidding firms do not make a significantly positive return. This striking observation raises the question of why so many takeovers and mergers are initiated. Roll (1986) offers a "hubris hypothesis" to explain why decision makers acquiring firms tend to pay too much for their targets. Roll cites optimistic estimates of "economies due to synergy and (any) assessments of weak management" as the primary causes of managerial hubris. The bidding firms are prone to overestimate the control they will have over the merged organization, and to underestimate the "weak" managers who are currently in charge.

Costs and Benefits. Optimism and the illusion of control increase risk taking in several ways. In a discussion of the Challenger disaster, Landau and Chisholm (1990) introduced a "law of increasing optimism" as a form of Russian roulette. Drawing on the same case, Starbuck and Milliken (1988) noted how quickly vigilance dissipates with repeated successes. Optimism in a competitive context may take the form of contempt for the capabilities of opponents (Roll 1986). In a bargaining situation, it will support a hard line that raises the risk of conflict. Neale and Bazerman (1983) observed a related effect in a final-offer arbitration setup, where the arbiter is constrained to choose between the final offers made by the contestants. The participants were asked to state their subjective probability that the final offer they presented would be preferred by the arbiter. The average of these probabilities was approximately 0.70; with a less sanguine view of the strength of their case the contestants would surely have made more concessions. In the context of capital investment decisions, optimism and the illusion of control manifest themselves in unrealistic forecasts and unrealizable plans (Arnold 1986).

Given the high cost of mistakes, it might appear obvious that a rational organization should want to base its decisions on unbiased odds, rather than on predictions painted in shades of rose. However, realism has its costs. In their review of the consequences of optimism and pessimism, Taylor and Brown (1988) reached the deeply disturbing conclusion that optimistic self-delusion is both a diagnostic indication of mental health and well-being, and a positive causal factor that contributes to successful coping with the challenges of life. The benefits of unrealistic optimism in increasing persistence in the face of difficulty have been documented by other investigators (Seligman 1991).

The observation that realism can be pathological and self-defeating raises troubling questions for the management of information and risk in organizations. Surely, no one would want to be governed entirely by wishful fantasies, but is there a point at which truth becomes destructive and doubt self-fulfilling? Should executives allow or even encourage unrealistic optimism among their subordinates? Should they willingly allow themselves to be caught up in productive enthusiasm, and to ignore discouraging portents? Should there be someone in the organization whose function it is to achieve forecasts free of optimistic bias, although such forecasts, if disseminated, would be demoralizing?

Should the organization maintain two sets of forecasting books (as some do, see Bromiley 1986)? Some authors in the field of strategy have questioned the value of realism, at least implicitly. Weick's famous story of the lost platoon that finds its way in the Alps by consulting a map of the Pyrenees indicates more respect for confidence and morale than for realistic appraisal. On the other hand, Landau and Chisholm (1990) pour withering scorn on the "arrogance of optimism" in organizations, and recommend a pessimistic failure-avoiding management strategy to control risk. Before further progress can be made on this difficult issue, it is important to recognize the existence of a genuine dilemma that will not yield to any simple rule

Concluding Remarks

Our analysis has suggested that many failures originate in the highly optimistic judgments of risks and opportunities that we label bold forecasts. In the words of March and Shapira (1987), "managers accept risks, in part, because they do not expect that they will have to bear them." March and Shapira emphasized the role of illusions of control in this bias. We have focused on another mechanism—the adoption of an inside view of problems, which leads to anchoring on plans and on the most available scenarios. We suggest that errors of intuitive prediction can sometimes be reduced by adopting an outside view, which forecasts the outcome without attempting to forecast its history (Kahneman and Tversky 1979b). This analysis identifies the strong intuitive preference for the inside view as a source of difficulties that are both grave and avoidable.

On the issue of risk we presented evidence that decision makers tend to deal with choices one at a time, and that their attitudes to risk exhibit risk-aversion and near-proportionality. The reluctance to take responsibility for possible losses is powerful, and can be very costly in the aggregate (for a discussion of its social costs see Wildavsky 1988). We claimed further that when the stakes are small or moderate relative to assets the aversion to risk is incoherent and substantively unjustified. Here again, the preference for treating decision problems as unique causes errors that could be avoided by a broader view.

Our analysis implies that the adoption of an outside view, in which the problem at hand is treated as an instance of a broader category, will generally reduce the optimistic bias and may facilitate the application of a consistent risk policy. This happens as a matter of course in problems of forecasting or decision that the organization recognizes as obviously recurrent or repetitive. However, we have suggested that people are strongly biased in favor of the inside view, and that they will normally treat significant decision problems as unique even when information that could support an outside view is available. The adoption of an outside view in such cases violates strong intuitions about the relevance of information. Indeed, the deliberate neglect of the features that make the current problem unique can appear irresponsible. A deliberate effort will therefore be required to foster the optimal use of outside and inside views in forecasting, and the maintenance of globally consistent risk attitudes in distributed decision systems.

Bold forecasts and timid attitudes to risk tend to have opposite effects. It would be fortunate if they canceled out precisely to yield optimal behavior in every situation, but there is little reason to expect such a perfect outcome. The conjunction of biases is less disastrous than either one would have been on its own, but there ought to be a better way to control choice under risk than pitting two mistakes against each other. The prescriptive implications of the relation between the biases in forecast and in risk taking is that corrective attempts should deal with these biases simultaneously. Increasing risk taking could easily go too far in the presence of optimistic forecasts, and a successful effort to improve the realism of assessments could do more harm than good in an organization that relies on unfounded optimism to ward off paralysis.[8]

[8] An earlier version of this paper was presented at a conference on Fundamental Issues in Strategy, held at Silverado, CA, in November 1990. The preparation of this article was supported by the Center for Management Research at the University of California, Berkeley, by the Russell Sage Foundation, and by grants from the Sloan Foundation and from AFOSR, under grant number 88-0206. The ideas presented here developed over years of collaboration with Amos Tversky, but he should not be held responsible for our errors. We thank Philip Bromiley, Colin Camerer, George Loewenstein, Richard Thaler, and Amos Tversky for their many helpful comments.

References

Arnold, J. III, "Assessing Capital Risk: You Can't Be Too Conservative," *Harvard Bus. Rev.*, 64 (1986), 113–121.

Bateman, T. S. and C. T. Zeithaml, "The Psychological Context of Strategic Decisions: A Model and Convergent Experimental Findings," *Strategic Management J.*, 10 (1989), 59–74.

Bazerman, M. H. and W. F. Samuelson, "I Won the Auction but Don't Want the Price," *J. Financial Econ.*, 27 (1983), 618–634.

Bowman, E., "Risk Seeking by Troubled Firms," *Sloan Management Rev.*, 23 (1982), 33–42.

Bromiley, P., *Corporate Capital Investment: A Behavioral Approach*, Cambridge University Press, New York, 1986.

Capen, E. C., R. V. Clapp and W. M. Campbell, "Competitive Bidding in High-Risk Situations," *J. Petroleum Technology*, 23 (1971), 641–653.

Cooper, A., C. Woo and W. Dunkelberg, "Entrepreneurs' Perceived Chances for Success," *J. Business Venturing*, 3 (1988), 97–108.

Curley, S. P., F. J. Yates and R. A. Abrams, "Psychological Sources of Ambiguity Avoidance," *Org. Behavior and Human Decision Processes*, 38 (1986), 230–256.

Davis, D., "New Projects: Beware of False Economies," *Harvard Bus. Rev.*, 63 (1985), 95–101.

Dawes, R. M., *Rational Choice in an Uncertain World*, Harcourt Brace Jovanovich, Orlando, FL, 1988.

Donaldson, G. and J. Lorsch, *Decision Making at the Top*, Basic Books, New York, 1983.

Duhaime, I. and C. Schwenk, "Conjectures on Cognitive Simplification in Acquisition and Divestment Decision Making," *Academy of Management Rev.*, 10 (1985), 287–295.

Dun and Bradstreet, *Patterns of Success in Managing a Business*, Dun and Bradstreet, New York, 1967.

Fiegenbaum, A., "Prospect Theory and the Risk-Return Association," *J. Econ. Behavior and Organization*, 14 (1990), 187–203.

—— and H. Thomas, "Attitudes Toward Risk and the Risk Return Paradox: Prospect Theory Explanations," *Academy of Management J.*, 31 (1988), 85–106.

Fishburn, P. C. and G. A. Kochenberger, "Two-Piece von Neumann-Morgenstern Utility Functions," *Decision Sci.*, 10 (1979), 503–518.

Gigerenzer, G., U. Hoffrage and H. Kleinbölting, "Probabilistic Mental Models: A Brunswikian Theory of Confidence," *Psychological Rev.*, 98 (1991), 506–528.

——, W. Hell and H. Blank, "Presentation and Content," *J. Experimental Psychology: Human Perception and Performance*, 14 (1988), 513–525.

Griffin, D. and H. Tversky, "The Weighting of Evidence and the Determinants of Confidence," *Cognitive Psychology*, 24 (1992), 411–435.

Harrison, J. R. and J. G. March, "Decision Making and Post-Decision Surprises," *Admin. Sci. Quarterly*, 29 (1984), 26–42.

Hogarth, R. M. and H. J. Einhorn, "Venture Theory: A Model of Decision Weights," *Management Sci.*, 36 (1990), 780–803.

Janis, I. L., *Groupthink* (2nd Ed.), Houghton-Mifflin, Boston, MA, 1982.

Kagel, J. H. and D. Levin, "The Winner's Curse and Public Information in Common Value Auctions," *American Econ. Rev.*, 76 (1986), 894–920.

Kahneman, D., J. L. Knetsch and R. H. Thaler, "The Endowment Effect, Loss Aversion, and Status Quo Bias," *J. Econ. Perspectives*, 5 (1991), 193–206.

—— and A. Tversky, "On the Psychology of Prediction," *Psychological Rev.*, 80 (1973), 237–251.

—— and ——, "Prospect Theory: An Analysis of Decision Under Risk," *Econometrica*, 47 (1979a), 263–290.

—— and ——, "Intuitive Prediction: Biases and Corrective Procedures," *Management Sci.*, 12 (1979b), 313–327.

Keeney, R. and A. Raiffa, *Decisions with Multiple Objectives: Preference and Value Tradeoffs*, Wiley, New York, 1976.

Kreps, D. M., "Static Choice in the Presence of Unforseen Contingencies," Working Paper: Stanford Graduate School of Business, Stanford, CA, 1988.

Landau, M. and D. Chisholm, "Fault Analysis, Professional Football, and the Arrogance of Optimism: An Essay on the Methodology of Administration," Working Paper: Univ. of California, 1990.

Larkey, P. and R. Smith, Eds., "Misrepresentation in Government Budgeting," *Advances in Information Processing in Organizations*, JAI Press, Greenwich, CT, 1984, 68–92.

Laughhunn, D., J. Payne and R. Crum, "Managerial Risk Preferences for Below-Target Returns," *Management Sci.*, 26 (1980), 1238–1249.

Lawler, E., "Control Systems in Organizations," *Handbook of Industrial and Organizational Psychology*, Rand-McNally, Chicago, IL, 1986, 1247–1291.

—— and J. Rhode, *Information and Control in Organizations*, Goodyear, Pacific Palisades, CA, 1976.

Lichtenstein, S., B. Fischhoff and L. D. Phillips, "Calibration of Probabilities: The State of the Art to 1980," in D. Kahneman, T. Slovic and A. Tversky (Eds.), *Judgment under Uncertainty: Heuristics and Biases*, Cambridge Univ. Press, New York, 1982, 1031.

Lopes, L., "Decision Making in the Short Run," *J. Experimental Psychology: Human Learning and Memory*, 7 (1981), 377–385.

Lowe, E. and R. Shaw, "An Analysis of Managerial Biasing: Evidence From a Company's Budgeting Process," *J. Management Studies*, 5 (1968), 304–315.

Lynch, J. G. and C. Ofir, "Effects of Cue Consistency and Value on Base-Rate Utilization," *J. Personality and Social Psychology*, 56 (1989), 170–181.

MacCrimmon, K. and D. Wehrung, *Taking Risks*, Free Press, New York, 1986.

March, J. and Z. Shapira, "Managerial Perspectives on Risk and Risk Taking," *Management Sci.*, 33 (1987), 1404–1418.

Merrow, E., K. Phillips and C. Myers, *Understanding Cost Growth and Performance Shortfalls in Pioneer Process Plants*, Rand Corporation, Santa Barbara, CA, 1981.

Neale, M. and M. Bazerman, "The Effects of Perspective-taking Ability under Alternate Forms of Arbitration on the Negotiation Process," *Industrial and Labor Relations Review*, 36 (1983), 378–388.

Redelmeier, D. A. and A. Tversky, "On the Framing of Multiple Prospects," *Psychological Sci.*, 3 (1992), 191–193.

Roll, L., "The Hubris Hypothesis of Corporate Takeovers," *J. Business*, 59 (1986), 197–218.

Ruefli, T. W., "Mean-Variance Approaches to Risk-Return Relationships in Strategy: Paradox Lost," *Management Sci.*, 36 (1990), 368–380.

Salancik, G. R. and J. R. Meindl, "Corporate Attributions as Strategic Illusions of Management Control," *Admin. Sci. Quarterly*, 29 (1984), 238–254.

Samuelson, P. A., "Risk and Uncertainty: A Fallacy of Large Numbers," *Scientia*, 98 (1963), 108–113.

Samuelson, W. and R. Zeckhauser, "Status Quo Bias in Decision Making," *J. Risk and Uncertainty*, 1 (1988), 7–59.

Seligman, M. E. P., *Learned Optimism*, Alfred A. Knopf, New York, 1991.

Shapira, Z., "Risk in Managerial Decision Making," Working Paper: Hebrew Univ. School of Business Administration, 1986.

Spence, M. and R. Zeckhauser, "The Effect of the Timing of Consumption Decisions and the Resolution of Lotteries on the Choice of Lotteries," *Econometrica*, 40 (1972), 401–403.

Starbuck, W. and F. Milliken, "Challenger: Fine-Tuning the Odds Until Something Breaks," *J. Management Studies*, 25 (1988), 319–340.

Staw, B. and J. Ross, "Understanding Behavior in Escalation Situations," *Science*, 246 (1989), 216–220.

Stevens, S. S., *Psychophysics*, John Wiley and Sons, New York, 1975.

Swalm, R. O., "Utility Theory: Insights into Risk Taking," *Harvard Bus. Rev.*, 44 (1966), 123–136.

Taylor, S. E. and J. D. Brown, "Illusion and Well-Being: A Social Psychological Perspective on Mental Health," *Psychological Bull.*, 103 (1988), 193–210.

Tetlock, P. E. and R. Boettger, "Accountability Amplifies the Status Quo Effect When Change Creates Victims," Working Paper: University of California at Berkeley, Berkeley, CA, 1992.

Tiger, L., *Optimism: The Biology of Hope*, Simon and Schuster, New York, 1979.

Tversky, A. and M. Bar-Hillel, "Risk: The Long and the Short," *J. Experimental Psychology: Learning, Memory, and Cognition*, 9 (1983), 713–717.

—— and D. Kahneman, "Extensional Verses Intuitive Reasoning: The Conjunction Fallacy in Probability Judgment," *Psychological Review*, 90 (1983), 293–315.

—— and ——, "Rational Choice and the Framing of Decisions," *J. Business*, 59 (1986), S251–S278.

—— and ——, "Reference Theory of Choice and Exchange," *Quart. J. Economics*, (1991), 1039–1061.

—— and ——, "Advances in Prospect Theory: Cumulative Representation of Uncertainty," *J. Risk and Uncertainty*, 5 (1992), 297–323.

Viscusi, K., W. Magat and J. Huber, "An Investigation of the Rationality of Consumer Valuations of Multiple Health Risks," *Rand J. Economics*, 18 (1987), 465–479.

Wehrung, D. A., "Risk Taking Over Gains and Losses: A Study of Oil Executives," *Ann. Oper. Res.*, 19 (1989), 115–139.

Wildavsky, A., *Searching for Safety*, Transaction Books, New Brunswick, 1988.

Accepted by Gregory W. Fischer; received April 3, 1991. This paper has been with the authors three months for one revision.

[27]

Prospect Theory in the Wild
Evidence from the Field

Colin F. Camerer

The workhorses of economic analysis are simple formal models that can explain naturally occurring phenomena. Reflecting this taste, economists often say they will incorporate more psychological ideas into economics if those ideas can parsimoniously account for field data better than standard theories do. Taking this statement seriously, this article describes 10 regularities in naturally occurring data that are anomalies for expected utility theory but can all be explained by three simple elements of prospect theory: loss aversion, reflection effects, and nonlinear weighting of probability; moreover, the assumption is made that people isolate decisions (or edit them) from others they might be grouped with (Read, Loewenstein, and Rabin 1999; cf. Thaler, 1999). I hope to show how much success has already been had applying prospect theory to field data and to inspire economists and psychologists to spend more time in the wild.

The 10 patterns are summarized in Table 16.1. To keep the article brief, I sketch expected utility and prospect theory very quickly. (Readers who want to know more should look elsewhere in this volume or in Camerer 1995 or Rabin 1998a). In expected utility, gambles that yield risky outcomes x_i with probabilities p_i are valued according to $\Sigma p_i u(x_i)$, where $u(x)$ is the *utility* of outcome x. In prospect theory they are valued by $\Sigma \pi(p_i) v(x_i - r)$, where $\pi(p)$ is a function that weights probabilities nonlinearly, overweighting probabilities below .3 or so and underweighting larger probabilities.[1] The value function $v(x - r)$ exhibits diminishing marginal sensitivity to deviations from the reference point r, creating a "reflection effect" because $v(x - r)$ is convex for losses and concave for gains (i.e., $v''(x - r) > 0$ for $x < r$ and $v''(x - r) < 0$ for $x > r$). The value function also exhibits *loss aversion* if the value of a loss $-x$ is larger in magnitude than the value of an equal-sized gain (i.e., $-v(-x) > v(x)$ for $x > 0$).

---

[1] In rank-dependent approaches, the weights attached to outcomes are differences in weighted cumulative probabilities. For example, if the outcomes are ordered $x_1 > x_2 > \cdots > x_n$, the weight on outcome x_i is $\pi(p_i + p_2 + \cdots p_i) - \pi(p_1 + p_2 + \cdots p_{i-1})$. (Notice that if $\pi(p) = p$ this weight is just the probability p_i). In cumulative prospect theory, gains and losses are ranked and weighted separately (by magnitude).

The research was supported by NSF grant SBR-9601236 and the hospitality of the Center for Advanced Study in Behavioral Sciences during 1997–98. Linda Babcock and Barbara Mellers gave helpful suggestions.

Table 16.1. Ten Field Phenomena Inconsistent with EU and Consistent with Cumulative Prospect Theory

Domain	Phenomenon	Description	Type of Data	Isolated Decision	Ingredients	References
Stock market	Equity premium	Stock returns are too high relative to bond returns	NYSE stock, bond returns	Single yearly return (not long-run)	Loss aversion	Benartzi and Thaler (1995)
Stock market	Disposition effect	Hold losing stocks too long, sell winners too early	Individual investor trades	Single stock (not portfolio)	Reflection effect	Odean (in press), Genesove and Mayer (in press)
Labor economics	Downward-sloping labor supply	NYC cabdrivers quit around daily income target	Cabdriver hours, earnings	Single day (not week or month)	Loss aversion	Camerer et al. (1997)
Consumer goods	Asymmetric price elasticities	Purchases more sensitive to price increases than to cuts	Product purchases (scanner data)	Single product (not shopping cart)	Loss aversion	Hardie, Johnson, Fader(1993)
Macro-economics	Insensitivity to bad income news	Consumers do not cut consumption after bad income news	Teachers' earnings, savings	Single year	Loss aversion, reflection effect	Shea (1995); Bowman, Minehart and Rabin (1999)
Consumer choice	Status quo bias, Default bias	Consumers do not switch health plans, choose default insurance	Health plan, insurance choices	Single choice	Loss aversion	Samuelson and Zeckhauser (1988), Johnson et al. (1993)
Horse race betting	Favorite-longshot bias	Favorites are underbet, longshots overbet	Track odds	Single race (not day)	Overweight low *p*(loss)	Jullien and Salánie (1997)
Horse race betting	End-of-the-day effect	Shift to longshots at the end of the day	Track odds	Single day	Reflection effect	McGlothlin (1956)
Insurance	Buying phone wire insurance	Consumers buy overpriced insurance	Phone wire insurance purchases	Single wire risk (not portfolio)	Overweight low *p*(loss)	Cicchetti and Dubin (1994)
Lottery betting	Demand for Lotto	More tickets sold as top prize rises	State lottery sales	Single lottery	Overweight low *p*(win)	Cook and Clotfelter (1993)

290   Colin F. Camerer

1. FINANCE: THE EQUITY PREMIUM

Two important anomalies in finance can be explained by elements of prospect theory. One anomaly is called the *equity premium*. Stocks – or equities – tend to have more variable annual price changes (or "returns") than bonds do. As a result, the average return to stocks is higher as a way of compensating investors for the additional risk they bear. In most of this century, for example, stock returns were about 8% per year higher than bond returns. This was accepted as a reasonable return premium for equities until Mehra and Prescott (1985) asked how large a degree of risk aversion is implied by this premium. The answer is surprising: under the standard assumptions of economic theory, investors must be absurdly risk averse to demand such a high premium. For example, a person with enough risk aversion to explain the equity premium would be indifferent between a coin flip paying either $50,000 or $100,000 and a sure amount of $51,209.

Explaining why the equity premium is so high has preoccupied financial economists for the last 15 years (see Siegel and Thaler 1997). Benartzi and Thaler (1997) suggested a plausible answer based on prospect theory. In their theory, investors are not averse to the variability of returns; they are averse to loss (the chance that returns are negative). Because annual stock returns are negative much more frequently than annual bond returns are, loss-averse investors will demand a large equity premium to compensate them for the much higher chance of losing money in a year. Keep in mind that the higher average return to stocks means that the cumulative return to stocks over a longer horizon is increasingly likely to be positive as the horizon lengthens. Therefore, to explain the equity premium Benartzi and Thaler must assume that investors take a short horizon over which stocks are more likely to lose money than bonds. They compute the expected prospect values of stock and bond returns over various horizons, using estimates of investor utility functions from Kahneman and Tversky (1992) and including a loss-aversion coefficient of 2.25 (i.e., the disutility of a small loss is 2.25 times as large as the utility of an equal gain). Benartzi and Thaler show that over a 1-year horizon, the prospect values of stock and bond returns are about the same if stocks return 8% more than bonds, which explains the equity premium.

Barberis, Huang, and Santos (1999) include loss-aversion in a standard general equilibrium model of asset pricing. They show that loss-aversion and a strong "house money effect" (an increase in risk-preference after stocks have risen) are both necessary to explain the equity premium.

2. FINANCE: THE DISPOSITION EFFECT

Shefrin and Statman (1985) predicted that because people dislike incurring losses much more than they like incurring gains and are willing to gamble in the domain of losses, investors will hold on to stocks that have lost value (relative to their purchase price) too long and will be eager to sell stocks that have risen in value. They called this the *disposition effect*. The disposition effect is anomalous because the purchase price of a stock should not matter much for whether you decided to sell it. If you think the stock will rise, you should keep it; if you think it will fall, you should sell it. In addition, tax laws encourage people to sell losers rather than winners because such sales generate losses that can be used to reduce the taxes owed on capital gains.

Disposition effects have been found in experiments by Weber and Camerer (1998).[2] On large exchanges, trading volume of stocks that have fallen in price is lower than for stocks that have risen. The best field study was done by Odean (in press). He obtained data from a brokerage firm about all the purchases and sales of a large sample of individual investors. He found that investors held losing stocks a median of 124 days and held winners only 104 days. Investors sometimes say they hold losers because they expect them to "bounce back" (or mean-revert), but in Odean's sample, the unsold losers returned only 5% in the subsequent year, whereas the winners that were sold later returned 11.6%. Interestingly, the winner–loser differences did disappear in December. In this month investors have their last chance to incur a tax advantage from selling losers (and selling winners generates a taxable capital gain), and thus their reluctance to incur losses is temporarily overwhelmed by their last chance to save on taxes.

Genovese and Meyer (in press) report a strong disposition effect in housing sales. Owners who may suffer a nominal loss (selling at a price below what they paid) set prices too high and, as a result, keep their houses too long before selling.

3. LABOR SUPPLY

Camerer, Babcock, Loewenstein, and Thaler (this volume) talked to cab drivers in New York City about when they decide to quit driving each day. Most of the drivers lease their cabs for a fixed fee for up to 12 hours. Many said they set an income target for the day and quit when they reach that target. Although daily income targeting seems sensible, it implies that drivers will work long hours on bad days when the per-hour wage is low and will quit earlier on good high-wage days. The standard theory of the supply of labor predicts the opposite: Drivers will work the hours that are most profitable, quitting early on bad days and making up the shortfall by working longer on good days.

The daily targeting theory and the standard theory of labor supply therefore predict opposite signs of the correlation between hours and the daily wage. To measure the correlation, we collected three samples of data on how many hours drivers worked on different days. The correlation between hours and

---

[2] In the Weber and Camerer experiment, subjects whose shares were automatically sold every period (but could be bought back with no transaction cost) did not buy back the shares of losers more than winners. This shows they are not optimistic about the losers but simply reluctant to sell them and lock in a realized loss.

292   Colin F. Camerer

wages was strongly negative for inexperienced drivers and close to zero for experienced drivers. This suggests that inexperienced drivers began using a daily income targeting heuristic, but those who did so either tended to quit or learned by experience to shift toward driving around the same number of hours every day.

Daily income targeting assumes loss aversion in an indirect way. To explain why the correlation between hours and wages for inexperienced drivers is so strongly negative, one needs to assume that drivers take a 1-day horizon and have a utility function for the day's income that bends sharply at the daily income target. This bend is an aversion to "losing" by falling short of an income reference point.

4. ASYMMETRIC PRICE ELASTICITIES OF CONSUMER GOODS

The price elasticity of a good is the change in quantity demanded, in percentage terms, divided by the percentage change in its price. Hundreds of studies estimate elasticities by looking at how much purchases change after prices change. Loss-averse consumers dislike price increases more than they like the windfall gain from price cuts and will cut back purchases more when prices rise compared with the extra amount they buy when prices fall. Loss aversion therefore implies elasticities will be asymmetric, that is, elasticities will be larger in magnitude after price increases than after price decreases. Putler (1992) first looked for such an asymmetry in price elasticities in consumer purchases of eggs and found it.

Hardie, Johnson, and Fader (1993) replicated the study using a typical model of brand choice in which a consumer's utility for a brand is unobserved but can be estimated by observing purchases. They included the possibility that consumers compare a good's current price to a reference price (the last price they paid) and get more disutility from buying when prices have risen than the extra utility they get when prices have fallen. For orange juice, they estimate a coefficient of loss aversion (the ratio of loss and gain disutilities) around 2.4.

Note that for loss aversion to explain these results, consumers must be narrowly bracketing purchases of a specific good (e.g., eggs or orange juice). Otherwise, the loss from paying more for one good would be integrated with gains or losses from other goods in their shopping cart and would not loom so large.

5. SAVINGS AND CONSUMPTION: INSENSITIVITY TO BAD NEWS

In economic models of lifetime savings and consumption decisions, people are assumed to have separate utilities for consumption in each period, denoted $u[c(t)]$, and discount factors that weight future consumption less than current consumption. These models are used to predict how much rational consumers will consume (or spend) now and how much they will save, depending on their current income, anticipations of future income, and their discount factors. The models make many predictions that seem to be empirically false. The central prediction is that people should plan ahead by anticipating future income to make a guess about their "permanent income" and consume a constant fraction of that total in any one year. Because most workers earn larger and larger incomes throughout their lives, this prediction implies that people will spend more than they earn when they are young – borrowing if they can – and will earn more than they spend when they are older. But in fact, spending on consumption tends to be close to a fixed fraction of current income and does not vary across the life cycle nearly as much as standard theory predicts. Consumption also drops steeply after retirement, which should not be the case if people anticipate retirement and save enough for it.

Shea (1995) pointed out another prediction of the standard life-cycle theory. Think of a group of workers whose wages for the next year are set in advance. In Shea's empirical analysis, these are unionized teachers whose contract is negotiated 1 year ahead. In the standard theory, if next year's wage is surprisingly good, then the teachers should spend more now, and if next year's wage is disappointingly low, the teachers should cut back on their spending now. In fact, the teachers in Shea's study did spend more when their future wages were expected to rise, but they *did not* cut back when their future wages were cut.

Bowman, Minehart, and Rabin (1999) can explain this pattern with a stylized two-period consumption–savings model in which workers have reference-dependent utility, $u(c(t) - r(t))$ (cf. Duesenberry, 1949). The utility they get from consumption in each period exhibits loss aversion (the marginal utility of consuming just enough to reach the reference point is always strictly larger than the marginal utility from exceeding it) and a reflection effect (if people are consuming below their reference point, the marginal utility of consumption rises as they get closer to it). Workers begin with some reference point $r(t)$ and save and consume in the first period. Their reference point in the second period is an average of their initial reference point and their first-period consumption, and thus $r(2) = \alpha r(1) + (1 - \alpha)c(1)$. The pleasure workers get from consuming in the second period depends on how much they consumed in the first period through the effect of previous consumption on the current reference point. If they consumed a lot at first, $r(2)$ will be high and they will be disappointed if their standard of living is cut and $c(2) < r(2)$.

Bowman et al. (1999) show formally how this simple model can explain the behavior of the teachers in Shea's study. Suppose teachers are consuming at their reference point and get bad news about future wages (in the sense that the distribution of possible wages next year shifts downward). Bowman et al. show that the teachers may not cut their current consumption at all. Consumption is "sticky downward" for two reasons: (1) Because they are loss averse, cutting current consumption means they will consume below their reference point this year, which feels awful. (2) Owing to reflection effects, they are willing to gamble that next year's wages might not be so low; thus, they would rather take a

294   Colin F. Camerer

gamble in which they either consume far below their reference point or consume right at it than accept consumption that is modestly below the reference point. These two forces make the teachers reluctant to cut their current consumption after receiving bad news about future income prospects, which explains Shea's finding.

6. STATUS QUO BIAS, ENDOWMENT EFFECTS, AND BUYING–SELLING PRICE GAPS

Samuelson and Zeckhauser (1988) coined the term *status quo bias* to refer to an exaggerated preference for the status quo and showed such a bias in a series of experiments. They also reported several observations in field data that are consistent with status quo bias.

When Harvard University added new health-care plan options, older faculty members who were hired previously when the new options were not available were, of course, allowed to switch to the new options. If one assumes that the new and old faculty members have essentially the same preferences for health-care plans, then the distribution of plans elected by new and old faculty should be the same. However, Samuelson and Zeckhauser found that older faculty members tended to stick to their previous plans; compared with the newer faculty members, fewer of the old faculty elected new options.

In cases in which there is no status quo, people may have an exaggerated preference for whichever option is the default choice. Johnson, Hershey, Meszaros, and Kunreuther (1993) observed this phenomenon in decisions involving insurance purchases. At the time of their study, Pennsylvania and New Jersey legislators were considering various kinds of tort reform allowing firms to offer cheaper automobile insurance that limited the rights of the insured person to sue for damages from accidents. Both states adopted very similar forms of limited insurance, but they chose different default options, creating a natural experiment. All insurance companies mailed forms to their customers asking them whether they wanted the cheaper limited-rights insurance or the more expensive unlimited-rights insurance. One state made the limited-rights insurance the default (the insured person would get that if they did not respond), and the other made unlimited-rights the default. In fact, the percentage of people actively electing the limited-rights insurance was higher in the state where that was the default. An experiment replicated the effect.

A closely related body of research on endowment effects established that buying and selling prices for a good are often quite different. The paradigmatic experimental demonstration of this is the "mugs" experiments of Kahneman, Knetsch, and Thaler (1990). In their experiments, some subjects are endowed (randomly) with coffee mugs, and others are not. Those who are given the mugs demand a price about 2–3 times as large as the price that those without mugs are willing to pay, even though in economic theory these prices should be extremely close together. In fact, the mugs experiments were inspired by field observations of large gaps in hypothetical buying and selling prices in "contingent valuations." Contingent valuations are measurements of the economic value of goods that are not normally traded – like clean air, environmental damage, and so forth. These money valuations are used for doing benefit–cost analysis and establishing economic damages in lawsuits. There is a huge literature establishing that selling prices are generally much larger than buying prices, although there is a heated debate among psychologists and economists about what the price gap means and how to measure "true" valuations in the face of such a gap.

All three phenomena (status quo biases, default preference, and endowment effects) are consistent with aversion to losses relative to a reference point. Making one option the status quo or default or endowing a person with a good (even hypothetically) seems to establish a reference point people move away from only reluctantly, or if they are paid a large sum.

7. RACETRACK BETTING: THE FAVORITE-LONGSHOT BIAS

In parimutuel betting on horse races, there is a pronounced bias toward betting on "longshots," which are horses with a relatively small chance of winning. That is, if one groups longshots with the same percentage of money bet on them into a class, the fraction of time horses in that class win is far smaller than the percentage of money bet on them. Longshot horses with 2% of the total money bet on them, for example, win only about 1% of the time (see Thaler and Ziemba 1988, Hausch and Ziemba 1995).

Overbetting longshots implies favorites are underbet. Indeed, some horses are so heavily favored that up to 70% of the win money is wagered on them. For these heavy favorites, the return for a dollar bet is very low if the horse wins. (Because the track keeps about 15% of the money bet for expenses and profit, bettors who bet on such a heavy favorite share only 85% of the money with 70% of the people, which results in a payoff of only about $2.40 for a $2 bet.) People dislike these bets so much that, in fact, if one makes those bets it is possible to earn a small positive profit (even accounting for the track's 15% take).

There are many explanations for the favorite-longshot bias, each of which probably contributes to the phenomenon. Horses that have lost many races in a row tend to be longshots, and thus a gambler's fallacious belief that such horses are due for a win may contribute to overbetting on them. Prospect-theoretic overweighting of low probabilities of winning will also lead to overbetting of longshots.

Within standard expected utility theory, the favorite-longshot bias can only be explained by assuming that people have convex utility functions for money outcomes. The most careful study comparing expected utility and prospect theory was done by Jullien and Salanié (1997). Their study used a huge sample of all the flat races run in England for 10 years (34,443 races). They assumed that bettors value bets on horses by using either expected utility theory,

296   Colin F. Camerer

rank-dependent utility theory, or cumulative prospect theory (see Kahneman and Tversky 1992). If the marginal bettor is indifferent among bets on all the horses at the odds established when the race is run, then indifference conditions can be used to infer the parameters of that bettor's utility and probability weighting functions.

Jullien and Salanié found that cumulative prospect theory fits much better than rank-dependent theory and expected utility theory. They estimated that the utility function for small money amounts is convex. Their estimate of the probability weighting function $\pi(p)$ for probabilities of gain is almost linear, but the weighting function for loss probabilities severely overweights low probabilities of loss (e.g., $\pi(.1) = .45$ and $\pi(.3) = .65$). These estimates imply a surprising new explanation for the favorite-longshot bias: Bettors like longshots because they have convex utility and weight their high chances of losing and small chances of winning roughly linearly. They hate favorites, however, because they like to gamble ($u(x)$ is convex) but are disproportionately afraid of the small chance of losing when they bet on a heavy favorite. (In my personal experience as a betting researcher I have found that losing on a heavy favorite is particularly disappointing – an emotional effect the Jullien-Salanié estimates capture.)

8. RACETRACK BETTING: THE END-OF-THE-DAY EFFECT

McGlothlin (1956) and Ali (1977) established another racetrack anomaly that points to the central role of reference points. They found that bettors tend to shift their bets toward longshots, and away from favorites, later in the racing day. Because the track takes a hefty bite out of each dollar, most bettors are behind by the last race of the day. These bettors really prefer longshots because a small longshot bet can generate a large enough profit to cover their earlier losses, enabling them to break even. The movement toward longshots, and away from favorites, is so pronounced that some studies show that conservatively betting on the favorite to show (to finish first, second, or third) in the last race is a profitable bet despite the track's take.

The end-of-the-day effect is consistent with using zero daily profit as a reference point and gambling in the domain of losses to break even. Expected utility theory cannot gracefully explain the shift in risk preferences across the day if bettors integrate their wealth because the last race on a Saturday is not fundamentally different than the first race on the bettor's next outing. Cumulative prospect theory can explain the shift by assuming people open a mental account at the beginning of the day, close it at the end, and hate closing an account in the red.

9. STATE LOTTERIES

Lotto is a special kind of lottery game in which players choose six different numbers from a set of 40–50 numbers. They win a large jackpot if their six choices match six numbers that are randomly drawn in public. If no player picks all six numbers correctly, the jackpot is rolled over and added to the next week's jackpot; several weeks of rollovers can build up jackpots up to $350 million or more. The large jackpots have made lotto very popular.[3] Lotto was introduced in several American states in 1980 and accounted for about half of all state lottery ticket sales by 1989.

Cook and Clotfelter (1993) suggest that the popularity of Lotto results from players' being more sensitive to the large jackpot than to the correspondingly low probability of winning. They write (p. 634):

> If players tend to judge the likelihood of winning based on the frequency with which someone wins, then a larger state can offer a game at longer odds but with the same perceived probability of winning as a smaller state. The larger population base in effect conceals the smaller probability of winning the jackpot, while the larger jackpot is highly visible. This interpretation is congruent with prospect theory.

Their regressions show that across states, ticket sales are strongly correlated with the size of a state's population (which is correlated with jackpot size). Within a state, ticket sales each week are strongly correlated with the size of the rollover. In expected utility, this can only be explained by utility functions for money that are convex. Prospect theory easily explains the demand for high jackpots, as Cook and Clotfelter suggest, by overweighting of, and insensitivity toward, very low probabilities.

10. TELEPHONE WIRE REPAIR INSURANCE

Ciccheti and Dubin (1994) conducted an interesting study of whether people purchase insurance against damage to their telephone wiring. The phone companies they studied either required customers to pay for the cost of wiring repair, about $60, or to buy insurance for $.45 per month. Given phone company estimates of the frequency of wire damage, the expected cost of wire damage is only $.26.

Ciccheti and Dubin looked across geographical areas with different probabilities of wire damage rates to see whether cross-area variation in the tendency to buy insurance was related to different probabilities. They did find a relation and exploited this to estimate parameters of an expected utility model. They found some evidence that people were weighting damage probabilities nonlinearly and also some evidence of status quo bias. (People who had previously been uninsured, when a new insurance option was introduced, were less likely to buy it than new customers were.)

More importantly, Ciccheti and Dubin never asked whether it is reasonable to purchase insurance against such a tiny risk. In standard expected utility, a

---

[3] A similar bet, the "pick six," was introduced at horse racing tracks in the 1980s. In the pick six, bettors must choose the winners of six races. This is extremely hard to do, and thus a large rollover occurs if nobody has picked all six winners several days in a row, just like lotto. Pick-six betting now accounts for a large fraction of overall betting.

298   Colin F. Camerer

person who is averse to very modest risks at all levels of wealth should be more risk averse to large risks. Rabin (in press) was the first to demonstrate how dramatic the implications of local risk aversion are for global risk aversion. He showed formally that a mildly risk-averse expected-utility maximizer who would turn down a coin flip (at all wealth levels) in which he or she is equally likely to win $11 or lose $10 should not accept a coin flip in which $100, could be lost, *regardless of how much he or she could win.* In expected utility terms, turning down the small-stakes flip implies a little bit of curvature in a $21 range of a concave utility function. Turning down the small-stakes flip for all wealth levels implies the utility function is slightly curved at all wealth levels, which mathematically implies a dramatic degree of global curvature.

Rabin's proof suggests a rejection of the joint hypotheses that consumers who buy wire repair insurance are integrating their wealth and valuing the insurance according to expected utility (and know the correct probabilities of damage). A more plausible explanation comes immediately from prospect theory – consumers are overweighting the probability of damage. (Loss aversion and reflection cannot explain their purchases because, if they are loss averse, they should dislike spending the $.45 per month, and reflection implies they will never insure unless they overestimate the probability of loss.) Once again, narrow bracketing is also required: consumers must be focusing only on wire repair risk; otherwise, the tiny probability of a modest loss would be absorbed into a portfolio of life's ups and downs and weighted more reasonably.

11. CONCLUSION

Economists value (1) mathematical formalism and econometric parsimony, and (2) the ability of theory to explain naturally occurring data. I share these tastes. This article has demonstrated that prospect theory is valuable in both ways because it can explain 10 patterns observed in a wide variety of economic domains with a small number of modeling features. Different features of prospect theory help explain different patterns. *Loss aversion* can explain the extra return on stocks compared with bonds (the equity premium), the tendency of cab drivers to work longer hours on low-wage days, asymmetries in consumer reactions to price increases and decreases, the insensitivity of consumption to bad news about income, and status quo and endowment effects. *Reflection effects* – gambling in the domain of a perceived loss – can explain holding losing stocks longer than winners and refusing to sell your house at a loss (disposition effects), insensitivity of consumption to bad income news, and the shift toward longshot betting at the end of a racetrack day. *Nonlinear weighting of probabilities* can explain the favorite-longshot bias in horse race betting, the popularity of lotto lotteries with large jackpots, and the purchase of telephone wire repair insurance. In addition, note that the disposition effect and downward-sloping labor supply of cab drivers were not simply observed but were also predicted in advance based on prospect theory.

In all these examples it is also necessary to assume people are isolating or narrowly bracketing the relevant decisions. Bracketing narrowly focuses attention most dramatically on the possibility of a loss or extreme outcome, or a low probability. With broader bracketing, outcomes are mingled with other gains and losses, diluting the psychological influence of any single outcome and making these phenomena hard to explain as a result of prospect theory valuation.

I have two final comments. First, I have chosen examples in which there are several studies, or one very conclusive one, showing regularities in field data that cannot be easily reconciled with expected utility theory. However, these regularities can be explained by adding extra assumptions. The problem is that these extras are truly ad hoc because each regularity requires a special assumption. Worse, an extra assumption that helps explain one regularity may contradict another. For example, assuming people are risk-preferring (or have convex utility for money) can explain the popularity of longshot horses and lotto, but that assumption predicts stocks should return *less* than bonds, which is wildly false. You can explain why cab drivers drive long hours on bad days by assuming they cannot borrow (they are liquidity constrained), but liquidity constraint implies teachers who get good income news should not be able to spend more, whereas those who get bad news can cut back, which is exactly the opposite of what they do.

Second, prospect theory is a suitable replacement for expected utility because it can explain anomalies like those listed above and can *also* explain the most basic phenomena expected utility is used to explain. A prominent example is pricing of financial assets discussed above in Sections 1 and 2. Another prominent example, which appears in every economics textbook, is the voluntary purchase of insurance by people. The expected utility explanation for why people buy actuarially unfair insurance is that they have concave utility, and thus they hate losing large amounts of money disproportionally compared with spending small amounts on insurance premiums.

In fact, many people *do not* purchase insurance voluntarily (e.g., most states require automobile insurance by law). The failure to purchase is inconsistent with the expected utility explanation and more easy to reconcile with prospect theory (because the disutility of loss is assumed to be convex). When people *do* buy insurance, people are probably avoiding low-probability disasters that they overweight (the prospect theory explanation) rather than avoiding a steep drop in a concave utility function (the expected utility theory explanation).

A crucial kind of evidence that distinguishes the two explanations comes from experiments on probabilistic insurance, which is insurance that does *not* pay a claim, if an accident occurs, with some probability r. According to expected utility theory, if r is small, people should pay approximately $(1 - r)$ times as much for probabilistic insurance as they pay for full insurance (Wakker, Thaler, and Tversky, 1997). But experimental responses show that people hate probabilistic insurance; they pay a multiple much less than $1 - r$ for it

300   Colin F. Camerer

(for example, they pay 80% as much when $r = .01$ when they should pay 99% as much). Prospect theory can explain their hatred easily: probabilistic insurance does not reduce the probability of loss all the way toward zero, and the low probability r is still overweighted. Prospect theory can therefore explain why people buy full insurance *and* why they do not buy probabilistic insurance. Expected utility cannot do both.

Because prospect theory can explain the basic phenomena expected utility was most fruitfully applied to, like asset pricing and insurance purchase, and can also explain field anomalies like the 10 listed in Table 16.1 (two of which were predicted), there is no good scientific reason why it should not be used alongside expected utility in current research and be given prominent space in economics textbooks.

References

Ali, M. (1977). Probability and utility estimates for racetrack bettors. *Journal of Political Economy, 85,* 803–815. [16]

Barberis, N., Hvary, M., & Santos, T. (1999). Prospect theory and asset prices. University of Chicago working paper. [26]

Benartzi, S., & Thaler, R. H. (1995). Myopic loss aversion and the equity premium puzzle. *Quarterly Journal of Economics, 110*(1), 73–92. [10, 11, 14, 16, 19, 20, 21]

Benartzi, S., & Thaler, R. H. (1998). Illusory diversification and retirement savings. Working paper, University of Chicago and UCLA. [14]

Bowman, D., **Minehart,** D., and Rabin, M. (1999). Loss aversion in a consumption/savings model. *Journal of Economic Behavior and Organization, 38*(2), 155–178. [16, 20]

Camerer, C. F. (1995). Individual decision making. In J. Kagel & A. E. Roth (Eds.), *Handbook of experimental economics* (pp. 587–703). Princeton: Princeton University Press. [6, 16, 23]

Camerer, C., Babcock, L. Loewenstein, G., & Thaler, R. H. (1997, May). Labor supply of New York cabdrivers: One day at a time. *Quarterly Journal of Economics, 112,* 407–442. [14, 16, 20]

Cicchetti, C. J., & Dubin, J. A. (1994). A micro-econometric analysis of risk-aversion and the decision to self-insure. *Journal of Political Economy, 102,* 169–186. [16]

Cook, P. J., & Clotfelter, C. T. (1993, June). The peculiar scale economies of lotto. *American Economic Review, 83,* 634–643. [16]

Duesenberry, J. S. (1949). *Income, saving and the theory of consumer behavior.* Cambridge, MA: Harvard University Press. [16, 19, 20, 33, 40]

Genesove, D., & Mayer, C. (in press). Loss aversion and seller behavior: Evidence from the housing market. *Quarterly Journal of Economics.* [16]

Hardie, B. G. S., Johnson, E. J., & Fader, P. S. (1993). Modeling loss aversion and reference dependence effects on brand choice. *Marketing Science, 12,* 378–394. [16, 42]

Hausch, D. B., & Ziemba, W. T. (1995). Efficiency in sports and lottery betting markets. In R. A. Jarrow, V. Maksimovic, & W. T. Ziemba (Eds.). *Handbook of Finance.* Amsterdam: North-Holland. [16]

Johnson, E. J., Hershey, J., Meszaros, J., & Kunreuther, H. (1992). Framing, probability distortions, and insurance decisions. *Journal of Risk and Uncertainty*, *7*, 35–51. **[5, 6, 16, 19]**

Jullien, B., & Salanié, B. (1997). Estimating preferences under risk: The case of racetrack bettors. IDEI and GREMAQ, Working paper, Toulouse University. **[16]**

Kahneman, D., Knetsch, J. L., & Thaler, R. (1990). Experimental tests of the endowment effect and the Coase theorem. *Journal of Political Economy*, *98*, 1325–1348. **[7, 8, 10, 13, 16, 17, 20, 24, 26, 40, 42]**

Kahneman, D., & Tversky, A. (1992, October). Advances in prospect theory: Cumulative representation of uncertainty. *Journal of Risk and Uncertainty*, *5*, 297–324. **[16]**

McGlothlin, W. H. (1956). Stability of choices among uncertain alternatives. *American Journal of Psychology*, *69*, 604–615. **[2, 15, 16, 20]**

Mehra, R., & Prescott, E. C. (1985). The equity premium: A puzzle. *Journal of Monetary Economics*, *15*, 145–161. **[14, 16, 17]**

Odean, T. (1998, October). Are investors reluctant to realise their losses? *Journal of Finance*, *53*, 1775–1798, Forthcoming. **[14, 16, 20]**

Putler, D. (1992). Incorporating reference prize effects into a theory of consumer choice. *Marketing Science*, *11*, 287–309. **[16]**

Rabin, M. (1998a). Psychology and economics. *Journal of Economic Literature*, *36*, 11–46. **[16]**

Rabin, M. (forthcoming), Risk Aversion and expected-utility theory: A calibration theorem. *Econometrica* (in press). **[11, 16]**

Read, D., Loewenstein, G., & Rabin, M. (1999). Choice bracketing. *Journal of Risk and Uncertainty*, *19*, 171–197. **[11, 14, 16]**

Samuelson, W., & Zeckhauser, R. (1988). Status Quo Bias in Decision Making. *Journal of Risk and Uncertainty*, *1*, 7–59. **[7, 8, 10, 13, 16, 17, 20, 22, 26]**

Shea, J. (1995). Union contracts and the life-cycle/permanent-income hypothesis. *American Economic Review*, *85*, 186–200. **[16, 20]**

Shefrin, H. M., & Statman, M., (1985). The disposition to sell winners too early and ride losers too long. *Journal of Finance*, *40*, 777–790. **[7, 14, 16, 20, 24, 33]**

Siegel, J., & Thaler, R. (1997). Anomalies: The equity premium puzzle. *Journal of Economic Perspectives*. *11*, 191–200. **[16]**

Thaler, R. H. (1999). Mental accounting matters. *Journal of Behavioral Decision Making*. *12*, 183–206. **[16]**

Thaler, R. H., & Ziemba, W. (1998). Pari-mutual betting markets: Racetracks and lotteries. *Journal of Economic Perspectives*, *2*, 161–174. **[14, 16]**

Wakker, P. P., Thaler, R. H., & Tversky, A. (1997). Probabilistic insurance. *Journal of Risk and Uncertainty*, *15*, 5–26. **[16]**

Weber, M., & Camerer, C. (1998). The disposition effect in securities trading: An experimental analysis. *Journal of Economic Behavior and Organization*, *33*, 167–184. **[16, 20, 21]**

[28]

Cognitive Biases and Organizational Correctives: Do Both Disease and Cure Depend on the Politics of the Beholder?

Philip E. Tetlock
The Ohio State University

The study reported here assessed the impact of managers' philosophies of human nature on their reactions to influential academic claims and counter-claims of when human judgment is likely to stray from rational-actor standards and of how organizations can correct these biases. Managers evaluated scenarios that depicted decision-making processes at micro, meso, and macro levels of analysis: alleged cognitive biases of individuals, strategies of structuring and coping with accountability relationships between supervisors and employees, and strategies that corporate entities use to cope with accountability demands from the broader society. Political ideology and cognitive style emerged as consistent predictors of the value spins that managers placed on decisions at all three levels of analysis. Specifically, conservative managers with strong preferences for cognitive closure were most likely (a) to defend simple heuristic-driven errors such as overattribution and overconfidence and to warn of the mirror-image mistakes of failing to hold people accountable and of diluting sound policies with irrelevant side-objectives; (b) to be skeptical of complex strategies of structuring or coping with accountability and to praise those who lay down clear rules and take decisive stands; (c) to prefer simple philosophies of corporate governance (the shareholder over stakeholder model) and to endorse organizational norms such as hierarchical filtering that reduce cognitive overload on top management by short-circuiting unnecessary argumentation. Intuitive theories of good judgment apparently cut across levels of analysis and are deeply grounded in personal epistemologies and political ideologies. •

Experimental research on judgment and choice casts us, human beings, in a less-than-flattering light (Goldstein and Hogarth, 1996; Gilovich, Griffin, and Kahneman, 2000). We fall prey, it has been claimed, to a wide assortment of errors and biases. We are too quick to draw conclusions about others, too slow to change our minds, excessively confident in our predictions, and prone to give too much weight to irrelevant cues (such as sunk costs) and too little weight to relevant ones (such as opportunity costs). Although this grim portrait has been qualified by the recent proliferation of dual-process models of judgment and choice that, in the spirit of Simon (1955), bestow on people some limited capacity to decide how to decide (see Chaiken and Trope, 1999, for a collection of current cognitive-manager models), the dominant emphasis in the last quarter century of experimental work has clearly been on judgmental shortcomings. The question remains, though, how organizational theorists should react to this burgeoning evidence of deviations from rationality at the individual level of analysis. March and Olsen (1989, 1995) have constructed a useful inventory of key conceptual stumbling blocks likely to trip up confident reductionists who propose one-size-fits-all normative frameworks for assessing rationality across levels of analysis. The relevant standards for gauging quality of decision making hinge on the relative importance that observers from varying organizational and political perspectives place on (1) making judgments and decisions in accord with utilitarian or rule-based models of human thought; (2) clarifying or obfuscating the underlying

I appreciate the support of National Science Foundation grant #SBR 9505680 and the Institute of Personality and Social Research at the University of California, Berkeley and the Mershon Center of The Ohio State University. I also thank the research participants and their employers for donating valuable time in completing a series of questionnaires that were admittedly a tad tedious. I hope that they feel the resulting contribution to knowledge justifies the cost. Finally, I thank Sara Bassett, Rachel Szteiter, Megan Berkowitz, Meaghan Quinn, Jeannette Poruban, Charles McGuire, Dan Newman, Orie Kristel, Mark Polifroni, and Beth Elson for research assistance, and Rod Kramer and Linda Johanson for valuable comments on the manuscript. Correspondence should be sent to Philip E. Tetlock, Department of Psychology, 142 Townshend Hall, 1885 Neil Avenue, Ohio State University, Columbus, OH 43210.

goals of decision making; and (3) treating the decision process as purely instrumental or a symbolic end in itself.

Utilitarian versus rule-based models of choice. Laboratory researchers stress the reality-appraisal and utility-maximizing functions of judgment and choice. People are posited to be intuitive scientists, engaged in a continuous struggle to achieve cognitive mastery of their world (Fiske and Taylor, 1991), and intuitive economists who use the resulting cognitive representations to identify courses of action that advance, if not maximize, their interests (Kagel and Roth, 1995). One's selection of functionalist metaphor should not be dismissed, however, as a mere matter of explanatory aesthetics; it is profoundly consequential. Tetlock (1992) has shown that our assessments of what counts as an error or bias are shaped by the metaphor-laden standards of rationality that we use to evaluate how people think. One example is the controversy surrounding the fundamental attribution error, the tendency to jump the inferential gun and to draw conclusions about the characters of others even when there are plausible alternative explanations for their conduct. This error looks most erroneous when we posit that people are intuitive scientists who dispassionately and rigorously evaluate evidence with the goal of identifying the true causes of behavior. A second example is base-rate neglect, the tendency to slight statistical generalizations and to give excessive weight to case-specific information in making predictions. This neglect counts most clearly as an error within a framework that posits people to be intuitive statisticians who use Bayesian or regression principles to minimize classification errors. A third example is trade-off aversion, the reluctance to acknowledge certain types of trade-offs or to treat certain values as fungible. This reluctance can be unequivocally classified as an error only within an intuitive-economist framework that insists that, in the search for utility-maximizing options, nothing is sacred or above calculation.

March and Olsen (1989, 1995) have urged us to step back and contemplate the possibility that these dominant functionalist metaphors do not capture real-world decision makers' conceptions of how they do or should make up their minds. As we move from the laboratory to actual organizations, decision makers may shift from quantitative utility-based logics to qualitative, rule-based logics of appropriateness that direct them to enact scripts linked to morally charged social identities. The refusal to factor base rates into one's calculations of likelihood of category membership, especially base rates that correlate with ethnicity or race, may reflect not our failings as intuitive statisticians but, rather, a principled defense of egalitarian values (Koehler, 1996; Tetlock et al., 2000). Outrage over taboo trade-offs—that affix monetary values to human life, loyalty, or integrity—may stem not from our shortcomings as intuitive economists but from our passionate desire as intuitive theologians to defend sacred values against secular encroachments (Tetlock, Peterson, and Lerner, 1996). Preferences for dispositional explanations for conduct, especially undesirable conduct, may derive not from our deficiencies as intuitive psychologists but from our shrewdness as intuitive prosecutors who recognize that one way to pressure

Biases and Correctives

people to live up to moral and performance expectations is to convey that one has a low threshold for drawing inferences about character from conduct. The no-excuses message is "Don't bother concocting ingenious stories for failure. I believe that what you do reveals a lot about who you are and your value to the organization."

Ambiguity about decision-making goals. Intuitive scientists seek clarity of understanding, and intuitive economists treat consistency as a minimal defining feature of rationality. In many organizational contexts, however, managers may function more like intuitive politicians whose guiding goal is to maintain good working relations with the diverse constituencies to whom they feel, for whatever reason, accountable. In this vein, Tetlock, Peterson, and Lerner (1996) documented that it is often adaptive for decision makers caught in accountability cross-pressures to find ways of fudging trade-offs (e.g., university administrators in late twentieth-century America who announced that excellence is diversity), of obfuscating where they stand on contested issues (e.g., by taking cover under moralistic platitudes and vague legalisms such as "we believe in fairness or equal opportunity"), and of convincing others that responsibility for controversial decisions lies elsewhere. Tetlock (1992) documented that it is often socially rational for decision makers confronted by complex or unfamiliar choice problems to select the most readily justifiable options, even if that means violating basic consistency axioms of rational-choice theory, such as ignoring irrelevant alternatives or violating the sure-thing principle (cf. Simonson, 1989).

Instrumental versus symbolic decision making. In many organizational settings, it is unclear when decision making is better viewed as a purely instrumental process or as a symbolic process that becomes a ritualistic end in itself for key constituencies. The intuitive-scientist metaphor depicts thought as a means to the end of understanding and solving problems, and the intuitive-economist metaphor depicts thought as a means to maximizing utility in competitive markets. A sound decision process yields good—ideally, the best possible—outcomes according to either an epistemic standard of evaluation such as Bayes' theorem or a utilitarian standard such as expected utility or game theory. Alternative functionalist metaphors alert us to the possibility that how decisions are made can be an important end in itself. In this vein, some observers defend multiple-advocacy, high-participation styles of decision making over more elitist, top-down styles not only on the consequentialist grounds that multiple advocacy leads to better outcomes (Janis and Mann, 1977; George, 1980), but also on the principled grounds that there is a moral imperative to give the full range of affected groups a voice in the process (Hirschman, 1970; Tetlock, 1999). Moreover, this moral argument for taking process seriously can be given an added consequentialist edge. People who feel that they have been treated unfairly become disaffected and more likely to protest, cheat, and resign (Tyler, 1990). Indeed, large parts of organizations may exist less for their instrumental rationality and more for their symbolic efficacy in convincing key internal and external constituencies that the organization is committed to sacrosanct societal values such as equal opportunity, environmental protection, or balancing work and family (Meyer, 1983).

Taken in its entirety, this Marchian inventory warns us that the normative standards that are useful in defining good judgment in the laboratory can be deeply misleading in organizational settings that are characterized by sharp contests for power and status, intense accountability pressures from conflicting constituencies, prickly principal-agent relationships, and enormous uncertainty about what should be done next. We should not be astonished, therefore, when work-a-day managers have the temerity to second-guess the normative pronouncements of high-profile experimental researchers. We should also not be astonished to discover systematic rifts in the opinions that managers themselves hold about what counts as a cognitive bias and about the types of organizational reforms that are likely to correct these biases, either by changing how employees think or by altering their thresholds for expressing particular thoughts.

Some theorists will treat disagreements over cognitive biases and organizational correctives as presumptive evidence that one camp must be right and the other wrong. Right and wrong take on clear-cut meanings within the intuitive-scientist framework, preoccupied as it is with maximizing epistemic goals, or within the intuitive-economist framework, preoccupied as it is with maximizing utilitarian goals in competitive markets that ruthlessly punish suboptimal practices. When the task is well-defined, there are rigorous mathematical baselines—derived from Bayes' theorem and decision theory—for gauging exactly how mistaken people are.

By contrast, right and wrong rapidly devolve into tendentious categorizations within a multifunctional theory of judgment and choice that incorporates less-well-defined goals and task constraints, such as projecting desired social identities to key constituencies, proclaiming fealty to sacred values, and defending the normative order. From a multifunctional perspective, disagreements over cognitive biases and organizational correctives count as presumptive evidence that the disputants subscribe to distinctive ideological worldviews that rest on diverging assumptions about human nature and the social order, about how to understand social reality and navigate oneself through it, and about the goals that give purpose to one's life and define one's relationship to various social structures. Confronted by disagreements over what is rational and how to fix alleged departures from rationality, the appropriate response is to trace these disagreements to their philosophical and ideological roots.

The current article proceeds from the premise that managers' opinions about cognitive biases and organizational correctives are rooted in competing epistemological and ideological worldviews, although most managers take pride in thinking of themselves as pragmatic problem solvers and resist characterizations of their views as either philosophical or ideological. Following research precedents in the literature on cognitive styles (Kruglanski and Webster, 1996; Tetlock, 1998), the study reported here assessed personal episte-

Biases and Correctives

mologies along a cognitive-style continuum that gauged strength of preference for conceptual simplicity and explanatory closure. At one end of the continuum are distaste for ambiguity and protracted debate and endorsements of the views that the social world is fundamentally simple, as are the most effective strategies of coping with it. At the other end are a high comfort level for dissonance and uncertainty and endorsements of the views that the social world is enormously complex and pluralistic and the most effective coping strategies for dealing with it require multifaceted perspective taking and trade-offs.

Following research precedents in the literature on political ideology in mass and elite samples (Lipsett and Raab, 1978; McClosky and Brill, 1983; Tetlock, 1984; Sniderman and Tetlock, 1986), ideological worldviews were assessed with a battery of items that tap views of human nature as well as endorsements of individualistic, egalitarian, environmentalist, and traditional conservative values. Consistent with past work on public attitudes, especially on elites (Kinder, 1998), it was impossible to forge a psychometrically defensible one-dimensional measure of ideology. A two-dimensional model did, however, fit the patterns of covariation among beliefs. The model includes (1) an authoritarianism factor, anchored at one end by authoritarian conservatism, characterized by an unapologetic defense of hierarchies and suspicions about the trustworthiness of the modal employee, and, at the anti-authoritarian egalitarian end by a distaste for hierarchy and a more benign view of humanity; and (2) a libertarianism factor, anchored at one end by libertarian conservatism, which is characterized by an enthusiastic embrace of market solutions, deep skepticism of government, and a view of humanity as resourceful, rational, and self-reliant, and, at the anti-libertarian egalitarian end, by a distaste for the cut-throat competition of capitalism, a fear of externalities, and a view of humanity as fragile and in need of protection by a caring state.

The guiding idea was that cognitive style and ideological worldview would jointly predict managerial reactions to a broad assortment of scenarios pitched at micro, meso, and macro levels of analysis. Predictions focused on (a) the soundness of strategies and styles of individual decision making; (b) the soundness of strategies of structuring and coping with accountability relationships; and (c) the soundness of competing political schemes for organizing accountability systems at the corporate or societal level.

Micro-level: Cognitive Biases

One possible predictor of what counts as a cognitive bias in social perception is baseline assumptions about the trustworthiness of other people. How prone are others to take advantage of the inevitable incompleteness of even the most formal contracts (not to mention informal understandings based on the proverbial handshake)? How wise is it to pressure others to live up to their ends of social bargains by indicating that one has a low threshold for drawing inferences about character even when extenuating circumstances exist? Other things being equal, the more pessimistic one's view of human nature, the more egoistic, calculating, and self-serving one should suppose others to be and the more likely one should be to approve of quickly drawing strong conclusions about the characters of employees who violate moral or performance norms of the organization. Drawing on past surveys of public opinion (McClosky and Brill, 1983; Sniderman and Tetlock, 1986), the following hypotheses are advanced:

H1: Authoritarian conservatives should subscribe to a more jaundiced view of humanity than do those on the ideological left.

H2: Authoritarian conservatives should rise to the normative defense of the fundamental attribution error by insisting both that the alleged error is not all that erroneous (people are often untrustworthy) and that it is often prudent (it is better, on average, to indict the occasional innocent soul than it is to fail to punish the sinful masses of defectors).

A second set of hypotheses highlight managers' opinions of the rationality and resilience of fellow human beings. The more doubts one harbors about the intellectual maturity of one's fellow human beings, about their tolerance for ambiguity and dissonance, the more prone one will be to adopt a hardball, authoritarian model of the ideal leader that springs right out of Machiavelli's advice to Renaissance princes. Drawing again on research on public opinion (Sniderman and Tetlock, 1986), as well as on cognitive style (Kruglanski and Webster, 1996), the following hypotheses are advanced:

H3: Authoritarian conservatives, especially those with strong preferences for cognitive closure, should most doubt the intellectual, emotional, and political maturity of subordinates.

H4: Authoritarian conservatives, especially those with strong preferences for cognitive closure, should display a pronounced affinity for leaders with simple, decisive styles of self-presentation that conceal private doubts and cloak imminent trade-offs under artful rhetoric.

At this juncture, skeptics might suspect that the apparent normative divergence between the laboratory classifications of effects as errors and biases and managers' assessments merely rests on a misunderstanding over levels of analysis. Conservative respondents may still see overconfidence, escalating commitment to sunk costs, and trade-off denial as private cognitive vices; they just also see them as public or political necessities. The disagreement revolves around what leaders need to do to sustain useful social illusions. To test whether authoritarian conservatives with strong preferences for closure subscribe to different theories of good judgment or of rhetorical manipulation, or perhaps both, we need to compare their reactions to private decision-making procedures as well as to public posturing. Here, though, there are reasons for predicting ideological effects in both private and public contexts. Drawing on survey research (Sniderman and Tetlock, 1986), archival content-analysis studies of political decision making (Tetlock, 1984), and laboratory studies of cognitive style (Kruglanski and Webster, 1996), it is hypothesized:

H5: Authoritarian conservatives should most strongly defend managers who (a) are confident in their private assessments of chal-

Biases and Correctives

lenges (even if they are systematically overconfident); (b) believe that failure to stay the course with fundamentally good ideas is a more common error than trying to recoup sunk costs by pouring resources into red-ink hemorrhaging projects; and (c) believe that exaggerating the complexity of problems is a more common error than overreliance on simple, intuitive rules of thumb.

A third dimension along which organizational theorists, and quite possibly managers, vary is their assumptions about the goals of judgment and choice (Tetlock, 1985; Tetlock and Boettger, 1989). Some subscribe to a monistic conception in which it is a bad idea to dilute core business objectives—efficiency and profit maximization—with ancillary goals that create unnecessary or distracting trade-offs (Jensen and Meckling, 1976); others subscribe to more pluralistic conceptions that place numerous moral and political constraints on the pursuit of efficiency (Etzioni, 1996). These observations lead to the following hypotheses:

H6: Anti-libertarian egalitarians should most object to factoring into policy deliberations statistical base rates that, however probative, work to the disadvantage of traditionally disadvantaged groups (e.g., setting insurance premiums in ways that reflect covariation between actuarial risk and racial/ethnic classification).

H7: Libertarian conservatives should take least umbrage at taboo trade-offs such as those that affix dollar values to human life.

Meso-level: Strategies for Accountability Systems

Opinions about what constitutes a cognitive bias or moral defect, and how pervasive those biases or defects are among the work force, should be closely coupled to opinions about how to design accountability systems that prevent these all-too-human shortcomings from impeding or tainting organizational functions. This argument leads to the tight-accountability-leash hypothesis:

H8: Authoritarian conservatives and those with strong preferences for cognitive closure should approve of bosses who give their subordinates well-defined job missions and monitor subordinates closely, whereas anti-authoritarian egalitarians should see good rationales for creating some degree of normative ambiguity and of encouraging imaginative thought experiments that undercut traditional ways of doing things.

A closely related argument is that these ideological and cognitive-stylistic preferences for order and discipline should seep into evaluations of how employees respond to accountability pressures from higher-ups:

H9: Authoritarian conservatives and those with strong preferences for cognitive closure should be more favorable to employees who have confident and decisive personas and who offer unequivocal recommendations, whereas anti-authoritarian egalitarians and those with weak closure preferences should favor employees with more self-critical and reflective personas who acknowledge uncertainty and enumerate complex trade-offs.

One recurring controversy in designing accountability systems concerns the relative emphasis to place on process accountability, which holds employees responsible for observing the correct decision-making procedures, and outcome accountability, which holds employees responsible for bottom-line performance indicators and permits considerable improvisation in pursuit of these objectives (cf. Chubb and Moe, 1990, on the accountability norms and relative bureaucratic overhead of private and public schools). Here the expectation is that egalitarians should favor process over outcome accountability but that authoritarian and libertarian conservatives should hold the opposite preference (Wilson, 1989):

H10: Anti-libertarian egalitarians fear the unfairness of holding people accountable for outcomes that are only partly under their control and, hence, are more willing to forgive those who fail but who followed the right procedures.

H11: Libertarian conservatives fear the perverse incentives created by shifting from a problem-solving focus on maximizing external outcomes to a ritualistic focus on observing prescribed routines. They tend to identify process accountability with the most notorious inefficiencies of public sector organizations. Authoritarian conservatives should share this concern but also worry about making performance appraisal unnecessarily cumbersome and opening the door to endless justifications and excuses for non-performance.

Yet another set of hypotheses predicts ideological variation in managerial reactions to accountability dilemmas that implicate classic problems of distributive and procedural justice. A recurring theme in the literature on distributive justice is the tension between efficiency, which requires directing resources to those who will use them most productively, and equality, which requires subsidizing the less productive (Messick, 1993). These ideological cleavages in the broader society should manifest themselves in managerial ideology:

H12: Anti-libertarian and anti-authoritarian egalitarians should resist concentrating budget cuts on the least productive, whereas libertarian and authoritarian conservatives should have no such compunctions.

With respect to procedural justice, there is the classic tension between the desire of authorities to enforce rules and the countervailing concern that everyone should feel that they had a fair say. The guiding hypotheses are:

H13: Anti-authoritarian and anti-libertarian egalitarians should be more sympathetic to employees who resisted decisions from above that ignored their point of view, sympathy that should extend not just to employees exercising the voice option (protest) and exit option (resignation) but even to employees engaging in conduct of dubious morality (loophole exploitation).

H14: Authoritarian conservatives should be more sympathetic to employees who defer to commands from above (conservatives are not embarrassed about talking about "subordinates") and more inclined to regard protestors as whiners and malcontents, quitters as disloyal, and loophole exploiters as cheaters.

H15: Libertarian conservatives should also back upper management, but less out of affinity for hierarchy and more out of deference to the core precepts of market pricing, formal contracts, and property rights. Their reactions to loophole exploiters should be harsh, but their reactions to protestors should be muted (they are less upset

Biases and Correctives

by insubordination), and their reactions to those who exit may even be positive (resourceful, self-reliant people don't passively accept ill-treatment, they find a better deal in the labor market).

Macro-level: Attitudes toward Corporate Governance

How should accountability relationships within the organization as a whole, and between the organization and the broader society, be structured? Working from the assumption that people who like simplicity in their immediate working environment prefer simplicity in the wider social universe, one hypothesis is that:

H16: Authoritarian conservatives and those with strong preferences for cognitive closure should be skeptical of multiple-advocacy systems that require soliciting and integrating inputs from a wide range of perspectives prior to reaching decisions and enthusiastic about hierarchical, top-down, decision systems that place a lot of authority in a few hands and permit rapid implementation of new initiatives.

This split between egalitarians and conservatives may be rooted in distinct cognitive and moral sources: those on the right should be both more dubious of the added utility of soliciting diverse inputs as a means to the end of better decisions (subordinates may actually detract from the quality of debate) and less committed to the egalitarian goal of giving voice, and the attendant sense that one has been heard, to the hoi polloi as a moral end in itself. Building on the same psycho-logic:

H17: Authoritarian conservatives who most value hierarchy and parsimony (seek rapid closure) will display stronger support for the shareholder model of corporate governance, a stringently monistic accountability regime that calls on management (the agents) to work single-mindedly toward the goal of greater financial returns to shareholders (the principals), and greater skepticism toward the stakeholder model, a more open-ended pluralistic accountability regime that calls on management to balance the contradictory demands of a cacophony of clamorous constituencies.

This preference for the shareholder model need not be rooted entirely in cognitive-stylistic affinity for accountability systems that make it easier to determine whether management is doing a good job. Libertarian as well as authoritarian conservatives should be especially sympathetic to the interests of the capitalized principals (who possess the moral trump card of rightful ownership and whose interests should be advanced as an end in itself), as well as more supportive of a single-minded focus on efficiency (Jensen and Meckling, 1976). Critical though they indisputably are to the long-term profitability of the enterprise, stakeholders "have not put their money where their mouths are" and occupy a distinctly secondary place in both the moral and pragmatic schemes of things. This argument leads to the following hypotheses:

H18: Libertarian and authoritarian conservatives will endorse the shareholder over the stakeholder model of corporate governance on the practical grounds that the shareholder model works better and on the moral grounds that property rights should trump other claims.

H19: Anti-libertarian and anti-authoritarian egalitarians will invoke mirror-image arguments to justify the stakeholder model: (a) given the pluralistic and interdependent character of modern business environments, it does not make practical sense to exclude key voices from the policy setting process; (b) economic underdogs and the traditionally disadvantaged have a moral right to be heard and won't be unless granted places on boards of directors (Etzioni, 1996).

In testing the above hypotheses, this study examined the patterns of consistency in managerial judgments of the soundness of decision-making practices and accountability procedures at micro, meso, and macro levels of analysis. The study focuses on the main and interactive effects of two key predictors of these patterns, ideological worldview and the cognitive-style construct of preference for simplicity and explanatory closure, but it also assessed a host of potential control variables, including private and public sector employment, gender, income, age, and education. Finally, although the current study is largely an exercise in hypothetico-deductive social science, there is an exploratory inductive dimension to the research design. In-depth interviews with ideological subsets of managers probed their justifications for their judgments at the different levels of analysis.

METHOD

Questionnaires were distributed to approximately 650 middle-managers in three public sector organizations (employing, on average, 5,000 persons) and three private-sector organizations (employing, on average, 4,500 persons). Of the managers in the target population, 39 percent ultimately responded to all or most of the questionnaire, yielding a sample of 259 managers who averaged 43.2 years of age, had 5.1 years of higher education, and had 8.2 years of experience in coordinating and supervising staffs that ranged in size from 4 to 210. The sex ratio was seven males to every three females. Data collection occurred in 1996 and 1997. The private-sector organizations included an insurance company and two high-technology firms; the public-sector organizations were civilian agencies of the federal government that specialized in national security or intelligence analysis and a state-level educational bureaucracy. Both individual respondents and organizational representatives were assured of the absolute confidentiality of all responses. The questionnaires were analytically partitioned into three components: ideological worldview, cognitive style, and preferred managerial styles, which measured reactions to micro, meso, and macro scenarios.

Ideological worldview. These items relied on 7-point semantic-differential-style scales to assess ideological self-identification, using a question adapted from the National Election Studies ("Overall, do you consider yourself to be a liberal or conservative?"), as well as views of the trustworthiness of other people ("Most people are looking for ways of getting away with something," and "When you treat employees with fairness and consideration, you can count on them to do the right thing even when no one is looking."), the resourcefulness and rationality of others ("People lower down in organizations generally understand a lot more than they are given credit for," "Even the strongest among us fall on hard times

Biases and Correctives

and need help from the community," and "A useful maxim in dealing with employees is KISS—keep it simple, stupid."), the willingness to defend explicit hierarchies ("I am not at all embarrassed to talk about 'subordinates' or 'people working under me in the chain of command,'" "It is not a perfect relationship but generally the higher in an organization you look, the more talented and hardworking the people tend to be," and "It sounds old-fashioned but obedience is an important virtue."), the willingness to defend the single-minded pursuit of profit-maximization ("It is a bad idea to mix business goals with concerns for social justice," and "Human progress owes a lot to innovators who had the courage of their convictions"), the relative importance of "avoiding being taken advantage of" versus "failing to reach mutually beneficial relationships with others," the necessity of strong leadership ("Most people are without direction in the absence of strong leadership."), enthusiasm for free markets (they "stimulate growth and prosperity"), wariness of markets ("We need government to protect us from the income inequality that results from unregulated free markets" or "to protect us from the damage to the natural environment that results from unregulated markets"), and attitudes toward government ("Overall, in our society today, government creates a lot more problems than it solves.").

Cognitive style. These cognitive style items were mostly adapted from Kruglanski and Webster's (1996) need-for-closure scale. They assessed tolerance for ambiguity ("I dislike questions that can be answered in many different ways," and "It is annoying to listen to someone who cannot seem to make up his or her mind.") and strength of personal preference for simple comprehensive explanations of phenomena, for working on problems with clear-cut solutions, and for working in homogeneous as opposed to heterogeneous social units ("The world is fundamentally a far simpler place than it initially seems to be"; "Even after I have made up my mind about something, I am always eager to consider a different opinion"; "I usually make important decisions quickly and confidently"; "When considering most conflict situations, I can usually see how both sides can be right"; "I prefer interacting with people whose opinions are very different from my own"; "It is better to accomplish one objective really well than it is to try to accomplish two or more objectives and do only a so-so job").

Micro Scenarios: Cognitive Biases

Fundamental attribution error. A pair of scenarios assessed approval of managers who varied in their receptiveness to employees' accounts for failure to achieve organizational goals. Half of the respondents were randomly assigned to the experimental condition in which they first read a scenario describing a prime managerial candidate for the fundamental attribution error—a manager with a low threshold for drawing strong conclusions about the character of his employees from performance data alone:

J. M. adopts a "no-excuses" approach to evaluating the people who report to him. He feels that most people are just far too inventive at concocting stories for failing to achieve organizational goals. He therefore holds people strictly accountable for objective performance indicators, taking into account only relatively extreme extenuating circumstances.

After rating the manager, these respondents then read a scenario that described an empathic manager who seemed a prime candidate for the flipside inferential bias, hyper-receptivity to any and all situational explanations that people might advance for their conduct:

L. V. thinks it a bad idea to base evaluations of the people reporting to him on so-called objective performance indicators. He needs to hear the employees' perspectives on why they failed or succeeded in achieving key organizational goals and always bases his evaluation primarily on the accounts that employees provide of what is actually going on in both the business and their personal lives.

The other half of the respondents read the scenarios in the opposite order. Dependent variables included eight descriptive phrases to which managers responded on 1–9 unipolar scales, ranging from "not at all characteristic" to "extremely characteristic." The traits were selected to capture the negative and positive value spins that could plausibly be attached to both managerial stances toward employees. The most negative value spin on the fundamental attribution error is that it reveals a "harsh" and "punitive" style of management; the most positive value spin is that it reveals "uncompromisingly high standards" and "a commitment to a no-nonsense, no-excuses working style" (alpha = .81). The most negative value spin on the flipside of the fundamental attribution error—hypersensitivity to situational accounts—is that such managers are "gullible" and "tolerant of low or inconsistent standards" (alpha = .84).

An additional single-item measure of attitude toward the fundamental attribution error was "Managers always run the risk in evaluating employees of two possible mistakes: (a) failing to hold them responsible for outcomes that they could and should have controlled; (b) holding them responsible for outcomes that they could not reasonably be expected to control." Participants then rated (on a 1–9 scale), the relative frequency and seriousness of these two errors in work settings today (with 9 representing the view that b is "by far the more common serious error").

Overconfidence. A second pair of counterbalanced scenarios explored evaluations of managers who viewed either over- or underconfidence as the more serious vice:

It is always possible to make one of two basic mistakes in decision-making: to be underconfident (to doubt that one has useful information in hand when one really does) or to be overconfident (to think one has useful information in hand when one really does not). But L. B./N. R. is convinced that underconfidence/overconfidence is much the more serious threat to high-quality decision-making and that [priority should be given to encouraging critical analysis of core assumptions, even if that slows decision making down] [priority should be given to advancing compelling arguments and mobilizing enthusiasm for what looks like the best option, even if it means acting too quickly].

Biases and Correctives

Dependent variables captured positive value spins on over-confidence (decisive, possesses a can-do attitude), as well as negative value spins (rigid/closed-minded, arrogant) (alpha = .76) and positive value spins on underconfidence (flexible/open-minded, possesses capacity for self-criticism), as well as negative value spins (indecisive, wishy-washy) (alpha = .78). In addition, a single-item measure of attitude toward over- and underconfidence explicitly distinguished between private thought and public self-presentation. Respondents rated their degree of preference (on a 9-point scale) for two styles of leadership: "M. V. believes that how-ever many doubts about a decision he may harbor privately, he needs to project confidence that he has the right answer to employees" versus "A. V. believes that if he has private doubts about a decision, it is a good idea to share those concerns with employees."

For *staying the course versus abandoning sunk costs,* participants rated the relative frequency of one of two mistakes that managers nowadays can make: they "are more likely to make the mistake of prematurely abandoning a good idea that runs into trouble" or "to make the flipside mistake of persevering too long with a bad idea and spending good money after bad." *Simple heuristics versus complex choice strategies* was assessed by the following item: "Which mistake do you think managers nowadays are more likely to make: to rely too heavily on simple, intuitive rules of thumb grounded in practical experience or to exaggerate the complexity of the issues at stake and to spend far too much time and energy seeking expert advice and developing complex decision-making procedures?" A single-item measure of *taboo trade-offs* explored reactions to a cost-benefit analysis that placed a dollar value on human life:

S. J. is an auto-industry executive who received a confidential cost-benefit analysis which indicated that the expected cost of correcting a potential safety defect is $900 million whereas the expected benefits (reduced legal liability from fewer injuries and deaths) is just $300 million, a 3:1 ratio in favor of taking no action. How do you think he should respond?: Should he go along with the recommendation and not undertake the repairs or reject the report's recommendation and order the potential safety defect corrected?

A single-item measure of morally suspect base rates explored the profit-maximization rooted in egalitarian/fairness concerns:

G. B. is an executive who discovered that, although the actuarial risk factors used to compute home-owners' insurance premiums are statistically and financially well designed to maximize profits and are not open to legal challenge, the net result of using these risk factors is that poor people, who come disproportionately from minority groups, wind up paying higher percentage premiums. How do you think he should respond?: Should he keep the current profit-maximizing policies in place or alter the current profit-maximizing policy and reduce the burden on the poor communities, notwithstanding the adverse effect on the corporate bottom line?

Meso Scenarios: Coping with Accountability

Preemptive self-criticism versus defensive bolstering was assessed with a pair of scenarios that posed the following problem:

Senior management has asked K. M. for his views on which projects in his division should be put on the "fast track." The "favorites" of senior management are at this point impossible to guess. He responds by [offering a complex and balanced appraisal of the pros and cons of each project, anticipating the key criticisms that can be leveled at each, and specifying the trade-offs that management confronts] [singling out the projects he considers most promising and making as powerful and compelling a case as he can for those options.]

Dependent variables included the same trait scales used in assessing reactions to over- and underconfidence, given that experimental evidence has shown that self-critical thought attenuates and bolstering amplifies overconfidence (Tetlock and Kim, 1987).

Open-ended versus directive accountability was assessed with the following pair of scenarios:

D. F. runs a policy planning group that consists of professionals with varying expertise. [He sees it as his job to guide the group by giving his opinion first and by laying out a clear discussion agenda that keeps meetings brief. He finds that this procedure helps to set definite boundaries on what it is and is not useful to consider.] [He sees it as his job to encourage the group members to think as creatively as possible and, to this end, he rarely reveals his opinion before everyone has had a say. Although meetings may be long, he believes that the process often reveals important new perspectives.]

Bipolar rating scales included positive and negative spins on open-ended accountability (open- versus closed-minded) and on directive accountability (well organized/poorly organized).

Process versus outcome accountability was assessed on the following pair of scenarios:

M. R. runs the purchasing department for his organization. [His philosophy is that employees are paid to implement carefully designed procedures for making deals with outside providers of goods and services. As long as employees follow the specified procedures for selecting high-quality products at competitive bids, employees know they won't get into trouble—even if the resulting price paid is too high.] [His philosophy is that employees are paid to get the best possible prices for high-quality products. The purchasing procedure guidelines are just that—guidelines, not fixed rules. Employees who pay too high a price or who buy defective merchandise jeopardize their careers. Following procedures is no defense.]

Positive value-spin descriptions of the process-accountability manager included fair and systematic; negative spins included rule-bound and bureaucratic (alpha = .75). Positive value spin descriptions of the outcome-accountability manager included resourceful and effective; negative value spins included excessively demanding and unfair (alpha = .83).

A pair of scenarios assessed managers' reactions to the necessity to concentrate or diffuse the pain of cuts:

Biases and Correctives

B. G. just learned that the department received a 10% cut in its annual operating budget. He responds [by trying to distribute the burden of the cuts fairly and equally across all employees who work for him] [by trying to maximize the efficiency of his organization—laying off those employees who contribute the least to productivity and streamlining operations by introducing new technology that reduces the need for future hiring].

Dependent variables captured positive and negative value spins that liberals and conservatives might place on the egalitarian versus efficiency responses to austerity. The positive value spin on concentrating the cuts on the least productive was that this policy "promotes profitability and efficiency" and "sends the right message to employees who take their jobs for granted"; the negative value spin was that this policy "violates the trust the workers have placed in the organization" (the implicit social contract) and "erodes the loyalty toward the organization and breeds cynicism and distrust." Alpha for the 4-item scale was .79. The positive value spin on diffusing the cuts is that sharing burdens equally was "morally right in itself" and also "promotes solidarity at the workplace"; the negative value spin was that this policy is merely "a cowardly dodge to avoid controversy" and "is short-sighted and likely to destroy the organization in the long term." Alpha for this 4-item scale was .76.

Scenarios assessing voice, exit, exploitation, and loyalty probed reactions to resistance to accountability that take the form of protest (exercising the voice option) looking for another job (exercising the exit option) and strategic exploitation of loopholes in the accountability guidelines:

P. T. learns that the work unit he manages will be expected in the coming year to achieve an increase in productivity he considers unreasonably and unfairly large. His unit was not consulted at all during the process of setting the new productivity standard. The firm is doing well and in no danger of insolvency. P. T. [protests by providing a detailed set of reasons why he considers the new standards to be both unreasonable and unfair to his work unit] [resigns to take another job] [looks for loopholes in the new accountability guidelines that allow him to "play games with numbers" in ways that artificially inflate the perceived productivity of his unit] [keeps his objections to himself and does the best he can do to achieve the new performance standards].

Dependent variables captured positive and negative value spins on voice (alpha = .75), exit (alpha = .82), subversion (alpha = .77), and compliance (alpha = .80): voice (whiny, ineffective/honest, principled), exit (disloyal, opportunistic/self-reliant, autonomous), subversion (cheater, fraud/reasonable response to unreasonable demands, resourceful), and compliance (easily bullied, submissive/can-do attitude, loyal worker).

Macro Scenarios: Accountability Regimes

A pair of scenarios assessed preferences for multiple advocacy versus hierarchical filtering as styles of organizational decision making:

Top management in this organization have worked together a long time and know each other well. [They think it most important to make decisions efficiently, minimizing unnecessary discussion and getting to the key points quickly. Accordingly, they have streamlined the decision process, requiring top managers to justify important decisions to the group but rarely requiring them to go outside the group to solicit critical suggestions.] [They think it most important to subject important decisions to thorough, critical analysis from a variety of viewpoints inside and outside the organization, even if it is time consuming. Accordingly, top managers can never be sure of the types of objections that might be raised to their proposals in decision-making meetings.]

Dependent variables included positive value spins on hierarchical filtering ("permits decisive action in rapidly changing situations," "preserves clear lines of authority") and on multiple advocacy ("compels decision makers to confront unpleasant facts," "prevents the error of acting impulsively") and negative spins on hierarchical filtering ("encourages an overconfident and clique-ish attitude at the top," "promotes a rigid, authoritarian structure") and on multiple advocacy ("creates a serious risk of waffling and paralysis," "promotes anarchy—everyone wants a say on everything"). Alpha for hierarchical-filtering scales was .79 and, for multiple advocacy, .86.

This pair of scenarios probed implicit philosophies of corporate governance with respect to shareholder versus stakeholder:

Corporation x is founded on the philosophy that it exists [for one overriding purpose—to maximize return to shareholders—and that, if every corporation were faithful to this mission, the net long-term result would be a vibrant economy that produces the greatest prosperity for the greatest number] [to achieve a variety of sometimes conflicting goals, including providing competitive returns to shareholders, ensuring all employees of good livelihoods and respectful treatment, maintaining good relations with customers, suppliers, and local communities, and pursuing sound social and environmental policies. In this view, if every corporation were faithful to these multiple missions, the net long-term result would be a fundamentally more decent and just society.]

Dependent variables included positive value spins on the two models of governance (shareholder: "keeps the faith with investors," "maximizes efficiency and long-term viability of the organization"; stakeholder: "keeps faith with the society as a whole," "promotes social justice") and negative value spins (shareholder: "short-sighted profit maximizing," "dehumanizes everyone but the investors"; stakeholder: "creates a blank check for lazy, inept, or corrupt managers," "prevents managers from making tough decisions critical for long-term survival"). Alpha for the shareholder scale was .84 and, for the stakeholder scale, .81.

Exploratory interviews. Priority was placed on intensively examining respondents with unusually coherent and well-defined ideological world views. Accordingly, libertarian conservatives who were interviewed had high scores on the factor by that name (preference for market-based solutions and distaste for government intervention, coupled with faith in people as rational and resilient) and low to moderate scores on the authoritarianism factor (an aversion to hierarchy). Egalitarians had low scores on both the libertarianism and

Biases and Correctives

authoritarianism factors. Authoritarian conservatives had high scores on the factor by that name and middle-range scores on the libertarianism factor (their scores on this factor should be inflated by their support for market solutions but should be deflated by their skepticism about the rationality of their fellow citizens). Finally, moderates or centrists scored in the middle range of both factors and were interviewed for comparison purposes. Interviews were conducted with 26 managers who represented four distinct political points of view: eight authoritarian conservatives, seven egalitarians, five libertarian conservatives, and six moderates or centrists. These interviews explored the explanations that managers offered for their reactions to each scenario from the structured questionnaire.

RESULTS

Independent-variable scales. Maximum-likelihood factor analysis indicated that the preference for simplicity and explanatory closure (PSEC) scale was reasonably unidimensional. The scale as a whole possessed adequate internal reliability (alpha = .77). By contrast, the same factor-analytic procedure indicated that the best representation of the underlying correlational structure of the measures of ideological worldview was two-dimensional. Table 1 presents the variable loadings that emerged from the two-factor oblimin rotated matrix. The first factor captured authoritarian conservatism. High-loading items included doubts about the trustworthiness of others, skepticism that even employees who have been treated fairly well will reciprocate by "doing the right thing when no one else is looking," placing a greater priority on avoiding exploitation (being taken for a sucker) than

Table 1

Variable Loadings in Rotated Factor Matrix from Maximum-likelihood Analysis

Variable	Authoritarian conservatism	Libertarian conservatism
Self-identification as conservative	.22	.19
Untrustworthiness of other people	.38	.04
Can count on employees doing right thing when no one is looking	−.35	.00
Underlings understand a lot	−.22	.02
Even the strong need help	.14	.27
"Keep it simple, stupid"	.41	.08
Embarrassed by talk of "subordinates"	−.27	−.10
System is meritocratic	.30	.26
Obedience is an underrated virtue	.29	.00
Don't mix business goals with social justice	.25	.41
Society owes much to courageous innovators	.16	.49
Avoiding exploitation less important than joint gain	−.37	.02
People are rudderless without leaders	.43	−.05
Free markets promote prosperity	.21	.46
Need government to check impact of free markets on inequality	−.20	−.35
Need governments to check impact of free markets on the environment	−.11	−.09
Government creates more problems than it solves	.24	.38

on failing to achieve mutually beneficial agreements, the belief that obedience is an important and underrated virtue, the belief that people are rudderless without strong leadership, and wariness of government intervention in the economy. Low scores captured anti-authoritarian egalitarianism: a distaste for obedience and hierarchies, a relatively benign view of people as decent and fair, and a willingness to give those lower down in the pecking order the benefit of the doubt.

The second factor captured libertarian conservatism, highlighting items that tapped into faith in free markets, wariness of government intervention in the economy, and a view of people as rational, resourceful, and self-reliant. Low scores captured anti-libertarian egalitarianism: support for a safety-net state that redistributes income and carefully watches for negative externalities of free-market behavior, doubts about how meritocratic society really is, doubts about great-man theories of social progress, and a view of individual human beings as fragile and in need of considerable social support. Interestingly, high scorers on both factors tended to label themselves as conservative and Republican, and low-scorers tended to label themselves as Democrats and liberal, in the conventional late-twentieth century sense of that term. Alphas for the resulting scales were .84 and .78, respectively.

Although scores on the two factors are moderately positively correlated ($r = .22$), it is a mistake to attribute much significance to that relationship, hinging as it does on the proportion of items pertaining to skepticism of government and support for markets (inflating the correlation) versus the proportion of items tapping views of human nature and support for authority and hierarchy (depressing the correlation). The low positive correlation between authoritarian conservatism and preference for cognitive closure ($r = .21$) is less easily dismissed, replicating as it does a long-standing body of work on the links between cognitive style and ideology (Lipsett and Raab, 1978; Tetlock, 1984). It is worth stressing, though, that confirmatory factor analysis applied to all individual-difference predictors supports that factorial distinctness of authoritarian conservatism and preference for cognitive closure.

Multiple regressions. Table 2 summarizes a series of multiple regressions that used the two-factor measure of ideological worldview and the measure of cognitive style as predictors of what counts as both cognitive bias and organizational corrective. Control variables included private-public sector employment, seniority, income, education, and gender. Table 3 presents the mean evaluative reactions of respondents who scored in the top and bottom tertiles of the measures of ideological worldview and need for closure (the most consistent predictors) to each of the scenarios and their variants.

As the regression coefficients in table 2 and the means in table 3 reveal, ideology in its two-factor form proved a robust predictor of reactions across levels of analysis. With respect to putative cognitive biases, support emerged for H1 and H2. Authoritarian conservatives were more favorable to the no-excuses manager (who committed the fundamental attribution error of insensitivity to situational explanations) and less

Biases and Correctives

Table 2

Coefficients of Multiple Regression Predictors of Evaluations of Micro, Meso, and Macro Scenarios

		Key Predictors (Standardized Betas)		
Scenarios	R^2	Authoritarian conservatism	Libertarian conservatism	Need closure
Cognitive biases				
Overattribution	.26	.38**	.10	.30*
Underattribution	.24	−.36**	−.07	−.24**
Overconfidence (private thought)	.22	.25**	.23*	.27**
Underconfidence (private thought)	.20	−.29**	−.22*	−.23**
Overconfidence (public self-presentation)	.19	.23*	.22*	.03
Sunk-cost justification serious problem	.18	−.29*	.01	−.25
Complex heuristics trump simple	.25	−.35*	−.02	−.32*
Use morally suspect base rate	.17	.25*	.27*	.02
Make taboo trade-off	.12	.08	.31*	−.01
Coping with accountability				
Preemptive self-criticism	.23	−.33**	.02	−.34**
Defensive bolstering	.22	.26**	.01	.23*
Directive accountability	.15	.22*	.03	.19*
Open-ended accountability	.14	−.23*	.00	−.19*
Process accountability	.11	.03	−.25*	.13
Outcome accountability	.13	.14	.28*	.09
Diffuse cuts/minimize protest	.24	−.28**	−.32**	−.07
Concentrate cuts/maximize efficiency	.23	.24*	.33**	−.10
Protest (voice)	.19	−.26**	−.18	−.14
Exit	.18	.02	.38**	.02
Loophole exploitation	.29	−.34**	−.33**	.00
Loyalty	.17	.26*	.18*	.02
Designing accountability systems				
Shareholder	.31	.31**	.39**	.10
Stakeholder	.27	−.29**	−.35**	−.08
Hierarchical filtering	.18	.30**	−.04	.26*
Multiple advocacy	.17	−.20*	.01	−.28*

* $p < .01$; ** $p < .05$.

favorable to the empathic manager (who committed the flip-side error of hypersensitivity to excuses that deflect responsibility for non-performance). There was also an unusually powerful association between certain single-item questions and reactions to the diverging attributional styles of managers. Respondents were especially positive toward the no-excuses manager and skeptical about the effectiveness of the sensitive manager to the degree that (a) they suspected "most people are continually looking for what they can get away with"; (b) they placed high importance on "preventing others from taking advantage of them"; and (c) they felt that managers erred far more often in the direction of letting employees off the hook for outcomes they could control than in wrongly blaming employees for outcomes they could control (all r's > .30). Indeed, the conservatism factor ceased to predict reactions to these scenarios after controlling for these three items [partial $r(240) = 0.09$]. Suspiciousness of human nature, which loads highly on the authoritarianism but not on the libertarianism factor, may thus be driving this effect.

Consistent with past psychological work on cognitive style, managers with strong preferences for cognitive closure, regardless of ideology, were more likely to defend the fundamental attribution error. This result suggests that the psychological appeal of the alleged error is also rooted in aversion to

Table 3

Mean Evaluations of Scenarios*

	Bottom and Top Tertiles		
Scenarios	Low/high conservatism	Low/high libertarianism	Low/high need closure
Overattribution	3.10 vs. 5.12	3.86 vs. 4.03	3.52 vs. 5.03
Underattribution	5.21 vs. 3.99	4.39 vs. 4.32	4.83 vs. 3.86
Overconfidence (private thought)	4.02 vs. 5.22	4.35 vs. 4.91	4.21 vs. 5.03
Underconfidence (private thought)	5.08 vs. 3.80	4.28 vs. 3.74	4.71 vs. 3.72
Overconfidence (public posturing)	3.86 vs. 6.02	4.12 vs. 5.73	4.41 vs. 5.55
Sunk-cost justification serious problem	6.02 vs. 3.52	5.05 vs. 5.37	6.15 vs. 3.71
Complex heuristics trump simple	6.33 vs. 3.66	5.14 vs. 5.01	5.99 vs. 3.18
Use morally suspect base rate	3.22 vs. 5.21	3.15 vs. 5.35	3.66 vs. 4.08
Make taboo trade-off	4.46 vs. 4.71	3.85 vs. 5.53	4.03 vs. 4.25
Preemptive self-criticism	5.39 vs. 4.21	4.78 vs. 4.98	5.54 vs. 4.22
Defensive bolstering	4.05 vs. 5.47	4.70 vs. 4.91	4.04 vs. 5.54
Directive accountability	4.72 vs. 6.05	5.15 vs. 5.25	4.42 vs. 5.89
Open-ended accountability	5.42 vs. 4.59	5.08 vs. 5.03	5.61 vs. 4.48
Process accountability	5.23 vs. 5.33	5.26 vs. 3.88	5.14 vs. 5.41
Outcome accountability	4.84 vs. 5.45	4.32 vs. 5.75	5.08 vs. 5.24
Diffuse cuts/minimize protest	4.85 vs. 2.80	5.04 vs. 2.71	3.76 vs. 4.03
Concentrate cuts/maximize efficiency	3.29 vs. 5.35	3.07 vs. 5.65	4.08 vs. 4.25
Protest (voice)	4.62 vs. 3.13	4.14 vs. 3.65	4.33 vs. 4.20
Exit	4.13 vs. 4.25	3.49 vs. 5.45	4.12 vs. 4.17
Loophole exploitation	3.76 vs. 2.83	3.80 vs. 2.70	3.53 vs. 3.55
Loyalty	4.93 vs. 5.38	4.62 vs. 5.17	4.31 vs. 4.86
Shareholder	3.37 vs. 5.21	3.16 vs. 5.37	4.20 vs. 4.31
Stakeholder	5.52 vs. 3.06	5.23 vs. 3.26	4.40 vs. 4.10
Hierarchical filtering	3.37 vs. 4.89	3.90 vs. 3.83	3.41 vs. 4.26
Multiple advocacy	5.45 vs. 4.21	4.73 vs. 4.59	4.99 vs. 4.32

*Higher scores indicate a more positive evaluation of the manager, coping strategy, or accountability regime.

the ambiguity that inevitably arises in weighing justifications and excuses for failure. Summary social justice simplifies life.

Authoritarian and libertarian conservatives had similar reactions to the over-/underconfidence scenarios. Consistent with H3, H4, and H5, both camps reacted favorably toward the manager who felt that overconfidence was, all other things being equal, a less serious error than underconfidence in both private decision making and public self-presentations to employees. Again, though, a more fine-grained analysis revealed especially powerful associations between certain items and reactions to the over- versus underconfident managers. Partial correlation analysis revealed that authoritarian conservatism ceased to predict reaction to the scenarios after controlling for endorsement of the maxim that, in dealing with employees, it is important to "keep it simple, stupid." Libertarian conservatism ceased to predict reactions after controlling for endorsement of the claim that human progress owed a lot to innovators with the courage of their convictions. Thus, although the two camps on the right agreed, they did not have the same reasons for taking this common stand. Support could be rooted in fear and distrust or in hope and techno-optimism.

Also consistent with H4 and H5, authoritarian conservatives were the most favorably disposed toward managers who thought that abandoning good ideas that had run into temporary trouble was a more common mistake than persevering

Biases and Correctives

with bad ideas (and vainly trying to save face and recoup sunk costs) and that excessive "complexification" was a more common mistake than excessive simplification in decision making. Libertarian conservatism predicted neither sentiment.

The cognitive-style predictions received more mixed support. As Kruglanski and Webster (1996) predicted, the stronger are managers' preferences for closure, the more support they offered for overconfidence, for staying the course, and for simplifying decision processes. But cognitive style did not predict support for overconfidence in public self-presentation, and none of the expected conservatism-by-cognitive-style interactions materialized.

Consistent with H6, authoritarian conservatives and libertarian conservatives were largely on the same ideological wavelength in their reactions to the morally suspect base rate. Unlike the anti-authoritarians and anti-libertarian egalitarians, these two groups refrained from condemning a business practice that, in pursuit of profit, harmed traditionally disadvantaged groups. This stance was rooted, according to partial-correlation analysis, in the degree to which respondents thought it a bad idea to mix business goals with concerns for social justice. There was also some support for H7: libertarian conservatives, not now joined by authoritarian conservatives, were virtually alone in refraining from condemning the executive who committed the taboo trade-off of affixing an explicit dollar value to human life.

Managers' reactions to strategies of structuring accountability were consistent with H8: authoritarian conservatives and those with strong closure preferences stood out as most critical of open-ended accountability (in which the boss keeps subordinates guessing about where he stands) and most supportive of directive accountability, in which the boss squarely assumes the mantle of responsibility for setting priorities. Partial correlation analysis suggested that this effect was partly rooted in the belief that people are rudderless without strong leadership.

With respect to strategies of coping with accountability, consistent with H9, both authoritarian conservatism and the preference for cognitive closure scale predicted the attribution of more positive traits to decision makers who coped with accountability by taking clear simple stands from which they could not be easily swayed. Authoritarian conservatism and preference for closure were also negatively associated with the attribution of more positive traits to decision makers who coped with accountability by engaging in preemptive self-criticism and by weighing legitimate competing perspectives against each other. The expected conservatism-by-cognitive-style interactions did not emerge.

There was only partial support for H10 and H11. As expected, libertarian conservatives were the stoutest defenders of outcome accountability and most critical of process accountability, which they disparaged as "just more bureaucracy" and "rules for the sake of rules." Unexpectedly, however, they were not joined by authoritarian conservatives who seemed quite ambivalent about the relative emphasis that should be placed on process and outcome accountability.

In the results for the more overtly political strategies of coping with accountability, support emerged for H12, that authoritarian and libertarian conservatives would be more likely than their egalitarian counterparts to (a) condemn the manager who, in their view, avoided the tough decisions by spreading budget cuts equally rather than targeting the cuts at the least productive and then restructuring to compensate for shifts in the division of labor; and (b) applaud the manager who "bit the bullet" and "allocated scarce resources more rationally."

The ideological agreement broke down somewhat, however, in reactions to the voice, exit, exploitation, and loyalty scenarios. Relative to the low scores on the two factors, authoritarian and libertarian conservatives were both more likely to deplore the subversive, loophole-exploiting response to rising accountability demands and, to a lesser extent, more likely to applaud the loyalty response (all in accord with H13 and H14). But, in accord with H15, libertarian conservatives had a much more positive reaction to the exit response (competent individuals exercising choices in self-correcting labor markets) than did the authoritarian conservatives, who saw the same conduct as rather opportunistic. Authoritarian conservatives also had a more negative reaction to protest than did the libertarians, but not a more negative reaction to cheaters, contrary to H15, a null result probably attributable to a floor effect on the rating scales for cheaters.

Finally, sharp ideological cleavages emerged in managers' evaluations of macro scenarios that explored the tensions between the hierarchical-filtering and multiple-advocacy models of internal corporate governance and the tensions between the shareholder-stakeholder models of external corporate governance. Consistent with H16, authoritarian but not libertarian conservatives judged top management more favorably when it relied on hierarchical filtering to simplify the decision process (screening out weak or irrelevant arguments), whereas anti-authoritarian egalitarians reserved the most praise for top managers who embraced a multiple-advocacy style of decision making that gave priority to considering inputs from a wide range of interest groups within the organization. Consistent with H17 and H18, authoritarian and libertarian conservatives alike judged top management more favorably when it favored a monistic accountability regime centered around shareholders, whereas low scorers on these two factor-analytic scales moved in the opposite direction, attributing the most positive traits to top managers who endorsed the pluralistic regime of accountability to stakeholders. Inconsistent with H17, the preference-for-closure scale failed to predict preferences for accountability regimes at this most macro level. The stands that middle-level managers took on the shareholder-stakeholder debate reflected abstract political sympathies (property rights of well-capitalized principals versus human rights of economic underdogs) more than personal cognitive style. Whether this result would hold up for top management—whose working lives are more tightly linked to the mode of corporate governance—is an open question.

Biases and Correctives

General observations. Overall, the measures of ideology, and to a lesser extent cognitive style, were the statistically dominant predictors. Moreover, the cognitive style results roughly paralleled those for authoritarian conservatism, with high scorers on the need-for-closure scale resembling authoritarian conservatives in their preference for simple decision-making styles across levels of analysis, but most noticeably at the micro and meso levels. The expected interactive effects of conservatism and cognitive style never emerged.

Among the control variables entered into the regressions, private-sector employment and gender had significant zero-order correlations with decision-style preferences. With only a few exceptions, however, the effects of these alternative predictors disappeared in the multiple regressions. The exceptions included a tendency for women to prefer an openness to situational explanations for performance shortfalls and for public-sector managers to prefer to avoid controversy by spreading the pain of budget cuts equally across constituencies. There was also some tendency for ideology effects to be larger (and justifications for policy preferences to be longer) the more years managers had spent in institutions of higher learning.

Supplementary Analyses of Qualitative Data

The interviews had three guiding objectives. The first was to assess the explanations that managers offered for preferring one or another style of making decisions or of structuring accountability. Could these free-flowing, stream-of-consciousness justifications be mapped onto the conceptual framework advanced earlier, which traces diverging conceptions of good judgment to more fundamental divergences in ideological worldview and in cognitive style? Does a qualitative analysis of the accounts that managers advance for their questionnaire responses point us in the same explanatory direction as do the multiple regression analyses reported earlier? The second objective was to assess the degree to which respondents possessed an intuitive awareness of the types of arguments that might be advanced for alternative answers to the questionnaire and the degree to which they accepted or disparaged these alternative outlooks. The third was to assess managers' willingness, in principle, to change their minds if it turned out that some of the factual arguments underpinning alternative answers were correct.

Fundamental attribution error. When queried, managers quite readily acknowledged the role of fundamental assumptions about human nature in shaping their openness to subordinates' accounts for failing to satisfy performance expectations. As the regression results led us to expect, the less trustworthy and committed they thought employees were ("to do the right thing when no one is looking"), the greater their reluctance to accept accounts. Managers with strong opinions on the perils of overattribution or underattribution virtually always had an accompanying horror story. Those who deplored overattribution usually had, ready at hand, there-but-for-the-grace-of-God-go-I parables in which decent, hardworking folks are temporarily overwhelmed by forces outside of their control—bad marriages, disease, depression, problem children—but eventually overcome these forces and become esteemed members of the organization, an outcome that would have been impossible if their bosses had not been caring and empathic ("open doors, open ears, open minds"). Sometimes, the managers recalled that they themselves were once in the role of the floundering subordinate. By contrast, those most concerned with the perils of underattribution came armed with stories that cut in the opposite direction: parables of free-riders exploiting gullible managers, in which shady characters concoct one cockamamie excuse or justification after another for non-performance and, in the process, harm coworkers, the managers in charge, and the organization as a whole. One manager waxed Shakespearian, "To be kind I must be cruel." One does no one any favors by pretending that poor performance is not poor or does not impose burdens on others who wind up suffering financial penalties or taking on extra work. A few of these tough managers even had stories about receiving thank-you notes from people they had fired. These reformed slackers and ne'er do wells eventually came to appreciate the wake-up call (cf. Rodgers, Taylor, and Foreman, 1992).

Styles of decision making and of structuring accountability. Managers justified their preferences for certain styles of decision making, in part, by invoking competing views of human nature. Some managers, especially authoritarian conservatives, subscribed to an implicit theory of leadership that stressed the importance of always projecting can-do confidence to others and not acknowledging errors as long as those errors can be "spun" into sound decisions: "If you don't believe in yourself, don't expect others to believe in you" (one defense of overconfidence at the level of private thought), and "Hamlets don't inspire confidence—you need to show a little bluster to get the troops moving" (a defense at the level of public self-presentation). Others, especially anti-authoritarian egalitarians, subscribed to the view that one gains the long-term respect of others by honestly admitting one's shortcomings and displaying a willingness to heed constructive criticism and make timely mid-course corrections.

But rationales for decision-making styles were also rooted in competing views of the challenges confronting the organization. Some managers, especially authoritarian conservatives, explicitly declared that, in many choice situations, one quickly reaches the point of diminishing marginal returns for further information search and analysis, whereas other managers, especially egalitarians, were equally explicit about the need to be wary of "premature closure." Popular refrains among those most skeptical of the value of protracted cognitive assessments of problems included "Time is money," "Real managers make decisions, they don't talk about them," "On-the-one-hand-and-on-the-other presentations get tiresome very quickly," and, most crudely, "S–t or get off the pot." Those more sympathetic to protracted cognitive assessments were equipped with fewer snappy aphorisms, but the gist of their comments was plain enough: "Learn to live with uncertainty," and "As soon as you stop hearing that little voice in the back of your mind saying 'you might be wrong,' you are definitely in trouble." These cleavages in managers'

Biases and Correctives

intuitive theories of decision making thus mirror themes in the now vast literature on contingency theories of social cognition and decision making (Chaiken and Trope, 1999) and the ongoing controversy over when simple heuristics generate as accurate assessments and as utility-enhancing decisions as do more complex and effort-demanding methods of making up one's mind (Gigerenzer and Todd, 1999).

Libertarian conservatives, with their dislike of rule-bound systems that constrain individual initiative, were harshest in their evaluations of the process-accountability manager ("He personifies what was wrong with the old approach to running businesses," and "That's how you get $1000 toilet seats.") and most favorable to the outcome-accountability manager ("who pays the people working for him the highest compliment: they are smart and they should use their smarts."). Authoritarian conservatives and egalitarian liberals had more mixed reactions, winding up on approximately the same locations on the rating scales but for somewhat different reasons. Moralistic conservatives rated both managers quite favorably. They resonated to the structure that the process-accountability manager gave employees and to the no-nonsense, results orientation of the outcome-accountability manager. Egalitarians were also quite favorable to both managers. They resonated to the procedural fairness of the process regime and to the autonomy to stray from guidelines in the outcome regime, although the latter reaction was qualified by concern that the outcome accountability regime might unfairly assume more potential employee control over outcomes than is humanly possible.

Authoritarian conservatives offered the most positive evaluations of the executive who ran meetings quickly and directed discussion down avenues he deemed productive ("Isn't this what leaders are supposed to do?") and the least positive evaluations of the executive who adopted a low profile in group discussions in order to stimulate creativity ("I understand the rationale but it looks like dilly-dallying and passing the buck to me."). Libertarian conservatives and egalitarians had one of their rare moments of convergence: they both made more positive character attributions to the manager who encouraged creativity among subordinates ("a reasonable strategy for encouraging open expression of unpopular opinions") and less positive attributions to the manager who played a more proactive role in steering the conversation ("He seems to want an echo chamber for his own views.").

Moral boundaries on the thinkable. Libertarian conservatives were least appalled by the life-money trade-off, often taking the position that no product is perfectly safe and that the market will punish manufacturers who sell particularly unsafe products. As one libertarian commented, "If people really wanted perfectly safe cars, they'd drive in tanks and accept 10-mile-per-hour speed limits. The hypocrisy . . . is overwhelming." Nonetheless, even this libertarian reluctantly endorsed recall, because "the public-relations hit could easily exceed the legal tab." The only other libertarian who thought the company should recall the cars with the potential defect did so not on the grounds that it was immoral to monetize life, a taboo trade-off (Tetlock, Peterson, and Lerner, 1996;

Fiske and Tetlock, 1997) but, rather, on the grounds that the company may not have been fully honest with its customers about the risks to their safety and thus prevented the customers from making money-life trade-offs of their own. By contrast, egalitarians were quite vehement in denouncing resistance to a vehicle recall, and their irritation focused on the taboo character of the trade-off ("Decent human beings just aren't supposed to dollarize human life," and "Who would want to do business with a company that doesn't care about your safety? It's just one more step and we start saying the lives of the poor are worth a lot less than those of the rich."). Authoritarian conservatives fell between libertarian conservatives and egalitarian. They shared the libertarian view that nothing is perfectly safe (and therefore that taboo trade-offs are an inevitable part of life) but shared the egalitarians' repugnance for the explicitness with which the cost-benefit analysis translated lives into money. Unlike the egalitarians, though, who invoked a secular morality to express their repugnance, authoritarian conservatives tended to use the religious language of "sin" and even "evil." One authoritarian conservative nicely captured the ambivalence of this faction toward taboo trade-offs: "I am not an idiot. I know that businesses and their customers can't put 100% emphasis on safety. But we shouldn't be so upfront about putting a dollar value on human life. Call it hypocrisy if you want, I think it is degrading. Society must treat some things as sacred."

Egalitarians were also most upset about the executive who kept in place a premium policy that boosted profits but hurt racial minorities and the poor, whereas libertarian and authoritarian conservatives were least bothered. Indeed, libertarians were unapologetic backers of the executive who retained the profit-maximizing scheme ("He was honoring his responsibilities to his firm and to the shareholders, not pandering to pressure groups. If he wants to give to charity, let him spend his own money, not other people's.").

Shareholder-stakeholder controversy. Managers for this study were drawn largely from the middle ranks of large organizations and had little experience making decisions that required answering directly either to shareholder or stakeholder representatives. Here, we thus entered a realm remote from the cognitive and interpersonal challenges that participants faced in their everyday lives—answering pressing questions such as "Is this person trustworthy or competent?" and "Should I decide now or give it more thought?" The tension between the two models of corporate governance struck many as a tad contrived. In the words of one skeptical centrist, "I don't get it. How can you please shareholders if everyone—from the customers to the politicians—is furious with you? And how can you keep stakeholders happy if you don't have any money to spread around?" That said, though, the interviews also revealed why ideology still predicted preferences for models of corporate accountability. Authoritarian and libertarian conservatives gravitated toward the shareholder model largely for the ideologically correct reason, the primacy of property rights: shareholders are owners of the corporation and managers are their agents.

Biases and Correctives

Authoritarian conservatives also occasionally added a procedural reason, an almost visceral distaste for messy accountability arrangements that blur lines of authority ("Where's the boss in this system and how will we ever know if he's doing a good job?") and that make it difficult to hold anyone accountable for anything ("Where does the buck stop in a setup like that?"). Egalitarians also arrived at the "right" answer (the stakeholder model) for largely the right political reasons: the need to protect the weak and control negative externalities ("There need to be some checks and balances on corporations," "How else can the little people be heard?" and "What's wrong with a bit more democracy in the workplace?").

Acknowledging the legitimacy of other perspectives.
Although many respondents were aware of arguments against the positions they preferred, awareness should not be confused with tolerance, less still, willingness to change one's mind. In the controversy over corporate governance, conservatives, both authoritarian and libertarian, understood stakeholder concerns and the necessity of taking them into account as a means to the end of profit maximization. But they feared that egalitarian efforts to promote the stakeholder vision rested on a fundamental misunderstanding both of human nature and of capitalism that would impair long-term growth by enmeshing corporate executives in ever more elaborate webs of communitarian regulations ("You can't do anything until the local politicians, labor unions, environmentalists, minority-rights activists, and other assorted opportunists have all had their palms crossed with silver.") and by creating an inexhaustible source of excuses for poorly performing managers to put off long-suffering shareholders. As one freshly minted M.B.A. pontificated, "The stakeholder model aggravates the principal-agent problem at the heart of corporate capitalism—it gives agents too much wiggle room to evade their responsibility to promote the principal's interest." Those on the egalitarian left often understood the value of "incentivizing" management to make the hard choices that are necessary to promote growth but felt that the concentration of power and wealth had just become too lopsided: "People who like the shareholder model are just out for number one and they really don't give a damn what happens to anybody else," and, more philosophically, "Society created corporations and it has the right to define the rules that they operate under."

At the micro end of the continuum of questions posed, there is also considerable awareness of the reasons for taking a position on the other side. In terms of the fundamental attribution error, authoritarian conservatives sometimes conceded that they might be too hard on employees (in this case, too slow to acknowledge legitimate excuses) but insisted that although many might think them hard-hearted, they had no difficulty living with themselves: "Somebody has to draw a line somewhere," and "It is only human nature to keep testing the limits." Egalitarians sometimes acknowledged that they might be "suckers" but thought the balance they were striking was best for themselves ("I can look myself in the

mirror.") and for the organization ("People who feel respect-
ed will respect the company.").

In the language of decision theory, most managers, when
challenged, acknowledged that there was no dominant
(trade-off-free) option. But this acknowledgment was rarely
spontaneous and tended to be grudging and perfunctory. In
the language of cognitive-consistency theory, managers
seem to have rather thoroughly rationalized their preferred
styles of thinking, evaluating, and acting. Perceptions of facts
and endorsements of values were in close alignment. If a
characteristic managerial stance emerged from the interviews, it appears to have been belief-system overkill, in
which participants insisted that their preferred working style
minimizes the more common type of error (factual claim) and
the more serious type of error (largely a moral or value judgment). Authoritarian conservatives put priority on minimizing
what, for convenience, might be called Type II errors, such as
failing to hold employees accountable for outcomes potentially under their control, exaggerating the complexity of fundamentally simple problems, pursuing additional information
beyond the point of diminishing marginal returns, abandoning
sound policies that run into temporary trouble, and resisting
misguided efforts to make the decision process more democratic, pluralistic, and, in their view, chaotic. This policy posture was justified by maintaining that these Type II errors
were both more likely and more serious than the logically
complementary errors that tend to preoccupy anti-authoritarian and anti-libertarian egalitarians and that do so for roughly
mirror-image reasons.

DISCUSSION

Opinions about cognitive biases and organizational correctives hinge on the ideological worldview and cognitive style
of the beholder. Most fundamentally, managers of varying
political persuasions subscribe to markedly different assumptions about human nature that, in turn, shape their underlying
philosophies of governance.[1] Authoritarian conservatives
believe that "most people" look for and exploit loopholes in
accountability systems, whereas anti-authoritarian egalitarians
believe that most people will refrain from exploiting loopholes as long as they feel fairly treated. These competing
views lead, among other things, to different assessments of
the fundamental attribution error. Authoritarian conservatives
deem it prudent managerial practice to communicate to subordinates a low tolerance for justifications and excuses that
invoke situational causes for conduct that falls short of organizational expectations. People will be more motivated to
behave properly if they believe that improper behavior will
almost automatically tarnish their reputations—a social variant of the legal doctrine of strict liability. From an authoritari-
an-conservative perspective, failing to hold people responsible for outcomes that they could have controlled is arguably a
more serious error than holding people responsible for outcomes that they could not control. By contrast, the anti-
authoritarian egalitarians see the fundamental attribution error
as punitive, not prudent. They disagree with conservatives
about both the frequency with which subordinates will invent
specious justifications and fictitious excuses for substandard

[1]
From Aristotle to the *Federalist Papers*,
there are numerous precedents for
assigning a foundational role to assumptions about human nature in philosophies
of governance. It is perhaps surprising,
therefore, that the topic has received as
little attention as it has in contemporary
behavioral and social science (for exceptions to this generalization, see Lane,
1973; Wrightsman, 1974).

Biases and Correctives

performance and the relative importance of avoiding Type I errors (condemning the innocent) versus Type II errors (acquitting the guilty), deploring the former error to a greater degree.

Authoritarian conservatives and those with a strong preference for cognitive closure were also more likely to concur with the sentiment that the world is often far simpler than it initially appears to be. They viewed simplicity as evidence of insight, not simple-mindedness, whereas low scorers on these scales viewed complexity as evidence of thoughtfulness, not confusion. Authoritarian conservatives also believed that lack of will power and of commitment to principles are common human failings, whereas anti-authoritarian egalitarians believed that an unwillingness to entertain self-critical thoughts and to reexamine basic assumptions are common human failings. Extending previous work in political psychology on the connections between political ideology and cognitive style, these competing views of the world translated quite directly into different evaluations of a host of putative biases, including the relative perils of over- and underconfidence, of staying the course versus escalating commitment to sunk costs, of simple versus complex choice heuristics, of preemptive self-criticism versus defensive bolstering as strategies of coping with accountability, and of directive versus open-ended strategies of structuring accountability. These two groups' markedly different evaluations of overconfidence and of staying the course are emblematic. Authoritarian conservatives believe that the can-do determination and optimism of the overconfident decision maker more than offsets the risk of persevering with a wrong assessment of the situation (cf. Staw and Ross, 1980). Anti-authoritarian egalitarians believe that the capacity of self-critical thinkers to realize quickly that they are on the wrong path more than offsets the risk of prematurely abandoning a good policy that has run into temporary difficulties. And, at the level of self-presentation, they think it a bad idea for managers to wear a worry-free mask and stress the benefits of keeping coworkers (they dislike the term "subordinates") reasonably fully informed.

Ideologically grounded disagreements over human nature and the causal structure of the social world parallel in key respects disagreements over how to manage people, at both a micro and macro level. Authoritarian conservatives and their high-preference-for-cognitive-closure allies approve of managers who communicate their policy preferences clearly to subordinates and approve of subordinates who respond equally decisively, whereas low scorers on these scales see advantages in encouraging open, balanced debate and cultivating an atmosphere of normative ambiguity that keeps coworkers guessing, at least for a while. Those on the political left—and this now includes both anti-authoritarian and anti-libertarian egalitarians—also offer more muted negative evaluations of the manager who responds in a borderline-dishonest, loophole-exploiting manner to an accountability regime perceived as unjust. Some egalitarian managers see such behavior as an understandable human bid to "empower oneself" when confronted by insensitive or arrogant authorities, with even occasional quasi-Marxist warnings about alienating and dehumanizing those lower in the pecking order.

At the most macro level, both authoritarian and libertarian conservatives favored the monistic regime of accountability solely to shareholders ("It is hard enough to do one thing well, less still half a dozen."), whereas the anti-authoritarian and anti-libertarian egalitarians embraced the value of accountability to a host of constituencies whose interests would often have to be combined in different ways in different situations ("Corporations can't be allowed just to focus on making money," and "There is more to running a society than just efficiency.").

Looking back on the full range of correlations between ideology and managerial policy preferences, it becomes clear that the more macro the issue domain, the more likely authoritarian and libertarian conservatives were to agree. As one might expect from the variable loadings in the rotated factor matrix, high scorers on both dimensions defended property rights and free markets (unless national security/sovereignty issues were implicated, in which case support from authoritarian conservatives quickly fades) and opposed what they frequently saw as misguided government efforts to help the less competitive and to dampen fictitious externalities. By contrast, the more micro the issue, the more likely authoritarian and libertarian conservatives were to be temperamentally and stylistically at odds with each other, agreeing strongly with each other only on the adaptive value of overconfidence and on the appropriateness of using morally suspect base rates. Libertarians tended to be more cognitively flexible (or, if one prefers, unprincipled), less preoccupied with precedent, status, and hierarchy (or, if one prefers, less loyal to existing organizational structures), and more prone to have an upbeat assessment of their fellow humans (or, if one prefers, an unrealistic or naive assessment). In certain respects, libertarian conservatives resembled anti-authoritarian egalitarians, especially in their lack of enthusiasm for deference and obedience to established ways, but breaking abruptly with this outlook when questions tapped into broader attitudes toward social equality, markets, and government. And, in certain respects, authoritarian conservatives resembled the anti-libertarian egalitarians, especially in their doubts about the self-sufficiency of the isolated individual, but breaking sharply with this camp on the more macro questions of societal and economic organization. In brief, this data set allows us to observe in a managerial microcosm the cross-cutting tensions documented by survey researchers in society at large between authoritarian conservatism/secular liberalism and economic individualism/egalitarianism (Kinder, 1998). If nothing else, the current results demonstrate that organizational behaviorists err if they suppose that these deep differences in worldviews do not insinuate themselves into a wide array of managerial preferences and practices. There is no "Chinese wall" between attitudes toward work and toward politics.[2]

Taken as a whole, the pattern of findings suggests the usefulness of revisiting a much maligned but still standing distinction in philosophy and social science: that between facts

2
The current approach to assessing managerial ideology draws on political psychological research on cognitive style and ideological worldviews. There are intriguing parallels, though, with sociological and cultural-anthropological work on rational and normative ideologies of control in managerial discourse (cf. Fiske, 1991; Barley and Kunda, 1992). Libertarian conservatives fall toward the rational extreme with their almost exclusive emphasis on market-pricing and calculated self-interest as the bases of working relationships inside and outside the organization. Authoritarian conservatives and anti-libertarian and anti-authoritarian egalitarians, each in their own fashion, put more emphasis on the normative bases of working relationships, with authoritarian conservatives stressing what Fiske (1991) called authority ranking (the organization as legitimate command hierarchy with superiors and subordinates), anti-libertarian egalitarians stressing communal sharing (the organization as extended family with obligations to care for needy members), and anti-authoritarian egalitarians stressing equality matching (the organization as a network of colleagues bound together in reciprocity networks).

Biases and Correctives

and values. One unresolved issue concerns the degree to which ideological disagreements over cognitive biases and organizational correctives are rooted either in competing views of the facts (How likely is this or that inferential error?) or in competing values (How important is it to avoid this or that inferential error?). Disagreements rooted in competing appraisals of a common reality should, in principle, be resolvable via recourse to evidence. From this standpoint, if we could persuade conservatives that they have exaggerated the degree to which people are inherently untrustworthy and prone to exploit empathic managers, conservatives should become less tolerant of the fundamental attribution error. Or if we could persuade low-need-for-closure respondents that simple heuristics perform as well as more complex decision rules developed through grueling hours of group discussion (cf. Gigerenzer and Todd, 1999), these respondents might be quicker to realize when they have reached the point of diminishing returns for further deliberation.

By contrast, disagreements rooted in values should be profoundly resistant to change. Authoritarian conservatives may so detest being suckers that they are willing to endure a high rate of falsely rejecting employees' accounts. Libertarian conservatives might oppose the (confiscatory) stakeholder model even when confronted by evidence that concessions in this direction have no adverse effects on profitability to shareholders. Expropriation is expropriation, no matter how prettified. And some egalitarians might well endorse the stakeholder model, even if shown compelling evidence that it reduces profits. Academics who rely on evidence-based appeals to change minds when the disagreements are rooted in values may be wasting everyone's time.

Placed in the broadest perspective, the current findings remind us that decision theorists are not the only people with strong opinions on the nature of good judgment and rationality. Decision theorists characteristically adopt an explicitly prescriptive stance to their subjects of study: there are right answers that can be derived from well-defined axiomatic systems of logic such as Bayes theorem or expected utility theory or game theory. To paraphrase John Milton in "Paradise Lost," their task is to explain the ways of God to man, not the ways of man to God, where God translates for early twenty-first-century audiences as the eternal truths of mathematical models of choice.

The intuitive theories of good judgment that many managers possess are not anchored in mathematical axioms and do not have a rigorous hypothetico-deductive structure. Rather, these intuitive theories are a conceptual mish-mash: loose amalgams of hunches that rest on speculative assumptions about human nature (How prone are people to exploit loopholes in rules and accountability regimes?), the efficacy of simple rules of thumb, and ultimately, the nature of the good society (How should we structure accountability ground rules so as to strike reasonable balances among such diverse values as efficiency, autonomy, equality, and fairness?). Insofar as this mish-mash coheres, and it often does not, psychological theory suggests that it does so in response to a combination of intrapsychic-consistency pressures to justify one's working style to oneself—Am I doing the right thing?—and self-presentational pressures to justify one's working style to others (cf. Schlenker, 1985).

Strictly speaking, there is no direct contradiction between logic and psycho-logic, between the formal prescriptivism of decision theory and the informal ideological hunches of decision makers who cope with messy human and organizational realities from day to day. Indeed, there is a rough complementarity. Formal prescriptive theories make minimal assumptions about the external world but extensive assumptions about how decision makers should integrate cues once they have been assigned likelihood or utility values, whereas intuitive theories make extensive assumptions about the world but are notoriously vague on the precise rules for combining elementary beliefs and preferences into final judgments. But there is also a palpable tension. Micro-economic reductionists might be tempted to argue that disagreements grounded in ideology and cognitive style are merely atavistic vestiges of a more primitive social order, soon to be swept away by the intensification of competitive market forces that have ever-closer-to-zero tolerance for obfuscation, fuzzy thinking, and self-serving posturing. What counts is what works, and it is only a matter of time before we are all converted into Bayesian belief updaters converging on common truths about human nature, the social world, and how best to go about understanding both. This is a crude but popular variant of the end-of-ideology and end-of-history theses (Friedman, 1999; Fukuyama, 1992). Other scholars, of a more pluralistic bent, might stubbornly insist, with Immanuel Kant and Isaiah Berlin, that from the crooked timber of humanity, no straight thing can be built, and that it will prove impossible to banish ideological posturing and human imperfections from business (Berlin, 1990). Even in perfectly competitive markets pulsating signals at the speed of light, there will be numerous niches of ever changing shape and size where each ideological worldview can survive, even thrive. In this view, if one is willing to concede that human nature is at least as bafflingly complex as that conceptual prototype of economic efficiency, the stock market, where bullish and bearish observers seem fated to co-exist indefinitely in dialectical interdependence, why should one resist the notion that an equally broad spectrum of managerial opinion on human nature will prove sustainable in the face of even ferocious market competition?

REFERENCES

Barley, S. R., and G. Kunda
1992 "Design and devotion: Surges of rational and normative ideologies of control in managerial discourse." Administrative Science Quarterly, 37: 363–399.

Berlin, I.
1990 The Crooked Timber of Humanity. New York: Knopf.

Chaiken, S., and Y. Trope
1999 Dual Process Models of Social Cognition. New York: Guilford.

Chubb, J. E., and T. Moe
1990 Politics, Markets, and America's Schools. Washington, DC: Brookings Institution.

Etzioni, A.
1996 Macro Socio-economics: From Theory to Activism. Armonk, NY: M. E. Sharpe.

Fiske, A. P.
1991 Structures of Social Life: The Four Elementary Forms of Human Relations. New York: Free Press.

Fiske, S., and S. Taylor
1991 Social Cognition. New York: McGraw-Hill.

Biases and Correctives

Fiske, S., and P. E. Tetlock
1997 "Taboo trade-offs: Reactions to transactions that transgress spheres of justice." Political Psychology, 18: 255–297.

Friedman, T.
1999 The Lexus and the Olive Tree. New York: Farrar, Strauss, & Giroux.

Fukuyama, F.
1992 The End of History and the Last Man. New York: Free Press.

George, A. L.
1980 Presidential Decision Making in Foreign Policy: The Effective Use of Information and Advice. Boulder, CO: Westview.

Gigerenzer, G., and P. M. Todd
1999 Simple Heuristics That Make Us Smart. New York: Oxford University Press.

Gilovich, T., D. Griffin, and D. Kahneman (eds.)
2000 Inferences, Heuristics and Biases: New Directions in Judgment under Uncertainty. New York: Cambridge University Press.

Goldstein, W., and R. Hogarth
1996 Research on Judgement and Decision Making: Currents, Connections, and Controversies. New York: Cambridge University Press.

Hirschman, A.
1970 Exit, Voice, and Loyalty: Responses to Decline in Firms, Organizations, and States. Cambridge, MA: Harvard University Press.

Janis, I. L., and L. Mann
1977 Decision Making: A Psychological Analysis of Conflict, Choice, and Commitment. New York: Free Press.

Jensen, M., and W. Meckling
1976 "Theory of the firm: Managerial behavior, agency costs, and ownership structure." Journal of Financial Economics, 3: 305–360.

Kagel, J. H., and A. E. Roth (eds.)
1995 The Handbook of Experimental Economics. Princeton, NJ: Princeton University Press.

Kinder, D.
1998 "Opinion and action in the realm of politics." In D. Gilbert et al. (eds.), Handbook of Social Psychology, 2: 778–867. New York: McGraw Hill.

Koehler, J.
1996 "The base rate fallacy reconsidered: Descriptive, normative and methodological challenges." Behavioral and Brain Sciences, 19: 1–53.

Kruglanski, A. W., and D. M. Webster
1996 "Motivated closing of the mind: 'Seizing' and 'freezing'." Psychological Review, 103: 263–268.

Lane, R.
1973 "Patterns of political belief." In J. Knutson (ed.), Handbook of Political Psychology: 83–116. San Francisco: Jossey-Bass.

Lipsett, S., and E. Raab
1978 The Politics of Unreason. Stanford, CA: Stanford University Press.

March, J. M., and J. P. Olsen
1989 Rediscovering Institutions. New York: Free Press.
1995 Democratic Governance. New York: Free Press.

McClosky, H., and A. Brill
1983 Dimensions of Tolerance. New York: Russell Sage Foundation.

Messick, D. M.
1993 "Equality as a decision heuristic." In B. Mellers and J. Baron (eds.), Psychological Perspectives on Justice: 11–31. New York: Cambridge University Press.

Meyer, J. W.
1983 "Conclusion: Institutionalization and the rationality of formal organizational structure." In J. W. Meyer and W. R. Scott (eds.), Organizational Environments: Ritual and Rationality: 266–299. Beverly Hills, CA: Sage.

Rodgers, T. J., W. Taylor, and R. Foreman
1992 No Excuses Management. New York: Doubleday.

Schlenker, B. R. (ed.)
1985 The Self and Social Life. New York: McGraw-Hill.

Simon, H.
1955 "A behavioral model of rational choice." Quarterly Journal of Economics, 69: 99–118.

Simonson, I.
1989 "Choice based on reasons: The case of attraction and compromise effects." Journal of Consumer Research, 16: 158–174.

Sniderman, P., and P. E. Tetlock
1986 "Interrelationship of political ideology and public opinion." In M. Herman (ed.), Handbook of Political Psychology: 62–96. San Francisco: Jossey-Bass.

Staw, B. M., and J. Ross
1980 "Commitment in an experimenting society: A study of the attribution of leadership from administrative scenarios." Journal of Applied Psychology, 65: 249–260.

Tetlock, P. E.
1984 "Cognitive style and political belief systems in the British House of Commons." Journal of Personality and Social Psychology: Personality Processes and Individual Differences, 46: 365–375.
1985 "Accountability: The neglected social context of judgment and choice." In B. M. Staw and L. L. Cummings (eds.), Research in Organizational Behavior, 7: 297–332. Greenwich, CT: JAI Press.
1992 "The impact of accountability on judgment and choice: Toward a social contingency model." Advances in Experimental Social Psychology, 25: 331–376.
1998 "Close-call counterfactuals and belief system defenses: 'I was not almost wrong but I was almost right.'" Journal of Personality and Social Psychology, 75: 230–242.
1999 "Accountability theory: Mixing properties of human agents with properties of social systems." In J. Levine, L. Thompson, and D. Messick (eds.), Shared Cognition in Organizations: The Management of Knowledge: 117–137. Hillsdale, NJ: Erlbaum.

Tetlock, P. E., and R. Boettger
1989 "Accountability: A social magnifier of the dilution effect." Journal of Personality and Social Psychology, 57: 388–398.

Tetlock, P. E., and J. Kim
1987 "Accountability and judgement in a personality prediction task." Journal of Personality and Social Psychology: Attitudes and Social Cognition, 52: 700–709.

Tetlock, P. E., O. Kristel, B. Elson, M. Green, and J. Lerner
2000 "The psychology of the unthinkable: Taboo trade-offs, forbidden base rates, and heretical counterfactuals." Journal of Personality and Social Psychology (in press).

Tetlock, P. E., R. Peterson, and J. Lerner
1996 "Revising the value pluralism model: Incorporating social content and context postulates." In C. Seligman, J. Olson, and M. Zanna (eds.), Ontario Symposium on Social and Personality Psychology: Values: 25–51. Hillsdale, NJ: Erlbaum.

Tyler, T. R.
1990 Why People Obey the Law. New Haven, CT: Yale University Press.

Wilson, J. Q.
1989 Bureaucracy: What Government Agencies Do and Why They Do It. New York: Basic Books.

Wrightsman, L. S.
1974 Assumptions about Human Nature: A Social-psychological Analysis. Monterey, CA: Brooks/Cole.

[29]

Organizational Behavior and Human Decision Processes
Vol. 82, No. 1, May, pp. 60–75, 2000
doi:10.1006/obhd.2000.2887, available online at http://www.idealibrary.com on **IDE&L**®

Avoiding Missed Opportunities in Managerial Life: Analogical Training More Powerful Than Individual Case Training

Leigh Thompson, Dedre Gentner, and Jeffrey Loewenstein

Northwestern University

We examined the ability of Masters of Management students to transfer knowledge gained from case studies to face-to-face negotiation tasks. During a study phase, students either read two cases and gave advice to the protagonist in each case ("Advice" condition) or derived an overall principle by comparing two cases ("Comparison" condition). Management students in the Comparison condition were nearly three times more likely to transfer the principle in an actual, face-to-face bargaining situation than those in the Advice condition. Further, content analysis of students' open-ended responses revealed that the quality of the advice given in the Advice condition did not predict subsequent behavior, whereas the quality of the principles given in the Comparison condition did predict successful transfer to the negotiation situation. Perhaps most striking is the fact that not a single person in the Advice condition drew a parallel between the two cases, even though they were presented on the same page. We conclude that the value of examples is far greater if analogical comparisons among examples are encouraged. We propose that this simple and cost-effective method can substantially improve the benefits of professional training and education. © 2000 Academic Press

Key Words: learning; transfer; negotiation; case study; comparison; advice; performance.

The research was supported by National Science Foundation Grant 9870892 awarded to the first author and National Science Foundation Grant SBR-9511757 and Office of Naval Research Grant N00014-92-J-1098 awarded to the second author. We thank the Similarity and Analogy group at Northwestern University for helpful discussions.

Address correspondence and reprint requests to Leigh Thompson, Management and Organizations Department, Kellogg Graduate School of Management, Northwestern University, 2001 Sheridan Road, Leverone Hall, Evanston, IL 60208-2011.

60

One of the more lamentable experiences in life is feeling that you knew something after the fact, but not when the opportunity presented itself. The assumption that we can use what we know underlies much of our intuition about how managers solve problems and make decisions. However, studies of problem solving reveal that people often do not retrieve their relevant knowledge at appropriate times (Bassok, 1990; Bassok & Holyoak, 1989; Gentner & Landers, 1985; Gentner, Rattermann, & Forbus, 1993; Gick & Holyoak, 1980; Ross, 1984, 1987; see Reeves & Weisberg, 1994, for a recent review). Thus knowledge transfer hinges on memory access. Our ability to access knowledge from memory depends crucially upon how we learned it.

Transfer of knowledge is of critical importance to managers who typically spend tens of thousands of dollars for an MBA degree and to companies who invest hundreds of thousands of dollars on the continuing management education of their employees. Typically, investigations of knowledge transfer have focused on dissemination and adoption of practices and knowledge between individuals or firms (e.g., Argote, 1993; Argote & Epple, 1990). A large body of research has examined the generalization of learned material to job behavior and the maintenance of trained skills over time (see Baldwin & Ford, 1988, for a review). The research reported here focused on cognitive processes involved in transfer. Virtually no research has dealt with the question of whether managers can transfer *their own* knowledge to novel-appearing organizational problems and challenges. In fact, the implicit assumption that underlies management training is that once presented and understood, managerial knowledge can be applied to future problems that managers may confront. There may be obstacles to implementing the knowledge, but not to retrieving it from memory. Our research investigation provides evidence that challenges this assumption. We argue that optimal learning processes leading to accessible knowledge available for transfer are not intuitively obvious. This may help explain why knowledge transfer is often so difficult.

Although retrieving previous experiences can help to solve novel-appearing problems, people appear to have limited ability to retrieve appropriate information. For example, Perfetto, Bransford, and Franks (1983) had people judge sentences for their validity (e.g., "A minister marries several people each week") and then had them solve riddles (e.g., "A man . . . married 20 different women of the same town. All are still living and he has never divorced one of them. Yet, he has broken no law. Can you explain?"). Participants who were not told that the initial sentences could help them solve the riddles not only solved fewer riddles but were no more likely to solve the riddles than participants who never read the initial sentences.

Furthermore, actively learning the initial information may not provide much advantage in knowledge transfer. Having solved one problem does not offer much help in solving an analogous problem when the two problems come from different contexts (e.g., Catrambone & Holyoak, 1989; Gick & Holyoak, 1980, 1983; Keane, 1988; Novick, 1988; Reed, Ernst, & Banerji, 1974; Ross, 1987, 1989; Schumacher & Gentner, 1988; Simon & Hayes, 1976; see Bransford, Franks, Vye, & Sherwood, 1989, and Reeves & Weisberg, 1994, for reviews).

For example, Ross taught students mathematical principles by having them solve problems embodying those principles. Students were then given a new set of problems from different contexts that required them to use the same principles they had just learned. Students solved less than 30% of the new problems correctly.

One key problem in knowledge transfer is that people tend to access previous knowledge that bears *surface*, rather than *structural*, similarity to the problem at hand. Consider the following example from Gentner and Schumacher (reported in Gentner & Medina, 1998). Gentner and Schumacher gave participants 100 proverbs, asking after each one if it reminded them of any of the previous proverbs. Very commonly, participants were reminded of proverbs with surface similarities. For example, the proverb "A hair from here, a hair from there will make a beard" reminded participants of "It is not the beard that makes the philosopher." However, participants were far less often reminded of proverbs with matching relational structure. For example, "Remove the dirt from your own eye before you wipe the speck from mine" is structurally similar to "He who laughs at the crooked man should walk very straight," but few people recalled these kinds of matches. Subsequently, participants judged the structurally similar pairs as both more sound and more similar than the surface similarity matches—even when they had failed to recall proverbs that were structurally similar to one another. Thus, the very matches judged by participants to be most useful in reasoning were the ones that came to mind least readily.

In another investigation involving more elaborate materials, Gentner, Rattermann, and Forbus (1993) gave students several stories prior to reading a target story. Some of the prior "source" stories bore a surface similarity to the critical target story (e.g., they shared similar characters or objects). In contrast, other stories did not bear much surface similarity, but were structurally equivalent. Stories containing surface feature matches were recalled 55% of the time, as compared with 12% of the time for recall based on purely analogical matches. Yet, when the same participants were presented with the original source stories, they clearly regarded those with structural similarity to be more useful for reasoning about the target story than those bearing only surface similarity. These results point to a striking dissociation between what is most accessible in memory and what is most useful in reasoning: We often fail to recall what is ultimately most valuable for solving new problems (Forbus, Gentner, & Law, 1995; Gentner & Landers, 1985; Gentner, Rattermann, & Forbus, 1993; Gick & Holyoak, 1980, 1983; Holyoak & Koh, 1987; Reeves & Weisberg, 1994; Ross, 1987, 1989).

Are there ways to foster analogical transfer, that is, to encourage knowledge transfer based on retrieving structurally similar, rather than superficially similar, instances? We think so. Successful analogical transfer relies on relational similarity between the current problem and stored experiences. If people abstract general schemas or principles during learning, perhaps these principles can form the basis for experiencing similarities with new cases involving the same principles (Forbus, Gentner, & Law, 1995). If so, it would allow people to better capitalize on their experiences. One method for promoting schema-abstraction is to draw a comparison between two or more instances (Gick & Holyoak, 1983). People seem to draw such abstractions readily when explicitly asked to compare (e.g., Brown, Kane, & Echols, 1986; Catrambone & Holyoak, 1989; Gick & Holyoak, 1983, Kotovsky & Gentner, 1996; Loewenstein & Gentner, 1997, submitted; Ross & Kennedy, 1990).

According to structure-mapping theory, comparison entails a structural alignment and mapping process that highlights the similar aspects of the two examples (Falkenhainer, Forbus, & Gentner, 1989; Gentner & Markman, 1997; Medin, Goldstone, & Gentner, 1993). Focusing on shared aspects between examples with different surface features promotes the abstraction of a common relational structure that can then be stored as a schema. Such a schema is useful for the learner because it is uncluttered with irrelevant surface information. In this way, judicious comparison can inform the learner as to which aspects of experience are relevant and which are causally irrelevant. Thus, our hypothesis is that comparing two or more instances during learning leads managers to derive a problem-solving schema that can be retrieved and applied to future instances. Analogical encoding fosters subsequent knowledge transfer.

To date, most studies of analogical reasoning of the kind we have described have used mathematical and logic puzzles. Because we were particularly interested in the role of analogical encoding in managerial life, we focused on negotiation, an important and complex managerial skill (Thompson, 1998). Negotiation is not only considered to be an essential skill in the managerial repertoire (Bazerman & Neale, 1992), but one that needs to be accessible in high-stress, cognitively demanding situations. Successful transfer in management situations requires that the principles and strategies underlying successful negotiation be accessed and adapted to vastly different contexts. Therefore, negotiation poses a serious challenge for cross-domain analogizing.

The cost of ineffective negotiation is dramatic. People often settle for suboptimal negotiation agreements, leaving large portions of money on the bargaining table. For example, the incidence of lose–lose outcomes is strikingly high: 50% of negotiators fail to realize that they have perfectly compatible interests with the other party and 20% of the pairs fail to settle on the value that both parties prefer (Thompson & Hrebec, 1996). These findings are particularly disturbing when viewed in light of research that suggests that people—even including managers—do not seem to know when they have negotiated well (Thompson, Valley, & Kramer, 1995). Further, when their mistakes are explained, people often feel that they understand fully, yet go on to repeat their errors in subsequent negotiations that have different surface (but similar deep) structures (Thompson & DeHarpport, 1994).

OVERVIEW OF RESEARCH

We conducted a research investigation to address whether and how analogical encoding during negotiation training promotes subsequent transfer. This experiment was a test of transfer from written case analysis to actual face-to-face negotiation. We compared the transfer ability of people who received analogical comparisons during learning with that of people who did not. In the learning phase, students read two cases. In the test phase, students had an opportunity to use what they had learned from the cases in a face-to-face negotiation.

We focused on an especially difficult, yet important, negotiation principle—the formation of contingency contracts (Lax & Sebenius, 1986; Bazerman & Gillespie, 1999). Most people tend to resolve negotiations through the use of compromise. However, compromise (or splitting-the-difference strategies) are suboptimal when negotiators have differing beliefs concerning relevant events. For example, suppose that an author is optimistic about book sales and wants a prospective publisher to agree to a high royalty rate. However, the prospective publisher is much less optimistic about book sales and consequently only wants to offer a standard minimal royalty rate. The two parties could compromise on the royalty rate. However, a more elegant solution would involve a contingency agreement, wherein the royalty rate is contingent upon book sales. Such an agreement has the beneficial effects of meeting both parties' interests, maximizing negotiators' profits, and allowing agreements to be reached in situations that might otherwise end in stalemate. As in betting, contingency contracts capitalize on parties' differing expectations regarding the outcome of a future event. Contingency contracts are effective in increasing negotiators' profits (and, hence, increasing joint profits) because they often allow negotiators to avoid impasse. Further, even though one person will eventually be right (and the other wrong) about the future, *at the time negotiators make the agreement*, they each believe in their own predictions.

In some areas of business—compensation, for example—contingent contracts are common, as with the case of book publishing. For example, when a CEO agrees to a salary tied to the company's stock price, that CEO is entering into a contingent contact. Similarly, an actor who takes points in a movie in return for a lower up-front payment is agreeing to a contingent contract. But in many business negotiations, contingent contracts are either ignored entirely or rejected outright for three reasons (Bazerman & Gillespie, 1999). First, many negotiators are simply unaware of the possibility of using contingent contracts. Second, contingent contracts are often seen as a form of gambling and are therefore antithetical to good business judgment. Finally, most companies lack a systematic way of thinking about the formulation of such contracts.

In an initial investigation, we tested the power of comparison in promoting subsequent knowledge transfer for contingent contracts (Loewenstein, Thompson, & Gentner, 1999). In a management class, half of the participants were instructed to compare training cases and draw out their common solution; the other half were asked to draw out the solution in each training case separately. In addition, we orthogonally examined whether providing participants with an explicit reference to a particular principle in the training phase would affect knowledge transfer. The results were dramatic and straightforward: managers who explicitly compared the cases were three times as likely to use contingency contracts in the subsequent negotiation case as those who did not compare the cases. Mentioning the principle during training had no effect.

The goal of the present experiment was to examine the efficacy of case comparison in a more realistic managerial context. Specifically, we contrasted the effectiveness of *comparing cases* versus *providing advice on a case-by-case basis*. Managers and executives, particularly those enrolled in MBA programs and consulting firms, are regularly in the position of giving advice. One view of advice is that it requires deep thinking about a specific case, particularly through an analysis of costs and benefits, and therefore should induce subsequent knowledge transfer. Another view is that giving advice may prevent comparison and abstraction, if the advice-giver becomes too focused on particulars present in a single instance, thereby inhibiting subsequent knowledge transfer.

All participants read two brief cases embodying the principle of contingency contracts prior to engaging in an actual face-to-face negotiation which contained the opportunity to apply this principle. Further, all participants received the two written cases presented on a single page. In the Advice condition, participants were asked to give advice to the protagonist for each of the two cases. In the Comparison condition, participants were asked to compare the two cases and draw out their similarities. We hypothesized that Management students in the Comparison condition would show superior transfer of the contingency contract principle to their face-to-face negotiation in the test phase because comparison entails a structural alignment process that promotes abstraction of a common schema (Gentner, 1983; Gentner & Medina, 1998; Markman & Gentner, 1997). In addition to measuring participant negotiation performance, we content-coded negotiators' responses so we could trace their paths of learning and reasoning.

METHOD

Participants

Participants were 88 Masters of Management students enrolled in a 10-week course in negotiation at Northwestern University's Kellogg Graduate School of Management. For their training in negotiation, the students were given a week to prepare for the face-to-face negotiation before spending up to an hour and a half at the bargaining table working out an agreement. Half of the students were randomly assigned to the Comparison condition ($n = 22$ dyads), and half were assigned to the Advice condition ($n = 22$ dyads). Students in the same condition were paired together to form dyads who negotiated with one another.[1]

Materials and Procedure

In the test phase, each student randomly received one of two roles to play in a face-to-face negotiation (buyer or seller) and was matched with a partner

---

[1] All data are analyzed at the level of the dyad.

who was to play the opposing role. The task concerned a negotiation between a general manager of a theater (buyer) and a producer of a Broadway show (seller).[2] The issues to be negotiated concerned the profit-sharing among parties, number of shows, salaries for cast and crew, and so on. Each party had different expectations about the profitability of the show—the seller anticipated sell-out performances; the buyer was much less optimistic. A contingency contract could be developed between parties concerning profit-sharing based on the number of ticket sales. For example, negotiators could agree to split profits 60/40 (buyer/seller) if ticket sales were in line with the buyer's conservative estimation; and 40/60 if the seller's optimistic prediction was borne out. This is an example of a contingency contract that is ultimately more beneficial for both parties than is a simple compromise agreement, such as splitting ticket revenues 50/50. For example, say that the producer of the show believes that ticket sales will gross $1M; however, the theater owner believes that ticket sales will barely gross $750K. One way to share profits would involve a compromise, wherein the parties agree to split ticket sales 50/50; this would mean an expected value of $500K for the producer and an expected value of $375K for the theater owner. However, a more elegant and mutually profitable solution would be for the parties to agree to a 60/40 split in the case of ticket sales over $1M and a 40/60 split in the case of ticket sales under $750K. Because the parties have different beliefs, the expected value of their profits is higher—in this case, $600K for the producer and $450K for the theater owner. Of course, both parties cannot be right about the future; however, because they each believe that they will be right at the time they form the contingency contract, their subjective value of the deal is greater. In hindsight, contingency contracts seem not only sensible but obvious; however, they rarely occur to the negotiator embroiled in the heat of conflict.

In the study phase, 1 week prior to the test phase, the students received a packet of materials to prepare for the negotiation. There were two pages of questions (all open-ended), the first of which asked students four questions concerning their expectations about the outcome of the negotiation and what strategies they planned to employ to reconcile differences of opinion, preference, and beliefs. The second page contained the training materials: two 225-word summaries of cases involving contingency contracts (see Appendix 1). We deliberately chose the two training cases with little or no surface similarity to the face-to-face negotiation case. Thus, to profit from their training experience, students would need to rely on relational, rather than surface-level, similarities.

In the Comparison condition, the cases were read one after another, and then the participants were asked to respond to the following question: "Think about the similarities between these two cases. What are the key parallels in the two negotiations? In the space below, identify an overall principle that

[2] The negotiation case *Oceania!* is available upon request through the Dispute Resolution Research Center, Kellogg School of Management, Northwestern University, 2001 Sheridan Road, Evanston, IL 60208-2011. E-mail: drrc@kellog.nwu.edu.

captures the essence of the strategy of betting on differences." In the Advice condition, the cases were read one at a time, after which the participants were asked to respond to the following question: "Suppose you are advising [the main character]. What should she do? Why?" Participants' responses to the Comparison/Advice questions were collected prior to the negotiation and coded for quality of response. Our key hypothesis was that negotiators who engaged in active comparison before the negotiation would be more likely to employ a contingency contract during the actual, face-to-face negotiation.

RESULTS

Negotiated Outcomes

The final contracts negotiated by participants were scored in terms of the inclusion of a contingency contract and also their overall monetary value to each negotiator. The results supported our prediction that making a comparison is crucial for encoding the relational commonalities necessary for analogical transfer. Specifically, only 5 (23%) of the 22 dyads in the Advice condition made contingency contracts; in contrast, 14 (64%) of the 22 dyads in the Comparison condition made contingency contracts. Thus, participants who explicitly compared the cases were nearly three times as likely to use contingency contracts as those who responded to separate cases: χ^2 (1, $N = 44$) = 7.503, $p < .01$. This held true despite the fact that all participants read the same two cases and both cases were presented on a single page.

A second indication of the influence of comparison is the monetary outcomes of the negotiations. As expected, using a contingency contract resulted in a higher gain than using a compromise solution. Negotiating dyads who compromised on ticket sales grossed, on average, \$987,500 from the negotiation, whereas dyads using a contingency contract grossed, on average, \$1,049,500, a \$52,000 (6%) gain, $t(42) = 2.484$, $p < .05$. Greater use of the contingency contract by participants in the Comparison condition meant an average gain of \$21,000 (2%) over the dyads in the Advice condition, a nonsignificant trend.

Content Coding

We examined participants' answers in the Advice and Comparison conditions. Although all participants in both conditions read the same two cases, the questions asked of them afterwards differed. Thus, we cannot compare the two conditions directly. Therefore, we performed a content analysis within each condition. We had complete data for 19 dyads in each condition. Two trained raters read all of the responses and rated the responses on several dimensions explained below. Although the coders were not blind to conditions (e.g., it was obvious whether a participant was in the Advice or Comparison condition), they had no knowledge of the hypotheses. For those cases in which there was a discrepancy, coders jointly resolved their differences. We report individual reliability statistics for each dimension below.

Advice Condition

Our first analysis concerned whether the quality of advice that participants gave in the Advice condition led to better negotiated agreements. If many people thought it unwise to accept the contingency proposed in the case, for example, then it would not be surprising that these participants did not develop contingency contracts in their actual negotiations. To examine this, we looked at only those participants in our Advice condition and coded their responses to the two cases in terms of whether they advised the protagonist to accept the contingency contract (or, in the language of the mini-case, "to take the bet") or not. Specifically, two raters coded the advice given on each particular case (0 = not to take the bet; 1 = indeterminate; 2 = to take the bet). The reliability measure was 87%. The results showed that the nature of the advice was unrelated to actual negotiation performance. Those dyads in which both people had advised taking the bet in 75% of the training cases (operationalized as at least one dyad member recommending the bet in both cases and the other member recommending the bet in at least one case) made contingency contracts in the actual face-to-face negotiation 25% of the time (2 of 8 dyads). Those dyads whose members had advised not taking the bet made contingency contracts 18% of the time (2 of 11 dyads). Thus, recognizing that the contingency contract was advisable was not related to transferring the betting principle to the face-to-face negotiation situation subsequently encountered by participants.

A second question is whether people in the Advice condition spontaneously noticed the parallels between the two cases. Not a single person in the Advice condition referenced the first case when talking about the second case in any meaningful way. Had participants noticed this common structure, it is reasonable to assume that they would have responded to the second case by referring to their advice for the first case. However, no suggestion of linking the cases was found among these participants' responses.

If participants offered what they regarded to be a better solution to the case, this was noted. A total of 85% of the dyads in the Advice condition made at least one suggestion that they considered to be a better solution to the case than the bet. These suggestions were often based on the particular idiosyncrasies of each case. In contrast, only three people in the Comparison condition suggested something they thought would be better than the bet.

Comparison Condition

We examined the quality of the principles articulated by participants in the Comparison condition. Each participant's response to the directive to "derive a principle that captures the essence of these two cases. . ." was rated on a 3-point scale in terms of depth of understanding, with 0 for little understanding (e.g., "Each party will pay what they think is fair after the event" $N = 2$), 1 for some understanding (e.g., "Both are negotiating with regard to their risks and are willing to pay a price if they are wrong" $N = 10$); and 2 for sophisticated understanding (e.g., "They are similar in that there are uncertain future events and different beliefs about the outcome of those events. The strategy is to

create a bet that hinges on the outcome of uncertain future events" $N = 7$).
The reliability measure was 82%. Developing contingency contracts in the
negotiation was highly related to the quality of the principles derived by the
participants. When only one member of the dyad abstracted a good principle,
development of a contingency contract was only moderately likely (45%, or 5
of 11 dyads). However, if one person stated the principle and the other person
stated at least elements of it, then making bets was extremely likely—88%,
or 7 of 8 of these dyads made bets. As in Gick and Holyoak's (1983) study,
better extraction of principles lead to greater tendency to apply the principles,
marginal by a Fisher's exact test, $p = .08$.

Despite the fact that the two cases were printed on the same page in both
conditions, we found widely different responses between groups. In the Advice
condition, there was no evidence that participants spontaneously compared
cases. Not one participant mentioned the first case when giving advice about
the second. In contrast, only 1 person (of 38) in the Comparison condition failed
to discuss the two cases together. What did participants in the Advice condition
do? Nearly everyone in the Advice condition attempted to come up with new
solutions to the cases, typically appealing to expected values when they were
trying to make the case for or against what to do. In contrast, virtually no one
in the Comparison condition mentioned expected values. Only 2 people in the
Comparison condition talked about the cases separately, and 1 of them first
stated an overall principle and then wrote how it played out in each case.
Comparing the cases led people to derive and understand the common betting
principle; in contrast, for people studying the cases separately, the common
principle did not emerge.

DISCUSSION

Management students who compared two cases were more likely to transfer
their knowledge to a face-to-face negotiation than students who read the same
two training cases but gave advice. In both the Advice and Comparison conditions, participants read the same two cases that were presented on a single
page. The cases were presented merely as an addendum to the role participants
were learning and in a written format quite unlike the actual face-to-face
negotiation scenario. Yet, the simple presence of explicit instructions to compare
the two cases and derive a principle led to a large advantage in negotiation
performance. Making a comparison enabled students to recognize the principle
in common to the cases and carry it forward to the negotiation nearly three
times as often as those students giving sequential advice. Moreover, in a related
study we found that simply giving instructions to compare two cases without
mentioning an abstract principle likewise led to superior performance in the
comparison group (54% of dyads transferred the principle to their negotiations)
over the advice group (13%) (Loewenstein, Thompson, & Gentner, 1999). Thus
the advantage of the comparison group in the current study does not appear
to stem from the directive to "derive a principle that captures the essence of

the two cases." These results support our hypothesis that comparison of instances can promote knowledge transfer.

Professional education in management, law, and medicine is often based on the case method. The traditional case method relies upon the belief that people can and will abstract higher order relations from the analysis of individual examples. The current findings cast doubt on this assumption. The present investigation corroborates and extends the findings of Loewenstein, Thompson, and Gentner (1999). Students showed little transfer of knowledge learned from individual examples. On the basis of the results of our experiments, we conclude that comparing cases does not automatically occur—even when cases are physically juxtaposed. It is not enough simply to be presented with multiple cases; rather, it is *comparing* multiple cases that leads to abstracting their common principles thereby facilitating later memory access and knowledge transfer. Given elaborate proposals for educational innovation and on-the-job training, our technique of simply encouraging people to compare available cases seems refreshingly cost-effective.

We might conjecture that the truly seasoned manager or executive would be able to retrieve appropriate experiences when confronted with a novel-appearing situation. However, an investigation of expertise in mathematics (Novick, 1988) suggests that although experts show somewhat more appropriate retrieval than novices, they too retrieve many surface-similar cases. The experts did show an advantage over novices in their ability to dismiss inappropriate cases quickly. However, although experts performed better than novices, they still failed to retrieve appropriate cases in many instances (Novick, 1988).

The available evidence suggests that although seasoned professionals will show a higher hit rate of accessing genuinely relevant prior experiences, they too are vulnerable to the problem of retrieval by surface similarities. The Management students in our experiment were not experts in negotiation—few people are—but they were not naive and they were highly motivated, intelligent, and competitive. Such people would seem to be an ideal group for recognizing parallels and connections. Yet, even when presented with relevant cases prior to a face-to-face negotiation, few of them drew upon principles embedded in the cases. Their difficulty (in the Advice condition) in transferring principles from a learning situation to a test situation shows that transfer difficulty holds even for highly motivated participants working on problems they find relevant.

Our own qualitative observations of our participants yield further insights about comparison and transfer. In a debriefing of the negotiation case after the fact, we asked participants whether they had thought about the two preceding mini-cases. Many of those in the Comparison condition said they had; fewer in the Advice condition reported doing so. Yet when we revealed the contingency solution to the negotiation case and pointed out the relational parallels to the test cases, participants often expressed regret. The conceptual parallels seemed completely obvious when pointed out to them, yet did not provoke spontaneous recall before the fact, a pattern reminiscent of Gentner, Rattermann, and Forbus' (1993) findings.

Mundane and Creative Analogy

Throughout this article, we have been arguing that managers need to access their relevant knowledge to apply to current problems they face. Many case-based retrievals are highly mundane (Gentner, Rattermann, & Forbus, 1993) and rightly so: If one is preparing an account statement, it is typical (and optimal) to be reminded of last quarter's account statement. Cases that share surface properties often share structural properties as well. But analogical retrieval processes can also yield distant analogies, as happens in scientific discovery. For example, Kepler's proposal that the sun causes planetary motion depended on positing an attractive force analogous to light: Like light, the attractive force diminishes with distance; and most importantly, like light, it shows "action at a distance": it travels unseen between the source and the distant object, yet has clear effects on the distant object (Gentner, Brem, Ferguson, Wolff, Markman, & Forbus, 1997). Reasoning by analogical comparison is most often ordinary, but can be extraordinary.

Analogical Reasoning in Individuals and Groups

There is a great deal of interest in team-based learning and transfer (Moreland, Argote, & Krishnan, 1996). Yet, little is known about analogical training in dyads and groups. Virtually all prior studies have involved individuals. To our knowledge, we are the first to examine the effect of analogical training on dyadic interaction. However, the analogical training in our study did in fact occur at an individual (nondyadic) level. It is interesting to speculate on the efficacy of dyadic versus individual analogical training effects. On the one hand, substantial evidence suggests that groups are poor at discussing noncommon information (Stasser & Stewart, 1992), which might result in poorer transfer of principles if comparison necessitates the discussion of unique examples. On the other hand, groups have access to a potentially richer source of experiences from which to compare. For example, Dunbar's (1994) direct observations of molecular biologists at work demonstrate that comparison is frequently used in the everyday practice of science. Dunbar's observations of the research process suggest three factors that make a lab creative: frequent use of comparison, attention to inconsistency, and heterogeneity of the research group (which contributes to the group's ability to think of many different analogs). Similarly, Hargadon and Sutton (1997) report qualitative evidence that teams of design engineers use analogies quite frequently in brainstorming sessions for new product design. Obviously, there is no connection necessarily between what makes for a creative organization and what makes for a creative manager. Nonetheless, there are some striking commonalities. The microbiology laboratories that showed the most progress were those that used analogies in quantity and took them seriously. Dunbar's analyses of transcripts show that in the successful lab groups, analogies are extended and "pushed" in group discussion.

Summary

We believe that ordinary case-based training may often leave learning on the table. We have introduced a method of training whereby students explicitly compare examples in order to derive common schemas or principles. Principles learned in this fashion have a greater likelihood of later being accessed and used than principles learned through the common practice of giving advice about individual examples. We suggest that this simple change in training procedures—to promote the opportunity to make fruitful comparisons—can dramatically improve people's ability to put their learning into practice.

APPENDIX 1

Cases Used in Advice and Comparison Conditions

Case 1: Syd, a recently-promoted head buyer of a major retail store, has bought some wholesale goods from an Asian merchant. All aspects of the deal have been successfully negotiated except the transfer of the goods. The merchant tells Syd that he will pay to ship the goods by boat. Syd is concerned because the U.S. has announced that a trade embargo is likely to be placed on all goods from that country in the near future. The Asian merchant tells Syd not to worry because the boat will arrive at the U.S. dock before the embargo occurs. Syd, however, thinks the boat will be late. Syd wants the merchant to pay to ship the goods by air freight (which is substantially more expensive). The merchant refuses because of the higher cost. They argue about when the boat will arrive.

The Asian merchant suggests that they "make a bet." The Asian merchant will ship the goods air freight but they will both watch when the boat actually docks in the U.S. If the boat arrives on time (as the Asian merchant believes it will), Syd will pay for all of the air freight. However, if the boat arrives late (as Syd believes it will), the Asian merchant will pay the entire air freight bill.

Advice Condition: Suppose that you are advising Syd. What should she/he do? Why?

Case 2: Two fairly poor brothers, Ben and Jerry, have just inherited a working farm whose main crop has a volatile price. Ben wants to sell rights to the farm's output under a long-term contract for a fixed amount rather than depend upon shares of an uncertain revenue stream. In short, Ben is risk-averse. Jerry, on the other hand is confident that the next season will be spectacular and revenues will be high. In short, Jerry is risk-seeking. The two argue for days and nights about the price of the crop for next season. Ben wants to sell now because he believes the price of the crop will fall; Jerry wants to hang onto the farm because he believes the price of the crop will increase. Jerry cannot afford to buy Ben out at this time.

Then, Jerry proposes a bet to his brother: They keep the farm for another season. If the price of the crop falls below a certain price (as Ben thinks it will), they will sell the farm and Ben will get 50% of today's value of its worth, adjusted for inflation; Jerry will get the rest. However, if the price of the crop rises (as Jerry thinks it will), Jerry will buy Ben out for 50% of today's value of the farm, adjusted for inflation, and keep all of the additional profits for himself.

Advice Condition: Suppose that you are advising Ben. What should he do? Why?

Comparison Condition: Think about the similarities between these two cases. What are the key parallels in the two negotiations? In the space below, identify an overall principle that captures the essence of the strategy of betting on differences.

REFERENCES

Argote, L. (1993). Group and organizational learning curves: Individual, system, and environmental components. *British Journal of Social Psychology*, **32**, 31–51.

Argote, L., & Epple, D. (1990). Learning curves in manufacturing. *Science*, **247**, 920–924.

Baldwin, T. T., & Ford, J. K. (1988). Transfer of training: A review and directions for future research. *Personnel Psychology*, **41**, 63–105.

Bassok, M. (1990). Transfer of domain-specific problem-solving procedures. *Journal of Experimental Psychology, Learning, Memory, & Cognition*, **16**(3), 522–533.

Bassok, M., & Holyoak, K. J. (1989). Interdomain transfer between isomorphic topics in algebra and physics. *Journal of Experimental Psychology, Learning, Memory, & Cognition*, **15**(1), 153–166.

Bazerman, M. H., & Gillespie, J. J. (1999). Betting on the future: The virtues of contingent contracts. *Harvard Business Review*, **77**(5), 155–160.

Bazerman, M. H., & Neale, M. A. (1992). *Negotiating rationally.* New York: Free Press.

Bransford, J. D., Franks, J. J., Vye, N. J., & Sherwood, R. D. (1989). New approaches to instruction: because wisdom can't be told. In S. Vosniadou & A. Ortony (Eds.), *Similarity and analogical reasoning* (pp. 470–497). New York: Cambridge Univ. Press.

Brown, A. L., Kane, M. J., & Echols, C. H. (1986). Young children's mental models determine analogical transfer across problems with a common goal structure. *Cognitive Development*, **1**, 103–121.

Catrambone, R., & Holyoak, K. J. (1989). Overcoming contextual limitations on problem-solving transfer. *Journal of Experimental Psychology: Learning, Memory and Cognition*, **15**(6), 1147–1156.

Dunbar, K. (1994). Scientific discovery heuristics: How current-day scientists generate new hypotheses and make scientific discoveries. In A. Ram & K. Eislet (Eds.), *Proceedings of the 16th Annual Conference of the Cognitive Science Society* (pp. 985–986). Atlanta, GA: Erlbaum.

Falkenhainer, B., Forbus, K. D., & Gentner, D. (1989). The structure-mapping engine: Algorithm and examples. *Artificial Intelligence*, **41**, 1–63.

Forbus, K. D., Gentner, D., & Law, K. (1995). MAC/FAC: A model of similarity-based retrieval. *Cognitive Science*, **19**, 141–205.

Gentner, D. (1983). Structure-mapping: A theoretical framework for comparison. *Cognitive Science*, **7**, 155–170.

Gentner, D. & Landers, R. (1985). Analogical reminding: A good match is hard to find. In *Proceedings of the International Conference on Cybernetics and Society* (pp. 607–613). New York: Institute of Electrical and Electronics Engineers.

Gentner, D., & Markman, A. B. (1997). Structure-mapping in analogy and similarity. *American Psychologist*, **52**(1) 45–56.

Gentner, D., & Medina, J. (1998). Similarity and the development of rules. *Cognition*, **65**(2–3), 263–297.

Gentner, D., Rattermann, M. J., & Forbus, K. D. (1993). The roles of similarity in transfer: Separating retrievability and inferential soundness. *Cognitive Psychology*, **25**, 524–575.

Gentner, D., Brem, S., Ferguson, R., Wolff, P., Markman, A. B., & Forbus, K. D. (1997). Comparison and creativity in the works of Johannes Kepler. In T. B. Ward, S. M. Smith, & J. Vaid (Eds.),

Creative thought: An investigation of conceptual structures and processes (pp.403–459). Washington, DC: American Psychological Association.

Gick, M. L., & Holyoak, K. J. (1980). Analogical problem solving. *Cognitive Psychology,* **12,** 306–355.

Gick, M. L., & Holyoak, K. J. (1983). Schema induction and analogical transfer. *Cognitive Psychology,* **15,** 1–38.

Hargadon, A., & Sutton, R. I. (1997). Technology brokering and innovation in a product development firm. *Administrative Science Quarterly,* **42**(4), 716–749.

Holyoak, K. J., & Koh, K. (1987). Surface and structural similarity in analogical transfer.*Memory & Cognition,* **15,** 332–340.

Keane, M. T. (1988). *Analogical problem solving.* Chichester, England: Ellis Horwood.

Kotovsky, L., & Gentner, D. (1996). Comparison and categorization in the development of relational similarity. *Child Development,* **67,** 2797–2822.

Lax, D. A., & Sebenius, J. K. (1986). *The manager as negotiator.* New York: Free Press.

Loewenstein, J., & Gentner, D. (1997). *Using comparison to improve preschoolers' spatial mapping ability.* Poster presented at the Biennial meeting of the Society for Research in Child Development, Washington, DC.

Loewenstein, J., & Gentner, D. (submitted). *Comparison promotes relational mapping in preschoolers.*

Loewenstein, J., Thompson, L., & Gentner, D. (1999). Analogical encoding facilitates knowledge transfer in negotiation. *Psychonomic Bulletin & Review,* **6**(4), 586–597.

Markman, A. B., & Gentner, D. (1997). The effects of alignability on memory. *Psychological Science,* **8**(5), 363–367.

Medin, D. L., Goldstone, R. L., & Gentner, D. (1993). Respects for similarity. *Psychological Review,* **100**(2), 254–278.

Moreland, R. L., Argote, L., & Krishnan, R. (1996). Socially shared cognition at work: Transactive memory and group performance. In J. L. Nye & A. M. Brower, (Eds.), *What's social about social cognition? Research on socially shared cognition in small groups* (pp. 57–84). Thousand Oaks, CA: Sage.

Novick, L. (1988). Analogical transfer, problem similarity, and expertise. *Journal of Experimental Psychology: Learning, Memory and Cognition,* **14,** 510–520.

Perfetto, G. A., Bransford, J. D., & Franks, J. J. (1983). Constraints on access in a problem solving context. *Memory & Cognition,* **11,** 24–31.

Reed, S. K., Ernst, G. W., & Banerji, R. (1974). The role of comparison in transfer between similar problem states. *Cognitive Psychology,* **6,** 436–450.

Reeves, L. M., & Weisberg, R. W. (1994). The role of content and abstract information in analogical transfer. *Psychological Bulletin,* **115**(3), 381–400.

Ross, B. H. (1984). Remindings and their effects in learning a cognitive skill. *Cognitive Psychology,* **16,** 371–416.

Ross, B. H. (1987). This is like that: The use of earlier problems and the separation of similarity effects. *Journal of Experimental Psychology: Learning, Memory & Cognition,* **13**(4), 629–639.

Ross, B. H. (1989). Distinguishing types of superficial similarities: Different effects on the access and use of earlier problems. *Journal of Experimental Psychology: Learning, Memory & Cognition,* **15,** 456–468.

Ross, B. H., & Kennedy, P. T. (1990). Generalizing from the use of earlier examples in problem-solving. *Journal of Experimental Psychology: Learning, Memory and Cognition,* **16**(1), 42–55.

Schumacher, R. M., & Gentner, D. (1988). Transfer of training as analogical mapping. *IEEE Transactions on Systems, Man, and Cybernetics,* **18**(4), 592–600.

Simon, H. A., & Hayes, J. R. (1976). The understanding process: Problem isomorphs. *Cognitive Psychology,* **8**(2), 165–190.

Stasser, G., & Stewart, D. (1992). The discovery of hidden profiles by decision making groups:

Solving a problem versus making a judgment. *Journal of Personality and Social Psychology,* **62,** 426–434.

Thompson, L. (1998). *The mind and heart of the negotiator.* Upper Saddle River, NJ: Prentice Hall.

Thompson, L., & DeHarpport, T. (1994). Social judgment, feedback, and interpersonal learning in negotiation. *Organization Behavior and Human Decision Processes,* **58,** 327–345.

Thompson, L., & Hrebec, D. (1996). Lose–lose agreements in interdependent decision making. *Psychological Bulletin,* **120**(3), 396–409.

Thompson, L., Valley, K. L., & Kramer, R. (1995). The bittersweet feeling of success: An examination of social perception in negotiation. *Journal of Experimental Social Psychology,* **31**(6), 467–492.

Received November 4, 1998

[30]

Games and Economic Behavior **38**, 127–155 (2002)
doi:10.1006/game.2001.0855, available online at http://www.idealibrary.com on **IDEAL**®

How Communication Improves Efficiency in Bargaining Games[1]

Kathleen Valley

Harvard Business School, Harvard University, Boston, Massachusetts 02163
E-mail: kvalley@hbs.edu

Leigh Thompson

*Kellogg Graduate School of Management, Northwestern University,
Evanston, Illinois 60208*

Robert Gibbons

*MIT Sloan School of Management and NBER, 50 Memorial Drive,
Cambridge, Massachusetts 02142*

and

Max H. Bazerman

Harvard Business School, Harvard University, Boston, Massachusetts 02163

Received December 22, 1998

We study a double auction with two-sided private information and preplay communication, for which Myerson and Satterthwaite (1983, *J. Econ. Theory* **28**, 265–281) showed that all equilibria are inefficient and the Chatterjee–Samuleson linear equilibrium is most efficient. Like several others, we find that players use communication to surpass equilibrium levels of efficiency, especially when the communication is face-to-face. Our main contribution is an analysis of *how* communication helps the parties achieve such high levels of efficiency. We find that when preplay communication is allowed, efficiency above equilibrium levels is a

[1] We are indebted to the Center for Advanced Study in the Behavioral Sciences for the opportunities it afforded us to spend time together and for fellowships to Gibbons and Thompson funded in part by National Science Foundation (NSF) grant SBR-90221192. Thompson also gratefully acknowledges NSF grants SES-9210298 and PYI-9157447. We thank the Harvard Business School for funding the experiment presented here, and seminar participants at Cal Tech, Cornell, Harvard, Northwestern, Pittsburgh, and Stanford for helpful comments. The reverse-alphabetical authorship order of this paper complements the alphabetical authorship order of our other papers.

127

128   VALLEY ET AL.

result of what we call "dyadic" strategies that allow the parties to coordinate on a single price that reflects both parties' valuations. *Journal of Economic Literature* Classification Numbers: C78, D82.   © 2002 Elsevier Science
   Key Words: private information games; preplay communication; coordination.

Private information can inspire communication or deception. In economic theory, mere words may achieve some communication, but the possibility of deception implies that full efficiency cannot be achieved (Myerson and Satterthwaite, 1983). In several experiments, however, communication allows bargaining parties in games with private information to capture greater gains from trade than can be obtained in any theoretical equilibrium (e.g., Hoffman and Spitzer, 1982; Radner and Schotter, 1989).

We provide further experimental support for the efficiency-enhancing effects of communication. More importantly, we analyze *how* the parties achieve this efficiency gain. We show that the conventional empirical representation of a player's strategy (such as buyer's bid as a function of buyer's value) is inadequate. Explaining our evidence requires what we call a "dyadic" strategy: a single mapping from the two players' value-cost types to their bid-ask actions.

We present an experiment involving a double auction with two-sided private information. A buyer and a seller simultaneously submit an offer and a demand, respectively. If the buyer's offer exceeds the seller's demand, then trade occurs at a price halfway between the two; otherwise, no trade occurs. After the parties learn their valuations but before they bargain, we allow written communication, face-to-face communication, or no communication. The written and face-to-face communication treatments allow "cheap talk" (Crawford and Sobel, 1982): the parties can make any claims that they like, including claims about their valuations, but they are not able to verify their claims.

We analyze the case in which the buyer's value and the seller's cost are independent draws from a uniform distribution. For this case, Chatterjee and Samuelson (1983) derived a linear equilibrium of the double auction without preplay communication, and Myerson and Satterthwaite derived an upper bound on the expected gains from trade in the double auction with preplay communication. Strikingly, Myerson and Satterthwaite showed that their upper bound on the expected gains from trade *with* communication can be achieved by the Chatterjee–Samuelson linear equilibrium *without* communication. Thus, cheap talk preceding a double auction may matter, in the sense of producing equilibrium outcomes that cannot arise as equilibria without communication (Farrell and Gibbons, 1989; Matthews and Postlewaite, 1989), but game theory predicts that talk cannot help, in the sense of capturing greater gains from trade than the best equilibrium available without communication.

We find that the incidence of trade in our communication conditions is higher than both the measured incidence in our no-communication condition and the theoretical incidence in the linear equilibrium. Our primary contribution is an analysis of *how* the players achieved this increased efficiency in the communication conditions. As a first step, we estimate the conventional empirical representations of the players' strategies, such as buyer's bid on buyer's value. This approach suggests that the parties played strategies akin to those of the linear equilibrium. But the players cannot have played anything like the linear equilibrium strategies, because they distinctly surpassed that equilibrium's predicted incidence of trade. Instead, we find that these conventional empirical representations of the parties' strategies suffer from omitted-variable and/or simultaneity bias, as follows. After communication, buyers base their bids not just on their own values, but also on their estimates of the seller's cost, so the latter is an omitted variable in the conventional strategy regression for buyers (and analogously for sellers). Furthermore, after communication, buyers and sellers often coordinate on a single price, so the buyer's bid can be seen as a function of the seller's ask and vice versa—a system of equations. Finally, and most importantly, we show that these omitted-variable and simultaneity biases in the conventional strategy regression are not just econometric niceties; such communication and coordination allow the parties to capture greater gains from trade than can be obtained in any equilibrium.

We proceed as follows. Section 1 presents the existing theory of double auctions with two-sided private information with and without communication. Section 2 describes our experimental design and the findings from our study. Section 3 discusses the mechanisms through which communication might increase efficiency in bargaining with private information in our experiment and beyond.

1. THEORY

Our experiments involve a trading game in which a buyer and a seller have private information about their valuations for a particular good. We focus on the role of communication in improving the efficiency of trading outcomes, but for ease of exposition we begin our theoretical analysis with the case in which communication is not possible.

1.1. *A Double Auction without Preplay Communication*

The trading game that we study is a double auction. The seller names an asking price, p_s, and the buyer simultaneously names an offer price, p_b; if $p_b \geq p_s$, then trade occurs at the midpoint price, $p = (p_b + p_s)/2$, but if $p_b < p_s$, then no trade occurs. We denote the buyer's valuation for the good by v_b; the seller's, by v_s. If the buyer gets the good for price p, then the buyer's payoff is $v_b - p$; if there is no trade, then the buyer's payoff is 0. If the seller sells the good for price p, then the seller's payoff is $p - v_s$; if there is no trade, then the seller's payoff is 0. We assume that both parties are risk neutral.

The parties' valuations are private information and are drawn from independent uniform distributions between 0 and 1. The presence of this private information means that a strategy for (say) the buyer in the double auction is a function specifying the price that the buyer will offer for each of the buyer's possible valuations. As in a game without private information, a pair of strategies is an equilibrium of the double auction if each party's strategy is a best response to the other party's strategy.

There are many equilibria of the double-auction game. For example, there is a continuum of so-called "one-price" equilibria, in which trade occurs at a single price if it occurs at all. To illustrate a particular one-price equilibrium, consider an arbitrary value x in [0, 1]. Let the buyer's strategy be to offer x if $v_b > x$ and to offer 0 otherwise, and let the seller's strategy be to demand x if $v_s > x$ and to demand 1 otherwise. Given the buyer's strategy, the seller's choices amount to trading at x or not trading; thus the seller's strategy is a best response to the buyer's strategy, because the seller types who prefer trading at x to not trading do so, and vice versa. The analogous argument shows that the buyer's strategy is a best response to the seller's, so these two strategies are an equilibrium. In this one-price equilibrium, trade occurs for the (v_s, v_b) pairs indicated in Figure 1; trade would be efficient for all (v_s, v_b) pairs such that $v_b \geq v_s$, but does not occur in the two shaded regions of the figure.

Chatterjee and Samuelson show that the following linear strategies are also an equilibrium of the double auction: the buyer's offer is

$$(1) \qquad\qquad p_b(v_b) = \frac{2}{3}v_b + \frac{1}{12},$$

and the seller's demand is

$$(2) \qquad\qquad p_s(v_s) = \frac{2}{3}v_s + \frac{1}{4}.$$

HOW COMMUNICATION IMPROVES EFFICIENCY   131

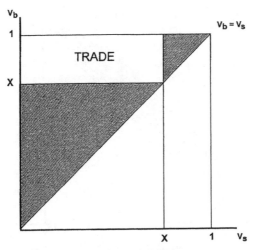

FIG. 1. One-price equilibrium.

Recall that trade occurs in the double auction if and only if $p_b \geq p_s$. Manipulating (1) and (2) shows that $p_b > p_s$ in the linear equilibrium if and only if $v_b - v_s \geq 1/4$, as shown in Figure 2.[2]

Figures 1 and 2 show that the most valuable possible trade (namely, $v_s = 0$ and $v_b = 1$) occurs in both the one-price equilibrium at price x and the linear equilibrium. But the one-price equilibrium at price x misses some valuable trades (e.g., $v_s = 0$ and $v_b = x - \varepsilon$, where ε is small) and achieves some trades that are worth next to nothing (e.g., $v_s = x - \varepsilon$ and $v_b = x + \varepsilon$). The linear equilibrium, in contrast, misses all trades worth next to nothing but achieves all trades worth at least $1/4$. This suggests that the linear equilibrium may dominate any one-price equilibrium, in terms of the total expected gains that the two players receive, but also raises the possibility that the players might achieve even higher expected gains from trade in an alternative equilibrium.

---

[2] The fact that trade occurs if and only if the buyer's value exceeds the seller's cost by at least $1/4$ implies that buyers with values below $1/4$ will not trade, and neither will sellers with costs above $3/4$. Figure 2 also illustrates this fact; seller types above $3/4$ make demands above the buyer's highest offer, $p_b(1) = 3/4$, and buyer types below $1/4$ make offers below the seller's lowest offer, $p_s(0) = 1/4$. Indeed, seller types above $3/4$ make demands below their costs, and buyer types below $1/4$ make offers above their values. These behaviors are rational only because such types know that they will not trade. It would also be equilibrium behavior for such types to offer/demand their values/costs.

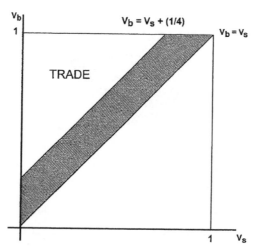

FIG. 2. Chatterjee-Samuelson linear equilibrium.

Our main focus is not on comparing equilibria in the absence of communication, but rather on the role of communication in improving the efficiency of trading outcomes. To study this, we conduct both the double auction described above and an expanded game in which a double auction is preceded by an opportunity for the players to communicate, as follows.

1.2. *A Double Auction with Preplay Communication*

There are again many equilibria of the double auction with preplay communication. Some of the equilibria are easy to characterize. If each side is either silent or uninformative in the communication phase, then the double auction proceeds as just analyzed without communication; therefore, all of the equilibria of the double auction without communication continue to be equilibria of the expanded game with communication. Of course, our interest in preplay communication stems from the possibility of accurate information exchange resulting in new equilibria, not from replicating no-communication equilibria when cheap talk is allowed. Unfortunately, deriving even one new equilibrium of the expanded game requires a formal model of the opportunity that the players are given to communicate —who can say what when. Such a derivation would be intractable for many of the rich communication opportunities of interest, but one simple case has been analyzed by Farrell and Gibbons (1989) and by Matthews and Postlewaite (1989), who allow one simultaneous exchange of messages to precede the double auction.

One potential role for such preplay communication is equilibrium creation. Farrell and Gibbons explore this role for communication; they show how communication can allow information exchange that changes the parties' beliefs, thereby making it rational to play strategies in the ensuing double auction that are not equilibrium strategies in the double auction without preplay communication. A second potential role for preplay communication is equilibrium selection. Matthews and Postlewaite exploit this role for communication; they show how communication can allow different (v_b, v_s) pairs to play different one-price equilibria, (as opposed to all (v_b, v_s) pairs playing a given one-price equilibrium, as described in the previous subsection).

Beyond the Farrell–Gibbons and Matthews–Postlewaite analyses, little has been done to derive new equilibria of double auctions preceded by specific communication opportunities. But Myerson and Satterthwaite (1983) prove a general result concerning all communication opportunities. They show that the linear equilibrium of the double auction without communication yields higher total expected gains for the two players than any other equilibrium of an expanded game in which a double auction is preceded by any opportunity for communication—whether the communication is simultaneous (as in Farrell–Gibbons and Matthews–Postlewaite), sequential, or anything else.

We now present an experiment in which participants play double auctions with and without preplay communication. We find that without communication, trade occurs roughly as predicted by the linear equilibrium. With communication, however, trade occurs more often, contrary to the Myerson–Satterthwaite theory. More importantly, we also find that players achieve this increased efficiency by coordinating on a single price (as a function of their value-cost types), reminiscent of the Matthews–Postlewaite analysis. Myerson and Satterthwaite's results imply that the increased efficiency in our data cannot arise in any equilibrium, so the coordination that we observe in our communication conditions must somehow go beyond the equilibrium selection argument of Matthews and Postlewaite. We explore this puzzle.

2. METHOD AND RESULTS

2.1. *Experimental Method*

One hundred and two undergraduates from five Boston-area universities participated in one of six experimental sessions. Participants were recruited through university newspaper advertisements and postings around the campuses. Each session involved students from several universities. At the beginning of each session, all of the participants (14 or more per session) were asked whether they knew anyone else in the room. The few participants who knew each other were then assigned the same role (e.g., buyer), so all interactions were carried out between strangers. Participants never bargained with the same partner more than once.

The experiment was a 3 × 2 design varying prebid communication (no prebid communication/written/face-to-face) and feedback (no-feedback/ feedback). Details regarding the six communication-feedback treatments are provided below. A given participant was assigned to a single role (buyer or seller) and a single treatment for the entire experiment. Only one treatment was run in each experimental session. The structure of the bargaining game was constant across treatments; regardless of the presence of feedback or the presence or medium of prebid communication, the bargaining game was a double auction involving private submission of sealed bids/asks.

At the beginning of each session, buyers and sellers were separated into two rooms. All participants received envelopes containing materials for the task.[3] Participants were told to read only the first sheet and to look at the next sheet in the envelope only when instructed to do so. The first sheet was an overview containing general information and describing the single communication-feedback treatment in which the player was participating.

The overview sheet stated that buyers would have the opportunity to purchase a fictitious commodity called Tynar from the sellers. Players were told they would participate in a number of rounds, each with a different partner. Each player participated in seven auctions, but players were not told the exact number of rounds they would play, to minimize end-game effects. The overview sheet stated that in each round the buyer's value and the seller's cost for Tynar were determined by independent draws from a uniform distribution from $0 to $50 in $1 increments. It was stated that the buyer's value could be above, below, or equal to the seller's cost. All participants were informed that the values and costs were private information. For example, the buyers were told, "Only you will know your value, and only the seller will know his or her cost."

The overview sheet explained the rules for a double auction, and stated that this mechanism would determine the final trading price: "The price at which Tynar is traded (if it is traded)...is determined jointly by the Buyer's Bid and the Seller's Asking Price. As long as the Buyer bids more than the Seller is asking, the trade will occur at the midpoint. For example, if the Buyer bids $10 and the Seller asks $5, the trade will occur at $7.50 [(10 + 5)/2]." Buyers were told that any positive difference between their

---

[3] See the Appendix for sample materials. A full set of experimental materials is available from the first author upon request.

value for Tynar and the trading price would be their profit for that round. Similarly, sellers were told that any positive difference between the trading price and their cost for the Tynar would be their profit for that round. The instructions stated that if the buyer bought Tynar at a price higher than his or her value, then he or she would lose money in that round. Analogously, sellers were told they would lose money if they sold the Tynar for less than their cost.[4] If no trade occurred, then no profit or loss would be realized. Participants in both roles were given three examples describing seller's cost, buyer's value, seller's ask, buyer's bid, seller's earnings, and buyer's earnings. In one example, both players made money. In another example, there was no trade. In the final example, one player lost money. (In the buyer's overview it was the buyer that lost money, and in the seller's overview it was the seller that lost money.)

The overview sheet explained that the participants would be rewarded with real money. Both hourly and incentive payments were provided. All participants were paid a base rate of approximately $6.67/hour for participating in the study.[5] Players were told that, in addition to the base pay, there was a potential for incentive earnings based on individual profits in three randomly selected payoff rounds. The expected value of the incentive payment was $6.25 per round, or $18.75 for the session. Actual incentive payments ranged from $0 to $68.

After everyone finished reading the overview sheet, there was a question-and-answer session, segregated by buyer or seller role. When all questions had been answered, players completed a short questionnaire to check their understanding of the double-auction mechanism. All participants answered the questions correctly.

Each round occurred in four stages. In the first stage, players read a sheet providing their private value or cost. The second stage contained the communication treatment. The third stage was the private submission of a sealed bid or ask. In the fourth and final stage, players were provided feedback about the outcome of the auction (in the feedback treatments only). At the end of this stage, a new round began. After all rounds had been completed, three rounds were randomly selected to be the payoff rounds.

The communication allowed between buyers and sellers in the second stage (if any) occurred after the players learned their values/costs but before they submitted their bids/asks. Participants in the *no-communication* treatment played anonymously, could not see one another, and could not communicate with one another at any time during the experiment.

---

[4] This information seemed clear to the players: No player lost money in any round.

[5] $10 base pay for approximately 1.5 hours in the no-communication treatments; $20 base pay for approximately 3 hours in the written and face-to-face treatments.

Players in this condition were given two minutes to think about their strategies before submitting their bids/asks. In the *written-communication* treatment, players were given a 13-minute communication period in which they were permitted to exchange written messages with their partner for the round, on sheets provided in their envelopes. The buyers and sellers in the written condition were physically separated, and all interactions were anonymous; couriers delivered all messages between the players. No constraints were placed on what players could write in these messages. All written messages were collected and saved. Participants in the *face-to-face-communication* treatment were allowed a 6-minute communication period, in which the buyer and the seller could meet and talk. No restrictions were placed on participants' conversations, but the players were restricted from bringing their valuation sheets with them to the discussion, to eliminate the potential for physical evidence that could document a claim about cost or value. All face-to-face interactions were audiotaped. Buyers and sellers in the face-to-face communication treatments returned to their separate rooms at the end of each 6-minute communication period to submit bids/asks.

The bid/ask stage was identical in all treatments and rounds. Buyers and sellers, separated by room and seated at desks spaced so that no one's submission was visible to anyone else, wrote their bid/ask on a sheet provided and gave it to the experimenter. Buyers were told that the bid should represent the maximum they would be willing to pay the seller for Tynar, and that the statement of a bid meant they would be willing to purchase Tynar for any price less than or equal to the price they listed. The instructions to sellers were entirely analogous. Players were told they could submit only a specific monetary value for a price; no other terms or conditions could be specified. Following the submission of a bid/ask, in each round each player was asked to write down his or her best estimate of the other party's valuation.

The timing and type of information provided in the final stage varied by feedback treatment; details for the appropriate treatment were provided in the overview sheet. In the *feedback* treatment, participants were given written feedback after each round stating (a) whether or not a trade occurred in the double auction just completed; (b) if so, at what price; and (c) his or her own profit for that round. Players in the *no-feedback* treatment received feedback regarding trade, price, and individual profit only after all rounds had been completed, and only for the three payoff rounds. Players in both treatments were informed that they would never be told the profit of the other party. Payments to participants were made in the separate buyer/seller rooms and were staggered—buyers first and sellers second—so that buyers and sellers exited the building at different times. Players were informed of these steps before the experiment, to make it clear that they would not have to meet the other party again after bargaining.

2.2. *Results*

We first present evidence about trade outcomes. We then turn to evidence regarding the bidding strategies used to achieve these trade outcomes.

2.2.1. Trade Outcomes. Because the parties' valuations were drawn randomly, the buyer's value was below the seller's cost in some observations, so trade was not expected to occur (and did not). Of the 343 observations, 192 had $v_b > v_s$. Unless noted otherwise, we restrict attention to these 192 observations.

Figure 3 plots the trade outcomes for the no-communication, written, and face-to-face treatments. (As we show below, neither feedback nor round affect efficiency, so both feedback conditions and all rounds are included in each figure.) Each graph in the figure shows the 45-degree line ($v_b = v_s$) and the line below which the Chatterjee–Samuelson linear equilibrium predicts that trade will not occur ($v_b = v_s + 12.5$). Figure 3(A) shows that the trade predictions of the linear equilibrium are fairly accurate for our no-communication condition, but Figures 3(B) and 3(C) show that the linear equilibrium fits the data less well for our communication conditions, largely because there are many trades in the Chatterjee–Samuleson no-trade region in these conditions. Table I presents these data in numeric form. In the no-communication treatments, 89% of the high-value ($v_b > v_s + 12.5$) trades were achieved but only 11% of the low-value ($v_s < v_b < v_s + 12.5$) trades were achieved. In aggregate over the no-communication observations, 82.3% of the total available surplus was captured through trade. In the written treatments, a slightly lower fraction (83%) of high-value trades was achieved, but a much higher fraction (44%) of low-value trades was achieved. We explore both of these differences between the no-communication and written treatments. In aggregate, 77.7% of the available surplus was captured in the written treatments, less than was captured in the no-communication treatments. In the face-to-face treatments, the fractions of trades achieved were significantly higher than equilibrium for both high-value and low-value trades (94% and 74%, respectively), and nearly all of the available surplus was captured (94.1%). We also explore these differences from the no-communication conditions.

Because we have random draws of value pairs, it is possible that any findings concerning trade incidence are confounded by differences in the gains from trade ($v_b - v_s$) across conditions. To assess this possibility, we ran logistic regressions on the 192 observations with positive gains from trade. The dependent variable is whether or not trade occurred. The

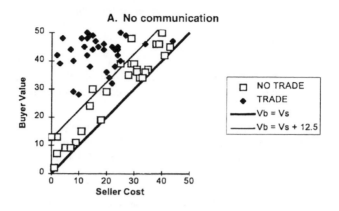

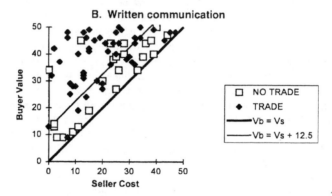

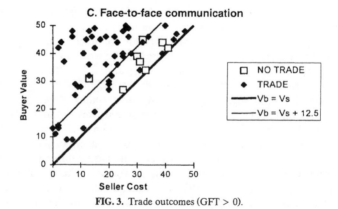

FIG. 3. Trade outcomes (GFT > 0).

TABLE I

Trade Outcomes by Communication Treatment

	$v_b > v_s + 12.5$	$v_s < v_b < v_s + 12.5$	Total
	No communication treatments (with and without feedback)		
No trade	4 (11%)	25 (89%)	29 (46%)
Trade	31 (89%)	3 (11%)	34 (54%)
Total	35	28	63
	Written treatments (with and without feedback)		
No trade	6 (17%)	19 (56%)	25 (36%)
Trade	30 (83%)	15 (44%)	45 (64%)
Total	36	34	70
	Face-to-face treatments (with and without feedback)		
No trade	2 (6%)	7 (26%)	9 (15%)
Trade	30 (94%)	20 (74%)	50 (85%)
Total	32	27	59

regressors are the gains from trade, two dummy variables for written and face-to-face communication conditions, a dummy variable for the feedback condition, and the round number (entered as a continuous variable). The results are presented in column 1 of Table II. The coefficient on face-to-face communication is positive and significant; the coefficient on written communication is positive but only marginally significant. The estimated coefficients on feedback and round are both positive but not significant. Adding the feedback*round interaction to this regression changed nothing of interest.

The insignificant coefficients on feedback and round in this logistic regression suggest that little learning occurs. This is a conservative test, however, since in the majority of the observations trade should occur and does; therefore, there is little opportunity for learning. As a less conservative test, we ran the same logistic regression on the subsample of observations where $v_s < v_b < v_s + 12.5$. As shown in column 2 of Table II, the estimated coefficients on feedback and round are again positive but not significant. On this subsample, however, the estimated coefficients on not only face-to-face but also written communication are positive and significant. Adding the feedback*round interaction to this regression changed nothing of interest.

2.2.2. Bidding Strategies. To determine how the parties achieved a higher incidence of trade in the communication conditions, we turn next to their bidding strategies. We first review "individual" strategies in the no-communication and communication conditions and then focus on "dyadic" strategies in the communication conditions. In all our analyses of

140   VALLEY ET AL.

TABLE II
Logistic Regressions of Trade Outcome

	(1)	(2)
	β	β
	z	z
	Pr > |z|	Pr > |z|
Constant	−3.133	−4.387
	−4.153	−3.587
	0.000	0.000
Gains from trade	0.167	0.190
	6.185	2.515
	0.000	0.012
Written dummy	0.843	1.922
	1.806	2.609
	0.071	0.009
Face-to-face dummy	2.295	3.395
	4.107	4.159
	0.000	0.000
Feedback dummy	0.326	0.515
	0.806	0.951
	0.420	0.342
Round	0.149	0.184
	0.418	1.281
	0.156	0.200
Number of observations	192	89
$\chi^2(5)$	84.01	33.17
Pr > χ^2	0.000	0.000

Note: Column (1) uses all observations with positive gains from trade; column (2) uses only those with $v_s < v_b < v_s + 12.5$.

individuals, the qualitative results for buyer behavior are identical to those for seller behavior. Thus we say nothing in the text about the results for the sellers, but provide full information about both parties in the figures. In our analysis of the no-communication condition we use data from all observations, not just the observations with positive gains from trade. In the communication conditions we restrict attention to the observations with positive gains from trade. Later we provide evidence that the parties often used the communication phase to exchange fairly accurate information on their valuations. We thus restrict attention to the observations with positive gains from trade, because bids and asks when gains from trade are known to be negative may be hard to interpret.

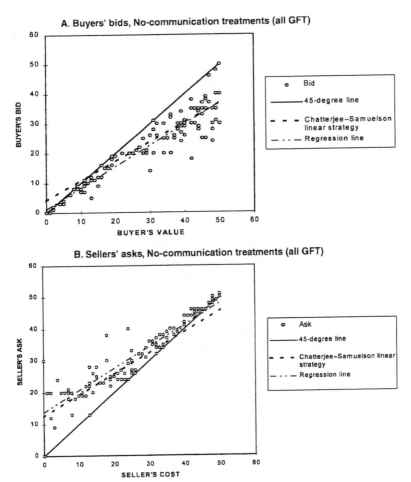

FIG. 4. Bidding strategies, no communication treatments.

We begin by comparing the players' strategies to those of the linear equilibrium. For observations in the no-communication treatment, Figure 4(A) shows the 45-degree line ($p_b = v_b$), the buyer's strategy in the linear equilibrium ($p_b = 0.67v_b + 4.16$), and the regression line through the buyers' bids ($p_b = 0.72v_b + 1.11$).[6] Figure 4(B) presents the analogous

---

[6] Because of the heteroscedasticity evident in the figure, standard errors in all strategy regressions are computed using White's (1980) estimator.

information for the seller; we follow this expositional convention hereafter. On the full sample, this buyer's strategy regression is statistically different from the linear equilibrium strategy ($F(2,110) = 49.27$, $p = 0.0000$), but the economic difference between the two is small. Furthermore, the buyer's strategy in the linear equilibrium has the counterintuitive feature that buyers with valuations $v_b < 12.5$ are indifferent about their bids as long as they do not exceed 12.5, so we reestimated the buyer's strategy on the subsample of buyer values satisfying $v_b > 12.5$. On this subsample (of 85 observations), the regression line is $p_b = 0.68v_b + 2.47$, which is again statistically different from the linear strategy ($F(2,83) = 6.40$, $p = 0.0026$) but is even closer economically.

Figure 5(A) shows buyers' bids in the written-communication treatment. Curiously, the strategy regressions for written communication are even closer to the linear equilibrium (both statistically and economically) than they were for no communication. On the entire sample, the regression line ($p_b = 0.69v_b + 2.50$) is not statistically different from the linear equilibrium ($F(2,68) = 1.33$, $p = 0.272$). But the parties cannot have produced the trading outcomes shown in Figure 3(B) and Table I by playing the linear equilibrium strategies in the written condition, because the linear equilibrium implies no trade when $v_s < v_b < v_s + 12.5$.

We find qualitatively similar results for face-to-face communication, as shown in Figure 6(A). For the whole sample, the regression line ($p_b = 0.60v_b + 4.06$) is statistically different from the buyer's strategy in the linear equilibrium ($F(2,57) = 5.21$, $p = 0.0084$). But this regression for the face-to-face treatments is approximately as close (both statistically and economically) to the linear equilibrium strategy as the no-communication regression was earlier. In particular, had the parties played these estimated strategies in the face-to-face treatments, the trade outcomes would not have been nearly as efficient as those reported in Figure 3(C) and Table I. Apparently, in our two communication conditions, something else is determining the players' bids, beyond their individual valuations.

2.2.3. *Dyadic Strategies.*   We now turn to analyses that investigate the strategies of the two players as a dyad, where the variable of interest is the relationship between the players' strategies. In 73 of the 129 dyads with positive gains from trade in the communication conditions, the buyer and seller named exactly the same price. We say that these dyads "coordinated on a single price." In 8 of the 129 dyads, the parties seemed to reveal their valuations to each other. (Recall that during the bid/ask phase in each round, each party was asked to estimate the other's valuation. In some cases, one party's estimate is equal to the other's valuation. We assume that such precise estimates result from truthful information exchange in

HOW COMMUNICATION IMPROVES EFFICIENCY   143

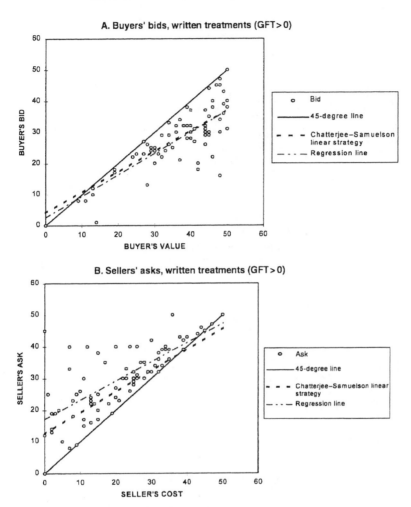

FIG. 5. Bidding strategies, written treatments.

the preplay communication stage.) When both parties in a given dyad gave precisely correct estimates of the other's valuation, we say that "mutual revelation" occurred. Figure 7 summarizes these dyadic behaviors. In total, 75 of the 129 dyads with positive gains from trade in the two communication conditions engaged in coordination on a single price and/or mutual revelation.

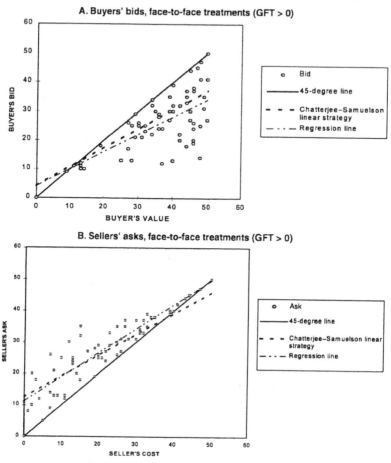

FIG. 6. Bidding strategies, face-to-face treatments.

These findings suggest potential omitted-variable and/or simultaneity biases in our earlier regressions of buyers' bids on their values. For example, if we regress buyer's bid on buyer's value for the 129 observations with communication and positive gains from trade, then the regression line is $p_b = 0.65v_b + 3.24$ and the $R^2 = 0.57$. But if we add seller's cost and seller's ask to this regression, then the regression line is $p_b = 0.25v_b + 0.10v_s + 0.57p_s - 0.52$ and the $R^2 = 0.85$ (and the two new regressors are individually significant). This regression is not intended as a structural

HOW COMMUNICATION IMPROVES EFFICIENCY   145

A. Dyadic strategies, written treatment ($v_b > v_s$, n = 59)

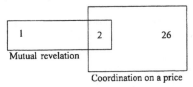

Mutual revelation

Coordination on a price

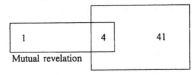

Neither

B. Dyadic strategies, face-to-face treatment ($v_b > v_s$, n = 59)

Mutual revelation

Coordination on a price

Neither

FIG. 7. Dyadic behaviors.

equation; rather, it reveals how misleading a conventional strategy regression (e.g., buyer's bid on buyer's value) is in the presence of dyadic behaviors such as coordination and mutual revelation.

2.2.4. Coordination. Figure 7 shows that coordination on a single price occurred in 28 of the 70 dyads with positive gains from trade in the written-communication treatment and in 45 of the 59 dyads with positive gains from trade in the face-to-face communication treatment. By chance, there was also coordination on a single price in 3 of the 63 observations in which trade occurred in the no-communication treatment. As discussed in Section 1.1, coordination on a single price is an equilibrium of a double auction without communication. Moreover, as discussed in Section 1.2,

Matthews and Postlewaite show how communication can allow different (v_b, v_s) pairs to play different one-price equilibria. But all of these equilibria (with and without communication) are still subject to Myerson and Satterthwaite's upper bound on the efficiency of any equilibrium (namely, the efficiency of the Chatterjee–Samuelson linear equilibrium), whereas our results suggest that coordination was a key factor in allowing our participants to outperform the Myerson–Satterthwaite upper bound.

Recall the logistic regressions reported in Table II, in which the dependent variable is whether trade occurred and the regressors of interest are gains from trade and dummy variables for the written and face-to-face conditions. On the full sample (of 192 observations with positive gains from trade), the estimated coefficient on written communication is positive and marginally significant, and the estimated coefficient on face-to-face communication is positive and highly significant. When we restrict this analysis to the subsample (116 observations) for which coordination did not occur, communication is not significant (written, $p = 0.197$; face-to-face, $p = 0.336$). That is, we find no significant differences between the no-communication and communication treatments for dyads who do not coordinate on a single price. In this sense, price coordination is key to our finding that communication yields higher efficiency.

As a further exploration of this issue, we also ran a linear-probability regression, i.e., an ordinary least squares (OLS) regression in which the dependent variable is whether trade occurred. As in Table II, here regressors are gains from trade and dummy variables for the written and face-to-face treatments. But in this regression we add the interactions of these three variables with a dummy variable equal to 1 if price coordination occurred. Now the coefficient for written communication is small, negative, and marginally significant and the coefficient for face-to-face is very small and insignificant, but the interaction of written and coordination is large, positive, and highly significant, as is the interaction of the face-to-face and coordination. Unlike the logistic regression (which cannot include a dummy variable for coordination, because it perfectly explains the dependent variable for all 76 observations in which coordination occurred), the linear probability model can include the coordination dummy, such as in the interaction terms reported earlier. Including variables reflecting coordination allows us to show that the written and face-to-face dummies are significantly different for the dyads that coordinate versus those that do not. Face-to-face and written communication increase the likelihood of trade only in those dyads that coordinate. This regression also suggests that for those who do not coordinate, written communication slightly *reduces* the likelihood of trade relative to no communication; we return to this later.

Given the importance of coordination in creating the efficiencies we observe, we examined how our treatments affected the likelihood of coordination. In a logistic regression on the 192 observations with positive gains from trade, the dependent variable is whether or not coordination occurred and the regressors are gains from trade, two dummy variables for written and face-to-face treatments, a dummy variable for feedback, and round number. The overall regression is significant ($\chi^2 = 91.10$, p < 0.0005), as are the coefficients for the communication treatments (written: $\beta = 2.932$, z = 4.392, p < 0.0005; face-to-face: $\beta = 4.540$, z = 6.420, p < 0.0005), feedback ($\beta = 1.170$, z = 2.944, p = 0.003), and round ($\beta = 0.248$, z = 2.454, p = 0.014). The coefficient for gains from trade is not significant ($\beta = 0.034$, z = 1.895, p = 0.058). The estimated coefficient for the written treatment is significantly different from that for face-to-face ($\chi^2 = 14.54$, p < 0.005). When the feedback*round interaction is added to the regression, the regression remains highly significant, as do the two coefficients for the communication, but feedback is no longer significant (z = 1.335, p = 0.182), and the round is only marginally significant (z = 1.835, p = 0.066). The coefficient for the interaction term is not significant (z = −0.034, p = 0.973). Both communication treatments make coordination more likely than no communication, but coordination is significantly more likely to occur face-to-face than in writing.

2.2.5. *Revelation and Deception.*   Mutual revelation occurred in 3 of the 70 observations in the written treatment and in 5 of the 59 observations in the face-to-face treatment. While mutual revelation of values does not determine the parties' bids, in 7 of the 8 cases of mutual revelation the parties traded at a price that equally distributed the profits between the two players (rounding to the nearest dollar). In 6 of these 7 cases, the parties coordinated on the single price that resulted in equal distribution of the surplus.

While we assume that a correct estimate of the other's valuation results from honest revelation, we cannot assume that an incorrect estimate results from deception. To measure deception directly, we used the transcripts of the written and face-to-face interactions using all observations, not just the 129 with positive gains from trade. We coded the behavior of each player into one of three categories of information exchange: (1) honest revelation of value; (2) no revelation but no misrepresentation; and (3) misrepresentation of value. There is a significant difference in the overall pattern between the two communication treatments ($\chi^2 = 6.198$, p = 0.045). This result is driven mainly by differences in misrepresentation ($\chi^2 = 5.611$(buyer), p = 0.018 and $\chi^2 = 15.581$(seller), p < 0.001). Simply put, players were more likely to lie in writing than face to face. An example from the written transcripts is illustrative. (Seller) "Let's get down

to business. We are here to earn money, right? So, we'll have to negotiate.
Let's be straight and honest. My cost is $19" (actual cost = $8). In writing,
48% of the sellers and 41% of the buyers explicitly misrepresented their
values. In contrast, in face-to-face communication, only 22% of the sellers
and 26% of the buyers misrepresented their values. This difference is also
reflected in dyadic behaviors. Using the costs and values revealed in the
transcripts, we find that 31% of the dyads mutually revealed when the
interaction was face-to-face, while only 17.9% of them mutually revealed
when the interaction was in writing ($\chi^2 = 11.692$, p < 0.001).

3. DISCUSSION

We take up the problem of communication in bargaining where most
earlier prior studies leave off. Others show that unstructured communication improves the outcome of bargaining games, but do not explore *how* it
matters. Our findings suggest that the bargaining pair works together to
achieve a mutually beneficial outcome. The bids and asks appear to be
determined dyadically, by the pair, rather than independently, by the
individuals. In light of this finding, we assert that a theory of interactive
bargaining with communication should incorporate not only individual, but
also dyadic behavior.

We document two efficiency-improving dyadic strategies: coordination
on a price and mutual revelation of values. We also explore how different
communication media (written versus face-to-face) affect bargaining efficiency. Recall that bargaining in the written treatment was more efficient
than that in the no-communication treatment only when potential gains
from trade were small. When potential gains from trade were large,
bargaining in the written treatment was less efficient than when no
communication was permitted. The sources of these differences between
the written and no-communication treatments are now clear: Higher
efficiency is the result of dyadic coordination, as shown in the regression
presented in Section 2.2.4, while lower efficiency is the result of high rates
of deception in the written treatment, as shown in Section 2.2.5. In
contrast, bargaining was more efficient in the face-to-face treatment than
in the no-communication treatment in both large and small zones of trade.
This increased efficiency is achieved through high levels of coordination,
not compromised by deception, when parties interact face-to-face.

In some of their experiments, Radner and Schotter (1989) studied
precisely our environment: two-sided private information about a buyer's
value and a seller's cost, each drawn independently from a uniform
distribution. Like us, they conducted double auctions without preplay
communication. They also conducted an experiment that allowed commu-

nication to occur, but did so using an unstructured negotiation in which face-to-face communication and bargaining occurred concurrently, rather than having communication precede a fixed bargaining game (in our case, a double auction). In the no-communication case, Radner and Schotter found behavior much like we found. In the communication case (with unstructured negotiation), they found essentially full efficiency—99% of the potential gains from trade were achieved. This finding about trade outcomes is again in keeping with ours: Face-to-face communication greatly improves performance.

But Radner and Schotter (1989) provide no analysis of the sources of this efficiency. Instead, they pose a series of questions (p. 210):

> The success of the face-to-face mechanism, if replicated, might lead to a halt in the search for better ways to structure bargaining in situations of incomplete information. It would create, however, a need for a theory of such unstructured bargaining in order to enable us to understand why the mechanism is so successful ... The answers to such questions will have to be pursued elsewhere.

Our experiments show that it is not unstructured bargaining, but rather the potential for coordination in interpersonal communication that produces the dramatic improvement in efficiency. We restricted communication to the preplay phase, but still found greatly enhanced efficiency effects.

Valley, Thompson, and Bazerman (2000) (hereafter VTB) also study a double auction with private information. The differences between our study and theirs suggest a refinement of the general conclusions that communication improves efficiency through dyadic strategies, and more so face-to-face than in writing. VTB used the same protocol that we present here, but they collected their data in a classroom, so that all interactions were carried out between acquaintances or friends. In our study, we observe higher levels of coordination and higher levels of trade with face-to-face communication than with written communication. But VTB observe no such differences across treatments; the parties achieved nearly full efficiency in both the written and the face-to-face treatments (but, as in our study, VTB find lower efficiency when no communication was allowed). Recall that the participants in our study were strangers, whereas the players in VTB had preestablished and ongoing relationships because of their participation in the same semester-long course. The differences between the two studies suggest a potential interactive effect between communication medium and social knowledge, where face-to-face and written communication forms are equally useful for promoting efficiency when social knowledge is present.

Valley, Moag, and Bazerman (1998) (hereafter VMB) also find that face-to-face bargaining involves not only greater efficiency, but also less deception than bargaining in other media. VMB studied a different environment—a variation on Akerlof's (1970) "lemons" environment, where (i) the seller knows v_s, (ii) the buyer knows that $v_b = (3/2)v_s$, but (iii) the buyer knows only the distribution of v_s (which is uniform on [0, 100]), not the actual value of v_s or v_b. VMB introduce written, telephone, and face-to-face communication into this variant of the "lemons" environment. As in Radner and Schotter's communication treatment, VMB allow unstructured negotiation rather than allowing only preplay communication before a specific bargaining game. They report direct measures of seller misrepresentation and buyer trust. VMB find a high incidence of seller misrepresentation and low levels of buyer trust in written bargaining; as a result, the modal outcome is impasse (as predicted in equilibrium). In telephone bargaining, seller misrepresentation is high, but so is buyer trust; the modal outcome is the winner's curse. In face-to-face bargaining, seller misrepresentation is low and buyer trust is high; the modal outcome is mutually profitable agreement. Notably, parties bargaining face to face achieved nearly full efficiency.

Prior explanations of the effects of communication on bargaining are often based on social utility effects from communication, especially face-to-face communication (Dawes, 1988; Sally, 1995). A social utility explanation suggests that trusting and trustworthy behavior occurs during social interactions because players who communicate with one another develop an interest in the welfare of the other party, especially if the communication takes place face to face. In many plausible formal models of such a social utility effect, face-to-face interaction would lead to more equal distribution of surplus across the two parties than would written interaction, and both would lead to more equal distribution than no communication. For example, with social utility, one might get more trade via bidding functions that were closer to bidding one's value, which would result in closer to equal splits of the surplus.

To explore the potential explanatory power of a social-utility explanation on our data, we created a variable indicating the distribution of profits across the two players, given agreement: absolute difference between buyer's profits and seller's profits, normalized by the total gains from trade. We regressed the profit-distribution variable on the two communication dummy variables, the feedback dummy, round, and dummy variables for coordination and mutual revelation. The overall regression is significant ($F(6,122) = 4.21$, $p = 0.0007$; $R^2 = 0.138$), as are the coefficients for face-to-face communication ($\beta = 0.183$, $p = 0.020$), written communication ($\beta = 0.188$, $p = 0.004$), and mutual revelation ($\beta = -0.275$, $p = 0.030$). Note that the estimated coefficients on the communication variables are positive, indicating that face-to-face and written communication *increase* the difference across the players' profits relative to no communication.

There is no significant difference between the written and face-to-face treatments $(F(1,122) = 0.03,\ p = 0.869)$. Only mutual revelation has a significant mitigating effect. Adding an interaction variable for feedback*round does not qualitatively affect the results. Similarly, Schotter (1995) reanalyzed Radner and Schotter's (1989) data and found that the variability of the buyer's share of surplus was substantially larger in unstructured face-to-face negotiations than in the sealed bid without communication. We find that both written and face-to-face treatments result in greater variability in distribution than no communication (Bartlett's test for equality of variances: $\chi^2 = 11.008,\ p = 0.001$, face-to-face; $\chi^2 = 11.713,\ p = 0.001$, written). We find no difference in variances between the written and face-to-face treatments. Thus, parties are using the communication phase to coordinate and ensure trade, but not to ensure equal distribution of the surplus. These findings suggest that social utility explanations provide little insight into the heightened efficiency in the communication treatments.

Our findings belong to the large body of research suggesting that actual bargaining behavior deviates from traditional game-theoretic models. Whereas much of the literature on behavioral decision theory suggests that people fall short of fully efficient outcomes, our findings add to the growing literature suggesting that real behavior can lead to *better* performance than is predicted by traditional notions of rationality. We hope that this research prompts further exploration of positive aspects of human behavior, specifically social interaction, in addition to the negative aspects that have been identified in behavioral decision theory. We believe that when observed behavior clashes with game-theoretic predictions, researchers face a decision of whether to dismiss the observed behavior as due to chance, mishap, or methodological flaw or to reformulate the theory. Bargaining often occurs with some communication between the parties. If, as our findings suggest, this communication substantially changes the strategies chosen by the players, then the critical consequences of communication—coordination and honest revelation—need to be considered in future theories of bargaining.

APPENDIX

Study II Materials[7]

Tynar Overview. In this exercise, you will participate in a series of negotiations. In each negotiation, there will be a Buyer and a Seller. You will remain the same role in all

---

[7] Only face-to-face seller materials are presented here. Written and no-communication materials vary in the last two pages. A full set of materials is available from the first author.

negotiations. You will negotiate with a different person in each negotiation. Please read closely all of the information below. You will have an opportunity to ask questions about anything you do not understand.

In each negotiation, you will bargain over a fictitious commodity called Tynar. Buyers value Tynar at a given value, which will change in each negotiation. The Seller has a cost for Tynar, which will also change in each negotiation. The Buyer makes money by buying Tynar at a price lower than the given value. The Seller makes money by selling Tynar at a price higher than the given cost.

The Buyer's value and the Seller's cost are independent. Both, however, will be randomly drawn from the same distribution—$0–$50 (integers only). Thus the Buyer's value will change in each negotiation and can vary across negotiations from $0 to $50, inclusive. Similarly, the Seller will be given a new cost for Tynar each round, and the cost can vary across negotiations from $0 to $50, inclusive. The Buyer's value in any negotiation may be above, below, or equal to Seller's cost. Only the Buyer will know the Buyer's value and only the Seller will know the Seller's cost.

Each negotiation has the potential for earnings or losses up to $50 across the Buyer and the Seller.

The price at which Tynar is traded (if it is traded) in any negotiation is determined jointly by the Buyer's Bid and the Seller's Asking Price. As long as the Buyer bids more than the Seller is asking, the trade will occur at the midpoint. For example, if the Buyer bids $10 and the Seller asks $5, the trade will occur at $7.50 [(10 + 5)/2].

If the Buyer bids $5 and the Seller asks $10, no trade occurs in that negotiation.

Buyers make a profit by trading at a price less than their value for the Tynar. Sellers make a profit by trading at a price higher than their costs.

Specifically:

$$\text{Buyer Profit} = \text{Buyer Value} - \text{Trading Price}$$

$$\text{Seller Profit} = \text{Trading Price} - \text{Seller Cost}$$

After the negotiations are over, a participant will randomly select 3 negotiations to be the payoff rounds. You will be paid whatever you earned in those 3 rounds. (This is in addition to the fee everyone will be paid for participating in the session.)

Below are some examples:

    Seller's Cost: $4.00
    Buyer's Value: $22.00
    Seller's Asking Price: $16.00
    Buyer's Bid: $20.00
    Buyer Bid > Seller Asking Price, so **Trading Price** = (16.00 + 20.00)/2 = $18.00
    Seller earns (trading price − cost) or $18.00 − $4.00 = $14.00
    Buyer earns (value − trading price) or $22.00 − 18.00 = $4.00

    Seller's Cost: $20.00
    Buyer's Value: $17.00
    Seller's Asking Price: $20.00
    Buyer's Bid: $17.00
    No sale takes place, since Buyer Bid < Seller Asking Price
    Seller earns: $0.00
    Buyer earns: $0.00

    Seller's Cost: $12.00
    Buyer's Value: $10.00
    Seller's Asking Price: $12.00

Buyer's Bid: $13.00

Buyer bid more than Seller asked, so **Trading price** = ($13.00 + 12.00)/2 = $12.50

Seller earns (trading price − cost) or $12.50 − 12.00 = $0.50

Buyer earns (value − trading price) or $10 − 12.50 = ⟨ − $2.50⟩ Notice: This is a loss to the Buyer. The Buyer lost only because s/he chose to make a Bid above his or her value for Tynar.

Be careful not to lose money in this exercise.

Please take this opportunity to ask the experimenter any questions you may have about the exercise.

After questions, before you begin the negotiations, please answer the questions on the next page.

Pre-negotiation Questions

1. If the Buyer's value is $4.00 and the Seller's cost is $5.00, is a mutually profitable trade possible?

2. If the Buyer's value is $46.00, what's the most s/he can bid for the Tynar and still be sure to make a profit if a trade occurs?

3. If the Seller's cost is $12, what's the lowest price s/he can ask and still be sure to make a profit if a trade occurs?

4. If the Buyer's value is $32.00 and the Seller's cost is $8.00, and the Buyer bids $26.00 while the Seller asks for $20.00, will a sale take place?

> If so, at what price?
> How much would the Buyer earn?
> How much would the Seller earn?

5. If the Buyer's value is $13.00 and the Seller's cost is $15.00, and a trade takes place at $16.00, how much does the Buyer earn?

> How much does the Seller earn?

Seller's Negotiation and Payment Details. Each negotiation takes place in three steps: (1) You will be given a cost on your Seller Report Form for this negotiation; (2) You will communicate face-to-face with the Buyer; (3) After the communication period is over, you will go back to the seller classroom and submit a private Asking Price for the Tynar.

Specifically:

1. You have been **given a cost** from a random number generator. All integer values between 0 and 50, inclusive, are possible values for the Tynar. This cost is recorded under "Cost" on the Seller's Record Sheet. These Record Sheets are on your assigned desk in the seller classroom. There is one Sheet for each negotiation. Look only at the Sheet for the upcoming negotiation. In other words, please do not look at the Record Sheet for any round other than the one you are about to negotiate.

2. The Record Sheet **is not to be taken out of the Seller Classroom.** You may want to note your partner's id # and your cost for Tynar for the upcoming negotiation before you go out of the room to the negotiation.

3. Each seller has a **pre-assigned negotiation space.** This is noted on the Map and the locations are clearly marked in the hallways. The buyers will be rotating across sellers, but the sellers will always be negotiating in the same spot, throughout all of the negotiations.

154					VALLEY ET AL.

4. You will need to **bring the tape recorder with you to the first negotiation.** After the first negotiation, and after all subsequent negotiations, please leave the recorder at the negotiation spot. Make sure you **turn the recorder on at the start of each negotiation and off when the negotiation is over.** Please announce the negotiation round number and the buyer's participant number at the beginning of each negotiation, after you have turned on the tape recorder.

5. You have 6 minutes to **communicate face-to-face with the Buyer.** You may talk about anything you would like during this communication period. After the 6 minutes are over, you must stop all communication.

6. At the end of the 6 minute communication period, please go back to the central seller classroom, to the seat you were assigned. On your desk is your Record Sheet for the negotiation just completed. **Record your Asking Price on the Seller's Record Sheet.** This Asking Price is the price at which you are willing to sell the Tynar. Your statement of Asking Price means you are willing to sell Tynar for any price more than or equal to the price you listed. This Asking Price is the minimum you are willing to accept for the Tynar. You may ask only a specific monetary value—in other words, no terms or conditions may be added to your Asking Price. Then, **complete the rest of the Record Sheet,** answering all the questions asked.

7. Bring the completed Record Sheet from the negotiation you just finished up to the front of the classroom. **Please put the completed Record Sheet into the manila folder labeled with your participant role and number (e.g., Seller #2).**

8. After turning in the Record Sheet for the negotiation you just finished, go back to your seat and **look at the Record Sheet for the next negotiation.** Look at your Pairing Sheet to see who will be your negotiation partner. On the Record Sheet, **note your participant number and your partner's participant number, along with your name.** Remember, you should NOT bring the Record Sheet for the upcoming negotiation with you to the negotiation.

At the same time as you submit your Asking Price, the Buyer will be submitting a private, sealed Bid for Tynar. The Bid will state the maximum s/he is willing to pay for the sale of Tynar. In order for any transaction to occur, the Buyer must bid as much as or more than the Seller is asking for the Tynar. If this occurs, the Tynar is sold at the price exactly midpoint between the Buyer's Bid and the Seller's Asking Price (the midpoint or average of the two values).

At the end of the series of negotiations, a participant will randomly select the 3 rounds for which you will be paid.

REFERENCES

Akerlof, G. (1970). "The Market for Lemons: Quality Uncertainty and the Market Mechanism," *Quart. J. Econ.* **84**, 488–500.

Chatterjee, K., and Samuelson, W. (1983). "Bargaining under Incomplete Information," *Oper. Res.* **31**, 835–851.

Crawford, V., and Sobel, J. (1982). "Strategic Information Transmission," *Econometrica* **50**, 1431–1451.

Dawes, R. (1988). *Rational Choice in an Uncertain World.* Orlando, FL.: Harcourt Brace Jovanovich.

Farrell, J., and Gibbons, R. (1989). "Cheap Talk Can Matter in Bargaining," *J. Econ. Theory* **48**, 221–237.

Hoffman, E., and Spitzer, M. (1982). "The Coase Theorem: Some Experimental Tests," *J. Law Econ.* **25**, 93–98.

Matthews, S., and. Postlewaite, A. (1989). "Pre-play Communication in Two-person Sealed-bid Double Auctions," *J. Econ. Theory* **48**, 238–263.

Myerson, R., and Satterthwaite, M. (1983). "Efficient mechanisms for bilateral trading," *J. Econ. Theory* **28**, 265–281.

Radner, R., and Schotter, A. (1989). "The Sealed-bid Mechanism: An Experimental Study," *J. Econ. Theory* **48**, 179–220.

Sally, D. F. (1995). "Conversation and Cooperation in Social Dilemmas: Experimental Evidence from 1958 to 1992," *Rationality and Society* **7**, 58–92.

Schotter, A. (1998). "Practical Criteria that Organizations Might Use for Mechanism Selection and Some Lessons from Experimental Economics," in *Organizations With Incomplete Information: Essays in Economic Analysis: A Tribute to Roy Radner* (M. Majumdar, Ed.), New York: Cambridge Univ. Press.

Valley, K. L., Moag, J., and Bazerman, M. H. (1998). "A Matter of Trust: Effects of Communication on the Efficiency and Distribution of Outcomes," *J. Econ. Behav. Organ.* **34**, 211–238.

Valley, K. L., Thompson, L., and Bazerman, M. H. (2000). "Social Improvements on Rationality: The Role of Social Closeness in Creating Positive Deviations from Rationality Based Expectations," Working Paper 01-028, Harvard Business School, Harvard, MA.

Name Index